Collins
German
Dictionary

HarperCollins Publishers
Westerhill Road
Bishopbriggs
Glasgow
G64 2QT
Great Britain

Ninth Edition 2007

Reprint 10 9 8 7 6 5 4 3 2 1 0

ISBN-13 978-0-00-725281-7
ISBN-10 0-00-725281-1

www.collins.co.uk

A catalogue record for this
book is available from the
British Library

Typeset by RefineCatch Ltd,
Bungay, Suffolk

Printed in Italy by
Legoprint S.p.A.

Acknowledgements
We would like to thank those
authors and publishers who
kindly gave permission for
copyright material to be used
in the Collins Word Web. We
would also like to thank Times
Newspapers Ltd for providing
valuable data.

CONTRIBUTORS/MITARBEITER
Howard Atkinson
Stuart Fortey
Helen Galloway
Silke Probst
Robin Sawers
Veronika Schnorr
Yvonne Stein
Karin Weindl

EDITORIAL STAFF/REDAKTION
Christine Bahr
Susie Beattie
Horst Kopleck
Joyce Littlejohn
Heike Pleisteiner

COMPUTING/
DATENVERARBEITUNG
Andreas Lang, context AG für
Informatik und
Kommunikation, Zürich
Oliver Schweiberer

This book is set in Collins
Fedra, a typeface specially
created for Collins Dictionarie
by Peter Bil'ak

INHALT

CONTENTS

WARENZEICHEN

Warenzeichen, die unseres Wissens eingetragene Warenzeichen darstellen, sind als solche gekennzeichnet. Es ist jedoch zu beachten, dass weder das Vorhandensein noch das Fehlen derartiger Kennzeichnungen die Rechtslage hinsichtlich eingetragener Warenzeichen berührt.

NOTE ON TRADEMARKS

Words which we have reason to believe constitute trademarks have been designated as such. However, neither the presence nor the absence of such designation should be regarded as affecting the legal status of any trademark.

William Collins' dream of knowledge for all began with the publication of his first book in 1819. A self-educated mill worker, he not only enriched millions of lives, but also founded a flourishing publishing house. Today, staying true to this spirit, Collins books are packed with inspiration, innovation, and practical expertise. They place you at the centre of a world of possibility and give you exactly what you need to explore it.

Language is the key to this exploration, and at the heart of Collins Dictionaries is language as it is really used. New words, phrases, and meanings spring up every day, and all of them are captured and analysed by the Collins Word Web. Constantly updated, and with over 2.5 billion entries, this living language resource is unique to our dictionaries.

Words are tools for life. And a Collins Dictionary makes them work for you.

Collins. Do more.

EINFÜHRUNG

Wir freuen uns sehr, dass Sie sich zum Kauf eines Collins Wörterbuchs Deutsch entschlossen haben. Wir wünschen Ihnen viel Spaß beim Gebrauch in der Schule, zu Hause, im Urlaub und im Beruf.

Diese Einführung wird Ihnen einige nützliche Hinweise dazu geben, wie Sie am besten von Ihrem neuen Wörterbuch profitieren. Schließlich bietet Ihnen das Wörterbuch nicht nur Stichwörter und Übersetzungen, sondern auch zahlreiche Zusatzinformationen in jedem einzelnen Eintrag. Mit Hilfe all dieser Informationen können Sie zum einen modernes Deutsch lesen und verstehen, zum anderen auch aktiv auf Deutsch kommunizieren.

Das Collins Wörterbuch Deutsch gibt Ihnen vor dem eigentlichen Wörterbuchtextteil selbst eine Liste aller verwendeten Abkürzungen sowie eine Übersicht zu Aussprache und Gebrauch phonetischer Umschrift. Darüber hinaus finden Sie noch eine Auflistung zu den regelmäßigen deutschen Substantivendungen sowie zu unregelmäßigen englischen und deutschen Verben. Auf den letzten Seiten Ihres Wörterbuchs finden Sie in einem „kleinen Reise-ABC" zahlreiche nützliche Phrasen für verschiedenste Situationen am Urlaubsort.

WIE FINDE ICH WAS?

Die verschiedenen Schriftarten, Schriftgrößen, Symbole, Abkürzungen und Klammern helfen Ihnen dabei, sich innerhalb der Informationen, die das Wörterbuch bietet, zurechtzufinden. Die Konventionen, die diesem Wörterbuch zugrunde liegen, sowie auch der Gebrauch verschiedener Symbole werden im Folgenden näher erläutert.

STICHWÖRTER

Die Wörter, die Sie in Ihrem Wörterbuch nachschlagen, die Stichwörter, sind in alphabetischer Reihenfolge angeordnet. Sie sind **fett** gedruckt und in blauer Farbe, sodass Sie sie schnell finden. Die Stichwörter, die rechts und links oben auf jeder Seite erscheinen, sind das jeweils erste Stichwort einer Seite, wenn es sich dabei um eine linke Seite handelt, bzw. das letzte Stichwort einer Seite, wenn es sich um eine rechte Seite handelt. Informationen zu Form und Gebrauch des jeweiligen Stichworts werden im Anschluss an die Lautschrift in Klammern angegeben. Normalerweise sind diese Angaben in abgekürzter Form und *kursiver Schrift* (z.B. *(fam)* für umgangssprachlich oder *(Comm)* als Sachgebietsangabe für Wirtschaft).

Wo es sich anbietet, werden zusammengehörige Wörter und Wortgruppen in einem Eintrag zusammengefasst (z.B. gather, gathering; höflich, Höflichkeit). Hierbei sind die Stichwörter innerhalb des Nests von der Schriftgröße etwas kleiner als das erste Stichwort. Geläufige Ausdrücke, in denen das Stichwort vorkommt, erscheinen ebenfalls **fett**, aber in einer anderen Schriftgröße. Die Tilde (~) steht hierbei für das Hauptstichwort am Anfang eines Eintrags. So steht beispielsweise im Eintrag ,Mitte' der Ausdruck ,~ Juni' für ,Mitte Juni'.

PHONETISCHE UMSCHRIFT

Die Aussprache jedes Stichworts findet sich in phonetischer Umschrift in eckigen Klammern jeweils direkt hinter dem Stichwort selbst (z.B. mountain ['maʊntɪn]). Eine Liste der Lautschriftzeichen mit Erklärungen finden Sie auf S. xi.

BEDEUTUNGEN

Die Übersetzung der Stichwörter ist in Normalschrift angegeben. Gibt es mehrere Bedeutungen oder Gebrauchsmöglichkeiten, so sind diese durch einen Strichpunkt voneinander zu unterscheiden. Sie finden ort weitere Angaben in Klammern vor der jeweiligen Übersetzungen. Diese zeigen Ihnen typische Kontexte auf, in denen das Stichwort verwendet werden kann (z.B. breakup *(of meeting, organisation)*), oder sie liefern Synonyme (z.B. fit *(suitable)*).

GRAMMATISCHE HINWEISE

Die Wortartangabe finden Sie als Abkürzung und in *kursiver Schrift* direkt hinter der Ausspracheinformation zum jeweiligen Stichwort (z.B. *vt, adj, n*).

Die Genusangaben zu deutschen Substantiven werden wie folg angegeben: *m* für Maskulinum, *f* für Femininum und *nt* für Neutrum. Darüber hinaus finden Sie neben dem Stichwort in Klammern Genitiv- und Pluralform (Abenteuer *(-s, -)*).

Die Genusangabe zur deutschen Übersetzung findet sich ebenfalls in *kursiver Schrift* direkt hinter dem Hauptbestandteil der Übersetzung.

INTRODUCTION

We are delighted you have decided to buy the Collins German Dictionary and hope you will enjoy and benefit from using it at school, at home, on holiday or at work.

This introduction gives you a few tips on how to get the most out of your dictionary - not simply from its comprehensive wordlist but also from the information provided in each entry. This will help you to read and understand modern German, as well as to communicate and express yourself in the language.

The Collins German Dictionary begins by listing the abbreviations used in the text and illustrating the sounds shown by the phonetic symbols. Next you will find regular German noun endings and English irregular verbs followed by a section on German irregular verbs. Finally, the new Phrasefinder supplement gives you hundreds of useful phrases which are intended to give you practical help in everyday situations when travelling.

USING YOUR COLLINS DICTIONARY

A wealth of information is presented in the dictionary, using various typefaces, sizes of type, symbols, abbreviations and brackets. The conventions and symbols used are explained in the following sections.

HEADWORDS

The words you look up in the dictionary - 'headwords' - are listed alphabetically. They are printed in **colour** for rapid identification. The headwords appearing at the top of each page indicate the first (if it appears on a left-hand page) and last word (if it appears on a right-hand page) dealt with on the page in question.

Information about the usage or form of certain headwords is given in brackets after the phonetic spelling. This usually appears in abbreviated form and in italics (e.g. (fam), (Comm)).

Where appropriate, words related to headwords are grouped in the same entry (gather, gathering; höflich, Höflichkeit) in a slightly smaller bold type than the headword. Common expressions in which the headword appears are shown in a different size of bold roman type. The swung dash, -, represents the main headword at the start of each entry. For example, in the entry for 'Mitte', the phrase '~ Juni' should be read '**Mitte Juni**'.

PHONETIC SPELLINGS

The phonetic spelling of each headword (indicating its pronunciation) is given in square brackets immediately after the headword (e.g. mountain ['mauntɪn]). A list of these spellings is given on page xi.

MEANINGS

Headword translations are given in ordinary type and, where more than one meaning or usage exists, they are separated by a semicolon. You will often find other words in italics in brackets before the translations. These offer suggested contexts in which the headword might appear (e.g. breakup (*of meeting, organisation*)) or provide synonyms (e.g. fit (*suitable*)).

GRAMMATICAL INFORMATION

Parts of speech are given in abbreviated form in italics after the phonetic spellings of headwords (e.g. *vt, adj, n*).

Genders of German nouns are indicated as follows: *m* for a masculine, *f* for a feminine, and *nt* for a neuter noun. Genitive and plural forms of nouns are also shown next to the headword (Abenteuer (*-s, -*)).

The gender of the German translation appears in *italics* immediately following the key element of the translation.

ABKÜRZUNGEN		ABBREVIATIONS
auch	a.	also
Abkürzung	abk, abbr	abbreviation
Akronym	acr	acronym
Adjektiv	adj	adjective
Adverb	adv	adverb
Landwirtschaft	Agr	agriculture
Akkusativ	akk	accusative
Akronym	akr	acronym
Anatomie	Anat	anatomy
Artikel	art	article
Bildende Künste	Art	fine arts
Astronomie, Astrologie	Astr	astronomy, astrology
Auto, Verkehr	Auto	automobiles, traffic
Luftfahrt	Aviat	aviation
Biologie	Bio	biology
Botanik	Bot	botany
britisch	BRIT	British
schweizerisch	CH	Swiss
Chemie	Chem	chemistry
Film	Cine	cinema
Wirtschaft	Comm	commerce
Konjunktion	conj	conjunction
Dativ	dat	dative
Eisenbahn	Eisenb	railways
Elektrizität	Elek, Elec	electricity
besonders	esp	especially
und so weiter	etc	et cetera
etwas	etw	
Femininum	f	feminine
umgangssprachlich	fam	familiar, informal
übertragen	fig	figurative
Finanzen, Börse	Fin	finance
Fotografie	Foto	photography
Gastronomie	Gastr	cooking, gastronomy
Genitiv	gen	genitive
Geographie, Geologie	Geo	geography, geology
Geschichte	Hist	history
Imperativ	imper	imperative
Imperfekt	imperf	past tense
Informatik und Computer	Inform	computing
Interjektion, Ausruf	interj	interjection
unveränderlich	inv	invariable
unregelmäßig	irr	irregular
jemand, jemandem	jd, jdm	
jemanden, jemandes	jdn, jds	
Rechtsprechung	Jur	law

Konjunktion	konj	conjunction
Bildende Künste	Kunst	fine arts
Sprachwissenschaft, Grammatik	Ling	linguistics, grammar
Maskulinum	m	masculine
Mathematik	Math	mathematics
Medizin	Med	medicine
Meteorologie	Meteo	meteorology
Maskulinum und Femininum	mf	masculine and feminine
Militär	Mil	military
Musik	Mus	music
Substantiv	n	noun
Seefahrt	Naut	nautical, naval
Neutrum	nt	neuter
Zahlwort	num	numeral
oder	o	or
pejorativ, abwertend	pej	pejorative
Physik	Phys	physics
Plural	pl	plural
Politik	Pol	politics
Partizip Perfekt	pp	past participle
Präfix	pref	prefix
Präposition	prep	preposition
Pronomen	pron	pronoun
1. Vergangenheit	pt	past tense
Eisenbahn	Rail	railways
Religion	Rel	religion
siehe	s.	see
	sb	someone, somebody
schottisch	Scot	Scottish
Singular	sing	singular
Skisport	Ski	skiing
	sth	something
Technik	Tech	technology
Nachrichtentechnik	Tel	telecommunications
Theater	Theat	theatre
Fernsehen	TV	television
Typographie, Buchdruck	Typo	printing
unpersönlich	unpers	impersonal
(nord)amerikanisch	US	(North) American
Verb	vb	verb
Hilfsverb	vb aux	auxiliary verb
intransitives Verb	vi	intransitive verb
reflexives Verb	vr	reflexive verb
transitives Verb	vt	transitive verb
vulgär	vulg	vulgar
Zoologie	Zool	zoology
ungefähre Entsprechung	≈	cultural equivalent
abtrennbares Präfix	|	separable prefix

[:] Längezeichen, length mark
['] Betonung, stress mark
[*] Bindungs-R, 'r' pronounced before a vowel

alle Vokallaute sind nur ungefähre Entsprechungen
all vowel sounds are approximate only

VOKALE UND DIPHTHONGE

plant, arm, father	[ɑ:]	Bahn
fiancé	[ɑ̃:]	Ensemble
life	[aɪ]	weit
house	[au]	Haut
man, sad	[æ]	
but, son	[ʌ]	Butler
get, bed	[e]	Metall
name, lame	[eɪ]	
ago, better	[ə]	bitte
bird, her	[ɜ:]	
there, care	[ɛə]	mehr
it, wish	[ɪ]	Bischof
bee, me, beat, belief	[i:]	viel
here	[ɪə]	Bier
no, low	[əʊ]	
not, long	[ɒ]	Post
law, all	[ɔ:]	Mond
boy, oil	[ɔɪ]	Heu
push, look	[ʊ]	Pult
you, do	[u:]	Hut
poor, sure	[ʊə]	

KONSONANTEN

been, blind	[b]	Ball
do, had	[d]	dann
jam, object	[dʒ]	
father, wolf	[f]	Fass
go, beg	[g]	Gast
house	[h]	Herr
youth, Indian	[j]	ja
keep, milk	[k]	kalt
lamp, oil, ill	[l]	Last
man, am	[m]	Mast
no, manner	[n]	Nuss
long, sing	[ŋ]	lang

El Niño	[ɲ]	El Niño
paper, happy	[p]	Pakt
red, dry	[r]	rot
stand, sand, yes	[s]	Rasse
ship, station	[ʃ]	Schal
tell, fat	[t]	Tal
thank, death	[θ]	
this, father	[ð]	
church, catch	[tʃ]	Rutsch
voice, live	[v]	was
water, we, which	[w]	
loch	[x]	Bach
zeal, these, gaze	[z]	Hase
pleasure	[ʒ]	Genie

REGULAR GERMAN NOUN ENDINGS

nominative		genitive	plural	nominative		genitive	plural
-ade	f	-ade	-aden	-ist	m	-isten	-isten
-ant	m	-anten	-anten	-ium	nt	-iums	-ien
-anz	f	-anz	-anzen	-ius	m	-ius	-iusse
-ar	m	-ars	-are	-ive	f	-ive	-iven
-är	m	-ärs	-äre	-keit	f	-keit	-keiten
-at	nt	-at(e)s	-ate	-lein	nt	-leins	-lein
-atte	f	-atte	-atten	-ling	m	-lings	-linge
-chen	nt	-chens	-chen	-ment	nt	-ments	-mente
-ei	f	-ei	-eien	-mus	m	-mus	-men
-elle	f	-elle	-ellen	-nis	f	-nis	-nisse
-ent	m	-enten	-enten	-nis	nt	-nisses	-nisse
-enz	f	-enz	-enzen	-nom	m	-nomen	-nomen
-ette	f	-ette	-etten	-rich	m	-richs	-riche
-eur	m	-eurs	-eure	-schaft	f	-schaft	-schaften
-euse	f	-euse	-eusen	-sel	nt	-sels	-sel
-heit	f	-heit	-heiten	-tät	f	-tät	-täten
-ie	f	-ie	-ien	-tiv	nt, m	-tivs	-tive
-ik	f	-ik	-iken	-tor	m	-tors	-toren
-in	f	-in	-innen	-tum	m, nt	-tums	-tümer
-ine	f	-ine	-inen	-ung	f	-ung	-ungen
-ion	f	-ion	-ionen	-ur	f	-ur	-uren

Substantive, die mit einem geklammerten 'r' oder 's' enden (z.B. **Angestellte(r)** *mf*, **Beamte(r)** *m*, **Gute(s)** *nt*) werden wie Adjektive dekliniert:

Nouns listed with an 'r' or an 's' in brackets (eg **Angestellte(r)** *mf*, **Beamte(r)** *m*, **Gute(s)** *nt*) take the same endings as adjectives:

der Angestellte *m*	**die Angestellte** *f*
ein Angestellter *m*	**eine Angestellte** *f*
der Beamte *m*	
ein Beamter *m*	
das Gute *nt*	
ein Gutes *nt*	

die Angestellten *pl*
Angestellte *pl*
die Beamten *pl*
Beamte *pl*

UNREGELMÄßIGE ENGLISCHE VERBEN

present	past tense	past participle	present	past tense	past participle
arise (arising)	arose	arisen	drink	drank	drunk
awake (awaking)	awoke	awaked	drive (driving)	drove	driven
be (am, is, are; being)	was, were	been	eat	ate	eaten
			fall	fell	fallen
bear	bore	born(e)	feed	fed	fed
beat	beat	beaten	feel	felt	felt
become (becoming)	became	become	fight	fought	fought
			find	found	found
begin (beginning)	began	begun	flee	fled	fled
bend	bent	bent	fling	flung	flung
bet (betting)	bet	bet	fly (flies)	flew	flown
bid (bidding)	bid	bid	forbid (forbidding)	forbade	forbidden
bind	bound	bound	foresee	foresaw	foreseen
bite (biting)	bit	bitten	forget (forgetting)	forgot	forgotten
bleed	bled	bled	forgive (forgiving)	forgave	forgiven
blow	blew	blown	freeze (freezing)	froze	frozen
break	broke	broken	get (getting)	got	got, (US) gotten
breed	bred	bred	give (giving)	gave	given
bring	brought	brought	go (goes)	went	gone
build	built	built	grind	ground	ground
burn	burnt (o burned)	burnt (o burned)	grow	grew	grown
			hang	hung (o hanged)	hung (o hanged)
burst	burst	burst	buy	bought	bought
buy	bought	bought	have (has; having)	had	had
can	could	(been able)	hear	heard	heard
cast	cast	cast	hide (hiding)	hid	hidden
catch	caught	caught	hit (hitting)	hit	hit
choose (choosing)	chose	chosen	hold	held	held
cling	clung	clung	hurt	hurt	hurt
come (coming)	came	come	keep	kept	kept
cost	cost	cost	kneel	knelt (o kneeled)	knelt (o kneeled)
creep	crept	crept	know	knew	known
cut (cutting)	cut	cut	lay	laid	laid
deal	dealt	dealt	lead	led	led
dig (digging)	dug	dug			
do (does)	did	done			
draw	drew	drawn			
dream	dreamed (o dreamt)	dreamed (o dreamt)			

present	past tense	past participle	present	past tense	past participle
lean	leant (o leaned)	leant (o leaned)	shoot	shot	shot
leap	leapt (o leaped)	leapt (o leaped)	show	showed	shown
			shrink	shrank	shrunk
learn	learnt (o learned)	learnt (o learned)	shut (shutting)	shut	shut
			sing	sang	sung
leave (leaving)	left	left	sink	sank	sunk
lend	lent	lent	sit (sitting)	sat	sat
let (letting)	let	let	sleep	slept	slept
lie (lying)	lay	lain	slide (sliding)	slid	slid
light	lit (o lighted)	lit (o lighted)	sling	slung	slung
			slit (slitting)	slit	slit
lose (losing)	lost	lost	smell	smelt (o smelled)	smelt (o smelled)
make (making)	made	made			
may	might	–	sow	sowed	sown (o sowed)
mean	meant	meant	speak	spoke	spoken
meet	met	met	speed	sped (o speeded)	sped (o speeded)
mow	mowed	mown (o mowed)	spell	spelt (o spelled)	spelt (o spelled)
must	(had to)	(had to)	spend	spent	spent
pay	paid	paid	spin (spinning)	spun	spun
put (putting)	put	put	spit (spitting)	spat	spat
quit (quitting)	quit (o quitted)	quit (o quitted)	split (splitting)	split	split
read	read	read	spoil	spoiled (o spoilt)	spoiled (o spoilt)
rid (ridding)	rid	rid			
ride (riding)	rode	ridden	spread	spread	spread
ring	rang	rung	spring	sprang	sprung
rise (rising)	rose	risen	stand	stood	stood
run (running)	ran	run	steal	stole	stolen
saw	sawed	sawn	stick	stuck	stuck
say	said	said	sting	stung	stung
see	saw	seen	stink	stank	stunk
seek	sought	sought	strike (striking)	struck	struck
sell	sold	sold	strive (striving)	strove	striven
send	sent	sent			
set (setting)	set	set	swear	swore	sworn
shake (shaking)	shook	shaken	sweep	swept	swept
shall	should	–	swell	swelled	swollen (o swelled)
shine (shining)	shone	shone			

present	past tense	past participle	present	past tense	past participle
swim (swimming)	swam	swum	wake (waking)	woke (o waked)	woken (o waked)
swing	swung	swung	wear	wore	worn
take (taking)	took	taken	weave (weaving)	wove (o weaved)	woven (o weaved)
teach	taught	taught	weep	wept	wept
tear	tore	torn	win (winning)	won	won
tell	told	told			
think	thought	thought	wind	wound	wound
throw	threw	thrown	write (writing)	wrote	written
thrust	thrust	thrust			
tread	trod	trodden			

IRREGULAR GERMAN VERBS

Infinitiv	Präsens 2., 3. Singular	Imperfekt	Partizip Perfekt
backen	bäckst, bäckt	backte o buk	gebacken
befehlen	befiehlst, befiehlt	befahl	befohlen
beginnen	beginnst, beginnt	begann	begonnen
beißen	beißt, beißt	biss	gebissen
bergen	birgst, birgt	barg	geborgen
betrügen	betrügst, betrügt	betrog	betrogen
biegen	biegst, biegt	bog	gebogen
bieten	bietest, bietet	bot	geboten
binden	bindest, bindet	band	gebunden
bitten	bittest, bittet	bat	gebeten
blasen	bläst, bläst	blies	geblasen
bleiben	bleibst, bleibt	blieb	geblieben
braten	brätst, brät	briet	gebraten
brechen	brichst, bricht	brach	gebrochen
brennen	brennst, brennt	brannte	gebrannt
bringen	bringst, bringt	brachte	gebracht
denken	denkst, denkt	dachte	gedacht
dringen	dringst, dringt	drang	gedrungen
dürfen	darfst, darf	durfte	gedurft
erschrecken	erschrickst, erschrickt	erschrak	erschrocken
essen	isst, isst	aß	gegessen
fahren	fährst, fährt	fuhr	gefahren
fallen	fällst, fällt	fiel	gefallen
fangen	fängst, fängt	fing	gefangen
finden	findest, findet	fand	gefunden
fliegen	fliegst, fliegt	flog	geflogen
fließen	fließt, fließt	floss	geflossen
fressen	frisst, frisst	fraß	gefressen
frieren	frierst, friert	fror	gefroren
geben	gibst, gibt	gab	gegeben
gehen	gehst, geht	ging	gegangen
gelingen	–, gelingt	gelang	gelungen
gelten	giltst, gilt	galt	gegolten
genießen	genießt, genießt	genoss	genossen
geschehen	–, geschieht	geschah	geschehen
gewinnen	gewinnst, gewinnt	gewann	gewonnen
gießen	gießt, gießt	goss	gegossen
gleichen	gleichst, gleicht	glich	geglichen
gleiten	gleitest, gleitet	glitt	geglitten
graben	gräbst, gräbt	grub	gegraben
greifen	greifst, greift	griff	gegriffen
haben	hast, hat	hatte	gehabt
halten	hältst, hält	hielt	gehalten
hängen	hängst, hängt	hing	gehangen

Infinitiv	Präsens 2., 3. Singular	Imperfekt	Partizip Perfekt
heben	hebst, hebt	hob	gehoben
heißen	heißt, heißt	hieß	geheißen
helfen	hilfst, hilft	half	geholfen
kennen	kennst, kennt	kannte	gekannt
klingen	klingst, klingt	klang	geklungen
kommen	kommst, kommt	kam	gekommen
können	kannst, kann	konnte	gekonnt
kriechen	kriechst, kriecht	kroch	gekrochen
laden	lädst, lädt	lud	geladen
lassen	lässt, lässt	ließ	gelassen
laufen	läufst, läuft	lief	gelaufen
leiden	leidest, leidet	litt	gelitten
leihen	leihst, leiht	lieh	geliehen
lesen	liest, liest	las	gelesen
liegen	liegst, liegt	lag	gelegen
lügen	lügst, lügt	log	gelogen
mahlen	mahlst, mahlt	mahlte	gemahlen
meiden	meidest, meidet	mied	gemieden
messen	misst, misst	maß	gemessen
mögen	magst, mag	mochte	gemocht
müssen	musst, muss	musste	gemusst
nehmen	nimmst, nimmt	nahm	genommen
nennen	nennst, nennt	nannte	genannt
pfeifen	pfeifst, pfeift	pfiff	gepfiffen
raten	rätst, rät	riet	geraten
reiben	reibst, reibt	rieb	gerieben
reißen	reißt, reißt	riss	gerissen
reiten	reitest, reitet	ritt	geritten
rennen	rennst, rennt	rannte	gerannt
riechen	riechst, riecht	roch	gerochen
rufen	rufst, ruft	rief	gerufen
saufen	säufst, säuft	soff	gesoffen
saugen	saugst, saugt	sog o saugte	gesogen o gesaugt
schaffen	schaffst, schafft	schuf	geschaffen
scheiden	scheidest, scheidet	schied	geschieden
scheinen	scheinst, scheint	schien	geschienen
schieben	schiebst, schiebt	schob	geschoben
schießen	schießt, schießt	schoss	geschossen
schlafen	schläfst, schläft	schlief	geschlafen
schlagen	schlägst, schlägt	schlug	geschlagen
schleichen	schleichst, schleicht	schlich	geschlichen
schließen	schließt, schließt	schloss	geschlossen
schmeißen	schmeißt, schmeißt	schmiss	geschmissen
schmelzen	schmilzt, schmilzt	schmolz	geschmolzen
schneiden	schneidest, schneidet	schnitt	geschnitten

Infinitiv	Präsens 2., 3. Singular	Imperfekt	Partizip Perfekt
schreiben	schreibst, schreibt	schrieb	geschrieben
schreien	schreist, schreit	schrie	geschrie(e)n
schweigen	schweigst, schweigt	schwieg	geschwiegen
schwellen	schwillst, schwillt	schwoll	geschwollen
schwimmen	schwimmst, schwimmt	schwamm	geschwommen
schwören	schwörst, schwört	schwor	geschworen
sehen	siehst, sieht	sah	gesehen
sein	bist, ist	war	gewesen
senden	sendest, sendet	sandte	gesandt
singen	singst, singt	sang	gesungen
sinken	sinkst, sinkt	sank	gesunken
sitzen	sitzt, sitzt	saß	gesessen
sollen	sollst, soll	sollte	gesollt
sprechen	sprichst, spricht	sprach	gesprochen
springen	springst, springt	sprang	gesprungen
stechen	stichst, sticht	stach	gestochen
stehen	stehst, steht	stand	gestanden
stehlen	stiehlst, stiehlt	stahl	gestohlen
steigen	steigst, steigt	stieg	gestiegen
sterben	stirbst, stirbt	starb	gestorben
stinken	stinkst, stinkt	stank	gestunken
stoßen	stößt, stößt	stieß	gestoßen
streichen	streichst, streicht	strich	gestrichen
streiten	streitest, streitet	stritt	gestritten
tragen	trägst, trägt	trug	getragen
treffen	triffst, trifft	traf	getroffen
treiben	treibst, treibt	trieb	getrieben
treten	trittst, tritt	trat	getreten
trinken	trinkst, trinkt	trank	getrunken
tun	tust, tut	tat	getan
verderben	verdirbst, verdirbt	verdarb	verdorben
vergessen	vergisst, vergisst	vergaß	vergessen
verlieren	verlierst, verliert	verlor	verloren
verschwinden	verschwindest, verschwindet	verschwand	verschwunden
verzeihen	verzeihst, verzeiht	verzieh	verziehen
wachsen	wächst, wächst	wuchs	gewachsen
wenden	wendest, wendet	wandte	gewandt
werben	wirbst, wirbt	warb	geworben
werden	wirst, wird	wurde	geworden
werfen	wirfst, wirft	warf	geworfen
wiegen	wiegst, wiegt	wog	gewogen
wissen	weißt, weiß	wusste	gewusst
wollen	willst, will	wollte	gewollt
ziehen	ziehst, zieht	zog	gezogen
zwingen	zwingst, zwingt	zwang	gezwungen

a

à prep +akk at ... each; **4 Tickets ~ 8 Euro** 4 tickets at 8 euros each

A abk = **Autobahn** ≈ M (Brit), ≈ I (US)

Aal (-(e)s, -e) m eel

⭕ SCHLÜSSELWORT

ab prep +dat from; **Kinder ab 12 Jahren** children from the age of 12; **ab morgen** from tomorrow; **ab sofort** as of now
▷ adv 1 off; **links ab** to the left; **der Knopf ist ab** the button has come off; **ab nach Hause!** off you go home
2 (zeitlich) **von da ab** from then on; **von heute ab** from today, as of today
3 (auf Fahrplänen) **München ab 12.20** leaving Munich 12.20
4 **ab und zu** o **an** now and then o again

ab|bauen vt (Zelt) to take down; (verringern) to reduce

ab|beißen irr vt to bite off

ab|bestellen vt to cancel

ab|biegen irr vi to turn off; (Straße) to bend; **nach links/rechts ~** to turn left/right

Abbildung f illustration

ab|blasen irr vt (fig) to call off

ab|blenden vt, vi (Auto) (**die Scheinwerfer**) **~** to dip (Brit) (o to dim (US)) one's headlights; **Abblendlicht** nt dipped (Brit) (o dimmed (US)) headlights pl

ab|brechen irr vt to break off; (Gebäude) to pull down; (aufhören) to stop; (Computerprogramm) to abort

ab|bremsen vi to brake, to slow down

ab|bringen irr vt: **jdn von einer Idee ~** to talk sb out of an idea; **jdn vom Thema ~** to get sb away from the subject; **davon lasse ich mich nicht ~** nothing will make me change my mind about it

ab|buchen vt to debit (von to)

ab|danken vi to resign

ab|drehen vt (Gas, Wasser) to turn off; (Licht) to switch off ▷ vi (Schiff, Flugzeug) to change course

Abend (-s, -e) m evening; **am ~** in the evening; **zu ~ essen** to have dinner; **heute/morgen/gestern** **~** this/tomorrow/yesterday evening; **guten ~!** good evening; **Abendbrot** nt supper; **Abendessen** nt dinner; **Abendgarderobe** f evening dress (o gown); **Abendkasse** f box office; **Abendkleid** nt evening dress (o gown); **Abendmahl** nt: **das ~** (Holy) Communion; **abends** adv in the evening; **montags ~** on Monday evenings

Abenteuer (-s, -) nt adventure; **Abenteuerurlaub** m adventure holiday

aber conj but; (jedoch) however; **oder ~** alternatively; **~ ja!** (but) of course; **das ist ~ nett von Ihnen** that's really nice of you

abergläubisch adj superstitious

ab|fahren irr vi to leave (o to depart) (nach for); (Ski) to ski down; **Abfahrt** f departure; (von Autobahn) exit; (Ski) descent; (Piste) run; **Abfahrtslauf** m (Ski) downhill; **Abfahrtszeit** f departure time

Abfall m waste; (Müll) rubbish (Brit), garbage (US); **Abfalleimer** m rubbish bin (Brit), garbage can (US)

abfällig adj disparaging; **~ von jdm sprechen** to make disparaging remarks about sb

ab|färben vi (Wäsche) to run; (fig) to rub off

ab|fertigen vt (Pakete) to prepare for dispatch; (an der Grenze) to clear; **Abfertigungsschalter** m (am Flughafen) check-in desk

ab|finden irr vt to pay off ▷ vr: **sich mit etw ~** to come to terms with sth; **Abfindung** f (Entschädigung) compensation; (von Angestellten) redundancy payment

ab|fliegen irr vi (Flugzeug) to take off; (Passagier a.) to fly off; **Abflug** m departure; (Start) takeoff; **Abflughalle** f departure lounge; **Abflugzeit** f departure time

Abfluss m drain; (am Waschbecken) plughole (Brit); **Abflussrohr** nt waste pipe; (außen) drainpipe

ab|fragen vt to test; (Inform) to call up

ab|führen vi (Med) to have a laxative effect ▷ vt (Steuern, Gebühren) to pay; **jdn ~ lassen** to take sb into custody; **Abführmittel** nt laxative

Abgabe f handing in; (von Ball) pass; (Steuer) tax; (einer Erklärung) making; **abgabenfrei** adj tax-free; **abgabenpflichtig** adj liable to tax

Abgase pl (Auto) exhaust fumes pl; **Abgas(sonder)untersuchung** f exhaust emission test

ab|geben irr vt (Gepäck, Schlüssel) to leave (bei with); (Schularbeit etc) to hand in; (Wärme) to give off; (Erklärung, Urteil) to make ▷ vr: **sich mit jdm ~** to associate with sb; **sich mit etw ~** to bother with sth

abgebildet adj: **wie oben ~** as shown above

ab|gehen irr vi (Post) to go; (Knopf etc) to come off; (abgezogen werden) to be taken off; (Straße) to branch off; **von der Schule ~** to leave school; **sie geht mir ab** I really miss her; **was geht denn hier ab?** (fam) what's going on here?

abgehetzt adj exhausted, shattered

abgelaufen adj (Pass) expired; (Zeit, Frist) up; **die Milch ist ~** the milk is past its sell-by date

abgelegen adj remote

abgemacht interj OK, it's a deal, that's settled, then

abgeneigt adj **einer Sache** (dat) **~ sein** to be averse to sth; **ich wäre nicht ~, das zu tun** I wouldn't mind doing that

Abgeordnete(r) mf Member of Parliament

abgepackt adj prepacked

abgerissen adj: **der Knopf ist ~** the button has come off

abgesehen adj: **es auf jdn/etw ~ haben** to be after sb/sth; **~ von** apart from

abgespannt adj (Person) exhausted, worn out

abgestanden adj stale; (Bier) flat

abgestorben adj (Pflanze) dead; (Finger) numb

abgestumpft adj (Person) insensitive

abgetragen adj (Kleidung) worn

ab|gewöhnen vt: **jdm etw ~** to cure sb of sth; **sich etw ~** to give sth up

ab|haken vt to tick off; **das (Thema) ist schon abgehakt** that's been dealt with

ab|halten irr vt (Versammlung) to hold; **jdn von etw ~** (fernhalten) to keep sb away from sth; (hindern) to keep sb from sth

abhanden adj: **~ kommen** to get lost

Abhang m slope

ab|hängen vt (Bild) to take down; (Anhänger) to uncouple; (Verfolger) to shake off ▷ irr vi: **von jdm/etw ~** to depend on sb/sth; **das hängt davon ab, ob ...** it depends (on) whether ...;

abhängig adj dependent (von on)

ab|hauen irr vt (abschlagen) to cut off ▷ vi (fam: verschwinden) to clear off; **hau ab!** get lost!, beat it!

ab|heben irr vt (Geld) to withdraw; (Telefonhörer, Spielkarten) to pick up ▷ vi (Flugzeug) to take off; (Rakete) to lift off; (Karten) to cut

ab|holen vt to collect; (am Bahnhof etc) to meet; (mit dem Auto) to pick up; **Abholmarkt** m cash and carry

ab|horchen vt (Med) to listen to

ab|hören vt (Vokabeln) to test; (Telefongespräch) to tap; (Tonband etc) to listen to

Abitur (-s, -e) nt German school-leaving examination, ≈ A-levels (Brit), ~ High School Diploma (US)

ab|kaufen vt: **jdm etw ~** to buy sth from sb; **das kauf ich dir nicht ab!** (fam: glauben) I don't believe you

ab|klingen irr vi (Schmerz) to ease; (Wirkung) to wear off

ab|kommen irr vi to get away; **von der Straße ~** to leave the road; **von einem Plan ~** to give up a plan; **vom Thema ~** to stray from the point

Abkommen (-s, -) nt agreement

ab|koppeln vt (Anhänger) to unhitch

ab|kratzen vt to scrape off ▷ vi (fam: sterben) to kick the bucket, to croak

ab|kühlen vi, vt to cool down ▷ vr: **sich ~** to cool down

ab|kürzen vt (Wort) to abbreviate; **den Weg ~** to take a short cut; **Abkürzung** f (Wort) abbreviation; (Weg) short cut

ab|laden irr vt to unload

Ablage f (für Akten) tray; (Aktenordnung) filing system

Ablauf m (Abfluss) drain; (von Ereignissen) course; (einer Frist, Zeit) expiry; **ab|laufen** irr vi (abfließen) to drain away; (Ereignisse) to happen; (Frist, Zeit, Pass) to expire

ab|legen vt to put down; (Kleider) to take off; (Gewohnheit) to get out of; (Prüfung) to take, to sit; (Akten) to file away ▷ vi (Schiff) to cast off

ab|lehnen vt to reject; (Einladung) to decline; (missbilligen) to disapprove of; (*Bewerber*) to turn down ▷ *vi* to decline

ab|lenken *vt* to distract; **jdn von der Arbeit ~** to distract sb from their work; **vom Thema ~** to change the subject; **Ablenkung** *f* distraction

ab|lesen *vt* (*Text, Rede*) to read; **das Gas/den Strom ~** to read the gas/electricity meter

ab|liefern *vt* to deliver

ab|machen *vt* (*entfernen*) to take off; (*vereinbaren*) to agree; **Abmachung** *f* agreement

ab|melden *vt* (*Zeitung*) to cancel; (*Auto*) to take off the road ▷ *vr*: **sich ~** to give notice of one's departure; (*im Hotel*) to check out; (*vom Verein*) to cancel one's membership

ab|messen *irr vt* to measure

ab|nehmen *irr vt* to take off, to remove; (*Hörer*) to pick up; (*Führerschein*) to take away; (*Geld*) to get (*jdm out of sb*); (*kaufen, umg: glauben*) to buy (*jdm from sb*) ▷ *vi* to decrease; (*schlanker werden*) to lose weight; (*Tel*) to pick up the phone; **fünf Kilo ~** to lose five kilos

Abneigung *f* dislike (*gegen* of); (*stärker*) aversion (*gegen* to)

ab|nutzen *vt* to wear out ▷ *vr*: **sich ~** to wear out

Abonnement (-s, -s) *nt* subscription; **Abonnent(in)** *m(f)* subscriber; **abonnieren** *vt* to subscribe to

ab|raten *irr vi*: **jdm von etw ~** to advise sb against sth

ab|räumen *vt*: **den Tisch ~** to clear the table; **das Geschirr ~** to clear away the dishes; (*Preis etc*) to walk off with

Abrechnung *f* settlement; (*Rechnung*) bill

ab|regen *vr*: **sich ~** (*fam*) to calm

(*o to cool*) down; **reg dich ab!** take it easy

Abreise *f* departure; **ab|reisen** *vi* to leave (*nach* for); **Abreisetag** *m* day of departure

ab|reißen *irr vt* (*Haus*) to pull down; (*Blatt*) to tear off; **den Kontakt nicht ~ lassen** to stay in touch ▷ *vi* (*Knopf etc*) to come off

ab|runden *vt*: **eine Zahl nach oben/unten ~** to round a number up/down

abrupt *adj* abrupt

ABS *nt abk* = **Antiblockiersystem** (*Auto*) ABS

Abs. *abk* = **Absender** from

ab|sagen *vt* to cancel, to call off; (*Einladung*) to turn down ▷ *vi* (*ablehnen*) to decline; **ich muss leider ~** I'm afraid I can't come

Absatz *m* (*Comm*) sales *pl*; (*neuer Abschnitt*) paragraph; (*Schuh*) heel

ab|schaffen *vt* to abolish, to do away with

ab|schalten *vt, vi* (*a. fig*) to switch off

ab|schätzen *vt* to estimate; (*Lage*) to assess

abscheulich *adj* disgusting

ab|schicken *vt* to send off

ab|schieben *irr vt* (*ausweisen*) to deport

Abschied (-(e)s, -e) *m* parting; **~ nehmen** to say good-bye (*von jdm* to sb); **Abschiedsfeier** *f* farewell party

Abschlagszahlung *f* interim payment

Abschleppdienst *m* (*Auto*) breakdown service; **ab|schleppen** *vt* to tow; **Abschleppseil** *nt* towrope; **Abschleppwagen** *m* breakdown truck (*Brit*), tow truck (*US*)

ab|schließen *irr vt* (*Tür*) to lock; (*beenden*) to conclude, to finish; (*Vertrag, Handel*) to conclude;

Abschluss m (Beendigung) close, conclusion; (von Vertrag, Handel) conclusion

ab|schmecken vt (kosten) to taste; (würzen) to season

ab|schminken vr: **sich ~** to take one's make-up off ▷ vt (fam) **sich** (dat) **etw ~** to get sth out of one's mind

ab|schnallen vr: **sich ~** to undo one's seatbelt

ab|schneiden irr vt to cut off ▷ vi: **gut/schlecht ~** to do well/badly

Abschnitt m (von Buch, Text) section; (Kontrollabschnitt) stub

ab|schrauben vt to unscrew

ab|schrecken vt to deter, to put off

ab|schreiben irr vt to copy (bei, von from, off); (verloren geben) to write off; (Comm: absetzen) to deduct

abschüssig adj steep

ab|schwächen vt to lessen; (Behauptung, Kritik) to tone down

ab|schwellen irr vi (Entzündung) to go down; (Lärm) to die down

absehbar adj foreseeable; **in ~er Zeit** in the foreseeable future; **ab|sehen** irr vt (Ende, Folgen) to foresee ▷ vi: **von etw ~** to refrain from sth

abseits adv out of the way; (Sport) offside ▷ prep +gen away from; **Abseits** nt (Sport) offside; **Abseitsfalle** f (Sport) offside trap

ab|senden irr vt to send off; (Post) to post; **Absender(in)** (-s, -) m(f) sender

ab|setzen vt (Glas, Brille etc) to put down; (aussteigen lassen) to drop (off); (Comm) to sell; (Fin) to deduct; (streichen) to drop ▷ vr: **sich ~** (sich entfernen) to clear off; (sich ablagern) to be deposited

Absicht f intention; **mit ~** on

purpose; **absichtlich** adj intentional, deliberate

absolut adj absolute

ab|specken vi (fam) to lose weight

ab|speichern vt (Inform) to save

ab|sperren vt to block (o to close) off; (Tür) to lock; **Absperrung** f (Vorgang) blocking (o closing) off; (Sperre) barricade

ab|spielen vt (CD etc) to play ▷ vr: **sich ~** to happen

ab|springen irr vi to jump down/off; (von etw Geplantem) to drop out (von of)

ab|spülen vt to rinse; (Geschirr) to wash (up)

Abstand m distance; (zeitlich) interval; **~ halten** to keep one's distance

ab|stauben vt, vi to dust; (fam: stehlen) to pinch

Abstecher (-s, -) m detour

ab|steigen irr vi (vom Rad etc) to get off, to dismount; (in Gasthof) to stay (in +dat at)

ab|stellen vt (niederstellen) to put down; (Auto) to park; (ausschalten) to turn (o to switch) off; (Missstand, Unsitte) to stop; **Abstellraum** m store room

Abstieg (-(e)s, -e) m (vom Berg) descent; (Sport) relegation

ab|stimmen vi to vote ▷ vt (Termine, Ziele) to fit in (auf +akk with); **Dinge aufeinander ~** to coordinate things ▷ vr: **sich ~** to come to an agreement (o arrangement)

abstoßend adj repulsive

abstrakt adj abstract

ab|streiten irr vt to deny

Abstrich m (Med) smear; **~e machen** to cut back (an +dat on); (weniger erwarten) to lower one's sights

Absturz m fall; (Aviat, Inform)

crash; ab|stürzen vi to fall;
(Aviat, Inform) to crash

absurd adj absurd

Abszess (-es, -e) m abscess

ab|tauen vt, vi to thaw;
(Kühlschrank) to defrost

Abtei (-, -en) f abbey

Abteil (-(e)s, -e) nt compartment

Abteilung f (in Firma, Kaufhaus)
department; (in Krankenhaus)
section

ab|treiben irr vt (Kind) to abort
▷ vi to be driven off course; (Med:
Abtreibung vornehmen) to carry out
an abortion; (Abtreibung vornehmen
lassen) to have an abortion;
Abtreibung f abortion

ab|trocknen vt to dry

ab|warten vt to wait for; das
bleibt abzuwarten that remains
to be seen ▷ vi to wait

abwärts adv down

Abwasch (-(e)s) m washing-up;
ab|waschen irr vt (Schmutz) to
wash off; (Geschirr) to wash (up)

Abwasser (-s, Abwässer) nt
sewage

ab|wechseln vr: sich ~ to
alternate; sich mit jdm ~ to take
turns with sb; abwechselnd adv
alternately; Abwechslung f
change; zur ~ for a change

ab|weisen irr vt to turn away;
(Antrag) to turn down; abweisend
adj unfriendly

abwesend adj absent;
Abwesenheit f absence

ab|wiegen irr vt to weigh (out)

ab|wimmeln vt (fam) jdn ~ to
get rid of sb, to give sb the elbow

ab|wischen vt (Gesicht, Tisch etc)
to wipe; (Schmutz) to wipe off

ab|zählen vt to count; (Geld) to
count out

Abzeichen nt badge

ab|zeichnen vt to draw, to copy;
(Dokument) to initial ▷ vr: sich

~ to stand out; (fig: bevorstehen) to
loom

ab|ziehen irr vt to take off; (Bett)
to strip; (Schlüssel) to take out;
(subtrahieren) to take away, to
subtract ▷ vi to go away

Abzug m (Foto) print; (Öffnung)
vent; (Truppen) withdrawal;
(Betrag) deduction; nach ~ der
Kosten charges deducted;
abzüglich prep +gen minus;
~ 20% Rabatt less 20% discount

ab|zweigen vi to branch off ▷ vt
to set aside; Abzweigung f
junction

Accessoires pl accessories pl

ach interj oh; ~ so! oh, I see;
~ was! (Überraschung) really?;
(Ärger) don't talk nonsense

Achse (-, -n) f axis; (Auto) axle

Achsel (-, -n) f shoulder;
(Achselhöhle) f armpit

Achsenbruch m (Auto) broken
axle

acht num eight; heute in ~ Tagen
in a week('s time), a week from
today

Acht (-) f: sich in ~ nehmen to be
careful (vor +dat of), to watch out
(vor +dat for); etw außer ~ lassen
to disregard sth

achte(r, s) adj eighth; siehe auch
dritte; Achtel (-s, -) nt (Bruchteil)
eighth; (Wein etc) eighth of a litre;
(Glas Wein) ~ small glass

achten vt to respect ▷ vi to pay
attention (auf +akk to)

Achterbahn f big dipper, roller
coaster

acht|geben irr vi to take care
(auf +akk of)

achthundert num eight
hundred; achtmal adv eight
times

Achtung f attention; (Ehrfurcht)
respect ▷ interj look out

achtzehn num eighteen;

achtzehnte(r, s) adj
eighteenth; *siehe auch* **dritte**;

achtzig num eighty; **in den ~er
Jahren** in the eighties;

achtzigste(r, s) adj eightieth

Acker (-s, Äcker) m field

Action (-, -) f (fam) action;
Actionfilm m action film

Adapter (-s, -) m adapter

addieren vt to add (up)

Adel (-s) m nobility; **adelig** adj
noble

Ader (-, -n) f vein

Adjektiv nt adjective

Adler (-s, -) m eagle

adoptieren vt to adopt;
Adoption f adoption;
Adoptiveltern pl adoptive
parents pl; **Adoptivkind** nt
adopted child

Adrenalin (-s) nt adrenalin

Adressbuch nt directory;
(*persönliches*) address book;
Adresse (-, -n) f address;
adressieren vt to address (an
+akk to)

Advent (-s, -) m Advent;
Adventskranz m Advent wreath

Adverb nt adverb

Aerobic (-s) nt aerobics sing

Affäre (-, -n) f affair

Affe (-n, -n) m monkey

Afghanistan (-s) nt
Afghanistan

Afrika (-s) nt Africa;
Afrikaner(in) (-s, -) m(f) African;
afrikanisch adj African

After (-s, -) m anus

Aftershave (-(s), -s) nt
aftershave

AG (-, -s) f abk =
Aktiengesellschaft plc (Brit),
corp. (US)

Agent(in) m(f) agent; **Agentur**
f agency

aggressiv adj aggressive

Ägypten (-s) nt Egypt

ah interj ah, ooh

äh interj (Sprechpause) er, um;
(angeekelt) ugh

aha interj I see, aha

ähneln vi +dat to be like, to
resemble ▷ vr: **sich ~** to be alike (o
similar)

ahnen vt to suspect; **du ahnst es
nicht!** would you believe it?

ähnlich adj similar (dat to); **jdm
~ sehen** to look like sb;
Ähnlichkeit f similarity

Ahnung f idea; (Vermutung)
suspicion; **keine ~!** no idea;
ahnungslos adj unsuspecting

Ahorn (-s, -e) m maple

Aids (-) nt Aids; **aidskrank** adj
suffering from Aids; **Aidstest** m
Aids test

Airbag (-s, -s) m (Auto) airbag;
Airbus m airbus

Akademie (-, -n) f academy;
Akademiker(in) (-s, -) m(f)
(university) graduate

akklimatisieren vr: **sich ~** to
acclimatize oneself

Akkordeon (-s, -s) nt accordion

Akku (-s, -s) m (storage) battery

Akkusativ m accusative (case)

Akne (-, -) f acne

Akrobat(in) (-s, -en) m(f) acrobat

Akt (-(e)s, -e) m act; (Kunst) nude

Akte (-, -n) f file; **etw zu den ~
legen** (a. fig) to file sth away;
Aktenkoffer m briefcase

Aktie (-, -n) f share;
Aktiengesellschaft f public
limited company (Brit),
corporation (US)

Aktion f (Kampagne) campaign;
(Einsatz) operation

Aktionär(in) (-s, -e) m(f)
shareholder

aktiv adj active; **aktivieren** vt
to activate

aktualisieren vt to update;
aktuell adj (Thema) topical;

(modern) up-to-date; (Problem) current; **nicht mehr ~** no longer relevant

Akupunktur f acupuncture

akustisch adj acoustic; **Akustik** f acoustics sing

akut adj acute

AKW (-s, -s) nt abk = **Atomkraftwerk** nuclear power station

Akzent (-(e)s, -e) m accent; (Betonung) stress; **mit starkem schottischen ~** with a strong Scottish accent

akzeptieren vt to accept

Alarm (-(e)s, -e) m alarm; **Alarmanlage** f alarm system; **alarmieren** vt to alarm; **die Polizei ~** to call the police

Albanien (-s) nt Albania

Albatros (-ses, -se) m albatross

albern adj silly

Albtraum m nightmare

Album (-s, Alben) nt album

Algen (Meeresalgen) seaweed sing

Algerien (-s) nt Algeria

Alibi (-s, -s) nt alibi

Alimente pl maintenance sing

Alkohol (-s, -e) m alcohol; **alkoholfrei** adj non-alcoholic; **-es Getränk** soft drink; **Alkoholiker(in)** (-s, -, m(f) alcoholic; **alkoholisch** adj alcoholic; **Alkoholtest** m breathalyser® test (Brit), alcohol test

All (-s) nt universe

O **SCHLÜSSELWORT**

alle(r, s) adj pron 1 (sämtliche) all; **wir alle** all of us; **alle Kinder waren da** all the children were there; **alle Kinder mögen ...** all children like ...; **alle beide** both of us/them; **sie kamen alle** they all came; **alles Gute** all the best; **alles**

in allem all in all

2 (mit Zeit- oder Maßangaben) every; **alle vier Jahre** every four years; **alle fünf Meter** every five metres

▷ pron everything; **alles, was er sagt** everything he says, all that he says

▷ adv (zu Ende, aufgebraucht) finished; **die Milch ist alle** the milk's all gone, there's no milk left; **etw alle machen** to finish sth up

Allee (-, -n) f avenue

allein adj, adv alone; (ohne Hilfe) on one's own, by oneself; **nicht ~** (nicht nur) not only; **allein-erziehend** adj; **-e Mutter** single mother; **Alleinerziehende(r)** mf single mother/father/parent; **alleinstehend** adj single, unmarried

allerbeste(r, s) adj very best

allerdings adv (zwar) admittedly; (gewiss) certainly, sure (US)

allererste(r, s) adj very first; **zu allererst** first of all

Allergie f allergy; **Allergiker(in)** (-s, -) m(f) allergy sufferer; **allergisch** adj allergic (gegen to)

allerhand adj inv (fam) all sorts of; **das ist doch ~!** (Vorwurf) that's the limit

Allerheiligen (-) nt All Saints' Day

allerhöchste(r, s) adj very highest; **allerhöchstens** adv at the very most; **allerlei** adj inv all sorts of; **allerletzte(r, s)** adj very last; **allerwenigste(r, s)** adj very least

alles pron everything; **~ in allem** all in all; siehe auch **alle**

Alleskleber (-s, -) m all-purpose glue

allgemein adj general; **im Allgemeinen** in general;

Allgemeinarzt m,

Allgemeinärztin f GP (Brit), family practitioner (US)
Alligator (-s, -en) m alligator
alljährlich adj annual
allmählich adj gradual ▷ adv gradually
Allradantrieb m all-wheel drive
Alltag m everyday life; **alltäglich** adj everyday; (gewöhnlich) ordinary; (tagtäglich) daily
allzu adv all too
Allzweckreiniger (-s, -) m multi-purpose cleaner
Alpen pl: **die** ~ the Alps pl
Alphabet (-(e)s, -e) nt alphabet; **alphabetisch** adj alphabetical
Alptraum m siehe Albtraum

○   ЅСHLÜ55ELWORT

als konj 1 (zeitlich) when; (gleichzeitig) as; **damals, als ...** (in the days) when ...; **gerade, als ...** just as ...
2 (in der Eigenschaft) than; **als Antwort** as an answer; **als Kind** as a child
3 (bei Vergleichen) than; **ich kam später als er** I came later than he (did) o later than him; **lieber ... als ...** rather ... than ...; **nichts als Ärger** nothing but trouble
4 **als ob/wenn** as if

also konj (folglich) so, therefore ▷ adv, interj so; ~ **gut** (o **schön**)! okay then
alt adj old; **wie ~ sind Sie?** how old are you?; **28 Jahre ~** 28 years old; **vier Jahre älter** four years older
Altar (-(e)s, Altäre) m altar
Alter (-s, -) nt age; (hohes) old age; **im ~ von** at the age of; **er ist in meinem ~** he's my age
alternativ adj alternative; (umweltbewusst) ecologically

minded; (Landwirtschaft) organic;
Alternative f alternative
Altersheim nt old people's home
Altglas nt used glass; **Altglascontainer** m bottle bank; **altmodisch** adj old-fashioned; **Altpapier** nt waste paper; **Altstadt** f old town
Alt-Taste f Alt key
Alufolie f tin (o kitchen) foil
Aluminium (-s) nt aluminium (Brit), aluminum (US)
Alzheimerkrankheit f Alzheimer's (disease)
am kontr von an dem, = **2. Januar** on January 2(nd); ~ **Morgen** in the morning; ~ **Strand** on the beach; ~ **Bahnhof** at the station; **was gefällt Ihnen ~ besten?** what do you like best?; ~ **besten bleiben wir hier** it would be best if we stayed here
Amateur(in) m(f) amateur
ambulant adj outpatient; **kann ich ~ behandelt werden?** can I have it done as an outpatient?; **Ambulanz** f (Krankenwagen) ambulance; (in der Klinik) outpatients' department
Ameise (-, -n) f ant
amen interj amen
Amerika (-s) nt America; **Amerikaner(in)** (-s, -) m(f) American; **amerikanisch** adj American
Ampel (-, -n) f traffic lights pl
Amphitheater nt amphitheatre
Amsel (-, -n) f blackbird
Amt (-(e)s, Ämter) nt (Dienststelle) office, department; (Posten) post; **amtlich** adj official; **Amtszeichen** nt (Tel) dialling tone (Brit), dial tone (US)
amüsant adj amusing; **amüsieren** vt to amuse ▷ vr: **sich ~** to enjoy oneself, to have a good time

○ SCHLÜSSELWORT

an prep +dat 1 (räumlich) (wo?) at; (auf, bei) on; (nahe bei) near; **an diesem Ort** at this place; **an der Wand** on the wall; **zu nahe an etw** too near to sth; **unten am Fluss** down by the river; **Köln liegt am Rhein** Cologne is on the Rhine

2 (zeitlich: wann?) on; **an diesem Tag** on this day; **an Ostern** at Easter

3 **arm an Fett** low in fat; **an etw sterben** to die of sth; **an (und für) sich** actually

▷ prep +akk 1 (räumlich: wohin?) to; **er ging ans Fenster** he went (over) to the window; **etw an die Wand hängen/schreiben** to hang/write sth on the wall

2 (woran?) **an etw denken** to think of sth

3 (gerichtet an) to; **ein Gruß/eine Frage an dich** greetings/a question to you

▷ adv 1 (ungefähr) about; **an die hundert** about a hundred

2 (auf Fahrplänen) Frankfurt an 18.30 arriving Frankfurt 18.30

3 (ab) from; **von dort/heute an** from there/today onwards

4 (angeschaltet, angezogen) on; **das Licht ist an** the light is on; **ohne etwas an** with nothing on; siehe auch **kann**

anal adj anal

analog adj analogous; (Inform) analog

Analyse (-, -n) f analysis; **analysieren** vt to analyse

Ananas (-, - o -se) f pineapple

an|baggern vt (fam) to chat up (Brit), to come on to (US)

Anbau m (Agr) cultivation;

(Gebäude) extension; **an|bauen** vt (Agr) to cultivate; (Gebäudeteil) to build on

an|behalten irr vt to keep on

anbei adv enclosed; **~ sende ich ...** please find enclosed ...

an|beten vt to worship

an|bieten irr vt to offer ▷ vr: **sich ~** to volunteer

an|binden irr vt to tie up

Anblick m sight

an|braten irr vt to brown

an|brechen irr vt to start; (Vorräte, Ersparnisse) to break into; (Flasche, Packung) to open ▷ vi to start; (Tag) to break; (Nacht) to fall

an|brennen irr vt, vi to burn; **das Fleisch schmeckt angebrannt** the meat tastes burnt

an|bringen irr vt (herbeibringen) to bring; (befestigen) to fix, to attach

Andacht (-, -en) f devotion; (Gottesdienst) prayers pl

an|dauern vi to continue, to go on; **andauernd** adj continual

Andenken (-s, -) nt memory; (Gegenstand) souvenir

andere(r, s) adj (weitere) other; (verschieden) different; (folgend) next; **am ~n Tag** the next day; **von etw/jmd ~m sprechen** to talk about sth/sb else; **unter ~m** among other things; **andererseits** adv on the other hand

ändern vt to alter, to change ▷ vr: **sich ~** to change

andernfalls adv otherwise

anders adv differently (als from); **jemand/irgendwo ~** someone/somewhere else; **sie ist ~ als ihre Schwester** she's not like her sister; **es geht nicht ~** there's no other way; **anders(he)rum** adv the other way round; **anderswo** adv somewhere else

anderthalb num one and a half

Änderung f change, alteration
an|deuten vt to indicate; (*Wink geben*) to hint at
Andorra (-s) nt Andorra
Andrang m: **es herrschte großer ~** there was a huge crowd
an|drohen vt: **jdm etw ~ to** threaten sb with sth
aneinander adv at/on/to one another (ó each other); **~ denken** think of each other; **sich ~ gewöhnen** to get used to each other; **aneinander|geraten** irr vi to clash; **aneinander|legen** vt to put together
an|erkennen irr vt (*Staat, Zeugnis etc*) to recognize; (*würdigen*) to appreciate; **Anerkennung** f recognition; (*Würdigung*) appreciation
an|fahren irr vt (*fahren gegen*) to run into; (*Ort, Hafen*) to stop (o call) at; (*liefern*) to deliver; **jdn ~** (*fig: schimpfen*) to jump on sb ▷ vi to start; (*losfahren*) to drive off
Anfall m (*Med*) attack; **anfällig** adj delicate; (*Maschine*) temperamental; **~ für** prone to
Anfang (-(e)s, Anfänge) m beginning, start; **zu/am ~** to start with; **~ Mai** at the beginning of May; **sie ist ~ 20** she's in her early twenties; **an|fangen** irr vt, vi to begin, to start; **damit kann ich nichts ~** that's no use to me; **Anfänger(in)** (-s, -) m(f) beginner; **anfangs** adv at first; **Anfangsbuchstabe** m first (o initial) letter
an|fassen vt (*berühren*) to touch ▷ vi: **kannst du mal mit ~?** can you give me a hand?
Anflug m (*Aviat*) approach; (*Hauch*) trace
an|fordern vt to demand; **Anforderung** f request (*von* for); (*Anspruch*) demand

Anfrage f inquiry
an|freunden vr: **sich mit jdm ~** to make (o to become) friends with sb
an|fühlen vr: **sich ~** to feel; **es fühlt sich gut an** it feels good
Anführungszeichen pl quotation marks pl
Angabe f (*Tech*) specification; (*fam: Prahlerei*) showing off; (*Tennis*) serve; **~n** pl (*Auskunft*) particulars pl; **die ~n waren falsch** (*Info*) the information was wrong; **an|geben** irr vt (*Name, Grund*) to give; (*zeigen*) to indicate; (*bestimmen*) to set ▷ vi (*fam: prahlen*) to boast; (*Sport*) to serve; **Angeber(in)** (-s, -) m(f) (*fam*) show-off; **angeblich** adj alleged
angeboren adj inborn
Angebot nt offer; (*Comm*) supply (*an +dat* of); **~ und Nachfrage** supply and demand
angebracht adj appropriate
angebunden adj: **kurz ~** curt
angeheitert adj tipsy
an|gehen irr vt to concern; **das geht dich nichts an** that's none of your business; **ein Problem ~** to tackle a problem; **was ihn angeht** as far as he's concerned, as for him ▷ vi (*Feuer*) to catch; (*fam: beginnen*) to begin; **angehend** adj prospective
Angehörige(r) mf relative
Angeklagte(r) mf accused, defendant
Angel (-, -n) f fishing rod; (*an der Tür*) hinge
Angelegenheit f affair, matter
Angelhaken m fish hook; **angeln** vt to catch ▷ vi to fish; **Angeln** (-s) nt angling, fishing; **Angelrute** (-, -n) f fishing rod
angemessen adj appropriate, suitable

angenehm adj pleasant; **~! (**bei Vorstellung**)** pleased to meet you

angenommen adj assumed ▷ conj: **~, es regnet, was machen wir dann?** suppose it rains, what do we do then?

angesehen adj respected

angesichts prep +gen in view of, considering

Angestellte(r) mf employee

angetan adj: **von jdm/etw ~ sein** to be impressed by (o taken with) sb/sth

angewiesen adj: **auf jdn/etw ~ sein** to be dependent on sb/sth

an|gewöhnen vt: **sich etw ~** to get used to doing sth; **Angewohnheit** f habit

Angina (-, Anginen) f tonsillitis; **Angina Pectoris** (-) f angina

Angler(in) (-s, -) m(f) angler

Angora (-s) nt angora

an|greifen irr vt to attack; (anfassen) to touch; (beschädigen) to damage; **Angriff** m attack; **etw in ~ nehmen** to get started on sth

Angst (-, Ängste) f fear; **~ haben** to be afraid (o scared) (vor +dat of); **jdm ~ machen** to scare sb; **ängstigen** vt to frighten ▷ vr: **sich ~** to worry (um, wegen +dat about); **ängstlich** adj nervous; (besorgt) worried

an|haben irr vt (Kleidung) to have on, to wear; (Licht) to have on

an|halten irr vi to stop; (andauern) to continue; **anhaltend** adj continuous; **Anhalter(in)** (-s, -) m(f) hitch-hiker; **per ~ fahren** to hitch-hike

anhand prep +gen with; **~ von** by means of

an|hängen vt to hang up; (Eisenb: Wagen) to couple; (Zusatz) to add (on); **jdm etw ~** (fam: unterschieben) to pin sth on sb;

Anhänger (-s, -) m (Auto) trailer; (am Koffer) tag; (Schmuck) pendant; **Anhänger(in)** (-s, -) m(f) supporter; **Anhängerkupplung** f towbar; **anhänglich** adj affectionate; (pej) clinging

Anhieb m: **auf ~** straight away; **das kann ich nicht auf ~ sagen** I can't say offhand

an|himmeln vt to worship, to idolize

an|hören vt to listen to ▷ vr: **sich ~** to sound; **das hört sich gut an** that sounds good

Animateur(in) m(f) host/hostess

Anis (-es, -e) m aniseed

Anker (-s, -) m anchor; **ankern** vt, vi to anchor; **Ankerplatz** m anchorage

an|klicken vt (Inform) to click on

an|klopfen vi to knock (an +akk on)

an|kommen irr vi to arrive; **bei jdm gut ~** to go down well with sb; **es kommt darauf an** it depends (ob on whether); **darauf kommt es nicht an** that doesn't matter

an|kotzen vt (vulg) **es kotzt mich an** it makes me sick

an|kreuzen vt to mark with a cross

an|kündigen vt to announce

Ankunft (-, Ankünfte) f arrival; **Ankunftszeit** f arrival time

Anlage f (Veranlagung) disposition; (Begabung) talent; (Park) gardens pl, grounds pl; (zu Brief etc) enclosure; (Stereoanlage) stereo (system); (Tech) plant; (Fin) investment

Anlass (-es, Anlässe) m cause (zu for); (Ereignis) occasion; **aus diesem ~** for this reason; **an|lassen** irr vt (Motor) to start; (Licht, Kleidung) to leave on;

Anlasser (-s, -) *m* (*Auto*) starter;
anlässlich *prep* +*gen* on the
occasion of

Anlauf *m* run-up; **an|laufen** *irr vi*
to begin; (*Film*) to open; (*Fenster*) to
mist up; (*Metall*) to tarnish

an|legen *vt* to put (*an +akk*
against/on); (*Schmuck*) to put on;
(*Garten*) to lay out; (*Geld*) to invest;
(*Gewehr*) to aim (*auf +akk* at); **es
auf etw** (*akk*) **~ to** be out for sth
▷ *vi* (*Schiff*) to berth, to dock ▷ *vr*:
sich mit jdm ~ (*fam*) to pick a
quarrel with sb; **Anlegestelle** *f*
moorings *pl*

an|lehnen *vt* to lean (*an +akk*
against); (*Tür*) to leave ajar
▷ *vr*: **sich ~** to lean (*an +akk*
against)

an|leiern *vt*: **etw ~** (*fam*) to get
sth going

Anleitung *f* instructions *pl*

Anliegen (-s, -) *nt* matter;
(*Wunsch*) request

Anlieger(in) (-s, -) *m(f)* resident,
~ frei residents only

an|lügen *irr vt* to lie to

an|machen *vt* (*befestigen*) to
attach; (*einschalten*) to switch
on; (*Salat*) to dress; (*fam: aufreizen*)
to turn on; (*fam: ansprechen*) to
chat up (*Brit*), to come on to
(*US*); (*fam: beschimpfen*) to have a
go at

Anmeldeformular *nt* application form; (*bei Amt*) registration
form; **an|melden** (*Besuch etc*)
to announce ▷ *vr*: **sich ~** (*beim
Arzt etc*) to make an appointment;
(*bei Amt, für Kurs etc*) to register;
Anmeldeschluss *m* deadline for
applications, registration
deadline; **Anmeldung** *f*
registration; (*Antrag*) application

an|nähen *vt*: **einen Knopf** (**an
den Mantel**) **~** to sew a button on
(one's coat)

annähernd *adv* roughly; **nicht
~** nowhere near

Annahme (-, -*n*) *f* acceptance;
(*Vermutung*) assumption;
annehmbar *adj* acceptable;
an|nehmen *irr vt* to accept;
(*Namen*) to take; (*Kind*) to adopt;
(*vermuten*) to suppose, to assume

Annonce (-, -*n*) *f* advertisement

an|öden *vt* (*fam*) to bore stiff (*o*
silly)

annullieren *vt* to cancel

anonym *adj* anonymous

Anorak (-s, -s) *m* anorak

an|packen *vt* (*Problem, Aufgabe*)
to tackle; **mit ~** to lend a hand

an|passen *vt* (*fig*) to adapt (*dat
to*) ▷ *vr*: **sich ~** to adapt (*an +akk
to*)

an|pfeifen *irr vt* (*Fußballspiel*)
das Spiel ~ to start the game;
Anpfiff *m* (*Sport*) (*starting*)
whistle; (*Beginn*) kick-off; (*fam:
Tadel*) roasting

an|probieren *vt* to try on

Anrede *f* form of address;
an|reden *vt* to address

an|regen *vt* to stimulate;
Anregung *f* stimulation;
(*Vorschlag*) suggestion

Anreise *f* journey; **an|reisen** *vi*
to arrive; **Anreisetag** *m* day of
arrival

Anreiz *m* incentive

an|richten *vt* (*Speisen*) to
prepare; (*Schaden*) to cause

Anruf *m* call; **Anrufbeantworter**
(-s, -) *m* answering machine,
answerphone; **an|rufen** *irr vt*
(*Tel*) to call, to phone, to ring (*Brit*)

ans *kontr von* an das

Ansage *f* announcement; (*auf
Anrufbeantworter*) recorded
message; **an|sagen** *vt* to
announce; **angesagt sein** to be
recommended; (*modisch sein*) to be
the in thing

an|schaffen vt to buy

an|schauen vt to look at

Anschein m appearance; dem (o allem) ~ nach ... it looks as if ...; den ~ erwecken, hart zu arbeiten to give the impression of working hard; anscheinend adj apparent ▷ adv apparently

an|schieben irr vt: könnten Sie mich mal ~? (Auto) could you give me a push?

Anschlag m notice; (Attentat) attack; an|schlagen irr vt (Plakat) to put up; (beschädigen) to chip ▷ vi (wirken) to take effect; mit etw an etw (akk) ~ to bang sth against sth

an|schließen irr vt (Elek, Tech) to connect (an +akk to); (mit Stecker) to plug in ▷ vi, vr (sich) an etw (akk) ~ (Gebäude etc) to adjoin sth; (zeitlich) to follow sth ▷ vr: sich ~ to join (jdm/einer Gruppe sb/a group); anschließend adj adjacent; (zeitlich) subsequent ▷ adv afterwards; ~ an (+akk) following; Anschluss m (Elek, Eisenb) connection; (von Wasser, Gas etc) supply; im ~ an (+akk) following; kein ~ unter dieser Nummer (Tel) the number you have dialled has not been recognized; Anschlussflug m connecting flight

an|schnallen vt (Skier) to put on ▷ vr: sich ~ to fasten one's seat belt

Anschrift f address

an|schwellen irr vi to swell (up)

an|schwindeln vt (umg): jdn/etw zuschauen) to watch; jdn/etw als etw ~ to look on sb/sth as sth; das sieht man ihm an he looks it

an sein irr vi siehe an

an|setzen vt (Termin) to fix; (zubereiten) to prepare ▷ vi (anfangen) to start, to begin; zu

etw ~ to prepare to do sth

Ansicht f (Meinung) view, opinion; (Anblick) sight; meiner ~ nach in my opinion; zur ~ on approval; Ansichtskarte f postcard

ansonsten adv otherwise

an|spielen vi auf etw (akk) ~ to allude to sth; Anspielung f allusion (auf +akk to)

an|sprechen irr vt to speak to; (gefallen) to appeal to ▷ vi auf etw (akk) ~ (Patient) to respond to sth; ansprechend adj attractive; Ansprechpartner(in) m(f) contact

an|springen irr vi (Auto) to start

Anspruch m claim; (Recht) right (auf +akk to); etw in ~ nehmen to take advantage of sth; ~ auf etw haben to be entitled to sth; anspruchslos adj undemanding; (bescheiden) modest; anspruchsvoll adj demanding

Anstalt (-, -en) f institution

Anstand m decency; anständig adj decent; (fig, fam) proper; (groß) considerable

an|starren vt to stare at

anstatt prep +gen instead of

an|stecken vt to pin on; (Med) to infect; jdn mit einer Erklärung ~ to pass one's cold on to sb ▷ vr: ich habe mich bei ihm angesteckt I caught it from him ▷ vi (fig) to be infectious; ansteckend adj infectious; Ansteckungsgefahr f danger of infection

an|stehen irr vi (in Warteschlange) to queue (Brit), to stand in line (US); (erledigt werden müssen) to be on the agenda

anstelle prep +gen instead of

an|stellen vt (einschalten) to turn on; (Arbeit geben) to employ; (machen) to do; was hast du

wieder angestellt? what have you been up to now? ▷ vr: **sich ~** to queue (Brit), to stand in line (US); (fam) **stell dich nicht so an!** stop making such a fuss

Anstoß m impetus; (Sport) kick-off; **an|stoßen** irr vt to push, (mit Fuß) to kick ▷ vi to knock, to bump; (mit Gläsern) to drink (a toast) (auf +akk to); **anstößig** adj offensive; (Kleidung etc) indecent

an|strengen vt to strain ▷ vr: **sich ~** to make an effort; **anstrengend** adj tiring

Antarktis f Antarctic

Anteil m share (an +dat in); **~ nehmen an** (+dat) (mitleidig) to sympathize with; (sich interessieren) to take an interest in

Antenne (-, -n) f aerial

Antibabypille f: **die ~** the pill; **Antibiotikum** (-s, Antibiotika) nt (Med) antibiotic

antik adj antique

Antilope (-, -n) f antelope

Antiquariat nt (für Bücher) second-hand bookshop

Antiquitäten pl antiques pl; **Antiquitätenhändler(in)** m(f) antique dealer

an|törnen vt (fam) to turn on

Antrag (-(e)s, Anträge) m proposal; (Pol) motion; (Formular) application form; **einen ~ stellen auf** (+akk) to make an application for

an|treffen irr vt to find

an|treiben irr vt (Tech) to drive; (anschwemmen) to wash up; **jdn zur Arbeit ~** to make sb work

an|treten irr vt: **eine Reise ~** to set off on a journey

Antrieb m (Tech) drive; (Motivation) impetus

an|tun irr vt: **jdm etwas ~** to do sth to sb; **sich** (dat) **etwas ~** (Selbstmord begehen) to kill

oneself

Antwort (-, -en) f answer, reply; **um ~ wird gebeten** RSVP (répondez s'il vous plaît); **antworten** vi to answer, to reply; **jdm ~** to answer sb; **auf etw** (akk) **~** to answer sth

an|vertrauen vt: **jdm etw ~** to entrust sb with sth

Anwalt (-s, Anwälte) m, **Anwältin** f lawyer

an|weisen irr vt (anleiten) to instruct; (zuteilen) to allocate (jdm etw sth to sb); **Anweisung** f instruction; (von Geld) money order

an|wenden irr vt to use; (Gesetz, Regel) to apply; **Anwender(in)** (-s, -) m(f) user; **Anwendung** f use; (Inform) application

anwesend adj present; **Anwesenheit** f presence

an|widern vt to disgust

Anwohner(in) (-s, -) m(f) resident

Anzahl f number (an +dat of); **an|zahlen** vt to pay a deposit on; **100 Euro ~** to pay 100 euros as a deposit; **Anzahlung** f deposit

Anzeichen nt sign; (Med) symptom

Anzeige (-, -n) f (Werbung) advertisement; (elektronisch) display; (bei Polizei) report; **an|zeigen** vt (Temperatur, Zeit) to indicate, to show; (elektronisch) to display; (bekannt geben) to announce; **jdn/einen Autodiebstahl bei der Polizei ~** to report sb/a stolen car to the police

an|ziehen irr vt to attract; (Kleidung) to put on; (Schraube, Seil) to tighten ▷ vr: **sich ~** to get dressed; **anziehend** adj attractive

Anzug m suit

anzüglich adj suggestive

an|zünden vt to light; (Haus etc)

to set fire to

an|zweifeln vt to doubt

Aperitif (-s, -s of (-s (o -e)) m aperitif

Apfel (-s, Äpfel) m apple;
Apfelbaum m apple tree;
Apfelkuchen m apple cake;
Apfelmus nt apple purée;
Apfelsaft m apple juice;
Apfelsine f orange; **Apfelwein**
m cider

Apostroph (-s, -e) m apostrophe

Apotheke (-, -n) f chemist's
(shop) (Brit), pharmacy (US);
apothekenpflichtig adj only
available at the chemist's (o
pharmacy); **Apotheker(in)** (-s, -)
m(f) chemist (Brit), pharmacist
(US)

Apparat (-(e)s, -e) m (piece of)
apparatus; (Tel) telephone; (Radio,
TV) set; **am ~!** (Tel) speaking; **am
~ bleiben** (Tel) to hold the line

Appartement (-s, -s) nt studio
flat (Brit) (o apartment (US))

Appetit (-(e)s, -e) m appetite;
guten ~! bon appétit; **appetitlich**
adj appetizing

Applaus (-es, -e) m applause

Aprikose (-, -n) f apricot

April (-(s), -e) m April; siehe auch
Juni; ~, ~! April fool!; **Aprilscherz**
(-es, -e) m April fool's joke

apropos adv by the way;
~ Urlaub ... while we're on the
subject of holidays ...

Aquajogging nt aqua jogging;
Aquaplaning (-(s)) nt
aquaplaning

Aquarell (-s, -e) nt watercolour

Aquarium (-s, Aquarien) nt
aquarium

Äquator (-s, -) m equator

Araber(in) (-s, -) m(f) Arab;
arabisch adj Arab; (Ziffer, Sprache)
Arabic; (Meer, Wüste) Arabian

Arbeit (-, -en) f work; (Stelle) job;
(Erzeugnis) piece of work; **arbeiten**

vi to work; **Arbeiter(in)** (-s, -) m(f)
worker; (ungelernt) labourer;
Arbeitgeber(in) (-s, -) m(f) employer;
Arbeitnehmer(in) (-s, -) m(f) employe
Arbeitsagentur f job agency
(Brit), unemployment agency (US);
Arbeitsamt nt job centre (Brit),
employment office (US);
Arbeitserlaubnis f work permit;
arbeitslos adj unemployed;
Arbeitslose(r) mf unemployed
person; **die ~n** pl the unemployed
pl; **Arbeitslosengeld** nt
(income-related) unemployment
benefit, job-seeker's allowance
(Brit); **Arbeitslosenhilfe** f
(non-income related)
unemployment benefit;
Arbeitslosigkeit f unemployment; **Arbeitsplatz** m job; (Ort)
workplace; **Arbeitsspeicher** m
(Inform) main memory;
Arbeitszeit f working hours pl;
Arbeitszimmer nt study

Archäologe (-n, -n) m,
Archäologin f archaeologist

Architekt(in) (-en, -en) m(f)
architect; **Architektur** f
architecture

Archiv (-s, -e) nt archives pl

arg adj bad; (schrecklich) awful
▷ adv (sehr) terribly

Argentinien (-s) nt Argentina

Ärger (-s) m annoyance; (stärker)
anger; (Unannehmlichkeiten)
trouble; **ärgerlich** adj (zornig)
angry; (lästig) annoying; **ärgern**
vt to annoy ▷ vr: **sich ~** to get
annoyed

Argument (-s, -e) nt argument

Arktis (-) f Arctic

arm adj poor

Arm (-(e)s, -e) m arm; (Fluss)
branch

Armaturenbrett nt instrument
panel; (Auto) dashboard

Armband nt bracelet;

Armbanduhr f (wrist)watch
Armee (-, -n) f army
Ärmel (-s, -) m sleeve;
Ärmelkanal m (English) Channel
Armut (-) f poverty
Aroma (-s, Aromen) nt aroma
arrogant adj arrogant
Arsch (-es, Ärsche) m (vulg) arse
(Brit), ass (US); **Arschloch** nt
(vulg: Person) arsehole (Brit),
asshole (US)
Art (-, -en) f (Weise) way; (Sorte)
kind, sort; (bei Tieren) species;
nach ~ des Hauses à la maison;
auf diese ~ (und Weise) in this
way; **das ist nicht seine ~** that's
not like him
Arterie (-, -n) f artery
artig adj good, well-behaved
Artikel (-s, -) m (Ware) article,
item; (Zeitung) article
Artischocke (-, -n) f artichoke
Artist(in) (-en, -en) m(f) (circus)
performer
Arznei f medicine; **Arzt** (-es,
Ärzte) m doctor; **Arzthelfer(in)**
m(f) doctor's assistant; **Ärztin** f
(female) doctor; **ärztlich** adj
medical; **sich ~ behandeln lassen**
to undergo medical treatment
Asche (-, -n) f ashes pl; (von
Zigarette) ash; **Aschenbecher** m
ashtray; **Aschermittwoch** m
Ash Wednesday
Asiat(in) (-en, -en) m(f) Asian;
asiatisch adj Asian; **Asien** (-s) nt
Asia
Aspekt (-(e)s, -e) m aspect
Asphalt (-(e)s, -e) m asphalt
Aspirin® (-s, -e) nt aspirin
aß imperf von **essen**
Ass (-es, -e) nt (Karten, Tennis) ace
Assistent(in) m(f) assistant
Ast (-(e)s, Äste) m branch
Asthma (-s) nt asthma
Astrologie f astrology;
Astronaut(in) (-en, -en) m(f)

astronaut; **Astronomie** f
astronomy
ASU (-, -s) f abk =
Abgassonderuntersuchung
exhaust emission test
Asyl (-s, -e) nt asylum; (Heim)
home; (für Obdachlose) shelter;
Asylant(in) m(f), **Asylbe-
werber(in)** m(f) asylum seeker
Atelier (-s, -s) nt studio
Atem (-s) m breath;
atemberaubend adj breathtaking; **Atembeschwerden** pl
breathing difficulties pl; **atemlos**
adj breathless; **Atempause** f
breather
Athen nt Athens
Äthiopien (-s) nt Ethiopia
Athlet(in) (-en, -en) m(f) athlete
Atlantik (-s) m Atlantic (Ocean)
Atlas (- o Atlasses, Atlanten) m
atlas
atmen vt, vi to breathe; **Atmung**
f breathing
Atom (-s, -e) nt atom;
Atombombe f atom bomb;
Atomkraftwerk nt nuclear
power station; **Atommüll** m
nuclear waste; **Atomwaffen** pl
nuclear weapons pl
Attentat (-(e)s, -e) nt
assassination (auf +akk of);
(Versuch) assassination attempt
Attest (-(e)s, -e) nt certificate
attraktiv adj attractive
Attrappe (-, -n) f dummy
ätzend adj (fam) revolting;
(schlecht) lousy
au interj ouch; **~ ja!** yeah
Aubergine (-, -n) f aubergine,
eggplant (US)

◯ SCHLÜSSELWORT

auch adv 1 (ebenfalls) also, too, as
well; **das ist auch schön** that's
nice too o as well; **er kommt — ich**

auch he's coming — so am I, me too; **auch nicht** not ... either; **ich auch nicht** nor I, me neither; **oder auch** or; **auch das noch!** not that as well!

2 (*selbst, sogar*) even; **auch wenn das Wetter schlecht ist** even if the weather is bad; **ohne auch nur zu fragen** without even asking

3 (*wirklich*) really; **du siehst müde aus—bin ich auch** you look tired— (so) I am; **so sieht es auch aus** it looks like it too

4 (*auch immer*) **wer auch** whoever; **was auch** whatever; **wie dem auch sei** be that as it may; **wie sehr er sich auch bemühte** however much he tried

audiovisuell *adj* audiovisual

○ SCHLÜSSELWORT

auf *prep* +*dat* (*wo?*) on; **auf dem Tisch** on the table; **auf der Reise** on the way; **auf der Post/dem Fest** at the post office/party; **auf der Straße** on the road; **auf dem Land/der ganzen Welt** in the country/the whole world

▷ *prep* +*akk* 1 (*wohin?*) on(to); **auf den Tisch** on(to) the table; **auf die Post gehen** to go to the post office; **etw auf einen Zettel schreiben** to write sth on a piece of paper

2 (*auf Deutsch*) in German; **auf Lebenszeit** for my/his lifetime; **bis auf ihn** except for him; **auf einmal** at once; **auf seinen Vorschlag (hin)** at his suggestion

▷ *adv* 1 (*offen*) open; **auf sein** (*fam*) (*Tür, Geschäft*) to be open; **das Fenster ist auf** the window is open

2 (*hinauf*) up; **auf und ab** up and down; **auf und davon** up and away; **auf!** (*los!*) come on!

3 (*aufgestanden*) up; **auf sein** to be up; **ist er schon auf?** is he up yet?

▷ *konj*: **auf dass** (so) that

auf|atmen *vi* to breathe a sigh of relief

auf|bauen *vt* (*errichten*) to put up; (*schaffen*) to build up; (*gestalten*) to construct; (*gründen*) to found, to base (*auf* +*akk* on); **sich eine Existenz ~** to make a life for oneself

auf|bewahren *vt* to keep, to store

auf|bleiben *irr vi* (*Tür, Laden etc*) to stay open; (*Mensch*) to stay up

auf|blenden *vi, vt*: (**die Scheinwerfer**) **~** to put one's headlights on full beam

auf|brechen *irr vt* to break open ▷ *vi* to burst open; (*gehen*) to leave; (*abreisen*) to set off

auf|drängen *vt*: **jdm etw ~** to force sth on sb ▷ *vr*: **sich ~** to intrude (*jdm* on sb); **aufdringlich** *adj* pushy

aufeinander *adv* (*übereinander*) on top of each other; **~ achten** to look after each other; **~ vertrauen** to trust each other; **aufeinander|folgen** *vi* to follow one another; **aufeinander|prallen** *vi* to crash into one another

Aufenthalt *m* stay; (*Zug*) stop; **Aufenthaltsgenehmigung** *f* residence permit; **Aufenthaltsraum** *m* lounge

auf|essen *irr vt* to eat up

auf|fahren *irr vi* (*Auto*) to run (*o* to crash) up (*auf* +*akk* into); (*herankommen*) to drive up; **Auffahrt** *f* (*am Haus*) drive; (*Autobahn*) slip road (*Brit*), ramp (*US*); **Auffahrunfall** *m* rear-end collision; (*mehrere Fahrzeuge*) pile-up

auffallen *irr vi* to stand out; **jdm ~** to strike sb; **das fällt gar nicht auf** nobody will notice; **auffallend** *adj* striking; **auffällig** *adj* conspicuous; (*Kleidung, Farbe*) striking

auffangen *irr vt* (*Ball*) to catch; (*Stoß*) to cushion

auffassen *vt* to understand; **Auffassung** *f* view; (*Meinung*) opinion; (*Auslegung*) concept; (*Auffassungsgabe*) grasp

auffordern *vt* (*befehlen*) to call upon; (*bitten*) to ask

auffrischen *vt* (*Kenntnisse*) to brush up

aufführen *vt* (*Theat*) to perform; (*in einem Verzeichnis*) to list; (*Beispiel*) to give ▷ *vr*: **sich ~** (*sich benehmen*) to behave; **Aufführung** *f* (*Theat*) performance

Aufgabe *f* job, task; (*Schule*) exercise; (*Hausaufgabe*) homework

Aufgang *m* (*Treppe*) staircase

aufgeben *irr vt* (*verzichten auf*) to give up; (*Paket*) to post; (*Gepäck*) to check in; (*Bestellung*) to place; (*Inserat*) to insert; (*Rätsel, Problem*) to set ▷ *vi* to give up

aufgehen *irr vi* (*Sonne, Teig*) to rise; (*sich öffnen*) to open; (*klar werden*) to dawn (**jdm** on sb)

aufgelegt *adj*: **gut/schlecht ~** in a good/bad mood

aufgeregt *adj* excited

aufgeschlossen *adj* open(minded)

aufgeschmissen *adj* (*fam*) in a fix

aufgrund, auf Grund *prep +gen* on the basis of; (*wegen*) because of

aufhaben *irr vt* (*Hut etc*) to have on; **viel ~** (*Schule*) to have a lot of homework to do ▷ *vi* (*Geschäft*) to be open

aufhalten *irr vt* (*jdn*) to detain; (*Entwicklung*) to stop; (*Tür, Hand*) to hold open; (*Augen*) to keep open ▷ *vr*: **sich ~** (*wohnen*) to live; (*vorübergehend*) to stay

aufhängen *irr vt* to hang up

aufheben *irr vt* (*vom Boden etc*) to pick up; (*aufbewahren*) to keep

aufholen *vt* (*Zeit*) to make up ▷ *vi* to catch up

aufhören *vi* to stop; **~, etw zu tun** to stop doing sth

aufklären *vt* (*Geheimnis etc*) to clear up; **jdn ~** to enlighten sb; (*sexuell*) to tell sb the facts of life

Aufkleber (*-s, -*) *m* sticker

aufkommen *irr vi* (*Wind*) to come up; (*Zweifel, Gefühl*) to arise; (*Mode etc*) to appear on the scene; **für den Schaden ~** to pay for the damage

aufladen *irr vt* to load; (*Handy etc*) to charge; (*Handykarte etc*) to top up; **Aufladegerät** *nt* charger

Auflage *f* edition; (*von Zeitung*) circulation; (*Bedingung*) condition

auflassen *vt* (*Hut, Brille*) to keep on; (*Tür*) to leave open

Auflauf *m* (*Menschen*) crowd; (*Speise*) bake

auflegen *vt* (*CD, Schminke etc*) to put on; (*Hörer*) to put down ▷ *vi* (*Tel*) to hang up

aufleuchten *vi* to light up

auflösen *vt* (*in Flüssigkeit*) to dissolve ▷ *vr*: **sich ~** (*in Flüssigkeit*) to dissolve; **der Stau hat sich aufgelöst** traffic is back to normal; **Auflösung** *f* (*von Rätsel*) solution; (*von Bildschirm*) resolution

aufmachen *vt* to open; (*Kleidung*) to undo ▷ *vr*: **sich ~** to set out (*nach for*)

aufmerksam *adj* attentive; **jdn auf etw** (*akk*) **~ machen** to draw sb's attention to sth;

Aufmerksamkeit f attention; (*Konzentration*) attentiveness; (*Geschenk*) small token

auf|muntern vt (*ermutigen*) to encourage; (*aufheitern*) to cheer up

Aufnahme (-, -n) f (*Foto*) photo(graph); (*einzelne*) shot; (*in Verein, Krankenhaus etc*) admission; (*Beginn*) beginning; (*auf Tonband etc*) recording; **Aufnahmeprüfung** f entrance exam; **auf|nehmen** *irr* vt (*in Krankenhaus, Verein etc*) to admit; (*Musik*) to record; (*beginnen*) to begin; (*in Liste*) to include; (*begreifen*) to take in; **mit jdm Kontakt ~** to get in touch with sb

auf|passen vi (*aufmerksam sein*) to pay attention; (*vorsichtig sein*) to take care; **auf jdn/etw ~** to keep an eye on sb/sth

Aufprall (-s, -e) m impact; **auf|prallen** vi **auf etw** (*akk*) **~** to hit sth, to crash into sth

Aufpreis m extra charge

auf|pumpen vt to pump up

Aufputschmittel nt stimulant

auf|räumen vt, vi (*Dinge*) to clear away; (*Zimmer*) to tidy up

aufrecht adj upright

auf|regen vt to excite; (*ärgern*) to annoy ▷ vr: **sich ~** to get worked up; **aufregend** adj exciting; **Aufregung** f excitement

auf|reißen *irr* vt (*Tüte*) to tear open; (*Tür*) to fling open; (*fam: Person*) to pick up

Aufruf m (*Aviat, Inform*) call; (*öffentlicher*) appeal; **auf|rufen** *irr* vt (*auffordern*) to call upon (*zu for*); (*Namen*) to call out; (*Aviat*) to call; (*Inform*) to call up

auf|runden vt (*Summe*) to round up

aufs *kontr von* **auf das**

Aufsatz m essay

auf|schieben *irr* vt (*verschieben*) to postpone; (*verzögern*) to put off; (*Tür*) to slide open

Aufschlag m (*auf Preis*) extra charge; (*Tennis*) service; **auf|schlagen** *irr* vt (*öffnen*) to open; (*verletzen*) to cut open; (*Zelt*) to pitch, to put up; (*Lager*) to set up ▷ vi (*Tennis*) to serve; **auf etw** (*+akk*) **~** (*aufprallen*) to hit sth

auf|schließen *irr* vt to unlock, to open up ▷ vi (*aufrücken*) to close up

auf|schneiden *irr* vt to cut open; (*in Scheiben*) to slice ▷ vi (*angeben*) to boast, to show off

Aufschnitt m (*slices pl of*) cold meat; (*bei Käse*) (assorted) sliced cheeses pl

auf|schreiben *irr* vt to write down

Aufschrift f inscription; (*Etikett*) label

Aufschub m (*Verzögerung*) delay; (*Vertagung*) postponement

Aufsehen (-s) nt stir; **großes ~ erregen** to cause a sensation; **Aufseher(in)** (-s, -) m(f) guard; (*im Betrieb*) supervisor; (*im Museum*) attendant; (*im Park*) keeper

auf sein *irr* vi *siehe* **auf**

auf|setzen vt to put on; (*Dokument*) to draw up ▷ vi (*Flugzeug*) to touch down

Aufsicht f supervision; (*bei Prüfung*) invigilation; **die ~ haben** to be in charge

auf|spannen vt (*Schirm*) to put up

auf|sperren vt (*Mund*) to open wide; (*aufschließen*) to unlock

auf|springen *irr* vi to jump (*auf +akk onto*); (*hochspringen*) to jump up; (*sich öffnen*) to spring open

auf|stehen *irr* vi to get up; (*Tür*) to be open

auf|stellen vt (*aufrecht stellen*) to

put up; (aufreihen) to line up;
(nominieren) to put up; (Liste,
Programm) to draw up; (Rekord) to
set up

Aufstieg (-(e)s, -e) m (auf Berg)
ascent; (Fortschritt) rise; (beruflich,
im Sport) promotion

Aufstrich m spread

auf|tanken vt, vi (Auto) to tank
up; (Flugzeug) to refuel

auf|tauchen vi to turn up; (aus
Wasser etc) to surface; (Frage,
Problem) to come up

auf|tauen vt (Speisen) to defrost
▷ vi to thaw; (fig: Person) to
unbend

Auftrag (-(e)s, Aufträge) m
(Comm) order; (Arbeit) job;
(Anweisung) instructions pl;
(Aufgabe) task; **im ~ von** on behalf
of; **auf|tragen** vt (Salbe etc) to
apply; (Essen) to serve

auf|treten irr vi to appear;
(Problem) to come up; (sich
verhalten) to behave; **Auftritt** m
(des Schauspielers) entrance; (fig:
Szene) scene

auf|wachen vi to wake up

auf|wachsen irr vi to grow up

Aufwand (-(e)s) m expenditure;
(Kosten a.) expense; (Anstrengung)
effort; **aufwändig** adj costly;
das ist zu ~ that's too much
trouble

auf|wärmen vt to warm up ▷ vr:
sich ~ to warm up

aufwärts adv upwards; **mit etw
geht es ~** things are looking up for
sth

auf|wecken vt to wake up

aufwendig adj siehe **aufwändig**

auf|wischen vt to wipe up;
(Fußboden) to wipe

auf|zählen vt to list

auf|zeichnen vt to sketch;
(schriftlich) to jot down; (auf Band
etc) to record; **Aufzeichnung** f

(schriftlich) note; (Tonband etc)
recording; (Film) record

auf|ziehen irr vt (öffnen) to pull
open; (Uhr) to wind (up); (fam:
necken) to tease; (Kinder) to bring
up; (Tiere) to rear ▷ vi (Gewitter) to
come up

Aufzug m (Fahrstuhl) lift (Brit),
elevator (US); (Kleidung) get-up;
(Theat) act

Auge (-s, -n) nt eye; **jdm etw
aufs ~ drücken** (fam) to force sth
on sb; **ins ~ gehen** (fam) to go
wrong; **unter vier ~n** in private;
etw im ~ behalten to keep sth in
mind; **Augenarzt** m,
Augenärztin f eye specialist, eye
doctor (US); **Augenblick** m
moment, **im ~** at the moment;
Augenbraue (-, -n) f eyebrow;
Augenbrauenstift m eyebrow
pencil; **Augenfarbe** f eye colour;
seine ~ the colour of his eyes;
Augenlid nt eyelid; **Augen-
optiker(in)** (-s, -) m(f) optician;
Augentropfen pl eyedrops pl;
Augenzeuge m, **Augenzeugin** f
eyewitness

August (-(e)s o -, -e) m August;
siehe auch **Juni**

Auktion f auction

○ SCHLÜSSELWORT

aus prep +dat **1** (räumlich) out of;
(von … her) from; **er ist aus Berlin**
he's from Berlin; **aus dem Fenster**
out of the window

2 (gemacht/hergestellt aus) made of;
ein Herz aus Stein a heart of
stone

3 (auf Ursache deutend) out of; **aus
Mitleid** out of sympathy; **aus
Erfahrung** from experience; **aus
Spaß** for fun

4 aus ihr wird nie etwas she'll
never get anywhere

▷ adv 1 (zu Ende) finished, over; **aus sein** to be over; **aus und vorbei** over and done with 2 (ausgeschaltet, ausgezogen) out; (Aufschrift an Geräten) off; **aus sein** (nicht brennen) to be out; (abgeschaltet sein: Radio, Herd) to be off; **Licht aus!** lights out! 3 (nicht zu Hause) **aus sein** to be out 4 (in Verbindung mit von) **von Rom aus** from Rome; **vom Fenster aus** out of the window; **von sich aus** (selbstständig) of one's own accord; **von ihm aus** as far as he's concerned

Aus (-) nt (Sport) touch; (fig) end
aus|atmen vi to breathe out
aus|bauen vt (Haus, Straße) to extend; (Motor etc) to remove
aus|bessern vt to repair; (Kleidung) to mend
aus|bilden vt to educate; (Lehrling etc) to train; (Fähigkeiten) to develop; **Ausbildung** f education; (von Lehrling etc) training; (von Fähigkeiten) development
Ausblick m view; (fig) outlook
aus|brechen irr vi to break out; **in Tränen ~** to burst into tears; **in Gelächter ~** to burst out laughing
aus|breiten vt to spread (out); (Arme) to stretch out ▷ vr: **sich ~** to spread
Ausbruch m (Krieg, Seuche etc) outbreak; (Vulkan) eruption; (Gefühle) outburst; (von Gefangenen) escape
aus|buhen vt to boo
Ausdauer f perseverance; (Sport) stamina
aus|dehnen vt to stretch; (fig: Macht) to extend
aus|denken irr vt **sich** (dat) **etw ~** to come up with sth

Ausdruck m (Ausdrücke) expression ▷ m (Ausdrucke, Computerausdruck) print-out;
aus|drucken vt (Inform) to print (out)
aus|drücken vt (formulieren) to express; (Zigarette) to put out; (Zitrone etc) to squeeze ▷ vr: **sich ~** to express oneself; **ausdrücklich** adj express ▷ adv expressly
auseinander adv (getrennt) apart; **~ schreiben** to write as separate words;
auseinander|gehen irr vi (Menschen) to separate; (Meinungen) to differ; (Gegenstand) to fall apart;
auseinander|halten irr vt to tell apart; **auseinander|setzen** vt (erklären) to explain;
auseinander|setzen vr: **sich ~** (sich beschäftigen) to look (mit at); (sich streiten) to argue (mit with); **Auseinandersetzung** f (Streit) argument; (Diskussion) debate
Ausfahrt f (des Zuges etc) departure; (Autobahn, Garage etc) exit
aus|fallen irr vi (Haare) to fall out; (nicht stattfinden) to be cancelled; (nicht funktionieren) to break down; (Strom) to be cut off; (Resultat haben) to turn out; **groß/klein ~** (Kleidung, Schuhe) to be too big/too small
ausfindig machen vt to discover
aus|flippen vi (fam) to freak out
Ausflug m excursion, outing; **Ausflugsziel** n destination
Ausfluss m (Med) discharge
aus|fragen vt to question
Ausfuhr (-, -en) f export
aus|führen vt (verwirklichen) to carry out; (Person) to take out; (Comm) to export; (darlegen) to explain

ausführlich *adj* detailed ▷ *adv* in detail

aus|füllen *vt* to fill up; *(Fragebogen etc)* to fill in *(o out)*

Ausgabe *f (Geld)* expenditure; *(Inform)* output; *(Buch)* edition; *(Nummer)* issue

Ausgang *m* way out, exit; *(Flugsteig)* gate; *(Ende)* end; *(Ergebnis)* result; **"kein ~"** "no exit"

aus|geben *irr vt (Geld)* to spend; *(austeilen)* to distribute; **jdm etw ~** *(spendieren)* to buy sb sth ▷ *vr*: **sich für etw/jdn ~** to pass oneself off as sth/sb

ausgebucht *adj* fully booked

ausgefallen *adj (ungewöhnlich)* unusual

aus|gehen *irr vi (abends etc)* to go out; *(Benzin, Kaffee etc)* to run out; *(Haare)* to fall out; *(Feuer, Licht etc)* to go out; *(Resultat haben)* to turn out; **davon ~, dass** to assume that; **ihm ging das Geld aus** he ran out of money

ausgelassen *adj* exuberant

ausgeleiert *adj* worn out

ausgenommen *conj, prep* +gen o dat except

ausgerechnet *adv*: **~ du** you of all people; **~ heute** today of all days

ausgeschildert *adj* signposted

ausgeschlafen *adj*: **bist du ~?** have you had enough sleep?

ausgeschlossen *adj (unmöglich)* impossible, out of the question

ausgesprochen *adj (absolut)* out-and-out; *(unverkennbar)* marked ▷ *adv* extremely; **~ gut** really good

ausgezeichnet *adj* excellent

ausgiebig *adj (Gebrauch)* thorough; *(Essen)* substantial

aus|gießen *irr vt (Getränk)* to pour out; *(Gefäß)* to empty

aus|gleichen *irr vt* to even out ▷ *vi (Sport)* to equalize

Ausguss *m (Spüle)* sink; *(Abfluss)* outlet

aus|halten *irr vt* to bear, to stand; **nicht auszuhalten sein** to be unbearable ▷ *vi* to hold out

aus|händigen *vt*: **jdm etw ~** to hand sth over to sb

Aushang *m* notice

Aushilfe *f* temporary help; *(im Büro)* temp

aus|kennen *irr vr*: **sich ~** to know a lot *(bei, mit about)*; *(an einem Ort)* to know one's way around

aus|kommen *irr vi*: **gut/schlecht mit jdm ~** to get on well/badly with sb; **mit etw ~** to get by with sth

Auskunft *f (~, Auskünfte)* information; *(nähere)* details *pl*; *(Schalter)* information desk; *(Tel)* (directory) enquiries *sing (kein Artikel, Brit)*, information *(US)*

aus|lachen *vt* to laugh at

aus|laden *irr vt (Gepäck etc)* to unload; **jdn ~** *(Gast)* to tell sb not to come

Auslage *f* window display; **~n** *pl (Kosten)* expenses

Ausland *nt* foreign countries *pl*; **im/ins ~** abroad; **Ausländer(in)** *(-s, -) m(f)* foreigner;

ausländerfeindlich *adj* hostile to foreigners, xenophobic;

ausländisch *adj* foreign;

Auslandsgespräch *nt* international call; **Auslandskrankenschein** *m* health insurance certificate for foreign countries, ≈ E111 *(Brit)*; **Auslandsschutzbrief** *m* international (motor) insurance cover (documents *pl*)

aus|lassen *irr vt* to leave out; *(Wort etc a.)* to omit; *(überspringen)* to skip; (*Wut, Ärger*) to vent (*an* +*dat* on); ▷ *vr* **sich über etw** (*akk*) ~ to speak one's mind about sth

aus|laufen *irr vi* (*Flüssigkeit*) to run out; (*Tank etc*) to leak; (*Schiff*) to leave port; (*Vertrag*) to expire

aus|legen *vt* (*Waren*) to display; (*Geld*) to lend; (*Text etc*) to interpret; (*technisch ausstatten*) to design (*für, auf* +*akk* for)

aus|leihen *irr vt* (*verleihen*) to lend; **sich** (*dat*) **etw** ~ to borrow sth

aus|loggen *vi* (*Inform*) to log out (*o off*)

aus|lösen *vt* (*Explosion, Alarm*) to set off; (*hervorrufen*) to cause; **Auslöser** (-*s*, -) *m* (*Foto*) shutter release

aus|machen *vt* (*Licht, Radio*) to turn off; (*Feuer*) to put out; (*Termin, Preis*) to fix; (*vereinbaren*) to agree; (*Anteil darstellen, betragen*) to represent; (*bedeuten*) to matter; **macht es Ihnen etwas aus, wenn ...?** would you mind if ...?; **das macht mir nichts aus** I don't mind

Ausmaß *nt* extent

Ausnahme (-, -*n*) *f* exception; **ausnahmsweise** *adv* as an exception, just this once

aus|nutzen *vt* (*Zeit, Gelegenheit, Einfluss*) to use; (*jdn, Gutmütigkeit*) to take advantage of

aus|packen *vt* to unpack

aus|probieren *vt* to try (out)

Auspuff (-(*e*)*s*, -*e*) *m* (*Tech*) exhaust; **Auspuffrohr** *nt* exhaust (pipe); **Auspufftopf** *m* (*Auto*) silencer (*Brit*), muffler (*US*)

aus|rauben *vt* to rob

aus|räumen *vt* (*Dinge*) to clear away; (*Schrank, Zimmer*) to empty; (*Bedenken*) to put aside

aus|rechnen *vt* to calculate, to work out

Ausrede *f* excuse

aus|reden *vi* to finish speaking ▷ *vt*: **jdm etw** ~ to talk sb out of sth

ausreichend *adj* sufficient, satisfactory; (*Schulnote*) ≈ D

Ausreise *f* departure; **bei der** ~ on leaving the country; **Ausreiseerlaubnis** *f* exit visa; **aus|reisen** *vi* to leave the country

aus|reißen *irr vt* to tear out ▷ *vi* to come off; (*fam: davonlaufen*) to run away

aus|renken *vt* **sich** (*dat*) **den Arm** ~ to dislocate one's arm

aus|richten *vt* (*Botschaft*) to deliver; (*Gruß*) to pass on; (*erreichen*) **ich konnte bei ihr nichts** ~ I couldn't get anywhere with her; **jdm etw** ~ to tell sb sth

aus|rufen *irr vt* (*über Lautsprecher*) to announce; **jdn** ~ **lassen** to page sb; **Ausrufezeichen** *nt* exclamation mark

aus|ruhen *vi* to rest ▷ *vr*: **sich** ~ to rest

Ausrüstung *f* equipment

aus|rutschen *vi* to slip

aus|schalten *vt* to switch off; (*fig*) to eliminate

Ausschau *f*: ~ **halten** to look out (*nach* for)

aus|scheiden *irr vt* (*Med*) to give off, to secrete ▷ *vi* to leave (*aus etw* sth); (*Sport*) to be eliminated

aus|schlafen *irr vi* to have a lie-in ▷ *vr*: **sich** ~ to have a lie-in ▷ *vt* to sleep off

Ausschlag *m* (*Med*) rash; **den** ~ **geben** (*fig*) to tip the balance; **aus|schlagen** *irr vt* (*Zahn*) to knock out; (*Einladung*) to turn down ▷ *vi* (*Pferd*) to kick out; **ausschlaggebend** *adj* decisive

aus|schließen *irr vt* to lock out; (*fig*) to exclude; **ausschließlich**

adv exclusively ▷ *prep* +*gen* excluding

Ausschnitt *m* (*Teil*) section; (*von Kleid*) neckline; (*aus Zeitung*) cutting

Ausschreitungen *pl* riots *pl*

aus|schütten *vt* (*Flüssigkeit*) to pour out; (*Gefäß*) to empty

aus|sehen *irr vi* to look; **krank ~** to look ill: **gut ~** (*Person*) to be good-looking; (*Sache*) to be looking good; **es sieht nach Regen aus** it looks like rain; **es sieht schlecht aus** things look bad

aus sein *irr vi siehe* **aus**

außen *adv* outside; **nach ~** outwards; **von ~** from (the) outside; **Außenbordmotor** *m* outboard motor; **Außenminister(in)** *m(f)* foreign minister, Foreign Secretary (Brit); **Außenseite** *f* outside; **Außenseiter(in)** *m(f)* outsider; **Außenspiegel** *m* wing mirror (Brit), side mirror (US)

außer *prep* +*dat* (*abgesehen von*) except (for); **nichts ~** nothing but; **~ Betrieb** out of order; **~ sich sein** to be beside oneself (*vor* with); **~ Atem** out of breath ▷ *conj* (*ausgenommen*) except; **~ wenn** unless; **~ dass** except; **außerdem** *conj* besides

äußere(r, s) *adj* outer, external

außergewöhnlich *adj* unusual ▷ *adv* exceptionally; **~ kalt** exceptionally cold; **außerhalb** *prep* +*gen* outside

äußerlich *adj* external

äußern *vt* to express; (*zeigen*) to show ▷ *vr:* **sich ~** to give one's opinion; (*sich zeigen*) to show itself

außerordentlich *adj* extraordinary; **außerplanmäßig** *adj* unscheduled

äußerst *adv* extremely;

äußerste(r, s) *adj* utmost; (*räumlich*) farthest; (*Termin*) last possible

Äußerung *f* remark

aus|setzen *vt* (*Kind, Tier*) to abandon; (*Belohnung*) to offer: **ich habe nichts daran auszusetzen** I have no objection to it ▷ *vi* (*aufhören*) to stop; (*Pause machen*) to drop out; (*beim Spiel*) to miss a turn

Aussicht *f* (*Blick*) view; (*Chance*) prospect; **aussichtslos** *adj* hopeless; **Aussichtsplattform** *f* observation platform; **Aussichtsturm** *m* observation tower

Aussiedler(in) (-s, -) *m(f)* émigré (*person of German descent from Eastern Europe*)

aus|spannen *vi* (*erholen*) to relax ▷ *vt:* **er hat ihm die Freundin ausgespannt** (*fam*) he's nicked his girlfriend

aus|sperren *vt* to lock out ▷ *vr:* **sich ~** to lock oneself out

Aussprache *f* (*von Wörtern*) pronunciation; (*Gespräch*) (frank) discussion; **aus|sprechen** *irr vt* to pronounce; (*äußern*) to express ▷ *vr:* **sich ~** to talk (*über* +*akk* about) ▷ *vi* (*zu Ende sprechen*) to finish speaking

aus|spülen *vt* to rinse (out)

Ausstattung *f* (*Ausrüstung*) equipment; (*Einrichtung*) furnishings *pl*; (*von Auto*) fittings *pl*

aus|stehen *irr vt* to endure; **ich kann ihn nicht ~** I can't stand him ▷ *vi* (*noch nicht da sein*) to be outstanding

aus|steigen *irr vi* to get out (*aus* of); **aus dem Bus/Zug ~** to get off the bus/train; **Austeiger(in)** *m(f)* dropout

aus|stellen *vt* to display; (*auf Messe, in Museum etc*) to exhibit;

(fam: ausschalten) to switch off;
(Scheck etc) to make out; (Pass etc)
to issue; **Ausstellung** f
exhibition

aus|sterben irr vi to die out

aus|strahlen vt to radiate;
(Programm) to broadcast;
Ausstrahlung f (Radio, TV)
broadcast; (fig: von Person)
charisma

aus|strecken vr: **sich ~** to
stretch out ▷ vt (Hand) to reach
out (nach for)

aus|suchen vt to choose

Austausch m exchange;
aus|tauschen vt to exchange
(gegen for)

aus|teilen vt to distribute;
(aushändigen) to hand out

Auster (-, -n) f oyster;
Austernpilz m oyster mushroom

aus|tragen irr vt (Post) to
deliver; (Wettkampf) to hold

Australien (-s) nt Australia;
Australier(in) (-s, -) m(f)
Australian; **australisch** adj
Australian

aus|trinken irr vt (Glas) to drain;
(Getränk) to drink up ▷ vi to finish
one's drink

aus|trocknen vi to dry out;
(Fluss) to dry up

aus|üben vt (Beruf, Sport) to
practise; (Einfluss) to exert

Ausverkauf m sale;
ausverkauft adj (Karten, Artikel)
sold out

Auswahl f selection, choice (an
+dat of); **aus|wählen** vt to
select, to choose

aus|wandern vi to emigrate

auswärtig adj (nicht am/vom Ort)
not local; (ausländisch) foreign;
auswärts adv (außerhalb der Stadt)
out of town; (Sport) **~ spielen** to
play away; **Auswärtsspiel** nt
away match

aus|wechseln vt to replace;
(Sport) to substitute

Ausweg m way out

aus|weichen irr vi to get out of
the way; **jdm/einer Sache ~** to
move aside for sb/sth; (fig) to
avoid sb/sth

Ausweis (-es, -e) m
(Personalausweis) identity card, ID;
(für Bibliothek etc) card; **aus|weisen**
irr vt to expel ▷ vr: **sich ~** to
prove one's identity;
Ausweiskontrolle f ID check;
Ausweispapiere pl identification documents pl

auswendig adv by heart

aus|wuchten vt (Auto: Räder) to
balance

aus|zahlen vt (Summe) to pay
(out); (Person) to pay off ▷ vr: **sich
~** to be worth it

aus|zeichnen vt (ehren) to
honour; (Comm) to price ▷ vr: **sich
~** to distinguish oneself

aus|ziehen irr vt (Kleidung) to
take off ▷ vr: **sich ~** to undress
▷ vi (aus Wohnung) to move out

Auszubildende(r) mf trainee

authentisch adj authentic,
genuine

Auto (-s, -s) nt car; **~ fahren** to
drive; **Autoatlas** m road atlas;
Autobahn f motorway (Brit),
freeway (US); **Autobahnauffahrt**
f motorway access road (Brit),
on-ramp (US); **Autobahnausfahrt**
f motorway exit (Brit), off-ramp
(US); **Autobahngebühr** f toll;
Autobahnkreuz nt motorway
interchange; **Autobahnring** m
motorway ring (Brit), beltway (US);
Autobombe f car bomb;
Autofähre f car ferry;
Autofahrer(in) m(f) driver,
motorist; **Autofahrt** f drive

Autogramm (-s, -e) nt
autograph

Automarke f make of car
Automat (-en, -en) m vending machine
Automatik (-, -en) f (Auto) automatic transmission; **Automatikschaltung** f automatic gear change (Brit) (o shift (US)); **Automatikwagen** m automatic
automatisch adj automatic ▷ adv automatically
Automechaniker(in) m(f) car mechanic; **Autonummer** f registration (Brit) (o license (US)) number; **Autoradio** nt car radio; **Autoreifen** m car tyre; **Autoreisezug** m Motorail train® (Brit), auto train (US); **Autorennen** nt motor racing; (einzelnes Rennen) motor race; **Autoschlüssel** m car key; **Autotelefon** nt car phone; **Autounfall** m car accident; **Autoverleih** m, **Autovermietung** f car hire (Brit) (o rental (US)); (Firma) car hire (Brit) (o rental (US)) company; **Autowaschanlage** f car wash; **Autowerkstatt** f car repair shop, garage; **Autozubehör** nt car accessories pl
Avocado (-, -s) f avocado
Axt (-, Äxte) f axe
Azubi (-s, -s) m (-, -s) f akr = **Auszubildende** trainee

B abk = **Bundesstraße**
Baby (-s, -s) nt baby; **Babybett** nt cot (Brit), crib (US); **Babyfläschchen** nt baby's bottle; **Babynahrung** f baby food; **Babysitter(in)** m(f) babysitter; **Babysitz** m child seat; **Babywickelraum** m baby-changing room
Bach (-(e)s, Bäche) m stream
Backblech nt baking tray (Brit), cookie sheet (US)
Backbord nt port (side)
Backe (-, -n) f cheek
backen (backte, gebacken) vt, vi to bake
Backenzahn m molar
Bäcker(in) (-s, -) m(f) baker; **Bäckerei** f bakery; (Laden) baker's (shop)
Backofen m oven; **Backpulver** nt baking powder
Backspace-Taste f (Inform)

backspace key
Backstein m brick
Backwaren pl bread, cakes and
pastries pl
Bad (-(e)s, *Bäder*) nt bath;
(*Schwimmen*) swim; (*Ort*) spa; **ein
~ nehmen** to have (o take) a bath;
Badeanzug m swimsuit,
swimming costume (Brit);
Badehose f swimming trunks pl;
Badekappe f swimming cap;
Bademantel m bathrobe;
Bademeister(in) m(f) pool
attendant; **Bademütze** f
swimming cap
baden vi to have a bath;
(*schwimmen*) to swim, to bathe
(Brit) ▷ vt to bath (Brit), to bathe
(US)
Baden-Württemberg (-s) nt
Baden-Württemberg
Badeort m spa; **Badesachen** pl
swimming things pl;
Badeschaum m bubble bath,
bath foam; **Badetuch** nt bath
towel; **Badewanne** f bath (tub);
Badezeug nt swimming gear;
Badezimmer nt bathroom
Badminton nt badminton
baff adj: **~ sein** (fam) to be
flabbergasted (o gobsmacked)
Bagger (-s, -) m excavator;
Baggersee m artificial lake in
quarry etc, used for bathing
Bahamas pl: **die ~** the Bahamas
pl
Bahn (-, -en) f (*Eisenbahn*) railway
(Brit), railroad (US); (*Rennbahn*)
track; (*für Läufer*) lane; (*Astr*) orbit;
Deutsche ~ Germany's main railway
operator; **bahnbrechend** adj
groundbreaking; **BahnCard®**
(-, -s) f rail card (allowing 50% or
25% reduction on tickets); **Bahnfahrt**
f railway (Brit) (o railroad (US))
journey; **Bahnhof** m station; **am**
(o **auf dem**) **~** at the station;

Bahnlinie f railway (Brit) (o
railroad (US)) line; **Bahnpolizei** f
railway (Brit) (o railroad (US))
police; **Bahnsteig** (-(e)s, -e) m
platform; **Bahnstrecke** f railway
(Brit) (o railroad (US)) line;
Bahnübergang m level crossing
(Brit), grade crossing (US)
Bakterien pl bacteria pl, germs pl
bald adv (zeitlich) soon; (beinahe)
almost; **bis ~!** see you soon (o
later); **baldig** adj quick, speedy
Balkan (-s) m: **der ~** the Balkans
pl
Balken (-s, -) m beam
Balkon (-s, -s o -e) m balcony
Ball (-(e)s, *Bälle*) m ball; (*Tanz*)
dance, ball
Ballett nt ballet
Ballon (-s, -s) m balloon
Ballspiel nt ball game
Ballungsgebiet nt conurbation
Baltikum (-s) nt: **das ~** the Baltic
States pl
Bambus (-ses, -se) m bamboo;
Bambussprossen pl bamboo
shoots pl
banal adj banal; (*Frage,
Bemerkung*) trite
Banane (-, -n) f banana
band imperf von **binden**
Band (-(e)s, *Bände*) m (Buch)
volume ▷ (-(e)s, *Bänder*) nt (aus
Stoff) ribbon, tape; (*Fließband*)
production line; (*Tonband*) tape;
(*Anat*) ligament; **etw auf
~ aufnehmen** to tape sth ▷ (-, -s) f
(*Musikgruppe*) band
Bandage (-, -n) f bandage;
bandagieren vt to bandage
Bande (-, -n) f (*Gruppe*) gang
Bänderriss m (Med) torn
ligament
Bandscheibe f (Anat) disc;
Bandwurm m tapeworm
Bank (-, *Bänke*) f (*Sitzbank*) bench
▷ (-, -en) f (Fin) bank

Bankautomat m cash dispenser; **Bankkarte** f bank card; **Bankkonto** nt bank account; **Bankleitzahl** f bank sort code; **Banknote** f banknote; **Bankverbindung** f (Kontonummer etc) banking (o account) details pl

bar adj: **~es Geld** cash; **etw (in) ~ bezahlen** to pay sth (in) cash

Bar (-, -s) f bar

Bär (-en, -en) m bear

barfuß adj barefoot

barg imperf von **bergen**

Bargeld nt cash; **bargeldlos** adj non-cash

Barkeeper (-s, -) m, **Barmann** m barman, bartender (US)

barock adj baroque

Barometer (-s, -) m barometer

barsch adj brusque

Barsch (-(e)s, -e) m perch

Barscheck m open (o uncrossed) cheque

Bart (-(e)s, Bärte) m beard; **bärtig** adj bearded

Barzahlung f cash payment

Basar (-s, -e) m bazaar

Baseballmütze f baseball cap

Basel (-s) nt Basle

Basilikum (-s) nt basil

Basis (-, Basen) f basis

Baskenland nt Basque region

Basketball m basketball

Bass (-es, Bässe) m bass

basta interj: **und damit ~!** and that's that

basteln vt to make ▷ vi to make things, to do handicrafts

bat imperf von **bitten**

Batterie f battery; **batteriebetrieben** adj battery-powered

Bau (-(e)s) m (Bauen) building, construction; (Aufbau) structure; (Baustelle) building site ▷ m (Baue) (Tier) burrow ▷ m (Bauten)

(Gebäude) building; **Bauarbeiten** pl construction work sing; (Straßenbau) roadworks pl (Brit), roadwork (US); **Bauarbeiter(in)** m(f) construction worker

Bauch ((o)s, Bäuche) m stomach, belly; **Bauchnabel** m navel; **Bauchredner(in)** m(f) ventriloquist; **Bauchschmerzen** pl stomach-ache sing; **Bauchspeicheldrüse** f pancreas; **Bauchtanz** m belly dance; (das Tanzen) belly dancing; **Bauchweh** (-s) nt stomach-ache

bauen vt, vi to build; (Tech) to construct

Bauer (-n o -s, -n) m farmer; (Schach) pawn; **Bäuerin** f farmer, (Frau des Bauern) farmer's wife; **Bauernhof** m farm

baufällig adj dilapidated; **Baujahr** adj year of construction; **der Wagen ist ~ 2002** the car is a 2002 model, the car was made in 2002

Baum (-(e)s, Bäume) m tree

Baumarkt m DIY centre

Baumwolle f cotton

Bauplatz m building site; **Baustein** m (für Haus) stone; (Spielzeug) brick; (fig) element; **elektronischer ~** chip; **Baustelle** f building site; (bei Straßenbau) roadworks pl (Brit), roadwork (US); **Bauteil** nt prefabricated part; **Bauunternehmer(in)** m(f) building contractor; **Bauwerk** nt building

Bayern (-s) nt Bavaria

beabsichtigen vt to intend

beachten vt (Aufmerksamkeit schenken) to pay attention to; (Vorschrift etc) to observe; **nicht ~** to ignore; **beachtlich** adj considerable

Beachvolleyball nt beach volleyball

Beamte(r) (-n, -n) *m*, **Beamtin** *f* official; (*Staatsbeamter*) civil servant

beanspruchen *vt* to claim; (*Zeit, Platz*) to take up; **jdn ~** to keep sb busy

beanstanden *vt* to complain about; **Beanstandung** *f* complaint

beantragen *vt* to apply for

beantworten *vt* to answer

bearbeiten *vt* to work; (*Material, Daten*) to process; (*Chem*) to treat; (*Fall etc*) to deal with; (*Buch etc*) to revise; (*fam: beeinflussen wollen*) to work on; **Bearbeitungsgebühr** *f* handling (*o service*) charge

beatmen *vt*: **jdn ~** to give sb artificial respiration

beaufsichtigen *vt* to supervise; (*bei Prüfung*) to invigilate

beauftragen *vt* to instruct; **jdn mit etw ~** to give sb the job of doing sth

Becher (-s, -) *m* mug; (*ohne Henkel*) tumbler; (*für Joghurt*) pot; (*aus Pappe*) tub

Becken (-s, -) *nt* basin; (*Spüle*) sink; (*zum Schwimmen*) pool; (*Mus*) cymbal; (*Anat*) pelvis

bedanken *vr*: **sich ~** to say thank you; **sich bei jdm für etw ~** to thank sb for sth

Bedarf (-(e)s) *m* need (*an +dat* for); (*Comm*) demand (*an +dat* for); **je nach ~** according to demand; **bei ~** if necessary; **Bedarfshaltestelle** *f* request stop, flag stop (US)

bedauerlich *adj* regrettable; **bedauern** *vt* to regret; (*bemitleiden*) to feel sorry for; **bedauernswert** *adj* (*Zustände*) regrettable; (*Mensch*) unfortunate

bedeckt *adj* covered; (*Himmel*) overcast

bedenken *irr vt* to consider;

Bedenken (-s, -) *nt* (*Überlegen*) consideration; (*Zweifel*) doubt; (*Skrupel*) scruples *pl*; **bedenklich** *adj* dubious; (*Zustand*) serious

bedeuten *vt* to mean; **jdm nichts/viel ~** to mean nothing/a lot to sb; **bedeutend** *adj* important; (*beträchtlich*) considerable; **Bedeutung** *f* meaning; (*Wichtigkeit*) importance

bedienen *vt* to serve; (*Maschine*) to operate ▷ *vr*: **sich ~** (*beim Essen*) to help oneself; **Bedienung** *f* service; (*Kellner/Kellnerin*) waiter/waitress; (*Verkäufer(in)*) shop assistant; (*Zuschlag*) service (charge); **Bedienungsanleitung** *f* operating instructions *pl*; **Bedienungshandbuch** *nt* instruction manual; **Bedingung** *f* condition; **unter der ~, dass** on condition that; **unter diesen ~en** under these circumstances

bedrohen *vt* to threaten

Bedürfnis *nt* need

beeilen *vr*: **sich ~** to hurry

beeindrucken *vt* to impress

beeinflussen *vt* to influence

beeinträchtigen *vt* to affect

beenden *vt* to end; (*fertigstellen*) to finish

beerdigen *vt* to bury; **Beerdigung** *f* burial; (*Feier*) funeral

Beere (-, -n) *f* berry; (*Traubenbeere*) grape

Beet (-(e)s, -e) *nt* bed

befahl *imperf von* **befehlen**

befahrbar *adj* passable; (*Naut*) navigable; **befahren** *irr vt* (*Straße*) to use; (*Pass*) to drive over; (*Fluss etc*) to navigate ▷ *adj*: **stark/wenig ~** busy/quiet

Befehl (-(e)s, -e) *m* order; (*Inform*) command; **befehlen** (*befahl, befohlen*) *vt* to order; **jdm ~, etw zu tun** to order sb to do sth ▷ *vi*

to give orders

befestigen vt to fix; (mit Schnur, Seil) to attach; (mit Klebestoff) to stick

befeuchten vt to moisten

befinden irr vr: **sich ~** to be

befohlen pp von **befehlen**

befolgen vt (Rat etc) to follow

befördern vt (transportieren) to transport; (beruflich) to promote; **Beförderung** f transport; (beruflich) promotion; **Beförderungsbedingungen** pl conditions pl of carriage

Befragung f questioning; (Umfrage) opinion poll

betreundet adj friendly; **~ sein** to be friends (mit jdm with sb)

befriedigen vt to satisfy; **befriedigend** adj satisfactory; (Schulnote) = C; **Befriedigung** f satisfaction

befristet adj limited (auf +akk to)

befruchten vt to fertilize; (fig) to stimulate

Befund (-(e)s, -e) m findings pl; (Med) diagnosis

befürchten vt to fear

befürworten vt to support

begabt adj gifted, talented; **Begabung** f talent, gift

begann imperf von **beginnen**

begegnen vi to meet (jdm sb), to meet with (einer Sache dat sth)

begehen irr vt (Straftat) to commit; (Jubiläum etc) to celebrate

begehrt adj sought-after; (Junggeselle) eligible

begeistern vt to fill with enthusiasm; (inspirieren) to inspire ▷ vr: **sich für etw ~** to be/get enthusiastic about sth; **begeistert** adj enthusiastic

Beginn (-(e)s) m beginning; **zu ~** at the beginning; **beginnen** (begann, begonnen) vt, vi to start, to begin

beglaubigen vt to certify; **Beglaubigung** f certification

begleiten vt to accompany; **Begleiter(in)** m(f) companion; **Begleitung** f company; (Mus) accompaniment

beglückwünschen vt to congratulate (zu on)

begonnen pp von **beginnen**

begraben irr vt to bury; **Begräbnis** nt burial; (Feier) funeral

begreifen irr vt to understand

Begrenzung f boundary; (fig) restriction

Begriff (-(e)s, -e) m concept; (Vorstellung) idea; **im ~ sein, etw zu tun** to be on the point of doing sth; **schwer von ~ sein** to be slow on the uptake

begründen vt (rechtfertigen) to justify; **Begründung** f explanation; (Rechtfertigung) justification

begrüßen vt to greet; (willkommen heißen) to welcome; **Begrüßung** f greeting; (Empfang) welcome

behaart adj hairy

behalten irr vt to keep; (im Gedächtnis) to remember; **etw für sich ~** to keep sth to oneself

Behälter (-s, -) m container

behandeln vt to treat; **Behandlung** f treatment

behaupten vt to claim, to maintain ▷ vr: **sich ~** to assert oneself; **Behauptung** f claim

beheizen vt to heat

behelfen irr vr: **sich mit/ohne etw ~** to make do with/without sth

beherbergen vt to accommodate

beherrschen vt (Situation, Gefühle) to control; (Instrument) to master ▷ vr: **sich ~** to control

oneself; **Beherrschung** f control (über +akk of); **die ~ verlieren** to lose one's self-control
behilflich adj helpful; **jdm ~ sein** to help sb (bei with)
behindern vt to hinder; (Verkehr, Sicht) to obstruct; **Behinderte(r)** mf disabled person; **behindertengerecht** adj suitable for disabled people
Behörde (-, -n) f authority; **die ~n** pl the authorities pl

○ SCHLÜSSELWORT

bei prep +dat **1** (nahe bei) near; (zum Aufenthalt) at, with; (unter, zwischen) among; **bei München** near Munich; **bei uns** at our place; **beim Friseur** at the hairdresser's; **bei seinen Eltern wohnen** to live with one's parents; **bei einer Firma arbeiten** to work for a firm; **etw bei sich haben** to have sth on one; **jdn bei sich haben** to have sb with one; **bei Goethe** in Goethe; **beim Militär** in the army **2** (zeitlich) at, on; (während) during; (Zustand, Umstand) in; **bei Nacht** at night; **bei Nebel** in fog; **bei Regen** if it rains; **bei solcher Hitze** in such heat; **bei meiner Ankunft** on my arrival; **bei der Arbeit** when I'm at working; **beim Fahren** while driving

bei|behalten irr vt to keep
Beiboot nt dinghy
bei|bringen irr vt: **jdm etw ~** (mitteilen) to break sth to sb; (lehren) to teach sb sth
beide(s) pron both; **meine ~n Brüder** my two brothers, both my brothers; **wir ~** both (o the two) of us; **keiner von ~n** neither of them; **alle ~** both (of them); **~s ist sehr schön** both are very nice; **30**

~ (beim Tennis) 30 all
beieinander adv together
Beifahrer(in) m(f) passenger; **Beifahrerairbag** m passenger airbag; **Beifahrersitz** m passenger seat
Beifall (-(e)s) m applause
beige adj inv beige
Beigeschmack m aftertaste
Beil (-(e)s, -e) nt axe
Beilage f (Gastr) side dish; (Gemüse) vegetables pl; (zu Buch etc) supplement
beiläufig adj casual ▷ adv casually
Beileid nt condolences pl; **(mein) herzliches ~** please accept my sincere condolences
beiliegend adj enclosed
beim kontr von **bei dem**
Bein (-(e)s, -e) nt leg
beinah(e) adv almost, nearly
beinhalten vt to contain
Beipackzettel m instruction leaflet
beisammen adv together; **Beisammensein** (-s) nt get-together
beiseite adv aside; **beiseite|legen** vt: **etw ~** (sparen) to put sth by
Beispiel (-(e)s, -e) nt example; **sich** (dat) **an jdm/etw ein ~ nehmen** to take sb/sth as an example; **zum ~** for example
beißen (biss, gebissen) vt to bite ▷ vi (stechen: Rauch, Säure) to sting ▷ vr: **sich ~** (Farben) to clash
Beitrag (-(e)s, Beiträge) m contribution; (für Mitgliedschaft) subscription; (Versicherung) premium; **bei|tragen** irr vt, vi to contribute (zu to)
bekannt adj well-known; (nicht fremd) familiar; **mit jdm ~ sein** to know sb; **~ geben** to announce;

jdn mit jdm ~ machen to introduce sb to sb; **Bekannte(r)** mf friend; (entfernter) acquaintance; **bekanntlich** adv as everyone knows; **Bekanntschaft** f acquaintance

bekiffen vr: **sich ~** (fam) to get stoned

beklagen vr: **sich ~** to complain

Bekleidung f clothing

bekommen irr vt to get; (erhalten) to receive; (Kind) to have; (Zug, Grippe) to catch, to get; **wie viel ~ Sie dafür?** how much is that? ▷ vi: **jdm ~** (Essen) to agree with sb; **wir ~ schon** (bedient werden) we're being served

beladen irr vt to load

Belag (-(e)s, Beläge) m coating; (auf Zähnen) plaque; (auf Zunge) fur

belasten vt to load; (Körper) to strain; (Umwelt) to pollute; (fig: mit Sorgen etc) to burden; (Comm: Konto) to debit; (Jur) to incriminate

belästigen vt to bother; (stärker) to pester; (sexuell) to harass; **Belästigung** f annoyance; **sexuelle ~** sexual harassment

belebt adj (Straße etc) busy

Beleg (-(e)s, -e) m (Comm) receipt; (Beweis) proof; **belegen** vt (Brot) to spread; (Platz) to reserve; (Kurs, Vorlesung) to register for; (beweisen) to prove

belegt adj (Tel) engaged (Brit), busy (US); (Hotel) full; (Zunge) coated; **~es Brötchen** sandwich; **der Platz ist ~** this seat is taken; **Belegtzeichen** nt (Tel) engaged tone (Brit), busy tone (US)

beleidigen vt to insult; (kränken) to offend; **Beleidigung** f insult; (Jur) slander; (schriftlich) libel

beleuchten vt to light; (bestrahlen) to illuminate; (fig) to examine; **Beleuchtung** f lighting; (Bestrahlung) illumination

Belgien (-s) nt Belgium; **Belgier(in)** (-s, -) m(f) Belgian; **belgisch** adj Belgian

belichten vt to expose; **Belichtung** f exposure; **Belichtungsmesser** (s, -) m light meter

Belieben nt: (ganz) **nach ~** (just) as you wish

beliebig adj: **jedes ~e Muster** any pattern; **jeder ~e** anyone ▷ adv: **~ lange** as long as you like; **~ viel** as many (o much) as you like

beliebt adj popular; **sich bei jdm ~ machen** to make oneself popular with sb

beliefern vt to supply

bellen vi to bark

Belohnung f reward

Belüftung f ventilation

belügen irr vt to lie to

bemerkbar adj noticeable; **sich ~ machen** (Mensch) to attract attention; (Zustand) to become noticeable; **bemerken** vt (wahrnehmen) to notice; (sagen) to remark; **bemerkenswert** adj remarkable; **Bemerkung** f remark

bemitleiden vt to pity

bemühen vr: **sich ~** to try (hard), to make an effort; **Bemühung** f effort

bemuttern vt to mother

benachbart adj neighbouring

benachrichtigen vt to inform; **Benachrichtigung** f notification

benachteiligen vt to (put at a) disadvantage; (wegen Rasse etc) to discriminate against

benehmen irr vr: **sich ~** to behave; **Benehmen** (-s, -) nt behaviour

beneiden vt to envy; **jdn um etw ~** to envy sb sth

Beneluxländer pl Benelux countries pl

benommen | 34

benommen *adj* dazed

benötigen *vt* to need

benutzen *vt* to use;
Benutzer(in) *(-s, -) m(f)* user;
benutzerfreundlich *adj* user-friendly; **Benutzerhandbuch** *nt* user's guide; **Benutzerkennung** *f* user ID; **Benutzeroberfläche** *f* (Inform) user/system interface;
Benutzung *f* use;
Benutzungsgebühr *f* (hire) charge

Benzin *(-s, -e) nt* (Auto) petrol (Brit), gas (US); **Benzingutschein** *m* petrol (Brit) (o gas (US)) coupon; **Benzinkanister** *m* petrol (Brit) (o gas (US)) can; **Benzinpumpe** *f* petrol (Brit) (o gas (US)) pump; **Benzintank** *m* petrol (Brit) (o gas (US)) tank; **Benzinuhr** *f* fuel gauge

beobachten *vt* to observe;
Beobachtung *f* observation

bequem *adj* comfortable;
(Ausrede) convenient; (faul) lazy;
machen Sie es sich ~ make yourself at home; **Bequemlichkeit** *f* comfort; (Faulheit) laziness

beraten *irr vt* to advise;
(besprechen) to discuss ▶ *vr*: **sich ~** to consult; **Beratung** *f* advice;
(bei Arzt etc) consultation

berauben *vt* to rob

berechnen *vt* to calculate;
(Comm) to charge; **berechnend** *adj* (Mensch) calculating

berechtigen *vt* to entitle (zu to);
(fig) to justify; **berechtigt** *adj* justified; **zu etw ~ sein** to be entitled to sth

bereden *vt* (besprechen) to discuss

Bereich *(-(e)s, -e) m* area;
(Ressort, Gebiet) field

bereisen *vt* to travel through

bereit *adj* ready; **by etw ~ sein** to be ready for sth; **sich ~ erklären, etw zu tun** to agree to do sth

bereiten *vt* to prepare; (Kummer) to cause; (Freude) to give

bereit|legen *vt* to lay out

bereit|machen *vr*: **sich ~** to get ready

bereits *adv* already

Bereitschaft *f* readiness;
~ haben (Arzt) to be on call

bereit|stehen *vi* to be ready

bereuen *vt* to regret

Berg *(-(e)s, -e) m* mountain;
(kleiner) hill; **in die ~e fahren** to go to the mountains; **bergab** *adv* downhill; **bergauf** *adv* uphill;
Bergbahn *f* mountain railway (Brit) (o railroad US)

bergen *(barg, geborgen) vt* (retten) to rescue; (enthalten) to contain

Bergführer(in) *m(f)* mountain guide; **Berghütte** *f* mountain hut;
bergig *adj* mountainous;
Bergschuh *m* climbing boot;
Bergsteigen *(-s) nt* mountaineering; **Bergsteiger(in)** *(-s, -) m(f)* mountaineer;
Bergtour *f* mountain hike

Bergung *f* (Rettung) rescue; (von Toten, Fahrzeugen) recovery

Bergwacht *(-, -en) f* mountain rescue service; **Bergwerk** *nt* mine

Bericht *(-(e)s, -e) m* report;
berichten *vt, vi* to report

berichtigen *vt* to correct

Bermudadreieck *nt* Bermuda triangle; **Bermudainseln** *pl* Bermuda *sing*; **Bermudashorts** *pl* Bermuda shorts *pl*

Bernstein *m* amber

berüchtigt *adj* notorious, infamous

berücksichtigen *vt* to take into account; (Antrag, Bewerber) to consider

Beruf *(-(e)s, -e) m* occupation; (akademischer) profession;
(Gewerbe) trade; **was sind Sie von**

~? what do you do (for a living)?;
beruflich *adj* professional

Berufsausbildung *f* vocational
training; **Berufsschule** *f*
vocational college; **berufstätig**
adj employed; **Berufsverkehr** *m*
commuter traffic

beruhigen *vt* to calm ▷ *vr:* **sich
~** (*Mensch, Situation*) to calm down;
beruhigend *adj* reassuring;
Beruhigungsmittel *nt* sedative

berühmt *adj* famous

berühren *vt* to touch;
(*gefühlsmäßig bewegen*) to move;
(*betreffen*) to affect; (*flüchtig
erwähnen*) to mention, to touch on
▷ *vr:* **sich ~** to touch

besaufen *irr vr:* **sich ~** (*fam*) to
get plastered

beschädigen *vt* to damage

beschäftigen *vt* to occupy;
(*beruflich*) to employ ▷ *vr:* **sich mit
etw ~** to occupy oneself with sth;
(*sich befassen*) to deal with sth;
beschäftigt *adj* busy, occupied;
Beschäftigung *f* (*Tätigkeit*)
employment; (*Tätigkeit*)
occupation; (*geistige*)
preoccupation (*mit* with)

Bescheid (*-(e)s, -e*) *m*
information; **~ wissen** to be
informed (*o know*) (*über* +*akk*
about); **ich weiß ~** I know; **jdm
~ geben** (*o* **sagen**) to let sb know

bescheiden *adj* modest

bescheinigen *vt* to certify;
(*bestätigen*) to acknowledge;
Bescheinigung *f* certificate;
(*Quittung*) receipt

bescheißen *irr vt* (*vulg*) to cheat
(*um* out of)

bescheuert *adj* (*fam, pej*) crazy

beschimpfen *vt* (*mit*
Kraftausdrücken) to swear at

Beschiss (*-es*) *m:* **das ist ~** (*vulg*)
that's a rip-off; **beschissen** *adj*
(*vulg*) shitty

beschlagnahmen *vt* to
confiscate

Beschleunigung *f* acceleration;
Beschleunigungsspur *f*
acceleration lane

beschließen *irr vt* to decide on,
(*beenden*) to end; **Beschluss** *m*
decision

beschränken *vt* to limit, to
restrict (*auf* +*akk* to) ▷ *vr:* **sich ~** to
restrict oneself (*auf* +*akk* to);
Beschränkung *f* limitation,
restriction

beschreiben *irr vt* to describe;
(*Papier*) to write on; **Beschreibung**
f description

beschuldigen *vt* to accuse (*gen*
of); **Beschuldigung** *f*
accusation

beschummeln *vt, vi* (*fam*) to
cheat (*um* out of)

beschützen *vt* to protect (*vor*
+*dat* from)

Beschwerde (*-, -n*) *f* complaint;
~n *pl* (*Leiden*) trouble *sing*;
beschweren *vt* to weight down;
(*fig*) to burden ▷ *vr:* **sich ~** to
complain

beschwipst *adj* tipsy

beseitigen *vt* to remove;
(*Problem*) to get rid of; (*Müll*) to
dispose of; **Beseitigung** *f*
removal; (*von Müll*) disposal

Besen (*-s, -*) *m* broom

besetzen *vt* (*Haus, Land*) to
occupy; (*Platz*) to take; (*Posten*) to
fill; (*Rolle*) to cast; **besetzt** *adj*
full; (*Tel*) engaged (*Brit*), busy (*US*);
(*Platz*) taken; (*WC*) engaged;
Besetztzeichen *nt* engaged tone
(*Brit*), busy tone (*US*)

besichtigen *vt* (*Museum*) to visit;
(*Sehenswürdigkeit*) to have a look at;
(*Stadt*) to tour

besiegen *vt* to defeat

Besitz (*-es*) *m* possession;
(*Eigentum*) property; **besitzen** *irr*

vt to own; (Eigenschaft) to have;
Besitzer(in) (-s, -) m(f) owner
besoffen adj (fam) plastered
besondere(r, s) adj special;
(bestimmt) particular;
(eigentümlich) peculiar; **nichts ~s**
nothing special; **Besonderheit** f
special feature; (besondere
Eigenschaft) peculiarity; **besonders**
adv especially, particularly;
(getrennt) separately
besorgen vt (beschaffen) to get
(jdm for sb); (kaufen a.) to purchase;
(erledigen: Geschäfte) to deal with
besprechen irr vt to discuss;
Besprechung f discussion;
(Konferenz) meeting; **Besprechungsraum** m consultation
room
besser adj better; **es geht ihm
~** he feels better; **~ gesagt** or
rather; **~ werden** to improve;
bessern vt to improve ▷ vr: **sich
~** to improve; (Mensch) to mend
one's ways; **Besserung** f
improvement; **gute ~!** get well
soon
beständig adj constant; (Wetter)
settled
Bestandteil m component
bestätigen vt to confirm;
(Empfang, Brief) to acknowledge;
Bestätigung f confirmation; (von
Brief) acknowledgement
beste(r, s) adj best; **das ~ wäre,
wir ...** it would be best if ...
▷ adv: **sie singt am ~n** she sings
best; **so ist es am ~n** it's best that
way; **am ~n gehst du gleich** you'd
better go at once
bestechen irr vt to bribe;
Bestechung f bribery
Besteck (-(e)s, -e) nt cutlery
bestehen irr vi to be, to exist;
(andauern) to last; **~ auf** (+dat) to
insist on; **~ aus** to consist of ▷ vt
(Probe, Prüfung) to pass; (Kampf) to

win
bestehlen irr vt to rob
bestellen vt to order; (reservieren)
to book; (Grüße, Auftrag) to pass on
(jdm to sb); (kommen lassen) to send
for; **Bestellnummer** f order
number; **Bestellung** f (Comm)
order; (das Bestellen) ordering
bestens adv very well
bestimmen vt to determine;
(Regeln) to lay down; (Tag, Ort) to
fix; (ernennen) to appoint;
(vorsehen) to mean (für for);
bestimmt adj definite; (gewiss)
certain; (entschlossen) firm ▷ adv
definitely; (wissen) for sure;
Bestimmung f (Verordnung)
regulation; (Zweck) purpose
Best.-Nr. abk = **Bestellnummer**
order number
bestrafen vt to punish
bestrahlen vt to illuminate;
(Med) to treat with radiotherapy
bestreiten irr vt (leugnen) to
deny
Bestseller (-s, -) m bestseller
bestürzt adj dismayed
Besuch (-(e)s, -e) m visit; (Mensch)
visitor; **~ haben** to have visitors/a
visitor; **besuchen** vt to visit;
(Schule, Kino etc) to go to;
Besucher(in) (-s, -) m(f) visitor;
Besuchszeit f visiting hours pl
betäuben vt (Med) to
anaesthetize; **Betäubung** f
anaesthetic; **örtliche ~** local
anaesthetic; **Betäubungsmittel**
nt anaesthetic
Bete (-, -n) f: **Rote ~** beetroot
beteiligen vr: **sich an etw** (dat)
~ to take part in sth, to participate
in sth ▷ vt: **jdn an etw** (dat) **~** to
involve sb in sth; **Beteiligung** f
participation; (Anteil) share;
(Besucherzahl) attendance
beten vi to pray
Beton (-s, -s) m concrete

betonen vt to stress;
(hervorheben) to emphasize;
Betonung f stress; (fig)
emphasis

Betr. abk = **Betreff**

Betracht m: **in ~ ziehen** to take
into consideration; **in ~ kommen**
to be a possibility; **nicht in
~ kommen** to be out of the
question; **betrachten** vt to look
at; **~ als** to regard as; **beträchtlich**
adj considerable

Betrag (-(e)s, Beträge) m amount,
sum; **betragen** irr vt to amount
(o come) to ▷ vr: **sich ~** to behave

betreffen irr vt to concern;
(Regelung etc) to affect; **was mich
betrifft** as for me; **betreffend** adj
relevant, in question

betreten irr vt to enter; (Bühne
etc) to step onto; „**Betreten
verboten**" "keep off/out"

betreuen vt to look after;
(Reisegruppe, Abteilung) to be in
charge of; **Betreuer(in)** (-s, -) m(f)
(Pfleger) carer; (von Kind) child
minder; (von Reisegruppe)
groupleader

Betrieb (-(e)s, -e) m (Firma) firm;
(Anlage) plant; (Tätigkeit)
operation; (Treiben) bustle; **außer
~ sein** to be out of order; **in ~ sein**
to be in operation; **betriebsbereit**
adj operational; **Betriebsrat** m
(Gremium) works council;
Betriebssystem nt (Inform)
operating system

betrinken irr vr: **sich ~** to get
drunk

betroffen adj (bestürzt) shaken;
von etw ~ werden/sein to be
affected by sth

betrog imperf von **betrügen**

betrogen pp von **betrügen**

Betrug (-(e)s) m deception; (Jur)
fraud; **betrügen** (betrog, betrogen)
vt to deceive; (Jur) to defraud;

(Partner) to cheat on; **Betrüger(in)**
(-s, -) m(f) cheat

betrunken adj drunk

Bett (-(e)s, -en) nt bed; **ins** (o **zu**)
~ gehen to go to bed; **das
~ machen** to make the bed;
Bettbezug m duvet cover;
Bettdecke f blanket

betteln vi to beg

Bettlaken nt sheet

Bettler(in) (-s, -) m(f) beggar

Bettsofa nt sofa bed; **Betttuch**
nt sheet; **Bettwäsche** f bed
linen; **Bettzeug** m bedding

beugen vt to bend ▷ vr: **sich ~** to
bend; (sich fügen) to submit (dat to)

Beule (-, -n) f (Schwellung) bump;
(Delle) dent

beunruhigen vt to worry ▷ vr:
sich ~ to worry

beurteilen vt to judge

Beute (-) f (von Dieb) booty, loot;
(von Tier) prey

Beutel (-s, -) m bag .

Bevölkerung f population

bevollmächtigt adj authorized
(zu etw to do sth)

bevor conj before; **bevor|stehen**
irr vi (Schwierigkeiten) to lie ahead;
(Gefahr) to be imminent; **jdm
~** (Überraschung etc) to be in store
for sb; **bevorstehend** adj
forthcoming; **bevorzugen** vt to
prefer

bewachen vt to guard; **bewacht**
adj: **~er Parkplatz** supervised car
park (Brit), guarded parking lot
(US)

bewegen vt to move; **jdn dazu ~,
etw zu tun** to get sb to do sth
▷ vr: **sich ~** to move; **es bewegt
sich etwas** (fig) things are
beginning to happen; **Bewegung**
f movement; (Phys) motion;
(innere) emotion; (körperlich)
exercise; **Bewegungsmelder**
(-s, -) m sensor (which reacts to

movement)

Beweis (*-es, -e*) *m* proof; (*Zeugnis*)
evidence; **beweisen** *irr vt* to
prove; (*zeigen*) to show

bewerben *irr vr:* **sich ~** to apply
(*um for*); **Bewerbung** *f*
application; **Bewerbungsun-
terlagen** *pl* application
documents *pl*

bewilligen *vt* to allow; (*Geld*) to
grant

bewirken *vt* to cause, to bring
about

bewohnen *vt* to live in;
Bewohner(in) (*-s, -*) *m(f)*
inhabitant; (*von Haus*) resident

bewölkt *adj* cloudy, overcast;
Bewölkung *f* clouds *pl*

bewundern *vt* to admire;
bewundernswert *adj* admirable

bewusst *adj* conscious;
(*absichtlich*) deliberate; **sich** (*dat*)
einer Sache (*gen*) **~ sein** to be
aware of sth ▷ *adv* consciously;
(*absichtlich*) deliberately;
bewusstlos *adj* unconscious;
Bewusstlosigkeit *f* unconsciousness; **Bewusstsein** (*-s*) *nt*
consciousness; **bei ~** conscious

bezahlen *vt* to pay; (*Ware,
Leistung*) to pay for; **kann ich
bar/mit Kreditkarte ~?** can I pay
cash/by credit card?; **sich bezahlt
machen** to be worth it;
Bezahlung *f* payment

bezeichnen *vt* (*kennzeichnen*) to
mark; (*nennen*) to call; (*beschreiben*)
to describe; **Bezeichnung** *f*
(*Name*) name; (*Begriff*) term

beziehen *irr vt* (*Bett*) to change;
(*Haus, Position*) to move into;
(*erhalten*) to receive; (*Zeitung*) to
take; **einen Standpunkt ~** to
take up a position ▷ *vr:* **sich ~** to
refer (*auf +akk* to); **Beziehung** *f*
(*Verbindung*) connection;
(*Verhältnis*) relationship; **~en**

haben (*vorteilhaft*) to have
connections (*o contacts*); **in dieser
~** in this respect;
beziehungsweise *adv* or;
(*genauer gesagt*) or rather

Bezirk (*-(e)s, -e*) *m* district

Bezug (*-(e)s, Bezüge*) *m* (*Überzug*)
cover; (*von Kopfkissen*) pillowcase;
in ~ auf (*+akk*) with regard to;
bezüglich *prep +gen* concerning

bezweifeln *vt* to doubt

BH (*-s, -s*) *m* bra

Bhf. *abk* = **Bahnhof** station

Biathlon (*-s, -s*) *m* biathlon

Bibel (*-, -n*) *f* Bible

Biber (*-s, -*) *m* beaver

Bibliothek (*-, -en*) *f* library

biegen (*bog, gebogen*) *vt* to bend
▷ *vr:* **sich ~** to bend ▷ *vi* to turn
(*in +akk* into); **Biegung** *f* bend

Biene (*-, -n*) *f* bee

Bier (*-(e)s, -e*) *nt* beer; **helles ~**
≈ lager (*Brit*), beer (*US*); **dunkles ~**
≈ brown ale (*Brit*), dark beer (*US*);
zwei ~, bitte! two beers, please;
Biergarten *m* beer garden;
Bierzelt *nt* beer tent

bieten (*bot, geboten*) *vt* to offer;
(*bei Versteigerung*) bid; **sich** (*dat*)
etw ~ lassen to put up with sth
▷ *vr:* **sich ~** (*Gelegenheit*) to present
itself (*dat* to)

Bikini (*-s, -s*) *m* bikini

Bild (*-(e)s, -er*) *nt* picture;
(*gedankliches*) image; (*Foto*) photo

bilden *vt* to form; (*geistig*) to
educate; (*ausmachen*) to constitute
▷ *vr:* **sich ~** (*entstehen*) to form;
(*lernen*) to educate oneself

Bilderbuch *nt* picture book

Bildhauer(in) (*-s, -*) *m(f)*
sculptor

Bildschirm *m* screen;
Bildschirmschoner (*-s, -*) *m*
screensaver; **Bildschirmtext** *m*
viewdata, videotext

Bildung *f* formation; (*Wissen,*

Benehmen) education;
Bildungsurlaub *m* educational holiday; (*von Firma*) study leave
Billard *nt* billiards *sing*
billig *adj* cheap; (*gerecht*) fair
Billigflieger *m* budget airline
Billigflug *m* cheap flight
Binde (-, -n) *f* bandage; (*Armbinde*) band; (*Damenbinde*) sanitary towel (*Brit*), sanitary napkin (*US*)
Bindehautentzündung *f* conjunctivitis
binden (*band, gebunden*) *vt* to tie; (*Buch*) to bind; (*Soße*) to thicken
Bindestrich *m* hyphen
Bindfaden *m* string
Bindung *f* bond, tie; (*Skibindung*) hinding
Bio- *in zW* bio-; **Biokost** *f* health food

○ **BIOLADEN**

- A **Bioladen** is a shop which
- specializes in selling
- environmentally friendly
- products such as
- phosphate-free washing
- powders, recycled paper and
- organically grown vegetables.

Biologie *f* biology; **biologisch** *adj* biological; (*Anbau*) organic
Birke (-, -n) *f* birch
Birne (-, -n) *f* (*Obst*) pear; (*Elek*) (light) bulb

 SCHLÜSSELWORT

bis *prep +akk, adv* 1 (*zeitlich*) till, until; (*bis spätestens*) by; **Sie haben bis Dienstag Zeit** you have until o till Tuesday; **bis Dienstag muss es fertig sein** it must be ready by Tuesday; **bis auf Weiteres** until further notice; **bis in die Nacht**

into the night; **bis bald/gleich** see you later/soon
2 (*räumlich*) (up) to; **ich fahre bis Köln** I'm going to o I'm going as far as Cologne; **bis an unser Grundstück** (right o up) to our plot; **bis hierher** this far
3 (*bei Zahlen*) up to; **bis zu** up to
4 **bis auf etw** *akk* (*außer*) except sth; (*einschließlich*) including sth
▷ *konj* 1 (*mit Zahlen*) to; **10 bis 20** 10 to 20
2 (*zeitlich*) till, until; **bis es dunkel wird** till o until it gets dark; **von ... bis ...** from ... to ...

Bischof (-s, *Bischöfe*) *m* bishop
bisher *adv* up to now, so far
Biskuit (-(*e*)s, -*s o* -*e*) *nt* sponge
biss *imperf von* **beißen**
Biss (-*es*, -*e*) *m* bite
bisschen *adj*: **ein ~** a bit of; **ein ~ Salz/Liebe** a bit of salt/love; **ich habe kein ~ Hunger** I'm not a bit hungry ▷ *adv*: **ein ~** a bit; **kein ~** not at all
bissig *adj* (*Hund*) vicious; (*Bemerkung*) cutting
Bit (-*s*, -*s*) *nt* (*Inform*) bit
bitte *interj* please; (**wie**) **~?** (I beg your) pardon?; **~ (schön)!** (*als Antwort auf Dank*) you're welcome, that's alright; **hier, ~** here you are; **Bitte** (-, -*n*) *f* request; **bitten** (*bat, gebeten*) *vt, vi* to ask (*um* for)
bitter *adj* bitter
Blähungen *pl* (*Med*) wind *sing*
blamieren *vr*: **sich ~** to make a fool of oneself ▷ *vt*: **jdn ~** to make sb look a fool
Blankoscheck *m* blank cheque
Blase (-, -*n*) *f* bubble; (*Med*) blister; (*Anat*) bladder
blasen (*blies, geblasen*) *vi* to blow; **jdm einen ~** (*vulg*) to give sb a blow job
Blasenentzündung *f* cystitis

blass adj pale

Blatt (-(e)s, Blätter) nt leaf; (von Papier) sheet; **blättern** vi (Inform) to scroll; **in etw** (dat) **~ to leaf through sth; Blätterteig** m puff pastry; **Blattsalat** m green salad; **Blattspinat** m spinach

blau adj blue; (fam: betrunken) plastered; (Gastr) boiled; **~es Auge** black eye; **~er Fleck** bruise; **Blaubeere** f bilberry, blueberry; **Blaulicht** nt flashing blue light; **blau|machen** vi to skip work; (in Schule) to skip school; **Blauschimmelkäse** m blue cheese

Blazer (-s, -) m blazer

Blech (-(e)s, -e) nt sheet metal; (Backblech) baking tray (Brit), cookie sheet (US); **Blechschaden** m (Auto) damage to the bodywork

Blei (-(e)s, -e) nt lead

bleiben (blieb, geblieben) vi to stay; **lass das ~!** stop it; **das bleibt unter uns** that's (just) between ourselves; **mir bleibt keine andere Wahl** I have no other choice

bleich adj pale; **bleichen** vt to bleach

bleifrei adj (Benzin) unleaded; **bleihaltig** adj (Benzin) leaded

Bleistift m pencil

Blende (-, -n) f (Foto) aperture

Blick (-(e)s, -e) m look; (kurz) glance; (Aussicht) view; **auf den ersten ~** at first sight; **einen ~ auf etw** (akk) **werfen** to have a look at sth; **blicken** vi to look; **sich ~ lassen** to show up

blieb imperf von **bleiben**

blies imperf von **blasen**

blind adj blind; (Glas etc) dull; **Blinddarm** m appendix; **Blinddarmentzündung** f appendicitis; **Blinde(r)** mf blind person/man/woman; **die ~n** pl

the blind pl; **Blindenhund** m guide dog; **Blindenschrift** f braille

blinken vi (Stern, Lichter) to twinkle; (aufleuchten) to shine; (Auto) to indicate; **Blinker** (-s, -) m (Auto) indicator (Brit), turn signal (US)

blinzeln vi (mit beiden Augen) to blink; (mit einem Auge) to wink

Blitz (-es, -e) m (flash of) lightning; (Foto) flash; **blitzen** vi (Foto) to use a/the flash; **es blitzte und donnerte** there was thunder and lightning; **Blitzlicht** nt flash

Block (-(e)s, Blöcke) m (a. fig) block; (von Papier) pad; **Blockflöte** f recorder; **Blockhaus** nt log cabin; **blockieren** vt to block ▷ vi to jam; (Räder) to lock; **Blockschrift** f block letters pl

blöd adj stupid; **blödeln** vi (fam) to fool around

Blog (-s, -s) nt (Inform) blog

blond adj blond; (Frau) blonde

○ SCHLÜSSELWORT

bloß adj **1** (unbedeckt) bare; (nackt) naked; **mit der bloßen Hand** with one's bare hand; **mit bloßem Auge** with the naked eye
2 (alleinig, nur) mere; **der bloße Gedanke** the very thought; **bloßer Neid** sheer envy
▷ adv only, merely; **lass das bloß!** just don't do that!; **wie ist das bloß passiert?** how on earth did that happen?

blühen vi to bloom; (fig) to flourish

Blume (-, -n) f flower; (von Wein) bouquet; **Blumengeschäft** nt florist's (shop); **Blumenkohl** m cauliflower; **Blumenladen** m flower shop; **Blumenstrauß** m bunch of flowers; **Blumentopf** m flowerpot; **Blumenvase** f vase

Bluse (-, -n) f blouse

Blut (-(e)s) nt blood; **Blutbild** nt blood count; **Blutdruck** m blood pressure; **Blutorange** f blood orange

Blüte (-, -n) f (Pflanzenteil) flower, bloom; (Baumblüte) blossom; (fig) prime

bluten vi to bleed

Blütenstaub m pollen

Bluter (-s, -) m (Med) haemophiliac; **Bluterguss** m haematoma; (blauer Fleck) bruise; **Blutgruppe** f blood group; **blutig** adj bloody; **Blutkonserve** f unit of stored blood; **Blutprobe** f blood sample; **Blutspende** f blood donation; **Bluttransfusion** f blood transfusion; **Blutung** f bleeding; **Blutvergiftung** f blood poisoning; **Blutwurst** f black pudding (Brit), blood sausage (US)

BLZ abk = **Bankleitzahl**

Bob (-s, -s) m bob(sleigh)

Bock (-(e)s, Böcke) m (Reh) buck; (Schaf) ram; (Gestell) trestle; (Sport) vaulting horse; **ich hab keinen ~ (drauf)** (fam) I don't feel like it

Boden (-s, Böden) m ground; (Fußboden) floor; (von Meer, Fass) bottom; (Speicher) attic; **Bodennebel** m ground mist; **Bodenpersonal** nt ground staff; **Bodenschätze** pl mineral resources pl

Bodensee m: **der ~** Lake Constance

Body (-s, -s) m body; **Bodybuilding** (-s) nt bodybuilding

bog imperf von **biegen**

Bogen (-s, -) m (Biegung) curve; (in der Architektur) arch; (Waffe, Instrument) bow; (Papier) sheet

Bohne (-, -n) f bean; **grüne ~n** pl green (o French (Brit)) beans pl; **weiße ~n** pl haricot beans pl; **Bohnenkaffee** m real coffee; **Bohnensprosse** f bean sprout

bohren vt to drill; **Bohrer** (-s, -) m drill

Boiler (-s, -) m water heater

Boje (-, -n) f buoy

Bolivien (-s) nt Bolivia

Bombe (-, -n) f bomb

Bon (-s, -s) m (Kassenzettel) receipt; (Gutschein) voucher, coupon

Bonbon (-s, -s) nt sweet (Brit), candy (US)

Bonus (- o -ses, -se o Boni) m bonus; (Punktvorteil) bonus points pl; (Schadenfreiheitsrabatt) no-claims bonus

Boot (-(e)s, -e) nt boat; **Bootsverleih** m boat hire (Brit) (o rental (US))

Bord (-(e)s, -e) m: **an ~ (eines Schiffes)** on board (a ship); **an ~ gehen** (Schiff) to go on board; (Flugzeug) to board; **von ~ gehen** to disembark; **Bordcomputer** m dashboard computer

Bordell (-s, -e) nt brothel

Bordkarte f boarding card

Bordstein m kerb (Brit), curb (US)

borgen vt to borrow; **jdm etw ~** to lend sb sth; **sich** (dat) **etw ~** to borrow sth

Börse (-, -n) f stock exchange; (Geldbörse) purse

bös adj siehe **böse**; **bösartig** adj malicious; (Med) malignant

Böschung f slope; (Uferböschung) embankment

böse adj bad; (stärker) evil; (Wunde) nasty; (zornig) angry; **bist du mir ~?** are you angry with me?

boshaft adj malicious

Bosnien (-s) nt Bosnia; **Bosnien-Herzegowina** (-s) nt

Bosnia-Herzegovina

böswillig *adj* malicious

bot *imperf von* **bieten**

botanisch *adj:* **~er Garten** botanical gardens *pl*

Botschaft *f* message; *(Pol)* embassy; **Botschafter(in)** *m(f)* ambassador

Botsuana *(-s) nt* Botswana

Bouillon *(-, -s) f* stock

Boutique *(-, -n) f* boutique

Bowle *(-, -n) f* punch

Box *(-, -en) f (Behälter, Pferdebox)* box; *(Lautsprecher)* speaker; *(bei Autorennen)* pit

boxen *vi* to box; **Boxer** *(-s, -) m (Hund, Sportler)* boxer;
. **Boxershorts** *pl* boxer shorts *pl*;
Boxkampf *m* boxing match

Boykott *(-s, -e) m* boycott

brach *imperf von* **brechen**

brachte *imperf von* **bringen**

Brainstorming *(-s) nt* brainstorming

Branchenverzeichnis *nt* yellow pages® *pl*

Brand *(-(e)s, Brände) m* fire; **einen ~ haben** *(fam)* to be parched

Brandenburg *(-s) nt* Brandenburg

Brandsalbe *f* ointment for burns

Brandung *f* surf

Brandwunde *f* burn

brannte *imperf von* **brennen**

Brasilien *(-s) nt* Brazil

braten *(briet, gebraten) vt* to roast; *(auf dem Rost)* to grill; *(in der Pfanne)* to fry; **Braten** *(-s, -) m* roast; *(roher)* joint; **Bratensoße** *f* gravy; **Brathähnchen** *nt* roast chicken; **Bratkartoffeln** *pl* fried potatoes *pl*; **Bratpfanne** *f* frying pan; **Bratspieß** *m* spit; **Bratwurst** *f* fried sausage; *(gegrillte)* grilled sausage

Brauch *(-s, Bräuche) m* custom

brauchen *vt (nötig haben)* to need

(für, zu for); *(erfordern)* to require; *(Zeit)* to take; *(gebrauchen)* to use; **wie lange wird er ~?** how long will it take him?; **du brauchst es nur zu sagen** you only need to say; **das braucht (seine) Zeit** it takes time; **ihr braucht es nicht zu tun** you don't have *(o* need) to do it; **sie hätte nicht zu kommen ~** she needn't have come

brauen *vt* to brew; **Brauerei** *f* brewery

braun *adj* brown; *(von Sonne)* tanned; **Bräune** *(-, -n) f* brownness; *(von Sonne)* tan; **Bräunungsstudio** *nt* tanning studio

Brause *(-, -n) f (Dusche)* shower; *(Getränk)* fizzy drink *(Brit)*, soda *(US)*

Braut *(-, Bräute) f* bride; **Bräutigam** *(-s, -e) m* bridegroom

brav *adj (artig)* good, well-behaved

bravo *interj* well done

BRD *(-) f abk = Bundesrepublik Deutschland* FRG

● **BRD**
●
● The **BRD** is the official name for
● the Federal Republic of
● Germany. It comprises 16
● **Länder** (see **Land**). It was the
● name given to the former West
● Germany as opposed to East
● Germany (the **DDR**). The two
● Germanies were reunited on 3rd
● October 1990.

brechen *(brach, gebrochen) vt* to break; *(erbrechen)* to bring up; **sich** *(dat)* **den Arm ~** to break one's arm ▷ *vi* to break; *(erbrechen)* to vomit, to be sick; **Brechreiz** *m* nausea

Brei *(-(e)s, -e) m (Breimasse)* mush, pulp; *(Haferbrei)* porridge; *(für*

Kinder) pap

breit *adj* wide; *(Schultern)* broad;
zwei Meter ~ two metres wide;
Breite (-, -n) *f* breadth; *(bei
Maßangaben)* width; *(Geo)* latitude;
der ~ nach widthways;
Breitengrad *m* (degree of)
latitude

Bremen (-s) *nt* Bremen

Bremsbelag *m* brake lining;
Bremse (, *n) f* brake, *(Zool)*
horsefly; **bremsen** *vi* to brake
▷ *vt (Auto)* to brake; *(fig)* to slow
down; **Bremsflüssigkeit** *f* brake
fluid; **Bremslicht** *nt* brake light;
Bremspedal *nt* brake pedal;
Bremsspur *f* tyre marks *pl*;
Bremsweg *m* braking distance

brennen *(brannte, gebrannt) vi* to
burn; *(in Flammen stehen)* to be on
fire; **es brennt!** fire!; **mir ~ die
Augen** my eyes are smarting; **das
Licht ~ lassen** to leave the light
on; **Brennholz** *nt* firewood;
Brennnessel *f* stinging nettle;
Brennspiritus *m* methylated
spirits *pl*; **Brennstab** *m* fuel rod;
Brennstoff *m* fuel

Brett (-(e)s, -er) *nt* board; *(länger)*
plank; *(Regal)* shelf; *(Spielbrett)*
board; **Schwarzes ~** notice board,
bulletin board (US); **~er** *pl* (ski) skis
pl; **Brettspiel** *nt* board game

Brezel (-, -n) *f* pretzel

Brief (-(e)s, -e) *m* letter;
Briefbombe *f* letter bomb;
Brieffreund(in) *m(f)* penfriend,
pen pal; **Briefkasten** *m* letterbox
(Brit), mailbox (US);
elektronischer ~ electronic
mailbox; **Briefmarke** *f* stamp;
Briefpapier *nt* writing paper;
Brieftasche *f* wallet;
Briefträger(in) *m(f)* post-
man/-woman; **Briefumschlag** *m*
envelope; **Briefwaage** *f* letter
scales *pl*

brief *imperf von* **braten**

Brille (-, -n) *f* glasses *pl*;
(Schutzbrille) goggles *pl*; **Brillenetui**
nt glasses case

bringen *(brachte, gebracht) vt*
(herbringen) to bring; *(mitnehmen,
vom Sprecher weg)* to take; *(holen,
herbringen)* to get, to fetch; *(Theat,
Cine)* to show; *(Radio, TV)* to
broadcast; **~ Sie mir bitte noch
ein Bier** could you bring me
another beer, please?; **jdn nach
Hause ~** to take sb home; **jdn
dazu ~, etw zu tun** to make sb do
sth; **jdn auf eine Idee ~** to give sb
an idea

Brise (-, -n) *f* breeze

Brite (-n, -n) *m*, **Britin** *f* British
person, Briton; **er ist ~** he is
British; **die ~n** the British; **britisch**
adj British

Brocken (-s, -) *m* bit; *(größer)*
lump, chunk

Brokkoli *m* broccoli

Brombeere *f* blackberry

Bronchitis (-) *f* bronchitis

Bronze (-, -n) *f* bronze

Brosche (-, -n) *f* brooch

Brot (-(e)s, -e) *nt* bread; *(Laib)* loaf;
Brotaufstrich *m* spread;
Brötchen *nt* roll; **Brotzeit** *f*
(Pause) break; *(Essen)* snack;
~ machen to have a snack

Browser (-s, -) *m (Inform)*
browser

Bruch (-(e)s, Brüche) *m (Brechen)*
breaking; *(Bruchstelle; mit Partei,
Tradition etc)* break; *(Med:
Eingeweidebruch)* rupture, hernia;
(Knochenbruch) fracture; *(Math)*
fraction; **brüchig** *adj* brittle

Brücke (-, -n) *f* bridge

Bruder (-s, Brüder) *m* brother

Brühe (-, -n) *f (Suppe)* (clear)
soup; *(Grundlage)* stock; *(pej:
Getränk)* muck; **Brühwürfel** *m*
stock cube

brüllen vi to roar; (Stier) to bellow; (vor Schmerzen) to scream (with pain)

brummen vi (Bär, Mensch) to growl; (brummeln) to mutter; (Insekt) to buzz; (Motor, Radio) to drone ▷ vt to growl

brünett adj brunette

Brunnen (-s, -) m fountain; (tief) well; (natürlich) spring

Brust (-, Brüste) f breast; (beim Mann) chest; **Brustschwimmen** (-s) nt breaststroke; **Brustwarze** f nipple

brutal adj brutal

brutto adv gross

BSE (-) nt abk = **bovine spongiforme Enzephalopathie** BSE

Bube (-n, -n) m boy, lad; (Karten) jack

Buch (-(e)s, Bücher) nt book

Buche (-, -n) f beech (tree)

buchen vt to book; (Betrag) to enter

Bücherei f library

Buchfink m chaffinch

Buchhalter(in) m(f) accountant

Buchhandlung f bookshop

Büchse (-, -n) f tin (Brit), can

Buchstabe (-ns, -n) m letter; **buchstabieren** vt to spell

Bucht (-, -en) f bay

Buchung f booking; (Comm) entry

Buckel (-s, -) m hump

bücken vr: **sich ~** to bend down

Buddhismus (-) m Buddhism

Bude (-, -en) f (auf Markt) stall; (fam: Wohnung) pad, place

Büfett (-s, -s) nt sideboard; **kaltes ~** cold buffet

Büffel (-s, -) m buffalo

Bügel (-s, -) m (Kleidung) hanger; (Steigbügel) stirrup; (Brille) sidepiece; (von Skilift) T-bar; **Bügelbrett** nt ironing board;

Bügeleisen nt iron; **Bügelfalte** f crease; **bügelfrei** adj non-iron; **bügeln** vt, vi to iron

buh interj boo

Bühne (-, -n) f stage; **Bühnenbild** nt set

Bulgare (-n, -n) m, **Bulgarin** f Bulgarian; **Bulgarien** (-s) nt Bulgaria; **bulgarisch** adj Bulgarian; **Bulgarisch** nt Bulgarian

Bulimie f bulimia

Bulle (-n, -n) m bull; (fam: Polizist) cop

Bummel (-s, -) m stroll; **bummeln** vi to stroll; (trödeln) to dawdle; (faulenzen) to loaf around; **Bummelzug** m slow train

bums interj bang

bumsen vi (vulg) to screw

Bund (-(e)s, Bünde) m (von Hose, Rock) waistband; (Freundschaftsbund) bond; (Organisation) association; (Pol) confederation; **der ~** (fam: Bundeswehr) the army ▷ (-(e)s, -e) nt bunch; (von Stroh etc) bundle

Bundes- in zW Federal; (auf Deutschland bezogen a.) German; **Bundeskanzler(in)** m(f) Chancellor; **Bundesland** nt state, Land; **Bundesliga** f: **erste/zweite ~** First/Second Division; **Bundespräsident(in)** m(f) President; **Bundesrat** m (in Deutschland) Upper House (of the German Parliament); (in der Schweiz) Council of Ministers; **Bundesregierung** f Federal Government; **Bundesrepublik** f Federal Republic; **~ Deutschland** Federal Republic of Germany; **Bundesstraße** f ≈ A road (Brit), ≈ state highway (US); **Bundestag** m Lower House (of the German Parliament); **Bundeswehr** f (German) armed forces pl

● **BUNDESWEHR**
●
● The **Bundeswehr** is the name
● for the German armed forces. It
● was established in 1955, first of
● all for volunteers, but since 1956
● there has been compulsory
● military service for all
● able-bodied young men of 18. In
● peacetime the Defence Minister
● is the head of the 'Bundeswehr',
● but in wartime the
● **Bundeskanzler** takes over. The
● 'Bundeswehr' comes under the
● jurisdiction of NATO.

Bündnis nt alliance
Bungalow (-s, -s) m bungalow
Bungeejumping (s) nt bungee
 jumping
bunt adj colourful; (von Programm
 etc) varied; **~e Farben** bright
 colours ▷ adv (anstreichen) in
 bright colours; **Buntstift** m
 crayon, coloured pencil
Burg (-, -en) f castle
Bürger(in) (-s, -) m(f) citizen;
 bürgerlich adj (Rechte, Ehe etc)
 civil; (vom Mittelstand)
 middle-class; (pej) bourgeois;
 Bürgermeister(in) m(f) mayor;
 Bürgersteig (-(e)s, -e) m
 pavement (Brit), sidewalk (US)
Büro (-s, -s) nt office;
 Büroklammer f paper clip
Bürokratie f bureaucracy
Bursche (-n, -n) m lad; (Typ) guy
Bürste (-, -n) f brush; **bürsten**
 vt to brush
Bus (-ses, -se) m bus; (Reisebus)
 coach (Brit); bus; **Busbahnhof** m
 bus station
Busch (-(e)s, Büsche) m bush;
 (Strauch) shrub
Busen (-s, -) m breasts pl, bosom
Busfahrer(in) m(f) bus driver;
 Bushaltestelle f bus stop

Businessclass (-) f business
 class
Busreise (-) f coach tour (Brit), bus
 tour
Bußgeld nt fine
Büstenhalter (-s, -) m bra
Busverbindung f bus
 connection
Butter (-) f butter; **Butterbrot**
 nt slice of bread and butter;
 Butterkäse m type of mild, full-fat
 cheese; **Buttermilch** f
 buttermilk; **Butterschmalz** nt
 clarified butter
Button (-s, -s) m badge (Brit),
 button (US)
b. w. abk = **bitte wenden** pto
Byte (-s, -s) nt byte
bzw. adv abk = **beziehungsweise**

C

ca. adv abk = **circa** approx

Cabrio (-s, -s) nt convertible

Café (-s, -s) nt café

Cafeteria (-, -s) f cafeteria

Call-Center (-s, -) nt call centre

campen vi to camp; **Camping** (-s) nt camping; **Campingbus** m camper; **Campingplatz** m campsite, camping ground (US)

Cappuccino (-s, -) m cappuccino

Carving (-s) nt (Ski) carving; **Carvingski** m carving ski

CD (-, -s) f abk = **Compact Disc** CD; **CD-Brenner** (-s, -) m CD burner, CD writer; **CD-Player** (-s, -) m CD player; **CD-ROM** (-, -s) f abk = **Compact Disc Read Only Memory** CD-ROM; **CD-ROM-Laufwerk** nt CD-ROM drive, **CD-Spieler** m CD player

Cello (-s, -s o Celli) nt cello

Celsius nt celsius; **20 Grad ~** 20 degrees Celsius, 68 degrees Fahrenheit

Cent (-, -s) m (von Dollar und Euro) cent

Chamäleon (-s, -s) nt chameleon

Champagner (-s, -) m champagne

Champignon (-s, -s) m mushroom

Champions League (-, -s) f Champions League

Chance (-, -n) f chance; **die ~n stehen gut** the prospects are good

Chaos (-) nt chaos; **Chaot(in)** (-en, -en) m(f) (fam) disorganized person, scatterbrain; **chaotisch** adj chaotic

Charakter (-s, -e) m character; **charakteristisch** adj characteristic (für of)

Charisma (-s, Charismen o Charismata) nt charisma

charmant adj charming

Charterflug m charter flight; **chartern** vt to charter

Chat (-s, -s) m (Inform) chat; **chatten** vi (Inform) to chat

checken vt (überprüfen) to check; (fam: verstehen) to get

Check-in (-s, -s) m check-in; **Check-in-Schalter** m check-in desk

Chef(in) (-s, -s) m(f) boss; **Chefarzt** m, **Chefärztin** f senior consultant (Brit), medical director (US)

Chemie (-) f chemistry; **chemisch** adj chemical; **~e Reinigung** dry cleaning

Chemotherapie f chemotherapy

Chicoree (-s) m chicory

Chiffre (-, -n) f (Geheimzeichen) cipher; (in Zeitung) box number

Chile (-s) nt Chile

Chili (-s, -s) m chilli

China (-s) nt China; **Chinakohl**
m Chinese leaves pl (Brit), bok
choy (US); **Chinarestaurant** nt
Chinese restaurant; **Chinese** (-n,
-n) m Chinese; **Chinesin** (-, -nen)
f Chinese (woman); **sie ist ~** she's
Chinese; **chinesisch** adj
Chinese; **Chinesisch** nt Chinese

Chip (-s, -s) m (Inform) chip;
Chipkarte f smart card

Chips pl (Kartoffelchips) crisps pl
(Brit), chips pl (US)

Chirurg(in) (-en, -en) m(f)
surgeon

Chlor (-s) nt chlorine

Choke (-s, -s) m choke

Cholera (-) f cholera

Cholesterin (-s) nt cholesterol

Chor (-(e), Chöre) m choir; (Theat)
chorus

Choreografie f choreography

Christ(in) (-en, -en) m(f)
Christian; **Christbaum** m
Christmas tree; **Christi
Himmelfahrt** f the Ascension (of
Christ); **Christkind** nt baby
Jesus; (das Geschenke bringt) ≈
Father Christmas, Santa Claus;
christlich adj Christian

Chrom (-s) nt chrome; (Chem)
chromium

chronisch adj chronic

chronologisch adj chronological ▷ adv in
chronological order

Chrysantheme (-, -n) f
chrysanthemum

circa adv about, approximately

City (-) f city centre, downtown
(US)

Clementine (-, -n) f clementine

clever adj clever, smart

Clique (-, -n) f group; (pej) clique;
David und seine ~ David and his
lot o crowd

Clown (-s, -s) m clown

Club (-s, -s) m club; **Cluburlaub**

m club holiday (Brit), club
vacation (US)

Cocktail (-s, -s) m cocktail;
Cocktailtomate f cherry tomato

Cognac (-s) m cognac

Cola (-, -s) f Coke®, cola

Comic (-s, -s) m comic strip;
(Heft) comic

Compact Disc (-, -s) f compact
disc

Computer (-s, -) m computer;
Computerfreak m computer
nerd; **computergesteuert** adj
computer-controlled; **Computer-
grafik** f computer graphics pl;
computerlesbar adj machine-
readable; **Computerspiel** nt
computer game; **Computer-
tomografie** f computer
tomography, scan; **Computer-
virus** m computer virus

Container (-s, -) m (zum
Transport) container; (für Bauschutt
etc) skip

Control-Taste f control key

Cookie (-s, -s) nt (Inform) cookie

cool adj (fam) cool

Cornflakes pl cornflakes pl

Couch (-, -en) f couch;
Couchtisch m coffee table

Coupé (-s, -s) nt coupé

Coupon (-s, -s) m coupon

Cousin (-s, -s) m cousin; **Cousine**
f cousin

Crack (-s) nt (Droge) crack

Creme (-, -s) f cream; (Gastr)
mousse

Creutzfeld-Jakob-Krankheit f
Creutzfeld-Jakob disease, CJD

Croissant (-s, -s) nt croissant

Curry (-s) m curry powder ▷ (-s)
nt (indisches Gericht) curry;
Currywurst f fried sausage with
ketchup and curry powder

Cursor (-s, -) m (Inform) cursor

Cybercafé nt cybercafé;
Cyberspace (-) m cyberspace

d

even though he has no idea; **ich finde nichts ~** I don't see anything wrong with it; **es bleibt ~** that's settled; **~ sein** (*anwesend*) to be present; (*beteiligt*) to be involved; **ich bin ~!** count me in; **er war gerade ~ zu gehen** he was just (*o* on the point of) leaving

dabei|bleiben *irr vi* to stick with it; **ich bleibe dabei** I'm not changing my mind

dabei|haben *irr vt*: **er hat seine Schwester dabei** he's brought his sister; **ich habe kein Geld dabei** I haven't got any money on me

Dach (*-(e)s, Dächer*) *nt* roof; **Dachboden** *m* attic, loft; **Dachgepäckträger** *m* roofrack; **Dachrinne** *f* gutter

Dachs (*-es, -e*) *m* badger

dachte *imperf von* **denken**

Dackel (*-s, -*) *m* dachshund

dadurch *adv* (*räumlich*) through it; (*durch diesen Umstand*) in that way; (*deshalb*) because of that, for that reason ▷ *conj*: **~, dass** because; **~, dass er hart arbeitete** (*indem*) by working hard

dafür *adv* for it; (*anstatt*) instead; **~ habe ich 50 Euro bezahlt** I paid 50 euros for it; **ich bin ~ zu bleiben** I'm for (*o* in favour of) staying; **~ ist er ja da** that's what he's there for; **er kann nichts ~** he can't help it

dagegen *adv* against it; (*im Vergleich damit*) in comparison; (*bei Tausch*) for it; **ich habe nichts ~** I don't mind

daheim *adv* at home

daher *adv* (*räumlich*) from there; (*Ursache*) that's why ▷ *conj* (*deshalb*) that's why

dahin *adv* (*räumlich*) there; (*zeitlich*) then; (*vergangen*) gone; **bis ~** (*zeitlich*) till then; (*örtlich*) up to there; **bis ~ muss die Arbeit fertig**

da *adv* **1** (*örtlich*) there; (*hier*) here; **da draußen** out there; **da sein** to be there; **da bin ich** here I am; **da, wo** where; **ist noch Milch da?** is there any milk left?
2 (*zeitlich*) then; (*folglich*) so
3 da haben wir Glück gehabt we were lucky there; **da kann man nichts machen** nothing can be done about it
▷ *konj* (*weil*) as, since

dabei *adv* (*räumlich*) close to it; (*zeitlich*) at the same time; (*obwohl, doch*) though; **sie hörte Radio und rauchte ~** she was listening to the radio and smoking (at the same time); **~ fällt mir ein ...** that reminds me ...; **~ kam es zu einem Unfall** this led to an accident; **... und ~ hat er gar keine Ahnung ...**

sein the work must be finished by then

dahinter adv behind it;
~ kommen to find out

dahinterkommen vi to find out

Dahlie f dahlia

Dalmatiner (-s, -) m dalmatian

damals adv at that time, then

Dame (-, -n) f lady; (Karten) queen; (Spiel) draughts sing (Brit), checkers sing (US); **Damenbinde** f sanitary towel (Brit), sanitary napkin (US); **Damenkleidung** f ladies' wear; **Damentoilette** f ladies' toilet (o restroom (US))

damit adv with it; (begründend) by that; **was meint er ~?** what does he mean by that?; **genug ~!** that's enough ▷ conj so that

Damm (-(e)s, Dämme) m dyke; (Staudamm) dam; (am Hafen) mole; (Bahn-, Straßendamm) embankment

Dämmerung f twilight; (am Morgen) dawn; (am Abend) dusk

Dampf (-(e)s, Dämpfe) m steam; (Dunst) vapour; **Dampfbad** nt Turkish bath; **Dampfbügeleisen** nt steam iron; **dampfen** vi to steam

dämpfen vt (Gastr) to steam; (Geräusch) to deaden; (Begeisterung) to dampen

Dampfer (-s, -) m steamer

Dampfkochtopf m pressure cooker

danach adv after that; (zeitlich a.) afterwards; (demgemäß) accordingly; **mir ist nicht ~** I don't feel like it; **~ sieht es aus** that's what it looks like

Däne (-n, -n) m Dane

daneben adv beside it; (im Vergleich) in comparison

Dänemark (-s) nt Denmark; **Dänin** f Dane, Danish

woman/girl; **dänisch** adj Danish; **Dänisch** nt Danish

dank prep +dat o gen thanks to; **Dank** (-(e)s) m thanks pl; **vielen ~!** thank you very much; **jdm ~ sagen** to thank sb; **dankbar** adj grateful; (Aufgabe) rewarding; **danke** interj thank you, thanks; **nein ~!** no, thank you; **~, gerne!** yes, please, **~, gleichfalls!** thanks, and the same to you; **danken** vi: **jdm für etw ~** to thank sb for sth; **nichts zu ~!** you're welcome

dann adv then; **bis ~!** see you (later); **~ eben nicht** okay, forget it, suit yourself

daran adv (räumlich) on it; (befestigen) to it; (stoßen) against it; **es liegt ~, dass ...** it's because ...

darauf adv (räumlich) on it; (zielgerichtet) towards it; (danach) afterwards; **es kommt ganz ~ an, ob ...** it all depends whether ...; **ich freue mich ~** I'm looking forward to it; **am Tag ~** the next day; **~folgend** (Tag, Jahr) next, following

darauffolgend adj (Tag, Jahr) next, following

daraus adv from it; **was ist ~ geworden?** what became of it?

darin adv in it; **das Problem liegt ~, dass ...** the basic problem is that ...

Darlehen (-s, -) nt loan

Darm (-(e)s, Därme) m intestine; (Wurstdarm) skin; **Darmgrippe** f gastroenteritis

dar|stellen vt to represent; (Theat) to play; (beschreiben) to describe; **Darsteller(in)** m(f) actor/actress; **Darstellung** f representation; (Beschreibung) description

darüber adv (räumlich) above it, over it; (fahren) over it; (mehr) more; (*währenddessen*) meanwhile; (*sprechen, streiten, sich freuen*) about it

darum *adv* (*deshalb*) that's why; **es geht ~, dass ...** the point (*o* thing) is that ...

darunter *adv* (*räumlich*) under it; (*dazwischen*) among them; (*weniger*) less; **was verstehen Sie ~?** what do you understand by that?; **~ fallen** to be included

darunterfallen *vi* to be included

das *art* the; **~ Auto da** that car; **er hat sich ~ Bein gebrochen** he's broken his leg; **vier Euro ~ Kilo** four euros a kilo ▷ *pron* that (one), this (one); (*relativ, Sache*) that, which; (*relativ, Person*) who, that; (*demonstrativ*) this/that one; **~ Auto da** that car; **ich nehme ~ da** I'll take that one; **~ Auto, ~ er kaufte** the car (that *o* which) he bought; **~ Mädchen, ~ nebenan wohnt** the girl who (*o* that) lives next door; **~ heißt** that is; **~ sind Amerikaner** they're American

da sein *irr vi siehe* **da**

dass *conj* that; **so ~** so that; **es sei denn, ~** unless; **ohne ~ er grüßte** without saying hello

dasselbe *pron* the same

Datei *f* (*Inform*) file; **Dateimanager** *m* file manager

Daten *pl* data *pl*; **Datenbank** *f* database; **Datenmissbrauch** *m* misuse of data; **Datenschutz** *m* data protection; **Datenträger** *m* data carrier; **Datenverarbeitung** *f* data processing

datieren *vt* to date

Dativ *m* dative (case)

Dattel (-, -*n*) *f* date

Datum (-*s*, **Daten**) *nt* date

Dauer (-, -*n*) *f* duration; (*Länge*) length; **auf die ~** in the long run; **für die ~ von zwei Jahren** for (a

period of) two years;

Dauerauftrag *m* (*Fin*) standing order; **dauerhaft** *adj* lasting; (*Material*) durable; **Dauerkarte** *f* season ticket; **dauern** *vi* to last; (*Zeit benötigen*) to take; **es hat sehr lange gedauert, bis er ...** it took him a long time to ...; **wie lange dauert es denn noch?** how much longer will it be?; **das dauert mir zu lange** I can't wait that long; **dauernd** *adj* lasting; (*ständig*) constant ▷ *adv* always, constantly; **er lachte ~** he kept laughing; **unterbrich mich nicht ~** stop interrupting me; **Dauerwelle** *f* perm (*Brit*), permanent (*US*)

Daumen (-*s*, -) *m* thumb

Daunendecke *f* eiderdown

davon *adv* of it; (*räumlich*) away; (*weg von*) from it; (*Grund*) because of it; **ich hätte gerne ein Kilo ~** I'd like one kilo of that; **~ habe ich gehört** I've heard of it; (*Geschehen*) I've heard about it; **das kommt ~, wenn ...** that's what happens when ...; **was habe ich ~?** what's the point?; **auf und ~** up and away; **davon|laufen** *irr vi* to run away

davor *adv* (*räumlich*) in front of it; (*zeitlich*) before; **ich habe Angst ~** I'm afraid of it

dazu *adv* (*zusätzlich*) on top of that, as well; (*zu diesem Zweck*) for it, for that purpose; **ich möchte Reis ~** I'd like rice with it; **und ~ noch** and in addition; **~ fähig sein, etw zu tun** to be capable of doing sth; **wie kam es ~?** how did it happen?; **dazu|gehören** *vi* to belong to it; **dazu|kommen** *irr vi* (*zu jdm ~*) to join sb; **kommt noch etwas dazu?** anything else?

dazwischen *adv* in between; (*Unterschieden etc*) between them; (*in einer Gruppe*) among them

dazwischen|kommen irr vi:
wenn nichts dazwischenkommt
if all goes well; **mir ist etwas
dazwischengekommen**
something has cropped up
DDR (-) f abk = **Deutsche
Demokratische Republik** (Hist)
GDR
dealen vi (fam: mit Drogen) to deal
in drugs; **Dealer(in)** (-s, -) m(f)
(fam) dealer, pusher
Deck (-(e)s, -s o -e) nt deck
Decke (-, -n) f cover; (für Bett)
blanket; (für Tisch) tablecloth; (von
Zimmer) ceiling
Deckel (-s, -) m lid
decken vt to cover; (Tisch) to lay,
to set ▷ vr: **sich ~** to coincide,
(Aussagen) to correspond
▷ vi (den Tisch decken) to lay (o set)
the table
Decoder (-s, -) m decoder
defekt adj faulty; **Defekt** (-(e)s,
-e) m fault, defect
definieren vt to define;
Definition (-, -en) f definition
deftig adj (Preise) steep; **ein ~es
Essen** a good solid meal
dehnbar adj flexible, elastic;
dehnen vt to stretch ▷ vr: **sich
~** to stretch
Deich (-(e)s, -e) m dyke
dein pron (adjektivisch) your;
deine(r, s) pron (substantivisch)
yours, of you; **deiner** pron gen
von **du**; of you; **deinetwegen** adv
(wegen dir) because of you; (dir
zuliebe) for your sake; (um dich)
about you
deinstallieren vt (Programm) to
uninstall
Dekolleté (-s, -s) nt low neckline
Dekoration f decoration; (in
Laden) window dressing;
dekorativ adj decorative;
dekorieren vt to decorate;
(Schaufenster) to dress

Delfin (-s, -e) m dolphin
delikat adj (lecker) delicious;
(heikel) delicate
Delikatesse (-, -n) f delicacy
Delle (-, -en) f (fam) dent
Delphin (-s, -e) m dolphin
dem dat sing von **der/das; wie
~ auch sein mag** be that as it may
demnächst adv shortly, soon
Demo (-, s) f (fam) demo
Demokratie (-, -n) f democracy;
demokratisch adj democratic
demolieren vt to demolish
Demonstration f demonstration; **demonstrieren** vt, vi to
demonstrate
den art akk sing, dat pl von **der; sie
hat sich ~ Arm gebrochen** she's
broken her arm ▷ pron him;
(Sache) that one; (relativ: Person)
who, that, whom; (relativ: Sache)
which, that; **~ hab ich schon ewig
nicht mehr gesehen** I haven't
seen him in ages ▷ pron (Person)
who, that, whom; (Sache) which,
that; **der Typ, auf ~ sie steht** the
guy (who) she fancies; **der Berg,
auf ~ wir geklettert sind** the
mountain (that) we climbed
denkbar adj: **das ist ~** that's
possible ▷ adv: **~ einfach**
extremely simple; **denken** (dachte,
gedacht) vt, vi to think (über +akk
about); **an jdn/etw ~** to think of
sb/sth; (sich erinnern,
berücksichtigen) to remember
sb/sth; **woran denkst Du?** what
are you thinking about?; **denk an
den Kaffee!** don't forget the coffee
▷ vr: **sich ~** (sich vorstellen) to
imagine; **das kann ich mir ~** I can
(well) imagine
Denkmal (-s, Denkmäler) nt
monument; **Denkmalschutz** m
monument preservation; **unter
~ stehen** to be listed
denn conj for, because ▷ adv

then; (*nach Komparativ*) than; **was ist ~?** what's wrong?; **ist das ~ so schwierig?** is it really that difficult?

dennoch *conj* still, nevertheless

Deo (-s, -s) *nt*, **Deodorant** (-s, -s) *nt* deodorant; **Deoroller** *m* roll-on deodorant; **Deospray** *m o nt* deodorant spray

Deponie (-, -n) *f* waste disposal site, tip

Depressionen *pl*: **an ~ leiden** to suffer from depression *sing*; **deprimieren** *vt* to depress

O SCHLÜSSELWORT

der (*f* **die**, *nt* **das**, *gen* **des**, **der**, **des**, *dat* **dem**, **der**, **dem**, *akk* **den**, **die**, **das**, *pl* **die**) *def art* the; **der Rhein** the Rhine; **der Klaus** (*fam*) Klaus; **die Frau** (*im Allgemeinen*) women; **der Tod/das Leben** death/life; **der Fuß des Berges** the foot of the hill; **gib es der Frau** give it to the woman; **er hat sich die Hand verletzt** he has hurt his hand

▷ *relativ pron* (*bei Menschen*) who, that; (*bei Tieren, Sachen*) which, that; **der Mann, den ich gesehen habe** the man who *o* whom *o* that I saw

▷ *demonstrativ pron* he/she/it (*jener, dieser*) that; (*pl*) those; **der/die war es** it was him/her; **der mit der Brille** the one with glasses; **ich will den (da)** I want that one

derart *adv* so; (*solcher Art*) such; **derartig** *adj*: **ein ~er Fehler** such a mistake, a mistake like that

deren *gen von* **die** ▷ *pron* (*Person*) her; (*Sache*) its; (*Plural*) their ▷ *pron* (*Person*) whose; (*Sache*) of which; **meine Freundin und ~ Mutter** my

friend and her mother; **das sind ~ Sachen** that's their stuff; **die Frau, ~ Tochter ...** the woman whose daughter ...; **ich bin mir ~ bewusst** I'm aware of that

dergleichen *pron*: **und ~ mehr** and the like, and so on; **nichts ~** no such thing

derjenige *pron* the one; **~, der** (*relativ*) the one who (*o* that)

dermaßen *adv* so much; (*mit Adj*) so

derselbe *pron* the same (person/thing)

deshalb *adv* therefore; **~ frage ich ja** that's why I'm asking

Design (-s, -s) *nt* design; **Designer(in)** (-s, -) *m(f)* designer

Desinfektionsmittel *nt* disinfectant; **desinfizieren** *vt* to disinfect

dessen *gen von* **der**, **das** ▷ *pron* (*Person*) his; (*Sache*) its; **ich bin mir ~ bewusst** I'm aware of that ▷ *pron* (*Person*) whose; (*Sache*) of which; **mein Freund und ~ Mutter** my friend and his mother; **der Mann, ~ Tochter ...** the man whose daughter ...; **ich bin mir ~ bewusst** I'm aware of that

Dessert (-s, -s) *nt* dessert; **zum** (*o* **als**) **~** for dessert

destilliert *adj* distilled

desto *adv*: **je eher, ~ besser** the sooner, the better

deswegen *conj* therefore

Detail (-s, -s) *nt* detail; **ins ~ gehen** to go into detail

Detektiv(in) (-s, -e) *m(f)* detective

deutlich *adj* clear; (*Unterschied*) distinct

deutsch *adj* German; **Deutsch** *nt* German; **auf ~** in German; **ins ~e übersetzen** to translate into German; **Deutsche(r)** *mf*

German; **Deutschland** nt
Germany

Devise (-, -n) f motto; **~n** pl (Fin)
foreign currency sing;
Devisenkurs m exchange rate

Dezember (-(s), -) m December;
siehe auch **Juni**

dezent adj discreet

d.h. abk von **das heißt** i.e.
(gesprochen: i.e. oder that is)

Dia (-s, -s) nt slide

Diabetes (-, -) m (Med) diabetes;
Diabetiker(in) (-s, -) m(f)
diabetic

Diagnose (-, -n) f diagnosis

diagonal adj diagonal

Dialekt (-(e)s, -e) m dialect

Dialog (-(e)s, -e) m dialogue;
(Inform) dialog

Dialyse (-, -n) f (Med) dialysis

Diamant m diamond

Diaprojektor m slide projector

Diät (-, -en) f diet; eine ~ machen
to be on a diet; (anfangen) to go on
a diet

dich pron akk von **du** you;
~ (selbst) (reflexiv) yourself; pass
auf ~ auf look after yourself; reg
~ nicht auf don't get upset

dicht adj dense; (Nebel) thick;
(Gewebe) close; (wasserdicht)
watertight; (Verkehr) heavy ▷ adv:
~ an/bei close to; ~ bevölkert
densely populated

Dichter(in) (-s, -) m(f) poet;
(Autor) writer

Dichtung f (Auto) gasket;
(Dichtungsring) washer; (Gedichte)
poetry

Dichtungsring m (Tech) washer

dick adj thick; (Person) fat; **jdn**
~ haben to be sick of sb;
Dickdarm m colon; **Dickkopf** m
stubborn (o pig-headed) person;
Dickmilch f sour milk

die art the; ~ arme Sarah poor
Sarah ▷ pron (sing, Person, als

Subjekt) she; (Person, als Subjekt,
Plural) they; (Person, als Objekt) her;
(Person, als Objekt, Plural) them;
(Sache) that (one), this (one);
(Plural) those (ones); (Sache, Plural)
those (ones); (relativ, auf Person)
who, that; (relativ, auf Sache)
which, that; ~ mit den langen
Haaren the one (o her) with the
long hair; **sie war ~ erste, die es**
erfuhr she was the first to know;
ich nehme ~ da I'll take that
one/those ▷ pl von **der, die, das**

Dieb(in) (-(e)s, -e) m(f) thief;
Diebstahl (-(e)s, Diebstähle) m
theft; **Diebstahlsicherung** f
burglar alarm

diejenige pron the one; ~, die
(relativ) the one who (o that); ~n pl
those pl, the ones

Diele (-, -n) f hall

Dienst (-(e)s, -e) m service; außer
~ retired; ~ haben to be on duty

Dienstag m Tuesday; siehe auch
Mittwoch; dienstags adv on
Tuesdays; siehe auch **mittwochs**

Dienstbereitschaft f: ~ haben
(Arzt) to be on call; **diensthabend**
adj: der ~e Arzt the doctor on
duty; **Dienstleistung** f service;
dienstlich adj official; er ist
~ unterwegs he's away on
business; **Dienstreise** f business
trip; **Dienststelle** f department;
Dienstwagen m company car;
Dienstzeit f office hours pl; (Mil)
period of service

diesbezüglich adj (formell) on
this matter

diese(r, s) pron this (one); pl
these; ~ Frau this woman; ~r
Mann this man; ~s Mädchen this
girl; ~ Leute these people; ich
nehme ~/~n/~s (hier) I'll take this
one; (dort) I'll take that one; ich
nehme ~ pl (hier) I'll take these
(ones); (dort) I'll take those (ones)

Diesel (-s, -) m (Auto) diesel

dieselbe pron the same; **es sind immer ~n** it's always the same people

Dieselmotor m diesel engine; **Dieselöl** nt diesel (oil)

diesig adj hazy, misty

diesmal adv this time

Dietrich (-s, -e) m skeleton key

Differenz (-, -en) f difference

digital adj digital; **Digital-** in zW (Anzeige etc) digital; **Digitalfernsehen** nt digital television, digital TV; **Digitalkamera** f digital camera

Diktat (-(e)s, -e) nt dictation

Diktatur f dictatorship

Dill (-s) m dill

DIN abk = **Deutsche Industrienorm** DIN; **~ A4** A4

Ding (-(e)s, -e) nt thing; **vor allen ~en** above all; **der Stand der ~e** the state of affairs; **das ist nicht mein ~** (fam) it's not my sort of thing (o cup of tea); **Dingsbums** (-) nt (fam) thingy, thingummybob

Dinkel (-s, -) m (Bot) spelt

Dinosaurier (-s, -) m dinosaur

Diphtherie (-, -n) f diphtheria

Diplom (-(e)s, -e) nt diploma

Diplomat(in) (-en, -en) m(f) diplomat

dir pron dat von **du** to you; **hat er ~ geholfen?** did he help you?; **ich werde es ~ erklären** I'll explain it to you; (reflexiv) **wasch ~ die Hände** go and wash your hands; **ein Freund von ~** a friend of yours

direkt adj direct; (Frage) straight; **~e Verbindung** through service ▷ adv directly; (sofort) immediately; **~ am Bahnhof** right next to the station; **Direktflug** m direct flight

Direktor(in) m(f) director; (Schule) headmaster/-mistress

(Brit), principal (US)

Direktübertragung f live broadcast

Dirigent(in) m(f) conductor; **dirigieren** vt to direct; (Mus) to conduct

Discman® (-s, -s) m Discman®

Diskette f disk, diskette; **Diskettenlaufwerk** nt disk drive

Diskjockey (-s, -s) m disc jockey; **Disko** (-, -s) f (fam) disco, club; **Diskothek** (-, -en) f discotheque, club

diskret adj discreet

diskriminieren vt to discriminate against

Diskussion f discussion; **diskutieren** vt, vi to discuss

Display (-s, -s) nt display

disqualifizieren vt to disqualify

Distanz f distance

Distel (-, -n) f thistle

Disziplin (-, -en) f discipline

divers adj various

dividieren vt to divide (durch by); **8 dividiert durch 2 ist 4** 8 divided by 2 is 4

DJ (-s, -s) m abk = **Diskjockey** DJ

🅞 SCHLÜSSELWORT

doch adv 1 (dennoch) after all; (sowieso) anyway; **er kam doch noch** he came after all; **du weißt es ja doch besser** you know better than I do anyway; **und doch ...** and yet ...

2 (als bejahende Antwort) yes I do/it does etc; **das ist nicht wahr — doch!** that's not true — yes it is!

3 (auffordernd) **komm doch** do come; **lass ihn doch** just leave him; **nicht doch!** oh no!

4 **sie ist doch noch so jung** but she's still so young; **Sie wissen doch, wie das ist** you know how

it is(, don't you?); **wenn doch** if
only
▷ *konj* (*aber*) but; (*trotzdem*) all the
same; **und doch hat er es getan**
but still he did it

Doktor(in) *m(f)* doctor
Dokument *nt* document;
Dokumentarfilm *m* docu-
mentary (film); **dokumentieren**
vt to document;
Dokumentvorlage *f* (*Inform*)
document template
Dolch (-(e)s, -e) *m* dagger
Dollar (-(s), -s) *m* dollar
dolmetschen *vt, vi* to interpret;
Dolmetscher(in) (-s, -) *m(f)*
interpreter
Dolomiten *pl* Dolomites *pl*
Dom (-(e)s, -e) *m* cathedral
Domäne (-, -n) *f* domain,
province; (*Inform: Domain*) domain
Dominikanische Republik *f*
Dominican Republic
Domino (-s, -s) *nt* dominoes *sing*
Donau (-) *f* Danube
Döner (-s, -) *m*, **Döner Kebab**
(-(s), -s) *m* doner kebab
Donner (-s, -) *m* thunder;
donnern *vi*: **es donnert** it's
thundering
Donnerstag *m* Thursday; *siehe
auch* **Mittwoch**; **donnerstags**
adv on Thursdays; *siehe auch*
mittwochs
doof *adj* (*fam*) stupid
dopen *vt* to dope; **Doping** (-s) *nt*
doping; **Dopingkontrolle** *f*
drugs test
Doppel (-s, -) *nt* duplicate; (*Sport*)
doubles *sing*; **Doppelbett** *nt*
double bed; **Doppeldecker** *m*
double-decker; **Doppelhaushälfte** *f* semi-detached house
(*Brit*), duplex (*US*); **doppelklicken**
vi to double-click; **Doppelname**
m double-barrelled name;

Doppelpunkt *m* colon;
Doppelstecker *m* two-way
adaptor; **doppelt** *adj* double; **in
~er Ausführung** in duplicate;
Doppelzimmer *nt* double room
Dorf (-(e)s, Dörfer) *nt* village
Dorn (-(e)s, -en) *m* (*Bot*) thorn
Dörrobst *nt* dried fruit
Dorsch ((-(e)s, -e) *m* cod
dort *adv* there; **~ drüben** over
there; **dorther** *adv* from there
Dose (-, -n) *f* box; (*Blechdose*) tin
(*Brit*), can; (*Bierdose*) can
dösen *vi* to doze
Dosenbier *nt* canned beer;
Dosenmilch *f* canned milk,
tinned milk (*Brit*); **Dosenöffner**
m tin opener (*Brit*), can opener
Dotter (-s, -) *m* (egg) yolk
downloaden *vt* to download
Downsyndrom (-(e)s, -e) *nt*
(*Med*) Down's syndrome
Dozent(in) *m(f)* lecturer
Dr. *abk* = **Doktor**
Drache (-n, -n) *m* dragon;
Drachen (-s, -) *m* (*Spielzeug*) kite;
(*Sport*) hang-glider;
Drachenfliegen (-s) *nt*
hang-gliding; **Drachenflieger(in)**
(-s, -) *m(f)* hang-glider
Draht (-(e)s, Drähte) *m* wire;
Drahtseilbahn *f* cable railway
Drama (-s, Dramen) *nt* drama;
dramatisch *adj* dramatic
dran *adv* (*fam*) *kontr von* **daran**;
gut ~ sein (*reich*) to be well-off;
(*glücklich*) to be fortunate;
(*gesundheitlich*) to be well;
schlecht ~ sein to be in a bad way;
wer ist ~? whose turn is it?; **ich
bin ~** it's my turn; **bleib ~!** (*Tel*)
hang on
drang *imperf von* **dringen**
Drang (-(e)s, Dränge) *m* (*Trieb*)
urge (*nach for*); (*Druck*) pressure
drängeln *vt, vi* to push
drängen *vt* (*schieben*) to push;

(antreiben) to urge ▷ vi (eilig sein) to be urgent; (Zeit) to press; **auf etw (akk) ~** to press for sth

dran|kommen irr vi: **wer kommt dran?** who's turn is it?, who's next?

drauf (fam) kontr von **darauf**; **gut/schlecht ~ sein** to be in a good/bad mood

Draufgänger(in) (-s, -) m(f) daredevil

drauf|kommen irr vi to remember; **ich komme nicht drauf** I can't think of it

drauf|machen vi (fam) **einen ~** to go on a binge

draußen adv outside

Dreck (-(e)s) m dirt, filth; **dreckig** adj dirty, filthy

drehen vt, vi to turn; (Zigaretten) to roll; (Film) to shoot ▷ vr: **sich ~** to turn; (um Achse) to rotate; **sich ~ um** (handeln von) to be about

Drehstrom m three-phase current; **Drehtür** f revolving door; **Drehzahlmesser** m rev counter

drei num three; **~ viertel voll** three-quarters full; **es ist ~ viertel neun** it's a quarter to nine; **Drei** (-, -en) f three; (Schulnote) ≈ C;

Dreieck nt triangle; **dreieckig** adj triangular; **dreifach** adj triple ▷ adv three times; **dreihundert** num three hundred; **Dreikönigstag** m Epiphany; **dreimal** adv three times; **Dreirad** nt tricycle; **dreispurig** adj three-lane

dreißig num thirty; **dreißigste(r, s)** adj thirtieth; siehe auch **dritte**

Dreiviertelstunde f: **eine ~** three quarters of an hour

dreizehn num thirteen; **dreizehnte(r, s)** adj thirteenth; siehe auch **dritte**

dressieren vt to train

Dressing (-s, -s) nt (salad) dressing

Dressman (-s, Dressmen) m (male) model

Dressur (-, -en) f training

drin (fam) kontr von **darin** in it; **mehr war nicht ~** that was the best I could do

dringen (Wasser, Licht, Kälte) to penetrate (durch through, in +akk into); **auf etw (akk) ~** to insist on sth; **dringend, dringlich** adj urgent

drinnen adv inside

dritt adv: **wir sind zu ~** there are three of us; **dritte(r, s)** adj third; **die Dritte Welt** the Third World; **7. Juni** 7(th) June (gesprochen: the seventh of June); **am 7. Juni** on 7(th) June, on June 7(th) (gesprochen: on the seventh of June); **München, den 7. Juni** Munich, June 7(th); **Drittel** (-s, -) nt (Bruchteil) third; **drittens** adv thirdly

Droge (-, -n) f drug; **drogenabhängig, drogensüchtig** adj addicted to drugs

Drogerie f chemist's (Brit), drugstore (US); **Drogeriemarkt** m discount chemist's (Brit (o drugstore (US))

● **DROGERIE**
●
● The **Drogerie** as opposed to the
● **Apotheke** sells medicines not
● requiring a prescription. It
● tends to be cheaper and also
● sells cosmetics, perfume and
● toiletries.

drohen vi to threaten (jdm sb); **mit etw ~** to threaten to do sth

dröhnen vi (Motor) to roar; (Stimme, Musik) to boom; (Raum) to resound

Drohung f threat

Drossel (-, -n) f thrush

drüben adv over there; (auf der anderen Seite) on the other side

drüber (fam) kontr von **darüber**

Druck (-(e)s, Drücke) m (Phys) pressure; (fig: Belastung) stress; **jdn unter ~ setzen** to put sb under pressure ▷ (-(e)s, -e) m (Typo: Vorgang) printing; (Produkt: Schriftart) print; **Druckbuchstabe** m block letter; **in ~n schreiben** to print; **drucken** vt, vi to print

drücken vt, vi (Knopf, Hand) to press; (zu eng sein) to pinch; (fig: Preise) to keep down; **jdm etw in die Hand ~** to press sth into sb's hand ▷ vr **sich vor etw** (dat) **~** to get out of sth; **drückend** adj oppressive

Drucker (-s, -) m (Inform) printer; **Druckertreiber** m printer driver

Druckknopf m press stud (Brit), snap fastener (US); **Drucksache** f printed matter; **Druckschrift** f block letters pl

drunten adv down there

drunter (fam) kontr von **darunter**

Drüse (-, -n) f gland

Dschungel (-s, -) m jungle

du pron you; **bist ~ es?** is it you?; **wir sind per ~** we're on first-name terms

Dübel (-s, -) m Rawlplug®

ducken vt to duck ▷ vr: **sich ~** to duck

Dudelsack m bagpipes pl

Duett (-s, -e) nt duet

Duft (-(e)s, Düfte) m scent; **duften** vi to smell nice; **es duftet nach ...** it smells of ...

dulden vt to tolerate

dumm adj stupid; **Dummheit** f stupidity; (Tat) stupid thing; **Dummkopf** m idiot

dumpf adj (Ton) muffled; (Erinnerung) vague; (Schmerz) dull

Düne (-, -n) f dune

Dünger (-s, -) m fertilizer

dunkel adj dark; (Stimme) deep; (Ahnung) vague; (rätselhaft) obscure; (verdächtig) dubious; **im Dunkeln tappen** (fig) to be in the dark; **dunkelblau** adj dark blue; **dunkelblond** adj light brown; **dunkelhaarig** adj dark-haired; **Dunkelheit** f darkness

dünn adj thin; (Kaffee) weak

Dunst (-es, Dünste) m haze; (leichter Nebel) mist; (Chem) vapour

dünsten vt (Gastr) to steam

Duo (-s, -s) nt duo

Dur (-) nt (Mus) major (key); **in G-~** in G major

○ **SCHLÜSSELWORT**

durch prep +akk **1** (hindurch) through; **durch den Urwald** through the jungle; **durch die ganze Welt reisen** to travel all over the world

2 (mittels) through, by (means of); (aufgrund) due to, owing to; **Tod durch Herzschlag/den Strang** death from a heart attack/by hanging; **durch die Post** by post; **durch seine Bemühungen** through his efforts ▷ adv **1** (hindurch) through; **die ganze Nacht durch** all through the night; **den Sommer durch** during the summer; **8 Uhr durch** past 8 o'clock; **durch und durch** completely

2 (durchgebraten etc) **(gut) durch** well-done

durchaus adv absolutely; **~ nicht** not at all

Durchblick m view; **den ~ haben** (fig) to know what's going on; **durch|blicken** vi to look through; (fam: verstehen) to understand (bei etw sth); **etw**

~ lassen (fig) to hint at sth
Durchblutung f circulation
durch|brennen irr vi (Sicherung) to blow; (Draht) to burn through; (fam: davonlaufen) to run away
durchdacht adv: **gut ~** well thought-out
durch|drehen vt (Fleisch) to mince ▷ vi (Räder) to spin; (fam: nervlich) to crack up
durcheinander adv in a mess; (fam: verwirrt) confused;
Durcheinander (-s) nt (Verwirrung) confusion; (Unordnung) mess;
durcheinander|bringen irr vt to mess up; (verwirren) to confuse;
durcheinander|reden vi to talk all at the same time;
durcheinander|trinken vi to mix one's drinks
Durchfahrt f way through;
„**~ verboten!**" "no thoroughfare"
Durchfall m (Med) diarrhoea
durch|fallen irr vi to fall through; (in Prüfung) to fail
durch|fragen vr: **sich ~** to ask one's way
durch|führen vt to carry out
Durchgang m passage; (Sport) round; (bei Wahl) ballot;
Durchgangsverkehr m through traffic
durchgebraten adj well done
durchgefroren adj frozen to the bone
durch|gehen irr vi to go through (durch etw sth); (ausreißen: Pferd) to break loose; (Mensch) to run away; **durchgehend** adj (Zug) through; **~ geöffnet** open all day
durch|halten irr vi to hold out ▷ vt (Tempo) to keep up; **etw ~** (bis zum Schluss) to see sth through
durch|kommen irr vi to get through; (Patient) to pull through

durch|lassen irr vt (jdn) to let through; (Wasser) to let in
durch|lesen irr vt to read through
durchleuchten vt to X-ray
durch|machen vt to go through; (Entwicklung) to undergo; **die Nacht ~** to make a night of it, to have an all-nighter
Durchmesser (-s, -) m diameter
Durchreise f journey through; **auf der ~** passing through; (Güter) in transit; **Durchreisevisum** nt transit visa
durch|reißen irr vt, vi to tear (in two)
durchs kontr von **durch das**
Durchsage (-, -n) f announcement
durchschauen vt (jdn, Lüge) to see through
durch|schlagen irr vr: **sich ~** to struggle through
durch|schneiden irr vt to cut (in two)
Durchschnitt m (Mittelwert) average; **im ~** on average; **durchschnittlich** adj average ▷ adv (im Durchschnitt) on average; **Durchschnittsgeschwindigkeit** f average speed
durch|setzen vt to get through ▷ vr: **sich ~** (Erfolg haben) to succeed; (sich behaupten) to get one's way
durchsichtig adj transparent, see-through
durch|stellen vt (Tel) to put through
durch|streichen irr vt to cross out
durchsuchen vt to search (nach for); **Durchsuchung** f search
durchwachsen adj (Speck) streaky; (fig: mittelmäßig) so-so
Durchwahl f direct dialling; (Nummer) extension

durch|ziehen irr vt (Plan) to carry through

Durchzug m draught

⬤ SCHLÜSSELWORT

dürfen unreg vi (Erlaubnis haben) to be allowed to; **ich darf das** I'm allowed to (do that); **darf ich?** may I?; **darf ich ins Kino?** can o may I go to the cinema?; **es darf geraucht werden** you may smoke
2 (in Verneinungen) **er darf das nicht** he's not allowed to (do that); **das darf nicht geschehen** that must not happen; **da darf sie sich nicht wundern** that shouldn't surprise her
3 (in Höflichkeitsformeln) **darf ich Sie bitten, das zu tun?** may o could I ask you to do that?; **was darf es sein?** what can I do for you?
4 (können) **das dürfen Sie mir glauben** you can believe me
5 (Möglichkeit) **das dürfte genug sein** that should be enough; **es dürfte Ihnen bekannt sein, dass ...** as you will probably know ...

dürftig adj (ärmlich) poor; (unzulänglich) inadequate

dürr adj dried-up; (Land) arid; (mager) skinny

Durst (-(e)s) m thirst; **~ haben** to be thirsty; **durstig** adj thirsty

Dusche (-, -n) f shower; **duschen** vi to have a shower ▷ vr: **sich ~ to** have a shower; **Duschgel** nt shower gel; **Duschvorhang** m shower curtain

Düse (-, -n) f nozzle; (Tech) jet; **Düsenflugzeug** nt jet (aircraft)

Dussel (-s, -) m (fam) dope; **duss(e)lig** adj (fam) stupid

düster adj dark; (Gedanken, Zukunft) gloomy

Dutyfreeshop (-s, -s) m duty-free shop

Dutzend (-s, -e) nt dozen

duzen vt to address as "du" ▷ vr: **sich ~ (mit jdm)** to address each other as "du", to be on first-name terms

DVD (-, -s) f abk = **Digital Versatile Disk** DVD; **DVD-Player** (-s, -) m DVD player; **DVD-Rekorder** (-s, -) m DVD recorder

dynamisch adj dynamic

Dynamo (-s, -s) m dynamo

D-Zug m fast train

e

Ebbe (-, -n) f low tide
eben adj level; (glatt) smooth ▷ adv just; (bestätigend) exactly
Ebene (-, -n) f plain; (fig) level
ebenfalls adv also, as well; (Antwort: gleichfalls!) you too; **ebenso** adv just as; **~ gut** just as well; **~ viel** just as much
Eber (-s, -) m boar
EC (-, -s) m abk = **Eurocityzug**
Echo (-s, -s) nt echo
echt adj (Leder, Gold) real, genuine; **ein ~er Verlust** a real loss
EC-Karte f = debit card
Ecke (-, -n) f corner; (Math) angle; **an der ~** at the corner; **gleich um die ~** just round the corner; **eckig** adj rectangular; **Eckzahn** m canine
Economyclass (-) f coach (class), economy class
Ecstasy (-) f (Droge) ecstasy
edel adj noble; **Edelstein** m precious stone

EDV (-) f abk = **elektronische Datenverarbeitung** EDP
Efeu (-s) m ivy
Effekt (-s, -e) m effect
egal adj: **das ist ~** it doesn't matter; **das ist mir ~** I don't care, it's all the same to me; **~ wie teuer** no matter how expensive
egoistisch adj selfish
ehe conj before
Ehe (-, -n) f marriage; **Ehefrau** f wife; (verheiratete Frau) married woman; **Eheleute** pl married couple sing
ehemalig adj former; **ehemals** adv formerly
Ehemann m husband; (verheirateter Mann) married man; **Ehepaar** nt married couple
eher adv (früher) sooner; (lieber) rather, sooner; (mehr) more; **je ~, desto besser** the sooner the better
Ehering m wedding ring
eheste(r, s) adj (früheste) first ▷ adv: **am ~n** (am wahrscheinlichsten) most likely
Ehre (-, -n) f honour; **ehren** vt to honour; **ehrenamtlich** adj voluntary; **Ehrengast** m guest of honour; **Ehrenwort** nt word of honour; **~! I** promise; **ich gebe dir mein ~** I give you my word
ehrgeizig adj ambitious
ehrlich adj honest
Ei (-(e)s, -er) nt egg; **hart gekochtes/weiches ~** hard-boiled/soft-boiled egg
Eiche (-, -n) f oak (tree); **Eichel** (-, -n) f acorn
Eichhörnchen nt squirrel
Eid (-(e)s, -e) m oath
Eidechse (-, -n) f lizard
Eierbecher m eggcup; **Eierstock** m ovary; **Eieruhr** f egg timer
Eifersucht f jealousy;

eifersüchtig adj jealous (auf +akk of)

Eigelb (-(e)s, -) nt egg yolk

eigen adj own; (typisch) characteristic (jdm of sb); (eigenartig) peculiar; **eigenartig** adj peculiar; **Eigenschaft** f quality; (Chem, Phys) property; (Merkmal) characteristic

eigentlich adj actual, real ▷ adv actually, really; **was denken Sie sich ~ dabei?** what on earth are you doing?

Eigentum nt property; **Eigentümer(in)** m(f) owner; **Eigentumswohnung** f owner-occupied flat (Brit), condominium (US)

eignen vr: **sich ~ für** to be suited for; **er würde sich als Lehrer ~** he'd make a good teacher

Eilbrief m express letter, special-delivery letter; **Eile** (-) f hurry; **eilen** vi (dringend sein) to be urgent; **es eilt nicht** there's no hurry; **eilig** adj hurried; (dringlich) urgent; **es ~ haben** to be in a hurry

Eimer (-s, -) m bucket

ein adv: **nicht ~ noch aus wissen** not to know what to do; **~ - aus** (Schalter) on - off

ein(e) art a; (vor gesprochenem Vokal) an; **~ Mann** a man; **~ Apfel** an apple; **~e Stunde** an hour; **~ Haus** a house; **~ (gewisser) Herr Miller** a (certain) Mr Miller; **~es Tages** one day

einander pron one another, each other

ein|arbeiten vt to train ▷ vr: **sich ~** to get used to the work

ein|atmen vt, vi to breathe in

Einbahnstraße f one-way street

ein|bauen vt to build in; (Motor etc) to install, to fit; **Einbauküche**

f fitted kitchen

ein|biegen irr vi to turn (in +akk into)

ein|bilden vt sich (dat) etw ~ to imagine sth

ein|brechen irr vi (in Haus) to break in; (Dach etc) to fall in, to collapse; **Einbrecher(in)** (-s, -) m(f) burglar

ein|bringen irr vt (Ernte) to bring in; (Gewinn) to yield; **jdm etw ~** to bring (o earn) sb sth ▷ vr **sich ~** (akk) **etw ~** to make a contribution to sth

Einbruch m (Haus) break-in, burglary; **bei ~ der Nacht** at nightfall

Einbürgerung f naturalization

ein|checken vt to check in

ein|cremen vt to put some cream on ▷ vr: **sich ~** to put some cream on

eindeutig adj clear, obvious ▷ adv clearly; **~ falsch** clearly wrong

ein|dringen irr vi (gewaltsam) to force one's way in (in +akk -to); (in Haus) to break in (in +akk -to); (Gas, Wasser) to get in (in +akk -to)

Eindruck m impression; **großen ~ auf jdn machen** to make a big impression on sb

eine(r, s) pron one; (jemand) someone; **~r meiner Freunde** one of my friends; **~r nach dem andern** one after the other

eineiig adj (Zwillinge) identical

eineinhalb num one and a half

einerseits adv on the one hand

einfach adj (nicht kompliziert) simple; (Mensch) ordinary; (Essen) plain; (nicht mehrfach) single; **~e Fahrkarte** single ticket (Brit), one-way ticket (US) ▷ adv simply; (nicht mehrfach) once

Einfahrt f (Vorgang) driving in; (eines Zuges) arrival; (Ort) entrance

Einfall m (Idee) idea; **ein|fallen** irr vi (Licht etc) to fall in; (einstürzen) to collapse; **ihm fiel ein, dass ...** it occurred to him that ...; **ich werde mir etwas ~ lassen** I'll think of something; **was fällt Ihnen ein!** what do you think you're doing?

Einfamilienhaus nt detached house

einfarbig adj all one colour; (Stoff etc) self-coloured

Einfluss m influence

ein|frieren irr vt, vi to freeze

ein|fügen vt to fit in; (zusätzlich) to add; (Inform) to insert; **Einfügetaste** f (Inform) insert key

Einfuhr (-, -en) f import; **Einfuhrbestimmungen** pl import regulations pl

ein|führen vt to introduce; (Ware) to import; **Einführung** f introduction

Eingabe f (Dateneingabe) input; **Eingabetaste** f (Inform) return (o enter) key

Eingang m entrance; **Eingangshalle** f entrance hall, lobby (US)

ein|geben irr vt (Daten etc) to enter, to key in

eingebildet adj imaginary; (eitel) arrogant

Eingeborene(r) mf native

ein|gehen irr vi (Sendung, Geld) to come in, to arrive; (Tier, Pflanze) to die; (Stoff) to shrink; **auf etw** (akk) **~ to agree to sth**; **auf jdn ~** to respond to sb ▷ vt (Vertrag) to enter into; (Wette) to make; (Risiko) to take

eingelegt adj (in Essig) pickled

eingeschaltet adj (switched) on

eingeschlossen adj locked in; (inklusive) included

ein|gewöhnen vr: **sich ~** to settle in

ein|gießen irr vt to pour

ein|greifen irr vi to intervene; **Eingriff** m intervention; (Operation) operation

ein|halten irr vt (Versprechen etc) to keep

einheimisch adj (Produkt, Mannschaft) local; **Einheimische(r)** mf local

Einheit f (Geschlossenheit) unity; (Maß) unit; **einheitlich** adj uniform

ein|holen vt (Vorsprung aufholen) to catch up with; (Verspätung) to make up for; (Rat, Erlaubnis) to ask for

Einhorn nt unicorn

einhundert num one (o a) hundred

einig adj (vereint) united; **sich** (dat) **~ sein** to agree

einige pron pl some; (mehrere) several ▷ adj some; **nach ~er Zeit** after some time; **~e hundert Euro** some hundred euros

einigen vr: **sich ~** to agree (auf +akk on)

einigermaßen adv fairly, quite; (leidlich) reasonably

einiges pron something; (ziemlich viel) quite a bit; (mehreres) a few things; **es gibt noch ~ zu tun** there's still a fair bit to do

Einkauf m purchase; **Einkäufe** (**machen**) (to do one's) shopping; **ein|kaufen** vt to buy ▷ vi to go shopping; **Einkaufsbummel** m shopping trip; **Einkaufstasche** f, **Einkaufstüte** f shopping bag; **Einkaufswagen** m shopping trolley (Brit) (o cart US); **Einkaufszentrum** nt shopping centre (Brit) (o mall US)

ein|klemmen vt to jam; **er hat sich** (dat) **den Finger eingeklemmt** he got his finger caught

Einkommen (-s, -) nt income

ein|laden *irr vt* (*jdn*) to invite; (*Gegenstände*) to load; **jdn zum Essen ~** to take sb out for a meal; **ich lade dich ein** (*bezahle*) it's my treat; **Einladung** *f* invitation

Einlass (*-es, Einlässe*) *m* admittance; **~ ab 18 Uhr** doors open at 6 pm; **ein|lassen** *irr vr* **sich mit jdm/auf etw** (*akk*) **~** to get involved with sb/sth

ein|leben *vr:* **sich ~** to settle down

ein|legen *vt* (*Film etc*) to put in; (*marinieren*) to marinate; **eine Pause ~** to take a break

ein|leiten *vt* to start; (*Maßnahmen*) to introduce; (*Geburt*) to induce; **Einleitung** *f* introduction; (*von Geburt*) induction

ein|leuchten *vi:* **jdm ~** to be (*o* become) clear to sb; **einleuchtend** *adj* clear

ein|loggen *vi* (*Inform*) to log on (*o* in)

ein|lösen *vt* (*Scheck*) to cash; (*Gutschein*) to redeem; (*Versprechen*) to keep

einmal *adv* once; (*früher*) before; (*in Zukunft*) some day; (*erstens*) first; **~ im Jahr** once a year; **noch ~** once more, again; **ich war schon ~ hier** I've been here before; **warst du schon ~ in London?** have you ever been to London?; **nicht ~** not even; **auf ~** suddenly; (*gleichzeitig*) at once; **einmalig** *adj* unique; (*einmal geschehend*) single; (*prima*) fantastic

ein|mischen *vr:* **sich ~** to interfere (*in +akk* with)

Einnahme (*-, -n*) *f* (*Geld*) takings *pl*; (*von Medizin*) taking; **ein|nehmen** *irr vt* (*Medizin*) to take; (*Geld*) to take in; (*Standpunkt, Raum*) to take up; **jdn für sich ~** to win sb over

ein|ordnen *vt* to put in order; (*klassifizieren*) to classify; (*Akten*) to file ▷ *vr:* **sich ~** (*Auto*) to get in lane; **sich rechts/links ~** to get into the right/left lane

ein|parken *vt* to pack (*up*)

ein|parken *vt, vi* to park

ein|planen *vt* to allow for

ein|prägen *vt* **sich** (*dat*) **etw ~** to remember (*o* memorize) sth

ein|räumen *vt* (*Bücher, Geschirr*) to put away; (*Schrank*) to put things in

ein|reden *vt:* **jdm/sich etw ~** to talk sb/oneself into (believing) sth

ein|reiben *irr vt:* **sich mit etw ~** to rub sth into one's skin

ein|reichen *vt* to hand in; (*Antrag*) to submit

Einreise *f* entry; **Einreisebestimmungen** *pl* entry regulations *pl*; **Einreiseerlaubnis** *f*, **Einreisegenehmigung** *f* entry permit; **ein|reisen** *vi* to enter (*in ein Land* a country); **Einreisevisum** *nt* entry visa

ein|renken *vt* (*Arm, Bein*) to set

ein|richten *vt* (*Wohnung*) to furnish; (*gründen*) to establish, to set up; (*arrangieren*) to arrange ▷ *vr:* **sich ~** (*in Haus*) to furnish one's home; (*sich vorbereiten*) to prepare oneself (*auf +akk* for); (*sich anpassen*) to adapt (*auf +akk* to); **Einrichtung** *f* (*Wohnung*) furnishings *pl*; (*öffentliche Anstalt*) institution; (*Schwimmbad etc*) facility

eins *num* one; **Eins** (*-, -en*) *f* one; (*Schulnote*) **~ A**

einsam *adj* lonely

ein|sammeln *vt* to collect

Einsatz *m* (*Teil*) insert; (*Verwendung*) use; (*Spieleinsatz*) stake; (*Risiko*) risk; (*Mus*) entry

ein|schalten *vt* (*Elek*) to switch on

ein|schätzen vt to estimate, to assess

ein|schenken vt to pour

ein|schiffen vr: **sich ~** to embark (nach for)

ein|schlafen irr vi to fall asleep, to drop off; **mir ist der Arm eingeschlafen** my arm's gone to sleep

ein|schlagen irr vt (Fenster) to smash; (Zähne, Schädel) to smash in; (Weg, Richtung) to take ▷ vi to hit (in etw akk sth, auf jdn sb); (Blitz) to strike; (Anklang finden) to be a success

ein|schließen irr vt (jdn) to lock in; (Gegenstand) to lock away; (umgeben) to surround; (fig: beinhalten) to include; **einschließlich** adv inclusive ▷ prep +gen including; **von Montag bis ~ Freitag** from Monday up to and including Friday, Monday through Friday (US)

ein|schränken vt to limit, to restrict; (verringern) to cut down on ▷ vr: **sich ~** to cut down (on expenditure)

ein|schreiben irr vr: **sich ~** to register; (Schule) to enrol; **Einschreiben** (-s, -) nt registered letter; **etw per ~ schicken** to send sth by special delivery

ein|schüchtern vt to intimidate

ein|sehen irr vt (verstehen) to see; (Fehler) to recognize; (Akten) to have a look at

einseitig adj one-sided

ein|senden irr vt to send in

ein|setzen vt to put in; (in Amt) to appoint; (Geld) to stake; (verwenden) to use ▷ vi (beginnen) to set in; (Mus) to enter, to come in ▷ vr: to work hard; **sich für jdn/etw ~** to support sb/sth

Einsicht f insight; **zu der**

~ kommen, dass ... to come to realize that ...

ein|sperren vt to lock up

ein|spielen vt (Geld) to bring in

ein|springen irr vi (aushelfen) to step in (für for)

Einspruch m objection (gegen to)

einspurig adj single-lane

Einstand m (Tennis) deuce

ein|stecken vt to pocket; (Elek: Stecker) to plug in; (Brief) to post, to mail (US); (mitnehmen) to take; (hinnehmen) to swallow

ein|steigen irr vi (in Auto) to get in; (in Bus, Zug, Flugzeug) to get on; (sich beteiligen) to get involved

ein|stellen vt (beenden) to stop; (Geräte) to adjust; (Kamera) to focus; (Sender, Radio) to tune in; (unterstellen) to put; (in Firma) to employ, to take on ▷ vr: **sich auf jdn/etw ~** to adapt to sb/prepare oneself for sth; **Einstellung** f (von Gerät) adjustment; (von Kamera) focusing; (von Arbeiter) taking on; (Meinung) attitude

ein|stürzen vi to collapse

eintägig adj one-day

ein|tauschen vt to exchange (gegen for)

eintausend num one (o a) thousand

ein|teilen vt (in Teile) to divide (up) (in +akk into); (Zeit) to organize

eintönig adj monotonous

Eintopf m stew

ein|tragen irr vt (in eine Liste) to put down, to enter ▷ vr: **sich ~** to put one's name down, to register

ein|treffen irr vi to happen; (ankommen) to arrive

ein|treten irr vi (hineingehen) to enter (in etw akk sth); (in Klub, Partei) to join (in etw akk sth); (sich ereignen) to occur; **~ für** to support; **Eintritt** m admission; **„~ frei"**

"admission free"; **Eintrittskarte**
f (entrance) ticket; **Eintrittspreis**
m admission charge
einverstanden interj okay, all
right ▷ adj: **mit etwas ~ sein** to
agree to sth, to accept sth
Einwanderer m, **Einwanderin**
f immigrant; **ein|wandern** vi to
immigrate
einwandfrei adj perfect, flawless
Einwegflasche f non-returnable
bottle
ein|weichen vt to soak
ein|weihen vt (Gebäude) to
inaugurate, to open; **jdn in etw**
(akk) **~** to let sb in on sth;
Einweihungsparty f house-
warming party
ein|werfen irr vt (Ball, Bemerkung
etc) to throw in; (Brief) to post, to
mail (US); (Geld) to put in, to
insert; (Fenster) to smash
ein|wickeln vt to wrap up; (fig)
jdn ~ to take sb in
Einwohner(in) (-s, -) m(f)
inhabitant; **Einwohnermeldeamt**
nt registration office for residents
Einwurf m (Öffnung) slot; (Sport)
throw-in
Einzahl f singular
ein|zahlen vt to pay in (auf ein
Konto -to an account)
Einzel (-s, -) nt (Tennis) singles
sing; **Einzelbett** nt single bed;
Einzelfahrschein m single ticket
(Brit), one-way ticket (US);
Einzelgänger(in) m(f) loner;
Einzelhandel m retail trade;
Einzelkind nt only child
einzeln adj individual; (getrennt)
separate; (einzig) single; **~e ...**
several ..., some ...; **der/die**
Einzelne the individual; **im**
Einzelnen in detail ▷ adv
separately; (verpacken, aufführen)
individually; **~ angeben** to
specify; **~ eintreten** to enter one

by one
Einzelzimmer nt single room;
Einzelzimmerzuschlag m
single-room supplement
ein|ziehen irr vt: **den Kopf ~** to
duck ▷ vi (in ein Haus) to move in
einzig adj only; (einzeln) single;
(einzigartig) unique; **kein ~er**
Fehler not a single mistake; **das**
Einzige the only thing, **der/die**
Einzige the only person ▷ adv
only; **die ~ richtige Lösung** the
only correct solution; **einzigartig**
adj unique
Eis (es, -) nt ice; (Speiseeis)
ice-cream; **Eisbahn** f
ice(skating) rink; **Eisbär** m polar
bear; **Eisbecher** m (ice-cream)
sundae; **Eisberg** m iceberg;
Eisbergsalat m iceberg lettuce;
Eiscafé nt, **Eisdiele** f ice-cream
parlour
Eisen (-s, -) nt iron; **Eisenbahn** f
railway (Brit), railroad (US); **eisern**
adj iron
eisgekühlt adj chilled;
Eishockey nt ice hockey;
Eiskaffee m iced coffee; **eiskalt**
adj ice-cold; (Temperatur) freezing;
Eiskunstlauf m figure skating;
eis|laufen irr vi to skate;
Eisschokolade f iced chocolate;
Eisschrank m fridge, ice-box
(US); **Eistee** m iced tea;
Eiswürfel m ice cube; **Eiszapfen**
m icicle
eitel adj vain
Eiter (-s) m pus
Eiweiß (-es, -e) nt egg white;
(Chem, Bio) protein
ekelhaft, **ek(e)lig** adj
disgusting, revolting; **ekeln** vr:
sich ~ to be disgusted (vor +dat at)
EKG (-s, -s) nt abk =
Elektrokardiogramm ECG
Ekzem (-s, -e) nt (Med) eczema
elastisch adj elastic

Elch (-(e)s, -e) m elk; (*nordamerikanischer*) moose

Elefant m elephant

elegant adj elegant

Elektriker(in) (-s, -) m(f) electrician; **elektrisch** adj electric; **Elektrizität** f electricity; **Elektroauto** nt electric car; **Elektrogerät** nt electrical appliance; **Elektrogeschäft** nt electrical shop; **Elektroherd** m electric cooker; **Elektromotor** m electric motor; **Elektronik** f electronics sing; **elektronisch** adj electronic; **Elektrorasierer** (-s, -) m electric razor

Element (-s, -e) nt element

elend adj miserable; **Elend** (-(e)s) nt misery

elf num eleven; **Elf** (-, -en) f (*Sport*) eleven

Elfenbein nt ivory

Elfmeter m (*Sport*) penalty (kick)

elfte(r, s) adj eleventh; *siehe auch* **dritte**

Ell(en)bogen m elbow

Elster (-, -n) f magpie

Eltern pl parents pl

EM f abk = **Europameisterschaft** European Championship(s)

E-Mail (-, -s) f (*Inform*) e-mail; **jdm eine ~ schicken** to e-mail sb, to send sb an e-mail; **jdm etwas per ~ schicken** to e-mail sth to sb; **E-Mail-Adresse** f e-mail address; **e-mailen** vt to e-mail

Emoticon (-s, -s) nt emoticon

emotional adj emotional

empfahl imperf von **empfehlen**

empfand imperf von **empfinden**

Empfang (-(e)s, Empfänge) m (*Rezeption; Veranstaltung*) reception; (*Erhalten*) receipt; **in ~ nehmen** to receive; **empfangen** (*empfing, empfangen*) vt to receive; **Empfänger(in)** (-s, -) m(f) recipient; (*Adressat*) addressee ▷ m

(*Tech*) receiver; **Empfängnisverhütung** f contraception; **Empfangshalle** f reception area

empfehlen (*empfahl, empfohlen*) vt to recommend; **Empfehlung** f recommendation

empfinden (*empfand, empfunden*) vt to feel; **empfindlich** adj (*Mensch*) sensitive; (*Stelle*) sore; (*reizbar*) touchy; (*Material*) delicate

empfing imperf von **empfangen**

empfohlen pp von **empfehlen**

empfunden pp von **empfinden**

empört adj indignant (*über +akk* at)

Ende (-s, -n) nt end; (*Film, Roman*) ending; **am ~** at the end; (*schließlich*) in the end; **~ Mai** at the end of May; **~ der Achtzigerjahre** in the late eighties; **sie ist ~ zwanzig** she's in her late twenties; **zu ~** over, finished; **enden** vi to end; **der Zug endet hier** this service (o train) terminates here; **endgültig** adj final; (*Beweis*) conclusive

Endivie f endive

endlich adv at last, finally; (*am Ende*) eventually; **Endspiel** nt final; (*Endrunde*) finals pl; **Endstation** f terminus; **Endung** f ending

Energie f energy; **~ sparend** energy-saving; **Energiebedarf** m energy requirement; **Energieverbrauch** m energy consumption

energisch adj (*entschlossen*) forceful

eng adj narrow; (*Kleidung*) tight; (*fig: Freundschaft, Verhältnis*) close; **das wird ~** (*fam: zeitlich*) we're running out of time, it's getting tight ▷ adv: **~ befreundet sein** to be close friends

engagieren vt to engage ▷ vr: **sich ~** to commit oneself, to be committed (für to)

Engel (-s, -) m angel

England nt England; **Engländer(in)** (-s, -) m(f) Englishman/-woman; **die ~** pl the English pl; **englisch** adj English; (Gastr) rare; **Englisch** nt English; **ins ~e übersetzen** to translate into English

Enkel (-s, -) m grandson; **Enkelin** f granddaughter

enorm adj enormous; (fig) tremendous

Entbindung f (Med) delivery

entdecken vt to discover; **Entdeckung** f discovery

Ente (-, -n) f duck

Enter-Taste f (Inform) enter (o return) key

entfernen vt to remove; (Inform) to delete ▷ vr: **sich ~** to go away; **entfernt** adj distant; **15 km von X ~** 15 km away from X; **20 km voneinander ~** 20 km apart; **Entfernung** f distance; **aus der ~** from a distance

entführen vt to kidnap; **Entführer(in)** m(f) kidnapper; **Entführung** f kidnapping

entgegen prep +dat contrary to ▷ adv towards; **dem Wind ~** against the wind; **entgegengesetzt** adj (Richtung) opposite; (Meinung) opposing; **entgegen|kommen** irr vi: **jdm ~** to come to meet sb; (fig) to accommodate sb; **entgegenkommend** adj (Verkehr) oncoming; (fig) obliging

entgegnen vt to reply (auf +akk to)

entgehen irr vi: **jdm ~** to escape sb's notice; **sich** (dat) **etw ~ lassen** to miss sth

entgleisen vi (Eisenb) to be derailed; (fig: Mensch) to misbehave

Enthaarungscreme f hair remover

enthalten irr vt (Behälter) to contain; (Preis) to include ▷ vr: **sich ~** to abstain (gen from)

entkoffeiniert adj decaffeinated

entkommen irr vi to escape

entkorken vt to uncork

entlang prep ⊕akk o dat ~ **dem Fluss, den Fluss ~** along the river; **entlang|gehen** irr vi to walk along

entlassen irr vt (Patient) to discharge; (Arbeiter) to dismiss

entlasten vt: **jdn ~** (Arbeit abnehmen) to relieve sb of some of his/her work

entmutigen vt to discourage

entnehmen vt to take (dat from)

entrahmt adj (Milch) skimmed

entschädigen vt to compensate; **Entschädigung** f compensation

entscheiden irr vt, vi to decide ▷ vr: **sich ~** to decide; **sich für/gegen etw ~** to decide on/against sth; **wir haben uns entschieden, nicht zu gehen** we decided not to go; **das entscheidet sich morgen** that'll be decided tomorrow; **entscheidend** adj decisive; (Stimme) casting; (Frage, Problem) crucial; **Entscheidung** f decision

entschließen irr vr: **sich ~** to decide (zu, für on), to make up one's mind; **Entschluss** m decision

entschuldigen vt to excuse ▷ vr: **sich ~** to apologize; **sich bei jdm für etw ~** to apologize to sb for sth ▷ vi: **entschuldige!, ~ Sie!** (vor einer Frage) excuse me; (Verzeihung!) (I'm) sorry, excuse me (US); **Entschuldigung** f apology;

(*Grund*) excuse; **jdn um ~ bitten** to apologize to sb; **~!** (*bei Zusammenstoß*) (I'm) sorry, excuse me (*US*); (*vor einer Frage*) excuse me; (*wenn man etw nicht verstanden hat*) (I beg your) pardon?

entsetzlich *adj* dreadful, appalling

entsorgen *vt* to dispose of

entspannen *vt* (*Körper*) to relax; (*Pol: Lage*) to ease ▷ *vr:* **sich ~** to relax; (*fam*) to chill out; **Entspannung** *f* relaxation

entsprechen *irr vi* +*dat* to correspond to; (*Anforderungen, Wünschen etc*) to comply with; **entsprechend** *adj* appropriate ▷ *adv* accordingly ▷ *prep* +*dat* according to, in accordance with

entstehen *vi* (*Schwierigkeiten*) to arise; (*gebaut werden*) to be built; (*hergestellt werden*) to be created

enttäuschen *vt* to disappoint; **Enttäuschung** *f* disappointment

entweder *conj:* **~ ... oder ...** either ... or ...; **~ oder!** take it or leave it

entwerfen *irr vt* (*Möbel, Kleider*) to design; (*Plan, Vertrag*) to draft

entwerten *vt* to devalue; (*Fahrschein*) to cancel; **Entwerter** (*-s, -*) *m* ticket-cancelling machine

entwickeln *vt* (*a. Foto*) to develop; (*Mut, Energie*) to show, to display ▷ *vr:* **sich ~** to develop; **Entwicklung** *f* development; (*Foto*) developing; **Entwicklungshelfer(in)** (*-s, -*) *m(f)* development worker; **Entwicklungsland** *nt* developing country

Entwurf *m* outline; (*Design*) design; (*Vertragsentwurf, Konzept*) draft

entzückend *adj* delightful, charming

Entzug *m* withdrawal;

(*Behandlung*) detox; **Entzugserscheinung** *f* withdrawal symptom

entzünden *vr:* **sich ~** to catch fire; (*Med*) to become inflamed; **Entzündung** *f* (*Med*) inflammation

Epidemie (*-, -n*) *f* epidemic

Epilepsie (*-, -n*) *f* epilepsy

epilieren *vt* to remove body hair, to depilate; **Epiliergerät** *nt* Ladyshave®

er *pron* (*Person*) he; (*Sache*) it; **er ist's** it's him; **wo ist mein Mantel? — ~ ist ...** where's my coat? — it's ...

Erbe (*-n, -n*) *m* heir ▷ (*-s*) *nt* inheritance; (*fig*) heritage; **erben** *vt* to inherit; **Erbin** *f* heiress; **erblich** *adj* hereditary

erbrechen *irr vt* to vomit ▷ *vr:* **sich ~** to vomit; **Erbrechen** *nt* vomiting

Erbschaft *f* inheritance

Erbse (*-, -n*) *f* pea

Erdapfel *m* potato; **Erdbeben** *nt* earthquake; **Erdbeere** *f* strawberry; **Erde** (*-, -n*) *f* (*Planet*) earth; (*Boden*) ground; **Erdgas** *nt* natural gas; **Erdgeschoss** *nt* ground floor (*Brit*), first floor (*US*); **Erdkunde** *f* geography; **Erdnuss** *f* peanut; **Erdöl** *nt* (mineral) oil; **Erdrutsch** *m* landslide; **Erdteil** *m* continent

ereignen *vr:* **sich ~** to happen, to take place; **Ereignis** *nt* event

erfahren *irr vt* to learn, to find out; (*erleben*) to experience ▷ *adj* experienced; **Erfahrung** *f* experience

erfinden *irr vt* to invent; **erfinderisch** *adj* inventive, creative; **Erfindung** *f* invention

Erfolg (*-(e)s, -e*) *m* success; (*Folge*) result; **~ versprechend** promising; **viel ~!** good luck;

erfolglos *adj* unsuccessful;
erfolgreich *adj* successful
erforderlich *adj* necessary
erforschen *vt* to explore;
(*untersuchen*) investigate
erfreulich *adj* pleasing, pleasant;
(*Nachricht*) good;
erfreulicherweise *adv*
fortunately
erfrieren *irr vi* to freeze to death;
(*Pflanzen*) to be killed by frost
Erfrischung *f* refreshment
erfüllen *vt* (*Raum*) to fill; (*Bitte,
Wunsch etc*) to fulfil ▷ *vr*: **sich ~** to
come true
ergänzen *vt* (*hinzufügen*) to add;
(*vervollständigen*) to complete ▷ *vr*:
sich ~ to complement one
another; **Ergänzung** *f*
completion; (*Zusatz*) supplement
ergeben *irr vt* (*Betrag*) to come
to; (*zum Ergebnis haben*) to result in
▷ *irr vr*: **sich ~** to surrender;
(*folgen*) to result (*aus from*) ▷ *adj*
devoted; (*demütig*) humble
Ergebnis *nt* result
ergreifen *irr vt* to seize; (*Beruf*) to
take up; (*Maßnahme, Gelegenheit*) to
take; (*rühren*) to move
erhalten *irr vt* (*bekommen*) to
receive; (*bewahren*) to preserve;
gut ~ sein to be in good
condition; **erhältlich** *adj*
available
erheblich *adj* considerable
erhitzen *vt* to heat (up)
erhöhen *vt* to raise; (*verstärken*)
to increase ▷ *vr*: **sich ~** to
increase
erholen *vr*: **sich ~** to recover; (*sich
ausruhen*) to have a rest; **erholsam**
adj restful; **Erholung** *f* recovery;
(*Entspannung*) relaxation, rest
erinnern *vt* to remind (*an +akk
of*) ▷ *vr*: **sich ~** to remember (*an
etw akk sth*); **Erinnerung** *f*
memory; (*Andenken*) souvenir;

(*Mahnung*) reminder
erkälten *vr*: **sich ~** to catch a
cold; **erkältet** *adj*: (**stark**) **~ sein**
to have a (bad) cold; **Erkältung** *f*
cold
erkennen *irr vt* to recognize;
(*sehen, verstehen*) to see; **~, dass ...**
to realize that ...; **erkenntlich**
adj: **sich ~ zeigen** to show one's
appreciation
Erker (*-s, -*) *m* bay
erklären *vt* to explain; (*kundtun*)
to declare; **Erklärung** *f*
explanation; (*Aussage*) declaration
erkundigen *vr*: **sich ~** to enquire
(*nach about*)
erlauben *vt* to allow, to permit;
jdm ~, etw zu tun to allow (*o
permit*) sb to do sth; **sich** (*dat*) **etw
~** to permit oneself sth; **~ Sie(,
dass ich rauche)?** do you mind (if I
smoke)?; **was ~ Sie sich?** what do
you think you're doing?; **Erlaubnis**
f permission
Erläuterung *f* explanation; (*zu
Text*) comment
erleben *vt* to experience; (*schöne
Tage etc*) to have; (*Schlimmes*) to go
through; (*miterleben*) to witness;
(*noch miterleben*) to live to see;
Erlebnis *nt* experience
erledigen *vt* (*Angelegenheit,
Aufgabe*) to deal with; (*fam:
ruinieren*) to finish; **erledigt** *adj*
(*beendet*) finished; (*gelöst*) dealt
with; (*fam: erschöpft*) whacked,
knackered (*Brit*)
erleichtert *adj* relieved
Erlös (*-es, -e*) *m* proceeds *pl*
ermahnen *vt* (*warnend*) to warn
ermäßigt *adj* reduced;
Ermäßigung *f* reduction
ermitteln *vt* to find out; (*Täter*)
to trace ▷ *vi* (*Jur*) to investigate
ermöglichen *vt* to make
possible (*dat for*)
ermorden *vt* to murder

ermüdend *adj* tiring

ermutigen *vt* to encourage

ernähren *vt* to feed; (*Familie*) to support ▷ *vr*: **sich ~** to support oneself; **sich ~ von** to live on; **Ernährung** *f* (*Essen*) food; **Ernährungsberater(in)** *m(f)* nutritional (*o* dietary) adviser

erneuern *vt* to renew; (*restaurieren*) to restore; (*renovieren*) to renovate; (*auswechseln*) to replace

ernst *adj* serious ▷ *adv*: **jdn/etw ~ nehmen** take sb/sth seriously; **Ernst** (*-es*) *m* seriousness; **das ist mein ~** I'm quite serious; **im ~?** seriously?; **ernsthaft** *adj* serious ▷ *adv* seriously

Ernte (*-, -n*) *f* harvest; **Erntedankfest** *nt* harvest festival (*Brit*); Thanksgiving (Day) (US: 4. *Donnerstag im November*); **ernten** *vt* to harvest; (*Lob etc*) to earn

erobern *vt* to conquer

eröffnen *vt* to open; **Eröffnung** *f* opening

erogen *adj* erogenous

erotisch *adj* erotic

erpressen *vt* (*jdn*) to blackmail; (*Geld etc*) to extort; **Erpressung** *f* blackmail; (*von Geld*) extortion

erraten *irr vt* to guess

erregen *vt* to excite; (*sexuell*) to arouse; (*ärgern*) to annoy; (*hervorrufen*) to arouse ▷ *vr*: **sich ~** to get worked up; **Erreger** (*-s, -*) *m* (*Med*) germ; (*Virus*) virus

erreichbar *adj*: **~ sein** to be within reach; (*Person*) to be available; **das Stadtzentrum ist zu Fuß/mit dem Wagen leicht ~** the city centre is within easy walking/driving distance; **erreichen** *vt* to reach; (*Zug etc*) to catch

Ersatz (*-es*) *m* replacement; (*auf*

Zeit) substitute; (*Ausgleich*) compensation; **Ersatzreifen** *m* (*Auto*) spare tyre; **Ersatzteil** *nt* spare (part)

erscheinen *irr vi* to appear; (*wirken*) to seem

erschöpft *adj* exhausted; **Erschöpfung** *f* exhaustion

erschrecken *vt* to frighten ▷ (*erschrak, erschrocken*) *vi* to get a fright; **erschreckend** *adj* alarming; **erschrocken** *adj* frightened

erschwinglich *adj* affordable

ersetzen *vt* to replace; (*Auslagen*) to reimburse

⭕ **SCHLÜSSELWORT**

erst *adv* **1** first; **mach erst mal die Arbeit fertig** finish your work first; **wenn du das erst mal hinter dir hast** once you've got that behind you
2 (*nicht früher als, nur*) only; (*nicht bis*) not till; **erst gestern** only yesterday; **erst morgen** not until tomorrow; **erst als** only when, not until; **wir fahren erst später** we're not going until later; **er ist (gerade) erst angekommen** he's only just arrived
3 **wäre er doch erst zurück!** if only he were back!

erstatten *vt* (*Kosten*) to refund; **Bericht ~** to report (*über +akk on*); **Anzeige gegen jdn ~** to report sb to the police

erstaunlich *adj* astonishing; **erstaunt** *adj* surprised

erstbeste(r, s) *adj*: **das ~ Hotel** any old hotel; **der Erstbeste** just anyone

erste(r, s) *adj* first; **siehe auch dritte**; **zum ~n Mal** for the first time; **er wurde Erster** he came first; **auf den ~n Blick** at first sight

erstens adv first(ly), in the first place

ersticken vi (Mensch) to suffocate: **in Arbeit ~** to be snowed under with work

erstklassig adj first-class; **erstmals** adv for the first time

erstrecken vr: **sich ~** to extend, to stretch (auf +akk to; über +akk over)

ertappen vt to catch

erteilen vt (Rat, Erlaubnis) to give

Ertrag ((e)s, Erträge) m yield; (Gewinn) proceeds pl; **ertragen** irr vt (Schmerzen) to bear, to stand; (dulden) to put up with; **erträglich** adj bearable; (nicht zu schlecht) tolerable

ertrinken irr vi to drown

erwachsen adj grown-up; **~ werden** to grow up; **Erwachsene(r)** mf adult, grown-up

erwähnen vt to mention

erwarten vt to expect; (warten auf) to wait for; **ich kann den Sommer kaum ~** I can hardly wait for the summer

erwerbstätig adj employed

erwidern vt to reply; (Gruß, Besuch) to return

erwischen vt (fam) to catch (bei etw doing sth)

erwünscht adj desired; (willkommen) welcome

Erz (-es, -e) nt ore

erzählen vt to tell (jdm etw sb sth); **Erzählung** f story, tale

erzeugen vt to produce; (Strom) to generate; **Erzeugnis** nt product

erziehen irr vt to bring up; (geistig) to educate; (Tier) to train; **Erzieher(in)** (-s, -) m(f) educator; (Kindergarten) (nursery school)

teacher; **Erziehung** f upbringing; (Bildung) education

es pron (Sache, im Nom und Akk) it; (Baby, Tier) he/she; **ich bin ~** it's me; **~ ist kalt** it's cold; **~ gibt ...** there is .../there are ...; **ich hoffe ~** I hope so; **ich kann ~** I can do it

Escape-Taste f (Inform) escape key

Esel (-s, -) m donkey

Espresso (-s, -) m espresso

essbar adj edible; **essen** (aß, gegessen) vt, vi to eat; **zu Mittag/Abend ~** to have lunch/dinner; **was gibt's zu ~?** what's for lunch/dinner?; **~ gehen** to eat out; **gegessen sein** (fig, fam) to be history; **Essen** (-s, -) nt (Mahlzeit) meal; (Nahrung) food

Essig (-s, -e) m vinegar

Esslöffel m dessert spoon; **Esszimmer** nt dining room

Estland nt Estonia

Etage (-, -n) f floor, storey; **in** (o **auf**) **der ersten ~** on the first (Brit) (o second (US)) floor; **Etagenbett** nt bunk bed

Etappe (-, -n) f stage

ethnisch adj ethnic

Etikett (-(e)s, -e) nt label

etliche pron pl several, quite a few; **etliches** pron quite a lot

etwa adv (ungefähr) about; (vielleicht) perhaps; (beispielsweise) for instance

etwas pron something; (verneinend, fragend) anything; (ein wenig) a little; **~ Neues** something/anything new; **~ zu essen** something to eat; **~ Salz** some salt; **wenn ich noch ~ tun kann ...** if I can do anything else ... ▸ adv a bit, a little; **~ mehr** a little more

EU (-) f abk = **Europäische Union** EU

euch pron akk, dat von **ihr**; you, (to)

you; ~ **(selbst)** (reflexiv) yourselves;
wo kann ich ~ treffen? where can
I meet you?; **sie schickt es ~** she'll
send it to you; **ein Freund von ~** a
friend of yours; **setzt ~ bitte**
please sit down; **habt ihr
~ amüsiert?** did you enjoy
yourselves?

euer pron (adjektivisch) your;
~ **David** (am Briefende) Yours, David
▷ pron gen von **ihr**; of you; **euere(r,
s)** pron siehe **eure**

Eule (-, -n) f owl

eure(r, s) pron (substantivisch)
yours; **das ist ~** that's yours;
euretwegen adv (wegen euch)
because of you; (euch zuliebe) for
your sake; (um euch) about you

Euro (-, -) m (Währung) euro;
Eurocent m eurocent; **Eurocity**
(-(s), -s) m, **Eurocityzug** m
European Intercity train; **Europa**
(-s) nt Europe; **Europäer(in)** (-s, -)
m(f) European; **europäisch** adj
European; **Europäische Union**
European Union;
Europameister(in) m(f) Euro-
pean champion; (Mannschaft)
European champions pl;
Europaparlament nt European
Parliament

Euter (-s, -) nt udder

evangelisch adj Protestant

eventuell adj possible ▷ adv
possibly, perhaps

ewig adj eternal; **er hat
~ gebraucht** it took him ages;
Ewigkeit f eternity

Ex mf ex

Ex- in zW ex-, former; **~frau**
ex-wife; **~freund** m ex-boyfriend;
~minister former minister

exakt adj precise

Examen (-s, -) nt exam

Exemplar (-s, -e) nt specimen;
(Buch) copy

Exil (-s, -e) nt exile

Existenz f existence; (Unterhalt)
livelihood, living; **existieren** vi
to exist

exklusiv adj exclusive; **exklusive**
adv, prep **+gen** excluding

exotisch adj exotic

Experte (-n, -n) m, **Expertin** f
expert

explodieren vi to explode;
Explosion f explosion

Export (-(e)s, -e) m export;
exportieren vt to export

Express (-es) m, **Expresszug** m
express (train)

extra adj inv (fam: gesondert)
separate; (zusätzlich) extra ▷ adv
(gesondert) separately; (speziell)
specially; (absichtlich) on purpose;
Extra (-s, -s) nt extra

extrem adj extreme ▷ adv extremely;
~ kalt extremely cold

exzellent adj excellent

Eyeliner (-s, -) m eyeliner

f

fabelhaft adj fabulous, marvellous

Fabrik f factory

Fach (-(e)s, Fächer) nt compartment; (Schulfach, Sachgebiet) subject; **Facharzt** m, **Fachärztin** f specialist; **Fachausdruck** (-s, Fachausdrücke) m technical term

Fächer (-s, -) m fan

Fachfrau f specialist, expert; **Fachmann** (-leute) m specialist, expert; **Fachwerkhaus** nt half-timbered house

Fackel (-, -n) f torch

fad(e) adj (Essen) bland; (langweilig) dull

Faden (-s, Fäden) m thread

fähig adj capable (zu, gen of); **Fähigkeit** f ability

Fahndung f search

Fahne (-, -n) f flag

Fahrausweis m ticket

Fahrbahn f road; (Spur) lane

Fähre (-, -n) f ferry

fahren (fuhr, gefahren) vt to drive; (Rad) to ride; (befördern) to drive, to take; **50 km/h ~** to drive at (o do) 50 kph ▷ vi (sich bewegen) to go; (Autofahrer) to drive; (Schiff) to sail; (abfahren) to leave; **mit dem Auto/Zug ~** to go by car/train; **rechts ~!** keep to the right; **Fahrer(in)** (-s, -) m(f) driver; **Fahrerairbag** m driver airbag; **Fahrerflucht** f: **~ begehen** to fail to stop after an accident; **Fahrersitz** m driver's seat

Fahrgast m passenger; **Fahrgeld** nt fare; **Fahrgemeinschaft** f car pool; **Fahrkarte** f ticket; **Fahrkartenautomat** m ticket machine; **Fahrkartenschalter** m ticket office

fahrlässig adj negligent

Fahrlehrer(in) m(f) driving instructor; **Fahrplan** m timetable; **Fahrplanauszug** m individual timetable; **fahrplanmäßig** adj (Eisenb) scheduled; **Fahrpreis** m fare; **Fahrpreisermäßigung** f fare reduction; **Fahrrad** nt bicycle; **Fahrradschlauch** m bicycle tube; **Fahrradschloss** nt bicycle lock; **Fahrradverleih** m cycle hire (Brit) (o rental (US)); **Fahrradweg** m cycle path; **Fahrschein** m ticket; **Fahrscheinautomat** m ticket machine; **Fahrscheinentwerter** m ticket-cancelling machine; **Fahrschule** f driving school; **Fahrschüler(in)** m(f) learner (driver) (Brit), student driver (US); **Fahrspur** f lane; **Fahrstreifen** m lane; **Fahrstuhl** m lift (Brit), elevator (US)

Fahrt (-, -en) f journey; (kurz) trip; (Auto) drive; **auf der ~ nach London** on the way to London; **nach drei Stunden ~** after travelling for three hours; **gute ~!** have a good trip; **Fahrtkosten** *pl* travelling expenses *pl*; **Fahrtrichtung** *f* direction of travel

fahrtüchtig *f* (*Person*) fit to drive; (*Fahrzeug*) roadworthy

Fahrtunterbrechung *f* break in the journey, stop

Fahrverbot *nt*: **~ erhalten/ haben** to be banned from driving; **Fahrzeug** *nt* vehicle; **Fahrzeugbrief** *m* (vehicle) registration document; **Fahrzeughalter(in)** *m(f)* registered owner; **Fahrzeugpapiere** *pl* vehicle documents *pl*

fair *adj* fair

Fakultät *f* faculty

Falke (-n, -n) *m* falcon

Fall (-(e)s, Fälle) *m* (*Sturz*) fall; (*Sachverhalt, juristisch*) case; **auf jeden ~, auf alle Fälle** in any case; (*bestimmt*) definitely; **auf keinen ~** on no account; **für den ~, dass ...** in case ...

Falle (-, -n) *f* trap

fallen (fiel, gefallen) *vi* to fall; **etw ~ lassen** to drop sth

fällig *adj* due

falls *adv* if; (*für den Fall, dass*) in case

Fallschirm *m* parachute; **Fallschirmspringen** *nt* parachuting, parachute jumping; **Fallschirmspringer(in)** *m(f)* parachutist

falsch *adj* (*unrichtig*) wrong; (*unehrlich, unecht*) false; (*Schmuck*) fake; **~ verbunden** sorry, wrong number; **fälschen** *vt* to forge; **Falschfahrer(in)** *m(f)* person driving the wrong way on the motorway; **Falschgeld** *nt* counterfeit money; **Fälschung** *f* forgery, fake

Faltblatt *nt* leaflet

Falte (-, -n) *f* (*Knick*) fold; (*Haut*) wrinkle; (*Rock*) pleat; (*Bügel*) crease; **falten** *vt* to fold; **faltig** *adj* (*zerknittert*) creased; (*Haut, Gesicht*) wrinkled

Familie *f* family; **Familien- angehörige(r)** *mf* family member; **Familienname** *m* surname; **Familienstand** *m* marital status

Fan (-s, -s) *m* fan

fand *imperf von* **finden**

fangen (fing, gefangen) *vt* to catch ▷ *vr*: **sich ~** (*nicht fallen*) to steady oneself; (*fig*) to compose oneself

Fantasie *f* imagination

fantastisch *adj* fantastic

Farbdrucker *m* colour printer; **Farbe** (-, -n) *f* colour; (*zum Malen etc*) paint; (*für Stoff*) dye; **färben** *vt* to colour; (*Stoff, Haar*) to dye; **Farbfernsehen** *nt* colour television; **Farbfilm** *m* colour film; **farbig** *adj* coloured; **Farbkopierer** *m* colour copier; **farblos** *adj* colourless; **Farbstoff** *m* dye; (*für Lebensmittel*) colouring

Farn (-(e)s, -e) *m* fern

Fasan (-(e)s, -e(n)) *m* pheasant

Fasching (-s, -e) *m* carnival, Mardi Gras (US); **Faschings- dienstag** (-s, -e) *m* Shrove Tuesday, Mardi Gras (US)

Faschismus *m* fascism

Faser (-, -n) *f* fibre

Fass (-es, Fässer) *nt* barrel; (*Öl*) drum

fassen *vt* (*ergreifen*) to grasp; (*enthalten*) to hold; (*Entschluss*) to take; (*verstehen*) to understand; **nicht zu ~!** unbelievable ▷ *vr*: **sich ~** to compose oneself; **Fassung** *f* (*Umrahmung*) mount; (*Brille*) frame; (*Lampe*) socket; (*Wortlaut*) version; (*Beherrschung*) composure; **jdn aus der ~ bringen**

to throw sb; **die ~ verlieren** to lose one's cool

fast adv almost, nearly

fasten vi to fast; **Fastenzeit** f: **die ~** (christlich) Lent; (muslimisch) Ramadan

Fast Food nt fast food

Fastnacht f (Fasching) carnival

fatal adj (verhängnisvoll) disastrous; (peinlich) embarrassing

faul adj (Obst, Gemüse) rotten; (Mensch) lazy; (Ausreden) lame; **faulen** vi to rot

faulenzen vi to do nothing, to hang around; **Faulheit** f laziness

faulig adj rotten; (Geruch, Geschmack) foul

Faust (-, Fäuste) f fist; **Fausthandschuh** m mitten

Fax (-, -(e)) nt fax; **faxen** vi, vt to fax; **Faxgerät** nt fax machine; **Faxnummer** f fax number

FCKW (-, -s) nt abk = **Fluorchlorkohlenwasserstoff** CFC

Februar (-(s), -e) m February; siehe auch **Juni**

Fechten nt fencing

Feder (-, -n) f feather; (Schreibfeder) (pen-)nib; (Tech) spring; **Federball** m (Ball) shuttlecock; (Spiel) badminton; **Federung** f suspension

Fee (-, -n) f fairy

fegen vi, vt to sweep

fehl adj: **~ am Platz** (o Ort) out of place

fehlen vi (abwesend sein) to be absent; **etw fehlt jdm** sb lacks sth; **was fehlt ihm?** what's wrong with him?; **du fehlst mir** I miss you; **es fehlt an ...** there's no...

Fehler (-s, -) m mistake, error; (Mangel, Schwäche) fault; **Fehlermeldung** f (Inform) error message

Fehlzündung f (Auto) misfire

Feier (-, -n) f celebration; (Party) party; **Feierabend** m end of the working day; **~ haben** to finish work; **nach ~** after work; **feierlich** adj solemn; **feiern** vt, vi to celebrate, to have a party; **Feiertag** m holiday; **gesetzlicher ~** public (o bank (Brit) o legal (US)) holiday

feig(e) adj cowardly

Feige (-, -n) f fig

Feigling m coward

Feile (-, -n) f file

fein adj fine; (vornehm) refined; **~!** great!; **das schmeckt ~** that tastes delicious

Feind(in) (-(e)s, -e) m(f) enemy; **feindlich** adj hostile

Feinkost (-) f delicacies pl, **Feinkostladen** m delicatessen; **Feinschmecker(in)** (-s, -) m(f) gourmet; **Feinstaub** m particulate matter; **Feinwaschmittel** nt washing powder for delicate fabrics

Feld (-(e)s, -er) nt field; (Schach) square; (Sport) pitch; **Feldsalat** m lamb's lettuce; **Feldweg** m path across the fields

Felge (-, -n) f (wheel) rim

Fell (-(e)s, -e) nt fur; (von Schaf) fleece

Fels (-en, -en) m, **Felsen** (-s, -) m rock; (Klippe) cliff; **felsig** adj rocky

feminin adj feminine; **Femininum** (-s, Feminina) nt (Ling) feminine noun

feministisch adj feminist

Fenchel (-s, -) m fennel

Fenster (-s, -) nt window; **Fensterbrett** nt windowsill; **Fensterladen** m shutter; **Fensterplatz** m windowseat; **Fensterscheibe** f windowpane

Ferien pl holidays pl (Brit), vacation sing (US); **~ haben/ machen** to be/go on holiday (Brit)

(o vacation (US)); **Ferienhaus** nt
holiday (Brit) (o vacation (US))
home; **Ferienkurs** m holiday
(Brit) (o vacation (US)) course;
Ferienlager nt holiday camp
(Brit), vacation camp (US); (für
Kinder im Sommer) summer camp;
Ferienort m holiday (Brit) (o
vacation (US)) resort;
Ferienwohnung f holiday flat
(Brit), vacation apartment (US)

Ferkel (-s, -) nt piglet

fern adj distant, far-off; **von
~ from** a distance; **Fernabfrage** f
remote-control access;
Fernbedienung f remote control;
Ferne f distance; **aus der ~ from**
a distance

ferner adj, adv further; (außerdem)
besides

Fernflug m long-distance flight;
Ferngespräch nt long-distance
call; **ferngesteuert** adj
remote-controlled; **Fernglas** nt
binoculars pl; **Fernlicht** nt full
beam (Brit), high beam (US)

Fernsehapparat m TV (set);
fern|sehen irr vi to watch
television; **Fernsehen** nt
television; **im ~ on** television;
Fernseher m TV (set);
Fernsehkanal m TV channel;
Fernsehprogramm nt (Sendung)
TV programme; (Zeitschrift) TV
guide; **Fernsehserie** f TV series
sing; **Fernsehturm** m TV tower;
Fernsehzeitschrift f TV guide

Fernstraße f major road;
Ferntourismus m long-haul
tourism; **Fernverkehr** m
long-distance traffic

Ferse (-, -n) f heel

fertig adj (bereit) ready; (beendet)
finished; (gebrauchsfertig)
ready-made; **~ machen** (beenden)
to finish; **sich ~ machen** to get
ready; **mit etw ~ werden** to be

able to cope with sth; **auf die
Plätze, ~, los!** on your marks, get
set, go!; **Fertiggericht** nt ready
meal; **fertig|machen** vt (jdn
kritisieren) to give sb hell; (jdn zur
Verzweiflung bringen) to drive sb
mad; (jdn deprimieren) to get sb
down

fest adj firm; (Nahrung) solid;
(Gehalt) regular; (Schuhe) sturdy;
(Schlaf) sound

Fest (-(e)s, -e) nt party; (Rel)
festival

Festbetrag m fixed amount

fest|binden irr vt to tie (an +dat
to); **fest|halten** irr vt to hold
onto ▷ vr: **sich ~** to hold on (an
+dat to)

Festiger (-s, -) m setting lotion

Festival (-s, -s) nt festival

Festland nt mainland; **das
europäische ~** the (European)
continent

fest|legen vt to fix ▷ vr: **sich
~** to commit oneself

festlich adj festive

fest|machen vt to fasten;
(Termin etc) to fix; **fest|nehmen** irr
vt to arrest; **Festnetz** nt (Tel)
fixed-line network; **Festplatte** f
(Inform) hard disk

fest|setzen vt to fix

Festspiele pl festival sing

fest|stehen irr vi to be fixed

fest|stellen vt to establish;
(sagen) to remark

Feststelltaste f shift lock

Festung f fortress

Festzelt nt marquee

Fete (-, -n) f party

fett adj (dick) fat; (Essen etc)
greasy; (Schrift) bold; **Fett** (-(e)s,
-e) nt fat; (Tech) grease; **fettarm**
adj low-fat; **fettig** adj fatty;
(schmierig) greasy

feucht adj damp; (Luft) humid;
Feuchtigkeit f dampness;

(*Luftfeuchtigkeit*) humidity;
Feuchtigkeitscreme f
moisturizing cream
Feuer (-s, -) nt fire; **haben Sie ~?**
have you got a light?; **Feueralarm**
m fire alarm; **feuerfest** adj
fireproof; **Feuerlöscher** (-s, -) m
fire extinguisher; **Feuermelder**
(-s, -) m fire alarm; **Feuertreppe**
f fire escape; **Feuerwehr** (-, -en) f
fire brigade; **Feuerwehrfrau** f
firewoman, fire fighter;
Feuerwehrmann m fireman, fire
fighter; **Feuerwerk** nt
fireworks pl; **Feuerzeug** nt
(cigarette) lighter
Fichte (-, -n) f spruce
ficken vt, vi (vulg) to fuck
Fieber (-s, -) nt temperature,
fever; **~ haben** to have a high
temperature; **Fieber-**
thermometer nt
thermometer
fiel imperf von **fallen**
fies adj (fam) nasty
Figur (-, -en) f figure; (im Schach)
piece
Filet (-s, -s) nt fillet; **filetieren**
vt to fillet; **Filetsteak** nt fillet
steak
Filiale (-, -n) f (Comm) branch
Film (-(e)s, -e) m film, movie;
filmen vt, vi to film
Filter (-s, -) m filter; **Filterkaffee**
m filter coffee; **filtern** vt to
filter; **Filterpapier** nt filter
paper
Filz (-es, -e) m felt; **Filzschreiber**
m, **Filzstift** m felt(-tip) pen,
felt-tip
Finale (-s, -) nt (Sport) final
Finanzamt nt tax office;
finanziell adj financial;
finanzieren vt to finance
finden (fand, gefunden) vt to find;
(meinen) to think; **ich finde nichts**
dabei, wenn ... I don't see what's

wrong if ...; **ich finde es**
gut/schlecht I like/don't like it
▷ vr: **es fanden sich nur wenige**
Helfer there were only a few
helpers
fing imperf von **fangen**
Finger (-s, -) m finger;
Fingerabdruck m fingerprint;
Fingerhandschuh m glove;
Fingernagel m fingernail
Fink (-en, -en) m finch
Finne (-n, -n) m, **Finnin** f Finn,
Finnish man/woman; **finnisch**
adj Finnish; **Finnisch** nt
Finnish; **Finnland** nt Finland
finster adj dark; (verdächtig)
dubious; (verdrossen) grim;
(Gedanke) dark; **Finsternis** f
darkness
Firewall (-, -s) f (Inform) firewall
Firma (-, Firmen) f firm
Fisch (-(e)s, -e) m fish; **~e** pl (Astr)
Pisces sing; **fischen** vt, vi to fish;
Fischer(in) (-s, -) m(f) fisherman,
-woman; **Fischerboot** nt
fishing boat; **Fischgericht** nt fish
dish; **Fischhändler(in)** m(f)
fishmonger; **Fischstäbchen** nt
fish finger (Brit) (o stick (US))
Fisole (-, -n) f French bean
fit adj fit; **Fitness** (-, -) f fitness;
Fitnesscenter (-s, -) nt fitness
centre; **Fitnesstrainer(in)** m(f)
fitness trainer, personal trainer
fix adj (schnell) quick; **~ und fertig**
exhausted
fixen vi (fam) to shoot up;
Fixer(in) (-s, -) m(f) (fam) junkie
FKK f abk = **Freikörperkultur**
nudism; **FKK-Strand** m nudist
beach
flach adj flat; (Gewässer; Teller)
shallow; **~er Absatz** low heel;
Flachbildschirm m flat screen
Fläche (-, -n) f area; (Oberfläche)
surface
Flagge (-, -n) f flag

flambiert adj flambé(ed)

Flamme (-, -n) f flame

Flanell (-s) m flannel

Flasche (-, -n) f bottle; **eine ~ sein** (fam) to be useless; **Flaschenbier** nt bottled beer; **Flaschenöffner** m bottle opener; **Flaschenpfand** nt deposit; **Flaschentomate** f plum tomato

flatterhaft adj fickle; **flattern** vi to flutter

flauschig adj fluffy

Flausen pl (fam) daft ideas pl

Flaute (-, -n) f calm; (Comm) recession

Flechte (-, -n) f plait; (Med) scab; (Bot) lichen; **flechten** (flocht, geflochten) vt to plait; (Kranz) to bind

Fleck (-(e)s, -e) m, **Flecken** (-s, -) m spot; (Schmutz) stain; (Stoff~) patch; (Makel) blemish; **Fleckentferner** (-s, -) m stain remover; **fleckig** adj spotted; (mit Schmutzflecken) stained

Fledermaus f bat

Fleisch (-(e)s) nt flesh; (Essen) meat; **Fleischbrühe** f meat stock; **Fleischer(in)** (-s, -) m(f) butcher; **Fleischerei** f butcher's (shop); **Fleischtomate** f beef tomato

fleißig adj diligent, hard-working

flennen vi (fam) to cry, to howl

flexibel adj flexible

flicken vt to mend; **Flickzeug** nt repair kit

Flieder (-s, -) m lilac

Fliege (-, -n) f fly; (Krawatte) bow tie

fliegen (flog, geflogen) vt, vi to fly

Fliese (-, -n) f tile

Fließband nt conveyor belt; (als Einrichtung) production (o assembly) line; **fließen** (floss, geflossen) vi to flow; **fließend** adj (Rede, Deutsch) fluent; (Übergänge) smooth; **~(es) Wasser** running water

Flipper (-s, -) m pinball machine; **flippern** vi to play pinball

flippig adj (fam) eccentric

flirten vi to flirt

Flitterwochen pl honeymoon sing

flocht imperf von **flechten**

Flocke (-, -n) f flake

flog imperf von **fliegen**

Floh (-(e)s, Flöhe) m flea; **Flohmarkt** m flea market

Flop (-s, -s) m flop

Floskel (-, -n) f empty phrase

floss imperf von **fließen**

Floß (-es, Flöße) nt raft

Flosse (-, -n) f fin; (Schwimmflosse) flipper

Flöte (-, -n) f flute; (Blockflöte) recorder

flott adj lively; (elegant) smart; (Naut) afloat

Fluch (-(e)s, Flüche) m curse; **fluchen** vi to swear, to curse

Flucht (-, -en) f flight; **flüchten** vi to flee (vor +dat from); **flüchtig** adj: **ich kenne ihn nur ~** I don't know him very well at all; **Flüchtling** m refugee

Flug (-(e)s, Flüge) m flight; **Flugbegleiter(in)** (-s, -) m(f) flight attendant; **Flugblatt** nt leaflet

Flügel (-s, -) m wing; (Mus) grand piano

Fluggast m passenger (on a plane); **Fluggesellschaft** f airline; **Flughafen** m airport; **Fluglotse** m air-traffic controller; **Flugnummer** f flight number; **Flugplan** m flight schedule; **Flugplatz** m airport; (klein) airfield; **Flugschein** m plane ticket; **Flugschreiber** m flight recorder, black box; **Flugsteig** (-s, -e) m gate; **Flugstrecke** f air route; **Flugticket** nt plane ticket; **Flugverbindung** f flight connection; **Flugverkehr** *m* air traffic; **Flugzeit** *f* flying time; **Flugzeug** *nt* plane; **Flugzeugentführung** *f* hijacking

Flunder (-, -*n*) *f* flounder

Fluor (-*s*) *nt* fluorine

Flur (-(*e*)*s*, -*e*) *m* hall

Fluss (-*es*, Flüsse) *m* river; (Fließen) flow

flüssig *adj* liquid, **Flüssigkeit** (-, -*en*) *f* liquid; **Flüssigseife** *f* liquid soap

flüstern *vt, vi* to whisper

Flut (-, -*en*) *f* (a. fig) flood; (Gezeiten) high tide; **Flutlicht** *nt* floodlight

Fohlen (-*s*, -) *nt* foal

Föhn ((*e*)*s*, -*e*) *m* hairdryer; (Wind) foehn; **föhnen** *vt* to dry; (beim Friseur) to blow-dry

Folge (-, -*n*) *f* (Reihe, Serie) series sing; (Aufeinanderfolge) sequence; (Fortsetzung eines Romans) instalment; (Fortsetzung einer Fernsehserie) episode; (Auswirkung) result; **etw zur ~ haben** to result in sth; **~n haben** to have consequences; **folgen** *vi* to follow (jdm sb); (gehorchen) to obey (jdm sb); **jdm ~ können** (fig) to be able to follow sb; **folgend** *adj* following; **folgendermaßen** *adv* as follows; **folglich** *adv* consequently

Folie *f* foil; (für Projektor) transparency

Fön® *m* siehe **Föhn**

Fondue (-*s*, -*s*) *nt* fondue

fönen *vt* siehe **föhnen**

fordern *vt* to demand

fördern *vt* to promote; (unterstützen) to help

Forderung *f* demand

Forelle *f* trout

Form (-, -*en*) *f* form; (Gestalt) shape; (Gussform) mould; (Backform) baking tin (Brit) (o pan

(US)); **in ~ sein** to be in good form; **Formalität** *f* formality; **Format** *nt* format; **von internationalem ~** of international standing; **formatieren** *vt* (Diskette) to format; (Text) to edit

Formblatt *nt* form; **formen** *vt* to form, to shape; **förmlich** *adj* formal; (buchstäblich) real; **formlos** *adj* informal; **Formular** (-*s*, -*e*) *nt* form; **formulieren** *vt* to formulate

forschen *vi* to search (nach for); (wissenschaftlich) to (do) research; **Forscher(in)** *m(f)* researcher; **Forschung** *f* research

Förster(in) (-*s*, -) *m(f)* forester; (für Wild) gamekeeper

fort *adv* away; (verschwunden) gone; **fort|bewegen** *vt* to move away ▷ *vr*: **sich ~** to move; **Fortbildung** *f* further education; (im Beruf) further training; **fort|fahren** *irr vi* to go away; (weitermachen) to continue; **fort|gehen** *irr vi* to go away; **fortgeschritten** *adj* advanced; **Fortpflanzung** *f* reproduction

Fortschritt *m* progress; **~e machen** to make progress; **fortschrittlich** *adj* progressive

fort|setzen *vt* to continue; **Fortsetzung** *f* continuation; (folgender Teil) instalment; **~ folgt** to be continued

Foto (-*s*, -*s*) *nt* photo ▷ (-*s*, -*s*) *m* (Fotoapparat) camera; **Fotograf(in)** (-*en*, -*en*) *m(f)* photographer; **Fotografie** *f* photography; (Bild) photograph; **fotografieren** *vt* to photograph ▷ *vi* to take photographs; **Fotohandy** *nt* camera phone; **Fotokopie** *f* photocopy; **fotokopieren** *vt* to photocopy

Foul (-*s*, -*s*) *nt* foul

Foyer (-*s*, -*s*) *nt* foyer

Fr. f abk = **Frau** Mrs; (unverheiratet, neutral) Ms

Fracht (-, -en) f freight; (Naut) cargo; (Preis) carriage; **Frachter** (-s, -) m freighter

Frack (-(e)s, Fräcke) m tails pl

Frage (-, -n) f question; **das ist eine ~ der Zeit** that's a matter (o question) of time; **das kommt nicht in ~** that's out of the question; **Fragebogen** m questionnaire; **fragen** vt, vi to ask; **Fragezeichen** nt question mark; **fragwürdig** adj dubious

Franken (-s, -) m (Schweizer Währung) Swiss franc ▷ (-s) nt (Land) Franconia

frankieren vt to stamp; (maschinell) to frank

Frankreich (-s) nt France; **Franzose** (-n, -n) m, **Französin** f Frenchman/-woman; **die ~n** pl the French pl; **französisch** adj French; **Französisch** nt French

fraß imperf von **fressen**

Frau (-, -en) f woman; (Ehefrau) wife; (Anrede) Mrs; (unverheiratet, neutral) Ms; **Frauenarzt** m, **Frauenärztin** f gynaecologist; **Frauenbewegung** f women's movement; **frauenfeindlich** adj misogynous; **Frauenhaus** nt refuge (for battered women)

Fräulein nt (junge Dame) young lady; (veraltet als Anrede) Miss

Freak (-s, -s) m (fam) freak

frech adj cheeky; **Frechheit** f cheek; **so eine ~!** what a cheek

Freeclimbing (-s) nt free climbing

frei adj free; (Straße) clear; (Mitarbeiter) freelance; **ein ~er Tag** a day off; **~e Arbeitsstelle** vacancy; **Zimmer ~** room(s) to let (Brit), room(s) for rent (US); **im Freien** in the open air; **Freibad** nt open-air (swimming) pool

freiberuflich adj freelance; **freig(i)ebig** adj generous; **Freiheit** f freedom; **Freikarte** f free ticket; **frei|lassen** irr vt to (set) free

freilich adv of course

Freilichtbühne f open-air theatre; **frei|machen** vr: **sich ~** to undress; **frei|nehmen** irr vt **sich** (dat) **einen Tag ~** to take a day off; **Freisprechanlage** f hands-free phone; **Freistoß** m free kick

Freitag m Friday; siehe auch **Mittwoch**; **freitags** adv on Fridays; siehe auch **mittwochs**

freiwillig adj voluntary

Freizeichen nt (Tel) ringing tone

Freizeit f spare (o free) time; **Freizeithemd** nt sports shirt; **Freizeitkleidung** f leisure wear; **Freizeitpark** m leisure park

fremd adj (nicht vertraut) strange; (ausländisch) foreign; (nicht eigen) someone else's; **Fremde(r)** mf (Unbekannter) stranger; (Ausländer) foreigner; **fremdenfeindlich** adj anti-foreigner, xenophobic; **Fremdenführer(in)** m(f) (Tourist) guide; **Fremdenverkehr** m tourism; **Fremdenverkehrsamt** nt tourist information office; **Fremdenzimmer** nt (guest) room; **Fremdsprache** f foreign language; **Fremdsprachen-kenntnisse** pl knowledge sing of foreign languages; **Fremdwort** nt foreign word

Frequenz f (Radio) frequency

fressen (fraß, gefressen) vt, vi (Tier) to eat; (Mensch) to guzzle

Freude (-, -n) f joy, delight; **freuen** vt to please; **es freut mich, dass ...** I'm pleased that ... ▷ vr: **sich ~** to be pleased (über +akk about); **sich auf etw** (akk) **~** to look forward to sth

Freund (-(e)s, -e) m friend; (in Beziehung) boyfriend; **Freundin** f friend; (in Beziehung) girlfriend; **freundlich** adj friendly; (liebenswürdig) kind; **freundlicherweise** adv kindly; **Freundlichkeit** f friendliness; (Liebenswürdigkeit) kindness; **Freundschaft** f friendship

Frieden (-s, -) m peace; **Friedhof** m cemetery; **friedlich** adj peaceful

frieren (fror, gefroren) vt, vi to freeze; **ich friere, es friert mich** I'm freezing

Frikadelle f rissole

Frisbee® nt, **Frisbeescheibe** f frisbee®

frisch adj fresh; (lebhaft) lively; **„~ gestrichen"** "wet paint"; **sich ~ machen** to freshen up; **Frischhaltefolie** f clingfilm® (Brit), plastic wrap (US); **Frischkäse** m cream cheese

Friseur(in) (-s, -e) m(f) hairdresser; **frisieren** vt: **jdn ~** to do sb's hair ▷ vr: **sich ~** to do one's hair

Frist (-, -en) f period; (Zeitpunkt) deadline; **innerhalb einer ~ von zehn Tagen** within a ten-day period; **eine ~ einhalten** to meet a deadline; **die ~ ist abgelaufen** the deadline has expired; **fristgerecht** adj, adv within the specified time; **fristlos** adj: **~e Entlassung** dismissal without notice

Frisur f hairdo, hairstyle

frittieren vt to deep-fry

Frl. f abk = **Fräulein** Miss

froh adj happy; **~e Weihnachten!** Merry Christmas

fröhlich adj happy, cheerful

Fronleichnam (-(e)s) m Corpus Christi

frontal adj frontal

fror imperf von **frieren**

Frosch (-(e)s, Frösche) m frog

Frost (-(e)s, Fröste) m frost; **bei ~** in frosty weather; **Frostschutzmittel** nt anti-freeze

Frottee nt terry(cloth); **Frottier(hand)tuch** nt towel

Frucht (-, Früchte) f (a. fig) fruit; (Getreide) corn; **Fruchteis** nt fruit-flavoured ice-cream; **Früchtetee** m fruit tea; **fruchtig** adj fruity; **Fruchtpresse** f juicer; **Fruchtsaft** m fruit juice; **Fruchtsalat** m fruit salad

früh adj, adv early; **heute ~** this morning; **um fünf Uhr ~** at five (o'clock) in the morning; **~ genug** soon enough; **früher** adj earlier; (ehemalig) former ▷ adv formerly, in the past; **frühestens** adv at the earliest

Frühjahr nt, **Frühling** m spring; **Frühlingsrolle** f spring roll; **Frühlingszwiebel** f spring onion (Brit), scallion (US)

frühmorgens adv early in the morning

Frühstück nt breakfast; **frühstücken** vi to have breakfast; **Frühstücksbüfett** nt breakfast buffet; **Frühstücksfernsehen** nt breakfast television; **Frühstücksspeck** m bacon

frühzeitig adj early

Frust (-s) m (fam) frustration; **frustrieren** vt to frustrate

Fuchs (-es, Füchse) m fox

fühlen vt, vi to feel ▷ vr: **sich ~** to feel

fuhr imperf von **fahren**

führen vt to lead; (Geschäft) to run; (Name) to bear; (Buch) to keep ▷ vi to lead, to be in the lead ▷ vr: **sich ~** to behave; **Führerschein** m driving licence (Brit), driver's license (US); **Führung** f leadership; (eines Unternehmens) management; (*Mil*) command; (*in Museum, Stadt*) guided tour; **in ~ liegen** to be in the lead

füllen *vt* to fill; (*Gastr*) to stuff
  ▷ *vr:* **sich ~** to fill

Füller (-s, -) *m*, **Füllfederhalter** (-s, -) *m* fountain pen

Füllung *f* filling

Fund (-(e)s, -e) *m* find; **Fundbüro** *nt* lost property office (*Brit*), lost and found (*US*); **Fundsachen** *pl* lost property *sing*

fünf *num* five; **Fünf** (-, -en) *f* five; (*Schulnote*) ≈ E; **fünfhundert** *num* five hundred; **fünfmal** *adv* five times; **fünfte(r, s)** *adj* fifth; *siehe auch* **dritte**; **Fünftel** (-s, -) *nt* (*Bruchteil*) fifth; **fünfzehn** *num* fifteen; **fünfzehnte(r, s)** *adj* fifteenth; *siehe auch* **dritte**; **fünfzig** *num* fifty; **fünfzigste(r, s)** *adj* fiftieth

Funk (-s) *m* radio; **über ~** by radio

Funke (-ns, -n) *m* spark; **funkeln** *vi* to sparkle

Funkgerät *nt* radio set; **Funktaxi** *nt* radio taxi, radio cab

Funktion *f* function; **funktionieren** *vi* to work, to function; **Funktionstaste** *f* (*Inform*) function key

für *prep* +*akk* for; **was ~ (ein) ...?** what kind (o sort) of ...?; **Tag ~ Tag** day after day

Furcht (-) *f* fear; **furchtbar** *adj* terrible; **fürchten** *vt* to be afraid of, to fear ▷ *vr:* **sich ~** to be afraid (*vor* +*dat* of); **fürchterlich** *adj* awful

füreinander *adv* for each other

fürs *kontr von* **für das**

Fürst(in) (-en, -en) *m(f)* prince/princess; **Fürstentum** *nt* principality; **fürstlich** *adj* (*fig*) splendid

Furunkel (-s, -) *nt* boil

Furz (-es, -e) *m* (*vulg*) fart; **furzen** *vi* (*vulg*) to fart

Fuß (-es, Füße) *m* foot; (*von Glas, Säule etc*) base; (*von Möbel*) leg; **zu ~ on** foot; **zu ~ gehen** to walk; **Fußball** *m* football (*Brit*), soccer; **Fußballmannschaft** *f* football (*Brit*) (o soccer) team; **Fußballplatz** *m* football pitch (*Brit*), soccer field (*US*); **Fußballspiel** *nt* football (*Brit*) (o soccer) match; **Fußballspieler(in)** *m(f)* footballer (*Brit*), soccer player; **Fußboden** *m* floor; **Fußgänger(in)** (-s, -) *m(f)* pedestrian; **Fußgängerüberweg** *m* pedestrian crossing (*Brit*), crosswalk (*US*); **Fußgängerzone** *f* pedestrian precinct (*Brit*) (o zone *US*); **Fußgelenk** *nt* ankle; **Fußpilz** *m* athlete's foot; **Fußtritt** *m* kick; **jdm einen ~ geben** to give sb a kick, to kick sb; **Fußweg** *m* footpath

Futon (-s, -s) *m* futon

Futter (-s, -) *nt* feed; (*Heu etc*) fodder; (*Stoff*) lining; **füttern** *vt* to feed; (*Kleidung*) to line

Futur (-s, -e) *nt* (*Ling*) future (tense)

Fuzzi (-s, -s) *m* (*fam*) guy

g

gab imperf von **geben**

Gabe (-, -n) f gift

Gabel (-, -n) f fork; **Gabelung** f fork

gaffen vi to gape

Gage (-, -n) f fee

gähnen vi to yawn

Galerie f gallery

Galle (-, -n) f gall; (Organ) gall bladder; **Gallenstein** m gallstone

Galopp (-s) m gallop; **galoppieren** vi to gallop

galt imperf von **gelten**

Gameboy® (-s, -s) m Gameboy®

gammeln vi to loaf (o hang) around; **Gammler(in)** (-s, -) m(f) layabout

gang adj: ~ **und gäbe sein** to be quite normal

Gang (-(e)s, Gänge) m walk; (im Flugzeug) aisle; (Essen, Ablauf) course; (Flur etc) corridor; (Durchgang) passage; (Auto) gear; **den zweiten ~ einlegen** to change into second (gear); **etw in ~ bringen** to get sth going; **Gangschaltung** f gears pl; **Gangway** (-, -s) f (Aviat) steps pl; (Naut) gangway

Gans (-, Gänse) f goose; **Gänseblümchen** nt daisy; **Gänsehaut** f goose pimples pl (Brit), goose bumps pl (US)

ganz adj whole; (vollständig) complete; ~ **Europa** all of Europe; **sein ~es Geld** all his money; **den ~en Tag** all day; **die ~e Zeit** all the time ▷ adv quite; (völlig) completely; **es hat mir ~ gut gefallen** I quite liked it; ~ **schön viel** quite a lot; ~ **und gar nicht** not at all; **das ist etwas ~ anderes** that's a completely different matter; **ganztägig** adj all-day; (Arbeit, Stelle) full-time

gar adj done, cooked ▷ adv at all; ~ **nicht/nichts/keiner** not/nothing/nobody at all; ~ **nicht schlecht** not bad at all

Garage (-, -n) f garage

Garantie f guarantee; **garantieren** vt to guarantee

Garderobe (-, -n) f (Kleidung) wardrobe; (Abgabe) cloakroom

Gardine f curtain

Garn (-(e)s, -e) nt thread

Garnele (-, -n) f shrimp

garnieren vt to decorate; (Speisen) to garnish

Garten (-s, Gärten) m garden; **Gärtner(in)** (-s, -) m(f) gardener; **Gärtnerei** f nursery; (Gemüsegärtnerei) market garden (Brit), truck farm (US)

Garzeit f cooking time

Gas (-es, -e) nt gas; ~ **geben** (Auto) to accelerate; (fig) to get a move on; **Gasanzünder** m gas lighter; **Gasbrenner** m gas burner;

Gasflasche f gas bottle;
Gasheizung f gas heating;
Gasherd m gas stove, gas cooker
(Brit); **Gaskocher** (-s, -) m
camping stove; **Gaspedal** nt
accelerator, gas pedal (US)
Gasse (-, -n) f alley
Gast (-es, Gäste) m guest; **Gäste**
haben to have guests;
Gastarbeiter(in) m(f) foreign
worker; **Gästebett** nt spare bed;
Gästebuch nt visitors' book;
Gästehaus nt guest house;
Gästezimmer nt guest room;
gastfreundlich adj hospitable;
Gastgeber(in) (-s, -) m(f) host/
hostess; **Gasthaus** nt, **Gasthof** m
inn; **Gastland** nt host country
Gastritis (-) f gastritis
Gastronomie f (Gewerbe)
catering trade
Gastspiel nt (Sport) away game;
Gaststätte f restaurant;
(Trinklokal) pub (Brit), bar;
Gastwirt(in) m(f) landlord/-lady
GAU (-s, -s) m abk = **größter**
anzunehmender Unfall MCA
Gaumen (-s, -) m palate
Gaze (-, -n) f gauze
geb. adj abk = **geboren** b. ▷ adj
abk = **geborene** née; siehe **geboren**
Gebäck (-(e)s, -e) nt pastries pl;
(Kekse) biscuits pl (Brit), cookies pl
(US)
gebacken pp von **backen**
Gebärdensprache f sign
language
Gebärmutter f womb
Gebäude (-s, -) nt building
geben (gab, gegeben) vt, vi to give
(jdm etw sb sth, sth to sb); (Karten)
to deal; **lass dir eine Quittung**
~ ask for a receipt; **es**
gibt there is/are; (in Zukunft) there
will be; **das gibt's nicht** I don't
believe it ▷ vr: **sich ~** (sich
verhalten) to behave, to act; **das**

gibt sich wieder it'll sort itself out
Gebet (-(e)s, -e) nt prayer
gebeten pp von **bitten**
Gebiet (-(e)s, -e) nt area;
(Hoheitsgebiet) territory; (fig) field
gebildet adj educated; (belesen)
well-read
Gebirge (-s, -) nt mountains pl;
gebirgig adj mountainous
Gebiss (-es, -e) nt teeth pl;
(künstlich) dentures pl; **gebissen**
pp von **beißen**; **Gebissreiniger** m
denture tablets pl
Gebläse (-s, -) nt fan, blower
geblasen pp von **blasen**
geblieben pp von **bleiben**
gebogen pp von **biegen**
geboren pp von **gebären** ▷ adj
born; **Andrea Jordan, geborene**
Christian Andrea Jordan, née
Christian
geborgen pp von **bergen** ▷ adj
secure, safe
geboten pp von **bieten**
gebracht pp von **bringen**
gebrannt pp von **brennen**
gebraten pp von **braten**
gebrauchen vt to use;
Gebrauchsanweisung f direc-
tions pl for use; **gebrauchsfertig**
adj ready to use; **gebraucht** adj
used; **etw ~ kaufen** to buy sth
secondhand; **Gebrauchtwagen**
m secondhand (o used) car
gebräunt adj tanned
gebrochen pp von **brechen**
Gebühr (-, -en) f charge; (Maut)
toll; (Honorar) fee; **Gebühren-**
einheit f (Tel) unit;
gebührenfrei adj free of charge;
(Telefonnummer) freefone® (Brit),
toll-free (US); **gebührenpflichtig**
adj subject to charges; **~e Straße**
toll road
gebunden pp von **binden**
Geburt (-, -en) f birth; **gebürtig**
adj: **er ist ~er Schweizer** he is

Swiss by birth; **Geburtsdatum**
nt date of birth; **Geburtsjahr** nt
year of birth; **Geburtsname** m
birth name; (einer Frau) maiden
name; **Geburtsort** m birthplace;
Geburtstag m birthday;
herzlichen Glückwunsch zum ~!
Happy Birthday; **Geburtsurkunde**
f birth certificate
Gebüsch (-(e)s, -e) nt bushes pl
gedacht pp von **denken**
Gedächtnis nt memory; **im**
~ behalten to remember
Gedanke (-ns, -n) m thought;
sich (dat) **über etw** (akk) **~n**
machen to think about sth;
(besorgt) to be worried about sth;
Gedankenstrich m dash
Gedeck (-(e)s, -e) nt place
setting; (Speisenfolge) set meal
Gedenkstätte f memorial;
Gedenktafel f commemorative
plaque
Gedicht (-(e)s, -e) nt poem
Gedränge (-s) nt crush, crowd
gedrungen pp von **dringen**
Geduld (-) f patience; **geduldig**
adj patient
gedurft pp von **dürfen**
geehrt adj: **Sehr ~er Herr Young**
Dear Mr Young
geeignet adj suitable
Gefahr (-, -en) f danger; **auf**
eigene ~ at one's own risk; **außer**
~ out of danger; **gefährden** vt to
endanger
gefahren pp von **fahren**
gefährlich adj dangerous
Gefälle (-s, -) nt gradient, slope
gefallen pp von **fallen** ▶ irr vi:
jdm ~ to please sb; **er/es gefällt**
mir I like him/it; **sich** (dat) **etw**
~ lassen to put up with sth
Gefallen (-s, -) nt favour; **jdm**
einen ~ tun to do sb a favour
gefälligst adv ..., will you!; **sei**
~ still! be quiet, will you!

gefangen pp von **fangen**
Gefängnis nt prison
Gefäß (-es, -e) nt (Behälter)
container, receptacle; (Anat, Bot)
vessel
gefasst adj composed, calm; **auf**
etw (akk) **~ sein** to be prepared (o
ready) for sth
geflochten pp von **flechten**
geflogen pp von **fliegen**
geflossen pp von **fließen**
Geflügel (-s) nt poultry
gefragt adj in demand
gefressen pp von **fressen**
Gefrierbeutel m freezer bag,
gefrieren irr vi to freeze;
Gefrierfach nt freezer
compartment; **Gefrierschrank**
m (upright) freezer; **Gefriertruhe**
f (chest) freezer
gefroren pp von **frieren**
Gefühl (-(e)s, -e) nt feeling
gefunden pp von **finden**
gegangen pp von **gehen**
gegeben pp von **geben**;
gegebenenfalls adv if need
be

⭕ SCHLÜSSELWORT

gegen prep +akk **1** against; **nichts**
gegen jdn haben to have nothing
against sb; **X gegen Y** (Sport, Jur) X
versus Y; **ein Mittel gegen**
Schnupfen something for colds
2 (in Richtung auf) towards; **gegen**
Osten to(wards) the east; **gegen**
Abend towards evening; **gegen**
einen Baum fahren to drive into a
tree
3 (ungefähr) round about; **gegen 3**
Uhr around 3 o'clock
4 (gegenüber) towards; (ungefähr)
around; **gerecht gegen alle** fair to
all
5 (im Austausch für) for; **gegen bar**
for cash; **gegen Quittung** against

a receipt
6 (*verglichen mit*) compared with

Gegend (-, -en) f area; **hier in der ~** around here
gegeneinander adv against one another
Gegenfahrbahn f opposite lane; **Gegenmittel** nt remedy (*gegen* for); **Gegenrichtung** f opposite direction; **Gegensatz** m contrast; **im ~ zu** in contrast to; **gegensätzlich** adj conflicting; **gegenseitig** adj mutual; **sich ~ helfen** to help each other
Gegenstand m object; (*Thema*) subject
Gegenteil nt opposite; **im ~** on the contrary; **gegenteilig** adj opposite, contrary
gegenüber prep +dat opposite; (*zu jdm*) to(wards); (*angesichts*) in the face of ▷ adv opposite; **gegenüber|stehen** vt to face; (*Problemen*) to be faced with; **gegenüber|stellen** vt to confront (*dat* with); (*fig*) compare (*dat* with)
Gegenverkehr m oncoming traffic; **Gegenwart** (-) f present (tense)
Gegenwind m headwind
gegessen pp von **essen**
geglichen pp von **gleichen**
geglitten pp von **gleiten**
Gegner(in) (-s, -) m(f) opponent
gegolten pp von **gelten**
gegossen pp von **gießen**
gegraben pp von **graben**
gegriffen pp von **greifen**
gehabt pp von **haben**
Gehackte(s) nt mince(d meat) (*Brit*), ground meat (*US*)
Gehalt (-(e)s, -e) m content ▷ -(e)s, Gehälter) nt salary
gehalten pp von **halten**
gehangen pp von **hängen**
gehässig adj spiteful, nasty

gehauen pp von **hauen**
gehbehindert adj: **sie ist ~** she can't walk properly
geheim adj secret; **etw ~ halten** to keep sth secret; **Geheimnis** nt secret; (*rätselhaft*) mystery; **geheimnisvoll** adj mysterious; **Geheimnummer** f, **Geheimzahl** f (*von Kreditkarte*) PIN number
geheißen pp von **heißen**
gehen (ging, gegangen) vt, vi to go; (*zu Fuß*) to walk; (*funktionieren*) to work; **über die Straße ~** to cross the street; **~ nach** (*Fenster*) to face ▷ vi impers: **wie geht es (dir)?** how are you (o things)?; **mir/ihm geht es gut** I'm/he's (doing) fine; **geht das?** is that possible?; **geht's noch?** can you still manage?; **es geht** not too bad, OK; **das geht nicht** that's not on; **es geht um ...** it's about ...
Gehirn (-(e)s, -e) nt brain; **Gehirnerschütterung** f concussion
gehoben pp von **heben**
geholfen pp von **helfen**
Gehör (-(e)s) nt hearing
gehorchen vi to obey (*jdm* sb)
gehören vi to belong (*jdm* to sb); **wem gehört das Buch?** whose book is this?; **gehört es dir?** is it yours? ▷ vr impers: **das gehört sich nicht** it's not done
gehörlos adj deaf
gehorsam adj obedient
Gehsteig m
Gehweg (-s, -e) m pavement (*Brit*), sidewalk (*US*)
Geier (-s, -) m vulture
Geige (-, -n) f violin
geil adj randy (*Brit*), horny (*US*); (*fam*: *toll*) fantastic
Geisel (-, -n) f hostage
Geist (-(e)s, -er) m spirit; (*Gespenst*) ghost; (*Verstand*) mind; **Geisterbahn** f ghost train, tunnel

of horror (US); **Geisterfahrer(in)**
m(f) person driving the wrong way on
the motorway

geizig adj stingy

gekannt pp von **kennen**

geklungen pp von **klingen**

geknickt adj (fig) dejected

gekniffen pp von **kneifen**

gekommen pp von **kommen**

gekonnt pp von **können** ▷ adj
skilful

gekrochen pp von **kriechen**

Gel (-s, -s) nt gel

Gelächter (-s, -) nt laughter

geladen pp von **laden** ▷ adj
loaded; (Elek) live; (fig) furious

gelähmt adj paralysed

Gelände (-s, -) nt land, terrain;
(Fabrik, Sportgelände) grounds pl;
(Baugelände) site

Geländer (-s, -) nt railing;
(Treppengeländer) banister

Geländewagen m off-road
vehicle

gelang imperf von **gelingen**

gelassen pp von **lassen** ▷ adj
calm, composed

Gelatine f gelatine

gelaufen pp von **laufen**

gelaunt adj: **gut/schlecht ~** in a
good/bad mood

gelb adj yellow; (Ampel) amber,
yellow (US); **gelblich** adj
yellowish; **Gelbsucht** f jaundice

Geld (-(e)s, -er) nt money;
Geldautomat m cash machine (o
dispenser (Brit)), ATM (US);
Geldbeutel m, **Geldbörse** f
purse; **Geldbuße** f fine;
Geldschein m (bank)note (Brit),
bill (US); **Geldstrafe** f fine;
Geldstück nt coin; **Geldwechsel**
m exchange of money; (Ort)
bureau de change;
Geldwechselautomat m,
Geldwechsler (-s, -) m change
machine

Gelee (-s, -s) nt jelly

gelegen pp von **liegen** ▷ adj
situated; (passend) convenient;
etw kommt jdm ~ sth is
convenient for sb

Gelegenheit f opportunity;
(Anlass) occasion

gelegentlich adj occasional
▷ adv occasionally; (bei
Gelegenheit) some time (or other)

Gelenk (-(e)s, -e) nt joint

gelernt adj skilled

gelesen pp von **lesen**

geliehen pp von **leihen**

gelingen (gelang, gelungen) vi to
succeed; **es ist mir gelungen, ihn
zu erreichen** I managed to get
hold of him

gelitten pp von **leiden**

gelockt adj curly

gelogen pp von **lügen**

gelten (galt, gegolten) vt (wert
sein) to be worth; **jdm viel/wenig
~** to mean a lot/not to mean much
to sb ▷ vi (gültig sein) to be valid;
(erlaubt sein) to be allowed; **jdm
~** (gemünzt sein auf) to be meant for
(o aimed at) sb; **etw ~ lassen** to
accept sth; **als etw ~** to be
considered to be sth;
Geltungsdauer f: **eine ~ von
fünf Tagen haben** to be valid for
five days

gelungen pp von **gelingen**

gemahlen pp von **mahlen**

Gemälde (-s, -) nt painting,
picture

gemäß prep +dat in accordance
with ▷ adj appropriate (dat to)

gemein adj (niederträchtig) mean,
nasty; (gewöhnlich) common

Gemeinde (-, -n) f district,
community; (Pfarrgemeinde)
parish; (Kirchengemeinde)
congregation

gemeinsam adj joint, common
▷ adv together, jointly; **das Haus**

gehört uns beiden ~ the house belongs to both of us

Gemeinschaft f community; **~ Unabhängiger Staaten** Commonwealth of Independent States

gemeint pp von **meinen**; **das war nicht so ~** I didn't mean it like that

gemessen pp von **messen**

gemieden pp von **meiden**

gemischt adj mixed

gemocht pp von **mögen**

Gemüse (-s, -) nt vegetables pl; **Gemüsehändler(in)** m(f) greengrocer

gemusst pp von **müssen**

gemustert adj patterned

gemütlich adj comfortable, cosy; (*Mensch*) good-natured, easy-going; **mach es dir ~** make yourself at home

genannt pp von **nennen**

genau adj exact, precise ▷ adv exactly, precisely; **~ in der Mitte** right in the middle; **es mit etw ~ nehmen** to be particular about sth; **~ genommen** strictly speaking; **ich weiß es ~** I know for certain (o for sure); **genauso adv** exactly the same (way); **~ gut/viel/viele Leute** just as well/much/many people (wie as)

genehmigen vt to approve; **sich** (dat) **etw ~** to indulge in sth; **Genehmigung** f approval

Generalkonsulat nt consulate general

Generation f generation

Genf (-s) nt Geneva; **~er See** Lake Geneva

Genforschung f genetic research

genial adj brilliant

Genick (-(e)s, -e) nt (back of the) neck

Genie (-s, -s) nt genius

genieren vr: **sich ~** to feel

awkward; **ich geniere mich vor ihm** he makes me feel embarrassed

genießen (genoss, genossen) vt to enjoy

Genitiv m genitive (case)

genmanipuliert adj genetically modified, GM

genommen pp von **nehmen**

genoss imperf von **genießen**

genossen pp von **genießen**

Gentechnik f genetic technology; **gentechnisch adv**: **~ verändert** genetically modified, GM

genug adv enough

genügen vi to be enough (jdm for sb); **danke, das genügt** thanks, that's enough (o that will do)

Genuss (-es, Genüsse) m pleasure; (*Zusichnehmen*) consumption

geöffnet adj (*Geschäft etc*) open

Geografie f geography

Geologie f geology

Georgien (-s) nt Georgia

Gepäck (-(e)s) nt luggage (Brit), baggage; **Gepäckabfertigung** f luggage (Brit) (o baggage) check-in; **Gepäckablage** f luggage (Brit) (o baggage) rack; **Gepäckannahme** f (zur Beförderung) luggage (Brit) (o baggage) office; (zur Aufbewahrung) left-luggage office (Brit), baggage checkroom (US); **Gepäckaufbewahrung** f left-luggage office (Brit), baggage checkroom (US); **Gepäckausgabe** f luggage (Brit) (o baggage) office; (am Flughafen) baggage reclaim; **Gepäckband** nt luggage (Brit) (o baggage) conveyor; **Gepäckkontrolle** f luggage (Brit) (o baggage) check; **Gepäckstück** nt item of luggage (Brit) (o baggage (US)); **Gepäckträger** m porter; (an Fahrrad) carrier;

Gepäckversicherung f luggage
(Brit) (o baggage) insurance;
Gepäckwagen m luggage van
(Brit), baggage car (US)
gepfiffen pp von **pfeifen**
gepflegt adj well-groomed; (Park)
well looked after
gequollen pp von **quellen**

○ SCHLÜSSELWORT

gerade adj straight; (aufrecht)
upright; **eine gerade Zahl** an even
number
▷ adv 1 (genau) just, exactly;
(speziell) especially; **gerade
deshalb** that's just o exactly why;
das ist es ja gerade! that's just it!
gerade du you especially; **warum
gerade ich?** why me (of all
people)?; **jetzt gerade nicht!** not
now!; **gerade neben** right next to
2 (eben, soeben) just; **er wollte
gerade aufstehen** he was just
about to get up; **gerade erst**
only just; **gerade noch** (only)
just

geradeaus adv straight ahead
gerannt pp von **rennen**
geraspelt adj grated
Gerät (-(e)s, -e) nt device, gadget;
(Werkzeug) tool; (Radio, Fernseher)
set; (Zubehör) equipment
geraten pp von **raten** ▷ irr vi to
turn out; **gut/schlecht ~** to turn
out well/badly; **an jdn ~** to come
across sb; **in etw** (akk) **~** to get into
sth
geräuchert adj smoked
geräumig adj roomy
Geräusch (-(e)s, -e) nt sound;
(unangenehm) noise
gerecht adj fair; (Strafe,
Belohnung) just; **jdm/einer Sache
~ werden** to do justice to sb/sth
gereizt adj irritable

Gericht (-(e)s, -e) nt (Jur) court;
(Essen) dish
gerieben pp von **reiben**
gering adj small; (unbedeutend)
slight; (niedrig) low; (Zeit) short;
geringfügig adj slight, minor
▷ adv slightly
gerissen pp von **reißen**
geritten pp von **reiten**
gern(e) adv willingly, gladly, **etw
~ tun** to like doing sth;
~ geschehen you're welcome;
gern|haben, gern mögen irr vt
to like
gerochen pp von **riechen**
Gerste (-, -n) f barley;
Gerstenkorn nt (im Auge) stye
Geruch (-(e)s, Gerüche) m smell
Gerücht (-(e)s, -e) nt rumour
gerufen pp von **rufen**
Gerümpel (-s) nt junk
gerungen pp von **ringen**
Gerüst (-(e)s, -e) nt (auf Bau)
scaffolding; (Gestell) trestle; (fig)
framework (zu of)
gesalzen pp von **salzen**
gesamt adj whole, entire;
(Kosten) total; (Werke) complete;
Gesamtschule f
comprehensive school
gesandt pp von **senden**
Gesäß (-es, -e) nt bottom
geschaffen pp von **schaffen**
Geschäft (-(e)s, -e) nt business;
(Laden) shop; (Geschäftsabschluss)
deal; **geschäftlich** adj commercial
▷ adv on business; **Geschäftsfrau**
f businesswoman; **Geschäfts-
führer(in)** m(f) managing
director; (von Laden) manager;
Geschäftsleitung f executive
board; **Geschäftsmann** m
businessman; **Geschäftsreise** f
business trip; **Geschäftsstraße** f
shopping street; **Geschäftszeiten**
pl business (o opening) hours
pl

geschehen (geschah, geschehen)
vi to happen

Geschenk (-(e)s, -e) nt present,
gift; **Geschenkgutschein** m gift
voucher; **Geschenkpapier** nt
gift-wrapping paper, giftwrap

Geschichte (-, -n) f story; (Sache)
affair; (Hist) history

geschickt adj skilful

▷ **geschieden** pp von **scheiden**

▷ adj divorced

▷ **geschienen** pp von **scheinen**

Geschirr (-(e)s, -e) nt crockery;
(zum Kochen) pots and pans pl; (von
Pferd) harness; ~ **spülen** to do (o
wash) the dishes, to do the
washing-up (Brit);
Geschirrspülmaschine f dishwasher; **Geschirrspülmittel** nt
washing-up liquid (Brit),
dishwashing liquid (US);
Geschirrtuch nt tea towel (Brit),
dish towel (US)

geschissen pp von **scheißen**

geschlafen pp von **schlafen**

geschlagen pp von **schlagen**

Geschlecht (-(e)s, -er) nt sex;
(Ling) gender; **Geschlechtskrankheit** f sexually transmitted
disease, STD; **Geschlechtsorgan**
nt sexual organ;
Geschlechtsverkehr m sexual
intercourse

geschlichen pp von **schleichen**

geschliffen pp von **schleifen**

geschlossen adj closed

Geschmack (-(e)s, Geschmäcke) m
taste; **geschmacklos** adj
tasteless; **Geschmack(s)sache** f:
das ist ~ that's a matter of taste;
geschmackvoll adj tasteful

geschmissen pp von **schmeißen**

geschmolzen pp von **schmelzen**

geschnitten pp von **schneiden**

geschoben pp von **schieben**

Geschoss (-es, -e) nt (Stockwerk)
floor

geschossen pp von **schießen**

Geschrei (-s) nt cries pl; (fig)
fuss

geschrieben pp von **schreiben**

geschrie(e)n pp von **schreien**

geschützt adj protected

Geschwätz (-es) nt chatter;
(Klatsch) gossip; **geschwätzig** adj
talkative, gossipy

geschweige adv: ~ **(denn)** let
alone

geschwiegen pp von **schweigen**

Geschwindigkeit f speed;
(Phys) velocity; **Geschwindigkeitsbegrenzung** f speed limit

Geschwister pl brothers and
sisters pl

geschwollen adj (angeschwollen)
swollen; (Rede) pompous

geschwommen pp von
schwimmen

geschworen pp von **schwören**

Geschwulst (-, Geschwülste) f
growth

Geschwür (-(e)s, -e) nt ulcer

gesehen pp von **sehen**

gesellig adj sociable;
Gesellschaft f society;
(Begleitung) company; (Abend~)
party; ~ **mit beschränkter
Haftung** limited company (Brit),
limited corporation (US)

gesessen pp von **sitzen**

Gesetz (-es, -e) nt law; **gesetzlich**
adj legal; **~er Feiertag** public (o
bank (Brit) o legal (US)) holiday;
gesetzwidrig adj illegal

Gesicht (-(e)s, -er) nt face; (Miene)
expression; **mach doch nicht so
ein ~!** stop pulling such a face;
Gesichtscreme f face cream;
Gesichtswasser nt toner

gesoffen pp von **saufen**

gesogen pp von **saugen**

gespannt adj tense; (begierig)
eager; **ich bin ~, ob ...** I wonder
if ...; **auf etw/jdn ~ sein** to look

forward to sth/to seeing sb

Gespenst (-(e)s, -er) nt ghost

gesperrt adj closed

gesponnen pp von **spinnen**

Gespräch (-(e)s, -e) nt talk, conversation; (Diskussion) discussion; (Anruf) call

gesprochen pp von **sprechen**

gesprungen pp von **springen**

Gestalt (-, -en) f form, shape; (Mensch) figure

gestanden pp von **stehen, gestehen**

Gestank (-(e)s) m stench

gestatten vt to permit, to allow; **~ Sie?** may I?

Geste (-, -n) f gesture

gestehen irr vt to confess

gestern adv yesterday; **~ Abend/Morgen** yesterday evening/morning

gestiegen pp von **steigen**

gestochen pp von **stechen**

gestohlen pp von **stehlen**

gestorben pp von **sterben**

gestört adj disturbed; (Empfang) poor

gestoßen pp von **stoßen**

gestreift adj striped

gestrichen pp von **streichen**

gestritten pp von **streiten**

gestunken pp von **stinken**

gesund adj healthy; **wieder ~ werden** to get better; **Gesundheit** f health; **~!** bless you!; **gesundheitsschädlich** adj unhealthy

gesungen pp von **singen**

gesunken pp von **sinken**

getan pp von **tun**

getragen pp von **tragen**

Getränk (-(e)s, -e) nt drink; **Getränkeautomat** m drinks machine; **Getränkekarte** f list of drinks

Getreide (-s, -) nt cereals pl, grain

getrennt adj separate; **~ leben** to live apart; **~ zahlen** to pay separately

getreten pp von **treten**

Getriebe (-s, -) nt (Auto) gearbox

getrieben pp von **treiben**

Getriebeschaden m gearbox damage

getroffen pp von **treffen**

getrunken pp von **trinken**

Getue nt fuss

geübt adj experienced

gewachsen pp von **wachsen** ▷ adj: **jdm/einer Sache ~ sein** to be a match for sb/up to sth

Gewähr (-) f guarantee; **keine ~ übernehmen für** to accept no responsibility for

Gewalt (-, -en) f (Macht) power; (Kontrolle) control; (große Kraft) force; (-taten) violence; **mit aller ~** with all one's might; **gewaltig** adj tremendous; (Irrtum) huge

gewandt pp von **wenden** ▷ adj (flink) nimble; (geschickt) skilful

gewann imperf von **gewinnen**

gewaschen pp von **waschen**

Gewebe (-s, -) nt (Stoff) fabric; (Bio) tissue

Gewehr (-(e)s, -e) nt rifle, gun

Geweih (-(e)s, -e) nt antlers pl

gewellt adj (Haare) wavy

gewendet pp von **wenden**

Gewerbe (-s, -) nt trade; **Gewerbegebiet** nt industrial estate (Brit) o park (US)); **gewerblich** adj commercial

Gewerkschaft f trade union

gewesen pp von **sein**

Gewicht (-(e)s, -e) nt weight; (fig) importance

gewiesen pp von **weisen**

Gewinn (-(e)s, -e) m profit; (bei Spiel) winnings pl; **gewinnen** (gewann, gewonnen) vt to win; (erwerben) to gain; (Kohle, Öl) to extract ▷ vi to win; (profitieren) to gain; **Gewinner(in)** (-s, -) m(f) winner

gewiss adj certain ▷ adv certainly

Gewissen (-s, -) nt conscience; **ein gutes/schlechtes ~ haben** to have a clear/bad conscience

Gewitter (-s, -) nt thunderstorm; **gewittern** vi impers: **es gewittert** it's thundering

gewogen pp von **wiegen**

gewöhnen vt **jdn an etw** (akk) **~** to accustom sb to sth ▷ vr: **sich an jdn/etw~** to get used (o accustomed) to sb/sth; **Gewohnheit** f habit; (Brauch) custom; **gewöhnlich** adj usual; (durchschnittlich) ordinary; (pej) common; **wie ~** as usual; **gewohnt** adj usual; **etw ~ sein** to be used to sth

Gewölbe (-s, -) nt (Deckengewölbe) vault

gewonnen pp von **gewinnen**

geworben pp von **werben**

geworden pp von **werden**

geworfen pp von **werfen**

Gewürz (-es, -e) nt spice; **Gewürznelke** f clove; **gewürzt** adj seasoned

gewusst pp von **wissen**

Gezeiten pl tides pl

gezogen pp von **ziehen**

gezwungen pp von **zwingen**

Gibraltar (-s) nt Gibraltar

Gicht (-) f gout

Giebel (-s, -) m gable

gierig adj greedy

gießen (goss, gegossen) vt to pour; (Blumen) to water; (Metall) to cast; **Gießkanne** f watering can

Gift (-(e)s, -e) nt poison; **giftig** adj poisonous

Gigabyte nt gigabyte

Gin (-s, -s) m gin

ging imperf von **gehen**

Gin Tonic (-(s), -s) m gin and tonic

Gipfel (-s, -) m summit, peak; (Pol) summit; (fig: Höhepunkt) height

Gips (-es, -e) m (a. Med) plaster; **Gipsbein** nt: **sie hat ein ~** she's got her leg in plaster; **Gipsverband** m plaster cast

Giraffe (-, -n) f giraffe

Girokonto nt current account (Brit), checking account (US)

Gitarre (-, -n) f guitar

Gitter (-s, -) nt bars pl

glänzen vi (a. fig) to shine; **glänzend** adj shining; (fig) brilliant

Glas (-es, Gläser) nt glass; (Marmelade) jar; **zwei ~ Wein** two glasses of wine; **Glascontainer** m bottle bank; **Glaser(in)** m(f) glazier; **Glasscheibe** f pane (of glass); **Glassplitter** m splinter of glass

Glasur f glaze; (Gastr) icing

glatt adj smooth; (rutschig) slippery; (Lüge) downright; **Glatteis** nt (black) ice

Glatze (-, -n) f bald head; (fam: Skinhead) skinhead

glauben vt, vi to believe (an +akk in); (meinen) to think; **jdm ~** to believe sb

gleich adj equal; (identisch) same, identical; **alle Menschen sind ~** all people are the same; **es ist mir ~** it's all the same to me ▷ adv equally; (sofort) straight away; (bald) in a minute; **~ groß/alt** the same size/age; **~ nach/an** right after/at; **Gleichberechtigung** f equal rights pl; **gleichen** (glich, geglichen) vi: **jdm/einer Sache ~** to be like sb/sth ▷ vr: **sich ~** to be alike; **gleichfalls** adv likewise; **danke ~!** thanks, and the same to you; **gleichgültig** adj indifferent; **gleichmäßig** adj regular; (Verteilung) even; equal;

gleichzeitig adj simultaneous
▷ adv at the same time

Gleis (-es, -e) nt track, rails pl; (Bahnsteig) platform

gleiten (glitt, geglitten) vi to glide; (rutschen) to slide;
Gleitschirmfliegen (-s) nt paragliding

Gletscher (-s, -) m glacier;
Gletscherskifahren nt glacier skiing; **Gletscherspalte** f crevasse

glich imperf von **gleichen**

Glied (-(e)s, -er) nt (Arm, Bein) limb; (von Kette) link; (Penis) penis;
Gliedmaßen pl limbs pl

glitschig adj slippery

glitt imperf von **gleiten**

glitzern vi to glitter; (Sterne) to twinkle

Glocke (-, -n) f bell; **Glockenspiel** nt chimes pl

Glotze (-, -n) f (fam: TV) box;
glotzen vi (fam) to stare

Glück (-(e)s) nt luck; (Freude) happiness; ~ **haben** to be lucky;
viel ~! good luck; **zum** ~ fortunately; **glücklich** adj lucky; (froh) happy;
glücklicherweise adv fortunately; **Glückwunsch** m congratulations pl; **herzlichen** ~ **zur bestandenen Prüfung** congratulations on passing your exam; **herzlichen** ~ **zum Geburtstag!** Happy Birthday

Glühbirne f light bulb; **glühen** vi to glow; **Glühwein** m mulled wine

GmbH (-, -s) f abk = **Gesellschaft mit beschränkter Haftung** ≈ Ltd (Brit), ≈ Inc (US)

Gokart (-(s), -s) m go-kart

Gold (-(e)s) nt gold; **golden** adj gold; (fig) golden; **Goldfisch** m goldfish; **Goldmedaille** f gold medal; **Goldschmied(in)** m(f)

goldsmith

Golf (-(e)s, -e) m gulf; **der** ~ **von Biskaya** the Bay of Biscay ▷ (-s) nt golf; **Golfplatz** m golf course;
Golfschläger m golf club

Gondel (-, -n) f gondola; (Seilbahn) cable-car

gönnen vt: **ich gönne es ihm** I'm really pleased for him; **sich** (dat) **etw** ~ to allow oneself sth

goss imperf von **gießen**

gotisch adj Gothic

Gott (-es, Götter) m God; (Gottheit) god; **Gottesdienst** m service;
Göttin f goddess

Grab (-(e)s, Gräber) nt grave

graben (grub, gegraben) vt to dig;
Graben (-s, Gräben) m ditch

Grabstein m gravestone

Grad (-(e)s, -e) m degree; **wir haben 30 ~ Celsius** it's 30 degrees Celsius, it's 86 degrees Fahrenheit;
bis zu einem gewissen ~ up to a certain extent

Graf (-en, -en) m count; (in Großbritannien) earl

Graffiti pl graffiti sing

Grafik (-, -en) f graph; (Kunstwerk) graphic; (Illustration) diagram; **Grafikkarte** f (Inform) graphics card; **Grafikprogramm** nt (Inform) graphics software

Gräfin (-, -nen) f countess

Gramm (-s) nt gram(me)

Grammatik f grammar

Grapefruit (-, -s) f grapefruit

Graphik (-, -s) f siehe **Grafik**

Gras (-es, Gräser) nt grass

grässlich adj horrible

Gräte (-, -n) f (fish)bone

gratis adj, adv free (of charge)

gratulieren vi: **jdm (zu etw)** ~ to congratulate sb (on sth); **(ich) gratuliere!** congratulations!

grau adj grey, gray (US);
grauhaarig adj grey-haired

grausam adj cruel

gravierend adj (Fehler) serious

greifen (griff, gegriffen) vt to
seize; **zu etw ~** (fig) to resort to
sth ▷ vi (Regel etc) to have an
effect (bei on)

grell adj harsh

Grenze (-, -n) f boundary; (Staat)
border; (Schranke) limit; **grenzen**
vi to border (an +akk on);
Grenzkontrolle f border control;
Grenzübergang m border
crossing point; **Grenzverkehr** m
border traffic

Grieche (-n, -n) m Greek;
Griechenland nt Greece;
Griechin f Greek; **griechisch** adj
Greek; **Griechisch** nt Greek

griesgrämig adj grumpy

Grieß (-es, -e) m (Gastr) semolina

griff imperf von **greifen**

Griff (-(e)s, -e) m grip; (Tür etc)
handle; **griffbereit** adj handy

Grill (-s, -s) m grill; (im Freien)
barbecue

Grille (-, -n) f cricket

grillen vt to grill ▷ vi to have a
barbecue; **Grillfest** nt, **Grillfete** f
barbecue; **Grillkohle** f charcoal

grinsen vi to grin; (höhnisch) to
sneer

Grippe (-, -n) f flu;
Grippeschutzimpfung f flu
vaccination

grob adj coarse; (Fehler, Verstoß)
gross; (Einschätzung) rough

Grönland (-s) nt Greenland

groß adj big, large; (hoch) tall;
(fig) great; (Buchstabe) capital;
(erwachsen) grown-up; **im Großen
und Ganzen** on the whole ▷ adv
greatly; **großartig** adj
wonderful

Großbritannien (-s) nt (Great)
Britain

Großbuchstabe m capital letter

Größe (-, -n) f size; (Länge)
height; (fig) greatness; **welche**

~ haben Sie? what size do you
take?

Großeltern pl grandparents pl;
Großhandel m wholesale trade;
Großmarkt m hypermarket;
Großmutter f grandmother;
Großraum m: **der ~ Manchester**
Greater Manchester;
groß|schreiben irr vt to write
with a capital letter; **Großstadt** f
city; **Großvater** m grandfather;
großzügig adj generous;
(Planung) on a large scale

Grotte (-, -n) f grotto

grub imperf von **graben**

Grübchen nt dimple

Grube (-, -n) f pit

grüezi interj (schweizerisch) hello

Gruft (-, -̈e) f vault

grün adj green; **~er Salat** lettuce;
~e Bohnen French beans; **der ~e
Punkt** symbol for recyclable
packaging; **im ~en Bereich**
hunky-dory

● **GRÜNER PUNKT**
●
● The **grüner Punkt** is the green
● spot symbol which appears on
● packaging, indicating that the
● packaging should not be
● thrown into the normal
● household refuse but kept
● separate to be recycled through
● the **DSD** (Duales System
● Deutschland) system. The
● recycling is financed by licences
● bought by the manufacturer
● from the 'DSD' and the cost of
● this is often passed on to the
● consumer.

Grünanlage f park

Grund (-(e)s, Gründe) m (Ursache)
reason; (Erdboden) ground; (See,
Gefäß) bottom; (Grundbesitz) land,
property; **aus gesundheitlichen**

Gründen for health reasons; **im ~e** basically; **aus diesem ~** for this reason

gründen vt to found; **Gründer(in)** m(f) founder

Grundgebühr f basic charge; **Grundgesetz** nt (German) Constitution

gründlich adj thorough

Gründonnerstag m Maundy Thursday

grundsätzlich adj fundamental, basic; **sie kommt ~ zu spät** she's always late; **Grundschule** f primary school; **Grundstück** nt plot; (Anwesen) estate; (Baugrundstück) site; **Grundwasser** nt ground water

Grüne(r) mf (Pol) Green; **die ~n** the Green Party

Gruppe (-, -n) f group; **Gruppenermäßigung** f group discount; **Gruppenreise** f group tour

Gruß (-es, Grüße) m greeting; **viele Grüße** best wishes; **Grüße an** (+akk) regards to; **mit freundlichen Grüßen** Yours sincerely (Brit), Sincerely yours (US); **sag ihm einen schönen ~ von mir** give him my regards; **grüßen** vt to greet; **grüß deine Mutter von mir** give your mother my regards; **Julia lässt (euch) ~** Julia sends (you) her regards

gucken vi to look

Gulasch (-(e)s, -e) nt goulash

gültig adj valid

Gummi (-s, -s) m o nt rubber; **Gummiband** nt rubber (o elastic (Brit)) band; **Gummibärchen** pl gums pl (in the shape of a bear) (Brit), gumdrops pl (in the shape of a bear) (US); **Gummihandschuhe** pl rubber gloves pl; **Gummistiefel** m wellington (boot) (Brit), rubber boot (US)

günstig adj favourable; (Preis) good

gurgeln vi to gurgle; (im Mund) to gargle

Gurke (-, -n) f cucumber; **saure ~** gherkin

Gurt (-(e)s, -e) m belt

Gürtel (-s, -) m belt; (Geo) zone; **Gürtelrose** f shingles sing

GUS (-) f abk = Gemeinschaft Unabhängiger Staaten CIS

O SCHLÜSSELWORT

gut adj good; **alles Gute** all the best; **also gut** all right then ▷ adv well; **gut gehen** to work, to come off; **es geht jdm gut** sb's doing fine; **gut gemeint** well meant; **gut schmecken** to taste good; **jdm guttun** to do sb good; **gut, aber ...** OK, but ...; **(na) gut, ich komme** all right, I'll come; **gut drei Stunden** a good three hours; **das kann gut sein** that may well be; **lass es gut sein** that'll do

Gutachten (-s, -) nt report; **Gutachter(in)** (-s, -) m(f) expert

gutartig adj (Med) benign

Güter pl goods pl; **Güterbahnhof** m goods station; **Güterzug** m goods train

gutgläubig adj trusting; **Guthaben** (-s) nt (credit) balance

gutmütig adj good-natured

Gutschein m voucher; **Gutschrift** f credit

Gymnasium nt = grammar school (Brit), = high school (US)

Gymnastik f exercises pl, keep-fit

Gynäkologe m, **Gynäkologin** f gynaecologist

Gyros (-, -) nt doner kebab

h

Haar (-(e)s, -e) nt hair; **um ein ~** nearly; **sich** (dat) **die ~e schneiden lassen** to have one's hair cut; **Haarbürste** f hairbrush; **Haarfestiger** m setting lotion; **Haargel** nt hair gel; **haarig** adj hairy; (fig) nasty; **Haarschnitt** m haircut; **Haarspange** f hair slide (Brit), barrette (US); **Haarspliss** m split ends pl; **Haarspray** nt hair spray; **Haartrockner** (-s, -) m hairdryer; **Haarwaschmittel** nt shampoo; **Haarwasser** nt hair tonic

haben (hatte, gehabt) vt, vaux to have; **Hunger/Angst ~** to be hungry/afraid; **Ferien ~** to be on holiday (Brit) (o vacation (US)); **welches Datum ~ wir heute?** what's the date today?; **ich hätte gerne ...** I'd like ...; **hätten Sie etwas dagegen, wenn ...?** would

you mind if ...?; **was hast du denn?** what's the matter (with you)?

Haben nt (Comm) credit

Habicht (-(e)s, -e) m hawk

Hacke (-, -n) f (im Garten) hoe; (Ferse) heel; **hacken** vt to chop; (Loch) to hack; (Erde) to hoe; **Hacker(in)** (-s, -) m(f) (Inform) hacker; **Hackfleisch** nt mince(d meat) (Brit), ground meat (US)

Hafen (-s, Häfen) m harbour; (großer) port; **Hafenstadt** f port

Hafer (-s, -) m oats pl; **Haferflocken** pl rolled oats pl

Haft (-) f custody; **haftbar** adj liable, responsible; **haften** vi to stick; **~ für** to be liable (o responsible) for; **Haftnotiz** f Post-it®; **Haftpflichtversicherung** f third party insurance; **Haftung** f liability

Hagebutte (-, -n) f rose hip

Hagel (-s) m hail; **hageln** vi impers to hail

Hahn (-(e)s, Hähne) m cock; (Wasserhahn) tap (Brit), faucet (US); **Hähnchen** nt cockerel; (Gastr) chicken

Hai(fisch) (-(e)s, -e) m shark

häkeln vi, vt to crochet; **Häkelnadel** f crochet hook

Haken (-s, -) m hook; (Zeichen) tick

halb adj half; **~ eins** half past twelve; (fam) half twelve; **eine ~e Stunde** half an hour; **~ offen** half-open; **Halbfinale** nt semifinal; **halbieren** vt to halve; **Halbinsel** f peninsula; **Halbjahr** nt half-year; **halbjährlich** adj half-yearly; **Halbmond** m (Astr) half-moon; (Symbol) crescent; **Halbpension** f half board; **halbseitig** adj: **~ gelähmt** paralyzed on one side; **halbtags**

adv (arbeiten) part-time; **halbwegs**
adv (leidlich) reasonably; **Halbzeit**
f half; (Pause) half-time
half *imperf von* **helfen; Hälfte**
(-, -n) *f* half
Halle (-, -n) *f* hall; **Hallenbad** *nt*
indoor (swimming) pool
hallo *interj* hello, hi
Halogenlampe *f* halogen lamp;
Halogenscheinwerfer *m* halogen headlight
Hals (-es, Hälse) *m* neck; (Kehle)
throat; **Halsband** *nt* (für Tiere)
collar; **Halsentzündung** *f* sore
throat; **Halskette** *f* necklace;
Hals-Nasen-Ohren-Arzt *m*,
Hals-Nasen-Ohren-Ärztin *f* ear,
nose and throat specialist;
Halsschmerzen *pl* sore throat
sing; **Halstuch** *nt* scarf
halt *interj* stop ▷ *adv:* **das ist ~ so**
that's just the way it is; **Halt** (-(e)s,
-e) *m* stop; (fester) hold; (innerer)
stability
haltbar *adj* durable; (Lebensmittel)
non-perishable; **Haltbarkeitsdatum** *nt* best-before
date
halten (hielt, gehalten) *vt* to keep;
(festhalten) to hold; **~ für** to regard
as; **~ von** to think of; **den
Elfmeter ~** to save the penalty;
eine Rede ~ to give (o make) a
speech ▷ *vi* to hold; (frisch bleiben)
to keep; (stoppen) to stop; **zu jdm
~** to stand by sb ▷ *vr:* **sich ~** (frisch
bleiben) to keep; (sich behaupten) to
hold out
Haltestelle *f* stop; **Halteverbot**
nt: **hier ist ~** you can't stop here
Haltung *f* (Körper) posture; (fig)
attitude; (Selbstbeherrschung)
composure; **~ bewahren** to keep
one's composure
Hamburg (-s) *nt* Hamburg;
Hamburger (-s, -) *m* (Gastr)
hamburger

Hammelfleisch *nt* mutton
Hammer (-s, Hämmer) *m* hammer; (fig. fam: Fehler) howler; **das
ist der ~** (unerhört) that's a bit
much
Hämorr(ho)iden *pl* haemorrhoids *pl*, piles *pl*
Hamster (-s, -) *m* hamster
Hand (-, Hände) *f* hand; **jdm die
~ geben** to shake hands with sb;
jdn bei der ~ nehmen to take sb
by the hand; **eine ~ voll
Reis/Leute** a handful of
rice/people; **zu Händen von**
attention; **Handarbeit** *f*
(Schulfach) handicraft; **~ sein** to be
handmade; **Handball** *m*
handball; **Handbremse** *f*
handbrake; **Handbuch** *nt*
handbook, manual; **Handcreme**
f hand cream; **Händedruck** *m*
handshake
Handel (-s) *m* trade; (Geschäft)
transaction; **handeln** *vi* to act,
(Comm) to trade; **~ von** to be
about ▷ *vr impers:* **sich ~ um** to
be about; **es handelt sich um ...**
it's about ...; **Handelskammer** *f*
chamber of commerce;
Handelsschule *f* business school
Handfeger (-s, -) *m* brush;
Handfläche *f* palm; **Handgelenk**
nt wrist; **handgemacht** *adj*
handmade; **Handgepäck** *nt*
hand luggage (Brit) (o baggage)
Händler(in) (-s, -) *m(f)* dealer
handlich *adj* handy
Handlung *f* act, action; (von
Roman, Film) plot
Handschellen *pl* handcuffs *pl;*
Handschrift *f* handwriting;
Handschuh *m* glove;
Handschuhfach *nt* glove
compartment; **Handtasche** *f*
handbag, purse (US); **Handtuch**
nt towel; **Handwerk** *nt* trade;
(Kunst~) craft; **Handwerker** (-s, -)

m workman

Handy (-s, -s) *nt* mobile (phone) (Brit), cell phone (US); **Handynummer** *f* mobile number (Brit), cell phone number (US)

Hanf (-(e)s) *m* hemp

Hang (-(e)s, Hänge) *m* (Abhang) slope; (fig) tendency

Hängebrücke *f* suspension bridge; **Hängematte** *f* hammock

hängen (hing, gehangen) *vi* to hang; **an der Wand/an der Decke ~** to hang on the wall/from the ceiling; **an jdm ~** (fig) to be attached to sb; **~ bleiben** to get caught (an +dat on); (fig) to get stuck ▷ *vt* to hang (an +akk on)

Hantel (-, -n) *f* dumbbell

Hardware (-, -s) *f* (Inform) hardware

Harfe (-, -n) *f* harp

harmlos *adj* harmless

harmonisch *adj* harmonious

Harn (-(e)s, -e) *m* urine; **Harnblase** *f* bladder

Harpune (-, -n) *f* harpoon

hart *adj* hard; (fig) harsh; **zu jdm ~ sein** to be hard on sb; **~ gekocht** (Ei) hard-boiled; **hartnäckig** *adj* stubborn

Haschee (-s, -s) *nt* hash

Haschisch (-) *nt* hashish

Hase (-n, -n) *m* hare

Haselnuss *f* hazelnut

Hasenscharte *f* (Med) harelip

Hass (-es) *m* hatred (auf, gegen +akk of), hate; **einen ~ kriegen** (fam) to see red; **hassen** *vt* to hate

hässlich *adj* ugly; (gemein) nasty

Hast (-) *f* haste, hurry; **hastig** *adj* hasty

hatte *imperf von* **haben**

Haube (-, -n) *f* hood; (Mütze) cap; (Auto) bonnet (Brit), hood (US)

Hauch (-(e)s, -e) *m* breath; (Luft~)

breeze; (fig) trace; **hauchdünn** *adj* (Schicht, Scheibe) wafer-thin

hauen (haute, gehauen) *vt* to hit

Haufen (-s, -) *m* pile; **ein ~ Geld** (viel Geld) a lot of money

häufig *adj* frequent ▷ *adv* frequently, often

Haupt- *in zW* main; **Hauptbahnhof** *m* central (o main) station; **Hauptdarsteller(in)** *m(f)* leading actor/lady; **Haupteingang** *m* main entrance; **Hauptgericht** *nt* main course; **Hauptgeschäftszeiten** *pl* peak shopping hours *pl*; **Hauptgewinn** *m* first prize

Häuptling *m* chief

Hauptquartier *nt* headquarters *pl*; **Hauptreisezeit** *f* peak tourist season; **Hauptrolle** *f* leading role; **Hauptsache** *f* main thing; **hauptsächlich** *adv* mainly, chiefly; **Hauptsaison** *f* high (o peak) season; **Hauptsatz** *m* main clause; **Hauptschule** *f* ≈ secondary school (Brit), ≈ junior high school (US); **Hauptspeicher** *m* (Inform) main storage (o memory); **Hauptstadt** *f* capital; **Hauptstraße** *f* main road; (im Stadtzentrum) main street; **Hauptverkehrszeit** *f* rush hour

Haus (-es, Häuser) *nt* house; **nach ~e** home; **zu ~e** at home; **jdn nach ~e bringen** to take sb home; **bei uns zu ~e** (Heimat) where we come from; (Familie) in my family; (Haus) at our place; **Hausarbeit** *f* housework; **Hausaufgabe** *f* (Schule) homework; **~n** *pl* homework *sing*; **Hausbesitzer(in)** (-s, -) *m(f)* house owner; (Vermieter) landlord/-lady; **Hausbesuch** *m* home visit; **Hausbewohner(in)** (-s, -) *m(f)* occupa[...]; **Hausflur** *m* hall; **Hausfrau** *f* housewife; **hausgemacht** adj homemade; **Haushalt** m household; (Pol) budget; **Hausherr(in)** m(f) host/hostess; (Vermieter) landlord/-lady

häuslich adj domestic

Hausmann m house-husband; **Hausmannskost** f good plain cooking; **Hausmeister(in)** m(f) caretaker (Brit), janitor (US); **Hausnummer** f house number; **Hausordnung** f (house) rules pl; **Hausschlüssel** m front-door key; **Hausschuh** m slipper; **Haustier** nt pet; **Haustür** f front door

Haut (-, Häute) f skin; (Tier) hide; **Hautarzt** m, **Hautärztin** f dermatologist; **Hautausschlag** m skin rash; **Hautcreme** f skin cream; **Hautfarbe** f skin colour; **Hautkrankheit** f skin disease

Hawaii (-s) nt Hawaii

Hbf. abk = **Hauptbahnhof** central station

Hebamme (-, -n) f midwife

Hebel (-s, -) m lever

heben (hob, gehoben) vt to raise, to lift

Hebräisch (-) nt Hebrew

Hecht (-(e)s, -e) m pike

Heck (-(e)s, -e) nt (von Boot) stern; (von Auto) rear; **Heckantrieb** m rear-wheel drive

Hecke (-, -n) f hedge

Heckklappe f tailgate; **Hecklicht** nt tail-light; **Heckscheibe** f rear window

Hefe (-, -n) f yeast

Heft (-(e)s, -e) nt notebook, exercise book; (Ausgabe) issue

heftig adj violent; (Kritik, Streit) fierce

Heftklammer f paper clip; **Heftpflaster** nt plaster (Brit), Band-Aid® (US)

Heide (-, -n) f heath, moor; **Heidekraut** nt heather

Heidelbeere f bilberry, blueberry

heidnisch adj (Brauch) pagan

heikel adj (Angelegenheit) awkward; (wählerisch) fussy

heil adj (Sache) in one piece, intact; (Person) unhurt; **heilbar** adj curable

Heilbutt (-(e)s, -e) m halibut

heilen vt to cure ▷ vi to heal

heilig adj holy; **Heiligabend** m Christmas Eve; **Heilige(r)** mf saint

Heilmittel nt remedy, cure (gegen for); **Heilpraktiker(in)** (-s, -) m(f) non-medical practitioner

heim adv home; **Heim** (-(e)s, -e) nt home

Heimat (-, -en) f home (town/country); **Heimatland** nt home country

heim|fahren irr vi to drive home; **Heimfahrt** f journey home; **heimisch** adj (Bevölkerung, Brauchtum) local; (Tiere, Pflanzen) native; **heim|kommen** irr vi to come (o return) home

heimlich adj secret

Heimreise f journey home; **Heimspiel** nt (Sport) home game; **Heimvorteil** m (Sport) home advantage; **Heimweg** m way home; **Heimweh** (-s) nt homesickness; **~ haben** to be homesick; **Heimwerker(in)** m(f) DIY enthusiast

Heirat (-, -en) f marriage; **heiraten** vi to get married ▷ vt to marry; **Heiratsantrag** m proposal; **er hat ihr einen ~ gemacht** he proposed to her

heiser adj hoarse

heiß adj hot; (Diskussion) heated; **mir ist ~** I'm hot

heißen (hieß, geheißen) vi to be called; (bedeuten) to mean; **ich heiße Tom** my name is Tom; **wie**

~ Sie? what's your name?; **wie heißt sie mit Nachnamen?** what's her surname?; **wie heißt das auf Englisch?** what's that in English? ▷ vi impers: **es heißt** (man sagt) it is said; **es heißt in dem Brief ...** it says in the letter ...; **das heißt** that is

Heißluftherd m fan-assisted oven

heiter adj cheerful; (Wetter) bright

heizen vt to heat; **Heizkissen** m (Med) heated pad; **Heizkörper** m radiator; **Heizöl** nt fuel oil; **Heizung** f heating

Hektar (-s, -) nt hectare

Hektik (-, -en) f: **nur keine ~!** take it easy; **hektisch** adj hectic

Held (-en, -en) m hero; **Heldin** f heroine

helfen (half, geholfen) vi to help (jdm bei etw sb with sth); (nützen) to be of use; **sie weiß sich** (dat) **zu ~** she can manage ▷ vi impers: **es hilft nichts, du musst ...** it's no use, you have to ...; **Helfer(in)** m(f) helper; (Mitarbeiter) assistant

Helikopter-Skiing (-s) nt heliskiing, helicopter skiing

hell adj bright; (Farbe) light; (Hautfarbe) fair; **hellblau** adj light blue; **hellblond** adj ash-blond; **hellgelb** adj pale yellow; **hellgrün** adj light green; **Hellseher(in)** m(f) clairvoyant

Helm (-(e)s, -e) m helmet; **Helmpflicht** f compulsory wearing of helmets

Hemd (-(e)s, -en) nt shirt; (Unter~) vest

hemmen vt to check; (behindern) to hamper; **gehemmt sein** to be inhibited; **Hemmung** f (psychisch) inhibition; **sie hatte keine ~, ihn zu betrügen** she had no scruples about deceiving him; (moralisch) scruple

Henkel (-s, -) m handle

Henna (-s) nt henna

Henne (-, -n) f hen

Hepatitis (-, Hepatitiden) f hepatitis

○ **SCHLÜSSELWORT**

her adv 1 (Richtung) **komm her zu mir** come here (to me); **von England her** from England; **von weit her** from a long way away; **her damit!** hand it over!; **wo hat er das her?** where did he get that from?; **wo bist du her?** where do you come from?
2 (Blickpunkt) **von der Form her** as far as the form is concerned
3 (zeitlich) **das ist 5 Jahre her** that was 5 years ago; **ich kenne ihn von früher her** I know him from before

herab adv down; **herablassend** adj (Bemerkung) condescending; **herab|sehen** irr vt: **auf jdn ~** to look down on sb; **herab|setzen** vt to reduce; (fig) to disparage

heran adv: **näher ~!** come closer; **heran|kommen** irr vi to approach; **~ an** (+akk) to be able to get at; (fig) to be able to get hold of; **heran|wachsen** irr vi to grow up

herauf adv up; **herauf|beschwören** irr vt to evoke; (verursachen) to cause; **herauf|ziehen** irr vt to pull up ▷ vi to approach; (Sturm) to gather

heraus adv out; **heraus|bekommen** irr vt (Geheimnis) to find out; (Rätsel) to solve; **ich bekomme noch zwei Euro heraus** I've got two euros change to come; **heraus|bringen** irr vt to bring out; **heraus|finden**

irr vt to find out; **heraus|fordern**
vt to challenge; **Herausforderung**
f challenge; **heraus|geben** irr vt
(Buch) to edit; (veröffentlichen) to
publish; **jdm zwei Euro ~** to give
sb two euros change; **geben Sie
mir bitte auf 20 Euro heraus**
could you give me change for 20
euros, please?; **heraus|holen** vt
to get out (aus of); **heraus|-
kommen** irr vi to come '
out; **dabei kommt nichts heraus**
nothing will come of it;
heraus|stellen vr: **sich ~** to turn
out (als to be); **heraus|ziehen** irr
vt to pull out

Herbst (-(e)s, -e) m autumn, fall
(US)
Herd (-(e)s, -e) m cooker, stove
Herde (-, -n) f herd; (Schafe) flock
herein adv in; **~!** come in;
herein|fallen irr vi: **wir sind auf
einen Betrüger hereingefallen**
we were taken in by a swindler;
herein|legen vt: **jdn ~** (fig) to
take sb for a ride
Herfahrt f journey here; **auf der
~** on the way here
Hergang m course (of events);
schildern Sie mir den ~ tell me
what happened
Hering (-s, -e) m herring
her|kommen irr vi to come; **wo
kommt sie her?** where does she
come from?
Heroin (-s) nt heroin
Herpes (-) m (Med) herpes
Herr (-(e)n, -en) m (vor Namen) Mr;
(Mann) gentleman; (Adliger, Gott)
Lord; **mein ~!** sir; **meine ~en!**
gentlemen; **Sehr geehrte Damen
und ~en** Dear Sir or Madam;
herrenlos adj (Gepäckstück)
abandoned; (Tier) stray;
Herrentoilette f men's toilet,
gents
her|richten vt to prepare

herrlich adj marvellous, splendid
Herrschaft f rule; (Macht) power;
meine ~en! ladies and gentlemen!
herrschen vi to rule; (bestehen) to
be
her|stellen vt to make;
(industriell) to manufacture;
Hersteller(in) m(f) manufacturer; **Herstellung** f
production
herüber adv over
herum adv around; (im Kreis)
round; **um etw ~** around sth; **du
hast den Pulli falsch ~ an** you're
wearing your sweater inside out;
anders ~ the other way round;
herum|fahren irr vi to drive
around; **herum|führen** vt: **jdn in
der Stadt ~** to show sb around the
town ▷ vi: **die Straße führt um
das Zentrum herum** the road
goes around the centre; **die Straße führt um
das Zentrum herum** the road
goes around the city centre;
herum|kommen irr vi: **sie ist
viel in der Welt herum-
gekommen** she's been
around the world; **um etw
~** (vermeiden) to get out of sth;
herum|kriegen vt to talk round;
herum|treiben irr vr: **sich ~** to
hang around
herunter adv down;
heruntergekommen adj (Gebäude,
Gegend) run-down; (Person)
down-at-heel; **herunter|handeln**
vt to get down; **herunter|holen**
vt to bring down;
herunter|kommen irr vi to come
down; **herunter|laden** irr vt
(Inform) to download
hervor adv out; **hervor|bringen**
irr vt to produce; (Wort) to utter;
hervor|heben irr vt to
emphasize, to stress;
hervorragend adj excellent;
hervor|rufen irr vt to cause, to
give rise to
Herz (-ens, -en) nt heart; (Karten)

hearts pl; **von ganzem ~en**
wholeheartedly; **sich** (dat) **etw zu
~en nehmen** to take sth to heart;
Herzanfall m heart attack;
Herzbeschwerden pl heart
trouble sing; **Herzfehler** m heart
defect; **herzhaft** adj (Essen)
substantial; **~ lachen** to have a
good laugh; **Herzinfarkt** m
heart attack; **Herzklopfen** (-s) nt
(Med) palpitations pl; **ich hatte
~** (vor Aufregung) my heart was
pounding (with excitement);
herzkrank adj: **sie ist ~** she's got
a heart condition; **herzlich** adj
(Empfang, Mensch) warm; **~en
Glückwunsch** congratulations

Herzog(in) (-s, Herzöge) m(f)
duke/duchess

Herzschlag m heartbeat;
(Herzversagen) heart failure;
Herzschrittmacher m pacemaker; **Herzstillstand** m
cardiac arrest

Hessen (-s) nt Hessen

heterosexuell adj heterosexual;
Heterosexuelle(r) mf
heterosexual

Hetze (-, -n) f (Eile) rush; **hetzen**
vt to rush ▷ vr: **sich ~** to rush

Heu (-(e)s) nt hay

heuer adv this year

heulen vi to howl; (weinen) to cry

Heuschnupfen m hay fever;
Heuschrecke (-, -n) f grasshopper; (größer) locust

heute adv today; **~ Abend/früh**
this evening/morning; **~ Nacht**
tonight; (letzte Nacht) last night;
~ in acht Tagen a week (from)
today; **sie hat bis ~ nicht bezahlt**
she hasn't paid to this day; **heutig**
adj: **die ~e Zeitung/Generation**
today's paper/generation;
heutzutage adv nowadays

Hexe (-, -n) f witch;
Hexenschuss m lumbago

hielt imperf von **halten**

hier adv here; **~ entlang** this way;
ich bin auch nicht von ~ I'm a
stranger here myself; **hier|bleiben**
irr vi to stay here; **hier|lassen** irr
vt to leave here; **hierher** adv
here; **das gehört nicht ~** that
doesn't belong here; **hiermit** adv
with this; **hierzulande** adv in
this country

hiesig adj local

hieß imperf von **heißen**

Hi-Fi-Anlage f hi-fi (system)

high adj (fam) high; **Highlife** (-s)
nt high life; **~ machen** to live it
up; **Hightech** (-s) nt high tech

Hilfe (-, -n) f help; (für Notleidende,
finanziell) aid; **~!** help!; **Erste
~ leisten** to give first aid; **um
~ bitten** to ask for help; **hilflos**
adj helpless; **hilfsbereit** adj
helpful; **Hilfsmittel** nt
aid

Himbeere f raspberry

Himmel (-s, -) m sky; (Rel)
heaven; **Himmelfahrt** f
Ascension; **Himmelsrichtung** f
direction; **himmlisch** adj
heavenly

⊙ SCHLÜSSELWORT

hin adv 1 (Richtung) **hin und zurück**
there and back; **hin und her** to
and fro; **bis zur Mauer hin** up to
the wall; **wo ist er hin?** where has
he gone?; **Geld hin, Geld her**
money or no money

2 (auf … hin) **auf meine Bitte hin**
at my request; **auf seinen Rat hin**
on the basis of his advice

3 mein Glück ist hin my happiness
has gone

hinab adv down; **hinab|gehen** irr
vi to go down

hinauf adv up; **hinauf|gehen** irr

vi, vt to go up; **hinauf|steigen** *irr vi* to climb (up)

hinaus *adv* out; **hinaus|gehen** *irr vi* to go out; **das Zimmer geht auf den See hinaus** the room looks out onto the lake; **~ über** (+*akk*) to exceed; **hinaus|laufen** *irr vi* to run out; **~ auf** (+*akk*) to come to, to amount to; **hinaus|schieben** *irr vi* to put off, to postpone; **hinaus|werfen** *irr vt* to throw out; (*aus Firma*) to fire, to sack (*Brit*); **hinaus|zögern** *vr*: **sich ~** to take longer than expected

Hinblick *m* (*o im*) **~ auf** (+*akk*) with regard to; **hin|bringen** *irr vt*: **ich bringe Sie hin** I'll take you there

hindern *vt* to prevent; **jdn daran ~, etw zu tun** to stop (*o prevent*) sb from doing sth; **Hindernis** *nt* obstacle

Hinduismus *m* Hinduism

hindurch *adv* through; **das ganze Jahr ~** throughout the year, all year round; **die ganze Nacht ~** all night (long)

hinein *adv* in; **hinein|gehen** *irr vi* to go in; **~ in** (+*akk*) to go into, to enter; **hinein|passen** *vi* to fit in; **~ in** (+*akk*) to fit into

hin|fahren *irr vi* to go there ▷ *vt* to take there; **Hinfahrt** *f* outward journey

hin|fallen *irr vi* to fall (down)

Hinflug *m* outward flight

hing *imperf von* **hängen**

hin|gehen *irr vi* to go there; (*Zeit*) to pass; **hin|halten** *irr vt* to hold out; (*warten lassen*) to put off

hinken *vi* to limp; **der Vergleich hinkt** the comparison doesn't work

hin|knien *vr*: **sich ~** to kneel down; **hin|legen** *vt* to put down ▷ *vr*: **sich ~** to lie down; **hin|nehmen** *irr vt* (*fig*) to put up

with, to take; **Hinreise** *f* outward journey; **hin|setzen** *vr*: **sich ~** to sit down; **hinsichtlich** *prep* +*gen* with regard to; **hin|stellen** *vt* to put (down) ▷ *vr*: **sich ~** to stand

hinten *adv* at the back; (*im Auto*) in the back; (*dahinter*) behind

hinter *prep* +*dat o akk* behind; (*nach*) after; **~ jdm her sein** to be after sb; **etw ~ sich** (*akk*) **bringen** to get sth over (and done) with; **Hinterachse** *f* rear axle; **Hinterausgang** *m* rear exit; **Hinterbein** *nt* hind leg; **Hinterbliebene(r)** *mf* dependant; **hintere(r, s)** *adj* rear, back; **hintereinander** *adv* (*in einer Reihe*) one behind the other; (*hintereinander her*) one after the other; **drei Tage ~** three days running (*o in a row*); **Hintereingang** *m* rear entrance; **Hintergedanke** *m* ulterior motive; **hintergehen** *irr vt* to deceive; **Hintergrund** *m* background; **hinterher** *adv* (*zeitlich*) afterwards; **los, ~!** come on, after him/her/them; **Hinterkopf** *m* back of the head; **hinterlassen** *vt* to leave; **jdm eine Nachricht ~** to leave a message for sb; **hinterlegen** *vt* to leave (*bei* with)

Hintern (*-, -*) *m* (*fam*) backside, bum

Hinterradantrieb *m* (*Auto*) rear-wheel drive; **Hinterteil** *nt* back (part); (*Hintern*) behind; **Hintertür** *f* back door

hinüber *adv* over; **~ sein** (*fam*: *kaputt*) to be ruined; (*verdorben*) to have gone bad; **hinüber|gehen** *irr vi* to go over

hinunter *adv* down; **hinunter|gehen** *irr vi, vt* to go down; **hinunter|schlucken** *vt* *(a. fig)* to swallow

Hinweg *m* outward journey

hinweg|setzen *vr* **sich über etw** *(akk)* ~ to ignore sth

Hinweis *(-es, -e) m (Andeutung)* hint; *(Anweisung)* instruction; *(Verweis)* reference; **hin|weisen** *irr vi* **jdn auf etw** *(acc)* ~ to point sth out to sb; **jdn nochmal auf etw** ~ to remind sb of sth

hinzu *adv* in addition; **hinzu|fügen** *vt* to add; **hinzu|kommen** *irr vi*: **zu jdm** ~ to join sb; **es war kalt, hinzu kam, dass es auch noch regnete** it was cold, and on top of that it was raining

Hirn *(-(e)s, -e) nt* brain; *(Verstand)* brains *pl;* **Hirnhautentzündung** *f* meningitis; **hirnverbrannt** *adj* crazy

Hirsch *(-(e)s, -e) m* deer; *(als Speise)* venison

Hirse *(-, -n) f* millet

Hirte *(-n, -n) m* shepherd

historisch *adj* historical

Hit *(-s, -s) m (fig, Mus, Inform)* hit; **Hitliste** *f,* **Hitparade** *f* charts *pl*

Hitze *(-) f* heat; **hitzebeständig** *adj* heat-resistant; **Hitzewelle** *f* heatwave; **hitzig** *adj* hot-tempered; *(Debatte)* heated; **Hitzschlag** *m* heatstroke

HIV *(-(s), -(s)) nt abk =* **Human Immunodeficiency Virus** HIV; **HIV-negativ** *adj* HIV-negative; **HIV-positiv** *adj* HIV-positive

H-Milch *f* long-life milk

hob *imperf von* **heben**

Hobby *(-s, -s) nt* hobby

Hobel *(-s, -) m* plane

hoch *adj* high; *(Baum, Haus)* tall; *(Schnee)* deep; **der Zaun ist drei Meter** ~ the fence is three metres high; ~ **auflösend** high-resolution; ~ **begabt** extremely gifted; **das ist mir zu** ~ that's above my head;

~ **soll sie leben!, sie lebe ~!** three cheers for her; **4 ~ 2 ist 16** 4 squared is 16; **4 ~ 5** 4 to the power of 5

Hoch *(-s, -s) nt (Ruf)* cheer; *(Meteo)* high; **hochachtungsvoll** *adv (in Briefen)* Yours faithfully; **Hochbetrieb** *m:* **es herrscht** ~ they/we are extremely busy; **Hochdeutsch** *nt* High German; **Hochgebirge** *nt* high mountains *pl;* **Hochgeschwindigkeitszug** *m* high-speed train; **Hochhaus** *nt* high rise; **hoch|heben** *irr vt* to lift (up); **hochprozentig** *adj (Alkohol)* high-proof; **Hochsaison** *f* high season; **Hochschule** *f* college; *(Universität)* university; **hochschwanger** *adj* heavily pregnant; **Hochsommer** *m* midsummer; **Hochspannung** *f* great tension; *(Elek)* high voltage; **Hochsprung** *m* high jump

höchst *adv* highly, extremely; **höchste(r, s)** *adj* highest; *(äußerste)* extreme; **höchstens** *adv* at the most; **Höchstgeschwindigkeit** *f* maximum speed; **Höchstparkdauer** *f* maximum stay

Hochstuhl *m* high chair

höchstwahrscheinlich *adv* very probably

Hochwasser *nt* high water; *(Überschwemmung)* floods *pl;* **hochwertig** *adj* high-quality

Hochzeit *(-, -en) f* wedding; **Hochzeitsnacht** *f* wedding night; **Hochzeitsreise** *f* honeymoon; **Hochzeitstag** *m* wedding day; *(Jahrestag)* wedding anniversary

hocken *vi* to squat, to crouch

Hocker *(-s, -) m* stool

Hockey *(-s) nt* hockey

Hoden *(-s, -) m* testicle

Hof *(-(e)s, Höfe) m (Hinterhof)* yard;

(*Innenhof*) courtyard; (*Bauernhof*) farm; (*Königshof*) court

hoffen *vi* to hope (*auf* +akk for); **ich hoffe es** I hope so; **hoffentlich** *adv* hopefully; **~ nicht** I hope not; **Hoffnung** *f* hope; **hoffnungslos** *adj* hopeless

höflich *adj* polite; **Höflichkeit** *f* politeness

hohe(r, s) *adj siehe* **hoch**

Höhe (-, -n) *f* height; (*Anhöhe*) hill; (*einer Summe*) amount; **in einer ~ von 5000 Metern** at an altitude of 5.000 metres; (*Flughöhe*) altitude; **Höhenangst** *f* vertigo

Höhepunkt *m* (*einer Reise*) high point; (*einer Veranstaltung*) highlight; (*eines Films*; *sexuell*) climax

höher *adj, adv* higher

hohl *adj* hollow

Höhle (-, -n) *f* cave

holen *vt* to get, to fetch; (*abholen*) to pick up; (*Atem*) to catch; **die Polizei ~** to call the police; **jdn/etw ~ lassen** to send for sb/sth

Holland *nt* Holland; **Holländer(in)** (-s, -) *m(f)* Dutchman/-woman; **holländisch** *adj* Dutch

Hölle (-, -n) *f* hell

Hologramm *nt* hologram

holperig *adj* bumpy

Holunder (-s, -) *m* elder

Holz (-es, Hölzer) *nt* wood; **Holzboden** *m* wooden floor; **hölzern** *adj* wooden; **holzig** *adj* (*Stängel*) woody; **Holzkohle** *f* charcoal

Homebanking (-s) *nt* home banking, online banking; **Homepage** (-, -s) *f* home page; **Hometrainer** *m* exercise machine

Homoehe *f* (*fam*) gay marriage

homöopathisch *adj* homeopathic

homosexuell *adj* homosexual; **Homosexuelle(r)** *mf* homosexual

Honig (-s, -e) *m* honey; **Honigmelone** *f* honeydew melon

Honorar (-s, -e) *nt* fee

Hopfen (-s, -) *m* (*Bot*) hop; (*beim Brauen*) hops *pl*

hoppla *interj* whoops, oops

horchen *vi* to listen (*auf* +akk to); (*an der Tür*) to eavesdrop

hören *vt, vi* (*passiv, mitbekommen*) to hear; (*zufällig*) to overhear; (*aufmerksam zuhören; Radio, Musik*) to listen to; **ich habe schon viel von Ihnen gehört** I've heard a lot about you; **Hörer** *m* (*Tel*) receiver; **Hörer(in)** *m(f)* listener; **Hörgerät** *nt* hearing aid

Horizont (-(e)s, -e) *m* horizon; **das geht über meinen ~** that's beyond me

Hormon (-s, -e) *nt* hormone

Hornhaut *f* hard skin; (*des Auges*) cornea

Hornisse (-, -n) *f* hornet

Horoskop (-s, -e) *nt* horoscope

Hörsaal *m* lecture hall; **Hörsturz** *m* acute hearing loss; **Hörweite** *f*: **in/außer ~** within/out of earshot

Höschenwindel (-, -n) *f* nappy (*Brit*), diaper (*US*)

Hose (-, -n) *f* trousers *pl* (*Brit*), pants *pl* (*US*); (*Unterhose*) (under)pants *pl*; **eine ~** a pair of trousers/pants; **kurze ~** (pair of) shorts *pl*; **Hosenanzug** *m* trouser suit (*Brit*), pantsuit (*US*); **Hosenschlitz** *m* fly, flies (*Brit*); **Hosentasche** *f* trouser pocket (*Brit*), pant pocket (*US*); **Hosenträger** *m* braces *pl* (*Brit*), suspenders *pl* (*US*)

Hospital (-s, Hospitäler) *nt* hospital

Hotdog (-s, -s) *nt o m* hot dog

Hotel (-s, -s) nt hotel; **in welchem ~ seid ihr?** which hotel are you staying at?; **Hoteldirektor(in)** m(f) hotel manager; **Hotelkette** f hotel chain; **Hotelzimmer** nt hotel room

Hotline (-, -s) f hot line

Hubraum m cubic capacity

hübsch adj (Mädchen, Kind, Kleid) pretty; (gutaussehend; Mann, Frau) good-looking, cute

Hubschrauber (-s, -) m helicopter

Huf (-(e)s, -e) m hoof; **Hufeisen** nt horseshoe

Hüfte (-, -n) f hip

Hügel (-s, -) m hill; **hügelig** adj hilly

Huhn (-(e)s, Hühner) nt hen; (Gastr) chicken; **Hühnchen** nt chicken; **Hühnerauge** nt corn; **Hühnerbrühe** f chicken broth

Hülle (-, -n) f cover; (für Ausweis) case; (Zellophan) wrapping

Hummel (-, -n) f bumblebee

Hummer (-s, -) m lobster; **Hummerkrabbe** f king prawn

Humor (-s) m humour; **~ haben** to have a sense of humour; **humorvoll** adj humorous

humpeln vi hobble

Hund (-(e)s, -e) m dog; **Hundeleine** f dog lead (Brit), dog leash (US)

hundert num hundred; **Hundertjahrfeier** f centenary; **hundertprozentig** adj, adv one hundred per cent; **hundertste(r, s)** adj hundredth

Hündin f bitch

Hunger (-s) m hunger; **~ haben/bekommen** to be/get hungry; **hungern** vi to go hungry; (ernsthaft, dauernd) to starve

Hupe (-, -n) f horn; **hupen** vi to sound one's horn

Hüpfburg f bouncy castle®; **hüpfen** vi to hop; (springen) to jump

Hürde (-, -n) f hurdle

Hure (-, -n) f whore

hurra interj hooray

husten vi to cough; **Husten** (-s) m cough; **Hustenbonbon** nt cough sweet; **Hustensaft** m cough mixture

Hut (-(e)s, Hüte) m hat

hüten vt to look after ▷ vr: **sich ~** to watch out; **sich ~, etw zu tun** to take care not to do sth; **sich ~ vor** (+dat) to beware of

Hütte (-, -n) f hut, cottage; **Hüttenkäse** m cottage cheese

Hyäne (-, -n) f hyena

Hydrant m hydrant

hygienisch adj hygienic

Hyperlink (-s, -s) m hyperlink

Hypnose (-, -n) f hypnosis; **Hypnotiseur(in)** m(f) hypnotist; **hypnotisieren** vt to hypnotize

Hypothek (-, -en) f mortgage

hysterisch adj hysterical

i

i. A. *abk* = **im Auftrag** pp

IC (-, -s) *m abk* = **Intercityzug**
Intercity (train)

ICE (-, -s) *m abk* =
Intercityexpresszug German
high-speed train

ich *pron* I; **~ bin's** it's me; **~ nicht**
not me; **du und ~** you and me; **hier
bin ~!** here I am; **~ Idiot!** stupid me

Icon (-s, -s) *nt* (*Inform*) icon

IC-Zuschlag *m* Intercity
supplement

ideal *adj* ideal; **Ideal** (-s, -e) *nt*
ideal

Idee (-, -n) *f* idea

identifizieren *vt* to identify
▷ *vr:* **sich mit jdm/etw ~** to
identify with sb/sth

identisch *adj* identical

Idiot(in) (-en, -en) *m(f)* idiot;
idiotisch *adj* idiotic

Idol (-s, -e) *nt* idol

Idylle *f* idyll; **idyllisch** *adj* idyllic

Igel (-s, -) *m* hedgehog

ignorieren *vt* to ignore

ihm *pron dat sing von* **er/es**; (to)
him, (to) it; **wie geht es ~?** how is
he?; **ein Freund von ~** a friend of
his ▷ *pron dat von* **es**; (to) it

ihn *pron akk sing von* **er**; (*Person*)
him; (*Sache*) it

ihnen *pron dat pl von* **sie**; (to)
them; **wie geht es ~?** how are
they?; **ein Freund von ~** a friend of
theirs

Ihnen *pron dat sing u pl von* **Sie**;
(to) you; **wie geht es ~?** how are
you?; **ein Freund von ~** a friend of
yours

○ SCHLÜSSELWORT

ihr *pron* **1** (*nom pl*) you; **ihr seid es**
it's you
2 (*dat von sie*) to her; **gib es ihr** give
it to her; **er steht neben ihr** he is
standing beside her
▷ *possessiv pron* **1** (*sg*) her; (*bei
Tieren, Dingen*) its; **ihr Mann** her
husband
2 (*pl*) their; **die Bäume und ihre
Blätter** the trees and their
leaves

Ihr *pron von* **Sie**; (*adjektivisch*) your;
~(e) XY (*am Briefende*) Yours, XY

ihre(r, s) *pron* (*substantivisch,
sing*) hers; (*pl*) theirs; **das ist
~/~r/ihr(e)s** that's hers; (*pl*) that's
theirs

Ihre(r, s) *pron* (*substantivisch*)
yours; **das ist ~/~r/Ihr(e)s** that's
yours

ihretwegen *adv* (*wegen ihr*)
because of her; (*ihr zuliebe*) for her
sake; (*um sie*) about her; (*von ihr
aus*) as far as she is concerned
▷ *adv* (*wegen ihnen*) because of
them; (*ihnen zuliebe*) for their sake;
(*um sie*) about them; (*von ihnen aus*)

as far as they are concerned;
Ihretwegen adv (wegen Ihnen)
because of you; (Ihnen zuliebe) for
your sake; (um Sie) about you; (von
Ihnen aus) as far as you are
concerned
Ikone (-, -n) f icon
illegal adj illegal
Illusion f illusion; **sich** (dat) **~en
machen** to delude oneself;
illusorisch adj illusory
Illustration f illustration
Illustrierte (-n, -n) f (glossy)
magazine
im kontr von **in dem**; **~ Bett** in bed;
~ Fernsehen on TV; **~ Radio** on
the radio; **~ Bus/Zug** on the
bus/train; **~ Januar** in January;
~ Stehen (while) standing up
Imbiss (-es, -e) m snack;
Imbissbude f, **Imbissstube** f
snack bar
Imbusschlüssel m hex key
immer adv always; **~ mehr** more
and more; **~ wieder** again and
again; **~ noch** still; **~ noch nicht**
still not; **für ~** forever; **~ wenn
ich ...** every time I ...; **~ schöner/
trauriger** more and
more beautiful/sadder and
sadder; **was/wer/wo/wann
(auch)** ~ whatever/whoever/
wherever/whenever; **immerhin**
adv after all; **immerzu** adv all the
time
Immigrant(in) m(f) immigrant
Immobilien pl property sing, real
estate sing; **Immobilien-
makler(in)** m(f) estate
agent (Brit), realtor (US)
immun adj immune (gegen to);
Immunschwäche f immunodeficiency; **Immun-
schwächekrankheit** f immune
deficiency syndrome;
Immunsystem nt immune
system

impfen vt to vaccinate; **ich muss
mich gegen Pocken ~ lassen** I've
got to get myself vaccinated
against smallpox; **Impfpass** m
vaccination card; **Impfstoff** m
vaccine; **Impfung** f vaccination
imponieren vi to impress (jdm
sb)
Import (-(e)s, -e) m import;
importieren vt to import
impotent adj impotent
imstande adj: **~ sein** to be
in a position; (fähig) to be
able

○ **SCHLÜSSELWORT**

in prep +akk 1 (räumlich: wohin?) in,
into; **in die Stadt** into town; **in die
Schule gehen** to go to school
2 (zeitlich) **bis ins 20. Jahrhundert**
into o up to the 20th century
▷ prep +dat 1 (räumlich: wo?) in; **in
der Stadt** in town; **in der Schule
sein** to be at school
2 (zeitlich: wann?) **in diesem Jahr**
this year, (in jenem Jahr) In that
year; **heute in zwei Wochen** two
weeks today

inbegriffen adj included
indem conj: **sie gewann, ~ sie
mogelte** she won by cheating
Inder(in) (-s, -) m(f) Indian
Indianer(in) (-s, -) m(f)
American Indian, Native
American; **indianisch** adj
American Indian, Native American
Indien (-s) nt India
indirekt adj indirect
indisch adj Indian
indiskret adj indiscreet
individuell adj individual
Indonesien (-s) nt Indonesia
Industrie f industry; **Industrie-**
in zW industrial; **Industriegebiet**
nt industrial area; **industriell** adj

industrial

ineinander adv in(to) one another (o each other)

Infarkt (-(e)s, -e) m (Herzinfarkt) heart attack

Infektion f infection; **Infektionskrankheit** f infectious disease; **infizieren** vt to infect
▷ vr: **sich ~** to be infected

Info (-, -s) f (fam) info

infolge prep +gen as a result of, owing to; **infolgedessen** adv consequently

Informaterial nt (fam) bumf, info

Informatik f computer science; **Informatiker(in)** (-s, -) m(f) computer scientist

Information f information; **Informationsschalter** m information desk; **informieren** vt to inform; **falsch ~** to misinform
▷ vr: **sich ~** to find out (über +akk about)

infrage adv: **das kommt nicht ~** that's out of the question; **etw ~ stellen** to question sth

Infrastruktur f infrastructure

Infusion f infusion

Ingenieur(in) m(f) engineer

Ingwer (-s) m ginger

Inhaber(in) (-s, -) m(f) owner; (Haus~) occupier; (von Lizenz) holder; (Fin) bearer

Inhalt (-(e)s, -e) m contents pl; (eines Buchs etc) content; (Math) volume; (Flächeninhalt) area; **Inhaltsangabe** f summary; **Inhaltsverzeichnis** nt table of contents

Initiative f initiative; **die ~ ergreifen** to take the initiative

Injektion f injection

inklusive adv, prep inclusive (gen of)

inkonsequent adj inconsistent

Inland nt (Pol, Comm) home; **im ~** at home; (Geo) inland;

inländisch adj domestic; **Inlandsflug** m domestic flight; **Inlandsgespräch** nt national call

Inliner pl, **Inlineskates** pl (Sport) Rollerblades® pl, in-line skates pl

innen adv inside; **Innenarchitekt(in)** m(f) interior designer; **Innenhof** m (inner) courtyard; **Innenminister(in)** m(f) minister of the interior, Home Secretary (Brit); **Innenseite** f inside; **Innenspiegel** m rearview mirror; **Innenstadt** f town centre; (von Großstadt) city centre

innere(r, s) adj inner; (im Körper, inländisch) internal; **innere(s)** nt inside; (Mitte) centre; (fig) heart

Innereien pl innards pl

innerhalb adv, prep +gen within; (räumlich) inside

innerlich adj internal; (geistig) inner

innerste(r, s) adj innermost

Innovation f innovation; **innovativ** adj innovative

inoffiziell adj unofficial; (zwanglos) informal

ins kontr von **in das**

Insasse (-n, -n) m, **Insassin** f (Auto) passenger; (Anstalt) inmate

insbesondere adv particularly, in particular

Inschrift f inscription

Insekt (-(e)s, -en) nt insect, bug (US); **Insektenschutzmittel** nt insect repellent; **Insektenstich** m insect bite

Insel (-, -n) f island

Inserat nt advertisement

insgesamt adv altogether, all in all

Insider(in) (-s, -) m(f) insider

insofern adv in that respect; (deshalb) (and) so ▷ conj if; **~ als** in so far as

Installateur(in) *m(f)* (*Klempner*)
plumber; (*Elektroinstallateur*)
electrician; **installieren** *vt*
(*Inform*) to install
Instinkt (-(*e*)*s*, -*e*) *m* instinct
Institut (-(*e*)*s*, -*e*) *nt* institute
Institution *f* institution
Instrument *nt* instrument
Insulin (-*s*) *nt* insulin
Inszenierung *f* production
intakt *adj* intact
intellektuell *adj* intellectual
intelligent *adj* intelligent;
Intelligenz *f* intelligence
intensiv *adj* (*gründlich*) intensive;
(*Gefühl, Schmerz*) intense;
Intensivkurs *m* crash course;
Intensivstation *f* intensive care
unit
interaktiv *adj* interactive
Intercityexpress(zug) *m* German
high-speed train; **Intercityzug** *m*
Intercity (train);
Intercityzuschlag *m* Intercity
supplement
interessant *adj* interesting;
Interesse (-*s*, -*n*) *nt* interest;
~ **haben an** (+*dat*) to be interested
in; **interessieren** *vt* to interest
▷ *vr:* **sich ~** to be interested (*für in*)
Interface (-, -*s*) *nt* (*Inform*)
interface
Internat *nt* boarding school
international *adj* international
Internet (-*s*) *nt* internet, net; **im**
~ **on** the internet; **im ~ surfen** to
surf the net; **Internetanschluss**
m internet connection;
Internetauktion *f* internet
auction; **Internetcafé** *nt*
internet café, cybercafé;
Internetfirma *f* dotcom
company; **Internethandel** *m*
e-commerce; **Internetseite** *f*
web page; **Internetzugang** *m*
internet access
interpretieren *vt* to interpret

(*als* as)
Interpunktion *f* punctuation
Interview (-*s*, -*s*) *nt* interview;
interviewen *vt* to interview
intim *adj* intimate
intolerant *adj* intolerant
investieren *vt* to invest
inwiefern *adv* in what way; (*in*
welchem Ausmaß) to what extent;
inwieweit *adv* to what extent
inzwischen *adv* meanwhile
Irak (-(*s*)) *m:* (**der**) ~ Iraq
Iran (-(*s*)) *m:* (**der**) ~ Iran
Ire (-*n*, -*n*) *m* Irishman
irgend *adv:* ~ **so ein Idiot** some
idiot; **wenn ~ möglich** if at all
possible; **irgendein** *pron*,
irgendeine(r, s) *adj* some;
(*fragend, im Bedingungssatz; beliebig*)
any; **irgendetwas** *pron*
something; (*fragend, im*
Bedingungssatz) anything;
irgendjemand *pron* somebody;
(*fragend, im Bedingungssatz*)
anybody; **irgendwann** *adv*
sometime; (*zu beliebiger Zeit*) any
time; **irgendwie** *adv* somehow;
irgendwo *adv* somewhere;
(*fragend, im Bedingungssatz*)
anywhere
Irin *f* Irishwoman; **irisch** *adj*
Irish; **Irland** *nt* Ireland
ironisch *adj* ironic
irre *adj* crazy, mad; (*toll*) terrific;
Irre(r) *mf* lunatic; **irreführen** *irr*
vt to mislead; **irremachen** *vt* to
confuse; **irren** *vi* to be mistaken;
(*umherirren*) to wander ▷ *vr:* **sich**
~ to be mistaken; **wenn ich mich**
nicht irre if I'm not mistaken; **sich**
in der Nummer ~ (*Telefon*) to get
the wrong number; **irrsinnig** *adj*
mad, crazy; **Irrtum** (-*s*, -*tümer*) *m*
mistake, error; **irrtümlich** *adj*
mistaken ▷ *adv* by mistake
ISBN (-) *nt* *abk* = **industrial**
standard business network ISBN

▷ (-) f abk = **Internationale Standard Buchnummer** ISBN

Ischias (-) m sciatica

ISDN (-) nt abk = **integrated services digital network** ISDN

Islam (-s) m Islam; **islamisch** adj Islamic

Island nt Iceland; **Isländer(in)** (-s, -) m(f) Icelander; **isländisch** adj Icelandic; **Isländisch** nt Icelandic

Isolierband nt insulating tape; **isolieren** vt to isolate; (Elek) to insulate

Isomatte f thermomat, karrymat®

Israel (-s) nt Israel; **Israeli** (-(s), -(s)) m (-, -(s)) f Israeli; **israelisch** adj Israeli

IT (-) f abk = **Informationstechnologie** IT

Italien (-s) nt Italy; **Italiener(in)** (-s, -) m(f) Italian; **italienisch** adj Italian; **Italienisch** nt Italian

j

SCHLÜSSELWORT

ja adv 1 yes; **haben Sie das gesehen? — ja** did you see it? — yes(, I did); **ich glaube ja** (yes,) I think so

2 (fragend) really?; **ich habe gekündigt — ja?** I've quit — have you?; **du kommst, ja?** you're coming, aren't you?

3 **sei ja vorsichtig** do be careful; **Sie wissen ja, dass ...** as you know, ...; **tu das ja nicht!** don't do that!; **ich habe es ja gewusst** I just knew it; **ja, also ...** well you see ...

Jacht (-, -en) f yacht; **Jachthafen** m marina

Jacke (-, -n) f jacket; (Wolljacke) cardigan

Jackett (-s, -s o -e) nt jacket

Jagd (-, -en) f hunt; (Jagen) hunting; **jagen** vi to hunt ▷ vt to hunt; (*verfolgen*) to chase; **Jäger(in)** *m(f)* hunter

Jaguar (-s, -e) *m* jaguar

Jahr (-(e)s, -e) *nt* year; **ein halbes ~** six months pl; **Anfang der neunziger ~e** in the early nineties; **mit sechzehn ~en** at (the age of) sixteen; **Jahrestag** *m* anniversary; **Jahreszahl** *f* date, year; **Jahreszeit** *f* season; **Jahrgang** *m* (*Wein*) year, vintage; **der ~ 1989** (*Personen*) those born in 1989; **Jahrhundert** (-s, -e) *nt* century; **jährlich** *adj* yearly, annual; **Jahrmarkt** *m* fair; **Jahrtausend** *nt* millennium; **Jahrzehnt** *nt* decade

jähzornig *adj* hot-tempered

Jakobsmuschel *f* scallop

Jalousie *f* (*venetian*) blind

Jamaika (-s) *nt* Jamaica

jämmerlich *adj* pathetic

jammern *vi* to moan

Januar (-(s), -e) *m* January; *siehe auch* **Juni**

Japan (-s) *nt* Japan; **Japaner(in)** (-s, -) *m(f)* Japanese; **japanisch** *adj* Japanese; **Japanisch** *nt* Japanese

jaulen *vi* to howl

jawohl *adv* yes (of course)

Jazz (-) *m* jazz

SCHLÜSSELWORT

je *adv* 1 (*jemals*) ever; **hast du so was je gesehen?** did you ever see anything like it?
2 (*jeweils*) every, each; **sie zahlten je 3 Euro** they paid 3 euros each
▷ *konj* 1 **je nach** depending on; **je nachdem** it depends; **je nachdem, ob ...** depending on whether ...
2 **je eher, desto** *o* **umso besser** the sooner the better

Jeans (-, -) *f* jeans pl

jede(r, s) *unbest Zahlwort* (*insgesamt gesehen*) every; (*einzeln gesehen*) each; (*jede(r, s) beliebige*) any; **~s Mal** every time, each time; **~n zweiten Tag** every other day; **sie hat an ~m Finger einen Ring** she's got a ring on each finger; **~r Computer reicht aus** any computer will do; **bei ~m Wetter** in any weather ▷ *pron* everybody; (*jeder Einzelne*) each; **~r von euch/uns** each of you/us; **jedenfalls** *adv* in any case; **jederzeit** *adv* at any time; **jedesmal** *adv* every time

jedoch *adv* however

jemals *adv* ever

jemand *pron* somebody; (*in Frage und Verneinung*) anybody

Jemen (-(s)) *m* Yemen

jene(r, s) *adj* that, those pl ▷ *pron* that (one), those pl

jenseits *adv* on the other side ▷ *prep* +*gen* on the other side of; (*fig*) beyond

Jetlag (-s) *m* jet lag

jetzig *adj* present

jetzt *adv* now; **erst ~** only now; **~ gleich** right now; **bis ~** so far, up to now; **von ~ an** from now on

jeweils *adv:* **~ zwei zusammen** two at a time; **zu ~ 5 Euro** at 5 euros each

Job (-s, -s) *m* job; **jobben** *vi* (*fam*) to work, to have a job

Jod (-(e)s) *nt* iodine

joggen *vi* to jog; **Jogging** (-s) *nt* jogging; **Jogginganzug** *m* jogging suit, tracksuit; **Jogginghose** *f* jogging pants pl

Jog(h)urt (-s, -s) *m o nt* yoghurt

Johannisbeere *f:* **Schwarze ~** blackcurrant; **Rote ~** redcurrant

Joint (-s, -s) *m* (*fam*) joint

jonglieren *vi* to juggle

Jordanien (-s) *nt* Jordan

Journalist(in) *m(f)* journalist

Joystick (-s, -s) m (Inform)
joystick
jubeln vi to cheer
Jubiläum (-s, Jubiläen) nt jubilee;
(Jahrestag) anniversary
jucken vi to itch ▷ vt: **es juckt
mich am Arm** my arm is itching;
das juckt mich nicht (fam) I
couldn't care less; **Juckreiz** m
itch
Jude (-n, -n) m, **Jüdin** f Jew; **sie
ist Jüdin** she's Jewish; **jüdisch** adj
Jewish
Judo (-(s)) nt judo
Jugend (-) f youth; **jugendfrei**
adj: **ein ~er Film** a U-rated film
(Brit), a G-rated film (US); **ein
nicht ~er Film** an X-rated film;
Jugendgruppe f youth group;
Jugendherberge (-, -n) f youth
hostel; **Jugendherbergsausweis**
m youth hostel card; **jugendlich**
adj youthful; **Jugendliche(r)** mf
young person; **Jugendstil** m art
nouveau; **Jugendzentrum** nt
youth centre
Jugoslawien (-s) nt (Hist)
Yugoslavia; **das ehemalige ~** the
former Yugoslavia
Juli (-(s), -s) m July; siehe auch **Juni**
jung adj young
Junge (-n, -n) m boy
Junge(s) (-n, -n) nt young animal;
die ~n pl the young pl
Jungfrau f virgin; (Astr) Virgo
Junggeselle (-n, -n) m bachelor;
Junggesellin f single woman
Juni (-(s), -s) m June; **im ~** in June;
am 4. ~ on 4(th) June, on June
4(th) (gesprochen: on the fourth of
June); **Anfang/Mitte/Ende ~** at
the beginning/in the middle/at
the end of June;
letzten/nächsten ~ last/next
June
Jupiter (-s) m Jupiter
Jura ohne Artikel (Studienfach) law;

~ studieren to study law;
Jurist(in) m(f) lawyer; **juristisch**
adj legal
Justiz (-) f justice;
Justizminister(in) m(f) minister
of justice
Juwel (-s, -en) nt jewel;
Juwelier(in) (-s, -e) m(f) jeweller

k

Kabel (-s, -) nt (Elek) wire; (stark) cable; **Kabelfernsehen** nt cable television

Kabeljau (-s, -e o -s) m cod

Kabine f cabin; (im Schwimmbad) cubicle

Kabrio (-s, -s) nt convertible

Kachel (-, -n) f tile; **Kachelofen** m tiled stove

Käfer (-s, -) m beetle, bug (US)

Kaff (-s, -s) nt dump, hole

Kaffee (-s, -s) m coffee; **~ kochen** to make some coffee; **Kaffeefilter** m coffee filter; **Kaffeekanne** f coffeepot; **Kaffeeklatsch** (-(e)s, -e) m chat over coffee and cakes, coffee klatch (US); **Kaffeelöffel** m coffee spoon; **Kaffeemaschine** f coffee maker (o machine); **Kaffeetasse** f coffee cup

Käfig (-s, -e) m cage

kahl adj (Mensch, Kopf) bald; (Baum, Wand) bare

Kahn (-(e)s, Kähne) m boat; (Lastkahn) barge

Kai (-s, -e o -s) m quay

Kaiser (-s, -) m emperor; **Kaiserin** f empress; **Kaiserschnitt** m (Med) caesarean (section)

Kajak (-s, -s) nt kayak; **Kajakfahren** nt kayaking

Kajal (-s) m kohl

Kajüte (-, -n) f cabin

Kakao (-s, -s) m cocoa; (Getränk) (hot) chocolate

Kakerlake (-, -n) f cockroach

Kaki (-, -s) f kaki

Kaktee (-, -n) f, **Kaktus** (-, -se) m cactus

Kalb (-(e)s, Kälber) nt calf; **Kalbfleisch** nt veal; **Kalbsbraten** m roast veal; **Kalbsschnitzel** nt veal cutlet; (paniert) escalope of veal

Kalender (-s, -) m calendar; (Taschenkalender) diary

Kalk (-(e)s, -e) m lime; (in Knochen) calcium

Kalorie f calorie; **kalorienarm** adj low-calorie

kalt adj cold; **mir ist (es) ~** I'm cold; **kaltblütig** adj cold-blooded; **Kälte** (-) f cold; (fig) coldness

kam imperf von **kommen**

Kambodscha (-s) nt Cambodia

Kamel (-(e)s, -e) nt camel

Kamera (-, -s) f camera

Kamerad(in) (-en, -en) m(f) friend; (als Begleiter) companion

Kamerafrau f, **Kameramann** m camerawoman/-man

Kamille (-, -n) f camomile; **Kamillentee** m camomile tea

Kamin (-s, -e) m (außen) chimney; (innen) fireplace

Kamm (-(e)s, Kämme) m comb; (Berg) ridge; (Hahn) crest; **kämmen** vr **sich ~, sich** (dat) **die Haare ~** to

comb one's hair; **Kammermusik**
f chamber music

Kampf (-(e)s, Kämpfe) m fight;
(Schlacht) battle; (Wettbewerb)
contest; (fig: Anstrengung)
struggle; **kämpfen** vi to fight
(für, um for); **Kampfsport** m
martial art

Kanada (-s) nt Canada;
Kanadier(in) (-s, -) m(f) Canadian; **kanadisch** adj Canadian

Kanal (-s, Kanäle) m (Fluss) canal;
(Rinne, TV) channel; (für Abfluss)
drain; **der ~** (Ärmelkanal) the
(English) Channel; **Kanalinseln**
pl Channel Islands pl;
Kanalisation f sewerage system;
Kanaltunnel m Channel Tunnel

Kanarienvogel m canary

Kandidat(in) (-en, -en) m(f)
candidate

Kandis(zucker) (-) m rock
candy

Känguru (-s, -s) nt kangaroo

Kaninchen nt rabbit

Kanister (-s, -) m can

Kännchen nt pot; **ein
~ Kaffee/Tee** a pot of coffee/tea;
Kanne (-, -n) f (Krug) jug;
(Kaffeekanne) pot; (Milchkanne)
churn; (Gießkanne) can

kannte imperf von **kennen**

Kante (-, -n) f edge

Kantine f canteen

Kanton (-s, -e) m canton

Kanu (-s, -s) nt canoe

Kanzler(in) (-s, -) m(f)
chancellor

Kap (-s, -s) nt cape

Kapazität f capacity; (Fachmann)
authority

Kapelle f (Gebäude) chapel; (Mus)
band

Kaper (-, -n) f caper

kapieren vt, vi (fam) to
understand; **kapiert?** got it?

Kapital (-s, -e o -ien) nt capital

Kapitän (-s, -e) m captain

Kapitel (-s, -) nt chapter

Kappe (-, -n) f cap

Kapsel (-, -n) f capsule

kaputt adj (fam) broken; (Mensch)
exhausted; **kaputtgehen** irr vi
to break; (Firma) to go bust; (Stoff) to wear
out; **kaputtmachen** vt to
break; (jdn) to wear out

Kapuze (-, -n) f hood

Kap Verde (-s) nt Cape Verde

Karaffe (-, -n) f carafe; (mit
Stöpsel) decanter

Karamell (-s) nt caramel, toffee

Karaoke (-(s)) nt karaoke

Karat (-s, -e) nt carat

Karate (-s) nt karate

Kardinal (-s, Kardinäle) m
cardinal

Karfreitag m Good Friday

kariert adj checked; (Papier)
squared

Karies (-) f (tooth) decay

Karikatur f caricature

Karneval (-s, -e o -s) m carnival

Kärnten (-s) nt Carinthia

Karo (-s, -s) nt square; (Karten)
diamonds pl

Karosserie f (Auto) body(work)

Karotte (-, -n) f carrot

Karpfen (-s, -) m carp

Karriere (-, -n) f career

Karte (-, -n) f card; (Landkarte) map; (Speisekarte) menu; (Eintrittskarte, Fahrkarte) ticket; **mit ~ bezahlen** to pay by credit card; **~n spielen** to play cards; **die ~n mischen/geben** to shuffle/deal the cards

Kartei f card index; **Karteikarte** f index card

Kartenspiel nt card game; **Kartentelefon** nt cardphone; **Kartenvorverkauf** m advance booking

Kartoffel (-, -n) f potato; **Kartoffelbrei** m mashed potatoes pl; **Kartoffelchips** pl crisps pl (Brit), chips pl (US); **Kartoffelpuffer** m potato cake (made from grated potatoes); **Kartoffelpüree** m mashed potatoes pl; **Kartoffelsalat** m potato salad

Karton (-s, -s) m cardboard; (Schachtel) (cardboard) box

Kartusche (-, -n) f cartridge

Karussell (-s, -s) nt roundabout (Brit), merry-go-round

Kaschmir (-s, e) m (Stoff) cashmere

Käse (-s, -) m cheese; **Käsekuchen** m cheesecake; **Käseplatte** f cheeseboard

Kasino (-s, -s) nt (Spielkasino) casino

Kaskoversicherung f comprehensive insurance

Kasper(l) (-s, -) m Punch; (fig) clown; **Kasperl(e)theater** nt (Vorstellung) Punch and Judy show; (Gebäude) Punch and Judy theatre

Kasse (-, -n) f (in Geschäft) till, cash register; (im Supermarkt) checkout; (Geldkasten) cashbox; (Theater) box office; (Kino) ticket office; (Krankenkasse) health insurance; (Spar~) savings bank; **Kassenbon** (-s, -s) m, **Kassenzettel** m receipt

Kassette f (small) box; (Tonband) cassette; **Kassettenrekorder** m cassette recorder

kassieren vt to take ▷ vi: **darf ich ~?** would you like to pay now?; **Kassierer(in)** m(f) cashier

Kastanie f chestnut

Kasten (-s, Kästen) m (Behälter) box; (Getränkekasten) crate

Kat m abk = **Katalysator**

Katalog (-(e)s, -e) m catalogue

Katalysator m (Auto) catalytic converter; (Phys) catalyst

Katar (-s) nt Qatar

Katarr(h) (-s, -e) m catarrh

Katastrophe (-, -n) f catastrophe, disaster

Kategorie (-, -n) f category

Kater (-s, -) m tomcat; (fam: nach zu viel Alkohol) hangover

Kathedrale (-, -n) f cathedral

Katholik(in) m(f) Catholic; **katholisch** adj Catholic

Katze (-, -n) f cat

Kauderwelsch (-(s)) nt (unverständlich) gibberish; (Fachjargon) jargon

kauen vt, vi to chew

Kauf (-(e)s, Käufe) m purchase; (Kaufen) buying; **ein guter ~** a bargain; **etw in ~ nehmen** to put up with sth; **kaufen** vt to buy; **Käufer(in)** m(f) buyer; **Kauffrau** f businesswoman; **Kaufhaus** nt department store; **Kaufmann** m businessman; (im Einzelhandel) shopkeeper (Brit), storekeeper (US); **Kaufpreis** m purchase price; **Kaufvertrag** m purchase agreement

Kaugummi m chewing gum

Kaulquappe (-, -n) f tadpole

kaum adv hardly, scarcely

Kaution f deposit; (Jur) bail

Kaviar m caviar

KB (-, -) nt, **Kbyte** (-, -) nt abk = **Kilobyte** KB

Kebab (-(s), -s) m kebab

Kegel (-s, -) m skittle; (beim Dowling) pin; (Math) cone; **Kegelbahn** f bowling alley; **kegeln** vi to play skittles; (bowlen) to bowl

Kehle (-, -n) f throat; **Kehlkopf** m larynx

Kehre (-, -n) f sharp bend

kehren vt (fegen) to sweep

Keilriemen m (Auto) fan belt

kein pron no, not ... any; **ich habe ~ Geld** I have no money; I don't have money; **~ Mensch** no one; **du bist ~ Kind mehr** you're not a child any more; **keine(r, s)** pron (Person) no one, nobody; (Sache) not ... any, none; **~r von ihnen** none of them; (bei zwei Personen/Sachen) neither of them; **ich will keins von beiden** I don't want either of them; **keinesfalls** adv on no account, under no circumstances

Keks (-es, -e) m biscuit (Brit), cookie (US); **jdm auf den ~ gehen** (fam) to get on sb's nerves

Keller (-s, -) m cellar; (Geschoss) basement

Kellner (-s, -) m waiter; **Kellnerin** f waitress

Kenia (-s) nt Kenya

kennen (kannte, gekannt) vt to know; **wir ~ uns seit 1990** we've known each other since 1990; **wir ~ uns schon** we've already met; **kennst du mich noch?** do you remember me?; **kennen|lernen** vt to get to know; **sich ~** to get to know each other; (zum ersten Mal) to meet

Kenntnis f knowledge; **seine ~se**

his knowledge

Kennwort nt (a. Inform) password; **Kennzeichen** nt mark, sign; (Auto) number plate (Brit), license plate (US); **besondere ~** distinguishing marks

Kerl (-s, -e) m guy, bloke (Brit)

Kern (-(e)s, -e) m (Obst) pip; (Pfirsich, Kirsche etc) stone; (Nuss) kernel; (Atomkern) nucleus; (fig) heart, core

Kernenergie f nuclear energy; **Kernkraft** f nuclear power; **Kernkraftwerk** nt nuclear power station

Kerze (-, -n) f candle; (Zündkerze) plug

Ket(s)chup (-(s), -s) m o nt ketchup

Kette (-, -n) f chain; (Halskette) necklace

keuchen vi to pant; **Keuchhusten** m whooping cough

Keule (-, -n) f club; (Gastr) leg; (von Hähnchen a.) drumstick

Keyboard (-s, -s) nt (Mus) keyboard

Kfz nt abk = **Kraftfahrzeug**

Kfz-Brief m ≈ logbook

Kfz-Steuer f ≈ road tax (Brit), vehicle tax (US)

KG (-, -s) f abk = **Kommanditgesellschaft** limited partnership

Kichererbse f chick pea

kichern vi to giggle

Kickboard® (-s, -s) nt micro scooter

Kicker (-s, -) m (Spiel) table football (Brit), foosball (US)

kidnappen vt to kidnap

Kidney-Bohne f kidney bean

Kiefer (-s, -) m jaw ▸ (-, -n) f pine; **Kieferchirurg(in)** m(f) oral surgeon

Kieme (-, -n) f gill

Kies (-es, -e) m gravel; **Kiesel**
(-s, -) m, **Kieselstein** m pebble

kiffen vi (fam) to smoke pot

Kilo (-s, -(s)) nt kilo; **Kilobyte** nt
kilobyte; **Kilogramm** nt
kilogram; **Kilometer** m
kilometre; **Kilometerstand** m
≈ mileage; **Kilometerzähler** m
≈ mileometer; **Kilowatt** nt
kilowatt

Kind (-(e)s, -er) nt child; **sie
bekommt ein ~** she's having a
baby; **Kinderarzt** m,
Kinderärztin f paediatrician;
Kinderbetreuung f childcare;
Kinderbett nt cot (Brit), crib (US);
Kinderfahrkarte f child's ticket;
Kindergarten m nursery school,
kindergarten; **Kindergärtner(in)**
m(f) nursery-school teacher;
Kindergeld nt child benefit;
Kinderkrankheit f children's
illness; **Kinderkrippe** f crèche
(Brit), daycare center (US);
Kinderlähmung f polio;
Kindermädchen nt nanny (Brit),
nurse(maid); **kindersicher** adj
childproof; **Kindersicherung** f
childproof safety catch; (an Flasche)
childproof cap; **Kindersitz** m
child seat; **Kindertagesstätte** nt
day nursery; **Kinderteller** m (im
Restaurant) children's portion;
Kinderwagen m pram (Brit),
baby carriage (US); **Kinderzimmer**
nt children's (bed)room; **Kindheit**
f childhood; **kindisch** adj
childish; **kindlich** adj childlike

Kinn (-(e)s, -e) nt chin

Kino (-s, -s) nt cinema (Brit),
movie theater (US); **ins ~ gehen** to
go to the cinema (Brit) (o to the
movies (US))

Kiosk (-(e)s, -e) m kiosk

Kippe f (fam: Zigarettenstummel)
cigarette end, fag end (Brit)

kippen vi to tip over ▷ vt to tilt;
(Regierung, Minister) to topple

Kirche (-, -n) f church;
Kirchturm m church tower; (mit
Spitze) steeple

Kirmes (-, -sen) f fair

Kirsche (-, -n) f cherry;
Kirschtomate f cherry tomato

Kissen (-s, -) nt cushion;
(Kopfkissen) pillow; **Kissenbezug**
m cushion cover; (für Kopfkissen)
pillowcase

Kiste (-, -n) f box; (Truhe) chest

KITA (-, -s) f abk =
Kindertagesstätte day-care
centre (Brit), day-care center (US)

kitschig adj kitschy, cheesy

kitzelig adj (a. fig) ticklish;
kitzeln vt, vi to tickle

Kiwi (-s, -s) f (Frucht) kiwi (fruit)

Klage (-, -n) f complaint; (Jur)
lawsuit; **klagen** vi to complain
(über +akk about, bei to); **kläglich**
adj wretched

Klammer (-, -n) f (in Text)
bracket; (Büroklammer) clip;
(Wäscheklammer) peg (Brit),
clothespin (US); (Zahnklammer)
brace; **Klammeraffe** m (fam)
at-sign, @; **klammern** vr: **sich
~ to cling** (an +akk to)

klang imperf von **klingen**

Klang (-(e)s, Klänge) m sound

Klappbett nt folding bed

klappen vi impers (gelingen) to
work; **es hat gut geklappt** it went
well

klappern vi to rattle; (Geschirr) to
clatter; **Klapperschlange** f
rattlesnake

Klappfahrrad nt folding bicycle;
Klappstuhl m folding chair

klar adj clear; **sich** (dat) **im Klaren
sein** to be clear (über +akk about);
alles ~? everything okay?

klären vt (Flüssigkeit) to purify;
(Probleme, Frage) to clarify ▷ vr:

sich ~ to clear itself up

Klarinette (-, -n) f clarinet

klar|kommen irr vi: **mit etw ~** to cope with something; **kommst du klar?** are you managing all right?; **mit jdm ~** to get along with sb; **klar|machen** vt: **jdm etw ~** to make sth clear to sb; **klar|stellen** vt to clarify

Klärung f (von Frage, Problem) clarification

klasse adj inv (fam) great, brilliant

Klasse (-, -n) f class; (Schuljahr) form (Brit), grade (US); **erster ~ reisen** to travel first class; **in welche ~ gehst du?** which form (Brit) (o grade (US)) are you in?; **Klassenarbeit** f test; **Klassenlehrer(in)** m(f) class teacher; **Klassenzimmer** nt classroom

Klassik f (Zeit) classical period; (Musik) classical music

Klatsch (-(e)s, -e) m (Gerede) gossip; **klatschen** vi (schlagen) to smack; (Beifall) to applaud, to clap; (reden) to gossip; **Klatschmohn** m (corn) poppy; **klatschnass** adj soaking (wet)

Klaue (-, -n) f claw; (fam: Schrift) scrawl; **klauen** vt (fam) to pinch

Klavier (-s, -e) nt piano

Klebeband nt adhesive tape; **kleben** vt to stick (an +akk to) ▷ vi (klebrig sein) to be sticky; **klebrig** adj sticky; **Klebstoff** m glue; **Klebstreifen** m adhesive tape

Klecks (-es, -e) m blob; (Tinte) blot

Klee (-s) m clover

Kleid (-(e)s, -er) nt (Frauen~) dress; **~er** pl (Kleidung) clothes pl; **Kleiderbügel** m coat hanger; **Kleiderschrank** m wardrobe (Brit), closet (US); **Kleidung** f clothing

klein adj small, little; (Finger) little; **mein ~er Bruder** my little (o

younger) brother; **als ich noch ~ war** when I was a little boy/girl; **etw ~ schneiden** to chop sth up; **Kleinanzeige** f classified ad; **Kleinbuchstabe** m small letter; **Kleinbus** m minibus; **Kleingeld** nt change; **Kleinigkeit** f trifle; (Zwischenmahlzeit) snack; **kleinkind** nt toddler; **klein|schreiben** vt (mit kleinem Anfangsbuchstaben) to write with a small letter; **Kleinstadt** f small town

Kleister (-s, -) m paste

Klempner(in) m(f) plumber

klettern vi to climb

Klettverschluss m Velcro® fastening

klicken vi (a. Inform) to click

Klient(in) (-en, -en) m(f) client

Klima nt climate; **Klimaanlage** f air conditioning; **klimatisiert** adj air-conditioned

Klinge (-, -n) f blade

Klingel (-, -n) f bell; **klingeln** vi to ring

klingen (klang, geklungen) vi to sound

Klinik f clinic; (Krankenhaus) hospital

Klinke (-, -n) f handle

Klippe (-, -n) f cliff; (im Meer) reef; (fig) hurdle

Klischee (-s, -s) nt (fig) cliché

Klo (-s, -s) nt (fam) loo (Brit), john (US); **Klobrille** f toilet seat; **Klopapier** nt toilet paper

klopfen vt, vi to knock; (Herz) to thump

Kloß (-es, Klöße) m (im Hals) lump; (Gastr) dumpling

Kloster (-s, Klöster) nt (für Männer) monastery; (für Frauen) convent

Klub (-s, -s) m club

klug adj clever

knabbern vt, vi to nibble

Knäckebrot nt crispbread
knacken vt, vi to crack
Knall (-(e)s, -e) m bang; **knallen** vi to bang
knapp adj (kaum ausreichend) scarce; (Sieg) narrow; ~ **bei Kasse sein** to be short of money; ~ **zwei Stunden** just under two hours
Knauf (-s, Knäufe) m knob
kneifen (kniff, gekniffen) vt, vi to pinch; (sich drücken) to back out (vor +dat of); **Kneifzange** f pincers pl
Kneipe (-, -n) f (fam) pub (Brit), bar
Knete (-) f (fam: Geld) dough; **kneten** vt to knead; (formen) to mould
knicken vt, vi (brechen) to break; (Papier) to fold; **geknickt sein** (fig) to be downcast
Knie (-s, -) nt knee; **in die ~ gehen** to bend one's knees; **Kniebeuge** f knee bend; **Kniegelenk** nt knee joint; **Kniekehle** f back of the knee; **knien** vi to kneel; **Kniescheibe** f kneecap; **Knieschoner** (-s, -) m, **Knieschützer** (-s, -) m knee pad; **Kniestrumpf** m knee-length sock
kniff imperf von **kneifen**
knipsen vt (fam) to punch; (Foto) to snap ▷ vi (Foto) to take snaps
knirschen vi (fam) to crunch; **mit den Zähnen ~** to grind one's teeth
knitterfrei adj non-crease; **knittern** vi to crease
Knoblauch m garlic; **Knoblauchbrot** nt garlic bread; **Knoblauchzehe** f clove of garlic
Knöchel (-s, -) m (Finger) knuckle; (Fuß) ankle
Knochen (-s, -) m bone; **Knochenbruch** m fracture; **Knochenmark** nt marrow
Knödel (-s, -) m dumpling
Knollensellerie m celeriac

Knopf (-(e)s, Knöpfe) m button; **Knopfdruck** m: **auf ~** at the touch of a button; **Knopfloch** nt buttonhole
Knospe (-, -n) f bud
knoten vt to knot; **Knoten** (-s, -) m knot; (Med) lump
Know-how (-(s)) nt know-how, expertise
knurren vi (Hund) to growl; (Magen) to rumble; (Mensch) to grumble
knusprig adj crisp; (Keks) crunchy
knutschen vi (fam) to smooch
k. o. adj inv (Sport) knocked out; (fig) knackered
Koalition f coalition
Koch (-(e)s, Köche) m cook; **Kochbuch** nt cookery book, cookbook; **kochen** vt, vi to cook; (Wasser) to boil; (Kaffee, Tee) to make; **Köchin** f cook; **Kochlöffel** m wooden spoon; **Kochnische** f kitchenette; **Kochplatte** f hotplate; **Kochrezept** nt recipe; **Kochtopf** m saucepan
Kode (-s, -s) m code
Köder (-s, -) m bait
Koffein (-s) nt caffeine; **koffeinfrei** adj decaffeinated
Koffer (-s, -) m (suit)case; **Kofferraum** m (Auto) boot (Brit), trunk (US)
Kognak (-s, -s) m brandy
Kohl (-(e)s, -e) m cabbage
Kohle (-, -n) f coal; (Holzkohle) charcoal; (Chem) carbon; (fam: Geld) cash, dough; **Kohlehydrat** nt carbohydrate; **Kohlendioxid** nt carbon dioxide; **Kohlensäure** f (in Getränken) fizz; **ohne ~** still, non-carbonated (US); **mit ~** sparkling, carbonated (US); **Kohletablette** f charcoal tablet
Kohlrabi (-(s), -(s)) m kohlrabi
Koje (-, -n) f cabin; (Bett) bunk

Kokain (-s) nt cocaine

Kokosnuss f coconut

Kolben (-s, -) m (Tech) piston; (Mais~) cob

Kolik (-, -en) f colic

Kollaps (-es, -e) m collapse

Kollege (-n, -n) m, **Kollegin** f colleague

Köln (-s) nt Cologne

Kolonne (-, -n) f convoy; **in ~ fahren** to drive in convoy

Kölsch (-, -) nt (Bier) (strong) lager (from the Cologne region)

Kolumbien (-s) nt Columbia

Koma (-s, -s) nt coma

Kombi (-(s), -s) m estate (car) (Brit), station wagon (US)

Kombination f combination; (Folgerung) deduction; (Hemdhose) combinations pl; (Aviat) flying suit; **kombinieren** vt to combine ▷ vi to reason; (vermuten) to guess; **Kombizange** f (pair of) pliers pl

Komfort (-s) m conveniences pl; (Bequemlichkeit) comfort

Komiker(in) m(f) comedian, comic; **komisch** adj funny

Komma (-s, -s) nt comma

Kommanditgesellschaft f limited partnership

kommen (kam, gekommen) vi to come; (näher kommen) to approach; (passieren) to happen; (gelangen, geraten) to get; (erscheinen) to appear; (in die Schule, das Gefängnis etc) to go; **~ lassen** to send for; **zu sich ~** to come round (o to); **zu etw ~** (bekommen) to acquire sth; (Zeit dazu finden) to get round to sth; **wer kommt zuerst?** who's first?; **kommend** adj coming; **~e Woche** next week; **in den ~en Jahren** in the years to come

Kommentar m commentary; **kein ~** no comment

Kommilitone (-n, -n) m, **Kommilitonin** f fellow student

Kommissar(in) m(f) inspector

Kommode (-, -n) f chest of drawers

Kommunikation f communication

Kommunion f (Rel) communion

Kommunismus m communism

Komödie f comedy

kompakt adj compact

Kompass (-es, -e) m compass

kompatibel adj compatible

kompetent adj competent

komplett adj complete

Kompliment nt compliment; **jdm ein ~ machen** to pay sb a compliment; **~!** congratulations

Komplize (-n, -n) m accomplice

kompliziert adj complicated

Komponist(in) m(f) composer

Kompost (-(e)s, -e) m compost; **Komposthaufen** m compost heap; **kompostierbar** adj biodegradable

Kompott (-(e)s, -e) nt stewed fruit

Kompresse (-, -n) f compress

Kompromiss (-es, -e) m compromise

Kondensmilch f condensed milk, evaporated milk

Kondition f (Leistungsfähigkeit) condition; **sie hat eine gute ~** she's in good shape

Konditorei f cake shop; (mit Café) café

Kondom (-s, -e) nt condom

Konfektionsgröße f size

Konferenz f conference

Konfession f religion; (christlich) denomination

Konfetti (-(s)) nt confetti

Konfirmation f (Rel) confirmation

Konfitüre (-, -n) f jam

Konflikt (-(e)s, -e) m conflict

konfrontieren vt to confront

Kongo (-s) m Congo

Kongress (-es, -e) m conference; **der ~** (Parlament der USA) Congress

König (-(e)s, -e) m king; **Königin** f queen; **königlich** adj royal; **Königreich** nt kingdom

Konkurrenz f competition

⬤ SCHLÜSSELWORT

können (pt **konnte**, pp **gekonnt** o (als Hilfsverb) **können**) vt, vi 1 to be able to; **ich kann es machen** I can do it, I am able to do it; **ich kann es nicht machen** I can't do it, I'm not able to do it; **ich kann nicht ...** I can't ..., I cannot ...; **ich kann nicht mehr** I can't go on
2 (wissen, beherrschen) to know; **können Sie Deutsch?** can you speak German?; **er kann gut Englisch** he speaks English well; **sie kann keine Mathematik** she can't do mathematics
3 (dürfen) to be allowed to; **kann ich gehen?** can I go?; **könnte ich ...?** could I ...?; **kann ich mit?** (fam) can I come with you?
4 (möglich sein) **Sie könnten recht haben** you may be right; **das kann sein** that's possible; **kann sein** maybe

konsequent adj consistent; **Konsequenz** f consequence

konservativ adj conservative

Konserven pl tinned food sing (Brit), canned food pl; **Konservendose** f tin (Brit), can

konservieren vt to preserve; **Konservierungsmittel** nt preservative

Konsonant m consonant

Konsul(in) (-s, -n) m(f) consul; **Konsulat** nt consulate

Kontakt (-(e)s, -e) m contact; **kontaktarm** adj: **er ist ~** he lacks contact with other people; **kontaktfreudig** adj sociable; **Kontaktlinsen** pl contact lenses pl

Kontinent m continent

Konto (-s, Konten) nt account; **Kontoauszug** m (bank) statement; **Kontoauszugsdrucker** m bank-statement machine; **Kontoinhaber(in)** m(f) account holder; **Kontonummer** f account number; **Kontostand** m balance

Kontrabass m double bass

Kontrast (-(e)s, -e) m contrast

Kontrolle (-, -n) f control; (Aufsicht) supervision; (Passkontrolle) passport control; **kontrollieren** vt to control; (nachprüfen) to check

Konzentration f concentration; **Konzentrationslager** nt (Hist) concentration camp; **konzentrieren** vt to concentrate ▷ vr: **sich ~** to concentrate

Konzept (-(e)s, -e) nt rough draft; **jdn aus dem ~ bringen** to put sb off

Konzern (-(e)s, -e) m firm

Konzert (-(e)s, -e) nt concert; (Stück) concerto; **Konzertsaal** m concert hall

koordinieren vt to coordinate

Kopf (-(e)s, Köpfe) m head; **pro ~ per** person; **sich den ~ zerbrechen** to rack one's brains; **Kopfhörer** m headphones pl; **Kopfkissen** nt pillow; **Kopfsalat** m lettuce; **Kopfschmerzen** pl headache sing; **Kopfstütze** f headrest; **Kopftuch** nt headscarf; **kopfüber** adv headfirst

Kopie f copy; **kopieren** vt (a. Inform) to copy; **Kopierer** (-s, -) m, **Kopiergerät** nt copier

Kopilot(in) m(f) co-pilot

Koralle (-, -n) f coral

Koran (-s) m (Rel) Koran

Korb (-(e)s, Körbe) m basket; **jdm einen ~ geben** (fig) to turn sb down

Kord (-(e)s, -e) m corduroy

Kordel (, n) f cord

Kork ((e)s, e) m cork; **Korken** (-s, -) m cork; **Korkenzieher** (-s, -) m corkscrew

Korn (-(e)s, Körner) nt grain; **Kornblume** f cornflower

Körper (-s, -) m body; **Körperbau** m build; **Körpergeruch** m body odour; **Körpergröße** f height; **körperlich** adj physical; **Körperteil** m part of the body; **Körperverletzung** f physical injury

korrekt adj correct

Korrespondent(in) m(f) correspondent; **Korrespondenz** f correspondence

korrigieren vt to correct

Kosmetik f cosmetics pl; **Kosmetikkoffer** m vanity case; **Kosmetiksalon** m beauty parlour; **Kosmetiktuch** m paper tissue

Kost (-) f (Nahrung) food; (Verpflegung) board

kostbar adj precious; (teuer) costly, expensive

kosten vt to cost ▷ vt, vi (versuchen) to taste; **to taste**; f costs pl, cost; (Ausgaben) expenses pl; **auf ~ von** at the expense of; **kostenlos** adj free (of charge); **Kostenvoranschlag** m estimate

köstlich adj (Essen) delicious; (Einfall) delightful; **sich ~ amüsieren** to have a marvellous time

Kostprobe f taster; (fig) sample; **kostspielig** adj expensive

Kostüm (-s, -e) nt costume;

(Damenkostüm) suit

Kot (-(e)s) m excrement

Kotelett (-(e)s, -e o -s) nt chop, cutlet

Koteletten pl sideboards pl (Brit), sideburns pl (US)

Kotflügel m (Auto) wing

kotzen vi (vulg) to puke, to throw up

Krabbe (-, -n) f shrimp; (großer prawn; (Krebs) crab

krabbeln vi to crawl

Krach (-(e)s, -s o -e) m crash; (andauernd) noise; (fam: Streit) row

Kraft (-, Kräfte) f strength; (Pol, Phys) force; (Fähigkeit) power; (Arbeits~) worker; **in ~ treten** to come into effect; **Kraftausdruck** m swearword; **Kraftfahrzeug** nt motor vehicle; **Kraftfahrzeugbrief** m ≈ logbook; **Kraftfahrzeugschein** m vehicle registration document; **Kraftfahrzeugsteuer** f ≈ road tax (Brit), vehicle tax (US); **Kraftfahrzeugversicherung** f car insurance; **kräftig** adj strong; (gesund) healthy; (Farben) intense, strong; **Kraftstoff** m fuel; **Kraftwerk** nt power station

Kragen (-s, -) m collar

Krähe (-, -n) f crow

Kralle (-, -n) f claw; (Parkkralle) wheel clamp

Kram (-(e)s) m stuff

Krampf (-(e)s, Krämpfe) m cramp; (zuckend) spasm; **Krampfader** f varicose vein

Kran (-(e)s, Kräne) m crane

Kranich (-s, -e) m (Zool) crane

krank adj ill, sick

kränken vt to hurt

Krankengymnastik f physiotherapy; **Krankenhaus** nt hospital; **Krankenkasse** f health insurance; **Krankenpfleger** (-s, -) m (male) nurse;

Krankenschein m health insurance certificate; **Krankenschwester** f nurse; **Krankenversicherung** f health insurance; **Krankenwagen** m ambulance; **Krankheit** f illness; (durch Infektion hervorgerufen) disease

Kränkung f insult

Kranz (-es, Kränze) m wreath

krass adj crass; (fam: toll) wicked

kratzen vt, vi to scratch; **Kratzer** (-s, -) m scratch

kraulen vi (schwimmen) to do the crawl ▷ vt (streicheln) to pet

Kraut (-(e)s, Kräuter) nt plant; (Gewürz) herb; (Gemüse) cabbage; **Kräuter** pl herbs pl; **Kräuterbutter** f herb butter; **Kräutertee** m herbal tea; **Krautsalat** m coleslaw

Krawatte f tie

kreativ adj creative

Krebs (-es, -e) m (Zool) crab; (Med) cancer; (Astr) Cancer

Kredit (-(e)s, -e) m credit; **auf ~** on credit; **einen ~ aufnehmen** to take out a loan; **Kreditkarte** f credit card

Kreide (-, -n) f chalk

Kreis (-es, -e) m circle; (Bezirk) district

kreischen vi to shriek; (Bremsen, Säge) to screech

Kreisel (-s, -) m (Spielzeug) top; (Verkehrskreisel) roundabout (Brit), traffic circle (US)

Kreislauf m (Med) circulation; (fig: der Natur etc) cycle; **Kreislaufstörungen** pl (Med) **ich habe ~** I've got problems with my circulation; **Kreisverkehr** m roundabout (Brit), traffic circle (US)

Kren (-s) m horseradish

Kresse (-, -n) f cress

Kreuz (-es, -e) nt cross; (Anat) small of the back; (Karten) clubs pl;

mir tut das ~ weh I've got backache; **Kreuzband** nt cruciate ligament; **kreuzen** vt to cross ▷ vr: **sich ~** to cross ▷ vi (Naut) to cruise; **Kreuzfahrt** f cruise; **Kreuzgang** m cloisters pl; **Kreuzotter** (-, -n) f adder; **Kreuzschlitzschraubenzieher** m Phillips® screwdriver; **Kreuzschlüssel** m (Auto) wheel brace; **Kreuzschmerzen** pl backache sing; **Kreuzung** f (Verkehrskreuzung) crossroads sing, intersection; (Züchtung) cross; **Kreuzworträtsel** nt crossword (puzzle)

kriechen (kroch, gekrochen) vi to crawl; (unauffällig) to creep; (fig, pej) (vor jdm) ~ to crawl (to sb); **Kriechspur** f crawler lane

Krieg (-(e)s, -e) m war

kriegen vt (fam) to get; (erwischen) to catch; **sie kriegt ein Kind** she's having a baby; **ich kriege noch Geld von dir** you still owe me some money

Krimi (-s, -s) m (fam) thriller; **Kriminalität** f criminality; **Kriminalpolizei** f detective force, ≈ CID (Brit), ≈ FBI (US); **Kriminalroman** m detective novel; **kriminell** adj criminal

Krippe (-, -n) f (Futterkrippe) manger; (Weihnachtskrippe) crib (Brit), crèche (US); (Kinderkrippe) crèche (Brit), daycare center (US)

Krise (-, -n) f crisis

Kristall (-s, -e) m crystal ▷ (-s) nt (Glas) crystal

Kritik f criticism; (Rezension) review; **Kritiker(in)** m(f) critic; **kritisch** adj critical

kritzeln vt, vi to scribble, to scrawl

Kroate (-n, -n) m Croat; **Kroatien** (-s) nt Croatia; **Kroatin** f Croat; **kroatisch** adj Croatian;

Kroatisch nt Croatian
kroch imperf von **kriechen**
Krokodil (-s, -e) nt crocodile
Krokus (-, -o -se) m crocus
Krone (-, -n) f crown;
Kronleuchter m chandelier
Kropf (-(e)s, Kröpfe) m (Med)
goitre; (von Vogel) crop
Kröte (-, -n) f toad
Krücke (-, -n) f crutch
Krug (-(e)s, Krüge) m jug;
(Bierkrug) mug
Krümel (-s, -) m crumb
krumm adj crooked
Krüppel (-s, -) m cripple
Kruste (-, -n) f crust
Kruzifix (es, e) nt crucifix
Kuba (-s) nt Cuba
Kübel (-s, -) m tub; (Eimer) bucket
Kubikmeter m cubic metre
Küche (-, -n) f kitchen; (Kochen)
cooking
Kuchen (-s, -) m cake; (mit
Teigdeckel) pie; **Kuchengabel** f
cake fork
Küchenmaschine f food
processor; **Küchenpapier** nt
kitchen roll; **Küchenschrank** m
(kitchen) cupboard
Kuckuck (-s, -e) m cuckoo
Kugel (-, -n) f ball; (Math) sphere;
(Mil) bullet; (Weihnachtskugel)
bauble; **Kugellager** nt ball
bearing; **Kugelschreiber** m
(ball-point) pen, biro® (Brit);
Kugelstoßen (-s) nt shot put
Kuh (-, Kühe) f cow
kühl adj cool; **Kühlakku** (-s, -s) m
ice pack; **Kühlbox** f cool box;
kühlen vt to cool; **Kühler** (-s, -)
m (Auto) radiator; **Kühlerhaube**
f (Auto) bonnet (Brit), hood (US);
Kühlschrank m fridge,
refrigerator; **Kühltasche** f cool
bag; **Kühltruhe** f freezer;
Kühlwasser nt (Auto) radiator
water

Kuhstall m cowshed
Küken (-s, -) nt chick
Kuli (-s, -s) m (fam: Kugelschreiber)
pen, biro® (Brit)
Kulisse (-, -n) f scenery
Kult (-s, -e) m cult; **Kultfigur** f
cult figure
Kultur f culture; (Lebensform)
civilization; **Kulturbeutel** m
toilet bag (Brit), washbag;
kulturell adj cultural
Kümmel (-s, -) m caraway
seeds pl
Kummer (-s) m grief, sorrow
kümmern vr: **sich um jdn ~** to
look after sb; **sich um etw ~** to see
to sth ▷ vt to concern; **das
kümmert mich nicht** that doesn't
worry me
Kumpel (-s, -) m (fam) mate, pal
Kunde (-, -n) m customer;
Kundendienst m after-sales (o
customer) service;
Kunden(kredit)karte f storecard, chargecard; **Kunden-
nummer** f customer number
kündigen vi to hand in one's
notice; (Mieter) to give notice that
one is moving out; **jdm ~** to give
sb his/her notice; (Vermieter) to
give sb notice to quit ▷ vt to
cancel; (Vertrag) to terminate; **jdm
die Stellung ~** to give sb his/her
notice; **jdm die Wohnung ~** to
give sb notice to quit; **Kündigung**
f (Arbeitsverhältnis) dismissal;
(Vertrag) termination;
(Abonnement) cancellation; (Frist)
notice; **Kündigungsfrist** f
period of notice
Kundin f customer; **Kundschaft**
f customers pl
künftig adj future
Kunst (-, Künste) f art; (Können)
skill; **Kunstausstellung** f art
exhibition; **Kunstgewerbe** nt arts
and crafts pl; **Künstler(in)** (-s, -)

m(f) artist; **künstlerisch** *adj* artistic

künstlich *adj* artificial

Kunststoff *m* synthetic material; **Kunststück** *nt* trick; **Kunstwerk** *nt* work of art

Kupfer (-s, -) *nt* copper

Kuppel (-, -n) *f* dome

kuppeln *vi* (*Auto*) to operate the clutch; **Kupplung** *f* coupling; (*Auto*) clutch

Kur (-, -en) *f* course of treatment; (*am Kurort*) cure

Kür (-, -en) *f* (*Sport*) free programme

Kurbel (-, -n) *f* crank; (*von Rollo, Fenster*) winder

Kürbis (-ses, -se) *m* pumpkin

Kurierdienst *m* courier service

kurieren *vt* to cure

Kurort *m* health resort

Kurs (-es, -e) *m* course; (*Fin*) rate; (*Wechselkurs*) exchange rate

kursiv *adj* italic ▷ *adv* in italics

Kursleiter(in) *m(f)* course tutor; **Kursteilnehmer(in)** *m(f)* (course) participant; **Kurswagen** *m* (*Eisenb*) through carriage

Kurve (-, -n) *f* curve; (*Straßenkurve*) bend; **kurvenreich** *adj* (*Straße*) winding

kurz *adj* short; (*zeitlich a.*) brief; **~ vorher/darauf** shortly before/after; **kannst du ~ kommen?** could you come here for a minute?; **~ gesagt** in short; **kurzärmelig** *adj* short-sleeved; **kürzen** *vt* to cut short; (*in der Länge*) to shorten; (*Gehalt*) to reduce; **kurzerhand** *adv* on the spot; **kurzfristig** *adj* short-term; **das Konzert wurde ~ abgesagt** the concert was called off at short notice; **Kurzgeschichte** *f* short story; **kurzhaarig** *adj* short-haired; **kürzlich** *adv* recently; **Kurzparkzone** *f*

short-stay (*Brit*) (*o* short-term (*US*)) parking zone; **Kurzschluss** *m* (*Elek*) short circuit; **kurzsichtig** *adj* short-sighted; **Kurztrip** *m* trip, break; **Kurzurlaub** *m* short holiday (*Brit*), short vacation (*US*); **Kurzwelle** *f* short wave

Kusine *f* cousin

Kuss (-es, *Küsse*) *m* kiss; **küssen** *vt* to kiss ▷ *vr*: **sich ~** to kiss

Küste (-, -n) *f* coast; (*Ufer*) shore; **Küstenwache** *f* coastguard

Kutsche (-, -n) *f* carriage; (*geschlossene*) coach

Kuvert (-s, -s) *nt* envelope

Kuvertüre (-, -n) *f* coating

Kuwait (-s) *nt* Kuwait

KZ (-s, -s) *nt* *abk* = **Konzentrationslager** (*Hist*) concentration camp

Labor (-s, -e o -s) nt lab

Labyrinth (-s, -e) nt maze

Lache (-, -n) f (Pfütze) puddle; (Blut-, Öl-) pool

lächeln vi to smile; **Lächeln** (-s) nt smile; **lachen** vi to laugh; **lächerlich** adj ridiculous

Lachs (-es, -e) m salmon

Lack (-(e)s, -e) m varnish; (Farblack) lacquer; (an Auto) paint; **lackieren** vt to varnish; (Auto) to spray; **Lackschaden** m scratch (on the paintwork)

Ladegerät nt (battery) charger; **laden** (lud, geladen) vt (a. Inform) to load; (einladen) to invite; (Handy etc) to charge

Laden (-s, Läden) m shop; (Fensterladen) shutter; **Ladendieb(in)** m(f) shoplifter; **Ladendiebstahl** m shoplifting; **Ladenschluss** m closing time

Ladung f load; (Naut, Aviat)

cargo; (Jur) summons sing

lag imperf von **liegen**

Lage (-, -n) f position, situation; (Schicht) layer; **in der ~ sein zu** to be in a position to

Lager (-s, -) nt camp; (Comm) warehouse; (Tech) bearing; **Lagerfeuer** nt campfire; **lagern** vi (Dinge) to be stored; (Menschen) to camp ▷ vt to store

Lagune f lagoon

lahm adj lame; (langweilig) dull; **lähmen** vt to paralyse; **Lähmung** f paralysis

Laib (-s, -e) m loaf

Laie (-n, -n) m layman

Laken (-s, -) nt sheet

Lakritze (-, -n) f liquorice

Lamm (-(e)s, Lämmer) nt lamb

Lampe (-, -n) f lamp; (Glühbirne) bulb; **Lampenfieber** nt stage fright; **Lampenschirm** m lampshade

Lampion (-s, -s) m Chinese lantern

Land (-(e)s, Länder) nt (Gelände) land; (Nation) country; (Bundesland) state, Land; **auf dem ~(e)** in the country

* **LAND**

* A Land (plural **Länder**) is a
* member state of the **BRD**. There
* are 16 **Länder**, namely
* Baden-Württemberg, Bayern,
* Berlin, Brandenburg, Bremen,
* Hamburg, Hessen,
* Mecklenburg-Vorpommern,
* Niedersachsen,
* Nordrhein-Westfalen,
* Rheinland-Pfalz, Saarland,
* Sachsen, Sachsen-Anhalt,
* Schleswig-Holstein and
* Thüringen. Each "Land" has its
* own parliament and
* constitution.

Landebahn f runway; **landen**
vt, vi to land; (Schiff) to dock

Länderspiel nt international
(match)

Landesgrenze f national
border, frontier; **Landesinnere**
nt interior; **landesüblich** adj
customary; **Landeswährung** f
national currency; **landesweit**
adj nationwide

Landhaus nt country house;
Landkarte f map; **Landkreis** m
administrative region, ≈ district

ländlich adj rural

Landschaft f countryside;
(schöne) scenery; (Kunst)
landscape; **Landstraße** f
country road, B road (Brit)

Landung f landing;
Landungsbrücke f,
Landungssteg m gangway

Landwirt(in) m(f) farmer;
Landwirtschaft f agriculture,
farming; **landwirtschaftlich** adj
agricultural

lang adj long; (Mensch) tall; **ein
zwei Meter ~er Tisch** a table two
metres long; **den ganzen Tag ~** all
day long; **die Straße ~** along the
street; **langärmelig** adj
long-sleeved; **lange** adv (for) a
long time; **ich musste ~ warten** I
had to wait (for) a long time; **ich
bleibe nicht ~** I won't stay long; **es
ist ~ her, dass wir uns gesehen
haben** it's a long time since we
saw each other; **Länge** (-, -n) f
length; (Geo) longitude

langen vi (fam: ausreichen) to be
enough; (fam: fassen) to reach (nach
for); **mir langt's** I've had enough

Langeweile f boredom

langfristig adj long-term ▷ adv in
the long term

Langlauf m cross-country skiing

längs prep +gen **die Bäume ~ der
Straße** the trees along(side) the
road ▷ adv: **die Streifen laufen
~ über das Hemd** the stripes run
lengthways down the shirt

langsam adj slow ▷ adv slowly

Langschläfer(in) (-s, -) m(f) late
riser

längst adv: **das ist ~ fertig** that
was finished a long time ago;
sie sollte ~ da sein she should
have been here long ago; **als
sie kam, waren wir ~ weg** when
she arrived we had long since
left

Langstreckenflug m long-haul
flight

Languste (-, -n) f crayfish,
crawfish (US)

langweilen vt to bore; **ich
langweile mich** I'm bored;
langweilig adj boring; **Langwelle**
f long wave

Laos (-) nt Laos

Lappen (-s, -) m cloth, rag;
(Staublappen) duster

läppisch adj silly; (Summe)
ridiculous

Laptop (-s, -s) m laptop

Lärche (-, -n) f larch

Lärm (-(e)s) m noise

las imperf von **lesen**

Lasche (-, -n) f flap

Laser (-s, -) m laser;
Laserdrucker m laser printer

SCHLÜSSELWORT

lassen (pt **ließ**, pp **gelassen** o (als
Hilfsverb) **lassen**) vt 1 (unterlassen)
to stop; (momentan) to leave; **lass
das (sein)!** don't (do it)!; (hör auf!)
stop it!; **lass mich!** leave me alone;
lassen wir das! let's leave it; **er
kann das Trinken nicht lassen** he
can't stop drinking
2 (zurücklassen) to leave; **etw
lassen, wie es ist** to leave sth
(just) as it is

3 (*überlassen*) **jdn ins Haus lassen**
to let sb into the house
▷ *vi* ; **lass mal, ich mache das schon** leave it, I'll do it
▷ *Hilfsverb* **1** (*veranlassen*) **etw machen lassen** to have *o* get sth done; **sich** *dat* **etw schicken lassen** to have sth sent (to one)
2 (*zulassen*) **jdn etw wissen lassen** to let sb know sth; **das Licht brennen lassen** to leave the light on; **jdn warten lassen** to keep sb waiting; **das lässt sich machen** that can be done
3 **lass uns gehen** let's go

lässig *adj* casual
Last (-, *-en*) *f* load; (*Bürde*) burden; (*Naut, Aviat*) cargo
Laster (*-s, -*) *nt* vice; (*fam*) truck, lorry (*Brit*)
lästern *vi*: **über jdn/etw ~** to make nasty remarks about sb/sth
lästig *adj* annoying; (*Person*) tiresome
Last-Minute-Angebot *nt* last-minute offer; **Last-Minute-Flug** *m* last-minute flight; **Last-Minute-Ticket** *nt* last-minute ticket
Lastwagen *m* truck, lorry (*Brit*)
Latein (*-s*) *nt* Latin
Laterne (-, *-n*) *f* lantern; (*Straßenlaterne*) streetlight
Latte (-, *-n*) *f* slat; (*Sport*) bar
Latz (*-es, Lätze*) *m* bib; **Latzhose** *f* dungarees *pl*
lau *adj* (*Wind, Luft*) mild
Laub (*-(e)s*) *nt* foliage; **Laubfrosch** *m* tree frog; **Laubsäge** *f* fretsaw
Lauch (*-(e)s, -e*) *m* leeks *pl*; **eine Stange ~** a leek; **Lauchzwiebel** *f* spring onions *pl* (*Brit*), scallions *pl* (*US*)
Lauf (*-(e)s, Läufe*) *m* run; (*Wettlauf*) race; (*Entwicklung*) course; (*von*

Gewehr) barrel; **Laufbahn** *f* career; **laufen** (*lief, gelaufen*) *vi, vt* to run; (*gehen*) to walk; (*funktionieren*) to work; **mir läuft die Nase** my nose is running; **was läuft im Kino?** what's on at the cinema?; **wie läuft's so?** how are things?; **laufend** *adj* running; (*Monat, Ausgaben*) current; **auf dem Laufenden sein/halten** to be/to keep up-to-date; **Läufer** (*-s, -*) *m* (*Teppich*) rug; (*Schach*) bishop; **Läufer(in)** *m(f)* (*Sport*) runner; **Laufmasche** *f* ladder (*Brit*), run (*US*); **Laufwerk** *nt* (*Inform*) drive
Laune (-, *-n*) *f* mood; **gute/schlechte ~ haben** to be in a good/bad mood; **launisch** *adj* moody
Laus (-, *Läuse*) *f* louse
lauschen *vi* to listen; (*heimlich*) to eavesdrop
laut *adj* loud ▷ *adv* loudly; (*lesen*) aloud ▷ *prep* +*gen o dat* according to
läuten *vt, vi* to ring
lauter *adv* (*fam: nichts als*) nothing but
Lautsprecher *m* loudspeaker; **Lautstärke** *f* loudness; (*Radio, TV*) volume
lauwarm *adj* lukewarm
Lava (-, *Laven*) *f* lava
Lavendel (*-s, -*) *m* lavender
Lawine *f* avalanche
LCD-Anzeige *f* LCD-display
leasen *vt* to lease; **Leasing** (*-s*) *nt* leasing
leben *vt, vi* to live; (*am Leben sein*) to be alive; **wie lange ~ Sie schon hier?** how long have you been living here?; **von ... ~** (*Nahrungsmittel etc*) to live on ...; (*Beruf, Beschäftigung*) to make one's living from ...; **Leben** (*-s, -*) *nt* life; **lebend** *adj* living; **lebendig** *adj* alive; (*lebhaft*) lively;

lebensgefährlich adj very dangerous; (Verletzung) critical;
Lebensgefährte m,
Lebensgefährtin f partner;
Lebenshaltungskosten pl cost sing of living; **lebenslänglich** adj for life; **~ bekommen** to get life;
Lebenslauf m curriculum vitae (Brit), CV (Brit), resumé (US);
Lebensmittel pl food sing;
Lebensmittelgeschäft nt grocer's (shop); **Lebensmittelvergiftung** f food poisoning;
lebensnotwendig adj vital;
Lebensretter(in) m(f) rescuer;
Lebensstandard m standard of living; **Lebensunterhalt** m livelihood; **Lebensversicherung** f life insurance (o assurance (Brit));
Lebenszeichen nt sign of life
Leber (-, -n) f liver; **Leberfleck** m mole; **Leberpastete** f liver pâté
Lebewesen nt living being
lebhaft adj lively; (Erinnerung, Eindruck) vivid; **Lebkuchen** m gingerbread; **ein ~** a piece of gingerbread; **leblos** adj lifeless
Leck nt leak
lecken vi (Loch haben) to leak ▷ vt, vi (schlecken) to lick
lecker adj delicious, tasty
Leder (-s, -) nt leather
ledig adj single
leer adj empty; (Seite) blank; (Batterie) dead; **leeren** vt to empty ▷ vr: **sich ~** to empty;
Leerlauf m (Gang) neutral;
Leertaste f space bar; **Leerung** f emptying; (Briefkasten) collection; **Leerzeichen** nt blank, space
legal adj legal, lawful
legen vt to put, to place; (Eier) to lay ▷ vr: **sich ~** to lie down; (Sturm, Begeisterung) to die down; (Schmerz, Gefühl) to wear off

Legende (-, -n) f legend
leger adj casual
Lehm (-(e)s, -e) m loam; (Ton) clay
Lehne (-, -n) f arm(rest); (Rückenlehne) back(rest); **lehnen** vt to lean ▷ vr: **sich ~** to lean (an/gegen +akk against); **Lehnstuhl** m armchair
Lehrbuch nt textbook; **Lehre** (-, -n) f teaching; (beruflich) apprenticeship; (moralisch) lesson; **lehren** vt to teach; **Lehrer(in)** (-s, -) m(f) teacher; **Lehrgang** m course; **Lehrling** m apprentice; **lehrreich** adj instructive
Leib (-(e)s, -er) m body; **Leibgericht** nt, **Leibspeise** f favourite dish; **Leibwächter(in)** m(f) bodyguard
Leiche (-, -n) f corpse; **Leichenhalle** f mortuary; **Leichenwagen** m hearse
leicht adj light; (einfach) easy, simple; (Erkrankung) slight; **es sich** (dat) **~ machen** to take the easy way out ▷ adv (mühelos, schnell) easily; (geringfügig) slightly; **Leichtathletik** f athletics sing; **leicht|fallen** irr vi: **jdm ~** to be easy for sb; **leichtsinnig** adj careless; (stärker) reckless
leid adj: **jdn/etw ~ sein** to be tired of sb/sth; **Leid** (-(e)s) nt grief, sorrow; **leiden** (litt, gelitten) vi, vt to suffer (an, unter +dat from); **ich kann ihn/es nicht ~** I can't stand him/it; **Leiden** (-s, -) nt suffering; (Krankheit) illness
Leidenschaft f passion; **leidenschaftlich** adj passionate
leider adv unfortunately; **wir müssen jetzt ~ gehen** I'm afraid we have to go now; **~ ja/nein** I'm afraid so/not
leid|tun irr vi: **es tut mir/ihm leid** I'm/he's sorry; **er tut mir leid** I'm sorry for him

Leihbücherei f lending library

leihen (lieh, geliehen) vt: **jdm etw ~** to lend sb sth; **sich** (dat) **etw von jdm ~** to borrow sth from sb; **Leihfrist** f lending period; **Leihgebühr** f hire charge; (für Buch) lending charge; **Leihwagen** m hire car (Brit), rental car (US)

Leim (-(e)s, -e) m glue

Leine (-, -n) f cord; (für Wäsche) line; (Hundeleine) lead (Brit), leash (US)

Leinen (-s, -) nt linen; **Leintuch** nt (für Bett) sheet; **Leinwand** f (Kunst) canvas; (Cine) screen

leise adj quiet; (sanft) soft ▷ adv quietly

Leiste (-, -n) f ledge; (Zierleiste) strip; (Anat) groin

leisten vt (Arbeit) to do; (vollbringen) to achieve; **jdm Gesellschaft ~** to keep sb company; **sich** (dat) **etw ~** (gönnen) to treat oneself to sth; **ich kann es mir nicht ~** I can't afford it

Leistenbruch m hernia

Leistung f performance; (gute) achievement

Leitartikel m leading article (Brit), editorial (US)

leiten vt to lead (Firma) to run; (in eine Richtung) to direct; (Elek) to conduct

Leiter (-, -n) f ladder

Leiter(in) (-s, -) m(f) (von Geschäft) manager

Leitplanke (-, -n) f crash barrier

Leitung f (Führung) direction; (Tel) line; (von Firma) management; (Wasserleitung) pipe; (Kabel) cable; **eine lange ~ haben** to be slow on the uptake; **Leitungswasser** nt tap water

Lektion f lesson

Lektüre (-, -n) f (Lesen) reading; (Lesestoff) reading matter

Lende (-, -n) f (Speise) loin; (vom Rind) sirloin; **die ~n** pl (Med) the lumbar region sing

lenken vt to steer; (Blick) to direct (auf +akk towards); **jds Aufmerksamkeit auf etw** (akk) **~** to draw sb's attention to sth; **Lenker** m (von Fahrrad, Motorrad) handlebars pl; **Lenkrad** nt steering wheel; **Lenkradschloss** nt steering lock; **Lenkstange** f handlebars pl

Leopard (-en, -en) m leopard

Lepra (-) f leprosy

Lerche (-, -n) f lark

lernen vt, vi to learn; (für eine Prüfung) to study, to revise

lesbisch adj lesbian

Lesebuch nt reader; **lesen** (las, gelesen) vi, vt to read; (ernten) to pick; **Leser(in)** m(f) reader; **Leserbrief** m letter to the editor; **leserlich** adj legible; **Lesezeichen** nt bookmark

Lettland nt Latvia

letzte(r, s) adj last; (neueste) latest; (endgültig) final; **zum ~n Mal** for the last time; **am ~n Montag** last Monday; **in ~r Zeit** lately, recently; **letztens** adv (vor kurzem) recently; **letztere(r, s)** adj the latter

Leuchtanzeige f illuminated display; **Leuchte** (-, -n) f lamp, light; **leuchten** vi to shine; (Feuer, Zifferblatt) to glow; **Leuchter** (-s, -) m candlestick; **Leuchtfarbe** f fluorescent colour; (Anstrichfarbe) luminous paint; **Leuchtreklame** f neon sign; **Leuchtstoffröhre** f strip light; **Leuchtturm** m lighthouse

leugnen vt to deny ▷ vi to deny everything

Leukämie f leukaemia (Brit), leukemia (US)

Leukoplast® (-(e)s, -e) nt
Elastoplast® (Brit), Band-Aid®
(US)

Leute pl people pl

Lexikon (-s, Lexika) nt encyclopaedia (Brit), encyclopedia (US);
(Wörterbuch) dictionary

Libanon (-s) m: **der ~** Lebanon

Libelle f dragonfly

liberal adj liberal

Libyen (-s) nt Libya

Licht (-(e)s, -er) nt light;
Lichtblick m ray of hope;
lichtempfindlich adj sensitive to
light; **Lichtempfindlichkeit** f
(Foto) speed; **Lichthupe** f: **die
~ betätigen** to flash one's lights;
Lichtjahr nt light year;
Lichtmaschine f dynamo;
Lichtschalter m light switch;
Lichtschranke f light barrier;
Lichtschutzfaktor m sun
protection factor, SPF

Lichtung f clearing

Lid (-(e)s, -er) nt eyelid;
Lidschatten m eyeshadow

lieb adj (nett) nice; (teuer, geliebt)
dear; (liebenswert) sweet; **das ist
~ von dir** that's nice of you; **Lieber
Herr X** Dear Mr X; **Liebe** (-, -n) f
love; **lieben** vt to love; (sexuell) to
make love to; **liebenswürdig** adj
kind; **lieber** adv rather; **ich
möchte ~ nicht** I'd rather not;
welches ist dir ~? which one do
you prefer?; siehe auch **gern, lieb**;
Liebesbrief m love letter;
Liebeskummer m: **~ haben** to be
lovesick; **Liebespaar** nt lovers pl;
liebevoll adj loving;
Liebhaber(in) (-s, -) m(f) lover;
lieblich adj lovely; (Wein) sweet;
Liebling m darling; (Günstling)
favourite; **Lieblings-** in zW
favourite; **liebste(r, s)** adj
favourite; **liebsten** adv: **am
~ esse ich ...** my favourite food

is ...; **am ~ würde ich bleiben** I'd
really like to stay

Liechtenstein (-s) nt
Liechtenstein

Lied (-(e)s, -er) nt song; (Rel) hymn

lief imperf von **laufen**

Lieferant(in) m(f) supplier

lieferbar adj available

liefern vt to deliver; (beschaffen)
to supply

Lieferschein m delivery note;
Lieferung f delivery;
Lieferwagen m delivery van

Liege (-, -n) f (beim Arzt) couch;
(Notbett) campbed; (Gartenliege)
lounger; **liegen** (lag, gelegen) vi to
lie; (sich befinden) to be; **mir liegt
nichts/viel daran** it doesn't
matter to me/it matters a lot to
me; **woran liegt es nur, dass ...?**
why is it that ...?; **~ bleiben**
(Mensch) to stay lying down; (im
Bett) to stay in bed; (Ding) to be left
(behind); **~ lassen** (vergessen) to
leave behind; **Liegestuhl** m deck
chair; **Liegestütz** m press-up
(Brit), push-up (US); **Liegewagen**
m (Eisenb) couchette car

lieh imperf von **leihen**

ließ imperf von **lassen**

Lift (-(e)s, -e o -s) m lift, elevator
(US)

Liga (-, Ligen) f league, division

light adj (Cola) diet; (fettarm)
low-fat; (kalorienarm) low-calorie;
(Zigaretten) mild

Likör (-s, -e) m liqueur

lila adj inv purple

Lilie f lily

Limette (, -n) f lime

Limo (-, -s) f (fam) fizzy drink
(Brit), soda (US); **Limonade** f
fizzy drink (Brit), soda (US); (mit
Zitronengeschmack) lemonade

Limone (-, -n) f lime

Limousine (-, -n) f saloon (car)
(Brit), sedan (US); (fam) limo

Linde (-, -n) f lime tree

lindern vt to relieve, to soothe

Lineal (-s, -e) nt ruler

Linie f line; **Linienflug** m scheduled flight; **liniert** adj ruled, lined

Link (-s, -s) m (Inform) link

Linke (-n, -n) f left-hand side; (Hand) left hand; (Pol) left (wing), **linke(r, s)** adj left; **auf der -n Seite** on the left, on the left-hand side; **links** adv on the left; **~ abbiegen** to turn left; **~ von** to the left of, **~ oben** at the top left; **Linkshänder(in)** (-s, -) m(f) left-hander; **linksherum** adv to the left, anticlockwise; **Linksverkehr** m driving on the left

Linse (-, -n) f lentil; (optisch) lens

Lippe (-, -n) f lip; **Lipgloss** nt lip gloss; **Lippenstift** m lipstick

lispeln vi to lisp

List (-, -en) f cunning; (Trick) trick

Liste (-, -n) f list

Litauen (-s) nt Lithuania

Liter (-s, -) m or nt litre

literarisch adj literary; **Literatur** f literature

Litschi (-, -s) f lychee, litchi

litt imperf von **leiden**

live adv (Radio, TV) live

Lizenz f licence

Lkw (-(s), -(s)) m abk = **Lastkraftwagen** truck, lorry (Brit); **Lkw-Maut** f heavy goods vehicle toll

Lob (-(e)s) nt praise; **loben** vt to praise

Loch (-(e)s, Löcher) nt hole; **lochen** vt to punch; **Locher** (-s, -) m (hole) punch

Locke (-, -n) f curl; **locken** vt (anlocken) to lure; (Haare) to curl; **Lockenstab** m curling tongs pl (Brit), curling irons pl (US); **Lockenwickler** (-s, -) m curler

locker adj (Schraube, Zahn) loose; (Haltung) relaxed; (Person) easy-going; **das schaffe ich ~** (fam) I'll manage it, no problem; **lockern** vt to loosen ▷ vr: **sich ~** to loosen

lockig adj curly

Löffel (-s, -) m spoon; **einen ~ Mehl zugeben** add a spoonful of flour; **Löffelbiskuit** (-(e)s, -s) m sponge finger

log imperf von **lügen**

Loge (-, -n) f (Theat) box

logisch adj logical

Logo (-s, -s) nt logo

Lohn (-(e)s, Löhne) m reward; (Arbeitslohn) pay, wages pl

lohnen vr: **sich ~** to be worth it; **es lohnt sich nicht zu warten** it's no use waiting

Lohnerhöhung f pay rise (Brit), pay raise (US); **Lohnsteuer** f income tax

Lokal (-(e)s, -e) nt (Gaststätte) restaurant; (Kneipe) pub (Brit), bar

Lokomotive f locomotive

London (-s) nt London

Lorbeer (-s, -en) m laurel; **Lorbeerblatt** nt (Gastr) bay leaf

los adj loose; **~!** go on!; **jdn/etw ~ sein** to be rid of sb/sth; **was ist ~?** what's the matter?, what's up?; **dort ist nichts/viel ~** there's nothing/a lot going on there

Los (-es, -e) nt (Schicksal) lot, fate; (Lotterie etc) ticket

losbinden irr vt to untie

löschen vt (Feuer, Licht) to put out, to extinguish; (Durst) to quench; (Tonband) to erase; (Daten, Zeile) to delete; **Löschtaste** f delete key

lose adj loose

Lösegeld nt ransom

losen vi to draw lots

lösen vt (lockern) to loosen; (Rätsel) to solve; (Chem) to dissolve; (Fahrkarte) to buy ▷ vr: **sich ~** (abgehen) to come off; (Zucker etc) to dissolve; (Problem, Schwierigkeit) to (re)solve itself

los|fahren irr vi to leave; **los|gehen** irr vi to set out; (anfangen) to start; **los|lassen** vt to let go

löslich adj soluble

Lösung f (eines Rätsels, Problems, Flüssigkeit) solution

los|werden irr vt to get rid of

Lotterie f lottery; **Lotto** (-s) nt National Lottery; **~ spielen** to play the lottery

Löwe (-n, -n) m (Zool) lion; (Astr) Leo; **Löwenzahn** m dandelion

Luchs (-es, -e) m lynx

Lücke (-, -n) f gap; **Lückenbüßer(in)** (-s, -) m(f) stopgap

lud imperf von **laden**

Luft (-, Lüfte) f air; (Atem) breath; **Luftballon** m balloon; **Luftblase** f (air) bubble; **luftdicht** adj airtight; **Luftdruck** m (Meteo) atmospheric pressure; (in Reifen) air pressure

lüften vt to air; (Geheimnis) to reveal

Luftfahrt f aviation; **Luftfeuchtigkeit** f humidity; **Luftfilter** m air filter; **Luftfracht** f air freight; **Luftkissenfahrzeug** nt hovercraft; **Luftlinie** f: **10 km ~** 10 km as the crow flies; **Luftmatratze** f airbed; **Luftpirat(in)** m(f) hijacker; **Luftpost** f airmail; **Luftpumpe** f (bicycle) pump; **Luftröhre** f windpipe

Lüftung f ventilation

Luftveränderung f change of air; **Luftverschmutzung** f air pollution; **Luftwaffe** f air force; **Luftzug** m draught (Brit), draft (US)

Lüge (-, -n) f lie; **lügen** (log, gelogen) vi to lie; **Lügner(in)** (-s, -) m(f) liar

Luke (-, -n) f hatch

Lumpen (-s, -) m rag

Lunchpaket nt packed lunch

Lunge (-, -n) f lungs pl; **Lungenentzündung** f pneumonia

Lupe (-, -n) f magnifying glass; **etw unter die ~ nehmen** (fig) to have a close look at sth

Lust (-, Lüste) f joy, delight; (Neigung) desire; **~ auf etw** (akk) **haben** to feel like sth; **~ haben, etw zu tun** to feel like doing sth

lustig adj (komisch) amusing, funny; (fröhlich) cheerful

lutschen vt to suck ▷ vi: **~ an** (+dat) to suck; **Lutscher** (-s, -) m lollipop

Luxemburg (-s) nt Luxembourg

luxuriös adj luxurious

Luxus (-) m luxury

Lymphdrüse f lymph gland; **Lymphknoten** m lymph node

Lyrik (-) f poetry

m

does that make?
5 was macht die Arbeit? how's the work going?; **was macht dein Bruder?** how is your brother doing?; **das Auto machen lassen** to have the car done; **mach's gut!** take care!; (viel Glück) good luck! ▷ vi: **mach schnell!** hurry up!; **Schluss machen** to finish (off); **mach schon!** come on!; **das macht müde** it makes you tired; **in etw** dat **machen** to be o dealing in sth ▷ vr to come along (nicely); **sich an etw** akk **machen** to set about sth; **sich verständlich machen** to make o.s. understood; **sich** dat **viel aus jdm/etw machen** to like sb/sth

Macho (-s, -s) m (fam) macho (type)

Macht (-s, Mächte) f power; **mächtig** adj powerful; (fam: ungeheuer) enormous; **machtlos** adj powerless; **da ist man ~** there's nothing you can do (about it)

Mädchen nt girl; **Mädchenname** m maiden name

Made (-, -n) f maggot

Magazin (-s, -e) nt magazine

Magen (-s, - o Mägen) m stomach; **Magenbeschwerden** pl stomach trouble sing; **Magen-Darm-Infektion** f gastroenteritis; **Magengeschwür** nt stomach ulcer; **Magenschmerzen** pl stomachache sing

mager adj (Fleisch, Wurst) lean; (Person) thin; (Käse, Joghurt) low-fat; **Magermilch** f skimmed milk; **Magersucht** f anorexia; **magersüchtig** adj anorexic

magisch adj magical

Magnet (-s o -en, -en) m magnet

mähen vt, vi to mow

machbar adj feasible

⊙ SCHLÜSSELWORT

machen vt **1** to do; (herstellen, zubereiten) to make; **was machst du da?** what are you doing (there)?; **das ist nicht zu machen** that can't be done; **das Radio leiser machen** to turn the radio down; **aus Holz gemacht** made of wood

2 (verursachen, bewirken) to make; **jdm Angst machen** to make sb afraid; **das macht die Kälte** it's the cold that does this

3 (ausmachen) to matter; **das macht nichts** that doesn't matter; **die Kälte macht mir nichts** I don't mind the cold

4 (kosten, ergeben) to be; **3 und 5 macht 8** 3 and 5 is o are 8; **was** o **wie viel macht das?** how much

mahlen (*mahlte, gemahlen*) *vt* to grind

Mahlzeit *f* meal; (*für Baby*) feed ▷ *interj* (*guten Appetit*) enjoy your meal

Mähne (-, -n) *f* mane

mahnen *vt* to urge; **jdn schriftlich ~** to send sb a reminder; **Mahngebühr** *f* fine; **Mahnung** *f* warning; (*schriftlich*) reminder

Mai (-(s), -e) *m* May; *siehe auch* **Juni**; **Maifeiertag** *m* May Day; **Maiglöckchen** *nt* lily of the valley; **Maikäfer** *m* cockchafer

Mail (-, -s) *f* e-mail; **jdm eine~ schicken** to mail sb, to e-mail sb; **Mailbox** *f* (*Inform*) mailbox; **mailen** *vi*, *vt* to e-mail

Mais (-es, -e) *m* maize, corn (*US*); **Maiskolben** *m* corn cob; (*Gastr*) corn on the cob

Majestät (-, -en) *f* Majesty

Majonäse (-, -n) *f* mayonnaise

Majoran (-s, -e) *m* marjoram

makaber *adj* macabre

Make-up (-s, -s) *nt* make-up

Makler(in) (-s, -) *m(f)* broker; (*Immobilienmakler*) estate agent (*Brit*), Realtor® (*US*)

Makrele (-, -n) *f* mackerel

Makro (-s, -s) *nt* (*Inform*) macro

Makrone (-, -n) *f* macaroon

mal *adv* (*beim Rechnen*) times, multiplied by; (*beim Messen*) by; (*fam: einmal = früher*) once; (*einmal = zukünftig*) some day; **4 ~ 3 ist 12** 4 times 3 is (*o equals*) twelve; **da habe ich ~ gewohnt** I'll go there one day; **irgendwann ~ werde ich dort hinfahren** I'll go there one day; **das ist nun ~ so** well, that's just the way it is (*o goes*); **Mal** (-(e)s, -e) *nt* (*Zeitpunkt*) time; (*Markierung*) mark; **jedes ~** every time; **ein paar ~** a few times; **ein einziges ~** just once

Malaria (-) *f* malaria

Malaysia (-s) *nt* Malaysia

Malbuch *nt* colouring book

Malediven *pl* Maldives *pl*

malen *vt*, *vi* to paint; **Maler(in)** (-s, -) *m(f)* painter; **Malerei** *f* painting; **malerisch** *adj* picturesque

Mallorca (-s) *nt* Majorca, Mallorca

mal|nehmen *irr vt* to multiply (*mit by*)

Malta (-s) *nt* Malta

Malventee *m* mallow tea

Malz (-es) *nt* malt; **Malzbier** *nt* malt beer

Mama (-, -s) *f* mum(my) (*Brit*), mom(my) (*US*)

man *pron* you; (*förmlich*) one; (*jemand*) someone, somebody; (*die Leute*) they, people *pl*; **wie schreibt ~ das?** how do you spell that?; **~ hat ihr das Fahrrad gestohlen** someone stole her bike; **~ sagt, dass ...** they (*o people*) say that ...

Mandant(in) *m(f)* client

Mandarine (-, -n) *f* mandarin, tangerine

Mandel (-, -n) *f* almond; **~n** (*Anat*) tonsils *pl*; **Mandelentzündung** *f* tonsillitis

Manege (-, -n) *f* ring

Mangel (-s, *Mängel*) *m* (*Fehlen*) lack; (*Knappheit*) shortage (*an +dat* of); (*Fehler*) defect, fault; **mangelhaft** *adj* (*Ware*) faulty; (*Schulnote*) ≈ E

Mango (-, -s) *f* mango

Mangold (-s) *m* mangel(wurzel)

Manieren pl manners pl

Maniküre (-, -n) f manicure

manipulieren vt to manipulate

Manko (-s, -s) nt deficiency

Mann (-(e)s, Männer) m man, (Ehemann) husband; **Männchen** nt: **es ist ein ~** (Tier) it's a he; **männlich** adj masculine; (Bio) male

Mannschaft f (Sport, fig) team; (Naut, Aviat) crew

Mansarde (-, -n) f attic

Manschettenknopf m cufflink

Mantel (-s, Mäntel) m coat; (Tech) casing, jacket

Mappe (-, -n) f briefcase; (Aktenmappe) folder

Maracuja (-, -s) f passion fruit

Marathon (-s, -s) m marathon

Märchen nt fairy tale

Marder (-s, -) m marten

Margarine f margarine

Marienkäfer m ladybird (Brit), ladybug (US)

Marihuana nt marijuana

Marille (-, -n) f apricot

Marinade f marinade

Marine f navy

marinieren vt to marinate

Marionette f puppet

Mark (-(e)s) nt (Knochenmark) marrow; (Fruchtmark) pulp

Marke (-, -n) f (Warensorte) brand; (Fabrikat) make; (Briefmarke) stamp; (Essenmarke) voucher, ticket; (aus Metall etc) disc; (Messpunkt) mark; **Markenartikel** m branded item, brand name product; **Markenzeichen** nt trademark

markieren vt to mark; **Markierung** f marking; (Zeichen) mark

Markise (-, -n) f awning

Markt (-(e)s, Märkte) m market; **auf den ~ bringen** to launch; **Markthalle** f covered market;

Marktlücke f gap in the market; **Marktplatz** m market place; **Marktwirtschaft** f market economy

Marmelade f jam; (Orangenmarmelade) marmalade

Marmor (-s, -e) m marble; **Marmorkuchen** m marble cake

Marokko (s) nt Morocco

Marone (-, -n) f chestnut

Mars (-) m Mars

Marsch (-(e)s, Märsche) m march

Märtyrer(in) (-s, -) m(f) martyr

März ((es), -e) m March; siehe auch **Juni**

Marzipan (-s, -e) nt marzipan

Maschine f machine; (Motor) engine, **maschinell** adj mechanical, machine-; **Maschinenbau** m mechanical engineering

Masern pl (Med) measles sing

Maske (-, -n) f mask; **Maskenball** m fancy-dress ball; **maskieren** vr: **sich ~** (Maske aufsetzen) to put on a mask; (verkleiden) to dress up

Maskottchen nt mascot

maß imperf von **messen**

Maß (-es, -e) nt measure; (Mäßigung) moderation; (Grad) degree, extent; **~e** (Person) measurements; (Raum) dimensions; **in gewissem/hohem ~e** to a certain/high degree; **in zunehmendem ~e** increasingly

Mass (-, -(en)) f (Bier) litre of beer

Massage (-, -n) f massage

Masse (-, -n) f mass; (von Menschen) crowd; (Großteil) majority; **massenhaft** adv masses (o loads) of; **am See sind ~ Mücken** there are masses of mosquitoes at the lake; **Massenkarambolage** f pile-up; **Massenmedien** pl mass media pl; **Massenproduktion** f mass

production; **Massentourismus**
m mass tourism
Masseur(in) *m(f)*
masseur/masseuse
maßgeschneidert *adj (Klei-dung)* made-to-measure
massieren *vt* to massage
mäßig *adj* moderate
massiv *adj* solid; *(fig)* massive
maßlos *adj* extreme
Maßnahme (-, -n) *f* measure,
step
Maßstab *m* rule, measure; *(fig)*
standard; **im ~ von 1:5** on a scale
of 1:5
Mast (-(e)s, -e(n)) *m* mast; *(Elek)*
pylon
Material (-s, -ien) *nt* material;
(Arbeitsmaterial) materials *pl*;
materialistisch *adj* materialistic
Materie *f* matter; **materiell** *adj*
material
Mathematik *f* mathematics
sing; **Mathematiker(in)** *m(f)*
mathematician
Matinee (-, -n) *f* = matinee
Matratze (-, -n) *f* mattress
Matrose (-n, -n) *m* sailor
Matsch (-(e)s) *m* mud; *(Schnee)*
slush; **matschig** *adj (Boden)*
muddy; *(Schnee)* slushy; *(Obst)*
mushy
matt *adj* weak; *(glanzlos)* dull;
(Foto) matt; *(Schach)* mate
Matte (-, -n) *f* mat
Matura (-) *f Austrian
school-leaving examination*; =
A-levels *(Brit)*, = High School
Diploma *(US)*
Mauer (-, -n) *f* wall
Maul (-(e)s, *Mäuler*) *nt* mouth;
(fam) gob; **halt's ~!** shut your face
(o gob); **Maulbeere** *f* mulberry;
Maulesel *m* mule; **Maulkorb** *m*
muzzle; **Maul- und Klauenseuche**
f foot-and-mouth disease;
Maulwurf *m* mole

Maurer(in) (-s, -) *m(f)* bricklayer
Mauritius (-) *nt* Mauritius
Maus (-, *Mäuse*) *f* mouse;
Mausefalle *f* mousetrap;
Mausklick (-s, -s) *m* mouse click;
Mauspad (-s, -s) *nt* mouse mat *(o*
pad); **Maustaste** *f* mouse key *(o*
button)
Maut (-, -en) *f* toll; **Mautgebühr**
f toll; **mautpflichtig** *adj*: **~e
Straße** toll road, turnpike *(US)*;
Mautstelle *f* tollbooth, tollgate;
Mautstraße *f* toll road, turnpike
(US)
maximal *adv*: **ihr habt ~ zwei
Stunden Zeit** you've got two
hours at (the) most; **~ vier Leute** a
maximum of four people
Mayonnaise *f siehe* **Majonäse**
Mazedonien (-s) *nt* Macedonia
MB (-, -) *nt*, **Mbyte** (-, -) *nt abk* =
Megabyte MB
Mechanik *f* mechanics *sing*;
(Getriebe) mechanics *pl*;
Mechaniker(in) (-s, -) *m(f)* mechanic;
mechanisch *adj* mechanical;
Mechanismus *m* mechanism
meckern *vi (Ziege)* to bleat; *(fam:
schimpfen)* to moan
Mecklenburg-Vorpommern
(-s) *nt* Mecklenburg-Western
Pomerania
Medaille (-, -n) *f* medal
Medien *pl* media *pl*
Medikament *nt* medicine
Meditation *f* meditation;
meditieren *vi* to meditate
medium *adj (Steak)* medium
Medizin (-, -en) *f* medicine *(gegen
für)*; **medizinisch** *adj* medical
Meer (-(e)s, -e) *nt* sea; **am ~** by
the sea; **Meerenge** *f* straits *pl*;
Meeresfrüchte *f* seafood *sing*;
Meeresspiegel *m* sea level;
Meerrettich *m* horseradish;
Meerschweinchen *nt* guinea
pig; **Meerwasser** *nt* seawater

Megabyte nt megabyte;
Megahertz nt megahertz

Mehl (-(e)s, -e) nt flour;
Mehlspeise f sweet dish made from
flour, eggs and milk

mehr pron, adv more; **~ will ich
nicht ausgeben** I don't want to
spend any more, that's as much as I
want to spend; **was willst du ~?**
what more do you want? ▷ adv:
immer ~ (Leute) more and more
(people); **~ als fünf Minuten** more
than five minutes; **je ~ ..., desto
besser** the more ..., the better; **Ich
kann nicht ~ stehen** I can't stand
any more (o longer); **es ist kein
Brot ~ da** there's no bread left; **nie
~** never again; **mehrdeutig** adj
ambiguous; **mehrere** pron
several; **mehreres** pron several
things; **mehrfach** adj multiple;
(wiederholt) repeated;
Mehrfachstecker m multiple
plug; **Mehrheit** f majority;
mehrmals adv repeatedly;
mehrsprachig adj multilingual;
Mehrwegflasche f returnable
bottle, deposit bottle;
Mehrwertsteuer f value added
tax, VAT; **Mehrzahl** f majority;
(Plural) plural

meiden (mied, gemieden) vt to
avoid

Meile (-, -n) f mile

mein pron (adjektivisch) my;
meine(r, s) pron (substantivisch)
mine

meinen vt, vi (glauben, der Ansicht
sein) to think; (sagen) to say; (sagen
wollen, beabsichtigen) to mean; **das
war nicht so gemeint** I didn't
mean it like that

meinetwegen adv (wegen mir)
because of me; (mir zuliebe) for my
sake; (von mir aus) as far as I'm
concerned

Meinung f opinion; **meiner**

~ nach in my opinion;
Meinungsumfrage f opinion
poll; **Meinungsverschiedenheit**
f disagreement (über +akk about)

Meise (-, -n) f tit; **eine ~ haben**
(fam) to be crazy

Meißel (-s, -) m chisel

meist adv mostly; **meiste(r, s)**
pron (adjektivisch) most; **die ~n**
(Leute) most people; **die ~ Zeit**
most of the time; **das ~** (davon)
most of it; **die ~n von ihnen** most
of them; (substantivisch) most of
them; **am ~n** (the) most;
meistens adv mostly; (zum
größten Teil) for the most part

Meister(in) (-s, -) m(f) master;
(Sport) champion; **Meisterschaft**
f championship; **Meisterwerk**
nt masterpiece

melden vt to report ▷ vr: **sich
~ to report** (bei to); (Schule) to put
one's hand up; (freiwillig) to
volunteer; (auf etw, am Telefon) to
answer; **Meldung** f
announcement; (Bericht) report;
(Inform) message

Melodie f tune, melody

Melone (-, -n) f melon

Memoiren pl memoirs pl

Menge (-, -n) f quantity;
(Menschen) crowd; **eine ~** (große
Anzahl) a lot (gen of);
Mengenrabatt m bulk discount

Meniskus (-, Menisken) m
meniscus

Mensa (-, Mensen) f canteen,
cafeteria (US)

Mensch (-en, -en) m human
being, man; (Person) person; **kein
~** nobody; **~!** (bewundernd) wow!;
(verärgert) bloody hell!;
Menschenmenge f crowd;
Menschenrechte pl human
rights pl; **Menschenverstand** m:
gesunder ~ common sense;
Menschheit f humanity,

mankind; **menschlich** adj
human; (human) humane

Menstruation f menstruation

Mentalität f mentality, mindset

Menthol (-s) nt menthol

Menü (-s, -s) nt set meal; (Inform)
menu; **Menüleiste** f (Inform)
menu bar

Merkblatt nt leaflet; **merken** vt
(bemerken) to notice; **sich** (dat) **etw**
~ to remember sth; **Merkmal** nt
feature

Merkur (-s) m Mercury

merkwürdig adj odd

Messbecher m measuring jug

Messe (-, -n) f fair; (Rel) mass;
Messebesucher(in) m(f) visitor
to a/the fair; **Messegelände** nt
exhibition site

messen (maß, gemessen) vt to
measure; (Temperatur, Puls) to take
▷ vr: **sich** ~ to compete; **sie kann**
sich mit ihm nicht ~ she's no
match for him

Messer (-s, -) nt knife

Messgerät nt measuring device,
gauge

Messing (-s) nt brass

Metall (-s, -e) nt metal

Meteorologe m, **Meteorologin**
f meteorologist

Meter (-s, -) m o nt metre;
Metermaß nt tape measure

Methode (-, -n) f method

Metzger(in) (-s, -) m(f) butcher;
Metzgerei f butcher's (shop)

Mexiko nt Mexico

MEZ f abk = **mitteleuropäische**
Zeit CET

miau interj miaow

mich pron akk von **ich** me;
~ (**selbst**) (reflexiv) myself; **stell**
dich hinter ~ stand behind me;
ich fühle ~ **wohl** I feel fine

mied imperf von **meiden**

Miene (-, -n) f look, expression

mies adj (fam) lousy

Miesmuschel f mussel

Mietauto nt siehe **Mietwagen**

Miete (-, -n) f rent; **mieten** vt to
rent; (Auto) to hire (Brit), to rent
(US); **Mieter(in)** (-s, -) m(f)
tenant; **Mietshaus** nt block of
flats (Brit), apartment house (US);
Mietvertrag m rental
agreement; **Mietwagen** m hire
car (Brit), rental car (US); **sich** (dat)
einen ~ **nehmen** to hire (Brit) (o
rent (US)) a car

Migräne (-, -n) f migraine

Migrant(in) (-en, -en) m(f)
migrant (worker)

Mikrofon (-s, -e) nt microphone

Mikrowelle (-, -n) f.
Mikrowellenherd m microwave
(oven)

Milch (-) f milk; **Milcheis** nt
ice-cream (made with milk);
Milchglas nt (dickes, trübes Glas)
frosted glass; **Milchkaffee** m
milky coffee; **Milchprodukte** pl
dairy products pl; **Milchpulver** nt
powdered milk; **Milchreis** m rice
pudding; **Milchshake** m milk
shake; **Milchstraße** f Milky Way

mild adj mild; (Richter) lenient;
(freundlich) kind

Militär (-s) nt military, army

Milliarde (-, -n) f billion;
Milligramm nt milligram;
Milliliter m millilitre; **Millimeter**
m millimetre; **Million** f million;
Millionär(in) m(f) millionaire

Milz (-, -en) f spleen

Mimik f facial expression(s)

Minderheit f minority

minderjährig adj underage

minderwertig adj inferior;
Minderwertigkeitskomplex m
inferiority complex

Mindest- in zW minimum;
mindeste(r, s) adj least;
mindestens adv at least;
Mindesthaltbarkeitsdatum nt

best-before date, sell-by date
(Brit)

Mine (-, -n) f mine; (Bleistift) lead;
(Kugelschreiber) refill

Mineralwasser nt mineral
water

Minibar f minibar; **Minigolf** nt
miniature golf, crazy golf (Brit)

minimal adj minimal

Minimum (-s, Minima) nt
minimum

Minirock m miniskirt

Minister(in) (-s, -) m(f) minister;
Ministerium nt ministry;
Ministerpräsident(in) m(f) (von
Bundesland) Minister President
(Prime Minister of a Bundesland)

minus adv minus; **Minus** (-, -) nt
deficit; **im ~ sein** to be in the red;
(Konto) to be overdrawn

Minute (-, -n) f minute

Minze (-, -n) f mint

Mio. nt abk von **Million(en)** m

mir pron dat von **ich** (to) me;
kannst du ~ helfen? can you help
me?; **kannst du es ~ erklären?** can
you explain it to me?; **ich habe
~ einen neuen Rechner gekauft** I
bought (myself) a new computer;
ein Freund von ~ a friend of mine

Mirabelle (-, -n) f mirabelle
(small yellow plum)

mischen vt to mix; (Karten) to
shuffle; **Mischmasch** m (fam)
hotchpotch; **Mischung** f
mixture (aus of)

missachten vt to ignore;
Missbrauch m abuse; (falscher
Gebrauch) misuse; **missbrauchen**
vt to misuse (zu for); (sexuell) to
abuse; **Misserfolg** m failure;
Missgeschick nt (Panne) mishap;
misshandeln vt to ill-treat

Mission f mission

misslingen (misslang, misslungen)
vi to fail; **der Versuch ist mir
misslungen** my attempt failed;

misstrauen vt +dat to distrust;
Misstrauen (-s) nt mistrust,
suspicion (gegenüber of);
misstrauisch adj distrustful;
(argwöhnisch) suspicious;

Missverständnis nt misunderstanding; **missverstehen** irr vt
to misunderstand

Mist (-(e)s) m (fam) rubbish; (von
Kühen) dung; (als Dünger) manure

Mistel (-, -n) f mistletoe

mit prep +dat with; (mittels) by;
~ der Bahn by train; **~ der
Kreditkarte bezahlen** to pay
by credit card; **~ 10 Jahren** at the
age of 10; **wie wärs ~ ...?** how
about ...? ▷ adv along, too; **wollen
Sie ~?** do you want to come along!

Mitarbeiter(in) m(f) (Angestellter) employee; (an Projekt)
collaborator; (freier) freelancer

mitbekommen irr vt (fam:
aufschnappen) to catch; (hören) to
hear; (verstehen) to get

mitbenutzen vt to share

Mitbewohner(in) m(f) (in
Wohnung) flatmate (Brit),
roommate (US)

mitbringen irr vt to bring
along; **Mitbringsel** (-s, -) nt small
present

miteinander adv with one
another; (gemeinsam) together

miterleben vt to see (with one's
own eyes)

Mitesser (-s, -) m blackhead

Mitfahrgelegenheit f = lift,
ride (US); **Mitfahrzentrale** f
agency for arranging lifts

mitgeben irr vt: **jdm etw ~** to
give sb sth (to take along)

Mitgefühl nt sympathy

mitgehen irr vi to go/come
along

mitgenommen adj worn out,
exhausted

Mitglied nt member

mithilfe *prep +gen* **- von** with the help of

mit|kommen *irr vi* to come along; *(verstehen)* to follow

Mitleid *nt* pity; **- haben mit** to feel sorry for

mit|machen *vt* to take part in ▷ *vi* to take part

mit|nehmen *irr vt* to take along; *(anstrengen)* to wear out, to exhaust

mit|schreiben *irr vi* to take notes ▷ *vt* to take down

Mitschüler(in) *m(f)* schoolmate

mit|spielen *vi* *(in Mannschaft)* to play; *(bei Spiel)* to join in; **in einem Film/Stück -** to act in a film/play

Mittag *m* midday; **gestern -** at midday yesterday, yesterday lunchtime; **über -** geschlossen closed at lunchtime; **zu - essen** to have lunch; **Mittagessen** *nt* lunch; **mittags** *adv* at lunchtime, at midday; **Mittagspause** *f* lunch break

Mitte *(-, -n)* *f* middle; **- Juni** in the middle of June; **sie ist - zwanzig** she's in her mid-twenties

mit|teilen *vt*: **jdm etw -** to inform sb of sth; **Mitteilung** *f* notification

Mittel *(-s -)* *nt* means *sing*; *(Maßnahme, Methode)* method; *(Med)* remedy *(gegen* for); **das ist ein gutes -, (um) junge Leute zu erreichen** that's a good way of engaging with young people

Mittelalter *nt* Middle Ages *pl*; **mittelalterlich** *adj* medieval; **Mittelamerika** *nt* Central America; **Mitteleuropa** *nt* Central Europe; **Mittelfeld** *nt* midfield; **Mittelfinger** *m* middle finger; **mittelmäßig** *adj* mediocre; **Mittelmeer** *nt* Mediterranean (Sea);

Mittelohrentzündung *f* inflammation of the middle ear; **Mittelpunkt** *m* centre; **im - stehen** to be the centre of attention

mittels *prep +gen* by means of

Mittelstreifen *m* central reservation *(Brit)*, median *(US)*; **Mittelstürmer(in)** *m(f)* striker, centre-forward; **Mittelwelle** *f* medium wave

mitten *adv* in the middle; **- auf der Straße/in der Nacht** in the middle of the street/night

Mitternacht *f* midnight

mittlere(r, s) *adj* middle; *(durchschnittlich)* average

mittlerweile *adv* meanwhile

Mittwoch *(-s, -e)* *m* Wednesday; **(am) -** on Wednesday; **(am) - Morgen/Nachmittag/Abend** (on) Wednesday morning/afternoon/evening; **diesen/letzten/nächsten -** this/last/next Wednesday; **jeden -** every Wednesday; **- in einer Woche** a week on Wednesday, Wednesday week; **mittwochs** *adv* on Wednesdays; **- abends** *(jeden Mittwochabend)* on Wednesday evenings

mixen *vt* to mix; **Mixer** *(-s, -)* *m* *(Küchengerät)* blender

MKS *f abk* = **Maul- und Klauenseuche** FMD

mobben *vt* to harass *(o* to bully) (at work)

Mobbing *(-s)* *nt* workplace bullying *(o* harassment)

Möbel *(-s, -)* *nt* piece of furniture; **die - pl** the furniture *sing*; **Möbelwagen** *m* removal van

mobil *adj* mobile

Mobilfunknetz *nt* cellular network; **Mobiltelefon** *nt* mobile phone

möblieren *vt* to furnish

mochte _imperf von_ **mögen**

Mode (-, -n) _f_ fashion

Model (-s, -s) _nt_ model

Modell (-s, -e) _nt_ model

Modem (-s, -s) _nt_ (_Inform_) modem

Mode(n)schau _f_ fashion show

Moderator(in) _m(f)_ presenter

modern _adj_ modern; (_modisch_) fashionable

Modeschmuck _m_ costume jewellery; **modisch** _adj_ fashionable

Modus (-, _Modi_) _m_ (_Inform_) mode; (_fig_) way

Mofa (-s, -s) _nt_ moped

mogeln _vi_ to cheat

⭕ **SCHLÜSSELWORT**

mögen (_pt_ **mochte**, _pp_ **gemocht** _o_ (_als Hilfsverb_) **mögen**) _vt, vi_ to like; **magst du/mögen Sie ihn?** do you like him?; **ich möchte ...** I would like ..., I'd like ...; **er möchte in die Stadt** he'd like to go into town; **ich möchte nicht, dass du ...** I wouldn't like you to ...; **ich mag nicht mehr** I've had enough ▷ _Hilfsverb_ to like to; (_wollen_) to want; **möchtest du etwas essen?** would you like something to eat?; **sie mag nicht bleiben** she doesn't want to stay; **das mag wohl sein** that may well be; **was mag das heißen?** what might that mean?; **Sie möchten zu Hause anrufen** could you please call home?

möglich _adj_ possible; **so bald wie ~** as soon as possible; **möglicherweise** _adv_ possibly; **Möglichkeit** _f_ possibility; **möglichst** _adv_ as ... as possible

Mohn (-(e)s, -e) _m_ (_Blume_) poppy; (_Samen_) poppy seed

Möhre (-, -n) _f_, **Mohrrübe** _f_ carrot

Mokka (-s, -s) _m_ mocha

Moldawien (-s) _nt_ Moldova

Molkerei (-, -en) _f_ dairy

Moll (-) _nt_ minor (key); **a-~** A minor

mollig _adj_ cosy; (_dicklich_) plump

Moment (-(e)s, -e) _m_ moment; **im ~** at the moment; **einen ~ bitte!** just a minute; **momentan** _adj_ momentary ▷ _adv_ at the moment

Monaco (-s) _nt_ Monaco

Monarchie _f_ monarchy

Monat (-(e)s, -e) _m_ month; **sie ist im dritten ~** (_schwanger_) she's three months pregnant; **monatlich** _adj, adv_ monthly; **~ 100 Euro zahlen** to pay 100 euros a month (_o_ every month); **Monatskarte** _f_ monthly season ticket

Mönch (-s, -e) _m_ monk

Mond (-(e)s, -e) _m_ moon; **Mondfinsternis** _f_ lunar eclipse

Mongolei (-) _f_: **die ~** Mongolia

Monitor _m_ (_Inform_) monitor

monoton _adj_ monotonous

Monsun (-s, -e) _m_ monsoon

Montag _m_ Monday; _siehe auch_ **Mittwoch**; **montags** _adv_ on Mondays; _siehe auch_ **mittwochs**

Montenegro (-s) _nt_ Montenegro

Monteur(in) (-s, -e) _m(f)_ fitter; **montieren** _vt_ to assemble, to set up

Monument _nt_ monument

Moor (-(e)s, -e) _nt_ moor

Moos (-es, -e) _nt_ moss

Moped (-s, -s) _nt_ moped

Moral (-) _f_ (_Werte_) morals _pl_; (_einer Geschichte_) moral; **moralisch** _adj_ moral

Mord (-(e)s, -e) _m_ murder;

Mörder(in) (-s, -) m(f) murderer/murderess

morgen adv tomorrow; ~ **früh** tomorrow morning

Morgen (-s, -) m morning; **am** ~ in the morning; **Morgenmantel** m, **Morgenrock** m dressing gown; **Morgenmuffel** m: **er ist ein** ~ he's not a morning person; **morgens** adv in the morning; **um 3 Uhr** ~ at 3 (o'clock) in the morning, at 3 am

Morphium (-s) nt morphine

morsch adj rotten

Mosaik (-s, -e(n)) nt mosaic

Mosambik (-s) nt Mozambique

Moschee (-, -n) f mosque

Moskau (-s) nt Moscow

Moskito (-s, -s) m mosquito; **Moskitonetz** nt mosquito net

Moslem (-s, -s) m, **Moslime** (-, -n) f Muslim

Most (-(e)s, -e) m (unfermented) fruit juice; (Apfelwein) cider

Motel (-s, -s) nt motel

motivieren vt to motivate

Motor m engine; (Elek) motor; **Motorboot** nt motorboat; **Motorenöl** nt engine oil; **Motorhaube** f bonnet (Brit), hood (US); **Motorrad** nt motorbike, motorcycle; **Motorradfahrer(in)** m(f) motorcyclist; **Motorroller** m (motor) scooter; **Motorschaden** m engine trouble

Motte (-, -n) f moth

Motto (-s, -s) nt motto

Mountainbike (-s, -s) nt mountain bike

Möwe (-, -n) f (sea)gull

MP3-Player (-s, -) m MP3 player

Mrd. f abk = **Milliarde(n)**

MS (-) f abk = **multiple Sklerose** MS

Mücke (-, -n) f midge; (tropische) mosquito; **Mückenstich** m mosquito bite

müde adj tired

muffig adj (Geruch) musty; (Gesicht, Mensch) grumpy

Mühe (-, -n) f trouble, pains pl; **sich** (dat) **große ~ geben** to go to a lot of trouble

muhen vi to moo

Mühle (-, -n) f mill; (Kaffeemühle) grinder

Müll (-(e)s) m rubbish (Brit), garbage (US); **Müllabfuhr** f rubbish (Brit) (o garbage (US)) disposal

Mullbinde f gauze bandage

Müllcontainer m waste container; **Mülldeponie** f rubbish (Brit) (o garbage (US)) dump; **Mülleimer** m rubbish bin (Brit), garbage can (US); **Mülltonne** f dustbin (Brit), garbage can (US); **Mülltrennung** f sorting and collecting household waste according to type of material; **Müllverbrennungsanlage** f incineration plant; **Müllwagen** m dustcart (Brit), garbage truck (US)

multikulturell adj multicultural

Multimedia- in zW multimedia

Multiple-Choice-Verfahren nt multiple choice

multiple Sklerose (-n, -n) f multiple sclerosis

Multiplexkino nt multiplex (cinema)

multiplizieren vt to multiply (mit by)

Mumie f mummy

Mumps (-) m mumps sing

München (-s) nt Munich

Mund (-(e)s, Münder) m mouth; **halt den ~!** shut up; **Mundart** f dialect; **Munddusche** f dental water jet

münden vi to flow (in +akk into)

Mundgeruch m bad breath; **Mundharmonika** (-, -s) f mouth organ

mündlich adj oral
Mundschutz m mask;
 Mundwasser nt mouthwash
Munition f ammunition
Münster (-s, -) nt minster,
 cathedral
munter adj lively
Münzautomat m vending
 machine; **Münze** (-, -n) f coin;
 Münzeinwurf m slot;
 Münzrückgabe f coin return;
 Münztelefon nt pay phone;
 Münzwechsler m change
 machine
murmeln vt, vi to murmur, to
 mutter
Murmeltier nt marmot
mürrisch adj sullen, grumpy
Mus (-es, -e) nt puree
Muschel (-, -n) f mussel; (~schale)
 shell
Museum (-s, Museen) nt
 museum
Musical (-s, -s) nt musical
Musik f music; **musikalisch** adj
 musical; **Musiker(in)** (-s, -) m(f)
 musician; **Musikinstrument** nt
 musical instrument; **musizieren**
 vi to play music
Muskat (-(e)s) m nutmeg
Muskel (-s, -n) m muscle;
 Muskelkater m: ~ **haben** to be
 stiff; **Muskelriss** m torn muscle;
 Muskelzerrung f pulled muscle;
 muskulös adj muscular
Müsli (-s, -) nt muesli
Muslim(in) (-s, -s) m(f) Muslim
Muss (-) nt must

○ **SCHLÜSSELWORT**

müssen (pt musste, pp gemusst
 o (als Hilfsverb) müssen) vi
 1 (Zwang) must; (nur im Präsens) to
 have to; **ich muss es tun** I must do
 it, I have to do it; **ich musste es
 tun** I had to do it; **er muss es**

nicht tun he doesn't have to do it;
 muss ich? must I?, do I have to?;
 wann müsst ihr zur Schule?
 when do you have to go to
 school?; **er hat gehen müssen** he
 (has) had to go; **muss das sein?** is
 that really necessary?; **ich muss
 mal** (fam) I need the toilet
 2 (sollen) **das musst du nicht tun!**
 you oughtn't to o shouldn't do
 that; **Sie hätten ihn fragen
 müssen** you should have asked
 him
 3 **es muss geregnet haben** it
 must have rained; **es muss nicht
 wahr sein** it needn't be true

Muster (-s, -) nt (Dessin) pattern,
 design; (Probe) sample; (Vorbild)
 model; **mustern** vt to have a
 close look at; **jdn ~** to look sb up
 and down
Mut (-(e)s) m courage; **jdm
 ~ machen** to encourage sb; **mutig**
 adj brave, courageous
Mutter (-, Mütter) f mother
 ▷ (-, -n) f (Schraubenmutter) nut;
 Muttersprache f mother
 tongue; **Muttertag** m Mother's
 Day; **Mutti** f mum(my) (Brit),
 mom(my) (US)
mutwillig adj deliberate
Mütze (-, -n) f cap
MwSt. abk = **Mehrwertsteuer**
 VAT
Myanmar (-s) nt Myanmar

n

SCHLÜSSELWORT

N *abk* = **Nord** N

na *interj*: ~ **also!**, ~ **bitte!** see?, what did I tell you?; ~ **ja** well; ~ **und?** so what?

Nabel (-s, -) *m* navel

nach *prep* +dat **1** (*örtlich*) to; **nach Berlin** to Berlin; **nach links/rechts** (to the) left/right; **nach oben/hinten** up/back **2** (*zeitlich*) after; **einer nach dem anderen** one after the other; **nach Ihnen!** after you!; **zehn (Minuten) nach drei** ten (minutes) past three **3** (*gemäß*) according to; **nach dem Gesetz** according to the law; **dem Namen nach** judging by his/her name; **nach allem, was ich weiß** as far as I know

▷ *adv*: **ihm nach!** after him!; **nach und nach** gradually, little by little; **nach wie vor** still

nach|ahmen *vt* to imitate

Nachbar(in) (-n, -n) *m(f)* neighbour; **Nachbarschaft** *f* neighbourhood

nach|bestellen *vt* to order some more

nachdem *conj* after; (*weil*) since; **je ~ (ob/wie)** depending on (whether/how)

nach|denken *irr vi* to think (*über* +akk about); **nachdenklich** *adj* thoughtful

nacheinander *adv* one after another (o the other)

Nachfolger(in) (-s, -) *m(f)* successor

nach|forschen *vt* to investigate

Nachfrage *f* inquiry; (*Comm*) demand; **nach|fragen** *vi* to inquire

nach|geben *irr vi* to give in (*jdm* to sb)

Nachgebühr *f* surcharge; (*für Briefe etc*) excess postage

nach|gehen *irr vi* to follow (*jdm* sb); (*erforschen*) to inquire (*einer Sache dat* into sth); **die Uhr geht (zehn Minuten) nach** this watch is (ten minutes) slow

nachher *adv* afterwards; **bis ~!** see you later

Nachhilfe *f* extra tuition

nach|holen *vt* to catch up with; (*Versäumtes*) to make up for

nach|kommen *irr vi* to follow; **einer Verpflichtung** (*dat*) ~ to fulfil an obligation

nach|lassen *irr vt* (*Summe*) to take off ▷ *vi* to decrease, to ease off; (*schlechter werden*) to deteriorate; **nachlässig** *adj* negligent, careless

nach|laufen *irr vi* to run after, to chase (*jdm* sb)

nach|lösen vt: **eine Fahrkarte ~** to buy a ticket on the bus/train
nach|machen vt to imitate, to copy (jdm etw sth from sb); (fälschen) to counterfeit
Nachmittag m afternoon; **heute ~** this afternoon; **am ~** in the afternoon; **nachmittags** adv in the afternoon; **um 3 Uhr ~** at 3 (o'clock) in the afternoon, at 3 pm
Nachnahme (-, -n) f cash on delivery; **per ~** COD
Nachname m surname
nach|prüfen vt to check
nach|rechnen vt to check
Nachricht (-, -en) f (piece of) news sing; (Mitteilung) message; **Nachrichten** pl news sing
Nachsaison f off-season
nach|schauen vi: **jdm ~** to gaze after sb ⊳ vt (prüfen) to check
nach|schicken vt to forward
nach|schlagen irr vt to look up
nach|sehen irr vt (prüfen) to check
Nachspeise f dessert
nächstbeste(r, s) adj: **der ~ Zug/Job** the first train/job that comes along; **nächste(r, s)** adj next; (nächstgelegen) nearest
Nacht (-, Nächte) f night; **in der ~** during the night; (bei Nacht) at night; **Nachtclub** m nightclub; **Nachtdienst** m night duty; **~ haben** (Apotheke) to be open all night
Nachteil m disadvantage
Nachtflug m night flight; **Nachtfrost** m overnight frost; **Nachthemd** nt (für Damen) nightdress; (für Herren) nightshirt
Nachtigall (-, -en) f nightingale
Nachtisch m dessert, sweet (Brit), pudding (Brit); **Nachtleben** nt nightlife

nach|tragen irr vt: **jdm etw ~** (übel nehmen) to hold sth against sb
nachträglich adv: **~ alles Gute zum Geburtstag!** Happy belated birthday
nachts adv at night; **um 11 Uhr ~** at 11 (o'clock) at night, at 11 pm; **um 2 Uhr ~** at 2 (o'clock) in the morning, at 2 am; **Nachtschicht** f night shift; **Nachttarif** m off-peak rate; **Nachttisch** m bedside table; **Nachtzug** m night train
Nachweis (-es, -e) m proof
Nachwirkung f after-effect
nach|zahlen vi to pay extra ⊳ vt: **20 Euro ~** to pay 20 euros extra
nach|zählen vt to check
Nacken (-s, -) m (nape of the) neck
nackt adj naked; (Tatsachen) plain, bare; **Nacktbadestrand** m nudist beach
Nadel (-, -n) f needle; (Stecknadel) pin; **Nadelstreifen** pl pinstripes pl
Nagel (-s, Nägel) m nail; **Nagelbürste** f nail brush; **Nagelfeile** f nail-file; **Nagellack** m nail varnish (o polish); **Nagellackentferner** (-s, -) m nail-varnish (o nail-polish) remover; **Nagelschere** f nail scissors pl
nah(e) adj, adv (räumlich) near(by); (zeitlich) near; (Verwandte, Freunde) close; **Nähe** (-) f (Umgebung) vicinity; **in der ~** nearby; **in der ~ von** near to; **nahe|gehen** irr vi: **jdm ~** to upset sb; **nahe|legen** vt: **jdm etw ~** to suggest sth to sb; **nahe|liegen** irr vi to be obvious ⊳ prep +dat near (to), close to
nähen vt, vi to sew
nähere(r, s) adj (Erklärung, Erkundung) more detailed; **die ~ Umgebung** the immediate area;

Nähere(s) nt details pl; **nähern**
vr: **sich** ~ to approach
nahezu adv virtually, almost
nahm imperf von **nehmen**
Nähmaschine f sewing
machine
nahrhaft adj nourishing,
nutritious; **Nahrung** f food;
Nahrungsmittel nt food
Naht (-, **Nähte**) f seam; (Med)
stitches pl, suture; (Tech) join
Nahverkehr m local traffic;
Nahverkehrszug m local train
Nähzeug nt sewing kit
naiv adj naive
Name (-ns, -n) m name
nämlich adv that is to say,
namely; (denn) since
nannte imperf von **nennen**
Napf (-(e)s, **Näpfe**) m bowl, dish
Narbe (-, -n) f scar
Narkose (-, -n) f anaesthetic
Narzisse (-, -n) f narcissus
naschen vt, vi to nibble;
Naschkatze f (fam) nibbler; **eine**
~ sein to have a sweet tooth
Nase (-, -n) f nose; **Nasenbluten**
(-s) nt nosebleed; **~ haben** to
have a nosebleed; **Nasenloch** nt
nostril; **Nasentropfen** pl nose
drops pl
Nashorn nt rhinoceros
nass adj wet; **Nässe** (-) f
wetness; **nässen** vi (Wunde) to
weep
Nation (-, -en) f nation; **national**
adj national; **Nationalfeiertag** m
national holiday; **Nationalhymne**
(-, -n) f national anthem;
Nationalität f nationality;
Nationalmannschaft f national
team; **Nationalpark** m National
Park; **Nationalspieler(in)** m(f)
international (player)
NATO (-) f abk = **North Atlantic**
Treaty Organization NATO, Nato
Natur f nature; **Naturkost** f

health food; **natürlich** adj natural
▷ adv naturally; (selbstverständlich)
of course; **Naturpark** m nature
reserve; **naturrein** adj natural,
pure; **Naturschutz** m
conservation; **Naturschutzgebiet**
nt nature reserve; **Naturwissen-**
schaft f (natural) science;
Naturwissenschaftler(in) m(f)
scientist
Navigationssystem nt (Auto)
navigation system
n. Chr. abk = **nach Christus** AD
Nebel (-s, -) m fog, mist; **neblig**
adj foggy, misty; **Nebelschein-**
werfer m foglamp; **Nebelschluss-**
leuchte f (Auto) rear foglight
neben prep +akk o dat next to;
(außer) apart from, besides;
nebenan adv next door;
Nebenausgang m side exit;
nebenbei adv at the same time;
(außerdem) additionally; (beiläufig)
incidentally; **nebeneinander** adv
side by side; **Nebeneingang** m
side entrance; **Nebenfach** nt
subsidiary subject
nebenher adv (zusätzlich)
besides; (gleichzeitig) at the same
time; (daneben) alongside
Nebenkosten pl extra charges
pl, extras pl; **Nebensache** f
minor matter; **nebensächlich**
adj minor; **Nebensaison** f low
season; **Nebenstraße** f side
street; **Nebenwirkung** f side
effect
neblig adj foggy, misty
necken vt to tease
Neffe (-n, -n) m nephew
negativ adj negative; **Negativ**
nt (Foto) negative
nehmen (nahm, genommen) vt to
take; **wie man's nimmt** it
depends on how you look at it;
den Bus/Zug ~ to take the
bus/train; **jdn/etw ernst ~** to

take sb/sth seriously; **etw zu sich ~** to eat sth; **jdn zu sich ~** to have sb come and live with one; **jdn an die Hand ~** to take sb by the hand

neidisch adj envious

neigen vi: **zu etw ~** to tend towards sth; **Neigung** f (des Geländes) slope; (Tendenz) inclination; (Vorliebe) liking

nein adv no

Nektarine f nectarine

Nelke (-, -n) f carnation; (Gewürz) clove

nennen (nannte, genannt) vt to name; (mit Namen) to call

Neonazi (-s, -s) m neo-Nazi

Nepal (-s) nt Nepal

Neptun (-s) m Neptune

Nerv (-s, -en) m nerve; **jdm auf die ~en gehen** to get on sb's nerves; **nerven** vt: **jdn ~** (fam) to get on sb's nerves; **Nerven-zusammenbruch** m nervous breakdown; **nervös** adj nervous

Nest (-(e)s, -er) nt nest; (pej: Ort) dump

nett adj nice; (freundlich) kind; **sei so ~ und ...** do me a favour and ...

netto adv net

Netz (-es, -e) nt (für Einkauf) string bag; (System) network; (Stromnetz) mains, power (US); **Netzanschluss** m mains connection; **Netzbetreiber(in)** m(f) network operator; (Inform) Internet (o Net) provider; **Netzgerät** nt power pack; **Netzkarte** f season ticket; **Netzwerk** nt (Inform) network; **Netzwerkkarte** f network card

neu adj new; (Sprache, Geschichte) modern; **die ~esten Nachrichten** the latest news; **Neubau** m new building; **neuerdings** adv recently; **Neueröffnung** f (Geschäft) new business;

Neuerung f innovation; (Reform) reform

Neugier f curiosity; **neugierig** adj curious (auf +akk about); **ich bin ~, ob ...** I wonder whether (o if) ...; **ich bin ~, was du dazu sagst** I'll be interested to hear what you have to say about it

Neuheit f novelty; **Neuigkeit** f news sing; **eine ~** a piece of news; **Neujahr** nt New Year; **prosit ~!** Happy New Year; **neulich** adv recently, the other day; **Neumond** m new moon

neun num nine; **neunhundert** num nine hundred; **neunmal** adv nine times; **neunte(r, s)** adj ninth; siehe auch **dritte**, **Neuntel** (-s, -) nt ninth; **neunzehn** num nineteen; **neunzehnte(r, s)** adj nineteenth; siehe auch **dritte**; **neunzig** num ninety; **in den ~er Jahren** in the nineties; **Neunzigerjahre** pl nineties pl; **neunzigste(r, s)** adj ninetieth

neureich adj nouveau riche

Neurologe m, **Neurologin** f neurologist; **Neurose** (-, -n) f neurosis; **neurotisch** adj neurotic

Neuseeland nt New Zealand

Neustart m (Inform) restart, reboot

neutral adj neutral

neuwertig adj nearly new

Nicaragua (-s) nt Nicaragua

O SCHLÜSSELWORT

nicht adv **1** (Verneinung) not; **er ist es nicht** it's not him, it isn't him; **er raucht nicht** (gerade) he isn't smoking; (gewöhnlich) he doesn't smoke; **ich kann das nicht — ich auch nicht** I can't do it — neither o nor can I; **es regnet nicht mehr** it's not raining any more, **nicht rostend** stainless

2 (*Bitte, Verbot*) **nicht!** don't!, no!;
nicht berühren! do not touch!;
nicht doch! don't!
3 (*rhetorisch*) **du bist müde, nicht
(wahr)?** you're tired, aren't you?;
das ist schön, nicht (wahr)? it's
nice, isn't it?
4 was du nicht sagst! the things
you say!

Nichte (-, -n) *f* niece
Nichtraucher(in) *m(f)* non-
smoker; **Nichtraucherabteil** *nt*
non-smoking compartment;
Nichtraucherzone *f* non-
smoking area
nichts *pron* nothing; **für ~ und
wieder ~** for nothing at all; **ich
habe ~ gesagt** I didn't say
anything; **macht ~** never mind
Nichtschwimmer(in) *m(f)*
non-swimmer
nichtssagend *adj* meaningless
nicken *vi* to nod
Nickerchen *nt* nap
nie *adv* never; **~ wieder** (*o mehr*)
never again; **fast ~** hardly ever
nieder *adj* (*niedrig*) low; (*gering*)
inferior ▷ *adv* down;
niedergeschlagen *adj* depressed;
Niederlage *f* defeat
Niederlande *pl* Netherlands *pl*;
Niederländer(in) *m(f)* Dutch-
man/Dutchwoman;
niederländisch *adj* Dutch;
Niederländisch *nt* Dutch
Niederlassung *f* branch
Niederösterreich *nt* Lower
Austria; **Niedersachsen** *nt*
Lower Saxony
Niederschlag *m* (*Meteo*)
precipitation; (*Regen*) rainfall
niedlich *adj* sweet, cute
niedrig *adj* low; (*Qualität*)
inferior
niemals *adv* never
niemand *pron* nobody, no one;

ich habe ~en gesehen I haven't
seen anyone; **~ von ihnen** none of
them
Niere (-, -n) *f* kidney;
Nierenentzündung *f* kidney
infection; **Nierensteine** *pl*
kidney stones *pl*
nieseln *vi impers* to drizzle;
Nieselregen *m* drizzle
niesen *vi* to sneeze
Niete (-, -n) *f* (*Los*) blank; (*Reinfall*)
flop; (*pej: Mensch*) failure; (*Tech*) rivet
Nigeria (-s) *nt* Nigeria
Nikotin (-s) *nt* nicotine
Nilpferd *nt* hippopotamus
nippen *vi* to sip; **an etw** (*dat*) **~** to
sip sth
nirgends *adv* nowhere
Nische (-, -n) *f* niche
Niveau (-s, -s) *nt* level; **sie hat
~** she's got class
nobel *adj* (*großzügig*) generous;
(*fam: luxuriös*) classy, posh;
Nobelpreis *m* Nobel Prize

⊙ SCHLÜSSELWORT

noch *adv* **1** (*weiterhin*) still; **noch
nicht** not yet; **noch nie** never
(yet); **noch immer** *o* **immer noch**
still; **bleiben Sie doch noch** stay a
bit longer
2 (*in Zukunft*) still, yet; **das kann
noch passieren** that might still
happen; **er wird noch kommen**
he'll come (yet)
3 (*nicht später als*) **noch vor einer
Woche** only a week ago; **noch am
selben Tag** the very same day;
noch im 19. Jahrhundert as late
as the 19th century; **noch heute**
today
4 (*zusätzlich*) **wer war noch da?**
who else was there?; **noch einmal**
once more, again; **noch dreimal**
three more times; **noch einer**
another one

5 (bei Vergleichen) **noch größer**
even bigger; **das ist noch besser**
that's better still; **und wenn es**
noch so schwer ist however hard
it is
6 Geld noch und noch heaps (and
heaps) of money; **sie hat noch**
und noch versucht, ... she tried
again and again to ...
▷ konj: **weder A noch B** neither A
nor B

nochmal(s) adv again, once
more
Nominativ m nominative (case)
Nonne (-, -n) f nun
Nonstop-Flug m nonstop flight
Nord north; **Nordamerika** nt
North America; **Norddeutschland**
nt Northern Germany; **Norden**
(-s) m north; **im ~ Deutschlands**
in the north of Germany;
Nordeuropa nt Northern Europe

Nordic Walking nt (Sport)
Nordic Walking
Nordirland nt Northern Ireland;
nordisch adj (Völker, Sprache)
Nordic; **Nordkorea** (-s) nt North
Korea; **nördlich** adj northern;
(Kurs, Richtung) northerly;
Nordost(en) m ,northeast;
Nordpol m North Pole;
Nordrhein-Westfalen (-s) nt
North Rhine-Westphalia; **Nordsee**
f North Sea; **nordwärts** adv
north, northwards; **Nordwest(en)**
m northwest; **Nordwind** m north
wind
nörgeln vi to grumble
Norm (-, -en) f norm;
(Größenvorschrift) standard
normal adj normal;
Normalbenzin nt regular (petrol
(Brit) o gas (US)); **normalerweise**
adv normally
normen vt to standardize
Norwegen (-s) nt Norway;

Norweger(in) m(f) Norwegian;
norwegisch adj Norwegian;
Norwegisch nt Norwegian
Not (-, Nöte) f need; (Armut)
poverty; (Elend) hardship;
(Bedrängnis) trouble; (Mangel)
want; (Mühe) trouble; (Zwang)
necessity; **zur ~** if necessary;
(gerade noch) just about
Notar(in) m(f) public notary;
notariell adj; **~ beglaubigt**
attested by a notary
Notarzt m, **Notärztin** f
emergency doctor;
Notarztwagen m emergency
ambulance; **Notaufnahme** f
A&E, casualty (Brit), emergency
room (US); **Notausgang** m
emergency exit; **Notbremse** f
emergency brake; **Notdienst** m
emergency service, after-hours
service; **notdürftig** adj scanty;
(behelfsmäßig) makeshift
Note (-, -n) f note; (in Schule)
mark, grade (US); (Mus) note
Notebook (-(s), -s) nt (Inform)
notebook
Notfall m emergency; **notfalls**
adv if necessary
notieren vt to note down
nötig adj necessary; **etw ~ haben**
to need sth
Notiz (-, -en) f note; (Zeitungs~)
item; **Notizblock** m notepad;
Notizbuch nt notebook
Notlage f crisis; (Elend) plight;
notlanden vi to make a forced (o
emergency) landing; **Notlandung**
f emergency landing; **Notruf** m
emergency call; **Notrufnummer**
f emergency number;
Notrufsäule f emergency
telephone
notwendig adj necessary
Nougat (-s, -s) m od nt nougat
November (-(s), -) m November;
siehe auch Juni

Nr. *abk* = **Nummer** No., no.

Nu *m*: **im ~** in no time

nüchtern *adj* sober; *(Magen)* empty

Nudel (-, -*n*) *f* noodle; **~n** *pl* *(italienische)* pasta *sing*

null *num* zero; *(Tel)* O *(Brit)*, zero *(US)*; **~ Fehler** no mistakes; **~ Uhr** midnight; **Null** (-, -*en*) *f* nought, zero; *(pej: Mensch)* dead loss; **Nulltarif** *m*: **zum ~** free of charge

Numerus clausus (- -) *m* restriction on the number of students allowed to study a particular subject

Nummer (-, -*n*) *f* number; **nummerieren** *vt* to number; **Nummernschild** *nt* *(Auto)* number plate *(Brit)*, license plate *(US)*

nun *adv* now; **von ~ an** from now on ▷ *interj* well; **~ gut!** all right, then; **es ist ~ mal so** that's the way it is

nur *adv* only; **nicht ~ ..., sondern auch ...** not only ..., but also ...; **~ Anna nicht** except Anna

Nürnberg (-*s*) *nt* Nuremberg

Nuss (-, Nüsse) *f* nut; **Nussknacker** (-*s*, -) *m* nutcracker; **Nuss-Nougat-Creme** *f* chocolate nut cream

Nutte (-, -*n*) *f* *(fam)* tart

nutz, nütze *adj*: **zu nichts ~ sein** to be useless; **nutzen, nützen** *vt* to use *(zu etw* for sth*)*; **was nützt es?** what use is it? ▷ *vi* to be of use; **das nützt nicht viel** that doesn't help much; **es nützt nichts(, es zu tun)** it's no use (doing it); **Nutzen** (-*s*, -) *m* usefulness; *(Gewinn)* profit; **nützlich** *adj* useful

Nylon (-*s*) *nt* nylon

o *interj* oh

O *abk* = **Ost** E

Oase (-, -*n*) *f* oasis

ob *conj* if, whether; **so als ~** as if; **er tut so, als ~ er krank wäre** he's pretending to be sick; **und ~!** you bet

obdachlos *adj* homeless

oben *adv* *(am oberen Ende)* at the top; *(obenauf)* on (the) top; *(im Haus)* upstairs; *(in einem Text)* above; **~ erwähnt** *(o genannt)* above-mentioned; **mit dem Gesicht nach ~** face up; **da ~** up there; **von ~ bis unten** from top to bottom; **siehe ~** see above

Ober (-*s*, -) *m* waiter

obere(r, s) *adj* upper, top

Oberfläche *f* surface; **oberflächlich** *adj* superficial; **Obergeschoss** *nt* upper floor

oberhalb *adv, prep* +*gen* above

Oberhemd *nt* shirt; **Oberkörper**

m upper body; **Oberlippe** *f* upper lip; **Oberösterreich** *nt* Upper Austria; **Oberschenkel** *m* thigh

oberste(r, s) *adj* very top, topmost

Oberteil *nt* top; **Oberweite** *f* bust/chest measurement

obig *adj* above(-mentioned)

Objekt (-(e)s, -e) *nt* object

objektiv *adj* objective; **Objektiv** *nt* lens

obligatorisch *adj* compulsory, obligatory

Oboe (-, -n) *f* oboe

Observatorium *nt* observatory

Obst (-(e)s) *nt* fruit; **Obstkuchen** *m* fruit tart; **Obstsalat** *m* fruit salad

obszön *adj* obscene

obwohl *conj* although

Ochse (-n, -n) *m* ox; **Ochsenschwanzsuppe** *f* oxtail soup

ocker *adj* ochre

öd(e) *adj* waste; (unbebaut) barren; (fig) dull

oder *conj* or; **~ aber** or else; **er kommt doch, ~?** he's coming, isn't he?

Ofen (-s, Öfen) *m* oven; (Heizofen) heater; (Kohleofen) stove; (Herd) cooker, stove; **Ofenkartoffel** *f* baked (o jacket) potato

offen *adj* open; (aufrichtig) frank; (Stelle) vacant ▷ *adv* frankly; **~ gesagt** to be honest

offenbar *adj* obvious; **offensichtlich** *adj* evident, obvious

öffentlich *adj* public; **Öffentlichkeit** *f* (Leute) public; (einer Versammlung etc) public nature

offiziell *adj* official

offline *adv* (Inform) offline

öffnen *vt* to open ▷ *vr*: **sich ~** to open; **Öffner** (-s, -) *m* opener;

Öffnung *f* opening; **Öffnungszeiten** *pl* opening times *pl*

oft *adv* often; **schon ~** many times; **öfter** *adv* more often (o frequently); **öfters** *adv* often, frequently

ohne *conj, prep* +akk without; **~ weiteres** without a second thought; (sofort) immediately; **~ ein Wort zu sagen** without saying a word; **~ mich** count me out

Ohnmacht (-machten) *f* unconsciousness; (Hilflosigkeit) helplessness; **in ~ fallen** to faint; **ohnmächtig** *adj* unconscious; **sie ist ~** she has fainted

Ohr (-(e)s, -en) *nt* ear; (Gehör) hearing

Öhr (-(e)s, -e) *nt* eye

Ohrenarzt *m*, **Ohrenärztin** *f* ear specialist; **Ohrenschmerzen** *pl* earache; **Ohrentropfen** *pl* ear drops *pl*; **Ohrfeige** *f* slap (in the face); **Ohrläppchen** *nt* earlobe; **Ohrringe** *pl* earrings *pl*

oje *interj* oh dear

okay *interj* OK, okay

Ökoladen *m* health food store; **ökologisch** *adj* ecological; **~e Landwirtschaft** organic farming

ökonomisch *adj* economic; (sparsam) economical

Ökosystem *nt* ecosystem

Oktanzahl *f* (bei Benzin) octane rating

Oktober (-(s), -) *m* October; *siehe auch* **Juni**

● **OKTOBERFEST**
●
●
● The annual October beer
● festival, the **Oktoberfest**,
● takes place in Munich on a
● huge field where beer tents,
● roller coasters and many other

amusements are set up. People
sit at long wooden tables, drink
beer from enormous litre beer
mugs, eat pretzels and listen
to brass bands. It is a great
attraction for tourists and locals
alike.

Öl (-(e)s, -e) nt oil; **Ölbaum** m
olive tree; **ölen** vt to oil; (Tech) to
lubricate; **Ölfarbe** f oil paint;
Ölfilter m oil filter; **Ölgemälde**
nt oil painting; **Ölheizung** f
oil-fired central heating; **ölig** adj
oily

oliv adj inv olive-green; **Olive**
(-, -n) f olive; **Olivenöl** nt olive
oil

Ölmessstab m dipstick; **Ölofen**
m oil stove; **Ölpest** f oil
pollution; **Ölsardine** f sardine in
oil; **Ölstandanzeiger** m (Auto)
oil gauge; **Ölteppich** m oil slick;
Ölwechsel m oil change

Olympiade f Olympic Games pl;
olympisch adj Olympic

Oma f, **Omi** (-s, -s) f grandma,
gran(ny)

Omelett (-(e)s, -s) nt, **Omelette**
f omelette

Omnibus m bus

onanieren vi to masturbate

Onkel (-s, -) m uncle

online adv (Inform) online;
Onlinedienst m (Inform) online
service

OP (-s, -s) m abk =
Operationssaal operating
theatre (Brit) (o room (US))

Opa m, **Opi** (-s, -s) m grandpa,
grandad

Open-Air-Konzert nt open-air
concert

Oper (-, -n) f opera; (Gebäude)
opera house

Operation f operation

Operette f operetta

operieren vi to operate ⊳ vt to
operate on

Opernhaus nt opera house,
opera; **Opernsänger(in)** m(f)
opera singer

Opfer (-s, -) nt sacrifice; (Mensch)
victim; **ein ~ bringen** to make a
sacrifice

Opium (-s) nt opium

Opposition f opposition

Optiker(in) (-s, -) m(f) optician

optimal adj optimal, optimum

optimistisch adj optimistic

oral adj oral; **Oralverkehr** m
oral sex

orange adj inv orange; **Orange**
(-, -n) f orange; **Orangenmarmelade** f marmalade;
Orangensaft m orange juice

Orchester (-s, -) nt orchestra

Orchidee (-, -n) f orchid

Orden (-s, -) m (Rel) order; (Mil)
decoration

ordentlich adj (anständig)
respectable; (geordnet) tidy, neat;
(fam: annehmbar) not bad; (fam:
tüchtig) proper ⊳ adv properly

ordinär adj common, vulgar;
(Witz) dirty

ordnen vt to sort out; **Ordner**
(-s, -) m (bei Veranstaltung)
steward; (Aktenordner) file;
Ordnung f order; (Geordnetsein)
tidiness; (geht) **in ~!** (that's) all
right; **mit dem Drucker ist etwas
nicht in ~** there's something
wrong with the printer

Oregano m oregano

Organ (-s, -e) nt organ; (Stimme)
voice

Organisation f organization;
organisieren vt to organize;
(fam: beschaffen) to get hold of
⊳ vr: **sich ~** to organize

Organismus m organism

Orgasmus m orgasm

Orgel (-, -n) f organ

Orgie f orgy
orientalisch adj oriental
orientieren vr: **sich** ~ to get
one's bearings; **Orientierung** f
orientation; **Orientierungssinn**
m sense of direction
original adj original; (echt)
genuine; **Original** (-s, -e) nt
original
originell adj original; (komisch)
witty
Orkan (-(e)s, -e) m hurricane
Ort (-(e)s, -e) m place; (Dorf)
village; **an ~ und Stelle, vor ~** on
the spot
Orthopäde (-n, -n) m,
Orthopädin f orthopaedist
örtlich adj local; **Ortschaft** f
village, small town; **Ortsgespräch**
nt local call; **Ortstarif** m local
rate; **Ortszeit** f local time

- **OSSI**

  - **Ossi** is a colloquial and rather
  - derogatory word used to
  - describe a German from the
  - former **DDR**.

Ost east; **Ostdeutschland** nt
(als Landesteil) Eastern Germany;
(Hist) East Germany; **Osten** (-s) m
east
Osterei nt Easter egg;
Osterglocke f daffodil;
Osterhase m Easter bunny;
Ostermontag m Easter Monday;
Ostern (-, -) nt Easter; **an** (o **zu**)
~ at Easter; **frohe** ~ Happy Easter
Österreich (-s) nt Austria;
Österreicher(in) (-s, -) m(f) Austrian;
österreichisch adj Austrian
Ostersonntag m Easter Sunday
Osteuropa nt Eastern Europe;
Ostküste f east coast; **östlich**
adj eastern; (Kurs, Richtung)
easterly; **Ostsee** f: **die** ~ the

Baltic (Sea); **Ostwind** m
east(erly) wind
OSZE (-) f abk = **Organisation für
Sicherheit und Zusammenarbeit
in Europa** OSCE
Otter (-s, -) m otter
out adj (fam) out; **outen** vt to
out
oval adj oval
Overheadprojektor m overhead projector
Ozean (-s, -e) m ocean; **der Stille
~** the Pacific (Ocean)
Ozon (-s) nt ozone;
Ozonbelastung f ozone level;
Ozonloch nt hole in the ozone
layer; **Ozonschicht** f ozone
layer; **Ozonwerte** pl ozone
levels pl

p

paar adj inv **ein ~** a few; **ein ~ Mal** a few times; **ein ~ Äpfel** some apples

Paar (-(e)s, -e) nt pair; (Ehepaar) couple; **ein ~ Socken** a pair of socks

pachten vt to lease

Päckchen nt package; (Zigaretten) packet; (zum Verschicken) small parcel; **packen** vt to pack; (fassen) to grasp, to seize; (fam: schaffen) to manage; (fig: fesseln) to grip; **Packpapier** nt brown paper; **Packung** f packet, pack (US); **Packungsbeilage** f package insert, patient information leaflet

Pädagoge (-n, -n) m, **Pädagogin** f teacher; **pädagogisch** adj educational; **~e Hochschule** college of education

Paddel (-s, -) nt paddle; **Paddelboot** nt canoe; **paddeln**
vi to paddle

Paket (-(e)s, -e) nt packet; (Postpaket) parcel; (Inform) package; **Paketbombe** f parcel bomb; **Paketkarte** f dispatch form (to be filled in with details of the sender and the addressee when handing in a parcel at the post office)

Pakistan (-s) nt Pakistan

Palast (-es, Paläste) m palace

Palästina (-s) nt Palestine; **Palästinenser(in)** (-s, -) m(f) Palestinian

Palatschinken pl filled pancakes pl

Palette f (von Maler) palette; (Ladepalette) pallet; (Vielfalt) range

Palme (-, -n) f palm (tree); **Palmsonntag** m Palm Sunday

Pampelmuse (-, -n) f grapefruit

pampig adj (fam: frech) cheeky; (breiig) gooey

Panda(bär) (-s, -s) m panda

Pandemie (-, -n) f pandemic

panieren vt (Gastr) to coat with breadcrumbs; **paniert** adj breaded

Panik f panic

Panne (-, -n) f (Auto) breakdown; (Missgeschick) slip; **Pannendienst** m, **Pannenhilfe** f breakdown (o rescue) service

Pant(h)er (-s, -) m panther

Pantomime (-, -n) f mime

Panzer (-s, -) m (Panzerung) armour (plating); (Mil) tank

Papa (-s, -s) m dad(dy), pa (US)

Papagei (-s, -en) m parrot

Papaya (-, -s) f papaya

Papier (-s, -e) nt paper; **~e** pl (Ausweispapiere) papers pl; (Dokumente, Urkunden) papers pl, documents pl; **Papiercontainer** m paper bank; **Papierformat** nt paper size; **Papiergeld** nt paper money; **Papierkorb** m wastepaper basket; (Inform)

recycle bin; **Papiertaschentuch**
nt (paper) tissue; **Papiertonne** f
paper bank
Pappbecher m paper cup;
Pappe (-, -n) f cardboard;
Pappkarton m cardboard box;
Pappteller m paper plate
Paprika (-s, -s) m (Gewürz)
paprika; (Schote) pepper
Papst (-(e)s, Päpste) m pope
Paradeiser (-s, -) m tomato
Paradies (-es, -e) nt paradise
Paragliding (-s) nt paragliding
Paragraph (-en, -en) m
paragraph; (Jur) section
parallel adj parallel
Paranuss f Brazil nut
Parasit (-en, -en) m parasite
parat adj ready; **etw ~ haben** to
have sth ready
Pärchen (-s, -) nt couple
Parfüm (-s, -s o -e) nt perfume;
Parfümerie f perfumery;
parfümieren vt to scent, to
perfume
Pariser (-s, -) m (fam: Kondom)
rubber
Park (-s, -s) m park
Park-and-ride-System nt
park-and-ride system; **Parkbank** f
park bench; **Parkdeck** nt parking
level; **parken** vt, vi to park
Parkett (-s, -e) nt parquet
flooring; (Theat) stalls pl (Brit),
parquet (US)
Parkhaus nt multi-storey car
park (Brit), parking garage (US)
parkinsonsche Krankheit f
Parkinson's disease
Parkkralle f (Auto) wheel clamp;
Parklicht nt parking light;
Parklücke f parking space;
Parkplatz m (für ein Auto) parking
space; (für mehrere Autos) car park
(Brit), parking lot (US);
Parkscheibe f parking disc;
Parkscheinautomat m pay

point; (Parkscheinausgabegerät)
ticket machine; **Parkuhr** f
parking meter; **Parkverbot** nt
(Stelle) no-parking zone; **hier ist**
you can't park here
Parlament nt parliament
Parmesan (-s) m Parmesan
(cheese)
Partei f party
Parterre (-s, -s) nt ground floor
(Brit), first floor (US)
Partie f part; (Spiel) game; (Mann,
Frau) catch; **mit von der ~ sein** to
be in on it
Partitur f (Mus) score
Partizip (-s, -ien) nt participle
Partner(in) (-s, -) m(f) partner;
Partnerschaft f partnership,
eingetragene ~ civil partnership;
Partnerstadt f twin town
Party (-, -s) f party; **Partymuffel**
(-s, -) m party pooper;
Partyservice m catering service
Pass (-es, Pässe) m pass; (Ausweis)
passport
passabel adj reasonable
Passagier (-s, -e) m passenger
Passamt nt passport office
Passant(in) m(f) passer-by;
Passbild nt passport photo
passen vi (Größe) to fit; (Farbe,
Stil) to go (zu with); (auf Frage) to
pass; **passt (es) dir morgen?** does
tomorrow suit you?; **das passt**
mir gut that suits me fine;
passend adj suitable;
(zusammenpassend) matching;
(angebracht) fitting; (Zeit)
convenient; **haben Sie es nicht ~?**
(Kleingeld) have you got the right
change?
passieren vi to happen
passiv adj passive
Passkontrolle f passport
control
Passwort nt password
Paste (-, -n) f paste

Pastellfarbe | 158

Pastellfarbe f pastel colour

Pastete (-, -n) f (warmes Gericht) pie; (Pastetchen) vol-au-vent; (ohne Teig) pâté

Pastor, in (-s, -en) m(f) minister, vicar

Pate (-n, -n) m godfather; **Patenkind** nt godchild

Patient(in) m(f) patient

Patin f godmother

Patrone (-, -n) f cartridge

patsch interj splat; **patschnass** adj soaking wet

pauschal adj (Kosten) inclusive; (Urteil) sweeping; **Pauschale** (-, -n) f, **Pauschalgebühr** f flat rate (charge); **Pauschalpreis** m flat rate; (für Hotel, Reise) all-inclusive price; **Pauschalreise** f package tour

Pause (-, -n) f break; (Theat) interval; (Kino etc) intermission; (Innehalten) pause

Pavian (-s, -e) m baboon

Pavillon (-s, -s) m pavilion

Pay-TV (-s) nt pay-per-view television, pay TV

Pazifik (-s) m Pacific (Ocean)

PC (-s, -s) m abk = **Personal Computer** PC

Pech (-s, -e) nt (fig) bad luck; ~ **haben** to be unlucky; ~ **gehabt!** tough (luck)

Pedal (-s, -e) nt pedal

Pediküre (-, -en) f pedicure

Peeling (-s, -s) nt (facial/body) scrub

peinlich adj (unangenehm) embarrassing, awkward; (genau) painstaking; **es war mir sehr ~** I was totally embarrassed

Peitsche (-, -n) f whip

Pelikan (-s, -e) m pelican

Pellkartoffeln pl potatoes pl boiled in their skins

Pelz (-es, -e) m fur; **pelzig** adj (Zunge) furred

pendeln vi (Zug, Bus) to shuttle; (Mensch) to commute; **Pendelverkehr** m shuttle traffic; (für Pendler) commuter traffic; **Pendler(in)** (-s, -) m(f) commuter

penetrant adj sharp; (Mensch) pushy

Penis (-, -se) m penis

Pension f (Geld) pension; (Ruhestand) retirement; (für Gäste) guesthouse, B&B; **pensioniert** adj retired; **Pensionsgast** m guest (in a guesthouse)

Peperoni (-, -) f chilli

per prep +akk by, per; (pro) per; (bis) by

perfekt adj perfect

Pergamentpapier nt grease-proof paper

Periode (-, -n) f period

Perle (-, -n) f (a. fig) pearl

perplex adj dumbfounded

Person (-, -en) f person; **ein Tisch für drei ~en** a table for three; **Personal** (-s) nt staff, personnel; (Bedienung) servants pl; **Personalausweis** m identity card; **Personalien** pl particulars pl; **Personenschaden** m injury to persons; **Personenwaage** f (bathroom) scales pl; **Personenzug** m passenger train; **persönlich** adj personal; (auf Briefen) private ▷ adv personally; (selbst) in person; **Persönlichkeit** f personality

Peru (-s) nt Peru

Perücke (-, -n) f wig

pervers adj perverted

pessimistisch adj pessimistic

Pest (-) f plague

Petersilie f parsley

Petroleum (-s) nt paraffin (Brit), kerosene (US)

Pfad (-(e)s, -e) m path; **Pfadfinder** (-s, -) m boy scout;

Pfadfinderin f girl guide
Pfahl (-(e)s, Pfähle) m post, stake
Pfand (-(e)s, Pfänder) nt security;
(Flaschenpfand) deposit; (im Spiel)
forfeit; **Pfandflasche** f
returnable bottle
Pfanne (-, -n) f (frying) pan
Pfannkuchen m pancake
Pfarrei f parish; **Pfarrer(in)**
(-s, -) m(f) priest
Pfau (-(e)s, -en) m peacock
Pfeffer (-s, -) m pepper;
Pfefferkuchen m gingerbread;
Pfefferminze (-e) f peppermint;
Pfefferminztee m peppermint
tea; **Pfeffermühle** f pepper mill;
pfeffern vt to put pepper on/in;
Pfefferstreuer (-s, -) m pepper
pot
Pfeife (-, -n) f whistle; (für Tabak,
von Orgel) pipe; **pfeifen** (pfiff,
gepfiffen) vt, vi to whistle
Pfeil (-(e)s, -e) m arrow
Pfeiltaste f (Inform) arrow key
Pferd (-(e)s, -e) nt horse;
Pferdeschwanz m (Frisur)
ponytail; **Pferdestall** m stable;
Pferdestärke f horsepower
pfiff imperf von **pfeifen**
Pfifferling m chanterelle
Pfingsten (-,) nt Whitsun,
Pentecost (US); **Pfingstmontag**
m Whit Monday; **Pfingstsonntag**
m Whit Sunday, Pentecost (US)
Pfirsich (-s, -e) m peach
Pflanze (-, -n) f plant; **pflanzen**
vt to plant; **Pflanzenfett** nt
vegetable fat
Pflaster (-s, -) nt (für Wunde)
plaster, Band Aid® (US);
(Straßenpflaster) road surface,
pavement (US)
Pflaume (-, -n) f plum
Pflege (-, -n) f care;
(Krankenpflege) nursing; (von Autos,
Maschinen) maintenance;
pflegebedürftig adj in need of

care; **pflegeleicht** adj easy-care;
(fig) easy to handle; **pflegen** vt
to look after; (Kranke) to nurse;
(Beziehungen) to foster; (Fingernägel,
Gesicht) to take care of; (Daten) to
maintain; **Pflegepersonal** nt
nursing staff; **Pflegeversicherung**
f long-term care insurance
Pflicht (-, -en) f duty, (Sport)
compulsory section; **pflicht-
bewusst** adj conscientious;
Pflichtfach nt (Schule)
compulsory subject; **Pflicht-
versicherung** f compulsory
insurance
pflücken vt to pick
Pforte (-, -n) f gate; **Pförtner(in)**
(-s, -) m(f) porter
Pfosten (-s, -) m post
Pfote (-, -n) f paw
pfui interj ugh
Pfund (-(e)s, -e) nt pound
pfuschen vi (fam) to be sloppy
Pfütze (-, -n) f puddle
Phantasie siehe **Fantasie**;
phantastisch adj siehe
fantastisch
Phase (-, -n) f phase
Philippinen pl Philippines pl
Philosophie f philosophy
Photo nt siehe **Foto**
pH-neutral adj pH-balanced;
pH-Wert m pH-value
Physalis (-, Physalis) f physalis
Physik f physics sing
physisch adj physical
Pianist(in) (-en, -en) m(f) pianist
Pickel (-s, -) m pimple; (Werkzeug)
pickaxe; (Berg~) ice-axe
Picknick (-s, -e o -s) nt picnic; **ein
~ machen** to have a picnic
piepsen vi to chirp
piercen vt: **sich die Nase
~ lassen** to have one's nose
pierced; **Piercing** (-s) nt (body)
piercing
pieseln vi (fam) to pee

Pik (-, -) nt (Karten) spades pl

pikant adj spicy

Pilates nt (Sport) Pilates

Pilger(in) m(f) pilgrim; **Pilgerfahrt** f pilgrimage

Pille (-, -n) f pill; **sie nimmt die ~** she's on the pill

Pilot(in) (-en, -en) m(f) pilot

Pilz (-es, -e) m (essbar) mushroom; (giftig) toadstool; (Med) fungus

PIN (-, -s) f PIN (number)

pingelig adj (fam) fussy

Pinguin (-s, -e) m penguin

Pinie f pine; **Pinienkern** m pine nut

pink adj shocking pink

pinkeln vi (fam) to pee

Pinsel (-s, -) m (paint)brush

Pinzette f tweezers pl

Pistazie f pistachio

Piste (-, -n) f (Ski) piste; (Aviat) runway

Pistole (-, -n) f pistol

Pixel (-s) nt (Inform) pixel

Pizza (-, -s) f pizza; **Pizzaservice** m pizza delivery service; **Pizzeria** (-, Pizzerien) f pizzeria

Pkw (-(s), -(s)) m abk = **Personenkraftwagen** car

Plakat nt poster

Plakette f (Schildchen) badge; (Aufkleber) sticker

Plan (-(e)s, Pläne) m plan; (Karte) map; **planen** vt to plan

Planet (-en, -en) m planet; **Planetarium** nt planetarium

planmäßig adj scheduled

Plan(t)schbecken nt paddling pool; **plan(t)schen** vi to splash around

Planung f planning

Plastik f sculpture ▷ (-s) nt (Kunststoff) plastic; **Plastikfolie** f plastic film; **Plastiktüte** f plastic bag

Platin (-s) nt platinum

platsch interj splash

platt adj flat; (fam: überrascht) flabbergasted; (fig: geistlos) flat, boring

Platte (-, -n) f (Foto, Tech, Gastr) plate; (Steinplatte) flag; (Schallplatte) record; **Plattenspieler** m record player

Plattform f platform; **Plattfuß** m flat foot; (Reifen) flat (tyre)

Platz (-es, Plätze) m place; (Sitzplatz) seat; (freier Raum) space, room; (in Stadt) square; (Sportplatz) playing field; **nehmen Sie ~** please sit down, take a seat; **ist dieser ~ frei?** is this seat taken?; **Platzanweiser(in)** m(f) usher/usherette

Plätzchen nt spot; (Gebäck) biscuit

platzen vi to burst; (Bombe) to explode

Platzkarte f seat reservation; **Platzreservierung** f seat reservation; **Platzverweis** m: **er erhielt einen ~** he was sent off; **Platzwunde** f laceration, cut

plaudern vi to chat, to talk

pleite adj (fam) broke; **Pleite** (-, -n) f (Bankrott) bankruptcy; (fam: Reinfall) flop

Plombe (-, -n) f lead seal; (Zahnplombe) filling; **plombieren** vt (Zahn) to fill

plötzlich adj sudden ▷ adv suddenly, all at once

plump adj clumsy; (Hände) ungainly; (Körper) shapeless

plumps interj thud; (in Flüssigkeit) plop

Plural (-s, -e) m plural

plus adv plus; **fünf ~ sieben ist zwölf** five plus seven is (o are) twelve; **zehn Grad ~** ten degrees above zero; **Plus** (-, -) nt plus; (Fin) profit; (Vorteil) advantage

Plüsch (-(e)s, -e) m plush

Pluto (-) m Pluto

PLZ *abk* = **Postleitzahl** postcode (Brit), zip code (US)

Po (-s, -s) *m* (*fam*) bottom, bum

Pocken *pl* smallpox *sing*

poetisch *adj* poetic

Pointe (-, -n) *f* punch line

Pokal (-s, -e) *m* goblet; (*Sport*) cup

pökeln *vt* to pickle

Pol (-s, -e) *m* pole

Pole (-n, -n) *m* Pole; **Polen** (-s) *nt* Poland

Police (-, -n) *f* (insurance) policy

polieren *vt* to polish

Polin *f* Pole, Polish woman

Politik *f* politics *sing*; (*eine bestimmte*) policy; **Politiker(in)** *m(f)* politician, **politisch** *adj* political

Politur *f* polish

Polizei *f* police *pl*; **Polizeibeamte(r)** *m*, **Polizeibeamtin** *f* police officer; **polizeilich** *adj* police; **sie wird ~ gesucht** the police are looking for her; **Polizeirevier** *nt*, **Polizeiwache** *f* police station; **Polizeistunde** *f* closing time; **Polizeiwache** *f* police station; **Polizist(in)** *m(f)* policeman/-woman

Pollen (-s, -) *m* pollen; **Pollenflug** (-s) *m* pollen count

polnisch *adj* Polish; **Polnisch** *nt* Polish

Polo (-s) *nt* polo; **Polohemd** *nt* polo shirt

Polster (-s, -) *nt* cushion; (*Polsterung*) upholstery; (*in Kleidung*) padding; (*fig: Geld*) reserves *pl*; **Polstergarnitur** *f* living-room suite; **Polstermöbel** *pl* upholstered furniture *sing*; **polstern** *vt* to upholster; (*Kleidung*) to pad

Polterabend *m* party prior to a wedding, at which old crockery is smashed to bring good luck

poltern *vi* (*Krach machen*) to crash; (*schimpfen*) to rant

Polyester (-s, -) *m* polyester

Polypen *pl* (*Med*) adenoids *pl*

Pommes frites *pl* chips (Brit), French fries (US)

Pony (-s, -s) *m* (*Frisur*) fringe (Brit), bangs *pl* (US) ▷ (-s, -s) *nt* (*Pferd*) pony

Popcorn (-s) *nt* popcorn

Popmusik *f* pop (music)

populär *adj* popular

Pore (-, -n) *f* pore

Pornografie *f* pornography

Porree (-s, -s) *m* leeks *pl*; **eine Stange ~** a leek

Portemonnaie, Portmonee (-s, -s) *nt* purse

Portier (-s, -s) *m* porter; *siehe auch* **Pförtner**

Portion *f* portion, helping

Porto (-s, -s) *nt* postage

Porträt, Porträt (-s, -s) *nt* portrait

Portugal (-s) *nt* Portugal; **Portugiese** (-n, -n) *m* Portuguese; **Portugiesin** (-, -nen) *f* Portuguese; **portugiesisch** *adj* Portuguese; **Portugiesisch** *nt* Portuguese

Portwein (-s, -e) *m* port

Porzellan (-s, -e) *nt* china

Posaune (-, -n) *f* trombone

Position *f* position

positiv *adj* positive

Post® (-, -en) *f* post office; (*Briefe*) post (Brit), mail; **Postamt** *nt* post office; **Postanweisung** *f* postal order (Brit), money order (US); **Postbank** *f* German post office bank; **Postbote** *m*, **-botin** *f* postman/-woman

Posten (-s, -) *m* post, position; (*Comm*) item; (*auf Liste*) entry

Poster (-s, -) *nt* poster

Postfach *nt* post-office box, PO box; **Postkarte** *f* postcard;

postlagernd adv poste restante; **Postleitzahl** f postcode (Brit), zip code (US)

postmodern adj postmodern

Postsparkasse f post office savings bank; **Poststempel** m postmark; **Postweg** m: **auf dem ~** by mail

Potenz f (Math) power; (eines Mannes) potency

PR (-, -s) f abk = **Public Relations** PR

prächtig adj splendid

prahlen vi to boast, to brag

Praktikant(in) m(f) trainee; **Praktikum** (-s, Praktika) nt practical training; **praktisch** adj practical; **~er Arzt** general practitioner

Praline f chocolate

Prämie f (bei Versicherung) premium; (Belohnung) reward; (von Arbeitgeber) bonus

Präparat nt (Med) medicine; (Bio) preparation

Präservativ nt condom

Präsident(in) m(f) president

Praxis (-, Praxen) f practice; (Behandlungsraum) surgery; (von Anwalt) office; **Praxisgebühr** f surgery surcharge

präzise adj precise, exact

predigen vt, vi to preach; **Predigt** (-, -en) f sermon

Preis (-es, -e) m (zu zahlen) price; (bei Sieg) prize; **den ersten ~ gewinnen** to win first prize; **Preisausschreiben** nt competition

Preiselbeere f cranberry

preisgünstig adj inexpensive; **Preislage** f price range; **Preisliste** f price list; **Preisschild** nt price tag; **Preisträger(in)** m(f) prizewinner; **preiswert** adj inexpensive

Prellung f bruise

Premiere (-, -n) f premiere, first night

Premierminister(in) m(f) prime minister, premier

Prepaidhandy nt prepaid mobile (Brit), prepaid cell phone (US); **Prepaidkarte** f prepaid card

Presse (-, -n) f press

pressen vt to press

prickeln vi to tingle

Priester(in) (-s, -) m(f) priest/(woman) priest

Primel (-, -n) f primrose

primitiv adj primitive

Prinz (-en, -en) m prince; **Prinzessin** f princess

Prinzip (-s, -ien) nt principle; **im ~ basically; aus ~** on principle

Priorität f priority

privat adj private; **Privatfernsehen** nt commercial television; **Privatgrundstück** nt private property; **privatisieren** vt to privatize

pro prep +akk per; **5 Euro ~ Stück/Person** 5 euros each/per person; **Pro** (-s) nt pro

Probe (-, -n) f test; (Teststück) sample; (Theat) rehearsal; **Probefahrt** f test drive; **eine ~ machen** to go for a test drive; **Probezeit** f trial period; **probieren** vt, vi to try; (Wein, Speise) to taste, to sample

Problem (-s, -e) nt problem

Produkt (-(e)s, -e) nt product; **Produktion** f production; (produzierte Menge) output; **produzieren** vt to produce

Professor(in) (-s, -en) m(f) professor

Profi (-s, -s) m pro

Profil (-s, -e) nt profile; (von Reifen, Schuhsohle) tread

Profit (-(e)s, -e) m profit; **profitieren** vi to profit (von from)

Prognose (-, -n) f prediction; (Wetter) forecast

Programm (-s, -e) nt programme; (Inform) program; (TV) channel; **Programmheft** nt programme; **programmieren** vt to program; **Programmierer(in)** (-s, -) m(f) programmer; **Programmkino** nt arts (o repertory (US)) cinema

Projekt (-(e)s, -e) nt project

Projektor m projector

Promenade (-, -n) f promenade

Promille (-(s), -) nt (Blood) alcohol level; **0,8 ~** 0,08 per cent; **Promillegrenze** f legal alcohol limit

prominent adj prominent; **Prominenz** f VIPs pl, prominent figures pl; (fam: Stars) the glitterati pl

Propeller (-s, -) m propeller

prosit interj cheers

Prospekt (-(e)s, -e) m leaflet, brochure

prost interj cheers

Prostituierte(r) mf prostitute

Protest (-(e)s, -e) m protest

Protestant(in) m(f) Protestant; **protestantisch** adj Protestant

protestieren vi to protest (gegen against)

Prothese (-, -n) f artificial arm/leg; (Gebiss) dentures pl

Protokoll (-s, -e) nt (bei Sitzung) minutes pl; (diplomatisch, Inform) protocol; (bei Polizei) statement

protzen vi to show off; **protzig** adj flashy

Proviant (-s, -e) m provisions pl

Provider (-s, -) m (Inform) (service) provider

Provinz (-, -en) f province

Provision f (Comm) commission

provisorisch adj provisional; **Provisorium** (-s, Provisorien) nt stopgap; (Zahn) temporary filling

provozieren vt to provoke

Prozent (-(e)s, -e) nt per cent

Prozess (-es, -e) m (Vorgang) process; (Jur) trial; (Rechtsfall) (court) case; **prozessieren** vi to go to law (mit against)

Prozession f procession

Prozessor (-s, -en) m (Inform) processor

prüde adj prudish

prüfen vt to test; (nachprüfen) to check; **Prüfung** f (Schule) exam; (Überprüfung) check; **eine ~ machen** (Schule) to take an exam

Prügelei f fight; **prügeln** vt to beat ▷ vr: **sich ~** to fight

PS abk = **Pferdestärke** hp; = **Postskript(um)** PS

pseudo- präf pseudo; **Pseudokrupp** (-s) m (Med) pseudocroup; **Pseudonym** (-s, -e) nt pseudonym

pst interj ssh

Psychiater(in) (-s, -) m(f) psychiatrist; **psychisch** adj psychological; (Krankheit) mental; **Psychoanalyse** f psychoanalysis; **Psychologe** (-n, -n) m, **Psychologin** f psychologist; **Psychologie** f psychology

Psychopharmaka pl mind-affecting drugs pl, psychotropic drugs pl; **psychosomatisch** adj psychosomatic; **Psychoterror** m psychological intimidation; **Psychotherapie** f psychotherapy

Pubertät f puberty

Publikum (-s) nt audience; (Sport) crowd

Pudding (-s, -e o -s) m blancmange

Pudel (-s, -) m poodle

Puder (-s, -) m powder; **Puderzucker** m icing sugar

Puerto Rico (-s) nt Puerto Rico

Pulli (-s, -s) m, **Pullover** (-s, -) m sweater, pullover, jumper (Brit)

Puls (-es, -e) m pulse

Pulver (-s, -) nt powder; **Pulverkaffee** m instant coffee; **Pulverschnee** m powder snow

pummelig adj chubby

Pumpe (-, -n) f pump; **pumpen** vt to pump; (fam: verleihen) to lend; (fam: sich ausleihen) to borrow

Pumps pl court shoes pl (Brit), pumps pl (US)

Punk (-s, -s) m (Musik, Mensch) punk

Punkt (-(e)s, -e) m point; (bei Muster) dot; (Satzzeichen) full stop (Brit), period (US); **~ zwei Uhr** at two o'clock sharp

pünktlich adj punctual, on time; **Pünktlichkeit** f punctuality

Punsch (-(e)s, -e) m punch

Pupille (-, -n) f pupil

Puppe (-, -n) f doll

pur adj pure; (völlig) sheer; (Whisky) neat

Püree (-s, -s) nt puree; (Kartoffelpüree) mashed potatoes pl

Puste (-) f (fam) puff; **außer ~ sein** to be puffed

Pustel (-, -n) f pustule; (Pickel) pimple; **pusten** vi to blow; (keuchen) to puff

Pute (-, -n) f turkey; **Putenschnitzel** nt turkey escalope

Putsch (-es, -e) m putsch

Putz (-es) m (Mörtel) plaster

putzen vt to clean; **sich** (dat) **die Nase ~** to blow one's nose; **sich** (dat) **die Zähne ~** to brush one's teeth; **Putzfrau** f cleaner; **Putzlappen** m cloth, **Putzmann** m cleaner; **Putzmittel** nt cleaning agent, cleaner

Puzzle (-s, -s) nt jigsaw (puzzle)

Pyjama (-s, -s) m pyjamas pl

Pyramide (-, -n) f pyramid

Python (-s, -s) m python

Quadrat nt square; **quadratisch** adj square; **Quadratmeter** m square metre

quaken vi (Frosch) to croak; (Ente) to quack

Qual (-, -en) f pain, agony; (seelisch) anguish; **quälen** vt to torment ▷ vr: **sich ~** to struggle; (geistig) to torment oneself; **Quälerei** f torture, torment

qualifizieren vt to qualify; (einstufen) to label ▷ vr: **sich ~** to qualify

Qualität f quality

Qualle (-, -n) f jellyfish

Qualm (-(e)s) m thick smoke; **qualmen** vt, vi to smoke

Quantität f quantity

Quarantäne (-, -n) f quarantine

Quark (-s) m quark; (fam: Unsinn) rubbish

Quartett (-s, -e) nt quartet; (Kartenspiel) happy families sing

Quartier (-s, -e) nt accommodation

quasi adv more or less

Quatsch (-es) m (fam) rubbish; **quatschen** vi (fam) to chat

Quecksilber nt mercury

Quelle (-, -n) f spring; (eines Flusses) source

quellen vi to pour

quer adv crossways, diagonally; (rechtwinklig) at right angles; **~ über die Straße** straight across the street; **querfeldein** adv across country; **Querflöte** f flute; **Querschnitt** m cross section; **querschnittsgelähmt** adj paraplegic, **Querstraße** f side street

quetschen vt to squash, to crush; (Med) to bruise; **Quetschung** f bruise

Queue (-s, -s) m (billiard) cue

quietschen vi to squeal; (Tür, Bett) to squeak; (Bremsen) to screech

quitt adj quits, even

Quitte (-, -n) f quince

Quittung f receipt

Quiz (-, -) nt quiz

Quote (-, -n) f rate; (Comm) quota

r

Rabatt (-(e)s, -e) m discount

Rabbi (-(s), -s) m rabbi; **Rabbiner** (-s, -) m rabbi

Rabe (-n, -n) m raven

Rache (-) f revenge, vengeance

Rachen (-s, -) m throat

rächen vt to avenge ▷ vr: **sich ~** to take (one's) revenge (an +dat on)

Rad (-(e)s, Räder) nt wheel; (Fahrrad) bike; **~ fahren** to cycle; **mit dem ~ fahren** to go by bike

Radar (-s) m o nt radar; **Radarfalle** f speed trap; **Radarkontrolle** f radar speed check

radeln vi (fam) to cycle; **Radfahrer(in)** m(f) cyclist; **Radfahrweg** m cycle track (o path)

Radicchio (-s) m (Salatsorte) radicchio

radieren vt to rub out, to erase;
Radiergummi m rubber (Brit),
eraser; **Radierung** f (Kunst)
etching

Radieschen nt radish

radikal adj radical

Radio (-s, -s) nt radio; **im ~** on
the radio

radioaktiv adj radioactive

Radiologe (-n, -n) m, **Radiologin**
f radiologist

Radiorekorder m radio cassette
recorder; **Radiosender** m radio
station; **Radiowecker** m radio
alarm (clock)

Radkappe f (Auto) hub cap

Radler(in) (-s, -) m(f) cyclist

Radler (-s, -) nt ≈ shandy

Radlerhose f cycling shorts pl;
Radrennen nt cycle racing;
(einzelnes Rennen) cycle race;
Radtour f cycling tour; **Radweg**
m cycle track (o path)

raffiniert adj crafty, cunning;
(Zucker) refined

Rafting (-s) nt white water
rafting

Ragout (-s, -s) nt ragout

Rahm (-s) m cream

rahmen vt to frame; **Rahmen**
(-s, -) m frame

Rakete (-, -n) f rocket

rammen vt to ram

Rampe (-, -n) f ramp

ramponieren vt (fam) to
damage, to batter

Ramsch (-(e)s, -e) m junk

ran (fam) kontr von **heran**

Rand (-(e)s, Ränder) m edge; (von
Brille, Tasse etc) rim; (auf Papier)
margin; (Schmutzrand, unter Augen)
ring; (fig) verge, brink

randalieren vi to (go on the)
rampage; **Randalierer(in)** (-s, -)
m(f) hooligan

Randstein m kerb (Brit), curb
(US); **Randstreifen** m shoulder

rang imperf von **ringen**

Rang (-(e)s, Ränge) m rank; (in
Wettbewerb) place; (Theat) circle

rannte imperf von **rennen**

ranzig adj rancid

Rap (-(s), -s) m (Mus) rap; **rappen**
vi (Mus) to rap; **Rapper(in)** (-s, -)
m(f) (Mus) rapper

rar adj rare, scarce

rasant adj quick, rapid

rasch adj quick

rascheln vi to rustle

rasen vi (sich schnell bewegen)
to race; (toben) to rave; **gegen
einen Baum ~** to crash into a
tree

Rasen (-s, -) m lawn

rasend adj (vor Wut) furious

Rasenmäher (-s, -) m
lawnmower

Rasierapparat m razor;
(elektrischer) shaver; **Rasiercreme**
f shaving cream; **rasieren** vt to
shave ▷ vr: **sich ~** to shave;
Rasierer m shaver; **Rasiergel** nt
shaving gel; **Rasierklinge** f
razor blade; **Rasiermesser** nt
(cutthroat) razor; **Rasierpinsel**
m shaving brush; **Rasierschaum**
m shaving foam; **Rasierzeug** nt
shaving tackle, shaving
equipment

Rasse (-, -n) f race; (Tiere) breed

Rassismus m racism;
Rassist(in) m(f) racist;
rassistisch adj racist

Rast (-, -en) f rest, break;
~ machen to have a rest (o break);
rasten vi to rest; **Rastplatz** m
(Auto) rest area; **Raststätte** f
(Auto) service area; (Gaststätte)
motorway (Brit) (o highway (US))
restaurant

Rasur f shave

Rat (-(e)s, Ratschläge) m (piece of)
advice; **sie hat mir einen
~ gegeben** she gave me some

advice; **um ~ fragen** to ask for advice

Rate (-, -n) f instalment; **etw auf ~n kaufen** to buy sth in instalments (Brit), to buy sth on the instalment plan (US)

raten (riet, geraten) vt, vi to guess; (empfehlen) to advise (jdm sb)

Rathaus nt town hall

Ration f ration

ratlos adj at a loss, helpless; **ratsam** adj advisable

Rätsel (-s, -) nt puzzle; (Worträtsel) riddle; **das ist mir ein ~** it's a mystery to me; **rätselhaft** adj mysterious

Ratte (-, -n) f rat

rau adj rough, coarse; (Wetter) harsh

Raub (-(e)s) m robbery; (Beute) loot, booty; **rauben** vt to steal; **jdm etw ~** to rob sb of sth; **Räuber(in)** (-s, -) m(f) robber; **Raubfisch** m predatory fish; **Raubkopie** f pirate copy; **Raubmord** m robbery with murder; **Raubtier** nt predator; **Raubüberfall** m mugging; **Raubvogel** m bird of prey

Rauch (-(e)s) m smoke; (Abgase) fumes pl; **rauchen** vt, vi to smoke; **Raucher(in)** (-s, -) m(f) smoker; **Raucherabteil** nt smoking compartment

Räucherlachs m smoked salmon; **räuchern** vt to smoke

rauchig adj smoky; **Rauchmelder** m smoke detector; **Rauchverbot** nt smoking ban; **hier ist ~** there's no smoking here

rauf (fam) kontr von **herauf**

rauh adj siehe **rau**; **Rauhreif** m siehe **Raureif**

Raum (-(e)s, Räume) m space; (Zimmer, Platz) room; (Gebiet) area

räumen vt to clear; (Wohnung, Platz) to vacate; (wegbringen) to

shift, to move; (in Schrank etc) to put away

Raumfähre f space shuttle; **Raumfahrt** f space travel; **Raumschiff** nt spacecraft, spaceship; **Raumsonde** f space probe; **Raumstation** f space station

Raumtemperatur f room temperature

Räumungsverkauf m clearance sale, closing-down sale

Raupe (-, -n) f caterpillar

Raureif m hoarfrost

raus (fam) kontr von **heraus**, **hinaus**; **~!** (get) out!

Rausch (-(e)s, Räusche) m intoxication; **einen ~ haben/kriegen** to be/get drunk

rauschen vi (Wasser) to rush; (Baum) to rustle; (Radio etc) to hiss; **Rauschgift** nt drug; **Rauschgiftsüchtige(r)** mf drug addict

raus|fliegen irr vi (fam) to be kicked out

raus|halten irr vr (fam) **halt du dich da raus!** you (just) keep out of it

räuspern vr: **sich ~** to clear one's throat

raus|schmeißen irr vt (fam) to throw out

Razzia (-, Razzien) f raid

reagieren vi to react (auf +akk to); **Reaktion** f reaction

real adj real; **realisieren** vt (merken) to realize; (verwirklichen) to implement; **realistisch** adj realistic; **Realität** (-, -en) f reality; **Reality-TV** (-s) nt reality TV

Realschule f ≈ secondary school, junior high (school) (US)

Rebe (-, -n) f vine

rebellieren vi to rebel

Rebhuhn nt partridge

rechnen *vt, vi* to calculate; **~ mit** to expect; (*bauen auf*) to count on ▷ *vr*: **sich ~** to pay off, to turn out to be profitable; **Rechner** (*-s, -*) *m* calculator; (*Computer*) computer; **Rechnung** *f* calculation(s); (*Comm*) bill (*Brit*), check (*US*); **die ~, bitte!** can I have the bill, please?; **das geht auf meine ~** this is on me

recht *adj* (*richtig, passend*) right; **~ haben** to be right; **jdm ~ geben** to agree with sb; **mir soll's ~ sein** it's alright by me; **mir ist es ~** I don't mind ▷ *adv* really, quite; (*richtig*) right(ly); **ich weiß nicht ~** I don't really know; **es geschieht ihm ~** it serves him right

Recht (*-(e)s, -e*) *nt* right; (*Jur*) law

Rechte (*-n, -n*) *f* right-hand side; (*Hand*) right hand; (*Pol*) right (wing); **rechte(r, s)** *adj* right; **auf der ~n Seite** on the right, on the right-hand side; **Rechte(s)** *nt* right thing; **etwas/nichts ~s** something/nothing proper

Rechteck (*-s, -e*) *nt* rectangle; **rechteckig** *adj* rectangular

rechtfertigen *vt* to justify ▷ *vr*: **sich ~** to justify oneself

rechtlich *adj* legal; **rechtmäßig** *adj* legal, lawful

rechts *adv* on the right; **~ abbiegen** to turn right; **~ von** to the right of; **~ oben** at the top right

Rechtsanwalt *m*, **-anwältin** *f* lawyer

Rechtschreibung *f* spelling

Rechtshänder(in) (*-s, -*) *m(f)* right-hander; **rechtsherum** *adv* to the right, clockwise; **rechtsradikal** *adj* (*Pol*) extreme right-wing

Rechtsschutzversicherung *f* legal costs insurance

Rechtsverkehr *m* driving on the right

rechtswidrig *adj* illegal

rechtwinklig *adj* right-angled; **rechtzeitig** *adj* timely ▷ *adv* in time

recycelbar *adj* recyclable; **recyceln** *vt* to recycle; **Recycling** (*-s*) *nt* recycling; **Recyclingpapier** *nt* recycled paper

Redakteur(in) *m(f)* editor; **Redaktion** *f* editing; (*Leute*) editorial staff; (*Büro*) editorial office(s)

Rede (*-, -n*) *f* speech; (*Gespräch*) talk; **eine ~ halten** to make a speech; **reden** *vi* to talk, to speak ▷ *vt* to say; (*Unsinn etc*) to talk; **Redewendung** *f* idiom; **Redner(in)** *m(f)* speaker

reduzieren *vt* to reduce

Referat (*-s, -e*) *nt* paper; **ein ~ halten** to give a paper (*über +akk* on)

reflektieren *vt* to reflect

Reform (*-, -en*) *f* reform; **Reformhaus** *nt* health food shop; **reformieren** *vt* to reform

Regal (*-s, -e*) *nt* shelf; (*Möbelstück*) shelves *pl*

Regel (*-, -n*) *f* rule; (*Med*) period; **regelmäßig** *adj* regular; **regeln** *vt* to regulate, to control; (*Angelegenheit*) to settle ▷ *vr*: **sich von selbst ~** to sort itself out; **Regelung** *f* regulation

Regen (*-s, -*) *m* rain; **Regenbogen** *m* rainbow; **Regenmantel** *m* raincoat; **Regenrinne** *f* gutter; **Regenschauer** *m* shower; **Regenschirm** *m* umbrella; **Regenwald** *m* rainforest; **Regenwurm** *m* earthworm

Regie *f* direction

regieren *vt, vi* to govern, to rule;

Regierung f government; (von Monarch) reign

Region f region; regional adj regional

Regisseur(in) m(f) director

registrieren vt to register; (bemerken) to notice

regnen vi impers to rain; regnerisch adj rainy

regulär adj regular; regulieren vt to regulate, to adjust

Reh (-(e)s, -e) nt deer; (Fleisch) venison

Rehabilitationszentrum nt (Med) rehabilitation centre

Reibe (-, -n) f, Reibeisen nt grater; reiben (rieb, gerieben) vt to rub; (Gastr) to grate; reibungslos adj smooth

reich adj rich

Reich (-(e)s, -e) nt empire; (eines Königs) kingdom

reichen vi to reach; (genügen) to be enough, to be sufficient (jdm for sb) ▷ vt to hold out; (geben) to pass, to hand; (anbieten) to offer

reichhaltig adj ample, rich; reichlich adj (Trinkgeld) generous; (Essen) ample; ~ Zeit plenty of time; Reichtum (-s, -tümer) m wealth

reif adj ripe; (Mensch, Urteil) mature

Reif (-(e)s) m (Raureif) hoarfrost ▷ (-(e)s, -e) m (Ring) ring, hoop

reifen vi to mature; (Obst) to ripen

Reifen (-s, -) m ring, hoop; (von Auto) tyre; Reifendruck m tyre pressure; Reifenpanne m puncture; Reifenwechsel m tyre change

Reihe (-, -n) f row; (von Tagen etc, fam: Anzahl) series sing; der ~ nach one after the other; er ist an der ~ it's his turn; Reihenfolge f order, sequence; Reihenhaus nt terraced house (Brit), row house (US)

Reiher (-s, -) m heron

rein (fam) kontr von herein, hinein ▷ adj pure; (sauber) clean

Reinfall m (fam) letdown; rein|fallen irr vi (fam) auf etw (akk) ~ to fall for sth

reinigen vt to clean; Reinigung f cleaning; (Geschäft) (dry) cleaner's; Reinigungsmittel nt cleaning agent, cleaner

rein|legen vt: jdn ~ to take sb for a ride

Reis (-es, -e) m rice

Reise (-, -n) f journey; (auf Schiff) voyage; Reiseapotheke f first-aid kit; Reisebüro nt travel agent's; Reisebus m coach; Reiseführer(in) m(f) (Mensch) courier; (Buch) guide(book); Reisegepäck nt luggage (Brit), baggage; Reisegesellschaft f (Veranstalter) tour operator; Reisegruppe f tourist party; (mit Reisebus) coach party; Reiseleiter(in) m(f) courier; reisen vi to travel; ~ nach to go to; Reisende(r) mf traveller; Reisepass m passport; Reiseroute f route, itinerary; Reiserücktrittversicherung f holiday cancellation insurance; Reisescheck m traveller's cheque; Reisetasche f holdall (Brit), carryall (US); Reiseveranstalter m tour operator; Reiseverkehr m holiday traffic; Reiseversicherung f travel insurance; Reiseziel nt destination

Reiskocher (-s, -) m rice steamer

reißen (riss, gerissen) vt, vi to tear; (ziehen) to pull, to drag; (Witz) to crack

Reißnagel *m* drawing pin (Brit),
thumbtack (US); **Reißverschluss**
m zip (Brit), zipper (US);
Reißzwecke *f* drawing pin (Brit),
thumbtack (US)

reiten (ritt, geritten) *vt, vi* to ride;
Reiter(in) *m(f)* rider; **Reithose** *f*
riding breeches *pl*; **Reitsport** *m*
riding; **Reitstiefel** *m* riding boot

Reiz (-es, -e) *m* stimulus;
(angenehm) charm; (Verlockung)
attraction; **reizen** *vt* to
stimulate; (unangenehm) to annoy;
(verlocken) to appeal to, to attract;
reizend *adj* charming; **Reizgas**
nt irritant gas; **Reizung** *f*
irritation

Reklamation *f* complaint

Reklame (-, -n) *f* advertising;
(Einzelwerbung) advertisement; (im
Fernsehen) commercial

reklamieren *vi* to complain
(wegen about)

Rekord (-(e)s, -e) *m* record

relativ *adj* relative ▷ *adv*
relatively

relaxen *vi* to relax, to chill out

Religion *f* religion; **religiös** *adj*
religious

Remoulade (-, -n) *f* tartar sauce

Renaissance *f* renaissance,
revival; (Hist) Renaissance

Rennbahn *f* racecourse; (Auto)
racetrack; **rennen** (rannte, gerannt)
vt, vi to run; **Rennen** (-s, -) *nt*
running; (Wettbewerb) race;
Rennfahrer(in) *m(f)* racing
driver; **Rennrad** *nt* racing bike;
Rennwagen *m* racing car

renommiert *adj* famous, noted
(wegen, für for)

renovieren *vt* to renovate;
Renovierung *f* renovation

rentabel *adj* profitable

Rente (-, -n) *f* pension;
Rentenversicherung *f* pension
scheme

Rentier *nt* reindeer

rentieren *vr*: **sich ~** to pay, to be
profitable

Rentner(in) (-s, -) *m(f)*
pensioner, senior citizen

Reparatur *f* repair;
Reparaturwerkstatt *f* repair
shop; (Auto) garage; **reparieren**
vt to repair

Reportage *f* report;
Reporter(in) (-s, -) *m(f)* reporter

Reptil (-s, -ien) *nt* reptile

Republik *f* republic

Reservat (-s, -e) *nt* nature
reserve; (für Ureinwohner)
reservation; **Reserve** (-, -n) *f*
reserve; **Reservekanister** *m*
spare can; **Reserverad** *nt* (Auto)
spare wheel; **reservieren** *vt* to
reserve; **Reservierung** *f*
reservation

resignieren *vi* to give up;
resigniert *adj* resigned

Respekt (-(e)s) *m* respect;
respektieren *vt* to respect

Rest (-(e)s, -e) *m* rest, remainder;
(Überreste) remains *pl*; **der ~ ist
für Sie** (zur Bedienung) keep the
change

Restaurant (-s, -s) *nt* restaurant

restaurieren *vt* to restore

Restbetrag *m* balance; **restlich**
adj remaining; **restlos** *adj*
complete

Resultat *nt* result

retten *vt* to save, to rescue

Rettich (-s, -e) *m* radish (large
white or red variety)

Rettung *f* rescue; (Hilfe) help;
(Rettungsdienst) ambulance
service; **Rettungsboot** *nt*
lifeboat; **Rettungshubschrauber**
m rescue helicopter;
Rettungsring *m* lifebelt, life
preserver (US); **Rettungswagen**
m ambulance

Reue (-) *f* remorse; (Bedauern)

regret; **reuen** vt: **es reut ihn** he regrets it

revanchieren vr: **sich ~** (*sich rächen*) to get one's back, to get one's revenge; (*für Hilfe etc*) to return the favour

Revolution f revolution

Rezept (-(e)s, -e) nt (*Gastr*) recipe; (*Med*) prescription; **rezeptfrei** adj over-the-counter, non-prescription

Rezeption f (*im Hotel*) reception

rezeptpflichtig adj available only on prescription

R-Gespräch nt reverse-charge (*Brit*) (*o collect* (*US*)) call

Rhabarber (-s) m rhubarb

Rhein (-s) m Rhine; **Rheinland-Pfalz** (-) nt Rhineland-Palatinate

Rheuma (-s) nt rheumatism

Rhythmus m rhythm

richten vt (*lenken*) to direct (*auf +akk* to); (*Waffe, Kamera*) to point (*auf +akk* at); (*Brief, Anfrage*) to address (*an +akk* to); (*einstellen*) to adjust; (*instand setzen*) to repair; (*zurechtmachen*) to prepare ▷ vr: **sich ~ nach** (*Regel etc*) to keep to; (*Mode, Beispiel*) to follow; (*abhängen von*) to depend on

Richter(in) (-s, -) m(f) judge

Richtgeschwindigkeit f recommended speed

richtig adj right, correct; (*echt*) proper ▷ adv (*fam: sehr*) really; **richtigstellen** vt: **etw ~** (*berichtigen*) to correct sth

Richtlinie f guideline

Richtung f direction; (*Tendenz*) tendency

rieb imperf von **reiben**

riechen (*roch, gerochen*) vt, vi to smell; **nach etw ~** to smell of sth; **an etw** (*dat*) **~** to smell sth

rief imperf von **rufen**

Riegel (-s, -) m bolt; (*Gastr*) bar

Riemen (-s, -) m strap; (*Gürtel*) belt

Riese (-n, -n) m giant; **Riesengarnele** f king prawn; **riesengroß** adj gigantic, huge; **Riesenrad** nt big wheel; **riesig** adj enormous, huge

riet imperf von **raten**

Riff (-(e)s, -e) nt reef

Rind (-(e)s, -er) nt cow; (*Bulle*) bull; (*Gastr*) beef; **~er** pl cattle pl

Rinde (-, -n) f (*Baum*) bark; (*Käse*) rind; (*Brot*) crust

Rinderbraten m roast beef; **Rinderwahn(sinn)** m mad cow disease; **Rindfleisch** nt beef

Ring (-(e)s, -e) m ring; (*Straße*) ring road, **Ringbuch** nt ring binder

ringen (*rang, gerungen*) vi to wrestle; **Ringer(in)** m(f) wrestler; **Ringfinger** m ring finger; **Ringkampf** m wrestling match; **ringsherum** adv round about

Rippe (-, -n) f rib; **Rippenfellentzündung** f pleurisy

Risiko (-s, -s *o* Risiken) nt risk; **auf eigenes ~** at one's own risk; **riskant** adj risky; **riskieren** vt to risk

riss imperf von **reißen**

Riss (-es, -e) m tear; (*in Mauer, Tasse etc*) crack; **rissig** adj cracked; (*Haut*) chapped

ritt imperf von **reiten**

Ritter (-s, -) m knight

Rivale (-n, -n) m, **Rivalin** f rival

Rizinusöl nt castor oil

Robbe (-, -n) f seal

Roboter (-s, -) m robot

robust adj robust

roch imperf von **riechen**

Rock (-(e)s, Röcke) m skirt

Rockband (-, Röcke) m skirt

Rockband (-, Röcke) m skirt

Rodelbahn f toboggan run;
rodeln vi to toboggan

Roggen (-s, -) m rye;
Roggenbrot nt rye bread

roh adj raw; (Mensch) coarse,
crude; **Rohkost** f raw vegetables
and fruit pl

Rohr (-(e)s, -e) nt pipe; (Bot) cane;
(Schilf) reed; **Röhre** (-, -n) f tube;
(Leitung) pipe; (Elek) valve;
(Backröhre) oven; **Rohrzucker** m
cane sugar

Rohstoff m raw material

Rokoko (-s) nt rococo

Rolle (-, -n) f (etw
Zusammengerolltes) roll; (Theat) role

rollen vt, vi to roll

Roller (-s, -) m scooter

Rollerblades® pl Rollerblades®
pl; **Rollerskates** pl roller skates
pl

Rollkragenpullover m polo-
neck (Brit) (o turtleneck (US))
sweater; **Rollladen** m, **Rollo**
(-s, -s) m (roller) shutters pl;
Rollschuh m roller skate;
Rollstuhl m wheelchair;
rollstuhlgerecht adj suitable
for wheelchairs; **Rolltreppe** f
escalator

Roman (-s, -e) m novel

Romantik f romance;
romantisch adj romantic

römisch-katholisch adj Roman
Catholic

röntgen vt to X-ray;
Röntgenaufnahme f,
Röntgenbild nt X-ray;
Röntgenstrahlen pl X-rays pl

rosa adj inv pink

Rose (-, -n) f rose

Rosenkohl m (Brussels) sprouts
pl

Rosé(wein) m rosé (wine)

rosig adj rosy

Rosine (-, -n) f raisin

Rosmarin (-s) m rosemary

Rosskastanie f horse chestnut

Rost (-(e)s, -e) m rust; (zum Braten)
grill, gridiron; **Rostbratwurst** f
grilled sausage; **rosten** vi to
rust; **rösten** vt to roast, to grill;
(Brot) to toast; **rostfrei** adj
rustproof; (Stahl) stainless; **rostig**
adj rusty; **Rostschutz** m
rustproofing

rot adj red; ~ **werden** to blush;
Rote Karte red card; **Rote Bete**
beetroot; **bei Rot über die Ampel
fahren** to jump the lights; **das
Rote Kreuz** the Red Cross

Röteln pl German measles sing

röten vt to redden ▷ vr: **sich ~** to
redden

rothaarig adj red-haired

rotieren vi to rotate; **am
Rotieren sein** (fam) to be rushing
around like a mad thing

Rotkehlchen nt robin; **Rotkohl**
m, **Rotkraut** nt red cabbage;
Rotlichtviertel nt red-light
district; **Rotwein** m red wine

Rouge (-s, -s) nt rouge

Route (-, -n) f route

Routine f experience; (Trott)
routine

Rubbellos nt scratchcard;
rubbeln vt to rub

Rübe (-, -n) f turnip; **Gelbe
~** carrot; **Rote ~** beetroot

rüber (fam) kontr von **herüber,
hinüber**

rückbestätigen vt (Flug etc) to
reconfirm

rücken vt, vi to move; **könntest
du ein bisschen ~?** could you
move over a bit?

Rücken (-s, -) m back;
Rückenlehne f back(rest);
Rückenmark nt spinal cord;
Rückenschmerzen pl backache
sing; **Rückenschwimmen** (-s) nt
backstroke; **Rückenwind** m
tailwind

Rückerstattung f refund;
Rückfahrkarte f return ticket
(Brit), round-trip ticket (US);
Rückfahrt f return journey;
Rückfall m relapse; **Rückflug** m
return flight; **Rückgabe** f return;
rückgängig adj: **etw ~ machen**
to cancel sth; **Rückgrat** (-(e)s, -e)
nt spine, backbone; **Rückkehr**
(-, -en) f return; **Rücklicht** nt
rear light; **Rückreise** f return
journey; **auf der ~** on the way
back

Rucksack m rucksack, backpack;
Rucksacktourist(in) m(f)
backpacker

Rückschritt m step back;
Rückseite f back; (hinterer Teil)
rear; **siehe ~** see overleaf;
Rücksicht f consideration;
~ nehmen auf (+akk) to show
consideration for; **rücksichtslos**
adj inconsiderate; (Fahren)
reckless; (unbarmherzig) ruthless;
rücksichtsvoll adj considerate;
Rücksitz m back seat;
Rückspiegel m (Auto) rear-view
mirror; **Rückstand** m: **sie sind
zwei Tore im ~** they're two goals
down; **im ~ sein mit** (Arbeit, Miete)
to be behind with; **Rücktaste** f
backspace key; **Rückvergütung**
f refund; **rückwärts** adv
backwards, back; **Rückwärtsgang** m (Auto) reverse (gear);
Rückweg m return journey, way
back; **Rückzahlung** f repayment

Ruder (-s, -) nt oar; (Steuer)
rudder; **Ruderboot** nt rowing
boat (Brit), rowboat (US); **rudern**
vt, vi to row

Ruf (-(e)s, -e) m call, cry; (Ansehen)
reputation; **rufen** (rief, gerufen) vt,
vi to call; (schreien) to cry;
Rufnummer f telephone number

Ruhe (-) f rest; (Ungestörtheit)
peace, quiet; (Gelassenheit, Stille)
calm; (Schweigen) silence; **lass
mich in ~!** leave me alone; **ruhen**
vi to rest; **Ruhestand** m
retirement; **im ~ sein** to be retired;
Ruhestörung f disturbance of
the peace; **Ruhetag** m closing
day; **montags ~ haben** to be
closed on Mondays

ruhig adj quiet; (bewegungslos)
still; (Hand) steady; (gelassen) calm

Ruhm (-(e)s) m fame, glory

Rührei nt scrambled egg(s);
rühren vt to move; (umrühren) to
stir ▸ vr: **sich ~** to move; (sich
bemerkbar machen) to say
something; **rührend** adj
touching, moving; **Rührung** f
emotion

Ruine (-, -n) f ruin; **ruinieren** vt
to ruin

rülpsen vi to burp, to belch

rum (fam) kontr von **herum**

Rum (-s, -s) m rum

Rumänien (-s) nt Romania

Rummel (-s) m (Trubel) hustle
and bustle; (Jahrmarkt) fair;
(Medienrummel) hype;
Rummelplatz m fairground

rumoren vi: **es rumort in
meinem Bauch/Kopf** my
stomach is rumbling/my head is
spinning

Rumpf (-(e)s, Rümpfe) m (Anat)
trunk; (Aviat) fuselage; (Naut)
hull

rümpfen vt: **die Nase ~** to turn
one's nose up (über at)

Rumpsteak nt rump steak

rund adj round ▸ adv (etwa)
around; **~ um etw** (a)round sth;
Runde (-, -n) f round; (in Rennen)
lap; **Rundfahrt** f tour (durch of);
Rundfunk m broadcasting;
(Rundfunkanstalt) broadcasting
service; **im ~** on the radio;
Rundgang m tour (durch of); (von
Wächter) round

rundlich _adj_ plump; **Rundreise** _f_ tour _(durch of)_

runter _(fam)_ kontr von **herunter, hinunter; runterscrollen** _vt_ _(Inform)_ to scroll down

runzeln _vt_: **die Stirn ~** to frown; **runzelig** _adj_ wrinkled

ruppig _adj_ gruff

Rüsche (-, -n) _f_ frill

Ruß (-es) _m_ soot

Russe (-n, -n) _m_ Russian

Rüssel (-s, -) _m_ _(Elefant)_ trunk; _(Schwein)_ snout

Russin _f_ Russian; **russisch** _adj_ Russian; **Russisch** _nt_ Russian; **Russland** _nt_ Russia

Rüstung _f_ _(mit Waffen)_ arming; _(Ritterrüstung)_ armour; _(Waffen)_ armaments _pl_

Rutsch (-(e)s, -e) _m_: **guten ~ (ins neue Jahr)!** Happy New Year; **Rutschbahn** _f_, **Rutsche** _f_ slide; **rutschen** _vi_ to slide; _(ausrutschen)_ to slip; **rutschig** _adj_ slippery

rütteln _vt, vi_ to shake

S _abk_ = **Süd** S

s. _abk_ = **siehe** see; = **Seite** p.

Saal (-(e)s, Säle) _m_ hall; _(für Sitzungen)_ room

Saarland _nt_ Saarland

sabotieren _vt_ to sabotage

Sache (-, -n) _f_ thing; _(Angelegenheit)_ affair, business; _(Frage)_ matter; **bei der ~ bleiben** to keep to the point; **sachkundig** _adj_ competent; **Sachlage** _f_ situation; **sachlich** _adj_ _(objektiv)_ objective; _(nüchtern)_ matter-of-fact; _(inhaltlich)_ factual; **sächlich** _adj_ _(Ling)_ neuter; **Sachschaden** _m_ material damage

Sachsen (-s) _nt_ Saxony; **Sachsen-Anhalt** (-s) _nt_ Saxony-Anhalt

sacht(e) _adv_ softly, gently

Sachverständige(r) _mf_ expert

Sack (-(e)s, Säcke) _m_ sack; _(pej:_

Mensch) bastard, bugger;
Sackgasse f dead end, cul-de-sac
Safe (-s, -s) m safe
Safer Sex m safe sex
Safran (-s, -e) m saffron
Saft (-(e)s, *Säfte*) m juice; **saftig**
adj juicy
Sage (-, -n) f legend
Säge (-, -n) f saw; **Sägemehl** nt
sawdust
sagen vt, vi to say (*jdm* to sb),
to tell (*jdm* sb); **wie sagt man ...
auf Englisch?** what's ... in
English?
sägen vt, vi to saw
sagenhaft adj legendary; (*fam:
großartig*) fantastic
sah imperf von **sehen**
Sahne (-) f cream
Saison (-, -s) f season;
außerhalb der ~ out of season
Saite (-, -n) f string
Sakko (-s, -s) nt jacket
Salami (-, -s) f salami
Salat (-(e)s, -e) m salad;
(*Kopfsalat*) lettuce; **Salatbar** f
salad bar; **Salatschüssel** f salad
bowl; **Salatsoße** f salad
dressing
Salbe (-, -n) f ointment
Salbei (-s) m sage
Salmonellenvergiftung f
salmonella (poisoning)
salopp adj (*Kleidung*) casual;
(*Sprache*) slangy
Salsamusik f salsa (music)
Salto (-s, -s) m somersault
Salz (-es, -e) nt salt; **salzarm** adj
low-salt; **salzen** (*salzte, gesalzen*)
vt to salt; **Salzgurke** f pickled
gherkin; **Salzhering** m pickled
herring; **salzig** adj salty;
Salzkartoffeln pl boiled potatoes
pl; **Salzstange** f pretzel stick;
Salzstreuer m salt cellar (Brit) (o
shaker (US)); **Salzwasser** nt salt
water

Samba (-, -s) f samba
Samen (-s, -) m seed; (*Sperma*)
sperm
sammeln vt to collect;
Sammler(in) m(f) collector;
Sammlung f collection,
(*Ansammlung, Konzentration*)
concentration
Samstag m Saturday; *siehe auch*
Mittwoch; **samstags** adv on
Saturdays; *siehe auch* **mittwochs**
samt prep +dat (along) with,
together with
Samt ((e)s, -e) m velvet
sämtliche(r, s) adj all (the)
Sanatorium (-s, *Sanatorien*) nt
sanatorium (Brit), sanitarium (US)
Sand (-(e)s, -e) m sand
Sandale (-, -n) f sandal
sandig adj sandy; **Sandkasten**
m sandpit (Brit), sandbox (US);
Sandpapier nt sandpaper;
Sandstrand m sandy beach
sandte imperf von **senden**
sanft adj soft, gentle
sang imperf von **singen**
Sänger(in) (-s, -) m(f) singer
Sangria (-, -s) f sangria
sanieren vt to redevelop;
(*Gebäude*) to renovate; (*Betrieb*) to
restore to profitability
sanitär adj sanitary; **~e Anlagen**
pl sanitation
Sanitäter(in) (-s, -) m(f) ambu-
lance man/woman, paramedic
sank imperf von **sinken**
Sankt Gallen (-s) nt St Gallen
Saphir (-s, -e) m sapphire
Sardelle f anchovy
Sardine f sardine
Sarg (-(e)s, *Särge*) m coffin
saß imperf von **sitzen**
Satellit (-en, -en) m satellite;
Satellitenfernsehen nt satellite
IV; **Satellitenschüssel** f (fam)
satellite dish
Satire (-, -n) f satire (*auf +akk* on)

satt *adj* full; (*Farbe*) rich, deep;
~ **sein** (*gesättigt*) to be full;
~ **machen** to be filling; **jdn/etw**
~ **sein** to be fed up with sb/sth
Sattel (-s, *Sättel*) *m* saddle
satt|haben *irr vt:* **jdn/etw**
~ (*nicht mehr mögen*) to be fed up
with sb/sth
Saturn (-s) *m* Saturn
Satz (-es, *Sätze*) *m* (*Ling*) sentence;
(*Mus*) movement; (*Tennis*) set;
(*Kaffee*) grounds pl; (*Comm*) rate
(*Sprung*) jump; (*Comm*) rate
Satzzeichen *nt* punctuation
mark
Sau (-, *Säue*) *f* sow; (*pej: Mensch*)
dirty bugger
sauber *adj* clean; (*ironisch*) fine;
~ **machen** to clean; **Sauberkeit** *f*
cleanness; (*von Person*) cleanliness;
säubern *vt* to clean
saublöd *adj* (*fam*) really stupid,
dumb
Sauce (-, *-n*) *f* sauce; (*zu Braten*)
gravy
Saudi-Arabien (-s) *nt* Saudi
Arabia
sauer *adj* sour; (*Chem*) acid; (*fam:
verärgert*) cross; **saurer Regen** acid
rain; **Sauerkirsche** *f* sour
cherry; **Sauerkraut** *nt*
sauerkraut; **säuerlich** *adj*
sligthhly sour; **Sauermilch** *f*
sour milk; **Sauerrahm** *m* sour
cream; **Sauerstoff** *m* oxygen
saufen (*soff, gesoffen*) *vt* to drink;
(*fam: Mensch*) to knock back ▷ *vi*
to drink; (*fam: Mensch*) to booze
saugen (*sog o saugte, gesogen o
gesaugt*) *vt, vi* to suck; (*mit
Staubsauger*) to vacuum, to hoover
(*Brit*); **Sauger** (-s, *-*) *m* (*auf Flasche*)
teat; **Säugetier** *nt* mammal;
Säugling *m* infant, baby
Säule (-, *-n*) *f* column, pillar
Saum (-s, *Säume*) *m* hem; (*Naht*)
seam

Sauna (-, *-s*) *f* sauna
Säure (-, *-n*) *f* acid
sausen *vi* (*Ohren*) to buzz; (*Wind*)
to howl; (*Mensch*) to rush
Saustall *m* pigsty; **Sauwetter**
nt: **was für ein** ~ (*fam*) what lousy
weather
Saxophon (-s, *-e*) *nt* saxophone
S-Bahn *f* suburban railway;
S-Bahn-Haltestelle *f,* **S-Bahnhof**
m suburban (train) station
scannen *vt* to scan; **Scanner**
(-s, *-*) *m* scanner
schäbig *adj* shabby
Schach (-s, *-s*) *nt* chess; (*Stellung*)
check; **Schachbrett** *nt*
chessboard; **Schachfigur** *f*
chess piece; **schachmatt** *adj*
checkmate
Schacht (-(*e*)s, *Schächte*) *m* shaft
Schachtel (-, *-n*) *f* box
schade *interj* what a pity
Schädel (-s, *-*) *m* skull;
Schädelbruch *m* fractured skull
schaden *vi* to damage, to harm
(*jdm sb*); **das schadet nichts** it
won't do any harm; **Schaden**
(-s, *Schäden*) *m* damage;
(*Verletzung*) injury; (*Nachteil*)
disadvantage; **einen**
~ **verursachen** to cause damage;
Schadenersatz *m* compensation, damages *pl*; **schadhaft** *adj*
faulty; (*beschädigt*) damaged;
schädigen *vt* to damage; (*jdn*) to
do harm to, to harm; **schädlich**
adj harmful (*für* to); **Schadstoff**
m harmful substance;
schadstoffarm *adj* low-emission
Schaf (-(*e*)s, *-e*) *nt* sheep;
Schafbock *m* ram; **Schäfer** (-s, *-*)
m shepherd; **Schäferhund** *m*
Alsatian (*Brit*), German shepherd;
Schäferin *f* shepherdess
schaffen (*schuf, geschaffen*) *vt* to
create; (*Platz*) to make ▷ *vt*
(*erreichen*) to manage, to do;

(erledigen) to finish; *(Prüfung)* to pass; *(transportieren)* to take; **jdm zu ~ machen** to cause sb trouble

Schaffner(in) (-s,) *m(f)* *(in Bus)* conductor/conductress; *(Eisenb)* guard

Schafskäse *m* sheep's (milk) cheese

schal *adj (Getränk)* flat

Schal (-s, -e o -s) *m* scarf

Schälchen *nt* (small) bowl

Schale (-, -n) *f* skin; *(abgeschält)* peel; *(Nuss, Muschel, Ei)* shell; *(Geschirr)* bowl, dish

schälen *vt* to peel; *(Tomate, Mandel)* to skin; *(Erbsen, Eier, Nüsse)* to shell; *(Getreide)* to husk ▷ *vr:* **sich ~** to peel

Schall (-(e)s, -e) *m* sound; **Schalldämpfer** (-s, -) *m (Auto)* silencer *(Brit)*, muffler *(US)*; **Schallplatte** *f* record

Schalotte (-, -n) *f* shallot

schalten *vt* to switch ▷ *vi (Auto)* to change gear; *(fam: begreifen)* to catch on; **Schalter** (-s, -) *m (auf Post, Bank)* counter; *(an Gerät)* switch; **Schalterhalle** *f* main hall; **Schalteröffnungszeiten** *pl* business hours *pl*

Schaltfläche *f (Inform)* button; **Schalthebel** *m* gear lever *(Brit)* (o shift *(US)*); **Schaltjahr** *nt* leap year; **Schaltknüppel** *m* gear lever *(Brit)* (o shift *(US)*); **Schaltung** *f* gear change *(Brit)*, gearshift *(US)*

Scham (-) *f* shame; *(Schamgefühl)* modesty; *(Schamteile)* private parts *pl*; **schämen** *vr:* **sich ~** to be ashamed

Schande (-) *f* disgrace

Schanze (-, -n) *f* ski jump

Schar (-, -en) *f (von Vögeln)* flock; *(Menge)* crowd; **in ~en** in droves

scharf *adj (Messer, Kritik)* sharp; *(Essen)* hot; **auf etw *(akk)* ~ sein** *(fam)* to be keen on sth

Schärfe (-, -n) *f* sharpness; *(Strenge)* rigour; *(Foto)* focus

Scharlach (-s) *m (Med)* scarlet fever

Scharnier (-s, -e) *nt* hinge

Schaschlik (-s, -s) *m o nt (shish)* kebab

Schatten (-s, -) *m* shadow; **30 Grad im ~** 30 degrees in the shade; **schattig** *adj* shady

Schatz (-es, Schätze) *m* treasure; *(Mensch)* love

schätzen *vt (abschätzen)* to estimate; *(Gegenstand)* to value; *(würdigen)* to value, to esteem; *(vermuten)* to reckon; **Schätzung** *f* estimate; *(von Schätzen)* estimation; *(von Wertgegenstand)* valuation; **schätzungsweise** *adv* roughly, approximately

Schau (-, -en) *f* show; *(Ausstellung)* exhibition

schauen *vi* to look; **ich schau mal, ob ...** I'll go and have a look whether ...; **schau, dass ...** see (to it) that ...

Schauer (-s, -) *m (Regen)* shower; *(Schreck)* shudder

Schaufel (-, -n) *f* shovel; **~ und Besen** dustpan and brush; **schaufeln** *vt* to shovel; **Schnee ~** to clear the snow away

Schaufenster *nt* shop window; **Schaufensterbummel** *m* window-shopping expedition

Schaukel (-, -n) *f* swing; **schaukeln** *vi* to rock; *(mit Schaukel)* to swing

Schaulustige(r) *mf* gawper *(Brit)*, rubbernecker *(US)*

Schaum (-(e)s, Schäume) *m* foam; *(Seifenschaum)* lather; *(Bierschaum)* froth; **Schaumbad** *nt* bubble bath; **schäumen** *vi* to foam; **Schaumfestiger** (-s, -) *m* styling mousse; **Schaumgummi** *m*

foam (rubber); **Schaumwein** m sparkling wine

Schauplatz m scene; **Schauspiel** nt spectacle; (Theat) play; **Schauspieler(in)** m(f) actor/actress

Scheck (-s, -s) m cheque; **Scheckheft** nt chequebook; **Scheckkarte** f cheque card

Scheibe (-, -n) f disc; (von Brot, Käse etc) slice; (Glasscheibe) pane; **Scheibenbremse** f (Auto) disc brake; **Scheibenwaschanlage** f (Auto) windscreen (Brit) (o windshield (US)) washer unit; **Scheibenwischer** (-s, -) m (Auto) windscreen (Brit) (o windshield (US)) wiper

Scheich (-s, -e) m sheik(h)

Scheide (-, -n) f (Anat) vagina

scheiden (schied, geschieden) vt (trennen) to separate; (Ehe) to dissolve; **sich ~ lassen** to get a divorce; **sie hat sich von ihm ~ lassen** she divorced him; **Scheidung** f divorce

Schein (-(e)s, -e) m light; (Anschein) appearance; (Geld) (bank)note; **scheinbar** adj apparent; **scheinen** (schien, geschienen) vi (Sonne) to shine; (den Anschein haben) to seem; **Scheinwerfer** (-s, -) m floodlight; (Theat) spotlight; (Auto) headlight

Scheiß- in zW (vulg) damned, bloody (Brit); **Scheiße** (-) f (vulg) shit, crap; **scheißegal** adj (vulg) **das ist mir ~** I don't give a damn (o toss); **scheißen** (schiss, geschissen) vi (vulg) to shit

Scheitel (-s, -) m parting (Brit), part (US)

scheitern vi to fail (an +dat because of)

Schellfisch m haddock

Schema (-s, -s o Schemata) nt

scheme, plan; (Darstellung) diagram

Schenkel (-s, -) m thigh

schenken vt to give; **er hat es mir geschenkt** he gave it to me (as a present); **sich** (dat) **etw ~** (fam: weglassen) to skip sth

Scherbe (-, -n) f broken piece, fragment

Schere (-, -n) f scissors pl; (groß) shears pl; **eine ~** a pair of scissors/shears

Scherz (-es, -e) m joke

scheu adj shy

scheuen vr **sich ~ vor** (+dat) to be afraid of, to shrink from ▷ vt to shun ▷ vi (Pferd) to shy

scheuern vt to scrub; **jdm eine ~** (fam) to slap sb in the face

Scheune (-, -n) f barn

scheußlich adj dreadful

Schi (-s, -er) m siehe **Ski**

Schicht (-, -en) f layer; (in Gesellschaft) class; (in Fabrik etc) shift

schick adj stylish, chic

schicken vt to send ▷ vr: **sich ~** (sich beeilen) to hurry up

Schickimicki (-(s), -s) m (fam) trendy

Schicksal (-s, -e) nt fate

Schiebedach nt (Auto) sunroof; **schieben** (schob, geschoben) vt, vi to push; **die Schuld auf jdn ~** to put the blame on sb; **Schiebetür** f sliding door

schied imperf von **scheiden**

Schiedsrichter(in) m(f) referee; (Tennis) umpire; (Schlichter) arbitrator

schief adj crooked; (Blick) funny ▷ adv crooked(ly); **schiefgehen** irr vi (fam: misslingen) to go wrong

schielen vi to squint

schien imperf von **scheinen**

Schienbein nt shin

Schiene (-, -n) f rail; (Med) splint

schier adj pure; (fig) sheer ▷ adv nearly, almost

schießen (schoss, geschossen) vt to shoot; (Ball) to kick; (Tor) to score; (Foto) to take ▷ vi to shoot (auf +akk at)

Schiff (-(e)s, -e) nt ship; (in Kirche) nave; **Schifffahrt** f shipping; **Schiffsreise** f voyage

schikanieren vt to harass; (Schule) to bully

Schild (-(e)s, -e) m (Schutz) shield ▷ (-(e)s, -er) nt sign; **was steht auf dem ~?** what does the sign say?

Schilddrüse f thyroid gland

schildern vt to describe

Schildkröte f tortoise; (Wasserschildkröte) turtle

Schimmel (-s, -) m mould; (Pferd) white horse; **schimmeln** vi to go mouldy

schimpfen vt to tell off ▷ vi (sich beklagen) to complain; **mit jdm ~** to tell sb off; **Schimpfwort** nt swearword

Schinken (-s, -) m ham

Schirm (-(e)s, -e) m (Regenschirm) umbrella; (Sonnenschirm) parasol, sunshade

schiss imperf von **scheißen**

Schlacht (-, -en) f battle; **schlachten** vt to slaughter; **Schlachter(in)** (-s, -) m(f) butcher

Schlaf (-(e)s) m sleep; **Schlafanzug** m pyjamas pl; **Schlafcouch** f bed settee

Schläfe (-, -n) f temple

schlafen (schlief, geschlafen) vi to sleep; **schlaf gut!** sleep well; **hast du gut geschlafen?** did you sleep all right?; **er schläft noch** he's still asleep; **~ gehen** to go to bed

schlaff adj slack; (kraftlos) limp; (erschöpft) exhausted

Schlafgelegenheit f place to sleep; **Schlaflosigkeit** f

sleeplessness; **Schlafmittel** nt sleeping pill; **schläfrig** adj sleepy

Schlafsaal m dormitory; **Schlafsack** m sleeping bag; **Schlaftablette** f sleeping pill; **er ist eine richtige ~** (fam: langweilig) he's such a bore; **Schlafwagen** m sleeping car, sleeper; **Schlafzimmer** nt bedroom

Schlag (-(e)s, Schläge) m blow; (Puls) beat; (Elek) shock; (fam: Portion) helping; (Art) kind, type; **Schlagader** f artery; **Schlaganfall** m (Med) stroke; **schlagartig** adj sudden

schlagen (schlug, geschlagen) vt to hit; (besiegen) to beat; (Sahne) to whip; **jdn zu Boden ~** to knock sb down ▷ vi (Herz) to beat; (Uhr) to strike; **mit dem Kopf gegen etw ~** to bang one's head against sth ▷ vr: **sich ~** to fight

Schläger (-s, -) m (Sport) bat; (Tennis) racket; (Golf) (golf) club; (Hockey) hockey stick; (Mensch) brawler; **Schlägerei** f fight, brawl

schlagfertig adj quick-witted; **Schlagloch** nt pothole; **Schlagsahne** f whipping cream; (geschlagen) whipped cream; **Schlagzeile** f headline; **Schlagzeug** nt drums pl; (in Orchester) percussion

Schlamm (-(e)s, -e) m mud; **schlampig** adj (fam) sloppy

schlang imperf von **schlingen**

Schlange (-, -n) f snake; (von Menschen) queue (Brit), line (US); **~ stehen** to queue (Brit), to stand in line (US); **Schlangenlinie** f wavy line; **in ~n fahren** to swerve about

schlank adj slim

schlapp adj limp; (locker) slack

Schlappe (-, -n) f (fam) setback

schlau adj clever, smart;
(raffiniert) crafty, cunning
Schlauch (-(e)s, Schläuche) m
hose; (in Reifen) inner tube;
Schlauchboot nt rubber dinghy
schlecht adj bad; **mir ist ~** I feel
sick; **die Milch ist ~** the milk has
gone off ▷ adv badly; **es geht ihm
~** he's having a hard time;
(gesundheitlich) he's not feeling
well; (finanziell) he's pretty hard
up; **schlecht|machen** vt: **jdn
~** (herabsetzen) to run sb down
schleichen (schlich, geschlichen) vi
to creep
Schleier (-s, -) m veil
Schleife (-, -n) f (Inform, Aviat,
Elek) loop; (Band) bow
schleifen vt (ziehen, schleppen) to
drag ▷ (schliff, geschliffen) vt
(schärfen) to grind; (Edelstein)
to cut
Schleim (-(e)s, -e) m slime; (Med)
mucus; **Schleimer** (-s, -) m (fam)
creep; **Schleimhaut** f mucous
membrane
schlendern vi to stroll
schleppen vt to drag; (Auto,
Schiff) to tow; (tragen) to lug;
Schlepplift m ski tow
Schleswig-Holstein (-s) nt
Schleswig-Holstein
Schleuder (-, -n) f catapult; (für
Wäsche) spin-dryer; **schleudern**
vt to hurl; (Wäsche) to spin-dry
▷ vi (Auto) to skid; **Schleudersitz**
m ejector seat
schlich imperf von **schleichen**
schlicht adj simple, plain
schlichten vt (Streit) to settle
schlief imperf von **schlafen**
schließen (schloss, geschlossen) vt,
vi to close, to shut; (beenden) to
close; (Freundschaft, Ehe) to enter
into; (folgern) to infer (aus from)
▷ vr: **sich ~** to close, to shut;
Schließfach nt locker

schließlich adv finally;
(schließlich doch) after all
schliff imperf von **schleifen**
schlimm adj bad; **schlimmer** adj
worse; **schlimmste(r, s)** adj
worst; **schlimmstenfalls** adv at
(the) worst
Schlinge (-, -n) f loop; (Med) sling
Schlips (-es, -e) m tie
Schlitten (-s, -) m sledge,
toboggan; (mit Pferden) sleigh;
Schlittenfahren (-s) nt
tobogganing
Schlittschuh (-s) m ice skate;
~ laufen to ice-skate
Schlitz (-es, -e) m slit; (für Münze)
slot; (an Hose) flies pl
schloss imperf von **schließen**
Schloss (-es, Schlösser) nt lock;
(Burg) castle
Schlosser(in) m(f) mechanic
Schlucht (-, -en) f gorge, ravine
schluchzen vi to sob
Schluck (-(e)s, -e) m swallow;
Schluckauf (-s) m hiccups pl;
schlucken vt, vi to swallow
schludern vi (fam) to do sloppy
work
schlug imperf von **schlagen**
Schlüpfer (-s, -) m panties pl
schlürfen vt, vi to slurp
Schluss (-es, Schlüsse) m end;
(Schlussfolgerung) conclusion; **am
~** at the end; **mit jdm ~ machen** to
finish (o split up) with sb
Schlüssel (-s, -) m (a. fig) key;
Schlüsselbein nt collarbone;
Schlüsselbund m bunch of keys;
Schlüsseldienst m key-cutting
service; **Schlüsselloch** nt keyhole
Schlussfolgerung f conclusion;
Schlusslicht nt tail-light; (fig)
tail-ender; **Schlussverkauf** m
clearance sale
schmächtig adj frail
schmal adj narrow; (Mensch, Buch
etc) slim; (karg) meagre

Schmalz *(-es, -e)* nt dripping, lard; *(fig: Sentimentalitäten)* schmaltz

schmatzen vi to eat noisily

schmecken vt, vi to taste *(nach of)*; **es schmeckt ihm** he likes it; **lass es dir ~!** bon appétit

Schmeichelei f flattery; **schmeichelhaft** adj flattering; **schmeicheln** vi: **jdm ~** to flatter sb

schmeißen *(schmiss, geschmissen)* vt *(fam)* to chuck, to throw

schmelzen *(schmolz, geschmolzen)* vt, vi to melt; *(Metall, Erz)* to smelt; **Schmelzkäse** m cheese spread

Schmerz *(-es, -en)* m pain; *(Trauer)* grief; **~en haben** to be in pain; **~en im Rücken haben** to have a pain in one's back; **schmerzen** vt, vi to hurt; **Schmerzensgeld** nt compensation; **schmerzhaft, schmerzlich** adj painful; **schmerzlos** adj painless; **Schmerzmittel** nt painkiller; **schmerzstillend** adj painkilling; **Schmerztablette** f painkiller

Schmetterling m butterfly

Schmied(in) *(-(e)s, -e)* m(f) blacksmith; **schmieden** vt to forge; *(Pläne)* to make

schmieren vt to smear; *(ölen)* to lubricate, to grease; *(bestechen)* to bribe ▷ vt, vi *(unsauber schreiben)* to scrawl; **Schmiergeld** nt *(fam)* bribe; **schmierig** adj greasy; **Schmierseife** f soft soap

Schminke *(-, -n)* f make-up; **schminken** vr: **sich ~** to put one's make-up on

schmiss *imperf von* **schmeißen**

schmollen vi to sulk; **schmollend** adj sulky

schmolz *imperf von* **schmelzen**

Schmuck *(-(e)s, -e)* m jewellery *(Brit)*, jewelry *(US)*; *(Verzierung)*

decoration; **schmücken** vt to decorate

schmuggeln vt, vi to smuggle

schmunzeln vi to smile

schmusen vi to (kiss and) cuddle

Schmutz *(-es)* m dirt, filth; **schmutzig** adj dirty

Schnabel *(-s, Schnäbel)* m beak, bill; *(Ausguss)* spout

Schnake *(-, -n)* f mosquito

Schnalle *(-, -n)* f buckle

Schnäppchen nt *(fam)* bargain; **schnappen** vt *(fangen)* to catch ▷ vi: **nach Luft ~** to gasp for breath; **Schnappschuss** m *(Foto)* snap(shot)

Schnaps *(-es, Schnäpse)* m schnapps

schnarchen vi to snore

schnaufen vi to puff, to pant

Schnauzbart m moustache; **Schnauze** *(-, -n)* f snout, muzzle; *(Ausguss)* spout; *(fam: Mund)* trap; **die ~ voll haben** to have had enough

schnäuzen vr: **sich ~** to blow one's nose

Schnecke *(-, -n)* f snail; **Schneckenhaus** nt snail's shell

Schnee *(-s)* m snow; **Schneeball** m snowball; **Schneebob** m snowmobile; **Schneebrille** f snow goggles pl; **Schneeflocke** f snowflake; **Schneegestöber** *(-s, -)* nt snow flurry; **Schneeglöckchen** nt snowdrop; **Schneegrenze** f snowline; **Schneekanone** f snow thrower; **Schneekette** f *(Auto)* snow chain; **Schneemann** m snowman; **Schneepflug** m snowplough; **Schneeregen** m sleet; **Schneeschmelze** f thaw; **Schneesturm** m snowstorm, blizzard; **Schneetreiben** nt light blizzards pl; **Schneewehe** f snowdrift

Schneide (-, -n) f edge; (Klinge)
blade; **schneiden** (schnitt,
geschnitten) vt to cut; **sich** (dat) **die
Haare ~ lassen** to have one's hair
cut ▷ vr: **sich ~ to** cut oneself;
Schneider(in) (-s, -) m(f) tailor;
(für Damenmode) dressmaker;
Schneiderin f dressmaker;
Schneidezahn m incisor

schneien vi impers to snow

schnell adj quick, fast ▷ adv
quickly, fast; **mach ~!** hurry up;
Schnelldienst m express service;
Schnellhefter m loose-leaf
binder; **Schnellimbiss** m snack
bar; **Schnellkochtopf** m
pressure cooker;
Schnellreinigung f express dry
cleaning; (Geschäft) express (dry)
cleaner's; **Schnellstraße** f
expressway; **Schnellzug** m fast
train

schneuzen vr siehe **schnäuzen**

schnitt imperf von **schneiden**

Schnitt (-(e)s, -e) m cut;
(Schnittpunkt) intersection;
(Querschnitt) (cross) section;
(Durchschnitt) style; **Schnitte** (-, -n) f
slice; (belegt) sandwich;
Schnittkäse m cheese slices pl;
Schnittlauch m chives pl;
Schnittmuster nt pattern;
Schnittstelle f (Inform, fig)
interface; **Schnittwunde** f cut,
gash

Schnitzel (-s, -) nt (Papier) scrap;
(Gastr) escalope

schnitzen vt to carve

Schnorchel (-s, -) m snorkel;
schnorcheln vi to go snorkelling,
to snorkel

schnüffeln vi to sniff

Schnuller (-s, -) m dummy (Brit),
pacifier (US)

Schnulze (-, -n) f (Film, Roman)
weepie

Schnupfen (-s, -) m cold

schnuppern vi to sniff

Schnur (-, Schnüre) f string, cord;
(Elek) lead; **schnurlos** adj
(Telefon) cordless

Schnurrbart m moustache

schnurren vi to purr

Schnürsenkel (-s, -) m shoelace

schob imperf von **schieben**

Schock (-(e)s, -e) m shock; **unter
~ stehen** to be in a state of shock;
schockieren vt to shock

Schokolade f chocolate;
Schokoriegel m chocolate bar

Scholle (-, -n) f (Fisch) plaice; (Eis)
ice floe

O   SCHLÜSSELWORT

schon adv **1** (bereits) already; **er ist
schon da** he's there already, he's
already there; **ist er schon da?** is
he there yet?; **warst du schon
einmal da?** have you ever been
there?; **ich war schon einmal da**
I've been there before; **das war
schon immer so** that has always
been the case; **schon oft** often;
hast du schon gehört? have you
heard?

2 (bestimmt) all right; **du wirst
schon sehen** you'll see (all right);
das wird schon noch gut that'll
be OK

3 (bloß) just; **allein schon das
Gefühl ...** just the very feeling ...;
schon der Gedanke the very
thought; **wenn ich das schon
höre** I only have to hear that

4 (einschränkend) **ja schon, aber ...**
yes (well), but ...

5 schon möglich possible; **schon
gut!** OK!; **du weißt schon** you
know; **komm schon!** come on!

schön adj beautiful; (nett) nice;
(Frau) beautiful, pretty; (Mann)

beautiful, handsome; (Wetter) fine;
~e Grüße best wishes; **~es
Wochenende** have a nice
weekend

schonen vt (pfleglich behandeln) to
look after ▷ vr: **sich ~** to take it
easy

Schönheit f beauty

Schonkost f light diet

schöpfen vt to scoop; (mit Kelle)
to ladle; **Schöpfkelle** f,
Schöpflöffel m ladle

Schöpfung f creation

Schoppen (-s, -) m glass (of
wine)

Schorf (-(e)s, -e) m scab

Schorle (-, -n) f spritzer

Schornstein m chimney;
Schornsteinfeger(in) (-s, -) m(f)
chimney sweep

schoss imperf von **schießen**

Schoß (-es, Schöße) m lap

Schotte (-n, -n) m Scot,
Scotsman; **Schottin** f Scot,
Scotswoman; **schottisch** adj
Scottish, Scots; **Schottland** nt
Scotland

schräg adj slanting; (Dach)
sloping; (Linie) diagonal; (fam:
unkonventionell) wacky

Schrank (-(e)s, Schränke) m
cupboard; (Kleiderschrank)
wardrobe (Brit), closet (US)

Schranke (-, -n) f barrier

Schrankwand f wall unit

Schraube (-, -n) f screw;
schrauben vt to screw; **Schrau-
bendreher** (-s, -) m screwdriver;
Schraubenschlüssel m spanner;
Schraubenzieher (-s, -) m screwdriver; **Schraubverschluss** m
screw top, screw cap

Schreck (-(e)s, -e) m terror; (Angst)
fright; **jdm
einen ~ einjagen** to give sb a
fright; **schreckhaft** adj jumpy;
schrecklich adj terrible, dreadful

Schrei (-(e)s, -e) m scream; (Ruf)
shout

Schreibblock m writing pad;
schreiben (schrieb, geschrieben) vt,
vi to write; (buchstabieren) to spell;
wie schreibt man ...? how do you
spell ...?; **Schreiben** (-s, -) nt
writing; (Brief) letter;
Schreibfehler m spelling
mistake; **schreibgeschützt** adj
(Diskette) write-protected;
Schreibtisch m desk;
Schreibwaren pl stationery sing;
Schreibwarenladen m
stationer's

schreien (schrie, geschrie(e)n) vt, vi
to scream; (rufen) to shout

Schreiner(in) m(f) joiner;
Schreinerei f joiner's workshop

schrie imperf von **schreien**

schrieb imperf von **schreiben**

Schrift (-, -en) f writing;
(Handschrift) handwriting;
(Schriftart) typeface; (Schrifttyp)
font; **schriftlich** adj written ▷ adv
in writing; **würden Sie uns das
bitte ~ geben?** could we have
that in writing, please?; **Schrift-
steller(in)** (-s, -) m(f) writer

Schritt (-(e)s, -e) m step; **~ für
~** step by step; **~e gegen etw
unternehmen** to take steps
against sth; **Schrittgeschwind-
igkeit** f walking speed;
Schrittmacher m (Med)
pacemaker

Schrott (-(e)s, -e) m scrap metal;
(fig) rubbish

schrubben vi, vt to scrub;
Schrubber (-s, -) m scrubbing
brush

schrumpfen vi to shrink

Schubkarren m wheel-
barrow; **Schublade** f drawer

schubsen vt to shove, to push

schüchtern adj shy

schuf imperf von **schaffen**

Schuh (-(e)s, -e) m shoe;
Schuhcreme f shoe polish;
Schuhgeschäft nt shoe shop;
Schuhgröße f shoe size;
Schuhlöffel m shoehorn

Schulabschluss m school-leaving qualification

schuld adj: **wer ist ~ daran?**
whose fault is it?; **er ist ~** it's his
fault, he's to blame; **Schuld** (-) f
guilt; (Verschulden) fault; **~ haben**
to be to blame (an +dat for); **er hat
~** it's his fault; **sie gibt mir die
~ an dem Unfall** she blames me
for the accident; **schulden** vt to
owe (jdm etw sb sth); **Schulden** pl
debts pl; **~ haben** to be in debt;
~ machen to run up debts; **seine
~ bezahlen** to pay off one's debts;
schuldig adj guilty (an +dat of);
(gebührend) due; **jdm etw ~ sein** to
owe sb sth

Schule (-, -n) f school; **in der ~** at
school; **in die ~ gehen** to go to
school; **Schüler(in)** (-s, -) m(f)
(jüngerer) pupil; (älterer) student;
Schüleraustausch m school
exchange; **Schulfach** nt subject;
Schulferien pl school holidays pl
(Brit) (o vacation (US)); **schulfrei**
adj: **morgen ist ~** there's no school
tomorrow; **Schulfreund(in)** m(f)
schoolmate; **Schuljahr** nt school
year; **Schulkenntnisse** pl: **~ in
Französisch** school-(level) French;
Schulklasse f class; **Schul-
leiter(in)** m(f) headmaster/
headmistress (Brit), principal (US)

Schulter (-, -n) f shoulder;
Schulterblatt nt shoulder blade

Schulung f training;
(Veranstaltung) training course

schummeln vi (fam) to cheat

Schuppe (-, -n) f (von Fisch) scale;
schuppen vt to scale ▷ vr: **sich
~ to peel; **Schuppen** pl (im Haar)
dandruff sing

Schürfwunde f graze

Schürze (-, -n) f apron

Schuss (-es, Schüsse) m shot; **mit
einem ~ Wodka** with a dash of
vodka

Schüssel (-, -n) f bowl

Schuster(in) (-s, -) m(f)
shoemaker

Schutt (-(e)s) m rubble

Schüttelfrost m shivering fit;
schütteln vt to shake ▷ vr: **sich
~ to shake

schütten vt to pour; (Zucker, Kies
etc) to tip ▷ vi impers to pour
(down)

Schutz (-es) m protection (gegen,
vor against, from); (Unterschlupf)
shelter; **jdn in ~ nehmen** to stand
up for sb; **Schutzblech** nt
mudguard; **Schutzbrief** m travel
insurance document for drivers;
Schutzbrille f (safety) goggles pl

Schütze (-n, -n) m (beim Fußball)
scorer; (Astr) Sagittarius

schützen vt: **jdn gegen/vor etw
~ to protect sb against/from sth;
Schutzimpfung f inoculation,
vaccination

schwach adj weak; **~e Augen**
poor eyesight sing; **Schwäche**
(-, -n) f weakness; **Schwachstelle**
f weak point; **Schwachstrom** m
low-voltage current

Schwager (-s, Schwäger) m
brother-in-law; **Schwägerin** f
sister-in-law

Schwalbe (-, -n) f swallow; (beim
Fußball) dive

schwamm imperf von
schwimmen

Schwamm (-(e)s, Schwämme) m
sponge; **~ drüber!** (fam) let's forget
it!

Schwan (-(e)s,
Schwäne) m swan

schwanger adj pregnant; **im
vierten Monat ~ sein** to be four

months pregnant; **Schwanger-schaft** f pregnancy; **Schwanger-schaftsabbruch** m abortion; **Schwangerschaftstest** m pregnancy test

schwanken vi to sway; (*Preise, Zahlen*) to fluctuate; (*zögern*) to hesitate; (*taumeln*) to stagger; **ich schwanke zwischen A und B** I can't decide between A and B

Schwanz (-es, *Schwänze*) m tail; (*vulg: Penis*) cock

Schwarm (-(e)s, *Schwärme*) m swarm; (*fam: angehimmelte Person*) heartthrob; **schwärmen** vi to swarm; **~ für** to be mad about

schwarz adj black, **nun wurde ~ vor Augen** everything went black; **Schwarzarbeit** f illicit work; **Schwarzbrot** nt black bread; **schwarz|fahren** irr vi to travel without a ticket; (*ohne Führerschein*) to drive without a licence; **Schwarzfahrer(in)** m(f) fare-dodger; **Schwarzmarkt** m black market; **schwarz|sehen** irr vi (*fam: pessimistisch sein*) to be pessimistic (*für* about); **Schwarzwald** m Black Forest; **schwarzweiß** adj black and white; **Schwarzwurzel** f salsify

schwatzen vi to chatter; **Schwätzer(in)** (-s, -) m(f) chatterbox; (*Schwafler*) gasbag; (*Klatschmaul*) gossip

Schwebebahn f suspension railway; **schweben** vi to float; (*hoch*) to soar

Schwede (-n, -n) m Swede; **Schweden** (-s) nt Sweden; **Schwedin** f Swede; **schwedisch** adj Swedish; **Schwedisch** nt Swedish

Schwefel (-s) m sulphur

schweigen (*schwieg, geschwiegen*) vi to be silent; (*nicht mehr reden*) to

stop talking; **Schweigen** (-s) nt silence; **Schweigepflicht** f duty of confidentiality; **die ärztliche ~** medical confidentiality

Schwein (-(e)s, -e) nt pig; (*fam: Glück*) luck; (*fam: gemeiner Mensch*) swine; **Schweinebraten** m roast pork; **Schweinefleisch** nt pork; **Schweinerei** f mess; (*Gemeinheit*) dirty trick

Schweiß (-es) m sweat

schweißen vt, vi to weld

Schweiz (-) f: **die ~** Switzerland; **Schweizer(in)** (-s, -) m(f) Swiss; **Schweizerdeutsch** nt Swiss German; **schweizerisch** adj Swiss

Schwelle (-, -n) f doorstep, (*u. fig*) threshold

schwellen vi to swell (up); **Schwellung** f swelling

schwer adj heavy; (*schwierig*) difficult, hard; (*schlimm*) serious, bad; **er ist ~ zu verstehen** it's difficult to understand what he's saying ▷ adv (*sehr*) really; (*verletzt etc*) seriously, badly; **etw ~ nehmen** to take sth hard; **Schwerbehinderte(r)** mf severely disabled person; **schwer|fallen** irr vi (*Schwierigkeiten bereiten*) **jdm ~** to be difficult for sb; **schwerhörig** adj hard of hearing

Schwert (-(e)s, -er) nt sword; **Schwertlilie** f iris

Schwester (-, -n) f sister; (*Med*) nurse

schwieg imperf von **schweigen**

Schwiegereltern pl parents-in-law pl; **Schwiegermutter** f mother-in-law; **Schwiegersohn** m son-in-law; **Schwiegertochter** f daughter-in-law; **Schwiegervater** m father-in-law

schwierig adj difficult, hard; **Schwierigkeit** f difficulty; **in ~en kommen** to get into trouble; **jdm**

~en machen to make things difficult for sb

Schwimmbad nt swimming pool; **Schwimmbecken** nt swimming pool; **schwimmen** (schwamm, geschwommen) vi to swim; (treiben) to float; (fig: unsicher sein) to be all at sea; **Schwimmer(in)** m(f) swimmer; **Schwimmflosse** f flipper; **Schwimmflügel** m water wing; **Schwimmreifen** m rubber ring; **Schwimmweste** f life jacket

Schwindel (-s) m dizziness; (Anfall) dizzy spell; (Betrug) swindle; **schwindelfrei** adj: **nicht ~ sein** to suffer from vertigo; **~ sein** to have a head for heights; **schwindlig** adj dizzy; **mir ist ~ I** feel dizzy

Schwips m: **einen ~ haben** to be tipsy

schwitzen vi to sweat

schwoll imperf von **schwellen**

schwor imperf von **schwören**

schwören (schwor, geschworen) vt, vi to swear; **einen Eid ~** to take an oath

schwul adj gay

schwül adj close

Schwung (-(e)s, Schwünge) m swing; (Triebkraft) momentum; (fig: Energie) energy; (fam: Menge) batch; **in ~ kommen** to get going

Schwur (-s, Schwüre) m oath

scrollen vi (Inform) to scroll

sechs num six; **Sechs** (-, -en) f six; (Schulnote) = F; **Sechserpack** m sixpack; **sechshundert** num six hundred; **sechsmal** adv six times; **sechste(r, s)** adj sixth; siehe auch **dritte; Sechstel** (-s, -) nt sixth; **sechzehn** num sixteen; **sechzehnte(r, s)** adj sixteenth; siehe auch **dritte; sechzig** num sixty; **in den ~er Jahren** in the

sixties; **sechzigste(r, s)** adj sixtieth

Secondhandladen m second-hand shop

See (-, -n) f sea; **an der ~** by the sea ▷ (-s, -n) m lake; **am ~** by the lake; **Seegang** m waves; **hoher/schwerer/leichter ~** rough/heavy/calm seas pl; **Seehund** m seal; **Seeigel** m sea urchin; **seekrank** adj seasick

Seele (-, -n) f soul

Seeleute pl seamen pl, sailors pl

seelisch adj mental, psychological

Seelöwe m sea lion; **Seemann** m sailor, seaman; **Seemeile** f nautical mile; **Seemöwe** f seagull; **Seenot** f distress (at sea); **Seepferdchen** nt sea horse; **Seerose** f water lily; **Seestern** m starfish; **Seezunge** f sole

Segel (-s, -) nt sail; **Segelboot** nt yacht; **Segelfliegen** (-s) nt gliding; **Segelflugzeug** nt glider; **segeln** vt, vi to sail; **Segelschiff** nt sailing ship

sehbehindert adj partially sighted

sehen (sah, gesehen) vt, vi to see; (in bestimmte Richtung) to look; **gut/schlecht ~** to have good/bad eyesight; **auf die Uhr ~** to look at one's watch; **kann ich das mal ~?** can I have a look at it?; **wir ~ uns morgen!** see you tomorrow; **ich kenne sie nur vom Sehen** I only know her by sight; **Sehenswürdigkeiten** pl sights pl

Sehne (-, -n) f tendon; (an Bogen) string

sehnen vr: **sich ~** to long (nach for)

Sehnenscheidenentzündung f (Med) tendovaginitis;

Sehnenzerrung f (Med) pulled tendon

Sehnsucht f longing; **sehnsüchtig** adj longing

sehr adv (vor Adjektiv, Adverb) very; (mit Verben) a lot, very much; **zu ~** too much

seicht adj shallow

Seide (-, -n) f silk

Seife (-, -n) f soap; **Seifenoper** f soap (opera); **Seifenschale** f soap dish

Seil (-(e)s, -e) nt rope; (Kabel) cable; **Seilbahn** f cable railway

○ SCHLÜSSELWORT

sein¹ (pt war, pp gewesen) vi 1 to be; **ich bin** I am; **du bist** you are; **er/sie/es ist** he/she/it is; **wir sind/ihr seid/sie sind** we/you/they are; **wir waren** we were; **wir sind gewesen** we have been

2 **seien Sie nicht böse** don't be angry; **sei so gut und …** be so kind as to …; **das wäre gut** that would o that'd be a good thing; **wenn ich Sie wäre** if I were o was you; **das wär's** that's all, that's it; **morgen bin ich in Rom** tomorrow I'll o I will o I shall be in Rome; **waren Sie mal in Rom?** have you ever been to Rome?

3 **wie ist das zu verstehen?** how is that to be understood?; **er ist nicht zu ersetzen** he cannot be replaced; **mit ihr ist nicht zu reden** you can't talk to her

4 **mir ist kalt** I'm cold; **was ist?** what's the matter?, what is it?; **ist was?** is something the matter?; **es sei denn, dass …** unless …; **wie dem auch sei** be that as it may; **wie wäre es mit …?** how o what about …?; **lass das sein!** stop that!

sein² pron possessiv von **er**; (adjektivisch) his ▷ pron possessiv von **es**; (adjektivisch) its; (adjektivisch, männlich) his; (weiblich) her; (sächlich) its; **das ist ~e Tasche** that's his bag; **jeder hat ~e Sorgen** everyone has their problems; **seine(r, s)** pron possessiv von **er**; (substantivisch) his ▷ pron possessiv von **es**; (substantivisch) its; (substantivisch, männlich) his; (weiblich) hers; **das ist ~r/~/~s** that's his/hers; **seiner** pron gen von **er**; of him ▷ pron gen von **es**; of it; **seinetwegen** adv (wegen ihm) because of him; (ihm zuliebe) for his sake; (um ihn) about him; (von ihm aus) as far as he is concerned

seit conj (bei Zeitpunkt) since; (bei Zeitraum) for; **er ist ~ Montag hier** he's been here since Monday; **er ist ~ einer Woche hier** he's been here for a week; **~ langem** for a long time; **seitdem** adv, conj since

Seite (-, -n) f side; (in Buch) page; **zur ~ gehen** to step aside; **Seitenairbag** m side-impact airbag; **Seitenaufprallschutz** m (Auto) side-impact protection; **Seitensprung** m affair; **Seitenstechen** (-s) nt: **~ haben/bekommen** to have/get a stitch; **Seitenstraße** f side street; **Seitenstreifen** m hard shoulder (Brit), shoulder (US); **Seitenwind** m crosswind

seither adv since (then)

seitlich adj side

Sekretär(in) m(f) secretary; **Sekretariat** (-s, -e) nt secretary's office

Sekt (-(e)s, -e) m sparkling wine (similar to champagne)

Sekte (-, -n) f sect

Sekunde (-, -n) f second;
Sekundenkleber (-s, -) m superglue; **Sekundenschnelle** f: **es
geschah alles in ~** it was all over
in a matter of seconds

○ **SCHLÜSSELWORT**

selbst pron 1 **ich/er/wir selbst** I
myself/he himself/we ourselves;
sie ist die Tugend selbst she's
virtue itself; **er braut sein Bier
selbst** he brews his own beer; **wie
geht's? — gut, und selbst?** how
are things? — fine, and yourself?
2 (ohne Hilfe) alone, on
my/his/one's etc own; **von selbst**
by itself; **er kam von selbst** he
came of his own accord; **selbst
gemacht** home-made
▷ adv even; **selbst wenn** even if;
selbst Gott even God (himself)

selbständig adj siehe
selbstständig
Selbstauslöser (-s, -) m (Foto)
self-timer; **Selbstbedienung** f
self-service; **Selbstbefriedigung** f
masturbation;
Selbstbeherrschung f
self-control; **Selbstbeteiligung** f
(einer Versicherung) excess;
selbstbewusst adj
(self-)confident; **Selbstbräuner**
(-s, -) m self-tanning lotion;
selbstgemacht adj self-made;
selbstklebend adj self-adhesive;
Selbstlaut m vowel; **Selbstmord**
m suicide; **Selbstmordattentat**
nt suicide bombing; **Selbstmord-
attentäter(in)** m(f) suicide
bomber; **selbstsicher** adj
self-assured; **selbstständig** adj
independent; (arbeitend)
self-employed; **Selbstverpflegung**
f self-catering;
selbstverständlich adj obvious;

ich halte das für ~ I take that for
granted ▷ adv naturally;
Selbstvertrauen nt
self-confidence

Sellerie (-s, -(s)) m (-, -n) f (Knollensellerie) celeriac; (Stangensellerie)
celery

selten adj rare ▷ adv seldom,
rarely

seltsam adj strange;
~ schmecken/riechen to
taste/smell strange

Semester (-s, -) nt semester;
Semesterferien pl vacation sing

Semikolon (-s, Semikola) nt
semicolon

Seminar (-s, -e) nt seminar

Semmel (-, -n) f roll;
Semmelbrösel pl breadcrumbs

Senat (-(e)s, -e) m senate

senden (sandte, gesandt) vt to
send ▷ vt, vi (Radio, TV) to
broadcast; **Sender** (-s, -) m (TV)
channel; (Radio) station; (Anlage)
transmitter; **Sendung** f (Radio,
TV) broadcasting; (Programm)
programme

Senf (-(e)s, -e) m mustard

Senior(in) m(f) senior citizen;
Seniorenpass m senior citizen's
travel pass

senken vt to lower ▷ vr: **sich
~** to sink

senkrecht adj vertical

Sensation (-, -en) f sensation

sensibel adj sensitive

sentimental adj sentimental

separat adj separate

September (-(s), -) m
September; siehe auch **Juni**

Serbien (-s) nt Serbia

Serie f series sing

seriös adj (ernsthaft) serious;
(anständig) respectable

Serpentine f hairpin (bend)

Serum (-s, Seren) nt serum

Server (-s, -) m (Inform) server

Service (-(s), -) nt (Geschirr)
service ▷ (-, -s) m service
servieren vt, vi to serve
Serviette f napkin, serviette
Servolenkung f (Auto) power
steering
Sesam (-s, -s) m sesame seeds pl
Sessel (-s, -) m armchair;
Sessellift m chairlift
Set (-(s), -s) m o nt set; (Tischset)
tablemat
setzen vt to put; (Baum etc) to
plant; (Segel) to set ▷ vr: **sich ~** to
settle; (hinsetzen) to sit down; **~ Sie
sich doch** please sit down
Seuche (-, -n) f epidemic
seufzen vt, vi to sigh
Sex (-(es)) m sex; **Sexismus** m
sexism; **sexistisch** adj sexist;
Sextourismus m sex tourism;
Sexualität f sexuality; **sexuell**
adj sexual
Seychellen pl Seychelles pl
sfr abk = **Schweizer Franken** Swiss
franc(s)
Shampoo (-s, -s) nt shampoo
Shareware (-, -s) f (Inform)
shareware
Shorts pl shorts pl
Shuttlebus m shuttle bus

○ **SCHLÜSSELWORT**

sich pron 1 (akk) **er/sie/es ... sich**
he/she/it ... himself/herself/itself;
sie pl/**man ... sich** they/one ...
themselves/oneself; **Sie ... sich**
you ... yourself/yourselves pl; **sich
wiederholen** to repeat
oneself/itself
2 (dat) **er/sie/es ... sich** he/she/it
... to himself/herself/itself; **sie**
pl/**man ... sich** they/one ... to
themselves/oneself; **Sie ... sich**
you ... to yourself/yourselves pl;
**sie hat sich einen Pullover
gekauft** she bought herself a

jumper; **sich die Haare waschen**
to wash one's hair
3 (mit Präposition) **haben Sie Ihren
Ausweis bei sich?** do you have
your pass on you?; **er hat nichts
bei sich** he's got nothing on him;
sie bleiben gern unter sich they
keep themselves to themselves
4 (einander) each other, one
another; **Sie ... sich** each other,
one another; **sie bekämpfen sich** they
fight each other o one another
5 **dieses Auto fährt sich gut** this
car drives well; **hier sitzt es sich
gut** it's good to sit here

sicher adj safe (vor +dat from);
(gewiss) certain (gen of);
(zuverlässig) reliable; (selbstsicher)
confident; **aber ~!** of course, sure;
Sicherheit f safety; (Aufgabe von
Sicherheitsbeamten) (Fin) security;
(Gewissheit) certainty;
(Selbstsicherheit) confidence; **mit
~** definitely; **Sicherheitsabstand**
m safe distance; **Sicherheitsgurt**
m seat belt; **sicherheitshalber**
adv just to be on the safe side;
Sicherheitsnadel f safety pin;
Sicherheitsvorkehrung f safety
precaution; **sicherlich** adv
certainly; (wahrscheinlich) probably
sichern vt to secure (gegen
against); (schützen) to protect;
(Daten) to back up; **Sicherung** f
(Sichern) securing; (Vorrichtung)
safety device; (an Waffen) safety
catch; (Elek) fuse; (Inform) backup;
die ~ ist durchgebrannt the fuse
has blown
Sicht (-) f sight; (Aussicht) view;
sichtbar adj visible; **sichtlich**
adj evident, obvious;
Sichtverhältnisse pl visibility
sing; **Sichtweite** f: **in/außer
~** within/out of sight
sie pron (3. Person sing) she; (3.
Person pl) they; (akk von sing) her;

(akk von pl) them; (für eine Sache) it;
da ist ~ ja there she is; **da sind ~ ja**
there they are; **ich kenne ~** (Frau) I
know her; (mehrere Personen) I
know them; **~ lag gerade noch
hier** (meine Jacke, Uhr) it was here
just a minute ago; **ich hab
~ gefunden** (meine Jacke, Uhr) I've
found it; **hast du meine
Brille/Hose gesehen? — ich kann
~ nirgends finden** have you seen
my glasses/trousers? — I can't
find them anywhere

Sie pron (Höflichkeitsform, Nom und
Akk) you

Sieb (-(e)s, -e) nt sieve; (Teesieb)
strainer

sieben num seven;
siebenhundert num seven
hundred; **siebenmal** adv seven
times; **siebte(r, s)** adj seventh;
siehe auch **dritte; Siebtel** (-s, -) nt
seventh; **siebzehn** num
seventeen; **siebzehnte(r, s)** adj
seventeenth; siehe auch **dritte;
siebzig** num seventy; **in den ~er
Jahren** in the seventies;
siebzigste(r, s) adj
seventieth

Siedlung (-, -en) f (Wohngebiet)
housing estate (Brit) (o
development (US))

Sieg (-(e)s, -e) m victory; **siegen**
vi to win; **Sieger(in)** (-s, -) m(f)
winner; **Siegerehrung** f
presentation ceremony

siehe imper see

siezen vt to address as "Sie"

Signal (-s, -e) nt signal

Silbe (-, -n) f syllable

Silber (-s) nt silver;
Silberhochzeit f silver wedding;
Silbermedaille f silver medal

Silikon (-s, -e) nt silicone

Silvester (-s) nt silver,
Silvesterabend m New Year's
Eve, Hogmanay (Scot)

● **SILVESTER**
●
● **Silvester** is the German name
● for New Year's Eve. Although
● not an official holiday, most
● businesses close early and
● shops shut at midday. Most
● Germans celebrate in the
● evening and at midnight they
● let off fireworks and rockets;
● the revelry usually lasts until the
● early hours of the morning.

Simbabwe (-s) nt Zimbabwe

simpel adj simple

simultan adj simultaneous

simsen vt, vi (fam) to text

Sinfonie (-, -n) f symphony;
Sinfonieorchester nt symphony
orchestra

Singapur (-s) nt Singapore

singen (sang, gesungen) vt, vi to
sing; **richtig/falsch ~** to sing in
tune/out of tune

Single (-, -s) f (CD) single ▷ (-s, -s)
m (Mensch) single

Singular (-s) m singular

sinken (sank, gesunken) vi to sink;
(Preise etc) to fall, to go down

Sinn (-(e)s, -e) m (Denken) mind;
(Wahrnehmung) sense; (Bedeutung)
sense, meaning; **~ machen** to
make sense; **das hat keinen ~** it's
no use; **sinnlich** adj sensuous;
(erotisch) sensual; (Wahrnehmung)
sensory; **sinnlos** adj (unsinnig)
stupid; (Verhalten) senseless;
(zwecklos) pointless; (bedeutungslos)
meaningless; **sinnvoll** adj
meaningful; (vernünftig) sensible

Sirup (-s, -e) m syrup

Sitte (-, -n) f custom

Situation f situation

Sitz (-es, -e) m seat; **sitzen** (saß,
gesessen) vi to sit; (Bemerkung,
Schlag) to strike home; (Gelerntes)
to have sunk in; **der Rock sitzt**

gut the skirt is a good fit;
Sitzgelegenheit f place to sit
down; **Sitzplatz** m seat; **Sitzung**
f meeting

Sizilien (-s) nt Sicily

Skandal (-s, -e) m scandal

Skandinavien (-s) nt
Scandinavia

Skateboard (-s, -s) nt
skateboard

Skelett (-s, -e) nt skeleton

skeptisch adj sceptical

Ski (-s, -er) m ski; **~ laufen** (o
fahren) to ski; **Skianzug** m ski
suit; **Skibrille** f ski goggles pl;
Skifahren (-s) nt skiing; **Skigebiet**
(-s, -e) nt skiing area; **Skihose** f
skiing trousers pl; **Skikurs** m
skiing course; **Skilanglauf** m
cross-country skiing; **Skiläufer(in)**
m(f) skier; **Skilehrer(in)** m(f) ski
instructor; **Skilift** m ski-lift

Skinhead (-s, -s) m skinhead

Skipiste f ski run; **Skischanze**
(-, -n) f ski jump; **Skischuh** m
ski boot; **Skischule** f ski school;
Skispringen (-s, -n) nt ski
jumping; **Skistiefel** (-s, -) m ski
boot; **Skistock** m ski pole;
Skiträger m ski rack; **Skiurlaub**
m skiing holiday (Brit) (o vacation
(US))

Skizze (-, -n) f sketch

Skonto (-s, -s) m o nt discount

Skorpion (-s, -e) m (Zool)
scorpion; (Astr) Scorpio

Skulptur (-, -en) f sculpture

S-Kurve f double bend

Slalom (-s, -s) m slalom

Slip (-s, -s) m (pair of) briefs pl;
Slipeinlage f panty liner

Slowakei (-) f Slovakia;
slowakisch adj Slovakian;
Slowakische Republik Slovak
Republic; **Slowakisch** nt
Slovakian

Slowenien (-s) nt Slovenia;

slowenisch adj Slovenian;
Slowenisch nt Slovenian

Smiley (-s, -s) m smiley

Smog (-s, -s) m smog; **Smogalarm**
m smog alert

Smoking (-s, -s) m dinner jacket
(Brit), tuxedo (US)

SMS nt abk = **Short Message
Service** ⊳ f (Nachricht) text
message; **ich schicke dir eine ~** I'll
text you, I'll send you a text
(message)

Snowboard (-s, -s) nt snowboard; **Snowboardfahren** (-s) nt
snowboarding;
Snowboardfahrer(in) m(f)
snowboarder

O   SCHLÜSSELWORT

so adv 1 (so sehr) so; **so groß/schön**
etc so big/nice etc; **so groß/schön
wie ...** as big/nice as ...; **so viel
(wie)** as much as; **rede nicht so
viel** don't talk so much; **so weit
sein** to be ready; **so weit wie** o **als
möglich** as far as possible; **ich bin
so weit zufrieden** by and large I'm
quite satisfied; **so wenig (wie)** as
little (as); **das hat ihn so
geärgert, dass ...** that annoyed
him so much that ...; **so etwas wie
ich** somebody like me; **na so was!**
well, well!

2 (auf diese Weise) like this; **mach
es nicht so** don't do it like that; **so
oder so** in one way or the other;
und so weiter and so on; **... oder
so was** ... or something like that;
das ist gut so that's fine

3 (fam) (umsonst) **ich habe es so
bekommen** I got it for nothing

⊳ konj: **sodass** so that; **so wie es
jetzt ist** as things are at the
moment

⊳ excl: **so?** really?; **so, das wär's**
so, that's it then

s. o. *abk* = **siehe oben** see above
sobald *conj* as soon as
Socke (-, -n) f sock
Sodbrennen (-s) nt heartburn
Sofa (-s, -s) nt sofa
sofern *conj* if, provided (that)
soff *imperf von* **saufen**
sofort *adv* immediately, at once;
Sofortbildkamera f instant
camera
Softeis nt soft ice-cream
Software (-, -s) f software
sog *imperf von* **saugen**
sogar *adv* even; **kalt, ~ sehr kalt**
cold, in fact very cold
sogenannt *adj* so-called
Sohle (-, -n) f sole
Sohn (-(e)s, Söhne) m son
Soja (-, Sojen) f soya;
Sojasprossen pl bean sprouts pl
solang(e) *conj* as long as
Solarium nt solarium
Solarzelle f solar cell
solche(r, s) *pron* such; **eine
~ Frau, solch eine Frau** such a
woman, a woman like that;
~ Sachen things like that, such
things; **ich habe ~ Kopfschmerz-
en** I've got such a headache; **ich
habe ~n Hunger** I'm so hungry
Soldat(in) (-en, -en) m(f) soldier
solidarisch *adj* showing
solidarity; **sich ~ erklären mit** to
declare one's solidarity with
solid(e) *adj* solid; (Leben, Mensch)
respectable
Soll (-(s), -(s)) nt (Fin) debit;
(Arbeitsmenge) quota, target

○ SCHLÜSSELWORT

sollen (*pt* **sollte**, *pp* **gesollt** o (*als
Hilfsverb*) **sollen**) Hilfsverb 1 (*Pflicht,
Befehl*) to be supposed to; **du
hättest nicht gehen sollen** you
shouldn't have gone, you oughtn't
to have gone; **soll ich?** shall I?; **soll**

ich dir helfen? shall I help you?;
sag ihm, er soll warten tell him
he's to wait; **was soll ich
machen?** what should I do?
2 (*Vermutung*) **sie soll verheiratet
sein** she's said to be married; **was
soll das heißen?** what's that
supposed to mean?; **man sollte
glauben, dass ...** you would think
that ...; **sollte das passieren, ...** if
that should happen ...
▷ *vt, vi*: **was soll das?** what's all
this?; **das sollst du nicht** you
shouldn't do that; **was soll's?**
what the hell!

Solo (-s, -) nt solo
Sommer (-s, -) m summer;
Sommerfahrplan m summer
timetable; **Sommerferien** pl
summer holidays pl (Brit) (o
vacation sing (US)); **sommerlich**
adj summery; (Sommer-) summer;
Sommerreifen m normal tyre;
Sommersprossen pl freckles pl;
Sommerzeit f summertime;
(Uhrzeit) daylight saving
time

Sonderangebot nt special
offer; **sonderbar** *adj* strange,
odd; **Sondermarke** f special
stamp; **Sondermaschine** f
special plane; **Sondermüll** m
hazardous waste
sondern *conj* but; **nicht nur ...,
~ auch** not only ..., but also
Sonderpreis m special price;
Sonderschule f special school;
Sonderzeichen nt (Inform)
special character; **Sonderzug** m
special train
Song (-s, -s) m song
Sonnabend m Saturday; *siehe
auch* **Mittwoch**; **sonnabends** *adv*
on Saturdays; **~ morgens** on
Saturday mornings; *siehe auch*
mittwochs

Sonne (-, -n) f sun; **sonnen** vr:
sich ~ to sunbathe;
Sonnenallergie f sun allergy;
Sonnenaufgang m sunrise;
Sonnenblume f sunflower;
Sonnenblumenkern m sunflower seed; **Sonnenbrand** m
sunburn; **Sonnenbrille** f
sunglasses pl, shades pl;
Sonnencreme f sun cream;
Sonnendach nt (an Haus)
awning; (Auto) sunroof; **Sonnendeck** nt sun deck; **Sonnenmilch** f
suntan lotion; **Sonnenöl** nt
suntan oil; **Sonnenschein** m
sunshine; **Sonnenschirm** m
parasol, sunshade; **Sonnenschutzcreme** f sunscreen; **Sonnenstich**
m sunstroke; **Sonnenstudio** nt
solarium; **Sonnenuhr** f sundial;
Sonnenuntergang m sunset;
sonnig adj sunny
Sonntag m Sunday; siehe auch
Mittwoch; **sonntags** adv on
Sundays; siehe auch **mittwochs**
sonst adv, conj (außerdem) else;
(andernfalls) otherwise; (or) else;
(mit Pron, in Fragen) else;
(normalerweise) normally, usually;
~ noch etwas? anything else?;
~ nichts nothing else
sooft conj whenever
Sopran (-s, -e) m soprano
Sorge (-, -n) f worry; (Fürsorge)
care; sich (dat) um jdn ~n machen
to be worried about sb; **sorgen**
vi: für jdn ~ to look after sb; für
etw ~ to take care of sth, to see to
sth ▷ vr: sich ~ to worry (um
about); **sorgfältig** adj careful
sortieren vt to sort (out)
Sortiment nt assortment
sosehr conj however much
Soße (-, -n) f sauce; (zu Braten)
gravy
Soundkarte f (Inform) sound
card

Souvenir (-s, -s) nt souvenir
soviel conj as far as
soweit conj as far as
sowie conj (wie auch) as well as;
(sobald) as soon as
sowohl conj: ~ ... als (o wie) auch
both ... and
sozial adj social; **Sozialhilfe** f
income support (Brit), welfare
(aid) (US); **Sozialismus** m
socialism; **Sozialversicherung** f
social security; **Sozialwohnung**
f council flat (Brit),
state-subsidized apartment (US)
Soziologie f sociology
sozusagen adv so to speak
Spachtel (-s, -) m spatula
Spag(h)etti pl spaghetti sing
Spalte (-, -n) f crack; (Gletscher)
crevasse; (in Text) column
spalten vt to split ▷ vr: sich ~ to
split
Spange (-, -n) f clasp;
(Haarspange) hair slide (Brit),
barrette (US)
Spanien (-s) nt Spain;
Spanier(in) (-s, -) m(f) Spaniard;
spanisch adj Spanish; **Spanisch**
nt Spanish
spann imperf von **spinnen**
spannen vt (straffen) to tighten;
(befestigen) to brace ▷ vi to be
tight
spannend adj exciting, gripping;
Spannung f tension; (Elek)
voltage; (fig) suspense
Sparbuch nt savings book;
(Konto) savings account; **sparen**
vt, vi to save
Spargel (-s, -) m asparagus;
Spargelsuppe f asparagus soup
Sparkasse f savings bank;
Sparkonto nt savings account
spärlich adj meagre; (Bekleidung)
scanty
sparsam adj economical;
Sparschwein nt piggy bank

Spaß (-es, Späße) m joke; (Freude) fun; **es macht mir ~** I enjoy it, it's (great) fun; **viel ~!** have fun

spät adj, adv late; **zu ~ kommen** to be late

Spaten (-s, -) m spade

später adj, adv later; **spätestens** adv at the latest; **Spätlese** f late vintage (wine); **Spätvorstellung** f late-night performance

Spatz (-en, -en) m sparrow

spazieren vi to stroll, to walk; **~ gehen** to go for a walk; **Spaziergang** m walk

Specht (-(e)s, -e) m woodpecker

Speck (-(e)s, -e) m bacon fat; (durchwachsen) bacon

Spedition f (für Umzug) removal firm

Speiche (-, -n) f spoke

Speichel (-s) m saliva

Speicher (-s, -) m storehouse; (Dachboden) attic; (Inform) memory; **speichern** vt (Inform) to store; (sichern) to save

Speise (-, -n) f food; (Gericht) dish; **Speisekarte** f menu; **Speiseröhre** f gullet, oesophagus; **Speisesaal** m dining hall; **Speisewagen** m dining car

Spende (-, -n) f donation; **spenden** vt to donate, to give

spendieren v: **jdm etw ~** to treat sb to sth

Sperre (-, -n) f barrier; (Verbot) ban; **sperren** vt to block; (Sport) to suspend; (verbieten) to ban

Sperrgepäck nt bulky luggage; **Sperrmüll** m bulky refuse; **Sperrstunde** f closing time; **Sperrung** f closing

Spesen pl expenses pl

spezialisieren vr: **sich ~** to specialize (auf +akk in); **Spezialist(in)** m(f) specialist; **Spezialität** f speciality (Brit),

specialty (US); **speziell** adj special ▷ adv especially

Spiegel (-s, -) m mirror; **Spiegelei** nt fried egg (sunny-side up (US)); **spiegelglatt** adj very slippery; **Spiegelreflexkamera** f reflex camera

Spiel (-(e)s, -e) nt game; (Tätigkeit) play(ing); (Karten) pack, deck; (Tech) (free) play; **Spielautomat** m (ohne Geldgewinn) gaming machine; (mit Geldgewinn) slot machine; **spielen** vt, vi to play; (um Geld) to gamble; (Theat) to perform, to act; **Klavier ~** to play the piano; **spielend** adv easily; **Spieler(in)** (-s, -) m(f) player; (um Geld) gambler; **Spielfeld** nt (für Fußball, Hockey) field; (für Basketball) court; **Spielfilm** m feature film; **Spielkasino** nt casino; **Spielplatz** m playground; **Spielraum** m room to manoeuvre; **Spielregel** f rule; **sich an die ~n halten** to stick to the rules; **Spielsachen** pl toys pl; **Spielzeug** nt toys pl; (einzelnes) toy

Spieß (-es, -e) m spear; (Bratspieß) spit; **Spießer(in)** (-s, -) m(f) square, stuffy type; **spießig** adj square, uncool

Spikes pl (Sport) spikes pl; (Auto) studs pl

Spinat (-(e)s, -e) m spinach

Spinne (-, -n) f spider; **spinnen** (spann, gesponnen) vt, vi to spin; (fam: Unsinn reden) to talk rubbish; (verrückt sein) to be crazy; **du spinnst!** you must be mad; **Spinnwebe** (-, -n) f cobweb

Spion(in) (-s, -e) m(f) spy; **spionieren** vi to spy; (fig) to snoop around

Spirale (-, -n) f spiral; (Med) coil

Spirituosen pl spirits pl, liquor sing (US)

Spiritus (-, -se) m spirit

spitz adj (Nase, Kinn) pointed; (Bleistift, Messer) sharp; (Winkel) acute; **Spitze** (-, -n) f point; (von Finger, Nase) tip; (Bemerkung) taunt, dig; (erster Platz) lead; (Gewebe) lace; **Spitzer** (-s, -) m pencil sharpener; **Spitzname** m nickname

Spliss (-) m split ends pl

sponsern vt to sponsor; **Sponsor(in)** (-s, -en) m(f) sponsor

spontan adj spontaneous

Sport (-(e)s, -e) m sport; ~ **treiben** to do sport; **Sportanlage** f sports grounds pl; **Sportart** f sport; **Sportbekleidung** f sportswear; **Sportgeschäft** nt sports shop; **Sporthalle** f gymnasium, gym; **Sportlehrer(in)** (-s, -) m(f) PE teacher; (Schule) PE teacher; **Sportler(in)** (-s, -) m(f) sportsman/-woman; **sportlich** adj sporting; (Mensch) sporty; **Sportplatz** m playing field; **Sporttauchen** nt (skin-)diving; (mit Gerät) scuba-diving; **Sportverein** m sports club; **Sportwagen** m sports car

sprach imperf von **sprechen**

Sprache (-, -n) f language; (Sprechen) speech; **Sprachenschule** f language school; **Sprachführer** m phrasebook; **Sprachkenntnisse** pl knowledge sing of languages; **gute englische ~ haben** to have a good knowledge of English; **Sprachkurs** m language course; **Sprachunterricht** m language teaching

sprang imperf von **springen**

Spray (-s, -s) m o nt spray

Sprechanlage f intercom; **sprechen** (sprach, gesprochen) vt, vi

to speak (jdn, mit jdm to sb); (sich unterhalten) to talk (mit to, über, von about); ~ **Sie Deutsch?** do you speak German?; **kann ich bitte mit David ~?** (am Telefon) can I speak to David, please?; **Sprecher(in)** m(f) speaker; (Ansager) announcer; **Sprechstunde** f consultation; (Arzt) surgery hours pl; (Anwalt etc) office hours pl; **Sprechzimmer** nt consulting room

Sprengstoff m explosive

Sprichwort nt proverb

Springbrunnen m fountain

springen (sprang, gesprungen) vi to jump; (Glas) to crack; (mit Kopfsprung) to dive

Sprit (-(e)s, -e) m (fam: Benzin) petrol (Brit), gas (US)

Spritze (-, -n) f (Gegenstand) syringe; (Injektion) injection; (an Schlauch) nozzle; **spritzen** vt to spray; (Med) to inject ▷ vi to splash; (Med) to give injections

Spruch (-(e)s, Sprüche) m saying

Sprudel (-s, -) m sparkling mineral water; (süßer) fizzy drink (Brit), soda (US); **sprudeln** vi to bubble

Sprühdose f aerosol (can); **sprühen** vt, vi to spray; (fig) to sparkle; **Sprühregen** m drizzle

Sprung (-(e)s, Sprünge) m jump; (Riss) crack; **Sprungbrett** nt springboard; **Sprungschanze** f ski jump; **Sprungturm** m diving platforms pl

Spucke (-) f spit; **spucken** vt, vi to spit; (fam: sich erbrechen) to vomit; **Spucktüte** f sick bag

spuken vi (Geist) to walk; **hier spukt es** this place is haunted

Spülbecken nt sink

Spule (-, -n) f spool; (Elek) coil

Spüle (-, -n) f sink; **spülen** vt, vi to rinse; (Geschirr) to wash up;

(*Toilette*) to flush; **Spülmaschine**
f dishwasher; **Spülmittel** nt
washing-up liquid (*Brit*),
dishwashing liquid (*US*); **Spültuch**
nt dishcloth; **Spülung** f (*von WC*)
flush

Spur (-, *-en*) f trace; (*Fußspur,
Radspur*) track; (*Fährte*) trail;
(*Fahrspur*) lane; **die ~ wechseln** to
change lanes pl

spüren vt to feel; (*merken*) to
notice; **Spürhund** m sniffer dog

Squash (-) nt squash;
Squashschläger m squash racket

Sri Lanka (-s) nt Sri Lanka

Staat (-(*e*)s, *-en*) m state;
staatlich adj state(-); (*vom Staat
betrieben*) state-run;
Staatsangehörigkeit f
nationality; **Staatsanwalt** m,
-anwältin f prosecuting counsel
(*Brit*), district attorney (*US*);
Staatsbürger(in) m(f) citizen;
Staatsbürgerschaft f nationality; **doppelte ~** dual nationality;
Staatsexamen nt final exam
taken by trainee teachers, medical and
law students

Stab (-(*e*)s, *Stäbe*) m rod; (*Gitter*)
bar; **Stäbchen** nt (*Essstäbchen*)
chopstick; **Stabhochsprung** m
pole vault

stabil adj stable; (*Möbel*) sturdy

stach imperf von **stechen**

Stachel (-s, *-n*) m spike; (*von Tier*)
spine; (*von Insekten*) sting;
Stachelbeere f gooseberry;
Stacheldraht m barbed wire;
stachelig adj prickly

Stadion (-s, *Stadien*) nt stadium

Stadt (-, *Städte*) f town; (*groß*)
city; **in der ~** in town;
Stadtautobahn f urban
motorway (*Brit*) (o expressway
(*US*)); **Stadtbummel** (-s, -) m:
einen ~ machen to go round
town; **Stadtführer** m (*Heft*) city

guide; **Stadtführung** f city
sightseeing tour; **Stadthalle** f
municipal hall; **städtisch** adj
municipal; **Stadtmauer** f city
wall(s); **Stadtmitte** f town/city
centre, downtown (*US*);
Stadtplan m (*street*) map;
Stadtrand m outskirts pl;
Stadtrundfahrt f city tour;
Stadtteil m, **Stadtviertel** nt
district, part of town;
Stadtzentrum nt town/city
centre, downtown (*US*)

stahl imperf von **stehlen**

Stahl (-(*e*)s, *Stähle*) m steel

Stall (-(*e*)s, *Ställe*) m stable;
(*Kaninchen*) hutch; (*Schweine*)
pigsty; (*Hühner*) henhouse

Stamm (-(*e*)s, *Stämme*) m (*Baum*)
trunk; (*von Menschen*) tribe;
stammen vi: **~ aus** to come from;
Stammgast m regular (guest);
Stammkunde m, **Stammkundin**
f regular (customer); **Stammtisch**
m table reserved for regulars

stampfen vt, vi to stamp; (*mit
Werkzeug*) to pound; (*stapfen*) to
tramp

stand imperf von **stehen**

Stand (-(*e*)s, *Stände*) m (*Wasser,
Benzin*) level; (*Stehen*) standing
position; (*Zustand*) state;
(*Spielstand*) score; (*auf Messe etc*)
stand; (*Klasse*) class; **im ~e sein** to
be in a position; (*fähig*) to be able

Stand-by-Betrieb m stand-by;
Stand-by-Ticket nt stand-by
ticket

Ständer (-s, -) m (*Gestell*) stand;
(*fam: Erektion*) hard-on

Standesamt nt registry office

ständig adj permanent;
(*ununterbrochen*) constant,
continual

Standlicht nt sidelights pl (*Brit*),
parking lights pl (*US*); **Standort**
m position; **Standpunkt** m

standpoint; **Standspur** f (Auto) hard shoulder (Brit), shoulder (US)

Stange (-, -n) f stick; (Stab) pole; (Metall) bar; (Zigaretten) carton; **Stangenbohne** f runner (Brit) (o string (US)) bean; **Stangenbrot** nt French stick; **Stangensellerie** m celery

stank imperf von **stinken**

Stapel (-s, -) m pile

Star (-(e)s, -e) m (Vogel) starling; (Med) cataract ▷ (-s, -s) m (in Film etc) star

starb imperf von **sterben**

stark adj strong; (heftig, groß) heavy; (Maßangabe) thick; **Stärke** (-, -n) f strength; (Dicke) thickness; (Wäschestärke, Speisestärke) starch; **stärken** vt to strengthen; (Wäsche) to starch; **Starkstrom** m high-voltage current; **Stärkung** f strengthening; (Essen) refreshment

starr adj stiff; (unnachgiebig) rigid; (Blick) staring

starren vi to stare

Start (-(e)s, -e) m start; (Aviat) takeoff; **Startautomatik** f automatic choke; **Startbahn** f runway; **starten** vt, vi to start; (Aviat) to take off; **Starthilfekabel** nt jump leads pl (Brit), jumper cables pl (US); **Startmenü** nt (Inform) start menu

Station f (Haltestelle) stop; (Bahnhof) station; (im Krankenhaus) ward; **stationär** adj stationary; **~e Behandlung** in-patient treatment; **jdn ~ behandeln** to treat sb as an in-patient

Statistik f statistics pl

Stativ nt tripod

statt conj, prep +gen o dat instead of; **~ zu arbeiten** instead of working

stattfinden irr vi to take place

Statue (-, -n) f statue

Statusleiste f, **Statuszeile** f (Inform) status bar

Stau (-(e)s, -e) m (im Verkehr) (traffic) jam; **im ~ stehen** to be stuck in a traffic jam

Staub (-(e)s, -) m dust; **~ wischen** to dust; **staubig** adj dusty; **staubsaugen** vt, vi to vacuum, to hoover (Brit); **Staubsauger** m vacuum cleaner, Hoover® (Brit); **Staubtuch** nt duster

Staudamm m dam

staunen vi to be astonished (über +akk at)

Stausee m reservoir; **Stauung** f (von Wasser) damming-up; (von Blut, Verkehr) congestion; **Stauwarnung** f traffic report

Std. abk = **Stunde** h

Steak (-s, -s) nt steak

stechen (stach, gestochen) vt, vi (mit Nadel etc) to prick; (mit Messer) to stab; (mit Finger) to poke; (Biene) to sting; (Mücke) to bite; (Sonne) to burn; (Kartenspiel) to trump; **Stechen** (-s, -) nt sharp pain, stabbing pain; **Stechmücke** f mosquito

Steckdose f socket; **stecken** vt to put; (Nadel) to stick; (beim Nähen) to pin ▷ vi (festsitzen) to be stuck; (Nadel) to be (sticking); **der Schlüssel steckt** the key is in the door; **Stecker** (-s, -) m plug; **Steckrübe** f swede (Brit), rutabaga (US)

Steg (-s, -e) m bridge

stehen (stand, gestanden) vi to stand (zu by); (sich befinden) to be; (stillstehen) to have stopped; **was steht im Brief?** what does it say in the letter?; **jdm (gut) ~** to suit sb; **~ bleiben** (Uhr) to stop; **~ lassen** to leave ▷ vi impers: **wie steht's?** (Sport) what's the score?

stehlen *(stahl, gestohlen)* vt to steal

Stehplatz *m (im Konzert etc)* standing ticket

Steiermark *(-)* f Styria

steif *adj* stiff

steigen *(stieg, gestiegen)* vi *(Preise, Temperatur)* to rise; *(klettern)* to climb; **~ in/auf** to get in/on

steigern vt to increase ▷ vr: **sich ~** to increase

Steigung f incline, gradient

steil *adj* steep; **Steilhang** *m* steep slope; **Steilküste** f steep coast

Stein *(-(e)s, -e)* m stone; **Steinbock** *m (Zool)* ibex; *(Astr)* Capricorn; **steinig** *adj* stony; **Steinschlag** *m* falling rocks pl

Stelle *(-, -n)* f place, spot; *(Arbeit)* post, job; *(Amt)* office; **ich an deiner ~** if I were you; **auf der ~** straightaway; **stellen** vt to put; *(Uhr etc)* to set *(auf +akk* to); *(zur Verfügung stellen)* to provide ▷ vr: **sich ~** *(bei Polizei)* to give oneself up; **sich schlafend ~** to pretend to be asleep; **Stellenangebot** *nt* job offer, vacancy; **stellenweise** *adv* in places; **Stellenwert** *m (fig)* status; **einen hohen ~ haben** to play an important role; **Stellplatz** *m* parking space; **Stellung** f position; **zu etw ~ nehmen** to comment on sth; **Stellvertreter(in)** *m(f)* representative; *(amtlich)* deputy; *(von Arzt)* locum *(Brit)*, locum tenens *(US)*

Stempel *(-s, -)* m stamp; **stempeln** vt to stamp; *(Briefmarke)* to cancel

sterben *(starb, gestorben)* vi to die

Stereoanlage f stereo *(system)*

steril *adj* sterile; **sterilisieren** vt to sterilize

Stern *(-(e)s, -e)* m star; **ein Hotel mit vier ~en** a four-star hotel; **Sternbild** *nt* constellation; *(Sternzeichen)* star sign, sign of the zodiac; **Sternfrucht** f star fruit; **Sternschnuppe** *(-, -n)* f shooting star; **Sternwarte** *(-e, -n)* f observatory; **Sternzeichen** *nt* star sign, sign of the zodiac; **welches ~ bist du?** what's your star sign?

stets *adv* always

Steuer *(-s, -)* nt *(Auto)* steering wheel ▷ *(-, -n)* f tax; **Steuerberater(in)** *m(f)* tax adviser; **Steuerbord** *nt* starboard; **Steuererklärung** f tax declaration; **steuerfrei** *adj* tax-free; *(Waren)* duty-free; **Steuerknüppel** *m* control column; *(Aviat, Inform)* joystick; **steuern** vt, vi to steer; *(Flugzeug)* to pilot; *(Entwicklung, Tonstärke)* *(Inform)* to control; **steuerpflichtig** *adj* taxable; **Steuerung** f *(Auto)* steering; *(Vorrichtung)* controls pl; *(Aviat)* piloting; *(fig)* control; **Steuerungstaste** f *(Inform)* control key

Stich *(-(e)s, -e)* m *(von Insekt)* sting; *(von Mücke)* bite; *(durch Messer)* stab; *(beim Nähen)* stitch; *(Färbung)* tinge; *(Kartenspiel)* trick; *(Kunst)* engraving

sticken vt, vi to embroider

Sticker *(-s, -)* m sticker

Stickerei f embroidery

stickig *adj* stuffy, close

Stiefbruder *m* stepbrother

Stiefel *(-s, -)* m boot

Stiefmutter f stepmother

Stiefmütterchen *nt* pansy

Stiefschwester f stepsister; **Stiefsohn** *m* stepson; **Stieftochter** f stepdaughter; **Stiefvater** *m* stepfather

stieg *imperf von* **steigen**

Stiege (-, -n) f steps pl

Stiel (-(e)s, -e) m handle; (Bot) stalk; **ein Eis am ~** an ice lolly (Brit), a Popsicle® (US)

Stier (-(e)s, -e) m (Zool) bull; (Astr) Taurus; **Stierkampf** m bullfight

stieß imperf von **stoßen**

Stift (-(e)s, -e) m (aus Holz) peg; (Nagel) tack; (zum Schreiben) pen; (Farbstift) crayon; (Bleistift) pencil

Stil (-s, -e) m style

still adj quiet; (unbewegt) still

stillen vt (Säugling) to breast-feed

still|halten irr vi to keep still; **still|stehen** irr vi to stand still

Stimme (-, -n) f voice; (bei Wahl) vote

stimmen vi to be right; **stimmt!** that's right; **hier stimmt was nicht** there's something wrong here; **stimmt so!** (beim Bezahlen) keep the change

Stimmung f mood; (Atmosphäre) atmosphere

Stinkefinger m (fam) **jdm den ~ zeigen** to give sb the finger (o bird (US))

stinken (stank, gestunken) vi to stink (nach of)

Stipendium nt scholarship; (als Unterstützung) grant

Stirn (-, -en) f forehead; **Stirnhöhle** f sinus

Stock (-(e)s, -Stöcke) m stick; (Bot) stock ▷ m (Stockwerke) floor, storey; **Stockbett** nt bunk bed; **Stöckelschuhe** pl high-heels; **Stockwerk** nt floor; **im ersten ~** on the first floor (Brit), on the second floor (US)

Stoff (-(e)s, -e) m (Gewebe) material; (Materie) matter; (von Buch etc) subject (matter); (fam: Rauschgift) stuff

stöhnen vi to groan (vor with)

stolpern vi to stumble, to trip

stolz adj proud

stopp interj hold it; (Moment mal!) hang on a minute; **stoppen** vt, vi to stop; (mit Uhr) to time; **Stoppschild** nt stop sign; **Stoppuhr** f stopwatch

Stöpsel (-s, -) m plug; (für Flaschen) stopper

Storch (-(e)s, Störche) m stork

stören vt to disturb; (behindern) to interfere with; **darf ich dich kurz ~?** can I trouble you for a minute?; **stört es dich, wenn ...?** do you mind if ...?

stornieren vt to cancel; **Stornogebühr** f cancellation fee

Störung f disturbance; (in der Leitung) fault

Stoß (-es, Stöße) m (Schub) push; (Schlag) blow; (mit Fuß) kick; (Haufen) pile; **Stoßdämpfer** (-s, -) m shock absorber

stoßen (stieß, gestoßen) vt (mit Druck) to shove, to push; (mit Schlag) to knock; (mit Fuß) to kick; (anstoßen) to bump; (zerkleinern) to pulverize ▷ vr: **sich ~** to bang oneself; **sich ~ an** (+dat) (fig) to take exception to

Stoßstange f (Auto) bumper

stottern vt, vi to stutter

Str. abk von **Straße** St, Rd

Strafe (-, -n) f punishment; (Sport) penalty; (Gefängnisstrafe) sentence; (Geldstrafe) fine; **strafen** vt to punish; **Straftat** f (criminal) offence; **Strafzettel** m ticket

Strahl (-s, -en) m ray, beam; (Wasser) jet; **strahlen** vi to radiate; (fig) to beam

Strähne (-, -n) f strand; (weiß, gefärbt) streak

Strand (-(e)s, Strände) m beach; **am ~** on the beach; **Strandcafé** nt beach café; **Strandkorb** m wicker beach chair with a hood; **Strandpromenade** f promenade

strapazieren vt (Material) to be hard on; (Mensch, Kräfte) to be a strain on

Straße (-, -n) f road; (in der Stadt) street; **Straßenarbeiten** pl roadworks pl (Brit), road repairs pl (US); **Straßenbahn** f tram (Brit), streetcar (US); **Straßencafé** nt pavement café (Brit), sidewalk café (US); **Straßenfest** nt street party; **Straßenglätte** f slippery roads pl; **Straßenkarte** f road map; **Straßenrand** m: **am ~** at the roadside; **Straßenschild** nt street sign; **Straßensperre** f roadblock; **Straßenverhältnisse** pl road conditions pl

Strategie (-, -n) f strategy

Strauch (-(e)s, Sträucher) m bush, shrub; **Strauchtomate** f vine-ripened tomato

Strauß (-es, Sträuße) m bunch; (als Geschenk) bouquet ▷ m (Strauße) (Vogel) ostrich

Strecke (-, -n) f route; (Entfernung) distance; (Eisenb) line

strecken vt to stretch ▷ vr: **sich ~** to stretch

streckenweise adv (teilweise) in parts; (zeitweise) at times

Streich (-(e)s, -e) m trick, prank

streicheln vt to stroke

streichen (strich, gestrichen) vt (anmalen) to paint; (berühren) to stroke; (auftragen) to spread; (durchstreichen) to delete; (nicht genehmigen) to cancel

Streichholz nt match; **Streichholzschachtel** f matchbox; **Streichkäse** m cheese spread

Streifen (-s, -) m (Linie) stripe; (Stück) strip; (Film) film

Streifenwagen m patrol car

Streik (-(e)s, -s) m strike; **streiken** vi to be on strike

Streit (-(e)s, -e) m argument (um, wegen about, over); **streiten** (stritt, gestritten) vi to argue (um, wegen about, over) ▷ vr: **sich ~** to argue (um, wegen about, over)

streng adj (Blick) severe; (Lehrer) strict; (Geruch) sharp

Stress (-es) m stress; **stressen** vt to stress (out); **stressig** adj (fam) stressful

Stretching (-s) nt (Sport) stretching exercises pl

streuen vt to scatter; **die Straßen ~** to grit the roads; (mit Salz) to put salt down on the roads; **Streufahrzeug** nt gritter lorry (Brit), salt truck (US)

strich imperf von **streichen**

Strich (-(e)s, -e) m (Linie) line; **Stricher** m (fam: Strichjunge) rent boy (Brit), boy prostitute; **Strichkode** (-s, -s) m bar code; **Stricherin** f (fam: Strichmädchen) hooker; **Strichpunkt** m semicolon

Strick (-(e)s, -e) m rope

stricken vt, vi to knit; **Strickjacke** f cardigan; **Stricknadel** f knitting needle

String (-s, -s) m, **Stringtanga** m G-string

Stripper(in) m(f) stripper; **Striptease** (-) m striptease

stritt imperf von **streiten**

Stroh (-(e)s) nt straw; **Strohdach** nt thatched roof; **Strohhalm** m (drinking) straw

Strom (-(e)s, Ströme) m river; (fig) stream; (Elek) current; **Stromanschluss** m connection; **Stromausfall** m power failure

strömen vi to stream, to pour; **Strömung** f current

Stromverbrauch m power consumption; **Stromzähler** m electricity meter

Strophe (-, -n) f verse

Strudel (-s, -) m (in Fluss) whirlpool; (Gebäck) strudel

Struktur f structure; (von Material) texture

Strumpf ((c)s, Strümpfe) m (Damenstrumpf) stocking; (Socke) sock; **Strumpfhose** f (pair of) tights pl (Brit), pantyhose (US)

Stück (-(e)s, -e) nt piece; (von Zucker) lump; (etwas) bit; (Zucker) lump; (Theat) play; **ein ~ Käse** a piece of cheese

Student(in) m(f) student; **Studentenausweis** m student card; **Studentenwohnheim** nt hall of residence (Brit), dormitory (US), **Studienabschluss** m qualification (at the end of a course of higher education); **Studienfahrt** f study trip; **Studienplatz** m university/college place; **studieren** vt, vi to study; **Studium** nt studies pl; **während seines ~s** while he is/was studying

Stufe (-, -n) f step; (Entwicklungsstufe) stage

Stuhl (-(e)s, Stühle) m chair

stumm adj silent; (Med) dumb

stumpf adj blunt; (teilnahmslos, glanzlos) dull; **stumpfsinnig** adj dull

Stunde (-, -n) f hour; (Unterricht) lesson; **eine halbe ~** half an hour; **Stundenkilometer** m: **80 ~** 80 kilometres an hour; **stundenlang** adv for hours; **Stundenlohn** m hourly wage; **Stundenplan** m timetable; **stündlich** adj hourly

Stuntman (-s, Stuntmen) m stuntman; **Stuntwoman** (-, Stuntwomen) f stuntwoman

stur adj stubborn; (stärker) pigheaded

Sturm (-(e)s, Stürme) m storm; **stürmen** vi (Wind) to blow hard; (rennen) to storm; **Stürmer(in)**

m(f) striker, forward; **Sturmflut** f storm tide; **stürmisch** adj stormy; (fig) tempestuous; (Zeit) turbulent; (Liebhaber) passionate; (Beifall, Begrüßung) tumultuous; **Sturmwarnung** f gale warning

Sturz (-es, Stürze) m fall; (Pol) overthrow; **stürzen** vt (werfen) to hurl; (Pol) to overthrow; (umkehren) to overturn ▷ vi to fall; (rennen) to dash; **Sturzhelm** m crash helmet

Stute (-, -n) f mare

Stütze (-, -n) f support; (Hilfe) help; (fam: Arbeitslosenunterstützung) dole (Brit), welfare (US)

stützen vt to support; (Ellbogen) to prop

stutzig adj perplexed, puzzled; (misstrauisch) suspicious

Styropor® (-s) nt polystyrene (Brit), styrofoam (US)

subjektiv adj subjective

Substanz (-, -en) f substance

subtrahieren vt to subtract

Subvention f subsidy; **subventionieren** vt to subsidize

Suche f search (nach for); **auf der ~ nach etw sein** to be looking for sth; **suchen** vt to look for; (Inform) to search ▷ vi to look, to search (nach for); **Suchmaschine** f (Inform) search engine

Sucht (-, Süchte) f mania; (Med) addiction; **süchtig** adj addicted; **Süchtige(r)** mf addict

Süd south; **Südafrika** nt South Africa; **Südamerika** nt South America; **Süddeutschland** nt Southern Germany; **Süden** (-s) m south; **im ~ Deutschlands** in the south of Germany; **Südeuropa** nt Southern Europe; **Südkorea** (-s) nt South Korea; **südlich** adj southern; (Kurs, Richtung) southerly; **Verkehr in ~er**

Richtung southbound traffic; **Südost(en)** m southeast; **Südpol** m South Pole; **Südstaaten** pl (der USA) the Southern States pl, the South sing; **südwärts** adv south, southwards; **Südwest(en)** m southwest; **Südwind** m south wind

Sülze (-, -n) f jellied meat

Summe (-, -n) f sum; (Gesamtsumme) total

summen vi, vt to hum; (Insekt) to buzz

Sumpf (-(e)s, Sümpfe) m marsh; (subtropischer) swamp; **sumpfig** adj marshy

Sünde (-, -n) f sin

super adj (fam) super, great; **Super** (-s) nt (Benzin) four star (petrol) (Brit), premium (US); **Supermarkt** m supermarket

Suppe (-, -n) f soup; **Suppengrün** nt bunch of herbs and vegetables for flavouring soup; **Suppenlöffel** m soup spoon; **Suppenschüssel** f soup tureen; **Suppentasse** f soup cup; **Suppenteller** m soup plate; **Suppenwürfel** m stock cube

Surfbrett nt surfboard; **surfen** vi to surf; **im Internet ~** to surf the Internet; **Surfer(in)** (-s, -) m(f) surfer

Surrealismus m surrealism

Sushi (-s, -s) nt sushi

süß adj sweet; **süßen** vt to sweeten; **Süßigkeit** f (Bonbon etc) sweet (Brit), candy (US); **Süßkartoffel** f sweet potato (Brit), yam (US); **süßsauer** adj sweet-and-sour; **Süßspeise** f dessert; **Süßstoff** m sweetener; **Süßwasser** nt fresh water

Sweatshirt (-s, -s) nt sweatshirt

Swimmingpool (-s, -s) m (swimming) pool

Sylvester nt siehe **Silvester**

Symbol (-s, -e) nt symbol; **Symbolleiste** f (Inform) toolbar

Symmetrie (-, -n) f symmetry; **symmetrisch** adj symmetrical

sympathisch adj nice; **jdn ~ finden** to like sb

Symphonie (-, -n) f symphony

Symptom (-s, -e) nt symptom (für of)

Synagoge (-, -n) f synagogue

synchronisiert adj (Film) dubbed; **Synchronstimme** f dubbing voice

Synthetik (-, -en) f synthetic (fibre); **synthetisch** adj synthetic

Syrien (-s) nt Syria

System (-s, -e) nt system; **systematisch** adj systematic; **Systemsteuerung** f (Inform) control panel

Szene (-, -n) f scene

t

Tabak (-s, -e) m tobacco;
Tabakladen m tobacconist's
Tabelle f table
Tablett (-s, -s) nt tray
Tablette f tablet, pill
Tabulator (-s, -) m tabulator, tab
Tacho(meter) (-s, -) m (Auto)
speedometer
Tafel (-, -n) f (a. Math) table;
(Anschlagtafel) board; (Wandtafel)
blackboard; (Schiefer~) slate;
(Gedenktafel) plaque; **eine**
~ Schokolade a bar of chocolate;
Tafelwasser nt table water;
Tafelwein m table wine
Tag (-(e)s, -e) m day; (Tageslicht)
daylight; **guten ~!** good
morning/afternoon; **am ~** during
the day; **sie hat ihre ~e** she's got
her period; **eines ~es** one day;
~ der Arbeit Labour Day;
Tagebuch nt diary; **tagelang**
adj for days (on end);

Tagesanbruch m daybreak;
Tagesausflug m day trip;
Tagescreme f day cream;
Tagesdecke f bedspread;
Tagesgericht nt dish of the day;
Tageskarte f (Fahrkarte) day
ticket; **die ~** (Speisekarte) today's
menu; **Tageslicht** nt daylight;
Tagesmutter f child minder;
Tagesordnung f agenda;
Tagestour f day trip;
Tageszeitung f daily newspaper;
täglich adj, adv daily; **tags(über)**
adv during the day; **Tagung** f
conference
Tai Chi (-) nt tai chi
Taille (-, -n) f waist
Taiwan (-s) nt Taiwan
Takt (-(e)s, -e) m (Taktgefühl) tact;
(Mus) time
Taktik (-, -en) f tactics pl
taktlos adj tactless; **taktvoll** adj
tactful
Tal (-(e)s, Täler) nt valley
Talent (-(e)s, -e) nt talent;
talentiert adj talented
Talkmaster(in) (-s, -) m(f) talk-show
host; **Talkshow** (-, -s) f talkshow
Tampon (-s, -s) m tampon
Tandem (-s, -s) nt tandem
Tang (-(e)s, -e) m seaweed
Tanga (-s, -s) m thong
Tank (-s, -s) m tank;
Tankanzeige f fuel gauge;
Tankdeckel m fuel cap; **tanken** vi
to get some petrol (Brit) (o gas
(US)); (Aviat) to refuel; **Tanker**
(-s, -) m (oil) tanker; **Tankstelle** f
petrol station (Brit), gas station
(US); **Tankwart(in)** (-s, -e) m(f)
petrol pump attendant (Brit), gas
station attendant (US)
Tanne (-, -n) f fir; **Tannenzapfen**
m fir cone
Tansania (s) nt Tanzania
Tante (-, -n) f aunt;
Tante-Emma-Laden m corner

shop (Brit), grocery store (US)

Tanz (-es, Tänze) m dance; **tanzen** vt, vi to dance; **Tänzer(in)** m(f) dancer; **Tanzfläche** f dance floor; **Tanzkurs** m dancing course; **Tanzlehrer(in)** m(f) dancing instructor; **Tanzstunde** f dancing lesson

Tapete (-, -n) f wallpaper; **tapezieren** vt, vi to wallpaper

Tarantel (-, -n) f tarantula

Tarif (-s, -e) m tariff, (scale of) fares/charges pl

Tasche (-, -n) f bag; (Hosentasche) pocket; (Handtasche) bag (Brit), purse (US)

Taschen- in zW pocket; **Taschenbuch** nt paperback; **Taschendieb(in)** m(f) pickpocket; **Taschengeld** nt pocket money; **Taschenlampe** f torch (Brit), flashlight (US); **Taschenmesser** nt penknife; **Taschenrechner** m pocket calculator; **Taschentuch** nt handkerchief

Tasse (-, -n) f cup; **eine ~ Kaffee** a cup of coffee

Tastatur f keyboard; **Taste** (-, -n) f button; (von Klavier, Computer) key; **Tastenkombination** f (Inform) shortcut

tat imperf von **tun**

Tat (-, -en) f action

Tatar (-s, -s) nt raw minced beef

Täter(in) (-s, -) m(f) culprit

tätig adj active; **in einer Firma ~ sein** to work for a firm; **Tätigkeit** f activity; (Beruf) occupation

tätowieren vt to tattoo; **Tätowierung** f tattoo (an +dat on)

Tatsache f fact; **tatsächlich** adj actual ▷ adv really

Tau (-(e)s, -e) nt (Seil) rope ▷ (-(e)s) m dew

taub adj deaf; (Füße etc) numb (vor Kälte with cold)

Taube (-, -n) f pigeon; (Turtel~, fig: Friedenssymbol) dove

taubstumm adj deaf-and-dumb; **Taubstumme(r)** mf deaf-mute

tauchen vt to dip ▷ vi to dive; (Naut) to submerge; **Tauchen** (-s) nt diving; **Taucher(in)** (-s, -) m(f) diver; **Taucheranzug** m diving (o wet) suit; **Taucherbrille** f diving goggles pl; **Tauchermaske** f diving mask; **Tauchkurs** m diving course; **Tauchsieder** (-s, -) m portable immersion coil for heating water

tauen vi impers to thaw

Taufe (-, -n) f baptism; **taufen** vt to baptize; (nennen) to christen

taugen vi to be suitable (für for); **nichts ~** to be no good

Tausch (-(e)s, -e) m exchange; **tauschen** vt to exchange, to swap

täuschen vt to deceive ▷ vi to be deceptive ▷ vr: **sich ~** to be wrong; **täuschend** adj deceptive; **Täuschung** f deception; (optisch) illusion

tausend num a thousand; **vier~** four thousand; **~ Dank!** thanks a lot; **tausendmal** adv a thousand times; **tausendste(r, s)** adj thousandth; **Tausendstel** (-s, -) nt (Bruchteil) thousandth

Taxi nt taxi; **Taxifahrer(in)** m(f) taxi driver; **Taxistand** m taxi rank (Brit), taxi stand (US)

Team (-s, -s) nt team; **Teamarbeit** f team work; **teamfähig** adj able to work in a team

Technik f technology; (angewandte) engineering; (Methode) technique; **Techniker(in)** (-s, -) m(f) engineer; (Sport, Mus) technician;

technisch adj technical

Techno (-s) m (Mus) techno

Teddybär m teddy bear

Tee (-s, -s) m tea; **Teebeutel** m teabag; **Teekanne** f teapot; **Teelöffel** m teaspoon

Teer (-(e)s, -e) m tar

Teesieb nt tea strainer; **Teetasse** f teacup

Teich (-(e)s, -e) m pond

Teig (-(e)s, -e) m dough; **Teigwaren** pl pasta sing

Teil (-(e)s, -e) m part; (Anteil) share; **zum** ~ partly ▷ (-(e)s, -e) nt part; (Bestandteil) component; **teilen** vt to divide; (mit jdm) to share (mit with); **20 durch 4** ~ to divide 20 by 4 ▷ vr: **sich** ~ to divide

Teilkaskoversicherung f third party, fire and theft insurance

teilmöbliert adj partly furnished

Teilnahme (-, -n) f participation (an +dat in); **teilnehmen** irr vi to take part (an +dat at); **Teilnehmer(in)** (-s, -) m(f) participant

teils adv partly; **teilweise** adv partially, in part; **Teilzeit** f: ~ **arbeiten** to work part-time

Teint (-s, -s) m complexion

Tel. abk von Telefon tel.

Telefon (-s, -e) nt telephone; **Telefonanruf** m, **Telefonat** nt (tele)phone call; **Telefonanschluss** m telephone connection; **Telefonauskunft** f directory enquiries pl (Brit), directory assistance (US); **Telefonbuch** nt telephone directory; **Telefongebühren** pl telephone charges pl; **Telefongespräch** nt telephone conversation; **telefonieren** vi: **ich telefoniere gerade (mit ...)** I'm on the phone (to ...), **telefonisch** adj telephone; (Benachrichtigung) by telephone;

Telefonkarte f phonecard; **Telefonnummer** f (tele)phone number; **Telefonrechnung** f phone bill; **Telefonverbindung** f telephone connection; **Telefonzelle** f phone box (Brit), phone booth; **Telefonzentrale** f switchboard; **über die** ~ through the switchboard

Telegramm nt telegram; **Teleobjektiv** nt telephoto lens; **Teleshopping** (-s) nt teleshopping; **Teleskop** (-s, -e) nt telescope

Teller (-s, -) m plate

Tempel (-s, -) m temple

Temperament nt temperament; (Schwung) liveliness; **temperamentvoll** adj lively

Temperatur f temperature; **bei ~en von 30 Grad** at temperatures of 30 degrees; ~ **haben** to have a temperature; ~ **bei jdm messen** to take sb's temperature

Tempo (-s, -s) nt (Geschwindigkeit) speed; **Tempolimit** (-s) nt speed limit

Tempotaschentuch® nt (Papiertaschentuch) (paper) tissue, ≈ Kleenex®

Tendenz f tendency; (Absicht) intention

Tennis (-) nt tennis; **Tennisball** m tennis ball; **Tennisplatz** m tennis court; **Tennisschläger** m tennis racket; **Tennisspieler(in)** m(f) tennis player

Tenor (-s, Tenöre) m tenor

Teppich (-s, -e) m carpet; **Teppichboden** m (wall-to-wall) carpet

Termin (-s, -e) m (Zeitpunkt) date; (Frist) deadline; (Arzttermin etc) appointment

Terminal (-s, -s) nt (Inform, Aviat) terminal

Terminkalender m diary;

Terminplaner m (in Buchform)
personal organizer, Filofax®;
(Taschencomputer) personal digital
assistant, PDA

Terpentin (-s, -e) nt turpentine,
turps sing

Terrasse (-, -n) f terrace; (hinter
einem Haus) patio

Terror (-s) m terror;
Terroranschlag m terrorist
attack; **terrorisieren** vt to
terrorize; **Terrorismus** m
terrorism; **Terrorist(in)** m(f)
terrorist

Tesafilm® m ≈ sellotape® (Brit),
≈ Scotch tape® (US)

Test (-s, -e) m test

Testament nt will; **das
Alte/Neue ~** the Old/New
Testament

testen vt to test; **Testergebnis**
nt test results pl

Tetanus (-) m tetanus;
Tetanusimpfung f (anti-)tetanus
injection

teuer adj expensive, dear (Brit)

Teufel (-s, -) m devil; **was/wo
zum ~** what/where the devil;
Teufelskreis m vicious circle

Text (-(e)s, -e) m text; (Liedertext)
words pl, lyrics pl; **Textmarker**
(-s, -) m highlighter;
Textverarbeitung f word
processing; **Textverarbeitungsprogramm** nt word processing
program

Thailand nt Thailand

Theater (-s, -) nt theatre; (fam)
fuss; **ins ~ gehen** to go to the
theatre; **Theaterkasse** f box
office; **Theaterstück** nt (stage)
play; **Theatervorstellung** f
(stage) performance

Theke (-, -n) f (Schanktisch) bar;
(Ladentisch) counter

Thema (-s, Themen) nt subject,
topic; **kein ~!** no problem

Themse (-) f Thames

Theologie f theology

theoretisch adj theoretical;
~ stimmt das that's right in
theory; **Theorie** f theory

Therapeut(in) m(f) therapist;
Therapie f therapy; **eine
~ machen** to undergo therapy

Thermalbad nt thermal bath;
(Ort) thermal spa; **Thermometer**
(-s, -) nt thermometer

Thermosflasche® f,
Thermoskanne® f Thermos®
(flask); **Thermostat** (-(e)s, -e) m
thermostat

These (-, -n) f theory

Thron (-(e)s, -e) m throne

Thunfisch m tuna

Thüringen (-s) nt Thuringia

Thymian (-s, -e) m thyme

Tick (-(e)s, -e) m tic; (Eigenart)
quirk; (Fimmel) craze; **ticken** vi
to tick; **er tickt nicht ganz richtig**
he's off his rocker

Ticket (-s, -s) nt (plane) ticket

tief adj deep; (Ausschnitt, Ton,
Sonne) low; **2 Meter ~** 2 metres
deep; **Tief** (-s, -s) nt (Meteo) low;
(seelisch) depression; **Tiefdruck**
m (Meteo) low pressure; **Tiefe**
(-, -n) f depth; **Tiefgarage** f
underground car park (Brit) (o
garage (US)); **tiefgekühlt** adj
frozen; **Tiefkühlfach** nt freezer
compartment; **Tiefkühlkost** f
frozen food; **Tiefkühltruhe** f
freezer; **Tiefpunkt** m low

Tier (-(e)s, -e) nt animal; **Tierarzt**
m, **Tierärztin** f vet; **Tiergarten** m
zoo; **Tierhandlung** f pet shop;
Tierheim nt animal shelter;
tierisch adj animal ▷ adv (fam)
really; **~ ernst** deadly serious; **ich
hatte ~ Angst** I was dead scared;
Tierkreiszeichen nt sign of the
zodiac; **Tierpark** m zoo;
Tierquälerei f cruelty to animals;

Tierschützer(in) (-s, -) m(f) animal rights campaigner; **Tierversuch** m animal experiment

Tiger (-s, -) m tiger

timen vt to time; **Timing** (-s) nt timing

Tinte (-, -n) f ink; **Tintenfisch** m cuttlefish; (klein) squid; (achtarmig) octopus; **Tintenfischringe** pl calamari pl; **Tintenstrahldrucker** m ink-jet printer

Tipp (-s, -s) m tip; **tippen** vt, vi to tap; (fam: schreiben) to type; (fam: raten) to guess

Tirol (-s) nt Tyrol

Tisch ((e)s, e) m table; **Tischdecke** f tablecloth; **Tischlerei** f joiner's workshop; (Arbeit) joinery; **Tischtennis** nt table tennis; **Tischtennisschläger** m table-tennis bat

Titel (-s, -) m title; **Titelbild** nt cover picture

Toast (-(e)s, -s) m toast; **toasten** vt to toast; **Toaster** (-s, -) m toaster

Tochter (-, Töchter) f daughter

Tod (-(e)s, -e) m death; **Todesopfer** nt casualty; **Todesstrafe** f death penalty; **todkrank** adj terminally ill; (sehr krank) seriously ill; **tödlich** adj deadly, fatal; **er ist ~ verunglückt** he was killed in an accident; **todmüde** adj (fam) dead tired; **todsicher** adj (fam) dead certain

Tofu (-(s)) m tofu, bean curd

Toilette f toilet, restroom (US); **Toilettenpapier** nt toilet paper

toi, toi, toi interj good luck

tolerant adj tolerant (gegen of)

toll adj mad; (Treiben) wild; (fam: großartig) great; **Tollkirsche** f deadly nightshade; **Tollwut** f rabies sing

Tomate (-, -n) f tomato; **Tomatenmark** nt tomato purée (Brit) (o paste (US)); **Tomatensaft** m tomato juice

Tombola (-, -s) f raffle, tombola (Brit)

Ton (-(e)s, -e) m (Erde) clay ▷ m (Töne; Laut) sound; (Mus) note; (Nedeweise) tone; (Farbton, Nuance) shade; **Tonband** nt tape; **Tonbandgerät** nt tape recorder

tönen vi to sound ▷ vt to shade; (Haare) to tint

Toner (-s, -) m toner; **Tonerkassette** f toner cartridge

Tonne (-, -n) f (Fass) barrel; (Gewicht) tonne, metric ton

Tontechniker(in) m(f) sound engineer

Tönung f hue; (für Haar) rinse

Top (-s, -s) nt top

Topf (-(e)s, Töpfe) m pot

Töpfer(in) (-s, -) m(f) potter; **Töpferei** f pottery; (Gegenstand) piece of pottery

Tor (-(e)s, -e) nt gate; (Sport) goal; **ein ~ schießen** to score a goal; **Torhüter(in)** m(f) goalkeeper

torkeln vi to stagger

Tornado (-s, -s) m tornado

Torschütze m, **Torschützin** f (goal)scorer

Torte (-, -n) f cake; (Obsttorte) flan; (Sahnetorte) gateau

Torwart(in) (-s, -e) m(f) goalkeeper

tot adj dead; **~er Winkel** blind spot

total adj total, complete; **Totalschaden** m complete write-off

Tote(r) mf dead man/woman; (Leiche) corpse; **töten** vt, vi to kill; **Totenkopf** m skull

tot|lachen vr: **sich ~** to kill oneself laughing

Toto (-s, -s) m o nt pools pl

tot|schlagen irr vt to beat to death; **die Zeit ~** to kill time

Touchscreen (-s, -s) m touch screen

Tour (-, -en) f trip; (Rundfahrt) tour; **eine ~ nach York machen** to go on a trip to York; **Tourenski** m touring ski

Tourismus m tourism; **Tourist(in)** m(f) tourist; **Touristenklasse** f tourist class; **touristisch** adj tourist; (pej) touristy

traben vi to trot

Tournee (-, -n) f tour

Tracht (-, -en) f (Kleidung) traditional costume

Trackball (-s, -s) m (Inform) trackball

Tradition f tradition; **traditionell** adj traditional

traf imperf von **treffen**

Trafik (-, -en) f tobacconist's

Tragbahre (-, -n) f stretcher

tragbar adj portable

träge adj sluggish, slow

tragen (trug, getragen) vt to carry; (Kleidung, Brille, Haare) to wear; (Namen, Früchte) to bear; **Träger** (-s, -) m (an Kleidung) strap; (Hosen~) braces pl (Brit), suspenders pl (US); (in der Architektur) beam; (Stahl~, Eisen~) girder

Tragfläche f wing; **Tragflügelboot** nt hydrofoil

tragisch adj tragic; **Tragödie** f tragedy

Trainer(in) (-s, -) m(f) trainer, coach; **trainieren** vt, vi to train; (jdn a.) to coach; (Übung) to practise; **Training** (-s, -s) nt training; **Trainingsanzug** m tracksuit

Traktor m tractor

Trambahn (-, -en) f tram (Brit), streetcar (US)

trampen vi to hitchhike; **Tramper(in)** m(f) hitchhiker

Träne (-, -n) f tear; **tränen** vi to water; **Tränengas** nt teargas

trank imperf von **trinken**

Transfusion f transfusion

Transitverkehr m transit traffic; **Transitvisum** nt transit visa

Transplantation f transplant; (Hauttransplantation) graft

Transport (-(e)s, -e) m transport; **transportieren** vt to transport; **Transportmittel** nt means sing of transport; **Transportunternehmen** nt haulage firm

Transvestit (-en, -en) m transvestite

trat imperf von **treten**

Traube (-, -n) f (einzelne Beere) grape; (ganze Frucht) bunch of grapes; **Traubensaft** m grape juice; **Traubenzucker** m glucose

trauen vi: **jdm/einer Sache ~** to trust sb/sth; **ich traute meinen Ohren nicht** I couldn't believe my ears ▷ vr: **sich ~** to dare ▷ vt to marry; **sich ~ lassen** to get married

Trauer (-) f sorrow; (für Verstorbenen) mourning

Traum (-(e)s, Träume) m dream; **träumen** vt, vi to dream (von of, about); **traumhaft** adj dreamlike; (fig) wonderful

traurig adj sad (über +akk about)

Trauschein m marriage certificate; **Trauung** f wedding ceremony; **Trauzeuge** m, **Trauzeugin** f witness (at wedding ceremony), ≈ best man/maid of honour

Travellerscheck m traveller's cheque

treffen (traf, getroffen) vr: **sich ~** to meet ▷ vt, vi to hit; (Bemerkung) to hurt; (begegnen) to meet; (*Entscheidung*) to make; (*Maßnahmen*) to take; **Treffen** (-s, -) *nt* meeting; **Treffer** (-s, -) *m* (*Tor*) goal; **Treffpunkt** *m* meeting place

treiben (*trieb, getrieben*) *vt* to drive; (*Sport*) to do ▷ *vi* (*im Wasser*) to drift; (*Pflanzen*) to sprout; (*Tee, Kaffee*) to be diuretic; **Treiber** (-s, -) *m* (*Inform*) driver

Treibgas *nt* propellant; **Treibhaus** *nt* greenhouse; **Treibstoff** *m* fuel

trennen *vt* to separate; (*teilen*) to divide ▷ *vr*: **sich ~** to separate; **sich von jdm ~** to leave sb; **mit jdm sich ~** to part with sth; **Trennung** *f* separation

Treppe (-, -n) *f* stairs *pl*; (*im Freien*) steps *pl*; **Treppengeländer** *nt* banister; **Treppenhaus** *nt* staircase

Tresen (-s, -) *m* (*in Kneipe*) bar; (*in Laden*) counter

Tresor (-s, -e) *m* safe

Tretboot *nt* pedal boat; **treten** (*trat, getreten*) *vi* to step; **mit jdm in Verbindung ~** to get in contact with sb ▷ *vt* to kick; (*nieder~*) to tread

treu *adj* (*gegenüber Partner*) faithful; (*Kunde, Fan*) loyal; **Treue** (-) *f* (*eheliche*) faithfulness; (*von Kunde, Fan*) loyalty

Triathlon (-s, -s) *m* triathlon

Tribüne (-, -n) *f* stand; (*Rednertribüne*) platform

Trick (-s, -e *o* -s) *m* trick; **Trickfilm** *m* cartoon

trieb *imperf von* **treiben**

Trieb (-(e)s, -e) *m* urge; (*Instinkt*) drive; (*Neigung*) inclination; (*an Baum etc*) shoot; **Triebwerk** *nt* engine

Trikot (-s, -s) *nt* shirt, jersey

Trimm-Dich-Pfad *m* fitness trail

trinkbar *adj* drinkable; **trinken** (*trank, getrunken*) *vt, vi* to drink; **einen ~ gehen** to go out for a drink; **Trinkgeld** *nt* tip; **Trinkhalm** *m* (*drinking*) straw; **Trinkwasser** *nt* drinking water

Trio (-s, -s) *nt* trio

Tripper (-s, -) *m* gonorrhoea

Tritt (-(e)s, -e) *m* (*Schritt*) step; (*Fußtritt*) kick; **Trittbrett** *nt* running board

Triumph (-(e)s, -e) *m* triumph; **triumphieren** *vi* to triumph (*über +akk* over)

trivial *adj* trivial

trocken *adj* dry; **Trockenhaube** *f* hair-dryer; **Trockenheit** *f* dryness; **trocken|legen** *vt* (*Baby*) to change; **trocknen** *vt, vi* to dry; **Trockner** (-s, -) *m* dryer

Trödel (-s, *kein pl*) *m* (*fam*) junk; **Trödelmarkt** *m* flea market

trödeln *vi* (*fam*) to dawdle

Trommel (-, -n) *f* drum; **Trommelfell** *nt* eardrum; **trommeln** *vt, vi* to drum

Trompete (-, -n) *f* trumpet

Tropen *pl* tropics *pl*

Tropf (-(e)s, -e) *m* (*Med*) drip; **am ~ hängen** to be on a drip; **tröpfeln** *vi* to drip; **es tröpfelt** it's drizzling; **tropfen** *vt, vi* to drip; **Tropfen** (-s, -) *m* drop; **tropfenweise** *adv* drop by drop; **tropfnass** *adj* dripping wet; **Tropfsteinhöhle** *f* stalactite cave

tropisch *adj* tropical

Trost (-es) *m* consolation, comfort; **trösten** *vt* to console, to comfort; **trostlos** *adj* bleak; (*Verhältnisse*) wretched; **Trostpreis** *m* consolation prize

Trottoir (-s, -s) *nt* pavement (*Brit*), sidewalk (*US*)

trotz *prep +gen o dat* in spite of; **Trotz** (-es) *m* defiance; **trotzdem** *adv* nevertheless ▷ *conj* although;

trotzig adj defiant

trüb adj dull; (Flüssigkeit, Glas) cloudy; (fig) gloomy

Trüffel (-, -n) f truffle

trug imperf von **tragen**

trügerisch adj deceptive

Truhe (-, -n) f chest

Trümmer pl wreckage sing; (Bau~) ruins pl

Trumpf (-(e)s, Trümpfe) m trump

Trunkenheit f intoxication; **~ am Steuer** drink driving (Brit), drunk driving (US)

Truthahn m turkey

Tscheche (-n, -n) m, **Tschechin** f Czech; **Tschechien** (-s) nt Czech Republic; **tschechisch** adj Czech; **Tschechische Republik** Czech Republic; **Tschechisch** nt Czech

Tschetschenien (-s) nt Chechnya

tschüs(s) interj bye

T-Shirt (-s, -s) nt T-shirt

Tube (-, -n) f tube

Tuberkulose (-, -n) f tuberculosis, TB

Tuch (-(e)s, Tücher) nt cloth; (Halstuch) scarf; (Kopftuch) headscarf

tüchtig adj competent; (fleißig) efficient; (fam: kräftig) good

Tugend (-, -en) f virtue; **tugendhaft** adj virtuous

Tulpe (-, -n) f tulip

Tumor (-s, -en) m tumour

tun (tat, getan) vt (machen) to do; (legen) to put; **was tust du da?** what are you doing?; **das tut man nicht** you shouldn't do that; **jdm etw ~** (antun) to do sth to sb; **das tut es auch** that'll do ▷ vi to act; **so ~, als ob** to act as if ▷ vr impers: **es tut sich etwas/viel** something/a lot is happening

Tuner (-s, -) m tuner

Tunesien (-s) nt Tunisia

Tunfisch m siehe **Thunfisch** tuna

Tunnel (-s, -s o -) m tunnel

Tunte (-, -n) f (pej, fam) fairy

tupfen vt, vi to dab; (mit Farbe) to dot; **Tupfen** (-s, -) m dot

Tür (-, -en) f door; **vor/an der ~** at the door; **an die ~ gehen** to answer the door

Türke (-n, -n) m Turk; **Türkei** (-) f: **die ~** Turkey; **Türkin** f Turk

Türkis (-es, -e) m turquoise

türkisch adj Turkish; **Türkisch** nt Turkish

Turm (-(e)s, Türme) m tower; (spitzer Kirchturm) steeple; (Sprung~) diving platform; (Schach) rook, castle

turnen vi to do gymnastics; **Turnen** (-s) nt gymnastics sing; (Schule) physical education, PE; **Turner(in)** m(f) gymnast; **Turnhalle** f gym(nasium); **Turnhose** f gym shorts pl

Turnier (-s, -e) nt tournament

Turnschuh m gym shoe, sneaker (US)

Türschild nt doorplate; **Türschloss** nt lock

tuscheln vt, vi to whisper

Tussi (-, -s) f (pej, fam) chick

Tüte (-, -n) f bag

TÜV (-s, -s) m akr = **Technischer Überwachungsverein** ≈ MOT (Brit), vehicle inspection (US)

⬤ TÜV
⬤
⬤ The **TÜV** is the organization
⬤ responsible for checking the
⬤ safety of machinery, particularly
⬤ vehicles. Cars over three years
⬤ old have to be examined every
⬤ two years for their safety and
⬤ for their exhaust emissions.
⬤ **TÜV** is also the name given to
⬤ the test itself.

TÜV-Plakette *f* badge attached to a vehicle's numberplate, indicating that it has passed the "TÜV"

Tweed (-s, -s) *m* tweed

Typ (-s, -en) *m* type; *(Auto)* model; *(Mann)* guy, bloke

Typhus (-) *m* typhoid

typisch *adj* typical (für of); **ein ~er Fehler** a common mistake; **~ Marcus!** that's just like Marcus; **~ amerikanisch!** that's so American

u. *abk* = **und**

u. a. *abk* = **und andere(s)** and others; = **unter anderem, unter anderen** among other things

u. A. w. g. *abk* = **um Antwort wird gebeten** RSVP

U-Bahn *f* underground *(Brit)*, subway *(US)*

übel *adj* bad; *(moralisch)* wicked; **mir ist ~** I feel sick; **diese Bemerkung hat er mir ~ genommen** he took offence at my remark; **Übelkeit** *f* nausea

üben *vt, vi* to practise

⬤ SCHLÜSSELWORT

über *prep* +*dat* **1** *(räumlich)* over, above; **zwei Grad über null** two degrees above zero

a *(zeitlich)* over; **über der Arbeit einschlafen** to fall asleep over one's work

▷ prep +akk **1** (räumlich) over; (hoch über auch) above; (quer über auch) across

2 (zeitlich) over; **über Weihnachten** over Christmas; **über kurz oder lang** sooner or later

3 (mit Zahlen) **Kinder über 12 Jahren** children over o above 12 years of age; **ein Scheck über 200 Euro** a cheque for 200 euros

4 (auf dem Wege) via; **nach Köln über Aachen** to Cologne via Aachen; **ich habe es über die Auskunft erfahren** I found out from information

5 (betreffend) about; **ein Buch über ...** a book about o on ...; **über jdn/etw lachen** to laugh about o at sb/sth

6 Macht über jdn haben to have power over sb; **sie liebt ihn über alles** she loves him more than everything

▷ adv over; **über und über** over and over; **den ganzen Tag über** all day long; **jdm in etw dat über sein** to be superior to sb in sth

überall adv everywhere
überanstrengen vr: **sich ~** to overexert oneself
überbacken adj: **(mit Käse) ~** au gratin; **überbelichten** vt (Foto) to overexpose; **überbieten** irr vt (übertreffen) to surpass; (Rekord) to break
Überbleibsel (-s, -) nt remnant
Überblick m overview; (fig: in Darstellung) survey; (Fähigkeit zu verstehen) grasp (über +akk of)
überbuchen vt to overbook; **Überbuchung** f overbooking
überdurchschnittlich adj above average
übereinander adv on top of each other; (sprechen etc) about

each other
übereinstimmen vi to agree (mit with)
überempfindlich adj hypersensitive
überfahren irr vt (Auto) to run over; **Überfahrt** f crossing
Überfall m (Banküberfall) robbery; (Mil) raid; (auf jdn) assault; **überfallen** irr vt to attack; (Bank) to raid
überfällig adj overdue
überfliegen irr vt to fly over; (Buch) to skim through
Überfluss m overabundance, excess (an +dat of); **überflüssig** adj superfluous
überfordern vt to demand too much of; (Kräfte) to overtax; **da bin ich überfordert** (bei Antwort) you've got me there
Überführung f (Brücke) flyover (Brit), overpass (US)
überfüllt adj overcrowded
Übergabe f handover
Übergang m crossing; (Wandel, Überleitung) transition; **Übergangslösung** f temporary solution, stopgap
übergeben irr vt to hand over
▷ vr: **sich ~** to be sick, to vomit
Übergepäck nt excess baggage
Übergewicht nt excess weight; **(10 Kilo) ~ haben** to be (10 kilos) overweight
überglücklich adj overjoyed; (fam) over the moon
Übergröße f outsize
überhaupt adv at all; (im Allgemeinen) in general; (besonders) especially; **was willst du ~?** what is it you want?
überheblich adj arrogant
überholen vt to overtake; (Tech) to overhaul; **Überholspur** f overtaking (Brit) (o passing (US)) lane; **überholt** adj outdated

Überholverbot nt: hier
herrscht ~ you can't overtake here
überhören vt to miss, not to
catch; (absichtlich) to ignore;
überladen irr vt to overload
▷ adj (fig) cluttered; **überlassen**
irr vt: **jdm etw** ~ to leave sth to
sb; **über|laufen** irr vi (Flüssigkeit)
to overflow
überleben vt, vi to survive;
Überlebende(r) mf survivor
überlegen vt to consider; **sich**
(dat) **etw** ~ to think about sth; **er
hat es sich** (dat) **anders überlegt**
he's changed his mind ▷ adj
superior (dat to); **Überlegung** f
consideration
überm kontr von **über dem**
übermäßig adj excessive
übermorgen adv the day after
tomorrow
übernächste(r, s) adj:
~ **Woche** the week after next
übernachten vi to spend the
night (bei jdm at sb's place);
übernächtigt adj bleary-eyed,
very tired; **Übernachtung** f
overnight stay; ~ **mit Frühstück**
bed and breakfast
übernehmen irr vt to take on;
(Amt, Geschäft) to take over ▷ vr:
sich ~ to take on too much
überprüfen vt to check;
Überprüfung f check;
(Überprüfen) checking
überqueren vt to cross
überraschen vt to surprise;
Überraschung f surprise
überreden vt to persuade; **er
hat mich überredet** he talked me
into it
überreichen vt to hand over
übers kontr von **über das**
überschätzen vt to
overestimate; **überschlagen** irr
vt (berechnen) to estimate;
(auslassen: Seite) to skip ▷ vr: **sich**

~ to somersault; (Auto) to
overturn; (Stimme) to crack;
überschneiden irr vr: **sich**
~ (Linien etc) to intersect; (Termine)
to clash
Überschrift f heading
Überschwemmung f flood
Übersee f: **nach/in** ~ overseas
übersehen irr vt (Gelände) to
look (out) over; (nicht beachten) to
overlook
übersetzen vt to translate (aus
from, in +akk into); **Übersetzer(in)**
(-s, -) m(f) translator;
Übersetzung f translation
Übersicht f overall view;
(Darstellung) survey; **übersichtlich**
adj clear
überstehen irr vt (durchstehen)
to get over; (Winter etc) to get
through
Überstunden pl overtime sing
überstürzt adj hasty
überteuert adj overpriced
übertragbar adj transferable;
(Med) infectious; **übertragen** irr
vt to transfer (auf +akk to); (Radio)
to broadcast; (Krankheit) to
transmit ▷ vr to spread (auf +akk
to) ▷ adj figurative;
Übertragung f (Radio) broadcast;
(von Daten) transmission
übertreffen irr vt to surpass
übertreiben irr vt, vi to
exaggerate, to overdo;
Übertreibung f exaggeration;
übertrieben adj exaggerated,
overdone
überwachen vt to supervise;
(Verdächtigen) to keep under
surveillance
überwand imperf von
überwinden
überweisen irr vt to transfer;
(Patienten) to refer (an +akk to);
Überweisung f transfer; (von
Patienten) referral

überwiegend adv mainly

überwinden (überwand, überwunden) vt to overcome ▷ vr: **sich ~** to make an effort, to force oneself; **überwunden** pp von **überwinden**

Überzelt nt flysheet

überzeugen vt to convince; **Überzeugung** f conviction

überziehen irr vt (bedecken) to cover; (Jacke etc) to put on; (Konto) to overdraw; **die Betten frisch ~** to change the sheets

üblich adj usual

übrig adj remaining; **ist noch Saft ~?** is there any juice left?; **die Übrigen** pl the rest pl; **im Übrigen** besides; **~ bleiben** to be left (over); **mir blieb nichts anderes ~, als zu gehen** I had no other choice (but to go); **übrigens** adv besides; (nebenbei bemerkt) by the way; **übrig**|**haben** vt: **für jdn etwas ~** (fam: jdn mögen) to have a soft spot for sb

Übung f practice; (im Sport, Aufgabe etc) exercise

Ufer (-s, -) nt (Fluss) bank; (Meer, See) shore; **am ~** on the bank/shore

Ufo (-(s), -s) nt akr = **unbekanntes Flugobjekt** UFO

Uhr (-, -en) f clock; (am Arm) watch; **wie viel ~ ist es?** what time is it?; **1 ~** 1 o'clock; **20 ~** 8 o'clock, 8 pm; **Uhrzeigersinn** m: **im ~** clockwise; **gegen den ~** anticlockwise (Brit), counterclockwise (US); **Uhrzeit** f time (of day)

Ukraine (-) f: **die ~** the Ukraine

UKW abk = **Ultrakurzwelle** VHF

Ulme (-, -n) f elm

Ultrakurzwelle f very high frequency; **Ultraschallaufnahme** f (Med) scan

○ **SCHLÜSSELWORT**

um prep +akk **1** (um herum) (a)round; **um Weihnachten** around Christmas; **er schlug um sich** he hit about him

2 (mit Zeitangabe) at; **um acht (Uhr)** at eight (o'clock)

3 (mit Größenangabe) by; **etw um 4 cm kürzen** to shorten sth by 4 cm; **um 10% teurer** 10% more expensive; **um vieles besser** better by far; **um so besser** so much the better

4 der Kampf um den Titel the battle for the title; **um Geld spielen** to play for money; **Stunde um Stunde** hour after hour; **Auge um Auge** an eye for an eye

▷ prep +gen: **um ... willen** for the sake of ...; **um Gottes willen** for goodness' o (stärker) God's sake

▷ konj: **um ... zu** (in order) to ...; **zu klug, um ... zu** too clever to ...; siehe **umso**

▷ adv **1** (ungefähr) about; **um (die) 30 Leute** about o around 30 people

2 (vorbei) **die 2 Stunden sind um** the two hours are up

umarmen vt to embrace

Umbau m rebuilding; (zu etwas) conversion (zu into); **um**|**bauen** vt to rebuild; (zu etwas) to convert (zu into)

um|**blättern** vt, vi to turn over

um|**bringen** irr vt to kill

um|**buchen** vi to change one's reservation/flight

um|**drehen** vt to turn (round); (obere Seite nach unten) to turn over ▷ vr: **sich ~** to turn (round); **Umdrehung** f turn; (Phys, Auto) revolution

um|**fahren** irr vt to knock down

um|fallen *irr vi* to fall over
Umfang *m* (*Ausmaß*) extent; (*von Buch*) size; (*Reichweite*) range; (*Math*) circumference; **umfangreich** *adj* extensive
Umfeld *nt* environment
Umfrage *f* survey
Umgang *m* company, (*mit jdm*) dealings *pl*; **umgänglich** *adj* sociable; **Umgangssprache** *f* colloquial language, slang
Umgebung *f* surroundings *pl*; (*Milieu*) environment; (*Personen*) people around one
umgehen *irr vi* (*Gerücht*) to go round; **~ (können) mit** (know how to) handle ▷ *irr vt* to avoid; (*Schwierigkeit, Verbot*) to get round
um|gehen *irr vi*: **mit etw ~** to handle sth; **Umgehungsstraße** *f* bypass
umgekehrt *adj* reverse; (*gegenteilig*) opposite ▷ *adv* the other way round; **und ~** and vice versa
um|hören *vr*: **sich ~** to ask around; **um|kehren** *vi* to turn back ▷ *vt* to reverse; (*Kleidungsstück*) to turn inside out; **um|kippen** *vt* to tip over ▷ *vi* to overturn; (*fig*) to change one's mind; (*fam: ohnmächtig werden*) to pass out
Umkleidekabine *f* changing cubicle (*Brit*), dressing room (*US*); **Umkleideraum** *m* changing room
Umkreis *m* neighbourhood; **im ~ von** within a radius of
um|leiten *vt* to divert; **Umleitung** *f* diversion
um|rechnen *vt* to convert (*in +akk into*); **Umrechnung** *f* conversion; **Umrechnungskurs** *m* rate of exchange
Umriss *m* outline
um|rühren *vi, vt* to stir

ums *kontr von* **um das**
Umsatz *m* turnover
um|schalten *vi* to turn over
Umschlag *m* cover; (*Buch*) jacket; (*Med*) compress; (*Brief*) envelope
Umschulung *f* retraining
um|sehen *irr vr*: **sich ~** to look around; (*suchen*) to look out (*nach for*)
umso *adv*: **je ..., ~ mehr** all the more; **~ besser** so much the better
umsonst *adv* (*vergeblich*) in vain; (*gratis*) for nothing
Umstand *m* circumstance; **Umstände** (*pl*) (*fig*) fuss; **in anderen Umständen sein** to be pregnant; **jdm Umstände machen** to cause sb a lot of trouble; **machen Sie bitte keine Umstände** please, don't put yourself out; **unter diesen/ keinen Umständen** under these/no circumstances; **unter Umständen** possibly; **umständlich** *adj* (*Methode*) complicated; (*Ausdrucksweise*) long-winded; (*Mensch*) ponderous; **Umstandsmode** *f* maternity wear
um|steigen *irr vi* to change (trains/buses)
um|stellen *vt* (*an anderen Ort*) to change round; (*Tech*) to convert ▷ *vr*: **sich ~** to adapt (*auf +akk to*); **Umstellung** *f* change; (*Umgewöhnung*) adjustment; (*Tech*) conversion
Umtausch *m* exchange; **um|tauschen** *vt* to exchange; (*Währung*) to change
Umweg *m* detour
Umwelt *f* environment; **Umweltbelastung** *f* ecological damage; **umweltbewusst** *adj* environmentally aware;

umweltfreundlich adj
environment-friendly;
Umweltpapier nt recycled paper;
umweltschädlich adj harmful to
the environment; **Umweltschutz**
m environmental protection;
Umweltschützer(in) (-s, -) m(f)
environmentalist;
Umweltverschmutzung f
pollution; **umweltverträglich** adj
environment-friendly

um|werfen irr vt to knock over;
(fig: ändern) to upset; (fig, fam: jdn)
to flabbergast

um|ziehen irr vt to change ▷ vr:
sich ~ to change ▷ vi to move
(house); **Umzug** m
(Straßenumzug) procession;
(Wohnungsumzug) move

unabhängig adj independent;
Unabhängigkeitstag m
Independence Day, Fourth of July
(US)

unabsichtlich adv
unintentionally

unangenehm adj unpleasant;
Unannehmlichkeit f inconvenience;
~en pl trouble sing

unanständig adj indecent;
unappetitlich (Essen)
unappetizing; (abstoßend)
off-putting; **unbeabsichtigt** adj
unintentional; **unbedeutend** adj
insignificant, unimportant;
(Fehler) slight

unbedingt adj unconditional
▷ adv absolutely

unbefriedigend adj unsatisfactory; **unbegrenzt** adj
unlimited; **unbekannt** adj
unknown; **unbeliebt** adj
unpopular; **unbemerkt** adj
unnoticed; **unbequem** adj
(Stuhl, Mensch) uncomfortable;
(Regelung) inconvenient;
unbeständig adj (Wetter)
unsettled; (Lage) unstable;

(Mensch) unreliable; **unbestimmt**
adj indefinite; **unbeteiligt** adj
(nicht dazugehörig) uninvolved;
(innerlich nicht berührt) indifferent,
unconcerned; **unbewacht** adj
unguarded; **unbewusst** adj
unconscious; **unbezahlt** adj
unpaid; **unbrauchbar** adj
useless

und conj and; **~ so weiter** and so
on; **na ~?** so what?

undankbar adj (Person)
ungrateful; (Aufgabe) thankless;
undenkbar adj inconceivable;
undeutlich adj indistinct;
undicht adj leaky; **uneben** adj
uneven; **unecht** adj (Schmuck etc)
fake; **unehelich** adj (Kind)
illegitimate; **unendlich** adj
endless; (Math) infinite;
unentbehrlich adj indispensable;
unentgeltlich adj free (of charge)

unentschieden adj undecided;
~ enden (Sport) to end in a draw

unerfreulich adj unpleasant

unerhört adj unheard-of; (Bitte)
outrageous; **unerlässlich** adj
indispensable; **unerträglich** adj
unbearable; **unerwartet** adj
unexpected

unerwünscht adj unwelcome;
(Eigenschaften) undesirable;
unfähig adj incompetent; **~ sein,
etw zu tun** to be incapable of
doing sth; **unfair** adj unfair

Unfall m accident; **Unfallbericht**
m accident report; **Unfallflucht** f
failure to stop after an accident;
Unfallhergang m: **den
~ schildern** to give details of the
accident; **Unfallstation** f
casualty ward; **Unfallstelle** f
scene of the accident;
Unfallversicherung f accident
insurance

unfreundlich adj unfriendly

Ungarn (-s) nt Hungary

Ungeduld f impatience;
  ungeduldig adj impatient
ungeeignet adj unsuitable
ungefähr adj approximate ▷ adv
  approximately; **~ 10 Kilometer**
  about 10 kilometres; **wann ~?**
  about what time?; **wo ~?**
  whereabouts?
ungefährlich adj harmless;
  (sicher) safe
ungeheuer adj huge ▷ adv (fam)
  enormously; **Ungeheuer** (-s, -) nt
  monster
ungehorsam adj disobedient
  (gegenüber to)
ungelegen adj inconvenient;
  ungemütlich adj unpleasant;
  (Mensch) disagreeable;
  ungenießbar adj inedible;
  (Getränk) undrinkable;
  ungenügend adj unsatisfactory;
  (Schulnote) = F; **ungepflegt** adj
  (Garten) untended; (Aussehen)
  unkempt; (Hände) neglected;
  ungerade adj odd
ungerecht adj unjust;
  ungerechtfertigt adj unjusti-
  fied; **Ungerechtigkeit** f
  injustice, unfairness
ungern adv reluctantly;
  ungeschickt adj clumsy;
  ungeschminkt adj without
  make-up; **ungesund** adj
  unhealthy; **ungewiss** adj
  uncertain; **ungewöhnlich** adj
  unusual
Ungeziefer (-s) nt vermin pl
ungezogen adj ill-mannered
ungezwungen adj relaxed
ungiftig adj non-toxic
unglaublich adj incredible
Unglück (-(e)s, -e) nt (Unheil)
  misfortune; (Pech) bad luck;
  (Unglücksfall) disaster; (Verkehrs~)
  accident; **das bringt ~** that's
  unlucky; **unglücklich** adj
  unhappy; (erfolglos) unlucky;

  (unerfreulich) unfortunate;
  unglücklicherweise adv
  unfortunately
ungültig adj invalid
ungünstig adj inconvenient
unheilbar adj incurable; **~ krank
  sein** to be terminally ill
unheimlich adj eerie ▷ adv (fam)
  incredibly
unhöflich adj impolite
uni adj plain
Uni (-, -s) f uni
Uniform (-, -en) f uniform
Universität f university
Unkenntnis f ignorance
unklar adj unclear
Unkosten pl expenses pl;
  Unkostenbeitrag m contribu
  tion (towards expenses)
Unkraut nt weeds pl, ~art, weed
unlogisch adj illogical
unmissverständlich adj
  unambiguous
unmittelbar adj immediate;
  ~ darauf immediately afterwards
unmöbliert adj unfurnished
unmöglich adj impossible
unnahbar adj unapproachable
unnötig adj unnecessary
UNO (-) f akr = **United Nations
  Organization** UN
unordentlich adj untidy;
  Unordnung f disorder
unpassend adj inappropriate;
  (Zeit) inconvenient; **unpersönlich**
  adj impersonal; **unpraktisch** adj
  impractical
Unrecht nt wrong; **zu ~** wrongly;
  im ~ sein to be wrong; **unrecht**
  adj wrong; **~ haben** to be
  wrong
unregelmäßig adj irregular;
  unreif adj unripe; **unruhig** adj
  restless; **~ schlafen** to have a bad
  night
uns pron akk, dat von **wir**; us, (to)
  us; **~ (selbst)** (reflexiv) ourselves;

sehen Sie ~? can you see us?; **er schickte es ~** he sent it to us; **lasst ~ in Ruhe** leave us alone; **ein Freund von ~** a friend of ours; **wir haben ~ hingesetzt** we sat down; **wir haben ~ amüsiert** we enjoyed ourselves; **wir mögen ~** we like each other

unscharf adj (Foto) blurred, out of focus

unscheinbar adj insignificant; (Aussehen) unprepossessing

unschlüssig adj undecided

unschuldig adj innocent

unser pron (adjektivisch) our ▷ pron gen von **wir**; of us; **unsere(r, s)** pron (substantivisch) ours; **unseretwegen** adv (wegen uns) because of us; (uns zuliebe) for our sake; (um uns) about us; (von uns aus) as far as we are concerned

unseriös adj dubious; **unsicher** adj (ungewiss) uncertain; (Person, Job) insecure

Unsinn m nonsense

unsterblich adj immortal; **~ verliebt** madly in love

unsympathisch adj unpleasant; **er ist mir ~** I don't like him

unten adv below; (im Haus) downstairs; (an der Treppe etc) at the bottom; **nach ~** down

○ **SCHLÜSSELWORT**

unter prep +dat 1 (räumlich, mit Zahlen) under; (drunter) underneath, below; **unter 18 Jahren** under 18 years
2 (zwischen) among(st); **sie waren unter sich** they were by themselves; **einer unter ihnen** one of them; **unter anderem** among other things
▷ prep +akk under, below

Unterarm m forearm

unterbelichtet adj (Foto) underexposed

Unterbewusstsein nt subconscious

unterbrechen irr vt to interrupt; **Unterbrechung** f interruption; **ohne ~** nonstop

unterdrücken vt to suppress; (Leute) to oppress

unterdurchschnittlich adj below average

untere(r, s) adj lower

untereinander adv (räumlich) one below the other; (gegenseitig) each other; (miteinander) among themselves/yourselves/ourselves

Unterführung f underpass

untergehen irr vi to go down; (Sonne) to set; (Volk) to perish; (Welt) to come to an end; (im Lärm) to be drowned out

Untergeschoss nt basement; **Untergewicht** nt: (3 Kilo) **~ haben** to be (3 kilos) underweight; **Untergrund** m foundation; (Pol) underground; **Untergrundbahn** f underground (Brit), subway (US)

unterhalb adv, prep +gen below; **~ von** below

Unterhalt m maintenance; **unterhalten** irr vt to maintain; (belustigen) to entertain ▷ vr: **sich ~** to talk; (sich belustigen) to enjoy oneself; **Unterhaltung** f (Belustigung) entertainment; (Gespräch) talk, conversation

Unterhemd nt vest (Brit), undershirt (US); **Unterhose** f underpants pl; (für Damen) briefs pl

unterirdisch adj underground

Unterkiefer m lower jaw

Unterkunft (-, -künfte) f accommodation

Unterlage f (Beleg) document; (Schreibunterlage) pad

unterlassen irr vt: **es ~, etw zu tun** (versäumen) to fail to do sth; (bleiben lassen) to refrain from doing sth

unterlegen adj inferior (dat to); (besiegt) defeated

Unterleib m abdomen

Unterlippe f lower lip

Untermiete f: **zur ~ wohnen** to be a subtenant; **Untermieter(in)** m(f) subtenant

unternehmen irr vt (Reise) to go on; (Versuch) to make; **etwas ~** to do something (gegen about); **Unternehmen** (-s, -) nt undertaking; (Comm) company; **Unternehmensberater(in)** (-s, -) m(f) management consultant; **Unternehmer(in)** (-s, -) m(f) entrepreneur

Unterricht (-(e)s, -e) m lessons pl; **unterrichten** vt to teach

unterschätzen vt to underestimate

unterscheiden irr vt to distinguish (von from, zwischen +dat between) ▷ vr: **sich ~** to differ (von from)

Unterschenkel m lower leg

Unterschied (-(e)s, -e) m difference; **im ~ zu dir** unlike you; **unterschiedlich** adj different

unterschreiben irr vt to sign; **Unterschrift** f signature

Untersetzer (-s, -) m tablemat; (für Gläser) coaster

unterste(r, s) adj lowest, bottom

unter|stellen vr: **sich ~** to take shelter

unterstellen vt (rangmäßig) to subordinate (dat to); (fig) to impute (jdm etw sth to sb)

unterstreichen irr vt (a. fig) to underline

Unterstrich m (Inform) underscore

unterstützen vt to support; **Unterstützung** f support

untersuchen vt (Med) to examine; (Polizei) to investigate; **Untersuchung** f examination; (polizeiliche) investigation

untertags adv during the day

Untertasse f saucer

Unterteil nt lower part, bottom

Untertitel m subtitle

untervermieten vt to sublet

Unterwäsche f underwear

unterwegs adv on the way

unterzeichnen vt to sign

untreu adj unfaithful

untröstlich adj inconsolable; **unüberlegt** adj ill-considered ▷ adv without thinking; **unüblich** adj unusual; **unverantwortlich** adj irresponsible; (unentschuldbar) inexcusable

unverbindlich adj not binding; (Antwort) noncommittal ▷ adv (Comm) without obligation

unverbleit adj unleaded; **unverheiratet** adj unmarried, single; **unvermeidlich** adj unavoidable; **unvernünftig** adj silly; **unverschämt** adj impudent; **unverständlich** adj incomprehensible; **unverträglich** adj (Person) quarrelsome; (Essen) indigestible

unverwüstlich adj indestructible; (Mensch) irrepressible

unverzeihlich adj unpardonable; **unverzüglich** adj immediate; **unvollständig** adj incomplete; **unvorsichtig** adj careless

unwahrscheinlich adj improbable, unlikely ▷ adv (fam) incredibly

Unwetter nt thunderstorm

unwichtig adj unimportant

unwiderstehlich adj irresistible

unwillkürlich adj involuntary ▷ adv instinctively; **ich musste ~ lachen** I couldn't help laughing
unwohl adj unwell, ill
unzählig adj innumerable, countless
unzerbrechlich adj unbreakable; **unzertrennlich** adj inseparable; **unzufrieden** adj dissatisfied; **unzugänglich** adj inaccessible; **unzumutbar** adj unacceptable
unzusammenhängend adj disconnected; (Äußerung) incoherent; **unzutreffend** adj inapplicable; (unwahr) incorrect; **unzuverlässig** adj unreliable
Update (-s, -s) nt (Inform) update
üppig adj (Essen) lavish; (Vegetation) lush
uralt adj ancient, very old
Uran (-s) nt uranium
Uranus (-) m Uranus
Uraufführung f premiere
Urenkel m great-grandson; **Urenkelin** f great-granddaughter; **Urgroßeltern** pl great-grandparents pl; **Urgroßmutter** f great-grandmother; **Urgroßvater** m great-grandfather
Urheber(in) (-s, -) m(f) originator; (Autor) author
Urin (-s, -e) m urine; **Urinprobe** f urine specimen
Urkunde (-, -n) f document
Urlaub (-(e)s, -e) m holiday (Brit), vacation (US); **im ~** on holiday (Brit), on vacation (US); **in ~ fahren** to go on holiday (Brit) (o vacation (US)); **Urlauber(in)** (-s, -) m(f) holiday-maker (Brit), vacationer (US); **Urlaubsort** m holiday resort; **urlaubsreif** adj ready for a holiday (Brit) (o vacation (US)); **Urlaubszeit** f holiday season (Brit), vacation period (US)

Urne (-, -n) f urn
Urologe m, **Urologin** f urologist
Ursache f cause (für of); **keine ~!** not at all; (bei Entschuldigung) that's all right
Ursprung m origin; (von Fluss) source; **ursprünglich** adj original ▷ adv originally; **Ursprungsland** adj country of origin
Urteil (-s, -e) nt (Meinung) opinion; (Jur) verdict; (Strafmaß) sentence; **urteilen** vi to judge
Uruguay (-s) nt Uruguay
Urwald m jungle
USA pl USA sing
User(in) (-s, -) m(f) (Inform) user
usw. abk = **und so weiter** etc
Utensilien pl utensils pl

V

vage *adj* vague
Vagina (-, *Vaginen*) *f* vagina
Valentinstag *m* St Valentine's Day
Vandalismus *m* vandalism
Vanille (-) *f* vanilla
variieren (-s, *-n*) vi to vary
Vase (-, *-n*) *f* vase
Vaseline (-) *f* Vaseline®
Vater (-s, *Väter*) *m* father;
väterlich *adj* paternal;
Vaterschaft *f* fatherhood; (*Jur*)
paternity; **Vatertag** *m* Father's
Day; **Vaterunser** *nt*: **das**
~ (**beten**) (to say) the Lord's Prayer
V-Ausschnitt *m* V-neck
v. Chr. *abk* = **vor Christus** BC
Veganer(in) (-s, -) *m(f)* vegan;
Vegetarier(in) (-s, -) *m(f)* vege-
tarian; **vegetarisch** *adj*
vegetarian
Veilchen *nt* violet
Velo (-s, -s) *nt* (*schweizerisch*)
bicycle
Vene (-, *-n*) *f* vein
Venedig (-s) *nt* Venice
Venezuela (-s) *nt* Venezuela
Ventil (-s, *-e*) *nt* valve
Ventilator *m* ventilator
Venus (-) *f* Venus
Venusmuschel *f* clam
verabreden vt to arrange ▷ vr:
sich ~ to arrange to meet (*mit jdm*
sb); **ich bin schon verabredet** I'm
already meeting someone;
Verabredung *f* arrangement;
(*Termin*) appointment; (*zum*
Ausgehen) date
verabschieden vt (*Gäste*) to say
goodbye to; (*Gesetz*) to pass ▷ vr:
sich ~ to say goodbye
verachten vt to despise;
verächtlich *adj* contemptuous;
(*verachtenswert*) contemptible;
Verachtung *f* contempt
verallgemeinern vt to
generalize
Veranda (-, *Veranden*) *f* veranda,
porch (US)
veränderlich *adj* changeable;
verändern vt to change ▷ vr:
sich ~ to change; **Veränderung** *f*
change
veranlassen vt to cause
veranstalten vt to organize;
Veranstalter(in) (-s, -) *m(f)*
organizer; **Veranstaltung** *f*
event; **Veranstaltungsort** *m*
venue
verantworten vt to take
responsibility for ▷ vr: **sich für**
etw ~ to answer for sth;
verantwortlich *adj* responsible
(*für* for); **Verantwortung** *f*
responsibility (*für* for)
verärgern vt to annoy
verarschen vt (*fam*) to take the
piss out of (*Brit*), to make a sucker
out of (US)
Verb (-s, *-en*) *nt* verb

Verband m (Med) bandage; (Bund) association; **Verband(s)kasten** m first-aid box; **Verband(s)zeug** nt dressing material

verbergen irr vt to hide (vor +dat from) ▷ vr: **sich ~** to hide (vor +dat from)

verbessern vt to improve; (berichtigen) to correct ▷ vr: **sich ~** to improve; (berichtigen) to correct oneself; **Verbesserung** f improvement; (Berichtigung) correction

verbiegen irr vi to bend ▷ vr: **sich ~** to bend

verbieten irr vt to forbid; **jdm ~, etw zu tun** to forbid sb to do sth

verbinden irr vt to connect; (kombinieren) to combine; (Med) to bandage; **können Sie mich mit ... ~?** (Tel) can you put me through to ...?; **ich verbinde** (Tel) I'm putting you through ▷ vr (Chem) **sich ~** to combine

verbindlich adj binding; (freundlich) friendly; **Verbindung** f connection

verbleit adj leaded

verblüffen vt to amaze

verblühen vi to fade

verborgen adj hidden

Verbot (-(e)s, -e) nt ban (für, von on); **verboten** adj forbidden; **es ist ~** it's not allowed; **es ist ~, hier zu parken** you're not allowed to park here; **Rauchen ~** no smoking

verbrannt adj burnt

Verbrauch (-(e)s) m consumption; **verbrauchen** vt to use up; **Verbraucher(in)** (-s, -) m(f) consumer

Verbrechen (-s, -) nt crime; **Verbrecher(in)** (-s, -) m(f) criminal

verbreiten vt to spread ▷ vr: **sich ~** to spread

verbrennen irr vt to burn; **Verbrennung** f burning; (in Motor) combustion

verbringen irr vt to spend

verbunden adj: **falsch ~** sorry, wrong number

Verdacht (-(e)s) m suspicion; **verdächtig** adj suspicious; **verdächtigen** vt to suspect

verdammt interj (fam) damn

verdanken vt: **jdm etw ~** to owe sth to sb

verdarb imperf von **verderben**

verdauen vt (a. fig) to digest; **verdaulich** adj digestible; **das ist schwer ~** that is hard to digest; **Verdauung** f digestion

Verdeck (-(e)s, -e) nt top

verderben (verdarb, verdorben) vt to spoil; (schädigen) to ruin; (moralisch) to corrupt; **es sich** (dat) **mit jdm ~** to get into sb's bad books; **ich habe mir den Magen verdorben** I've got an upset stomach ▷ vi (Lebensmittel) to go off

verdienen vt to earn; (moralisch) to deserve; **Verdienst** (-(e)s, -e) m earnings pl ▷ (-(e)s, -e) nt merit; (Leistung) service (um to)

verdoppeln vt to double

verdorben pp von **verderben** ▷ adj spoilt; (geschädigt) ruined; (moralisch) corrupt

verdrehen vt to twist; (Augen) to roll; **jdm den Kopf ~** (fig) to turn sb's head

verdünnen vt to dilute

verdunsten vi to evaporate

verdursten vi to die of thirst

verehren vt to admire; (Rel) to worship; **Verehrer(in)** (-s, -) m(f) admirer

Verein (-(e)s, -e) m association; (Klub) club

vereinbar adj compatible

vereinbaren vt to arrange;
Vereinbarung f agreement,
arrangement

vereinigen vt to unite ▷ vr: **sich
~** to unite; **Vereinigtes
Königreich** nt United Kingdom;
**Vereinigte Staaten (von
Amerika)** pl United States sing
(of America); **Vereinigung** f
union; (Verein) association;
Vereinte Nationen pl United
Nations pl

vereisen vi (Straße) to freeze
over; (Fenster) to ice up ▷ vt (Méd)
to freeze

vererben vt: **jdm etw ~** to leave
sth to sb; (Bio) to pass sth on to sb
▷ vr: **sich ~** to be hereditary;
vererblich adj hereditary

verfahren irr vi to proceed ▷ vr:
sich ~ to get lost; **Verfahren** (-s, -)
nt procedure; (Tech) method; (Jur)
proceedings pl

verfallen irr vi to decline; (Haus)
to be falling apart; (Fin) to lapse;
(Fahrkarte etc) to expire; **~ in** (+akk)
to lapse into; **Verfallsdatum** nt
expiry (Brit) (o expiration (US))
date; (von Lebensmitteln)
best-before date

verfärben vr: **sich ~** to change
colour; (Wäsche) to discolour

Verfasser(in) (-s, -) m(f) author,
writer; **Verfassung** f
(gesundheitlich) condition; (Pol)
constitution

verfaulen vi to rot

verfehlen vt to miss

verfeinern vt to refine

Verfilmung f film (o screen)
version

verfluchen vt to curse

verfolgen vt to pursue; (Pol) to
persecute

verfügbar adj available;
verfügen vi **über etw** (akk) **~** to
have sth at one's disposal;

Verfügung f order; **jdm zur
~ stehen** to be at sb's disposal;
jdm etw zur ~ stellen to put sth
at sb's disposal

verführen vt to tempt; (sexuell)
to seduce; **verführerisch** adj
seductive

vergangen adj past; **~e Woche**
last week; **Vergangenheit** f past

Vergaser (-s, -) m (Auto)
carburettor

vergaß imperf von **vergessen**

vergeben irr vt to forgive (jdm
etw sb for sth); (weggeben) to
award, to allocate; **vergebens**
adv in vain; **vergeblich** adv in
vain ▷ adj vain, futile

vergehen irr vi to pass ▷ vr:
sich an jdm ~ to indecently
assault sb; **Vergehen** (-s, -) nt
offence

Vergeltung f retaliation

vergessen (vergaß, vergessen) vt
to forget; **vergesslich** adj
forgetful

vergeuden vt to squander, to
waste

vergewaltigen vt to rape;
Vergewaltigung f rape

vergewissern vr: **sich ~** to make
sure

vergiften vt to poison;
Vergiftung f poisoning

Vergissmeinnicht (-(e)s, -e) nt
forget-me-not

Vergleich (-(e)s, -e) m
comparison; (Jur) settlement; **im
~ zu** compared to (o with);
vergleichen irr vt to compare
(mit to, with)

Vergnügen (-s, -) nt pleasure;
viel ~! enjoy yourself; **vergnügt**
adj cheerful; **Vergnügungspark**
m amusement park

vergoldet adj gold-plated

vergriffen adj (Buch) out of print;
(Ware) out of stock

vergrößern vt to enlarge;
(Menge) to increase; (mit Lupe) to
magnify; **Vergrößerung** f
enlargement; (Menge) increase;
(mit Lupe) magnification;
Vergrößerungsglas nt magnifying glass

verh. adj abk = **verheiratet**
married

verhaften vt to arrest

verhalten irr vr: **sich ~** (sich
benehmen) to behave; (Sache) to be;
Verhalten (-s) nt behaviour

Verhältnis nt relationship (zu
with); (Math) ratio; **~se** pl
circumstances pl, conditions pl; **im
~ von 1 zu 2** in a ratio of 1 to 2;
verhältnismäßig adj relative
▷ adv relatively

verhandeln vi to negotiate (über
etw akk sth); **Verhandlung** f
negotiation

verheimlichen vt to keep secret
(jdm from sb)

verheiratet adj married

verhindern vt to prevent; **sie
ist verhindert** she can't make
it

Verhör (-(e)s, -e) nt
interrogation; (gerichtlich)
examination; **verhören** vt to
interrogate; (bei Gericht) to
examine ▷ vr: **sich ~** to mishear

verhungern vi to starve to
death

verhüten vt to prevent;
Verhütung f prevention; (mit
Pille, Kondom etc) contraception;
Verhütungsmittel nt
contraceptive

verirren vr: **sich ~** to get lost

Verkauf m sale; **verkaufen** vt to
sell; **zu ~** for sale; **Verkäufer(in)**
m(f) seller; (beruflich) salesperson;
(in Laden) shop assistant (Brit),
salesperson (US); **verkäuflich** adj
for sale

Verkehr (-s, -e) m traffic; (Sex)
intercourse; (Umlauf) circulation;
verkehren vi (Bus etc) to run; **~ in**
to frequent; **~ mit** to associate (o
mix) with; **Verkehrsampel** f
traffic lights pl; **Verkehrsamt** nt
tourist information office;
verkehrsfrei adj traffic-free;
Verkehrsfunk m travel news sing;
Verkehrsinsel f traffic island;
Verkehrsmeldung f traffic
report; **Verkehrsmittel** nt means
sing of transport; **öffentliche ~** pl
public transport sing;
Verkehrsschild nt traffic sign;
Verkehrstote(r) mf road
casualty; **die Zahl der ~n** the
number of deaths on the road;
Verkehrsunfall m road accident;
Verkehrszeichen nt traffic sign

verkehrt adj wrong; (verkehrt
herum) the wrong way round;
(Pullover etc) inside out; **du machst
es ~** you're doing it wrong

verklagen vt to take to court

verkleiden vt to dress up (als as)
▷ vr: **sich ~** to dress up (als as); (um
unerkannt zu bleiben) to disguise
oneself; **Verkleidung** f (Karneval)
fancy dress; (um nicht erkannt zu
werden) disguise

verkleinern vt to reduce;
(Zimmer, Gebiet etc) to make smaller

verkneifen irr vr: **sich** (dat) **etw
~** (Lachen) to stifle sth; (Schmerz) to
hide sth; (sich versagen) to do
without sth; **verkommen** irr vi
to deteriorate; (Mensch) to go
downhill ▷ adj (Haus) dilapidated;
(moralisch) depraved; **verkraften**
vt to cope with

verkratzt adj scratched

verkühlen vr: **sich ~** to get a chill

verkürzen vt to shorten

Verlag (-(e)s, -e) m publishing
company

verlangen vt (fordern) to

demand; (wollen) to want; (Preis) to ask; (Qualifikation) to require; (erwarten) to ask (von of); (fragen nach) to ask for; (Pass etc) to ask to see; **~ Sie Herrn X** ask for Mr X ▷ vi: **~ nach** to ask for

verlängern vt to extend; (Pass, Erlaubnis) renew; **Verlängerung** f extension; (Sport) extra time; (von Pass, Erlaubnis) renewal; **Verlängerungsschnur** f extension cable; **Verlängerungswoche** f extra week

verlassen irr vt to leave ▷ irr vr: **sich ~** to rely (auf +akk on) ▷ adj desolate; (Mensch) abandoned; **verlässlich** adj reliable

Verlauf m course; **verlaufen** irr vi (Weg, Grenze) to run (entlang along); (zeitlich) to run ▷ vr: **sich ~** to get lost; (Farben) to run ▷ vr: **sich ~** to get lost; (Menschenmenge) to disperse

verlegen vt to move; (verlieren) to mislay; (Buch) to publish ▷ adj embarrassed; **Verlegenheit** f embarrassment; (Situation) difficulty

Verleih (-(e)s, -e) m (Firma) hire company (Brit), rental company (US); **verleihen** irr vt to lend; (vermieten) to hire (out) (Brit), to rent (out) (US); (Preis, Medaille) to award

verleiten vt: **jdn dazu ~, etw zu tun** to induce sb to do sth

verlernen vt to forget

verletzen vt to hurt; (fig) to hurt; **Verletzte(r)** mf injured person; **Verletzung** f injury; (Verstoß) violation

verlieben vr: **sich ~** to fall in love (in jdn with sb); **verliebt** adj in love

verlieren (verlor, verloren) vt, vi to lose

verloben vr: **sich ~** to get engaged (mit to); **Verlobte(r)** mf

fiancé/fiancée; **Verlobung** f engagement

verlor imperf von **verlieren**

verloren pp von **verlieren** ▷ adj lost; (Eier) poached; **~ gehen** to go missing

verlosen vt to raffle; **Verlosung** f raffle

Verlust (-(e)s, -e) m loss

vermehren vt to multiply; (Menge) to increase ▷ vr: **sich ~** to multiply; (Menge) to increase

vermeiden irr vt to avoid

vermeintlich adj supposed

vermieten vt to rent (out), to let (out) (Brit); (Auto) to hire (out) (Brit), to rent (out) (US); **Vermieter(in)** m(f) landlord/-lady

vermischen vt to mix ▷ vr: **sich ~** to mix

vermissen vt to miss; **vermisst** adj missing; **jdn als ~ melden** to report sb missing

Vermittlung f (bei Streit) mediation; (Herbeiführung) arranging; (Stelle) agency

Vermögen (-s, -) nt fortune

vermuten vt to suppose; (argwöhnen) to suspect; **vermutlich** adj probable ▷ adv probably; **Vermutung** f supposition; (Verdacht) suspicion

vernachlässigen vt to neglect

vernichten vt to destroy; **vernichtend** adj (fig) crushing; (Blick) withering; (Kritik) scathing

Vernunft (-) f reason; **ich kann ihn nicht zur ~ bringen** I can't make him see reason; **vernünftig** adj sensible; (Preis) reasonable

veröffentlichen vt to publish

verordnen vt (Med) to prescribe; **Verordnung** f order; (Med) prescription

verpachten vt to lease (out) (an +akk to)

verpacken vt to pack; (einwickeln) to wrap up

Verpackung f packaging; **Verpackungskosten** pl packing charges pl

verpassen vt to miss

verpflegen vt to feed; **Verpflegung** f feeding; (Kost) food; (in Hotel) board

verpflichten vt to oblige; (anstellen) to engage ▷ vr: **sich ~** to commit oneself (etw zu tun to doing sth)

verprügeln vt to beat up

verraten irr vt to betray; (Geheimnis) to divulge; **aber nicht ~!** but don't tell anyone ▷ vr: **sich ~** to give oneself away

verrechnen vt: **~ mit** to set off against ▷ vr: **sich ~** to miscalculate; **Verrechnungsscheck** m crossed cheque (Brit), check for deposit only (US)

verregnet adj rainy

verreisen vi to go away (nach to); **sie ist (geschäftlich) verreist** she's away (on business); **verrenken** vt to contort; (Med) to dislocate; **sich** (dat) **den Knöchel ~** to sprain (o twist) one's ankle; **verringern** vt to reduce

verrostet adj rusty

verrückt adj mad, crazy; **es macht mich ~** it's driving me mad

versagen vi to fail; **Versagen** (-s) nt failure; **Versager(in)** (-s, -) m(f) failure

versalzen irr vt to put too much salt in/on

versammeln vt to assemble, to gather ▷ vr: **sich ~** to assemble, to gather; **Versammlung** f meeting

Versand (-(e)s) m dispatch; (Abteilung) dispatch department; **Versandhaus** nt mail-order company

versäumen vt to miss; (unterlassen) to neglect; **~, etw zu tun** to fail to do sth

verschätzen vr: **sich ~** to miscalculate

verschenken vt to give away; (Chance) to waste

verschicken vt to send off

verschieben vt irr (auf später) to postpone, to put off; (an anderen Ort) to move

verschieden adj (unterschiedlich) different; (mehrere) various; **sie sind ~ groß** they are of different sizes; **Verschiedene** pl various people/things pl; **Verschiedenes** various things pl

verschimmelt adj mouldy

verschlafen irr vt to sleep through; (fig) to miss ▷ vi to oversleep

verschlechtern vr: **sich ~** to deteriorate, to get worse; **Verschlechterung** f deterioration

Verschleiß (-es) m wear and tear

verschließbar adj lockable; **verschließen** vt irr to close; (mit Schlüssel) to lock

verschlimmern vt to make worse ▷ vr: **sich ~** to get worse

verschlossen adj locked; (fig) reserved

verschlucken vt to swallow ▷ vr: **sich ~** to choke (an +dat on)

Verschluss m lock; (von Kleid) fastener; (Foto) shutter; (Stöpsel) stopper

verschmutzen vt to get dirty; (Umwelt) to pollute

verschnaufen vi: **ich muss mal ~** I need to get my breath back

verschneit adj snow-covered

verschnupft adj: **~ sein** to have a cold; (fam: beleidigt) to be peeved

verschonen vt to spare (jdn mit etw sb sth)

verschreiben irr vt (Med) to prescribe;
verschreibungspflichtig adj available only on prescription

verschwand Imperf von **verschwinden**

verschweigen irr vt to keep secret; **jdm etw ~** to keep sth from sb

verschwenden vt to waste; **Verschwendung** f waste

verschwiegen adj discreet; (Ort) secluded

verschwinden (verschwand, verschwunden) vi to disappear, to vanish; **verschwinde!** get lost!; **verschwunden** pp von **verschwinden**

Versehen (-s, -) nt: **aus ~** by mistake; **versehentlich** adv by mistake

versenden irr vt to send off

versessen adj **~ auf** (+akk) mad about

versetzen vt to transfer; (verpfänden) to pawn; (fam: bei Verabredung) to stand up ▷ vr: **sich in jdn** (o jds Lage) **~** to put oneself in sb's place

verseuchen vt to contaminate

versichern vt to insure; (bestätigen) to assure; **versichert sein** to be insured; **Versichertenkarte** f health-insurance card; **Versicherung** f insurance; **Versicherungskarte** f: **grüne ~** green card (Brit), insurance document for driving abroad; **Versicherungspolice** f insurance policy

versilbert adj silver-plated

versinken irr vi to sink

Version f version

versöhnen vt to reconcile ▷ vr: **sich ~** to become reconciled

versorgen vt to provide, to supply (mit with); (Familie) to look after ▷ vr: **sich ~** to look after oneself; **Versorgung** f provision; (Unterhalt) maintenance; (für Alter etc) benefit

verspäten vr: **sich ~** to be late; **verspätet** adj late; **Verspätung** f delay; **(eine Stunde) ~ haben** to be (an hour) late

versprechen irr vt to promise ▷ vr: **ich habe mich versprochen** I didn't mean to say that

Verstand m mind; (Vernunft) (common) sense; **den ~ verlieren** to lose one's mind; **verständigen** vt to inform ▷ vr: **sich ~** to communicate; (sich einigen) to come to an understanding; **Verständigung** f communication; **verständlich** adj understandable; **Verständnis** nt understanding (für of); (Mitgefühl) sympathy; **verständnisvoll** adj understanding

verstauchen vt to sprain; **verstaucht** pp von **verstauchen** sprained

Versteck (-(e)s, -e) nt hiding place; **~ spielen** to play hide-and-seek; **verstecken** vt to hide (vor +dat from) ▷ vr: **sich ~** to hide (vor +dat from)

verstehen irr vt to understand; **falsch ~** to misunderstand ▷ vr: **sich ~** to get on (mit with)

Versteigerung f auction

verstellbar adj adjustable; **verstellen** vt to move; (Uhr) to adjust; (versperren) to block; (Stimme, Handschrift) to disguise ▷ vr: **sich ~** to pretend, to put on an act

verstopfen vt to block up; (Med) to constipate; **Verstopfung** f obstruction; (Med) constipation

Verstoß m infringement, violation (gegen of)

Versuch (-(e)s, -e) m attempt; (wissenschaftlich) experiment; **versuchen** vt to try

vertauschen vt to exchange; (versehentlich) to mix up

verteidigen vt to defend; **Verteidiger(in)** (-s, -) m(f) (Sport) defender; (Jur) defence counsel; **Verteidigung** f defence

verteilen vt to distribute

Vertrag (-(e)s, Verträge) m contract; (Pol) treaty

vertragen irr vt to stand, to bear ▷ vr: **sich ~** to get along (with each other); (sich aussöhnen) to make it up

verträglich adj (Mensch) good-natured; (Speisen) digestible

vertrauen vi: **jdm/einer Sache ~** to trust sb/sth; **Vertrauen** (-s) nt trust (in +akk in, zu in); **ich habe kein ~ zu ihm** I don't trust him; **ich hab's ihm im ~ gesagt** I told him in confidence; **vertraulich** adj (geheim) confidential; **vertraut** adj: **sich mit etw ~ machen** to familiarize oneself with sth

vertreten irr vt to represent; (Ansicht) to hold; **Vertreter(in)** (-s, -) m(f) representative

Vertrieb (-(e)s, -e) m (Abteilung) sales department

vertrocknen vi to dry up

vertun irr vr: **sich ~** to make a mistake

vertuschen vt to cover up

verunglücken vi to have an accident; **tödlich ~** to be killed in an accident

verunsichern vt to make uneasy

verursachen vt to cause

verurteilen vt to condemn

vervielfältigen vt to make copies of

verwählen vr: **sich ~** to dial the wrong number

verwalten vt to manage; (behördlich) to administer; **Verwalter(in)** (-s, -) m(f) manager; (Vermögens~) trustee; **Verwaltung** f management; (amtlich) administration

verwandt adj related (mit to); **Verwandte(r)** mf relative, relation; **Verwandtschaft** f relationship; (Menschen) relations pl

verwarnen vt to warn; (Sport) to caution

verwechseln vt to confuse (mit with); (halten für) to mistake (mit for)

verweigern vt to refuse

verwenden vt to use; (Zeit) to spend; **Mühe auf etw ~** to take trouble over sth; **Verwendung** f use

verwirklichen vt to realize; **sich selbst ~** to fulfil oneself

verwirren vt to confuse; **Verwirrung** f confusion

verwitwet adj widowed

verwöhnen vt to spoil

verwunderlich adj surprising; **Verwunderung** f astonishment

verwüsten vt to devastate

verzählen vr: **sich ~** to miscount

verzehren vt to consume

Verzeichnis nt (Liste) list; (Katalog) catalogue; (in Buch) index; (Inform) directory

verzeihen (verzieh, verziehen) vt, vi to forgive (jdm etw sb for sth); **~ Sie bitte, ...** (vor Frage etc) excuse me, ...; **~ Sie die Störung** sorry to disturb you; **Verzeihung** f: **~!** sorry; **~, ...** (vor Frage etc) excuse me, ...; **(jdn) um ~ bitten** to apologize (to sb)

verzichten vi: **auf etw** (akk) **~** to do without sth; (aufgeben) to give sth up

verzieh *imperf von* **verzeihen**

verziehen *pp von* **verzeihen**

verziehen *irr vt (Kind)* to spoil; **das Gesicht ~** to pull a face ▷ *vr:* **sich ~** to go out of shape; *(Gesicht)* to contort; *(verschwinden)* to disappear

verzieren *vt* to decorate

verzögern *vt* to delay ▷ *vr:* **sich ~** to be delayed; **Verzögerung** *f* delay

verzweifeln *vi* to despair *(an +dat of)*; **verzweifelt** *adj* desperate; **Verzweiflung** *f* despair

Veterinär(in) *(-s, -e) m(f)* veterinary surgeon *(Brit)*, veterinarian *(US)*

Vetter *(-s, -n) m* cousin

vgl. *abk = vergleiche* cf

Viagra® *(-s) nt* Viagra®

Vibrator *(-s, -en) m* vibrator; **vibrieren** *vi* to vibrate

Video *(-s, -s) nt* video; **auf ~ aufnehmen** to video; **Videoclip** *(-s, -s) m* video clip; **Videofilm** *m* video; **Videogerät** *nt* video (recorder); **Videokamera** *f* video camera; **Videokassette** *f* video (cassette); **Videorekorder** *m* video recorder; **Videospiel** *nt* video game; **Videothek** *(-, -en) f* video library

Vieh *(-(e)s) nt* cattle

viel *pron* a lot (of), lots of; **~ Arbeit** a lot of work, lots of work; **~e** **Leute** a lot of people, lots of people, many people; **zu ~** too much; **zu ~e** too many; **sehr ~** a great deal of; **sehr ~e** a great many; **ziemlich ~/~e** quite a lot of; **nicht ~** not much, not a lot of; **nicht ~e** not many, not a lot of ▷ *pron* a lot; **sie sagt nicht ~** she doesn't say a lot; **nicht ~** not much, not a lot of; **nicht ~e** not many, not a lot of; **gibt es ~?** is

there much?, is there a lot?; **gibt es ~e?** are there many?, are there a lot? ▷ *adv* a lot; **er geht ~ ins Kino** he goes a lot to the cinema; **sehr ~** a great deal; **ziemlich ~** quite a lot; **~ besser** much better; **~ teurer** much more expensive; **~ zu ~** far too much

vielleicht *adv* perhaps; **~ ist sie krank** perhaps she's ill, she might be ill; **weißt du ~, wo er ist?** do you know where he is (by any chance)?

vielmal(s) *adv* many times; **danke ~s** many thanks; **vielmehr** *adv* rather; **vielseitig** *adj* very varied *(Mensch, Gerät)* versatile

vier *num* four; **auf allen ~en** on all fours; **unter ~ Augen** in private, privately; **Vier** *(-, -en) f* four; *(Schulnote)* ≈ D; **Vierbettzimmer** *nt* four-bed room; **Viereck** *(-(e)s, -e) nt* four-sided figure; *(Quadrat)* square; **viereckig** *adj* four-sided; *(quadratisch)* square; **vierfach** *adj:* **die ~e Menge** four times the amount; **vierhundert** *num* four hundred; **viermal** *adv* four times; **vierspurig** *adj* four-lane

viert *adv:* **wir sind zu ~** there are four of us; **vierte(r, s)** *adj* fourth; *siehe auch* **dritte**

Viertel *(-s, -) nt (Stadtviertel)* quarter, district; *(Bruchteil)* quarter; *(Viertelliter)* quarter-litre; *(Uhrzeit)* quarter; **~ vor/nach drei** a quarter to/past three; **viertel drei** a quarter past two; **viertel drei** a quarter to three; **Viertelfinale** *nt* quarter-final; **vierteljährlich** *adj* quarterly; **Viertelstunde** *f* quarter of an hour

vierzehn *num* fourteen; **in ~ Tagen** in two weeks, in a fortnight *(Brit)*; **vierzehntägig** *adj* two-week, fortnightly *(Brit)*

vierzehnte(r, s) adj fourteenth;
siehe auch **dritte**; **vierzig** num
forty; **vierzigste(r, s)** adj
fortieth

Vietnam (-s) nt Vietnam

Vignette f (Autobahn~)
motorway (Brit) (o freeway (US))
permit

Villa (-, Villen) f villa

violett adj purple

Violine f violin

Virus (-, Viren) m o nt virus

Visitenkarte f card

Visum (-s, Visa o Visen) nt visa

Vitamin (-s, -e) nt vitamin

Vitrine (-, -n) f (glass) cabinet;
(Schaukasten) display case

Vogel (-s, Vögel) m bird;
Vogelgrippe f bird flu, avian flu;
vögeln vi, vt (vulg) to screw

Voicemail (-, -s) f voice mail

Vokal (-s, -e) m vowel

Volk (-(e)s, Völker) nt people pl;
(Nation) nation; **Volksfest** nt
festival; (Jahrmarkt) funfair;
Volkshochschule f adult
education centre; **Volkslied** nt
folksong; **Volksmusik** f folk
music; **volkstümlich** adj (einfach
und beliebt) popular; (herkömmlich)
traditional; (Kunst) folk

voll adj full (von of); **voll|machen**
vt to fill (up); **voll|tanken** vi to
fill up

Vollbart m beard; **Vollbremsung**
f: **eine ~ machen** to slam on
the brakes; **vollends** adv
completely

Volleyball m volleyball

Vollgas nt: **mit ~** at full throttle;
~ geben to step on it

völlig adj complete ▷ adv
completely

volljährig adj of age;
Vollkaskoversicherung f fully
comprehensive insurance;
vollklimatisiert adj fully

air-conditioned; **vollkommen**
adj perfect; **~er Unsinn** complete
rubbish ▷ adv completely

Vollkornbrot nt wholemeal
(Brit) (o whole wheat (US)) bread

Vollmacht (-, -en) f authority;
(Urkunde) power of attorney

Vollmilch f full-fat milk (Brit),
whole milk (US);
Vollmilchschokolade f milk
chocolate; **Vollmond** m full
moon; **Vollnarkose** f general
anaesthetic; **Vollpension** f full
board

vollständig adj complete

Volltreffer m direct hit;
Vollwertkost f wholefood;
vollzählig adj complete

Volt (-, -) nt volt

Volumen (-s, -) nt volume

vom kontr von **von dem** (räumlich,
zeitlich, Ursache) from; **ich kenne
sie nur ~ Sehen** I only know her by
sight

⊙ SCHLÜSSELWORT

von prep +dat 1 (Ausgangspunkt)
from; **von ... bis** from ... to; **von
morgens bis abends** from
morning till night; **von ... nach ...**
from ... to ...; **von ... an** from ...;
von ... aus from ...; **von dort aus**
from there; **etw von sich aus** tun
to do sth of one's own accord; **von
mir aus** (fam) if you like, I don't
mind; **von wo/wann ...?**
where/when ... from?
2 (Ursache, im Passiv) by; **ein
Gedicht von Schiller** a poem by
Schiller; **von etw müde** tired from
sth
3 (als Genitiv) of; **ein Freund von
mir** a friend of mine; **nett von dir**
nice of you; **jeweils zwei von zehn**
two out of every ten
4 (über) about; **er erzählte vom**

Urlaub he talked about his holiday
5 von wegen! *(fam)* no way!

voneinander *adv* from each
other

○ SCHLÜSSELWORT

vor *prep* +*dat* **1** *(räumlich)* in front
of; **vor der Kirche links abbiegen**
turn left before the church
2 *(zeitlich)* before; **ich war vor ihm
da** I was there before him; **vor 2
Tagen** 2 days ago; **5 (Minuten) or
4 5** (minutes) to 4; **vor Kurzem**
a little while ago
3 *(Ursache)* with; **vor Wut/Liebe**
with rage/love; **vor Hunger
sterben** to die of hunger; **vor
lauter Arbeit** because of work
4 vor allem, vor allen Dingen
most of all
▷ *prep* +*akk (räumlich)* in front of
▷ *adv*: **vor und zurück** backwards
and forwards

voran|gehen *irr vi* to go ahead;
einer Sache *(dat)* **~** to precede sth;
voran|kommen *irr vi* to make
progress

Vorarlberg (-s) *nt* Vorarlberg

voraus *adv* ahead; **im Voraus** in
advance; **voraus|fahren** *irr vi* to
drive on ahead; **vorausgesetzt**
conj provided (that); **Voraussage**
f prediction; *(Wetter)* forecast;
voraus|sagen *vt* to predict;
voraus|sehen *irr vt* to foresee;
voraus|sein *irr vi*: **jdm ~** to be
ahead of sb; **voraus|setzen** *vt* to
assume; **Voraussetzung** *f*
requirement, prerequisite;
voraussichtlich *adj* expected
▷ *adv* probably; **voraus|zahlen**
vt to pay in advance

Vorbehalt (-(e)s, -e) *m*
reservation; **vor|behalten** *irr vt*:

sich/jdm etw ~ to reserve sth (for
oneself)/for sb

vorbei *adv* past, over, finished;
vorbei|bringen *irr vt* to drop by
(o in); **vorbei|fahren** *irr vi* to
drive past; **vorbei|gehen** *irr vi* to
pass by, to go past; *(verstreichen,
aufhören)* to pass; **vorbei|kommen**
irr vi: **U** to drop by; **vorbei|lassen** *irr
vt*: **kannst du die Leute ~?** would
you let these people pass?; **lässt
du mich bitte mal vorbei?** can I
get past, please?; **vorbei|reden**
vi: **aneinander ~** to talk at
cross-purposes

vor|bereiten *vt* to prepare ▷ *vr*:
sich ~ to get ready *(auf +akk, für*
for); **Vorbereitung** *f* preparation

vor|bestellen *vt* to book in
advance; *(Essen)* to order in
advance; **Vorbestellung** *f*
booking, reservation

vor|beugen *vi* to prevent *(dat*
sth); **vorbeugend** *adj* preven-
tive; **Vorbeugung** *f* prevention

Vorbild *nt* (role) model;
vorbildlich *adj* model, ideal

Vorderachse *f* front axle;
vordere(r, s) *adj* front;
Vordergrund *m* foreground;
Vorderradantrieb *m* *(Auto)*
front-wheel drive; **Vorderseite** *f*
front; **Vordersitz** *m* front seat;
Vorderteil *m o nt* front (part)

Vordruck *m* form

voreilig *adj* hasty, rash; **~e
Schlüsse ziehen** to jump to
conclusions; **voreingenommen**
adj biased

vor|enthalten *vt*: **jdm etw
~** to withhold sth from sb

vorerst *adv* for the moment

vor|fahren *irr vi* *(vorausfahren)* to
drive on ahead; **vor das Haus ~** to
drive up to the house; **fahren Sie
bis zur Ampel vor** drive as far as
the traffic lights

Vorfahrt f (Auto) right of way; **~ achten** give way (Brit), yield (US); **Vorfahrtsschild** nt give way (Brit) (o yield (US)) sign; **Vorfahrtsstraße** f major road

Vorfall m incident

vor|führen vt to demonstrate; (Film) to show; (Theaterstück, Trick) to perform

Vorgänger(in) m(f) predecessor

vor|gehen irr vi (vorausgehen) to go on ahead; (nach vorn) to go forward; (handeln) to act, to proceed; (Uhr) to be fast; (Vorrang haben) to take precedence; (passieren) to go on; **Vorgehen** (-s) nt procedure

Vorgesetzte(r) mf superior

vorgestern adv the day before yesterday

vor|haben irr vt to plan; **hast du schon was vor?** have you got anything on?; **ich habe vor, nach Rom zu fahren** I'm planning to go to Rome

vor|halten irr vt: **jdm etw ~** to accuse sb of sth

Vorhand f forehand

vorhanden adj existing; (erhältlich) available

Vorhang m curtain

Vorhaut f foreskin

vorher adv before; **zwei Tage ~** two days before; **~ essen wir** we'll eat first; **Vorhersage** f forecast; **vorher|sehen** irr vt to foresee

vorhin adv just now, a moment ago

Vorkenntnisse pl previous knowledge sing

vor|kommen irr vi (nach vorne kommen) to come forward; (geschehen) to happen; (sich finden) to occur; (scheinen) to seem (to be); **sich** (dat) **dumm ~** to feel stupid

Vorlage f model

vor|lassen irr vt: **jdn ~** to let sb go first

vorläufig adj temporary

vor|lesen irr vt to read out

Vorlesung f lecture

vorletzte(r, s) adj last but one; **am ~n Samstag** (on) the Saturday before last

Vorliebe f preference

vor|machen vt: **kannst du es mir ~?** can you show me how to do it?; **jdm etwas ~** (fig: täuschen) to fool sb

vor|merken vt to note down; (Plätze) to book

Vormittag m morning; **am ~** in the morning; **heute ~** this morning; **vormittags** adv in the morning; **um 9 Uhr ~** at 9 (o'clock) in the morning, at 9 am

vorn(e) adv in front; **von ~ anfangen** to start at the beginning; **nach ~** to the front; **weiter ~** further up; **von ~ bis hinten** from beginning to end

Vorname m first name; **wie heißt du mit ~** what's your first name?

vornehm adj (von Rang) distinguished; (Benehmen) refined; (fein, elegant) elegant

vor|nehmen irr vt **sich** (dat) **etw ~** to start on sth; **sich** (dat) **~, etw zu tun** (beschließen) to decide to do sth

vornherein adv: **von ~** from the start

Vorort m suburb

vorrangig adj priority

Vorrat m stock, supply; **vorrätig** adj in stock

Vorrecht nt privilege

Vorruhestand m early retirement

Vorsaison f early season

Vorsatz m intention; (Jur) intent;

vorsätzlich adj intentional; (Jur) premeditated

Vorschau f preview; (Film) trailer

Vorschlag m suggestion, proposal, **vorschlagen** irr vt to suggest, to propose; **ich schlage vor, dass wir gehen** I suggest we go

vor|schreiben irr vt (befehlen) to stipulate; **jdm etw ~** to dictate sth to sb

Vorschrift f regulation, rule; (Anweisung) instruction; **vorschriftsmäßig** adj correct

Vorschule f nursery school, pre-school (US)

Vorsicht f care, **~!** look out; (Schild) caution; **~ Stufe!** mind the step; **vorsichtig** adj careful; **vorsichtshalber** adv just in case

Vorsorge f precaution; (Vorbeugung) prevention; **Vorsorgeuntersuchung** f checkup; **vorsorglich** adv as a precaution

Vorspann (-(e)s, -e) m credits pl

Vorspeise f starter

Vorsprung m projection; (Abstand) lead

vor|stellen vt (bekannt machen) to introduce; (Uhr) to put forward; (vor etw) to put in front; **sich** (dat) **etw ~** to imagine sth; **Vorstellung** f (Bekanntmachen) introduction; (Theat) performance; (Gedanke) idea; **Vorstellungsgespräch** nt interview

vor|täuschen vt to feign

Vorteil m advantage (gegenüber over); **die Vor- und Nachteile** the pros and cons; **vorteilhaft** adj advantageous

Vortrag (-(e)s, Vorträge) m talk (über +akk on); (akademisch) lecture; **einen ~ halten** to give a talk

vorüber adv over; **vorüber|gehen** irr vi to pass; **vorübergehend** adj temporary

▷ adv temporarily, for the time being

Vorurteil nt prejudice

Vorverkauf m advance booking

vor|verlegen vt to bring forward

Vorwahl f (Tel) dialling code (Brit), area code (US)

Vorwand (-(e)s, Vorwände) m pretext, excuse; **unter dem ~, dass** with the excuse that

vorwärts adv forward; **vorwärts|gehen** irr vi (fig) to progress

vorweg adv in advance; **vorweg|nehmen** irr vt to anticipate

Vorweihnachtszeit f pre-Christmas period, run-up to Christmas (Brit)

vor|werfen irr vt; **jdm etw ~** to accuse sb of sth

vorwiegend adv mainly

Vorwort nt preface

Vorwurf m reproach; **sich** (dat) **Vorwürfe machen** to reproach oneself; **jdm Vorwürfe machen** to accuse sb; **vorwurfsvoll** adj reproachful

vor|zeigen vt to show

vorzeitig adj premature, early

vor|ziehen irr vt (lieber haben) to prefer

Vorzug m preference; (gute Eigenschaft) merit; (Vorteil) advantage

vorzüglich adj excellent

vulgär adj vulgar

Vulkan (-s, -e) m volcano; **Vulkanausbruch** m volcanic eruption

W

W abk = **West** W

Waage (-, -n) f scales pl; (Astr) Libra; **waagerecht** adj horizontal

wach adj awake; **~ werden** to wake up; **Wache** (-, -n) f guard

Wachs (-es, -e) nt wax

wachsen (wuchs, gewachsen) vi to grow

wachsen vt (Skier) to wax

Wachstum nt growth

Wachtel (-, -n) f quail

Wächter(in) (-s, -) m(f) guard; (auf Parkplatz) attendant

wackelig adj wobbly; (fig) shaky; **Wackelkontakt** m loose connection; **wackeln** vi (Stuhl) to be wobbly; (Zahn, Schraube) to be loose; **mit dem Kopf ~** to waggle one's head

Wade (-, -n) f (Anat) calf

Waffe (-, -n) f weapon

Waffel (-, -n) f waffle; (Keks, Eiswaffel) wafer

wagen vt to risk; **es ~, etw zu tun** to dare to do sth

Wagen (-s, -) m (Auto) car; (Eisenb) carriage; **Wagenheber** (-s, -) m jack; **Wagentyp** m model, make

Wahl (-, -en) f choice; (Pol) election

wählen vt to choose; (Tel) to dial; (Pol) to vote for; (durch Wahl ermitteln) to elect ▷ vi to choose; (Tel) to dial; (Pol) to vote; **Wähler(in)** (-s, -) m(f) voter; **wählerisch** adj choosy

Wahlkampf m election campaign; **wahllos** adv at random; **Wahlwiederholung** f redial

Wahnsinn m madness; **~!** amazing!; **wahnsinnig** adj insane, mad ▷ adv (fam) incredibly

wahr adj true; **das darf doch nicht ~ sein!** I don't believe it; **nicht ~?** that's right, isn't it?

während prep +gen during ▷ conj while; **währenddessen** adv meanwhile, in the meantime

Wahrheit f truth

wahrnehmbar adj noticeable, perceptible; **wahr|nehmen** irr vt to perceive

Wahrsager(in) (-s, -) m(f) fortune-teller

wahrscheinlich adj probable, likely ▷ adv probably; **ich komme ~ zu spät** I'll probably be late; **Wahrscheinlichkeit** f probability

Währung f currency

Wahrzeichen nt symbol

Waise (-, -n) f orphan

Wal (-(e)s, -e) m whale

Wald (-(e)s, Wälder) m wood; (groß) forest; **Waldbrand** m forest fire; **Waldsterben** (-s) nt forest dieback

Wales (-) nt Wales; **Waliser(in)** m(f) Welshman/Welshwoman; **walisisch** adj Welsh; **Walisisch** nt Welsh

Walkie-Talkie (-(s), -s) nt walkie-talkie

Walkman® (-s, -s) m walkman®, personal stereo

Wall (-(e)s, Wälle) m embankment

Wallfahrt f pilgrimage; **Wallfahrtsort** m place of pilgrimage

Walnuss f walnut

Walross (-es, -e) nt walrus

wälzen vt to roll; (Bücher) to pore over; (Probleme) to deliberate on ▷ vr: **sich ~** to wallow; (vor Schmerzen) to roll about; (im Bett) to toss and turn

Walzer (-s, -) m waltz

Wand (-, Wände) f wall; (Trenn~) partition; (Berg~) (rock) face

Wandel (-s) m change; **wandeln** vt to change ▷ vr: **sich ~** to change

Wanderer (-s, -) m, **Wanderin** f hiker; **Wanderkarte** f hiking map; **wandern** vi to hike; (Blick) to wander; (Gedanken) to stray; **Wanderschuh** m walking shoe; **Wanderstiefel** m hiking boot; **Wanderung** f hike; **eine ~ machen** to go on a hike; **Wanderweg** m walking (o hiking) trail

Wandleuchte f wall lamp; **Wandmalerei** f mural; **Wandschrank** m built-in cupboard (Brit), closet (US)

wandte imperf von **wenden**

Wange (-, -n) f cheek

wann adv when; **seit ~ ist sie da?** how long has she been here?; **bis ~ bleibt ihr?** how long are you staying?

Wanne (-, -n) f (bath) tub

Wappen (-s, -) nt coat of arms

war imperf von **sein**

warb imperf von **werben**

Ware (-, -n) f product; **~n** goods pl; **Warenhaus** nt department store; **Warenprobe** f sample; **Warenzeichen** nt trademark

warf imperf von **werfen**

warm adj warm; (Essen) hot; **~ laufen** to warm up; **mir ist es zu ~** I'm too warm; **Wärme** (-, -n) f warmth; **wärmen** vt to warm; (Essen) to warm (o to heat) up ▷ vi (Kleidung, Sonne) to be warm ▷ vr: **sich ~** to warm up; (gegenseitig) to keep each other warm; **Wärmflasche** f hot-water bottle; **Warmstart** m (Inform) warm start

Warnblinkanlage f (Auto) warning flasher; **Warndreieck** nt (Auto) warning triangle; **warnen** vt to warn (vor +dat about, of); **Warnung** f warning

Warteliste f waiting list; **warten** vi to wait (auf +akk for); **warte mal!** wait (o hang on) a minute ▷ vt (Tech) to service

Wärter(in) m(f) attendant

Wartesaal m, **Wartezimmer** nt waiting room

Wartung f service; (das Warten) servicing

warum adv why

Warze (-, -n) f wart

was pron what; (fam: etwas) something; **~ kostet das?** what does it cost? how much is it?; **~ für ein Auto ist das?** what kind of car is that?; **~ für eine Farbe/Größe?** what colour/size?; **~?** (fam: wie bitte?) what?; **~ ist/gibt's?** what is it? what's up? **du weißt, ~ ich meine** you know what I mean; **~ (auch) immer** whatever; **soll ich dir ~ mitbringen?** do you want me to bring you anything?; **alles, ~ er hat** everything he's got

Waschanlage f (Auto) car wash;
waschbar adj washable;
Waschbär m raccoon;
Waschbecken nt washbasin
Wäsche (-, -n) f washing;
(schmutzig) laundry; (Bettwäsche)
linen; (Unterwäsche) underwear; **in
der ~** in the wash;
Wäscheklammer f clothes peg
(Brit) (o pin (US)); **Wäscheleine** f
clothesline
waschen (wusch, gewaschen) vt, vi
to wash; **Waschen und Legen**
shampoo and set ▷ vr: **sich ~** to
(have a) wash; **sich** (dat) **die Haare
~** to wash one's hair
Wäscherei f laundry;
Wäscheständer m clothes horse;
Wäschetrockner m tumble-drier
Waschgelegenheit f washing
facilities pl; **Waschlappen** m
flannel (Brit), washcloth (US); (fam:
Mensch) wet blanket;
Waschmaschine f washing
machine; **Waschmittel** nt,
Waschpulver nt washing
powder; **Waschraum** m
washroom; **Waschsalon** (-s, -s) m
launderette (Brit), laundromat
(US); **Waschstraße** f car wash
Wasser (-s, -) nt water;
fließendes ~ running water;
Wasserball m (Sport) water polo;
Wasserbob m jet ski;
wasserdicht adj watertight; (Uhr
etc) waterproof; **Wasserfall** m
waterfall; **Wasserfarbe** f
watercolour; **wasserfest** adj
watertight, waterproof;
Wasserhahn m tap (Brit), faucet
(US); **wässerig** adj watery;
Wasserkessel (-s, -) m kettle;
Wasserkocher (-s, -) m electric
kettle; **Wasserleitung** f water
pipe; **wasserlöslich** adj
water-soluble; **Wassermann** m
(Astr) Aquarius; **Wassermelone** f

water melon; **Wasserrutschbahn**
f water chute; **Wasserschaden**
m water damage; **wasserscheu**
adj scared of water; **Wasserski**
nt water-skiing; **Wasserspiegel**
m surface of the water;
(Wasserstand) water level;
Wassersport m water sports pl;
wasserundurchlässig adj
watertight, waterproof;
Wasserverbrauch m water
consumption;
Wasserversorgung f water
supply; **Wasserwaage** f spirit
level; **Wasserwerk** nt
waterworks pl
waten vi to wade
Watt (-(e)s, -en) nt (Geo) mud flats
pl ▷ (-s, -) nt (Elek) watt
Watte (-, -n) f cotton wool;
Wattepad (-s, -s) m cotton pad;
Wattestäbchen nt cotton bud,
Q-tip® (US)
WC (-s, -s) nt toilet, restroom
(US); **WC-Reiniger** m toilet
cleaner
Web (-s) nt (Inform) Web;
Webseite f (Inform) web page
Wechsel (-s, -) m change;
(Spieler~: Sport) substitution;
Wechselgeld nt change;
wechselhaft adj (Wetter)
changeable; **Wechseljahre** pl
menopause sing; **Wechselkurs** m
exchange rate; **wechseln** vt to
change; (Blicke) to exchange; **Geld
~** to change some money; (in
Kleingeld) to get some change;
Euro in Pfund ~ to change euros
into pounds ▷ vi to change;
kannst du ~? can you change
this?; **Wechselstrom** m
alternating current, AC;
Wechselstube f bureau de
change
Weckdienst m wake-up call
service; **wecken** vt to wake (up);

Wecker (-s, -) m alarm clock;
Weckruf m wake-up call

wedeln vi (Ski) to wedel; **mit etw ~** to wave sth; **mit dem Schwanz ~** to wag its tail; **der Hund wedelte mit dem Schwanz** the dog wagged its tail

weder conj: **~ ... noch ...** neither ... nor ...

weg adv (entfernt, verreist) away; (los, ab) off; **er war schon ~** he had already left (o gone); **Hände ~!** hands off; **weit ~** a long way away (o off)

Weg (-(e)s, -e) m way; (Pfad) path; (Route) route; **jdn nach dem ~ fragen** to ask sb the way; **auf dem ~ sein** to be on the way

weg|bleiben irr vi to stay away; **weg|bringen** irr vt to take away

wegen prep +gen o dat because of

weg|fahren irr vi to drive away; (abfahren) to leave; (in Urlaub) to go away; **Wegfahrsperre** f (Auto) (engine) immobilizer; **weg|kommen** irr vi to go away; (fig) **gut/schlecht ~** to come off well/badly; **weg|lassen** irr vt to leave out; **weg|laufen** irr vi to run away; **weg|legen** vt to put aside; **weg|machen** vt (fam) to get rid of; **weg|müssen** irr vi: **ich muss weg** I've got to go; **weg|nehmen** irr vt to take away; **weg|räumen** vt to clear away; **weg|rennen** irr vi to run away; **weg|schicken** vt to send away; **weg|schmeißen** irr vt to throw away; **weg|sehen** irr vi to look away; **weg|tun** irr vt to put away

Wegweiser (-s, -) m signpost

weg|werfen irr vt to throw away; **weg|wischen** vt to wipe off; **weg|ziehen** irr vi to move (away)

weh adj sore; siehe auch **wehtun**

wehen vt, vi to blow; (Fahne) to flutter

Wehen pl labour pains pl

Wehrdienst m military service

wehren vr: **sich ~** to defend oneself

weh|tun irr vt to hurt; **jdm/sich ~** to hurt sb/oneself

Welbchen nt: **es ist ein ~** (Tier) it's a she; **weiblich** adj feminine; (Bio) female

weich adj soft; **~ gekocht** (Ei) soft-boiled

Weichkäse m soft cheese; (Streichkäse) cheese spread; **weichlich** adj soft; (körperlich) weak; **Weichspüler** (-s, -) m (für Wäsche) (fabric) softener

Weide (-, -n) f (Baum) willow; (Grasfläche) meadow

weigern vr: **sich ~** to refuse; **Weigerung** f refusal

Weiher (-s, -) m pond

Weihnachten (-, -) nt Christmas; **Weihnachtsabend** m Christmas Eve; **Weihnachtsbaum** m Christmas tree; **Weihnachtsfeier** f Christmas party; **Weihnachtsferien** pl Christmas holidays pl (Brit), Christmas vacation sing (US); **Weihnachtsgeld** nt Christmas bonus; **Weihnachtsgeschenk** nt Christmas present; **Weihnachtskarte** f Christmas card; **Weihnachtslied** nt Christmas carol; **Weihnachtsmann** m Father Christmas, Santa (Claus)

● **WEIHNACHTSMARKT**
●
● The **Weihnachtsmarkt** is a
● market held in most large
● towns in Germany in the weeks
● prior to Christmas. People visit
● it to buy presents, toys and

- Christmas decorations, and to
- enjoy the festive atmosphere.
- Food and drink associated with
- the Christmas festivities can
- also be eaten and drunk then,
- for example, gingerbread and
- mulled wine.

Weihnachtsstern m (Bot)
poinsettia; **Weihnachtstag** m:
erster ~ Christmas Day; **zweiter
~** Boxing Day; **Weihnachtszeit** f
Christmas season

weil conj because

Weile (-) f while, short time; **es
kann noch eine ~ dauern** it could
take some time

Wein (-(e)s, -e) m wine; (Pflanze)
vine; **Weinbeere** f grape;
Weinberg m vineyard;
Weinbergschnecke f snail;
Weinbrand m brandy

weinen vt, vi to cry

Weinglas nt wine glass;
Weinkarte f wine list;
Weinkeller m wine cellar;
Weinlese (-, -n) f vintage;
Weinprobe f wine tasting;
Weintraube f grape

weise adj wise

Weise (-, -n) f manner, way; **auf
diese (Art und) ~** this way

weisen (wies, gewiesen) vt to
show

Weisheit f wisdom;
Weisheitszahn m wisdom
tooth

weiß adj white; **Weißbier** nt ~
wheat beer; **Weißbrot** nt white
bread; **weißhaarig** adj
white-haired; **Weißkohl** m,
Weißkraut nt (white) cabbage;
Weißwein m white wine

weit adj wide; (Begriff) broad;
(Reise, Wurf) long; (Kleid) loose; **wie
~ ist es ...?** how far is it ...?; **so
~ sein** to be ready ▷ adv far;

~ verbreitet widespread;
~ gereist widely travelled; **~ offen**
wide open; **das geht zu ~** that's
going too far, that's pushing it

weiter adj wider; (~ weg) farther
(away); (zusätzlich) further; **~e
Informationen** further
information sing ▷ adv further; **~!**
go on; (weitergehen!) keep moving;
~ nichts/niemand
nothing/nobody else; **und so
~** and so on; **weiter|arbeiten** vi
to carry on working;
Weiterbildung f further training
(o education); **weiter|empfehlen**
irr vt to recommend;
weiter|erzählen vt: **nicht ~!**
don't tell anyone; **weiter|fahren**
irr vi to go on (nach to, bis as far
as); **weiter|geben** irr vt to pass
on; **weiter|gehen** irr vi to pass on;
weiter|helfen irr vi: **jdm ~** to
help sb; **weiterhin** adv: **etw
~ tun** to go on doing sth;
weiter|machen vt, vi to
continue; **weiter|reisen** vi to
continue one's journey

weitgehend adj considerable
▷ adv largely; **weitsichtig** adj
long-sighted; (fig) far-sighted;
Weitsprung m long jump;
Weitwinkelobjektiv nt (Foto)
wide-angle lens

Weizen (-s, -) m wheat;
Weizenbier nt ~ wheat beer

⭕ **SCHLÜSSELWORT**

welche(r, s) interrogativ pron
which; **welcher von beiden?**
which (one) of the two?; **welchen
hast du genommen?** which (one)
did you take?; **welche eine ...!**
what a ...!; **welche Freude!** what
joy! ▷ indef pron some; (in Fragen)
any; **ich habe welche** I have some;
haben Sie welche? do you have

any? ▷ *relativ pron* (*bei Menschen*)
who; (*bei Sachen*) which, that;
welche(r, s) auch immer
whoever/whichever/whatever

welk *adj* withered; **welken** *vi* to
wither

Welle (-, -n) *f* wave; **Wellengang**
m waves *pl*; **starker ~** heavy seas
pl; **Wellenlänge** *f* (*a. fig*)
wavelength; **Wellenreiten** *nt*
surfing; **Wellensittich** (-s, -e) *m*
budgerigar, budgie; **wellig** *adj*
wavy

Wellness *f* health and beauty
(*Brit*), wellness (*US*)

Welpe (-n, -n) *m* puppy

Welt (-, -en) *f* world; **auf der ~** in
the world; **auf die ~ kommen** to
be born; **Weltall** *nt* universe;
weltbekannt, weltberühmt
world-famous; **Weltkrieg** *m*
world war; **Weltmacht** *f* world
power; **Weltmeister(in)** *m(f)*
world champion;
Weltmeisterschaft *f* world
championship; (*im Fußball*) World
Cup; **Weltraum** *m* space;
Weltreise *f* trip round the world;
Weltrekord *m* world record;
Weltstadt *f* metropolis;
weltweit *adj* worldwide, global

wem *pron dat von* **wer** who ... to,
(to) whom; **~ hast du's gegeben?**
who did you give it to?; **~ gehört
es?** who does it belong to?, whose
is it?; **~ auch immer es gehört**
whoever it belongs to

wen *pron akk von* **wer** who, whom;
~ hast du besucht? who did you
visit?; **~ möchten Sie sprechen?**
who would you like to speak to?

Wende (-, -n) *f* turning point;
(*Veränderung*) change; **die ~** (*Hist*)
the fall of the Berlin Wall; **Wende-
kreis** *m* (*Auto*) turning circle

Wendeltreppe *f* spiral staircase

wenden (*wendete o wandte,
gewendet o gewandt*) *vt, vi* to turn
(round); (*um 180°*) to make a
U-turn; **sich an jdn ~** to turn to sb;
bitte ~! please turn over, PTO ▷ *vr*;
sich ~ to turn; **sich an jdn ~** to
turn to sb

wenig *pron, adv* little; **~(e)** *pl* few;
(nur) ein (klein) ~ (*Just*) a little
(bit); **ein ~ Zucker** a little bit of
sugar, a little sugar; **wir haben
~ Zeit** we haven't got much time;
zu ~ too little; *pl* too few; **nur
~ wissen** only a few know ▷ *adv*;
er spricht ~ he doesn't talk much;
~ bekannt little known; **wenige**
pron pl few *pl*; **wenigste(r, s)** *adj*
least; **wenigstens** *adv* at least

○ **SCHLÜSSELWORT**

wenn *konj* **1** (*falls, bei Wünschen*) if;
wenn auch ..., selbst wenn ...
even if ...; **wenn ich doch ...** if
only I ...
2 (*zeitlich*) when; **immer wenn**
whenever

wennschon *adv*: **na ~** so what?

wer *pron* who; **~ war das?** who
was that?; **~ von euch?** which
(one) of you? ▷ *pron* whoever
who, anyone who; **~ das glaubt,
ist dumm** anyone who believes
that is stupid; **~ auch immer**
whoever ▷ *pron* somebody,
someone; (*in Fragen*) anybody,
anyone; **ist da ~?** is (there)
anybody there?

Werbefernsehen *nt* TV
commercials *pl*; **Werbegeschenk**
nt promotional gift; **werben**
(*warb, geworben*) *vt* to win;
(*Mitglied*) to recruit ▷ *vi* to
advertise; **Werbespot** (-s, -s) *m*
commercial; **Werbung** *f*
advertising

🔵 SCHLÜSSELWORT

werden (*pt* **wurde**, *pp* **geworden**
o (*bei Passiv*) **worden**) *vi* to
become; **was ist aus ihm/aus der
Sache geworden?** what became
of him/it?; **es ist nichts/gut
geworden** it came to
nothing/turned out well; **es wird
Nacht/Tag** it's getting dark/light;
mir wird kalt I'm getting cold; **mir
wird schlecht** I feel ill; **Erster
werden** to come *o* be first; **das
muss anders werden** that'll have
to change; **rot/zu Eis werden** to
turn red/to ice; **was willst du
(mal) werden?** what do you want
to be?; **die Fotos sind gut
geworden** the photos have come
out nicely
▷ *als Hilfsverb* **1** (*bei Futur*) **er wird
es tun** he will *o* he'll do it; **er wird
das nicht tun** he will not *o* he
won't do it; **es wird gleich regnen**
it's going to rain
2 (*bei Konjunktiv*) **ich würde ...** I
would ...; **er würde gern ...** he
would *o* he'd like to ...; **ich würde
lieber ...** I would *o* I'd rather ...
3 (*bei Vermutung*) **sie wird in der
Küche sein** she will be in the
kitchen
4 (*bei Passiv*) **gebraucht werden** to
be used; **er ist erschossen
worden** he has *o* he's been shot;
mir wurde gesagt, dass ... I was
told that ...

werfen (*warf, geworfen*) *vt* to
throw
Werft (-, -en) *f* shipyard,
dockyard
Werk (-(e)s, -e) *nt* (*Kunstwerk, Buch
etc*) work; (*Fabrik*) factory;
(*Mechanismus*) works *pl*; **Werkstatt**
(-, -stätten) *f* workshop; (*Auto*)

garage; **Werktag** *m* working
day; **werktags** *adv* on weekdays,
during the week; **Werkzeug** *nt*
tool; **Werkzeugkasten** *m*
toolbox

wert *adj* worth; **es ist etwa 50
Euro ~** it's worth about 50 euros;
das ist nichts ~ it's worthless;
Wert (-(e)s, -e) *m* worth; (*Zahlen~*)
(*Fin*) value; **~ legen auf** (+*akk*) to
attach importance to; **es hat
doch keinen ~** (*Sinn*) it's pointless;
Wertangabe *f* declaration of
value; **Wertbrief** *m* insured
letter; **Wertgegenstand** *m*
valuable object; **wertlos** *adj*
worthless; **Wertmarke** *f* token;
Wertpapiere *pl* securities *pl*;
Wertsachen *pl* valuables *pl*;
Wertstoff *m* recyclable waste;
wertvoll *adj* valuable
Wesen (-s, -) *nt* being; (*Natur,
Charakter*) nature
wesentlich *adj* significant;
(*beträchtlich*) considerable ▷ *adv*
considerably
weshalb *adv* why
Wespe (-, -n) *f* wasp;
Wespenstich *m* wasp sting
wessen *pron gen von* **wer**; whose

⬤ **WESSI**

⬤ A **Wessi** is a colloquial and often
⬤ derogatory word used to
⬤ describe a German from the
⬤ former West Germany. The
⬤ expression 'Besserwessi' is used
⬤ by East Germans to describe a
⬤ West German who is considered
⬤ to be a know-all.

West west; **Westdeutschland**
nt (*als Landesteil*) Western
Germany; (*Hist*) West Germany
Weste (-, -n) *f* waistcoat (*Brit*),
vest (*US*); (*Wollweste*) cardigan

Westen (-s) m west; **im ~ Englands** in the west of England; **der Wilde ~** the Wild West; **Westeuropa** nt Western Europe; **Westküste** f west coast; **westlich** adj western; (Kurs, Richtung) westerly; **Westwind** m west(erly) wind

weswegen adv why

Wettbewerb m competition; **Wettbüro** nt betting office; **Wette** (-, -n) f bet; **eine ~ abschließen** to make a bet; **die ~ gilt!** you're on; **wetten** vt, vi to bet (auf +akk on); **ich habe mit ihm gewettet, dass ...** I bet him that ...; **ich wette mit dir um 50 Euro** I'll bet you 50 euros; **~, dass?** wanna bet?

Wetter (-s, -) nt weather; **Wetterbericht** m, **Wettervorhersage** f weather forecast; **Wetterkarte** f weather map; **Wetterlage** f weather situation; **Wettervorhersage** f weather forecast

Wettkampf m contest; **Wettlauf** m race; **Wettrennen** nt race

WG (-, -s) f abk = **Wohngemeinschaft**

Whirlpool® (-s, -s) m jacuzzi®

Whisky (-s, -s) m (schottisch) whisky; (irisch, amerikanisch) whiskey

wichtig adj important

wickeln vt (Schnur) to wind (um round); (Schal, Decke) to wrap (um round); **ein Baby ~** to change a baby's nappy (Brit) (o diaper (US)); **Wickelraum** m baby-changing room; **Wickeltisch** m baby-changing table

Widder (-s, -) m (Zool) ram; (Astr) Aries sing

wider prep +akk against

widerlich adj disgusting

widerrufen irr vt to withdraw; (Auftrag, Befehl etc) to cancel

widersprechen irr vi to contradict (jdm sb); **Widerspruch** m contradiction

Widerstand m resistance; **widerstandsfähig** adj resistant (gegen to)

widerwärtig adj disgusting

widerwillig adj unwilling, reluctant

widmen vt to dedicate ▷ vr. **sich jdm/etw ~** to devote oneself to sb/sth; **Widmung** f dedication

🔘 SCHLÜSSELWORT

wie adv how; **wie groß/schnell?** how big/fast?; **wie wär's?** how about it?; **wie ist er?** what's he like?; **wie gut du das kannst!** you're very good at it; **wie bitte?** pardon?; (entrüstet) I beg your pardon!; **und wie!** and how!; **wie viel** how much; **wie viele Menschen** how many people; **wie weit** to what extent

▷ konj **1** (bei Vergleichen) **so schön wie ...** as beautiful as ...; **wie ich schon sagte** as I said; **wie du** like you; **singen wie ein ...** to sing like a ...; **wie (zum Beispiel)** such as (for example)

2 (zeitlich) **wie er das hörte, ging er** when he heard that he left; **er hörte, wie der Regen fiel** he heard the rain falling

wieder adv again; **~ ein(e) ...** another ...; **~ erkennen** to recognize; **etw ~ gutmachen** to make up for sth; **~ verwerten** to recycle

wieder|bekommen irr vt to get back

wiederholen vt to repeat;
Wiederholung f repetition
Wiederhören nt (Tel) **auf**
~ goodbye
wieder|kommen irr vi to come
back
wieder|sehen irr vt to see
again; (wieder treffen) to meet
again; **Wiedersehen** (-s) nt
reunion; **auf ~!** goodbye
Wiedervereinigung f
reunification
Wiege (-, -n) f cradle; **wiegen**
(wog, gewogen) vt, vi (Gewicht) to
weigh
Wien (-s) nt Vienna
wies imperf von **weisen**
Wiese (-, -n) f meadow
Wiesel (-s, -) nt weasel
wieso adv why
wievielmal adv how often;
wievielte(r, s) adj: **zum ~n Mal?**
how many times?; **den**
Wievielten haben wir heute?
what's the date today?; **am**
Wievielten hast du Geburtstag?
which day is your birthday?
wieweit conj to what extent
wild adj wild
Wild (-(e)s) nt game
wildfremd adj (fam) **ein ~er**
Mensch a complete (o total)
stranger; **Wildleder** nt suede;
Wildpark m game park;
Wildschwein nt (wild) boar;
Wildwasserfahren (-s) nt
whitewater canoeing (o
rafting)
Wille (-ns, -n) m will
willen prep +gen **um ... ~** for the
sake of ...; **um Himmels ~!**
(vorwurfsvoll) for heaven's sake;
(betroffen) goodness me
willkommen adj welcome
Wimper (-, -n) f eyelash;
Wimperntusche f mascara
Wind (-(e)s, -e) m wind

Windel (-, -n) f nappy (Brit),
diaper (US)
windgeschützt adj sheltered
from the wind; **windig** adj windy;
(fig) dubious; **Windjacke** f
windcheater; **Windmühle** f
windmill; **Windpocken** pl
chickenpox sing;
Windschutzscheibe f (Auto)
windscreen (Brit), windshield (US);
Windstärke f wind force;
Windsurfen (-s) nt windsurfing;
Windsurfer(in) m(f) windsurfer
Winkel (-s, -) m (Math) angle;
(Gerät) set square; (in Raum)
corner; **im rechten ~ zu** at right
angles to
winken vt, vi to wave
Winter (-s, -) m winter;
Winterausrüstung f (Auto)
winter equipment;
Winterfahrplan m winter
timetable; **winterlich** adj
wintry; **Wintermantel** m winter
coat; **Winterreifen** m winter
tyre; **Winterschlussverkauf** m
winter sales pl; **Wintersport** m
winter sports pl
Winterzeit f (Uhrzeit) winter
time (Brit), standard time (US)
winzig adj tiny
wir pron we; **~ selbst** we
ourselves; **~ alle** all of us; **~ drei**
the three of us; **~ sind's** it's us;
~ nicht not us
Wirbel (-s, -) m whirl; (Trubel)
hurly-burly; (Aufsehen) fuss; (Anat)
vertebra; **Wirbelsäule** f spine
wirken vi to be effective;
(erfolgreich sein) to work; (scheinen)
to seem
wirklich adj real; **Wirklichkeit** f
reality
wirksam adj effective; **Wirkung**
f effect
wirr adj confused; **Wirrwarr** (-s)
m confusion

Wirsing (-s) m savoy cabbage
Wirt (-(e)s, -e) m landlord; **Wirtin**
f landlady
Wirtschaft f (Comm) economy;
(Gaststätte) pub; **wirtschaftlich**
adj (Pol, Comm) economic;
(sparsam) economical
Wirtshaus nt pub
wischen vt, vi to wipe; **Wischer**
(s, -) m wiper
wissen (wusste, gewusst) vt to
know; **weißt du schon, ...?** did
you know ...?; **woher weißt du
das?** how do you know?; **das
musst du selbst ~** that's up to
you; **Wissen** (-s) nt knowledge
Wissenschaft f science;
Wissenschaftler(in) (-s, -) m(f)
scientist; (Geisteswissenschaftler)
academic; **wissenschaftlich** adj
scientific; (geisteswissenschaftlich)
academic
Witwe (-, -n) f widow; **Witwer**
(-s, -) m widower
Witz (-(e)s, -e) m joke; **mach
keine ~e!** you're kidding!; **das soll
wohl ein ~ sein** you've got to be
joking; **witzig** adj funny
wo adv where; **zu einer Zeit, ~ ...**
at a time when ...; **überall, ~ ...**
hingehe wherever I go ▷ conj:
jetzt, ~ du da bist now that you're
here; **~ ich dich gerade spreche**
while I'm talking to you;
woanders adv somewhere else
wobei adv: **~ mir einfällt ...**
which reminds me ...
Woche (-, -n) f week; **während** (o
unter) **der ~** during the week;
einmal die ~ once a week;
Wochenende nt weekend; **am
~** at (Brit) (o on (US)) the weekend;
wir fahren übers ~ weg we're
going away for the weekend;
Wochenendhaus nt weekend
cottage; **Wochenendtrip** m
weekend trip; **Wochenendurlaub**

m weekend break; **Wochenkarte**
f weekly (season) ticket;
wochenlang adv for weeks (on
end); **Wochenmarkt** m weekly
market; **Wochentag** m
weekday; **wöchentlich** adj, adv
weekly
Wodka (-s, -s) m vodka
wodurch adv: **~ unterscheiden
sie sich?** what's the difference
between them?; **~ hast du es
gemerkt?** how did you notice?;
wofür adv (relativ) for which;
(Frage) what ... for; **~ brauchst du
das?** what do you need that for?
wog imperf von **wiegen**
woher adv where ... from; **wohin**
adv where ... to

⊘ SCHLÜSSELWORT

wohl adv 1 **wohl oder übel**
whether one likes it or not
2 (wahrscheinlich) probably; (gewiss)
certainly; (vielleicht) perhaps; **sie
ist wohl zu Hause** she's probably
at home; **das ist doch wohl nicht
dein Ernst!** surely you're not
serious; **das mag wohl sein** that
may well be; **ob das wohl stimmt?**
I wonder if that's true; **er weiß das
sehr wohl** he knows that perfectly
well

Wohl (-(e)s) nt: **zum ~!** cheers;
wohlbehalten adv safe and
sound; **wohl|fühlen** vr: **sich
~** (zufrieden) to feel happy;
(gesundheitlich) to feel well;
Wohlstand m prosperity,
affluence; **wohl|tun** irr vi: **jdm
~** to do sb good; **Wohlwollen** nt
goodwill
Wohnblock m block of flats
(Brit), apartment house (US);
wohnen vi to live;
Wohngemeinschaft f shared flat

(Brit) (o apartment (US)); **ich wohne in einer ~ I** share a flat (o apartment); **wohnhaft** adj resident; **Wohnküche** f kitchen-cum-living-room; **Wohnmobil** (-s, -e) nt camper, RV (US); **Wohnort** m place of residence; **Wohnsitz** m place of residence; **Wohnung** f flat (Brit), apartment (US); **Wohnungstür** f front door; **Wohnwagen** m caravan; **Wohnzimmer** nt living room

Wolf (-(e)s, Wölfe) m wolf

Wolke (-, -n) f cloud; **Wolkenkratzer** m skyscraper; **wolkenlos** adj cloudless; **wolkig** adj cloudy

Wolldecke f (woollen) blanket; **Wolle** (-, -n) f wool

SCHLÜSSELWORT

wollen (pt **wollte**, pp **gewollt** o (als Hilfsverb) **wollen**) vt, vi to want; **ich will nach Hause** I want to go home; **er will nicht** he doesn't want to; **er wollte das nicht** he didn't want it; **wenn du willst** if you like; **ich will, dass du mir zuhörst** I want you to listen to me
▷ Hilfsverb: **er will ein Haus kaufen** he wants to buy a house; **ich wollte, ich wäre ...** I wish I were ...; **etw gerade tun wollen** to be going to do sth

Wolljacke f cardigan

womit adv what ... with; **~ habe ich das verdient?** what have I done to deserve that?

womöglich adv possibly

woran adv: **~ denkst du?** what are you thinking of?; **~ ist er gestorben?** what did he die of?; **~ sieht man das?** how can you tell?

worauf adv: **~ wartest du?** what are you waiting for?

woraus adv: **~ ist das gemacht?** what is it made of?

Workshop (-s, -s) m workshop

World Wide Web nt World Wide Web

Wort (-(e)s, Wörter) nt (Vokabel) word ▷ (-(e)s, -e) nt (Äußerung) word; **mit anderen -en** in other words; **jdn beim ~ nehmen** to take sb at his/her word; **Wörterbuch** nt dictionary; **wörtlich** adj literal

worüber adv: **~ redet sie?** what is she talking about?

worum adv: **~ gehts?** what is it about?

worunter adv: **~ leidet er?** what is he suffering from?

wovon adv (relativ) from which; **~ redest du?** what are you talking about?; **wozu** adv (relativ) to/for which; (interrogativ) what ... for/to; (warum) why; **~?** what for?; **~ brauchst du das?** what do you need it for?; **~ soll das gut sein?** what's it for?; **~ hast du Lust?** what do you feel like doing?

Wrack (-(e)s, -s) nt wreck

Wucher (-s) m profiteering; **das ist ~!** that's daylight robbery!

wuchs imperf von **wachsen**

wühlen vi to rummage; (Tier) to root; (Maulwurf) to burrow

Wühltisch m bargain counter

wund adj sore; **Wunde** (-, -n) f wound

Wunder (-s, -) nt miracle; **es ist kein ~** it's no wonder; **wunderbar** adj wonderful, marvellous; **Wunderkerze** f sparkler; **Wundermittel** nt wonder cure; **wundern** vr: **sich ~** to be surprised (über +akk at) ▷ vt to surprise; **wunderschön** adj beautiful; **wundervoll** *adj* wonderful

Wundsalbe *f* antiseptic ointment; **Wundstarrkrampf** *m* tetanus

Wunsch (-(e)s, Wünsche) *m* wish (nach for); **wünschen** *vt* to wish; **sich** (*dat*) **etw ~** to want sth; **ich wünsche dir alles Gute** I wish you all the best; **wünschenswert** *adj* desirable

wurde *imperf von* **werden**

Wurf (-s, Würfe) *m* throw; (Zool) litter

Würfel (-s, -) *m* dice; (Math) cube; **würfeln** *vi* to throw (the dice), (Würfel spielen) to play dice ▷ *vt* (Zahl) to throw; (Gastr) to dice; **Würfelzucker** *m* lump sugar

Wurm (-(e)s, Würmer) *m* worm

Wurst (-, Würste) *f* sausage; **das ist mir ~** (*fam*) I couldn't care less

Würstchen *nt* frankfurter

Würze (-, -n) *f* seasoning, spice

Wurzel (-, -n) *f* root; **Wurzelbehandlung** *f* root canal treatment

würzen *vt* to season, to spice; **würzig** *adj* spicy

wusch *imperf von* **waschen**

wusste *imperf von* **wissen**

wüst *adj* (unordentlich) chaotic; (ausschweifend) wild; (öde) desolate; (*fam*: heftig) terrible

Wüste (-, -n) *f* desert

Wut (-) *f* rage, fury; **ich habe eine ~ auf ihn** I'm really mad at him; **wütend** *adj* furious

WWW (-) *nt abk =* **World Wide Web** WWW

X-Beine *pl* knock-knees *pl*; **x-beinig** *adj* knock-kneed

x-beliebig *adj*: **ein ~es Buch** any book (you like)

x-mal *adv* umpteen times

Xylophon (-s, -e) *nt* xylophone

Yoga (-(s)) *m* nt yoga
Yuppie (-s, -s) *m* (-, -s) *f* yuppie

zackig *adj* (*Linie etc*) jagged; (*fam: Tempo*) brisk
zaghaft *adj* timid
zäh *adj* tough; (*Flüssigkeit*) thick
Zahl (-, -en) *f* number; **zahlbar** *adj* payable; **zahlen** *vt, vi* to pay; **~ bitte!** could I have the bill (*Brit*) (*o* check (*US*)) please?; **bar ~** to pay cash; **zählen** *vt, vi* to count (*auf +akk* on); **~ zu** to be one of; **Zahlenschloss** *nt* combination lock; **Zähler** (-s, -) *m* (*Gerät*) counter; (*für Strom, Wasser*) meter; **zahlreich** *adj* numerous; **Zahlung** *f* payment; **Zahlungsanweisung** *f* money order; **Zahlungsbedingungen** *pl* terms *pl* of payment
zahm *adj* tame; **zähmen** *vt* to tame
Zahn (-(e)s, *Zähne*) *m* tooth; **Zahnarzt** *m*, **Zahnärztin** *f* dentist; **Zahnbürste** *f*

toothbrush; **Zahncreme** f
toothpaste; **Zahnersatz** m
dentures pl; **Zahnfleisch** nt gums
pl; **Zahnfleischbluten** nt bleeding
gums pl; **Zahnfüllung** f filling;
Zahnklammer f brace;
Zahnpasta f, **Zahnpaste** f
toothpaste; **Zahnradbahn** f rack
railway (Brit) (o railroad (US));
Zahnschmerzen pl toothache
sing; **Zahnseide** f dental floss;
Zahnspange f brace;
Zahnstocher (-s, -) m toothpick
Zange (-, -n) f pliers pl;
(Zuckerzange) tongs pl; (Beißzange,
Zool) pincers pl; (Med) forceps pl
zanken vi to quarrel ▷ vr: **sich**
~ to quarrel
Zäpfchen nt (Anat) uvula; (Med)
suppository
zapfen vt (Bier) to pull; **Zapfsäule**
f petrol (Brit) (o gas (US)) pump
zappeln vi to wriggle; (unruhig
sein) to fidget
zappen vi to zap, to channel-hop
zart adj (weich, leise) soft; (Braten
etc) tender; (fein, schwächlich)
delicate; **zartbitter** adj
(Schokolade) plain, dark
zärtlich adj tender, affectionate;
Zärtlichkeit f tenderness; **~en** pl
hugs and kisses pl
Zauber (-s, -) m magic; (Bann)
spell; **Zauberei** f magic; **Zauberer**
(-s, -) m magician; (Künstler)
conjuror; **Zauberformel** f (magic)
spell; **zauberhaft** adj enchanting;
Zauberin f sorceress;
Zauberkünstler(in) m(f)
magician, conjuror; **Zaubermittel**
nt magic cure; **zaubern** vi to do
magic; (Künstler) to do conjuring
tricks; **Zauberspruch** m (magic)
spell
Zaun (-(e)s, Zäune) m fence
z. B. abk = **zum Beispiel** e.g., eg
Zebra (-s, -s) nt zebra;

Zebrastreifen m zebra crossing
(Brit), crosswalk (US)
Zecke (-, -n) f tick
Zehe (-, -n) f toe; (Knoblauch)
clove; **Zehennagel** m toenail;
Zehenspitze f tip of the toes
zehn num ten; **Zehnerkarte** f
ticket valid for ten trips; **Zehnkampf**
m decathlon; **Zehnkämpfer(in)**
m(f) decathlete; **zehnmal** adv ten
times; **zehntausend** num ten
thousand; **zehnte(r, s)** adj
tenth; siehe auch **dritte**; **Zehntel**
(-s, -) nt (Bruchteil) tenth;
Zehntelsekunde f tenth of a
second
Zeichen (-s, -) nt sign;
(Schriftzeichen) character;
Zeichenblock m sketch pad;
Zeichenerklärung f key;
Zeichensetzung f punctuation;
Zeichensprache f sign language;
Zeichentrickfilm m cartoon
zeichnen vt, vi to draw;
Zeichnung f drawing
Zeigefinger m index finger;
zeigen vt to show; **sie zeigte uns**
die Stadt she showed us around
the town; **zeig mal!** let me see
▷ vi to point (auf +akk to, at) ▷ vr:
sich ~ to show oneself; **es wird**
sich ~ time will tell; **Zeiger** (-s, -)
m pointer; (Uhr) hand
Zeile (-, -n) f line
Zeit (-, -en) f time; **ich habe keine**
~ I haven't got time; **lass dir ~** take
your time; **das hat ~** there's no
rush; **von ~ zu ~** from time to
time; **Zeitansage** f (Tel)
speaking clock (Brit), correct time
(US); **Zeitarbeit** f temporary
work; **zeitgenössisch** adj
contemporary, modern; **zeitgleich**
adj simultaneous ▷ adv at exactly
the same time; **zeitig** adj early;
Zeitkarte f season ticket;
zeitlich adj (Reihenfolge)

chronological; **es passt ~ nicht** it isn't a convenient time; **ich schaff es ~ nicht** I'm not going to make it; **Zeitlupe** f slow motion; **Zeitplan** m schedule; **Zeitpunkt** m point in time; **Zeitraum** m period (of time); **Zeitschrift** f magazine; (*wissenschaftliche*) periodical

Zeitung f newspaper; **es steht in der ~** it's in the paper(s); **Zeitungsanzeige** f newspaper advertisement; **Zeitungsartikel** m newspaper article; **Zeitungskiosk** m, **Zeitungsstand** m newsstand

Zeitunterschied m time difference; **Zeitverschiebung** f time lag; **Zeitvertreib** (-(e)s, -e) m: **zum ~** to pass the time; **zeitweise** adv occasionally; **Zeitzone** f time zone

Zelle (-, -n) f cell

Zellophan® (-s) nt cellophane®

Zelt (-(e)s, -e) nt tent; **zelten** vi to camp, to go camping; **Zeltplatz** m campsite, camping site

Zement (-(e)s, -e) m cement

Zentimeter m o nt centimetre

Zentner (-s, -) m (metric) hundredweight; (*in Deutschland*) fifty kilos; (*in Österreich und der Schweiz*) one hundred kilos

zentral adj central; **Zentrale** (-, -n) f central office; (*Tel*) exchange; **Zentralheizung** f central heating; **Zentralverriegelung** f (*Auto*) central locking; **Zentrum** (-s, Zentren) nt centre

zerbrechen irr vt, vi to break; **zerbrechlich** adj fragile

Zeremonie (-, -n) f ceremony

zergehen irr vi to dissolve; (*schmelzen*) to melt

zerkleinern vt to cut up; (*zerhacken*) to chop (up);

zerkratzen vt to scratch;

zerlegen vt to take to pieces; (*Fleisch*) to carve; (*Gerät, Maschine*) to dismantle; **zerquetschen** vt to squash; **zerreißen** irr vt to tear to pieces ▷ vi to tear

zerren vt to drag; **sich** (dat) **einen Muskel ~** to pull a muscle ▷ vi to tug (*an* +dat *at*); **Zerrung** f (*Med*) pulled muscle

zerschlagen irr vt to smash ▷ vr: **sich ~** to come to nothing

zerschneiden irr vt to cut up

zerstören vt to destroy; **Zerstörung** f destruction

zerstreuen vt to scatter; (*Menge*) to disperse; (*Zweifel etc*) to dispel ▷ vr: **sich ~** (*Menge*) to disperse; **zerstreut** adj scattered; (*Mensch*) absent-minded; (*kurzfristig*) distracted

zerteilen vt to split up

Zertifikat (-(e)s, -e) nt certificate

Zettel (-s, -) m piece of paper; (*Notizzettel*) note

Zeug (-(e)s, -e) nt (*fam*) stuff; (*Ausrüstung*) gear; **dummes ~** nonsense

Zeuge (-n, -n) m, **Zeugin** f witness

Zeugnis nt certificate; (*Schule*) report; (*Referenz*) reference

z. H(d). abk = **zu Händen von** attn

zickig adj (*fam*) touchy, bitchy

Zickzack (-(e)s, -e) m: **im ~ fahren** to zigzag (across the road)

Ziege (-, -n) f goat

Ziegel (-s, -) m brick; (*Dach*) tile

Ziegenkäse m goat's cheese; **Ziegenpeter** m mumps

ziehen (zog, gezogen) vt to draw; (*zerren*) to pull; (*Spielfigur*) to move; (*züchten*) to rear ▷ vi (*zerren*) to pull; (*sich bewegen*) to move; (*Rauch, Wolke etc*) to drift; **den Tee**

~ lassen to let the tea stand ▷ vi impers: **es zieht** there's a draught ▷ vr: **sich ~** (Treffen, Rede) to drag on

Ziel (-(e)s, -e) nt (Reise) destination; (Sport) finish; (Absicht) goal, aim; **zielen** vi to aim (auf +akk at); **Zielgruppe** f target group; **ziellos** adj aimless; **Zielscheibe** f target

ziemlich adj considerable; **ein ~es Durcheinander** quite a mess; **mit ~er Sicherheit** with some certainty ▷ adv rather, quite; **~ viel** quite a lot

zierlich adj dainty; (Frau) petite

Ziffer (-, -n) f figure, **arabische/römische ~n** pl Arabic/Roman numerals pl; **Zifferblatt** nt dial, face

zig adj (fam) umpteen

Zigarette f cigarette; **Zigarettenautomat** m cigarette machine; **Zigarettenpapier** nt cigarette paper; **Zigarettenschachtel** f cigarette packet; **Zigarettenstummel** m cigarette end; **Zigarillo** (-s, -s) m cigarillo; **Zigarre** (-, -n) f cigar

Zigeuner(in) (-s, -) m(f) gipsy

Zimmer (-s, -) nt room; **haben Sie ein ~ für zwei Personen?** do you have a room for two?; **Zimmerlautstärke** f reasonable volume; **Zimmermädchen** nt chambermaid; **Zimmermann** m carpenter; **Zimmerpflanze** f house plant; **Zimmerschlüssel** m room key; **Zimmerservice** m room service; **Zimmervermittlung** f accommodation agency

Zimt (-(e)s, -e) m cinnamon; **Zimtstange** f cinnamon stick

Zink (-(e)s) nt zinc

Zinn (-(e)s) nt (Element) tin; (legiertes) pewter

Zinsen pl interest sing

Zipfel (-s, -) m corner; (spitz) tip; (Hemd) tail; (Wurst) end; **Zipfelmütze** f pointed hat

zirka adv about, approximately

Zirkel (-s, -) m (Math) (pair of) compasses pl

Zirkus (-, -se) m circus

zischen vi to hiss

Zitat (-(e)s, -e) nt quotation (aus from); **zitieren** vt to quote

Zitronat nt candied lemon peel; **Zitrone** (-, -n) f lemon; **Zitronenlimonade** f lemonade; **Zitronensaft** m lemon juice

zittern vi to tremble (vor +dat with)

zivil adj civilian; (Preis) reasonable; **Zivil** (-s) nt plain clothes pl; (Mil) civilian clothes pl; **Zivildienst** m community service (for conscientious objectors)

zocken vi (fam) to gamble

Zoff (-s) m (fam) trouble

zog imperf von **ziehen**

zögerlich adj hesitant; **zögern** vi to hesitate

Zoll (-(e)s, Zölle) m customs pl; (Abgabe) duty; **Zollabfertigung** f customs clearance; **Zollamt** nt customs office; **Zollbeamte(r)** m, **-beamtin** f customs official; **Zollerklärung** f customs declaration; **zollfrei** adj duty-free; **Zollgebühren** pl customs duties pl; **Zollkontrolle** f customs check; **Zöllner(in)** m(f) customs officer; **zollpflichtig** adj liable to duty

Zone (-, -n) f zone

Zoo (-s, -s) m zoo

Zoom (-s, -s) nt zoom (shot); (Objektiv) zoom (lens)

Zopf (-(e)s, Zöpfe) m plait (Brit), braid (US)

Zorn (-(e)s) m anger; **zornig** adj angry (über etw akk about sth, auf jdn with sb)

○ SCHLÜSSELWORT

zu prep +dat **1** (örtlich) to; **zum Bahnhof/Arzt gehen** to go to the station/doctor; **zur Schule/Kirche gehen** to go to school/church; **sollen wir zu euch gehen?** shall we go to your place?; **sie sah zu ihm hin** she looked towards him; **zum Fenster herein** through the window; **zu meiner Linken** to o on my left

2 (zeitlich) at; **zu Ostern** at Easter; **bis zum 1. Mai** until May 1st; (nicht später als) by May 1st; **zu meiner Zeit** in my time

3 (Zusatz) with; **Wein zum Essen trinken** to drink wine with one's meal; **sich zu jdm setzen** to sit down beside sb; **setz dich doch zu uns** (come and) sit with us; **Anmerkungen zu etw** notes on sth

4 (Zweck) for; **Wasser zum Waschen** water for washing; **Papier zum Schreiben** paper to write on; **etw zum Geburtstag bekommen** to get sth for one's birthday

5 (Veränderung) into; **zu etw werden** to turn into sth; **jdn zu etw machen** to make sb (into) sth; **zu Asche verbrennen** to burn to ashes

6 (mit Zahlen) **3 zu 2** (Sport) 3-2; **das Stück zu 5 Euro** at 5 euros each; **zum ersten Mal** for the first time

7 **zu meiner Freude** etc to my joy etc; **zum Glück** luckily; **zu Fuß** on foot; **es ist zum Weinen** it's enough to make you cry

▷ konj to; **etw zu essen** sth to eat; **um besser sehen zu können** in order to see better; **ohne es zu wissen** without knowing it; **noch zu bezahlende Rechnungen** bills

that are still to be paid
▷ adv **1** (allzu) too; **zu sehr** too much; **zu viel** too much; **zu wenig** too little

2 (örtlich) toward(s); **er kam auf mich zu** he came up to me

3 (geschlossen) shut, closed; **die Geschäfte haben zu** the shops are closed; **„auf/zu"** (Wasserhahn etc) "on/off"

4 (fam) (los) **nur zu!** just keep on!; **mach zu!** hurry up!

zuallererst adv first of all; **zuallerletzt** adv last of all

Zubehör (-(e)s, -e) nt accessories pl

zu|**bereiten** vt to prepare; **Zubereitung** f preparation

zu|**binden** irr vt to do (o tie) up

Zucchini pl courgettes pl (Brit), zucchini pl (US)

züchten vt (Tiere) to breed; (Pflanzen) to grow

zucken vi to jerk; (krampfhaft) to twitch; (Strahl etc) to flicker; **mit den Schultern ~** to shrug (one's shoulders)

Zucker (-s, -) m sugar; (Med) diabetes sing; **Zuckerdose** f sugar bowl; **zuckerkrank** adj diabetic; **Zuckerrohr** nt sugar cane; **Zuckerrübe** f sugar beet; **Zuckerwatte** f candy-floss (Brit), cotton candy (US)

zu|**decken** vt to cover up

zu|**drehen** vt to turn off

zueinander adv to one another; (mit Verb) together; **zueinander**|**halten** irr vi to stick together

zuerst adv first; (zu Anfang) at first; **~ einmal** first of all

Zufahrt f access; (Einfahrt) drive(way); **Zufahrtsstraße** f access road; (Autobahn) slip road (Brit), ramp (US)

Zufall m chance; (Ereignis) coincidence; **durch ~** by accident; **so ein ~!** what a coincidence; **zufällig** adj chance ▷ adv by chance; **weißt du ~, ob ...?** do you happen to know whether ...?

zufrieden adj content(ed); (befriedigt) satisfied; **lass sie ~** leave her alone (o in peace); **zufrieden|geben** irr vr: **sich mit etw ~** to settle for sth; **Zufriedenheit** f contentment; (Befriedigtsein) satisfaction; **zufrieden|stellen** vt: **sie ist schwer zufriedenzustellen** she is hard to please

zu|fügen vt to add (dat to); **jdm Schaden/Schmerzen ~** to cause sb harm/pain

Zug (-(e)s, Züge) m (Eisenb) train; (Luft) draught; (Ziehen) pull; (Gesichtszug) feature; (Schach) move; (Charakterzug) trait; (an Zigarette) puff, drag; (Schluck) gulp

Zugabe f extra; (in Konzert etc) encore

Zugabteil nt train compartment

Zugang m access; **„kein ~!"** "no entry!"

Zugauskunft f (Stelle) train information office/desk;

Zugbegleiter(in) m(f) guard (Brit), conductor (US)

zu|geben irr vt (zugestehen) admit; **zugegeben** adv admittedly

zu|gehen irr vi (schließen) to shut; **auf jdn/etw ~** to walk towards sb/sth; **dem Ende ~** to be coming to a close ▷ vi impers (sich ereignen) to happen; **es ging lustig zu** we/they had a lot of fun; **dort geht es streng zu** it's strict there

Zügel (-s, -) m rein

Zugführer(in) m(f) guard (Brit), conductor (US)

zugig adj draughty

zügig adj speedy

Zugluft f draught

Zugpersonal nt train staff

zu|greifen irr vi (fig) to seize the opportunity; (beim Essen) to help oneself; **~ auf** (+akk) (Inform) to access

Zugrestauraunt nt dining car, diner (US)

Zugriffsberechtigung f (Inform) access right

zugrunde adv: **~ gehen** to perish; **~ gehen an** (+dat) (sterben) to die of

Zugschaffner(in) m(f) ticket inspector; **Zugunglück** nt train crash

zugunsten prep +gen o dat in favour of

Zugverbindung f train connection

zu|haben irr vi to be closed

zu|halten irr vt: **sich** (dat) **die Nase ~** to hold one's nose; **sich** (dat) **die Ohren ~** to hold one's hands over one's ears; **die Tür ~** to hold the door shut

Zuhause (-s) nt home

zu|hören vi to listen (dat to); **Zuhörer(in)** m(f) listener

zu|kleben vt to seal

zu|kommen irr vi to come up (auf +akk to); **jdm etw ~ lassen** to give/send sb sth; **etw auf sich** (akk) **~ lassen** to take sth as it comes

zu|kriegen vt: **ich krieg den Koffer nicht zu** I can't shut the case

Zukunft (-, Zukünfte) f future; **zukünftig** adj future ▷ adv in future

zu|lassen irr vt (hereinlassen) to admit; (erlauben) to permit; (Auto) to license; (fam: nicht öffnen) to keep shut; **zulässig** adj permissible, permitted

zuletzt adv finally, at last
zuliebe adv: **jdm ~** for sb's sake
zum kontr von **zu dem**; **~ dritten Mal** for the third time; **~ Scherz** as a joke; **~ Trinken** for drinking
zu|machen vt to shut; (Kleidung) to do up ▷ vi to shut
zumindest adv at least
zu|muten vt: **jdm etw ~** to expect sth of sb ▷ vr **sich** (dat) **zu viel ~** to overdo things
zunächst adv first of all; **~ einmal** to start with
Zunahme (-, -n) f increase
Zuname m surname, last name
zünden vt, vi (Auto) to ignite, to fire; **Zündkabel** f (Auto) ignition cable; **Zündkerze** f (Auto) spark plug; **Zündschloss** nt ignition lock; **Zündschlüssel** m ignition key; **Zündung** f ignition
zu|nehmen irr vi to increase; (Mensch) to put on weight ▷ vt: **5 Kilo ~** to put on 5 kilos
Zunge (-, -n) f tongue
Zungenkuss m French kiss
zunichte|machen vt (zerstören) to ruin
zunutze vr **sich** (dat) **etw ~ machen** to make use of sth
zu|parken vt to block
zur kontr von **zu der**
zurecht|finden irr vr: **sich ~** to find one's way around;
zurecht|kommen irr vi to cope (mit etw with sth);
zurecht|machen vt to prepare ▷ vr: **sich ~** to get ready
Zürich (-s) nt Zurich
zurück adv back
zurück|bekommen irr vt to get back; **zurück|blicken** vi to look back (auf +akk at); **zurück|bringen** irr vt (hierhin) to bring back; (woandershin) to take back; **zurück|erstatten** vt to refund; **zurück|fahren** irr vi to go back;

zurück|geben irr vt to give back; (antworten) to answer; **zurück|gehen** irr vi to go back; (zeitlich) to date back (auf +akk to) **zurück|halten** irr vt to hold back; (hindern) to prevent ▷ vr: **sich ~** to hold back; **zurückhaltend** adj reserved **zurück|holen** irr vt to fetch back; **zurück|kommen** irr vi to come back; **auf etw** (akk) **~** to return (o get back) to sth; **zurück|lassen** irr vt to leave behind; **zurück|legen** vt to put back; (reservieren) to keep back; (Strecke) to cover; **zurück|nehmen** irr vt to take back; **zurück|rufen** irr vt to call back; **zurück|schicken** vt to send back; **zurück|stellen** vt to put back; **zurück|treten** irr vi to step back; (von Amt) to retire; **zurück|verlangen** vt: **etw ~** to ask for sth back; **zurück|zahlen** vt to pay back
zurzeit adv at present
Zusage f promise; (Annahme) acceptance; **zu|sagen** vt to promise ▷ vi to accept; **jdm ~** (gefallen) to appeal to sb
zusammen adv together
Zusammenarbeit f collaboration; **zusammen|arbeiten** vi to work together
zusammen|brechen irr vi to collapse; (psychisch) to break down; **Zusammenbruch** m collapse; (psychischer) breakdown
zusammen|fassen vt to summarize; (vereinigen) to unite; **zusammenfassend** adj summarizing ▷ adv to summarize; **Zusammenfassung** f summary
zusammen|gehören vi to belong together; **zusammen|halten** irr vi to stick together

Zusammenhang m connection; **im/aus dem ~** in/out of context; **zusammen|hängen** irr vi to be connected; **zusammenhängend** adj coherent; **zusammenhang(s)los** adj incoherent

zusammen|klappen vi, vt to fold up

zusammen|knüllen vt to screw up

zusammen|kommen irr vi to meet; (sich ereignen) to happen together; **zusammen|legen** vt to fold up ▷ vi (Geld sammeln) to club together; **zusammen|nehmen** irr vt to summon up; **alles zusammengenommen** all in all ▷ vr: **sich ~** to pull oneself together; (fam) to get a grip, to get one's act together; **zusammen|passen** vi to go together; (Personen) to be suited; **zusammen|rechnen** vt to add up

Zusammensein (-s) nt get-together

zusammen|setzen vt to put together ▷ vr: **sich ~ aus** to be composed of; **Zusammensetzung** f composition

Zusammenstoß m crash, collision; **zusammen|stoßen** irr vi to crash (mit into)

zusammen|zählen vt to add up **zusammen|ziehen** irr vi (in Wohnung etc) to move in together

Zusatz m addition; **zusätzlich** adj additional ▷ adv in addition

zu|schauen vi to watch; **Zuschauer(in)** (-s, -) m(f) spectator; **die ~** (pl) (Theat) the audience sing; **Zuschauertribüne** f stand

zu|schicken vt to send

Zuschlag m extra charge; (Fahrkarte) supplement

zuschlagpflichtig adj subject to an extra charge; (Eisenb) subject to a supplement

zu|schließen irr vt to lock up

zu|sehen irr vi to watch (jdm sb); **~, dass** (dafür sorgen) to make sure that

zu|sichern vt: **jdm etw ~** to assure sb of sth

Zustand m state, condition; **sie bekommt Zustände, wenn sie das sieht** (fam) she'll have a fit if she sees that

zustande adv: **~ bringen** to bring about; **~ kommen** to come about

zuständig adj (Behörde) relevant, **~ für** responsible for

Zustellung f delivery

zu|stimmen vi to agree (einer Sache dat to sth, jdm with sb); **Zustimmung** f approval

zu|stoßen irr vi (fig) to happen (jdm to sb)

Zutaten pl ingredients pl

zu|trauen vt: **jdm etw ~** to think sb is capable of sth; **das hätte ich ihm nie zugetraut** I'd never have thought he was capable of it; **ich würde es ihr ~** (etw Negatives) I wouldn't put it past her; **Zutrauen** (-s) nt confidence (zu in); **zutraulich** adj trusting; (Tier) friendly

zu|treffen irr vi to be correct; **~ auf** (+akk) to apply to; **Zutreffendes bitte streichen** please delete as applicable

Zutritt m entry; (Zugang) access; **~ verboten!** no entry

zuverlässig adj reliable; **Zuverlässigkeit** f reliability

Zuversicht f confidence; **zuversichtlich** adj confident

zuvor adv before; (zunächst) first; **zuvor|kommen** irr vi: **jdm ~** to

beat sb to it; **zuvorkommend**
adj obliging

Zuwachs (-es, Zuwächse) m
increase, growth; (fam: Baby)
addition to the family

zuwider adv: **es ist mir ~** I hate (o
detest) it

zuzüglich prep +gen plus

zwang imperf von **zwingen**

Zwang (-(e)s, Zwänge) m (innerer)
compulsion; (Gewalt) force

zwängen vt to squeeze (in +akk
into) ▷ vr: **sich ~** to squeeze (in
+akk into)

zwanglos adj informal

zwanzig num twenty;
zwanzigste(r, s) adj twentieth;
siehe auch **dritte**

zwar adv: **und ~ ...** (genauer) ...,
to be precise; **das ist ~ schön,
aber ...** it is nice, but ...; **ich kenne
ihn ~, aber ...** I know him all right,
but ...

Zweck (-(e)s, -e) m purpose;
zwecklos adj pointless

zwei num two; **Zwei** (-, -en) f
two; (Schulnote) ≈ B;
Zweibettzimmer nt twin room;
zweideutig adj ambiguous;
(unanständig) suggestive;
zweifach adj, adv double

Zweifel (-s, -) m doubt;
zweifellos adv undoubtedly;
zweifeln vi to doubt (an etw dat
sth); **Zweifelsfall** m: **im ~** in case
of doubt

Zweig (-(e)s, -e) m branch

Zweigstelle f branch

zweihundert num two hundred;
zweimal adv twice; **zweisprachig**
adj bilingual; **zweispurig** adj
(Auto) two-lane; **zweit** adv: **wir
sind zu ~** there are two of us;
zweite(r, s) adj second; siehe
auch **dritte eine ~ Portion** a
second helping; **zweitens** adv
secondly; (bei Aufzählungen)

second; **zweitgrößte(r, s)** adj
second largest; **Zweitschlüssel**
m spare key

Zwerchfell nt diaphragm

Zwerg(in) (-(e)s, -e) m(f) dwarf

Zwetschge (-, -n) f plum

zwicken vt to pinch

Zwieback (-(e)s, -e) m rusk

Zwiebel (-, -n) f onion; (von
Blume) bulb; **Zwiebelsuppe** f
onion soup

Zwilling (-s, -e) m twin; **~e** (pl)
(Astr) Gemini sing

zwingen (zwang, gezwungen) vt
to force

zwinkern vi to blink; (absichtlich)
to wink

zwischen prep +akk o dat
between

Zwischenablage f (Inform)
clipboard

zwischendurch adv in between

Zwischenfall m incident

Zwischenlandung f stopover

zwischenmenschlich adj
interpersonal

Zwischenraum m space

Zwischenstopp (-s, -s) m
stopover

Zwischensumme f subtotal

Zwischenzeit f: **in der ~** in the
meantime

zwitschern vt, vi to twitter, to
chirp

zwölf num twelve; **zwölfte(r, s)**
adj twelfth; siehe auch **dritte**

Zylinder (-s, -) m cylinder; (Hut)
top hat

zynisch adj cynical

Zypern (-s) nt Cyprus

Zyste (-, -n) f cyst

a

a [eɪ, ə; æn, ən] (*before vowel or silent h:* **an**) *indef art* **1** ein, eine; **a woman** eine Frau; **a book** ein Buch; **an eagle** ein Adler; **she's a doctor** sie ist Ärztin

2 (*instead of the number "one"*) ein, eine; **a year ago** vor einem Jahr; **a hundred/thousand** *etc* **pounds** (ein) hundert/(ein) tausend *etc* Pfund

3 (*in expressing ratios, prices etc*) pro; **3 a day/week** 3 pro Tag/Woche, 3 am Tag/in der Woche; **10 km an hour** 10 km pro Stunde/in der Stunde

AA *abbr* = **Automobile Association** britischer Automobilklub, ≈ ADAC *m*

aback *adv:* **taken ~** erstaunt

abandon [əˈbændən] *vt* (*desert*) verlassen; (*give up*) aufgeben

abbey [ˈæbɪ] *n* Abtei *f*

abbreviate [əbriːˈvɪeɪt] *vt* abkürzen; **abbreviation** [əbriːvɪˈeɪʃən] *n* Abkürzung *f*

ABC [ˈeɪbiːˈsiː] *n* (*a. fig*) Abc *nt*

abdicate [ˈæbdɪkeɪt] *vi* (*king*) abdanken; **abdication** [æbdɪˈkeɪʃən] *n* Abdankung *f*

abdomen [ˈæbdəmən] *n* Unterleib *m*

ability [əˈbɪlɪtɪ] *n* Fähigkeit *f*; **able** [ˈeɪbl] *adj* fähig; **to be ~ to do sth** etw tun können

abnormal [æbˈnɔːml] *adj* anormal

aboard [əˈbɔːd] *adv, prep* an Bord +*gen*

abolish [əˈbɒlɪʃ] *vt* abschaffen

aborigine [æbəˈrɪdʒɪniː] *n* Ureinwohner(in) *m(f)* (Australiens)

abort [əˈbɔːt] *vt* (*Med: foetus*) abtreiben; (*Space: mission*) abbrechen; **abortion** [əˈbɔːʃən] *n* Abtreibung *f*

about [əˈbaʊt] *adv* **1** (*approximately*) etwa, ungefähr; **about a hundred/thousand** *etc* etwa hundert/tausend etc; **at about 2 o'clock** etwa um 2 Uhr; **I've just about finished** ich bin gerade fertig

2 (*referring to place*) herum, umher; **to leave things lying about** Sachen herumliegen lassen; **to run/walk** *etc* **about** herumrennen/gehen etc

3 to be about to do sth im Begriff sein, etw zu tun; **he was about to go to bed** er wollte gerade ins Bett gehen

▷ prep **1** (relating to) über +akk; **a book about London** ein Buch über London; **what is it about?** worum geht es?; (book etc) wovon handelt es?; **we talked about it** wir haben darüber geredet; **what o how about doing this?** wollen wir das machen?
2 (referring to place) um (... herum); **to walk about the town** in der Stadt herumgehen; **her clothes were scattered about the room** ihre Kleider waren über das ganze Zimmer verstreut

above [ə'bʌv] adv oben; **children aged 8 and ~** Kinder ab 8 Jahren; **on the floor ~** im Stockwerk höher ▷ prep über; **~ 40 degrees** über 40 Grad; **~ all** vor allem ▷ adj obig

abroad [ə'brɔːd] adv im Ausland; **to go ~** ins Ausland gehen

abrupt [ə'brʌpt] adj (sudden) plötzlich, abrupt

abscess ['æbsɪs] n Geschwür nt

absence ['æbsəns] n Abwesenheit f; **absent** ['æbsənt] adj abwesend; **to be ~** abwesend sein; **absent-minded** adj zerstreut

absolute ['æbsəluːt] adj absolut; (power) unumschränkt; (rubbish) vollkommen, total; **absolutely** adv absolut; (true, stupid) vollkommen; **~! genau!; you're ~ right** du hast/Sie haben völlig recht

absorb [əb'zɔːb] vt absorbieren; (fig: information) in sich aufnehmen; **absorbed** adj: **~ in sth** in etw vertieft; **absorbent** adj absorbierend; **~ cotton** (US) Watte f; **absorbing** adj (fig) faszinierend, fesselnd

abstain [əb'steɪn] vi: **to ~ (from voting)** sich (der Stimme) enthalten

abstract ['æbstrækt] adj abstrakt

absurd [əb'sɜːd] adj absurd

abundance [ə'bʌndəns] n Reichtum m (of an +dat)

abuse [ə'bjuːs] n (rude language) Beschimpfungen pl; (mistreatment) Missbrauch m ▷ [ə'bjuːz] vt (misuse) missbrauchen; **abusive** [ə'bjuːsɪv] adj beleidigend

AC abbr = **alternating current** Wechselstrom m ▷ abbr = **air conditioning** Klimaanlage

a/c abbr = **account** Kto.

academic [ækə'demɪk] n Wissenschaftler(in) m(f) ▷ adj akademisch, wissenschaftlich

accelerate [æk'seləreɪt] vi (car etc) beschleunigen; (driver) Gas geben; **acceleration** [ækselə'reɪʃən] n Beschleunigung f; **accelerator** [æk'seləreɪtə°] n Gas(pedal) nt

accent ['æksent] n Akzent m

accept [ək'sept] vt annehmen; (agree to) akzeptieren; (responsibility) übernehmen; **acceptable** [ək'septəbl] adj annehmbar

access ['ækses] n Zugang m; (Inform) Zugriff m; **accessible** [æk'sesəbl] adj (leicht) zugänglich/erreichbar; (place) (leicht) erreichbar

accessory [æk'sesərɪ] n Zubehörteil nt

access road n Zufahrtsstraße f

accident ['æksɪdənt] n Unfall m; **by ~** zufällig; **accidental** [æksɪ'dentl] adj unbeabsichtigt; (meeting) zufällig; (death) durch Unfall; **~ damage** Unfallschaden m; **accident-prone** adj vom Pech verfolgt

acclimatize [ə'klaɪmətaɪz] vt: **to ~ oneself** sich gewöhnen (to an +akk)

accommodate [əˈkɒmədeɪt] vt
unterbringen;
accommodation(s)
[əkɒməˈdeɪʃən(z)] n Unterkunft f

accompany [əˈkʌmpənɪ] vt
begleiten

accomplish [əˈkʌmplɪʃ] vt
erreichen

accord [əˈkɔːd] n: **of one's own
~** freiwillig; **according to** prep
nach, laut +dat

account [əˈkaʊnt] n (in bank etc)
Konto nt; (narrative) Bericht m; **on
~ of** wegen; **on no ~** auf keinen
Fall; **to take into ~**
berücksichtigen, in Betracht
ziehen; **accountant** [əˈkaʊntənt]
n Buchhalter(in) m(f); **account for**
vt (explain) erklären; (expenditure)
Rechenschaft ablegen für;
account number n
Kontonummer f

accumulate [əˈkjuːmjʊleɪt] vt
ansammeln ▷ vi sich ansammeln

accuracy [ˈækjʊrəsɪ] n
Genauigkeit f; **accurate** [ˈækjʊrɪt]
adj genau

accusation [ækjʊˈzeɪʃən] n
Anklage f, Beschuldigung f

accusative [əˈkjuːzətɪv] n
Akkusativ m

accuse [əˈkjuːz] vt beschuldigen;
(Jur) anklagen (of wegen +gen); **~ sb
of doing sth** jdn beschuldigen,
etw getan zu haben; **accused** n
(Jur) Angeklagte(r) mf

accustom [əˈkʌstəm] vt
gewöhnen (to an +akk);
accustomed adj gewohnt; **to get
~ to sth** sich an etw akk gewöhnen

ace [eɪs] n Ass nt ▷ adj Star-

ache [eɪk] n Schmerz m ▷ vi
wehtun

achieve [əˈtʃiːv] vt erreichen;
achievement n Leistung f

acid [ˈæsɪd] n Säure f ▷ adj sauer;
~ rain saurer Regen

acknowledge [əkˈnɒlɪdʒ] vt
(recognize) anerkennen; (admit)
zugeben; (receipt of letter etc)
bestätigen; **acknowledgement** n
Anerkennung f; (of letter)
Empfangsbestätigung f

acne [ˈæknɪ] n Akne f

acorn [ˈeɪkɔːn] n Eichel f

acoustic [əˈkuːstɪk] adj akustisch; **acoustics** [əˈkuːstɪks] npl
Akustik f

acquaintance [əˈkweɪntəns] n
(person) Bekannte(r) mf

acquire [əˈkwaɪəʳ] vt erwerben,
sich aneignen; **acquisition**
[ækwɪˈzɪʃn] n (of skills etc) Erwerb
m; (object) Anschaffung f

acrobat [ˈækrəbæt] n Akrobat(in)
m(f)

across [əˈkrɒs] prep über +akk; **he
lives ~ the street** er wohnt auf der
anderen Seite der Straße ▷ adv
hinüber, herüber; **100m ~** 100m
breit

act [ækt] n (deed) Tat f; (Jur: law)
Gesetz nt; (Theat) Akt m; (fig:
pretence) Schau f; **it's all an ~** es ist
alles nur Theater; **to be in the ~ of
doing sth** gerade dabei sein, etw
zu tun ▷ vi (take action) handeln;
(behave) sich verhalten; (Theat) spielen
to ~ as (person) fungieren als; (thing)
dienen als ▷ vt (a part) spielen

action [ˈækʃən] n (of play, novel
etc) Handlung f; (in film etc) Action
f; (Mil) Kampf m; **to take ~**
unternehmen; **out of ~** (machine)
außer Betrieb; **to put a plan into
~** einen Plan in die Tat umsetzen;
action replay n (Sport, TV)
Wiederholung f

activate [ˈæktɪveɪt] vt aktivieren;
active [ˈæktɪv] adj aktiv; (child)
lebhaft; **activity** [ækˈtɪvɪtɪ] n
Aktivität f; (occupation)
Beschäftigung f; (organized event)
Veranstaltung f

actor ['æktə*] n Schauspieler(in) m(f); **actress** ['æktrıs] n Schauspielerin f

actual ['æktjuəl] adj wirklich; **actually** adv eigentlich; (said in surprise) tatsächlich

acupuncture ['ækjupʌŋktʃə*] n Akupunktur f

acute [ə'kju:t] adj (pain) akut; (sense of smell) fein; (Math: angle) spitz

ad [æd] abbr = **advertisement**

AD abbr = **Anno Domini** nach Christi, n. Chr.

adapt [ə'dæpt] vi sich anpassen (to +dat) ▷ vt anpassen (to +dat); (rewrite) bearbeiten (for für); **adaptable** adj anpassungsfähig; **adaptation** n (of book etc) Bearbeitung f; **adapter** n (Elec) Zwischenstecker m, Adapter m

add [æd] vt (ingredient) hinzufügen; (numbers) addieren; **add up** vi (make sense) stimmen ▷ vt (numbers) addieren

addict ['ædıkt] n Süchtige(r) mf; **addicted** [ə'dıktıd] adj: **~ to alcohol/drugs** alkohol-/ drogensüchtig

addition [ə'dıʃən] n Zusatz m; (to bill) Aufschlag m; (Math) Addition f; **in ~** außerdem, zusätzlich (to zu); **additional** adj zusätzlich, weiter; **additive** ['ædıtıv] n Zusatz m; **add-on** ['ædɒn] n Zusatzgerät nt

address [ə'dres] n Adresse f ▷ vt (letter) adressieren; (person) anreden

adequate ['ædıkwıt] adj (appropriate) angemessen; (sufficient) ausreichend; (time) genügend

adhesive [əd'hi:sıv] n Klebstoff m; **adhesive tape** n Klebstreifen m

adjacent [ə'dʒeısənt] adj benachbart

adjective ['ædʒəktıv] n Adjektiv nt

adjoining [ə'dʒɔınıŋ] adj benachbart, Neben-

adjust [ə'dʒʌst] vt einstellen; (put right also) richtig stellen; (speed, flow) regulieren; (in position) verstellen ▷ vi sich anpassen (to +dat); **adjustable** adj verstellbar

admin [əd'mın] n (fam) Verwaltung f; **administration** [ədmınıs'treıʃən] n Verwaltung f; (Pol) Regierung f

admirable ['ædmərəbl] adj bewundernswert; **admiration** [ædmı'reıʃən] n Bewunderung f; **admire** [əd'maıə*] vt bewundern

admission [əd'mıʃən] n (entrance) Zutritt m; (to university etc) Zulassung f; (fee) Eintritt m; (confession) Eingeständnis nt; **admission charge**, **admission fee** n Eintrittspreis m; **admit** [əd'mıt] vt (let in) hereinlassen (to in +akk); (to university etc) zulassen; (confess) zugeben, gestehen; **to be ~ted to hospital** ins Krankenhaus eingeliefert werden

adolescent [ædə'lesnt] n Jugendliche(r) mf

adopt [ə'dɒpt] vt (child) adoptieren; (idea) übernehmen; **adoption** [ə'dɒptʃn] n (of child) Adoption f; (of idea) Übernahme f

adorable [ə'dɔ:rəbl] adj entzückend; **adore** [ə'dɔ:*] vt anbeten; (person) über alles lieben, vergöttern

adult ['ædʌlt] adj (person) erwachsen; (film etc) für Erwachsene ▷ n Erwachsene(r) mf

adultery [ə'dʌltərı] n Ehebruch m

advance [əd'va:ns] n (money) Vorschuss m; (progress) Fortschritt

m; **in ~** im Voraus; **to book in ~**
vorbestellen ▷ vi (move forward)
vorrücken ▷ vt (money)
vorschießen; **advance booking** *n*
Reservierung *f*; (Theat) Vorverkauf
m; **advanced** *adj* (modern)
fortschrittlich; (course, study) für
Fortgeschrittene; **advance
payment** *n* Vorauszahlung *f*

advantage [əd'vɑ:ntɪdʒ] *n*
Vorteil *m*, **to take ~ of** (exploit)
ausnutzen; (profit from) Nutzen
ziehen aus; **it's to your ~** es ist in
deinem/Ihrem Interesse

adventure [əd'ventʃə°] *n*
Abenteuer *nt*; **adventure holiday**
n Abenteuerurlaub *m*; **adventure
playground** *n* Abenteuerspiel-
platz *m*; **adventurous**
[əd'ventʃərəs] *adj* (person)
abenteuerlustig

adverb ['ædvɜ:b] *n* Adverb *nt*

adverse ['ædvɜ:s] *adj* (conditions
etc) ungünstig; (effect, comment etc)
negativ

advert ['ædvɜ:t] *n* Anzeige *f*;
advertise ['ædvətaiz] *vt* werben
für; (in newspaper) inserieren; (job)
ausschreiben ▷ vi Reklame
machen; (in newspaper)
annoncieren (for für);
advertisement
[əd'vɜ:tısmənt] *n* Werbung *f*; (announcement)
Anzeige *f*; **advertising** *n*
Werbung *f*

advice [əd'vais] *n* Rat(schlag) *m*;
word o **piece of ~** Ratschlag *m*;
take my ~ hör auf mich;
advisable [əd'vaizəbl] *adj* ratsam; **advise** [əd'vaiz] *vt* raten
(sb jdm); **to ~ sb to do sth/not to
do sth** jdm zuraten/abraten, etw
zu tun

Aegean [i:'dʒi:ən] *n*: **the ~ (Sea)**
die Ägäis

aerial ['eəriəl] *n* Antenne *f* ▷ *adj*
Luft-

aerobatics [eərəʊ'bætıks] *npl*
Kunstfliegen *nt*

aerobics [eə'rəʊbıks] *nsing*
Aerobic *nt*

aeroplane ['eərəpleın] *n*
Flugzeug *nt*

afaik *abbr* ~ **as far as I know**;
(SMS) ≈ soweit ich weiß

affair [ə'feə°] *n* (matter, business)
Sache *f*, Angelegenheit *f*; (scandal)
Affäre *f*; (love affair) Verhältnis *nt*

affect [ə'fekt] *vt* (influence)
(ein)wirken auf+akk; (health,
organ) angreifen; (move deeply)
berühren; (concern) betreffen;
affection [ə'fekʃən] *n* Zuneigung
f; **affectionate** [ə'fekʃənıt] *adj*
liebevoll

affluent ['æfluənt] *adj*
wohlhabend

afford [ə'fɔ:d] *vt* sich leisten; **I
can't ~ it** ich kann es mir nicht
leisten; **affordable** [ə'fɔ:dəbl]
adj erschwinglich

Afghanistan [æf'gænıstæn] *n*
Afghanistan *nt*

aforementioned
[əfɔ:'menʃənd] *adj* oben genannt

afraid [ə'freɪd] *adj*: **to be ~** Angst
haben (of vor+dat); **to be ~ that ...**
fürchten, dass ...; **I'm ~ I don't
know** das weiß ich leider nicht

Africa ['æfrɪkə] *n* Afrika *nt*;
African *adj* afrikanisch ▷ *n*
Afrikaner(in) *m(f)*; **African
American, Afro-American** *n*
Afroamerikaner(in) *m(f)*

after ['ɑ:ftə°] *prep* nach; **ten
~ five** (US) zehn nach fünf; **to be
~ sb/sth** (following, seeking) hinter
jdm/etw her sein; **~ all**
schließlich; (in spite of everything)
(schließlich) doch ▷ *conj*
nachdem ▷ *adv*: **soon ~** bald
danach; **aftercare** *n*
Nachbehandlung *f*; **after-effect** *n*
Nachwirkung *f*

afternoon n Nachmittag m; ~, **good ~** guten Tag!; **in the ~** nachmittags

afters npl Nachtisch m; **after-sales service** n Kundendienst m; **after-shave (lotion)** n Rasierwasser nt; **afterwards** adv nachher; (after that) danach

again [ə'gen] adv wieder; (one more time) noch einmal; **not ~!** (nicht) schon wieder; **~ and ~** immer wieder; **the same ~ please** das Gleiche noch mal bitte

against [ə'genst] prep gegen; **~ my will** wider Willen; **~ the law** unrechtmäßig, illegal

age [eɪdʒ] n Alter nt; (period of history) Zeitalter nt; **at the ~ of four** im Alter von vier (Jahren); **what ~ is she?, what is her ~?** wie alt ist sie?; **to come of ~** volljährig werden; **under ~** minderjährig ▷ vi altern, alt werden; **aged** adj: **~ thirty** dreißig Jahre alt; **a son ~ twenty** ein zwanzigjähriger Sohn ▷ adj ['eɪdʒɪd] (elderly) betagt; **age group** n Altersgruppe f; **ageism** n Diskriminierung f aufgrund des Alters; **age limit** n Altersgrenze f

agency ['eɪdʒənsɪ] n Agentur f

agenda [ə'dʒendə] n Tagesordnung f

agent ['eɪdʒənt] n (Comm) Vertreter(in) m(f); (for writer, actor etc) Agent(in) m(f)

aggression [ə'greʃn] n Aggression f; **aggressive** [ə'gresɪv] adj aggressiv

agitated adj aufgeregt; **to get ~** sich aufregen

AGM abbr = **Annual General Meeting** JHV f

ago [ə'gəʊ] adv: **two days ~** heute vor zwei Tagen; **not long ~** (erst) vor Kurzem

agonize ['ægənaɪz] vi sich den Kopf zerbrechen (over über dat); **agonizing** adj qualvoll; **agony** ['ægənɪ] n Qual f

agree [ə'griː] vt (date, price etc) vereinbaren; **to ~ to do sth** sich bereit erklären, etw zu tun; **to ~ that ...** sich dat einig sein, dass ...; (decide) beschließen, dass ...; (admit) zugeben, dass ... ▷ vi (have same opinion, correspond) übereinstimmen (with mit); (consent) zustimmen; (come to an agreement) sich einigen (about, on auf +akk); (food) **not to ~ with sb** jdm nicht bekommen; **agreement** n (agreeing) Übereinstimmung f; (contract) Abkommen nt, Vereinbarung f

agricultural [ægrɪ'kʌltʃərəl] adj landwirtschaftlich, Landwirtschafts-; **agriculture** ['ægrɪkʌltʃə°] n Landwirtschaft f

ahead [ə'hed] adv: **to be ~** führen, vorne liegen; **~ of** vor +dat; **to be ~ of sb** (person) jdm voraus sein; (thing) vor jdm liegen; **to be 3 metres ~** 3 Meter Vorsprung haben

aid [eɪd] n Hilfe f; **in ~ of** zugunsten +gen; **with the ~ of** mithilfe +gen ▷ vt helfen +dat; (support) unterstützen

Aids [eɪdz] n acr = **acquired immune deficiency syndrome** Aids nt

aim [eɪm] vt (gun, camera) richten (at auf +akk) ▷ vi: **to ~ at** (with gun etc) zielen auf +akk; (fig) abzielen auf +akk; **to ~ to do sth** beabsichtigen, etw zu tun ▷ n Ziel nt

air [eə°] n Luft f; **in the open ~** im Freien; (Radio, TV) **to be on the ~** (programme) auf Sendung sein;

(*station*) senden ▷ vt lüften;
airbag n (Auto) Airbag m;
air-conditioned adj mit
Klimaanlage, **air conditioning** n
Klimaanlage f; **aircraft** n
Flugzeug nt; **airfield** n Flugplatz
m; **air force** n Luftwaffe f;
airgun n Luftgewehr nt;
airline n Fluggesellschaft f;
airmail n Luftpost f; **by** ~ mit
Luftpost; **airplane** n (US)
Flugzeug nt; **air pollution** n
Luftverschmutzung f; **airport** n
Flughafen m; **airsick** adj
luftkrank; **airtight** adj luftdicht;
air-traffic controller n Fluglotse
m, Fluglotsin f; **airy** adj luftig;
(*manner*) lässig

aisle [aɪl] n Gang m; (in church)
Seitenschiff nt; ~ **seat** Sitz m am
Gang

ajar [ə'dʒɑː°] adj (door) angelehnt

alarm [ə'lɑːm] n (warning) Alarm
m; (bell etc) Alarmanlage f ▷ vt
beunruhigen; **alarm clock** n
Wecker m; **alarmed** adj (protected)
alarmgesichert; **alarming** adj
beunruhigend

Albania [æl'beɪnɪə] n Albanien
nt; **Albanian** adj albanisch ▷ n
(person) Albaner(in) m(f); (language)
Albanisch nt

album ['ælbəm] n Album nt

alcohol ['ælkəhɒl] n Alkohol m;
alcohol-free adj alkoholfrei;
alcoholic [ælkə'hɒlɪk] adj (drink)
alkoholisch ▷ n Alkoholiker(in)
m(f); **alcoholism** n Alkoholismus
m

ale [eɪl] n Ale nt (helles englisches
Bier)

alert [ə'lɜːt] adj wachsam ▷ n
Alarm m ▷ vt warnen (to vor +dat)

algebra ['ældʒɪbrə] n Algebra f

Algeria [æl'dʒɪərɪə] n Algerien nt

alibi ['ælɪbaɪ] n Alibi nt

alien ['eɪlɪən] n (foreigner)
Ausländer(in) m(f); (from space)
Außerirdische(r) mf

align [ə'laɪn] vt ausrichten (with
auf +akk)

alike [ə'laɪk] adj, adv gleich;
(similar) ähnlich

alive [ə'laɪv] adj lebendig; **to
keep sth** ~ etw am Leben
erhalten; **he's still** ~ er lebt noch

O **KEYWORD**

all [ɔːl] adj alle(r, s); **all day/night**
den ganzen Tag/die ganze Nacht;
all men are equal alle Menschen
sind gleich; **all five came** alle fünf
kamen; **all the books/food** die
ganzen Bücher/das ganze Essen;
all the time die ganze Zeit (über);
all his life sein ganzes Leben
(lang)

▷ pron 1 alles; **I ate it all, I ate all of
it** ich habe alles gegessen; **all of
us/the boys went** wir gingen
alle/alle Jungen gingen; **we all sat
down** wir setzten uns alle

2 (in phrases) **above all** vor allem;
after all schließlich; **at all: not at
all** (in answer to question)
überhaupt nicht; (in answer to
thanks) gern geschehen; **I'm not at
all tired** ich bin überhaupt nicht
müde; **anything at all will do** es
ist egal, welche(r, s); **all in all** alles
in allem

▷ adv ganz; **all alone** ganz allein;
it's not as hard as all that so
schwer ist es nun auch wieder
nicht; **all the more/the better**
umso mehr/besser; **all but** fast;
the score is 2 all es steht 2 zu 2

allegation [ælɪ'ɡeɪʃən] n
Behauptung f; **alleged** adj
angeblich

allergic [ə'lɜːdʒɪk] adj allergisch

(to gegen); **allergy** ['ælədʒɪ] n
Allergie f

alleviate [ə'liːvɪeɪt] vt (pain)
lindern

alley ['ælɪ] n (enge) Gasse;
(passage) Durchgang m; (bowling)
Bahn f

alliance [ə'laɪəns] n Bündnis nt

alligator ['ælɪgeɪtə°] n Alligator
m

all-night adj (café, cinema) die
ganze Nacht geöffnet

allocate ['æləkeɪt] vt zuweisen,
zuteilen (to dat)

allotment n (plot)
Schrebergarten m

allow [ə'laʊ] vt (permit) erlauben
(sb jdm); (grant) bewilligen; (time)
einplanen; **allow for** vt
berücksichtigen; (cost etc)
einkalkulieren; **allowance** n (from
state) Beihilfe f; (from parent)
Unterhaltsgeld nt

all right ['ɔːl'raɪt] adj okay, in
Ordnung; **I'm ~** mir geht's gut
▷ adv (satisfactorily) ganz gut
▷ interj okay

all-time adj (record, high) aller
Zeiten

allusion [ə'luːʒn] n Anspielung f
(to auf +akk)

ally ['ælaɪ] n Verbündete(r) mf;
(Hist) Alliierte(r) mf

almond ['ɑːmənd] n Mandel f

almost ['ɔːlməʊst] adv fast

alone [ə'ləʊn] adj, adv allein

along [ə'lɒŋ] prep entlang
+akk; **~ the river** den Fluss
entlang; (position) am Fluss
entlang ▷ adv (onward) weiter;
~ with zusammen mit; **all ~** die
ganze Zeit, von Anfang an;
alongside prep neben +dat ▷ adv
(walk) nebenher

aloud [ə'laʊd] adv laut

alphabet ['ælfəbet] n Alphabet
nt

alpine ['ælpaɪn] adj alpin; **Alps**
[ælps] npl: **the ~** die Alpen

already [ɔːl'redɪ] adv schon,
bereits

Alsace ['ælsæs] n Elsass nt;
Alsatian [æl'seɪʃən] adj
elsässisch ▷ n Elsässer(in) m(f);
(Brit: dog) Schäferhund m

also ['ɔːlsəʊ] adv auch

altar ['ɔːltə°] n Altar m

alter ['ɔːltə°] vt ändern;
alteration [ɔːltə'reɪʃən] n
Änderung f; **~s** (to building) Umbau
m

alternate [ɔːl'tɜːnət] adj
abwechselnd ▷ ['ɔːltəneɪt] vi
abwechseln (with mit);
alternating current n
Wechselstrom m

alternative [ɔːl'tɜːnətɪv] adj
Alternativ- ▷ n Alternative f

although [ɔːl'ðəʊ] conj obwohl

altitude ['æltɪtjuːd] n Höhe f

altogether [ɔːltə'geðə°] adv (in
total) insgesamt; (entirely) ganz
und gar

aluminium [æljʊ'mɪnɪəm], **aluminum** (US)
[ə'luːmɪnəm] n
Aluminium nt

always ['ɔːlweɪz] adv immer

am [æm] present of **be**; bin

am, **a.m.** abbr = **ante meridiem**
vormittags, vorm.

amateur ['æmətə°] n Ama-
teur(in) m(f) ▷ adj Amateur-;
(theatre, choir) Laien-

amaze [ə'meɪz] vt erstaunen;
amazed adj erstaunt (at über
+akk); **amazing** adj erstaunlich

Amazon ['æməzən] n: **~ (river)**
Amazonas m

ambassador [æm'bæsədə°] n
Botschafter m

amber ['æmbə°] n Bernstein m

ambiguity [æmbɪ'gjuːɪtɪ] n
Zweideutigkeit f; **ambiguous**
[æm'bɪgjʊəs] adj zweideutig

ambition [æmˈbɪʃən] n Ambition f; (ambitious nature) Ehrgeiz m; **ambitious** [æmˈbɪʃəs] adj ehrgeizig

ambulance [ˈæmbjʊləns] n Krankenwagen m

amend [əˈmend] vt (law etc) ändern

America [əˈmerɪkə] n Amerika nt; **American** adj amerikanisch ▷ n Amerikaner(in) m(f); **native ~** Indianer(in) m(f)

amiable [ˈeɪmɪəbl] adj liebenswürdig

amicable [ˈæmɪkəbl] adj freundlich; (relations) freundschaftlich; (Jur: settlement) gütlich

amnesia [æmˈniːzɪə] n Gedächtnisverlust m

among(st) [əˈmʌŋ(st)] prep unter +dat

amount [əˈmaʊnt] n (quantity) Menge f; (of money) Betrag m; **a large/small ~ of ...** ziemlich viel/wenig ... ▷ vi: **to ~ to** (total) sich belaufen auf +akk

amp, ampere [æmp, ˈæmpeəˀ] n Ampere nt

amplifier [ˈæmplɪfaɪəˀ] n Verstärker m

amputate [ˈæmpjʊteɪt] vt amputieren

Amtrak® [ˈæmtræk] n amerikanische Eisenbahngesellschaft f

amuse [əˈmjuːz] vt amüsieren; (entertain) unterhalten; **amused** adj: **I'm not ~** das finde ich gar nicht lustig; **amusement** n (enjoyment) Vergnügen nt; (recreation) Unterhaltung f; **amusement arcade** n Spielhalle f; **amusement park** n Vergnügungspark m; **amusing** adj amüsant

an [æn, ən] art ein(e)

anaemic [əˈniːmɪk] adj blutarm

anaesthetic [ænɪsˈθetɪk] n

Narkose f; (substance) Narkosemittel nt

analyse, analyze [ˈænəlaɪz] vt analysieren; **analysis** [əˈnælɪsɪs] n Analyse f

anatomy [əˈnætəmɪ] n Anatomie f; (structure) Körperbau m

ancestor [ˈænsestəˀ] n Vorfahr m

anchor [ˈæŋkəˀ] n Anker m ▷ vt verankern; **anchorage** n Ankerplatz m

anchovy [ˈæntʃəvɪ] n Sardelle f

ancient [ˈeɪnʃənt] adj alt; (fam: person, clothes etc) uralt

and [ænd, ənd] conj und

Andorra [ænˈdɔːrə] n Andorra nt

anemic [əˈniːmɪk] adj (US) see **anaemic**

anesthetic n (US) see **anaesthetic**

angel [ˈeɪndʒəl] n Engel m

anger [ˈæŋgəˀ] n Zorn m ▷ vt ärgern

angina, angina pectoris [ænˈdʒaɪnə(ˈpektərɪs)] n Angina Pectoris f

angle [ˈæŋgl] n Winkel m; (fig) Standpunkt m

angler [ˈæŋgləˀ] n Angler(in) m(f); **angling** [ˈæŋglɪŋ] n Angeln nt

angry [ˈæŋgrɪ] adj verärgert; (stronger) zornig; **to be ~ with sb** auf jdn böse sein

angular [ˈæŋgjʊləˀ] adj eckig; (face) kantig

animal [ˈænɪməl] n Tier nt; **animal rights** npl Tierrechte pl

animated [ˈænɪmeɪtɪd] adj lebhaft; **~ film** Zeichentrickfilm m

aniseed [ˈænɪsiːd] n Anis m

ankle [ˈæŋkl] n (Fuß)knöchel m

annex [ˈæneks] n Anbau m

anniversary [ænɪˈvɜːsərɪ] n Jahrestag m

announce [əˈnaʊns] vt bekannt geben; (officially) bekannt machen; (on radio, TV etc) (Radio,

TV) ansagen; **announcement** n
Bekanntgabe f; *(official)*
Bekanntmachung f; *(Radio, TV)*
Ansage f; **announcer** n *(Radio, TV)*
Ansager(in) m(f)

annoy [əˈnɔɪ] vt ärgern;
annoyance n Ärger m; **annoyed**
adj ärgerlich; **to be ~ with sb
(about sth)** sich über jdn (über
etw) ärgern; **annoying** *adj*
ärgerlich; *(person)* lästig, nervig

annual [ˈænjʊəl] *adj* jährlich
▷ n Jahrbuch nt

anonymous [əˈnɒnɪməs] *adj*
anonym

anorak [ˈænəræk] n Anorak m;
(Brit fam: pej) Freak m

anorexia [ænəˈreksɪə] n Magersucht f; **anorexic** *adj*
magersüchtig

another [əˈnʌðəʳ] *adj, pron*
(different) ein(e) andere(r, s);
(additional) noch eine(r, s); **let me
put it ~ way** lass es mich anders
sagen

answer [ˈɑːnsəʳ] n Antwort f *(to
auf +akk)*; *(solution)* Lösung f *+gen*
▷ vi antworten; *(on phone)* sich
melden ▷ vt *(person)* antworten
+dat; *(letter, question)* beantworten;
(telephone) gehen an *+akk,*
abnehmen; *(door)* öffnen; **answer
back** vi widersprechen;
**answering machine,
answerphone** n Anrufbeantworter m

ant [ænt] n Ameise f

Antarctic [æntˈɑːktɪk] n
Antarktis f; **Antarctic Circle** n
südlicher Polarkreis

antelope [ˈæntɪləʊp] n Antilope f

antenna [ænˈtenə] *(pl **antennae**)*
n *(Zool)* Fühler m; *(Radio)* Antenne f

anti- [ˈæntɪ] *pref* Anti-, anti-;
antibiotic [ˈæntɪbaɪˈɒtɪk] n
Antibiotikum nt

anticipate [ænˈtɪsɪpeɪt] vt *(expect:*

trouble, question) erwarten,
rechnen mit; **anticipation**
[æntɪsɪˈpeɪʃən] n Erwartung f

anticlimax [æntɪˈklaɪmæks] n
Enttäuschung f; **anticlockwise**
[æntɪˈklɒkwaɪz] *adv* entgegen
dem Uhrzeigersinn

antidote [ˈæntɪdəʊt] n Gegenmittel nt; **antifreeze** n
Frostschutzmittel nt

Antipodes [ænˈtɪpədiːz] *npl*
Australien und Neuseeland

antiquarian [æntɪˈkwɛərɪən]
adj: **~ bookshop** Antiquariat nt

antique [ænˈtiːk] n Antiquität f
▷ *adj* antik; **antique shop** n
Antiquitätengeschäft nt

anti-Semitism [æntɪˈsemɪtɪzm]
n Antisemitismus m; **antiseptic**
[æntɪˈseptɪk] n Antiseptikum nt
▷ *adj* antiseptisch; **antisocial** *adj*
(person) ungesellig; *(behaviour)*
unsozial, asozial

antlers [ˈæntləz] *npl* Geweih nt

anxiety [æŋˈzaɪətɪ] n Sorge f
(about um); **anxious** [ˈæŋkʃəs] *adj*
besorgt *(about* um); *(apprehensive)*
ängstlich

○ **KEYWORD**

any [ˈenɪ] *adj* **1** *(in questions etc)*
have you any butter? haben Sie
(etwas) Butter?; **have you any
children?** haben Sie Kinder?; **if
there are any tickets left** falls
noch Karten da sind
2 *(with negative)* **I haven't any
money/books** ich habe kein
Geld/keine Bücher
3 *(no matter which)* jede(r, s)
(beliebige); **any colour (at all)**
jede beliebige Farbe; **choose any
book you like** nehmen Sie ein
beliebiges Buch
4 *(in phrases)* **in any case** in jedem

Fall; **any day now** jeden Tag; **at any moment** jeden Moment; **at any rate** auf jeden Fall
▷ *pron* **1** (*in questions etc*) **have you got any?** haben Sie welche?; **can any of you sing?** kann (irgend)einer von euch singen? **2** (*with negative*) **I haven't any (of them)** ich habe keinen/keines (davon) **3** (*no matter which one(s)*): **take any of those books (you like)** nehmen Sie irgendeines dieser Bücher
▷ *adv* **1** (*in questions etc*) **do you want any more soup/sandwiches?** möchten Sie noch Suppe/Brote?; **are you feeling any better?** fühlen Sie sich etwas besser? **2** (*with negative*) **I can't hear him any more** ich kann ihn nicht mehr hören

anybody *pron* (*whoever one likes*) irgendjemand; (*everyone*) jeder; (*in question*) jemand; **anyhow** *adv*: **I don't want to talk about it, not now ~** ich möchte nicht darüber sprechen, jedenfalls nicht jetzt; **they asked me not to go, but I went ~** sie baten mich, nicht hinzugehen, aber ich bin trotzdem hingegangen; **anyone** *pron* (*whoever one likes*) irgendjemand; (*everyone*) jeder; (*in question*) jemand; **isn't there ~ you can ask?** gibt es denn niemanden, den du fragen kannst/den Sie fragen können?; **anyplace** *adv* (*US*) irgendwo; (*direction*) irgendwohin; (*everywhere*) überall

○ **KEYWORD**

anything ['enιθιη] *pron* **1** (*in questions etc*) (irgend)etwas; **can**

you see anything? können Sie etwas sehen? **2** (*with negative*) **I can't see anything** ich kann nichts sehen **3** (*no matter what*) **you can say anything you like** Sie können sagen, was Sie wollen; **anything will do** irgendetwas (wird genügen), irgendeine(r, s) (wird genügen); **he'll eat anything** er isst alles

anytime *adv* jederzeit; **anyway** *adv*: **I didn't want to go there ~** ich wollte da sowieso nicht hingehen; **thanks ~** trotzdem danke; **~, as I was saying, ...** jedenfalls, wie ich schon sagte, ...; **anywhere** *adv* irgendwo; (*direction*) irgendwohin; (*everywhere*) überall

apart [ə'pɑːt] *adv* auseinander; **~ from** außer; **live ~** getrennt leben

apartment [ə'pɑːtmənt] *n* (*esp US*) Wohnung *f*; **apartment block** *n* (*esp US*) Wohnblock *m*

ape [eɪp] *n* (Menschen)affe *m*

aperitif [ə'perιtιf] *n* Aperitif *m*

aperture ['æpətjuə°] *n* Öffnung *f*; (*Foto*) Blende *f*

apologize [ə'pɒlədʒaɪz] *vi* sich entschuldigen; **apology** *n* Entschuldigung *f*

apostrophe [ə'pɒstrəfι] *n* Apostroph *m*

appalled [ə'pɔːld] *adj* entsetzt (*at* über +*akk*); **appalling** *adj* entsetzlich

apparatus [æpə'reιtəs] *n* Apparat *m*; (*piece of apparatus*) Gerät *nt*

apparent [ə'pærənt] *adj* (*obvious*) offensichtlich (*to* für); (*seeming*) scheinbar; **apparently** *adv* anscheinend

appeal [ə'piːl] *vi* (dringend)

bitten (for um, to +akk); (Jur) Berufung einlegen; **to ~ to sb** (be attractive) jdm zusagen ▷ n Aufruf m (to an +akk); (Jur) Berufung f; (attraction) Reiz m; **appealing** adj ansprechend, attraktiv

appear [ə'pɪə°] vi erscheinen; (Theat) auftreten; (seem) scheinen; **appearance** n Erscheinen nt; (Theat) Auftritt m; (look) Aussehen nt

appendicitis [əpendɪ'saɪtɪs] n Blinddarmentzündung f; **appendix** [ə'pendɪks] n Blinddarm m; (to book) Anhang m

appetite ['æpɪtaɪt] n Appetit m; (fig: desire) Verlangen nt; (sexual) Lust f; **appetizing** ['æpɪtaɪzɪŋ] adj appetitlich, appetitanregend

applause [ə'plɔːz] n Beifall m, Applaus m

apple ['æpl] n Apfel m; **apple crumble** n mit Streuseln bestreutes Apfeldessert; **apple juice** n Apfelsaft m; **apple pie** n gedeckter Apfelkuchen m; **apple puree**, **apple sauce** n Apfelmus nt; **apple tart** n Apfelkuchen m; **apple tree** n Apfelbaum m

appliance [ə'plaɪəns] n Gerät nt; **applicable** [ə'plɪkəbl] adj anwendbar; (on forms) zutreffend; **applicant** ['æplɪkənt] n Bewerber(in) m(f); **application** [æplɪ'keɪʃən] n (request) Antrag m (for auf +akk); (for job) Bewerbung f (for um); **application form** n Anmeldeformular nt; **apply** [ə'plaɪ] vi (be relevant) zutreffen (to auf +akk); (for job etc) sich bewerben (for um) ▷ vt (cream, paint etc) auftragen; (put into practice) anwenden; (brakes) betätigen

appoint [ə'pɔɪnt] vt (to post) ernennen; **appointment** n Verabredung f; (at doctor, hairdresser

etc, in business) Termin m; **by ~** nach Vereinbarung

appreciate [ə'priːʃɪeɪt] vt (value) zu schätzen wissen; (understand) einsehen; **to be much ~d** gewürdigt werden ▷ vi (increase in value) im Wert steigen; **appreciation** [əpriːʃɪ'eɪʃən] n (esteem) Anerkennung f, Würdigung f; (of person also) Wertschätzung f

apprehensive [æprɪ'hensɪv] adj ängstlich

apprentice [ə'prentɪs] n Lehrling m

approach [ə'prəʊtʃ] vi sich nähern ▷ vt (place) sich nähern +dat; (person) herantreten an +akk; (problem) angehen

appropriate [ə'prəʊprɪət] adj passend; (to occasion) angemessen; (remark) treffend; **appropriately** adv passend; (expressed) treffend

approval [ə'pruːvəl] n (show of satisfaction) Anerkennung f; (permission) Zustimmung f (of zu); **approve** [ə'pruːv] vt billigen ▷ vi: **to ~ of sth/sb** etw billigen/von jdm etwas halten; **I don't ~** ich missbillige das

approx [ə'prɒks] abbr = **approximately** ca.; **approximate** [ə'prɒksɪmɪt] adj ungefähr; **approximately** adv ungefähr, circa

apricot ['eɪprɪkɒt] n Aprikose f

April ['eɪprəl] n April m; see also **September**

apron ['eɪprən] n Schürze f

aptitude ['æptɪtjuːd] n Begabung f

aquaplaning ['ækwəpleɪnɪŋ] n (Auto) Aquaplaning nt

aquarium [ə'kweərɪəm] n Aquarium nt

Aquarius [ə'kweərɪəs] n (Astr) Wassermann m

Arab ['ærəb] n Araber(in) m(f); (horse) Araber m; **Arabian** [ə'reɪbɪən] adj arabisch; **Arabic** ['ærəbɪk] n (language) Arabisch nt ▷ adj arabisch

arbitrary ['ɑːbɪtrərɪ] adj willkürlich

arcade [ɑː'keɪd] n Arkade f; (shopping arcade) Einkaufspassage f

arch [ɑːtʃ] n Bogen m

archaeologist, archeologist (US) [ɑːkɪ'ɒlədʒɪst] n Archäologe m, Archäologin f; **archaeology, archeology** (US) [ɑːkɪ'ɒlədʒɪ] n Archäologie f

archaic [ɑː'keɪɪk] adj veraltet

archbishop [ɑːtʃ'bɪʃəp] n Erzbischof m

archery ['ɑːtʃərɪ] n Bogenschießen nt

architect ['ɑːkɪtekt] n Architekt(in) m(f); **architecture** [ɑːkɪ'tektʃə] n Architektur f

archive(s) ['ɑːkaɪv(z)] n(pl) Archiv nt

archway ['ɑːtʃweɪ] n Torbogen m

Arctic ['ɑːktɪk] n Arktis f; **Arctic Circle** n nördlicher Polarkreis

are [ə, unstressed ɑː°] present of **be**

area ['eərɪə] n (region, district) Gebiet nt, Gegend f; (amount of space) Fläche f; (part of building etc) Bereich m, Zone f; (fig: field) Bereich m; **the London ~** der Londoner Raum; **area code** n (US) Vorwahl f

aren't [ɑːnt] contr of **are not**

Argentina [ɑːdʒən'tiːnə] n Argentinien n

argue ['ɑːgjuː] vi streiten (about, over über +akk); to ~; that ... behaupten, dass ...; to ~ for/against ... sprechen für/gegen ...; **argument** n (reasons) Argument nt; (quarrel)

Streit m; **to have an ~** sich streiten

Aries ['eəriːz] nsing (Astr) Widder m

arise [ə'raɪz] (**arose, arisen**) vi sich ergeben, entstehen; (problem, question, wind) aufkommen

aristocracy [ærɪs'tɒkrəsɪ] n (class) Adel m; **aristocrat** ['ærɪstəkræt] n Adlige(r) mf; **aristocratic** [ærɪstə'krætɪk] adj aristokratisch, adlig

arm [ɑːm] n Arm m; (sleeve) Ärmel m; (of armchair) Armlehne f ▷ vt bewaffnen; **armchair** [ɑːmtʃeə°] n Lehnstuhl m

armed [ɑːmd] adj bewaffnet

armpit ['ɑːmpɪt] n Achselhöhle f

arms [ɑːmz] npl Waffen pl

army ['ɑːmɪ] n Armee f, Heer nt

A road ['eɪrəʊd] n (Brit) = Bundesstraße f

aroma [ə'rəʊmə] n Duft m, Aroma nt; **aromatherapy** [ərəʊmə'θerəpɪ] n Aromatherapie f

arose [ə'rəʊz] pt of **arise**

around [ə'raʊnd] adv herum, umher; (present) hier (irgendwo); (approximately) ungefähr; (with time) gegen; **he's ~ somewhere** er ist hier irgendwo in der Nähe ▷ prep (surrounding) um ... (herum); (about in) in ... herum

arr. abbr = **arrival, arrives** Ank.

arrange [ə'reɪndʒ] vt (put in order) (an)ordnen; (alphabetically) ordnen; (artistically) arrangieren; (agree to: meeting etc) vereinbaren, festsetzen; (holidays) festlegen; (organize) planen; **to ~ that ...** es so einrichten, dass ...; **we ~d to meet at eight o'clock** wir haben uns für acht Uhr verabredet; **it's all ~d** es ist alles arrangiert; **arrangement** n (layout) Anordnung f; (agreement)

Vereinbarung f; Plan m; **make ~s**
Vorbereitungen treffen
arrest [ə'rest] vt (person)
verhaften ▷ n Verhaftung f;
under ~ verhaftet
arrival [ə'raɪvəl] n Ankunft f;
new ~ (person) Neuankömmling
m; **arrivals** n (airport) Ankunftshalle
f; **arrive** [ə'raɪv] vi ankommen
(at bei, in +dat); **to ~ at a solution**
eine Lösung finden
arrogant ['ærəgənt] adj arrogant
arrow ['ærəʊ] n Pfeil m
arse [ɑːs] n (vulg) Arsch m
art [ɑːt] n Kunst f, **the ~s** (pl)
Geisteswissenschaften pl
artery ['ɑːtəri] n Schlagader f,
Arterie f
art gallery n Kunstgalerie f,
Kunstmuseum nt
arthritis [ɑː'θraɪtɪs] n Arthritis f
artichoke ['ɑːtɪtʃəʊk] n
Artischocke f
article ['ɑːtɪkl] n Artikel m;
(object) Gegenstand m
artificial [ɑːtɪ'fɪʃəl] adj künstlich,
Kunst-; (smile etc) gekünstelt
artist ['ɑːtɪst] n Künstler(in) m(f);
artistic [ɑː'tɪstɪk] adj
künstlerisch

○ **KEYWORD**

as [æz, əz] conj 1 (referring to time)
als; **as the years went by** mit den
Jahren; **he came in as I was
leaving** als er hereinkam, ging ich
gerade; **as from tomorrow** ab
morgen
2 (in comparisons) **as big as** so groß
wie; **twice as big as** zweimal so
groß wie; **as much/many as** so
viel/so viele wie; **as soon as**
sobald
3 (since, because) da; **he left early
as he had to be home by 10** er

ging früher, da er um 10 zu Hause
sein musste
4 (referring to manner, way) wie; **do
as you wish** mach was du willst;
as she said wie sie sagte
5 (concerning) **as for** o **to that** was
das betrifft o angeht
6 as if o **though** als ob
▷ prep als; as against o long; **he
works as a driver** er arbeitet als
Fahrer; see also **such**; **he gave it
to me as a present** er hat es
mir als Geschenk gegeben; see
also **well**

asap [eɪeseɪ'piː, 'eɪsæp] acr = **as
soon as possible** möglichst bald
ascertain [æsə'teɪn] vt
feststellen
ash [æʃ] n (dust) Asche f; (tree)
Esche f
ashamed [ə'ʃeɪmd] adj beschämt;
to be ~ (of sb/sth) sich (für
jdn/etw) schämen
ashore [ə'ʃɔː°] adv an Land
ashtray ['æʃtreɪ] n Aschenbecher
m
Asia ['eɪʃə] n Asien nt; **Asian** adj
asiatisch ▷ n Asiat(in) m(f)
aside [ə'saɪd] adv beiseite, zur
Seite; **~ from** (esp US) außer
ask [ɑːsk] vt, vi fragen; (question)
stellen; (request) bitten um; (invite)
einladen; **to ~ sb the way** jdn
nach dem Weg fragen; **to ~ sb to
do sth** jdn darum bitten, etw zu
tun; **ask for** bitten um
asleep [ə'sliːp] adj, adv; **to be
~** schlafen; **to fall ~** einschlafen
asparagus [əs'pærəgəs] n
Spargel m
aspect ['æspekt] n Aspekt m
aspirin ['æsprɪn] n Aspirin® nt
ass [æs] n (a. fig) Esel m; (US vulg)
Arsch m
assassinate [ə'sæsɪneɪt] vt
ermorden; **assassination**

[ə'sæsɪneɪʃn] n Ermordung f;
~ attempt Attentat nt

assault [ə'sɔːlt] n Angriff m; (Jur)
Körperverletzung f ▸ vt
überfallen, herfallen über +akk

assemble [ə'sembl] vt (parts)
zusammensetzen; (people)
zusammenrufen ▸ vi sich
versammeln; **assembly**
[ə'semblɪ] n (of people)
Versammlung f; (putting together)
Zusammensetzen nt; **assembly
hall** n Aula f

assert [ə'sɜːt] vt behaupten;
assertion [ə'sɜːʃən] n Behauptung f

assess [ə'ses] vt einschätzen;
assessment n Einschätzung f

asset ['æset] n Vermögenswert
m; (fig) Vorteil m; **~s** pl Vermögen
nt

assign [ə'saɪn] vt zuweisen;
assignment n Aufgabe f;
(mission) Auftrag m

assist [ə'sɪst] vt helfen +dat;
assistance n Hilfe f; **assistant**
n Assistent(in) m(f), Mitarbeiter(in)
m(f); (in shop) Verkäufer(in) m(f);
assistant referee n (Sport)
Schiedsrichterassistent(in) m(f)

associate [ə'səʊʃɪeɪt] vt
verbinden (with mit); **association**
[əsəʊsɪ'eɪʃən] n (organization)
Verband m, Vereinigung f; **in
~ with ...** in Zusammenarbeit
mit ...

assorted [ə'sɔːtɪd] adj gemischt;
assortment n Auswahl f (of an
+dat); (of sweets) Mischung f

assume [ə'sjuːm] vt annehmen
(that ... dass ...); (role, responsibility)
übernehmen; **assumption**
[ə'sʌmpʃən] n Annahme f

assurance [ə'ʃʊərəns] n Versicherung f; (confidence) Zuversicht
f; **assure** [ə'ʃʊə˟] vt (say
confidently) versichern +dat; **to**

~ sb of sth jdm etw zusichern; **to
be ~d of sth** einer Sache sicher
sein

asterisk ['æstərɪsk] n Sternchen
nt

asthma ['æsmə] n Asthma nt

astonish [ə'stɒnɪʃ] vt erstaunen;
astonished adj erstaunt (at
über); **astonishing** adj
erstaunlich; **astonishment** n
Erstaunen nt

astound [ə'staʊnd] vt sehr
erstaunen; **astounding** adj
erstaunlich

astray [ə'streɪ] adv: **to go ~**
(letter etc) verloren gehen;
(person) vom Weg abkommen; **to
lead ~** irreführen, verführen

astrology [ə'strɒlədʒɪ] n
Astrologie f

astronaut ['æstrənɔːt] n Astro-
naut(in) m(f)

astronomy [ə'strɒnəmɪ] n
Astronomie f

asylum [ə'saɪləm] n (home)
Anstalt f; (political asylum) Asyl nt;
asylum seeker n
Asylbewerber(in) m(f)

⭕ **KEYWORD**

at [æt] prep **1** (referring to position,
direction) an +dat; bei +dat; (with
place) in +dat; **at the top** an der
Spitze; **at home/school** zu Hause,
zuhause (österreichisch,
schweizerisch)/in der Schule; **at the
baker's** beim Bäcker; **to look at
sth** auf etw akk blicken; **to throw
sth at sb** etw nach jdm werfen
2 (referring to time) **at 4 o'clock** um
4 Uhr; **at night** bei Nacht; **at
Christmas** zu Weihnachten; **at
times** manchmal
3 (referring to rates, speed etc) **at £1 a
kilo** zu £1 pro Kilo; **two at a time**

zwei auf einmal; **at 50 km/h** mit 50 km/h

4 (referring to manner) **at a stroke** mit einem Schlag; **at peace** in Frieden

5 (referring to activity) **to be at work** bei der Arbeit sein; **to play at cowboys** Cowboy spielen; **to be good at sth** gut in etw dat sein

6 (referring to cause) **shocked/surprised/annoyed at sth** schockiert/überrascht/verärgert über etw akk; **I went at his suggestion** ich ging auf seinen Vorschlag hin

ate [et, eɪt] pt of **eat**

athlete ['æθliːt] n Athlet(in) m(f); (track and field) Leichtathlet(in) m(f); (sportsman) Sportler(in) m(f); **~'s foot** Fußpilz m; **athletic** [æθ'letɪk] adj sportlich; (build) athletisch; **athletics** npl Leichtathletik f

Atlantic [ət'læntɪk] n: **the ~ (Ocean)** der Atlantik

atlas ['ætləs] n Atlas m

ATM abbr = **automated teller machine** Geldautomat m

atmosphere ['ætməsfɪə] n Atmosphäre f; (fig) Stimmung f

atom ['ætəm] n Atom nt; **atom(ic) bomb** n Atombombe f; **atomic** [ə'tɒmɪk] adj Atom-; **~ energy** Atomenergie f; **~ power** Atomkraft f

A to Z® ['eɪtə'zed] n Stadtplan m (in Buchform)

atrocious [ə'trəʊʃəs] adj grauenhaft; **atrocity** [ə'trɒsɪtɪ] n Grausamkeit f; (deed) Gräueltat f

attach [ə'tætʃ] vt befestigen, anheften (to an +akk); **to ~ importance to sth** Wert auf etw akk legen; **to be ~ed to sb/sth** an jdm/etw hängen; **attachment** [ə'tætʃmənt] n (affection)

Zuneigung f; (Inform) Attachment nt, Anhang m, Anlage f

attack [ə'tæk] vt, vi angreifen ▷ n Angriff +akk (on sb/m); (Med) Anfall m

attempt [ə'tempt] n Versuch m; **to make an ~ to do sth** versuchen, etw zu tun ▷ vt versuchen

attend [ə'tend] vt (go to) teilnehmen an +dat; (lectures, school) besuchen ▷ vi (be present) anwesend sein; **attend to** vt sich kümmern um; (customer) bedienen; **attendance** n (presence) Anwesenheit f; (people present) Teilnehmerzahl f; **attendant** n (in car park etc) Wächter(in) m(f); (in museum) Aufseher(in) m(f)

attention [ə'tenʃən] n Aufmerksamkeit f; **(your) ~ please** Achtung!; **to pay ~ to sth** beachten; **to pay ~ to sb** jdm aufmerksam zuhören; (listen) jdm/etw aufmerksam zuhören; **for the ~ of ...** zu Händen von ...; **attentive** [ə'tentɪv] adj aufmerksam

attic ['ætɪk] n Dachboden m; (lived in) Mansarde f

attitude ['ætɪtjuːd] n (mental) Einstellung f (to, towards zu); (more general, physical) Haltung f

attorney [ə'tɜːnɪ] n (US: lawyer) Rechtsanwalt m, Rechtsanwältin f

attract [ə'trækt] vt anziehen; (attention) erregen; **to be ~ed to o by sb** sich zu jdm hingezogen fühlen; **attraction** [ə'trækʃən] n Anziehungskraft f; (thing) Attraktion f; **attractive** adj attraktiv; (thing, idea) reizvoll

aubergine ['əʊbəʒiːn] n Aubergine f

auction ['ɔːkʃən] n Versteigerung f, Auktion f ▷ vt versteigern

audible [ˈɔːdɪbl] *adj* hörbar

audience [ˈɔːdɪəns] *n* Publikum *nt*; (*Radio*) Zuhörer *pl*; (*TV*) Zuschauer *pl*

audio [ˈɔːdɪəʊ] *adj* Ton-

audition [ɔːˈdɪʃən] *n* Probe *f* ▷ *vi* (*Theat*) vorspielen, vorsingen

auditorium [ɔːdɪˈtɔːrɪəm] *n* Zuschauerraum *m*

Aug *abbr* = **August**

August [ˈɔːgəst] *n* August *m*; *see also* **September**

aunt [ɑːnt] *n* Tante *f*

au pair [əʊˈpɛəˈ] *n* Aupairmädchen *nt*, Aupairjunge *m*

Australia [ɒˈstreɪlɪə] *n* Australien *nt*; **Australian** *adj* australisch ▷ *n* Australier(in) *m(f)*

Austria [ˈɒstrɪə] *n* Österreich *nt*; **Austrian** *adj* österreichisch ▷ *n* Österreicher(in) *m(f)*

authentic [ɔːˈθentɪk] *adj* echt; (*signature*) authentisch; **authenticity** [ɔːθenˈtɪsɪtɪ] *n* Echtheit *f*

author [ˈɔːθəˈ] *n* Autor(in) *m(f)*; (*of report etc*) Verfasser(in) *m(f)*

authority [ɔːˈθɒrɪtɪ] *n* (*power, expert*) Autorität *f*; **an ~ on sth** eine Autorität auf dem Gebiet einer Sache; **the authorities** (*pl*) die Behörden *pl*; **authorize** [ˈɔːθəraɪz] *vt* (*permit*) genehmigen; **to be ~d to do sth** offiziell berechtigt sein, etw zu tun

auto [ˈɔːtəʊ] (*pl* **-s**) *n* (*US*) Auto *nt*

autobiography [ɔːtəbaɪˈɒgrəfɪ] *n* Autobiographie *f*; **autograph** [ˈɔːtəgrɑːf] *n* Autogramm *nt*

automatic [ɔːtəˈmætɪk] *adj* automatisch; **~ gear change** (*Brit*), **~ gear shift** (*US*) Automatikschaltung *f* ▷ *n* (*car*) Automatikwagen *m*

automobile [ˈɔːtəməbiːl] *n* (*US*) Auto(mobil) *nt*; **autotrain**

[ˈɔːtəʊtreɪn] *n* (*US*) Autoreisezug *m*

autumn [ˈɔːtəm] *n* (*Brit*) Herbst *m*

auxiliary [ɔːgˈzɪlɪərɪ] *adj* Hilfs-; **~ verb** Hilfsverb *nt* ▷ *n* Hilfskraft *f*

availability [əveɪləˈbɪlɪtɪ] *n* (*of product*) Lieferbarkeit *f*; (*of resources*) Verfügbarkeit *f*; **available** *adj* erhältlich; (*existing*) vorhanden; (*product*) lieferbar; (*person*) erreichbar; **to be/make ~ to sb** jdm zur Verfügung stehen/stellen; **they're only ~ in black** es gibt sie nur in Schwarz, sie sind nur in Schwarz erhältlich

avalanche [ˈævəlɑːnʃ] *n* Lawine *f*

Ave *abbr* = **avenue**

avenue [ˈævənjuː] *n* Allee *f*

average [ˈævərɪdʒ] *n* Durchschnitt *m*; **on ~** im Durchschnitt ▷ *adj* durchschnittlich; **~ speed** Durchschnittsgeschwindigkeit *f*; **of ~ height** von mittlerer Größe

avian flu [ˈeɪvɪənˈfluː] *n* Vogelgrippe *f*

aviation [eɪvɪˈeɪʃən] *n* Luftfahrt *f*

avocado [ævəˈkɑːdəʊ] (*pl* **-s**) *n* Avocado *f*

avoid [əˈvɔɪd] *vt* vermeiden; **to ~ sb** jdm aus dem Weg gehen; **avoidable** *adj* vermeidbar

awake [əˈweɪk] (**awoke**, **awoken**) *vi* aufwachen ▷ *adj* wach

award [əˈwɔːd] *n* (*prize*) Preis *m*; (*for bravery etc*) Auszeichnung *f* ▷ *vt* zuerkennen (*to sb* jdm); (*present*) verleihen (*to sb* jdm)

aware [əˈwɛəˈ] *adj* bewusst; **to be ~ of sth** sich *dat* einer Sache *gen* bewusst sein; **I was not ~ that ...** es war mir nicht klar, dass ...

away [əˈweɪ] *adv* weg; **to look ~** wegsehen; **he's ~** er ist nicht da; (*on a trip*) er ist verreist; (*from school, work*) er fehlt; (*Sport*) **they**

are (**playing**) ~ sie spielen
auswärts; (*with distance*) **three
miles** ~ drei Meilen (von hier)
entfernt; **to work** ~ drauflos
arbeiten
awful ['ɔːfʊl] *adj* schrecklich,
furchtbar; **awfully** *adv* furchtbar
awkward ['ɔːkwəd] *adj* (*clumsy*)
ungeschickt; (*embarrassing*)
peinlich; (*difficult*) schwierig
awning ['ɔːnɪŋ] *n* Markise f
awoke [ə'wəʊk] *pt of* **awake**;
awoken [ə'wəʊkən] *pp of* **awake**
ax (*US*), **axe** [æks] *n* Axt f
axle ['æksl] *n* (*Tech*) Achse f

BA *abbr* = **Bachelor of Arts**
BSc *abbr* = **Bachelor of Science**
babe [beɪb] *n* (*fam*) Baby *nt*;
(*fam: affectionate*) Schatz m,
Kleine(r) *mf*
baby ['beɪbɪ] *n* Baby *nt*; (*of animal*)
Junge(s) *nt*; (*fam: affectionate*)
Schatz m, Kleine(r) *mf*; **to have a**
~ ein Kind bekommen; **it's your**
~ (*fam: responsibility*) das ist dein
Bier; **baby carriage** *n* (*US*)
Kinderwagen m; **baby food** *n*
Babynahrung f; **babyish** *adj*
kindisch; **baby shower** *n* (*US*)
Party für die werdende Mutter;
baby-sit *irr vi* babysitten;
baby-sitter *n* Babysitter(in) *m(f)*
bachelor ['bætʃələ°] *n* Junggeselle *m*; **Bachelor of**
Arts/Science *erster akademischer*
Grad, ≈ Magister/Diplom;
bachelorette *n* Junggesellin f;
bachelorette party *n* (*US*)

Junggesellinnenabschied; **bachelor party** *n (US) Junggesellenabschied m*

back [bæk] *n (of person, animal)* Rücken *m; (of house, coin etc)* Rückseite *f, (of chair)* Rückenlehne *f; (of car)* Rücksitz *m; (of train)* Ende *nt; (Sport: defender)* Verteidiger(in) *m(f);* **at the ~ of ...,** *(US)* **in ~ of** *(inside)* hinten in ...; *(outside)* hinter ...; **~ to front** verkehrt herum ▷ *vt (support)* unterstützen; *(car)* rückwärtsfahren ▷ *vi (go backwards)* rückwärtsgehen *o* rückwärtsfahren ▷ *adj* Hinter-; **~ wheel** Hinterrad *nt ▷ adv zurück;* **they're ~** sie sind wieder da; **back away** *vi* sich zurückziehen; **back down** *vi* nachgeben; **back up** *vi (car etc)* zurücksetzen ▷ *vt (support)* unterstützen; *(Inform)* sichern; *(car)* zurückfahren

backache *n* Rückenschmerzen *pl;* **backbone** *n* Rückgrat *nt;* **backdate** *vt* zurückdatieren; **backdoor** *n* Hintertür *f;* **backfire** *vi (plan)* fehlschlagen; *(Auto)* fehlzünden; **background** *n* Hintergrund *m;* **backhand** *n (Sport)* Rückhand *f;* **backlog** *(of work)* Rückstand *m;* **backpack** *n (US)* Rucksack *m;* **backpacker** *n* Rucksacktourist(in) *m(f);* **backpacking** *n* Rucksacktourismus *m;* **back seat** *n* Rücksitz *m;* **backside** *n (fam)* Po *m;* **back street** *n* Seitenstraßen *nt,* **backstroke** *n* Rückenschwimmen *nt;* **back up** *n (support)* Unterstützung *f;* **~ copy** *(Inform)* Sicherungskopie *f;* **backward** *adj (child)* zurückgeblieben; *(region)* rückständig; **~ movement** Rückwärtsbewegung *f;* **backwards** *adv* rückwärts; **backyard** *n* Hinterhof *m*

bacon ['beɪkən] *n* Frühstücksspeck *m*

bacteria [bæk'tɪərɪə] *npl* Bakterien *pl*

bad [hæd] *adj (worse, worst) adj* schlecht, schlimm; *(smell)* übel; **I have a ~ back** mir tut der Rücken weh; **I'm ~ at maths/sport** ich bin schlecht in Mathe/Sport; **to go ~** schlecht werden, verderben

badge [bædʒ] *n* Abzeichen *nt*

badger ['bædʒə*] *n* Dachs *m*

badly ['bædlɪ] *adv* schlecht; **~ wounded** schwer verwundet; **to need sth ~** etw dringend brauchen; **had-tempered** ['bæd'tempəd] *adj* schlecht gelaunt

bag [bæg] *n (small)* Tüte *f; (larger)* Beutel *m; (handbag)* Tasche *f;* **my ~s** *(luggage)* mein Gepäck

baggage ['bægɪdʒ] *n* Gepäck *nt;* **baggage allowance** *n* Freigepäck *nt;* **baggage (re)claim** *n* Gepäckrückgabe *f*

baggy ['bægɪ] *adj (zu)* weit; *(trousers, suit)* ausgebeult

bag lady ['bægleɪdɪ] *n* Stadtstreicherin *f*

bagpipes ['bægpaɪps] *npl* Dudelsack *m*

Bahamas [bə'hɑːməz] *npl:* **the ~** die Bahamas *pl*

bail [beɪl] *n (money)* Kaution *f*

bait [beɪt] *n* Köder *m*

bake [beɪk] *vt, vi* backen; **baked beans** *npl* weiße Bohnen in Tomatensoße; **baked potato** *(pl -es) n* in der Schale gebackene Kartoffel, Ofenkartoffel *f;* **baker** *n* Bäcker(in) *m(f);* **bakery** ['beɪkərɪ] *n* Bäckerei *f;* **baking powder** *n* Backpulver *nt*

balance ['bæləns] *n (equilibrium)* Gleichgewicht *nt ▷ vt (make up for)* ausgleichen; **balanced** *adj*

ausgeglichen; **balance sheet** n
Bilanz f
balcony ['bælkənɪ] n Balkon m
bald [bɔːld] adj kahl; **to be ~** eine
Glatze haben
Balkans ['bɔːlkənz] npl: **the ~**
der Balkan, die Balkanländer pl
ball [bɔːl] n Ball m; **to have a ~**
(fam) sich prima amüsieren
ballet ['bæleɪ] n Ballett nt; **ballet
dancer** n Balletttänzer(in) m(f)
balloon [bə'luːn] n (Luft)ballon
m
ballot ['bælət] n (geheime)
Abstimmung; **ballot box** n
Wahlurne f; **ballot paper** n
Stimmzettel m
ballpoint (pen) ['bɔːlpɔɪnt] n
Kugelschreiber m
ballroom ['bɔːlruːm] n Tanzsaal
m
Baltic ['bɔːltɪk] adj: **~ Sea** Ostsee
f; **the ~ States** die baltischen
Staaten
Baltics ['bɔːltɪks] n: **the ~** das
Baltikum nt
bamboo [bæm'buː] n Bambus m;
bamboo shoots npl
Bambussprossen pl
ban [bæn] n Verbot nt ▷ vt
verbieten
banana [bə'nɑːnə] n Banane f;
he's ~s er ist völlig durchgeknallt;
banana split n Bananensplit m
band [bænd] n (group) Gruppe f;
(of criminals) Bande f; (Mus) Kapelle
f; (pop, rock etc) Band f; (strip) Band
nt
bandage ['bændɪdʒ] n Verband
m; (elastic) Bandage f ▷ vt
verbinden
B & B abbr = **bed and breakfast**
bang [bæŋ] n (noise) Knall m;
(blow) Schlag m ▷ vt, vi knallen;
(door) zuschlagen, zuknallen;
banger ['bæŋə°] n (Brit fam:
firework) Knallkörper m; (sausage)

Würstchen nt; (fam: old car)
Klapperkiste f
bangs [bæŋz] npl (US: of hair)
Pony m
banish ['bænɪʃ] vt verbannen
banister(s) ['bænɪstə°] n (Treppen)geländer nt
bank [bæŋk] n (Fin) Bank f; (of
river etc) Ufer nt; **bank account** n
Bankkonto nt; **bank balance** n
Kontostand m; **bank card** n
Bankkarte f; **bank code** n
Bankleitzahl f; **bank holiday** n
gesetzlicher Feiertag

● **BANK HOLIDAY**

● Als **bank holiday** wird in
● Großbritannien ein gesetzlicher
● Feiertag bezeichnet, an dem die
● Banken geschlossen sind. Die
● meisten dieser Feiertage,
● abgesehen von Weihnachten
● und Ostern, fallen auf Montage
● im Mai und August. An diesen
● langen Wochenenden (bank
● holiday weekends) fahren viele
● Briten in Urlaub, sodass dann
● auf den Straßen, Flughäfen und
● bei der Bahn sehr viel Betrieb
● ist.

bank manager n Filialleiter(in)
m(f); **banknote** n Banknote f
bankrupt vt ruinieren; **to go
~** Pleite gehen
bank statement n
Kontoauszug m
baptism ['bæptɪzəm] n Taufe f;
baptize ['bæptaɪz] vt taufen
bar [bɑː°] n (for drinks) Bar f; (less
smart) Lokal nt; (rod) Stange f; (of
chocolate etc) Riegel m, Tafel f; (of
soap) Stück nt; (counter) Theke f
▷ prep außer; **~ none** ohne
Ausnahme
barbecue ['bɑːbɪkjuː] n (device)

belief [bɪ'liːf] n Glaube m (in an +akk); (conviction) Überzeugung f; **it's my ~ that ...** ich bin der Überzeugung, dass ...; **believe** [bɪ'liːv] vt glauben; **believe in** vi glauben an +akk; **believer** n (Rel) Gläubige(r) mf

bell [bel] n (church) Glocke f; (bicycle, door) Klingel f; **bellboy** ['belbɔɪ] n (esp US) Page m

bellows ['beləʊz] npl (for fire) Blasebalg m

belly ['belɪ] n Bauch m; **bellyache** n Bauchweh nt ⊳ vi (fam) meckern; **belly button** n (fam) Bauchnabel m; **bellyflop** n (fam) Bauchklatscher m

belong [bɪ'lɒŋ] vi gehören (to sb jdm); (to club) angehören +dat; **belongings** npl Habe f

below [bɪ'ləʊ] prep unter ⊳ adv unten

belt [belt] n (round waist) Gürtel m; (safety belt) Gurt m; **below the ~** unter die Gürtellinie ⊳ vi (fam: go fast) rasen, düsen; **beltway** n (US) Umgehungsstraße f

bench [bentʃ] n Bank f

bend [bend] n Biegung f; (in road) Kurve f ⊳ vt (bent, bent) (curve) biegen; (head, arm) beugen ⊳ vi sich biegen; (person) sich beugen; **bend down** vi sich bücken

beneath [bɪ'niːθ] prep unter ⊳ adv darunter

beneficial [benɪ'fɪʃl] adj gut, nützlich (to für); **benefit** ['benɪfɪt] n (advantage) Vorteil m; (profit) Nutzen m; **for your/his ~** deinetwegen/seinetwegen; **unemployment ~** Arbeitslosengeld nt ⊳ vt guttun +dat ⊳ vi Nutzen ziehen (from aus)

benign [bɪ'naɪn] adj (person) gütig; (climate) mild; (Med) gutartig

bent [bent] pt, pp of **bend** krumm; (fam) korrupt

beret ['bereɪ] n Baskenmü[...]

Bermuda [bə'mjuːdə] n t[...] pl die Bermudas pl ⊳ adj t[...] pl Bermudashorts pl; **the** [...] **~ triangle** das Bermudadrei[...]

berry ['berɪ] n Beere f

berth [bɜːθ] n (for ship) Ankerplatz m; (in ship) Koje f[...] train) Bett nt ⊳ vt am Kai festmachen ⊳ vi anlegen

beside [bɪ'saɪd] prep neben[...] **~ the sea/lake** am Meer/See[...] **besides** [bɪ'saɪdz] prep außer[...] ⊳ adv außerdem

besiege [bɪ'siːdʒ] vt belager[...]

best [best] adj beste(r, s); m[...] **~ friend** mein bester o engst[...] Freund; **the ~ thing (to do) w[...] be to ...** das Beste wäre zu ...[...] food packaging) **~ before ...** m[...] mindestens haltbar bis ...; **der/die/das Beste; all the ~ a[...]** Gute; **to make the ~ of it** das[...] Beste daraus machen ⊳ adv a[...] besten; **I like this ~** das mag ic[...] am liebsten; **best-before dat[...]** Mindesthaltbarkeitsdatum nt; **best man** ['best'mæn] (pl me[...] Trauzeuge m; **bestseller** ['bestselə°] n Bestseller m

bet [bet] (bet, bet) vt, vi wett[...] (on auf +akk); **I ~ him £5 that ..[...]** ich habe mit ihm um 5 Pfund gewettet, dass ...; **you ~** (fam) und ob!; **I ~ he'll be late** er kommt mit Sicherheit zu spät ⊳ n Wette f

betray [bɪ'treɪ] vt verraten; **betrayal** n Verrat m

better ['betə°] adj, adv besser; **get ~** (healthwise) sich erholen, wieder gesund werden; (improv[...] sich verbessern; **I'm much ~ today** es geht mir heute viel besser; **you'd ~ go** du solltest/S[...]

Grill m; (party) Barbecue nt, Grillfete f; **barbecue ~** grillen

barbed wire ['bɑːbd'waɪə°] n Stacheldraht m

barber ['bɑːbə°] n (Herren)friseur m

bar code ['bɑːkəʊd] n Strichcode m

bare [beə°] adj nackt, **~ patch** kahle Stelle; **barefoot** adj, adv barfuß; **bareheaded** adj, adv ohne Kopfbedeckung; **barely** adv kaum; (with age) knapp

bargain ['bɑːɡɪn] n (cheap offer) günstiges Angebot, Schnäppchen nt; (transaction) Geschäft nt; **what a ~** das ist aber günstig! ⊳ vi (ver)handeln

barge [bɑːdʒ] n (for freight) Lastkahn m; (unpowered) Schleppkahn m

bark [bɑːk] n (of tree) Rinde f; (of dog) Bellen nt ⊳ vi (dog) bellen

barley ['bɑːlɪ] n Gerste f

barmaid ['bɑːmeɪd] n Barkeeperin f, Barmann ['bɑːmən] (pl -men) n Barkeeper m

barn [bɑːn] n Scheune f

barometer [bə'rɒmɪtə°] n Barometer nt

baroque [bə'rɒk] adj barock, Barock-

barracks ['bærəks] npl Kaserne f

barrel ['bærəl] n Fass nt; **barrel organ** n Drehorgel f

barricade [bærɪ'keɪd] n Barrikade f

barrier ['bærɪə°] n (obstruction) Absperrung f, Barriere f; (across road etc) Schranke f

barrow ['bærəʊ] n (cart) Schubkarren m

bartender ['bɑːtendə°] n (US) Barkeeper(in) m(f)

base [beɪs] n Basis f; (of lamp, pillar etc) Fuß m; (Mil) Stützpunkt m

---

⊳ vt gründen (on auf +akk); **to be ~d on sth** auf etw dat basieren; **baseball** n Baseball m; **baseball cap** n Baseballmütze f; **basement** n Kellergeschoss nt

bash [bæʃ] (fam) n Schlag m; (fam) Party f ⊳ vt hauen

basic ['beɪsɪk] adj einfach; (fundamental) Grund-; (importance, difference) grundlegend; (in principle) grundsätzlich; **the accomodation is very ~** die Unterkunft ist sehr bescheiden; **basically** adv im Grunde; **basics** npl: **the ~** das Wesentliche

basil ['bæzl] n Basilikum nt

basin ['beɪsn] n (for washing, valley) (Wasch)becken nt

basis ['beɪsɪs] n Basis f; **on the ~ of** aufgrund +gen; **on a monthly ~** monatlich

basket ['bɑːskɪt] n Korb m; **basketball** n Basketball m

Basque [bæsk] n (person) Baske m, Baskin f; (language) Baskisch nt ⊳ adj baskisch

bass [beɪs] n (Mus) Bass m; (Zool) Barsch m ⊳ adj (Mus) Bass-

bastard ['bɑːstəd] n (vulg: awful person) Arschloch nt

bat [bæt] n (Zool) Fledermaus f; (Sport: cricket, baseball) Schlagholz nt; (table tennis) Schläger m

batch [bætʃ] n Schwung m; (fam: of letters, books etc) Stoß m

bath [bɑːθ] n Bad nt; (tub) Badewanne f; **to have a ~** baden ⊳ vt (child etc) baden

bathe [beɪð] vt, vi (wound etc) baden; **bath foam** ['bɑːθfəʊm] n Badeschaum m; **bathing cap** n Badekappe f; **bathing costume, bathing suit** (US) n Badeanzug m

bathmat ['bɑːθmæt] n Badevorleger m; **bathrobe** n Bademantel m; **bathroom** n Bad(ezimmer) nt; **baths** [bɑːðz] npl (Schwimm)bad

nt; **bath towel** n Badetuch nt;
bathtub n Badewanne f
baton ['bætən] n (Mus) Taktstock m; (police) Schlagstock m
batter ['bætə'] n Teig m ▷ vt heftig schlagen; **battered** adj übel zugerichtet; (hat, car) verbeult; (wife, baby) misshandelt
battery ['bætərɪ] n (Elec) Batterie f; **battery charger** n Ladegerät nt
battle ['bætl] n Schlacht f; (fig) Kampf m (for um +akk); **battlefield** n Schlachtfeld nt; **battlements** npl Zinnen pl
Bavaria [bə'veərɪə] n Bayern nt; **Bavarian** adj bay(e)risch ▷ n Bayer(in) m(f)
bay [beɪ] n (of sea) Bucht f; (on house) Erker m; (tree) Lorbeerbaum m; **bay leaf** n Lorbeerblatt nt; **bay window** n Erkerfenster nt
BBC abbr = **British Broadcasting Corporation** BBC f
BC abbr = **before Christ** vor Christi Geburt, v. Chr.

○ **KEYWORD**

be [biː] (pt **was**, **were**, pp **been**) vb aux **1** (with present participle: forming continuous tenses): **what are you doing?** was machst du (gerade)?; **it is raining** es regnet; **I've been waiting for you for hours** ich warte schon seit Stunden auf dich
2 (with pp: forming passives): **to be killed** getötet werden; **the thief was nowhere to be seen** der Dieb war nirgendwo zu sehen
3 (in tag questions) **it was fun, wasn't it?** es hat Spaß gemacht, nicht wahr?
4 (+to +infin) **the house is to be sold** das Haus soll verkauft werden; **he's not to open it** er darf es nicht öffnen
▷ vb +complement **1** (usu) sein; **I'm tired** ich bin müde; **I'm hot/cold** mir ist heiß/kalt; **he's a doctor** er ist Arzt; **2 and 2 are 4** 2 und 2 ist o sind 4; **she's tall/pretty** sie ist groß/hübsch; **be careful/quiet** sei vorsichtig/ruhig
2 (of health) **how are you?** wie geht es dir?; **he's very ill** er ist sehr krank; **I'm fine now** jetzt geht es mir gut
3 (of age) **how old are you?** wie alt bist du?; **I'm sixteen (years old)** ich bin sechzehn (Jahre alt)
4 (cost) **how much was the meal?** was o wie viel hat das Essen gekostet?; **that'll be £5.75, please** das macht £5.75, bitte
▷ vi **1** (exist, occur etc) sein; **is there a God?** gibt es einen Gott?; **be that as it may** wie dem auch sei; **so be it** also gut
2 (referring to place) sein; **I won't be here tomorrow** ich werde morgen nicht hier sein
3 (referring to movement) **where have you been?** wo bist du gewesen?; **I've been in the garden** ich war im Garten
▷ impers vb **1** (referring to time, distance, weather) sein; **it's 5 o'clock** es ist 5 Uhr; **it's 10 km to the village** es sind 10 km bis zum Dorf; **it's too hot/cold** es ist zu heiß/kalt
2 (emphatic) **it's me** ich bin's; **it's the postman** es ist der Briefträger

beach [biːtʃ] n Strand m; **beachwear** n Strandkleidung f
bead [biːd] n (of glass, wood etc) Perle f; (drop) Tropfen m
beak [biːk] n Schnabel m
beam [biːm] n (of wood etc) Balken m; (of light) Strahl m ▷ vi (smile etc) strahlen
bean [biːn] n Bohne f; **bean curd** n Tofu m

bear [beə'] (bore, borne) vt (carry) tragen; (tolerate) ertragen ▷ n Bär m; **bearable** adj erträglich
beard [bɪəd] n Bart m
beast [biːst] n Tier nt; (brutal person) Bestie f; (disliked person) Biest nt
beat [biːt] (beat, beaten) vt schlagen; (as punishment) prügeln; **to ~ sb at tennis** jdn im Tennis schlagen ▷ n (of heart, drum etc) Schlag m; (Mus) Takt m; (type of music) Beat m; **beat up** vt zusammenschlagen
beaten ['biːtn] pp of **beat**; **off the ~ track** abgelegen
beautiful ['bjuːtɪful] adj schön; (splendid) herrlich; **beauty** ['bjuːtɪ] n Schönheit f; **beauty spot** n (place) lohnendes Ausflugsziel
beaver ['biːvə'] n Biber m
became [bɪ'keɪm] pt of **become**
because [bɪ'kɒz] adv, conj weil ▷ prep: **~ of** wegen +gen o dat
become [bɪ'kʌm] (became, become) vt werden; **what's ~ of him?** was ist aus ihm geworden?
bed [bed] n Bett nt; (in garden) Beet nt; **bed and breakfast** n Übernachtung f mit Frühstück; **bedclothes** npl Bettwäsche f; **bedding** n Bettzeug nt; **bed linen** n Bettwäsche f; **bedroom** n Schlafzimmer nt; **bed-sit(ter)** n (fam) möblierte Einzimmerwohnung; **bedspread** n Tagesdecke f; **bedtime** n Schlafenszeit f
bee [biː] n Biene f
beech [biːtʃ] n Buche f
beef [biːf] n Rindfleisch nt; **beefburger** n Hamburger m; **beef tomato** (pl **-es**) n Fleischtomate f
beehive ['biːhaɪv] n Bienenstock m

been [biːn] pp of **be**
beer [bɪə'] n Bier nt; **beer garden** n Biergarten m
beetle ['biːtl] n Käfer m
beetroot ['biːtruːt] n Rote Bete
before [bɪ'fɔː'] prep vor; **the year ~ last** vorletztes Jahr; **the day ~ yesterday** vorgestern ▷ conj bevor ▷ adv (of time) vorher; **have you been there ~?** waren Sie/warst du schon einmal dort?; **beforehand** adv vorher
beg [beg] vt: **to ~ sb to do sth** jdn inständig bitten, etw zu tun ▷ vi (beggar) betteln (for um +akk)
began [bɪ'gæn] pt of **begin**
beggar ['begə'] n Bettler(in) m(f)
begin [bɪ'gɪn] (began, begun) vt, vi anfangen, beginnen; **to ~ to do sth** anfangen, etw zu tun; **beginner** n Anfänger(in) m(f); **beginning** n Anfang m
begun [bɪ'gʌn] pp of **begin**
behalf [bɪ'hɑːf] n: **on ~ of, in ~ of** (US) im Namen/Auftrag von; **on my ~** für mich
behave [bɪ'heɪv] vi sich benehmen; **~ yourself!** benimm dich!; **behavior** (US), **behaviour** [bɪ'heɪvjə'] n Benehmen nt
behind [bɪ'haɪnd] prep hinter; **to be ~ time** Verspätung haben ▷ adv hinten; **to be ~ with one's work** mit seiner Arbeit im Rückstand sein ▷ n (fam) Hinterteil nt
beige [beɪʒ] adj beige
being ['biːɪŋ] n (existence) Dasein nt; (person) Wesen nt
Belarus [belə'rʊs] n Weißrussland nt
belch [beltʃ] n Rülpser m ▷ vi rülpsen
belfry ['belfrɪ] n Glockenturm m
Belgian ['beldʒən] adj belgisch ▷ n Belgier(in) m(f); **Belgium** ['beldʒəm] n Belgien nt

sollten lieber gehen; **a change for the** ~ eine Wendung zum Guten

betting ['betɪŋ] n Wetten pl; **betting shop** n Wettbüro nt

between [bɪ'twiːn] prep zwischen; (among) unter; ~ **you and me, ...** unter uns gesagt, ... ▷ adv (in) ~ dazwischen

beverage ['bevərɪdʒ] n (formal) Getränk nt

beware [bɪ'weə'] vt: **to ~ of sth** sich vor etw +dat hüten; **"~ of the dog"** „Vorsicht, bissiger Hund!"

bewildered [bɪ'wɪldəd] adj verwirrt

beyond [bɪ'jɒnd] prep (place) jenseits +gen; (time) über ... hinaus; (out of reach) außerhalb +gen; **it's ~ me** da habe ich keine Ahnung, da geht über mein Begreifen hinaus

bias ['baɪəs] n (prejudice) Vorurteil nt, Voreingenommenheit f

bias(s)ed adj voreingenommen

bib [bɪb] n Latz m

Bible ['baɪbl] n Bibel f

bicycle ['baɪsɪkl] n Fahrrad nt

bid [bɪd] (bid, bid) vt (offer) bieten ▷ n (attempt) Versuch m; (offer) Gebot nt

big [bɪg] adj groß; **it's no ~ deal** (fam) es ist nichts Besonderes; **big dipper** n (Brit) Achterbahn f; **big-headed** [bɪg'hedɪd] adj eingebildet

bike [baɪk] n (fam) Rad nt

bikini [bɪ'kiːnɪ] n Bikini m

bilberry ['bɪlbərɪ] n Heidelbeere f

bilingual [baɪ'lɪŋgwəl] adj zweisprachig

bill [bɪl] n (account) Rechnung f; (US: banknote) Banknote f; (Pol) Gesetzentwurf m; (Zool) Schnabel m; **billfold** ['bɪlfəʊld] n (US) Brieftasche f

billiards ['bɪlɪədz] nsing Billard nt; **billiard table** Billardtisch m

billion ['bɪlɪən] n Milliarde f

bin [bɪn] n Behälter m; (rubbish bin) (Müll)eimer m; (for paper) Papierkorb m

bind [baɪnd] (bound, bound) vt binden; (bind together) zusammenbinden; (wound) verbinden; **binding** n (ski) Bindung f; (book) Einband m

binge [bɪndʒ] n (fam: drinking) Sauferei f; **to go on a ~** auf Sauftour gehen

bingo ['bɪŋgəʊ] n Bingo nt

binoculars [bɪ'nɒkjʊləz] npl Fernglas nt

biodegradable ['baɪəʊdɪ'greɪdəbl] adj biologisch abbaubar

biography [baɪ'ɒgrəfɪ] n Biografie f

biological [baɪə'lɒdʒɪkəl] adj biologisch; **biology** [baɪ'ɒlədʒɪ] n Biologie f

birch [bɜːtʃ] n Birke f

bird [bɜːd] n Vogel m; (Brit fam: girl, girlfriend) Tussi f; **bird flu** n Vogelgrippe f; **bird watcher** n Vogelbeobachter(in) m(f)

birth [bɜːθ] n Geburt f; **birth certificate** n Geburtsurkunde f; **birth control** n Geburtenkontrolle f; **birthday** n Geburtstag m; **happy ~** herzlichen Glückwunsch zum Geburtstag; **birthday card** n Geburtstagskarte f; **birthday party** n Geburtstagsfeier f; **birthplace** n Geburtsort m

biscuit ['bɪskɪt] n (Brit) Keks m

bisexual [baɪ'seksjʊəl] adj bisexuell

bishop ['bɪʃəp] n Bischof m; (in chess) Läufer m

bit [bɪt] pt of **bite** ▷ n (piece) Stück(chen) nt; (Inform) Bit nt; **a ~ (of ...)** (small amount) ein bisschen ...; **a ~ tired** etwas müde;

~ by ~ allmählich; (*time*) **for a ~** ein Weilchen; **quite a ~** (*a lot*) ganz schön viel

bitch [bɪtʃ] *n* (*dog*) Hündin *f*; (*pej: woman*) Miststück *nt*, Schlampe *f*; **son of a ~** (*US: vulg*) Hurensohn *m*, Scheißkerl *m*; **bitchy** *adj* gemein, zickig

bite [baɪt] (**bit, bitten**) *vt, vi* beißen ▷ *n* Biss *m*; (*mouthful*) Bissen *m*; (*insect*) Stich *m*; **to have a ~** eine Kleinigkeit essen; **bitten** *pp* of **bite**

bitter [ˈbɪtəʳ] *adj* bitter; (*memory etc*) schmerzlich ▷ *n* (*Brit: beer*) halbdunkles Bier; **bitter lemon** *nt* Bitter Lemon *nt*

bizarre [bɪˈzɑː] *adj* bizarr

black [blæk] *adj* schwarz; **blackberry** *n* Brombeere *f*; **blackbird** *n* Amsel *f*; **blackboard** *n* (*Wand*)tafel *f*; **black box** *n* (*Aviat*) Flugschreiber *m*; **blackcurrant** *n* Schwarze Johannisbeere; **black eye** *n* blaues Auge; **Black Forest** *n* Schwarzwald *m*; **Black Forest gateau** *n* Schwarzwälder Kirschtorte *f*; **blackmail** *n* Erpressung *f* ▷ *vt* erpressen; **black market** *n* Schwarzmarkt *m*; **blackout** *n* (*Med*) Ohnmacht *f*; **to have a ~** ohnmächtig werden; **black pudding** *n* ≈ Blutwurst *f*; **Black Sea** *n*: **the ~** das Schwarze Meer; **blacksmith** *n* Schmied(in) *m(f)*; **black tie** *n* Abendanzug *m*, Smoking *m*; **is it ~?** ist/besteht da Smokingzwang?

bladder [ˈblædəʳ] *n* Blase *f*

blade [bleɪd] *n* (*of knife*) Klinge *f*; (*of propeller*) Blatt *nt*; (*of grass*) Halm *m*

blame [bleɪm] *n* Schuld *f* ▷ *vt*: **to ~ sth on sb** jdm die Schuld an etw *dat* geben; **he is to ~** er ist daran schuld

bland [blænd] *adj* (*taste*) fade; (*comment*) nichtssagend

blank [blæŋk] *adj* (*page, space*) leer, unbeschrieben; (*look*) ausdruckslos; **~ cheque** *n* Blankoscheck *m*

blanket [ˈblæŋkɪt] *n* (*Woll*)decke *f*

blast [blɑːst] *n* (*of wind*) Windstoß *m*; (*of explosion*) Druckwelle *f* ▷ *vt* (*blow up*) sprengen; **~!** (*fam*) Mist!, verdammt!

blatant [ˈbleɪtənt] *adj* (*undisguised*) offen; (*obvious*) offensichtlich

blaze [bleɪz] *vi* lodern; (*sun*) brennen ▷ *n* (*building*) Brand *m*; (*other fire*) Feuer *nt*; **a ~ of colour** eine Farbenpracht

blazer [ˈbleɪzəʳ] *n* Blazer *m*

bleach [bliːtʃ] *n* Bleichmittel *nt* ▷ *vt* bleichen

bleak [bliːk] *adj* öde, düster; (*future*) trostlos

bleary [ˈblɪərɪ] *adj* (*eyes*) trübe, verschlafen

bleed [bliːd] (**bled, bled**) *vi* bluten

blend [blend] *n* Mischung *f* ▷ *vt* mischen ▷ *vi* sich mischen; **blender** *n* Mixer *m*

bless [bles] *vt* segnen; **~ you!** Gesundheit!; **blessing** *n* Segen *m*

blew [bluː] *pt* of **blow**

blind [blaɪnd] *adj* blind; (*corner*) unübersichtlich; **to turn a ~ eye to sth** bei etw ein Auge zudrücken ▷ *n* (*for window*) Rollo *nt* ▷ *vt* blenden; **blind alley** *n* Sackgasse *f*; **blind spot** *n* (*Auto*) toter Winkel; (*fig*) schwacher Punkt

blink [blɪŋk] *vi* blinzeln; (*light*) blinken

bliss [blɪs] *n* (*Glück*)seligkeit *f*

blister [ˈblɪstəʳ] *n* Blase *f*

blizzard ['blɪzəd] *n* Schneesturm *m*

bloated ['bləʊtɪd] *adj* aufgedunsen

block [blɒk] *n* (of wood, stone, ice) Block *m*, Klotz *m*; (of buildings) Häuserblock *m*; **~ of flats** (Brit) Wohnblock *m* ▷ *vt* (road etc) blockieren; (pipe, nose) verstopfen; **blockage** ['blɒkɪdʒ] *n* Verstopfung *f*; **blockbuster** ['blɒkbʌstə] *n* Knüller *m*; **block letters** *npl* Blockschrift *f*

blog [blɒg] *n* (Inform) Blog *nt*

bloke [bləʊk] *n* (Brit fam) Kerl *m*, Typ *m*

blond(e) [blɒnd] *adj* blond ▷ *n* (person) Blondine *f*, blonder Typ *m*

blood [blʌd] *n* Blut *nt*; **blood count** *n* Blutbild *nt*; **blood donor** *n* Blutspender(in) *m(f)*; **blood group** *n* Blutgruppe *f*; **blood orange** *n* Blutorange *f*; **blood poisoning** *n* Blutvergiftung *f*; **blood pressure** *n* Blutdruck *m*; **blood sample** *n* Blutprobe *f*; **bloodsports** *npl* Sportarten, bei denen Tiere getötet werden; **bloodthirsty** *adj* blutrünstig; **bloody** *adj* (Brit fam) verdammt, Scheiß-; (literal sense) blutig

bloom [bluːm] *n* Blüte *f* ▷ *vi* blühen

blossom ['blɒsəm] *n* Blüte *f* ▷ *vi* blühen

blot [blɒt] *n* (of ink) Klecks *m*; (fig) Fleck *m*

blouse [blaʊz] *n* Bluse *f*; **big girl's ~** (fam) Schwächling *m*, femininer Typ

blow [bləʊ] *n* Schlag *m* ▷ *vi, vt* (blew, blown) (wind) wehen, blasen; (person: trumpet etc) blasen; **to ~ one's nose** sich die Nase putzen; **blow out** *vt* (candle etc) ausblasen; **blow up** *vi* explodieren ▷ *vt* sprengen;

(balloon, tyre) aufblasen; (Foto: enlarge) vergrößern; **blow-dry** *vt* föhnen; **blowjob** *n* (fam) **to give sb a ~** jdm einen blasen; **blown** [bləʊn] *pp* of **blow**; **blow-out** *n* (Auto) geplatzter Reifen

BLT *n abbr* = **bacon, lettuce and tomato sandwich** mit Frühstücksspeck, Kopfsalat und Tomaten belegtes Sandwich

blue [bluː] *adj* blau; (fam: unhappy) trübsinnig, niedergeschlagen; (film) pornografisch; (joke) anzüglich; (language) derb; **bluebell** *n* Glockenblume *f*; **blueberry** *n* Blaubeere *f*; **blue cheese** *n* Blauschimmelkäse *m*; **blues** *npl* **the ~** (Mus) der Blues; **to have the ~** (fam) niedergeschlagen sein

blunder ['blʌndə] *n* Schnitzer *m*

blunt [blʌnt] *adj* (knife) stumpf; (fig) unverblümt; **bluntly** *adv* geradeheraus

blurred [blɜːd] *adj* verschwommen, unklar

blush [blʌʃ] *vi* erröten

board [bɔːd] *n* (of wood) Brett *nt*; (committee) Ausschuss *m*; (of firm) Vorstand *m*; **~ and lodging** Unterkunft und Verpflegung; **on ~** an Bord ▷ *vt* (train, bus) einsteigen in +akk; (ship) an Bord +gen gehen; **boarder** *n* Pensionsgast *m*; (school) Internatsschüler(in) *m(f)*; **board game** *n* Brettspiel *nt*; **boarding card, boarding pass** *n* Bordkarte *f*, Einsteigekarte *f*; **boarding school** *n* Internat *nt*; **board meeting** *n* Vorstandssitzung *f*; **boardroom** *n* Sitzungssaal *m* (des Vorstands)

boast [bəʊst] *vi* prahlen (about mit) ▷ *n* Prahlerei *f*

boat [bəʊt] *n* Boot *nt*; (ship) Schiff *nt*; **boatman** *n* (hirer)

Bootsverleiher m; **boat race** n
Regatta f; **boat train** n Zug m mit
Schiffsanschluss
bob(sleigh) ['bɒbsleɪ] n Bob m
bodily ['bɒdɪlɪ] adj körperlich
▷ adv (forcibly) gewaltsam; **body**
['bɒdɪ] n Körper m; (of car) Karosserie f; **bodybuilding**
n Bodybuilding nt; **bodyguard** n
Leibwächter m; (group) Leibwache
f; **body jewellery** n
Intimschmuck m; **body odour** n
Körpergeruch m; **body piercing** n
Piercing nt; **bodywork** n
Karosserie f
boil [bɔɪl] vt, vi kochen ▷ n (Med)
Geschwür nt; **boiler** n Boiler m;
boiling adj (water etc) kochend
(heiß); **I was ~** (hot) mir war
fürchterlich heiß; (with rage) ich
kochte vor Wut; **boiling point** n
Siedepunkt m
bold [bəʊld] adj kühn, mutig;
(colours) kräftig; (type) fett
Bolivia [bə'lɪvɪə] n Bolivien nt
bolt [bəʊlt] n (lock) Riegel m;
(screw) Bolzen m ▷ vt verriegeln
bomb [bɒm] n Bombe f ▷ vt
bombardieren
bond [bɒnd] n (link) Bindung f;
(Fin) Obligation f
bone [bəʊn] n Knochen m; (of
fish) Gräte f; **boner** n (US fam)
Schnitzer m; (vulg: erection) Ständer
m
bonfire ['bɒnfaɪə°] n Feuer nt
(im Freien)
bonnet ['bɒnɪt] n (Brit Auto)
Haube f; (for baby) Häubchen nt
bonny ['bɒnɪ] adj (esp Scottish)
hübsch
bonus ['bəʊnəs] n Bonus m,
Prämie f
boo [bu:] vt auspfeifen,
ausbuhen ▷ vi buhen ▷ n Buhruf
m
book [bʊk] n Buch nt; (of tickets,

stamps) Heft nt ▷ vt (ticket etc)
bestellen; (hotel, flight etc) buchen;
(Sport) verwarnen; **fully ~ed (up)**
ausgebucht; (performance)
ausverkauft; **to be ~ed in at a hotel**
ein Zimmer in einem Hotel
bestellt haben; **bookcase** n
Bücherregal nt; **booking** n
Buchung f; **booking office** n
(Rail) Fahrkartenschalter m; (Theat)
Vorverkaufsstelle f; **book-keeping**
n Buchhaltung f; **booklet** n
Broschüre f; **bookmark** n (a.
Inform) Lesezeichen nt; **bookshelf**
n Bücherbord nt; **bookshelves**
Bücherregal nt; **bookshop,
bookstore** n (esp US)
Buchhandlung f
boom [bu:m] n (of business)
Boom m; (noise) Dröhnen nt ▷ vi
(business) boomen; (fam) florieren;
(voice etc) dröhnen
boomerang ['bu:məræŋ] n
Bumerang m
boost [bu:st] n Auftrieb m ▷ vt
(production, sales) ankurbeln;
(power, profits etc) steigern;
booster (injection) n
Wiederholungsimpfung f
boot [bu:t] n Stiefel m; (Brit Auto)
Kofferraum m ▷ vt (Inform) laden,
booten
booth [bu:ð] n (at fair etc) Bude f;
(at trade fair etc) Stand m
booze [bu:z] n (fam) Alkohol m
▷ vi (fam) saufen
border ['bɔ:də°] n Grenze f; (edge)
Rand m; **north/south of the
Border** in Schottland/England;
borderline n Grenze f
bore [bɔ:°] pt of **bear** ▷ vt (hole
etc) bohren; (person) langweilen
▷ n (person) Langweiler(in) m(f),
langweiliger Mensch; (thing)
langweilige Sache; **bored** adj: **to
be ~** sich langweilen; **boredom** n

Langeweile f; **boring** adj langweilig

born [bɔːn] adj: **he was ~ in London** er ist in London geboren

borne [bɔːn] pp of **bear**

borough ['bʌrə] n Stadtbezirk m

borrow ['bɒrəʊ] vt borgen

Bosnia-Herzegovina ['bɒznɪəhɜːtsəɡəʊviːnə] n Bosnien-Herzegowina nt; **Bosnian** ['bɒznɪən] adj bosnisch ▷ n Bosnier(in) m(f)

boss [bɒs] n Chef(in) m(f), Boss m; **boss around** vt herumkommandieren; **bossy** adj herrisch

botanical [bə'tænɪkəl] adj botanisch; **~ garden(s)** botanischer Garten

both [bəʊθ] adj beide; **~ the books** beide Bücher ▷ pron (people) beide; (things) beides; **~ (of) the boys** die beiden Jungs; **I like ~ of them** ich mag sie (alle) beide ▷ adv: **~ X and Y** sowohl X als auch Y

bother ['bɒðə] vt ärgern, belästigen; **it doesn't ~ me** das stört mich nicht; **he can't be ~ with details** mit Details gibt er sich nicht ab; **I'm not ~ed** das ist mir egal ▷ vi sich kümmern (about um); **don't ~** (das ist) nicht nötig, lass es! ▷ n (trouble) Mühe f; (annoyance) Ärger m

bottle ['bɒtl] n Flasche f ▷ vt (in Flaschen) abfüllen; **bottle out** vi (fam) den Mut verlieren, aufgeben; **bottle bank** n Altglascontainer m; **bottled** adj in Flaschen; **~ beer** Flaschenbier nt; **bottleneck** n (fig) Engpass m; **bottle opener** n Flaschenöffner m

bottom ['bɒtəm] n (of container) Boden m; (underside) Unterseite f; (fam: of person) Po m; **at the ~ of the sea/table/page** auf dem Meeresgrund/am Tabellenende/unten auf der Seite ▷ adj unterste(r, s); **to be ~ of the class/league** Klassenletzte(r)/Tabellenletzte(r) sein; **~ gear** (Auto) erster Gang

bought [bɔːt] pt, pp of **buy**

bounce [baʊns] vi (ball) springen, aufprallen; (cheque) platzen; **~ up and down** (person) herumhüpfen; **bouncy** adj (ball) gut springend; (person) munter; **bouncy castle®** n Hüpfburg f

bound [baʊnd] pt, pp of **bind** ▷ adj (tied up) gebunden; (obliged) verpflichtet; **to be ~ to do sth** (certain) tun etw tun müssen; (likely) es ist wahrscheinlich, dass sie (wohl) tun müssen; **it's ~ to happen** es muss so kommen; **to be ~ for ...** auf dem Weg nach ... sein; **boundary** ['baʊndərɪ] n Grenze f

bouquet [bʊ'keɪ] n (flowers) Strauß m; (of wine) Blume f

boutique [buːˈtiːk] n Boutique f

bow [bəʊ] n (ribbon) Schleife f; (instrument, weapon) Bogen m ▷ [baʊ] vi sich verbeugen ▷ [baʊ] n (with head) Verbeugung f; (of ship) Bug m

bowels ['baʊəlz] npl Darm m

bowl [bəʊl] n (basin) Schüssel f; (shallow) Schale f; (for animal) Napf m ▷ v, vt (in cricket) werfen

bowler ['bəʊlə°] n (in cricket) Werfer(in) m(f); (hat) Melone f

bowling ['bəʊlɪŋ] n Kegeln nt; **bowling alley** n Kegelbahn f; **bowling green** n Rasen m zum Bowling-Spiel; **bowls** [bəʊlz] nsing (game) Bowling-Spiel nt

bow tie [bəʊ'taɪ] n Fliege f

box [bɒks] n Schachtel f; (cardboard) Karton m; (bigger) Kasten m; (space on form) Kästchen nt; (Theat) Loge f; **boxer** n Boxer(in) m(f); **boxers, boxer**

shorts *npl* Boxershorts *pl*; **boxing**
n (*Sport*) Boxen *nt*; **Boxing Day** *n*
zweiter Weihnachtsfeiertag

● **BOXING DAY**

● **Boxing Day** ist ein Feiertag in
● Großbritannien. Fällt
● Weihnachten auf ein
● Wochenende, wird der Feiertag
● am nächsten Wochentag
● nachgeholt. Der Name geht auf
● einen alten Brauch zurück:
● früher erhielten Händler und
● Lieferanten an diesem Tag ein
● Geschenk, die sogenannte
● Christmas Box.

boxing gloves *npl*
Boxhandschuhe *pl*; **boxing ring** *n*
Boxring *m*
box number *n* Chiffre *f*
box office *n* (*cinema, theatre*)
Kasse *f*
boy [bɔɪ] *n* Junge *m*
boycott ['bɔɪkɒt] *n* Boykott *m*
▷ *vt* boykottieren
boyfriend ['bɔɪfrɛnd] *n* (*fester*)
Freund *m*; **boy scout** *n*
Pfadfinder *m*
bra [brɑː] *n* BH *m*
brace [breɪs] *n* (*on teeth*) Spange *f*
bracelet ['breɪslɪt] *n* Armband *nt*
braces ['breɪsɪz] *npl* (*Brit*)
Hosenträger *pl*
bracket ['brækɪt] *n* (*in text*)
Klammer *f*; (*Tech*) Träger *m* ▷ *vt*
einklammern
brag [bræɡ] *vi* angeben
Braille [breɪl] *n* Blindenschrift *f*
brain [breɪn] *n* (*Anat*) Gehirn *nt*;
(*mind*) Verstand *m*, **-s** (*pl*)
(*intelligence*) Grips *m*; **brainwave** *n*
Geistesblitz *m*; **brainy** *adj* schlau,
clever
braise [breɪz] *vt* schmoren
brake [breɪk] *n* Bremse *f* ▷ *vi*

bremsen; **brake fluid** *n*
Bremsflüssigkeit *f*; **brake light** *n*
Bremslicht *nt*; **brake pedal** *n*
Bremspedal *nt*
branch [brɑːntʃ] *n* (*of tree*) Ast *m*;
(*of family, subject*) Zweig *m*; (*of firm*)
Filiale *f*, Zweigstelle *f*; **branch off**
vi (*road*) abzweigen
brand [brænd] *n* (*Comm*) Marke *f*
brand-new ['brænd'njuː] *adj*
(funkel)nagelneu
brandy ['brændɪ] *n* Weinbrand *m*
brass [brɑːs] *n* Messing *nt*; (*Brit
fam: money*) Knete *f*; **brass band** *n*
Blaskapelle *f*
brat [bræt] *n* (*pej, fam*) Gör *nt*
brave [breɪv] *adj* tapfer, mutig;
bravery ['breɪvərɪ] *n* Mut *m*
brawl [brɔːl] *n* Schlägerei *f*
brawn [brɔːn] *n* (*strength*)
Muskelkraft *f*; (*Gastr*) Sülze *f*;
brawny *adj* muskulös
Brazil [brə'zɪl] *n* Brasilien *nt*;
Brazilian *adj* brasilianisch ▷ *n*
Brasilianer(in) *m(f)*; **brazil nut** *n*
Paranuss *f*
bread [brɛd] *n* Brot *nt*; **breadbin** *n*
(*Brit*), **breadbox** (*US*) *n*
Brotkasten *m*; **breadcrumbs** *npl*
Brotkrumen *pl*; (*Gastr*) Paniermehl
nt; **breaded** *adj* paniert;
breadknife *n* Brotmesser *nt*
breadth [brɛdθ] *n* Breite *f*
break [breɪk] *n* (*fracture*) Bruch
m; (*rest*) Pause *f*; (*short holiday*)
Kurzurlaub *m*; **give me a ~** gib mir
eine Chance, hör auf damit! ▷ *vt*
(**broke, broken**) (*fracture*) brechen;
(*in pieces*) zerbrechen; (*toy, device*)
kaputt machen; (*promise*) nicht
halten; (*silence*) brechen; (*law*)
verletzen; (*journey*) unterbrechen;
(*news*) mitteilen (*to sb* jdm); **I
broke my leg** ich habe mir das
Bein gebrochen; **he broke it to
her gently** er hat es ihr schonend
beigebracht ▷ *vi* (*come apart*)

(auseinander)brechen; (in pieces) zerbrechen; (toy, device) kaputtgehen; (person) zusammenbrechen; (day, dawn) anbrechen; (news) bekannt werden; **break down** vi (car) eine Panne haben; (machine) versagen; (person) zusammenbrechen; **break in** vt (burglar) einbrechen; **break into** vt einbrechen in +akk; **break off** vi, vt abbrechen; **break out** vi ausbrechen; **to ~ in a rash** einen Ausschlag bekommen; **break up** vi aufbrechen; (meeting, organisation) sich auflösen; (marriage) in die Brüche gehen; (couple) sich trennen; **school breaks up on Friday** am Freitag beginnen die Ferien ▷ vt aufbrechen; (marriage) zerstören; (meeting) auflösen; **breakable** adj zerbrechlich; **breakage** n Bruch m; **breakdown** n (of car) Panne f; (of machine) Störung f; (of person, relations, system) Zusammenbruch m; **breakdown service** n Pannendienst m; **breakdown truck** n Abschleppwagen m

breakfast ['brekfəst] n Frühstück nt; **to have ~** frühstücken; **breakfast cereal** n Cornflakes, Muesli etc; **breakfast television** n Frühstücksfernsehen nt

break-in ['breikin] n Einbruch m; **breakup** ['breikʌp] n (of meeting, organization) Auflösung f; (of marriage) Zerrüttung f

breast [brest] n Brust f; **breastfeed** vt stillen; **breaststroke** n Brustschwimmen m

breath [breθ] n Atem m; **out of ~** außer Atem; **breathalyze** ['breθəlaiz] vt (ins Röhrchen) blasen lassen; **breathalyser, breathalyzer** n Promillemesser m; **breathe** [bri:ð]

vt, vi atmen; **breathe in** vt, vi einatmen; **breathe out** vt, vi ausatmen; **breathless** ['breθlis] adj atemlos; **breathtaking** ['breθteikiŋ] adj atemberaubend

bred [bred] pt, pp of **breed**

breed [bri:d] n (race) Rasse f ▷ vt (bred, bred) sich vermehren ▷ vt züchten; **breeder** n Züchter(in) m(f); (fam) Hetero m; **breeding** n (of animals) Züchtung f; (of person) (gute) Erziehung f

breeze [bri:z] n Brise f

brevity ['breviti] n Kürze f

brew [bru:] vt (beer) brauen; (tea) kochen; **brewery** n Brauerei f

bribe ['braib] n Bestechungsgeld nt ▷ vt bestechen; **bribery** ['braibəri] n Bestechung f

brick [brik] n Backstein m; **bricklayer** n Maurer(in) m(f)

bride [braid] n Braut f; **bridegroom** n Bräutigam m; **bridesmaid** n Brautjungfer f

bridge [bridʒ] n Brücke f; (cards) Bridge nt

brief [bri:f] adj kurz ▷ vt instruieren (on über +akk); **briefcase** n Aktentasche f; **briefs** npl Slip m

bright [brait] adj hell; (colour) leuchtend; (cheerful) heiter; (intelligent) intelligent; (idea) glänzend; **brighten up** vt aufhellen; (person) aufheitern ▷ vi sich aufheitern; (person) fröhlicher werden

brilliant ['briljənt] adj (sunshine, colour) strahlend; (person) brillant; (idea) glänzend; (Brit fam) **it was ~** es war fantastisch

brim [brim] n Rand m

bring [briŋ] (brought, brought) vt bringen; (with one) mitbringen; **bring about** vt herbeiführen, bewirken; **bring back** vt zurückbringen; (memories) wecken; **bring down** vt (reduce) senken; (*government etc*) zu Fall bringen; **bring in** vt hereinbringen; (*introduce*) einführen; **bring out** vt herausbringen; **bring round**, **bring to** vt wieder zu sich bringen; **bring up** vt (*child*) aufziehen; (*question*) zur Sprache bringen

brisk [brɪsk] *adj* (*trade*) lebhaft; (*wind*) frisch

bristle ['brɪsl] *n* Borste *f*

Brit [brɪt] *n* (*fam*) Brite *m*, Britin *f*; **Britain** ['brɪtn] *n* Großbritannien *nt*; **British** ['brɪtɪʃ] *adj* britisch; **the ~ Isles** (*pl*) die Britischen Inseln *pl* ▷ *n* **the ~** (*pl*) die Briten *pl*

brittle ['brɪtl] *adj* spröde

broad [brɔːd] *adj* breit; (*accent*) stark; **in ~ daylight** am helllichten Tag ▷ (*US fam*) Frau *f*

B road ['biːrəʊd] *n* (*Brit*) ≈ Landstraße *f*

broadcast ['brɔːdkɑːst] *n* Sendung *f* ▷ *irr* vt, vi senden; (*event*) übertragen

broaden ['brɔːdn] vt: **to ~ the mind** den Horizont erweitern; **broad-minded** *adj* tolerant

broccoli ['brɒkəlɪ] *n* Brokkoli *pl*

brochure ['brəʊʃjʊə²] *n* Prospekt *m*, Broschüre *f*

broke [brəʊk] *pt of* **break** ▷ *adj* (*Brit fam*) pleite; **broken** ['brəʊkən] *pp of* **break**; **broken-hearted** *adj* untröstlich

broker ['brəʊkə²] *n* Makler(in) *m(f)*

brolly ['brɒlɪ] *n* (*Brit*) Schirm *m*

bronchitis [brɒŋ'kaɪtɪs] *n* Bronchitis *f*

bronze [brɒnz] *n* Bronze *f*

brooch [brəʊtʃ] *n* Brosche *f*

broom [bruːm] *n* Besen *m*

Bros [brɒs] *abbr* = **brothers** Gebr.

broth [brɒθ] *n* Fleischbrühe *f*

brothel ['brɒθl] *n* Bordell *nt*

brother ['brʌðə²] *n* Bruder *m*; **~s** (*pl*) (*Comm*) Gebrüder *pl*; **brother-in-law** (*pl* **brothers-in-law**) *n* Schwager *m*

brought [brɔːt] *pt*, *pp of* **bring**

brow [braʊ] *n* (*eyebrow*) (Augen)braue *f*; (*forehead*) Stirn *f*

brown [braʊn] *adj* braun; **brown bread** *n* Mischbrot *nt*; (*wholemeal*) Vollkornbrot *nt*; **brownie** ['braʊnɪ] *n* (*Gastr*) Brownie *f*; (*Brit*) junge Pfadfinderin; **brown paper** *n* Packpapier *nt*; **brown rice** *n* Naturreis *m*; **brown sugar** *n* brauner Zucker

browse [braʊz] vi (*in book*) blättern; (*in shop*) schmökern, herumschauen; **browser** *n* (*Inform*) Browser *m*

bruise [bruːz] *n* blauer Fleck ▷ vt: **to ~ one's arm** sich dat einen blauen Fleck (am Arm) holen

brunette [bruː'net] *n* Brünette *f*

brush [brʌʃ] *n* Bürste *f*; (*for sweeping*) Handbesen *m*; (*for painting*) Pinsel *m* ▷ vt bürsten; (*sweep*) fegen; **to ~ one's teeth** sich dat die Zähne putzen; **brush up** vt (*French etc*) auffrischen

Brussels sprouts [brʌsl'spraʊts] *npl* Rosenkohl *m*, Kohlsprossen *pl*

brutal ['bruːtl] *adj* brutal; **brutality** [bruː'tælɪtɪ] *n* Brutalität *f*

BSE *abbr* = **bovine spongiform encephalopathy** BSE *f*

bubble ['bʌbl] *n* Blase *f*; **bubble bath** *n* Schaumbad *nt*, Badeschaum *m*; **bubbly** ['bʌblɪ] *adj* sprudelnd; (*person*) temperamentvoll ▷ *n* (*fam*) Schampus *m*

buck [bʌk] *n* (*animal*) Bock *m*; (*US fam*) Dollar *m*

bucket ['bʌkɪt] *n* Eimer *m*

BUCKINGHAM PALACE

Der **Buckingham Palace** ist die offizielle Londoner Residenz der britischen Monarchen und liegt am St James's Park. Der Palast wurde 1703 für den Herzog von Buckingham erbaut, 1762 von George III gekauft, zwischen 1821 und 1836 von John Nash umgebaut und Anfang des 20. Jahrhunderts teilweise neu gestaltet. Teile des Buckingham Palace sind heute der Öffentlichkeit zugänglich.

buckle ['bʌkl] n Schnalle f ▷ vi (Tech) sich verbiegen ▷ vt zuschnallen

bud [bʌd] n Knospe f

Buddhism ['budɪzəm] n Buddhismus m; **Buddhist** adj buddhistisch ▷ n Buddhist(in) m(f)

buddy ['bʌdɪ] n (fam) Kumpel m

budget ['bʌdʒɪt] n Budget nt ▷ adj preisgünstig; **budget airline** n Billigflieger m

budgie ['bʌdʒɪ] n Wellensittich m

buff [bʌf] adj (US) muskulös; **in the ~** nackt ▷ n (enthusiast) Fan m

buffalo ['bʌfələʊ] n (pl -es) n Büffel m

buffer ['bʌfə°] n (a. Inform) Puffer m

buffet ['bʊfeɪ] n (food) (kaltes) Büfett nt

bug [bʌg] n (Inform) Bug m, Programmfehler m; (listening device) Wanze f; (US: insect) Insekt nt; (fam: illness) Infektion f ▷ vt (fam) nerven

bugger ['bʌgə°] n (vulg) Scheißkerl m ▷ intrj (vulg) Scheiße f; **bugger off** vi (vulg) abhauen, Leine ziehen

buggy® ['bʌgɪ] n (for baby) Buggy® m

build [bɪld] (built, built) vt bauen; **build up** vt aufbauen; **builder** n Bauunternehmer(in) m(f); **building** n Gebäude nt; **building site** n Baustelle f; **building society** n Bausparkasse f

built pt, pp of build; **built-in** adj (cupboard) Einbau-, eingebaut

bulb [bʌlb] n (Bot) (Blumen)zwiebel f; (Elec) Glühbirne f

Bulgaria [bʌl'gɛərɪə] n Bulgarien nt; **Bulgarian** adj bulgarisch ▷ n (person) Bulgare m, Bulgarin f; (language) Bulgarisch nt

bulimia [bə'lɪmɪə] n Bulimie f

bulk [bʌlk] n (mass) Masse f; (greater part) Großteil m (of +gen), **in ~** en gros; **bulky** adj (goods) sperrig; (person) stämmig

bull [bʊl] n Stier m; **bulldog** n Bulldogge f; **bulldoze** ['bʊldəʊz] vt planieren; **bulldozer** n Planierraupe f

bullet ['bʊlɪt] n Kugel f

bulletin ['bʊlɪtɪn] n Bulletin nt; (announcement) Bekanntmachung f; (Med) Krankenbericht m; **bulletin board** n (US: Inform) schwarzes Brett

bullfight ['bʊlfaɪt] n Stierkampf m; **bullshit** n (fam) Scheiß m

bully ['bʊlɪ] n Tyrann m

bum [bʌm] n (Brit fam: backside) Po m; (US: vagrant) Penner m; (worthless person) Rumtreiber m; **bum around** vi herumgammeln

bumblebee ['bʌmblbiː] n Hummel f

bumf [bʌmf] (fam) n Infomaterial nt, Papierkram m

bump [bʌmp] n (fam: swelling) Beule f; (road) Unebenheit f; (blow) Stoß m ▷ vt stoßen, **to ~ one's head** sich den Kopf anschlagen (on an +dat); **bump into** vt stoßen gegen; (fam: meet)

(zufällig) begegnen +dat; **bumper**
n (Auto) Stoßstange f ▷ adj
(edition etc) Riesen-; (crop etc)
Rekord-; **bumpy** ['bʌmpɪ] adj
holp(e)rig

bun [bʌn] n süßes Brötchen
bunch [bʌntʃ] n (of flowers)
Strauß m; (fam: of people) Haufen m;
~ **of keys** Schlüsselbund m; ~ **of
grapes** Weintraube f
bundle ['bʌndl] n Bündel nt
bungalow ['bʌŋgələʊ] n Bungalow m
bungee jumping ['bʌndʒɪ-
dʒʌmpɪŋ] n Bungeejumping nt
bunk [bʌŋk] n Koje f; **bunk
bed(s)** n(pl) Etagenbett nt
bunker ['bʌŋkəᵊ] n (Mil) Bunker
m
bunny ['bʌnɪ] n Häschen nt
buoy [bɔɪ] n Boje f; **buoyant**
['bɔɪənt] adj (floating)
schwimmend
BUPA ['bu:pə] abbr (Brit) private
Krankenkasse
burden ['bɜ:dn] n Last f
bureau ['bjʊərəʊ] n Büro nt;
(government department) Amt nt;
bureaucracy [bjʊ'rɒkrəsɪ] n
Bürokratie f; **bureaucratic**
[bjʊərə'krætɪk] adj bürokratisch;
bureau de change ['bjʊərəʊ də
'ʃɑ̃:ʒ] n Wechselstube f
burger ['bɜ:gəᵊ] n Hamburger m
burglar ['bɜ:gləᵊ] n Einbre-
cher(in) m(f); **burglar alarm** n
Alarmanlage f; **burglarize** vt (US)
einbrechen in +akk; **burglary** n
Einbruch m; **burgle** ['bɜ:gl] vt
einbrechen in +akk
burial ['berɪəl] n Beerdigung f
burn [bɜ:n] (**burnt** o **burned**,
burnt o **burned**) vt verbrennen;
(food, slightly) anbrennen; **to
~ one's hand** sich auf die Hand
verbrennen ▷ vi brennen ▷ n
(injury) Brandwunde f; (on material)

verbrannte Stelle; **burn down** vt,
vi abbrennen
burp [bɜ:p] vi rülpsen ▷ vt (baby)
aufstoßen lassen
bursary ['bɜ:sərɪ] n Stipendium nt
burst [bɜ:st] (**burst, burst**) vt
platzen lassen ▷ vi platzen;
to ~ into tears in Tränen
ausbrechen
bury ['berɪ] vt begraben; (in grave)
beerdigen; (hide) vergraben
bus [bʌs] n Bus m; **bus driver** n
Busfahrer(in) m(f)
bush [bʊʃ] n Busch m
business ['bɪznɪs] n Geschäft nt;
(enterprise) Unternehmen nt;
(concern, affair) Sache f; **I'm here on
~** ich bin geschäftlich hier; **it's
none of your ~** das geht dich
nichts an; **business card** n
Visitenkarte f; **business class** n
(Aviat) Businessclass f;
businessman (pl **-men**) n
Geschäftsmann m; **business
studies** npl Betriebswirtschaft-
slehre f; **businesswoman** (pl
-women) n Geschäftsfrau f
bus service n Busverbindung f;
bus shelter n Wartehäuschen nt;
bus station n Busbahnhof m; **bus
stop** n Bushaltestelle f
bust [bʌst] n Büste f ▷ adj
(broken) kaputt; **to go ~** Pleite
gehen; **bust-up** n (fam) Krach m
busy ['bɪzɪ] adj beschäftigt;
(street, place) belebt; (esp US:
telephone) besetzt; **~ signal** (US)
Besetztzeichen nt

KEYWORD

but [bʌt, bət] conj **1** (yet) aber; **not
X but Y** nicht X sondern Y
2 (however) **I'd love to come, but
I'm busy** ich würde gern kommen,
bin aber beschäftigt
3 (showing disagreement, surprise etc)

but that's fantastic! (aber) das ist ja fantastisch!

▷ *prep (apart from, except)*: **nothing but trouble** nichts als Ärger; **no-one but him can do it** niemand außer ihm kann es machen; **but for you/your help** ohne dich/deine Hilfe; **anything but that** alles, nur das nicht

▷ *adv (just, only)* **she's but a child** sie ist noch ein Kind; **had I but known** wenn ich es nur gewusst hätte; **I can but try** ich kann es immerhin versuchen; **all but finished** so gut wie fertig

butcher ['bʊtʃə'] *n* Fleischer(in) *m(f)*, Metzger(in) *m(f)*

butler ['bʌtlə'] *n* Butler *m*

butt [bʌt] *(cigarette)* *n* Hintern *m*

butter ['bʌtə'] *n* Butter *f* ▷ *vt* buttern; **buttercup** *n* Butterblume *f*; **butterfly** *n* Schmetterling *m*

buttocks ['bʌtəks] *npl* Gesäß *nt*

button ['bʌtn] *n* Knopf *m*; *(badge)* Button *m* ▷ *vt* zuknöpfen; **buttonhole** *n* Knopfloch *nt*

buy [baɪ] *n* Kauf *m* ▷ *vt (bought, bought)* kaufen *(from von)*; **he bought me a ring** er hat mir einen Ring gekauft; **buyer** *n* Käufer(in) *m(f)*

buzz [bʌz] *n* Summen *nt*; **to give sb a ~** *(fam)* jdn anrufen ▷ *vi* summen; **buzzer** ['bʌzə'] *n* Summer *m*; **buzz word** *n (fam)* Modewort *nt*

KEYWORD

by [baɪ] *prep* **1** *(referring to cause, agent)* von, durch; **killed by lightning** vom Blitz getötet; **a painting by Picasso** ein Gemälde von Picasso

2 *(referring to method, manner)* **by**

bus/car/train mit dem Bus/Auto/Zug; **to pay by cheque** per Scheck bezahlen; **by moonlight** bei Mondschein; **by saving hard, he ...** indem er eisern sparte, ... er ...

3 *(via, through)* über +*akk*; **he came in by the back door** er kam durch die Hintertür herein

4 *(close to, past)* bei, an +*dat*; **a holiday by the sea** ein Urlaub am Meer; **she rushed by** sie eilte an mir vorbei

5 *(not later than)* **by 4 o'clock** bis 4 Uhr; **by this time tomorrow** morgen um diese Zeit; **by the time I got here it was too late** als ich hier ankam, war es zu spät

6 *(during)* **by day** bei Tag

7 *(amount)* **by the kilo/metre** kiloweise/meterweise; **paid by the hour** stundenweise bezahlt

8 *(math, measure)* **to divide by 3** durch 3 teilen; **to multiply by 3** mit 3 malnehmen; **a room 3 metres by 4** ein Zimmer 3 mal 4 Meter; **it's broader by a metre** es ist (um) einen Meter breiter

9 *(according to)* nach; **it's all right by me** von mir aus gern

10 *(all) by oneself etc* ganz allein

11 by the way übrigens

▷ *adv* **1** *see* **go**; **pass** *etc*

2 by and by irgendwann; *(with past tenses)* nach einiger Zeit; **by and large** *(on the whole)* im Großen und Ganzen

bye-bye ['baɪ'baɪ] *interj (fam)* Wiedersehen, tschüss

by-election *n* Nachwahl *f*; **bypass** *n* Umgehungsstraße *f*; *(Med)* Bypass *m*; **byproduct** *n* Nebenprodukt *nt*; **byroad** *n* Nebenstraße *f*; **bystander** *n* Zuschauer(in) *m(f)*

byte [baɪt] *n* Byte *nt*

C

C [siː] *abbr* = **Celsius** C
c *abbr* = **circa** ca
cab [kæb] *n* Taxi *nt*
cabbage ['kæbɪdʒ] *n* Kohl *m*
cabin ['kæbɪn] *n* (Naut) Kajüte *f*; (Aviat) Passagierraum *m*; (wooden house) Hütte *f*; **cabin crew** *n* Flugbegleitpersonal *nt*; **cabin cruiser** *n* Kajütboot *nt*
cabinet ['kæbɪnɪt] *n* Schrank *m*; (for display) Vitrine *f*; (Pol) Kabinett *nt*
cable ['keɪbl] *n* (Elec) Kabel *nt*; **cable-car** *n* Seilbahn *f*; **cable railway** *n* Drahtseilbahn *f*; **cable television**, **cablevision** (US) *n* Kabelfernsehen *nt*
cactus ['kæktəs] *n* Kaktus *m*
CAD *abbr* = **computer-aided design** CAD *nt*
Caesarean [siːˈzɛərɪən] *adj*: **~ (section)** Kaiserschnitt *m*
café ['kæfeɪ] *n* Café *nt*; **cafeteria** [kæfɪˈtɪərɪə] *n* Cafeteria *f*; **cafetiere** [kæfəˈtjɛəʳ] *n* Kaffeebereiter *m*
cage [keɪdʒ] *n* Käfig *m*
Cairo ['kaɪərəʊ] *n* Kairo *nt*
cake [keɪk] *n* Kuchen *m*; **cake shop** *n* Konditorei *f*
calamity [kəˈlæmɪtɪ] *n* Katastrophe *f*
calculate ['kælkjʊleɪt] *vt* berechnen; (estimate) kalkulieren; **calculating** *adj* berechnend; **calculation** [kælkjʊˈleɪʃən] *n* Berechnung *f*; (estimate) Kalkulation *f*; **calculator** ['kælkjʊleɪtəʳ] *n* Taschenrechner *m*
calendar ['kælɪndəʳ] *n* Kalender *m*
calf [kɑːf] (*pl* **calves**) *n* Kalb *nt*; (Anat) Wade *f*
California [kælɪˈfɔːnɪə] *n* Kalifornien *nt*
call [kɔːl] *vt* rufen; (name, describe as) nennen; (Tel) anrufen; (Inform, Aviat) aufrufen; **what's this ~ed?** wie heißt das?; **that's what I ~ service** das nenne ich guten Service ▷ *vi* (shout) rufen (for help um Hilfe); (visit) vorbeikommen; **to ~ at the doctor's** beim Arzt vorbeigehen; (of train) **to ~ at ...** in ... halten ▷ *n* (shout) Ruf *m*; (Tel) Anruf; (Inform, Aviat) Aufruf *m*; **to make a ~** telefonieren; **to give sb a ~** jdn anrufen; **to be on ~** Bereitschaftsdienst haben; **call back** *vt, vi* zurückrufen; **call for** *vt* (come to pick up) abholen; (demand, require) verlangen; **call off** *vt* absagen
call centre *n* Callcenter *nt*; **caller** *n* Besucher(in) *m(f)*; (Tel) Anrufer(in) *m(f)*
calm [kɑːm] *n* Stille *f*; (also of person) Ruhe *f*; (of sea) Flaute *f* ▷ *vt*

beruhigen ▷ adj ruhig; **calm down** vi sich beruhigen

calorie ['kælərɪ] n Kalorie f

calves [kɑːvz] pl of **calf**

Cambodia [kæm'bəʊdɪə] n Kambodscha nt

camcorder ['kæmkɔːdə°] n Camcorder m

came [keɪm] pt of **come**

camel ['kæməl] n Kamel nt

camera ['kæmərə] n Fotoapparat m, Kamera f; **camera phone** ['kæmərəfəʊn] n Fotohandy nt

camomile ['kæməmaɪl] n Kamille f

camouflage ['kæməflɑːʒ] n Tarnung f

camp [kæmp] n Lager nt; (camping place) Zeltplatz m ▷ vi zelten, campen ▷ adj (fam) theatralisch, tuntig

campaign [kæm'peɪn] n Kampagne f; (Pol) Wahlkampf m ▷ vi sich einsetzen (for/against für/gegen)

campbed ['kæmpbed] n Campingliege f; **camper** ['kæmpə°] n (person) Camper(in) m(f); (van) Wohnmobil nt; **camping** ['kæmpɪŋ] n Zelten nt, Camping nt; **campsite** ['kæmpsaɪt] n Zeltplatz m, Campingplatz m

campus ['kæmpəs] n (of university) Universitätsgelände nt, Campus m

KEYWORD

can [kæn] (negative **cannot, can't**, conditional **could**) vb aux **1** (be able to, know how to) können; **I can see you tomorrow, if you like** ich könnte Sie morgen sehen, wenn Sie wollen; **I can swim** ich kann schwimmen; **can you speak German?** sprechen Sie Deutsch?

2 (may) können, dürfen; **could I have a word with you?** könnte ich Sie kurz sprechen?

Canada ['kænədə] n Kanada nt; **Canadian** [kə'neɪdɪən] adj kanadisch ▷ n Kanadier(in) m(f)

canal [kə'næl] n Kanal m

canary [kə'neərɪ] n Kanarienvogel m

cancel ['kænsəl] vt (plans) aufgeben; (meeting, event) absagen; (Comm: order etc) stornieren; (contract) kündigen; (inform) löschen; (Aviat: flight) streichen; **to be ~led** (event, train, bus) ausfallen; **cancellation** [kænsə'leɪʃən] n Absage f; (Comm) Stornierung f; (Aviat) gestrichener Flug

cancer ['kænsə°] n (Med) Krebs m; **Cancer** n (Astr) Krebs m

candid ['kændɪd] adj (person, conversation) offen

candidate ['kændɪdət] n (for post) Bewerber(in) m(f); (Pol) Kandidat(in) m(f)

candle ['kændl] n Kerze f; **candlelight** n Kerzenlicht nt; **candlestick** n Kerzenhalter m

candy ['kændɪ] n (US) Bonbon nt; (quantity) Süßigkeiten pl; **candy-floss** n (Brit) Zuckerwatte f

cane [keɪn] n Rohr nt; (stick) Stock m

cannabis ['kænəbɪs] n Cannabis m

canned [kænd] adj Dosen-

cannot ['kænɒt] contr of **can not**

canny ['kænɪ] adj (shrewd) schlau

canoe [kə'nuː] n Kanu nt; **canoeing** n Kanufahren nt

can opener ['kænəʊpnə°] n Dosenöffner m

canopy ['kænəpɪ] n Baldachin m; (awning) Markise f; (over entrance) Vordach nt

can't [kɑːnt] *contr of* **can not**

canteen [kæn'tiːn] *n (in factory)* Kantine *f*; *(in university)* Mensa *f*

canvas ['kænvəs] *n (for sails, shoes)* Segeltuch *nt*; *(for tent)* Zeltstoff *m*; *(for painting)* Leinwand *f*

canvass ['kænvəs] *vi* um Stimmen werben *(for* für)

canyon ['kænjən] *n* Felsenschlucht *f*; **canyoning** ['kænjənɪŋ] *n* Canyoning *nt*

cap [kæp] *n* Mütze *f*; *(lid)* Verschluss *m*, Deckel *m*

capability [keɪpə'bɪlɪtɪ] *n* Fähigkeit *f*; **capable** ['keɪpəbl] *adj* fähig; **to be ~ of sth** zu etw fähig (*o* imstande) sein; **to be ~ of doing sth** etw tun können

capacity [kə'pæsɪtɪ] *n (of building, container)* Fassungsvermögen *nt*; *(ability)* Fähigkeit *f*; *(function)* **in his ~ as ...** in seiner Eigenschaft als ...

cape [keɪp] *n (garment)* Cape *nt*, Umhang *m*; *(Geo)* Kap *nt*

caper ['keɪpə°] *n (for cooking)* Kaper *f*

capital ['kæpɪtl] *n (Fin)* Kapital *nt*; *(letter)* Großbuchstabe *m*; **~ (city)** Hauptstadt *f*; **capitalism** *n* Kapitalismus *m*; **capital punishment** *n* die Todesstrafe

Capricorn ['kæprɪkɔːn] *n (Astr)* Steinbock *m*

capsize [kæp'saɪz] *vi* kentern

capsule ['kæpsjuːl] *n* Kapsel *f*

captain ['kæptɪn] *n* Kapitän *m*; *(army)* Hauptmann *m*

caption ['kæpʃən] *n* Bildunterschrift *f*

captive ['kæptɪv] *n* Gefangene(r) *mf*; **capture** ['kæptʃə°] *vt (person)* fassen, gefangen nehmen; *(town etc)* einnehmen; *(Inform: data)* erfassen ▷ *n* Gefangennahme *f*; *(Inform)* Erfassung *f*

car [kɑː°] *n* Auto *nt*; *(US Rail)* Wagen *m*

carafe [kə'ræf] *n* Karaffe *f*

caramel ['kærəmel] *n* Karamelle *f*

caravan ['kærəvæn] *n* Wohnwagen *m*; **caravan site** *n* Campingplatz *m* für Wohnwagen

caraway (seed) ['kærəweɪ] *n* Kümmel *m*

carbohydrate [kɑːbəʊ'haɪdreɪt] *n* Kohle(n)hydrat *nt*

car bomb *n* Autobombe *f*

carbon ['kɑːbən] *n* Kohlenstoff *m*

car boot sale *n auf einem Parkplatz stattfindender Flohmarkt*

carburettor, carburetor (US) ['kɑːbjʊretə°] *n* Vergaser *m*

card [kɑːd] *n* Karte *f*; *(material)* Pappe *f*; **cardboard** *n* Pappe *f*; **~ (box)** Karton *m (smaller)* Pappschachtel *f*; **card game** *n* Kartenspiel *nt*

cardigan ['kɑːdɪgən] *n* Strickjacke *f*

card index *n* Kartei *f*; **cardphone** ['kɑːdfəʊn] *n* Kartentelefon *nt*

care [keə°] *n (worry)* Sorge *f*; *(carefulness)* Sorgfalt *f*; *(looking after things, people)* Pflege *f*; **with ~** sorgfältig; *(cautiously)* vorsichtig; **to take ~ (watch out)** vorsichtig sein; *(in address)* **~ of** bei; **to take ~ of** sorgen für, sich kümmern um ▷ *vi*: **I don't ~** es ist mir egal; **to ~ about sth** Wert auf etw akk legen; **he ~s about her** sie liegt ihm am Herzen; **care for** *vt (look after)* sorgen für, sich kümmern um; *(like)* mögen

career [kə'rɪə°] *n* Karriere *f*, Laufbahn *f*; **career woman** *(pl* **women)** *n* Karrierefrau *f*; **careers adviser** *n* Berufsberater(in) *m(f)*

carefree ['keəfriː] *adj* sorgenfrei; **careful, carefully** *adj, adv* sorgfältig; *(cautious, cautiously)*

vorsichtig; **careless, carelessly**
adj, adv nachlässig; (driving etc)
leichtsinnig; (remark)
unvorsichtig; **carer** ['kɛərə°] n
Betreuer(in) m(f), Pfleger(in) m(f);
caretaker ['kɔɔteɪkə°] n Haus-
meister(in) m(f); **careworker** n
Pfleger(in) m(f)
car-ferry ['kɑːferɪ] n Autofähre f
cargo ['kɑːgəʊ] (pl -(e)s) n
Ladung f
car hire, car hire company n
Autovermietung f
Caribbean [kærɪ'biːən] n Karibik
f ▷ adj karibisch
caring ['kɛərɪŋ] adj mitfühlend;
(parent, partner) liebevoll; (looking
after sb) fürsorglich
car insurance n
Kraftfahrzeugversicherung f
carnation [kɑː'neɪʃən] n Nelke f
carnival ['kɑːnɪvəl] n Volksfest
nt; (before Lent) Karneval m
carol ['kærəl] n Weihnachtslied nt
carp [kɑːp] n (fish) Karpfen m
car park n (Brit) Parkplatz m;
(multi-storey car park) Parkhaus nt
carpenter ['kɑːpəntə°] n Zimmermann m
carpet ['kɑːpɪt] n Teppich m
car phone n Autotelefon nt;
carpool n Fahrgemeinschaft f
(vehicles) Fuhrpark m ▷ vi eine
Fahrgemeinschaft bilden; **car
rental** n Autovermietung f
carriage ['kærɪdʒ] n (Brit Rail:
coach) Wagen m; (compartment)
Abteil nt; (horse-drawn) Kutsche f;
(transport) Beförderung f;
carriageway n (Brit: on road)
Fahrbahn f
carrier ['kærɪə°] n (Comm)
Spediteur(in) m(f); **carrier bag** n
Tragetasche f
carrot ['kærət] n Karotte f
carry ['kærɪ] vt tragen; (in vehicle)
befördern; (have on one) bei sich

haben; **carry on** vi (continue)
weitermachen; (fam: make a scene)
ein Theater machen ▷ vt
(continue) fortführen; **to ~ on
working** weiter arbeiten; **carry
out** vt (orders, plan) ausführen,
durchführen
carrycot n Babytragetasche f
carsick ['kɑːsɪk] adj: **he gets
~** ihm wird beim Autofahren übel
cart [kɑːt] n Wagen m, Karren m;
(US: shopping trolley)
Einkaufswagen m
carton ['kɑːtən] n (Papp)karton
m; (of cigarettes) Stange f
cartoon [kɑː'tuːn] n Cartoon m o
nt; (one drawing) Karikatur f; (film
[Zeichen])trickfilm m
cartridge ['kɑːtrɪdʒ] n (for film)
Kassette f; (for gun, pen, printer)
Patrone f; (for copier) Kartusche f
carve [kɑːv] vt, vi (wood)
schnitzen; (stone) meißeln; (meat)
schneiden, tranchieren; **carving** n
(in wood) Schnitzerei f; (in stone)
Skulptur f; (Ski) Carving nt
car wash n Autowaschanlage f
case [keɪs] n (crate) Kiste f; (box)
Schachtel f; (for jewels) Schatulle f;
(for spectacles) Etui nt; (Jur, matter)
Fall m; **in ~** falls; **in that ~** in dem
Fall; **in ~ of fire** bei Brand; **it's a
~ of ...** es handelt sich hier um ...
cash [kæʃ] n Bargeld nt; **in ~** bar;
~ on delivery per Nachnahme
▷ vt (cheque) einlösen; **cash desk**
n Kasse f; **cash dispenser** n
Geldautomat m; **cashier** [kæ'ʃɪə°]
n Kassierer(in) m(f); **cash
machine** n (Brit) Geldautomat m
cashmere ['kæʃmɪə°] n Kasch-
mirwolle f
cash payment n Barzahlung f;
cashpoint n (Brit) Geldautomat m
casing ['keɪsɪŋ] n Gehäuse nt
casino [kə'siːnəʊ] (pl -s) n
Kasino nt

cask [kɑːsk] n Fass nt

casserole ['kæsərəʊl] n Kasserole f; (food) Schmortopf m

cassette [kæ'set] n Kassette f; **cassette recorder** n Kassettenrekorder m

cast [kɑːst] (**cast, cast**) vt (throw) werfen; (Theat, Cine) besetzen; (roles) verteilen ▷ n (Theat, Cine) Besetzung f; (Med) Gipsverband m; **cast off** vi (Naut) losmachen

caster ['kɑːstə°] n: ~ **sugar** Streuzucker m

castle ['kɑːsl] n Burg f

castrate [kæs'treɪt] vt kastrieren

casual ['kæʒjʊəl] adj (arrangement, remark) beiläufig; (attitude, manner) (nach)lässig, zwanglos; (dress) leger; (work, earnings) Gelegenheits-; (look, glance) flüchtig; ~ **wear** Freizeitkleidung f; ~ **sex** Gelegenheitssex m; **casually** adv (remark, say) beiläufig; (meet) zwanglos; (dressed) leger

casualty ['kæʒjʊəltɪ] n Verletzte(r) mf; (dead) Tote(r) mf; (department in hospital) Notaufnahme f

cat [kæt] n Katze f; (male) Kater m

catalog (US), **catalogue** ['kætəlɒg] n Katalog m ▷ vt katalogisieren

cataract ['kætərækt] n Wasserfall m; (Med) grauer Star

catarrh [kə'tɑː°] n Katarr(h) m

catastrophe [kə'tæstrəfɪ] n Katastrophe f

catch [kætʃ] n (fish etc) Fang m ▷ vt (**caught, caught**) fangen; (thief) fassen; (train, bus etc) nehmen; (not miss) erreichen; **to ~ a cold** sich erkälten; **to ~ fire** Feuer fangen; **I didn't ~ that** das habe ich nicht verstanden; **catch on** vi (become popular) Anklang finden; **catch up** vt, vi: **to ~ with**

sb jdn einholen; **to ~ on sth** etw nachholen; **catching** adj ansteckend

category ['kætɪgərɪ] n Kategorie f

cater ['keɪtə°] vi die Speisen und Getränke liefern (for für); **cater for** vt (have facilities for) eingestellt sein auf +akk; **catering** n Versorgung f mit Speisen und Getränken, Gastronomie f; **catering service** n Partyservice m

caterpillar ['kætəpɪlə°] n Raupe f

cathedral [kə'θiːdrəl] n Kathedrale f, Dom m

Catholic ['kæθəlɪk] adj katholisch ▷ Katholik(in) m(f)

cat nap n (Brit) kurzer Schlaf; **cat's eyes** ['kætsaɪz] npl (in road) Katzenaugen pl, Reflektoren pl

catsup ['kætsəp] n (US) Ketchup nt o m

cattle ['kætl] npl Vieh nt

caught [kɔːt] pt, pp of **catch**

cauliflower ['kɒlɪflaʊə°] n Blumenkohl m; **cauliflower cheese** n Blumenkohl m in Käsesoße

cause [kɔːz] n (origin) Ursache f (of für); (reason) Grund m (for zu); (purpose) Sache f; **for a good ~** für wohltätige Zwecke; **no ~ for alarm/complaint** kein Grund zur Aufregung/Klage ▷ vt verursachen

causeway ['kɔːzweɪ] n Damm m

caution ['kɔːʃən] n Vorsicht f; (Jur, Sport) Verwarnung f ▷ vt (ver)warnen; **cautious** ['kɔːʃəs] adj vorsichtig

cave [keɪv] n Höhle f; **cave in** vi einstürzen

cavity ['kævɪtɪ] n Hohlraum m; (in tooth) Loch nt

cayenne (pepper) ['keɪ'en] n Cayennepfeffer m

chart [tʃɑːt] n Diagramm nt;
(map) Karte f; **the ~s** pl die Charts,
die Hitliste

charter ['tʃɑːtə°] n Urkunde f
▷ vt (Naut, Aviat) chartern;
charter flight n Charterflug m

chase [tʃeɪs] vt jagen, verfolgen
▷ n Verfolgungsjagd f; (hunt) Jagd f

chassis ['ʃæsɪ] n (Auto)
Fahrgestell nt

chat [tʃæt] vi plaudern; (Inform)
chatten ▷ n Plauderei f; **chat up**
vt anmachen, anbaggern;
chatroom n (Inform) Chatroom
m; **chat show** n Talkshow f;
chatty adj geschwätzig

chauffeur ['ʃəʊfə°] n Chauf-
feur(in) m(f), Fahrer(in) m(f)

cheap [tʃiːp] adj billig; (of poor
quality) minderwertig

cheat [tʃiːt] vt, vi betrügen; (in
school, game) mogeln

Chechen ['tʃetʃen] adj
tschetschenisch ▷ n Tschet-
schene m, Tschetschenin f;
Chechnya ['tʃetʃnɪə] n Tschetschenien nt

check [tʃek] vt (examine)
überprüfen (for auf +akk); (Tech:
adjustment etc) kontrollieren; (US:
tick) abhaken; (Aviat: luggage)
einchecken; (US: coat) abgeben
▷ n (examination, restraint)
Kontrolle f; (US: restaurant bill)
Rechnung f; (pattern) Karo(muster)
nt; (US) see **cheque**; **check in** vi, vt
(Aviat) einchecken; (into hotel) sich
anmelden; **check out** vi sich
abmelden, auschecken; **check up**
vi nachprüfen; **to ~ on sb**
Nachforschungen über jdn
anstellen

checkers ['tʃekəz] nsing (US)
Damespiel nt

check-in ['tʃekɪn] n (airport)
Check-in m; (hotel) Anmeldung f;
check-in desk n

Abfertigungsschalter m; **checking
account** n (US) Scheckkonto nt;
check list n Kontrollliste f;
checkout n (supermarket) Kasse f;
checkout time n (hotel)
Abreise(zeit) f; **checkpoint** n
Kontrollpunkt m; **checkroom** n
(US) Gepäckaufbewahrung f;
checkup n (Med) (ärztliche)
Untersuchung

cheddar ['tʃedə°] n Cheddarkäse
m

cheek [tʃiːk] n Backe f, Wange f;
(insolence) Frechheit f; **what a ~** so
eine Frechheit!; **cheekbone** n
Backenknochen m; **cheeky** adj
frech

cheer [tʃɪə°] n Beifallsruf m,
(when drinking) prost!; (Brit fam:
thanks) danke; (Brit: goodbye)
tschüs ▷ vt zujubeln +dat ▷ vi
jubeln; **cheer up** vt aufmuntern
▷ vi fröhlicher werden; **~!** Kopf
hoch!; **cheerful** ['tʃɪəfʊl] adj
fröhlich

cheese [tʃiːz] n Käse m;
cheeseboard n Käsebrett nt; (as
course) (gemischte) Käseplatte;
cheesecake n Käsekuchen m

chef [ʃef] n Koch m; (in charge of
kitchen) Küchenchef(in) m(f)

chemical ['kemɪkəl] adj chemisch ▷ Chemikalie f; **chemist**
['kemɪst] n (pharmacist)
Apotheker(in) m(f); (industrial
chemist) Chemiker(in) m(f); **~'s**
(shop) Apotheke f; **chemistry** n
Chemie f

cheque [tʃek] n (Brit) Scheck m;
cheque account n (Brit)
Girokonto nt; **cheque book** n
(Brit) Scheckheft nt; **cheque card**
n (Brit) Scheckkarte f

chequered ['tʃekəd] adj kariert

cherish ['tʃerɪʃ] vt (look after)
liebevoll sorgen für; (hope) hegen;
(memory) bewahren

cherry ['tʃerɪ] n Kirsche f; **cherry tomato** (pl **-es**) n Kirschtomate f

chess [tʃes] n Schach nt; **chessboard** n Schachbrett nt

chest [tʃest] n Brust f; (box) Kiste f; **~ of drawers** Kommode f

chestnut ['tʃesnʌt] n Kastanie f

chew [tʃuː] vt, vi kauen; **chewing gum** n Kaugummi m

chick [tʃɪk] n Küken nt; **chicken** n Huhn nt; (food: roast) Hähnchen nt; (coward) Feigling m; **chicken breast** n Hühnerbrust f; **chicken Kiev** n paniertes Hähnchen, mit Knoblauchbutter gefüllt; **chickenpox** n Windpocken pl; **chickpea** n Kichererbse f

chicory ['tʃɪkərɪ] n Chicorée f

chief [tʃiːf] n (of department etc) Leiter(in) m(f); (boss) Chef(in) m(f); (of tribe) Häuptling m ▷ adj Haupt-; **chiefly** adv hauptsächlich

child [tʃaɪld] (pl **children**) n Kind nt; **child abuse** n Kindesmisshandlung f; **child allowance**, **child benefit** (Brit) n Kindergeld nt; **childbirth** n Geburt f, Entbindung f; **childhood** n Kindheit f; **childish** adj kindisch; **child lock** n Kindersicherung f; **childproof** adj kindersicher; **children** ['tʃɪldrən] pl of **child**; **child seat** n Kindersitz m

Chile ['tʃɪlɪ] n Chile nt

chill [tʃɪl] n Kühle f; (Med) Erkältung f ▷ vt (wine) kühlen; **chill out** vi (fam) chillen, relaxen; **chilled** adj gekühlt

chilli ['tʃɪlɪ] n Pepperoni pl; (spice) Chili m; **chilli con carne** ['tʃɪlɪkɒn'kɑːnɪ] n Chili con carne nt

chilly ['tʃɪlɪ] adj kühl, frostig

chimney ['tʃɪmnɪ] n Schornstein m; **chimneysweep** n Schornsteinfeger(in) m(f)

chimpanzee [tʃɪmpæn'ziː] n Schimpanse m

chin [tʃɪn] n Kinn nt

china ['tʃaɪnə] n Porzellan nt

China ['tʃaɪnə] n China nt; **Chinese** [tʃaɪ'niːz] adj chinesisch ▷ n (person) Chinese m, Chinesin f; (language) Chinesisch nt; **Chinese leaves** npl Chinakohl m

chip [tʃɪp] n (of wood etc) Splitter m; (damage) angeschlagene Stelle; (Inform) Chip m; **~s** (Brit: potatoes) Pommes (frites) pl; (US: crisps) Kartoffelchips pl ▷ vt anschlagen, beschädigen; **chippie** (fam), **chip shop** n Frittenbude f

chiropodist [kɪ'rɒpədɪst] n Fußpfleger(in) m(f)

chirp [tʃɜːp] vi zwitschern

chisel ['tʃɪzl] n Meißel m

chitchat ['tʃɪttʃæt] n Gerede nt

chives ['tʃaɪvz] npl Schnittlauch m

chlorine ['klɔːriːn] n Chlor nt

chocaholic, **chocoholic** [tʃɒkə'hɒlɪk] n Schokoladenfreak m; **choc-ice** ['tʃɒkaɪs] n Eis nt mit Schokoladenüberzug; **chocolate** ['tʃɒklɪt] n Schokolade f; (chocolate-coated sweet) Praline f; **a bar of ~** eine Tafel Schokolade; **a box of ~s** eine Schachtel Pralinen; **chocolate cake** n Schokoladenkuchen m; **chocolate sauce** n Schokoladensoße f

choice [tʃɔɪs] n Wahl f; (selection) Auswahl f ▷ adj auserlesen; (product) Qualitäts-

choir ['kwaɪə] n Chor m

choke [tʃəʊk] vi sich verschlucken; (Sport) die Nerven verlieren ▷ vt erdrosseln ▷ n (Auto) Choke m

cholera ['kɒlərə] n Cholera f

cholesterol [kə'lestərəl] n Cholesterin nt

choose [tʃuːz] (**chose, chosen**) vt wählen; (pick out) sich aussuchen; **there are three to ~ from** es stehen drei zur Auswahl

chop [tʃɒp] vt (7er)hacken; (meat etc) klein schneiden ▷ n (meat) Kotelett nt; **to get the ~** gefeuert werden; **chopper** n Hackbeil nt; (fam: helicopter) Hubschrauber m; **chopsticks** npl Essstäbchen pl

chorus ['kɔːrəs] n Chor m; (in song) Refrain m

chose, chosen [tʃəʊz, 'tʃəʊzn] pt, pp of **choose**

chowder ['tʃaʊdə°] n (US) dicke Suppe mit Meeresfrüchten

christen ['krɪsn] vt taufen; **christening** n Taufe f; **Christian** ['krɪstɪən] adj christlich ▷ n Christ(in) m(f); **Christian name** n (Brit) Vorname m

Christmas ['krɪsməs] n Weihnachten pl; **Christmas bonus** n Weihnachtsgeld nt; **Christmas card** n Weihnachtskarte f; **Christmas carol** n Weihnachtslied nt; **Christmas Day** n der erste Weihnachtstag; **Christmas Eve** n Heiligabend m; **Christmas pudding** n Plumpudding m; **Christmas tree** n Weihnachtsbaum m

chronic ['krɒnɪk] adj (Med, fig) chronisch; (fam: very bad) miserabel

chrysanthemum [krɪ'sænθɪməm] n Chrysantheme f

chubby ['tʃʌbɪ] adj (child) pummelig; (adult) rundlich

chuck [tʃʌk] vt (fam) schmeißen; **chuck in** vt (fam: job) hinschmeißen; **chuck out** vt (fam) rausschmeißen; **chuck up** vi (fam) kotzen

chunk [tʃʌŋk] n Klumpen m; (of bread) Brocken m; (of meat) Batzen m; **chunky** adj (person) stämmig

Chunnel ['tʃʌnəl] n (fam) Kanaltunnel m

church [tʃɜːtʃ] n Kirche f; **churchyard** n Kirchhof m

chute [ʃuːt] n Rutsche f

chutney ['tʃʌtnɪ] n Chutney m

CIA abbr = **Central Intelligence Agency** (US) CIA f

CID abbr = **Criminal Investigation Department** (Brit) ≈ Kripo f

cider ['saɪdə°] n ≈ Apfelmost m

cigar [sɪ'gɑː°] n Zigarre f; **cigarette** [sɪgə'ret] n Zigarette f

cinema ['sɪnəmə] n Kino nt

cinnamon ['sɪnəmən] n Zimt m

circle ['sɜːkl] n Kreis m ▷ vi kreisen; **circuit** ['sɜːkɪt] n Rundfahrt f; (on foot) Rundgang m; (for racing) Rennstrecke f; (Elec) Stromkreis m; **circular** ['sɜːkjʊlə°] adj (kreis)rund, kreisförmig ▷ n Rundschreiben nt; **circulation** [sɜːkjʊ'leɪʃən] n (of blood) Kreislauf m; (of newspaper) Auflage f

circumstances ['sɜːkəmstənsəz] npl (facts) Umstände pl; (financial condition) Verhältnisse pl; **in/under the ~** unter den Umständen; **under no ~** auf keinen Fall

circus ['sɜːkəs] n Zirkus m

cissy ['sɪsɪ] n (fam) Weichling m

cistern ['sɪstən] n Zisterne f; (of WC) Spülkasten m

citizen ['sɪtɪzn] n Bürger(in) m(f); (of nation) Staatsangehörige(r) mf; **citizenship** n Staatsangehörigkeit f

city ['sɪtɪ] n Stadt f; (large) Großstadt f; **the ~** (London's financial centre) die (Londoner)

City; **city centre** n Innenstadt f, Zentrum nt

civil ['sɪvl] adj (of town) Bürger-; (of state) staatsbürgerlich; (not military) zivil; **civil ceremony** n standesamtliche Hochzeit; **civil engineering** n Hoch- und Tiefbau m, Bauingenieurwesen nt; **civilian** [sɪ'vɪljən] n Zivilist(in) m(f); **civilization** [sɪvɪlaɪ'zeɪʃən] n Zivilisation f, Kultur f; **civilized** ['sɪvɪlaɪzd] adj zivilisiert, kultiviert; **civil partnership** n eingetragene Partnerschaft; **civil rights** npl Bürgerrechte pl; **civil servant** n (Staats)beamte(r) m, (Staats)beamtin f; **civil service** n Staatsdienst m; **civil war** n Bürgerkrieg m

CJD abbr = **Creutzfeld-Jakob disease** Creutzfeld-Jakob-Krankheit f

cl abbr = **centilitre(s)** cl

claim [kleɪm] vt beanspruchen; (apply for) beantragen; (demand) fordern; (assert) behaupten (that dass) ▷ n (demand) Forderung f (for für); (right) Anspruch m (to auf +akk); **~ for damages** Schadensersatzforderung f; **to make** o **put in a ~** (insurance) Ansprüche geltend machen; **claimant** n Antragsteller(in) m(f)

clam [klæm] n Venusmuschel f; **clam chowder** n (US) dicke Muschelsuppe (mit Sellerie, Zwiebeln etc)

clap [klæp] vi (Beifall) klatschen

claret ['klærɪt] n roter Bordeaux(wein)

clarify ['klærɪfaɪ] vt klären

clarinet [klærɪ'net] n Klarinette f

clarity ['klærɪtɪ] n Klarheit f

clash [klæʃ] n (physically) zusammenstoßen (with mit); (argue) sich auseinandersetzen (with mit); (fig: colours) sich beißen ▷ n Zusammenstoß m; (argument) Auseinandersetzung f

clasp [klɑːsp] n (on belt) Schnalle f

class [klɑːs] n Klasse f ▷ vt einordnen, einstufen

classic ['klæsɪk] adj (mistake, example etc) klassisch ▷ n Klassiker m; **classical** ['klæsɪkəl] adj (music, ballet etc) klassisch

classification [klæsɪfɪ'keɪʃn] n Klassifizierung f; **classify** ['klæsɪfaɪ] vt klassifizieren; **classified advertisement** Kleinanzeige f

classroom ['klɑːsrʊm] n Klassenzimmer nt

classy ['klɑːsɪ] adj (fam) nobel, exklusiv

clatter ['klætə*] vi klappern

clause [klɔːz] n (Ling) Satz m; (Jur) Klausel f

claw [klɔː] n Kralle f

clay [kleɪ] n Lehm m; (for pottery) Ton m

clean [kliːn] adj sauber; **~ driving licence** Führerschein ohne Strafpunkte ▷ vt sauber machen; (carpet etc) reinigen; (window, shoes, vegetables) putzen; (wound) säubern; **clean up** vt sauber machen o vi aufräumen; **cleaner** n (person) Putzmann m, Putzfrau f; (substance) Putzmittel nt; **~'s** (firm) Reinigung f

cleanse [klenz] vt reinigen; (wound) säubern; **cleanser** n Reinigungsmittel nt

clear [klɪə*] adj klar; (distinct) deutlich; (conscience) rein; (free, road etc) frei; **to be ~ about sth** sich über etw im Klaren sein ▷ adv: **to stand ~** zurücktreten ▷ vt (road, room etc) räumen; (table) abräumen; (Jur: find innocent) freisprechen (of von) ▷ vi (fog, mist) sich verziehen; (weather) aufklaren; **clear away** vt wegräumen; (dishes) abräumen; **clear off** vi (fam) abhauen; **clear up** vi (tidy up) aufräumen; (weather) sich aufklären ▷ vt (room) aufräumen; (litter) wegräumen; (matter) klären

clearance sale n Räumungsverkauf m; **clearing** n Lichtung f; **clearly** adv klar; (speak, remember) deutlich; (obviously) eindeutig; **clearout** n Entrümpelungsaktion f; **clearway** n (Brit) Straße f mit Halteverbot nt

clench [klentʃ] vt (fist) ballen; (teeth) zusammenbeißen

clergyman ['klɜ:dʒɪmæn] (pl ▪▪▪▪▪▪) n Geistliche(r) m; **clergywoman** ['klɜ:dʒɪwʊmən] (pl -women) n Geistliche f

clerk [klɑ:k], (US) [klɜ:k] n (in office) Büroangestellte(r) m/f; (US: salesperson) Verkäufer(in) m(f)

clever ['klevə°] adj schlau, klug; (idea) clever

cliché ['kli:ʃeɪ] n Klischee nt

click [klɪk] n Klicken nt; (Inform) Mausklick m ▷ vi klicken; **to ~ on sth** (Inform) etw anklicken; **it ~ed** (fam) ich hab's/er hat's etc geschnallt, es hat gefunkt, es hat Klick gemacht; **they ~ed** sie haben sich gleich verstanden; **click on** vt (Inform) anklicken

client ['klaɪənt] n Kunde m, Kundin f; (Jur) Mandant(in) m(f)

cliff [klɪf] n Klippe f

climate ['klaɪmɪt] n Klima nt

climax ['klaɪmæks] n Höhepunkt m

climb [klaɪm] vi (person) klettern; (aircraft, sun) steigen; (road) ansteigen ▷ vt (mountain) besteigen; (tree etc) klettern auf +akk ▷ n Aufstieg m; **climber** n (mountaineer) Bergsteiger(in) m(f); **climbing** n Klettern nt,

Bergsteigen nt; **climbing frame** n Klettergerüst nt

cling [klɪŋ] (**clung, clung**) vi sich klammern (to an +akk); **cling film®** n Frischhaltefolie f

clinic ['klɪnɪk] n Klinik f; **clinical** adj klinisch

clip [klɪp] n Klammer f ▷ vt (fix) anklemmen (to an +akk); (fingernails) schneiden; **clipboard** n Klemmbrett nt; **clippers** npl Schere f; (for nails) Zwicker m

cloak [kləʊk] n Umhang m; **cloakroom** n (for coats) Garderobe f

clock [klɒk] n Uhr f; (Auto: fam) Tacho m; **round the ~** rund um die Uhr, ▪▪▪▪▪▪▪▪ adv im Uhrzeigersinn

clog [klɒg] n Holzschuh m ▷ vt verstopfen

cloister ['klɔɪstə°] n Kreuzgang m

clone [kləʊn] n Klon m ▷ vt klonen

close [kləʊs] adj nahe (to +dat); (friend, contact) eng; (resemblance) groß; **~ to the beach** in der Nähe des Strandes; **~ win** knapper Sieg; **on ~r examination** bei näherer genauerer Untersuchung ▷ adv [kləʊs] dicht; **he lives ~ by** er wohnt ganz in der Nähe ▷ vt [kləʊz] schließen; (road) sperren; (discussion, matter) abschließen ▷ vi [kləʊz] schließen rtri; n [kləʊz] Ende nt; **close down** vi (factory) stillgelegt werden ▷ vt (shop) schließen; (factory) stilllegen; **closed** adj (road) gesperrt; (shop etc) geschlossen; **closed circuit television** n Videoüberwachungsanlage f; **closely** adv (related) eng, nah; (packed, follow) dicht; (attentively) genau

closet ['klɒzɪt] n (esp US) Schrank m

close-up ['kləʊsʌp] n Nahaufnahme f

closing ['kləʊzɪŋ] adj: ~ **date** letzter Termin; (for competition) Einsendeschluss m; ~ **time** (of shop) Ladenschluss m; (Brit: of pub) Polizeistunde f

closure ['kləʊʒə°] n Schließung f; Abschluss m; **to look for ~** mit etw abschließen wollen

clot [klɒt] (**blood**) ~ Blutgerinnsel nt; (fam: idiot) Trottel m ▷ vi (blood) gerinnen

cloth [klɒθ] n (material) Tuch nt; (for cleaning) Lappen m

clothe [kləʊð] vt kleiden; **clothes** [kləʊðz] npl Kleider pl, Kleidung f; **clothes line** n Wäscheleine f; **clothes peg**, **clothespin** (US) n Wäscheklammer f; **clothing** ['kləʊðɪŋ] n Kleidung f

clotted ['klɒtɪd] adj: ~ **cream** dicke Sahne (aus erhitzter Milch)

cloud [klaʊd] n Wolke f; **cloudy** adj (sky) bewölkt; (liquid) trüb

clove [kləʊv] n Gewürznelke f; ~ **of garlic** Knoblauchzehe f

clover ['kləʊvə°] n Klee m; **cloverleaf** (pl **-leaves**) n Kleeblatt f

clown [klaʊn] n Clown m

club [klʌb] n (weapon) Knüppel m; (society) Klub m, Verein m; (nightclub) Disko f; (golf club) Golfschläger m; ~**s** (Cards) Kreuz nt; **clubbing**: **to go ~** in die Disko gehen; **club class** n (Aviat) Businessclass f

clue [klu:] n Anhaltspunkt m, Hinweis m; **he hasn't a ~** er hat keine Ahnung

clumsy ['klʌmzi] adj unbeholfen, ungeschickt

clung [klʌŋ] pt, pp of **cling**

clutch [klʌtʃ] n (Auto) Kupplung f ▷ vt umklammern; (book etc) an sich akk klammern

cm abbr = **centimetre(s)** cm

c/o abbr = **care of** bei

Co abbr = **company** Co

coach [kəʊtʃ] n (Brit: bus) Reisebus m; (Rail) (Personen)wagen m; (Sport: trainer) Trainer(in) m(f) ▷ vt Nachhilfeunterricht geben +dat; (Sport) trainieren; **coach (class)** n (Aviat) Economyclass f; **coach driver** n Busfahrer(in) m(f); **coach party** n Reisegruppe f (Bus); **coach station** n Busbahnhof m; **coach trip** n Busfahrt f; (tour) Busreise f

coal [kəʊl] n Kohle f

coalition [kəʊəˈlɪʃən] n (Pol) Koalition f

coalmine ['kəʊlmaɪn] n Kohlenbergwerk nt; **coalminer** n Bergarbeiter m

coast [kəʊst] n Küste f; **coastguard** n Küstenwache f; **coastline** n Küste f

coat [kəʊt] n Mantel m; (jacket) Jacke f; (on animals) Fell m, Pelz m; (of paint) Schicht f; ~ **of arms** Wappen nt; **coathanger** n Kleiderbügel m; **coating** n Überzug m; (layer) Schicht f

cobble(stone)s ['kɒbl(stəʊn)z] npl Kopfsteine pl; (surface) Kopfsteinpflaster nt

cobweb ['kɒbweb] n Spinnennetz nt

cocaine [kəˈkeɪn] n Kokain nt

cock [kɒk] n (vulg: penis) Schwanz m; **cock up** vt (Brit fam) vermasseln, versauen; **cockerel** ['kɒkərəl] n junger Hahn

cockle ['kɒkl] n Herzmuschel f

cockpit ['kɒkpɪt] n (in plane, racing car) Cockpit nt; **cockroach** ['kɒkrəʊtʃ] n Kakerlake f; **cocktail**

['kɒkteɪl] n Cocktail m; **cock-up** n (Brit fam) **to make a ~ of sth** bei etw Mist bauen; **cocky** ['kɒkɪ] adj großspurig, von sich selbst überzeugt

cocoa ['kəʊkəʊ] n Kakao m

coconut ['kəʊkənʌt] n Kokosnuss f

cod [kɒd] n Kabeljau m

COD abbr = **cash on delivery** per Nachnahme

code [kəʊd] n Kode m

coeducational [kəʊedjʊ'keɪʃənl] adj (school) gemischt

coffee ['kɒfɪ] n Kaffee m; **coffee bar** n Café nt; **coffee break** n Kaffeepause f; **coffee machine** n Kaffeemaschine f; **coffee pot** n Kaffeekanne f; **coffee shop** n Café nt; **coffee table** n Couchtisch m

coffin ['kɒfɪn] n Sarg m

coil [kɔɪl] n Rolle f; (Elec) Spule f; (Med) Spirale f

coin [kɔɪn] n Münze f

coincide [kəʊɪn'saɪd] vi (happen together) zusammenfallen (with mit); **coincidence** [kəʊ'ɪnsɪdəns] n Zufall m

coke [kəʊk] n Koks m; **Coke®** Cola f

cola ['kəʊlə] n Cola f

cold [kəʊld] adj kalt; **I'm ~** mir ist kalt, ich friere ▷ n Kälte f; (illness) Erkältung f, Schnupfen m; **to catch a ~** sich erkälten; **cold box** n Kühlbox f; **cold sore** n Herpes m; **cold turkey** n (fam) Totalentzug m; (symptoms) Entzugserscheinungen pl

coleslaw ['kəʊlslɔː] n Krautsalat m

collaborate [kə'læbəreɪt] vi zusammenarbeiten (with mit); **collaboration** [kəlæbə'reɪʃən] n Zusammenarbeit f; (of one party) Mitarbeit f

collapse [kə'læps] vi zusammenbrechen; (building etc) einstürzen ▷ n Zusammenbruch m; (of building) Einsturz m; **collapsible** [kə'læpsəbl] adj zusammenklappbar, Klapp-

collar ['kɒlə'] n Kragen m; (for dog, cat) Halsband nt; **collarbone** n Schlüsselbein nt

colleague ['kɒliːg] n Kollege m, Kollegin f

collect [kə'lekt] vt sammeln; (fetch) abholen ▷ vi sich sammeln; **collect call** n (US) R-Gespräch nt; **collected** adj (works) gesammelt; (person) gefasst; **collector** n Sammler(in) m(f); **collection** [kə'lekʃən] n Sammlung f; (in church) Kollekte f; (from postbox) Leerung f

college ['kɒlɪdʒ] n (residential) College nt; (specialist) Fachhochschule f; (vocational) Berufsschule f; (US: university) Universität f; **to go to ~** (US) studieren

collide [kə'laɪd] vi zusammenstoßen; **collision** [kə'lɪʒən] n Zusammenstoß m

colloquial [kə'ləʊkwɪəl] adj umgangssprachlich

Cologne [kə'ləʊn] n Köln nt

colon ['kəʊlən] n (punctuation mark) Doppelpunkt m

colonial [kə'ləʊnɪəl] adj Kolonial-; **colonize** ['kɒlənaɪz] vt kolonisieren; **colony** ['kɒlənɪ] n Kolonie f

color n (US, colour ['kʌlə']) n Farbe f; (of skin) Hautfarbe f ▷ vt anmalen; (bias) färben; **colour-blind** adj farbenblind; **coloured** adj farbig; (biased) gefärbt; **colour film** n Farbfilm m; **colourful** adj (lit, fig) bunt; (life, past) bewegt; **colouring** n (in food etc) Farbstoff m; (complexion) Gesichtsfarbe f; **colourless** adj (*lit, fig*) farblos; **colour photo(graph)** n Farbfoto nt; **colour television** n Farbfernsehen nt

column ['kɒləm] n Säule f; (*of print*) Spalte f

comb [kəʊm] n Kamm m ⊳ vt kämmen; **to ~ one's hair** sich kämmen

combination [kɒmbɪ'neɪʃən] n Kombination f; (*mixture*) Mischung f (*of* aus); **combine** [kəm'baɪn] vt verbinden (*with* mit); (*two things*) kombinieren

come [kʌm] (**came, come**) vi kommen; (*arrive*) ankommen; (*on list, in order*) stehen; (*with adjective: become*) werden; **~ and see us** besuchen Sie uns mal; **coming** ich komm ja schon!; **to ~ first/second** erster/zweiter werden; **to ~ true** wahr werden; **to ~ loose** sich lockern; **the years to ~** die kommenden Jahre; **there's one more to ~** es kommt noch eins/noch einer; **how ~ ...?** (*fam*) wie kommt es, dass ...?; **~ to think of it** (*fam*) wo es mir gerade einfällt; **come across** vt (*find*) stoßen auf +akk; **come back** vi zurückkommen; **I'll ~ to that** ich komme darauf zurück; **come down** vi herunterkommen; (*rain, snow, price*) fallen; **come from** vt (*result*) kommen von; **where do you ~?** wo kommen Sie her?; **I ~ London** ich komme aus London; **come in** vi hereinkommen; (*arrive*) ankommen; (*in race*) **to ~ fourth** Vierter werden; **come off** vi (*button, handle etc*) abgehen; (*succeed*) gelingen; **to ~ well/badly** gut/schlecht wegkommen; **come on** vi (*progress*) vorankommen; **~!** komm!; (*hurry*) beeil dich!; (*encouraging*) los!; **come out** vi

herauskommen; (*photo*) was werden; (*homosexual*) sich outen; **come round** vi (*visit*) vorbeikommen; (*regain consciousness*) wieder zu sich kommen; **come to** vi (*regain consciousness*) wieder zu sich kommen ⊳ vt (*sum*) sich belaufen auf +akk; **when it comes to ...** wenn es um ... geht; **come up** vi hochkommen; (*sun, moon*) aufgehen; **to ~ (for discussion)** zur Sprache kommen; **come up to** vt (*approach*) zukommen auf +akk; (*water*) reichen bis zu; (*expectations*) entsprechen +dat; **come up with** vt (*idea*) haben; (*solution, answer*) kommen auf +akk; **to ~ a suggestion** einen Vorschlag machen

comedian [kə'miːdɪən] n Komiker(in) m(f)

comedown ['kʌmdaʊn] n Abstieg m

comedy ['kɒmədɪ] n Komödie f, Comedy f

comfort ['kʌmfət] n Komfort m; (*consolation*) Trost m ⊳ vt trösten; **comfortable** adj bequem; (*income*) ausreichend; (*temperature, life*) angenehm; **comforting** adj tröstlich

comic ['kɒmɪk] n (*magazine*) Comic(heft) nt; (*comedian*) Komiker(in) m(f) ⊳ adj komisch

coming ['kʌmɪŋ] adj kommend; (*event*) bevorstehend

comma ['kɒmə] n Komma nt

command [kə'mɑːnd] n Befehl m; (*control*) Führung f; (*Mil*) Kommando nt ⊳ vt befehlen +dat

commemorate [kə'meməreɪt] vt gedenken +gen; **commemoration** [kəmemə'reɪʃən] n: **in ~ of** in Gedenken an +akk

comment ['kɒment] n (*remark*)

Bemerkung f; (note) Anmerkung f; (official) Kommentar m (on zu); **no ~** kein Kommentar ▷ vi sich äußern (on zu); **commentary** ['kɔməntrɪ] n Kommentar m (on zu); (TV, Sport) Livereportage f; **commentator** ['kɔmənteɪtə°] n Kommentator(in) m(f); (TV, Sport) Reporter(in) m(f)

commerce ['kɔmɜːs] n Handel m; **commercial** [kə'mɜːʃəl] adj kommerziell; (training) kaufmännisch; **~ break** Werbepause f; **~ vehicle** Lieferwagen m ▷ n (TV) Werbespot m

commission [kə'mɪʃən] n Auftrag m; (fee) Provision f; (reporting body) Kommission f ▷ vt beauftragen

commit [kə'mɪt] vt (crime) begehen ▷ vr: **to ~ oneself** (undertake) sich verpflichten (to zu); **commitment** n Verpflichtung f; (Pol) Engagement nt

committee [kə'mɪtɪ] n Ausschuss m, Komitee nt

commodity [kə'mɔdɪtɪ] n Ware f

common ['kɔmən] adj (experience) allgemein, alltäglich; (shared) gemeinsam; (widespread, frequent) häufig; (pej) gewöhnlich, ordinär; **to have sth in ~** etw gemein haben ▷ n (Brit: land) Gemeindewiese f; **commonly** adv häufig, allgemein; **commonplace** adj alltäglich; (pej) banal; **commonroom** n Gemeinschaftsraum m; **Commons** n (Brit Pol) **the (House of) ~** das Unterhaus; **common sense** n gesunder Menschenverstand; **Commonwealth** n Commonwealth nt; **~ of Independent**

States Gemeinschaft f Unabhängiger Staaten

communal ['kɔmjunl] adj gemeinsam; (of a community) Gemeinschafts-, Gemeinde-

communicate [kə'mjuːnɪkeɪt] vi kommunizieren (with mit); **communication** [kəmjuːnɪ'keɪʃən] n Kommunikation f, Verständigung f; **communications satellite** n Nachrichtensatellit m; **communications technology** n Nachrichtentechnik f; **communicative** adj gesprächig

communion [kə'mjuːnɪən] n: **(Holy) Communion** Heiliges Abendmahl; (Catholic) Kommunion f

communism ['kɔmjunɪzəm] n Kommunismus m; **communist** ['kɔmjunɪst] adj kommunistisch ▷ n Kommunist(in) m(f)

community [kə'mjuːnɪtɪ] n Gemeinschaft f; **community centre** n Gemeindezentrum nt; **community service** n (Jur) Sozialdienst m

commutation ticket [kɔmjuː'teɪʃəntɪkɪt] n (US) Zeitkarte f; **commute** [kə'mjuːt] vi pendeln; **commuter** n Pendler(in) m(f)

compact [kəm'pækt] adj kompakt ▷ ['kɔmpækt] n (for make-up) Puderdose f; (US: car) **~** Mittelklassewagen m; **compact camera** n Kompaktkamera f; **compact disc** n Compact Disc f, CD f

companion [kəm'pænɪən] n Begleiter(in) m(f)

company ['kʌmpənɪ] n Gesellschaft f; (Comm) Firma f; **to keep sb ~** jdm Gesellschaft leisten; **company car** n Firmenauto nt

comparable ['kɒmpərəbl] adj
vergleichbar (with, to mit)
comparative [kəm'pærətɪv] adj
relativ ▷ n (Ling) Komparativ m;
comparatively adv
verhältnismäßig
compare [kəm'pɛə°] vt vergleichen (with, to mit); **~d with** o
to im Vergleich zu; **beyond**
~ unvergleichlich; **comparison**
[kəm'pærɪsn] n Vergleich m; **in**
~ with im Vergleich mit (o zu)
compartment [kəm'pɑːtmənt]
n (Rail) Abteil nt; (in desk etc) Fach
nt
compass ['kʌmpəs] n Kompass
m; **~es** pl Zirkel m
compassion [kəm'pæʃən] n
Mitgefühl nt
compatible [kəm'pætɪbl] adj
vereinbar (with mit); (Inform)
kompatibel; **we're not ~** wir
passen nicht zueinander
compensate ['kɒmpenseɪt] vt
(person) entschädigen (for für) ▷ vi:
to ~ for sth Ersatz für etw leisten;
(make up for) etw ausgleichen;
compensation [kɒmpen'seɪʃən]
n Entschädigung f; (money)
Schadenersatz m; (Jur) Abfindung f
compete [kəm'piːt] vi konkur-
rieren (for um); (Sport) kämpfen (for
um); (take part) teilnehmen (in an
+dat)
competence ['kɒmpɪtəns] n
Fähigkeit f; (Jur) Zuständigkeit f;
competent adj fähig; (Jur)
zuständig
competition [kɒmpɪ'tɪʃən] n
(contest) Wettbewerb m; (Comm)
Konkurrenz f (for um);
competitive [kəm'petɪtɪv] adj
(firm, price, product)
konkurrenzfähig; **competitor**
[kəm'petɪtə°] n (Comm)
Konkurrent(in) m(f); (Sport)
Teilnehmer(in) m(f)

complain [kəm'pleɪn] vi klagen;
(formally) sich beschweren (about
über +akk); **complaint** n Klage f;
Beanstandung f; (formal)
Beschwerde f; (med) Leiden nt
complement vt ergänzen
complete [kəm'pliːt] adj vollständig; (finished) fertig; (failure,
disaster) total; (happiness)
vollkommen; **are we ~?** sind wir
vollzählig? ▷ vt vervollständigen;
(finish) beenden; (form) ausfüllen;
completely adv völlig; **not ~ ...**
nicht ganz ...
complex ['kɒmpleks] adj komplex; (task, theory etc) kompliziert
▷ n Komplex m
complexion [kəm'plekʃən] n
Gesichtsfarbe f, Teint m
complicated ['kɒmplɪkeɪtɪd] adj
kompliziert; **complication**
['kɒmplɪkeɪʃən] n Komplikation
f
compliment ['kɒmplɪmənt] n
Kompliment nt; **complimentary**
[kɒmplɪ'mentərɪ] adj lobend;
(free of charge) Gratis-; **~ ticket**
Freikarte f
comply [kəm'plaɪ] vi: **to ~ with**
the regulations den Vorschriften
entsprechen
component [kəm'pəʊnənt] n
Bestandteil m
compose [kəm'pəʊz] vt (music)
komponieren; **to ~ oneself** sich
zusammennehmen; **composed**
adj gefasst; **to be ~ of** bestehen
aus; **composer** n Komponist(in)
m(f); **composition** [kɒmpə'zɪʃən]
n (of a group) Zusammensetzung f;
(Mus) Komposition f
comprehend [kɒmprɪ'hend] vt
verstehen; **comprehension**
[kɒmprɪ'henʃən] n Verständnis nt
comprehensive
[kɒmprɪ'hensɪv] adj umfassend;
~ school Gesamtschule f

compress [kəm'pres] vt
komprimieren

comprise [kəm'praɪz] vt
umfassen, bestehen aus

compromise ['kɒmprəmaɪz] n
Kompromiss m ▷ vi einen
Kompromiss schließen

compulsory [kəm'pʌlsərɪ] adj
obligatorisch; **~ subject**
Pflichtfach nt

computer [kəm'pju:tə°] n
Computer m; **computer-aided** adj
computergestützt;
computer-controlled adj rech-
nergesteuert; **computer game** n
Computerspiel nt;
computer-literate adj: **to be
~ mit dem Computer umgehen
können; computer scientist** n
Informatiker(in) m(f); **computing**
n (subject) Informatik f

con [kɒn] (fam) n Schwindel m
▷ vt betrügen (out of um)

conceal [kən'si:l] vt verbergen
(from vor +dat)

conceivable [kən'si:vəbl] adj
denkbar, vorstellbar; **conceive**
[kən'si:v] vt (imagine) sich
vorstellen; (child) empfangen

concentrate ['kɒnsəntreɪt] vi
sich konzentrieren (on auf +akk);
concentration [kɒnsən'treɪʃən]
n Konzentration f

concept ['kɒnsept] n Begriff m

concern [kən'sɜːn] n (affair)
Angelegenheit f; (worry) Sorge f;
(Comm: firm) Unternehmen nt; **it's
not my ~** das geht mich nichts an;
there's no cause for ~ kein Grund
zur Beunruhigung ▷ vt (affect)
angehen; (have connection with)
betreffen; (be about) handeln von;
those ~ed die Betroffenen; **as far
as I'm ~ed** was mich betrifft;
concerned adj (anxious) besorgt;
concerning prep bezüglich,
hinsichtlich +gen

concert ['kɒnsət] n Konzert nt;
~ hall Konzertsaal m

concession [kən'seʃən] n Zu-
geständnis nt; (reduction)
Ermäßigung f

concise [kən'saɪs] adj knapp
gefasst, prägnant

conclude [kən'kluːd] vt (end)
beenden, (ab)schließen; (infer)
folgern (from aus); **to ~ that ...** zu
dem Schluss kommen, dass ...;
conclusion [kən'kluːʒən] n
Schluss m, Schlussfolgerung f

concrete ['kɒnkriːt] n Beton m
▷ adj konkret

concussion [kən'kʌʃən] n
Gehirnerschütterung f

condemn [kən'dem] vt
verdammen; (esp Jur)
verurteilen

condensed milk [kən'denst-]
Kondensmilch f, Dosenmilch f

condition [kən'dɪʃən] n (state)
Zustand m; (requirement)
Bedingung f; **on ~ that ...** unter
der Bedingung, dass ...; **~s** pl
(circumstances, weather)
Verhältnisse pl; **conditional** adj
bedingt; (Ling) Konditional-;
conditioner n Weichspüler m; (for
hair) Pflegespülung f

condo ['kɒndəʊ] (pl **-s**) n see
condominium

condolences [kən'dəʊlənsɪz]
npl Beileid nt

condom ['kɒndəm] n Kondom nt

condominium [kɒndə'mɪnɪəm]
n (US: apartment)
Eigentumswohnung f

conduct ['kɒndʌkt] n (behaviour)
Verhalten nt ▷ [kən'dʌkt] vt
führen, leiten; (orchestra)
dirigieren; **conductor**
[kən'dʌktə°] n (of orchestra)
Dirigent(in) m(f); (Brit: in bus)
Schaffner(in) m(f); (US: on train)
Zugführer(in) m(f)

cone [kəʊn] *n* Kegel *m; (for ice cream)* Waffeltüte *f; (fir cone)* (Tannen)zapfen *m*

conference ['kɒnfərəns] *n* Konferenz *f*

confess [kən'fes] *vt, vi*: **to ~ that ...** gestehen, dass ...; **confession** [kən'feʃən] *n* Geständnis *nt; (Rel)* Beichte *f*

confetti [kən'fetɪ] *n* Konfetti *nt*

confidence ['kɒnfɪdəns] *n* Vertrauen *nt (in zu); (assurance)* Selbstvertrauen *nt;* **confident** *adj (sure)* zuversichtlich *(that ... dass ...),* überzeugt *(of von); (self-assured)* selbstsicher; **confidential** [kɒnfɪ'denʃəl] *adj* vertraulich

confine [kən'faɪn] *vt* beschränken *(to auf +akk)*

confirm [kən'fɜːm] *vt* bestätigen; **confirmation** [kɒnfə'meɪʃən] *n* Bestätigung *f; (Rel)* Konfirmation *f;* **confirmed** *adj* überzeugt; *(bachelor)* eingefleischt

confiscate ['kɒnfɪskeɪt] *vt* beschlagnahmen, konfiszieren

conflict ['kɒnflɪkt] *n* Konflikt *m*

confuse [kən'fjuːz] *vt* verwirren; *(sth with sth)* verwechseln *(with mit); (several things)* durcheinanderbringen; **confused** *adj (person)* konfus, verwirrt; *(account)* verworren; **confusing** *adj* verwirrend; **confusion** [kən'fjuːʒən] *n* Verwirrung *f; (of two things)* Verwechslung *f; (muddle)* Chaos *nt*

congested [kən'dʒestɪd] *adj* verstopft; *(overcrowded)* überfüllt; **congestion** [kən'dʒestʃən] *n* Stau *m*

congratulate [kən'dʒætjʊleɪt] *vt* gratulieren *(on zu);* **congratulations** [kəngrætjʊ'leɪʃənz] *npl* Glück-

wünsche *pl;* **~!** gratuliere!, herzlichen Glückwunsch!

congregation [kɒngrɪ'geɪʃən] *n (Rel)* Gemeinde *f*

congress ['kɒngres] *n* Kongress *m; (US)* **Congress** der Kongress; **congressman** *(pl* **-men)** *n,* **congresswoman** *(pl* **-women)** *n (US)* Mitglied *nt* des Repräsentantenhauses

conifer ['kɒnɪfəʳ] *n* Nadelbaum *m*

conjunction [kən'dʒʌŋkʃən] *n (Ling)* Konjunktion *f;* **in ~ with** in Verbindung mit

conk out [kɒŋk 'aʊt] *vi (fam: appliance, car)* den Geist aufgeben, streiken; *(person: die)* ins Gras beißen

connect [kə'nekt] *vt* verbinden *(with, to mit); (Elec, Tech: appliance etc)* anschließen *(to an +akk)* ▷ *vi (train, plane)* Anschluss haben *(with an +akk);* **~ing flight** Anschlussflug *m;* **~ing train** Anschlusszug *m;* **connection** [kə'nekʃən] *n* Verbindung *f; (link)* Zusammenhang *m; (for train, plane, electrical appliance)* Anschluss *m (with, to an +akk); (business etc)* Beziehung *f;* **in ~ with** in Zusammenhang mit; **bad ~** *(Tel)* schlechte Verbindung; *(Elec)* Wackelkontakt *m;* **connector** *n (Inform: computer)* Stecker *m*

conscience ['kɒnʃəns] *n* Gewissen *nt;* **conscientious** [kɒnʃɪ'enʃəs] *adj* gewissenhaft

conscious ['kɒnʃəs] *adj (act)* bewusst; *(Med)* bei Bewusstsein; **to be ~** bei Bewusstsein sein; **consciousness** *n* Bewusstsein *nt*

consecutive [kən'sekjʊtɪv] *adj* aufeinanderfolgend

consent [kən'sent] *n* Zustimmung *f* ▷ *vi* zustimmen *(to dat)*

consequence ['kɒnsɪkwəns] n Folge f, Konsequenz f; **consequently** ['kɒnsɪkwəntlɪ] adv folglich, deshalb

conservation [kɒnsə'veɪʃən] n Erhaltung f; (nature conservation) Naturschutz m; **conservation area** n Naturschutzgebiet nt

conservative (Pol) **Conservative** [kən'sɜːvətɪv] adj konservativ

conservatory [kən'sɜːvətrɪ] n (greenhouse) Gewächshaus nt; (room) Wintergarten m

consider [kən'sɪdə°] vt (reflect on) nachdenken über, sich überlegen; (take into account) in Betracht ziehen; (regard) halten für; **he is ~ed (to be)** ... er gilt als ...; **considerable** [kən'sɪdərəbl] adj beträchtlich; **considerate** [kən'sɪdərɪt] adj aufmerksam, rücksichtsvoll; **consideration** [kənsɪdə'reɪʃən] n (thoughtfulness) Rücksicht f; (thought) Überlegung f; **to take sth into ~** etw in Betracht ziehen; **considering** [kən'sɪdərɪŋ] prep in Anbetracht ▷ conj da

consist [kən'sɪst] vi: **to ~ of** ... bestehen aus ...

consistent [kən'sɪstənt] adj (behaviour, process etc) konsequent; (statements) übereinstimmend; (argument) folgerichtig; (performance, results) beständig

consolation [kɒnsə'leɪʃən] n Trost m; **console** [kən'səʊl] vt trösten

consolidate [kən'sɒlɪdeɪt] vt festigen

consonant ['kɒnsənənt] n Konsonant m

conspicuous [kən'spɪkjʊəs] adj auffällig, auffallend

conspiracy [kən'spɪrəsɪ] n Komplott nt; **conspire**

[kən'spaɪə°] vi sich verschwören (against gegen)

constable ['kʌnstəbl] n (Brit) Polizist(in) m(f)

Constance ['kɒnstəns] n Konstanz nt; **Lake ~** der Bodensee

constant ['kɒnstənt] adj (continual) ständig, dauernd; (unchanging: temperature etc) gleichbleibend; **constantly** adv dauernd

consternation [kɒnstə'neɪʃən] n (dismay) Bestürzung f

constituency [kən'stɪtjʊənsɪ] n Wahlkreis m

constitution [kɒnstɪ'tjuːʃən] n Verfassung f; (of person) Konstitution f

construct [kən'strʌkt] vt bauen; **construction** [kən'strʌkʃən] n (process, result) Bau m; (method) Bauweise f; **under ~** im Bau befindlich; **construction site** n Baustelle f; **construction worker** n Bauarbeiter(in) m(f)

consulate ['kɒnsjʊlət] n Konsulat nt

consult [kən'sʌlt] vt um Rat fragen; (doctor) konsultieren; (book) nachschlagen in +dat; **consultant** n (Med) Facharzt m, Fachärztin f; **consultation** [kɒnsəl'teɪʃən] n Beratung f; (Med) Konsultation f; **~ room** n Besprechungsraum; Sprechzimmer

consume [kən'sjuːm] vt verbrauchen; (food) konsumieren; **consumer** n Verbraucher(in) m(f); **consumer-friendly** adj verbraucherfreundlich

contact ['kɒntækt] n (touch) Kontakt m; (person) Kontaktperson f; (communication) Kontakt m; **to be/keep in ~ (with sb)** (mit jdm) in Kontakt sein/bleiben ▷ vt sich in Verbindung setzen mit;

contact lenses npl Kontaktlinsen pl

contagious [kənˈteɪdʒəs] adj ansteckend

contain [kənˈteɪn] vt enthalten; **container** n Behälter m; (for transport) Container m

contaminate [kənˈtæmɪneɪt] vt verunreinigen; (chemically) verseuchen; **~d by radiation** strahlenverseucht, verstrahlt; **contamination** [kənˌtæmɪˈneɪʃən] n Verunreinigung f; (by radiation) Verseuchung f

contemporary [kənˈtempərərɪ] adj zeitgenössisch

contempt [kənˈtempt] n Verachtung f; **contemptuous** adj verächtlich; **to be ~** voller Verachtung sein (of für)

content [kənˈtent] adj zufrieden

content(s) [ˈkɒntent(s)] n pl Inhalt m

contest [ˈkɒntest] n (Wett)kampf m (for um); (competition) Wettbewerb m ▷ [kənˈtest] vt kämpfen um +akk; (dispute) bestreiten; **contestant** [kənˈtestənt] n Teilnehmer(in) m(f)

context [ˈkɒntekst] n Zusammenhang m; **out of ~** aus dem Zusammenhang gerissen

continent [ˈkɒntɪnənt] n Kontinent m, Festland nt; **the Continent** (Brit) das europäische Festland, der Kontinent; **continental** [kɒntɪˈnentl] adj kontinental; **~ breakfast** kleines Frühstück mit Brötchen und Marmelade, Kaffee oder Tee

continual [kənˈtɪnjʊəl] adj (endless) ununterbrochen; (constant) dauernd, ständig; **continually** adv dauernd; (again and again) immer wieder; **continuation** [kəntɪnjʊˈeɪʃən] n

Fortsetzung f; **continue** [kənˈtɪnjuː] vi weitermachen (with mit); (esp talking) fortfahren (with mit); (travelling) weiterfahren; (state, conditions) fortdauern, anhalten ▷ vt fortsetzen; **to be ~d** Fortsetzung folgt; **continuous** [kənˈtɪnjʊəs] adj (endless) ununterbrochen; (constant) ständig

contraceptive [kɒntrəˈseptɪv] n Verhütungsmittel nt

contract [ˈkɒntrækt] n Vertrag m

contradict [kɒntrəˈdɪkt] vt widersprechen +dat; **contradiction** [kɒntrəˈdɪkʃən] n Widerspruch m

contrary [ˈkɒntrərɪ] n Gegenteil nt; **on the ~** im Gegenteil ▷ adj: **~ to** entgegen +dat

contrast [ˈkɒntrɑːst] n Kontrast m, Gegensatz m; **in ~ to** im Gegensatz zu ▷ [kənˈtrɑːst] vt entgegensetzen

contribute [kənˈtrɪbjuːt] vt, vi beitragen (to zu); (money) spenden (to für); **contribution** [kɒntrɪˈbjuːʃən] n Beitrag m

control [kənˈtrəʊl] vt (master) beherrschen; (temper etc) im Griff haben; (esp Tech) steuern; **to ~ oneself** sich beherrschen ▷ n Kontrolle f; (mastery) Beherrschung f; (esp Tech) Steuerung f; **~s** pl (knobs, switches etc) Bedienungselemente pl; (collectively) Steuerung f; **to be out of ~** außer Kontrolle sein; **control knob** n Bedienungsknopf m; **control panel** n Schalttafel f

controversial [kɒntrəˈvɜːʃəl] adj umstritten

convalesce [kɒnvəˈles] vi gesund werden; **convalescence** n Genesung f

convenience [kənˈviːnɪəns] n (quality, thing) Annehmlichkeit f; **at**

your ~ wann es Ihnen passt; **with all modern ~s** mit allem Komfort; **convenience food** n Fertiggericht nt; **convenient** adj günstig, passend

convent ['kɒnvənt] n Kloster nt

convention [kən'venʃən] n (custom) Konvention f; (meeting) Konferenz f; **the Geneva Convention** die Genfer Konvention; **conventional** adj herkömmlich, konventionell

conversation [kɒnvə'seɪʃən] n Gespräch nt, Unterhaltung f

conversion [kən'vɜːʃən] n Umwandlung f (into in +akk); (of building) Umbau m (into zu); (Religion) Umstellung f; **conversion table** n Umrechnungstabelle f; **convert** [kən'vɜːt] vt umwandeln; (person) bekehren; (Inform) konvertieren; **to ~ into euros** in Euro umrechnen; **convertible** n (Auto) Kabrio nt ▷ adj umwandelbar

convey [kən'veɪ] vt (carry) befördern; (feelings) vermitteln; **conveyor belt** n Förderband nt, Fließband nt

convict [kən'vɪkt] vt verurteilen (of wegen) ▷ ['kɒnvɪkt] n Strafgefangene(r) mf; **conviction** n (Jur) Verurteilung f; (strong belief) Überzeugung f

convince [kən'vɪns] vt überzeugen (of von); **convincing** adj überzeugend

cook [kʊk] n, vi kochen ▷ n Koch m, Köchin f; **cookbook** n Kochbuch nt; **cooker** n Herd m; **cookery** n Kochkunst f; **~ book** Kochbuch nt; **cookie** n (US) Keks m; **cooking** n Kochen nt; (style of cooking) Küche f

cool [kuːl] adj kühl, gelassen; (fam: brilliant) cool, stark ▷ vt, vi (ab)kühlen; **~ it** reg dich ab! ▷ n:

to keep/lose one's ~ (fam) ruhig bleiben/durchdrehen; **cool down** vi abkühlen; (calm down) sich beruhigen

cooperate [kəʊ'ɒpəreɪt] vi zusammenarbeiten, kooperieren; **cooperation** [kəʊɒpə'reɪʃən] n Zusammenarbeit f, Kooperation f; **cooperative** [kəʊ'ɒpərətɪv] adj hilfsbereit ▷ n Genossenschaft f

coordinate [kəʊ'ɔːdɪneɪt] vt koordinieren

cop [kɒp] n (fam: policeman) Bulle m

cope [kəʊp] vi zurechtkommen, fertig werden (with mit)

Copenhagen [kəʊpən'heɪgən] n Kopenhagen nt

copier ['kɒpɪə] n Kopierer m

copper ['kɒpə] n Kupfer nt; (Brit fam: policeman) Bulle m; (fam: coin) Kupfermünze f; **~s** Kleingeld nt

copy ['kɒpɪ] n Kopie f; (of book) Exemplar nt ▷ vt kopieren; (imitate) nachahmen; **copyright** n Urheberrecht nt

coral ['kɒrəl] n Koralle f

cord [kɔːd] n Schnur f; (material) Kordsamt m; **cordless** ['kɔːdlɪs] adj (phone) schnurlos

core [kɔː] n (a. fig) Kern m; (of apple, pear) Kerngehäuse nt; **core business** n Kerngeschäft nt

cork [kɔːk] n (material) Kork m; (stopper) Korken m; **corkscrew** ['kɔːkskruː] n Korkenzieher m

corn [kɔːn] n Getreide nt, Korn nt; (US: maize) Mais m; (on foot) Hühnerauge nt; **~ on the cob** (gekochter) Maiskolben; **corned beef** n Cornedbeef nt

corner ['kɔːnə] n Ecke f; (on road) Kurve f; (Sport) Eckstoß m ▷ vt in die Enge treiben; **corner shop** n Laden m an der Ecke

cornflakes ['kɔːfleɪks] npl Cornflakes pl

Cornish [ˈkɔːnɪʃ] adj kornisch;
~ **pasty** mit Fleisch und Kartoffeln
gefüllte Pastete; **Cornwall**
[ˈkɔːnwəl] n Cornwall nt

coronation [kɒrəˈneɪʃən] n
Krönung f

corporation [kɔːpəˈreɪʃən] n
(US Comm) Aktiengesellschaft f

corpse [kɔːps] n Leiche f

correct [kəˈrekt] adj (accurate)
richtig; (proper) korrekt ▷ vt
korrigieren, verbessern;
correction n (esp written)
Korrektur f

correspond [kɒrɪˈspɒnd] vi
entsprechen (to dat); (two things)
übereinstimmen; (exchange letters)
korrespondieren; **corresponding**
adj entsprechend

corridor [ˈkɒrɪdɔː°] n (in building)
Flur m; (in train) Gang m

corrupt [kəˈrʌpt] adj korrupt

cosmetic [kɒzˈmetɪk] adj kos-
metisch; **cosmetics** npl
Kosmetika pl; **cosmetic surgeon**
n Schönheitschirurg(in) m(f);
cosmetic surgery n
Schönheitschirurgie f

cosmopolitan [kɒzməˈpɒlɪtən]
adj international; (attitude)
weltoffen

cost [kɒst] (**cost, cost**) vt kosten
▷ n Kosten pl; **at all ~s, at any**
~ um jeden Preis; ~ **of living**
Lebenshaltungskosten pl; **costly**
adj kostspielig

costume [ˈkɒstjuːm] n (Theat)
Kostüm nt

cosy [ˈkəʊzɪ] adj gemütlich

cot [kɒt] n (Brit) Kinderbett nt;
(US) Campingliege f

cottage [ˈkɒtɪdʒ] n kleines Haus;
(country cottage) Landhäuschen nt;
cottage cheese n Hüttenkäse m;
cottage pie n Hackfleisch mit
Kartoffelbrei überbacken

cotton [ˈkɒtn] n Baumwolle f;

cotton candy n (US) Zuckerwatte
f; **cotton wool** n (Brit) Watte f

couch [kaʊtʃ] n Couch f; (sofa)
Sofa nt; **couchette** [kuːˈʃet] n
Liegewagen(platz) m

cough [kɒf] vi husten ▷ n Hus-
ten m; **cough mixture** n
Hustensaft m; **cough sweet** n
Hustenbonbon nt

could [kʊd] pt of **can** konnte;
conditional könnte; ~ **you come
earlier?** könntest du/könnten Sie
früher kommen?

couldn't contr of **could not**

council [ˈkaʊnsl] n (Pol) Rat m;
(local ~) Gemeinderat m; (town ~)
Stadtrat m; **council estate** n
Siedlung f des sozialen
Wohnungsbaus; **council house** n
Sozialwohnung f; **councillor**
[ˈkaʊnsɪləª] n Gemeinderat m,
Gemeinderätin f; **council tax** n
Gemeindesteuer f

count [kaʊnt] vt, vi zählen;
(include) mitrechnen ▷ n Zählung
f; (noble) Graf m; **count on** vt (rely
on) sich verlassen auf +akk; (expect)
rechnen mit

counter [ˈkaʊntəª] n (in shop)
Ladentisch m; (in café) Theke f; (in
bank, post office) Schalter m;
counter attack n Gegenangriff m
▷ vi zurückschlagen;
counter-clockwise adv (US)
entgegen dem Uhrzeigersinn

counterpart [ˈkaʊntəpɔːt] n
Gegenstück nt (of zu)

countess n Gräfin f

countless [ˈkaʊntlɪs] adj zahl-
los, unzählig

country [ˈkʌntrɪ] n Land nt; **in
the** ~ auf dem Land(e); **in this**
~ hierzulande; **country cousin** n
(fam) Landei nt; **country dancing**
n Volkstanz m; **country house** n
Landhaus nt; **countryman** n
(compatriot) Landsmann m;

country music n Countrymusic f;
country road n Landstraße f;
countryside n Landschaft f; (rural area) Land nt

county ['kauntɪ] n (Brit) Grafschaft f; (US) Verwaltungsbezirk m; **county town** n (Brit) = Kreisstadt f

couple ['kʌpl] n Paar nt; **a ~ of** ein paar

coupon ['ku:pɒn] n (voucher) Gutschein m

courage ['kʌrɪdʒ] n Mut m; **courageous** [kə'reɪdʒəs] adj mutig

courgette [kuə'ʒet] n (Brit) Zucchini f

courier ['kurɪə'] n (for tourists) Reiseleiter(in) m(f); (messenger) Kurier m

course [kɔ:s] n (of study) Kurs m; (for race) Strecke f; (Naut, Aviat) Kurs m; (at university) Studiengang m; (in meal) Gang m; **of** ~ natürlich; **in the ~ of** während

court [kɔ:t] n (Sport) Platz m; (Jur) Gericht nt

courteous ['kɜ:tɪəs] adj höflich; **courtesy** ['kɜ:təsɪ] n Höflichkeit f; **~ bus/coach** (gebührenfreier) Zubringerbus

courthouse ['kɔ:thaus] n (US) Gerichtsgebäude nt; **court order** n Gerichtsbeschluss m; **courtroom** n Gerichtssaal m; **courtyard** ['kɔ:tjɑ:d] n Hof m

cousin ['kʌzn] n (male) Cousin m; (female) Cousine f

cover ['kʌvə'] vt bedecken (in, with mit); (distance) zurücklegen; (loan, costs) decken ▷ n (for bed etc) Decke f; (of cushion) Bezug m; (lid) Deckel m; (of book) Umschlag m; (insurance) ~ Versicherungsschutz m; **cover up** vt zudecken; (error etc) vertuschen; **coverage** n Berichterstattung f (of über +akk)

cover charge n Kosten pl für ein Gedeck; **covering** n Decke f; **covering letter** n Begleitbrief m; **cover story** n (newspaper) Titelgeschichte f

cow [kau] n Kuh f

coward ['kauəd] n Feigling m; **cowardly** adj feig(e)

cowboy ['kaubɔɪ] n Cowboy m

coy [kɔɪ] adj gespielt schüchtern, kokett

cozy ['kəuzɪ] adj (US) gemütlich

CPU abbr = **central processing unit** Zentraleinheit f

crab [kræb] n Krabbe f

crabby ['kræbɪ] adj mürrisch, reizbar

crack [kræk] n (in pottery, glass) Sprung m; (drug) Crack nt; **to have a ~ at sth** etw ausprobieren ▷ vi (pottery, glass) einen Sprung bekommen; (wood, ice etc) einen Riss bekommen; **to get ~ing** (fam) loslegen ▷ vt (bone) anbrechen; (nut, code) knacken

cracker ['krækə'] n (biscuit) Kräcker m; (Christmas ~) Knallbonbon nt; **crackers** adj (fam) verrückt, bekloppt; **he's ~** er hat nicht alle Tassen im Schrank

crackle ['krækl] vi knistern; (telephone, radio) knacken; **crackling** n (Gastr) Kruste f (des Schweinebratens)

cradle ['kreɪdl] n Wiege f

craft [krɑ:ft] n Handwerk nt; (art) Kunsthandwerk nt; (Naut) Boot nt; **craftsman** (pl -men) n Handwerker m; **craftsmanship** n Handwerkskunst f; (ability) handwerkliches Können

crafty ['krɑ:ftɪ] adj schlau

cram [kræm] vt stopfen (into in +akk); **to be ~med with ...** mit ... vollgestopft sein ▷ vi (revise for exam) pauken (für für)

cramp [kræmp] n Krampf m

cranberry ['krænbərɪ] n Preiselbeere f

crane [kreɪn] n (machine) Kran m; (bird) Kranich m

crap [kræp] n (vulg) Scheiße f; (rubbish) Mist m ▷ adj beschissen, Scheiß-

crash [kræʃ] vi einen Unfall haben; (two vehicles) zusammenstoßen; (plane, computer) abstürzen; (economy) zusammenbrechen; **to ~ into sth** gegen etw knallen ▷ vt einen Unfall haben mit ▷ n (car) Unfall m; (train) Unglück nt; (collision) Zusammenstoß m; (Aviat, Inform) Absturz m; (noise) Krachen nt; **crash barrier** n Leitplanke f; **crash course** n Intensivkurs m; **crash helmet** n Sturzhelm m; **crash landing** n Bruchlandung f

crate [kreɪt] n Kiste f; (of beer) Kasten m

crater ['kreɪtə°] n Krater m

craving ['kreɪvɪŋ] n starkes Verlangen, Bedürfnis nt

crawl [krɔːl] vi kriechen; (baby) krabbeln ▷ n (swimming) Kraul nt; **crawler lane** n Kriechspur f

crayfish ['kreɪfɪʃ] n Languste f

crayon ['kreɪən] n Buntstift m

crazy ['kreɪzɪ] adj verrückt (about nach)

cream [kriːm] n (from milk) Sahne f, Rahm m; (polish, cosmetic) Creme f ▷ adj cremefarben; **cream cake** n (small) Sahnetörtchen nt; (big) Sahnetorte f; **cream cheese** n Frischkäse m; **creamer** n Kaffeeweißer m; **cream tea** n (Brit) Nachmittagstee mit Törtchen, Marmelade und Schlagsahne; **creamy** adj sahnig

crease [kriːs] n Falte f ▷ vt falten; (untidy) zerknittern

create [kriː'eɪt] vt schaffen; (cause) verursachen; **creative**

[kriː'eɪtɪv] adj schöpferisch; (person) kreativ; **creature** ['kriːtʃə°] n Geschöpf nt

crèche [kreɪʃ] n Kinderkrippe f

credible ['kredɪbl] adj (person) glaubwürdig; **credibility** n Glaubwürdigkeit f

credit ['kredɪt] n (Fin: amount allowed) Kredit m; (amount possessed) Guthaben nt; (recognition) Anerkennung f; **~s** (of film) Abspann m; **credit card** n Kreditkarte f

creep [kriːp] (crept, crept) vi kriechen; **creeps** n: **he gives me the ~** er ist mir nicht ganz geheuer; **creepy** ['kriːpɪ] adj (frightening) gruselig, unheimlich

crept [krept] pt, pp of **creep**

cress [kres] n Kresse f

crest [krest] n Kamm m; (coat of arms) Wappen nt

crew [kruː] n Besatzung f, Mannschaft f

crib [krɪb] n (US) Kinderbett nt

cricket ['krɪkɪt] n (insect) Grille f; (game) Kricket nt

crime [kraɪm] n Verbrechen nt; **criminal** ['krɪmɪnl] n Verbrecher(in) m(f) ▷ adj kriminell, strafbar

cripple ['krɪpl] n Krüppel m ▷ vt verkrüppeln, lähmen

crisis ['kraɪsɪs] n (pl **crises**) n Krise f

crisp [krɪsp] adj knusprig; **crisps** npl (Brit) Chips pl; **crispbread** n Knäckebrot nt

criterion [kraɪ'tɪərɪən] n Kriterium nt; **critic** ['krɪtɪk] n Kritiker(in) m(f); **critical** adj kritisch; **critically** adv kritisch; **~ ill/injured** schwer krank/verletzt; **criticism** ['krɪtɪsɪzm] n Kritik f; **criticize** ['krɪtɪsaɪz] vt kritisieren

Croat ['krəʊæt] n Kroate m,

Kroatin f; **Croatia** [krəʊˈeɪʃə] n Kroatien nt; **Croatian** [krəʊˈeɪʃən] adj kroatisch

crockery [ˈkrɒkərɪ] n Geschirr nt

crocodile [ˈkrɒkədaɪl] n Krokodil nt

crocus [ˈkrəʊkəs] n Krokus m

crop [krɒp] n (harvest) Ernte f; **crops** npl Getreide nt; **crop up** vi auftauchen

croquette [krəˈket] n Krokette f

cross [krɒs] n Kreuz nt; **to mark sth with a ~** etw ankreuzen ▷ vt (road, river etc) überqueren; (legs) übereinanderschlagen; **it ~ed my mind** es fiel mir ein, **to ~ one's fingers** die Daumen drücken ▷ vi (roads) sich kreuzen; **cross out** vt durchstreichen

crossbar n (of bicycle) Stange f; (Sport) Querlatte f; **cross-country** adj: **~ running** Geländelauf m; **~ skiing** Langlauf m; **cross-examination** n Kreuzverhör nt; **cross-eyed** adj: **to be ~** schielen; **crossing** n (crossroads) (Straßen)kreuzung f; (for pedestrians) Fußgängerüberweg m; (on ship) Überfahrt f; **crossroads** nsing o pl Straßenkreuzung f; **cross section** n Querschnitt m; **crosswalk** n (US) Fußgängerüberweg m; **crossword (puzzle)** n Kreuzworträtsel nt

crouch [kraʊtʃ] vi hocken

crouton [ˈkruːtɒn] n Croûton m

crow [krəʊ] n Krähe f

crowbar [ˈkrəʊbɑː] n Brecheisen nt

crowd [kraʊd] n Menge f ▷ vi sich drängen (into in +akk; round um); **crowded** adj überfüllt

crown [kraʊn] n Krone f ▷ vt krönen; (fam) **and to ~ it all ...** und als Krönung ...

crucial [ˈkruːʃəl] adj entscheidend

crude [kruːd] adj primitiv; (humour, behaviour) derb, ordinär ▷ n: **~ (oil)** Rohöl nt

cruel [ˈkruːəl] adj grausam (to zu, gegen); (unfeeling) gefühllos; **cruelty** (n) Grausamkeit f; **~ to animals** Tierquälerei f

cruise [kruːz] n Kreuzfahrt f ▷ vi (ship) kreuzen; (car) mit Reisegeschwindigkeit fahren; **cruise liner** n Kreuzfahrtschiff nt; **cruise missile** n Marschflugkörper m; **cruising speed** n Reisegeschwindigkeit f

crumb [krʌm] n Krume f

crumble [ˈkrʌmbl] vt, vi zerbröckeln ▷ n mit Streuseln überbackenes Kompott

crumpet [ˈkrʌmpɪt] n weiches Hefegebäck zum Toasten; (fam: attractive woman) Schnecke f

crumple [ˈkrʌmpl] vt zerknittern

crunchy [ˈkrʌntʃɪ] adj (Brit) knusprig

crusade [kruːˈseɪd] n Kreuzzug m

crush [krʌʃ] vt zerdrücken; (finger etc) quetschen; (spices, stone) zerstoßen ▷ n: **to have a ~ on sb** in jdn verknallt sein; **crushing** adj (defeat, remark) vernichtend

crust [krʌst] n Kruste f; **crusty** adj knusprig

crutch [krʌtʃ] n Krücke f

cry [kraɪ] vi (call) rufen; (scream) schreien; (weep) weinen ▷ n (call) Ruf m; (louder) Schrei m

crypt [krɪpt] n Krypta f

crystal [ˈkrɪstl] n Kristall m

cu abbr **= see you** (SMS, e-mail) bis bald

Cuba [ˈkjuːbə] n Kuba nt

cube [kjuːb] n Würfel m

cubic [ˈkjuːbɪk] adj Kubik-

cubicle [ˈkjuːbɪkl] n Kabine f

cuckoo ['kʊkuː] n Kuckuck m

cucumber ['kjuːkʌmbə°] n Salatgurke f

cuddle ['kʌdl] vt in den Arm nehmen; (amorously) schmusen mit ▷ n Liebkosung f, Umarmung f; **to have a ~** schmusen; **cuddly** adj verschmust; **cuddly toy** n Plüschtier m

cuff [kʌf] n Manschette f; (US: trouser ~) Aufschlag m; **off the ~** aus dem Stegreif; **cufflink** n Manschettenknopf m

cuisine [kwɪˈziːn] n Kochkunst f, Küche f

cul-de-sac ['kʌldəsæk] n (Brit) Sackgasse f

culprit ['kʌlprɪt] n Schuldige(r) mf; (fig) Übeltäter(in) m(f)

cult [kʌlt] n Kult m

cultivate ['kʌltɪveɪt] vt (Agr: land) bebauen; (crop) anbauen; **cultivated** adj (person) kultiviert, gebildet

cultural ['kʌltʃərəl] adj kulturell, Kultur-; **culture** ['kʌltʃə°] n Kultur f; **cultured** adj gebildet, kultiviert; **culture vulture** (Brit fam) n Kulturfanatiker(in) m(f)

cumbersome ['kʌmbəsəm] adj (object) unhandlich

cumin ['kʌmɪn] n Kreuzkümmel m

cunning ['kʌnɪŋ] adj schlau; (person a.) gerissen

cup [kʌp] n Tasse f; (prize) Pokal m; **it's not his ~ of tea** das ist nicht sein Fall; **cupboard** ['kʌbəd] n Schrank m; **cup final** n Pokalendspiel nt; **cup tie** n Pokalspiel nt

cupola ['kjuːpələ] n Kuppel f

curable ['kjʊərəbl] adj heilbar

curb [kɜːb] n (US) see **kerb**

curd [kɜːd] n: ~ **cheese**, **~s** ~ Quark m

cure [kjʊə°] n Heilmittel nt (for

gegen); (process) Heilung f ▷ vt heilen; (Gastr) pökeln; (smoke) räuchern

curious ['kjʊərɪəs] adj neugierig; (strange) seltsam

curl [kɜːl] n Locke f ▷ vi sich kräuseln; **curly** adj lockig

currant ['kʌrənt] n (dried) Korinthe f; (red, black) Johannisbeere f

currency ['kʌrənsɪ] n Währung f; **foreign ~** Devisen pl

current ['kʌrənt] n (in water) Strömung f; (electric ~) Strom m ▷ adj (issue, affairs) aktuell, gegenwärtig; (expression) gängig; **current account** n Girokonto nt; **currently** adv zur Zeit

curriculum [kəˈrɪkjʊləm] n Lehrplan m; **curriculum vitae** [kəˈrɪkjʊləmˈviːtaɪ] n (Brit) Lebenslauf m

curry ['kʌrɪ] n Currygericht nt; **curry powder** n Curry(pulver) nt

curse [kɜːs] vi (swear) fluchen (at auf +akk) ▷ n Fluch m

cursor ['kɜːsə°] n (Inform) Cursor m

curt [kɜːt] adj schroff, kurz angebunden

curtain ['kɜːtn] n Vorhang m; **it was ~s for Benny** für Benny war alles vorbei

curve [kɜːv] n Kurve f ▷ vi einen Bogen machen; **curved** adj gebogen

cushion ['kʊʃən] n Kissen nt

custard ['kʌstəd] n dicke Vanillesoße, die warm oder kalt zu vielen englischen Nachspeisen gegessen wird

custom ['kʌstəm] n Brauch m; (habit) Gewohnheit f; **customary** ['kʌstəmrɪ] adj üblich; **custom-built** adj nach Kundenangaben gefertigt; **customer** ['kʌstəmə°] n Kunde *m*, Kundin *f*: **customer loyalty card** *n* Kundenkarte *f*: **customer service** *n* Kundendienst *m*

customs ['kʌstəmz] *npl* (*organization, location*) Zoll *m*; **to pass through ~** durch den Zoll gehen; **customs officer** *n* Zollbeamte(r) *m*, Zollbeamtin *f*

cut [kʌt] (**cut, cut**) *vt* schneiden; (*cake*) anschneiden; (*wages, benefits*) kürzen; (*prices*) heruntersetzen; **I ~ my finger** ich habe mir in den Finger geschnitten ▷ *n* Schnitt *m*; (*wound*) Schnittwunde *f*; (*reduction*) Kürzung *f* (*in gen*); **price/tax ~** Preissenkung/Steuersenkung *f*; **to be a ~ above the rest** eine Klasse besser als die anderen sein; **cut back** *vt* (*workforce etc*) reduzieren; **cut down** *vt* (*tree*) fällen; **to ~ on sth** etwas einschränken; **cut in** *vi* (*Auto*) scharf einscheren; **to ~ on sb** jdn schneiden; **cut off** *vt* abschneiden; (*gas, electricity*) abdrehen, abstellen; (*Tel*) **I was ~** ich wurde unterbrochen

cutback *n* Kürzung *f*

cute [kjuːt] *adj* putzig, niedlich; (*US: shrewd*) clever

cutlery ['kʌtlərɪ] *n* Besteck *nt*

cutlet ['kʌtlɪt] *n* (*pork*) Kotelett *nt*; (*veal*) Schnitzel *nt*

cut-price *adj* verbilligt

cutting ['kʌtɪŋ] *n* (*from paper*) Ausschnitt *m*; (*of plant*) Ableger *m* ▷ *adj* (*comment*) verletzend

CV *abbr* = **curriculum vitae**

cwt *abbr* = **hundredweight** = Zentner, Ztr.

cybercafé [saɪbə'kæfeɪ] *n* Internetcafé *nt*; **cyberspace** *n* Cyberspace *m*

cycle ['saɪkl] *n* Fahrrad *nt* ▷ *vi* Rad fahren; **cycle lane, cycle path** *n* Radweg *m*; **cycling** *n*

Radfahren *nt*; **cyclist** ['saɪklɪst] *n* Radfahrer(in) *m(f)*

cylinder ['sɪlɪndə°] *n* Zylinder *m*

cynical ['sɪnɪkəl] *adj* zynisch

cypress ['saɪprɪs] *n* Zypresse *f*

Cypriot ['sɪprɪət] *adj* zypriotisch ▷ *n* Zypriote *m*, Zypriotin *f*; **Cyprus** ['saɪprəs] *n* Zypern *nt*

czar [zɑː°] *n* Zar *m*; **czarina** [zɑː'riːnə] *n* Zarin *f*

Czech [tʃek] *adj* tschechisch ▷ *n* (*person*) Tscheche *m*, Tschechin *f*; (*language*) Tschechisch *nt*; **Czech Republic** *n* Tschechische Republik, Tschechien *nt*

d

dab [dæb] vt (wound, nose etc) betupfen (with mit)

dachshund ['dækshʊnd] n Dackel m

dad(dy) ['dæd(ɪ)] n Papa m, Vati m; **daddy-longlegs** nsing (Brit) Schnake; (US) Weberknecht m

daffodil ['dæfədɪl] n Osterglocke f

daft [dɑːft] adj (fam) blöd, doof

dahlia ['deɪlɪə] n Dahlie f

daily ['deɪlɪ] adj, adv täglich ▷ n (paper) Tageszeitung f

dairy ['dɛərɪ] n (on farm) Molkerei f; **dairy products** npl Milchprodukte pl

daisy ['deɪzɪ] n Gänseblümchen nt

dam [dæm] n Staudamm m ▷ vt stauen

damage ['dæmɪdʒ] n Schaden m; **~s** pl (Jur) Schadenersatz m ▷ vt beschädigen; (reputation, health) schädigen, schaden +dat

damn [dæm] adj (fam) verdammt ▷ vt (condemn) verurteilen; **~ (it)!** verflucht! ▷ n: **he doesn't give a ~** es ist ihm völlig egal

damp [dæmp] adj feucht ▷ n Feuchtigkeit f; **dampen** ['dæmpən] vt befeuchten

dance [dɑːns] n Tanz m; (event) Tanzveranstaltung f ▷ vi tanzen; **dance floor** n Tanzfläche f; **dancer** n Tänzer(in) m(f); **dancing** n Tanzen nt

dandelion ['dændɪlaɪən] n Löwenzahn m

dandruff ['dændrəf] n Schuppen pl

Dane [deɪn] n Däne m, Dänin f

danger ['deɪndʒə*] n Gefahr f; **~ (sign)** Achtung!; **to be in ~** in Gefahr sein; **dangerous** adj gefährlich

Danish ['deɪnɪʃ] adj dänisch ▷ n (language) Dänisch nt; **the ~** pl die Dänen; **Danish pastry** n Plundergebäck nt

Danube ['dænjuːb] n Donau f

dare [dɛə*] vi: **to ~ (to) do sth** es wagen, etw zu tun; **I didn't ~ ask** ich traute mich nicht, zu fragen; **how ~ you** was fällt dir ein!; **daring** adj (person) mutig; (film, clothes etc) gewagt

dark [dɑːk] adj dunkel; (gloomy) düster, trübe; (sinister) finster; **~ chocolate** Bitterschokolade f; **~ green/blue** dunkelgrün/dunkelblau ▷ n: **in the ~** im Dunkeln; **dark glasses** npl Sonnenbrille f; **darkness** n Dunkelheit f

darling ['dɑːlɪŋ] n Schatz m; (also favourite) Liebling m

darts [dɑːts] nsing (game) Darts nt

dash [dæʃ] vi stürzen, rennen

▷ vt: **to ~ hopes** Hoffnungen zerstören ▷ n (in text) Gedankenstrich m; (of liquid) Schuss m; **dashboard** n Armaturenbrett nt

data ['deɪtə] npl Daten pl; **data bank, data base** n Datenbank f; **data capture** n Datenerfassung f; **data processing** n Datenverarbeitung f; **data protection** n Datenschutz m

date [deɪt] n Datum nt; (for meeting, delivery etc) Termin m; (with person) Verabredung f; (with girlfriend/boyfriend etc) Date nt; (fruit) Dattel f; **what's the ~ (today)?** der Wievielte ist heute? **out of ~** adj veraltet; **up to ~** adj (news) aktuell; (fashion) zeitgemäß ▷ vt (letter etc) datieren; (person) gehen mit; **dated** adj altmodisch; **date of birth** n Geburtsdatum nt; **dating agency** n Partnervermittlung f

dative ['deɪtɪv] n Dativ m

daughter ['dɔːtə*] n Tochter f; **daughter-in-law** (pl **daughters-in-law**) n Schwiegertochter f

dawn [dɔːn] n Morgendämmerung f ▷ vi dämmern; **it ~ed on me** mir ging ein Licht auf

day [deɪ] n Tag m; **one ~** eines Tages; **by ~** bei Tage; **~ after ~, ~ by ~** Tag für Tag; **the ~ after/before** am Tag danach/zuvor; **the ~ before yesterday** vorgestern; **the ~ after tomorrow** übermorgen; **these ~s** damals; heutzutage; **in those ~s** damals; **let's call it a ~** Schluss für heute!; **daybreak** n Tagesanbruch m; **day-care center** (US), **day-care centre** n (Brit) Kita f (Kindertagesstätte); **daydream** n Tagtraum m ▷ vi (mit offenen Augen) träumen; **daylight** n

Tageslicht nt; **in ~** bei Tage; **day nursery** n Kita f (Kindertagesstätte); **day return** n (Brit Rail) Tagesrückfahrkarte f; **daytime** n: **in the ~** bei Tage, tagsüber; **daytrip** n Tagesausflug m

dazed [deɪzd] adj benommen

dazzle ['dæzl] vt blenden; **dazzling** adj blendend, glänzend

dead [ded] adj tot; (limb) abgestorben ▷ adv genau; (fam) total, völlig; **~ tired** adj todmüde; **~ slow** (sign) Schritt fahren; **dead end** n Sackgasse f; **deadline** n Termin m; (period) Frist f; **~ for applications** Anmeldeschluss m; **deadly** adj tödlich n ▷ adv: **~ dull** todlangweilig

deaf [def] adj taub; **deafen** vt taub machen; **deafening** adj ohrenbetäubend

deal [diːl] n (dealt, dealt) vt, vi (cards) geben, austeilen ▷ n (business~) Geschäft nt; (agreement) Abmachung f; **it's a ~** abgemacht!; **a good/great ~ of** ziemlich/sehr viel; **deal in** vt handeln mit; **deal with** vt (matter) sich beschäftigen mit; (book, film) behandeln; (successfully: person, problem) fertig werden mit; (matter) erledigen; **dealer** n (Comm) Händler(in) m(f); (drugs) Dealer(in) m(f); **dealings** npl (Comm) Geschäfte pl

dealt [delt] pt, pp of **deal**

dear [dɪə*] adj lieb, teuer; **Dear Sir or Madam** Sehr geehrte Damen und Herren; **Dear David** Lieber David ▷ n Schatz m; (as address) mein Schatz, Liebling; **dearly** adv (love) (heiß und) innig; (pay) teuer

death [deθ] n Tod m; (in accident etc) Todesfall m, Todesopfer nt; **death certificate** n Totenschein m;

death penalty n Todesstrafe f;
death toll n Zahl f der
Todesopfer; **death trap** n
Todesfalle f

debatable [dɪ'beɪtəbl] adj
fraglich; (question) strittig; **debate**
[dɪ'beɪt] n Debatte f ▷ vt
debattieren

debauched [dɪ'bɔːtʃt] adj
ausschweifend

debit ['debɪt] n Soll nt ▷ vt
(account) belasten; **debit card** n
Geldkarte f

debris ['debriː] n Trümmer pl

debt [det] n Schuld f; **to be in
~** verschuldet sein

decade ['dekeɪd] n Jahrzehnt nt

decadent ['dekədənt] adj
dekadent

decaff ['diːkæf] n (fam)
koffeinfreier Kaffee;
decaffeinated [diː'kæfɪneɪtɪd]
adj koffeinfrei

decanter [dɪ'kæntə°] n Dekanter
m, Karaffe f

decay [dɪ'keɪ] n Verfall m;
(rotting) Verwesung f; (of tooth)
Karies f ▷ vi verfallen; (rot)
verwesen; (wood) vermodern;
(teeth) faulen; (leaves) vermodern

deceased [dɪ'siːst] n: **the ~**
der/die Verstorbene

deceit [dɪ'siːt] n Betrug m;
deceive [dɪ'siːv] vt täuschen

December [dɪ'sembə°] n
Dezember m; see also **September**

decent ['diːsənt] adj anständig

deception [dɪ'sepʃən] n Betrug
m; **deceptive** [dɪ'septɪv] adj
täuschend, irreführend

decide [dɪ'saɪd] vt (question)
entscheiden; (body of people)
beschließen; **I can't ~ what to do**
ich kann mich nicht entscheiden,
was ich tun soll ▷ vi sich
entscheiden; **to ~ on sth** (in favour
of sth) sich für etw entscheiden,

sich zu etw entschließen; **decided**
adj entschieden; (clear) deutlich;
decidedly adv entschieden

decimal ['desɪməl] adj Dezimal-;
decimal system n
Dezimalsystem nt

decipher [dɪ'saɪfə°] vt entziffern

decision [dɪ'sɪʒən] n Entscheidung f (on über +akk); (of committee,
jury etc) Beschluss m; **to make a
~** eine Entscheidung treffen;
decisive [dɪ'saɪsɪv] adj entscheidend; (person)
entscheidungsfreudig

deck [dek] n (Naut) Deck nt; (of
cards) Blatt nt; **deckchair** n
Liegestuhl m

declaration [deklə'reɪʃən] n
Erklärung f; **declare** [dɪ'kleə°] vt
erklären; (state) behaupten (that
dass); (at customs) **have you
anything to ~?** haben Sie etwas
zu verzollen?

decline [dɪ'klaɪn] n Rückgang m
▷ vt (invitation, offer) ablehnen ▷ vi
(become less) sinken, abnehmen;
(health) sich verschlechtern

decode [diː'kəʊd] vt
entschlüsseln

decompose [diːkəm'pəʊz] vi sich
zersetzen

decontaminate
[diːkən'tæmɪneɪt] vt entgiften;
(from radioactivity) entseuchen

decorate [dɪ'dekəreɪt] vt
(aus)schmücken; (wallpaper)
tapezieren; (paint) anstreichen;
decoration [dekə'reɪʃən] n
Schmuck m; (process) Schmücken
nt; (wallpapering) Tapezieren nt;
(painting) Anstreichen nt;
Christmas ~s Weihnachts-
schmuck m; **decorator** n
Maler(in) m(f)

decrease ['diːkriːs] n Abnahme f
▷ [diː'kriːs] vi abnehmen

dedicate ['dedɪkeɪt] vt widmen

(to sb jdm); **dedicated** adj (person) engagiert; **dedication** [dedɪˈkeɪʃən] n Widmung f; (commitment) Hingabe f, Engagement nt

deduce [dɪˈdjuːs] vt folgern, schließen (from aus, that dass)

deduct [dɪˈdʌkt] vt abziehen (from von); **deduction** [dɪˈdʌkʃən] n (of money) Abzug m; (conclusion) (Schluss)folgerung f

deed [diːd] n Tat f

deep [diːp] adj tief; **deepen** vt vertiefen; **deep-freeze** n Tiefkühltruhe f; (upright) Gefrierschrank m; **deep-fry** vt frittieren

deer [dɪəʳ] n inv (with stag) Hirsch m

defeat [dɪˈfiːt] n Niederlage f; **to admit ~** sich geschlagen geben ▷ vt besiegen

defect [ˈdiːfekt] n Defekt m, Fehler m; **defective** [dɪˈfektɪv] adj fehlerhaft

defence [dɪˈfens] n Verteidigung f; **defend** [dɪˈfend] vt verteidigen; **defendant** [dɪˈfendənt] n (Jur) Angeklagte(r) mf; **defender** n (Sport) Verteidiger(in) m(f); **defensive** [dɪˈfensɪv] adj defensiv

deficiency [dɪˈfɪʃənsɪ] n Mangel m; **deficient** adj mangelhaft; **deficit** [ˈdefɪsɪt] n Defizit nt

define [dɪˈfaɪn] vt (word) definieren; (duties, powers) bestimmen; **definite** [ˈdefɪnɪt] adj (clear) klar, eindeutig; (certain) sicher; **it's ~** es steht fest; **definitely** adv bestimmt; **definition** [defɪˈnɪʃən] n Definition f; (Foto) Schärfe f

defrost [diːˈfrɒst] vt (fridge) abtauen; (food) auftauen

degrading [dɪˈɡreɪdɪŋ] adj erniedrigend

degree [dɪˈɡriː] n Grad m; (at university) akademischer Grad; **a certain/high ~ of** ein gewisses/hohes Maß an +dat; **to a certain ~** einigermaßen; **the ~ in chemistry** = ich habe einen Abschluss in Chemie

dehydrated [diːhaɪˈdreɪtɪd] adj (food) getrocknet, Trocken-; (person) ausgetrocknet

de-ice [diːˈaɪs] vt enteisen

delay [dɪˈleɪ] vt (postpone) verschieben, aufschieben; **to be ~ed** (event) sich verzögern; **the train/flight was ~ed** der Zug/die Maschine hatte Verspätung ▷ vi warten; (hesitate) zögern ▷ n Verzögerung f; (of train etc) Verspätung f; **without ~** unverzüglich; **delayed** adj (train etc) verspätet

delegate n [ˈdelɪɡət] Delegierte(r) mf ▷ [ˈdelɪɡeɪt] vt delegieren; **delegation** [delɪˈɡeɪʃən] n Abordnung f; (foreign) Delegation f

delete [dɪˈliːt] vt (aus)streichen; (Inform) löschen; **deletion** n Streichung f; (Inform) Löschung f

deli [ˈdelɪ] n (fam) Feinkostgeschäft nt

deliberate [dɪˈlɪbərət] adj (intentional) absichtlich; **deliberately** adv mit Absicht, extra

delicate [ˈdelɪkət] adj (fine) fein; (fragile) zart; (a. Med) empfindlich; (situation) heikel

delicatessen [delɪkəˈtesn] nsing Feinkostgeschäft nt

delicious [dɪˈlɪʃəs] adj köstlich, lecker

delight [dɪˈlaɪt] n Freude f ▷ vt entzücken; **delighted** adj sehr erfreut; (with über +akk); **delightful** adj entzückend; (weather, meal etc) herrlich

deliver [dɪ'lɪvə°] vt (goods) liefern (to sb jdm); (letter, parcel) zustellen; (speech) halten; (baby) entbinden; **delivery** n Lieferung f; (of letter, parcel) Zustellung f; (of baby) Entbindung f; **delivery van** n Lieferwagen m

delude [dɪ'luːd] vt täuschen; **don't ~ yourself** mach dir nichts vor; **delusion** n Irrglaube m

de luxe [dɪ'lʌks] adj Luxus-

demand [dɪ'mɑːnd] vt verlangen (from von); (time, patience etc) erfordern ▷ n (request) Forderung f, Verlangen nt (for nach); (Comm: for goods) Nachfrage f (for nach); **on ~** auf Wunsch; **very much in ~** sehr gefragt; **demanding** adj anspruchsvoll

demented [dɪ'mentɪd] adj wahnsinnig

demerara [demə'reərə] n: **~ (sugar)** brauner Zucker

demister n Defroster m

demo ['deməʊ] (pl -s) n (fam) Demo f

democracy [dɪ'mɒkrəsɪ] n Demokratie f; **democrat, Democrat** (US Pol) ['deməkræt] n Demokrat(in) m(f); **democratic** adj demokratisch; **the Democratic Party** (US Pol) die Demokratische Partei

demolish [dɪ'mɒlɪʃ] vt abreißen; (fig) zerstören; **demolition** [demə'lɪʃən] n Abbruch m

demonstrate ['demənstreɪt] vt, vi demonstrieren, beweisen; **demonstration** n Demonstration f

demoralize [dɪ'mɒrəlaɪz] vt demoralisieren

denial [dɪ'naɪəl] n Leugnung f; (official ~) Dementi nt

denim ['denɪm] n Jeansstoff m; **denim jacket** n Jeansjacke f; **denims** npl Bluejeans pl

Denmark ['denmɑːk] n Dänemark nt

denomination [dɪnɒmɪ'neɪʃən] n (Rel) Konfession f; (Comm) Nennwert m

dense [dens] adj dicht; (fam: stupid) schwer von Begriff; **density** ['densɪtɪ] n Dichte f

dent [dent] n Beule f, Delle f ▷ vt einbeulen

dental ['dentl] adj Zahn-; **~ floss** Zahnseide f; **dentist** ['dentɪst] n Zahnarzt m, Zahnärztin; **dentures** ['dentʃəz] npl Zahnprothese f; (full) Gebiss nt

deny [dɪ'naɪ] vt leugnen, bestreiten; (refuse) ablehnen

deodorant [diː'əʊdərənt] n Deo(dorant) nt

depart [dɪ'pɑːt] vi abreisen; (bus, train) abfahren (for nach, from von); (plane) abfliegen (for nach, from von)

department [dɪ'pɑːtmənt] n Abteilung f; (at university) Institut nt; (Pol: ministry) Ministerium nt; **department store** n Kaufhaus nt

departure [dɪ'pɑːtʃə°] n (of person) Weggang m; (on journey) Abreise f (for nach); (of train etc) Abfahrt f (for nach); (of plane) Abflug m (for nach); **departure lounge** n (Aviat) Abflughalle f; **departure time** n Abfahrtzeit f; (Aviat) Abflugzeit f

depend [dɪ'pend] vi: **it ~s** es kommt darauf an (whether, if ob); **depend on** vt (thing) abhängen von; (person: rely on) sich verlassen auf +akk; (person, area etc) angewiesen sein auf +akk; **it ~s on the weather** es kommt auf das Wetter an; **dependable** adj zuverlässig; **dependence** n Abhängigkeit f (on von); **dependent** adj abhängig (on von)

deport [dɪ'pɔːt] vt ausweisen,

abschieben; **deportation**
[di:pɔːˈteɪʃən] n Abschiebung f

deposit [dɪˈpɒzɪt] n (down
payment) Anzahlung f; (security)
Kaution f; (for bottle) Pfand nt; (to
bank account) Einzahlung f; (in river
etc) Ablagerung f ▷ vt (put down)
abstellen, absetzen; (to bank
account) einzahlen; (sth valuable)
deponieren; **deposit account** n
Sparkonto nt

depot [ˈdepəʊ] n Depot nt

depreciate [dɪˈpriːʃɪeɪt] vi an
Wert verlieren

depress [dɪˈpres] vt (in mood)
deprimieren; **depressed** adj
(person) niedergeschlagen,
deprimiert; **~ area**
Notstandsgebiet nt; **depressing**
adj deprimierend; **depression**
[dɪˈpreʃən] n (of mind) Depression f;
(Meteo) Tief nt

deprive [dɪˈpraɪv] vt: **to ~ sb of
sth** jdn einer Sache berauben;
deprived (child) (sozial)
benachteiligt

dept abbr = **department** Abt.

depth [depθ] n Tiefe f

deputy [ˈdepjʊtɪ] adj stell-
vertretend, Vize- ▷ n
Stellvertreter(in) m(f); (US Pol)
Abgeordnete(r) mf

derail [dɪˈreɪl] vt entgleisen
lassen; **to be ~ed** entgleisen

deranged [dɪˈreɪndʒd] adj
geistesgestört

derivation [derɪˈveɪʃən] n
Ableitung f; **derive** [dɪˈraɪv] vt
ableiten (from von) ▷ abstammen
(from von)

dermatitis [dɜːməˈtaɪtɪs] n
Hautentzündung f

derogatory [dɪˈrɒgətərɪ] adj
abfällig

descend [dɪˈsend] vt, vi
hinabsteigen, hinuntergehen;
(person) **to ~ o** be **~ed from**

abstammen von; **descendant** n
Nachkomme m; **descent** [dɪˈsent]
n (coming down) Abstieg m; (origin)
Abstammung f

describe [dɪsˈkraɪb] vt beschreiben; **description**
[dɪsˈkrɪpʃən] n Beschreibung f

desert [ˈdezət] n Wuste f
▷ [dɪˈzɜːt] vt verlassen; (abandon)
im Stich lassen; **deserted** adj
verlassen; (empty) menschenleer

deserve [dɪˈzɜːv] vt verdienen

design [dɪˈzaɪn] n (plan) Entwurf
m; (of vehicle, machine)
Konstruktion f; (of object) Design
nt; (planning) Gestaltung f ▷ vt
entwerfen; (machine etc)
konstruieren; **~ed for sb/sth**
(intended) für jdn/etw konzipiert

designate [ˈdezɪgneɪt] vt
bestimmen

designer [dɪˈzaɪnə°] n
Designer(in) m(f); (Tech)
Konstrukteur(in) m(f); **designer
drug** n Designerdroge f

desirable [dɪˈzaɪərəbl] n
wünschenswert; (person)
begehrenswert; **desire** [dɪˈzaɪə°]
n Wunsch m (for nach); (esp sexual)
Begierde f (for nach) ▷ vt
wünschen; (ask for) verlangen; **if
~d** auf Wunsch

desk [desk] n Schreibtisch m;
(reception ~) Empfang m; (at airport
etc) Schalter m; **desktop
publishing** n Desktoppublishing
nt

desolate [ˈdesəlɪt] adj trostlos

despair [dɪsˈpeə°] n Verzweiflung f (at über +akk) ▷ vi
verzweifeln (of an +dat)

despatch [dɪsˈpætʃ] see **dispatch**

desperate [ˈdespərɪt] adj
verzweifelt; (situation)
hoffnungslos; **to be ~ for sth** etw
dringend brauchen; unbedingt
wollen; **desperation**

[despə'reɪʃən] n Verzweiflung f

despicable [dɪ'spɪkəbl] adj verachtenswert; **despise** [dɪ'spaɪz] vt verachten

despite [dɪ'spaɪt] prep trotz +gen

dessert [dɪ'zɜːt] n Nachtisch m; **dessert spoon** n Dessertlöffel m

destination [destɪ'neɪʃən] n (of person) (Reise)ziel nt; (of goods) Bestimmungsort m

destiny ['destɪnɪ] n Schicksal nt

destroy [dɪ'strɔɪ] vt zerstören; (completely) vernichten; **destruction** [dɪ'strʌkʃən] n Zerstörung f; (complete) Vernichtung f; **destructive** [dɪ'strʌktɪv] adj zerstörerisch; (esp fig) destruktiv

detach [dɪ'tætʃ] vt abnehmen; (from form etc) abtrennen; (free) lösen (from von); **detachable** adj abnehmbar; (from form etc) abtrennbar; **detached** adj (attitude) distanziert, objektiv; **~ house** Einzelhaus nt

detail ['diːteɪl, (US) dɪ'teɪl] n Einzelheit f, Detail nt; (further) **~s from ...** Näheres erfahren Sie bei ...; **to go into ~** ins Detail gehen; **in ~** ausführlich; **detailed** adj detailliert, ausführlich

detain [dɪ'teɪn] vt aufhalten; (police) in Haft nehmen

detect [dɪ'tekt] vt entdecken; (notice) wahrnehmen; **detective** [dɪ'tektɪv] n Detektiv(in) m(f); **detective story** n Krimi m

detention [dɪ'tenʃən] n Haft f; (Sch) Nachsitzen nt

deter [dɪ'tɜː°] vt abschrecken (from von)

detergent [dɪ'tɜːdʒənt] n Reinigungsmittel nt; (soap powder) Waschmittel nt

deteriorate [dɪ'tɪərɪəreɪt] vi sich verschlechtern

determination [dɪtɜːmɪ'neɪʃən] n Entschlossenheit f; **determine** [dɪ'tɜːmɪn] vt bestimmen; **determined** adj (fest) entschlossen

deterrent [dɪ'terənt] n Abschreckungsmittel nt

detest [dɪ'test] vt verabscheuen; **detestable** adj abscheulich

detour ['diːtʊə°] n Umweg m; (of traffic) Umleitung f

deuce [djuːs] n (Tennis) Einstand m

devalue [diː'væljuː] vt abwerten

devastate ['devəsteɪt] vt verwüsten; **devastating** ['devəsteɪtɪŋ] adj verheerend

develop [dɪ'veləp] vt entwickeln; (illness) bekommen ▷ vi sich entwickeln; **developing country** n Entwicklungsland nt; **development** n Entwicklung f; (of land) Erschließung f

device [dɪ'vaɪs] n Vorrichtung f, Gerät nt

devil ['devl] n Teufel m; **devilish** adj teuflisch

devote [dɪ'vəʊt] vt widmen (to dat); **devoted** adj liebend; (servant etc) treu ergeben; **devotion** n Hingabe f

devour [dɪ'vaʊə°] vt verschlingen

dew [djuː] n Tau m

diabetes [daɪə'biːtiːz] n Diabetes m, Zuckerkrankheit f; **diabetic** [daɪə'betɪk] adj zuckerkrank, für Diabetiker ▷ n Diabetiker(in) m(f)

diagnosis [daɪəg'nəʊsɪs] n (pl **diagnoses**) n Diagnose f

diagonal [daɪ'ægənl] adj diagonal

diagram ['daɪəgræm] n Diagramm nt

dial ['daɪəl] n Skala f; (of clock)

Zifferblatt nt ▷ vt (Tel) wählen; **dial code** n (US) Vorwahl f

dialect ['daɪəlekt] n Dialekt m

dialling code n (Brit) Vorwahl f; **dialling tone** n (Brit) Amtszeichen nt

dialogue, dialog (US) ['daɪəlɒg] n Dialog m

dial tone n (US) Amtszeichen nt

dialysis [daɪˈæləsɪs] n (Med) Dialyse f

diameter [daɪˈæmɪtə°] n Durchmesser m

diamond ['daɪəmənd] n Diamant m; (Cards) Karo nt

diaper ['daɪpə°] n (US) Windel f

diarrhoea [daɪəˈriːə] n Durchfall m

diary ['daɪərɪ] n (Taschen)kalender m; (account) Tagebuch nt

dice [daɪs] npl Würfel pl; **diced** adj in Würfel geschnitten

dictate [dɪkˈteɪt] vt diktieren;
dictation [dɪkˈteɪʃən] n Diktat nt

dictator [dɪkˈteɪtə°] n Diktator(in) m(f); **dictatorship** [dɪkˈteɪtəʃɪp] n Diktatur f

dictionary ['dɪkʃənrɪ] n Wörterbuch nt

did [dɪd] pt of **do**

didn't ['dɪdnt] contr of **did not**

die [daɪ] vi sterben (of an +dat); (plant, animal) eingehen; (engine) absterben; **to be dying to do sth** darauf brennen, etw zu tun; **I'm dying for a drink** ich brauche unbedingt was zu trinken; **die away** vi schwächer werden; (wind) sich legen; **die down** vi nachlassen; **die out** vi aussterben

diesel ['diːzəl] n (fuel, car) Diesel m; ~ **engine** n Dieselmotor m

diet ['daɪət] n Kost f, (special food) Diät f ▷ vi eine Diät machen

differ ['dɪfə°] vi (be different) sich unterscheiden; (disagree) anderer Meinung sein; **difference** ['dɪfrəns] n Unterschied m; **it makes no ~ (to me)** es ist (mir) egal; **it makes a big ~** es macht viel aus; **different** adj andere(r, s); (with pl) verschieden; **to be ~** ganz anders sein (from als); (two people, things) verschieden sein; **a ~ person** ein anderer Mensch; **differentiate** [dɪfəˈrenʃɪeɪt] vt, vi unterscheiden; **differently** ['dɪfrəntlɪ] adv anders (from als); (from one another) unterschiedlich

difficult ['dɪfɪkəlt] adj schwierig; **I find it ~** es fällt mir schwer; **difficulty** n Schwierigkeit f; **with ~** nur schwer; **to have ~ in doing sth** etw nur mit Mühe machen können

dig [dɪg] (dug, dug) vt, vi (hole) graben; **dig in** vi (fam: to food) reinhauen; **~! I** greif(t) zu!; **dig up** vt ausgraben

digest [daɪˈdʒest] vt (a. fig) verdauen; **digestible** [dɪˈdʒestəbl] adj verdaulich; **digestion** [dɪˈdʒestʃən] n Verdauung f; **digestive** [dɪˈdʒestɪv] adj: ~ **biscuit** (Brit) Vollkornkeks m

digit ['dɪdʒɪt] n Ziffer f; **digital** ['dɪdʒɪtəl] adj digital; ~ **computer** Digitalrechner m; ~ **watch/clock** Digitaluhr f; **digital camera** n Digitalkamera f; **digital television, digital TV** n Digitalfernsehen nt

dignified ['dɪgnɪfaɪd] adj würdevoll; **dignity** ['dɪgnɪtɪ] n Würde f

dilapidated [dɪˈlæpɪdeɪtɪd] adj baufällig

dilemma [daɪˈlemə] n Dilemma nt

dill [dɪl] n Dill m

dilute [daɪˈluːt] vt verdünnen

dim [dɪm] adj (light) schwach; (outline) undeutlich; (stupid)

schwer von Begriff ▷ vt
verdunkeln; (US Auto) abblenden;
~med headlights (US)
Abblendlicht nt

dime [daɪm] n (US)
Zehncentstück nt

dimension [daɪˈmenʃən] n
Dimension f; **~s** pl Maße pl

diminish [dɪˈmɪnɪʃ] vt
verringern ▷ vi sich verringern

dimple [ˈdɪmpl] n Grübchen nt

dine [daɪn] vi speisen; **dine out**
vi außer Haus essen; **diner** n Gast
m; (Rail) Speisewagen m; (US)
Speiselokal nt

dinghy [ˈdɪŋgɪ] n Ding(h)i nt;
(inflatable) Schlauchboot nt

dingy [ˈdɪndʒɪ] adj düster; (dirty)
schmuddelig

dining car [ˈdaɪnɪŋkaːʳ] n
Speisewagen m; **dining room** n
Esszimmer nt; (in hotel)
Speiseraum m; **dining table** n
Esstisch m

dinner [ˈdɪnəʳ] n Abendessen nt;
(lunch) Mittagessen nt; (public)
Diner nt; **to be at ~** beim Essen
sein; **to have ~** zu Abend/Mittag
essen; **dinner jacket** n Smoking
m; **dinner party** n
Abendgesellschaft f (mit Essen);
dinnertime n Essenszeit f

dinosaur [ˈdaɪnəsɔːʳ] n Dinosaurier m

dip [dɪp] vt tauchen (in in +akk);
to ~ (one's headlights (Brit Auto)
abblenden; **~ped headlights**
Abblendlicht nt ▷ n (in ground)
Bodensenke f; (sauce) Dip m

diploma [dɪˈpləʊmə] n Diplom nt

diplomat [ˈdɪpləmæt] n Diplo-
mat(in) m(f); **diplomatic**
[dɪpləˈmætɪk] adj diplomatisch

dipstick [ˈdɪpstɪk] n Ölmessstab
m

direct [daɪˈrekt] adj direkt;

(cause, consequence) unmittelbar;
~ debit (mandate)
Einzugsermächtigung f;
(transaction) Abbuchung f im
Lastschriftverfahren; **~ train**
durchgehender Zug ▷ vt (aim,
send) richten (at, to an +akk); (film)
die Regie führen bei; (traffic)
regeln; **direct current** n (Elec)
Gleichstrom m

direction [dɪˈrekʃən] n (course)
Richtung f; (Cine) Regie f; **in
the ~ of ...** in Richtung ...; **~s**
pl (to a place) Wegbeschreibung f

directly [dɪˈrektlɪ] adv direkt; (at
once) sofort

director [dɪˈrektəʳ] n Direk-
tor(in) m(f), Leiter(in) m(f); (of film)
Regisseur(in) m(f)

directory [dɪˈrektərɪ] n Adressbuch nt; (Tel) Telefonbuch nt;
~ enquiries o (US) **assistance** (Tel)
Auskunft f

dirt [dɜːt] n Schmutz m, Dreck m;
dirt cheap adj spottbillig; **dirt
road** n unbefestigte Straße; **dirty**
adj schmutzig

disability [dɪsəˈbɪlɪtɪ] n
Behinderung f; **disabled**
[dɪsˈeɪbld] adj behindert,
Behinderten- ▷ npl: **the ~** die
Behinderten

disadvantage [dɪsədˈvaːntɪdʒ]
n Nachteil m; **at a ~** benachteiligt;
disadvantageous [dɪsædvaːn-
ˈteɪdʒəs] adj unvorteilhaft,
ungünstig

disagree [dɪsəˈgriː] vi anderer
Meinung sein; (two people) sich
nicht einig sein; (two reports etc)
nicht übereinstimmen; **to ~ with
sb** mit jdm nicht übereinstimmen;
(food) jdm nicht bekommen;
disagreeable adj unangenehm;
(person) unsympathisch;
disagreement n Meinungsverschiedenheit f

disappear [dɪsə'pɪə⁰] vi verschwinden; **disappearance** n Verschwinden nt

disappoint [dɪsə'pɔɪnt] vt enttäuschen; **disappointing** adj enttäuschend; **disappointment** n Enttäuschung f

disapproval [dɪsə'pruːvl] n Missbilligung f; **disapprove** [dɪsə'pruːv] vi missbilligen (of akk)

disarm [dɪs'aːm] vt entwaffnen ▷ vi (Pol) abrüsten; **disarmament** n Abrüstung f; **disarming** adj (smile, look) gewinnend

disaster [dɪ'zaːstə⁰] n Katastrophe f; **disastrous** [dɪ'zaːstrəs] adj katastrophal

disbelief [dɪsbə'liːf] n Ungläubigkeit f

disc [dɪsk] n Scheibe f, CD f; see also **disk**; (Anat) Bandscheibe f; **disc brake** n Scheibenbremse f

discharge [dɪstʃaːdʒ] n (Med) Ausfluss m ▷ [dɪs'tʃaːdʒ] vt (person) entlassen; (emit) ausstoßen; (Med) ausscheiden

discipline ['dɪsɪplɪn] n Disziplin f

disc jockey ['dɪskdʒɒkɪ] n Diskjockey m

disclose [dɪs'kləʊz] vt bekannt geben; (secret) enthüllen

disco ['dɪskəʊ] (pl -s) n Disko f, Diskomusik f

discomfort [dɪs'kʌmfət] n (slight pain) leichte Schmerzen pl; (unease) Unbehagen nt

disconnect [dɪskə'nekt] vt (electricity, gas, phone) abstellen; (unplug) **to ~ the TV (from the mains)** den Stecker des Fernsehers herausziehen; (Tel) **I've been ~ed** das Gespräch ist unterbrochen worden

discontent [dɪskən'tent] n Unzufriedenheit f; **discontented** adj unzufrieden

discontinue [dɪskən'tɪnjuː] vt einstellen; (product) auslaufen lassen

discount [dɪskaʊnt] n Rabatt m

discover [dɪs'kʌvə⁰] vt entdecken; **discovery** n Entdeckung f

discredit [dɪs'kredɪt] vt in Verruf bringen ▷ n Misskredit m

discreet [dɪs'kriːt] adj diskret

discrepancy [dɪs'krepənsɪ] n Unstimmigkeit f, Diskrepanz f

discriminate [dɪs'krɪmɪneɪt] vi unterscheiden; **to ~ against sb** jdn diskriminieren; **discrimination** [dɪskrɪmɪ'neɪʃən] n (different treatment) Diskriminierung f

discus ['dɪskəs] n Diskus m

discuss [dɪs'kʌs] vt diskutieren, besprechen; **discussion** [dɪs'kʌʃən] n Diskussion f

disease [dɪ'ziːz] n Krankheit f

disembark [dɪsɪm'baːk] vi von Bord gehen

disentangle ['dɪsɪn'tæŋgl] vt entwirren

disgrace [dɪs'greɪs] n Schande f ▷ vt Schande machen +dat; (family etc) Schande bringen über +akk; (less strong) blamieren; **disgraceful** adj skandalös

disguise [dɪs'gaɪz] vt verkleiden; (voice) verstellen ▷ n Verkleidung f; **in ~** verkleidet

disgust [dɪs'gʌst] n Abscheu m; (physical) Ekel m ▷ vt anekeln, anwidern; **disgusting** adj widerlich; (physically) ekelhaft

dish [dɪʃ] n Schüssel f; (food) Gericht nt; **~es** pl (crockery) Geschirr nt; **to do/wash the ~es** abwaschen; **dishcloth** n (for washing) Spültuch nt; (for drying) Geschirrtuch nt

dishearten [dɪsˈhɑːtən] vt
entmutigen; **don't be ~ed** lass den
Kopf nicht hängen!

dishonest [dɪsˈɒnɪst] adj
unehrlich

dishonour [dɪsˈɒnəʳ] n Schande
f

dish towel n (US) Geschirrtuch
nt; **dish washer** n
Geschirrspülmaschine f

dishy [ˈdɪʃɪ] adj (Brit fam) gut
aussehend

disillusioned [dɪsɪˈluːʒənd] adj
desillusioniert

disinfect [dɪsɪnˈfekt] vt desinfizieren; **disinfectant** n
Desinfektionsmittel nt

disintegrate [dɪsˈɪntɪgreɪt]
vi zerfallen; (group) sich
auflösen

disjointed [dɪsˈdʒɔɪntɪd] adj
unzusammenhängend

disk [dɪsk] n (Inform: floppy)
Diskette f; **disk drive** n
Diskettenlaufwerk nt; **diskette**
[dɪsˈket] n Diskette f

dislike [dɪsˈlaɪk] n Abneigung f
▷ vt nicht mögen; **to ~ doing sth**
etw ungern tun

dislocate [ˈdɪsləkeɪt] vt (Med)
verrenken, ausrenken

dismal [ˈdɪzməl] adj trostlos

dismantle [dɪsˈmæntl] vt
auseinandernehmen; (machine)
demontieren

dismay [dɪsˈmeɪ] n Bestürzung f;
dismayed adj bestürzt

dismiss [dɪsˈmɪs] vt (employee)
entlassen; **dismissal** n
Entlassung f

disobedience [dɪsəˈbiːdɪəns] n
Ungehorsam m; **disobedient** adj
ungehorsam; **disobey** [dɪsəˈbeɪ]
vt nicht gehorchen +dat

disorder [dɪsˈɔːdəʳ] n (mess)
Unordnung f; (riot) Aufruhr m;
(Med) Störung f, Leiden nt

disorganized [dɪsˈɔːgənaɪzd] adj
chaotisch

disparaging adj geringschätzig

dispatch [dɪsˈpætʃ] vt abschicken, abfertigen

dispensable [dɪsˈpensəbl] adj
entbehrlich; **dispense** vt
verteilen; **dispense with** vt
verzichten auf +akk; **dispenser** n
Automat m

disperse [dɪsˈpɜːs] vi sich
zerstreuen

display [dɪsˈpleɪ] n (exhibition)
Ausstellung f, Show f; (of goods)
Auslage f; (Tech) Anzeige f, Display
nt ▷ vt zeigen; (goods) ausstellen

disposable [dɪsˈpəʊzəbl] adj
(container, razor etc) Wegwerf-;
~ nappy Wegwerfwindel f;
disposal [dɪsˈpəʊzəl] n Loswerden nt; (of waste) Beseitigung f; **to
be at sb's ~** jdm zur Verfügung
stehen; **to have at one's
~** verfügen über; **dispose of** vt
loswerden; (waste etc) beseitigen

dispute [dɪsˈpjuːt] n Streit m;
(industrial) Auseinandersetzung f
▷ vt bestreiten

disqualification
[dɪskwɒlɪfɪˈkeɪʃən] n Disquali-
fikation f; **disqualify**
[dɪsˈkwɒlɪfaɪ] vt disqualifizieren

disregard [dɪsrɪˈgɑːd] vt nicht
beachten

disreputable [dɪsˈrepjʊtəbl] adj
verrufen

disrespect [dɪsrɪˈspekt] n
Respektlosigkeit f

disrupt [dɪsˈrʌpt] vt stören;
(interrupt) unterbrechen;
disruption [dɪsˈrʌpʃən] n
Störung f; (interruption)
Unterbrechung f

dissatisfied [dɪsˈsætɪsfaɪd] adj
unzufrieden

dissent [dɪˈsent] n Widerspruch
m

dissolve [dɪ'zɒlv] vt auflösen
▷ vi sich auflösen

dissuade [dɪ'sweɪd] vt (davon abbringen) **to ~ sb from doing sth** jdn davon abbringen, etw zu tun

distance ['dɪstəns] n Entfernung f; **in the/from a ~** in/aus der Ferne; **distant** adj (a. in time) fern; (relative etc) entfernt; (person) distanziert

distaste [dɪs'teɪst] n Abneigung f (for gegen)

distil [dɪs'tɪl] vt destillieren; **distillery** n Brennerei f

distinct [dɪs'tɪŋkt] adj verschieden; (clear) klar, deutlich; **distinction** [dɪs'tɪŋkʃən] n (difference) Unterscheidung f; (in exam etc) Auszeichnung f; **distinctive** adj unverkennbar; **distinctly** adv deutlich

distinguish [dɪs'tɪŋɡwɪʃ] vt unterscheiden (sth from sth etw von etw)

distort [dɪs'tɔːt] vt verzerren; (truth) verdrehen

distract [dɪs'trækt] vt ablenken; **distraction** [dɪs'trækʃən] n Ablenkung f; (diversion) Zerstreuung f

distress [dɪs'tres] n (need, danger) Not f; (suffering) Leiden nt; (mental) Qual f; (worry) Kummer m ▷ vt mitnehmen, erschüttern; **distressed area** n Notstandsgebiet nt; **distress signal** n Notsignal nt

distribute [dɪs'trɪbjuːt] vt verteilen; (Comm: goods) vertreiben; **distribution** [dɪstrɪ'bjuːʃən] n Verteilung f; (Comm: of goods) Vertrieb m; **distributor** [dɪs'trɪbjʊtə°] n (Auto) Verteiler m; (Comm) Händler(in) m(f)

district ['dɪstrɪkt] n Gegend f; (administrative) Bezirk m; **district attorney** n (US) Staatsanwalt m, Staatsanwältin f

distrust [dɪs'trʌst] vt misstrauen +dat ▷ n Misstrauen f

disturb [dɪs'tɜːb] vt stören; (worry) beunruhigen; **disturbance** n Störung f, **disturbing** adj beunruhigend

ditch [dɪtʃ] n Graben m ▷ vt (fam: person) den Laufpass geben +dat; (plan etc) verwerfen

ditto ['dɪtəʊ] adv dito, ebenfalls

dive [daɪv] n (into water) Kopfsprung m; (Aviat) Sturzflug m; (fam) zwielichtiges Lokal ▷ vi (under water) tauchen; **diver** n Taucher(in) m(f)

diverse [daɪ'vɜːs] adj verschieden; **diversion** [daɪ'vɜːʃən] n (of traffic) Umleitung f; (distraction) Ablenkung f; **divert** [daɪ'vɜːt] vt ablenken; (traffic) umleiten

divide [dɪ'vaɪd] vt teilen; (in several parts, between people) aufteilen ▷ vi sich teilen; **dividend** ['dɪvɪdend] n Dividende f

divine [dɪ'vaɪn] adj göttlich

diving ['daɪvɪŋ] n (Sport)-tauchen nt; (jumping in) Springen nt; (Sport: from board) Kunstspringen nt; **diving board** n Sprungbrett nt; **diving goggles** npl Taucherbrille f; **diving mask** n Tauchmaske f

division [dɪ'vɪʒən] n Teilung f; (Math) Division f; (department) Abteilung f; (Sport) Liga f

divorce [dɪ'vɔːs] n Scheidung f ▷ vt sich scheiden lassen von; **divorced** adj geschieden; **to get ~** sich scheiden lassen; **divorcee** [dɪvɔː'siː] n Geschiedene(r) mf

DIY [diːaɪ'waɪ] abbr =

do-it-yourself; **DIY centre** n
Baumarkt m

dizzy ['dɪzɪ] adj schwindlig

DJ [di:'dʒeɪ] abbr = **dinner jacket**
Smoking m ▷ abbr = **disc jockey**
Diskjockey m, DJ m

DNA abbr = **desoxyribonucleic
acid** DNS f

○ **KEYWORD**

do [du:] (pt **did**, pp **done**) n (inf)
(party etc) Fete f
▷ vb aux 1 (in negative constructions
and questions) **I don't understand**
ich verstehe nicht; **didn't you
know?** wusstest du das nicht?;
what do you think? was meinen
Sie?
2 (for emphasis, in polite phrases) **she
does seem rather tired** sie
scheint wirklich sehr müde zu
sein; **so sit down/help yourself**
setzen Sie sich doch hin/greifen
Sie doch zu
3 (used to avoid repeating vb) **she
swims better than I do** sie
schwimmt besser als ich; **she
lives in Glasgow — so do I** sie
wohnt in Glasgow — ich auch
4 (in tag questions) **you like him,
don't you?** du magst/Sie mögen
ihn doch, oder?
▷ vt 1 (carry out, perform etc) tun,
machen; **what are you doing
tonight?** was machst du/machen
Sie heute Abend?; **I've got
nothing to do** ich habe nichts zu
tun; **to do one's hair/nails** sich
die Haare/Nägel machen
2 (car etc) fahren
▷ vi 1 (act, behave) **do as I do** mach
es wie ich
2 (get on, fare) **he's doing
well/badly at school** er ist
gut/schlecht in der Schule; **how
do you do?** guten Tag

3 (be suitable) gehen; (be sufficient)
reichen; **to make do (with)**
auskommen mit
do away with vt (kill)
umbringen; (abolish: law etc)
abschaffen
do up vt (laces, dress, buttons)
zumachen; (renovate: room, house)
renovieren
do with vt (need) brauchen; (be
connected) zu tun haben mit
do without vt, vi auskommen
ohne
do up vt (fasten) zumachen;
(parcel) verschnüren; (renovate)
wiederherrichten
do with vt (need) brauchen; **I
could ~ a drink** ich könnte einen
Drink gebrauchen
do without vt auskommen
ohne; **I can ~ your comments**
auf deine Kommentare kann ich
verzichten

dock [dɒk] n Dock nt; (Jur)
Anklagebank f; **docker** n
Hafenarbeiter m; **dockyard** n
Werft f

doctor ['dɒktə*] n Arzt m, Ärztin;
(in title, also academic) Doktor m

document ['dɒkjʊmənt] n
Dokument nt; **documentary**
[dɒkjʊ'mentərɪ] n Dokumentarfilm m; **documentation**
[dɒkjʊmən'teɪʃən] n Dokumen-
tation f

docusoap ['dɒkjʊsəʊp] n
Reality-Serie f, Dokusoap f

doddery ['dɒdərɪ] adj tatterig

dodgem ['dɒdʒəm] n Auto-
skooter m

dodgy ['dɒdʒɪ] adj nicht ganz in
Ordnung; (dishonest, unreliable)
zwielichtig; **he has a ~ stomach**
er hat sich den Magen verdorben

dog [dɒg] n Hund m; **dog food** n
Hundefutter nt; **doggie bag**

['dɒgɪˌbæg] n Tüte oder Box, in der
Essensreste aus dem Restaurant
mit nach Hause genommen werden
können

do-it-yourself ['duːɪtjəˈself] n
Heimwerken nt, Do-it-yourself nt
▷ adj Heimwerker-;
do-it-yourselfer n Bastler(in)
m(f), Heimwerker(in) m(f)

doll [dɒl] n Puppe f

dollar ['dɒlə*] n Dollar m

dolphin ['dɒlfɪn] n Delphin m

domain n Domäne f; (Inform)
Domain f

dome [dəʊm] n Kuppel f

domestic [dəˈmestɪk] adj häuslich; (within country) Innen-,
Binnen-; **domestic animal** n
Haustier nt, **domesticated**
[dəˈmestɪkeɪtɪd] adj (person)
häuslich; (animal) zahm; **domestic
flight** n Inlandsflug m

domicile ['dɒmɪsaɪl] n (ständi-
ger) Wohnsitz

dominant ['dɒmɪnənt] adj
dominierend, vorherrschend;
dominate ['dɒmɪneɪt] vt
beherrschen

dominoes ['dɒmɪnəʊz] npl
Domino(spiel) nt

donate [dəʊˈneɪt] vt spenden;
donation n Spende f

done [dʌn] pp of **do** ▷ adj (cooked)
gar; **well ~** durchgebraten

doner (kebab) ['dɒnəkəˈbæb] n
Döner (Kebab) m

donkey ['dɒŋkɪ] n Esel m

donor ['dəʊnə*] n Spender(in)
m(f)

don't [dəʊnt] contr of **do not**

doom [duːm] n Schicksal nt;
(downfall) Verderben nt

door [dɔː*] n Tür f; **doorbell** n
Türklingel f; **door handle** n
Türklinke f; **doorknob** n Türknauf
m; **doormat** n Fußabtreter m;
doorstep n Türstufe f; **right**

on our ~ direkt vor unserer
Haustür

dope [dəʊp] (Sport) n (for athlete)
Aufputschmittel nt ▷ vt dopen

dormitory ['dɔːmɪtrɪ] n Schlafsaal m; (US) Studentenwohnheim
nt

dosage ['dəʊsɪdʒ] n Dosierung f;
dose [dəʊs] n Dosis f ▷ vt
dosieren

dot [dɒt] n Punkt m; **on the ~** auf
die Minute genau, pünktlich

dotcom ['dɒtkɒm] n: **~ (company)** Internetfirma f,
Dotcom-Unternehmen nt

dote on [dəʊt ɒn] vt abgöttisch
lieben

dotted line n punktierte Linie

double ['dʌbl] adj, adv doppelt;
~ the quantity die zweifache
Menge, doppelt so viel ▷ vt
verdoppeln ▷ n (person)
Doppelgänger(in) m(f); (Cine)
Double nt; **double bass** n
Kontrabass m; **double bed** n
Doppelbett nt; **double-click** vt
(Inform) doppelklicken; **double
cream** n Sahne mit hohem
Fettgehalt; **doubledecker** n
Doppeldecker m; **double glazing**
n Doppelverglasung f;
double-park vi in zweiter Reihe
parken; **double room** n
Doppelzimmer nt; **doubles** npl
(Sport: also match) Doppel nt

doubt [daʊt] n Zweifel m; **no
~** ohne Zweifel, zweifellos,
wahrscheinlich; **to have one's ~s**
Bedenken haben ▷ vt bezweifeln;
(statement, word) anzweifeln; **I ~ it**
das bezweifle ich; **doubtful** adj
zweifelhaft, zweifelnd; **it is
~ whether ...** es ist fraglich, ob ...;
doubtless adv ohne Zweifel,
sicherlich

dough [dəʊ] n Teig m; **doughnut**
n Donut m (runder Hefegebäck)

dove [dʌv] n Taube f
down [daʊn] n Daunen pl; (fluff)
Flaum m ▷ adv unten; (motion)
nach unten; (towards speaker)
herunter; (away from speaker)
hinunter; ~ **here/there** hier/dort
unten; (downstairs) **they came
~ for breakfast** sie kamen zum
Frühstück herunter; (southwards)
he came ~ from Scotland er kam
von Schottland herunter ▷ prep
(towards speaker) herunter; (away
from speaker) hinunter; **to drive
~ the hill/road** den Berg/die
Straße hinunter fahren; (along) **to
walk ~ the street** die Straße
entlang gehen; **he's ~ the pub**
(fam) er ist in der Kneipe ▷ vt
(fam: drink) runterkippen ▷ adj
niedergeschlagen, deprimiert
down-and-out adj
heruntergekommen ▷ n
Obdachlose(r) mf, Penner(in) m(f);
downcast adj niedergeschlagen;
downfall n Sturz m;
down-hearted adj entmutigt;
downhill adv bergab; **he's going
~** (fig) mit ihm geht es bergab

○ **DOWNING STREET**

○ **Downing Street** ist die Straße
○ in London, die von Whitehall
○ zum St James's Park führt, und
○ in der sich der offizielle
○ Wohnsitz des Premierministers
○ (Nr. 10) und des Finanzministers
○ (Nr. 11) befindet. Im weiteren
○ Sinne bezieht sich der Begriff
○ „Downing Street" auf die
○ britische Regierung.

download ['daʊnləʊd] vt
downloaden, herunterladen;
downmarket adj für den
Massenmarkt; **down payment** n
Anzahlung f; **downpour** n

Platzregen m; **downs** npl
Hügelland nt; **downsize** vt
(business) verkleinern ▷ vi sich
verkleinern

Down's syndrome
['daʊnz'sɪndrəʊm] n (Med)
Downsyndrom nt
downstairs ['daʊn'steəz] adv
unten; (motion) nach unten;
downstream adv flussabwärts;
downtime n Ausfallzeit f;
downtown adv (be, work etc) in
der Innenstadt; (go) in die
Innenstadt ▷ adj (US) in die
Innenstadt; ~ **Chicago** die
Innenstadt von Chicago; **down
under** adv (fam: in/to Australia)
in/nach Australien; (in/to New
Zealand) in/nach Neuseeland;
downwards adv, adj nach unten;
(movement, trend) Abwärts-
doze [dəʊz] vi dösen ▷ n Nickerchen nt
dozen ['dʌzn] n Dutzend nt; **two
~ eggs** zwei Dutzend Eier; **~s of
times** x-mal
DP abbr = **data processing** DV f
drab [dræb] adj trist; (colour)
düster
draft [drɑːft] n (outline) Entwurf
m; (US Mil) Einberufung f
drag [dræg] vt schleppen ▷ n (fam)
to be a ~ (boring) stinklangweilig
sein; (laborious) ein ziemlicher
Schlauch sein; **drag on** vi sich in
die Länge ziehen
dragon ['drægən] n Drache m;
dragonfly n Libelle f
drain [dreɪn] n Abfluss m ▷ vt
(water, oil) ablassen; (vegetables etc)
abgießen; (land) entwässern,
trockenlegen ▷ vi (of water)
abfließen; **drainpipe** n
Abflussrohr nt
drama ['drɑːmə] n (a. fig) Drama
nt; **dramatic** [drə'mætɪk] adj
dramatisch

drank [dræŋk] pt of drink

drapes [dreips] npl (US) Vorhänge pl

drastic ['dræstik] adj drastisch

draught [drɑːft] n (Luft)zug m; there's a ~ es zieht; on ~ (beer) vom Fass; draughts nsing Damespiel nt; draughty adj zugig

draw [drɔː] (drew, drawn) vt (pull) ziehen; (crowd) anlocken, anziehen; (picture) zeichnen ▷ vi (Sport) unentschieden spielen ▷ n (Sport) Unentschieden nt; (attraction) Attraktion f; (for lottery) Ziehung f; draw out vi herausziehen; (money) abheben; draw up vi (formulate) entwerfen; (list) eisstellen ▷ vi (car) anhalten; drawback n Nachteil m; drawbridge n Zugbrücke f

drawer ['drɔː°] n Schublade f

drawing ['drɔːiŋ] n Zeichnung f; drawing pin n Reißzwecke f

drawn [drɔːn] pp of draw

dread [dred] n Furcht f (of vor +dat) ▷ vt sich fürchten vor +dat; dreadful adj furchtbar; dreadlocks npl Rastalocken pl

dream [driːm] (dreamed o dreamt, dreamed o dreamt) vt, vi träumen (about von) ▷ n Traum m; dreamt [dremt] pt, pp of dream

dreary ['driəri] adj (weather, place) trostlos; (book etc) langweilig

drench [drentʃ] vt durchnässen

dress [dres] n Kleidung f; (garment) Kleid nt ▷ vt anziehen; (Med: wound) verbinden; to get ~ed sich anziehen; dress up vi sich fein machen; (in costume) sich verkleiden (as als); dress circle n (Theat) erster Rang; dresser n Anrichte f; (US: dressing table) (Fisier)kommode f; dressing n (Gastr) Dressing nt, Soße f; (Med) Verband m; dressing gown n

Bademantel m; dressing room n (Theat) Künstlergarderobe f; dressing table n Frisierkommode f; dress rehearsal n (Theat) Generalprobe f

drew [druː] pt of draw

dried [draid] adj getrocknet; (milk, flowers) Trocken-; ~ fruit Dörrobst nt; drier ['draiə°] n see dryer

drift [drift] vi treiben ▷ n (of snow) Verwehung f; (fig) Tendenz f; if you get my ~ wenn du mich richtig verstehst/wenn Sie mich richtig verstehen

drill [dril] n Bohrer m ▷ vt, vi bohren

drink [driŋk] (drank, drunk) vt, vi trinken ▷ n Getränk nt; (alcoholic) Drink m; drink-driving n (Brit) Trunkenheit f am Steuer; drinking water n Trinkwasser nt

drip [drip] n Tropfen m ▷ vi tropfen; drip-dry adj bügelfrei; dripping n Bratenfett nt ▷ adj: ~ (wet) tropfnass

drive [draiv] (drove, driven) vt (car, person in car) fahren; (force: person, animal) treiben; (Tech) antreiben; to ~ sb mad jdn verrückt machen ▷ vi fahren ▷ n Fahrt f; (entrance) Einfahrt f, Auffahrt f; (Inform) Laufwerk nt; to go for a ~ spazieren fahren; drive away, drive off vi wegfahren ▷ vt vertreiben

drive-in adj Drive-in-; ~ cinema n (US) Autokino nt

driven ['drivn] pp of drive

driver ['draivə°] n Fahrer(in) m(f); (Inform) Treiber m; ~'s license n (US) Führerschein m; ~'s seat n Fahrersitz m; driving ['draiviŋ] n (Auto)fahren nt; he likes ~ er fährt gern Auto; driving lesson n

drizzle | 334

Fahrstunde f; **driving licence** n (Brit) Führerschein m; **driving school** n Fahrschule f; **driving seat** n (Brit) Fahrersitz m; **to be in the ~** alles im Griff haben; **driving test** n Fahrprüfung f

drizzle ['drɪzl] n Nieselregen m ▷ vi nieseln

drop [drɒp] n (of liquid) Tropfen m; (fall in price etc) Rückgang m ▷ vt (a. fig: give up) fallen lassen ▷ vi (fall) herunterfallen; (figures, temperature) sinken, zurückgehen; **drop by, drop in** vi vorbeikommen; **drop off** vi (to sleep) einnicken; **drop out** vi (withdraw) aussteigen; (university) das Studium abbrechen; **dropout** n Aussteiger(in) m(f)

drought [draʊt] n Dürre f

drove [drəʊv] pt of **drive**

drown [draʊn] vi ertrinken ▷ vt ertränken

drowsy ['draʊzɪ] adj schläfrig

drug [drʌg] n (Med) Medikament nt, Arznei f; (addictive) Droge f; (narcotic) Rauschgift nt; **to be on ~s** drogensüchtig sein ▷ vt (mit Medikamenten) behandeln; **drug addict** n Rauschgiftsüchtige(r) mf; **drug dealer** n Drogenhändler(in) m(f); **druggist** n (US) Drogist(in) m(f); **drugstore** n (US) Drogerie f

drum [drʌm] n Trommel f nt; **~s pl** Schlagzeug nt; **drummer** n Schlagzeuger(in) m(f)

drunk [drʌŋk] pp of **drink** ▷ adj betrunken; **to get ~** sich betrinken ▷ n Betrunkene(r) mf; (alcoholic) Trinker(in) m(f); **drunk-driving** n (US) Trunkenheit f am Steuer; **drunken** adj betrunken, besoffen

dry [draɪ] adj trocken ▷ vt trocknen; (dishes, oneself, one's hands etc) abtrocknen ▷ vi trocknen, trocken werden; **dry out**

vi trocknen; **dry up** vi austrocknen; **dry-clean** vt chemisch reinigen; **dry-cleaning** n chemische Reinigung; **dryer** n Trockner m; (for hair) Föhn m; (over head) Trockenhaube f

DTP abbr = **desktop publishing** DTP nt

dual ['djuːal] adj doppelt; **~ carriageway** (Brit) zweispurige Schnellstraße f; **~ nationality** doppelte Staatsangehörigkeit

dubbed [dʌbd] adj (film) synchronisiert

dubious ['djuːbɪəs] adj zweifelhaft

duchess ['dʌtʃəs] n Herzogin f

duck [dʌk] n Ente f

dude [duːd] n (US fam) Typ m; **a cool ~** ein cooler Typ

due [djuː] adj (time) fällig; (fitting) angemessen; **in ~ course** zu gegebener Zeit; **~ to** infolge +gen, wegen +gen ▷ adv: **~ south/north** etc direkt nach Norden/Süden etc

dug [dʌg] pt, pp of **dig**

duke [djuːk] n Herzog m

dull [dʌl] adj (colour, light, weather) trübe; (boring) langweilig

duly ['djuːlɪ] adv ordnungsgemäß; (as expected) wie erwartet

dumb [dʌm] adj stumm; (fam: stupid) doof, blöde

dumb-bell ['dʌmbel] n Hantel f

dummy ['dʌmɪ] n (sham) Attrappe f; (in shop) Schaufensterpuppe f; (Brit: teat) Schnuller m; (fam: person) Dummkopf m ▷ adj unecht, Schein-; **~** run Testlauf m

dump [dʌmp] n Abfallhaufen m; (fam: place) Kaff nt ▷ vt (lit, fig) abladen; (fam) **he ~ed her** er hat mir ihr Schluss gemacht

dumpling ['dʌmplɪŋ] n Kloß m, Knödel m

dune [djuːn] n Düne f

dung [dʌŋ] n (manure) Mist m

dungarees [dʌŋgəˈriːz] npl
Latzhose f

dungeon [ˈdʌndʒən] n Kerker m

duplex [ˈdjuːpleks] n
zweistöckige Wohnung; (US)
Doppelhaushälfte f

duplicate [ˈdjuːplɪkɪt] n Dup-
likat nt ▷ [ˈdjuːplɪkeɪt] vt (make
copies of) kopieren; (repeat)
wiederholen

durable [ˈdjʊərəbl] adj haltbar;
duration [djʊəˈreɪʃən] n Dauer f

during [ˈdjʊərɪŋ] prep (time)
während +gen

dusk [dʌsk] n Abenddämmerung f

dust [dʌst] n Staub m ▷ vt
abstauben; **dustbin** n (Brit)
Mülleimer m; **dustcart** n (Brit)
Müllwagen m; **duster** n
Staubtuch nt; **dust jacket** n
Schutzumschlag m; **dustman** n
(Brit) Müllmann m; **dustpan** n
Kehrschaufel f; **dusty** adj staubig

Dutch [dʌtʃ] adj holländisch ▷ n
(language) Holländisch nt; **to
speak/talk double ~** (fam)
Quatsch reden; **the ~** pl die
Holländer; **Dutchman** (pl -men)
n Holländer m; **Dutchwoman** (pl
-women) n Holländerin f

duty [ˈdjuːtɪ] n Pflicht f; (task)
Aufgabe f; (tax) Zoll m; **on/off ~** im
Dienst/nicht im Dienst; **to be on
~** Dienst haben; **duty-free** adj
zollfrei; **~ shop** Dutyfreeshop m

duvet [ˈduːveɪ] n Federbett nt

DVD n abbr = **digital versatile
disk** DVD f; **DVD player** n
DVD-Player m; **DVD recorder** n
DVD-Rekorder m

dwelling [ˈdwelɪŋ] n Wohnung f

dwindle [ˈdwɪndl] vi schwinden

dye [daɪ] n Farbstoff m ▷ vt
färben

dynamic [daɪˈnæmɪk] adj
dynamisch

dynamo [ˈdaɪnəməʊ] n Dynamo m

dyslexia [dɪsˈleksɪə] n Legasthenie
f; **dyslexic** adj legasthenisch; **to
be ~** Legastheniker(in) sein

e

E [iː] *abbr* = **east** (geo) O; *abbr* = **ecstasy** (drug) Ecstasy *nt*

E111 form *n* ≈ Auslandskrankenschein *m*

each [iːtʃ] *adj* jeder/jede/jedes ▷ *pron* jeder/jede/jedes; **I'll have one of ~** ich nehme von jedem eins; **they ~ have a car** jeder von ihnen hat ein Auto; **~ other** einander, sich; **for/against ~ other** füreinander/gegeneinander ▷ *adv* je; **they cost 10 euros** sie kosten je 10 Euro, sie kosten 10 Euro das Stück

eager ['iːɡə°] *adj* eifrig; **to be ~ to do sth** darauf brennen, etw zu tun

eagle ['iːɡl] *n* Adler *m*

ear [ɪə°] *n* Ohr *nt*; **earache** *n* Ohrenschmerzen *pl*; **eardrum** *n* Trommelfell *nt*

earl [ɜːl] *n* Graf *m*

early ['ɜːlɪ] *adj*, *adv* früh; **to be 10 minutes ~** 10 Minuten zu früh

kommen; **at the earliest** frühestens; **in ~ June/2008** Anfang Juni/2008; **~ retirement** vorzeitiger Ruhestand; **~ warning system** Frühwarnsystem *nt*

earn [ɜːn] *vt* verdienen

earnest ['ɜːnɪst] *adj* ernst; **in ~** im Ernst

earnings ['ɜːnɪŋz] *npl* Verdienst *m*, Einkommen *nt*

earplug *n* Ohrenstöpsel *m*, Ohropax® *nt*; **earring** *n* Ohrring *m*

earth [ɜːθ] *n* Erde *f*; **what on ~ ...?** was in aller Welt ...? ▷ *vt* erden; **earthenware** *n* Tonwaren *pl*; **earthquake** *n* Erdbeben *nt*

earwig ['ɪəwɪɡ] *n* Ohrwurm *m*

ease [iːz] *vt* (pain) lindern; (burden) erleichtern ▷ *n* (easiness) Leichtigkeit *f*; **to feel at ~** sich wohlfühlen; **to feel ill at ~** sich nicht wohlfühlen; **easily** ['iːzɪlɪ] *adv* leicht; **he is ~ the best** er ist mit Abstand der Beste

east [iːst] *n* Osten *m*; **to the ~ of** östlich von ▷ *adv* (go, face) nach Osten ▷ *adj* Ost-; **~ wind** Ostwind *m*; **eastbound** *adj* (in) Richtung Osten

Easter ['iːstə°] *n* Ostern *nt*; **at ~** zu Ostern; **Easter egg** *n* Osterei *nt*; **Easter Sunday** *n* Ostersonntag *m*

eastern ['iːstən] *adj* Ost-, östlich; **Eastern Europe** *n* Osteuropa *nt*; **East Germany** *n* Ostdeutschland *nt*; **former ~** die ehemalige DDR, die neuen Bundesländer; **eastwards** ['iːstwədz] *adv* nach Osten

easy ['iːzɪ] *adj* leicht; (task, solution) einfach; (life) bequem; (manner) ungezwungen; **easy-going** *adj* gelassen

eat [iːt] (ate, eaten) *vt* essen; (animal) fressen; **eat out** *vi* zum

Essen ausgehen; **eat up** vt
aufessen; (animal) auffressen
eaten ['iːtn] pp of **eat**
eavesdrop ['iːvzdrɒp] vi (heimlich) lauschen; **to ~ on sb** jdn
belauschen
eccentric [ɪk'sentrɪk] adj
exzentrisch
echo ['ekəʊ] (pl **-es**) n Echo nt
▷ vi widerhallen
ecological [iːkə'lɒdʒɪkl] adj
ökologisch; **~ disaster**
Umweltkatastrophe f; **ecology**
[ɪ'kɒlədʒɪ] n Ökologie f
economic [iːkə'nɒmɪk] adj
wirtschaftlich, Wirtschafts-; **~ aid**
Wirtschaftshilfe f, **economical** adj
wirtschaftlich; (person) sparsam;
economics n Betriebs-
Wirtschaftswissenschaft f,
economist [ɪ'kɒnəmɪst] n
Wirtschaftswissenschaftler(in)
m(f); **economize** [ɪ'kɒnəmaɪz] vi
sparen (on an +dat); **economy**
[ɪ'kɒnəmɪ] n (of state) Wirtschaft
f; (thrift) Sparsamkeit f; **economy
class** n (Aviat) Economyclass f
ecstasy ['ekstəsɪ] n Ekstase f;
(drug) Ecstasy f
eczema ['eksɪmə] n Ekzem nt
edge [edʒ] n Rand m; (of knife)
Schneide f; **on ~** nervös; **edgy**
['edʒɪ] adj nervös
edible ['edɪbl] adj essbar
Edinburgh ['edɪnbərə] n Edin-
burg nt
edit ['edɪt] vt (series, newspaper
etc) herausgeben; (text) redigieren;
(film) schneiden; (Inform)
editieren; **edition** [ɪ'dɪʃən] n
Ausgabe f; **editor** n Redakteur(in)
m(f); (of series etc) Herausgeber(in)
m(f); **editorial** [edɪ'tɔːrɪəl] adj
Redaktions- ▷ n Leitartikel m
educate ['edjʊkeɪt] vt (child)
erziehen; (at school, university)
ausbilden; (public) aufklären;

educated adj gebildet,
education [edjʊ'keɪʃən] n
Erziehung f; (studies, training)
Ausbildung f; (subject of study)
Pädagogik f; (system) Schulwesen
nt; (knowledge) Bildung f;
educational adj pädagogisch;
(instructive) lehrreich; **~ television**
Schulfernsehen nt
eel [iːl] n Aal m
eerie ['ɪərɪ] adj unheimlich
effect [ɪ'fekt] n Wirkung f (on auf
+akk); **to come into ~** in Kraft
treten; **effective** adj wirksam,
effektiv
effeminate [ɪ'femɪnət] adj (of
man) tuntig
efficiency [ɪ'fɪʃənsɪ] n Leistungsfähigkeit f; (of method)
Wirksamkeit f; **efficient** adj
(Tech) leistungsfähig; (method)
wirksam, effizient
effort ['efət] n Anstrengung f;
(attempt) Versuch m; **to make an
~** sich anstrengen; **effortless** adj
mühelos
e.g. abbr = exempli gratia (for
example) z. B.
egg [eg] n Ei nt; **eggcup** n
Eierbecher m; **eggplant** n (US)
Aubergine f; **eggshell** n
Eierschale f
ego ['iːgəʊ] (pl **-s**) n Ich nt;
(self-esteem) Selbstbewusstsein nt;
ego(t)ist ['egəʊ(t)ɪst] n Ego-
zentriker(in) m(f)
Egypt ['iːdʒɪpt] n Ägypten nt;
Egyptian [ɪ'dʒɪpʃən] adj
ägyptisch ▷ n Ägypter(in) m(f)
eiderdown ['aɪdədaʊn] n
Daunendecke f
eight [eɪt] num acht; **at the age
of ~** im Alter von acht Jahren; **it's
~ (o'clock)** es ist acht Uhr ▷ n (a.
bus etc) Acht f; (boat) Achter m;
eighteen [eɪ'tiːn] num achtzehn
▷ n Achtzehn f; see also **eight**;

eighteenth adj achtzehnte(r, s); see also **eighth**; **eighth** [eɪtθ] adj achte(r, s); **the ~ of June** der achte Juni ▷ n (fraction) Achtel nt; **an ~ of a litre** ein Achtelliter; **eightieth** ['eɪtɪəθ] adj achtzigste(r, s); see also **eighth**; **eighty** ['eɪtɪ] num achtzig ▷ n Achtzig f; see also **eight**

Eire ['eərə] n die Republik Irland

either ['aɪðə²] conj: **~ ... or** entweder ... oder ▷ pron: **~ of the two** eine(r, s) von beiden ▷ adj: **on ~ side** auf beiden Seiten ▷ adv: **I won't go ~** ich gehe auch nicht

eject [ɪ'dʒekt] vt ausstoßen; (person) vertreiben

elaborate [ɪ'læbərət] adj (complex) kompliziert; (plan) ausgeklügelt; (decoration) kunstvoll ▷ vi [ɪ'læbəreɪt] **could you ~ on that?** könntest du/könnten Sie mehr darüber sagen?

elastic [ɪ'læstɪk] adj elastisch; **~ band** Gummiband nt

elbow ['elbəu] n Ellbogen m; **to give sb the ~** (fam) jdm den Laufpass geben

elder ['eldə²] adj (of two) älter ▷ n Ältere(r) mf; (Bot) Holunder m; **elderly** ['eldəlɪ] adj ältere(r, s) ▷ n: **the ~** die älteren Leute; **eldest** ['eldɪst] adj älteste(r, s)

elect [ɪ'lekt] vt wählen; **he was ~ed chairman** er wurde zum Vorsitzenden gewählt; **election** [ɪ'lekʃən] n Wahl f; **election campaign** n Wahlkampf m; **electioneering** [ɪlekʃə'nɪərɪŋ] n Wahlpropaganda f; **electorate** [ɪ'lektərɪt] n Wähler pl

electric [ɪ'lektrɪk] adj elektrisch; (car, motor, razor etc) Elektro-; **~ blanket** Heizdecke f; **~ cooker** Elektroherd m; **~ current** elektrischer Strom; **~ shock**

Stromschlag m; **electrical** adj elektrisch; **~ goods/appliances** Elektrogeräte; **electrician** [ɪlek'trɪʃən] n Elektriker(in) m(f); **electricity** [ɪlek'trɪsɪtɪ] n Elektrizität f; **electrocute** [ɪ'lektrəʊkjuːt] vt durch einen Stromschlag töten; **electronic** [ɪlek'trɒnɪk] adj elektronisch

elegance ['elɪɡəns] n Eleganz f; **elegant** adj elegant

element ['elɪmənt] n Element nt; **an ~ of truth** ein Körnchen Wahrheit; **elementary** [elɪ'mentərɪ] adj einfach; (basic) grundlegend; **~ stage** Anfangsstadium nt; **~ school** (US) Grundschule f; **~ maths/French** Grundkenntnisse in Mathematik/Französisch

elephant ['elɪfənt] n Elefant m

elevator ['elɪveɪtə²] n (US) Fahrstuhl m

eleven [ɪ'levn] num elf ▷ n (team, bus etc) Elf f see **eight**; **eleventh** [ɪ'levnθ] adj elfte(r, s) ▷ n (fraction) Elftel nt see **eighth**

eligible ['elɪdʒəbl] adj infrage kommend; (for grant etc) berechtigt; **~ for a pension/competition** pensions-/teilnahmeberechtigt; **~ bachelor** begehrter Junggeselle

eliminate [ɪ'lɪmɪneɪt] vt ausschließen (from aus), ausschalten; (problem etc) beseitigen; **elimination** n Ausschluss m (from aus); (of problem etc) Beseitigung f

elm [elm] n Ulme f

elope [ɪ'ləʊp] vi durchbrennen (with sb mit jdm)

eloquent ['eləkwənt] adj redegewandt

else [els] adv: **anybody/anything ~** (in addition) sonst (noch) jemand/etwas: (other) ein anderer/etwas anderes; **somebody ~** jemand anders; **everyone ~** alle anderen; **or ~** sonst; **elsewhere** adv anderswo, woanders; (direction) woandershin

ELT abbr = **English Language Teaching**

e-mail, E-mail ['i:meɪl] vi, vt mailen (sth to sb jdm etw) ▷ n E-Mail f; **e-mail address** n E-Mail-Adresse f

emancipated [ɪ'mænsɪpeɪtɪd] adj emanzipiert

embankment [ɪm'bæŋkmənt] n Böschung f; (for railway) Bahndamm m

embargo [ɪm'bɑːgəʊ] (pl -es) n Embargo nt

embark [ɪm'bɑːk] vi an Bord gehen

embarrass [ɪm'bærəs] vt in Verlegenheit bringen; **embarrassed** adj verlegen; **embarrassing** adj peinlich

embassy ['embəsɪ] n Botschaft f

embrace [ɪm'breɪs] vt umarmen ▷ n Umarmung f

embroider [ɪm'brɔɪdə°] vt besticken; **embroidery** n Stickerei f

embryo ['embrɪəʊ] (pl -s) n Embryo m

emerald ['emərəld] n Smaragd m

emerge [ɪ'mɜːdʒ] vi auftauchen; **it ~d that ...** es stellte sich heraus, dass ...

emergency [ɪ'mɜːdʒənsɪ] n Notfall m ▷ adj Not-; **~ exit** Notausgang m; **~ landing** Notlandung f; **~ room** (US) Unfallstation f; **~ service** Notdienst m; **~ stop** Vollbremsung f

emigrate ['emɪgreɪt] vi auswandern

emit [ɪ'mɪt] vt ausstoßen; (heat) abgeben

emotion [ɪ'məʊʃən] n Emotion f, Gefühl nt; **emotional** adj (person) emotional; (experience, moment, scene) ergreifend

emperor ['empərə°] n Kaiser m

emphasis ['emfəsɪs] n Betonung f; **emphasize** ['emfəsaɪz] vt betonen; **emphatic**; **emphatically** [ɪm'fætɪk, -lɪ] adj, adv nachdrücklich

empire ['empaɪə°] n Reich nt

employ [ɪm'plɔɪ] vt beschäftigen; (hire) anstellen; (use) anwenden; **employee** [emplɔɪ'i:] n Angestellte(r) mf; **employer** [ɪm'plɔɪə°] n Arbeitgeber(in) m(f); **employment** n Beschäftigung f, (position) Stellung f; **employment agency** n Stellenvermittlung f

empress ['empris] n Kaiserin f

empty ['emptɪ] adj leer ▷ vt (contents) leeren; (container) ausleeren

enable [ɪ'neɪbl] vt: **to ~ sb to do sth** jdm ermöglichen, etw zu tun

enamel [ɪ'næməl] n Email nt; (of teeth) Zahnschmelz m

enchanting [ɪn'tʃɑːntɪŋ] adj bezaubernd

enclose [ɪn'kləʊz] vt einschließen; (in letter) beilegen (in, with dat); **enclosure** [ɪn'kləʊʒə°] n (for animals) Gehege nt; (in letter) Anlage f

encore ['ɒŋkɔː°] n Zugabe f

encounter [ɪn'kaʊntə°] n Begegnung f ▷ vt (person) begegnen +dat; (difficulties) stoßen auf +akk

encourage [ɪn'kʌrɪdʒ] vt ermutigen; **encouragement** n Ermutigung f

encyclopaedia
[ensaɪkləʊˈpiːdɪə] n Lexikon nt, Enzyklopädie f

end [end] n Ende nt; (of film, play etc) Schluss m; (purpose) Zweck m; **at the ~ of** May Ende Mai; **in the ~** schließlich; **to come to an ~** zu Ende gehen ▷ vt beenden ▷ vi enden; **end up** vi enden

endanger [ɪnˈdeɪndʒəʳ] vt gefährden; **~ed species** vom Aussterben bedrohte Art

endeavour [ɪnˈdevəʳ] n Bemühung f ▷ vi sich bemühen (to do sth etw zu tun)

ending [ˈendɪŋ] n (of book) Ausgang m; (last part) Schluss m; (of word) Endung f; **endless** [ˈendlɪs] adj endlos; (possibilities) unendlich

endurance [ɪnˈdjʊərəns] n Ausdauer f; **endure** [ɪnˈdjʊəʳ] vt ertragen

enemy [ˈenɪmɪ] n Feind(in) m(f) ▷ adj feindlich

energetic [enəˈdʒetɪk] adj energiegeladen; (active) aktiv; **energy** [ˈenədʒɪ] n Energie f

enforce [ɪnˈfɔːs] vt durchsetzen; (obedience) erzwingen

engage [ɪnˈɡeɪdʒ] vt (employ) einstellen; (singer, performer) engagieren; **engaged** adj verlobt; (toilet, telephone line) besetzt; **to get ~** sich verloben (to mit); **engaged tone** n (Brit Tel) Belegtzeichen nt; **engagement** n (to marry) Verlobung f; **~ ring** Verlobungsring m; **engaging** adj gewinnend

engine [ˈendʒɪn] n (Auto) Motor m; (Rail) Lokomotive f; **~ failure** (Auto) Motorschaden m; **~ trouble** (Auto) Defekt m am Motor; **engineer** [endʒɪˈnɪəʳ] n Ingenieur(in) m(f); (US Rail) Lokomotivführer(in) m(f);

engineering [endʒɪˈnɪərɪŋ] n Technik f; (mechanical ~) Maschinenbau m; (subject) Ingenieurwesen nt; **engine immobilizer** n (Auto) Wegfahrsperre f

England [ˈɪŋɡlənd] n England nt; **English** adj englisch; **he's ~** er ist Engländer; **the ~ Channel** der Ärmelkanal ▷ n (language) Englisch nt; **in ~** auf Englisch; **to translate into ~** ins Englische übersetzen; (people) **the ~** pl die Engländer; **Englishman** (pl **-men**) n Engländer m; **Englishwoman** (pl **-women**) n Engländerin f

engrave [ɪnˈɡreɪv] vt eingravieren; **engraving** n Stich m

engrossed [ɪnˈɡrəʊst] adj vertieft (in sth in etw akk)

enigma [ɪˈnɪɡmə] n Rätsel nt

enjoy [ɪnˈdʒɔɪ] vt genießen; **I ~ reading** ich lese gern; **he ~s teasing her** es macht ihm Spaß, sie aufzuziehen; **did you ~ the film?** hat dir der Film gefallen?; **enjoyable** adj angenehm; (entertaining) unterhaltsam; **enjoyment** n Vergnügen nt; (stronger) Freude f (of an +dat)

enlarge [ɪnˈlɑːdʒ] vt vergrößern; (expand) erweitern; **enlargement** n Vergrößerung f

enormous, enormously [ɪˈnɔːməs, -lɪ] adj, adv riesig, ungeheuer

enough [ɪˈnʌf] adj genug; **that's ~ das reicht!**; (stop it) Schluss damit!; **I've had ~** das hat mir gereicht; (to eat) ich bin satt ▷ adv genug, genügend

enquire [ɪnˈkwaɪəʳ] vi sich erkundigen (about nach); **enquiry** [ɪnˈkwaɪərɪ] n (question) Anfrage f; (for information) Erkundigung f (about über +akk); (investigation)

Untersuchung f; **"Enquiries"** „Auskunft"

enrol [ɪn'rəʊl] vi sich einschreiben; (for course, school) sich anmelden; (for vehicles) einfahren in +akk; (country) einreisen in +akk; (in list) eintragen; (Inform) eingeben; (race, contest) teilnehmen an +dat ▷ vi (towards speaker) hereinkommen; (away from speaker) hineingehen

enterprise ['entəpraɪz] n (Comm) Unternehmen nt

entertain [entə'teɪn] vt (guest) bewirten; (amuse) unterhalten; **entertaining** adj unterhaltsam; **entertainment** n (amusement) Unterhaltung f

enthusiasm [ɪn'θju:zɪæzəm] n Begeisterung f; **enthusiastic** [ɪnθju:zɪ'æstɪk] adj begeistert (about von)

entice [ɪn'taɪs] vt locken; (lead astray) verleiten

entire [ɪn'taɪə], **-ly** adj, adv ganz

entitle [ɪn'taɪtl] vt (qualify) berechtigen (to zu); (name) betiteln

entrance ['entrəns] n Eingang m; (for vehicles) Einfahrt f; (entering) Eintritt m; (Theat) Auftritt m; **entrance exam** n Aufnahmeprüfung f; **entrance fee** n Eintrittsgeld nt

entrust [ɪn'trʌst] vt: **to ~ sb with sth** jdm etw anvertrauen

entry ['entrɪ] n (way in) Eingang m; (entering) Eintritt m; (in vehicle) Einfahrt f; (into country) Einreise f;

(admission) Zutritt m; (in diary, accounts) Eintrag m; **"no ~"** „Eintritt verboten"; (for vehicles) „Einfahrt verboten"; **entry phone** n Türsprechanlage f

E-number n (food additive) E-Nummer f

envelope ['envələʊp] n (Brief)umschlag m

enviable ['envɪəbl] adj beneidenswert; **envious** ['envɪəs] adj neidisch

environment [ɪn'vaɪərənmənt] n Umgebung f; (ecology) Umwelt f; **environmental** [ɪnvaɪərən'məntl] adj Umwelt-; **~ pollution** Umweltverschmutzung f; **environmentalist** n Umweltschützer(in) m(f)

envy ['envɪ] n Neid m (of auf +akk) ▷ vt beneiden (sb sth jdm etw)

epic ['epɪk] n Epos nt; (film) Monumentalfilm m

epidemic [epɪ'demɪk] n Epidemie f

epilepsy ['epɪlepsɪ] n Epilepsie f; **epileptic** [epɪ'leptɪk] adj epileptisch

episode ['epɪsəʊd] n Episode f; (TV) Folge f

epoch ['i:pɒk] n Zeitalter nt, Epoche f

equal ['i:kwl] adj gleich (to +dat) ▷ n Gleichgestellte(r) mf ▷ vt gleichen; (match) gleichkommen +dat; **two times two ~s four** zwei mal zwei ist gleich vier; **equality** [ɪ'kwɒlɪtɪ] n Gleichheit f; (equal rights) Gleichberechtigung f; **equalize** vi (Sport) ausgleichen; **equalizer** n (Sport) Ausgleichstreffer m; **equally** adv gleich; (on the other hand) andererseits; **equation** [ɪ'kweɪʒən] n (Math) Gleichung f

equator [ɪ'kweɪtə°] n Äquator m

equilibrium [i:kwɪ'lɪbrɪəm] n
Gleichgewicht nt

equip [ɪ'kwɪp] vt ausrüsten;
(kitchen) ausstatten; **equipment** n
Ausrüstung f; (for kitchen)
Ausstattung f; **electrical**
~ Elektrogeräte pl

equivalent [ɪ'kwɪvələnt] adj
gleichwertig (to dat);
(corresponding) entsprechend (to
dat) ▷ n Äquivalent nt; (amount)
gleiche Menge; (in money)
Gegenwert m

era ['ɪərə] n Ära f, Zeitalter nt

erase [ɪ'reɪz] vt ausradieren;
(tape, disk) löschen; **eraser** n
Radiergummi m

erect [ɪ'rekt] adj aufrecht ▷ vt
(building, monument) errichten;
(tent) aufstellen; **erection** n
Errichtung f; (Anat) Erektion f

erode [ɪ'rəud] vt zerfressen;
(land) auswaschen; (rights, power)
aushöhlen; **erosion** [ɪ'rəuʒən] n
Erosion f

erotic [ɪ'rɒtɪk] adj erotisch

err [ɜ:°] vi sich irren

errand ['erənd] n Besorgung f

erratic [ɪ'rætɪk] adj (behaviour)
unberechenbar; (bus link etc)
unregelmäßig; (performance)
unbeständig

error ['erə°] n Fehler m; **in**
~ irrtümlicherweise; **error**
message n (Inform)
Fehlermeldung f

erupt [ɪ'rʌpt] vi ausbrechen

escalator ['eskəleɪtə°] n Rolltreppe f

escalope ['eskələp] n Schnitzel
nt

escape [ɪ'skeɪp] n Flucht f; (from
prison etc) Ausbruch m; **to have a
narrow** ~ gerade noch
davonkommen; **there's no** ~ (fig)
es gibt keinen Ausweg ▷ vt
(pursuers) entkommen +dat;

(punishment etc) entgehen +dat ▷ vi
(from pursuers) entkommen (from
dat); (from prison etc) ausbrechen
(from dat); (leak: gas) ausströmen;
(water) auslaufen

escort ['eskɔ:t] n (companion)
Begleiter(in) m(f); (guard) Eskorte f
▷ vt [ɪ'skɔ:t] (lady) begleiten

especially [ɪ'speʃəlɪ] adv
besonders

espionage ['espɪənɑ:ʒ] n Spio-
nage f

Esquire [ɪ'skwaɪə°] n (Brit: in
address): **J. Brown, Esq** Herrn J.
Brown

essay ['eseɪ] n Aufsatz m;
(literary) Essay m

essential [ɪ'senʃəl] adj (necessary) unentbehrlich,
unverzichtbar; (basic) wesentlich
▷ n **the ~s** pl das Wesentliche;
essentially adv im Wesentlichen

establish [ɪ'stæblɪʃ] vt (set up)
gründen; (introduce) einführen;
(relations) aufnehmen; (prove)
nachweisen; **to ~ that ...**
feststellen, dass ...;
establishment n Institution f;
(business) Unternehmen nt

estate [ɪ'steɪt] n Gut nt; (of
deceased) Nachlass m; (housing ~)
Siedlung f; (country house) Landsitz
m; **estate agent** n (Brit)
Grundstücksmakler(in) m(f),
Immobilienmakler(in) m(f); **estate
car** n (Brit) Kombiwagen m

estimate ['estɪmət] n Schätzung
f; (Comm: of price)
Kostenvoranschlag m ▷ ['estɪmeɪt]
vt schätzen

Estonia [e'stəunɪə] n Estland nt;
Estonian [e'stəunɪən] adj
estnisch; ▷ n (person) Este m;
Estin f; (language) Estnisch nt

estuary ['estjuərɪ] n Mündung f

etching ['etʃɪŋ] n Radierung f

eternal, eternally [ɪ'tɜ:nl, -nəlɪ]

adj, adv ewig; **eternity** n
Ewigkeit f

ethical ['eθɪkəl] adj ethisch;
ethics ['eθɪks] npl Ethik f

Ethiopia [iːθɪˈəʊpɪə] n Äthiopien
nt

ethnic ['eθnɪk] adj ethnisch;
(clothes etc) landesüblich;
~ **minority** ethnische Minderheit

EU abbr = **European Union** EU f

euphemism ['juːfɪmɪzəm] n
Euphemismus m

euro ['jʊərəʊ] (pl -s) n (Fin) Euro
m; ~ **symbol** Eurozeichen nt;
Eurocheque ['jʊərəʊtʃek] n
Euroscheck m; **Europe** ['jʊərəp]
n Europa nt; **European**
[jʊərə'piːən] adj europäisch;
~ **Parliament** Europäisches
Parlament; ~ **Union** Europäische
Union ⊳ n Europäer(in) m(f);
Eurosceptic ['jʊərəʊskeptɪk] n
Euroskeptiker(in) m(f);
Eurotunnel n Eurotunnel m

evacuate [ɪˈvækjʊeɪt] vt (place)
räumen; (people) evakuieren

evade [ɪˈveɪd] vt ausweichen
+dat; (pursuers) sich entziehen +dat

evaluate [ɪˈvæljʊeɪt] vt
auswerten

evaporate [ɪˈvæpəreɪt] vi ver-
dampfen; (fig) verschwinden; ~**d**
milk Kondensmilch f

even ['iːvən] adj (flat) eben;
(regular) gleichmäßig; (equal)
gleich; (number) gerade; **the score**
is ~ es steht unentschieden ⊳ adv
sogar; ~ **you** selbst (o sogar)
du/Sie; ~ **if** selbst wenn, wenn
auch; ~ **though** obwohl; **not**
~ nicht einmal; ~ **better** noch
besser; **even out** vi (prices) sich
einpendeln

evening ['iːvnɪŋ] n Abend m; **in**
the ~ abends, am Abend; **this**
~ heute Abend; **evening class** n
Abendkurs m; **evening dress** n

(generally) Abendkleidung f;
(woman's) Abendkleid nt

evenly ['iːvənlɪ] adv gleichmäßig

event [ɪˈvent] n Ereignis nt;
(organized) Veranstaltung f; (Sport:
discipline) Disziplin f; **in the - of** im
Falle +gen; **eventful** adj
ereignisreich

eventual [ɪˈventʃʊəl] adj (final)
letztendlich; **eventually**
[ɪˈventʃʊəlɪ] adv (at last) am Ende;
(given time) schließlich

ever ['evə°] adv (at any time)
je(mals); **don't - do that again** tu
das ja nie wieder; **he's the best**
~ er ist der Beste, den es je
gegeben hat; **have you - been to**
the States? bist du schon einmal
in den Staaten gewesen?; **for**
~ (für) immer; **for** ~ **and** ~ auf
immer und ewig; ~ **so ...** (fam)
äußerst ...; ~ **so drunk** ganz schön
betrunken

every ['evrɪ] adj jeder/jede/
jedes; ~ **day** jeden Tag; ~ **other**
day jeden zweiten Tag; ~ **five**
days alle fünf Tage; **I have**
~ **reason to believe that ...** ich
habe allen Grund anzunehmen,
dass ...; **everybody** pron jeder,
alle pl; **everyday** adj
(commonplace) alltäglich; (clothes,
language etc) Alltags-; **everyone**
pron jeder, alle pl; **everything**
pron alles; **everywhere** adv
überall; (with direction) überallhin

evidence ['evɪdəns] n Beweise
pl; (single piece) Beweis m;
(testimony) Aussage f; (signs)
Spuren pl; **evident, evidently** adj,
adv offensichtlich

evil ['iːvl] adj böse ⊳ n Böse(s) nt;
an ~ ein Übel

evolution [iːvə'luːʃən] n Entwicklung f; (of life) Evolution f;
evolve [ɪˈvɒlv] vi sich entwickeln

ex- [eks] pref Ex-, ehemalig;

~boyfriend Exfreund *m*; **~wife** frühere Frau, Exfrau *f*; **ex n** (*fam*) Verflossene(r) *mf*, Ex *mf*
exact [ɪgˈzækt] *adj* genau; **exactly** *adv* genau; **not ~ fast** nicht gerade schnell
exaggerate [ɪgˈzædʒəreɪt] *vt, vi* übertreiben; **exaggerated** *adj* übertrieben; **exaggeration** *n* Übertreibung *f*
exam [ɪgˈzæm] *n* Prüfung *f*; **examination** [ɪgzæmɪˈneɪʃən] *n* (*Med etc*) Untersuchung *f*, Prüfung *f*; (*at university*) Examen *nt*; (*at customs etc*) Kontrolle *f*; **examine** [ɪgˈzæmɪn] *vt* untersuchen (*for* auf +*akk*); (*check*) kontrollieren, prüfen; **examiner** *n* Prüfer(in) *m(f)*
example [ɪgˈzɑːmpl] *n* Beispiel *nt* (*of* für +*akk*); **for ~** zum Beispiel
excavation [ekskəˈveɪʃən] *n* Ausgrabung *f*
exceed [ɪkˈsiːd] *vt* überschreiten, übertreffen; **exceedingly** *adv* äußerst
excel [ɪkˈsel] *vt* übertreffen; **he ~led himself** er hat sich selbst übertroffen ▷ *vi* sich auszeichnen (*in* in +*dat*, *at* bei); **excellent, excellently** [ˈeksələnt, -lɪ] *adj, adv* ausgezeichnet
except [ɪkˈsept] *prep*: **~ außer** +*dat*; **~ for** abgesehen von ▷ *vt* ausnehmen; **exception** [ɪkˈsepʃən] *n* Ausnahme *f*; **exceptional, exceptionally** [ɪkˈsepʃənl, -nəlɪ] *adj, adv* außergewöhnlich
excess [ekˈses] *n* Übermaß *nt* (*of* an +*dat*); **excess baggage** *n* Übergepäck *nt*; **excesses** *npl* Exzesse *pl*; (*drink, sex*) Ausschweifungen *pl*; **excessive, excessively** *adj, adv* übermäßig; **excess weight** *n* Übergewicht *nt*

exchange [ɪksˈtʃeɪndʒ] *n* Austausch *m* (*for* gegen); (*of bought items*) Umtausch *m* (*for* gegen); (*Fin*) Wechsel *m*; (*Tel*) Vermittlung *f*, Zentrale *f* ▷ *vt* austauschen; (*goods*) tauschen; (*bought items*) umtauschen (*for* gegen); (*money, blows*) wechseln; **exchange rate** *n* Wechselkurs *m*
excite [ɪkˈsaɪt] *vt* erregen; **excited** *adj* aufgeregt; **to get ~** sich aufregen; **exciting** *adj* aufregend; (*book, film*) spannend
exclamation [ekskləˈmeɪʃən] *n* Ausruf *m*; **exclamation mark, exclamation point** (*US*) *n* Ausrufezeichen *nt*
exclude [ɪksˈkluːd] *vt* ausschließen; **exclusion** [ɪksˈkluːʒən] *n* Ausschluss *m*; **exclusive** [ɪksˈkluːsɪv] *adj* (*select*) exklusiv; (*sole*) ausschließlich; **exclusively** *adv* ausschließlich
excrement [ˈekskrɪmənt] *n* Kot *m*, Exkremente *pl*
excruciating [ɪksˈkruːʃɪeɪtɪŋ] *adj* fürchterlich, entsetzlich
excursion [ɪksˈkɜːʃən] *n* Ausflug *m*
excusable [ɪksˈkjuːzəbl] *adj* entschuldbar; **excuse** [ɪksˈkjuːz] *vt* entschuldigen; **~ me** Entschuldigung!; **to ~ sb for sth** jdm etw verzeihen; **to ~ sb from sth** jdn von etw befreien ▷ [ɪksˈkjuːs] *n* Entschuldigung *f*, Ausrede *f*
ex-directory [eksdaɪˈrektərɪ] *adj*: **to be ~** (*Brit Tel*) nicht im Telefonbuch stehen
execute [ˈeksɪkjuːt] *vt* (*carry out*) ausführen; (*kill*) hinrichten; **execution** *n* (*killing*) Hinrichtung *f*; (*carrying out*) Ausführung *f*; **executive** [ɪgˈzekjʊtɪv] *n* (*Comm*) leitender Angestellter, leitende Angestellte

exemplary [ɪgˈzempları] adj
beispielhaft

exempt [ɪgˈzempt] adj befreit
(from von) ▷ vt befreien

exercise [ˈeksəsaɪz] n (in school,
sports) Übung f; (movement)
Bewegung f; **to get more ~** mehr
Sport treiben; **exercise bike** n
Heimtrainer m; **exercise book** n
Heft nt

exert [ɪgˈzɜːt] vt (influence)
ausüben

exhaust [ɪgˈzɔːst] n (fumes)
Abgase pl; (Auto) Auspuff
m; **exhausted** adj erschöpft;
exhausting adj anstrengend

exhibit [ɪgˈzɪbɪt] n (in exhibition)
Ausstellungsstück nt; **exhibition**
[eksɪˈbɪʃən] n Ausstellung f;
exhibitionist [eksɪˈbɪʃənɪst] n
Selbstdarsteller(in) m(f); **exhibitor**
n Aussteller(in) m(f)

exhilarating [ɪgˈzɪləreɪtɪŋ] adj
belebend, erregend

exile [ˈeksaɪl] n Exil nt; (person)
Verbannte(r) m(f) ▷ vt verbannen

exist [ɪgˈzɪst] vi existieren; (live)
leben (on von); **existence** n
Existenz f; **to come into**
~ entstehen; **existing** adj
bestehend

exit [ˈeksɪt] n Ausgang m; (for
vehicles) Ausfahrt f; **exit poll** n
Umfrage direkt nach dem Wahlgang

exorbitant [ɪgˈzɔːbɪtənt] adj
astronomisch

exotic [ɪgˈzɒtɪk] adj exotisch

expand [ɪksˈpænd] vt ausdehnen, erweitern ▷ vi sich
ausdehnen; **expansion**
[ɪksˈpænʃən] n Expansion f,
Erweiterung f

expect [ɪksˈpekt] vt erwarten;
(suppose) annehmen; **he ~s me to**
do it er erwartet, dass ich es
mache; **I ~ it'll rain** es wird wohl
regnen; **I ~ so** ich denke schon

▷ vi: **she's ~ing** sie bekommt ein
Kind

expedition [ekspɪˈdɪʃən] n
Expedition f

expenditure [ɪksˈpendɪtʃəᵊ] n
Ausgaben pl

expense [ɪksˈpens] n Kosten pl;
(single cost) Ausgabe f; **(business)**
~s pl Spesen pl; **at sb's ~** auf jds
Kosten; **expensive** [ɪksˈpensɪv]
adj teuer

experience [ɪksˈpɪərɪəns] n
Erfahrung f; (particular incident)
Erlebnis nt; **by/from ~** aus
Erfahrung ▷ vt erfahren, erleben;
(hardship) durchmachen;
experienced adj erfahren

experiment [ɪksˈperɪmənt] n
Versuch m, Experiment nt ▷ vi
experimentieren

expert [ˈekspɜːt] n Experte m,
Expertin f; (professional) Fachmann
m, Fachfrau f; (jur)
Sachverständige(r) mf ▷ adj
fachmännisch, Fach-; **expertise**
[ekspɜːˈtiːz] n Sachkenntnis f

expire [ɪksˈpaɪəᵊ] vi (end)
ablaufen; **expiry date**
[ɪksˈpaɪərɪdeɪt] n Verfallsdatum
nt

explain [ɪksˈpleɪn] vt erklären
(sth to sb jdm etw); **explanation**
[ekspləˈneɪʃən] n Erklärung f

explicit [ɪksˈplɪsɪt] adj aus-
drücklich, eindeutig

explode [ɪksˈpləʊd] vi
explodieren

exploit [ɪksˈplɔɪt] vt ausbeuten

explore [ɪksˈplɔːᵊ] vt erforschen

explosion [ɪksˈpləʊʒən] n
Explosion f; **explosive**
[ɪksˈpləʊsɪv] adj explosiv ▷ n
Sprengstoff m

export [eksˈpɔːt] vt, vi
exportieren ▷ [ˈekspɔːt] n Export
m ▷ adj (trade) Export-

expose [ɪksˈpəʊz] vt (to danger)

etc) aussetzen (*to dat*); (*uncover*) freilegen; (*imposter*) entlarven; **exposed** *adj* (*position*) ungeschützt; **exposure** [ɪkˈspəʊʒəʳ] *n* (*Med*) Unterkühlung *f*; (*Foto: time*) Belichtung(szeit) *f*; **24 ~s** 24 Aufnahmen

express [ɪkˈspres] *adj* (*speedy*) Express-, Schnell-; **~ delivery** Eilzustellung *f* ▷ *n* (*Rail*) Schnellzug *m* ▷ *vt* ausdrücken ▷ *vr*: **to ~ oneself** sich ausdrücken; **expression** [ɪkˈspreʃən] *n* (*phrase*) Ausdruck *m*; (*look*) Gesichtsausdruck *m*; **expressive** *adj* ausdrucksvoll; **expressway** *n* (*US*) Schnellstraße *f*

extend [ɪkˈstend] *vt* (*arms*) ausstrecken; (*lengthen*) verlängern; (*building*) vergrößern, ausbauen; (*business, limits*) erweitern; **extension** [ɪkˈstenʃən] *n* (*lengthening*) Verlängerung *f*; (*of building*) Anbau *m*; (*Tel*) Anschluss *m*; (*of business, limits*) Erweiterung *f*; **extensive** [ɪkˈstensɪv] *adj* (*knowledge*) umfangreich; (*use*) häufig; **extent** [ɪkˈstent] *n* (*length*) Länge *f*; (*size*) Ausdehnung *f*; (*scope*) Umfang *m*, Ausmaß *nt*; **to a certain/large ~** in gewissem/hohem Maße

exterior [ekˈstɪərɪəʳ] *n* Äußere(s) *nt*

external [ekˈstɜːnl] *adj* äußere(r, s), Außen-; **externally** *adv* äußerlich

extinct [ɪkˈstɪŋkt] *adj* (*species*) ausgestorben

extinguish [ɪkˈstɪŋgwɪʃ] *vt* löschen; **extinguisher** *n* Löschgerät *nt*

extra [ˈekstrə] *adj* zusätzlich; **~ charge** Zuschlag *m*; **~ time** (*Sport*) Verlängerung *f* ▷ *adv*

besonders; **~ large** (*clothing*) übergroß ▷ *npl*: **~s** zusätzliche Kosten *pl*; (*food*) Beilagen *pl*; (*accessories*) Zubehör *nt*; (*for car etc*) Extras *pl*

extract [ɪkˈstrækt] *vt* herausziehen (*from aus*); (*tooth*) ziehen ▷ [ˈekstrækt] *n* (*from book etc*) Auszug *m*

extraordinary [ɪkˈstrɔːdnrɪ] *adj* außerordentlich; (*unusual*) ungewöhnlich; (*amazing*) erstaunlich

extreme [ɪkˈstriːm] *adj* äußerste(r, s); (*drastic*) extrem ▷ *n* Extrem *nt*; **extremely** *adv* äußerst, höchst; **extreme sports** *npl* Extremsportarten *pl*; **extremist** [ɪkˈstriːmɪst] *adj* extremistisch ▷ *n* Extremist *m*

extricate [ˈekstrɪkeɪt] *vt* befreien (*from aus*)

extrovert [ˈekstrəʊvɜːt] *adj* extrovertiert

exuberance [ɪgˈzuːbərəns] *n* Überschwang *m*; **exuberant** *adj* überschwänglich

exultation [egzʌlˈteɪʃən] *n* Jubel *m*

eye [aɪ] *n* Auge *nt*; **to keep an ~ on sb/sth** auf jdn/etw aufpassen ▷ *vt* mustern; **eyebrow** *n* Augenbraue *f*; **eyelash** *n* Wimper *f*; **eyelid** *n* Augenlid *nt*; **eyeliner** *n* Eyeliner *m*; **eyeopener** *n*: **that was an ~** das hat mir die Augen geöffnet; **eyeshadow** *n* Lidschatten *m*; **eyesight** *n* Sehkraft *f*; **eyesore** *n* Schandfleck *m*; **eye witness** *n* Augenzeuge *m*, Augenzeugin *f*

f

fabric ['fæbrɪk] n Stoff m
fabulous ['fæbjʊləs] adj
sagenhaft
façade [fə'sɑːd] n (a. fig) Fassade
f
face [feɪs] n Gesicht nt; (of clock)
Zifferblatt nt; (of mountain) Wand f;
in the ~ of trotz +gen; **to be ~ to
~** (people)
gegenüberstehen ▷ vt, vi (person)
gegenüberstehen +dat; (at table)
gegenübersitzen +dat; **to ~ north**
(room) nach Norden gehen; **to
~ (up to) the facts** den Tatsachen
ins Auge sehen; **to be ~d with sth**
mit etw konfrontiert sein; **face lift**
n Gesichtsstraffung f; (fig)
Verschönerung f; **face powder** n
Gesichtspuder m
facet ['fæsɪt] n (fig) Aspekt m
face value n Nennwert m
facial ['feɪʃəl] adj Gesichts- ▷ n
(fam) kosmetische
Gesichtsbehandlung f

facilitate [fə'sɪlɪteɪt] vt
erleichtern
facility [fə'sɪlɪtɪ] n (building etc to
be used) Einrichtung f, Möglichkeit
f; (installation) Anlage f; (skill)
Gewandtheit f
fact [fækt] n Tatsache f; **as a
matter of ~, in ~** eigentlich,
tatsächlich
factor ['fæktə] n Faktor m
factory ['fæktərɪ] n Fabrik f;
factory outlet n Fabrikverkauf m
factual ['fæktjʊəl] adj sachlich
faculty ['fækəltɪ] n Fähigkeit f;
(at university) Fakultät f; (US:
teaching staff) Lehrkörper m
fade [feɪd] vi (a. fig) verblassen;
faded adj verblasst, verblichen
faff about ['fæfəbaʊt] vi (Brit
fam) herumwursteln
fag [fæg] (Brit fam) n Zigarette,
Kippe f; (US fam pej) Schwule(r) fn
Fahrenheit ['færənhaɪt] n
Fahrenheit
fail [feɪl] vt (exam) nicht bestehen
▷ vi versagen; (plan, marriage)
scheitern; (student) durchfallen;
(eyesight) nachlassen; **words ~ me**
ich bin sprachlos; **failing** n
Schwäche f, Fehler m ▷ **failure** ['feɪljə] n
(person) Versager(in) m(f); (act, a.
Tech) Versagen nt; (of engine etc)
Ausfall m; (of plan, marriage)
Scheitern nt
faint [feɪnt] adj schwach; (sound)
leise; (fam) **I haven't the ~est
(idea)** ich habe keinen blassen
Schimmer ▷ vi ohnmächtig
werden (with +dat); **faintness**
n (Med) Schwächegefühl nt
fair [fɛə] adj (hair) (dunkel)blond;
(skin) hell; (just) gerecht, fair;
(reasonable) ganz ordentlich; (in
school) befriedigend; (weather)
schön; (wind) günstig; **a
~ number/amount of** ziemlich
viele/viel ▷ adv: **to play ~** fair

spielen; *(fig)* fair sein; **~ enough** in
Ordnung! ▷ *n (fun~)* Jahrmarkt *m*;
(Comm) Messe *f*; **fair-haired** *adj*
(dunkel)blond; **fairly** *adv*
(honestly) fair; *(rather)* ziemlich

fairy ['fεərɪ] *n* Fee *f*; **fairy tale** *n*
Märchen *nt*

faith [feɪθ] *n (trust)* Vertrauen *nt*
(in sb zu jdm); *(Rel)* Glaube *m*;
faithful, faithfully *adj, adv* treu;
Yours ~ly Hochachtungsvoll

fake [feɪk] *n (thing)* Fälschung *f*
▷ *adj* vorgetäuscht ▷ *vt* fälschen

falcon ['fɔːlkən] *n* Falke *m*

fall [fɔːl] *(fell, fallen) vi* fallen;
(from a height, badly) stürzen; **to
~ ill** krank werden; **to ~ asleep**
einschlafen; **to ~ in love** sich
verlieben ▷ *n* Fall *m*; *(accident, fig:
of regime)* Sturz *m*; *(decrease)* Sinken
nt (in +gen); *(US: autumn)* Herbst *m*;
fall apart *vi* auseinanderfallen;
fall behind *vi* zurückbleiben;
(with work, rent) in Rückstand
geraten; **fall down** *vi (person)*
hinfallen; **fall off** *vi*
herunterfallen; *(decrease)*
zurückgehen; **fall out** *vi*
herausfallen; *(quarrel)* sich
streiten; **fall over** *vi* hinfallen;
fall through *vi (plan etc)* ins
Wasser fallen

fallen ['fɔːlən] *pp of* **fall**

fallout ['fɔːlaʊt] *n* radioaktiver
Niederschlag, Fall-out *m*

false [fɔːls] *adj* falsch; *(artificial)*
künstlich; **false alarm** *n* blinder
Alarm; **false start** *n (Sport)*
Fehlstart *m*; **false teeth** *npl*
(künstliches) Gebiss

fame [feɪm] *n* Ruhm *m*

familiar [fə'mɪlɪə*] *adj* vertraut,
bekannt; **to be ~ with** vertraut
sein mit, gut kennen; **familiarity**
[fəmɪlɪ'ærɪtɪ] *n* Vertrautheit *f*

family ['fæmɪlɪ] *n* Familie *f*;
(including relations) Verwandtschaft

f; **family man** *n* Familienvater *m*;
family name *n* Familienname *m*,
Nachname *m*; **family practitioner**
n (US) Allgemeinarzt *m*,
Allgemeinärztin *f*

famine ['fæmɪn] *n* Hungersnot *f*;
famished ['fæmɪʃt] *adj*
ausgehungert

famous ['feɪməs] *adj* berühmt

fan [fæn] *n (hand-held)* Fächer *m*;
(Elec) Ventilator *m*; *(admirer)* Fan *m*

fanatic [fə'nætɪk] *n* Fanatiker(in)
m(f)

fancy ['fænsɪ] *adj (elaborate)*
kunstvoll; *(unusual)* ausgefallen
▷ *vt (like)* gernhaben; **he fancies
her** er steht auf sie; **~ that** stell dir
vor!, so was!; **fancy dress** *n*
Kostüm *nt*, Verkleidung *f*

fan heater ['fænhiːtə*] *n*
Heizlüfter *m*; **fanlight** *n*
Oberlicht *nt*

fan mail *n* Fanpost *f*

fantasise ['fæntəsaɪz] *vi* träumen *(about* von*)*; **fantastic**
[fæn'tæstɪk] *adj (a. fam)*
fantastisch; **that's ~** *(fam)* das ist
ja toll!; **fantasy** ['fæntəzɪ] *n*
Fantasie *f*

far [fɑː*] *(further o* farther*,
furthest o* farthest*) adj* weit; **the
~ end of the room** das andere
Ende des Zimmers; **the Far East**
der Ferne Osten ▷ *adv* weit;
~ better viel besser; **by ~ the best**
bei weitem der/die/das Beste;
~ as ... bis zum o zur ...; *(with place
name)* bis nach ...; **as ~ as I'm
concerned** was mich betrifft, von
mir aus; **so ~** soweit, bisher;
faraway *adj* weit entfernt; *(look)*
verträumt

fare [fεə*] *n* Fahrpreis *m*; *(money)*
Fahrgeld *nt*

farm [fɑːm] *n* Bauernhof *m*, Farm
f; **farmer** *n* Bauer *m*, Bäuerin *f*,
Landwirt(in) *m(f)*; **farmhouse** *n*

Bauernhaus nt; **farming** n
Landwirtschaft f; **farmland** n
Ackerland nt; **farmyard** n Hof m

far-reaching ['fɑː'riːtʃɪŋ] adj
weit reichend; **far-sighted** adj
weitsichtig, (fig) weitblickend

fart [fɑːt] n (fam) Furz m; old
~ (fam: person) alter Sack ▷ vi (fam)
furzen

farther ['fɑːðəʳ] adj, adv
comparative of **far**; see **further**

farthest ['fɑːðɪst] adj, adv
superlative of **far**; see **furthest**

fascinating ['fæsɪneɪtɪŋ] adj
faszinierend; **fascination** n
Faszination f

fascism ['fæʃɪzəm] n Faschismus
m; **fascist** ['fæʃɪst] adj
faschistisch ▷ Faschist(in) m(f)

fashion ['fæʃən] n (clothes) Mode
f; (manner) Art (und Weise) f; **to be
in ~** (in) Mode sein; **out of
~** unmodisch; **fashionable,
fashionably** adj, adv (clothes,
person) modisch; (author, pub etc) in
Mode

fast [fɑːst] adj schnell; **to be
~** (clock) vorgehen ▷ adv schnell;
(firmly) fest; **to be ~ asleep** fest
schlafen ▷ n Fasten nt ▷ vi
fasten; **fastback** n (Auto)
Fließheck nt

fasten ['fɑːsn] vt (attach)
befestigen (to an +dat); (do up)
zumachen; **~ your seatbelts** bitte
anschnallen; **fastener, fastening**
n Verschluss m

fast food n Fast Food nt; **fast
forward** n (for tape)
Schnellvorlauf m; **fast lane** n
Überholspur f

fat [fæt] adj dick; (meat) fett ▷ n
Fett nt

fatal ['feɪtl] adj tödlich

fate [feɪt] n Schicksal nt

fat-free adj (food) fettfrei

father ['fɑːðəʳ] n Vater m; (priest)

Pfarrer m ▷ vt (child) zeugen;
Father Christmas n der
Weihnachtsmann; **father-in-law**
(pl **fathers-in-law**) n
Schwiegervater m

fatigue [fə'tiːg] n Ermüdung
f

fattening ['fætnɪŋ] adj: **to be
~** dick machen; **fatty** ['fætɪ] adj
(food) fettig

faucet ['fɔːsɪt] n (US)
Wasserhahn m

fault [fɔːlt] n Fehler m; (Tech)
Defekt m; (Elec) Störung f; (blame)
Schuld f; **it's your ~** du bist daran
schuld; **faulty** adj fehlerhaft;
(Tech) defekt

favor (US), **favour** ['feɪvəʳ] n
(approval) Gunst f; (kindness)
Gefallen m; **in ~ of** für; **I'm in ~ (of
going)** ich bin dafür, (dass wir
gehen); **to do sb a ~** jdm einen
Gefallen tun ▷ vt (prefer)
vorziehen; **favourable** adj
günstig (to, for für); **favourite**
['feɪvərɪt] n Liebling m,
Favorit(in) m(f) ▷ adj Lieblings-

fax [fæks] vt faxen ▷ n Fax nt;
fax number n Faxnummer f

faze [feɪz] vt (fam) aus der
Fassung bringen

FBI abbr = **Federal Bureau of
Investigation** FBI nt

fear [fɪəʳ] n Angst f (of vor +dat)
▷ vt befürchten; **fearful** adj
(timid) ängstlich, furchtsam;
(terrible) fürchterlich; **fearless** adj
furchtlos

feasible ['fiːzəbl] adj machbar

feast [fiːst] n Festessen nt

feather ['feðəʳ] n Feder f

feature ['fiːtʃəʳ] n (facial)
(Gesichts)zug m; (characteristic)
Merkmal nt; (of car etc)
Ausstattungsmerkmal nt; (in the
press) (Cine) Feature nt ▷ vt
bringen, (als Besonderheit)

zeigen; **feature film** n Spielfilm m

February ['februərı] n Februar m; see also **September**

fed [fed] pt, pp of **feed**

federal ['fedərəl] adj Bundes-; **the Federal Republic of Germany** die Bundesrepublik Deutschland

fed-up [fed'ʌp] adj: **to be ~ with sth** etw satthaben; **I'm ~** ich habe die Nase voll

fee [fiː] n Gebühr f; (of doctor, lawyer) Honorar nt

feeble ['fiːbl] adj schwach

feed [fiːd] (fed, fed) vt (baby, animal) füttern; (support) ernähren ▷ n (for baby) Mahlzeit f; (for animals) Futter nt; (Inform: paper ~) Zufuhr f; **feed in** vt (information) eingeben; **feedback** n (information) Feed-back nt

feel [fiːl] (felt, felt) vt (sense) fühlen; (pain) empfinden; (touch) anfassen; (think) meinen ▷ vi (person) sich fühlen; **I ~ cold** mir ist kalt; **do you ~ like a walk?** hast du Lust, spazieren zu gehen?; **feeling** n Gefühl nt

feet [fiːt] pl of **foot**

fell [fel] pt of **fall** ▷ vt (tree) fällen

fellow ['feləu] n Kerl m, Typ m; **~ citizen** Mitbürger(in) m(f); **~ countryman** Landsmann m; **~ worker** Mitarbeiter(in) m(f)

felt [felt] pt, pp of **feel** ▷ n Filz m; **felt tip**, **felt-tip pen** n Filzstift m

female ['fiːmeɪl] n (of animals) Weibchen nt ▷ adj weiblich; **~ doctor** Ärztin f; **feminine** ['femɪnɪn] adj weiblich; **feminist** ['femɪnɪst] n Feminist(in) m(f) ▷ adj feministisch

fence [fens] n Zaun m

fencing n (Sport) Fechten nt

fender ['fendə°] n (US Auto) Kotflügel m

fennel ['fenl] n Fenchel m

fern [fɜːn] n Farn m

ferocious [fə'rəuʃəs] adj wild

ferry ['ferı] n Fähre f ▷ vt übersetzen

fertile ['fɜːtaɪl] adj fruchtbar; **fertility** [fə'tɪltɪ] n Fruchtbarkeit f; **fertilize** ['fɜːtɪlaɪz] vt (Bio) befruchten; (Agr: land) düngen; **fertilizer** n Dünger m

festival ['festɪvəl] n (Rel) Fest nt; (Art, Mus) Festspiele pl; (pop music) Festival nt; **festive** ['festɪv] adj festlich; **festivities** [fe'stɪvɪtɪz] n Feierlichkeiten pl

fetch [fetʃ] vt holen; (collect) abholen; (in sale, money) einbringen; **fetching** adj reizend

fetish ['fetɪʃ] n Fetisch m

fetus ['fiːtəs] n (US) Fötus m

fever ['fiːvə°] n Fieber nt; **feverish** adj (Med) fiebrig; (fig) fieberhaft

few [fjuː] adj, pron pl wenige pl; **a ~** pl ein paar; **fewer** adj weniger; **fewest** adj wenigste(r, s)

fiancé [fɪ'ãːnseɪ] n Verlobte(r) m; **fiancée** n Verlobte f

fiasco [fɪ'æskəu] (pl **-s** o US **-es**) n Fiasko nt

fiber (US), **fibre** ['faɪbə°] n Faser f; (material) Faserstoff m

fickle ['fɪkl] adj unbeständig

fiction ['fɪkʃən] n (novels) Prosaliteratur f; **fictional** adj erfunden; **fictitious** [fɪk'tɪʃəs] adj erfunden

fiddle ['fɪdl] n Geige f; (trick) Betrug m ▷ vt (accounts, results) frisieren; **fiddle with** vt herumfummeln an +dat; **fiddly** adj knifflig

fidelity [fɪ'delɪtɪ] n Treue f

fidget ['fɪdʒɪt] vi zappeln; **fidgety** adj zappelig

field [fiːld] n Feld nt; (grass-covered) Wiese f; (fig: of work) (Arbeits)gebiet nt

fierce [fɪəs] *adj* heftig; (*animal, appearance*) wild; (*criticism, competition*) scharf

fifteen [fɪfˈtiːn] *num* fünfzehn ▷ n Fünfzehn f; *see also* **eight**; **fifteenth** *adj* fünfzehnte(r, s); *see also* **eighth**; **fifth** [fɪfθ] *adj* fünfte(r, s) ▷ n (*fraction*) Fünftel *nt*; *see also* **eighth**; **fifty** [ˈfɪftɪ] *num* fünfzig ▷ n Fünfzig f; *see also* **eight**; **fiftieth** *adj* fünfzigste(r, s); *see also* **eighth**

fig [fɪg] *n* Feige f

fight [faɪt] (*fought, fought*) *vi* kämpfen (*with, against* gegen; *for, over* um) ▷ vt (*person*) kämpfen mit; (*fig: disease, fire etc*) bekämpfen ▷ n Kampf *m*; (*brawl*) Schlägerei f; (*argument*) Streit *m*; **fight back** *vi* zurückschlagen; **fight off** *vt* abwehren; **fighter** *n* Kämpfer(in) *m(f)*

figurative [ˈfɪɡərətɪv] *adj* übertragen

figure [ˈfɪɡəʳ] *n* (*person*) Gestalt f; (*of person*) Figur f; (*number*) Zahl f, Ziffer f; (*amount*) Betrag *m*; **a four-figure sum** eine vierstellige Summe ▷ vt (*US: think*) glauben ▷ vi (*appear*) erscheinen; **figure out** *vt* (*work out*) herausbekommen; **I can't figure him out** ich werde aus ihm nicht schlau; **figure skating** *n* Eiskunstlauf *m*

file [faɪl] *n* (*tool*) Feile f; (*dossier*) Akte f; (*Inform*) Datei f; (*folder*) Aktenordner *m*; **on ~** in den Akten ▷ vt (*metal, nails*) feilen; (*papers*) ablegen (*under* unter) ▷ vi: **to ~ in/out** hintereinander hereinkommen/hinausgehen; **filing cabinet** *n* Aktenschrank *m*

fill [fɪl] *vt* füllen; (*tooth*) plombieren; (*post*) besetzen; **fill in** *vt* (*hole*) auffüllen; (*form*) ausfüllen; (*tell*) informieren (*on* über); **fill out**

vt (*form*) ausfüllen; **fill up** *vi* (*Auto*) volltanken

fillet [ˈfɪlɪt] *n* Filet *nt*

filling [ˈfɪlɪŋ] *n* (*Gastr*) Füllung f; (*for tooth*) Plombe f; **filling station** *n* Tankstelle f

film [fɪlm] *n* Film *m* ▷ vt (*scene*) filmen; **film star** *n* Filmstar *m*; **film studio** *n* Filmstudio *nt*

filter [ˈfɪltəʳ] *n* Filter *m*; (*traffic lane*) Abbiegespur f ▷ vt filtern

filth [fɪlθ] *n* Dreck *m*; **filthy** *adj* dreckig

fin [fɪn] *n* Flosse f

final [ˈfaɪnl] *adj* letzte(r, s); (*stage, round*) End-; (*decision, version*) endgültig; **~ score** Schlussstand *m* ▷ n (*Sport*) Endspiel *nt*; (*competition*) Finale *nt*, **~s** *pl* Abschlussexamen *nt*; **finalize** *vt* die endgültige Form geben +*dat*; **finally** *adv* (*lastly*) zuletzt; (*eventually*) schließlich, endlich

finance [faɪˈnæns] *n* Finanzwesen *nt*; **~s** *pl* Finanzen *pl* ▷ vt finanzieren; **financial** [faɪˈnænʃəl] *adj* finanziell; (*adviser, crisis, policy etc*) Finanz-

find [faɪnd] (*found, found*) *vt* finden; **he was found dead** er wurde tot aufgefunden; **I ~ myself in difficulties** ich befinde mich in Schwierigkeiten; **she ~s it difficult/easy** es fällt ihr schwer/leicht; **find out** *vt* herausfinden; **findings** *npl* (*Jur*) Ermittlungsergebnis *nt*; (*of report, Med*) Befund *m*

fine [faɪn] *adj* (*thin*) dünn, fein; (*good*) gut; (*splendid*) herrlich; (*clothes*) elegant; (*weather*) schön; **I'm ~** es geht mir gut; **that's ~** das ist OK ▷ adv (*well*) gut ▷ n (*Jur*) Geldstrafe f ▷ vt (*Jur*) mit einer Geldstrafe belegen; **fine arts** *npl*: **the ~** die schönen Künste *pl*;

finely adv (cut) dünn; (ground) fein

finger ['fɪŋɡə°] n Finger m ▷ vt herumfingern an +dat; **fingernail** n Fingernagel m; **fingerprint** n Fingerabdruck m; **fingertip** n Fingerspitze f

finicky ['fɪnɪkɪ] adj (person) pingelig; (work) knifflig

finish ['fɪnɪʃ] n Ende nt; (Sport) Finish nt; (line) Ziel nt; (of product) Verarbeitung f ▷ vt beenden; (book etc) zu Ende lesen; (food aufessen; (drink) austrinken ▷ vi zu Ende gehen; (song, story) enden; (person) fertig sein; (stop) aufhören; **have you ~ed?** bist du fertig?; **to ~ first/second** (Sport) als erster/zweiter durchs Ziel gehen; **finishing line** n Ziellinie f

Finland ['fɪnlənd] n Finnland nt; **Finn** n Finne m, Finnin f; **Finnish** adj finnisch ▷ n (language) Finnisch nt

fir [fɜː°] n Tanne f

fire [faɪə°] n Feuer nt; (house etc) Brand m; **to set ~ to sth** etw in Brand stecken; **to be on ~** brennen ▷ vt (bullets, rockets) abfeuern; (fam: dismiss) feuern ▷ vi (Auto: engine) zünden; **to ~ at sb** auf jdn schießen; **fire alarm** n Feuermelder m; **fire brigade** n Feuerwehr f; **fire engine** n Feuerwehrauto nt; **fire escape** n Feuerleiter f; **fire extinguisher** n Feuerlöscher m; **firefighter** n Feuerwehrmann m, Feuerwehrfrau f; **fireman** n Feuerwehrmann m; **fireplace** n (offener) Kamin; **fireproof** adj feuerfest; **fire station** n Feuerwache f; **firewood** n Brennholz nt; **fireworks** npl Feuerwerk nt

firm [fɜːm] adj fest; (person) **to be ~** entschlossen auftreten ▷ n Firma f

first [fɜːst] adj erste(r, s) ▷ adv (at first) zuerst; (firstly) erstens; (arrive, finish) als erste(r); (begin) zum ersten Mal; **~ of all** zuallererst ▷ n (person) Erste(r) mf; (Auto: gear) erster Gang; **at ~** zuerst, anfangs; **first aid** n erste Hilfe; **first-class** adj erstklassig; (compartment, ticket) erster Klasse; **~ mail** (Brit) bevorzugt beförderte Post ▷ adv (travel) erster Klasse; **first floor** n (Brit) erster Stock; (US) Erdgeschoss nt; **first lady** n (US) Frau f des Präsidenten; **firstly** adv erstens; **first name** n Vorname m; **first night** n (Theat) Premiere f; **first-rate** adj erstklassig

fir tree n Tannenbaum m

fish [fɪʃ] n Fisch m; **~ and chips** (Brit) frittierter Fisch mit Pommes frites ▷ vi fischen; (with rod) angeln; **to go ~ing** fischen/angeln gehen; **fishbone** n Gräte f; **fishcake** n Fischfrikadelle f; **fish farm** n Fischzucht f; **fish finger** n (Brit) Fischstäbchen nt; **fishing** ['fɪʃɪŋ] n Fischen nt; (with rod) Angeln nt; (as industry) Fischerei f; **fishing boat** n Fischerboot nt; **fishing line** n Angelschnur f; **fishing rod** n Angelrute f; **fishing village** n Fischerdorf nt; **fishmonger** ['fɪʃmʌŋɡə°] n Fischhändler(in) m(f); **fish stick** n (US) Fischstäbchen nt; **fish tank** n Aquarium nt

fishy ['fɪʃɪ] adj (fam: suspicious) faul

fist [fɪst] n Faust f

fit [fɪt] adj (Med) gesund; (Sport) in Form, fit; (suitable) geeignet; **to keep ~** sich in Form halten ▷ vt passen +dat; (attach) anbringen (to an +dat); (install) einbauen (in in +akk) ▷ vi passen; (in space, gap) hineinpassen ▷ n (of clothes) Sitz m; (Med) Anfall m; **it's a good ~** es

passt gut; **fit in** vt (accommodate)
unterbringen; (find time for)
einschieben ▷ vi (in space)
hineinpassen; (plans, ideas) passen;
he doesn't ~ (here) er passt nicht
hierher; **to ~ with sb's plans** sich
mit jds Plänen vereinbaren lassen;
fitness n (Med) Gesundheit f;
(Sport) Fitness f; **fitness trainer** n
(Sport) Fitnesstrainer(in) m(f);
fitted carpet n Teppichboden m;
fitted kitchen n Einbauküche f;
fitting adj passend ▷ n (of dress)
Anprobe f; **~s** pl Ausstattung f

five [faɪv] num fünf ▷ n Fünf f;
see also **eight**; **fiver** n (Brit fam)
Fünfpundschein m

fix [fɪks] vt befestigen (to an
+dat); (settle) festsetzen (fixity,
time) ausmachen; (repair)
reparieren; **fixer** n (drug addict)
Fixer(in) m(f); **fixture** ['fɪkstʃə°]
n (Sport) Veranstaltung f; (match)
Spiel nt; (in building)
Installationsteil nt; **~s (and
fittings)** pl Ausstattung f

fizzy ['fɪzɪ] adj sprudelnd;
~ drink Limo f

flabbergasted ['flæbəgɑːstɪd]
adj (fam) platt

flabby ['flæbɪ] adj (fat) wabbelig

flag [flæg] n Fahne f; **flagstone** n
Steinplatte f

flake [fleɪk] n Flocke f ▷ vi: **to
~ (off)** abblättern

flamboyant [flæm'bɔɪənt] adj
extravagant

flame [fleɪm] n Flamme f; (person)
an old ~ eine alte Liebe

flan [flæn] n (fruit ~) Obstkuchen
m

flannel ['flænl] n Flanell m; (Brit:
face ~) Waschlappen m; (fam: waffle)
Geschwafel nt ▷ vi herumlabern

flap [flæp] n Klappe f (fam) **to be
in a ~** rotieren ▷ vt (wings)
schlagen mit ▷ vi flattern

flared [flɛəd] adj (trousers) mit
Schlag; **flares** npl Schlaghose f

flash [flæʃ] n Blitz m; (news ~)
Kurzmeldung f; (Foto) Blitzlicht nt;
in a ~ im Nu ▷ vt: **to ~ one's
(head)lights** die Lichthupe
betätigen ▷ vi aufblitzen;
(brightly) aufblitzen; **flashback** n
Rückblende f, Flashback m;
flashlight ['flæʃlaɪt] n (Photo)
Blitzlicht nt; (US: torch)
Taschenlampe f; **flashy** adj grell,
schrill; (pej) protzig

flat [flæt] adj flach; (surface) eben;
(drink) abgestanden; (tyre) platt;
(battery) leer; (refusal) glatt ▷ n
(Brit: rooms) Wohnung f; (Auto)
Reifenpanne f; **flat screen** n
(Inform) Flachbildschirm m; **flatten**
vt platt machen, einebnen

flatter ['flætə°] vt schmeicheln
+dat; **flattering** adj
schmeichelhaft

flatware ['flætweə] n (US)
Besteck nt

flavor (US), **flavour** ['fleɪvə°] n
Geschmack m ▷ vt Geschmack
geben +dat; (with spices) würzen;
flavouring n Aroma nt

flaw [flɔː] n Fehler m; **flawless**
adj fehlerlos; (complexion) makellos

flea [fliː] n Floh m

fled [fled] pt, pp of **flee**

flee [fliː] (**fled, fled**) vi fliehen

fleece [fliːs] n (of sheep) Vlies nt;
(soft material) Fleece m; (jacket)
Fleecejacke f

fleet [fliːt] n Flotte f

Flemish ['flemɪʃ] adj flämisch
▷ n (language) Flämisch nt

flesh [fleʃ] n Fleisch nt

flew [fluː] pt of **fly**

flex [fleks] n (Brit Elec) Schnur
f

flexibility [fleksɪ'bɪlɪtɪ] n Bieg-
samkeit f (fig) Flexibilität f;
flexible ['fleksɪbl] adj biegsam;

(plans, person) flexibel; **flexitime** n
gleitende Arbeitszeit, Gleitzeit f
flicker ['flɪkə°] vi flackern; (TV)
flimmern
flies [flaɪz] pl of **fly** ▷ n
flight [flaɪt] n Flug m; (escape)
Flucht f; **~ of stairs** Treppe f; **flight
attendant** n Flugbegleiter(in)
m(f); **flight recorder** n
Flugschreiber m
flimsy ['flɪmzɪ] adj leicht gebaut,
nicht stabil; (thin) hauchdünn;
(excuse) fadenscheinig
fling [flɪŋ] (flung, flung) vt
schleudern ▷ n: **to have a ~** eine
(kurze) Affäre haben
flip [flɪp] vt schnippen; **to ~ a
coin** eine Münze werfen; **flip
through** n (book) durchblättern;
flipchart n Flipchart nt
flipper ['flɪpə°] n Flosse f
flirt [flɜːt] vi flirten
float [fləʊt] n (for fishing)
Schwimmer m; (in procession)
Festwagen m; (money)
Wechselgeld nt ▷ vi schwimmen;
(in air) schweben
flock [flɒk] n (of sheep) (Rel) Herde
f; (of birds) Schwarm m; (of people)
Schar f
flog [flɒg] vt auspeitschen; (Brit
fam) verscheuern
flood [flʌd] n Hochwasser nt,
Überschwemmung f; (fig) Flut f
▷ vt überschwemmen; **floodlight**
n Flutlicht nt; **floodlit** adj
(building) angestrahlt
floor [flɔː°] n Fußboden m;
(storey) Stock m; **ground ~** (Brit),
first ~ (US) Erdgeschoss nt; **first
~** (Brit), **second ~** (US) erster Stock;
floorboard n Diele f
flop [flɒp] n (fam: failure) Reinfall
m, Flop m ▷ vi misslingen, floppen
floppy disk ['flɒpɪ'dɪsk] n
Diskette f
Florence ['flɒrəns] n Florenz nt

florist ['flɒrɪst] n Blumenhänd-
ler(in) m(f); **florist's (shop)**
['flɒrɪsts] n Blumengeschäft
m(f)
flounder ['flaʊndə°] n (fish)
Flunder f
flour ['flaʊə°] n Mehl nt
flourish ['flʌrɪʃ] vi gedeihen;
(business) gut laufen; (boom)
florieren ▷ vt (wave about)
schwenken; **flourishing** adj
blühend
flow [fləʊ] n Fluss m; **to go with
the ~** mit dem Strom schwimmen
▷ vi fließen
flower ['flaʊə°] n Blume f ▷ vi
blühen; **flower bed** n Blumenbeet
nt; **flowerpot** n Blumentopf
m
flown [fləʊn] pp of **fly**
flu [fluː] n (fam) Grippe f
fluent adj (Italian etc) fließend; **to
be ~ in German** fließend Deutsch
sprechen
fluid ['fluːɪd] n Flüssigkeit f ▷ adj
flüssig
flung [flʌŋ] pt, pp of **fling**
fluorescent [flʊə'resnt] adj fluo-
reszierend, Leucht-
flush [flʌʃ] n (lavatory)
Wasserspülung f; (blush) Röte f
▷ vi (lavatory) spülen
flute [fluːt] n Flöte f
fly [flaɪ] (flew, flown) vt, vi
fliegen; **how time flies** wie die Zeit
vergeht! ▷ n (insect) Fliege f;
~/flies (pl) (on trousers)
Hosenschlitz m; **fly-drive** n
Urlaub m mit Flug und
Mietwagen; **flyover** n (Brit)
Straßenüberführung f;
Eisenbahnüberführung f; **flysheet**
n Überzelt nt
FM abbr = **frequency modulation**
≈ UKW
FO abbr = **Foreign Office** ≈ AA nt
foal [fəʊl] n Fohlen nt

foam [fəʊm] n Schaum m ▷ vi schäumen

fob off [fɒb ɒf] vt: **to fob sb off with sth** jdm etw andrehen

focus ['fəʊkəs] n Brennpunkt m; **in/out of ~** (photo) scharf/unscharf; (camera) scharf/unscharf eingestellt ▷ vt (camera) scharf stellen ▷ vi sich konzentrieren (on auf +akk)

foetus ['fiːtəs] n Fötus m

fog [fɒg] n Nebel m; **foggy** adj neblig; **fog light** n (Auto: at rear) Nebelschlussleuchte f

foil [fɔɪl] vt vereiteln ▷ n Folie f

fold [fəʊld] vt falten ▷ vi (fam: business) eingehen ▷ n Falte f; **fold up** vi (map etc) zusammenfalten, (chair etc) zusammenklappen ▷ vi (fam: business) eingehen; **folder** n (portfolio) Aktenmappe f; (pamphlet) Broschüre f; (Inform) Ordner m; **folding** adj zusammenklappbar; (bicycle, chair) Klapp-

folk [fəʊk] n Leute pl; (Mus) Folk m, **my ~s** pl (fam) meine Leute ▷ adj Volks-

follow ['fɒləʊ] vt folgen +dat; (pursue) verfolgen; (understand) folgen können +dat; (career, news etc) verfolgen; **as ~s** wie folgt ▷ vi folgen; (result) sich ergeben (from aus); **follow up** vt (request, rumour) nachgehen +dat, weiter verfolgen; **follower** n Anhänger(in) m(f); **following** adj folgend; **the ~ day** am (darauf)folgenden Tag ▷ prep nach; **follow up** n (event, book etc) Fortsetzung f

fond [fɒnd] adj: **to be ~ of** gernhaben; **fondly** adv (with love) liebevoll; **fondness** n Vorliebe f, (for people) Zuneigung f

fondue ['fɒnduː] n Fondue nt

font [fɒnt] n Taufbecken nt, (Typo) Schriftart f

food [fuːd] n Essen nt, Lebensmittel pl; (for animals) Futter nt; (groceries) Lebensmittel pl; **food poisoning** n Lebensmittelvergiftung f; **food processor** n Küchenmaschine f; **foodstuff** n Lebensmittel nt

fool [fuːl] n Idiot m, Narr m; **to make a ~ of oneself** sich blamieren ▷ vt (deceive) hereinlegen ▷ vi: **to ~ around** herumalbern; (waste time) herumtrödeln; **foolish** adj dumm; **foolproof** adj idiotensicher

foot [fʊt] n (pl feet [fiːt]) n Fuß m; (measure) Fuß m (30,48 cm); **on ~** zu Fuß ▷ vt (bill) bezahlen; **foot and mouth disease** n Maul- und Klauenseuche f; **football** n Fußball m; (US: American ~) Football m; **footballer** n Fußballspieler(in) m(f); **footbridge** n Fußgängerbrücke f; **footing** n (hold) Halt m; **footlights** npl Rampenlicht nt; **footnote** n Fußnote f; **footpath** n Fußweg m; **footprint** n Fußabdruck m; **footwear** n Schuhwerk nt

○ **KEYWORD**

for [fɔː°] prep **1** für; **is this for me?** ist das für mich?; **the train for London** der Zug nach London; **he went for the paper** er ging die Zeitung holen; **give it to me — what for?** gib es mir — warum? **2** (because of) wegen; **for this reason** aus diesem Grunde **3** (referring to distance) **there are roadworks for 5 km** die Baustelle ist 5 km lang; **we walked for miles** wir sind meilenweit gegangen

4 (referring to time) seit; (with future sense) für; **he was away for 2 years** er war zwei Jahre lang weg **5** (+infin clauses) **it is not for me to decide** das kann ich nicht entscheiden; **for this to be possible ...** damit dies möglich wird/wurde ... **6** (in spite of) trotz +gen o (inf) dat; **for all his complaints** obwohl er sich ständig beschwert ▷ conj denn

forbade [fə'bæd] pt of **forbid**
forbid [fə'bɪd] (**forbade, forbidden**) vt verbieten
force [fɔːs] n Kraft f; (compulsion) Zwang m, Gewalt; **to come into ~** in Kraft treten; **the Forces** pl die Streitkräfte pl vt zwingen; **forced** adj (smile) gezwungen; **~ landing** Notlandung f; **forceful** adj kraftvoll
forceps ['fɔːseps] npl Zange f
forearm ['fɔːrɑːm] n Unterarm m
forecast ['fɔːkɑːst] vt voraussagen; (weather) vorhersagen ▷ n Vorhersage f
forefinger ['fɔːfɪŋgə²] n Zeigefinger m
foreground ['fɔːgraʊnd] n Vordergrund m
forehand ['fɔːhænd] n (Sport) Vorhand f
forehead ['fɔːhed, 'fɒrɪd] n Stirn f
foreign ['fɒrən] adj ausländisch; **foreigner** n Ausländer(in) m(f); **foreign exchange** n Devisen pl; **foreign language** n Fremdsprache f; **foreign minister** n Außenminister(in) m(f); **Foreign Office** n (Brit) Außenministerium nt; **Foreign Secretary** n (Brit) Außenminister(in) m(f); **foreign policy** n Außenpolitik f

foremost ['fɔːməʊst] adj erste(r, s); (leading) führend
forerunner ['fɔːrʌnə²] n Vorläufer(in) m(f)
foresee [fɔː'siː] irr vt vorhersehen; **foreseeable** adj absehbar
forest ['fɒrɪst] n Wald m; **forestry** ['fɒrɪstrɪ] n Forstwirtschaft f
forever [fə'revə²] adv für immer
forgave [fə'geɪv] pt of **forgive**
forge [fɔːdʒ] n Schmiede f ▷ vt schmieden; (fake) fälschen; **forger** n Fälscher(in) m(f); **forgery** n Fälschung f
forget [fə'get] (**forgot, forgotten**) vt, vi vergessen; **to ~ about sth** etw vergessen; **forgetful** adj vergesslich; **forgetfulness** n Vergisslichkeit f; **forget-me-not** n Vergissmeinnicht nt
forgive [fə'gɪv] (**forgave, forgiven**) irr vt verzeihen; **to ~ sb for sth** jdm etw verzeihen
forgot [fə'gɒt] pt of **forget**
forgotten [fə'gɒtn] pp of **forget**
fork [fɔːk] n Gabel f; (in road) Gabelung f ▷ vi (road) sich gabeln
form [fɔːm] n (shape) Form f, Klasse f; (document) Formular nt; (person) **to be in (good) ~** in Form sein ▷ vt bilden
formal ['fɔːməl] adj förmlich, formell; **formality** [fɔː'mælɪtɪ] n Formalität f
format ['fɔːmæt] n Format nt ▷ vt (Inform) formatieren
former ['fɔːmə²] adj frühere(r, s); (opposite of latter) erstere(r, s); **formerly** adv früher
formidable ['fɔːmɪdəbl] adj gewaltig; (opponent) stark
formula ['fɔːmjʊlə] n Formel f
formulate ['fɔːmjʊleɪt] vt formulieren

forth [fɔ:θ] *adv*: **and so ~** und so weiter; **forthcoming** [fɔ:θ'kʌmɪŋ] *adj* kommend, bevorstehend

fortify ['fɔ:tɪfaɪ] *vt* verstärken; *(for protection)* befestigen

fortieth ['fɔ:tɪəθ] *adj* vierzigste(r, s); *see also* **eighth**

fortnight ['fɔ:tnaɪt] *n* vierzehn Tage *pl*

fortress ['fɔ:trɪs] *n* Festung *f*

fortunate ['fɔ:tʃənɪt] *adj* glücklich; **I was ~** ich hatte Glück; **fortunately** *adv* zum Glück; **fortune** ['fɔ:tʃən] *n (money)* Vermögen *nt*; **good ~** Glück *nt*; **fortune-teller** *n* Wahrsager(in) *m(f)*

forty ['fɔ:tɪ] *num* vierzig *n* Vierzig *f*; *see also* **eight**

forward ['fɔ:wəd] *adv* vorwärts ▷ *n (Sport)* Stürmer(in) *m(f)* ▷ *vt (send on)* nachsenden; *(Inform)* weiterleiten; **forwards** *adv* vorwärts

foster child ['fɒstətʃaɪld] *n* Pflegekind *nt*; **foster parents** *npl* Pflegeeltern *pl*

fought [fɔ:t] *pt, pp of* **fight**

foul [faʊl] *adj (weather)* schlecht; *(smell)* übel ▷ *n (Sport)* Foul *nt*

found [faʊnd] *pt, pp of* **find** ▷ *vt (establish)* gründen; **foundations** [faʊn'deɪʃənz] *npl* Fundament *nt*

fountain ['faʊntɪn] *n* Springbrunnen *m*; **fountain pen** *n* Füller *m*

four [fɔ:] *num* vier ▷ *n* Vier *f*; *see also* **eight**; **fourteen** ['fɔ:ti:n] *num* vierzehn ▷ *n* Vierzehn *f*; *see also* **eight**; **fourteenth** *adj* vierzehnte(r, s); *see also* **eighth**; **fourth** [fɔ:θ] *adj* vierte(r, s); *see also* **eighth**

four-wheel drive *n* Allradantrieb *m*; *(car)* Geländewagen *m*

fowl [faʊl] *n* Geflügel *nt*

fox [fɒks] *n (a. fig)* Fuchs *m*

fraction ['frækʃən] *n (Math)* Bruch *m*; *(part)* Bruchteil *m*; **fracture** ['fræktʃə°] *n (Med)* Bruch *m* ▷ *vt* brechen

fragile ['frædʒaɪl] *adj* zerbrechlich

fragment ['frægmənt] *n* Bruchstück *nt*

fragrance ['freɪgrəns] *n* Duft *m*; **fragrant** *adj* duftend

frail [freɪl] *adj* gebrechlich

frame [freɪm] *n* Rahmen *m*; *(of spectacles)* Gestell *nt*; **~ of mind** Verfassung *f* ▷ *vt* einrahmen; **to ~ sb** *(fam: incriminate)* jdm etwas anhängen; **framework** *n* Rahmen *m*, Struktur *f*

France [frɑ:ns] *n* Frankreich *nt*

frank [fræŋk] *adj* offen

frankfurter ['fræŋkfɜ:tə°] *n* (Frankfurter) Würstchen *nt*

frankly ['fræŋklɪ] *adv* offen gesagt; **quite ~** ganz ehrlich; **frankness** *n* Offenheit *f*

frantic ['fræntɪk] *adj (activity)* hektisch; *(effort)* verzweifelt; **~ with worry** außer sich vor Sorge

fraud [frɔ:d] *n (trickery)* Betrug *m*; *(person)* Schwindler(in) *m(f)*

freak [fri:k] *n* Anomalie *f*; *(animal, person)* Missgeburt *f*; *(fam: fan)* Fan *m*, Freak *m* ▷ *adj (conditions)* außergewöhnlich, seltsam; **freak out** *vi (fam)* ausflippen

freckle ['frekl] *n* Sommersprosse *f*

free [fri:] *adj, adv* frei; *(without payment)* gratis, kostenlos; **for ~** umsonst ▷ *vt* befreien; **freebie** ['fri:bɪ] *n (fam)* Werbegeschenk *nt*; **it was a ~** es war gratis; **freedom** ['fri:dəm] *n* Freiheit *f*; **freefone** ['fri:fəʊn] *adj*: **a ~ number** eine gebührenfreie

Nummer; **free kick** n (Sport) Freistoß m

freelance ['friːlɑːns] adj freiberuflich tätig; (artist) freischaffend ▷ n Freiberufler(in) m(f)

free-range ['friːreɪndʒ] adj (hen) frei laufend; **~ eggs** pl Freilandeier pl

freeway ['friːweɪ] n (US) (gebührenfreie) Autobahn

freeze [friːz] (froze, frozen) vi (feel cold) frieren; (of lake etc) zufrieren; (water etc) gefrieren ▷ vt einfrieren; **freezer** n Tiefkühltruhe f; (in fridge) Gefrierfach nt; **freezing** adj eiskalt; **I'm ~** mir ist eiskalt; **freezing point** n Gefrierpunkt m

freight [freɪt] n (goods) Fracht f; (money charged) Frachtgebühr f; **freight car** n (US) Güterwagen m; **freight train** n (US) Güterzug m

French [frentʃ] adj französisch ▷ n (language) Französisch nt; **the ~** pl die Franzosen; **French bean** n grüne Bohne; **French bread** n Baguette f; **French dressing** n Vinaigrette f; **French fries** (US) npl Pommes frites pl; **French kiss** n Zungenkuss m; **Frenchman** (pl -men) n Franzose m; **French toast** n (US) in Ei und Milch getunktes gebratenes Brot; **French window(s)** n(pl) Balkontür f, Terrassentür f; **Frenchwoman** (pl -women) n Französin f

frequency ['friːkwənsɪ] n Häufigkeit f; (Phys) Frequenz f; **frequent** ['friːkwənt] adj häufig; **frequently** adv häufig

fresco ['freskəʊ] (pl -es) n Fresko nt

fresh [freʃ] adj frisch; (new) neu; **freshen** vi: **to ~ (up)** (person) sich frisch machen; **fresher, freshman** (pl -men) n Erstsemester nt;

freshwater fish n Süßwasserfisch m

Fri abbr = **Friday** Fr

friction ['frɪkʃən] n (a. fig) Reibung f

Friday ['fraɪdeɪ] n Freitag m; see also **Tuesday**

fridge [frɪdʒ] n Kühlschrank m

fried [fraɪd] adj gebraten; **~ potatoes** Bratkartoffeln pl; **~ egg** Spiegelei nt; **~ rice** gebratener Reis

friend [frend] n Freund(in) m(f); (less close) Bekannte(r) mf; **to make ~s with sb** sich mit jdm anfreunden; **we're good ~s** wir sind gut befreundet; **friendly** adj freundlich; **to be ~ with sb** mit jdm befreundet sein ▷ n (Sport) Freundschaftsspiel nt; **friendship** ['frendʃɪp] n Freundschaft f

fright [fraɪt] n Schrecken m; **frighten** vt erschrecken; **to be ~ed** Angst haben; **frightening** adj beängstigend

frill [frɪl] n Rüsche f; **~s** (fam) Schnickschnack

fringe [frɪndʒ] n (edge) Rand m; (on shawl etc) Fransen pl; (hair) Pony m

frivolous ['frɪvələs] adj leichtsinnig; (remark) frivol

frizzy ['frɪzɪ] adj kraus

frog [frɒg] n Frosch m

KEYWORD

from [frɒm] prep 1 (indicating starting place) von; (indicating origin etc) aus +dat; **a letter/telephone call from my sister** ein Brief/Anruf von meiner Schwester; **where do you come from?** woher kommen Sie?; **to drink from the bottle** aus der Flasche trinken

2 (*indicating time*) von ... an; (*past*)
seit; **from one o'clock to 0 until 0
till two** von ein Uhr bis zwei; **from
January (on)** ab Januar
3 (*indicating distance*) von ...
(entfernt)
4 (*indicating price, number etc*) ab
+dat; **from £10** ab £10; **there were
from 20 to 30 people there** es
waren zwischen 20 und 30 Leute
da
5 (*indicating difference*) **he can't tell
red from green** er kann nicht
zwischen Rot und Grün
unterscheiden; **to be different
from sb/sth** anders sein als
jd/etw
f (because of, owing to) **from what
he says** aus dem, was er sagt;
weak from hunger schwach vor
Hunger

front [frʌnt] *n* Vorderseite *f*; (*of
house*) Fassade *f*; (*in war, of weather*)
Front *f*; (*at seaside*) Promenade *f*; **in
~, at the ~** vorne; **in ~ of** vor; **up
~** (*in advance*) vorher, im Voraus
▷ *adj* vordere(r, s), Vorder-; (*first*)
vorderste(r, s); **~ door** Haustür *f*;
~ page Titelseite *f*; **~ seat**
Vordersitz *m*; **~ wheel** Vorderrad *nt*

frontier ['frʌntɪə*] *n* Grenze *f*

front-wheel drive *n* (*Auto*)
Frontantrieb *m*

frost [frɒst] *n* Frost *m*; (*white ~*)
Reif *m*; **frosting** *n* (*US*)
Zuckerguss *m*; **frosty** *adj*
frostig

froth [frɒθ] *n* Schaum *m*; **frothy**
adj schaumig

frown [fraʊn] *vi* die Stirn
runzeln

froze [frəʊz] *pt of* **freeze**

frozen [ˈfrəʊzn] *pp of* **freeze** ▷ *adj*
(*food*) tiefgekühlt, Tiefkühl-

fruit [fruːt] *n* (*as collective, a. type*)
Obst *nt*; (*single ~, a. fig*) Frucht *f*;

fruit machine *n* Spielautomat *m*;
fruit salad *n* Obstsalat *m*

frustrated [frʌˈstreɪtɪd] *adj*
frustriert; **frustratration** *n*
Frustration *f*, Frust *m*

fry [fraɪ] *vt* braten; **frying pan** *n*
Bratpfanne *f*

fuchsia [ˈfjuːʃə] *n* Fuchsie *f*

fuck [fʌk] *vt* (*vulg*) ficken; **~ off**
verpiss dich!; **fucking** *adj* (*vulg*)
Scheiß-

fudge [fʌdʒ] *n* weiche
Karamellsüßigkeit

fuel [fjʊəl] *n* Kraftstoff *m*; (*for
heating*) Brennstoff *m*; **fuel
consumption** *n* Kraftstoffver-
brauch *m*; **fuel gauge** *n*
Benzinuhr *f*; **fuel oil** *n* Gasöl *nt*;
fuel rod *n* Brennstab *m*; **fuel tank**
n Tank *m*; (*for oil*) Öltank *m*

fugitive [ˈfjuːdʒɪtɪv] *n* Flüchtling
m

fulfil [fʊlˈfɪl] *vt* erfüllen

full [fʊl] *adj* voll; (*person: satisfied*)
satt; (*member, employment*)
Voll(zeit)-; (*complete*) vollständig;
~ of ... voller ... gen; **full beam** *n*
(*Auto*) Fernlicht *nt*; **full moon** *n*
Vollmond *m*; **full stop** *n* Punkt *m*;
full-time *adj:* **~ job**
Ganztagsarbeit *f*; **fully** *adv* völlig;
(*recover*) voll und ganz; (*discuss*)
ausführlich

fumble [ˈfʌmbl] *vi* herumfummeln (*with, at an* +dat)

fumes [fjuːmz] *npl* Dämpfe *pl*; (*of
car*) Abgase *pl*

fun [fʌn] *n* Spaß *m*; **for ~** zum
Spaß; **it's ~** es macht Spaß; **to
make ~ of** sich lustig machen
über +akk

function [ˈfʌŋkʃən] *n* Funktion *f*;
(*event*) Feier *f*; (*reception*) Empfang
m ▷ *vi* funktionieren; **function
key** *n* (*Inform*) Funktionstaste *f*

fund [fʌnd] *n* Fonds *m*; **~s** *pl*
Geldmittel *pl*

fundamental [fʌndə'mentl] *adj* grundlegend; **fundamentally** *adv* im Grunde

funding ['fʌndɪŋ] *n* finanzielle Unterstützung

funeral ['fju:nərəl] *n* Beerdigung *f*

funfair ['fʌnfeə°] *n* Jahrmarkt *m*

fungus ['fʌŋgəs] (*pl* **fungi** o **funguses**) *n* Pilz *m*

funicular [fju:'nɪkjʊlə°] *n* Seilbahn *f*

funnel ['fʌnl] *n* Trichter *m*; (*of steamer*) Schornstein *m*

funny ['fʌnɪ] *adj* (*amusing*) komisch, lustig; (*strange*) seltsam

fur [fɜ:°] *n* Pelz *m*; (*of animal*) Fell *nt*

furious ['fjʊərɪəs] *adj* wütend (*with sb* auf jdn)

furnished ['fɜ:nɪʃd] *adj* möbliert; **furniture** ['fɜ:nɪtʃə°] *n* Möbel *pl*; **piece of ~** Möbelstück *nt*

further ['fɜ:ðə°] *comparative of* **far** ▷ *adj* weitere(r, s); **~ education** Weiterbildung *f*; **until ~ notice** bis auf weiteres ▷ *adv* weiter; **furthest** ['fɜ:ðɪst] *superlative of* **far** ▷ *adj* am weitesten entfernt ▷ *adv* am weitesten

fury ['fjʊərɪ] *n* Wut *f*

fuse [fju:z] *n* (*Elec*) Sicherung *f* ▷ *vi* (*Elec*) durchbrennen; **fuse box** *n* Sicherungskasten *m*

fuss [fʌs] *n* Theater *nt*; **to make a ~** (*ein*) Theater machen; **fussy** *adj* (*difficult*) schwierig, kompliziert; (*attentive to detail*) pingelig

future ['fju:tʃə°] *adj* künftig ▷ *n* Zukunft *f*

fuze (*US*) *see* **fuse**

fuzzy ['fʌzɪ] *adj* (*indistinct*) verschwommen; (*hair*) kraus

g

gable ['geɪbl] *n* Giebel *m*

gadget ['gædʒɪt] *n* Vorrichtung *f*, Gerät *nt*

Gaelic ['geɪlɪk] *adj* gälisch ▷ *n* (*language*) Gälisch *nt*

gain [geɪn] *vt* (*obtain, win*) gewinnen; (*advantage, respect*) sich verschaffen; (*wealth*) erwerben; (*weight*) zunehmen ▷ *vi* (*improve*) gewinnen (*in* an +dat); (*clock*) vorgehen ▷ *n* Gewinn *m* (*in* an +dat)

gale [geɪl] *n* Sturm *m*

gall bladder ['gɔ:lblædə°] *n* Gallenblase *f*

gallery ['gælərɪ] *n* Galerie *f*, Museum *nt*

gallon ['gælən] *n* Gallone *f*; ((Brit) 4,546 l, (US) 3,79 l)

gallop ['gæləp] *n* Galopp *m* ▷ *vi* galoppieren

gallstone ['gɔ:lstəʊn] *n* Gallenstein *m*

Gambia ['gæmbɪə] n Gambia nt

gamble ['gæmbl] vi um Geld spielen, wetten ▷ n: **it's a ~ es ist riskant; gambling** f Glücksspiel nt

game [geɪm] n Spiel nt; (animals) Wild nt; **a ~ of chess** eine Partie Schach; **~s** (in school) Sport m; **game show** n (TV) Gameshow f

gammon ['gæmən] n geräucherter Schinken

gang [gæŋ] n (of criminals, youths) Bande f, Gang f, Clique f ▷ vt: **to ~ up on** sich verschwören gegen

gangster ['gæŋstə*] n Gangster m

gangway ['gæŋweɪ] n (for ship) Laufplanke f; (Brit: aisle) Gang m, Gangway f

gap [gæp] n (hole) Lücke f; (in time) Pause f; (in age) Unterschied m

gape [geɪp] vi (mit offenem Mund) starren

gap year n Jahr zwischen Schulabschluss und Studium, das oft zu Auslandsaufenthalten genutzt wird

garage ['gærɑːʒ] n Garage f; (for repair) (Auto)werkstatt f; (for fuel) Tankstelle f

garbage ['gɑːbɪdʒ] n (US) Müll m; (fam: nonsense) Quatsch m; **garbage can** n (US) Mülleimer m; (outside) Mülltonne f; **garbage truck** n (US) Müllwagen m

garden ['gɑːdn] n Garten m; (public) **~s** Park m; **garden centre** n Gartencenter nt; **gardener** n Gärtner(in) m(f); **gardening** n Gartenarbeit f

gargle ['gɑːgl] vi gurgeln

gargoyle ['gɑːgɔɪl] n Wasserspeier m

garlic ['gɑːlɪk] n Knoblauch m; **garlic bread** n Knoblauchbrot nt; **garlic butter** n Knoblauchbutter f

gas [gæs] n Gas nt; (US: petrol)

Benzin nt; **to step on the ~** Gas geben; **gas cooker** n Gasherd m; **gas cylinder** n Gasflasche f; **gas fire** n Gasofen m

gasket ['gæskɪt] n Dichtung f

gas lighter n (for cigarettes) Gasfeuerzeug nt; **gas mask** n Gasmaske f; **gas meter** n Gaszähler m

gasoline ['gæsəliːn] n (US) Benzin nt

gasp [gɑːsp] vi keuchen; (in surprise) nach Luft schnappen

gas pedal n (US) Gaspedal nt; **gas pump** n (US) Zapfsäule f; **gas station** n (US) Tankstelle f; **gas tank** n (US) Benzintank m

gastric ['gæstrɪk] adj Magen-; **~ flu** Magen-Darm-Grippe f; **gastroenteritis** n Magen-Darm-Infektion f

gasworks ['gæswɜːks] n Gaswerk nt

gate [geɪt] n Tor nt; (barrier) Schranke f; (Aviat) Gate nt, Flugsteig m

gateau ['gætəʊ] n (pl gateaux) n Torte f

gateway n Tor nt

gather ['gæðə*] vt (collect) sammeln; **to ~ speed** beschleunigen ▷ vi (assemble) sich versammeln; (understand) schließen (from aus); **gathering** n Versammlung f

gauge [geɪdʒ] n Meßgerät nt

gauze [gɔːz] n Gaze f; (for bandages) Mull m

gave [geɪv] pt of **give**

gay [geɪ] adj (homosexual) schwul; **~ marriage** (fam) Homoehe f

gaze [geɪz] n Blick m ▷ vi starren

GCSE abbr = **general certificate of secondary education** (school) Abschlussprüfung f der Sekundarstufe, ≈ mittlere Reife

gear [gɪə*] n (Auto) Gang m; (equipment) Ausrüstung f; (clothes)

Klamotten pl; **to change ~** schalten; **gearbox** n Getriebe nt; **gear change, gear shift** (US) n Gangschaltung f; **gear lever, gear stick** (US) n Schalthebel m

geese [giːs] pl of **goose**

gel [dʒel] n Gel nt ▷ vi gelieren; **they really ~led** sie verstanden sich auf Anhieb

gem [dʒem] n Edelstein m; (fig) Juwel nt

Gemini ['dʒeminiː] nsing (Astr) Zwillinge pl

gender ['dʒendə°] n Geschlecht nt

gene [dʒiːn] n Gen nt

general ['dʒenərəl] adj allgemein; **~ knowledge** Allgemeinbildung f; **~ election** Parlamentswahlen pl; **generalize** ['dʒenrəlaiz] vi verallgemeinern; **generally** ['dʒenrəli] adv im Allgemeinen

generation [dʒenə'reiʃən] n Generation f; **generation gap** n Generationsunterschied m

generator ['dʒenəreitə°] n Generator m

generosity [dʒenə'rɔsiti] n Großzügigkeit f; **generous** ['dʒenərəs] adj großzügig; (portion) reichlich

genetic [dʒi'netik] adj genetisch; **~ research** Genforschung f; **~ technology** Gentechnik f; **genetically modified** adj gentechnisch verändert, genmanipuliert; see also **GM**

Geneva [dʒi'niːvə] n Genf nt; **Lake ~** der Genfer See

genitals ['dʒenitlz] npl Geschlechtsteile pl

genitive ['dʒenitiv] n Genitiv m

genius ['dʒiːniəs] n Genie nt

gentle ['dʒentl] adj sanft; (touch) zart; **gentleman** (pl **-men**)

Herr m; (polite man) Gentleman m

gents [dʒents] n: **"~"** (lavatory) „Herren"; **the ~** pl die Herrentoilette

genuine ['dʒenjuin] adj echt

geographical [dʒiə'græfikəl] adj geografisch; **geography** [dʒi'ɔgrəfi] n Geografie f; (at school) Erdkunde f

geological [dʒiə'lɔdʒikəl] adj geologisch; **geology** [dʒi'ɔlədʒi] n Geologie f

geometry [dʒi'ɔmitri] n Geometrie f

geranium [dʒi'reiniəm] n Geranie f

gerbil ['dʒɜːbəl] n (Zool) Wüstenrennmaus f

germ [dʒɜːm] n Keim m; (Med) Bazillus m

German ['dʒɜːmən] adj deutsch; **she's ~** sie ist Deutsche; **~ shepherd** Deutscher Schäferhund m ▷ n (person) Deutsche(r) mf; (language) Deutsch nt; **in ~** auf Deutsch; **German measles** n sing Röteln pl; **Germany** ['dʒɜːməni] n Deutschland nt

gesture ['dʒestʃə°] n Geste f

O **KEYWORD**

get [get] (pt, pp **got**, pp **gotten** (US)) vi 1 (become, be) werden; **to get old/tired** alt/müde werden; **to get married** heiraten

2 (go) (an)kommen, gehen

3 (begin) **to get to know sb** jdn kennenlernen; **let's get going** o **started!** fangen wir an!

4 (modal vb aux) **you've got to do it** du musst/Sie müssen es tun

▷ vt 1 **to get sth done** (do) etw machen; (have done) etw machen lassen; **to get sth going** o **to go** etw in Gang bringen o bekommen;

to get sb to do sth jdn dazu bringen, etw zu tun

2 (obtain: money, permission, results) erhalten; (find: job, flat) finden; (fetch: person, object) holen; **to get sth for sb** jdm etw besorgen; **get me Mr Jones, please** (Tel) verbinde/verbinden Sie mich bitte mit Mr Jones; **get a life!** (annoyed) mach dich mal locker!, reg dich bloß ab!

3 (receive: present, letter) bekommen, kriegen; (acquire: reputation etc) erwerben

4 (catch) bekommen, kriegen; (hit) (target etc) treffen, erwischen; **get him!** (to dog) fass!

5 (take, move) kriegen; **to get sth to sb** jdm etw bringen

6 (understand) verstehen; (hear) mitbekommen; **I've got it!** ich hab's!

7 (have, possess) **to have got sth** etw haben

get about vi herumkommen; (news) sich verbreiten

get across vi: **to sth** über etw akk kommen; vt: **to get sth across** (communicate) etw klarmachen

get along vi (people) (gut) zurecht-/auskommen (with) mit; (depart) sich akk auf den Weg machen

get at vt (reach) herankommen an +akk; (facts) herausbekommen; **what are you getting at?** worauf wollen Sie hinaus?, was meinst du damit?; **to get at sb** (nag) an jdm herumnörgeln

get away vi (leave) sich akk davonmachen, wegkommen (escape); **to get away from sth** von etw abkommen; **to get away with sth** mit etw davonkommen

get back vi (return) zurückkommen; (Tel) **to get back**

to s.o. jdn zurückrufen
▷ vt zurückbekommen

get by vi (pass) vorbeikommen; (manage) zurecht-/auskommen (on) mit

get down vi (her)untergehen; **to get down to** in Angriff nehmen, (find time to do) kommen zu; ▷ vt (depress) fertigmachen; **it gets me down** (fam) es macht mich fertig; **to get sth down** (write) etw aufschreiben

get in vi (train) ankommen; (arrive home) heimkommen

get into vt (enter) hinein-/ hereinkommen in +akk; (car, train etc) einsteigen in +akk; (clothes) anziehen; (rage, panic etc) geraten in +akk; **to get into trouble** in Schwierigkeiten kommen

get off vi (from train etc) aussteigen; (from horse etc) absteigen; (fam: be enthusiastic) **to get off on sth** auf etw abfahren; ▷ vt (nail, sticker) los-/abbekommen; (clothes) ausziehen

get on vi (progress) vorankommen; (be friends) auskommen; (age) alt werden; (onto train etc) einsteigen; (onto horse etc) aufsteigen
▷ vt etw +akk vorantreiben, mit etw akk loslegen

get out vi (of house) herauskommen; (of vehicle) aussteigen; **get out!** raus! ▷ vt (take out) herausholen; (stain, nail) herausbekommen

get out of vt (duty etc) herumkommen um

get over vi (illness) sich akk erholen von; (surprise) verkraften; (news) fassen; (loss) sich abfinden mit

get round vi herumkommen um; vt (fig) (person) herumkriegen

get through vi (Tel)
durchkommen (to) zu
get together vi
zusammenkommen
get up vi aufstehen
▷ vt hinaufbringen; (go up)
hinaufgehen; (organize) auf die
Beine stellen
get up to vi (reach) erreichen;
(prank etc) anstellen

getaway n Flucht f;
get-together n Treffen nt
Ghana ['gɑːnə] n Ghana nt
gherkin ['gɜːkɪn] n Gewürzgurke
f
ghetto ['getəʊ] (pl -es) n Ghetto
nt
ghost [gəʊst] n Gespenst nt; (of
sb) Geist m
giant ['dʒaɪənt] n Riese m ▷ adj
riesig
giblets ['dʒɪblɪts] npl Geflü-
gelinnereien pl
Gibraltar [dʒɪ'brɔːltə⁰] n
Gibraltar nt
giddy ['gɪdɪ] adj schwindlig
gift [gɪft] n Geschenk nt; (talent)
Begabung f; **gifted** adj begabt;
giftwrap vt als Geschenk
verpacken
gigantic [dʒaɪ'gæntɪk] adj riesig
giggle ['gɪgl] vi kichern ▷ n
Gekicher nt
gill [gɪl] n (of fish) Kieme f
gimmick ['gɪmɪk] n (for sales,
publicity) Gag m
gin [dʒɪn] n Gin m
ginger ['dʒɪndʒə⁰] n Ingwer m
▷ adj (colour) kupferrot; (cat)
rötlichgelb; **ginger ale** n
Gingerale nt; **ginger beer** n
Ingwerlimonade f; **gingerbread** n
Lebkuchen m (mit
Ingwergeschmack); **ginger-(haired)**
adj rotblond; **gingerly** adv (move)
vorsichtig

gipsy ['dʒɪpsɪ] n Zigeuner(in)
m(f)
giraffe [dʒɪ'rɑːf] n Giraffe f
girl [gɜːl] n Mädchen nt;
girlfriend n (feste) Freundin f;
girl guide n (Brit), **girl scout** (US)
Pfadfinderin f
gist [dʒɪst] n: **to get the ~ (of it)**
das Wesentliche verstehen
give [gɪv] (gave, given) vt
geben; (as present) schenken (to sb
jdm); (state: name etc) angeben;
(speech) halten; (blood) spenden; **to
~ sb sth** jdm etw geben/schenken
▷ vi (yield) nachgeben; **give away**
vt (give free) verschenken; (secret)
verraten; **give back** vt
zurückgeben; **give in** vi
aufgeben; **give up** vt, vi
aufgeben; **give way** vi (collapse,
yield) nachgeben; (traffic) die
Vorfahrt beachten
given ['gɪvn] pp of **give** ▷ adj
(fixed) festgesetzt; (certain)
bestimmt; **~ name** (US) Vorname
m ▷ conj: **~ that ...** angesichts der
Tatsache, dass ...
glacier ['glæsɪə⁰] n Gletscher
m
glad [glæd] adj froh (about über;
I was ~ (to hear) that ... es hat
mich gefreut, dass ...; **gladly**
['glædlɪ] adv gerne
glance [glɑːns] n Blick m ▷ vi
einen Blick werfen (at auf +akk)
gland [glænd] n Drüse f;
glandular fever n Drüsenfieber
nt
glare [gleə⁰] n grelles Licht;
(stare) stechender Blick ▷ vi
(angrily) **to ~ at sb** jdn böse
anstarren; **glaring** adj (mistake)
krass
glass [glɑːs] n Glas nt; **~es** pl
Brille f
glen [glen] n (Scot) (enges)
Bergtal nt

glide [glaɪd] vi gleiten; (hover) schweben; **glider** n Segelflugzeug nt; **gliding** n Segelfliegen nt

glimmer ['glɪmə°] n (of hope) Schimmer m

glimpse [glɪmps] n flüchtiger Blick

glitter ['glɪtə°] vi glitzern; (eyes) funkeln

glitzy [glɪtsɪ] adj (fam) glanzvoll, Schickimicki-

global ['gləʊbəl] adj global, Welt-; **~ warming** die Erwärmung der Erdatmosphäre; **globe** [gləʊb] spz; n (sphere) Kugel f; (world) Erdball m; (map) Globus m

gloomily ['gluːmɪlɪ], **gloomy** adj, adj düster

glorious ['glɔːrɪəs] adj (victory, past) ruhmreich; (weather, day) herrlich; **glory** ['glɔːrɪ] n Herrlichkeit f

gloss [glɒs] n (shine) Glanz m

glossary ['glɒsərɪ] n Glossar nt

glossy ['glɒsɪ] adj (surface) glänzend ▷ n (magazine) Hochglanzmagazin nt

glove [glʌv] n Handschuh m; **glove compartment** n Handschuhfach nt

glow [gləʊ] vi glühen

glucose ['gluːkəʊs] n Traubenzucker m

glue [gluː] n Klebstoff m ▷ vt kleben

glutton ['glʌtn] n Vielfraß m; **a ~ for punishment** (fam) Masochist m

GM abbr = **genetically modified** Gen-; **~ foods** gentechnisch veränderte Lebensmittel

GMT abbr = **Greenwich Mean Time** WEZ f

go [gəʊ] (**went, gone**) vi gehen; (in vehicle, travel) fahren; (plane) fliegen; (road) führen (to nach); (depart: train, bus) (ab)fahren;

(person) (fort)gehen; (disappear) verschwinden; (time) vergehen; (function) gehen, funktionieren; (machine, engine) laufen; (fit, suit) passen (with zu); (fail) nachlassen; **I have to ~ to the doctor/to London** ich muss zum Arzt/nach London; **to ~ shopping** einkaufen gehen; **to ~ for a walk/swim** spazieren/schwimmen gehen; **has he gone yet?** ist er schon weg?; **the wine ~es in the cupboard** der Wein kommt in den Schrank; **to get sth ~ing** etw in Gang setzen; **to keep ~ing** weitermachen; (machine etc) weiterlaufen; **how's the job ~ing?** was macht der Job?; **his memory/eyesight is going** sein Gedächtnis lässt ihn im Stich/seine Augen werden schwach; **to ~ deaf/mad/grey** taub/verrückt/grau werden ▷ vb aux: **to be ~ing to do sth** etw tun werden; **I was ~ing to do it** ich wollte es tun ▷ n (pl **-es**) (attempt) Versuch m; **can I have another ~?** darf ich noch mal (probieren)?; **it's my ~** ich bin dran; **in one ~** auf einen Schlag; (drink) in einem Zug; **go after** vt nachlaufen +dat; (in vehicle) nachfahren +dat, **go ahead** vi (in front) vorausgehen; (start) anfangen; **go away** vi weggehen; (on holiday, business) verreisen; **go back** vi (return) zurückgehen; **we ~ a long way** (fam) wir kennen uns schon ewig; **go by** vi vorbeigehen; (vehicle) vorbeifahren; (years, time) vergehen ▷ vt (judge by) gehen nach; **go down** vi (sun, ship) untergehen; (flood, temperature) zurückgehen; (price) sinken; **to ~ well/badly** gut/schlecht ankommen; **go in** vi hineingehen; **go into** vt (enter) hineingehen in +akk; (crash) fahren gegen, hineinfahren in +akk; **to ~ teaching/politics/the army** Lehrer werden/in die Politik gehen/zum Militär gehen; **go off** vi (depart) weggehen; (in vehicle) wegfahren; (lights) ausgehen; (milk etc) sauer werden; (gun, bomb, alarm) losgehen ▷ vt (dislike) nicht mehr mögen; **go on** vi (continue) weitergehen; (lights) angehen; **to ~ with o doing sth** etw weitermachen; **go out** vi (leave house) hinausgehen; (fire, light, person socially) ausgehen; **to ~ for a meal** essen gehen; **go up** vi (temperature, price) steigen; (lift) hochfahren; **go without** vt verzichten auf +akk; (food, sleep) auskommen ohne

go-ahead ['gəʊəhɛd] adj (progressive) fortschrittlich ▷ n grünes Licht

goal [gəʊl] n (aim) Ziel nt; (Sport) Tor nt; **goalie, goalkeeper** n Torwart m, Torfrau f; **goalpost** n Torpfosten m

goat [gəʊt] n Ziege f

gob [gɒb] n (Brit fam) Maul nt; **shut your ~** halt's Maul! ▷ vi spucken; **gobsmacked** (fam: surprised) platt

god [gɒd] n Gott m; **thank God** Gott sei Dank; **godchild** (pl -children) n Patenkind nt; **goddaughter** n Patentochter f; **goddess** ['gɒdɛs] n Göttin f; **godfather** n Pate m; **godmother** n Patin f; **godson** n Patensohn m

goggles npl Schutzbrille f; (for skiing) Skibrille f; (for diving) Taucherbrille f

going ['gəʊɪŋ] adj (rate) üblich; **goings-on** npl Vorgänge pl

go-kart ['gəʊkɑːt] n Gokart m

gold [gəʊld] n Gold nt; **golden**

adj golden; **goldfish** n Goldfisch m; **gold-plated** adj vergoldet

golf [gɒlf] n Golf nt; **golf ball** n Golfball m; **golf club** n Golfschläger m; (association) Golfklub m; **golf course** n Golfplatz m; **golfer** n Golfspieler(in) m(f)

gone [gɒn] pp of **go**; **he's ~** er ist weg ▷ prep: **just ~ three** kurz nach drei

good [gʊd] n (benefit) Wohl nt; (morally good things) Gute(s) nt; **for the ~ of** zum Wohle +gen; **it's for your own ~** es ist zu deinem/Ihrem Besten o Vorteil; **it's no ~ (doing sth)** es hat keinen Sinn o Zweck; (thing) es taugt nichts; **for ~** für immer ▷ adj (better, best) gut; (suitable) passend; (thorough) gründlich; (well-behaved) brav; (kind) nett, lieb; **to be ~ at sport/maths** gut in Sport/Mathe sein; **to be no ~ at sport/maths** schlecht in Sport/Mathe sein; **it's ~ for you** es tut dir gut; **this is ~ for colds** das ist gut gegen Erkältungen; **too ~ to be true** zu schön, um wahr zu sein; **this is just not ~ enough** so geht das nicht; **a ~ three hours** gute drei Stunden; **~ morning/evening** guten Morgen/Abend; **~ night** gute Nacht; **to have a ~ time** sich gut amüsieren

goodbye [gʊdˈbaɪ] interj auf Wiedersehen

Good Friday n Karfreitag m

good-looking adj gut aussehend

goods [gʊdz] npl Waren pl, Güter pl; **goods train** n (Brit) Güterzug m

goodwill [gʊdˈwɪl] n Wohlwollen nt

goose [guːs] n (pl **geese**) n Gans f

▷ vt (fam) **to ~ s.o.** jdn in den Arsch kneifen; **gooseberry** ['guzbərɪ] n Stachelbeere f; **goose bumps** n, **goose pimples** npl Gänsehaut f

gorge [gɔːdʒ] n Schlucht f

gorgeous ['gɔːdʒəs] adj wunderschön; **he's ~** er sieht toll aus

gorilla [gə'rɪlə] n Gorilla m

gossip ['gɒsɪp] n (talk) Klatsch m; (person) Klatschtante f ▷ vi klatschen, tratschen

got [gɒt] pt, pp of **get**

gotten ['gɒtn] (US) pp of **get**

govern ['gʌvən] vt regieren; (province etc) verwalten; **government** n Regierung f; **governor** n Gouverneur(in) m(f); **govt** abbr = **government** Regierung f

gown [gaʊn] n Abendkleid nt; (academic) Robe f

GP abbr = **General Practitioner** Allgemeinarzt, Allgemeinärztin f

GPS n abbr = **global positioning system** GPS nt

grab [græb] vt packen; (person) schnappen

grace [greɪs] n Anmut f; (prayer) Tischgebet nt; **5 days'** ~ 5 Tage Aufschub; **graceful** adj anmutig

grade [greɪd] n Niveau nt; (of goods) Güteklasse f; (mark) Note f; (US: year) Klasse f; **to make the ~** es schaffen; **grade crossing** n (US) Bahnübergang m; **grade school** n (US) Grundschule f

gradient ['greɪdɪənt] n (upward) Steigung f; (downward) Gefälle nt

gradual, gradually ['grædjʊəl, -lɪ] adj, adv allmählich

graduate ['grædjʊɪt] n Unlabsolvent(in) m(f), Hochschulabsolvent(in) m(f) ▷ ['grædjʊeɪt] vi einen akademischen Grad erwerben

grain [greɪn] n (cereals) Getreide nt; (of corn, sand) Korn nt; (in wood) Maserung f

gram [græm] n Gramm nt

grammar ['græmə] n Grammatik f; **grammar school** n (Brit) ≈ Gymnasium nt

gran [græn] n (fam) Oma f

grand [grænd] adj (esp) hochnäsig; (posh) vornehm ▷ n (fam) 1000 Pfund bzw 1000 Dollar

grand(d)ad n (fam) Opa m; **granddaughter** n Enkelin f; **grandfather** n Großvater m; **grandma** n (fam) Oma f; **grandmother** n Großmutter f; **grandpa** n (fam) Opa m; **grandparents** npl Großeltern pl; **grandson** n Enkel m

grandstand n (Sport) Tribüne f

granny ['grænɪ] n (fam) Oma f

grant [grɑːnt] vt gewähren (sb sth jdm etw); **to take sb/sth for ~ed** jdn/etw als selbstverständlich hinnehmen ▷ n Subvention f, finanzielle Unterstützung f; (for university) Stipendium nt

grape [greɪp] n Weintraube f; **grapefruit** n Grapefruit f; **grape juice** n Traubensaft m

graph [grɑːf] n Diagramm nt; **graphic** ['græfɪk] adj grafisch; (description) anschaulich

grasp [grɑːsp] vt ergreifen; (understand) begreifen

grass [grɑːs] n (lawn) Rasen m; **grasshopper** n Heuschrecke f

grate [greɪt] n Feuerrost m ▷ vi kratzen ▷ vt (cheese) reiben

grateful, gratefully ['greɪtfʊl, -fəlɪ] adj, adv dankbar

grater ['greɪtə] n Reibe f

gratifying ['grætɪfaɪɪŋ] adj erfreulich

gratitude ['grætɪtjuːd] n Dankbarkeit f

grave [greɪv] n Grab nt ▷ adj
ernst; (mistake) schwer

gravel ['grævəl] n Kies m

graveyard ['greɪvjɑːd] n Friedhof m

gravity ['grævɪtɪ] n Schwerkraft
f; (seriousness) Ernst m

gravy ['greɪvɪ] n Bratensoße
f

gray [greɪ] adj (US) grau

graze [greɪz] vi (of animals)
grasen ▷ vt (touch) streifen; (Med)
abschürfen ▷ n (Med)
Abschürfung f

grease [griːs] n (fat) Fett nt;
(lubricant) Schmiere f ▷ vt
einfetten; (Tech) schmieren;
greasy ['griːsɪ] adj fettig; (hands,
tools) schmierig; (fam: person)
schleimig

great [greɪt] adj groß; (fam: good)
großartig, super; **a ~ deal of** viel;
Great Britain ['greɪt'brɪtn] n
Großbritannien nt;
great-grandfather n Urgroßvater m; **great-grandmother** n
Urgroßmutter f; **greatly** adv sehr;
~ disappointed zutiefst
enttäuscht

Greece [griːs] n Griechenland nt

greed [griːd] n (also: ~ for) Gier f (for nach);
(for food) Gefräßigkeit f; **greedy**
adj gierig; (for food) gefräßig

Greek [griːk] adj griechisch ▷ n
(person) Grieche m, Griechin f;
(language) Griechisch nt; **it's all
~ to me** ich verstehe nur
Bahnhof

green [griːn] adj grün; **~ with
envy** grün/gelb vor Neid ▷ n
(colour; for golf) Grün nt; (village ~)
Dorfwiese f; **~s** (vegetables) grünes
Gemüse; **the Greens, the Green
Party** (Pol) die Grünen; **green card**
n (US: work permit)
Arbeitserlaubnis f; (Brit: for car)
grüne Versicherungskarte;

greengage n Reneklode f;
greengrocer n Obst- und
Gemüsehändler(in) m(f);
greenhouse n Gewächshaus nt;
~ effect Treibhauseffekt m;
Greenland n Grönland nt; **green
pepper** n grüner Paprika; **green
salad** n grüner Salat

Greenwich Mean Time
['grenɪdʒ'miːntaɪm] n west-
europäische Zeit

greet [griːt] vt grüßen; **greeting**
n Gruß m

grew [gruː] pt of **grow**

grey [greɪ] adj grau; **grey-haired**
adj grauhaarig; **greyhound** n
Windhund m

grid [grɪd] n Gitter nt; **gridlock** n
Verkehrsinfarkt m; **gridlocked**
(roads) völlig verstopft; (talks)
festgefahren

grief [griːf] n Kummer m; (over
loss) Trauer f

grievance ['griːvəns] n
Beschwerde f

grieve [griːv] vi trauern (for um)

grill [grɪl] n (on cooker) Grill m ▷ vt
grillen

grim [grɪm] adj (face, humour)
grimmig; (situation, prospects)
trostlos

grin [grɪn] n Grinsen nt ▷ vi
grinsen

grind [graɪnd] (**ground, ground**)
vt mahlen; (sharpen) schleifen; (US:
meat) durchdrehen, hacken

grip [grɪp] n Griff m; **get a
~** nimm dich zusammen!; **to get
to ~s with sth** etw in den Griff
bekommen ▷ vt packen; **gripping**
adj (exciting) spannend

groan [grəʊn] vi stöhnen (with
vor +dat)

grocer ['grəʊsə*] n Lebensmit-
telhändler(in) m(f); **groceries** npl
Lebensmittel pl

groin [grɔɪn] n (Anat) Leiste f;

groin strain n (Med) Leistenbruch m

groom [gru:m] n Bräutigam m
▷ vt: **well -ed** gepflegt

grope [grəʊp] vi tasten ▷ vt
(sexually harrass) befummeln

gross [grəʊs] adj (coarse) derb;
(extreme: negligence, error) grob;
(disgusting) ekelhaft; (Comm)
brutto; **~ national product**
Bruttosozialprodukt nt; **~ salary**
Bruttogehalt nt

grotty ['grɒtɪ] adj (fam) mies,
vergammelt

ground [graʊnd] pt, pp of **grind**
▷ n Boden m, Erde f; (Sport) Platz
m; **~s** pl (around house)
(Garten)anlagen pl; (reasons)
Gründe pl; (of coffee) Satz m; **on
(the) ~s of** aufgrund von, **ground
floor** n (Brit) Erdgeschoss nt;
ground meat n (US) Hackfleisch
nt

group [gru:p] n Gruppe f ▷ vt
gruppieren

grouse [graʊs] (pl **-**) n (bird)
Schottisches Moorhuhn;
(complaint) Nörgelei f

grow [grəʊ] (**grew, grown**) vi
wachsen; (increase) zunehmen (in
an); (become) werden; **to ~ old** alt
werden; **to ~ into** ... sich
entwickeln zu ... ▷ vt (crop, plant)
ziehen; (commercially) anbauen;
I'm ~ing a beard ich lasse mir
einen Bart wachsen; **grow up** vi
aufwachsen; (mature) erwachsen
werden; **growing** adj wachsend;
a ~ number of people immer
mehr Leute

growl [graʊl] vi knurren

grown [grəʊn] pp of **grow**

grown-up [grəʊn'ʌp] adj
erwachsen ▷ n Erwachsene(r) mf;
growth [grəʊθ] n Wachstum nt;
(increase) Zunahme f; (Med)
Wucherung f

grubby ['grʌbɪ] adj schmuddelig

grudge [grʌdʒ] n Abneigung f
(against gegen) ▷ vt: **to ~ sb sth**
jdm etw nicht gönnen

gruelling ['grʊəlɪŋ] adj
aufreibend; (pace) mörderisch

gruesome ['gru:səm] adj
grausig

grumble ['grʌmbl] vi murren
(about über +akk)

grumpy ['grʌmpɪ] adj (fam)
mürrisch, grantig

grunt [grʌnt] vi grunzen

G-string ['dʒi:strɪŋ] n String m,
Stringtanga m

guarantee [ˌgærən'ti:] n Garantie f (of für); **it's still under ~** es ist
noch Garantie darauf ▷ vt
garantieren

guard [gɑ:d] n (sentry) Wache f;
(in prison) Wärter(in) m(f); (Brit
Rail) Schaffner(in) m(f) ▷ vt
bewachen; **a closely ~ed
secret** ein streng gehütetes
Geheimnis

guardian ['gɑ:dɪən] n Vormund
m; **~ angel** Schutzengel m

guess [ges] n Vermutung f;
(estimate) Schätzung f; **have a
~ rate mal** ▷ vt, vi raten;
(estimate) schätzen; **I ~ you're
right** du hast wohl recht; **I ~ so**
glaube schon

guest [gest] n Gast m; **be my
~** nur zu!; **guest-house** n Pension
f; **guest room** n Gästezimmer
nt

guidance ['gaɪdəns] n (direction)
Leitung f; (advice) Rat m;
(counselling) Beratung f; **for your
~** zu Ihrer Orientierung; **guide**
[gaɪd] n (person) Führer(in) m(f);
(tour) Reiseleiter(in) m(f); (book)
Führer m; (girl ~) Pfadfinderin f
▷ vt führen; **guidebook** n
Reiseführer m; **guide dog** n
Blindenhund m; **guided tour** n

Führung f *(of* durch); **guidelines**
npl Richtlinien *pl*
guilt [gɪlt] *n* Schuld f; **guilty** *adj*
schuldig *(of* gen); *(look)*
schuldbewusst; **to have a**
~ conscience ein schlechtes
Gewissen haben
guinea pig ['gɪnɪ pɪg] *n*
Meerschweinchen *nt*; *(person)*
Versuchskaninchen *nt*
guitar [gɪ'taː°] *n* Gitarre f
gulf [gʌlf] *n* Golf m; *(gap)* Kluft f;
Gulf States *npl* Golfstaaten *pl*
gull [gʌl] *n* Möwe f
gullible ['gʌlɪbl] *adj*
leichtgläubig
gulp [gʌlp] *n* (kräftiger) Schluck
▷ *vi* schlucken
gum [gʌm] *n (around teeth, usu pl)*
Zahnfleisch *nt*; *(chewing ~)*
Kaugummi m
gun [gʌn] *n* Schusswaffe f; *(rifle)*
Gewehr *nt*; *(pistol)* Pistole f;
gunfire *n* Schüsse *pl*,
Geschützfeuer *nt*; **gunpowder** *n*
Schießpulver *nt*; **gunshot** *n*
Schuss m
gush [gʌʃ] *vi* (heraus)strömen
(from aus)
gut [gʌt] *n* Darm m; **~s** *pl*
(intestines) Eingeweide; *(courage)*
Mumm m
gutter ['gʌtə°] *n (for roof)*
Dachrinne f; *(in street)* Rinnstein m,
Gosse f; **gutter press** *n*
Skandalpresse f
guy [gaɪ] *n (man)* Typ m, Kerl m; **~s**
pl (US) Leute *pl*
gym [dʒɪm] *n* Turnhalle f; *(for*
working out) Fitnesscenter *nt*;
gymnasium [dʒɪm'neɪzɪəm] *n*
Turnhalle f; **gymnastics**
[dʒɪm'næstɪks] *nsing* Turnen *nt*;
gym-toned *adj* durchtrainiert
gynaecologist [gaɪnɪ'kɒlədʒɪst]
n Frauenarzt m, Frauenärztin f,
Gynäkologe m, Gynäkologin f;

gynaecology *n* Gynäkologie f,
Frauenheilkunde f
gypsy ['dʒɪpsɪ] *n* Zigeuner(in)
m(f)

h

habit ['hæbɪt] n Gewohnheit f;
habitual [hə'bɪtjʊəl] adj
gewohnt; (drinker, liar)
gewohnheitsmäßig
hack [hæk] vt hacken; **hacker** n
(Inform) Hacker(in) m(f)
had [hæd] pt, pp of **have**
haddock ['hædək] n Schellfisch
m
hadn't ['hædnt] contr of **had not**
haemophiliac, hemophiliac (US)
[hi:məʊ'fɪlɪæk] n Bluter(in) m(f);
haemorrhage, hemorrhage (US)
['hemərɪdʒ] n Blutung f ▷ vi
bluten; **haemorrhoids,
hemorrhoids** (US) ['hemərɔɪdz]
npl Hämorrhoiden pl
haggis ['hægɪs] n (Scot) mit
gehackten Schafsinnereien und
Haferschrot gefüllter Schafsmagen
Hague [heɪg] n: the ~ Den Haag
hail [heɪl] n Hagel m ▷ vi hageln
▷ vt: **to ~ sb as sth** jdn als etw

feiern; **hailstone** n Hagelkorn nt;
hailstorm n Hagelschauer m
hair [heə°] n Haar nt, Haare pl; **to
do one's ~** sich frisieren; **to get
one's ~ cut** sich dat die Haare
schneiden lassen; **hairbrush** n
Haarbürste f; **hair conditioner** n
Haarspülung f; **haircut** n
Haarschnitt m; **to have a ~** sich
dat die Haare schneiden lassen;
hairdo (pl -s) n Frisur f;
hairdresser n Friseur m, Friseuse
f; **hairdryer** n Haartrockner m;
(hand-held) Fön® m; (over head)
Trockenhaube f; **hair gel** n
Haargel nt; **hairpin** n Haarnadel f;
hair remover n
Enthaarungsmittel nt; **hair spray**
n Haarspray nt; **hair style**
Frisur f; **hairy** adj haarig,
behaart; (fam: dangerous) brenzlig
hake [heɪk] n Seehecht m
half [hɑ:f] n (pl **halves**) n Hälfte f;
(Sport: of game) Halbzeit f; **to cut in
~** halbieren ▷ adj halb; **three and
a ~ pounds** dreieinhalb Pfund;
~ an hour, a ~ hour eine halbe
Stunde; **one and a ~** eineinhalb,
anderthalb ▷ adv halb, zur Hälfte;
~ past three, ~ three halb vier; **at
~ past** um halb; **~ asleep** fast
eingeschlafen; **she's ~ German** sie
ist zur Hälfte Deutsche; **~ as big
(as)** halb so groß (wie); **half board**
n Halbpension f; **half fare** n
halber Fahrpreis; **half-hearted**
adj halbherzig; **half-hour** n halbe
Stunde; **half moon** n Halbmond
m; **half pint** n = Viertelliter m o nt;
half price n: (at) **~** zum halben
Preis; **half-term** n (at school)
Ferien pl in der Mitte des
Trimesters; **half-time** n Halbzeit
f; **halfway** adv auf halbem Wege;
halfwit n (fam) Trottel m
halibut ['hælɪbət] n Heilbutt m
hall [hɔ:l] n (building) Halle f; (for

audience) Saal *m*; *(entrance ~)* Flur *m*; *(large)* Diele *f*; **~ of residence** *(Brit)* Studentenwohnheim *nt*

hallmark ['hɔːlmɑːk] *n* Stempel *m*; *(fig)* Kennzeichen *nt*

hallo [hʌ'ləu] *interj* hallo

Hallowe'en [hæləu'iːn] *n* Halloween *nt* *(Tag vor Allerheiligen, an dem sich Kinder verkleiden und von Tür zu Tür gehen)*

● **HALLOWE'EN**

● **Hallowe'en** ist der 31. Oktober,
● der Vorabend von Allerheiligen,
● und nach alten Glauben der
● Abend, an dem man Geister und
● Hexen sehen kann. In
● Großbritannien und vor allem in
● den USA feiern die Kinder
● Hallowe'en, indem sie sich
● verkleiden und mit selbst
● gemachten Laternen aus
● Kürbissen von Tür zu Tür
● ziehen.

halo ['heɪləu] *(pl* **-es)** *n (of saint)* Heiligenschein *m*

halt [hɔːlt] *n* Pause *f*, Halt *m*; **to come to a ~** zum Stillstand kommen ▷ *vt, vi* anhalten

halve [hɑːv] *vt* halbieren

ham [hæm] *n* Schinken *m*; **~ and eggs** Schinken mit Spiegelei

hamburger ['hæmbɜːgə°] *n (Gastr)* Hamburger *m*

hammer ['hæmə°] *n* Hammer *m* ▷ *vt, vi* hämmern

hammock ['hæmək] *n* Hängematte *f*

hamper ['hæmpə°] *vt* behindern ▷ *n (as gift)* Geschenkkorb *m*; *(for picnic)* Picknickkorb *m*

hamster ['hæmstə°] *n* Hamster *m*

hand [hænd] *n* Hand *f*; *(of clock, instrument)* Zeiger *m*; *(in card game)* Blatt *nt*; **to be made by**

~ Handarbeit sein; **~s up!** Hände hoch!; *(at school)* meldet euch!; **~s off!** Finger weg!; **on the one ~ ..., on the other ~...** einerseits ..., andererseits ...; **to give sb a ~** jdm helfen *(with* bei); **it's in his ~s** er hat es in der Hand; **to be in good ~s** gut aufgehoben sein; **to get out of ~** außer Kontrolle geraten ▷ *vt (pass)* reichen *(to sb* jdm); **hand down** *vt (tradition)* überliefern; *(heirloom)* vererben; **hand in** *vt* einreichen; *(at school, university etc)* abgeben; **hand out** *vt* verteilen; **hand over** *vt* übergeben

handbag *n* Handtasche *f*; **handbook** *n* Handbuch *nt*; **handbrake** *n (Brit)* Handbremse *f*; **handcuffs** *npl* Handschellen *pl*; **handful** *n* Handvoll *f*; **handheld PC** *n* Handheld-PC *m*

handicap ['hændɪkæp] *n* Behinderung *f*, Handikap *nt* ▷ *vt* benachteiligen; **handicapped** *adj* behindert; **the ~** die Behinderten

handicraft ['hændɪkrɑːft] *n* Kunsthandwerk *nt*

handkerchief ['hæŋkətʃɪf] *n* Taschentuch *nt*

handle ['hændl] *n* Griff *m*; *(of door)* Klinke *f*; *(of cup etc)* Henkel *m*; *(for winding)* Kurbel *f* ▷ *vt (touch)* anfassen; *(deal with: matter)* sich befassen mit; *(people, machine etc)* umgehen mit; *(situation, problem)* fertig werden mit; **handlebars** *npl* Lenkstange *f*

hand luggage ['hændlʌgɪdʒ] *n* Handgepäck *nt*; **handmade** *adj* handgefertigt; **to be ~** Handarbeit sein; **handout** *n (sheet)* Handout *nt*, Thesenpapier *nt*; **handset** *n* Hörer *m*; **please replace the ~** bitte legen Sie auf; **hands-free phone** *n* Freisprechanlage *f*; **handshake** *n* Händedruck *m*

handsome [ˈhænsəm] *adj (man)*
gut aussehend

hands-on [hændzˈɒn] *adj* praxisorientiert; **~ experience**
praktische Erfahrung

handwriting [ˈhændraɪtɪŋ] *n*
Handschrift f

handy [ˈhændɪ] *adj (useful)*
praktisch

hang [hæŋ] **(hung, hung)** *vt*
(auf)hängen; *(execute: hanged,
hanged)* hängen; **to ~ sth on sth**
etw an etw *akk* hängen ▷ *vi*
hängen ▷ *n:* **he's got the ~ of it**
er hat den Dreh raus; **hang about**
vi sich herumtreiben, rumhängen;
hang on *vi* sich festhalten *(to an
+dat)*; *(fam: wait)* warten; **to ~
sth** etw behalten; **hang up** *vi (Tel)*
auflegen ▷ *vt* aufhängen

hangar [ˈhæŋəˀ] *n* Flugzeughalle
f

hanger [ˈhæŋəˀ] *n* Kleiderbügel
m

hang glider [ˈhæŋɡlaɪdəˀ] *n*
(Flug)drachen m; *(person)*
Drachenflieger(in) m(f);
hang-gliding *n* Drachenfliegen nt

hangover [ˈhæŋəʊvəˀ] *n (bad
head)* Kater m; *(relic)* Überbleibsel
nt

hankie [ˈhæŋkɪ] *n (fam)*
Taschentuch nt

happen [ˈhæpən] *vi* geschehen,
(sth strange, unpleasant) passieren;
if anything should ~ to me wenn
mir etwas passieren sollte; **it
won't ~ again** es wird nicht
wieder vorkommen; **I ~ed to be
passing** ich kam zufällig vorbei;
happening *n* Ereignis nt,
Happening nt

happily [ˈhæpɪlɪ] *adv* fröhlich,
glücklich; *(luckily)*
glücklicherweise; **happiness**
[ˈhæpɪnəs] *n* Glück nt; **happy**
[ˈhæpɪ] *adj* glücklich; *(satisfied)*

~ with sth mit etw zufrieden,
(willing) **to be ~ to do sth** etw
gerne tun; **Happy Christmas**
fröhliche Weihnachten!; **Happy
New Year** ein glückliches Neues
Jahr!; **Happy Birthday** herzlichen
Glückwunsch zum Geburtstag!;
happy hour *n* Happy Hour f *(Zeit,
in der man in Bars Getränke zu
günstigeren Preisen bekommt)*

harass [ˈhærəs] *vt (ständig)*
belästigen; **harassment** *n*
Belästigung f; *(at work)* Mobbing
nt; **sexual ~** sexuelle Belästigung

harbor *(US)*, **harbour** [ˈhɑːbəˀ] *n*
Hafen m

hard [hɑːd] *adj* hart; *(difficult)*
schwer, schwierig; *(harsh)*
hart(herzig); **don't be ~ on him**
sei nicht so streng zu ihm; **it's ~ to
believe** es ist kaum zu glauben
▷ *adv (work)* schwer; *(run)* schnell;
(rain, snow) stark; **to try ~/~er** sich
dat große/mehr Mühe geben;
hardback *n* gebundene Ausgabe;
hard-boiled *adj (egg)* hart
gekocht; **hard copy** *n (Inform)*
Ausdruck m; **hard disk** *n (Inform)*
Festplatte f; **harden** *vt* härten
▷ *vi* hart werden; **hardened** *adj
(person)* abgehärtet *(to gegen)*;
hard-hearted *adj* hartherzig;
hardliner *n* Hardliner(in) m(f);
hardly [ˈhɑːdlɪ] *adv* kaum;
~ ever fast nie; **hardship**
[ˈhɑːdʃɪp] *n* Not f; **hard shoulder**
n (Brit) Standspur f; **hardware** *n
(Inform)* Hardware f, Haushalts-
und Eisenwaren *pl*; **hard-working**
adj fleißig, tüchtig

hare [hɛəˀ] *n* Hase m

harm [hɑːm] *n* Schaden m;
(bodily) Verletzung f; **it wouldn't
do any ~** es würde nicht schaden
▷ *vt* schaden +*dat*; *(person)*
verletzen; **harmful** *adj* schädlich;
harmless *adj* harmlos

harp [hɑːp] n Harfe f

harsh [hɑːʃ] adj (climate, voice) rau; (light, sound) grell; (severe) hart, streng

harvest ['hɑːvɪst] n Ernte f; (time) Erntezeit f ▷ vt ernten

has [hæz] pres of **have**

hash [hæʃ] n (Gastr) Haschee nt; (fam: hashish) Haschisch nt; **to make a ~ of sth** etw vermasseln; **hash browns** npl (US) ~ Kartoffelpuffer/Rösti mit Zwiebeln pl

hassle ['hæsl] n Ärger m; (fuss) Theater nt; **no ~** kein Problem ▷ vt bedrängen

hasn't ['hæznt] contr of **has not**

haste [heɪst] n Eile f; **hastily, hasty** adv, adj hastig; (rash) vorschnell

hat [hæt] n Hut m

hatch [hætʃ] n (Naut) Luke f; (in house) Durchreiche f; **hatchback** ['hætʃbæk] n (car) Wagen m mit Hecktür

hate [heɪt] vt hassen; **I ~ doing this** ich mache das sehr ungern ▷ n Hass m (of auf +akk)

haul [hɔːl] vt ziehen, schleppen ▷ n (booty) Beute f; **haulage** ['hɔːlɪdʒ] n Transport m; (trade) Spedition f; **haunted** adj: **a ~ house** ein Haus, in dem es spukt

⊙ **KEYWORD**

have [hæv] (pt, pp **had**) vb aux **1** haben; (esp with vbs of motion) sein; **to have arrived/slept** angekommen sein/geschlafen haben; **to have been** gewesen sein; **having eaten** ▷ **when he had eaten, he left** nachdem er gegessen hatte, ging er

2 (in tag questions) **you've done it, haven't you?** du hast/Sie haben es doch gemacht, oder nicht?

3 (in short answers and questions) **you've made a mistake — so I have/no I haven't** du hast/Sie haben einen Fehler gemacht — ja, stimmt/nein; **we haven't paid — yes we have!** wir haben nicht bezahlt — doch!; **I've been there before, have you?** ich war schon einmal da, du/Sie auch?

▷ modal vb aux (be obliged): **to have (got) to do sth** etw tun müssen; **you haven't to tell her** du darfst es ihr nicht erzählen

▷ vt **1** (possess) haben; **he has (got) blue eyes** er hat blaue Augen; **I have (got) an idea** ich habe eine Idee

2 (referring to meals etc) **to have breakfast/a cigarette** frühstücken/eine Zigarette rauchen

3 (receive, obtain etc) haben; **may I have your address?** kann ich deine/Ihre Adresse haben?; **to have a baby** ein Kind bekommen

4 (maintain, allow) **he will have it that he is right** er besteht darauf, dass er recht hat; **I won't have it** das lasse ich mir nicht bieten

5 to have sth done etw machen lassen; **to have sb do sth** jdn etw machen lassen; **he soon had them all laughing** er brachte sie alle zum Lachen

6 (experience, suffer) **she had her bag stolen** man hat ihr die Tasche gestohlen; **he had his arm broken** er hat sich den Arm gebrochen

7 (+noun: take, hold etc) **to have a walk/rest** spazieren gehen/sich ausruhen; **to have a meeting/party** eine Besprechung/Party haben; **have on** vt (be wearing) anhaben; (have arranged) vorhaben; (Brit) **you're having me on** du verarschst mich doch;

have out vt: **to have it out with sb** (settle problem) etw mit jdm bereden

Hawaii [həˈwaɪiː] n Hawaii nt
hawk [hɔːk] n Habicht m
hay [heɪ] n Heu nt; **hay fever** n Heuschnupfen m
hazard [ˈhæzəd] n Gefahr f; (risk) Risiko nt; **hazardous** adj gefährlich; **~ waste** Sondermüll m; **hazard warning lights** npl Warnblinkanlage f
haze [heɪz] n Dunst m
hazelnut [ˈheɪzlnʌt] n Haselnuss f
hazy [ˈheɪzɪ] adj (misty) dunstig; (vague) verschwommen
he [hiː] pron er

head [hed] n Kopf m (leader) Leiter(in) m(f); (at school) Schulleiter(in) m(f); **~ of state** Staatsoberhaupt nt; **at the ~ of** an der Spitze von; (tossing coin) **~s or tails?** Kopf oder Zahl? ▷ adj (leading) Ober-; **~ boy** Schulsprecher m; **~ girl** Schulsprecherin f ▷ vt anführen; (organization) leiten; **head for** vt zusteuern auf +akk; **he's heading for trouble** er wird Ärger bekommen
headache [ˈhedeɪk] n Kopfschmerzen pl, Kopfweh nt; **header** n (football) Kopfball m; (dive) Kopfsprung m; **headfirst** adj kopfüber; **headhunt** vt (Comm) abwerben; **heading** n Überschrift f; **headlamp, headlight** n Scheinwerfer m; **headline** n Schlagzeile f; **headmaster** n Schulleiter m; **headmistress** n Schulleiterin f; **head-on collision** adj Frontalzusammenstoß m; **headphones** npl Kopfhörer m; **headquarters** npl (of firm) Zentrale f; **headrest, head**

restraint n Kopfstütze f; **headscarf** (pl **-scarves**) n Kopftuch nt; **head teacher** n Schulleiter(in) m(f)

heal [hiːl] vt, vi heilen
health [helθ] n Gesundheit f; **good/bad for one's ~** gesund/ungesund; **your ~!** zum Wohl!; **~ and beauty** Wellness, **health centre** n Ärztezentrum nt; **health club** n Fitnesscenter nt; **health food** n Reformkost f; **~ shop, ~ store** Bioladen m; **health insurance** n Krankenversicherung f; **health service** n Gesundheitswesen nt; **healthy** adj gesund
heap [hiːp] n Haufen m; **~s of** (fam) jede Menge ▷ vt, vi häufen
hear [hɪəʳ] (heard, heard) vt, vi hören; **to ~ about sth** von etw erfahren; **I've ~d of it/him** ich habe schon davon/von ihm gehört; **hearing** n Gehör nt; (Jur) Verhandlung f; **hearing aid** n Hörgerät nt; **hearsay** n: **from ~** vom Hörensagen
heart [hɑːt] n Herz nt; **to lose/take ~** den Mut verlieren/Mut fassen; **to learn by ~** auswendig lernen; (cards) **~s** Herz nt; **queen of ~s** Herzdame f; **heart attack** n Herzanfall m; **heartbeat** n Herzschlag m; **heartbreaking** adj herzzerreißend; **heartbroken** adj todunglücklich, untröstlich; **heartburn** n Sodbrennen nt; **heart failure** n Herzversagen nt; **heartfelt** adj tief empfunden; **heartless** adj herzlos; **heart-throb** n (fam) Schwarm m; **heart-to-heart** n offene Aussprache; **hearty** [ˈhɑːtɪ] adj (meal, appetite) herzhaft; (welcome) herzlich
heat [hiːt] n Hitze f; (pleasant) Wärme f; (temperature) Temperatur

f; (Sport) Vorlauf m ▷ vt (house,
room) heizen; **heat up** vi warm
werden ▷ vt aufwärmen; **heated**
adj beheizt; (fig) hitzig; **heater** n
Heizofen m; (Auto) Heizung f
heath [hi:θ] n (Brit) Heide f;
heather ['hεðə*] n Heidekraut
nt
heating ['hi:tɪŋ] n Heizung f;
heat resistant adj
hitzebeständig; **heatwave** n
Hitzewelle f
heaven ['hεvn] n Himmel m;
heavenly adj himmlisch
heavily ['hεvɪlɪ] adv (rain, drink
etc) stark; **heavy** ['hεvɪ] adj
schwer; (rain, traffic, smoker etc)
stark; **heavy goods vehicle** n
Lastkraftwagen m
Hebrew ['hi:bru:] adj hebräisch
▷ n (language) Hebräisch nt
hectic ['hεktɪk] adj hektisch
he'd [hi:d] contr of **he had**; **he
would**
hedge [hεdʒ] n Hecke f
hedgehog ['hεdʒhɒg] n Igel
m
heel [hi:l] n (Anat) Ferse f; (of
shoe) Absatz m
hefty ['hεftɪ] adj schwer; (person)
stämmig; (fine, amount) saftig
height [haɪt] n Höhe f; (of person)
Größe f
heir [εə*] n Erbe m; **heiress**
['εərɪs] n Erbin f
held [hεld] pt, pp of **hold**
helicopter ['hεlɪkɒptə*] n
Hubschrauber m; **heliport**
['hεlɪpɔ:t] n Hubschrauber-
landeplatz m
hell [hεl] n Hölle f; **go to ~** scher
dich zum Teufel ▷ interj
verdammt; **that's a ~ of a lot of
money** das ist verdammt viel Geld
he'll [hi:l] contr of **he will**; **he
shall**
hello [hʌ'ləʊ] interj hallo

helmet ['hεlmɪt] n Helm m
help [hεlp] n Hilfe f ▷ vt, vi
helfen +dat (with bei); **to ~ sb** (to)
do sth jdm helfen, etw zu tun; **can
I ~?** kann ich (Ihnen) behilflich
sein?; **I couldn't ~ laughing** ich
musste einfach lachen; **I can't ~ it**
ich kann nichts dafür; **~ yourself**
bedienen Sie sich; **helpful** adj
(person) hilfsbereit; (useful)
nützlich; **helping** n Portion f;
helpless adj hilflos
hem [hεm] n Saum m
hemophiliac [hi:məʊ'fɪlɪæk] n
(US) Bluter m; **hemorrhage**
['hεmərɪdʒ] n (US) Blutung f;
hemorrhoids ['hεmərɔɪdz] npl
(US) Hämorrhoiden pl
hen [hεn] n Henne f
hen night n (Brit)
Junggesellinnenabschied m
hence [hεns] adv (reason) daher
henpecked ['hεnpεkt] adj: **to
be ~** unter dem Pantoffel stehen
hepatitis [hεpə'taɪtɪs] n Hepatitis f
her [hɜ:*] adj ihr; **she's hurt - leg**
sie hat sich dat das Bein verletzt
▷ pron (direct object) sie; (indirect
object) ihr; **do you know ~?** kennst
du sie?; **can you help ~?** kannst du
ihr helfen?; **it's ~** sie ist's
herb [hɜ:b] n Kraut nt
herbal medicine ['hɜ:bəl-] n
Pflanzenheilkunde f; **herbal tea** n
Kräutertee m
herd [hɜ:d] n Herde f; **herd
instinct** n Herdentrieb m
here [hɪə*] adv hier; (to this place)
hierher; **come ~** komm her; **I
won't be ~ for lunch** ich bin zum
Mittagessen nicht da; **~ and there**
hier und da, da und dort
hereditary [hɪ'rεdɪtərɪ] adj
erblich; **hereditary disease** n
Erbkrankheit f; **heritage**
['hεrɪtɪdʒ] n Erbe nt

hernia ['hɜːnɪə] n Leistenbruch m, Eingeweidebruch m

hero ['hɪərəʊ] (pl -es) n Held m

heroin ['herəʊɪn] n Heroin nt

heroine ['herəʊɪn] n Heldin f; **heroism** ['herəʊɪzəm] n Heldentum nt

herring ['herɪŋ] n Hering m

hers [hɜːz] pron ihre(r, s); **this is ~** das gehört ihr; **a friend of ~** ein Freund von ihr

herself [hɜːˈself] pron (reflexive) sich; **she's bought ~ a flat** sie hat sich eine Wohnung gekauft; **she needs it for ~** sie braucht es für sich (selbst); (emphatic) **she did it ~** sie hat es selbst gemacht; **(all) by ~** allein

he's [hiːz] contr of **he is, he has**

hesitant ['hezɪtənt] adj zögernd; **hesitate** ['hezɪteɪt] vi zögern; **don't ~ to ask** fragen Sie ruhig; **hesitation** n Zögern nt; **without ~** ohne zu zögern

heterosexual [hetərəʊˈseksʊəl] adj heterosexuell ▷ n Heterosexuelle(r) mf

HGV abbr = **heavy goods vehicle** LKW m

hi [haɪ] interj hi, hallo

hiccup ['hɪkʌp] n Schluckauf m, (minor problem) Problemchen nt; **to have (the) ~s** Schluckauf haben

hid [hɪd] pt of **hide**

hidden ['hɪdn] pp of **hide**

hide [haɪd] (**hid, hidden**) vt verstecken (from vor +dat); (feelings, truth) verbergen; (cover) verdecken ▷ vi sich verstecken (from vor +dat)

hideous ['hɪdɪəs] adj scheußlich

hiding ['haɪdɪŋ] n (beating) Tracht f Prügel; (concealment) **to be in ~** sich versteckt halten; **hiding place** n Versteck nt

hi-fi ['haɪfaɪ] n Hi-Fi nt; (system) Hi-Fi-Anlage f

high [haɪ] adj hoch; (wind) stark;

(living) im großen Stil; (on drugs) high ▷ adv hoch ▷ n (Meteo) Hoch nt; **highchair** n Hochstuhl m; **higher** adj höher; **higher education** n Hochschulbildung f; **high flier** n Hochbegabte(r) (m)f; **high heels** npl Stöckelschuhe pl; **high jump** n Hochsprung m; **Highlands** npl (schottisches) Hochland nt; **highlight** n (in hair) Strähnchen nt; (fig) Höhepunkt m ▷ vt (with pen) hervorheben; **highlighter** n Textmarker m; **highly** adv hoch, sehr; **~ paid** hoch bezahlt; **I think ~ of him** ich habe eine hohe Meinung von ihm; **high-performance** adj Hochleistungs-; **high school** n (US) Highschool f, ~ Gymnasium nt; **high speed** adj schnell; **~ train** Hochgeschwindigkeitszug m; **high street** n Hauptstraße f; **high tech** adj Hightech- ▷ n Hightech nt; **high tide** n Flut f; **highway** n (US) = Autobahn f; (Brit) Landstraße f

hijack ['haɪdʒæk] vt entführen, hijacken; **hijacker** n Entführer(in) m(f), Hijacker m

hike [haɪk] vi wandern ▷ n Wanderung f; **hiker** n Wanderer m, Wanderin f; **hiking** n Wandern nt

hilarious [hɪˈlɛərɪəs] adj zum Schreien komisch

hill [hɪl] n Hügel m; (higher) Berg m; **hilly** adj hügelig

him [hɪm] pron (direct object) ihn; (indirect object) ihm; **do you know ~?** kennst du ihn?; **can you help ~?** kannst du ihm helfen?; **it's ~** er ist's; **~ too** er auch

himself [hɪmˈself] pron (reflexive) sich; **he's bought ~ a flat** er hat sich eine Wohnung gekauft; **he needs it for ~** er braucht es für sich (selbst); (emphatic) **he did it ~**

~ er hat es selbst gemacht; **(all) by ~** allein

hinder ['hɪndə°] vt behindern; **hindrance** ['hɪndrəns] n Behinderung f

Hindu ['hɪnduː] adj hinduistisch ▷ n Hindu m; **Hinduism** ['hɪnduːɪzəm] n Hinduismus m

hinge [hɪndʒ] n Scharnier nt; (on door) Angel f

hint [hɪnt] n Wink m, Andeutung f; (trace) Spur f ▷ vi andeuten (at akk)

hip [hɪp] n Hüfte f

hippopotamus [hɪpə'pɒtəməs] n Nilpferd nt

hire ['haɪə°] vt (worker) anstellen; (car, bike etc) mieten ▷ n Miete f; **for ~** (taxi) frei; **hire car** n Mietwagen m; **hire charge** n Benutzungsgebühr f; **hire purchase** n Ratenkauf m

his [hɪz] adj sein; **he's hurt ~ leg** er hat sich auf das Bein verletzt ▷ pron seine(r, s); **it's ~** es gehört ihm; **a friend of ~** ein Freund von ihm

historic [hɪ'stɒrɪk] adj (significant) historisch; **historical** adj (monument etc) historisch; (studies etc) geschichtlich; **history** ['hɪstərɪ] n Geschichte f

hit [hɪt] n (blow) Schlag m; (on target) Treffer m; (successful film, CD etc) Hit m ▷ vt (pt, pp **hit, hit**) schlagen; (bullet, stone etc) treffen; **the car ~ the tree** das Auto fuhr gegen einen Baum; **to ~ one's head on sth** sich dat den Kopf an etw dat stoßen; **hit (up)on** vt sich stoßen auf +akk; **hit-and-run** adj: **~ accident** Unfall m mit Fahrerflucht

hitch [hɪtʃ] vt (pull up) hochziehen ▷ n Schwierigkeit f; **without ~** reibungslos

hitch-hike ['hɪtʃhaɪk] vi trampen; **hitch-hiker** n Tramper(in)

m(f); **hitchhiking** n Trampen n

HIV abbr = **human immunodeficiency virus** HIV nt; **~ positive/negative** HIV-positiv/negativ

hive [haɪv] n Bienenstock m

HM abbr = **His/Her Majesty**

HMS abbr = **His/Her Majesty's Ship**

hoarse [hɔːs] adj heiser

hoax [həʊks] n Streich m, Jux m; (false alarm) blinder Alarm

hob [hɒb] n (of cooker) Kochfeld nt

hobble ['hɒbl] vi humpeln

hobby ['hɒbɪ] n Hobby nt

hobo ['həʊbəʊ] (pl **-es**) n (US) Penner(in) m(f)

hockey ['hɒkɪ] n Hockey nt

hold [həʊld] (held, held) vt halten; (contain) enthalten; (be able to contain) fassen; (post, office) innehaben; (value) behalten; (meeting) abhalten; (person as prisoner) gefangen halten; **to ~ one's breath** den Atem anhalten; **to ~ hands** Händchen halten; **~ the line** (Tel) bleiben Sie am Apparat ▷ vi halten; (weather) sich halten ▷ n (grasp) Halt m; (of ship, aircraft) Laderaum m; **hold back** vt zurückhalten; (keep secret) verheimlichen; **hold on** vi sich festhalten; (wait) warten; (Tel) dranbleiben; **to ~ to sth** etw festhalten; **hold out** vt ausstrecken; (offer) hinhalten; (offer) bieten ▷ vi durchhalten; **hold up** vt hochhalten; (support) stützen; (delay) aufhalten; **holdall** n Reisetasche f; **holder** n (person) Inhaber(in) m(f); **holdup** n (in traffic) Stau m; (robbery) Überfall m

hole [həʊl] n Loch nt; (of fox, rabbit) Bau m; **~ in the wall** (cash dispenser) Geldautomat m

holiday ['hɒlɪdəɪ] n (day off)
freier Tag; (public ~) Feiertag m;
(vacation) Urlaub m; (at school)
Ferien pl; **on ~** im Urlaub; **to go on
~** Urlaub machen; **holiday camp**
n Ferienlager nt; **holiday home** n
Ferienhaus nt; (flat)
Ferienwohnung f; **holidaymaker**
n Urlauber(in) m(f); **holiday
resort** n Ferienort m

Holland ['hɒlənd] n Holland nt

hollow ['hɒləʊ] adj hohl; (words)
leer ▷ n Vertiefung f

holly ['hɒlɪ] n Stechpalme f

holy ['həʊlɪ] adj heilig; **Holy
Week** n Karwoche f

home [həʊm] n Zuhause nt;
(area, country) Heimat f; (institution)
Heim nt; **at ~** zu Hause; **to make
oneself at ~** es sich dat bequem
machen; **away from ~** verreist
▷ adv: **to go ~** nach Hause
gehen/fahren; **home address** n
Heimatadresse f; **home country**
n Heimatland nt; **home game** n
(Sport) Heimspiel nt; **homeless** adj
obdachlos; **homely** adj häuslich;
(US: ugly) unscheinbar;
home-made adj selbst gemacht;
home movie n Amateurfilm m;
Home Office n (Brit)
Innenministerium nt

homeopathic adj (US) see
homoeopathic

home page ['həʊmpeɪdʒ] n
(Inform) Homepage f; **Home
Secretary** n (Brit)
Innenminister(in) m(f); **homesick**
adj: **to be ~** Heimweh haben;
home town n Heimatstadt f;
homework n Hausaufgaben pl

homicide ['hɒmɪsaɪd] n (US)
Totschlag m

homoeopathic
[həʊmɪəʊ'pæθɪk] adj
homöopathisch

homosexual [hɒməʊ'sekʃʊəl]

adj homosexuell ▷ n Homosex-
uelle(r) mf

Honduras [hɒn'djʊərəs] n
Honduras nt

honest ['ɒnɪst] adj ehrlich;
honesty n Ehrlichkeit f

honey ['hʌnɪ] n Honig m;
honeycomb n Honigwabe f;
honeydew melon n
Honigmelone f; **honeymoon** n
Flitterwochen pl

Hong Kong [hɒŋ 'kɒŋ] n
Hongkong nt

honor (US) see **honour**; **honorary**
['ɒnərərɪ] adj (member, title etc)
Ehren-, ehrenamtlich; **honour**
['ɒnə] vt ehren; (cheque) einlösen;
(contract) einhalten ▷ n Ehre f; **in
~ of** zu Ehren von; **honourable** adj
ehrenhaft; **honours degree** n
akademischer Grad mit Prüfung im
Spezialfach

hood [hʊd] n Kapuze f; (Auto)
Verdeck nt; (US Auto) Kühlerhaube
f

hoof [huːf] (pl **hooves**) n Huf
m

hook [hʊk] n Haken m; **hooked**
adj (keen) besessen (on von);
(drugs) abhängig sein (on von)

hooligan ['huːlɪgən] n Hooligan
m

hoot [huːt] vi (Auto) hupen

Hoover® ['huːvə] n Staubsauger
m; **hoover** vi, vt staubsaugen

hop [hɒp] vi hüpfen ▷ n (Bot)
Hopfen m

hope [həʊp] vi, vt hoffen (for auf
+akk); **I ~ so/~ not**
hoffentlich/hoffentlich nicht; **I
~ (that) we'll meet** ich hoffe, dass
wir uns sehen werden ▷ n
Hoffnung f; **there's no ~** es ist
aussichtslos; **hopeful** adj
hoffnungsvoll; **hopefully** adv (full
of hope) hoffnungsvoll; (I hope so)
hoffentlich; **hopeless** adj

hoffnungslos; (*incompetent*) miserabel

horizon [hə'raɪzn] n Horizont m;
horizontal [hɒrɪ'zɒntl] adj horizontal

hormone ['hɔ:məʊn] n Hormon nt

horn [hɔ:n] n Horn nt; (*Auto*) Hupe f

hornet ['hɔ:nɪt] n Hornisse f

horny ['hɔ:nɪ] adj (*fam*) geil

horoscope ['hɒrəskəʊp] n Horoskop nt

horrible, horribly ['hɒrɪbl, -blɪ] adj, adv schrecklich; **horrid,
horridly** ['hɒrɪd, -lɪ] adj, adv abscheulich; **horrify** ['hɒrɪfaɪ] vt entsetzen; **horror** ['hɒrə⁰] n Entsetzen nt; **~s** (*things*) Schrecken pl

hors d'oeuvre [ɔ:'dɜ:vr] n Vorspeise f

horse [hɔ:s] n Pferd nt; **horse chestnut** n Rosskastanie f;
horsepower n Pferdestärke f, PS nt; **horse racing** n Pferderennen nt; **horseradish** n Meerrettich m; **horse riding** n Reiten nt; **horseshoe** n Hufeisen nt

horticulture ['hɔ:tɪkʌltʃə⁰] n Gartenbau m

hose, hosepipe [həʊz, 'həʊzpaɪp] n Schlauch m

hospitable [hɒ'spɪtəbl] adj gastfreundlich

hospital ['hɒspɪtl] n Krankenhaus nt

hospitality [hɒspɪ'tælɪtɪ] n Gastfreundschaft f

host [həʊst] n Gastgeber m; (*TV: of show*) Moderator(in) m(f), Talkmaster(in) m(f) ▷ vt (*party*) geben; (*TV: TV show*) moderieren

hostage ['hɒstɪdʒ] n Geisel f

hostel ['hɒstəl] n Wohnheim nt; (*youth ~*) Jugendherberge f

hostess ['həʊstɪs] n (*of a party*) Gastgeberin f

hostile ['hɒstaɪl] adj feindlich;
hostility [hɒs'tɪlɪtɪ] n Feindseligkeit f

hot [hɒt] adj heiß; (*drink, food, water*) warm; (*spiced*) scharf; **I'm (feeling)** ~ mir ist heiß; **hot cross bun** n Rosinenbrötchen mit einem Kreuz darauf, hauptsächlich zu Ostern gegessen; **hot dog** n Hotdog nt

hotel [həʊ'tel] n Hotel nt; **hotel room** n Hotelzimmer nt

hothouse n Treibhaus nt; **hotline** n Hotline f; **hotplate** n Kochplatte f; **hotpot** n Fleischeintopf mit Kartoffeleinlage; **hot-water bottle** n Wärmflasche f

hour ['aʊə⁰] n Stunde f; **to wait for ~s** stundenlang warten; **~s** pl (*of shops etc*) Geschäftszeiten pl; **hourly** adj adv stündlich

house [haʊs] (*pl* **houses**) n Haus nt; **at my** ~ bei mir (zu Hause); **to my** ~ zu mir (nach Hause); **on the** ~ auf Kosten des Hauses; **the House of Commons/Lords** das britische Unterhaus/Oberhaus; **the Houses of Parliament** das britische Parlamentsgebäude ▷ [haʊz] vt unterbringen; **houseboat** n Hausboot nt; **household** n Haushalt m; **~ appliance** Haushaltsgerät nt; **house-husband** n Hausmann m; **housekeeping** n Haushaltung f; (*money*) Haushaltsgeld nt; **house-trained** adj stubenrein; **house-warming (party)** n Einzugsparty f; **housewife** (*pl* **-wives**) n Hausfrau f; **house wine** n Hauswein m; **housework** n Hausarbeit f

housing ['haʊzɪŋ] n (*houses*) Wohnungen pl; (*house building*) Wohnungsbau m; **housing**

benefit n Wohngeld nt; **housing development, housing estate** (Brit) n Wohnsiedlung f

hover ['hɒvə] vi schweben; **hovercraft** n Luftkissenboot nt

how [hau] adv wie; **~ many** wie viele; **~ much** wie viel; **~ are you?** wie geht es Ihnen?; **~ are things?** wie geht's?; **~'s work?** was macht die Arbeit?; **~ about ...?** wie wäre es mit ...?; **however** [hau'evə] conj (but) jedoch, aber ⊳ adv (no matter how) wie ... auch; **~ much it costs** wie viel es auch kostet; **~ you do it** wie man es auch macht

howl [haul] vi heulen; **howler** ['haulə°] n (fam) grober Schnitzer

HP, hp n (Brit) abbr = **hire purchase** Ratenkauf m ⊳ abbr = **horsepower** PS

HQ abbr = **headquarters**

hubcap ['hʌbkæp] n Radkappe f

hug [hʌg] vt umarmen ⊳ n Umarmung f

huge [hju:dʒ] adj riesig

hum [hʌm] vi, vt summen

human ['hju:mən] adj menschlich; **~ rights** Menschenrechte pl ⊳ n: **~ (being)** Mensch m; **humanitarian** [hju:mænɪ'teərɪən] adj humanitär; **humanity** [hju:'mænɪtɪ] n Menschheit f; (kindliness) Menschlichkeit f; **humanities** n Geisteswissenschaften pl

humble ['hʌmbl] adj demütig; (modest) bescheiden

humid ['hju:mɪd] adj feucht; **humidity** [hju:'mɪdɪtɪ] n (Luft)feuchtigkeit f

humiliate [hju:'mɪlɪeɪt] vt demütigen; **humiliation** [hju:mɪlɪ'eɪʃn] n Erniedrigung f, Demütigung f

humor (US) see **humour**;

humorous ['hju:mərəs] adj humorvoll; (story) lustig, witzig; **humour** ['hju:mə°] n Humor m; **sense of ~** Sinn m für Humor

hump [hʌmp] n Buckel m

hunch [hʌntʃ] n Gefühl nt, Ahnung f ⊳ vt (back) krümmen; **hunchback** n Bucklige(r) mf

hundred ['hʌndrəd] num: **one ~, a ~** (ein)hundert; **a ~ and one** hundert(und)eins; **two ~** zweihundert; **hundredth** adj hundertste(r, s) ⊳ n (fraction) Hundertstel nt; **hundredweight** n Zentner m (50,8 kg)

hung [hʌŋ] pt, pp of **hang**

Hungarian [hʌŋ'geərɪən] adj ungarisch ⊳ n (person) Ungar(in) m(f); (language) Ungarisch nt; **Hungary** ['hʌŋgərɪ] n Ungarn nt

hunger ['hʌŋgə°] n Hunger m; **hungry** ['hʌŋgrɪ] adj hungrig; **to be ~** Hunger haben

hunk [hʌŋk] n (fam) gut gebauter Mann; **hunky** ['hʌŋkɪ] adj (fam) gut gebaut

hunt [hʌnt] n Jagd f; (search) Suche f (for nach) ⊳ vt, vi jagen; (search) suchen (for nach); **hunting** n Jagen nt, Jagd f

hurdle ['hɜ:dl] n (a. fig) Hürde f; **the 400m ~s** der 400m-Hürdenlauf m

hurl [hɜ:l] vt schleudern

hurricane ['hʌrɪkən] n Orkan m

hurried ['hʌrɪd] adj eilig; **hurry** ['hʌrɪ] n Eile f; **to be in a ~** es eilig haben; **there's no ~** es eilt nicht ⊳ vi sich beeilen; **~ (up)** mach schnell ⊳ vt antreiben

hurt [hɜ:t] (hurt, hurt) vt wehtun +dat; (wound: person, feelings) verletzen; **I've ~ my arm** ich habe mir am Arm wehgetan ⊳ vi wehtun; **my arm ~s** mir tut der Arm weh

husband ['hʌzbənd] n Ehemann m

husky ['hʌskɪ] adj rau ▷ n Schlittenhund m

hut [hʌt] n Hütte f

hyacinth ['haɪəsɪnθ] n Hyazinthe f

hybrid ['haɪbrɪd] n Kreuzung f

hydroelectric ['haɪdrəʊ'lektrɪk] adj: ~ **power station** Wasserkraftwerk nt

hydrofoil ['haɪdrəʊfɔɪl] n Tragflächenboot nt

hydrogen ['haɪdrədʒən] n Wasserstoff m

hygiene ['haɪdʒiːn] n Hygiene f; **hygienic** [haɪ'dʒiːnɪk] adj hygienisch

hymn [hɪm] n Kirchenlied nt

hypermarket ['haɪpəmɑːkɪt] n Großmarkt m; **hypersensitive** adj überempfindlich

hyphen ['haɪfən] n Bindestrich m

hypnosis [hɪp'nəʊsɪs] n Hypnose f; **hypnotize** ['hɪpnətaɪz] vt hypnotisieren

hypochondriac [haɪpəʊ'kɒndrɪæk] n eingebildete(r) Kranke(r), eingebildete Kranke

hypocrisy [hɪ'pɒkrəsɪ] n Heuchelei f; **hypocrite** ['hɪpəkrɪt] n Heuchler(in) m(f)

hypodermic [haɪpə'dɜːmɪk] adj, n: ~ **(needle)** Spritze f

hypothetical [haɪpəʊ'θetɪkəl] adj hypothetisch

hysteria [hɪ'stɪərɪə] n Hysterie f; **hysterical** [hɪ'sterɪkəl] adj hysterisch; (amusing) zum Totlachen

I

I [aɪ] pron ich

ice [aɪs] n Eis nt ▷ vt (cake) glasieren; **iceberg** n Eisberg m; **iceberg lettuce** n Eisbergsalat m; **icebox** n (US) Kühlschrank m; **icecold** adj eiskalt; **ice cream** n Eis nt; **ice cube** n Eiswürfel m; **iced** adj eisgekühlt; (coffee, tea) Eis-; (cake) glasiert; **ice hockey** n Eishockey nt

Iceland ['aɪslənd] n Island nt; **Icelander** n Isländer(in) m(f); **Icelandic** [aɪs'lændɪk] adj isländisch ▷ n (language) Isländisch nt

ice lolly n (Brit) Eis nt am Stiel; **ice rink** n Kunsteisbahn f; **ice skating** n Schlittschuhlaufen nt

icing ['aɪsɪŋ] n (on cake) Zuckerguss m

icon ['aɪkɒn] n Ikone f; (Inform) Icon nt, Programmsymbol nt

icy ['aɪsɪ] adj (slippery) vereist; (cold) eisig

I'd [aɪd] contr of **I would; I had**

ID abbr = **identification** Ausweis m

idea [aɪ'dɪə] n Idee f; **I've no ~** (ich habe) keine Ahnung; **that's my ~ of ...** so stelle ich mir ... vor

ideal [aɪ'dɪəl] n Ideal nt ▷ adj ideal; **ideally** adv ideal; (before statement) idealerweise

identical [aɪ'dentɪkəl] adj identisch; **~ twins** eineiige Zwillinge

identify [aɪ'dentɪfaɪ] vt identifizieren, **identity** [aɪ'dentɪtɪ] n Identität f; **identity card** n Personalausweis m

idiom ['ɪdɪəm] n Redewendung f; **idiomatic** adj idiomatisch

idiot ['ɪdɪət] n Idiot(in) m(f)

idle ['aɪdl] adj (doing nothing) untätig; (worker) unbeschäftigt; (machines) außer Betrieb; (lazy) faul; (promise, threat) leer

idol ['aɪdl] n Idol nt; **idolize** ['aɪdəlaɪz] vt vergöttern

idyllic [ɪ'dɪlɪk] adj idyllisch

i.e. abbr = **id est** d.h.

KEYWORD

if [ɪf] conj 1 wenn; (in case also) falls; **if I were you** wenn ich Sie wäre
2 (although) (even) if (selbst o auch) wenn
3 (whether) ob
4 **if so/not** wenn ja/nicht; **if only ...** wenn ... doch nur ...; **if only I could** wenn ich doch nur könnte; see also **as**

ignition [ɪg'nɪʃən] n Zündung f; **ignition key** n (Auto) Zündschlüssel m

ignorance ['ɪgnərəns] n Unwissenheit f; **ignorant** adj

unwissend; **ignore** [ɪg'nɔː] vt ignorieren, nicht beachten

I'll [aɪl] contr of **I will; I shall**

ill [ɪl] adj krank; **~ at ease** unbehaglich

illegal [ɪ'liːgəl] adj illegal

illegitimate [ɪlɪ'dʒɪtɪmət] adj unzulässig; (child) unehelich

illiterate [ɪ'lɪtərət] adj: **to be ~** Analphabet(in) sein

illness ['ɪlnəs] n Krankheit f

illuminate [ɪ'luːmɪneɪt] vt beleuchten; **illuminating** adj (remark) aufschlussreich

illusion [ɪ'luːʒən] n Illusion f; **to be under the ~ that ...** sich einbilden, dass ...

illustrate ['ɪləstreɪt] vt illustrieren; **illustration** n Abbildung f, Bild nt

I'm [aɪm] contr of **I am**

image ['ɪmɪdʒ] n Bild nt; (public ~) Image nt; **imaginable** ['ɪmædʒɪnəbl] adj denkbar; **imaginary** [ɪ'mædʒɪnərɪ] adj eingebildet; **~ world** Fantasiewelt f; **imagination** [ɪmædʒɪ'neɪʃən] n Fantasie f; (mistaken) Einbildung f; **imaginative** [ɪ'mædʒɪnətɪv] adj fantasievoll; **imagine** [ɪ'mædʒɪn] vt sich vorstellen; (wrongly) sich einbilden; **~!** stell dir vor!

imbecile ['ɪmbəsiːl] n Trottel m

imitate ['ɪmɪteɪt] vt nachahmen, nachmachen; **imitation** n Nachahmung f ▷ adj imitiert, Kunst-

immaculate [ɪ'mækjʊlɪt] adj tadellos; (spotless) makellos

immature [ɪmə'tjʊə] adj unreif

immediate [ɪ'miːdɪət] adj unmittelbar; (instant) sofortig; (reply) umgehend; **immediately** adv sofort

immense, immensely [ɪ'mens, -lɪ] adj, adv riesig, enorm

immersion heater [ɪˈmɜːʃn
hiːtə] n Boiler m
immigrant [ˈɪmɪɡrənt] n Einwanderer m, Einwanderin f;
immigration [ɪmɪˈɡreɪʃən] n
Einwanderung f; (facility)
Einwanderungskontrolle f
immobilize [ɪˈməʊbɪlaɪz] vt
lähmen; **immobilizer** n (Auto)
Wegfahrsperre f
immoral [ɪˈmɒrəl] adj
unmoralisch
immortal [ɪˈmɔːtl] adj
unsterblich
immune [ɪˈmjuːn] adj (Med)
immun (from, to gegen); **immune
system** n Immunsystem nt
impact [ˈɪmpækt] n Aufprall m;
(effect) Auswirkung f (on auf +akk)
impatience [ɪmˈpeɪʃəns] n
Ungeduld f; **impatient**,
impatiently adj, adv ungeduldig
impeccable [ɪmˈpekəbl] adj
tadellos
impede [ɪmˈpiːd] vt behindern
imperative [ɪmˈperətɪv] adj
unbedingt erforderlich ▷ n (Ling)
Imperativ m
imperfect [ɪmˈpɜːfɪkt] adj
unvollkommen; (goods) fehlerhaft
▷ n (Ling) Imperfekt nt;
imperfection [ɪmpəˈfekʃən] n
Unvollkommenheit f; (fault) Fehler
m
imperial [ɪmˈpɪərɪəl] adj kaiser-
lich, Reichs-; **imperialism** n
Imperialismus m
impertinence [ɪmˈpɜːtɪnəns] n
Unverschämtheit f, Zumutung f;
impertinent adj unverschämt
implant [ˈɪmplɑːnt] n (Med)
Implantat nt
implausible [ɪmˈplɔːzəbl] adj
unglaubwürdig
implement [ˈɪmplɪmənt] n
Werkzeug nt, Gerät nt
▷ [ɪmplɪˈment] vt durchführen

implication [ɪmplɪˈkeɪʃən] n
Folge f, Auswirkung f; (logical)
Schlussfolgerung f; **implicit**
[ɪmˈplɪsɪt] adj implizit,
unausgesprochen; **imply**
[ɪmˈplaɪ] vt (indicate) andeuten;
(mean) bedeuten; **are you -ing
that ...** wollen Sie damit sagen,
dass ...
impolite [ɪmpəˈlaɪt] adj
unhöflich
import [ɪmˈpɔːt] vt einführen,
importieren ▷ n [ˈɪmpɔːt] Einfuhr f, Import m
importance [ɪmˈpɔːtəns] n
Bedeutung f; **of no ~** unwichtig;
important adj wichtig (to sb für
jdn); (significant) bedeutend;
(influential) einflussreich
import duty n [ˈɪmpɔːt djuːtɪ] n
Einfuhrzoll m; **import licence** n
Einfuhrgenehmigung f
impose [ɪmˈpəʊz] vt (conditions)
auferlegen (on dat); (penalty,
sanctions) verhängen (on gegen);
imposing [ɪmˈpəʊzɪŋ] adj eindrucksvoll, imposant
impossible [ɪmˈpɒsəbl] adj
unmöglich
impotence [ˈɪmpətəns] n
Machtlosigkeit f; (sexual)
Impotenz f; **impotent** adj
machtlos; (sexually) impotent
impractical [ɪmˈpræktɪkəl] adj
unpraktisch; (plan)
undurchführbar
impress [ɪmˈpres] vt beeindrucken; **impression** [ɪmˈpreʃən]
n Eindruck m; **impressive** adj
eindrucksvoll
imprison [ɪmˈprɪzn] vt inhaf-
tieren; **imprisonment** n
Inhaftierung f
improbability [ɪmprɒbəˈbɪlɪtɪ]
n Unwahrscheinlichkeit f;
improbable [ɪmˈprɒbəbl] adj
unwahrscheinlich

improper [ɪmˈprɒpə⁰] *adj*
(*indecent*) unanständig; (*use*)
unsachgemäß

improve [ɪmˈpruːv] *vt*
verbessern ▷ *vi* sich verbessern,
besser werden; (*patient*)
Fortschritte machen;
improvement *n* Verbesserung f
(*in +gen*; *on* gegenüber); (*in*
appearance) Verschönerung f

improvise [ˈɪmprəvaɪz] *vt, vi*
improvisieren

impulse [ˈɪmpʌls] *n* Impuls m;
impulsive [ɪmˈpʌlsɪv] *adj*
impulsiv

○ **KEYWORD**

in [ɪn] *prep* 1 (*indicating place,*
position) in +dat; (*with motion*) in
+akk; **in here/there** hier/dort; **in**
London in London; **in the United**
States in den Vereinigten Staaten
2 (*indicating time: during*) in +dat; **in**
summer im Sommer; **in 1988** (im
Jahre) 1988; **in the afternoon**
nachmittags, am Nachmittag
3 (*indicating time: in the space of*)
innerhalb von; **I'll see you in 2**
weeks o **in 2 weeks' time** ich sehe
dich/Sie in zwei Wochen
4 (*indicating manner, circumstances,*
state etc) in +dat; **in the sun/rain**
in der Sonne/im Regen; **in**
English/French auf
Englisch/Französisch; **in a**
loud/soft voice mit lauter/leiser
Stimme
5 (*with ratios, numbers*) **1 in 10** jeder
Zehnte; **20 pence in the pound** 20
Pence pro Pfund; **they lined up in**
twos sie stellten sich in
Zweierreihe auf
6 (*referring to people, works*) **the**
disease is common in children
die Krankheit ist bei Kindern
häufig; **in Dickens** bei Dickens;

we have a loyal friend in him er
ist uns ein treuer Freund
7 (*indicating profession etc*) **to be in**
teaching/the army Lehrer,
Lehrerin/beim Militär sein; **to be**
in publishing im Verlagswesen
arbeiten
8 (*with present participle*) **in saying**
this, I ... wenn ich das sage, ... ich;
in accepting this view, he ... weil
er diese Meinung akzeptierte, ...
er
▷ *adv*: **to be in** (*person: at home,*
work) da sein; (*train, ship, plane*)
angekommen sein; (*in fashion*) in
sein; **to ask sb in** jdn hereinbitten;
to run/limp etc in
hereingerannt/gehumpelt etc
kommen
▷ *n*: **the ins and outs** (*of proposal,*
situation etc) die Feinheiten

inability [ɪnəˈbɪlɪtɪ] *n* Unfähig-
keit f

inaccessible [ɪnækˈsesəbl] *adj*
(*a. fig*) unzugänglich

inaccurate [ɪnˈækjʊrɪt] *adj*
ungenau

inadequate [ɪnˈædɪkwət] *adj*
unzulänglich

inapplicable [ɪnəˈplɪkəbl] *adj*
unzutreffend

inappropriate [ɪnəˈprəʊprɪət]
adj unpassend; (*clothing*)
ungeeignet; (*remark*)
unangebracht

inborn [ˈɪnˈbɔːn] *adj* angeboren

incapable [ɪnˈkeɪpəbl] *adj*
unfähig (*of* zu); **to be ~ of doing**
sth nicht imstande sein, etw zu
tun

incense [ˈɪnsens] *n* Weihrauch
m

incentive [ɪnˈsentɪv] *n* Anreiz m

incessant, incessantly [ɪnˈsesnt,
-lɪ] *adj, adv* unaufhörlich

incest [ˈɪnsest] *n* Inzest m

inch [ɪntʃ] n Zoll m (2,54 cm)
incident ['ɪnsɪdənt] n Vorfall m; (disturbance) Zwischenfall m; **incidentally** [ɪnsɪ'dentlɪ] adv nebenbei bemerkt, übrigens
inclination [ɪnklɪ'neɪʃən] n Neigung f; **inclined** ['ɪnklaɪnd] adj: **to be ~ to do sth** dazu neigen, etw zu tun
include [ɪn'kluːd] vt einschließen; (on list, in group) aufnehmen; **including** prep einschließlich (+gen); **not ~ service** Bedienung nicht inbegriffen; **inclusive** [ɪn'kluːsɪv] adj einschließlich (of +gen); (price) Pauschal-
incoherent [ɪnkəʊ'hɪərənt] adj zusammenhanglos
income ['ɪnkʌm] n Einkommen nt; (from business) Einkünfte pl; **income tax** n Einkommensteuer f; (on wages, salary) Lohnsteuer f; **incoming** ['ɪnkʌmɪŋ] adj ankommend; (mail) eingehend
incompatible [ɪnkəm'pætəbl] adj unvereinbar; (people) unverträglich; (Inform) nicht kompatibel
incompetent [ɪn'kɒmpɪtənt] adj unfähig
incomplete [ɪnkəm'pliːt] adj unvollständig
incomprehensible [ɪnkɒmprɪ'hensəbl] adj unverständlich
inconceivable [ɪnkən'siːvəbl] adj unvorstellbar
inconsiderate [ɪnkən'sɪdərət] adj rücksichtslos
inconsistency [ɪnkən'sɪstənsɪ] n Inkonsequenz f; (contradictory) Widersprüchlichkeit f; **inconsistent** adj inkonsequent; (contradictory) widersprüchlich; (work) unbeständig

inconvenience [ɪnkən'viːnɪəns] n Unannehmlichkeit f; (trouble) Umstände pl; **inconvenient** adj ungünstig, unbequem; (time) **it's ~ for me** es kommt mir ungelegen; **if it's not too ~ for you** wenn es dir/Ihnen passt
incorporate [ɪn'kɔːpəreɪt] vt aufnehmen (into +akk); (include) enthalten
incorrect [ɪnkə'rekt] adj falsch; (improper) inkorrekt
increase ['ɪnkriːs] n Zunahme f (in an +dat); (in amount, speed) Erhöhung f (in +gen) ▷ [ɪn'kriːs] vt (price, taxes, salary, speed etc) erhöhen; (wealth) vermehren; (number) vergrößern; (business) erweitern ▷ vi zunehmen (in an +dat); (prices) steigen; (in size) größer werden; (in number) sich vermehren; **increasingly** [ɪn'kriːsɪŋlɪ] adv zunehmend
incredible, incredibly [ɪn'kredəbl, -blɪ] adj, adv unglaublich; (very good) fantastisch
incredulous [ɪn'kredjʊləs] adj ungläubig, skeptisch
incriminate [ɪn'krɪmɪneɪt] vt belasten
incubator ['ɪnkjʊbeɪtə°] n Brutkasten m
incurable [ɪn'kjʊərəbl] adj unheilbar
indecent [ɪn'diːsnt] adj unanständig
indecisive [ɪndɪ'saɪsɪv] adj (person) unentschlossen; (result) nicht entscheidend
indeed [ɪn'diːd] adv tatsächlich; (as answer) allerdings; **very hot ~** wirklich sehr heiß
indefinite [ɪn'defɪnɪt] adj unbestimmt; **indefinitely** adv endlos; (postpone) auf unbestimmte Zeit

independence [ˌɪndɪˈpendəns]
n Unabhängigkeit f

● **INDEPENDENCE DAY**
●
● Der **Independence Day**, der 4.
● Juli, ist in den USA ein
● gesetzlicher Feiertag zum
● Gedenken an die
● Unabhängigkeitserklärung am
● 4. Juli 1776, mit der die 13
● amerikanischen Kolonien ihre
● Freiheit und Unabhängigkeit
● von Großbritannien erklärten.

independent [ˌɪndɪˈpendənt]
adj unabhängig (of von); (person)
selbstständig

indescribable [ˌɪndɪˈskraɪbəbl]
adj unbeschreiblich

index [ˈɪndeks] n Index m,
Verzeichnis nt; **index finger** n
Zeigefinger m

India [ˈɪndɪə] n Indien nt; **Indian**
[ˈɪndɪən] adj indisch; ▷ n (Native
American) indianisch ▷ n Inder(in)
m(f); (Native American) Indianer(in)
m(f); **Indian Ocean** n Indischer
Ozean; **Indian summer** n Spät-
sommer m, Altweibersommer m

indicate [ˈɪndɪkeɪt] vt (show)
zeigen; (instrument) anzeigen;
(suggest) hinweisen auf +akk ▷ vi
(Auto) blinken; **indication**
[ˌɪndɪˈkeɪʃn] n (sign) Anzeichen nt
(of für); **indicator** [ˈɪndɪkeɪtəʳ] n
(Auto) Blinker m

indifferent [ɪnˈdɪfrənt] adj (not
caring) gleichgültig (to, towards
gegenüber); (mediocre)
mittelmäßig

indigestible [ˌɪndɪˈdʒestəbl] adj
unverdaulich; **indigestion**
[ˌɪndɪˈdʒestʃən] n Verdau-
ungsstörung f

indignity [ɪnˈdɪgnɪtɪ] n Demütigung f

indirect, indirectly [ˌɪndɪˈrekt, -lɪ]
adj, adv indirekt

indiscreet [ˌɪndɪˈskriːt] adj
indiskret

indispensable [ˌɪndɪˈspensəbl]
adj unentbehrlich

indisposed [ˌɪndɪˈspəʊzd] adj
unwohl

indisputable [ˌɪndɪˈspjuːtəbl]
adj unbestreitbar; (evidence)
unanfechtbar

individual [ˌɪndɪˈvɪdjʊəl] n
Einzelne(r) mf ▷ adj einzeln;
(distinctive) eigen, individuell;
~ **case** Einzelfall m; **individually**
adv (separately) einzeln

Indonesia [ˌɪndəʊˈniːzjə] n
Indonesien nt

indoor [ˈɪndɔːʳ] adj (shoes)
Haus-; (plant, games) Zimmer-;
(Sport: football, championship, record
etc) Hallen-; **indoors** adv drinnen,
im Haus

indulge [ɪnˈdʌldʒ] vi: **to ~ in** sth
sich dat etw gönnen; **indulgence**
n Nachsicht f; (enjoyment)
(übermäßiger) Genuss; (luxury)
Luxus m; **indulgent** adj
nachsichtig (with gegenüber)

industrial [ɪnˈdʌstrɪəl] adj
Industrie-, industriell; ~ **estate**
Industriegebiet nt; **industry**
[ˈɪndəstrɪ] n Industrie f

inedible [ɪnˈedɪbl] adj nicht
essbar, ungenießbar

ineffective [ˌɪnɪˈfektɪv] adj
unwirksam, wirkungslos;
inefficient adj unwirksam; (use,
machine) unwirtschaftlich; (method
etc) unrationell

ineligible [ɪnˈelɪdʒəbl] adj nicht
berechtigt (for zu)

inequality [ˌɪnɪˈkwɒlɪtɪ] n
Ungleichheit f

inevitable [ɪnˈevɪtəbl] adj
unvermeidlich; **inevitably** adv
zwangsläufig

inexcusable [ɪnɪks'kjuːzəbl]
adj unverzeihlich; **that's ~** das
kann man nicht verzeihen

inexpensive [ɪnɪks'pensɪv] *adj*
preisgünstig

inexperience [ɪnɪks'pɪərɪəns]
n Unerfahrenheit f;
inexperienced *adj* unerfahren

inexplicable [ɪnɪks'plɪkəbl] *adj*
unerklärlich

infallible [ɪn'fæləbl] *adj*
unfehlbar

infamous ['ɪnfəməs] *adj* (person)
berüchtigt (for wegen); (deed)
niederträchtig

infancy ['ɪnfənsɪ] *n* frühe
Kindheit; **infant** ['ɪnfənt] *n*
Säugling m; (small child)
Kleinkind nt; **infant school** *n*
Vorschule f

infatuated [ɪn'fætjʊeɪtɪd] *adj*
vernarrt (with in +akk), verknallt
(with in +akk)

infect [ɪn'fekt] *vt* (person)
anstecken; (wound) infizieren;
infection [ɪn'fekʃən] *n* Infektion
f; **infectious** [ɪn'fekʃəs] *adj*
ansteckend

inferior [ɪn'fɪərɪə°] *adj* (in quality)
minderwertig; (in rank)
untergeordnet; **inferiority**
[ɪnfɪərɪ'ɒrɪtɪ] *n* Minderwertigkeit
f; **~ complex** Minderwertigkeitskomplex m

infertile [ɪn'fɜːtaɪl] *adj*
unfruchtbar

infidelity [ɪnfɪ'delɪtɪ] *n* Untreue
f

infinite ['ɪnfɪnɪt] *adj* unendlich

infinitive [ɪn'fɪnɪtɪv] *n* (Ling)
Infinitiv m

infinity [ɪn'fɪnɪtɪ] *n* Unend-
lichkeit f

infirmary [ɪn'fɜːmərɪ] *n*
Krankenhaus nt

inflame [ɪn'fleɪm] *vt* (Med)
entzünden; **inflammation**

[ɪnflə'meɪʃən] *n* (Med)
Entzündung f

inflatable [ɪn'fleɪtəbl] *adj* auf-
blasbar; **~ dinghy** Schlauchboot
nt; **inflate** [ɪn'fleɪt] *vt*
aufpumpen; (by blowing)
aufblasen; (prices) hochtreiben

inflation [ɪn'fleɪʃən] *n* Inflation
f

inflexible [ɪn'fleksəbl] *adj*
unflexibel

inflict [ɪn'flɪkt] *vt*: **to ~ sth on sb**
jdm etw zufügen; **~** (punishment)
jdm etw auferlegen; (wound) jdm
etw beibringen

in-flight [ɪn'flaɪt] *adj* (catering,
magazine) Bord-; **~ entertainment**
Bordprogramm nt

influence ['ɪnflʊəns] *n* Einfluss
m (on auf +akk) ▷ *vt* beeinflussen;
influential [ɪnflʊ'enʃəl] *adj*
einflussreich

influenza [ɪnflʊ'enzə] *n* Grippe
f

inform [ɪn'fɔːm] *vt* informieren
(of, about über +akk); **to keep sb
~ed** jdn auf dem Laufenden halten

informal [ɪn'fɔːməl] *adj* zwanglos, ungezwungen

information [ɪnfə'meɪʃən] *n*
Auskunft f, Informationen pl; **for
your ~** zu deiner/Ihrer
Information; **further ~** weitere
Informationen, Weiteres;
information desk *n*
Auskunftsschalter m; **information
technology** *n* Informations-
technik f; **informative**
[ɪn'fɔːmətɪv] *adj* aufschlussreich

infra-red [ɪnfrə'red] *adj* infrarot

infrastructure *n* Infrastruktur
f

infuriate [ɪn'fjʊərɪeɪt] *vt* wütend
machen; **infuriating** *adj* äußerst
ärgerlich

infusion [ɪn'fjuːʒən] *n* (herbal
tea) Aufguss m; (Med) Infusion f

ingenious [in'dʒi:niəs] adj (person) erfinderisch; (device) raffiniert; (idea) genial

ingredient [in'gri:diənt] n (Gastr) Zutat f

inhabit [in'hæbit] vt bewohnen; **inhabitant** n Einwohner(in) m(f)

inhale [in'heil] vt einatmen; (cigarettes, Med) inhalieren; **inhaler** n Inhalationsgerät nt

inherit [in'herit] vt erben; **inheritance** n Erbe nt

inhibited [in'hibitid] adj gehemmt; **inhibition** [inhi'biʃən] n Hemmung f

in-house [in'haus] adj intern

inhuman [in'hju:mən] adj unmenschlich

initial [i'niʃəl] adj anfänglich; *stage* Anfangsstadium nt ▷ vt mit Initialen unterschreiben; **initially** adv anfangs; **initials** npl Initialen pl

initiative [i'niʃətiv] n Initiative f

inject [in'dʒekt] vt (drug etc) einspritzen; **to ~ sb with sth** jdm etw (ein)spritzen; **injection** n Spritze f, Injektion f

in-joke ['indʒəuk] vt verletzen; **to ~ one's leg** sich dat das Bein verletzen; **injury** ['indʒəri] n Verletzung f

injustice [in'dʒʌstis] n Ungerechtigkeit f

ink [iŋk] n Tinte f; **ink-jet printer** n Tintenstrahldrucker m

inland ['inlənd] adj Binnen- ▷ adv landeinwärts; **inland revenue** n (Brit) Finanzamt nt

in-laws ['inlɔ:z] npl (fam) Schwiegereltern pl

inline skates ['inlainskeits] npl Inlineskates pl, Inliner pl

inmate ['inmeit] n Insasse m

inn [in] n Gasthaus nt

innate [i'neit] adj angeboren

inner ['inə°] adj innere(r, s); **~ city** Innenstadt f

innocence ['inəsns] n Unschuld f; **innocent** adj unschuldig

innovation [inəu'veiʃən] n Neuerung f

innumerable [i'nju:mərəbl] adj unzählig

inoculate [i'nɒkjuleit] vt impfen (against gegen); **inoculation** [inɒkju'leiʃən] n Impfung f

in-patient ['inpeiʃənt] n stationärer Patient, stationäre Patientin

input ['input] n (contribution) Beitrag m; (Inform) Eingabe f

inquest ['inkwest] n gerichtliche Untersuchung (einer Todesursache)

inquire [in'kwaiə°] see **enquire**; **inquiry** [in'kwaiəri] see **enquiry**

insane [in'sein] adj wahnsinnig; (Med) geisteskrank; **insanity** [in'sæniti] n Wahnsinn m

insatiable [in'seiʃəbl] adj unersättlich

inscription [in'skripʃən] n (on stone etc) Inschrift f

insect ['insekt] n Insekt nt; **insecticide** [in'sektisaid] n Insektenbekämpfungsmittel nt; **insect repellent** n Insektenschutzmittel nt

insecure [insi'kjuə°] adj (person) unsicher; (shelves) instabil

insensitive [in'sensitiv] adj unempfindlich (to gegen); (unfeeling) gefühllos; **insensitivity** [insensi'tiviti] n Unempfindlichkeit f (to gegen); (unfeeling nature) Gefühllosigkeit f

inseparable [in'sepərəbl] adj unzertrennlich

insert [in'sɜ:t] vt einfügen; (coin) einwerfen; (key etc) hineinstecken

▷ *n* (*in magazine*) Beilage *f*;
insertion *n* (*in text*) Einfügen *nt*
inside ['ɪn'saɪd] *n*: **the ~** das
Innere; (*surface*) die Innenseite;
from the ~ von innen ▷ *adj*
innere(r, s), Innen-; **~ lane** (*Auto*)
Innenspur *f*; (*Sport*) Innenbahn *f*
▷ *adv* (*place*) innen; (*direction*)
hinein; **to go ~** hineingehen
▷ *prep* (*place*) in +*dat*; (*into*) in +*akk*
... hinein; (*time, within*) innerhalb
+*gen*; **inside out** *adv* verkehrt
herum; (*know*) in- und auswendig;
insider *n* Eingeweihte(r) *mf*,
Insider(in) *m(f)*
insight ['ɪnsaɪt] *n* Einblick *m*
(*into* in +*akk*)
insignificant [ɪnsɪg'nɪfɪkənt]
adj unbedeutend
insincere [ɪnsɪn'sɪə°] *adj* un-
aufrichtig, falsch
insinuate [ɪn'sɪnjʊeɪt] *vt*
andeuten; **insinuation**
[ɪnsɪnjʊ'eɪʃən] *n* Andeutung *f*
insist [ɪn'sɪst] *vi* darauf bestehen;
to ~ on sth auf etw *dat* bestehen;
insistent *adj* hartnäckig
insoluble [ɪn'sɒljʊbl] *adj*
unlösbar
insomnia [ɪn'sɒmnɪə] *n* Schlaflosigkeit *f*
inspect [ɪn'spekt] *vt* prüfen,
kontrollieren; **inspection** *n*
Prüfung *f*; (*check*) Kontrolle *f*;
inspector *n* (*police ~*)
Inspektor(in) *m(f)*; (*senior*)
Kommissar(in) *m(f)*; (*on bus etc*)
Kontrolleur(in) *m(f)*
inspiration [ɪnspɪ'reɪʃən] *n*
Inspiration *f*; **inspire** [ɪn'spaɪə°]
vt (*respect*) einflößen (*in dat*);
(*person*) inspirieren
install [ɪn'stɔ:l] *vt* (*software*)
installieren; (*furnishings*) einbauen
installment, instalment
[ɪn'stɔ:lmənt] *n* Rate *f*; (*of story*)
Folge *f*; **to pay in ~s** auf Raten

zahlen; **installment plan** *n* (*US*)
Ratenkauf *m*
instance ['ɪnstəns] *n* (*of
discrimination*) Fall *m*; (*example*)
Beispiel *nt* (*of* für +*akk*); **for ~** zum
Beispiel
instant ['ɪnstənt] *n* Augenblick
m ▷ *adj* sofortig; **instant coffee**
n löslicher Kaffee *m*; **instantly** *adv*
sofort
instead [ɪn'sted] *adv* stattdes-
sen; **instead of** *prep* (an)statt
+*gen*; **~ of me** an meiner Stelle;
~ of going (an)statt zu gehen
instinct ['ɪnstɪŋkt] *n* Instinkt *m*;
instinctive, instinctively
[ɪn'stɪŋktɪv, -lɪ] *adj, adv*
instinktiv
institute ['ɪnstɪtju:t] *n* Institut
nt; **institution** [ɪnstɪ'tju:ʃən] *n*
(*organisation*) Institution *f*,
Einrichtung *f*; (*home*) Anstalt *f*
instruct [ɪn'strʌkt] *vt* anweisen;
instruction [ɪn'strʌkʃən] *n*
(*teaching*) Unterricht *m*; (*command*)
Anweisung *f*; **~s for use**
Gebrauchsanweisung *f*;
instructor *n* Lehrer(in) *m(f)*; (*US*)
Dozent(in) *m(f)*
instrument ['ɪnstrəmənt] *n*
Instrument *nt*; **instrument panel**
n Armaturenbrett *nt*
insufficient [ɪnsə'fɪʃənt] *adj*
ungenügend
insulate ['ɪnsjʊleɪt] *vt* (*Elec*)
isolieren; **insulating tape** *n*
Isolierband *nt*; **insulation**
[ɪnsjʊ'leɪʃən] *n* Isolierung *f*
insulin ['ɪnsjʊlɪn] *n* Insulin *nt*
insult ['ɪnsʌlt] *n* Beleidigung *f*
▷ [ɪn'sʌlt] *vt* beleidigen;
insulting [ɪn'sʌltɪŋ] *adj*
beleidigend
insurance [ɪn'ʃʊərəns] *n* Versicherung *f*; **~ company** *n*
Versicherungsgesellschaft *f*;
~ policy Versicherungspolice *f*;

invigorating [ɪnˈvɪɡəreɪtɪŋ] *adj* erfrischend, belebend; (*tonic*) stärkend

invisible [ɪnˈvɪzəbl] *adj* unsichtbar

invitation [ɪnvɪˈteɪʃən] *n* Einladung *f*; **invite** [ɪnˈvaɪt] *vt* einladen

invoice [ˈɪnvɔɪs] *n* (*bill*) Rechnung *f*

involuntary [ɪnˈvɒləntərɪ] *adj* unbeabsichtigt

involve [ɪnˈvɒlv] *vt* verwickeln (*in sth* in etw akk); (*entail*) zur Folge haben; **to be ~d in sth** (*participate in*) an etw dat beteiligt sein; **I'm not ~d** (*affected*) ich bin nicht betroffen

inward [ˈɪnwəd] *adj* innere(r, s); **inwardly** *adv* innerlich; **inwards** *adv* nach innen

iodine [ˈaɪədiːn] *n* Jod *nt*

IOU [aɪəʊˈjuː] *abbr* = **I owe you** Schuldschein *m*

IQ *abbr* = **intelligence quotient** IQ *m*

Iran [ɪˈrɑːn] *n* der Iran

Iraq [ɪˈrɑːk] *n* der Irak

Ireland [ˈaɪələnd] *n* Irland *nt*

iris [ˈaɪrɪs] *n* (*flower*) Schwertlilie *f*; (*of eye*) Iris *f*

Irish [ˈaɪrɪʃ] *adj* irisch; **~ coffee** Irish Coffee *m*; **~ Sea** die Irische See ▷ *n* (*language*) Irisch *nt*; **the ~pl** die Iren *pl*; **Irishman** (*pl* **-men**) *n* Ire *m*; **Irishwoman** (*pl* **-women**) *n* Irin *f*

iron [ˈaɪən] *n* Eisen *nt*; (*for ironing*) Bügeleisen *nt* ▷ *adj* eisern ▷ *vt* bügeln

ironic(al) [aɪˈrɒnɪk(əl)] *adj* ironisch

ironing board *n* Bügelbrett *nt*

irony [ˈaɪrənɪ] *n* Ironie *f*

irrational [ɪˈræʃənl] *adj* irrational

irregular [ɪˈreɡjʊlə*] *adj* unregelmäßig; (*shape*) ungleichmäßig

irrelevant [ɪˈreləvənt] *adj* belanglos, irrelevant

irreplaceable [ɪrɪˈpleɪsəbl] *adj* unersetzlich

irresistible [ɪrɪˈzɪstəbl] *adj* unwiderstehlich

irrespective of [ɪrɪˈspektɪv ɒv] *prep* ungeachtet +*gen*

irresponsible [ɪrɪˈspɒnsəbl] *adj* verantwortungslos

irretrievable [ɪrɪˈtriːvəbl] *adv* unwiederbringlich; (*loss*) unersetzlich

irritable [ˈɪrɪtəbl] *adj* reizbar; **irritate** [ˈɪrɪteɪt] *vt* (*annoy*) ärgern; (*deliberately*) reizen; **irritation** [ɪrɪˈteɪʃən] *n* (*anger*) Ärger *m*; (*Med*) Reizung *f*

IRS *abbr* = **Internal Revenue Service** (US) Finanzamt *nt*

is [ɪz] *present of* **be** ist

Islam [ˈɪzlɑːm] *n* Islam *m*; **Islamic** [ɪzˈlæmɪk] *adj* islamisch

island [ˈaɪlənd] *n* Insel *f*; **Isle** [aɪl] *n* (*in names*) **the ~ of Man** die Insel Man; **the ~ of Wight** die Insel Wight; **the British ~s** die Britischen Inseln

isn't [ˈɪznt] *contr of* **is not**

isolate [ˈaɪsəleɪt] *vt* isolieren; **isolated** *adj* (*remote*) abgelegen; (*cut off*) abgeschnitten (*from* von); **an ~ case** ein Einzelfall; **isolation** [aɪsəˈleɪʃən] *n* Isolierung *f*

Israel [ˈɪzreɪl] *n* Israel *nt*; **Israeli** [ɪzˈreɪlɪ] *adj* israelisch ▷ *n* Israeli *m* of

issue [ˈɪʃuː] *n* (*matter*) Frage *f*; (*problem*) Problem *nt*; (*subject*) Thema *nt*; (*of newspaper etc*) Ausgabe *f*; **that's not the ~** darum geht es nicht ▷ *vt* ausgeben; (*document*) ausstellen; (*orders*) erteilen; (*book*) herausgeben

it [It] pron 1 (specific: subject)
er/sie/es; (direct object) ihn/sie/es;
(indirect object) ihm/ihr/ihm;
about/from/in/of it
darüber/davon/darin/davon
2 (impers) es; **it's raining** es regnet;
it's Friday tomorrow morgen ist
Freitag; **who is it? — it's me** wer ist
da? — ich (bin's)

IT abbr = **information technology**
IT f

Italian [ɪˈtæljən] adj italienisch
▷ n Italiener(in) m(f); (language)
Italienisch nt

italic [ɪˈtælɪk] adj kursiv ▷ npl: **in
~s** kursiv

Italy [ˈɪtəlɪ] n Italien nt

itch [Itʃ] n Juckreiz m; **I have an
~** mich juckt es ▷ vi jucken; **he is
~ing to ...** es juckt ihn, zu ...; **itchy**
adj juckend

it'd [ˈItd] contr of **it would; it had**

item [ˈaɪtəm] n (article)
Gegenstand m; (in catalogue)
Artikel m; (on list, in accounts)
Posten m; (on agenda) Punkt m; (in
show programme) Nummer f; (in
news) Bericht m; (TV, radio)
Meldung f

itinerary [aɪˈtɪnərərɪ] n Reiseroute f

it'll [ˈItl] contr of **it will; it shall**

its [Its] pron sein; (feminine form)
ihr

it's [Its] contr of **it is; it has**

itself [Itˈself] pron (reflexive) sich;
(emphatic) **the house ~** das Haus
selbst o an sich; **by ~** allein; **the
door closes (by) ~** die Tür schließt
sich von selbst

I've [aIv] contr of **I have**

ivory [ˈaɪvərɪ] n Elfenbein nt

ivy [ˈaɪvɪ] n Efeu m

jab [dʒæb] vt (needle, knife)
stechen (into in +akk) ▷ n (fam)
Spritze f

jack [dʒæk] n (Auto) Wagenheber
m; (Cards) Bube m; **jack in** vt (fam)
aufgeben, hinschmeißen; **jack up**
vt (car etc) aufbocken

jacket [ˈdʒækɪt] n Jacke f; (of
man's suit) Jackett nt; (of book)
Schutzumschlag m; **jacket potato**
(pl **-es**) n (in der Schale)
gebackene Kartoffel

jack-knife [ˈdʒæknaɪf] (pl
jack-knives) n Klappmesser nt
▷ vi (truck) sich quer stellen

jackpot [ˈdʒækpɒt] n Jackpot m

jacuzzi® [dʒəˈkuːzɪ] n (bath)
Whirlpool® m

jail [dʒeɪl] n Gefängnis nt ▷ vt
einsperren

jam [dʒæm] n Konfitüre f,
Marmelade f; (traffic ~) Stau m ▷ vt
(street) verstopfen; (machine)

blockieren; **to be ~med** (*stuck*) klemmen; **to ~ on the brakes** eine Vollbremsung machen

Jamaica [dʒəˈmeɪkə] n Jamaika nt

jam-packed adj proppenvoll

janitor [ˈdʒænɪtəʳ] n (US) Hausmeister(in) m(f)

Jan abbr = **January** Jan

January [ˈdʒænjʊərɪ] n Januar m

Japan [dʒəˈpæn] n Japan nt; **Japanese** [dʒæpəˈniːz] adj japanisch ▷ n (person) Japaner(in) m(f); (language) Japanisch nt

jar [dʒɑːʳ] n Glas nt

jaundice [ˈdʒɔːndɪs] n Gelbsucht f

javelin [ˈdʒævlɪn] n Speer m; (Sport) Speerwerfen nt

jaw [dʒɔː] n Kiefer m

jazz [dʒæz] n Jazz m

jealous [ˈdʒeləs] adj eifersüchtig (of auf +akk); **don't make me ~** mach mich nicht neidisch; **jealousy** n Eifersucht f

jeans [dʒiːnz] npl Jeans pl

jeep® [dʒiːp] n Jeep® m

jelly [ˈdʒelɪ] n Gelee nt; (on meat) Gallert nt; (dessert) Götterspeise f; (US: jam) Marmelade f; **jelly baby** n (sweet) Gummibärchen nt; **jellyfish** n Qualle f

jeopardize [ˈdʒepədaɪz] vt gefährden

jerk [dʒɜːk] n Ruck m; (fam: idiot) Trottel m ▷ vt ruckartig bewegen ▷ vi (rope) rucken; (muscles) zucken

Jerusalem [dʒəˈruːsələm] n Jerusalem n

jet [dʒet] n (of water etc) Strahl m; (nozzle) Düse f; (aircraft) Düsenflugzeug nt; **jet foil** n Tragflächenboot nt; **jetlag** n Jetlag m (Müdigkeit nach langem Flug)

Jew [dʒuː] n Jude m, Jüdin f

jewel [ˈdʒuːəl] n Edelstein m; (esp fig) Juwel nt; **jeweller, jeweler** (US) n Juwelier(in) m(f); **jewellery, jewelry** (US) n Schmuck m

Jewish [ˈdʒuːɪʃ] adj jüdisch; **she's ~** sie ist Jüdin

jigsaw (puzzle) [ˈdʒɪgsɔː(ˌpʌzl)] n Puzzle nt

jilt [dʒɪlt] vt den Laufpass geben +dat

jingle [ˈdʒɪŋgl] n (advert) Jingle m; (verse) Reim m

jitters [ˈdʒɪtərz] npl (fam) **to have the ~** Bammel haben; **jittery** adj (fam) ganz nervös

job [dʒɒb] n (piece of work) Arbeit f; (task) Aufgabe f; (occupation) Stellung f, Job m; **what's your ~?** was machen Sie beruflich?; **it's a good ~ you did that** gut, dass du das gemacht hast; **jobcentre** n Arbeitsvermittlungsstelle f, Arbeitsamt nt; **job-hunting** n: **to go ~** auf Arbeitssuche gehen; **jobless** adj arbeitslos; **job seeker** n Arbeitssuchende(r) mf; **jobseeker's allowance** n Arbeitslosengeld nt; **job-sharing** n Arbeitsplatzteilung f

jockey [ˈdʒɒkɪ] n Jockey m

jog [dʒɒg] vt (person) anstoßen ▷ vi (run) joggen; **jogging** n Jogging nt; **to go ~** joggen gehen

john [dʒɒn] n (US fam) Klo nt

join [dʒɔɪn] vt (put together) verbinden (to mit); (club etc) beitreten +dat; **to ~ sb** sich jdm anschließen; (sit with) sich zu jdm setzen ▷ vi (unite) sich vereinigen; (rivers) zusammenfließen ▷ n Verbindungsstelle f; (seam) Naht f; **join in** vi, vt mitmachen (sth bei etw)

joint [dʒɔɪnt] n (of bones) Gelenk nt; (in pipe etc) Verbindungsstelle f; (of meat) Braten m; (of marijuana)

Joint *m* ▷ *adj* gemeinsam; **joint account** *n* Gemeinschaftskonto *nt*; **jointly** *adv* gemeinsam

joke [dʒəuk] *n* Witz *m*; (*prank*) Streich *m*; **for a ~** zum Spaß; **it's no ~** das ist nicht zum Lachen ▷ *vi* Witze machen; **you must be joking** das ist ja wohl nicht dein Ernst!

jolly ['dʒɒlɪ] *adj* lustig, vergnügt

Jordan ['dʒɔːdən] *n* (*country*) Jordanien *nt*; (*river*) Jordan *m*

jot down [dʒɒt daun] *vt* sich notieren; **jotter** *n* Notizbuch *nt*

journal ['dʒɜːnl] *n* (*diary*) Tagebuch *nt*; (*magazine*) Zeitschrift *f*; **journalism** *n* Journalismus *m*; **journalist** *n* Journalist(in) *m(f)*

journey ['dʒɜːnɪ] *n* Reise *f*; (*esp on stage, by car, train*) Fahrt *f*

joy [dʒɔɪ] *n* Freude *f* (*at über* +*akk*); **joystick** *n* (*Inform*) Joystick *m*; (*Aviat*) Steuerknüppel *m*

judge [dʒʌdʒ] *n* Richter(in) *m(f)*; (*Sport*) Punktrichter(in) *m(f)* ▷ *vt* beurteilen (*by nach*); **as far as I can ~** meinem Urteil nach ▷ *vi* urteilen (*by nach*); **judg(e)ment** *n* (*Jur*) Urteil *nt*; (*opinion*) Ansicht *f*; **an error of ~** Fehleinschätzung *f*

judo ['dʒuːdəu] *n* Judo *nt*

jug [dʒʌg] *n* Krug *m*

juggle ['dʒʌgl] *vi* (*lit, fig*) jonglieren (*with mit*)

juice [dʒuːs] *n* Saft *m*; **juicy** *adj* saftig; (*story, scandal*) pikant

July [dʒuː'laɪ] *n* Juli *m*; *see also* **September**

jumble ['dʒʌmbl] *n* Durcheinander *nt* ▷ *vt*: **to ~ (up)** durcheinanderwerfen; (*facts*) durcheinanderbringen; **jumble sale** *n* (*for charity*) Flohmarkt *m*; Wohltätigkeitsbasar *m*

jumbo ['dʒʌmbəu] *adj* (*sausage etc*) Riesen-; **jumbo jet** *n* Jumbojet *m*

jump [dʒʌmp] *vi* springen; (*nervously*) zusammenzucken; **to ~ to conclusions** voreilige Schlüsse ziehen; **to ~ from one thing to another** dauernd das Thema wechseln ▷ *vt* (*a. fig: omit*) überspringen; **to ~ the lights** bei Rot über die Kreuzung fahren; **to ~ the queue** sich vordrängen ▷ *n* Sprung *m*; (*for horses*) Hindernis *nt*; **jumper** *n* Pullover *m*; (*US: dress*) Trägerkleid *nt*; (*person, horse*) Springer(in) *m(f)*; **jumper cable** *n* (*US*), **jump lead** *n* (*Brit Auto*) Starthilfekabel *nt*

junction ['dʒʌŋkʃən] *n* (*of roads*) Kreuzung *f*; (*Rail*) Knotenpunkt *m*

June [dʒuːn] *n* Juni *m*; *see also* **September**

jungle ['dʒʌŋgl] *n* Dschungel *m*

junior ['dʒuːnɪə*] *adj* (*younger*) jünger; (*lower position*) untergeordnet (*to sb jdm*) ▷ *n*: **she's two years my ~** sie ist zwei Jahre jünger als ich; **junior high (school)** *n* (*US*) = Mittelschule *f*; **junior school** *n* (*Brit*) Grundschule *f*

junk [dʒʌŋk] *n* (*trash*) Plunder *m*; **junk food** *n* Nahrungsmittel *pl* mit geringem Nährwert, Junkfood *nt*; **junkie** *n* (*fam*) Junkie *m*, Fixer(in) *m(f)*; (*fig: fan*) Freak *m*; **junk mail** *n* Reklame *f*; (*Inform*) Junkmail *f*; **junk shop** *n* Trödelladen *m*

jury ['dʒuərɪ] *n* Geschworene *pl*; (*in competition*) Jury *f*

just [dʒʌst] *adj* gerecht ▷ *adv* (*recently*) gerade; (*exactly*) genau; **~ as expected** genau wie erwartet; **~ as nice** genauso nett; (*barely*) **~ in time** gerade noch rechtzeitig; (*immediately*) **~ before/after …** gleich vor/nach …; (*small distance*) **~ round the corner** gleich um die Ecke; (*a little*)

~ over an hour etwas mehr als eine
Stunde; *(only)* **~ the two of us** nur
wir beide; **~ a moment** Moment
mal; *(absolutely, simply)* **it was
~ fantastic** es war einfach klasse;
~ about so etwa; *(more or less)*
mehr oder weniger; **~ about
ready** fast fertig

justice ['dʒʌstɪs] *n* Gerechtigkeit
f; **justifiable** [dʒʌstɪ'faɪəbl] *adj*
berechtigt; **justifiably** *adv* zu
Recht; **justify** ['dʒʌstɪfaɪ] *vt*
rechtfertigen

jut [dʒʌt] *vi*: **to ~ (out)**
herausragen

juvenile ['dʒuːvənaɪl] *n adj*
Jugend-, jugendlich ▷ *n*
Jugendliche(r) *mf*

k *abbr* = **thousand**; **15k** 15 000

K *abbr* = **kilobyte** KB

kangaroo [kæŋgə'ruː] *n* Känguru
nt

karaoke [kærɪ'əʊkɪ] *n* Karaoke *nt*

karate [kə'rɑːtɪ] *n* Karate *nt*

kart [kɑːt] *n* Gokart *m*

kayak ['kaɪæk] *n* Kajak *m o nt*;
kayaking ['kaɪækɪŋ] *n* Kajakfahren *nt*

Kazakhstan [kæzæk'stɑːn] *n*
Kasachstan *nt*

kebab [kə'bæb] *n* *(shish ~)*
Schaschlik *nt o m*; *(doner ~)* Kebab
m

keel [kiːl] *n* *(Naut)* Kiel *m*; **keel
over** *vi* *(boat)* kentern; *(person)*
umkippen

keen [kiːn] *adj* begeistert *(on*
von); *(hardworking)* eifrig; *(mind,
wind)* scharf; *(interest, feeling)* stark;
to be ~ on sb von jdm angetan
sein; **she's ~ on riding** sie reitet

gern; **to be ~ to do sth** darauf erpicht sein, etw zu tun

keep [ki:p] (**kept, kept**) vt (retain) behalten; (secret) für sich behalten; (observe) einhalten; (promise) halten; (run: shop, diary, accounts) führen; (animals) halten; (support, family etc) unterhalten, versorgen; (store) aufbewahren; **to ~ sb waiting** jdn warten lassen; **to ~ sb from doing sth** jdn davon abhalten, etw zu tun; **to ~ sth clean/secret** etw sauber/geheim halten; **"~ clear"** „(bitte) frei halten"; **~ this to yourself** behalten Sie das für sich ▷ vi (food) sich halten; (remain, with adj) bleiben; **~ quiet** sei ruhig!; **~ left** links fahren; **to ~ doing sth** (repeatedly) etw immer wieder tun; **~ at it** mach weiter so!; **it ~s happening** es passiert immer wieder ▷ n (livelihood) Unterhalt m; **keep back** vi zurückbleiben ▷ vt zurückhalten; (information) verschweigen (from sb jdm); **keep off** vt (person, animal) fernhalten; **"~ off the grass"** „Betreten des Rasens verboten"; **keep on** vi weitermachen; (walking) weitergehen; (in car) weiterfahren; **to ~ doing sth** (persistently) etw immer wieder tun ▷ vt (coat etc) anbehalten; **keep out** vt nicht hereinlassen ▷ vi draußen bleiben; **~ (on sign)** Eintritt verboten; **keep to** vt (road, path) bleiben auf +dat; (plan etc) sich halten an +akk; **to ~ the point** bei der Sache bleiben; **keep up** vi Schritt halten (with mit) ▷ vt (maintain) aufrechterhalten; (speed) halten; **to ~ appearances** den Schein wahren; **keep it up!** (fam) weiter so!

keeper n (museum etc) Aufseher(in) m(f); (goal-) Torwart

m; (zoo ~) Tierpfleger(in) m(f); **keep-fit** n Fitnesstraining nt; **~ exercises** Gymnastik f

kennel ['kɛnl] n Hundehütte f; **kennels** n Hundepension f

Kenya ['kɛnjə] n Kenia nt

kept [kɛpt] pt, pp of **keep**

kerb ['kɜːb] n Randstein m

kerosene ['kɛrəsiːn] n (US) Petroleum nt

ketchup ['kɛtʃəp] n Ketchup nt o m

kettle ['kɛtl] n Kessel m

key [kiː] n Schlüssel m; (of piano, computer) Taste f; (Mus) Tonart f; (for map etc) Zeichenerklärung f ▷ vt: **to ~ (in)** (Inform) eingeben ▷ adj entscheidend; **keyboard** n (piano, computer) Tastatur f; **keyhole** n Schlüsselloch nt; **keypad** n (Inform) Nummernblock m; **keyring** n Schlüsselring m

kick [kik] n (Sport) Stoß m; **I get a ~ out of it** (fam) es turnt mich an ▷ vt, vi treten; **kick out** vt rausschmeißen (of aus); **kick-off** n (Sport) Anstoß m

kid [kid] n (child) Kind nt ▷ vt (tease) auf den Arm nehmen ▷ vi Witze machen; **you're ~ding** das ist doch nicht dein Ernst!; **no ~ding** aber echt!

kidnap ['kidnæp] vt entführen; **kidnapper** n Entführer(in) m(f); **kidnapping** n Entführung f

kidney ['kidni] n Niere f; **kidney machine** n künstliche Niere

kill [kil] vt töten; (esp intentionally) umbringen; (weeds) vernichten; **killer** n Mörder(in) m(f)

kilo ['kiːləu] (pl -s) n Kilo nt; **kilobyte** n Kilobyte nt; **kilogramme** n Kilogramm nt; **kilometer** (US), **kilometre** n Kilometer m; **~s per hour**

Stundenkilometer pl; **kilowatt** n
Kilowatt nt

kilt [kɪlt] n Schottenrock m

kind [kaɪnd] adj nett, freundlich
(to zu) ▷ n Art f; (of coffee, cheese
etc) Sorte f; **what ~ of ...?** was für
ein(e) ...?; **this ~ of ...** so ein(e) ...;
~ of (+ adj) irgendwie

kindergarten ['kɪndəgɑːtn] n
Kindergarten m

kindly ['kaɪndlɪ] adj nett,
freundlich ▷ adv liebenswürdi-
gerweise; **kindness** ['kaɪndnəs]
n Freundlichkeit f

king [kɪŋ] n König m; **kingdom** n
Königreich nt; **kingfisher** n
Eisvogel m; **king-size** adj im
Großformat; (bed) extra groß

kipper ['kɪpə*] n Räucherhering
m

kiss [kɪs] n Kuss m; **~ of life**
Mund-zu-Mund-Beatmung f ▷ vt
küssen

kit [kɪt] n (equipment) Ausrüstung
f; (fam) Sachen pl; (sports ~)
Sportsachen pl; (belongings, clothes)
Sachen pl; (for building sth) Bausatz
m

kitchen ['kɪtʃɪn] n Küche f;
kitchen foil n Alufolie f; **kitchen
scales** n Küchenwaage f; **kitchen
unit** n Küchenschrank m;
kitchenware n Küchengeschirr
nt

kite [kaɪt] n Drachen m

kitten ['kɪtn] n Kätzchen nt

kiwi ['kiːwiː] n (fruit) Kiwi f

km abbr = **kilometres** km

knack [næk] n Dreh m, Trick m; **to
get/have got the ~** den Dreh
herauskriegen/heraushaben;
knackered ['nækəd] adj (Brit fam)
fix und fertig, kaputt

knee [niː] n Knie nt; **kneecap** n
Kniescheibe f; **knee-jerk** adj
(reaction) reflexartig; **kneel** [niːl]
(knelt o kneeled, knelt o kneeled)

vi knien; (action, **~ down**) sich
hinknien

knelt [nelt] pt, pp of **kneel**

knew [njuː] pt of **know**

knickers ['nɪkəz] npl (Brit fam)
Schlüpfer m

knife [naɪf] (pl **knives**) n Messer
nt

knight [naɪt] n Ritter m; (in
chess) Pferd nt, Springer m

knit [nɪt] vt, vi stricken; **knitting**
n (piece of work) Strickarbeit f;
(activity) Stricken nt; **knitting
needle** n Stricknadel f; **knitwear**
n Strickwaren pl

knob [nɒb] n (on door) Knauf m;
(on radio etc) Knopf m

knock [nɒk] vt (with hammer etc)
schlagen; (accidentally) stoßen; **to
~ one's head** sich dat den Kopf
anschlagen ▷ vi klopfen (on, at an
+akk) ▷ n (blow) Schlag m; (on door)
Klopfen nt; **there was a ~ (at the
door)** es hat geklopft; **knock
down** vt (object) umstoßen;
(person) niederschlagen; (with car)
anfahren; (building) abreißen;
knock out vt (stun) bewusstlos
schlagen; (boxer) k.o. schlagen;
knock over vt umstoßen; (with
car) anfahren; **knocker** n
Türklopfer m; **knockout** n
Knockout m, K.o. m

knot [nɒt] n Knoten m

know [nəʊ] (knew, known) vt, vi
wissen; (be acquainted with: people,
places) kennen; (recognize)
erkennen; (language) können; **I'll
let you ~** ich sage dir Bescheid; **I
~ some French** ich kann etwas
Französisch; **to get to ~ sb** jdn
kennenlernen; **to be ~n as** als
bekannt sein als; **know about** vt
Bescheid wissen über +akk;
(subject) sich auskennen in +dat;
(cars, horses etc) sich auskennen
mit; **know of** vt kennen; **not that**

I ~ nicht dass ich wüsste;
know-all n (fam) Klugscheißer m;
know-how n Kenntnis f,
Know-how nt; **knowing** adj
wissend; (look, smile) vielsagend;
knowledge ['nɒlɪdʒ] n Wissen
nt; (of a subject) Kenntnisse pl; **to
(the best of) my ~** meines
Wissens

known [nəʊn] pp of know
knuckle ['nʌkl] n (Fin-
ger)knöchel m; (Gastr) Hachse f;
knuckle down vi sich an die
Arbeit machen
Koran [kɒˈrɑːn] n Koran m
Korea [kəˈrɪə] n Korea nt
Kosovo ['kɒsɒvəʊ] n der Kosovo
kph abbr = kilometres per hour
km/h
Kremlin ['kremlɪn] n: **the ~** der
Kreml
Kurd [kɜːd] n Kurde m, Kurdin f;
Kurdish adj kurdisch
Kuwait [kʊˈweɪt] n Kuwait nt

L abbr (Brit Auto) = **learner**
LA abbr = **Los Angeles**
lab [læb] n (fam) Labor nt
label ['leɪbl] n Etikett nt; (tied)
Anhänger m; (adhesive) Aufkleber
m; (record ~) Label nt ⊳ vt
etikettieren; (pej) abstempeln
laboratory [ləˈbɒrətərɪ] n Labor
nt

- LABOR DAY

- Der **Labor Day** ist in den USA
- und Kanada der Name für den
- Tag der Arbeit. Er wird dort als
- gesetzlicher Feiertag am ersten
- Montag im September
- begangen.

laborious [ləˈbɔːrɪəs] adj
mühsam; **labor** (US), **labour**
['leɪbə°] n Arbeit f; (Med) Wehen
pl; **to be in ~** Wehen haben ⊳ adj

(Pol) Labour-; **~ Party** Labour Party
f; **labor union** n *(US)*
Gewerkschaft f; **labourer** n
Arbeiter(in) m(f)

lace [leɪs] n *(fabric)* Spitze f; *(of
shoe)* Schnürsenkel m ▷ vt: **to
~ (up)** zuschnüren; **lace-up** n
Schnürschuh m

lack [læk] vt, vi: **to be ~ing** fehlen;
sb ~s o is ~ing in sth es fehlt jdm
an etw dat; **we ~ the time** uns
fehlt die Zeit ▷ n Mangel m (*of* an
+dat)

lacquer ['lækə°] n Lack m; *(Brit:
hair ~)* Haarspray nt

lad [læd] n Junge m

ladder ['lædə°] n Leiter f; *(in tight)*
Laufmasche f

laddish ['lædɪʃ] adj *(Brit)*
machohaft

laden ['leɪdn] adj beladen *(with*
mit)

ladies ['leɪdɪz], **ladies' room** n
Damentoilette f

lad mag n Männerzeitschrift f

lady ['leɪdɪ] n Dame f; *(as title)*
Lady f; **ladybird, ladybug** *(US)* n
Marienkäfer m; **Ladyshave®** n
Epiliergerät nt

lag [læg] vi: **to ~ (behind)**
zurückliegen ▷ vt *(pipes)* isolieren

lager ['lɑːgə°] n helles Bier;
~ lout betrunkener Rowdy

lagging ['lægɪŋ] n Isolierung f

laid [leɪd] pt, pp of **lay**; **laid-back**
adj *(fam)* cool, gelassen

lain [leɪn] pp of **lie**

lake [leɪk] n See m; **the Lake
District** Seengebiet im Nordwesten
Englands

lamb [læm] n Lamm nt; *(meat)*
Lammfleisch nt; **lamb chop** n
Lammkotelett nt

lame [leɪm] adj lahm; *(excuse)*
faul; *(argument)* schwach

lament [lə'ment] n Klage f ▷ vt
beklagen

laminated ['læmɪneɪtɪd] adj
beschichtet

lamp [læmp] n Lampe f; *(in street)*
Laterne f; *(in car)* Licht nt,
Scheinwerfer m; **lamppost** n
Laternenpfahl m; **lampshade** n
Lampenschirm m

land [lænd] n Land nt ▷ vi *(from
ship)* an Land gehen; *(Aviat)* landen
▷ vt *(passengers)* absetzen; *(goods)*
abladen; *(plane)* landen; **landing** n
Landung f; *(on stairs)*
Treppenabsatz m; **landing stage**
n Landesteg m; **landing strip** n
Landebahn f

landlady n Hauswirtin f,
Vermieterin f; **landlord** n *(of
house)* Hauswirt m, Vermieter m;
(of pub) Gastwirt m; **landmark** n
Wahrzeichen nt; *(event)*
Meilenstein m; **landowner** n
Grundbesitzer(in) m(f); **landscape**
n Landschaft f; *(format)*
Querformat nt; **landslide** n *(Geo)*
Erdrutsch m

lane [leɪn] n *(in country)* enge
Landstraße, Weg m; *(in town)* Gasse
f; *(of motorway)* Spur f; *(Sport)* Bahn
f **to get in ~** *(in car)* sich einordnen

language ['læŋgwɪdʒ] n Sprache
f; *(style)* Ausdrucksweise f

lantern ['læntən] n Laterne f

lap [læp] n Schoß m; *(in race)*
Runde f ▷ vt *(in race)* überholen

lapse [læps] n *(mistake)* Irrtum m;
(moral) Fehltritt m ▷ vi ablaufen

laptop ['læptɒp] n Laptop m

large [lɑːdʒ] adj groß; **by and
~** im Großen und Ganzen; **largely**
adv zum größten Teil; **large-scale**
adj groß angelegt, Groß-

lark [lɑːk] n *(bird)* Lerche f

laryngitis [lærɪn'dʒaɪtɪs] n Kehl-
kopfentzündung f; **larynx**
['lærɪŋks] n Kehlkopf m

laser ['leɪzə°] n Laser m; **laser
printer** n Laserdrucker m

lash [læʃ] vt peitschen; **lash out**
vi (with fists) um sich schlagen;
(spend money) sich in Unkosten
stürzen (on mit)

lass [læs] n Mädchen nt

last [lɑːst] adj letzte(r, s); **the
~ but one** der/die/das vorletzte;
~ night gestern Abend; **~ but not
least** nicht zuletzt ▷ adv zuletzt;
(last time) das letzte Mal; **at
~** endlich ▷ n (person) Letzte(r) m/f;
(thing) Letzte(s) nt; **he was the
~ to leave** er ging als Letzter ▷ vi
(continue) dauern; (remain in good
condition) durchhalten; (remain
good) sich halten; (money)
ausreichen; **lasting** adj
dauerhaft; (impression) nachhaltig;
lastly adv schließlich;
last-minute adj in letzter
Minute; **last name** n Nachname
m

late [leɪt] adj spät; (after proper
time) zu spät; (train etc) verspätet;
(dead) verstorben; **to be ~** zu spät
kommen; (train etc) Verspätung
haben ▷ adv spät; (after proper
time) zu spät; **late availibility
flight** n Last-Minute-Flug m;
lately adv in letzter Zeit; **late
opening** n verlängerte
Öffnungszeiten pl; **later** ['leɪtə°]
adj, adv später; **see you ~** bis
später; **latest** ['leɪtɪst] adj
späteste(r, s); (most recent)
neueste(r, s) ▷ n (~ news) das
Neueste; **at the ~** spätestens

Latin ['lætɪn] n Latein nt ▷ adj
lateinisch; **Latin America** n
Lateinamerika nt;
Latin-American adj
lateinamerikanisch ▷ n Latein-
amerikaner(in) m(f)

Latvia ['lætvɪə] n Lettland nt;

Latvian ['lætvɪən] ▷ adj lettisch;
▷ n (person) Lette m, Lettin f;
(language) Lettisch nt

laugh [lɑːf] n Lachen nt; **for a
~** aus Spaß ▷ vi lachen (at, about
über +akk); **to ~ at sb** sich über jdn
lustig machen; **it's no ~ing
matter** es ist nicht zum Lachen;
laughter [lɑːftə°] n Gelächter nt

launch [lɔːntʃ] n (launching, of
ship) Stapellauf m; (of rocket)
Abschuss m; (of product)
Markteinführung f; (with hype)
Lancierung f; (event)
Eröffnungsfeier f ▷ vt (ship) vom
Stapel lassen; (rocket) abschießen;
(product) einführen; (with hype)
lancieren; (project) in Gang setzen
launder ['lɔːndə°] vt waschen
und bügeln; (fig: money) waschen;
laundrette [lɔːn'dret] n (Brit),
laundromat ['lɔːndrəmæt] n (US)
Waschsalon m; **laundry** ['lɔːndrɪ]
n (place) Wäscherei f; (clothes)
Wäsche f

lavatory ['lævətrɪ] n Toilette f

lavender ['lævɪndə°] n Lavendel
m

lavish ['lævɪʃ] adj verschwende-
risch; (furnishings etc) üppig; (gift)
großzügig

law [lɔː] n Gesetz nt; (system)
Recht nt; (for study) Jura; (of sport)
Regel f; **against the
~** gesetzwidrig; **law-abiding** adj
gesetzestreu; **law court** n
Gerichtshof m; **lawful** adj
rechtmäßig

lawn [lɔːn] n Rasen m;
lawnmower n Rasenmäher m

lawsuit ['lɔːsuːt] n Prozess m;
lawyer ['lɔːjə°] n Rechtsanwalt
m, Rechtsanwältin f

laxative ['læksətɪv] n Abführ-
mittel nt

lay [leɪ] pt of **lie** ▷ vt (**laid, laid**)
legen; (table) decken; (vulg)

poppen, bumsen; (egg) legen ▷ adj
Laien-; **lay down** vt hinlegen; **lay
off** vt (workers) (vorübergehend)
entlassen; (stop attacking) in Ruhe
lassen; **lay on** vt (provide)
anbieten; (organize) veranstalten,
bereitstellen; **layabout** n
Faulenzer(in) m(f); **lay-by** n
Parkbucht f; (bigger) Parkplatz m

layer ['leɪə*] n Schicht f

layman ['leɪmən] n Laie m

layout ['leɪaʊt] n Gestaltung f;
(of book etc) Lay-out nt

laze [leɪz] vi faulenzen; **laziness**
['leɪzɪnɪs] n Faulheit f; **lazy**
['leɪzɪ] adj faul; (day, time)
gemütlich

lb abbr = **pound** Pfd.

lead [led] n Blei nt ▷ vt, vi [liːd]
(lead, led) führen; (group etc) leiten;
to ~ the way vorangehen; **this is
~ing us nowhere** das bringt uns
nicht weiter ▷ [liːd] n (race)
Führung f; (distance, time ahead)
Vorsprung m (over vor +dat); (for
police) Spur f; (Theat) Hauptrolle f;
(dog's) Leine f; (Elec: flex) Leitung f;
lead astray vt irreführen; **lead
away** vt wegführen; **lead back** vi
zurückführen; **lead on** vt
anführen; **lead to** vt (street)
hinführen nach; (result in) führen
zu; **lead up to** vt (drive) führen zu

leaded ['ledɪd] adj (petrol)
verbleit

leader ['liːdə*] n Führer(in) m(f);
(of party) Vorsitzende(r) mf; (of
project, expedition) Leiter(in) m(f);
(Sport: in race) der/die Erste; (in
league) Tabellenführer m;
leadership ['liːdəʃɪp] n Führung
f

lead-free ['ledfriː] adj (petrol)
bleifrei

leading ['liːdɪŋ] adj führend,
wichtig

leaf [liːf] (pl **leaves**) n Blatt nt;

leaflet ['liːflɪt] n Prospekt m;
(pamphlet) Flugblatt nt; (with
instructions) Merkblatt nt

league [liːg] n Bund m; (Sport)
Liga f

leak [liːk] n (gap) undichte Stelle;
(escape) Leck nt; **to take a ~** (fam)
pinkeln gehen ▷ vi (pipe etc)
undicht sein; (liquid etc) auslaufen;
leaky adj undicht

lean [liːn] adj (meat) mager; (face)
schmal; (person) drahtig ▷ vi
(**leant** o **leaned**, **leant** o **leaned**)
(not vertical) sich neigen; (rest) **to
~ against sth** sich an etw akk
lehnen; (support oneself) **to ~ on
sth** sich auf etw akk stützen ▷ vt
lehnen (on, against an +akk); **lean
forward** vi sich vorbeugen; **lean
over** vi sich hinüberbeugen; **lean
towards** vt tendieren zu

leant [lent] pt, pp of **lean**

leap [liːp] n Sprung m ▷ vi (**leapt**
o **leaped**, **leapt** o **leaped**)
springen; **leapt** [lept] pt, pp of
leap; **leap year** n Schaltjahr nt

learn [lɜːn] (**learnt** o **learned**,
learnt o **learned**) vt, vi lernen;
(find out) erfahren; **to ~ (how) to
swim** schwimmen lernen;
learned ['lɜːnɪd] adj gelehrt;
learner n Anfänger(in) m(f);
(Brit: driver) Fahrschüler(in) m(f)

learnt [lɜːnt] pt, pp of **learn**

lease [liːs] n (of land, premises etc)
Pacht f; (contract) Pachtvertrag m;
(of house, car etc) Miete f; (contract)
Mietvertrag m ▷ vt pachten;
(house, car etc) mieten; **lease out**
vt vermieten; **leasing** ['liːsɪŋ] n
Leasing nt

least [liːst] adj wenigste(r, s);
(slightest) geringste(r, s) ▷ adv am
wenigsten; **~ expensive**
billigste(r, s) ▷ n: **the ~** das
Mindeste; **not in the ~** nicht im

geringsten; **at ~** wenigstens; (with number) mindestens

leather ['leðə'] n Leder nt ▷ adj ledern, Leder-

leave [li:v] n (time off) Urlaub m; **on ~** auf Urlaub; **to take one's ~** Abschied nehmen (of von) ▷ vt (**left, left**) (place, person) verlassen; (not remove, not change) lassen; (~ behind: message, scar etc) hinterlassen; (forget) hinter sich lassen; (after death) hinterlassen (to sb jdm); (entrust) überlassen (to sb jdm); **to be left** (remain) übrig bleiben; **~ me alone** lass mich in Ruhe!; **don't ~ it to the last minute** warte nicht bis zur letzten Minute ▷ vi (weg)gehen, (weg)fahren; (on journey) abreisen; (bus, train) abfahren (for nach); **leave behind** vt zurücklassen; (scar etc) hinterlassen; (forget) hinter sich lassen; **leave out** vt auslassen; (person) ausschließen (of von)

leaves [li:vz] pl of **leaf**

leaving do [li:viŋ du:] n Abschiedsfeier f

Lebanon ['lebənən] n: **the ~** der Libanon

lecture ['lektʃə'] n Vortrag m; (at university) Vorlesung f; **to give a ~** einen Vortrag/eine Vorlesung halten; **lecturer** n Dozent(in) m(f); **lecture theatre** n Hörsaal m

led [led] pt, pp of **lead**

LED abbr = **light-emitting diode** Leuchtdiode f

ledge [ledʒ] n Leiste f; (window ~) Sims m or nt

leek [li:k] n Lauch m

left [left] pt, pp of **leave** ▷ adj linke(r, s) ▷ adv (position) links; (movement) nach links ▷ n (side) linke Seite; **the Left** (Pol) die Linke; **on/to the ~** links (of von); **move/fall to the ~** nach links

rücken/fallen; **left-hand** adj linke(r, s); **~ bend** Linkskurve f; **~ drive** Linkssteuerung f; **left-handed** adj linkshändig; **left-hand side** n linke Seite

left-luggage locker n Gepäckschließfach nt; **left-luggage office** n Gepäckaufbewahrung f

leftovers npl Reste pl

left wing n linker Flügel; **left-wing** adj (Pol) linksgerichtet

leg [leg] n Bein nt; (of meat) Keule f

legacy ['legəsɪ] n Erbe nt, Erbschaft f

legal ['li:gəl] adj Rechts-, rechtlich; (allowed) legal; (limit, age) gesetzlich; **~ aid** Rechtshilfe f; **legalize** vt legalisieren; **legally** adv legal

legend ['ledʒənd] n Legende f

legible, legibly ['ledʒɪbl, -blɪ] adj, adv leserlich

legislation [ledʒɪs'leɪʃn] n Gesetze pl

legitimate [lɪ'dʒɪtɪmət] adj rechtmäßig, legitim

legroom ['legrʊm] n Beinfreiheit f

leisure ['leʒə'] n (time) Freizeit f ▷ adj Freizeit-; **~ centre** Freizeitzentrum nt; **leisurely** ['leʒəlɪ] adj gemächlich

lemon ['lemən] n Zitrone f; **lemonade** [lemə'neɪd] n Limonade f; **lemon curd** n Brotaufstrich aus Zitronen, Butter, Eiern und Zucker; **lemon juice** n Zitronensaft m; **lemon sole** n Seezunge f

lend [lend] (**lent, lent**) vt leihen; **to ~ sb sth** jdm etw leihen; **to (sb) ~ a hand** (jdm) behilflich sein; **lending library** n Leihbücherei f

length [leŋθ] n Länge f; **4 metres in ~** 4 Meter lang; **what**

~ is it? wie lange ist es?; **for any ~ of time** für längere Zeit; **at ~** *(lengthily)* ausführlich; **lengthen** ['leŋθən] *vt* verlängern; **lengthy** *adj* sehr lange; *(dragging)* langwierig

lenient ['li:nɪənt] *adj* nachsichtig

lens [lenz] *n* Linse *f*; *(Foto)* Objektiv *nt*

lent [lent] *pt, pp of* **lend**

Lent [lent] *n* Fastenzeit *f*

lentil ['lentl] *n (Bot)* Linse *f*

Leo ['li:əʊ] *(pl* **-s)** *n (Astr)* Löwe *m*

leopard ['lepəd] *n* Leopard *m*

lesbian ['lezbɪən] *adj* lesbisch ▷ *n* Lesbe *f*

less [les] *adj, adv, n* weniger; **~ and ~** immer weniger; **(~ often)** immer seltener; **lessen** ['lesn] *vi* abnehmen, nachlassen ▷ *vt* verringern; *(pain)* lindern; **lesser** ['lesə°] *adj* geringer; *(amount)* kleiner

lesson ['lesn] *n (at school)* Stunde *f*; *(unit of study)* Lektion *f*; *(fig)* Lehre *f*; *(Rel)* Lesung *f*; **~s start at 9** der Unterricht beginnt um 9

let [let] *(let, let)* *vt* lassen; *(lease)* vermieten; **to ~ sb have sth** jdm etw geben; **~'s go** gehen wir; **to ~ go (of sth)** (etw) loslassen; **let down** *vt* herunterlassen; *(fail to help)* im Stich lassen; *(disappoint)* enttäuschen; **let in** *vt* hereinlassen; **let off** *vt (bomb)* hochgehen lassen; *(person)* laufen lassen; **let out** *vt* hinauslassen; *(secret)* verraten; *(scream etc)* ausstoßen; **let up** *vi* nachlassen; *(stop)* aufhören

lethal ['li:θəl] *adj* tödlich

let's *contr =* **let us**

letter ['letə°] *n (of alphabet)* Buchstabe *m*; *(message)* Brief *m*; *(official ~)* Schreiben *nt*; **letter bomb** *n* Briefbombe *f*; **letterbox** *n* Briefkasten *m*

lettuce ['letɪs] *n* Kopfsalat *m*

leukaemia, leukemia *(US)* [lu:'ki:mɪə] *n* Leukämie *f*

level ['levl] *adj (horizontal)* waagerecht; *(ground)* eben; *(two things, two runners)* auf selber Höhe; **to be ~ with sb/sth** mit jdm/etw auf gleicher Höhe sein; **~ on points** punktgleich ▷ *adv (run etc)* auf gleicher Höhe, gleich auf; **to draw ~** *(in race)* gleichziehen *(with* mit); *(in game)* ausgleichen ▷ *n (altitude)* Höhe *f*; *(standard)* Niveau *nt*; *(amount, degree)* Grad *m*; **to be on a ~ with** auf gleicher Höhe sein mit *f*; *(ground)* Ebene *f*; **level crossing** *n (Brit)* Bahnübergang *m*; **level-headed** *adj* vernünftig

lever ['li:və°, *(US)* 'levə°] *n* Hebel *m*; *(fig)* Druckmittel *nt*; **lever up** *vt* hochstemmen

liability [laɪə'bɪlɪtɪ] *n* Haftung *f*; *(responsibility)* Belastung *f*; *(obligation)* Verpflichtung *f*; **liable** ['laɪəbl] *adj:* **to be ~ for sth** *(responsible)* für etw haften; **~ for tax** steuerpflichtig

liar ['laɪə°] *n* Lügner(in) *m(f)*

Lib Dem [lɪb'dem] *abbr =* **Liberal Democrat**

liberal ['lɪbərəl] *adj (generous)* großzügig; *(broad-minded)* liberal; **Liberal Democrat** *n (Brit Pol)* Liberaldemokrat(in) *m(f)* ▷ *adj* liberaldemokratisch

liberate ['lɪbəreɪt] *vt* befreien; **liberation** [lɪbə'reɪʃn] *n* Befreiung *f*

Liberia [laɪ'bɪərɪə] *n* Liberia *nt*

liberty ['lɪbətɪ] *n* Freiheit *f*

Libra ['li:brə] *n (Astr)* Waage *f*

library ['laɪbrərɪ] *n* Bibliothek *f*; *(lending ~)* Bücherei *f*

Libya ['lɪbɪə] n Libyen nt

lice [laɪs] pl of **louse**

licence ['laɪsəns] n (permit)
Genehmigung f; (Comm) Lizenz f;
(driving ~) Führerschein m; **license
plate** ['laɪsəns] n (US) see **licence** ▷ vt
genehmigen; **licensed** adj
(restaurant etc) mit
Schankerlaubnis; **license plate** n
(US Auto) Nummernschild nt;
licensing hours npl
Ausschankzeiten pl

lick [lɪk] vt lecken ▷ n Lecken nt

licorice ['lɪkərɪs] n Lakritze f

lid [lɪd] n Deckel m; (eye~) Lid nt

lie [laɪ] n Lüge f; **~ detector**
Lügendetektor m ▷ vi lügen; **to
~ sb** jdn belügen ▷ vi (**lay, lain**)
(rest, be situated) liegen; (~ down)
sich legen; (snow) liegen bleiben;
to be lying third an dritter Stelle
liegen; **lie about** vi herumliegen;
lie down vi sich hinlegen

Liechtenstein ['lɪktənstaɪn] n
Liechtenstein nt

lie in [laɪ'ɪn] n: **to have a
~ ausschlafen**

life [laɪf] n (pl **lives**) n Leben nt; **to
get ~** lebenslänglich bekommen;
there isn't much ~ here hier ist
nicht viel los; **how many lives
were lost?** wie viele sind ums
Leben gekommen?; **life assurance**
n Lebensversicherung f; **lifebelt** n
Rettungsring m; **lifeboat** n
Rettungsboot nt; **lifeguard** n
Bademeister(in) m(f),
Rettungsschwimmer(in) m(f); **life
insurance** n Lebensversicherung
f; **life jacket** n Schwimmweste f;
lifeless adj (dead) leblos; **lifelong**
adj lebenslang; **life preserver** n
(US) Rettungsring m; **life-saving**
adj lebensrettend; **life-size(d)** adj
in Lebensgröße; **life span** n
Lebensspanne f; **life style** n

Lebensstil m; **lifetime** n
Lebenszeit f

lift [lɪft] vt (hoch)heben; (ban)
aufheben ▷ n (Brit: elevator)
Aufzug m, Lift m; **to give sb a ~** jdn
im Auto mitnehmen; **lift up** vt
hochheben; **lift-off** n Start m

ligament ['lɪgəmənt] n Band nt

light [laɪt] (lit o **lighted, lit** o
lighted) vt beleuchten; (fire,
cigarette) anzünden ▷ n Licht nt;
(lamp) Lampe f; **~s** pl (Auto)
Beleuchtung f; (traffic ~s) Ampel f;
in the ~ of angesichts +gen ▷ adj
(bright) hell; (not heavy, easy) leicht;
(punishment) milde; (taxes) niedrig;
~ blue/green hellblau/hellgrün;
light up vt (illuminate) beleuchten
▷ vi (a. eyes) aufleuchten

light bulb n Glühbirne f

lighten ['laɪtn] vi hell werden
▷ vt (give light to) erhellen; (make
less heavy) leichter machen; (fig)
erleichtern

lighter ['laɪtə°] n (cigarette ~)
Feuerzeug nt

light-hearted adj unbeschwert;
lighthouse n Leuchtturm m;
lighting n Beleuchtung f; **lightly**
adv leicht; **light meter** n (Foto)
Belichtungsmesser m

lightning ['laɪtnɪŋ] n Blitz m

lightweight adj leicht

like [laɪk] vt mögen, gernhaben;
he ~s swimming er schwimmt
gern; **would you ~ ...?** hättest
du/hätten Sie gern ...?; **I'd ~ to go
home** ich möchte nach Hause
(gehen); **I don't ~ the film** der
Film gefällt mir nicht ▷ prep wie;
what's it/he ~? wie ist es/er?; **he
looks ~ you** er sieht dir/Ihnen
ähnlich; **~ that/this** so; **likeable**
['laɪkəbl] adj sympathisch

likelihood ['laɪklɪhʊd] n Wahrscheinlichkeit f; **likely** ['laɪklɪ]
adj wahrscheinlich; **the bus is**

~ to be late der Bus wird wahrscheinlich Verspätung haben; **he's not (at all) ~ to come** (höchst)wahrscheinlich kommt er nicht

like-minded [laɪkˈmaɪndɪd] adj gleich gesinnt

likewise [ˈlaɪkwaɪz] adv ebenfalls; **to do ~** das Gleiche tun

liking [ˈlaɪkɪŋ] n (for person) Zuneigung f; (for type, things) Vorliebe f (for für)

lilac [ˈlaɪlək] n Flieder m ⊳ adj fliederfarben

lily [ˈlɪlɪ] n Lilie f; **~ of the valley** Maiglöckchen nt

limb [lɪm] n Glied nt

limbo [ˈlɪmbəʊ] n: **in ~** (plans) auf Eis gelegt

lime [laɪm] n (tree) Linde f; (fruit) Limone f; (substance) Kalk m; **lime juice** n Limonensaft m; **limelight** n (fig) Rampenlicht nt

limerick [ˈlɪmərɪk] n Limerick m (fünfzeiliges komisches Gedicht)

limestone [ˈlaɪmstəʊn] n Kalkstein m

limit [ˈlɪmɪt] n Grenze f; (for pollution etc) Grenzwert m; **there's a ~ to that** dem sind Grenzen gesetzt; **to be over the ~** (speed) das Tempolimit überschreiten; (alcohol consumption) fahruntüchtig sein; **that's the ~** jetzt reicht's!, das ist die Höhe! ⊳ vt beschränken (to auf +akk); (freedom, spending) einschränken; **limitation** [lɪmɪˈteɪʃən] n Beschränkung f; (of freedom, spending) Einschränkung f; **limited** adj begrenzt; **~ liability company** Gesellschaft f mit beschränkter Haftung, GmbH f; **public ~ company** Aktiengesellschaft f

limousine [ˈlɪməziːn] n Limousine f

limp [lɪmp] vi hinken ⊳ adj schlaff

line [laɪn] n Linie f; (written) Zeile f; (rope) Leine f; (on face) Falte f; (row) Reihe f; (US: queue) Schlange f; (Rail) Bahnlinie f; (between A and B) Strecke f; (Tel) Leitung f; (range of items) Kollektion f; **hold the ~** bleiben Sie am Apparat; **to stand in ~** Schlange stehen; **in ~ with** in Übereinstimmung mit; **something along those ~s** etwas in dieser Art; **drop me a ~** schreib mir ein paar Zeilen; **~s** (Theat) Text m ⊳ vt (clothes) füttern; (streets) säumen; **lined** adj (paper) liniert; (face) faltig; **line up** vi sich aufstellen; (US: form queue) sich anstellen

linen [ˈlɪnɪn] n Leinen nt; (sheets etc) Wäsche f

liner [ˈlaɪnə°] n Überseedampfer m, Passagierschiff nt

linger [ˈlɪŋgə°] vi verweilen; (smell) nicht weggehen

lingerie [ˈlænʒəriː] n Damenunterwäsche f

lining [ˈlaɪnɪŋ] n (of clothes) Futter nt; (brake ~) Bremsbelag m

link [lɪŋk] n (connection) Verbindung f; (of chain) Glied nt; (relationship) Beziehung f (with zu); (between events) Zusammenhang m; (Internet) Link m ⊳ vt verbinden

lion [ˈlaɪən] n Löwe m; **lioness** n Löwin f

lip [lɪp] n Lippe f; **lipstick** n Lippenstift m

liqueur [lɪˈkjʊə°] n Likör m

liquid [ˈlɪkwɪd] n Flüssigkeit f ⊳ adj flüssig

liquidate [ˈlɪkwɪdeɪt] vt liquidieren

liquidizer [ˈlɪkwɪdaɪzə°] n Mixer m

liquor [ˈlɪkə°] n Spirituosen pl

liquorice ['lɪkərɪs] n Lakritze f
Lisbon ['lɪzbən] n Lissabon nt
lisp [lɪsp] vt, vi lispeln
list [lɪst] n Liste f ▷ vi (ship)
Schlagseite haben ▷ vt auflisten,
aufzählen; **~ed building** unter
Denkmalschutz stehendes
Gebäude
listen ['lɪsn] vi zuhören, horchen
(for sth auf etw akk); **listen to** vt
(person) zuhören +dat; (radio)
hören; (advice) hören auf; **listener**
n Zuhörer(in) m(f); (to radio)
Hörer(in) m(f)
lit [lɪt] pt, pp of **light**
liter ['liːtə] n (US) Liter m
literacy ['lɪtərəsɪ] n Fähigkeit f
zu lesen und zu schreiben; **literal**
['lɪtərəl] adj (translation, meaning)
wörtlich; (actual) buchstäblich;
literally adv (translate, take sth)
wörtlich; (really) buchstäblich,
wirklich; **literary** ['lɪtərərɪ] adj
literarisch; (critic, journal etc)
Literatur-; (language) gehoben;
literature ['lɪtrətʃə] n Literatur
f; (brochures etc)
Informationsmaterial nt
Lithuania [lɪθjuː'eɪnjə] n Litauen
nt; **Lithuanian** [lɪθjuː'eɪnjən]
▷ adj litauisch; ▷ n (person)
Litauer(in) m(f); (language)
Litauisch nt
litre ['liːtə] n Liter m
litter ['lɪtə] n Abfälle pl; (of
animals) Wurf m ▷ vt: **to be ~ed
with** übersät sein mit; **litter bin** n
Abfalleimer m
little ['lɪtl] adj (smaller,
smallest) klein; (in quantity)
wenig; **a ~ while ago** vor kurzer
Zeit ▷ adv, n (fewer, fewest)
wenig; **a ~** ein bisschen, ein
wenig; **as ~ as possible** so wenig
wie möglich; **for as ~ as £5** ab nur
5 Pfund; **I see very ~ of them** ich
sehe sie sehr selten; **~ by ~** nach

und nach; **little finger** n kleiner
Finger
live [laɪv] adj lebendig; (Elec)
geladen, unter Strom; (TV, Radio:
event) live; **~ broadcast**
Direktübertragung f ▷ [lɪv] vi
leben; (not die) überleben; (dwell)
wohnen; **you ~ and learn** man
lernt nie aus ▷ vt (life) führen; **to
~ a life of luxury** im Luxus leben;
live on vi weiterleben ▷ vt: **to
~ sth** von etw leben; (feed) sich von
etw ernähren; **to earn enough to
~** genug verdienen, um davon zu
leben; **live together** vi
zusammenleben; **live up to** vt
(reputation) gerecht werden +dat;
(expectations) entsprechen +dat;
live with vt (parents etc) wohnen
bei; (partner) zusammenleben mit;
(difficulty) **you'll just have to ~ it**
du musst dich/Sie müssen sich
eben damit abfinden
liveliness ['laɪvlɪnɪs] n Lebhaf-
tigkeit f; **lively** ['laɪvlɪ] adj
lebhaft
liver ['lɪvə] n Leber f
lives [laɪvz] pl of **life**
livestock ['laɪvstɒk] n Vieh nt
living ['lɪvɪŋ] n Lebensunterhalt
m; **what do you do for a ~?** was
machen Sie beruflich? ▷ adj
lebend; **living room** n
Wohnzimmer nt
lizard ['lɪzəd] n Eidechse f
llama ['lɑːmə] n (Zool) Lama nt
load [ləʊd] n Last f; (cargo)
Ladung f; (Tech, fig) Belastung f; **~s
of** (fam) massenhaft; **it was a ~ of
rubbish** (fam) es war
grottenschlecht ▷ vt (vehicle)
beladen; (Inform) laden; (film)
einlegen
loaf [ləʊf] (pl **loaves**) n: **a ~ of
bread** ein (Laib) Brot (m)nt
loan [ləʊn] n (item leant)
Leihgabe f; (Fin) Darlehen nt; **on**

~ geliehen ▷ vt leihen (to sb jdm)

loathe [ləʊð] vt verabscheuen

loaves [ləʊvz] pl of **loaf**

lobby ['lɒbɪ] n Vorhalle f; (Pol) Lobby f

lobster ['lɒbstə°] n Hummer m

local ['ləʊkəl] adj (traffic, time etc) Orts-; (radio, news, paper) Lokal-; (government, authority) Kommunal-; (anaesthetic) örtlich; ~ **call** (Tel) Ortsgespräch nt; ~ **elections** Kommunalwahlen pl; ~ **time** Ortszeit f; ~ **train** Nahverkehrszug m; **the ~ shops** die Geschäfte am Ort ▷ n (pub) Stammlokal nt; **the ~s** pl die Ortsansässigen pl, **locally** adv örtlich, am Ort

locate [ləʊ'keɪt] vt (find) ausfindig machen; (position) legen; (establish) errichten; **to be ~d** sich befinden (in, at in +dat); **location** [ləʊ'keɪʃən] n (position) Lage f; (Cine) Drehort m

loch [lɒx] n (Scot) See m

lock [lɒk] n Schloss nt; (Naut) Schleuse f; (of hair) Locke f ▷ vt (door etc) abschließen ▷ vi (door etc) sich abschließen lassen; (wheels) blockieren; **lock in** vt einschließen, einsperren; **lock out** vt aussperren; **lock up** vt (house) abschließen; (person) einsperren

locker ['lɒkə°] n Schließfach nt; **locker room** n (US) Umkleideraum m

locksmith ['lɒksmɪθ] n Schlosser(in) m(f)

locust ['ləʊkəst] n Heuschrecke f

lodge [lɒdʒ] n (small house) Pförtnerhaus nt; (porter's ~) Pförtnerloge f ▷ vi in Untermiete wohnen (with bei); (get stuck) stecken bleiben; **lodger** n Untermieter(in) m(f); **lodging** n Unterkunft f

loft [lɒft] n Dachboden m

log [lɒg] n Klotz m; (Naut) Log nt; **to keep a ~ of sth** über ein Buch führen; **log in** vi (Inform) sich einloggen; **log off** vi (Inform) sich ausloggen; **log on** vi (Inform) sich einloggen; **log out** vi (Inform) sich ausloggen

logic ['lɒdʒɪk] n Logik f; **logical** adj logisch

logo ['ləʊgəʊ] (pl ~s) n Logo nt

loin [lɔɪn] n Lende f

loiter ['lɔɪtə°] vi sich herumtreiben

lollipop ['lɒlɪpɒp] n Lutscher m; ~ **man/lady** (Brit) Schülerlotse m, Schülerlotsin f

lolly ['lɒlɪ] n Lutscher m

London ['lʌndən] n London nt; **Londoner** n Londoner(in) m(f)

loneliness ['ləʊnlɪnɪs] n Einsamkeit f; **lonely** ['ləʊnlɪ], (esp US) **lonesome** ['ləʊnsəm] adj einsam

long [lɒŋ] adj lang; (distance) weit; **it's a ~ way** es ist weit (to nach); **for a ~ time** lange; **how ~ is the film?** wie lange dauert der Film?; **in the ~ run** auf die Dauer ▷ adv lange; **not for ~** nicht lange; ~ **ago** vor langer Zeit; **before ~** bald; **all day ~** den ganzen Tag; **no ~er** nicht mehr; **as ~ as** solange ▷ vi sich sehnen (for nach); (be waiting) sehnsüchtig warten (for auf); **long-distance call** n Ferngespräch nt; **long drink** n Longdrink m; **long-haul flight** n Langstreckenflug m; **longing** n Sehnsucht f (for nach); **longingly** adv sehnsüchtig; **longitude** ['lɒŋgɪtjuːd] n Länge f; **long jump** n Weitsprung m; **long-life milk** n H-Milch f; **long-range** adj Langstrecken-, Fern-; ~ **missile** Langstreckenrakete f; **long-sighted** adj weitsichtig; **long-standing** adj alt, langjährig; **long-term** adj

langfristig: (car park, effect etc)
Langzeit-; ~ **unemployment**
Langzeitarbeitslosigkeit f; **long
wave** n Langwelle f
loo [luː] n (Brit fam) Klo nt
look [lʊk] n Blick m; (appearance)
~(s) pl Aussehen nt; **I'll have a
~** ich schau mal nach; **to have a
~ at sth** sich dat etw ansehen; **can
I have a ~?** darf ich mal sehen?
▷ vi schauen, gucken; (with prep)
sehen; (search) nachsehen; (appear)
aussehen; **(I'm) just ~ing** ich
schaue nur; **it ~s like rain** es sieht
nach Regen aus ▷ vt: ~ **what
you've done** sieh dir mal an, was
du da angestellt hast; (appear) **he
~s his age** man sieht ihm sein Alter
an; **to ~ one's best** sehr vorteilhaft
aussehen; **look after** vt (care for)
sorgen für; (keep an eye on) aufpassen auf +akk; **look at** vt
ansehen, anschauen; **look back** vi
sich umsehen; (fig) zurückblicken;
look down on vt (fig) herabsehen
auf +akk; **look for** vt suchen; **look
forward to** vt sich freuen auf +akk;
look into vt (investigate) untersuchen; **look out** vi hinaussehen
(of the window zum Fenster); (watch
out) Ausschau halten (for nach); (be
careful) aufpassen, Acht geben (for
auf +akk); ~! Vorsicht!; **look up** vi
aufsehen ▷ vt (word etc)
nachschlagen; **look up to** vt
aufsehen zu
loony ['luːnɪ] adj (fam) bekloppt
loop [luːp] n Schleife f
loose [luːs] adj locker (knot,
button) lose; **loosen** vt lockern;
(knot) lösen
loot [luːt] n Beute f
lop-sided ['lɒp'saɪdɪd] adj schief
lord [lɔːd] n (ruler) Herr m; (Brit:
title) Lord m; **the Lord** (God) Gott
der Herr; **the (House of) Lords**
(Brit) das Oberhaus

lorry ['lɒrɪ] n (Brit) Lastwagen m
lose [luːz] (pt, lost) vt
verlieren; (chance) verpassen; **to
~ weight** abnehmen; **to ~ one's
life** umkommen ▷ vi verlieren;
(clock, watch) nachgehen; **loser** n
Verlierer(in) m(f); **loss** [lɒs] n
Verlust m; **lost** [lɒst] pt, pp of **lose**;
we're ~ wir haben uns verlaufen
▷ adj verloren; **lost-and-found**
(US), **lost property (office)** n
Fundbüro nt
lot [lɒt] n (fam: batch) Menge f,
Haufen m, Stoß m; **this is the first
~** das ist die erste Ladung; **a
~** viel(e); **a ~ of money** viel Geld;
~**s of people** viele Leute; **the
(whole) ~** alles; (people) alle
lotion ['ləʊʃən] n Lotion f
lottery ['lɒtərɪ] n Lotterie f
loud [laʊd] adj laut; (colour)
schreiend; **loudspeaker** n
Lautsprecher m; (of stereo) Box f
lounge [laʊndʒ] n Wohnzimmer
nt; (in hotel) Aufenthaltsraum m;
(at airport) Warteraum m ▷ vi sich
herumlümmeln
louse [laʊs] n (pl lice) n Laus f;
lousy ['laʊzɪ] adj (fam) lausig
lout [laʊt] n Rüpel m
lovable ['lʌvəbl] adj liebenswert
love [lʌv] n Liebe f (of zu); (person,
address) Liebling m, Schatz m;
(Sport) null; **to be in ~** verliebt sein
(with sb in jdn); **to fall in ~** sich
verlieben (with sb in jdn); **to make
~** (with sb) mit jdm schlafen;
(in letter) **he sends his ~** er lässt
grüßen; **give her my ~** grüße sie
von mir; ~, **Tom** liebe Grüße, Tom
▷ vt (person) lieben; (activity) sehr
gerne mögen; **to ~ to do sth** etw
für sein Leben gerne tun; **I'd ~ a
cup of tea** ich hätte liebend gern
eine Tasse Tee; **love affair** n
(Liebes)verhältnis nt; **love letter** n

Liebesbrief m; **love life** n
Liebesleben nt; **lovely** ['lʌvlɪ] adj
schön, wunderschön; (charming)
reizend; **we had a ~ time** es war
sehr schön; **lover** ['lʌvə] n Lieb-
haber(in) m(f); **loving** adj liebevoll
low [ləʊ] adj niedrig; (rank)
niedere(r, s); (level, note, neckline)
tief; (intelligence, density) gering;
(quality, standard) schlecht; (not
loud) leise; (depressed)
niedergeschlagen; **we're ~ on
petrol** wir haben kaum noch
Benzin ▷ n (Meteo) Tief nt;
low-calorie adj kalorienarm;
low-cut adj (dress) tief
ausgeschnitten; **low-emission**
adj schadstoffarm; **lower** ['ləʊə]
adj niedriger; (storey, class etc)
untere(r, s) ▷ vt herunterlassen;
(eyes, price) senken; (pressure)
verringern; **low-fat** adj fettarm;
low tide [ləʊ'taɪd] n Ebbe f
loyal ['lɔɪəl] adj treu; **loyalty** n
Treue f
lozenge ['lɒzɪndʒ] n Pastille f

● **L-PLATES**

Als **L-Plates** werden in
Großbritannien die weißen
Schilder mit einem roten „L"
bezeichnet, die vorn und hinten
an jedem von einem
Fahrschüler gesteuerten
Fahrzeug befestigt werden
müssen. Fahrschüler müssen
einen vorläufigen Führerschein
beantragen und dürfen damit
unter der Aufsicht eines
erfahrenen Autofahrers auf
allen Straßen außer
Autobahnen fahren.

Ltd abbr = **limited** ≈ GmbH f
lubricant ['luːbrɪkənt] n
Schmiermittel nt, Gleitmittel nt
luck [lʌk] n Glück nt; **bad ~** Pech

nt; **luckily** adv glücklicherweise,
zum Glück; **lucky** adj (number, day
etc) Glücks-; **to be ~** Glück haben
ludicrous ['luːdɪkrəs] adj
grotesk
luggage ['lʌgɪdʒ] n Gepäck nt;
luggage compartment n
Gepäckraum m; **luggage rack** n
Gepäcknetz nt
lukewarm ['luːkwɔːm] adj
lauwarm
lullaby ['lʌləbaɪ] n Schlaflied nt
lumbago [lʌm'beɪgəʊ] n Hexenschuss m
luminous ['luːmɪnəs] adj
leuchtend
lump [lʌmp] n Klumpen m; (Med)
Schwellung f; (in breast) Knoten m;
(of sugar) Stück m; **lump sum** n
Pauschalsumme f; **lumpy** adj
klumpig
lunacy ['luːnəsɪ] n Wahnsinn m;
lunatic ['luːnətɪk] adj wahnsinnig ▷ n Wahnsinnige(r) mf
lunch, **luncheon** [lʌntʃ, -ən] n
Mittagessen nt; **to have ~** zu
Mittag essen; **lunch break**, **lunch
hour** n Mittagspause f;
lunchtime n Mittagszeit f
lung [lʌŋ] n Lunge f
lurch [lɜːtʃ] n: **to leave sb in the
~** jdn im Stich lassen
lurid ['ljʊərɪd] adj (colour) grell;
(details) widerlich
lurk [lɜːk] vi lauern
lust [lʌst] n (sinnliche) Begierde
(for nach)
Luxembourg ['lʌksəmbɜːg] n
Luxemburg nt; **Luxembourger**
[lʌksəm'bɜːgə°] n Luxemburger(in)
m(f)
luxurious [lʌg'zʊərɪəs] adj luxuriös, Luxus-; **luxury** ['lʌkʃərɪ] n
(a. luxuries pl) Luxus m; **~ goods**
Luxusgüter pl
lynx [lɪŋks] n Luchs m
lyrics ['lɪrɪks] npl Liedtext m

m

m *abbr* = **metre** m

M *abbr* (street) = **Motorway** A; (size)
= **medium** M

MA *abbr* = **Master of Arts**
Magister Artium m

ma [maː] *n* (fam) Mutti f

mac [mæk] *n* (Brit fam)
Regenmantel m

macaroon [mækə'ruːn] *n*
Makrone f

Macedonia [mæsɪdəʊnɪə] *n*
Mazedonien nt

machine [mə'ʃiːn] *n* Maschine f;
machine gun n
Maschinengewehr nt; **machinery**
[mə'ʃiːnərɪ] n Maschinen pl; (fig)
Apparat m; **machine washable**
adj waschmaschinenfest

mackerel ['mækrəl] *n* Makrele f

macro ['mækrəʊ] (pl **-s**) *n*
(Inform) Makro nt

mad [mæd] *adj* wahnsinnig,
verrückt; (dog) tollwütig; (angry)
wütend, sauer (at auf +akk); (fam)
~ about (fond of) verrückt nach; **to
work like ~** wie verrückt arbeiten;
are you ~? spinnst du/spinnen
Sie?

madam ['mædəm] *n* gnädige
Frau

mad cow disease
[mæd'kaʊdɪ'ziːz] *n* Rinder-
wahnsinn m; **maddening** adj
zum Verrücktwerden

made [meɪd] *pt, pp of* **make**

made-to-measure
['meɪdtə'meʒə°] *adj* nach Maß;
~ suit Maßanzug m

madly ['mædlɪ] *adv* wie verrückt;
(with adj) wahnsinnig; **madman**
['mædmən] (pl **-men**) n
Verrückte(r) m; **madwoman**
['mædwʊmən] (pl **-women**) n
Verrückte f; **madness** ['mædnɪs]
n Wahnsinn m

magazine ['mægəziːn] *n*
Zeitschrift f

maggot ['mægət] *n* Made f

magic ['mædʒɪk] *n* Magie f;
(activity) Zauberei f; (fig: effect)
Zauber m; **as if by ~** wie durch
Zauberei ▷ *adj* Zauber-; (powers)
magisch; **magician** [mə'dʒɪʃən]
n Zauberer m, Zaub(r)erin f

magnet ['mægnɪt] *n* Magnet m;
magnetic [mæg'netɪk] adj
magnetisch; **magnetism**
['mægnɪtɪzəm] n (fig)
Anziehungskraft f

magnificent, magnificently
[mæg'nɪfɪsənt, -lɪ] *adj, adv*
herrlich, großartig

magnify ['mægnɪfaɪ] *vt* vergrößern; **magnifying glass** n
Vergrößerungsglas nt, Lupe f

magpie ['mægpaɪ] *n* Elster f

maid [meɪd] *n* Dienstmädchen
nt; **maiden name** n
Mädchenname m; **maiden
voyage** n Jungfernfahrt f

mail [meɪl] n Post f; (e-mail) Mail
f ▷ vt (post) aufgeben; (send) mit
der Post schicken (to an +akk);
mailbox n (US) Briefkasten m;
(Inform) Mailbox f; **mailing list** n
Adressenliste f; **mailman** n (pl
-men) (US) Briefträger m; **mail
order** n Bestellung f per Post;
mail order firm n Versandhaus
nt; **mailshot** n Mailing nt

main [meɪn] adj Haupt-;
~ **course** Hauptgericht nt; **the
~ thing** die Hauptsache ▷ n (pipe)
Hauptleitung f; **mainframe** n
Großrechner m; **mainland** n
Festland nt; **mainly** adv
hauptsächlich; **main road** n
Hauptverkehrsstraße f; **main
street** n (US) Hauptstraße f

maintain [meɪnˈteɪn] vt (keep
up) aufrechterhalten; (machine,
roads) instand halten; (service)
warten; (claim) behaupten;
maintenance [ˈmeɪntənəns] n
Instandhaltung f; (Tech) Wartung f

maize [meɪz] n Mais m

majestic [məˈdʒɛstɪk] adj
majestätisch; **majesty**
[ˈmædʒɪstɪ] n Majestät f;
Your/His/Her Majesty
Eure/Seine/Ihre Majestät

major [ˈmeɪdʒə°] adj (bigger)
größer; (important) bedeutend;
~ **part** Großteil m; (role) wichtige
Rolle; ~ **road** Hauptverkehrsstraße
f; (Mus) **A** ~ A-Dur nt ▷ vi (US) **to
~ in sth** etw als Hauptfach
studieren

Majorca [məˈjɔːkə] n Mallorca
nt

majority [məˈdʒɒrɪtɪ] n Mehrheit f; **to be in the ~** in der
Mehrzahl sein

make [meɪk] n Marke f ▷ vt
(**made**, **made**) machen;
(manufacture) herstellen; (clothes)
anfertigen; (dress) nähen; (soup)

zubereiten; (bread, cake) backen;
(tea, coffee) kochen; (speech) halten;
(earn) verdienen; (decision) treffen;
it's made of gold es ist aus Gold;
to ~ sb do sth jdn dazu bringen,
etw zu tun; (force) jdn zwingen,
etw zu tun; **she made us wait** sie
ließ uns warten; **what ~s you
think that?** wie kommen Sie
darauf?; **it ~s the room look
smaller** es lässt den Raum kleiner
wirken; **to ~ (it to) the airport**
(reach) den Flughafen erreichen; (in
time) es zum Flughafen schaffen;
he never really made it er hat es
nie zu etwas gebracht; **she didn't
~ it through the night** sie hat die
Nacht nicht überlebt; (calculate) **I
~ it €5/a quarter to six** nach
meiner Rechnung kommt es auf 5
Pfund/nach meiner Uhr ist es
dreiviertel sechs; **he's just made
for this job** er ist für diese Arbeit
wie geschaffen; **make for** vt
zusteuern auf +akk; **make of** vt
(think of) halten von; **I couldn't
~ anything of it** ich wurde daraus
nicht schlau; **make off** vi sich
davonmachen (with mit); **make
out** vi zurechtkommen ▷ vt
(cheque) ausstellen; (list)
aufstellen; (understand) verstehen;
(discern) erkennen; **to ~ (that) ...**
es so hinstellen, als ob ...; **make
up** vt (team etc) bilden; (face)
schminken; (invent: story etc)
erfinden; **to ~ one's mind** sich
entscheiden; **to make (it) up with
sb** sich mit jdm aussöhnen ▷ vi
sich versöhnen; **make up for** vt
ausgleichen; (time) aufholen

make-believe adj Fantasie-;
makeover n gründliche
Veränderung, Verschönerung f;
maker n (Comm) Hersteller(in)
m(f); **makeshift** adj
behelfsmäßig; **make-up** n

Make-up nt, Schminke f; **making**
['meɪkɪŋ] n Herstellung f
maladjusted [mæləˈdʒʌstɪd] adj
verhaltensgestört
malaria [məˈlɛərɪə] n Malaria f
Malaysia [məˈleɪzɪə] n Malaysia
nt
male [meɪl] n Mann m; (animal)
Männchen nt ▷ adj männlich;
~ chauvinist Chauvi m, Macho m;
~ nurse Krankenpfleger m
malfunction [mælˈfʌŋkʃən] vi
nicht richtig funktionieren ▷ n
Defekt m
malice ['mælɪs] n Bosheit f;
malicious [məˈlɪʃəs] adj boshaft;
(behaviour, action) böswillig;
(damage) mutwillig
malignant [məˈlɪɡnənt] adj
bösartig
mall [mɔːl] n (US)
Einkaufszentrum nt
malnutrition [mælnjuːˈtrɪʃən] n
Unterernährung f
malt [mɔːlt] n Malz nt
Malta ['mɔːltə] n Malta nt;
Maltese [mɔːlˈtiːz] adj
maltesisch ▷ n (person)
Malteser(in) m(f); (language)
Maltesisch nt
maltreat [mælˈtriːt] vt schlecht
behandeln; (violently) misshandeln
mammal ['mæməl] n Säugetier
nt
mammoth ['mæməθ] adj
Mammut-, Riesen-
man [mæn] (pl **men**) n (male)
Mann m; (human race) der Mensch,
die Menschen pl; (in chess) Figur f
▷ vt besetzen
manage ['mænɪdʒ] vi zurechtkommen; **can you ~?** schaffst du
es?; **to ~ without sth** ohne etw
auskommen, auf etw verzichten
können ▷ vt (control) leiten;
(musician, sportsman) managen;
(cope with) fertig werden mit; (task,

portion, climb etc) schaffen; **to ~ to
do sth** es schaffen, etw zu tun;
manageable adj (object)
handlich; (task) zu bewältigen;
management n Leitung f;
(directors) Direktion f; (subject)
Management nt,
Betriebswirtschaft f;
management consultant n
Unternehmensberater(in) m(f);
manager n Geschäftsführer(in)
m(f); (departmental ~)
Abteilungsleiter(in) m(f); (of
branch, bank) Filialleiter(in) m(f); (of
musician, sportsman) Manager(in)
m(f); **managing director** n
Geschäftsführer(in) m(f)
mane [meɪn] n Mähne f
maneuver (US) see manoeuvre
mango ['mæŋɡəʊ] (pl **-es**) n
Mango f
man-hour n Arbeitsstunde f
manhunt n Fahndung f
mania ['meɪnɪə] n Manie f;
maniac ['meɪnɪæk] n Wahnsin-
nige(r) mf; (fan) Fanatiker(in)
m(f)
manicure ['mænɪkjʊə°] n
Maniküre f
manipulate [məˈnɪpjʊleɪt] vt
manipulieren
mankind [mænˈkaɪnd] n
Menschheit f
manly ['mænlɪ] adj männlich
man-made ['mænmeɪd] adj
(product) künstlich
manner ['mænə°] n Art f; **in this
~** auf diese Art und Weise; **~s** pl
Manieren pl
manoeuvre [məˈnuːvə°] n
Manöver n ▷ vt, vi manövrieren
manor ['mænə°] n: **~ (house)**
Herrenhaus nt
manpower ['mænpaʊə°] n
Arbeitskräfte pl
mansion ['mænʃən] n Villa f; (of
old family) Herrenhaus nt

415 | **mascara**

manslaughter ['mænslɔ:tə°] n
Totschlag m

mantelpiece ['mæntlpi:s] n
Kaminsims m

manual ['mænjʋəl] adj manuell,
Hand- ▷ n Handbuch nt

manufacture [mænjʋ'fæktʃə°]
vt herstellen ▷ n Herstellung f;
manufacturer n Hersteller m

manure [mə'njʋə°] n Dung m;
(esp artificial) Dünger m

many ['menɪ] (**more**, **most**) adj,
pron viele; **~ times** oft; **not
~ people** nicht viele Leute; **too
~ problems** zu viele Probleme

map [mæp] n Landkarte f; (of
town) Stadtplan m

maple ['meɪpl] n Ahorn m

marathon ['mærəθən] n Marathon m

marble ['mɑ:bl] n Marmor m; (for
playing) Murmel f

march [mɑ:tʃ] vi marschieren
▷ n Marsch m; (protest)
Demonstration f

March [mɑ:tʃ] n März m; see also
September

mare [meə] n Stute f

margarine [mɑ:dʒə'ri:n] n
Margarine f

margin ['mɑ:dʒɪn] n Rand m;
(extra amount) Spielraum m;
(Comm) Gewinnspanne f;
marginal adj (difference etc)
geringfügig

marijuana [mærjʋ'ɑ:nə] n
Marihuana nt

marine [mə'ri:n] adj Meeres-

marital ['mærɪtl] adj ehelich;
~ status Familienstand m

maritime ['mærɪtaɪm] adj See-

marjoram ['mɑ:dʒərəm] n
Majoran m

mark [mɑ:k] n (spot) Fleck m; (at
school) Note f; (sign) Zeichen nt
▷ vt (make ~) Flecken machen auf
+akk; (indicate) markieren;

(schoolwork) benoten, korrigieren,
Flecken machen auf +akk;
markedly ['mɑ:kɪdlɪ] adv merk-
lich; (with comp adj) wesentlich;
marker n (in book) Lesezeichen nt;
(pen) Marker m

market ['mɑ:kɪt] n Markt m;
(stock ~) Börse f ▷ vt (Comm: new
product) auf den Markt bringen;
(goods) vertreiben; **marketing** n
Marketing nt; **market leader** n
Marktführer m; **market place** n
Marktplatz m; **market research** n
Marktforschung f

marmalade ['mɑ:məleɪd] n
Orangenmarmelade f

maroon [mə'ru:n] adj rötlich
braun

marquee [mɑ:'ki:] n großes Zelt

marriage ['mærɪdʒ] n Ehe f;
(wedding) Heirat f (to mit);
married ['mærɪd] adj (person)
verheiratet

marrow ['mærəʋ] n (bone ~)
Knochenmark nt; (vegetable) Kürbis
m

marry ['mærɪ] vt heiraten; (join)
trauen; (take as husband, wife)
heiraten ▷ vi: **to ~ / to get
married** heiraten

marsh [mɑ:ʃ] n Marsch f, Sumpf
m

marshal ['mɑ:ʃəl] n (at rally etc)
Ordner m; (US: police)
Bezirkspolizeichef m

martial arts ['mɑ:ʃəl'ɑ:ts] npl
Kampfsportarten pl

martyr ['mɑ:tə°] n Märtyrer(in)
m(f)

marvel ['mɑ:vəl] n Wunder nt
▷ vi staunen (at über +akk);
marvellous, **marvelous** (US) adj
wunderbar

marzipan [mɑ:zɪ'pæn] n Marzipan m or nt

mascara [mæ'skɑ:rə] n Wimperntusche f

mascot ['mæskɒt] n Maskottchen nt

masculine ['mæskjʊlɪn] adj männlich

mashed [mæʃt] adj ~ potatoes pl Kartoffelbrei m, Kartoffelpüree nt

mask [mɑːsk] n (a. Inform) Maske f ▷ vt (feelings) verbergen

masochist ['mæsəʊkɪst] n Masochist(in) m(f)

mason ['meɪsn] n (stone~) Steinmetz(in) m(f); (freemason) Freimaurer m; **masonry** n Mauerwerk nt

mass [mæs] n Masse f; (of people) Menge f; (Rel) Messe f; ~es of massenhaft

massacre ['mæsəkə°] n Blutbad nt

massage ['mæsɑːʒ] n Massage f ▷ vt massieren

massive ['mæsɪv] adj (powerful) gewaltig; (very large) riesig

mass media ['mæs'miːdɪə] npl Massenmedien pl; **mass-produce** vt in Massenproduktion herstellen; **mass production** n Massenproduktion f

master ['mɑːstə°] n Herr m; (of dog) Besitzer m, Herrchen nt; (teacher) Lehrer m; (artist) Meister m ▷ vt meistern; (language etc) beherrschen; **masterly** adj meisterhaft; **masterpiece** n Meisterwerk nt

masturbate ['mæstəbeɪt] vi masturbieren

mat [mæt] n Matte f; (for table) Untersetzer m

match [mætʃ] n Streichholz nt; (Sport) Wettkampf m; (ball games) Spiel nt; (tennis) Match nt ▷ vt (be like, suit) passen zu; (equal) gleichkommen +dat ▷ vi zusammenpassen; **matchbox** n Streichholzschachtel f; **matching** adj (one item)

passend; (two items) zusammenpassend

mate [meɪt] n (companion) Kumpel m; (of animal) Weibchen nt/Männchen m ▷ vi sich paaren

material [mə'tɪərɪəl] n Material nt; (for book etc, cloth) Stoff m; **materialistic** [mətɪərɪə'lɪstɪk] adj materialistisch; **materialize** [mə'tɪərɪəlaɪz] vi zustande kommen; (hope) wahr werden

maternal [mə'tɜːnl] adj mütterlich; **maternity** [mə'tɜːnɪtɪ] adj: ~ dress Umstandskleid nt; ~ leave Elternzeit f (der Mutter); ~ ward Entbindungsstation f

math [mæθ] n (US fam) Mathe f; **mathematical** [mæθə'mætɪkəl] adj mathematisch; **mathematics** [mæθə'mætɪks] nsing Mathematik f; **maths** [mæθs] nsing (Brit fam) Mathe f

matinée ['mætɪneɪ] n Nachmittagsvorstellung f

matter ['mætə°] n (substance) Materie f; (affair) Sache f; a personal ~ eine persönliche Angelegenheit; a ~ of taste eine Frage des Geschmacks; no ~ how/what egal wie/was; what's the ~? was ist los?; as a ~ of fact eigentlich; a ~ of time eine Frage der Zeit ▷ vi darauf ankommen, wichtig sein; it doesn't ~ es macht nichts; **matter-of-fact** adj sachlich, nüchtern

mattress ['mætrəs] n Matratze f

mature [mə'tjʊə°] adj reif ▷ vi reif werden; **maturity** [mə'tjʊərɪtɪ] n Reife f

maximum ['mæksɪməm] adj Höchst-, höchste(r, s); ~ speed Höchstgeschwindigkeit f ▷ n Maximum nt

may [meɪ] (**might**) vb aux (be

possible) können; *(have permission)* dürfen; **it ~ rain** es könnte regnen; **~ I smoke?** darf ich rauchen?; **it ~ not happen** es passiert vielleicht gar nicht; **we ~ as well go** wir können ruhig gehen

May [meɪ] *n* Mai *m*; *see also* **September**

maybe ['meɪbɪ] *adv* vielleicht

May Day ['meɪdeɪ] *n* der erste Mai

mayo ['meɪəʊ] *(US fam)* *n* Mayo *f*, Mayonnaise *f*

mayonnaise [meɪə'neɪz] *n* Mayo *f*, Mayonnaise *f*, Majonäse *f*

mayor [mɛə*] *n* Bürgermeister *m*

maze [meɪz] *n* Irrgarten *m*; *(fig)* Wirrwarr *nt*

MB *abbr* = **megabyte** MB *nt*

○ **KEYWORD**

me [miː] *pron* **1** *(direct)* mich; **it's me** ich bin's
2 *(indirect)* mir; **give them to me** gib sie mir
3 *(after prep)* (+akk) mich; (+dat) mir; **with/without me** mit mir/ohne mich

meadow ['medəʊ] *n* Wiese *f*

meal [miːl] *n* Essen *nt*, Mahlzeit *f*; **to go out for a ~** essen gehen; **meal pack** *n* *(US)* tiefgekühltes Fertiggericht; **meal time** *n* Essenszeit *f*

mean [miːn] *(pt, pp* **meant, meant)** *vt* *(signify)* bedeuten; *(have in mind)* meinen; *(intend)* vorhaben; **I ~ it** ich meine das ernst; **what do you ~ (by that)?** was willst du damit sagen?; **to ~ to do sth** etw tun wollen; **it was ~t for you** es war für dich bestimmt (o gedacht); **it was ~t to be a joke** es sollte ein Witz sein ▷ *vi:* **he ~s well** er

meint es gut ▷ *adj* *(stingy)* geizig; *(spiteful)* gemein *(to zu)*; **meaning** ['miːnɪŋ] *n* Bedeutung *f*; *(of life, poem)* Sinn *m*; **meaningful** *adj* sinnvoll; **meaningless** *adj* *(text)* ohne Sinn

means [miːnz] *(pl* **means)** *n* Mittel *nt*; *(pl: funds)* Mittel *pl*; **by ~ of** durch, mittels; **by all ~** selbstverständlich; **by no ~** keineswegs; **~ of transport** Beförderungsmittel

meant [ment] *pt, pp of* **mean**

meantime ['miːntaɪm] *adv:* **in the ~** inzwischen; **meanwhile** ['miːnwaɪl] *adv* inzwischen

measles ['miːzlz] *nsing* Masern *pl*; **German ~** Röteln *pl*

measure ['meʒə*] *vt, vi* messen ▷ *n* *(unit, device for measuring)* Maß *nt*; *(step)* Maßnahme *f*; **to take ~s** Maßnahmen ergreifen; **measurement** *n* *(amount measured)* Maß *nt*

meat [miːt] *n* Fleisch *nt*; **meatball** *n* Fleischbällchen *nt*

mechanic [mɪ'kænɪk] *n* Mechaniker(in) *m(f)*; **mechanical** *adj* mechanisch; **mechanics** *nsing* Mechanik *f*; **mechanism** ['mekənɪzəm] *n* Mechanismus *m*

medal ['medl] *n* Medaille *f*; *(decoration)* Orden *m*; **medalist** *(US)*, **medallist** ['medəlɪst] *n* Medaillengewinner(in) *m(f)*

media ['miːdɪə] *npl* Medien *pl*

median strip ['miːdɪən strɪp] *n* *(US)* Mittelstreifen *m*

mediate ['miːdɪeɪt] *vi* vermitteln

medical ['medɪkəl] *adj* medizinisch; *(treatment etc)* ärztlich; **~ student** Medizinstudent(in) *m(f)* ▷ *n* Untersuchung *f*; **Medicare** ['medɪkeə*] *n* *(US)* Krankenkasse *f* für ältere Leute; **medication**

medieval [medɪ'keɪʃən] n Medikamente pl; **to be on ~** Medikamente nehmen; **medicinal** [me'dɪsɪnl] adj Heil-; **~ herbs** Heilkräuter pl; **medicine** ['medsɪn] n Arznei f; (science) Medizin f

medieval [medɪ'iːvəl] adj mittelalterlich

mediocre [miːdɪ'əʊkə°] adj mittelmäßig

meditate ['medɪteɪt] vi meditieren; (fig) nachdenken (on über +akk)

Mediterranean [medɪtə'reɪnɪən] n (sea) Mittelmeer nt; (region) Mittelmeerraum m

medium ['miːdɪəm] adj (quality, size) mittlere(r, s); (steak) halbdurch; **~ (dry)** (wine) halbtrocken; **~ sized** mittelgroß; **~ wave** Mittelwelle f ▷ n (pl **media**) Medium nt; (means) Mittel nt

meet [miːt] (**met, met**) vt treffen; (by arrangement) sich treffen mit; (difficulties) stoßen auf +akk; (get to know) kennenlernen; (requirement, demand) gerecht werden +dat; (deadline) einhalten; **pleased to ~ you** sehr angenehm!; **to ~ sb at the station** jdn vom Bahnhof abholen ▷ vi sich treffen; (become acquainted) sich kennenlernen; **we've met** (before) wir kennen uns schon; **meet up** vi sich treffen (with mit); **meet with** vt (group) zusammenkommen mit; (difficulties, resistance etc) stoßen auf +akk; **meeting** n Treffen nt; (business ~) Besprechung f; (of committee) Sitzung f; (assembly) Versammlung f; **meeting place**, **meeting point** n Treffpunkt m

megabyte ['megəbaɪt] n Megabyte nt

melody ['melədɪ] n Melodie f

melon ['melən] n Melone f

melt [melt] vt, vi schmelzen

member ['membə°] n Mitglied nt; (of tribe, species) Angehörige(r) mf; **Member of Parliament** Parlamentsabgeordnete(r) mf; **membership** n Mitgliedschaft f; **membership card** n Mitgliedskarte f

memento [mə'mentəʊ] (pl **-es**) n Andenken nt (of an +akk)

memo ['meməʊ] (pl **-s**) n Mitteilung f, Memo nt; **memo pad** n Notizblock m

memorable ['memərəbl] adj unvergesslich; **memorial** [mɪ'mɔːrɪəl] n Denkmal nt (to für); **memorize** ['meməraɪz] vt sich einprägen, auswendig lernen; **memory** ['memərɪ] n Gedächtnis nt; (Inform: of computer) Speicher m; (sth recalled) Erinnerung f; **in ~ of** zur Erinnerung an +akk

men [men] pl of **man**

menace ['menɪs] n Bedrohung f; (danger) Gefahr f

mend [mend] vt reparieren; (clothes) flicken ▷ n: **to be on the ~** auf dem Wege der Besserung sein

meningitis [menɪn'dʒaɪtɪs] n Hirnhautentzündung f

menopause ['menəʊpɔːz] n Wechseljahre pl

mental ['mentl] adj geistig; **mentality** [men'tælɪtɪ] n Mentalität f; **mentally** ['mentəlɪ] adv geistig; **~ handicapped** geistig behindert; **~ ill** geisteskrank

mention ['menʃən] n Erwähnung f ▷ vt erwähnen (to sb jdm gegenüber); **don't ~ it** bitte sehr, gern geschehen

menu ['menjuː] n Speisekarte f; (Inform) Menü nt

merchandise ['mɜːtʃəndaɪz] n
Handelsware f; **merchant**
['mɜːtʃənt] adj Handels-

merciful ['mɜːsɪfʊl] adj gnädig;
mercifully adv glücklicherweise

mercury ['mɜːkjʊrɪ] n Quecksilber nt

mercy ['mɜːsɪ] n Gnade f

mere [mɪə°] adj bloß; **merely**
['mɪəlɪ] adv bloß, lediglich

merge [mɜːdʒ] vi verschmelzen;
(Auto) sich einfädeln; (Comm)
fusionieren; **merger** n (Comm)
Fusion f

meringue [məˈræŋ] n Baiser m

merit ['merɪt] n Verdienst nt;
(advantage) Vorzug m

merry ['merɪ] adj fröhlich; (fam:
tipsy) angeheitert; **Merry
Christmas** Fröhliche
Weihnachten!; **merry-go-round** n
Karussell nt

mess [mes] n Unordnung f;
(muddle) Durcheinander nt; (dirty)
Schweinerei f; (trouble)
Schwierigkeiten pl; **in a
~** (muddled) durcheinander; (untidy)
unordentlich; (fig: person) in der
Klemme; **to make a ~ of sth** etw
verpfuschen; **to look a
~** unmöglich aussehen; **mess
about** vi (tinker with)
herummurksen (with an +dat);
(play the fool) herumalbern; (do
nothing in particular)
herumgammeln; **mess up** vt
verpfuschen; (make untidy) in
Unordnung bringen; (dirty)
schmutzig machen

message ['mesɪdʒ] n Mitteilung
f, Nachricht f; (meaning) Botschaft
f; **can I give him a ~?** kann ich
ihm etwas ausrichten?; **please
leave a ~** (on answerphones)
bitte hinterlassen Sie eine
Nachricht; **I get the ~** ich hab's
verstanden

messenger ['mesɪndʒə°] n Bote
m

messy ['mesɪ] adj (untidy)
unordentlich; (situation etc)
verfahren

met [met] pt, pp of **meet**

metal ['metl] n Metall nt;
metallic [mɪˈtælɪk] adj
metallisch

meteorology [miːtɪəˈrɒlədʒɪ] n
Meteorologie f

meter ['miːtə°] n Zähler m;
(parking meter) Parkuhr f; (US) see
metre

method ['meθəd] n Methode f;
methodical [mɪˈθɒdɪkəl] adj
methodisch

meticulous [mɪˈtɪkjʊləs] adj
(peinlich) genau

metre ['miːtə°] n Meter m o nt;
metric ['metrɪk] adj metrisch;
~ system Dezimalsystem nt

Mexico ['meksɪkəʊ] n Mexiko nt

mice [maɪs] pl of **mouse**

mickey ['mɪkɪ] n: **to take the
~ (out of sb)** (fam) (jdn) auf den
Arm nehmen

microchip ['maɪkrəʊtʃɪp] n
(Inform) Mikrochip m; **microphone**
n Mikrofon nt; **microscope** n
Mikroskop nt; **microwave (oven)**
n Mikrowelle(nherd) f(m)

mid [mɪd] adj: **in ~** January
Mitte Januar; **he's in his ~-**forties
er ist Mitte vierzig

midday ['mɪddeɪ] n Mittag m;
at ~ mittags

middle ['mɪdl] n Mitte f; (waist)
Taille f; **in the ~ of** mitten in +dat;
to be in the ~ of doing sth gerade
dabei sein, etw zu tun ▷ adj
mittlere(r, s), Mittel-; **the ~ one**
der/die/das Mittlere;
middle-aged adj mittleren
Alters, **Middle Ages** npl: **the
~** das Mittelalter; **middle-class**
adj mittelständisch; (bourgeois)

bürgerlich; **middle classes** npl:
the ~ der Mittelstand; **Middle
East** n: **the ~** der Nahe Osten;
middle name n zweiter
Vorname

Midlands ['mɪdləndz] npl: **the
~** Mittelengland nt

midnight ['mɪdnaɪt] n Mitternacht f

midst [mɪdst] n: **in the ~ of**
mitten in +dat

midsummer ['mɪdsʌmə°] n
Hochsommer m; **Midsummer's
Day** Sommersonnenwende f

midway [mɪd'weɪ] adv auf
halbem Wege; **~ through the film**
nach der Hälfte des Films;
midweek [mɪd'wiːk] adj, adv in
der Mitte der Woche

midwife ['mɪdwaɪf] (pl -wives) n
Hebamme f

midwinter [mɪd'wɪntə°] n
tiefster Winter

might [maɪt] pt of **may**;
(possibility) könnte; (permission)
dürfte; (would) würde; **they ~ still
come** sie könnten noch kommen;
he ~ have let me know er hätte
mir doch Bescheid sagen können;
I thought she ~ change her mind
ich dachte schon, sie würde sich
anders entscheiden ▷ n Macht f,
Kraft f

mighty ['maɪtɪ] adj gewaltig;
(powerful) mächtig

migraine ['miːgreɪn] n Migräne
f

migrant ['maɪgrənt] n (bird)
Zugvogel m; **~ worker**
Gastarbeiter(in) m(f); Migrant(in)
m(f); **migrate** [maɪ'greɪt] vi
abwandern; (birds) nach Süden
ziehen

mike [maɪk] n (fam) Mikro nt

Milan [mɪ'læn] n Mailand nt

mild [maɪld] adj mild; (person)
sanft; **mildly** adv: **to put it**

~ gelinde gesagt; mildness n
Milde f

mile [maɪl] n Meile f (= 1,609 km);
for ~s (and ~s) = kilometerweit; **~s
per hour** Meilen pro Stunde; **~s
better than** hundertmal besser
als; **mileage** n Meilen pl,
Meilenzahl f; **mileometer**
[maɪ'lɒmɪtə°] n =
Kilometerzähler m; **milestone** n
(a. fig) Meilenstein m

militant ['mɪlɪtənt] adj militant;
military ['mɪlɪtərɪ] adj Militär-,
militärisch

milk [mɪlk] n Milch f ▷ vt
melken; **milk chocolate** n
Vollmilchschokolade f; **milkman**
(pl -men) n Milchmann m; **milk
shake** n Milkshake m,
Milchmixgetränk nt

mill [mɪl] n Mühle f; (factory)
Fabrik f

millennium [mɪ'lenɪəm] n
Jahrtausend n

milligramme ['mɪlɪgræm] n
Milligramm nt; **milliliter** (US),
millilitre n Milliliter m;
millimeter (US), **millimetre** n
Millimeter m

million ['mɪljən] n Million f; **five
~** fünf Millionen; **~s of people**
Millionen von Menschen;
millionaire [mɪljə'neə°] n Mil-
lionär(in) m(f)

mime [maɪm] n Pantomime f
▷ vt, vi mimen; **mimic** ['mɪmɪk]
n Imitator(in) m(f) ▷ vt, vi
nachahmen; **mimicry** ['mɪmɪkrɪ]
n Nachahmung f

mince [mɪns] vt (zer)hacken
▷ n (meat) Hackfleisch nt;
mincemeat n süße Gebäckfüllung
aus Rosinen, Äpfeln, Zucker, Gewürzen
und Talg; **mince pie** n mit
'mincemeat' gefülltes süßes
Weihnachtsgebäck

mind [maɪnd] n (intellect)

Verstand m; (also person) Geist m; **out of sight, out of ~** aus dem Augen, aus dem Sinn; **he is out of his ~** er ist nicht bei Verstand; **to keep sth in ~** etw im Auge behalten; **do you have sth in ~?** denken Sie an etwas Besonderes?; **I've a lot on my ~** mich beschäftigt so vieles im Moment; **to change one's ~** es sich dat anders überlegen ▷ vt (look after) aufpassen auf +akk; (object to) etwas haben gegen; **~ you, ...** allerdings ...; **I wouldn't ~** ... ich hätte nichts gegen ...; **"~ the step"** "Vorsicht Stufe!" ▷ vi etwas dagegen haben; **do you ~ if I ...** macht es Ihnen etwas aus, wenn ich ...; **I don't ~** es ist mir egal, meinetwegen; **never ~** macht nichts

mine [maɪn] pron meine(r, s); **this is ~** das gehört mir; **a friend of ~** ein Freund von mir ▷ n (coalmine) Bergwerk nt; (Mil) Mine f; **miner** n Bergarbeiter(in) m(f)

mineral ['mɪnərəl] n Mineral nt; **mineral water** n Mineralwasser nt

mingle ['mɪŋgl] vi sich mischen (with unter +akk)

miniature ['mɪnɪtʃə] adj Miniatur-

minibar ['mɪnɪbɑː] n Minibar f; **minibus** n Kleinbus m; **minicab** n Kleintaxi n

minimal ['mɪnɪml] adj minimal; **minimize** ['mɪnɪmaɪz] vt auf ein Minimum reduzieren; **minimum** ['mɪnɪməm] n Minimum nt ▷ adj Mindest-

mining ['maɪnɪŋ] n Bergbau m

miniskirt n Minirock m

minister ['mɪnɪstə] n (Pol) Minister(in) m(f); (Rel) Pastor(in) m(f), Pfarrer(in) m(f); **ministry** ['mɪnɪstrɪ] n (Pol) Ministerium nt

minor ['maɪnə] adj kleiner; (insignificant) unbedeutend; (operation, offence) harmlos; **~ road** Nebenstraße f; (Mus) **A ~** a-Moll nt ▷ n (Brit: under 18) Minderjährige(r) mf; **minority** [maɪ'nɒrɪtɪ] n Minderheit f

mint [mɪnt] n Minze f; (sweet) Pfefferminz(bonbon) nt; **mint sauce** n Minzsoße f

minus ['maɪnəs] prep minus, (without) ohne

minute [maɪ'njuːt] adj winzig; **in ~ detail** genauestens ▷ ['mɪnɪt] n Minute f; **just a ~** Moment mal!; **any ~** jeden Augenblick; **~s** pl (of meeting) Protokoll nt

miracle ['mɪrəkl] n Wunder nt; **miraculous** [mɪ'rækjʊləs] adj unglaublich

mirage ['mɪrɑːʒ] n Fata Morgana f, Luftspiegelung f

mirror ['mɪrə] n Spiegel m

misbehave [mɪsbɪ'heɪv] vi sich schlecht benehmen

miscalculation ['mɪskælkjʊ'leɪʃən] n Fehlkalkulation f; (misjudgement) Fehleinschätzung f

miscarriage [mɪs'kærɪdʒ] n (Med) Fehlgeburt f

miscellaneous [mɪsɪ'leɪnɪəs] adj verschieden

mischief ['mɪstʃɪf] n Unfug m; **mischievous** ['mɪstʃɪvəs] adj (person) durchtrieben; (glance) verschmitzt

misconception [mɪskən'sepʃən] n falsche Vorstellung

misconduct [mɪs'kɒndʌkt] n Vergehen nt

miser ['maɪzə] n Geizhals m

miserable ['mɪzərəbl] adj (person) todunglücklich; (conditions, life) elend; (pay, weather) miserabel

miserly ['maɪzəlɪ] adj geizig

misery ['mɪzərɪ] n Elend nt; (suffering) Qualen pl

misfit ['mɪsfɪt] n Außenseiter(in) m(f)

misfortune [mɪs'fɔːtʃən] n Pech nt

misguided [mɪs'gaɪdɪd] adj irrig; (optimism) unangebracht

misinform [mɪsɪn'fɔːm] vt falsch informieren

misinterpret [mɪsɪn'tɜːprɪt] vt falsch auslegen

misjudge [mɪs'dʒʌdʒ] vt falsch beurteilen

mislay [mɪs'leɪ] irr vt verlegen

mislead [mɪs'liːd] irr vt irreführen; **misleading** adj irreführend

misprint ['mɪsprɪnt] n Druckfehler m

mispronounce [mɪsprə'naʊns] vt falsch aussprechen

miss [mɪs] vt (fail to hit, catch) verfehlen; (not notice, hear) nicht mitbekommen; (be too late for) verpassen; (chance) versäumen; (regret the absence of) vermissen; **I ~ you** du fehlst mir ▷ vi nicht treffen; (shooting) danebenschießen; (ball, shot etc) danebengehen; **miss out** vt auslassen ▷ vi: **to ~ on sth** etw verpassen

Miss [mɪs] n (unmarried woman) Fräulein nt

missile ['mɪsaɪl] n Geschoss nt; (rocket) Rakete f

missing ['mɪsɪŋ] adj (person) vermisst; (thing) fehlend; **to be/go ~** vermisst werden, fehlen

mission ['mɪʃən] n (Pol, Mil, Rel) Auftrag m, Mission f; **missionary** ['mɪʃənrɪ] n Missionar(in) m(f)

mist [mɪst] n (feiner) Nebel m; (haze) Dunst m; **mist over, mist up** vi sich beschlagen

mistake [mɪs'teɪk] n Fehler m; **by ~** aus Versehen ▷ irr vt

(**mistook, mistaken**) (misunderstand) falsch verstehen; (mix up) verwechseln (for mit); **there's no mistaking ...** ... ist unverkennbar; (meaning) ... ist unmissverständlich;

mistaken adj (idea, identity) falsch; **to be ~** sich irren, falschliegen

mistletoe ['mɪsltəʊ] n Mistel f

mistreat [mɪs'triːt] vt schlecht behandeln

mistress ['mɪstrɪs] n (lover) Geliebte f

mistrust [mɪs'trʌst] n Misstrauen nt (of gegen) ▷ vt misstrauen +dat

misty ['mɪstɪ] adj neblig; (hazy) dunstig

misunderstand [mɪsʌndə'stænd] irr vt, vi falsch verstehen; **misunderstanding** n Missverständnis nt; (disagreement) Differenz f

mitten ['mɪtn] n Fausthandschuh m

mix [mɪks] n (mixture) Mischung f ▷ vt mischen; (blend) vermischen (with mit); (drinks, music) mixen; **to ~ business with pleasure** das Angenehme mit dem Nützlichen verbinden ▷ vi (liquids) sich vermischen lassen; **mix up** vt (mix) zusammenmischen; (confuse) verwechseln (with mit); **mixed** adj gemischt; **a ~ bunch** eine bunt gemischte Truppe; **~ grill** Mixed Grill m; **~ vegetables** Mischgemüse nt; **mixer** n (for food) Mixer m; **mixture** ['mɪkstʃə*] n Mischung f; (Med) Saft m; **mix-up** n Durcheinander nt, Missverständnis nt

ml abbr = **millilitre** ml

mm abbr = **millimetre** mm

moan [məʊn] n Stöhnen nt; (complaint) Gejammer nt ▷ vi

stöhnen; (complain) jammern,
meckern (about über +akk)

mobile ['məʊbaɪl] adj beweglich;
(on wheels) fahrbar ▷ n (phone)
Handy nt; **mobile phone** n
Mobiltelefon nt, Handy nt

mobility [məʊ'bɪlɪtɪ] n Beweg-
lichkeit f

mock [mɒk] vt verspotten ▷ adj
Schein-; **mockery** n Spott m

mod cons ['mɒd'kɒnz] abbr =
modern conveniences
(moderner) Komfort

mode [məʊd] n Art f; (Inform)
Modus m

model ['mɒdl] n Modell nt;
(example) Vorbild nt; (fashion ~)
Model nt ▷ adj (miniature) Modell-;
(perfect) Muster- ▷ vt (make)
formen ▷ vi: **she ~s for Versace**
sie arbeitet als Model bei Versace

modem ['məʊdem] n Modem nt

moderate ['mɒdərət] adj mäßig;
(views, politics) gemäßigt; (income,
success) mittelmäßig ▷ n (Pol)
Gemäßigte(r) mf ▷ ['mɒdəreɪt] vt
mäßigen; **moderation**
[mɒdə'reɪʃən] n Mäßigung f; **in
~** mit Maßen

modern ['mɒdən] adj modern;
~ history neuere Geschichte;
~ Greek Neugriechisch nt;
modernize ['mɒdənaɪz] vt
modernisieren

modest ['mɒdɪst] adj bescheiden; **modesty** n Bescheidenheit f

modification [mɒdɪfɪ'keɪʃən]
n Abänderung f; **modify**
['mɒdɪfaɪ] vt abändern

moist [mɔɪst] adj feucht;
moisten ['mɔɪsn] vt befeuchten;
moisture ['mɔɪstʃə°] n
Feuchtigkeit f; **moisturizer** n
Feuchtigkeitscreme f

molar ['məʊlə°] n Backenzahn
m

mold (US) see **mould**

mole [məʊl] n (spot) Leberfleck
m; (animal) Maulwurf m

molecule ['mɒlɪkju:l] n Molekül
nt

molest [məʊ'lest] vt belästigen

molt (US) see **moult**

molten ['məʊltən] adj
geschmolzen

mom [mɒm] n (US) Mutti f

moment ['məʊmənt] n Moment
m, Augenblick m; **just a ~** Moment
mal!; **at (o for) a ~** im
Augenblick; **in a ~** gleich

momentous [məʊ'mentəs] adj
bedeutsam

Monaco ['mɒnəkəʊ] n Monaco
nt

monarchy ['mɒnəkɪ] n Monarchie f

monastery ['mɒnəstrɪ] n (for
monks) Kloster nt

Monday ['mʌndeɪ] n Montag m;
see also **Tuesday**

monetary ['mʌnɪtərɪ] adj
(reform, policy, union) Währungs-;
~ unit Geldeinheit f

money ['mʌnɪ] n Geld nt; **to get
one's ~'s worth** auf seine Kosten
kommen; **money order** n
Postanweisung f

mongrel ['mʌŋɡrəl] n
Promenadenmischung f

monitor ['mɒnɪtə°] n (screen)
Monitor m ▷ vt (progress etc)
überwachen; (broadcasts) abhören

monk [mʌŋk] n Mönch m

monkey ['mʌŋkɪ] n Affe m;
~ business Unfug m

monopolize [mə'nɒpəlaɪz] vt
monopolisieren; (fig: person, thing)
in Beschlag nehmen; **monopoly**
[mə'nɒpəlɪ] n Monopol nt

monotonous [mə'nɒtənəs] adj
eintönig, monoton

monsoon [mɒn'su:n] n Monsun
m

monster ['mɒnstə°] n (animal,

thing) Monstrum *nt* ▷ *adj* Riesen-;
monstrosity [mɒnˈstrɒsɪtɪ] *n*
Monstrosität *f*; *(thing)* Ungetüm
nt

Montenegro [mɒntɪˈniːɡrəʊ] *n*
Montenegro *nt*

month [mʌnθ] *n* Monat *m*;
monthly *adj* monatlich; *(ticket,
salary)* Monats- ▷ *adv* monatlich
▷ *n (magazine)* Monatsschrift *f*

monty [ˈmɒntɪ] *n*: **to go the full
~** *(fam: strip)* alle Hüllen fallen
lassen; *(go the whole hog)* aufs
Ganze gehen

monument [ˈmɒnjʊmənt] *n*
Denkmal *nt (to* für); **monumental**
[mɒnjʊˈmentl] *adj (huge)*
gewaltig

mood [muːd] *n (of person)*
Laune *f*; *(a. general)* Stimmung *f*;
**to be in a good/bad
~** gute/schlechte Laune haben;
to be in the ~ for sth zu etw
aufgelegt sein; **I'm not in the
~** ich fühle mich nicht danach;
moody *adj* launisch

moon [muːn] *n* Mond *m*; **to be
over the ~** *(fam)* überglücklich
sein; **moonlight** *n* Mondlicht *nt*
▷ *vi* schwarzarbeiten; **moonlit**
adj (night, landscape) mondhell

moor [mɔː] *n* Moor *nt* ▷ *vt, vi*
festmachen; **moorings** *npl*
Liegeplatz *m*; **moorland** *n*
Moorland *nt*, Heideland *nt*

moose [muːs] *(pl -)* *n* Elch *m*

mop [mɒp] *n* Mopp *m*; **mop up**
vt aufwischen

mope [məʊp] *vi* Trübsal blasen

moped [ˈməʊped] *n (Brit)* Moped
nt

moral [ˈmɒrəl] *adj* moralisch;
(values) sittlich ▷ *n* Moral *f*; **~s** *pl*
Moral *f*; **morale** [mɒˈrɑːl] *n*
Stimmung *f*, Moral *f*; **morality**
[məˈrælɪtɪ] *n* Moral *f*, Ethik *f*

morbid [ˈmɔːbɪd] *adj* krankhaft

◯ **KEYWORD**

more [mɔː°] *adj (greater in number
etc)* mehr; *(additional)* noch mehr;
do you want (some) more tea?
möchtest du/möchten Sie noch
etwas Tee?; **I have no** o **I don't
have any more money** ich habe
kein Geld mehr
▷ *pron (greater amount)* mehr;
(further o *additional amount)* noch
mehr; **is there any more?** gibt es
noch mehr?; *(left over)* ist noch
etwas da?; **there's no more** es ist
nichts mehr da
▷ *adv* mehr; **more
dangerous/easily** *etc* **(than)**
gefährlicher/einfacher *etc* (als);
more and more immer mehr;
more and more excited immer
aufgeregter; **more or less** mehr
oder weniger; **more than ever**
mehr denn je; **more beautiful
than ever** schöner denn je

moreish *adj (food)* **these
crisps are really ~** ich kann mit
diesen Chips einfach nicht
aufhören; **moreover** *adv*
außerdem

morgue [mɔːɡ] *n* Leichen-
schauhaus *nt*

morning [ˈmɔːnɪŋ] *n* Morgen *m*;
in the ~ am Morgen, morgens;
(tomorrow) morgen früh; **this
~** heute morgen ▷ *adj* Morgen-;
(early) Früh-; *(walk etc)*
morgendlich; **morning after pill**
n die Pille danach; **morning
sickness** *n* Schwangerschafts-
übelkeit *f*

Morocco [məˈrɒkəʊ] *n* Marokko
nt

moron [ˈmɔːrɒn] *n* Idiot(in) *m(f)*

morphine [ˈmɔːfiːn] *n* Morphium *nt*

morsel ['mɔːsl] n Bissen m

mortal ['mɔːtl] adj sterblich; (wound) tödlich ▷ n Sterbliche(r) mf; **mortality** [mɔːˈtælɪtɪ] n (death rate) Sterblichkeitsziffer f; **mortally** adv tödlich

mortgage ['mɔːgɪdʒ] n Hypothek f ▷ vt mit einer Hypothek belasten

mortified ['mɔːtɪfaɪd] adj: **I was ~** es war mir schrecklich peinlich

mortuary ['mɔːtjʊərɪ] n Leichenhalle f

mosaic [məˈzeɪɪk] n Mosaik nt

Moscow ['mɒskəʊ] n Moskau nt

Moslem ['mɒzləm] adj, n see **Muslim**

mosque [mɒsk] n Moschee f

mosquito [mɒsˈkiːtəʊ] (pl -es) n (Stech)mücke f; (tropical) Moskito m; **~ net** Moskitonetz nt

moss [mɒs] n Moos nt

most [məʊst] adj meiste pl, die meisten; **in ~ cases** in den meisten Fällen ▷ adv (with verbs) am meisten; (with adj) ...ste; (with adv) am ...sten; (very) äußerst, höchst; **he ate (the) ~** er hat am meisten gegessen; **the ~ beautiful/interesting** der/die/das schönste/interessanteste; **~ interesting** hochinteressant! ▷ n das meiste, der größte Teil; (people) die meisten; **~ of the money/players** das meiste Geld/die meisten Spieler; **for the ~ part** zum größten Teil; **five at the ~** höchstens fünf; **to make the ~ of sth** etw voll ausnützen; **mostly** adv (most of the time) meistens; (mainly) hauptsächlich; (for the most part) größtenteils

MOT abbr = Ministry of Transport; **~ (test)** = TÜV m

motel [məʊˈtel] n Motel nt

moth [mɒθ] n Nachtfalter m; (wool-eating) Motte f; **mothball** n Mottenkugel f

mother ['mʌðə*] n Mutter f ▷ vt bemuttern; **mother-in-law** (pl **mothers-in-law**) n Schwiegermutter f; **mother-to-be** (pl **mothers-to-be**) n werdende Mutter

motif [məʊˈtiːf] n Motiv nt

motion ['məʊʃən] n Bewegung f; (in meeting) Antrag m; **motionless** adj bewegungslos

motivate ['məʊtɪveɪt] vt motivieren; **motive** ['məʊtɪv] n Motiv nt

motor ['məʊtə*] n Motor m; (fam: car) Auto nt ▷ adj Motor-; **Motorail train®** n (Brit) Autoreisezug m; **motorbike** n Motorrad nt; **motorboat** n Motorboot nt; **motorcycle** n Motorrad nt; **motor industry** n Automobilindustrie f; **motoring** ['məʊtərɪŋ] n Autofahren nt; **~ organization** Automobilklub m; **motorist** ['məʊtərɪst] n Autofahrer(in) m(f); **motor oil** n Motorenöl nt; **motor racing** n Autorennsport nt; **motor scooter** n Motorroller m; **motor show** n Automobilausstellung f; **motor vehicle** n Kraftfahrzeug nt; **motorway** n (Brit) Autobahn f

motto ['mɒtəʊ] (pl -es) n Motto nt

mould [məʊld] n Form f; (mildew) Schimmel m ▷ vt (a. fig) formen; **mouldy** ['məʊldɪ] adj schimmelig

moult [məʊlt] vi sich mausern, haaren

mount [maʊnt] vt (horse) steigen auf +akk; (exhibition etc) organisieren; (painting) mit einem Passepartout versehen ▷ vi: **to ~ (up)** (an)steigen ▷ n Passepartout nt

mountain ['mauntɪn] n Berg m;
mountain bike n Mountainbike
nt; **mountaineer** [mauntɪ'nɪə°]
n Bergsteiger(in) m(f);
mountaineering [mauntɪ'nɪərɪŋ]
n Bergsteigen nt; **mountainous**
adj bergig; **mountainside** n
Berghang m

mourn [mɔːn] vt betrauern ▷ vi
trauern (for um); **mourner** n
Trauernde(r) mf; **mournful** adj
trauervoll; **mourning** n Trauer f;
to be in ~ trauern (for um)

mouse [maus] (pl **mice**) n (a.
Inform) Maus f; **mouse mat**,
mouse pad (US) n Mauspad nt;
mouse trap n Mausefalle f

mousse [muːs] n (Gastr) Creme f;
(styling ~) Schaumfestiger m

moustache [mə'stɑːʃ] n
Schnurrbart m

mouth [mauθ] n Mund m; (of
animal) Maul nt; (of cave) Eingang
m; (of bottle etc) Öffnung f; (of river)
Mündung f; **to keep one's ~ shut**
(fam) den Mund halten; **mouthful**
n (of drink) Schluck m; (of food)
Bissen m; **mouth organ** n
Mundharmonika f; **mouthwash** n
Mundwasser nt; **mouthwatering**
adj appetitlich, lecker

move [muːv] n (movement)
Bewegung f; (in game) Zug m; (step)
Schritt m; (moving house) Umzug m;
to make a ~ (in game) ziehen;
(leave) sich auf den Weg machen;
to get a ~ on (with sth) sich (mit
etw) beeilen ▷ vt bewegen;
(object) rücken; (car) wegfahren;
(transport: goods) befördern; (people)
transportieren; (in job)
versetzen; (emotionally) bewegen,
rühren; **I can't ~ it** (stuck, too heavy)
ich bringe es nicht von der Stelle;
to ~ (house) (change place) gehen;
(vehicle, ship) fahren; (move house,

town etc) umziehen; (in game)
ziehen; **move about** vi sich
bewegen; (travel) unterwegs sein;
move away vi weggehen; (move
town) wegziehen; **move in** vi (to
house) einziehen; **move off** vi
losfahren; **move on** vi
weitergehen; (vehicle)
weiterfahren; **move out** vi
ausziehen; **move up** vi (in queue
etc) aufrücken; **movement** n
Bewegung f

movie ['muːvɪ] n Film m; **the ~s**
(the cinema) das Kino; **movie
theatre** n (US) Kino nt

moving ['muːvɪŋ] adj (emotionally) ergreifend, berührend

mow [məʊ] (**mowed**, **mown** o
mowed) vt mähen; **mower** n
(lawn~) Rasenmäher m

mown [məʊn] pp of **mow**

Mozambique [məʊzæm'biːk] n
Mosambik nt

MP abbr = **Member of Parliament**
Parlamentsabgeordnete(r) mf

mph abbr = **miles per hour** Meilen
pro Stunde

MPV abbr = **multi-purpose
vehicle** Mehrzweckfahrzeug nt

MP3 player [empiː'θriː'pleɪə°]
n MP₃-Player m

Mr [mɪstə°] n (written form of
address) Herr

Mrs ['mɪsɪz] n (written form of
address) Frau

Ms [mɪz] n (written form of address
for any woman, married or unmarried)
Frau

MS n abbr = **multiple sclerosis** MS
f

Mt abbr = **Mount** Berg m

much [mʌtʃ] (**more**, **most**) adj
viel; **we haven't got ~ time** wir
haben nicht viel Zeit; **how
~ money?** wie viel Geld? ▷ adv
viel; (with verb) sehr; **~ better** viel
besser; **I like it very ~** es gefällt

mir sehr gut; **I don't like it** ~ ich mag es nicht besonders; **thank you very** ~ danke sehr; **I thought as** ~ das habe ich mir gedacht; ~ **as I like him** so sehr ich ihn mag; **we don't see them** ~ wir sehen sie nicht sehr oft; ~ **the same** fast gleich ▷ *n* viel; **as** ~ **as you want** so viel du willst; **he's not** ~ **of a cook** er ist kein großer Koch

muck [mʌk] *n* (*fam*) Dreck *m*; **muck about** *vi* (*fam*) herumalbern; **muck up** *vt* (*fam*) dreckig machen; (*spoil*) vermasseln; **mucky** *adj* dreckig

mucus ['mjuːkəs] *n* Schleim *m*

mud [mʌd] *n* Schlamm *m*

muddle ['mʌdl] *n* Durcheinander *nt*; **to be in a** ~ ganz durcheinander sein ▷ *vt*: **to** ~ **(up)** durcheinanderbringen; **muddled** *adj* konfus

muddy ['mʌdɪ] *adj* schlammig; (*shoes*) schmutzig; **mudguard** ['mʌdɡɑːd] *n* Schutzblech *nt*

muesli ['muːzlɪ] *n* Müsli *nt*

muffin ['mʌfɪn] *n* (*Brit*) weiches, flaches Milchbrötchen aus Hefeteig, das meist getoastet und mit Butter gegessen wird

muffle ['mʌfl] *vt* (*sound*) dämpfen; **muffler** *n* (*US*) Schalldämpfer *m*

mug [mʌɡ] *n* (*cup*) Becher *m*; (*fam: fool*) Trottel *m* ▷ *vt* (*attack and rob*) überfallen; **mugging** *n* Raubüberfall *m*

muggy ['mʌɡɪ] *adj* (*weather*) schwül

mule [mjuːl] *n* Maulesel *m*

mull over [mʌl 'əʊvə°] *vt* nachdenken über +*akk*

mulled [mʌld] *adj*: ~ **wine** Glühwein *m*

multicolored (*US*), **multicoloured** ['mʌltɪ'kʌləd] *adj* bunt; **multicultural** *adj*

multikulturell; **multi-grade** *adj*: ~ **oil** Mehrbereichsöl *nt*; **multilingual** *adj* mehrsprachig; **multinational** *n* (*company*) Multi *m*

multiple ['mʌltɪpl] *n* Vielfache(s) *nt* ▷ *adj* mehrfach; (*several*) mehrere; **multiple-choice (method)** *n* Multiple-Choice-Verfahren *nt*; **multiple sclerosis** ['mʌltɪplskle'rəʊsɪs] *n* Multiple Sklerose *f*

multiplex ['mʌltɪpleks] *adj*, *n*: ~ **(cinema)** Multiplexkino *nt*

multiplication [mʌltɪplɪ'keɪʃən] *n* Multiplikation *f*; **multiply** ['mʌltɪplaɪ] *vt* multiplizieren (*by* mit) ▷ *vi* sich vermehren

multi-purpose ['mʌltɪ'pɜːpəs] *adj* Mehrzweck-; **multistorey (car park)** *n* Parkhaus *nt*; **multitasking** *n* (*Inform*) Multitasking *nt*

mum [mʌm] *n* (*fam: mother*) Mutti *f*, Mami *f*

mumble ['mʌmbl] *vt*, *vi* murmeln

mummy ['mʌmɪ] *n* (*dead body*) Mumie *f*; (*fam: mother*) Mutti *f*, Mami *f*

mumps [mʌmps] *nsing* Mumps *m*

munch [mʌntʃ] *vt*, *vi* mampfen

Munich ['mjuːnɪk] *n* München *nt*

municipal [mjuː'nɪsɪpəl] *adj* städtisch

mural ['mjʊərəl] *n* Wandgemälde *nt*

murder ['mɜːdə°] *n* Mord *m*; **the traffic was** ~ der Verkehr war die Hölle ▷ *vt* ermorden; **murderer** *n* Mörder(in) *m(f)*

murky ['mɜːkɪ] *adj* düster; (*water*) trüb

murmur ['mɜːmə°] *vt*, *vi* murmeln

muscle ['mʌsl] n Muskel m;
muscular ['mʌskjʊlə°] adj (strong)
muskulös; (cramp, pain etc) Muskel-
nt
museum [mju:'zɪəm] n Museum
nt
mushroom ['mʌʃru:m] n (ess-
barer) Pilz; (button ~) Champignon
m ▷ vi (fig) emporschießen
mushy ['mʌʃi] adj breiig; ~ **peas**
Erbsenmus nt
music ['mju:zɪk] n Musik f;
(printed) Noten pl; **musical** adj
(sound) melodisch; (person)
musikalisch; ~ **instrument**
Musikinstrument nt ▷ n (show)
Musical nt; **musically** adv
musikalisch; **musician**
[mju:'zɪʃən] n Musiker(in) m(f)
Muslim ['mʊzlɪm] adj
moslemisch ▷ n Moslem m,
Muslime f
mussel ['mʌsl] n Miesmuschel f
must [mʌst] (had to, had to) vb
aux (need to) müssen; (in negation)
dürfen; **I ~n't forget** ich darf
das nicht vergessen; (certainty) **he
~ be there by now** er ist
inzwischen bestimmt schon da;
(assumption) **I ~ have lost it** ich
habe es wohl verloren; ~ **you?**
muss das sein? ▷ n Muss nt
mustache ['mʌstæʃ] n (US)
Schnurrbart m
mustard ['mʌstəd] n Senf m; **to
cut the ~** es bringen
mustn't ['mʌsnt] contr of **must
not**
mute [mju:t] adj stumm
mutter ['mʌtə°] vt, vi murmeln
mutton ['mʌtn] n Ham-
melfleisch nt
mutual ['mju:tjʊəl] adj gegenseitig; **by ~ consent** in
gegenseitigem Einvernehmen
my [maɪ] adj mein; **I've hurt
~ leg** ich habe mir das Bein
verletzt

Myanmar ['maɪænma:] n
Myanmar nt
myself [maɪ'self] pron (reflexive)
mich akk, mir dat; **I've hurt ~** ich
habe mich verletzt; **I've bought
~ a flat** ich habe mir eine
Wohnung gekauft; **I need it for
~** ich brauche es für mich (selbst);
(emphatic) **I did it ~** ich habe es
selbst gemacht; (all) **by ~** allein
mysterious [mɪ'stɪərɪəs] adj
geheimnisvoll, mysteriös;
(inexplicable) rätselhaft; **mystery**
['mɪstərɪ] n Geheimnis nt; (puzzle)
Rätsel nt; **it's a ~ to me** es ist mir
schleierhaft; **mystify** ['mɪstɪfaɪ]
vt verblüffen
myth [mɪθ] n Mythos m; (fig:
untrue story) Märchen nt; **mythical**
adj mythisch; (fig: untrue)
erfunden; **mythology**
[mɪ'θɒlədʒɪ] n Mythologie f

n

N *abbr* = **north** N

nag [næg] *vt, vi* herumnörgeln (sb an jdm); **nagging** *n* Nörgelei f

nail [neɪl] *n* Nagel *m* ▷ *vt* nageln (to an); **nail down** *vt* festnageln; **nailbrush** *n* Nagelbürste f; **nail clippers** *npl* Nagelknipser m; **nailfile** *n* Nagelfeile f; **nail polish** *n* Nagellack m; **nail polish remover** *n* Nagellackentferner m; **nail scissors** *npl* Nagelschere f; **nail varnish** *n* Nagellack m

naive [naɪˈiːv] *adj* naiv

naked [ˈneɪkɪd] *adj* nackt

name [neɪm] *n* Name *m*; **his ~ is ...** er heißt ...; **what's your ~?** wie heißen Sie?; (*reputation*) **to have a good/bad ~** einen guten/schlechten Ruf haben ▷ *vt* nennen (*after nach*); (*sth how*) benennen; (*nominate*) ernennen (*as als/zu*); **a boy ~d ...** ein Junge

namens ...; **namely** *adv* nämlich; **name plate** *n* Namensschild *nt*

nan bread [ˈnɑːnˈbred] *n* (*warm serviertes*) *indisches Fladenbrot*

nanny [ˈnænɪ] *n* Kindermädchen *nt*

nap [næp] *n*: **to have/take a ~** ein Nickerchen machen

napkin [ˈnæpkɪn] *n* (*at table*) Serviette f

Naples [ˈneɪplz] *n* Neapel *nt*

nappy [ˈnæpɪ] *n* (*Brit*) Windel f

narcotic [nɑːˈkɒtɪk] *n* Rauschgift *nt*

narrate [nəˈreɪt] *vt* erzählen; **narration** [nəˈreɪʃən], **narrative** [ˈnærətɪv] *n* Erzählung f; **narrator** [nəˈreɪtə°] *n* Erzähler(in) m(f)

narrow [ˈnærəʊ] *adj* eng, schmal; (*victory, majority*) knapp; **to have a ~ escape** mit knapper Not davonkommen ▷ *vi* sich verengen; **narrow down** *vt* einschränken (*to sth auf etw akk*); **narrow-minded** *adj* engstirnig

nasty [ˈnɑːstɪ] *adj* ekelhaft; (*person*) fies; (*remark*) gehässig; (*accident, wound etc*) schlimm

nation [ˈneɪʃən] *n* Nation f; **national** [ˈnæʃənl] *adj* national; **~ anthem** Nationalhymne f; **National Health Service** (*Brit*) staatlicher Gesundheitsdienst; **~ insurance** (*Brit*) Sozialversicherung f; **~ park** Nationalpark m; **~ service** Wehrdienst m; **~ socialism** (*Hist*) Nationalsozialismus m ▷ *n* Staatsbürger(in) m(f)

● **NATIONAL TRUST**
●
● Der **National Trust** ist ein 1895
● gegründeter Natur- und
● Denkmalschutzverband in
● Großbritannien, der Gebäude
● und Gelände von besonderem

• historischen oder ästhetischen
• Interesse erhält und der
• Öffentlichkeit zugänglich
• macht.

nationality [næʃˈnælɪtɪ] n
Staatsangehörigkeit f,
Nationalität f; **nationalize**
[ˈnæʃnəlaɪz] vt verstaatlichen;
nationwide adj, adv landesweit
native [ˈneɪtɪv] adj einheimisch;
(inborn) angeboren, natürlich;
Native American Indianer(in)
m(f); ~ **country** Heimatland nt; **a**
~ **German** ein gebürtiger
Deutscher, eine gebürtige
Deutsche; ~ **language**
Muttersprache f; ~ **speaker**
Muttersprachler(in) m(f) ▷ n
Einheimische(r) mf; (in colonial
context) Eingeborene(r) mf
nativity play [nəˈtɪvɪtɪpleɪ] n
Krippenspiel nt
NATO [ˈneɪtəʊ] acr = **North
Atlantic Treaty Organization**
Nato f
natural [ˈnætʃrəl] adj natürlich;
(law, science, forces etc) Natur-;
(inborn) angeboren; ~ **gas** Erdgas
nt; ~ **resources** Bodenschätze pl;
naturally adv natürlich; (by
nature) von Natur aus; **it comes**
~ **to her** es fällt ihr leicht
nature [ˈneɪtʃə⁰] n Natur f;
(type) Art f; **it is not in my** ~ es
entspricht nicht meiner Art;
by ~ von Natur aus; **nature
reserve** n Naturschutzgebiet nt
naughty [ˈnɔːtɪ] adj (child)
ungezogen; (cheeky) frech
nausea [ˈnɔːsɪə] n Übelkeit f
nautical [ˈnɔːtɪkəl] adj nautisch;
~ **mile** Seemeile f
nave [neɪv] n Hauptschiff nt
navel [ˈneɪvəl] n Nabel m
navigate [ˈnævɪgeɪt] vi navi-
gieren; (in car) lotsen, dirigieren;

navigation [nævɪˈgeɪʃən] n
Navigation f; (in car) Lotsen nt
navy [ˈneɪvɪ] n Marine f; ~ **blue**
Marineblau nt
Nazi [ˈnɑːtsɪ] n Nazi m
NB abbr = **nota bene** NB
NE abbr = **northeast** NO
near [nɪə⁰] adj nahe; **in the**
~ **future** in nächster Zukunft; **that
was a** ~ **miss** (o thing) das war
knapp; (with price) **... or ~est offer**
Verhandlungsbasis ... ▷ adv in der
Nähe; **so** ~ so nahe; **come ~er**
näher kommen; (event) näher
rücken ▷ prep: ~ **(to)** (space) nahe
an +dat; (vicinity) in der Nähe +gen;
~ **the sea** nahe am Meer; ~ **the
station** in der Nähe des Bahnhofs,
in Bahnhofsnähe; **nearby** adj
nahe gelegen ▷ adv in der Nähe;
nearly adv fast; **nearside** n
(Auto) Beifahrerseite f;
near-sighted adj kurzsichtig
neat [niːt] adj ordentlich; (work,
writing) sauber; (undiluted) pur
necessarily [nesəˈserəlɪ] adv
notwendigerweise; **not** ~ nicht
unbedingt; **necessary** [ˈnesəsərɪ]
adj notwendig, nötig; **it's ~ to ...**
man muss ...; **it's not ~ for him to
come** er braucht nicht
mitzukommen; **necessity**
[nɪˈsesɪtɪ] n Notwendigkeit f; **the
bare necessities** das absolut
Notwendigste; **there is no ~ to ...**
man braucht nicht (zu) ..., man
muss nicht ...
neck [nek] n Hals m; (size)
Halsweite f; **back of the ~** Nacken
m; **necklace** [ˈneklɪs] n
Halskette f; **necktie** n (US)
Krawatte f
nectarine [ˈnektərɪn] n Nektarine f
née [neɪ] adj geborene
need [niːd] n (requirement)
Bedürfnis nt (for für); (necessity)

Notwendigkeit f; (poverty) Not f; **to be in ~ of** sth etw brauchen; **if ~(s) be** wenn nötig; **there is no ~ to ...** man braucht nicht (zu) ..., man muss nicht ... ▷ vt brauchen; **I ~ to speak to you** ich muss mit dir reden; **you ~n't go** du brauchst nicht (zu) gehen, du musst nicht gehen

needle ['niːdl] n Nadel f

needless, needlessly ['niːdlɪs, -lɪ] adj, adv unnötig; **~ to say** selbstverständlich

needy ['niːdɪ] adj bedürftig

negative ['negətɪv] n (Ling) Verneinung f; (Foto) Negativ nt ▷ adj negativ (answer) verneinend

neglect [nɪ'glekt] n Vernachlässigung f ▷ vt vernachlässigen; **to ~ to do** sth es versäumen, etw zu tun; **negligence** ['neglɪdʒəns] n Nachlässigkeit f; **negligent** adj nachlässig

negligible ['neglɪdʒəbl] adj unbedeutend; (amount) geringfügig

negotiate [nɪ'gəʊʃɪeɪt] vi verhandeln; **negotiation** [nɪgəʊʃɪ'eɪʃən] n Verhandlung f

neigh [neɪ] vi (horse) wiehern

neighbor (US), **neighbour** ['neɪbə°] n Nachbar(in) m(f); **neighbo(u)rhood** n Nachbarschaft f; **neighbo(u)ring** adj benachbart

neither ['naɪðə°] adj, pron keine(r,s) von beiden; **~ of you/us** keiner von euch/uns beiden ▷ adv: **~ ... nor ...** weder ... noch ... ▷ conj: **I'm not going - ~ am I** ich gehe nicht - ich auch nicht

neon ['niːɒn] n Neon nt; **~ sign** (advertisement) Leuchtreklame f

nephew ['nefjuː] n Neffe m

nerd [nɜːv] n (fam) Schwachkopf m; **he's a real computer ~** er ist ein totaler Computerfreak

nerve [nɜːv] n Nerv m; **he gets on my ~s** er geht mir auf die Nerven; (courage) **to keep/lose one's ~** die Nerven behalten/verlieren; (cheek) **to have the ~ to do** sth die Frechheit besitzen, etw zu tun; **nerve-racking** adj nervenaufreibend; **nervous** ['nɜːvəs] adj (apprehensive) ängstlich; (on edge) nervös; **nervous breakdown** n Nervenzusammenbruch m

nest [nest] n Nest nt ▷ vi nisten

net [net] n Netz nt; **the Net** (Internet) das Internet, **on the ~** im Netz ▷ adj (price, weight) Netto-; **~ profit** Reingewinn m, **netball** n Netzball m

Netherlands ['neðələndz] npl: **the ~** die Niederlande pl

nettle ['netl] n Nessel f

network ['netwɜːk] n Netz nt; (TV, Radio) Sendenetz nt; (Inform) Netzwerk nt; **networking** n Networking nt (das Knüpfen und Pflegen von Kontakten, die dem beruflichen Fortkommen dienen)

neurosis [njʊə'rəʊsɪs] n Neurose f; **neurotic** [njʊə'rɒtɪk] adj neurotisch

neuter ['njuːtə°] adj (Bio) geschlechtslos; (Ling) sächlich

neutral ['njuːtrəl] adj neutral ▷ n (gear in car) Leerlauf m

never ['nevə°] adv nie(mals); **~ before** noch nie; **~ mind** macht nichts!; **never-ending** adj endlos; **nevertheless** [nevəðə'les] adv trotzdem

new [njuː] adj neu; **this is all ~ to me** das ist für mich noch ungewohnt; **newcomer** n Neuankömmling m; (in job, subject) Neuling m

New England [njuː'ɪŋglənd] n Neuengland nt

Newfoundland ['nju:fəndlənd]
n Neufundland nt

newly ['nju:lɪ] adv neu; ~ made
(cake) frisch gebacken;
newly-weds npl Frischvermählte
pl; **new moon** n Neumond m

news [nju:z] nsing (item of ~)
Nachricht f; (Radio, TV)
Nachrichten pl; **good** ~ ein
erfreuliche Nachricht; **what's the**
~? was gibt's Neues?; **have you**
heard the ~? hast du das Neueste
gehört?; **that's ~ to me** das ist mir
neu; **newsagent**, **news dealer**
(US) n Zeitungshändler(in) m(f);
news bulletin n
Nachrichtensendung f; **news flash**
n Kurzmeldung f; **newsgroup** n
(Inform) Diskussionsforum nt,
Newsgroup f; **newsletter** n
Mitteilungsblatt nt; **newspaper**
['nju:speɪpə] n Zeitung f

New Year ['nju:'jɪə] n das
neue Jahr; **Happy ~** (ein) frohes
Neues Jahr!; (toast) Prosit
Neujahr!; **~'s Day** Neujahr nt,
Neujahrstag m; **~'s Eve**
Silvesterabend m; **~'s resolution**
guter Vorsatz fürs neue Jahr

New York [nju:'jɔ:k] n New
York nt

New Zealand [nju:'zi:lənd] n
Neuseeland nt ▷ adj
neuseeländisch; **New Zealander**
n Neuseeländer(in) m(f)

next [nekst] adj nächste(r, s);
the week after ~ übernächste
Woche; **~ time I see him** wenn ich
ihn das nächste Mal sehe; **you're**
~ du bist jetzt dran ▷ adv als
Nächstes; (then) dann, darauf; **~ to**
neben +dat; **~ to last** vorletzte(r,
s); **~ to impossible** nahezu
unmöglich; **the ~ best thing** das
Nächstbeste; **~ door** nebenan

NHS abbr = **National Health**
Service

Niagara Falls [naɪ'ægrə'fɔ:lz]
npl Niagarafälle pl

nibble ['nɪbl] vt knabbern an
+dat; **nibbles** npl Knabberzeug nt

Nicaragua [nɪkə'rægjʊə] n
Nicaragua nt

nice [naɪs] adj nett, sympathisch;
(taste, food, drink) gut; (weather)
schön; **~ and ...** schön ...; **be ~ to**
him sei nett zu ihm; **have a ~ day**
(US) schönen Tag noch!; **nicely** adv
nett; (well) gut; **that'll do ~** das
genügt vollauf

nick [nɪk] vt (fam: steal) klauen;
(capture) schnappen

nickel ['nɪkl] n (Chem) Nickel nt;
(US: coin) Nickel m

nickname ['nɪkneɪm] n
Spitzname m

nicotine ['nɪkəti:n] n Nikotin nt;
nicotine patch n Nikotinpflaster
nt

niece [ni:s] n Nichte f

Nigeria [naɪ'dʒɪərɪə] n Nigeria
nt

night [naɪt] n Nacht f; (before bed)
Abend m; **good ~** gute Nacht!; **at**
(o by) ~ nachts; **to have an early**
~ früh schlafen gehen; **nightcap** n
Schlummertrunk m; **nightclub** n
Nachtklub m; **nightdress** n
Nachthemd nt; **nightie** ['naɪtɪ] n
(fam) Nachthemd nt

nightingale ['naɪtɪŋgeɪl] n
Nachtigall f

night life ['naɪtlaɪf] n
Nachtleben nt; **nightly** adv (every
evening) jeden Abend; (every night)
jede Nacht; **nightmare**
['naɪtmeə] n Albtraum m;
nighttime n Nacht f; **at ~** nachts

nil [nɪl] n (Sport) null

Nile [naɪl] n Nil m

nine [naɪn] num neun; **~ times**
out of ten so gut wie immer ▷ n
(a. bus etc) Neun f; see also **eight**;
nineteen [naɪn'ti:n] num

neunzehn ▷ n (a. bus etc)
Neunzehn f; see also **eight**;
nineteenth adj neunzehnte(r, s);
see also **eighth**; **ninetieth**
['naɪntɪəθ] adj neunzigste(r, s);
see also **eighth**; **ninety** ['naɪntɪ]
num neunzig ▷ n Neunzig f; see
also **eight**; **ninth** [naɪnθ] adj
neunte(r, s) ▷ n (fraction) Neuntel
nt; see also **eighth**

nipple ['nɪpl] n Brustwarze f
nitrogen ['naɪtrədʒən] n Stick-
stoff m

O   **KEYWORD**

no [nəʊ] (pl noes) adv (opposite of
yes) nein; **to answer no** (to
question) mit Nein antworten; (to
request) Nein o nein sagen; **no
thank you** nein, danke
▷ adj (not any) kein(e); **I have no
money/time** ich habe kein
Geld/keine Zeit; **"no smoking"**
„Rauchen verboten"
▷ n Nein nt; (no vote) Neinstimme f

nobility [nəʊ'bɪlɪtɪ] n Adel m;
noble ['nəʊbl] adj (rank) adlig;
(quality) edel ▷ n Adlige(r)
mf
nobody ['nəʊbədɪ] pron niemand; (emphatic) keiner; ~ **knows**
keiner weiß es; ~ **else** sonst
niemand, kein anderer ▷ n
Niemand m
no-claims bonus
[nəʊ'kleɪmzbəʊnəs] n Schadenfreiheitsrabatt m
nod [nɒd] vi, vt nicken; **nod off** vi
einnicken
noise [nɔɪz] n (loud) Lärm m;
(sound) Geräusch nt; **noisy** adj
laut; (crowd) lärmend
nominate ['nɒmɪneɪt] vt (in
election) aufstellen; (appoint)
ernennen

nominative ['nɒmɪnətɪv] n
(Ling) Nominativ m
nominee [nɒmɪ'niː] n Kandi-
dat(in) m(f)
non- [nɒn] pref Nicht-; (with adj)
nicht-, un-; **non-alcoholic** adj
alkoholfrei
none [nʌn] pron keine(r, s); ~ **of
them** keiner von ihnen; ~ **of it is
any use** nichts davon ist
brauchbar; **there are** ~ **left** es sind
keine mehr da; (with comparative)
to be ~ **the wiser** auch nicht
schlauer sein; **I was** ~ **the worse
for it** es hat mir nichts geschadet
nonentity [nɒ'nentɪtɪ] n Null
f
nonetheless [nʌnðə'les] adv
nichtsdestoweniger, dennoch
non-event n Reinfall m;
non-existent adj nicht
vorhanden; **non-fiction** n
Sachbücher pl; **non-iron** adj
bügelfrei; **non-polluting** adj
schadstofffrei; **non-resident** n:
"open to ~**s"** „auch für
Nichthotelgäste"; **non-returnable**
adj: ~ **bottle** Einwegflasche f
nonsense ['nɒnsəns] n Unsinn
m; **don't talk** ~ red keinen Unsinn
non-smoker [nɒn'sməʊkə°] n
Nichtraucher(in) m(f);
non-smoking adj Nichtraucher-;
~ **area** Nichtraucherbereich m;
nonstop adj (train) durchgehend;
(flight) Nonstop- ▷ adv (talk)
ununterbrochen; (travel) ohne
Unterbrechung; (fly) ohne
Zwischenlandung; **non-violent**
adj gewaltfrei
noodles ['nuːdlz] npl Nudeln pl
noon [nuːn] n Mittag m; **at** ~ um
12 Uhr mittags
no one ['nəʊwʌn] pron
niemand; (emphatic) keiner; ~ **else**
sonst niemand, kein anderer
nor [nɔː] conj: **neither ... ~ ...**

weder ... noch ...; **I don't smoke, ~ does he** ich rauche nicht, er auch nicht

norm [nɔːm] n Norm f

normal ['nɔːməl] adj normal; **to get back to ~** sich wieder normalisieren; **normally** adv (usually) normalerweise

north [nɔːθ] n Norden m; **to the ~ of** nördlich von ▷ adv (go, face) nach Norden ▷ adj Nord-; **~ wind** Nordwind m; **North America** n Nordamerika nt; **northbound** adj (in) Richtung Norden; **northeast** n Nordosten m; **to the ~ of** nordöstlich von ▷ adj (go, face) nach Nordosten ▷ adj Nordost-; **northern** ['nɔːðən] adj nördlich; **~ France** Nordfrankreich nt; **Northern Ireland** n Nordirland nt; **North Pole** n Nordpol m; **North Sea** n Nordsee f; **northwards** adv nach Norden; **northwest** n Nordwesten m; **to the ~ of** nordwestlich von ▷ adj (go, face) nach Nordwesten ▷ adj Nordwest-

Norway ['nɔːweɪ] n Norwegen nt; **Norwegian** [nɔːˈwiːdʒən] adj norwegisch ▷ n (person) Norweger(in) m(f); (language) Norwegisch nt

nos. abbr = **numbers** Nr.

nose [nəʊz] n Nase f; **nose around** vi herumschnüffeln; **nosebleed** n Nasenbluten nt; **nose-dive** n Sturzflug m; **to take a ~** abstürzen

nosey ['nəʊzɪ] see **nosy**

nostalgia [nɒˈstældʒɪə] n Nostalgie f (for nach); **nostalgic** adj nostalgisch

nostril ['nɒstrɪl] n Nasenloch nt

nosy ['nəʊzɪ] adj neugierig

not [nɒt] adv nicht; **~ a** kein; **~ one of them** kein einziger von ihnen; **he is ~ an expert** er ist kein

Experte; **I told him ~ to (do it)** ich sagte ihm, er solle es nicht tun; **~ at all** überhaupt nicht, keineswegs; (don't mention it) gern geschehen; **~ yet** noch nicht

notable ['nəʊtəbl] adj bemerkenswert; **note** [nəʊt] n (written) Notiz f; (short letter) paar Zeilen pl; (on scrap of paper) Zettel m; (comment in book etc) Anmerkung f; (bank~) Schein m; (Mus: sign) Note f; (sound) Ton m; **to make a ~ of sth** sich dat etw notieren; **~s** (of lecture etc) Aufzeichnungen pl; **to take ~s** sich dat Notizen machen (of über +akk) ▷ vt (notice) bemerken (that dass); (write down) notieren; **notebook** n Notizbuch nt; (Inform) Notebook nt; **notepad** n Notizblock m; **notepaper** n Briefpapier nt

nothing ['nʌθɪŋ] n nichts; **~ but ... lauter ...; for ~** umsonst; **he thinks ~ of it** er macht sich nichts daraus

notice ['nəʊtɪs] n (announcement) Bekanntmachung f; (on ~ board) Anschlag m; (attention) Beachtung f; (advance warning) Ankündigung f; (to leave job, flat etc) Kündigung f; **at short ~** kurzfristig; **until further ~** bis auf weiteres; **to give sb ~** jdm kündigen; **to hand in one's ~** kündigen; **to take (no) ~ of (sth)** etw (nicht) beachten; **take no ~** kümmere dich nicht darum! ▷ vt bemerken; **noticeable** adj erkennbar; (visible) sichtbar; **to be ~** auffallen; **notice board** n Anschlagtafel f

notification [nəʊtɪfɪˈkeɪʃən] n Benachrichtigung f (of von); **notify** ['nəʊtɪfaɪ] vt benachrichtigen (of von)

notion ['nəʊʃən] n Idee f

notorious [nəʊˈtɔːrɪəs] adj berüchtigt

nought [nɔːt] n Null f
noun [naʊn] n Substantiv nt
nourish ['nʌrɪʃ] vt nähren;
nourishing adj nahrhaft;
nourishment n Nahrung f
novel ['nɒvəl] n Roman m ▷ adj
neuartig; **novelist** n
Schriftsteller(in) m(f); **novelty** n
Neuheit f
November [nəʊ'vembə⁰] n
November m; see also **September**
novice ['nɒvɪs] n Neuling m
now [naʊ] adv (at the moment)
jetzt; (introductory phrase) also;
right ~ jetzt gleich; **just ~** gerade;
by ~ inzwischen; **from ~ on** ab
jetzt; **~ and again** o (then) ab und
zu; **nowadays** adv heutzutage
nowhere ['nəʊweə⁰] adv nirgends; **we're getting ~** wir
kommen nicht weiter; **~ near**
noch lange nicht
nozzle ['nɒzl] n Düse f
nuclear ['njuːklɪə⁰] adj (energy
etc) Kern-; **~ power station**
Kernkraftwerk nt; **nuclear waste**
n Atommüll m
nude [njuːd] adj nackt ▷ n (person) Nackte(r) mf; (painting etc) Akt
m
nudge [nʌdʒ] vt stupsen; **nudist**
['njuːdɪst] n Nudist(in) m(f),
FKK-Anhänger(in) m(f); **nudist
beach** n FKK-Strand m
nuisance ['njuːsns] n Ärgernis
nt; (person) Plage f; **what a ~** wie
ärgerlich!
nuke [njuːk] (US fam) n (bomb)
Atombombe f ▷ vt eine
Atombombe werfen auf +akk
numb [nʌm] adj taub, gefühllos
▷ vt betäuben
number ['nʌmbə⁰] n Nummer f;
(Math) Zahl f; (quantity) (An)zahl f;
in small/large ~s in
kleinen/großen Mengen; **a ~ of
times** mehrmals ▷ vt (give a

number to) nummerieren; (count)
zählen (among zu); **his days are
~ed** seine Tage sind gezählt;
number plate n (Brit Auto)
Nummernschild nt
numeral ['njuːmərəl] n Ziffer f;
numerical [njuː'merɪkəl] adj
numerisch; (superiority)
zahlenmäßig; **numerous**
['njuːmərəs] adj zahlreich
nun [nʌn] n Nonne f
Nuremberg ['njuərəmbɜːg] n
Nürnberg nt
nurse [nɜːs] n Krankenschwester
f; (male ~) Krankenpfleger m ▷ vt
(patient) pflegen, (baby) stillen;
nursery n Kinderzimmer nt; (for
infants) Kinderkrippe f, (for
children) Kindergarten m;
Baumschule f; **nursery rhyme** n
Kinderreim m; **nursery school** n
Kindergarten m; **~ teacher**
Kindergärtner(in) m(f),
Erzieher(in) m(f); **nursing** n
(profession) Krankenpflege f;
~ home Privatklinik f
nut [nʌt] n Nuss f; (Tech: for bolt)
Mutter f; **nutcase** n (fam)
Spinner(in) m(f); **nutcracker** n,
nutcrackers npl Nussknacker m
nutmeg ['nʌtmeg] n Muskat m,
Muskatnuss f
nutrient ['njuːtrɪənt] n Nährstoff
m
nutrition [njuː'trɪʃən] n Ernährung f; **nutritious** [njuː'trɪʃəs]
adj nahrhaft
nuts [nʌts] (fam) adj verrückt; **to
be ~ about sth** nach etw verrückt
sein ▷ npl (testicles) Eier pl
nutshell ['nʌtʃel] n Nussschale f;
in a ~ kurz gesagt
nutter ['nʌtə⁰] n (fam)
Spinner(in) m(f); **nutty** ['nʌtɪ]
adj (fam) verrückt
NW abbr = **northwest** NW
nylon ['naɪlɒn] n Nylon® nt
▷ adj Nylon-

O

O [əʊ] n (Tel) Null f

oak [əʊk] n Eiche f ▷ adj Eichen-

OAP abbr = **old-age pensioner**
Rentner(in) m(f)

oar [ɔː°] n Ruder nt

oasis [əʊˈeɪsɪs] n (pl **oases**) n Oase f

oatcake [ˈəʊtkeɪk] n Haferkeks m

oath [əʊθ] n (statement) Eid m

oats [əʊts] npl Hafer m; (Gastr) Haferflocken pl

obedience [əˈbiːdɪəns] n Gehorsam m; **obedient** adj gehorsam; **obey** [əˈbeɪ] vt, vi gehorchen +dat

object [ˈɒbdʒekt] n Gegenstand m; (abstract) Objekt nt; (purpose) Ziel n ▷ [əbˈdʒekt] vi dagegen sein; (raise objection) Einwände erheben (to gegen); (morally) Anstoß nehmen (to an +dat); **do you ~ to my smoking?** haben Sie etwas dagegen, wenn ich rauche?; **objection** [əbˈdʒekʃən] n Einwand m

objective [əbˈdʒektɪv] n Ziel nt ▷ adj objektiv; **objectivity** [ɒbdʒekˈtɪvɪtɪ] n Objektivität f

obligation [ɒblɪˈgeɪʃən] n (duty) Pflicht f; (commitment) Verpflichtung f; **no ~** unverbindlich; **obligatory** [əˈblɪɡətərɪ] adj obligatorisch; **oblige** [əˈblaɪdʒ] vt: **to ~ sb to do sth** jdn (dazu) zwingen, etw zu tun; **he felt ~d to accept the offer** er fühlte sich verpflichtet, das Angebot anzunehmen

oblique [əˈbliːk] adj schräg; (angle) schief

oboe [ˈəʊbəʊ] n Oboe f

obscene [əbˈsiːn] adj obszön

obscure [əbˈskjʊə°] adj unklar; (unknown) unbekannt

observant [əbˈzɜːvənt] adj aufmerksam; **observation** [ɒbzəˈveɪʃən] n (watching) Beobachtung f; (remark) Bemerkung f; **observe** [əbˈzɜːv] vt (notice) bemerken; (watch) beobachten; (customs) einhalten

obsessed [əbˈsest] adj besessen (with an idea etc von einem Gedanken etc); **obsession** [əbˈseʃən] n Manie f

obsolete [ˈɒbsəliːt] adj veraltet

obstacle [ˈɒbstəkl] n Hindernis nt (to für); **to be an ~ to sth** einer Sache im Weg stehen

obstinate [ˈɒbstɪnət] adj hartnäckig

obstruct [əbˈstrʌkt] vt versperren; (pipe) verstopfen; (hinder) behindern, aufhalten; **obstruction** [əbˈstrʌkʃən] n Blockierung f; (of pipe) Verstopfung f; (obstacle) Hindernis nt

obtain [əbˈteɪn] vt erhalten; **obtainable** adj erhältlich

obvious [ˈɒbvɪəs] *adj* offensichtlich; **it was ~ to me that ...** es war mir klar, dass ...; **obviously** *adj* offensichtlich

occasion [əˈkeɪʒən] *n* Gelegenheit *f*; (*special event*) (großes) Ereignis; **on the ~ of** anlässlich +*gen*; **special** ~ besonderer Anlass; **occasional, occasionally** *adj, adv* gelegentlich

occupant [ˈɒkjʊpənt] *n* (*of house*) Bewohner(in) *m(f)*; (*of vehicle*) Insasse *m*, Insassin *f*; **occupation** [ɒkjʊˈpeɪʃən] *n* Beruf *m*; (*pastime*) Beschäftigung *f*; (*of country etc*) Besetzung *f*; **occupied** *adj* (*country, seat, toilet*) besetzt; (*person*) beschäftigt; **to keep sb/oneself ~** jdn/sich beschäftigen; **occupy** [ˈɒkjʊpaɪ] *vt* (*country*) besetzen; (*time*) beanspruchen; (*mind, person*) beschäftigen

occur [əˈkɜː] *vi* vorkommen; **~ to sb** jdm einfallen; **occurrence** [əˈkʌrəns] *n* (*event*) Ereignis *nt*; (*presence*) Vorkommen *nt*

ocean [ˈəʊʃən] *n* Ozean *m*; (*US: sea*) das Meer *nt*

o'clock [əˈklɒk] *adv*: **5 ~** 5 Uhr; **at 10 ~** um 10 Uhr

octagon [ˈɒktəgən] *n* Achteck *nt*

October [ɒkˈtəʊbə] *n* Oktober *m*; *see also* **September**

octopus [ˈɒktəpəs] *n* Tintenfisch *m*

odd [ɒd] *adj* (*strange*) sonderbar; (*not even*) ungerade; (*one missing*) einzeln; **to be the ~ one out** nicht dazugehören; **~ jobs** Gelegenheitsarbeiten *pl*; **odds** *npl* Chancen *pl*; **against all ~** entgegen allen Erwartungen; **~ and ends** (*fam*) Kleinkram *pl*

odometer [əʊˈdɒmətə°] *n* (*US Auto*) Meilenzähler *m*

odor (*US*), **odour** [ˈəʊdə°] *n* Geruch *m*

O KEYWORD

of [ɒv, əv] *prep* **1** von +*dat* = use of gen; **the history of Germany** die Geschichte Deutschlands; **a friend of ours** ein Freund von uns; **a boy of 10** ein 10-jähriger Junge; **that was kind of you** das war sehr freundlich von Ihnen **2** (*expressing quantity, amount, dates etc*) **a kilo of flour** ein Kilo Mehl; **how much of this do you need?** wie viel brauchst Sie (davon)?; **there were 3 of them** (*people*) sie waren zu dritt; (*objects*) es gab 3 (davon); **a cup of tea/vase of flowers** eine Tasse Tee/Vase mit Blumen; **the 5th of July** der 5. Juli **3** (*from, out of*) aus; **a bridge made of wood** eine Holzbrücke, eine Brücke aus Holz

off [ɒf] *adv* (*away*) weg, fort; (*free*) frei; (*switch*) ausgeschaltet; (*milk*) sauer; **a mile ~** eine Meile entfernt; **I'll be ~ now** ich gehe jetzt; **to have the day/Monday ~** heute/Montag freihaben; **the lights are ~** die Lichter sind aus; **the concert is ~** das Konzert fällt aus; **I get 10 % ~** ich habe 10 % Nachlass bekommen ▸ *prep* (*away from*) von; **to jump/fall ~ the roof** vom Dach springen/fallen; **to get ~ the bus** aus dem Bus aussteigen; **he's ~ work/school** er hat frei/schulfrei; **to take £20 ~ the price** den Preis um 20 Pfund herabsetzen

offence [əˈfens] *n* (*crime*) Straftat *f*; (*minor*) Vergehen *nt*; (*to feelings*) Kränkung *f*; **to cause/take ~** Anstoß

erregen/nehmen; **offend** [əˈfend]
vt kränken; (eye, ear) beleidigen;
offender n Straffällige(r) mf;
offense (US) see offence
offensive [əˈfensɪv] adj anstößig;
(insulting) beleidigend; (smell) übel,
abstoßend ⊳ n (Mil) Offensive f
offer [ˈɒfə°] n Angebot nt; **on**
~ (Comm) im Angebot ⊳ vt
anbieten (to sb jdm); (money, a
chance etc) bieten
offhand [ɒfˈhænd] adj lässig
⊳ adv (say) auf Anhieb
office [ˈɒfɪs] n Büro nt; (position)
Amt nt; **doctor's** ~ (US) Arztpraxis
f; **office block** n Bürogebäude nt;
office hours npl Dienstzeit f;
(notice) Geschäftszeiten pl; **officer**
[ˈɒfɪsə°] n (Mil) Offizier(in) m(f);
(official) Polizeibeamte(r) m,
Polizeibeamtin f; **office worker**
[ˈɒfɪsˌwɜːkə°] n Büroangestellte/r
mf; **official** [əˈfɪʃəl] adj offiziell;
(report etc) amtlich; ~ **language**
Amtssprache f ⊳ n Beamte(r) m,
Beamtin f, Repräsentant(in)
m(f)
off-licence [ˈɒflaɪsəns] n (Brit)
Wein- und Spirituosenhandlung f
off-line adj (Inform) offline;
off-peak adj außerhalb der
Stoßzeiten; (rate, ticket) verbilligt;
off-putting adj abstoßend,
entmutigend, irritierend;
off-season adj außerhalb der
Saison
offshore [ˈɒfʃɔː°] adj küstennah,
Küsten-; (oil rig) im Meer; **offside**
[ˈɒfˈsaɪd] n (Auto) Fahrerseite f;
(Sport) Abseits nt
often [ˈɒfən] adv oft; **every so**
~ von Zeit zu Zeit
oil [ɔɪl] n Öl nt ⊳ vt ölen; **oil level**
n Ölstand m; **oil painting** n
Ölgemälde nt; **oil-rig** n
(Öl)bohrinsel f; **oil slick** n
Ölteppich m; **oil tanker** n

Öltanker m; (truck) Tankwagen m;
oily adj ölig; (skin, hair) fettig
ointment [ˈɔɪntmənt] n Salbe f
OK, okay [əʊˈkeɪ] adj (fam) okay,
in Ordnung; **that's ~ by** (o **with**)
me das ist mir recht
old [əʊld] adj alt; **old age** n Alter
nt; ~ **pension** Rente f; ~ **pensioner**
Rentner(in) m(f); **old-fashioned**
adj altmodisch; **old people's**
home n Altersheim nt
olive [ˈɒlɪv] n Olive f; **olive oil** n
Olivenöl nt
Olympic [əʊˈlɪmpɪk] adj olympisch; **the ~ Games, the ~s** pl die
Olympischen Spiele pl, die
Olympiade
omelette [ˈɒmlət] n Omelett nt
omission [əʊˈmɪʃən] n Auslas-
sung f; **omit** [əʊˈmɪt] vt
auslassen

⬤ **KEYWORD**

on [ɒn] prep **1**(indicating position)
auf +dat; (with vb of motion) auf
+akk; (on vertical surface, part of
body) an +dat/akk; **it's on the table**
es ist auf dem Tisch; **she put the**
book on the table sie legte das
Buch auf den Tisch; **on the left**
links

2 (indicating means, method,
condition etc) **on foot** (go, be) zu
Fuß; **on the train/plane** (go) mit
dem Zug/Flugzeug; (be) im
Zug/Flugzeug; **on the**
telephone/television am
Telefon/im Fernsehen; **to be on**
drugs Drogen nehmen; **to be on**
holiday/business im Urlaub/auf
Geschäftsreise sein

3 (referring to time) **on Friday** (am)
Freitag; **on Fridays** freitags; **on**
June 20th am 20. Juni; **a week on**
Friday Freitag in einer Woche; **on**
arrival he ... als er ankam, ... er ...

4 (about, concerning) über +akk
▷ adv **1** (referring to dress) an; **she put her boots/hat on** sie zog ihre Stiefel an/setzte ihren Hut auf **2** (further, continuously) weiter; **to walk on** weitergehen
▷ adj **1** (functioning, in operation: machine, TV, light) an; (tap) aufgedreht; (brakes) angezogen; **is the meeting still on?** findet die Versammlung noch statt?; **there's a good film on** es läuft ein guter Film
2 that's not on! (inf) (of behaviour) das ist nicht drin!

once [wʌns] adv (one time, in the past) einmal; **at ~** sofort; (at the same time) gleichzeitig; **~ more** noch einmal; **for ~** ausnahmsweise (einmal); **~ in a while** ab und zu mal ▷ conj wenn ... einmal; **~ you've got used to it** sobald Sie sich daran gewöhnt haben

oncoming ['ɒnkʌmɪŋ] adj entgegenkommend; **~ traffic** Gegenverkehr m

KEYWORD

one [wʌn] num eins; (with noun, referring back to noun) ein/eine/ein; **it is one (o'clock)** es ist eins, es ist ein Uhr; **one hundred and fifty** einhundertfünfzig
▷ adj **1** (sole) einzige(r, s); **the one book which** das einzige Buch, welches
2 (same) derselbe/dieselbe/dasselbe; **they came in the one car** sie kamen alle in dem einen Auto
3 (indef) **one day I discovered** eines Tages bemerkte ich ...
▷ pron **1** eine(r, s); **do you have a red one?** haben Sie einen

roten/eine rote/ein rotes?; **this one** diese(r, s); **that one** der/die/das; **which one?** welche(r, s)?; **one by one** einzeln
2 one another einander; **do you two ever see one another?** seht ihr beide euch manchmal?
3 (impers) man; **one never knows** man kann nie wissen; **to cut one's finger** sich in den Finger schneiden

one-off adj einmalig ▷ n: **a ~** etwas Einmaliges; **one-parent family** n Einelternfamilie f; **one-piece** adj einteilig; **oneself** pron (reflexive) sich; **one-way** adj: **~ street** Einbahnstraße f; **~ ticket** (US) einfache Fahrkarte

onion ['ʌnjən] n Zwiebel f

on-line ['ɒnlaɪn] adj (Inform) online; **~ banking** Homebanking nt

only ['əʊnlɪ] adv nur; (with time) erst; **~ yesterday** erst gestern; **he's ~ four** er ist erst vier; **~ just arrived** gerade erst angekommen
▷ adj einzige(r, s); **~ child** Einzelkind nt

o.n.o. abbr = **or nearest offer** VB

onside ['ɒn'saɪd] adj (Sport) nicht im Abseits

onto ['ɒntu] prep auf +akk; (vertical surface) an +akk; **to be ~ sb** jdm auf die Schliche gekommen sein

onwards ['ɒnwədz] adv voran, vorwärts; **from today ~** von heute an, ab heute

open ['əʊpən] adj offen; **in the ~ air** im Freien; **~ to the public** für die Öffentlichkeit zugänglich; **the shop is ~ all day** das Geschäft hat den ganzen Tag offen ▷ vt öffnen, aufmachen; (meeting, account, new building) eröffnen; (*road*) dem Verkehr übergeben ▷ *vi* (*door, window etc*) aufgehen, sich öffnen; (*shop, bank*) öffnen, aufmachen; (*begin*) anfangen (*with* mit); **open-air** *adj* Freiluft-; **open day** *n* Tag *m* der offenen Tür; **opening** *n* Öffnung *f*; (*beginning*) Anfang *m*; (*official, of exhibition etc*) Eröffnung *f*; (*opportunity*) Möglichkeit *f*; **~ hours** (*o* **times**) Öffnungszeiten *pl*; **openly** *adv* offen; **open-minded** *adj* aufgeschlossen; **open-plan** *adj*: **~ office** Großraumbüro *nt*

opera ['ɒpərə] *n* Oper *f*; **opera glasses** *npl* Opernglas *nt*; **opera house** *n* Oper *f*, Opernhaus *nt*; **opera singer** *n* Opernsänger(in) *m(f)*

operate ['ɒpəreɪt] *vt* (*machine*) bedienen; (*brakes, lights*) betätigen ▷ *vi* (*machine*) laufen; (*bus etc*) verkehren (*between* zwischen); **to ~ (on sb)** (*Med*) (jdn) operieren; **operating theatre** *n* Operationssaal *m*; **operation** [ɒpə'reɪʃən] *n* (*of machine*) Bedienung *f*; (*functioning*) Funktionieren *nt*; (*Med*) Operation *f* (*on* an *+dat*); (*undertaking*) Unternehmen *nt*; **in ~** (*machine*) in Betrieb; **to have an ~** operiert werden (*for* wegen); **operator** ['ɒpəreɪtə*] *n*: **to phone the ~** die Vermittlung anrufen

opinion [ə'pɪnjən] *n* Meinung *f* (*on* zu); **in my ~** meiner Meinung nach

opponent [ə'pəʊnənt] *n* Gegner(in) *m(f)*

opportunity [ɒpə'tju:nɪtɪ] *n* Gelegenheit *f*

oppose [ə'pəʊz] *vt* sich widersetzen *+dat*; (*idea*) ablehnen; **opposed** *adj*: **to be ~ to sth** gegen etw sein; **as ~ to** im Gegensatz zu; **opposing** *adj* (*team*) gegnerisch; (*points of view*) entgegengesetzt

opposite ['ɒpəzɪt] *adj* (*house*) gegenüberliegend; (*direction*) entgegengesetzt; **the ~ sex** das andere Geschlecht ▷ *adv* gegenüber ▷ *prep* gegenüber *+dat*; **~ me** mir gegenüber ▷ *n* Gegenteil *nt*

opposition [ɒpə'zɪʃən] *n* Widerstand *m* (*to* gegen); (*Pol*) Opposition *f*

oppress [ə'pres] *vt* unterdrücken; **oppressive** *adj* (*heat*) drückend

opt [ɒpt] *vi*: **to ~ for sth** sich für etw entscheiden; **to ~ to do sth** sich entscheiden, etw zu tun

optician [ɒp'tɪʃən] *n* Optiker(in) *m(f)*

optimist ['ɒptɪmɪst] *n* Optimist(in) *m(f)*; **optimistic** [ɒptɪ'mɪstɪk] *adj* optimistisch

option ['ɒpʃən] *n* Möglichkeit *f*; (*Comm*) Option *f*; **to have no ~** keine Wahl haben; **optional** *adj* freiwillig; **~ extras** (*Auto*) Extras *pl*

or [ɔ:*] *conj* oder; (*otherwise*) sonst; (*after neg*) noch; **hurry up, ~ (else) we'll be late** beeil dich, sonst kommen wir zu spät

oral ['ɔ:rəl] *adj* mündlich; **~ sex** Oralverkehr *m* ▷ *n* (*exam*) Mündliche(s) *nt*; **oral surgeon** *n* Kieferchirurg(in) *m(f)*

orange ['ɒrɪndʒ] *n* Orange *f* ▷ *adj* orangefarben; **orange juice** *n* Orangensaft *m*

orbit ['ɔ:bɪt] *n* Umlaufbahn *f*; **to be out of ~** (*fam*) nicht zu erreichen sein ▷ *vt* umkreisen

orchard ['ɔ:tʃəd] *n* Obstgarten *m*

orchestra ['ɔ:kɪstrə] *n* Orchester *nt*; (*US Theat*) Parkett *nt*

orchid ['ɔ:kɪd] *n* Orchidee *f*

ordeal [ɔːˈdiːl] n Tortur f; (emotional) Qual f

order [ˈɔːdəʳ] n (sequence) Reihenfolge f; (good arrangement) Ordnung f; (command) Befehl m; (Jur) Anordnung f; (condition) Zustand m; (Comm) Bestellung f; **out of ~** (not functioning) außer Betrieb; (unsuitable) nicht angebracht; **in ~** (items) richtig geordnet; (all right) in Ordnung; **in ~ to do sth** um etw zu tun ▷ vt (arrange) ordnen; (command) befehlen; **to ~ sb to do sth** jdm befehlen, etw zu tun; (food, product) bestellen; **order form** n Bestellschein m

ordinary [ˈɔːdnⁱr] adj gewöhnlich, normal; (average) durchschnittlich

ore [ɔːʳ] n Erz nt

organ [ˈɔːgən] n (Mus) Orgel f; (Anat) Organ nt

organic [ɔːˈgænɪk] adj organisch; (farming, vegetables) Bio-, Öko-; **~ farmer** Biobauer m, Biobäuerin f; **~ food** Biokost f

organization [ɔːgənaɪˈzeɪʃən] n Organisation f; (arrangement) Ordnung f; **organize** [ˈɔːgənaɪz] vt organisieren; **organizer** n (elektronisches) Notizbuch

orgasm [ˈɔːgæzəm] n Orgasmus m

orgy [ˈɔːdʒɪ] n Orgie f

oriental [ɔːrɪˈɛntəl] adj orientalisch

orientation [ɔːrɪɛnteɪʃən] n Orientierung f

origin [ˈɒrɪdʒɪn] n Ursprung m; (of person) Herkunft f; **original** [əˈrɪdʒɪnl] adj (first) ursprünglich; (painting) original; (idea) originell ▷ n Original nt; **originality** [ərɪdʒɪˈnælɪtɪ] n Originalität f; **originally** adv ursprünglich

Orkneys [ˈɔːknɪz] npl, **Orkney Islands** npl Orkneyinseln pl

ornament [ˈɔːnəmənt] n Schmuckgegenstand m; **ornamental** [ɔːnəˈmɛntl] adj dekorativ

orphan [ˈɔːfən] n Waise f, Waisenkind nt; **orphanage** [ˈɔːfənɪdʒ] n Waisenhaus nt

orthodox [ˈɔːθədɒks] adj orthodox

orthopaedic, orthopedic (US) [ɔːθəʊˈpiːdɪk] adj orthopädisch

ostentatious [ɒstɛnˈteɪʃəs] adj protzig

ostrich [ˈɒstrɪtʃ] n (Zool) Strauß m

other [ˈʌðəʳ] adj pron andere(r, s), any **~ questions?** weitere Fragen?; **the ~ day** neulich; **every ~ day** jeden zweiten Tag; **any person ~ than him** alle außer ihm; **someone/something or ~** irgendjemand/irgendetwas; **otherwise** adv sonst; (differently) anders

OTT adj abbr = **over the top** übertrieben

otter [ˈɒtəʳ] n Otter m

ought [ɔːt] vb aux (obligation) sollte; (probability) dürfte; (stronger) müsste; **you ~ to do that** du solltest/Sie sollten das tun; **he ~ to win** er müsste gewinnen; **that ~ to do** das müsste reichen

ounce [aʊns] n Unze f (28,35 g)

our [aʊəʳ] adj unser; **ours** pron unsere(r, s); **this is ~** das gehört uns; **a friend of ~** ein Freund von uns; **ourselves** pron (reflexive) uns; **we enjoyed ~** wir haben uns amüsiert; **we've got the house to ~** wir haben das Haus für uns; (emphatic) **we did it ~** wir haben es selbst gemacht; **(all) by ~** allein

out [aʊt] adv hinaus/heraus; (not

indoors) draußen; (*not at home*) nicht zu Hause; (*not alight*) aus; (*unconscious*) bewusstlos; (*published*) herausgekommen; (*results*) bekannt gegeben; **have you been ~ yet?** warst du/waren Sie schon draußen?; **I was ~ when they called** ich war nicht da, als sie vorbeikamen; **to be ~ and about** unterwegs sein; **the sun is ~** die Sonne scheint; **the fire is ~** das Feuer ist ausgegangen; (*wrong*) **the calculation is (way) ~** die Kalkulation stimmt (ganz und gar) nicht; **they're ~ to get him** sie sind hinter ihm her ▷ *vt* (*fam*) outen

outback ['autbæk] *n* (*in Australia*) **the ~** das Hinterland

outboard ['autbɔːd] *adj*: **~ motor** Außenbordmotor *m*

outbreak ['autbreık] *n* Ausbruch *m*

outburst ['autbɜːst] *n* Ausbruch *m*

outcome ['autkʌm] *n* Ergebnis *nt*

outcry ['autkraı] *n* (*public protest*) Protestwelle *f* (*against* gegen)

outdo [aut'duː] *irr vt* übertreffen

outdoor ['autdɔː°] *adj* Außen-; (*Sport*) im Freien; **~ swimming pool** Freibad *nt*; **outdoors** [aut'dɔːz] *adv* draußen, im Freien

outer ['autə°] *adj* äußere(r, s); **outer space** *n* Weltraum *m*

outfit ['autfıt] *n* Ausrüstung *f*; (*clothes*) Kleidung *f*

outgoing ['autgəuıŋ] *adj* kontaktfreudig

outgrow [aut'grəu] *irr vt* (*clothes*) herauswachsen aus

outing ['autıŋ] *n* Ausflug *m*

outlet ['autlet] *n* Auslass *m*, Abfluss *m*; (*US*) Steckdose *f*; (*shop*) Verkaufsstelle *f*

outline ['autlaın] *n* Umriss *m*; (*summary*) Abriss *m*

outlive [aut'lıv] *vt* überleben

outlook ['autluk] *n* Aussicht(en) *f(pl)*; (*prospects*) Aussichten *pl*; (*attitude*) Einstellung *f* (*on zu*)

outnumber [aut'nʌmbə°] *vt* zahlenmäßig überlegen sein +*dat*; **~ed** zahlenmäßig unterlegen

out of ['autəv] *prep* (*motion, motive, origin*) aus; (*position, away from*) außerhalb +*gen*; **~ danger/sight/breath** außer Gefahr/Sicht/Atem; **made ~ wood** aus Holz gemacht; **we are ~ bread** wir haben kein Brot mehr; **out-of-date** *adj* veraltet; **out-of-the-way** *adj* abgelegen

outpatient ['autpeıʃənt] *n* ambulanter Patient, ambulante Patientin

output ['autput] *n* Produktion *f*; (*of engine*) Leistung *f*; (*Inform*) Ausgabe *f*

outrage ['autreıdʒ] *n* (*great anger*) Empörung *f* (*at* über); (*wicked deed*) Schandtat *f*; (*crime*) Verbrechen *nt*; (*indecency*) Skandal *m*; **outrageous** [aut'reıdʒəs] *adj* unerhört; (*clothes, behaviour etc*) unmöglich, schrill

outright ['autraıt] *adv* (*killed*) sofort ▷ *adj* total; (*denial*) völlig; (*winner*) unbestritten

outside [aut'saıd] *n* Außenseite *f*; **on the ~** außen ▷ *adj* äußere(r, s), Außen-; (*chance*) sehr gering ▷ *adv* außen; **to go ~** nach draußen gehen ▷ *prep* außerhalb +*gen*; **outsider** *n* Außenseiter(in) *m(f)*

outskirts ['autskɜːts] *npl* (*of town*) Stadtrand *m*

outstanding [aut'stændıŋ] *adj* hervorragend; (*debts etc*) ausstehend

outward ['autwəd] *adj* äußere(r, s); **~ journey** Hinfahrt *f*;

outwardly adv nach außen hin;
outwards adv nach außen
oval ['əʊvəl] adj oval
ovary ['əʊvərɪ] n Eierstock m
ovation [əʊ'veɪʃən] n Ovation f,
Applaus m
oven ['ʌvn] n Backofen m; **oven
glove** n Topfhandschuh m;
ovenproof adj feuerfest;
oven-ready adj bratfertig
over ['əʊvə°] prep (position) über
+dat; (motion) über; ~ **here** sie haben
lange dazu gebraucht; **from all
~ England** aus ganz England; ~
£20 mehr als 20 Pfund; ~ **the
phone/radio** am Telefon/im
Radio; **to talk ~ a glass of wine**
sich bei einem Glas Wein
unterhalten; ~ **and above this**
darüber hinaus; ~ **the summer**
während des Sommers ▷ adv
(across) hinüber/herüber; (finished)
vorbei; (match, play etc) zu Ende;
(left) übrig; (more) mehr;
~ **there/in America** da
drüben/drüben in Amerika, ~ **to
you** du bist/Sie sind dran; **it's (all)
~ between us** es ist aus zwischen
uns; ~ **and ~ again** immer wieder;
to start (all) ~ again noch einmal
von vorn anfangen; **children of 8
and ~** Kinder ab 8 Jahren
over- ['əʊvə°] pref über-
overall ['əʊvərɔːl] n (Brit) Kittel
m ▷ adj (situation) allgemein;
(length) Gesamt-; ~ **majority**
absolute Mehrheit ▷ adv
insgesamt; **overalls** npl Overall
m
overboard [əʊvə'bɔːd] adv über
Bord
overbooked [əʊvə'bʊkt] adj
überbucht; **overbooking** n
Überbuchung f
overcharge [əʊvə'tʃɑːdʒ] vt zu
viel verlangen von

overcoat ['əʊvəkəʊt] n Wintermantel m
overcome [əʊvə'kʌm] irr vt
überwinden; ~ **by sleep/emotion**
von Schlaf/Rührung übermannt;
we shall ~ wir werden siegen
overcooked [əʊvə'kʊkt] adj
verkocht; (meat) zu lange gebraten
overcrowded [əʊvə'kraʊdɪd]
adj überfüllt
overdo [əʊvə'duː] irr vt übertreiben; **overdone** adj
übertrieben; (food) zu lange
gekocht; (meat) zu lange gebraten
overdose ['əʊvədəʊs] n Über-
dosis f
overdraft ['əʊvədrɑːft] n Kon-
toüberziehung f; **overdrawn**
[əʊvə'drɔːn] adj überzogen
overdue [əʊvə'djuː] adj
überfällig
overestimate [əʊvər'estɪmeɪt]
vt überschätzen
overexpose [əʊvərɪks'pəʊz] vt (Foto)
überbelichten
overflow [əʊvə'fləʊ] vi
überlaufen
overhead ['əʊvəhed] adj (Aviat)
~ **locker** Gepäckfach nt;
~ **projector** Overheadprojektor m;
~ **railway** Hochbahn f
▷ [əʊvə'hed] adv oben;
overhead, (Brit) **overheads** n
(Comm) allgemeine
Geschäftskosten pl
overhear [əʊvə'hɪə°] irr vt zufällig
mit anhören
overheat [əʊvə'hiːt] vi (engine)
heiß laufen
overjoyed [əʊvə'dʒɔɪd] adj
überglücklich (at über)
overland ['əʊvəlænd] adj Über-
land- ▷ [əʊvə'lænd] adv (travel)
über Land
overlap [əʊvə'læp] vi (dates etc)
sich überschneiden; (objects) sich
teilweise decken

overload [əʊvə'ləʊd] *vt*
überladen

overlook [əʊvə'lʊk] *vt* (view from
above) überblicken; (not notice)
übersehen; (pardon) hinwegsehen
über +akk

overnight [əʊvə'naɪt] *adj* (jour-
ney, train) Nacht-; **~ bag**
Reisetasche f; **~ stay**
Übernachtung f ▷ *adv* über Nacht

overpass ['əʊvəpɑ:s] *n*
Überführung f

overpay [əʊvə'peɪ] *vt*
überbezahlen

overrule [əʊvə'ru:l] *vt* verwerfen; (decision) aufheben

overseas [əʊvə'si:z] *adj* Über-
see-; ausländisch; (fam) Auslands-
▷ *adv* (go) nach Übersee; (live,
work) in Übersee

oversee [əʊvə'si:] *irr vt*
beaufsichtigen

overshadow [əʊvə'ʃædəʊ] *vt*
überschatten

overshoot [əʊvə'ʃu:t] *irr vt*
(runway) hinausschießen über
+akk; (turning) vorbeifahren
+dat

oversight ['əʊvəsaɪt] *n* Versehen nt

oversimplify [əʊvə'sɪmplɪfaɪ]
vt zu sehr vereinfachen

oversleep [əʊvə'sli:p] *irr vi*
verschlafen

overtake [əʊvə'teɪk] *irr vt, vi*
überholen

overtime ['əʊvətaɪm] *n* Überstunden pl

overturn [əʊvə'tɜ:n] *vt, vi*
umkippen

overweight [əʊvə'weɪt] *adj*: **to
be ~** Übergewicht haben

overwhelm [əʊvə'welm] *vt*
überwältigen; **overwhelming** *adj*
überwältigend

overwork [əʊvə'wɜ:k] *n*
Überarbeitung f ▷ *vi* sich

überarbeiten; **overworked** *adj*
überarbeitet

owe [əʊ] *vt* schulden; **to ~ sth to
sb** (money) jdm etw schulden;
(favour etc) jdm etw verdanken;
how much do I ~ you? was bin ich
dir/Ihnen schuldig?; **owing to**
prep wegen +gen

owl [aʊl] *n* Eule f

own [əʊn] *vt* besitzen ▷ *adj* eigen;
on one's ~ allein; **he has a flat of
his ~** er hat eine eigene Wohung;
own up *vi*: **to ~ to sth** etw
zugeben; **owner** *n* Besitzer(in)
m(f); (of business) Inhaber(in) m(f);
ownership *n* Besitz m; **under
new ~** unter neuer Leitung

ox [ɒks] (*pl* **oxen**) *n* Ochse m;
oxtail ['ɒksteɪl] *n* Ochsen-
schwanz m; **~ soup**
Ochsenschwanzsuppe f; **oxygen**
['ɒksɪdʒən] *n* Sauerstoff m

oyster ['ɔɪstə*] *n* Auster f

oz *abbr* = **ounces** Unzen pl

Oz ['ɒz] *n* (fam) Australien nt

ozone ['əʊzəʊn] *n* Ozon nt;
~ layer Ozonschicht f

p

p abbr = **page** S.; abbr = **penny, pence**

p.a. abbr = **per annum**

pace [peɪs] n (speed) Tempo nt; (step) Schritt m; **pacemaker** n (Med) Schrittmacher m

Pacific [pəˈsɪfɪk] n: **the ~ (Ocean)** der Pazifik; **Pacific Standard Time** n pazifische Zeit

pacifier [ˈpæsɪfaɪə] n (US: for baby) Schnuller m

pack [pæk] n (of cards) Spiel m; (esp US: of cigarettes) Schachtel f; (gang) Bande f; (US: backpack) Rucksack m ▷ vt (case) packen; (clothes) einpacken ▷ vi (for holiday) packen; **pack in** vt (Brit fam: job) hinschmeißen; **package** [ˈpækɪdʒ] n (a. Inform, fig) Paket nt; **package deal** n Pauschalangebot nt; **package holiday**, **package tour** n Pauschalreise f; **packaging** n

(material) Verpackung f; **packed lunch** n (Brit) Lunchpaket nt; **packet** n Päckchen nt; (of cigarettes) Schachtel f

pad [pæd] n (of paper) Schreibblock m; (padding) Polster nt; **padded envelope** n wattierter Umschlag; **padding** n (material) Polsterung f

paddle [ˈpædl] n (for boat) Paddel nt ▷ vi (in boat) paddeln; **paddling pool** n (Brit) Planschbecken nt

padlock [ˈpædlɒk] n Vorhängeschloss nt

page [peɪdʒ] n (of book etc) Seite f

paper [ˈpeɪdʒə°] n Pieper m

paid [peɪd] pt, pp of **pay** ▷ adj bezahlt

pain [peɪn] n Schmerz m; **to be in ~** Schmerzen haben; **she's a (real) ~** sie nervt; **painful** adj (physically) schmerzhaft; (embarrassing) peinlich; **painkiller** n schmerzstillendes Mittel

painstaking adj sorgfältig

paint [peɪnt] n Farbe f ▷ vt anstreichen; (picture) malen; **paintbrush** n Pinsel m; **painter** n Maler(in) m(f); **painting** n (picture) Bild nt, Gemälde nt

pair [peə°] n Paar nt; **a ~ of shoes** ein Paar Schuhe; **a ~ of scissors** eine Schere; **a ~ of trousers** eine Hose

pajamas [pəˈdʒɑːməz] npl (US) Schlafanzug m

Pakistan [ˌpɑːkɪˈstɑːn] n Pakistan nt

pal [pæl] n (fam) Kumpel m

palace [ˈpæləs] n Palast m

pale [peɪl] adj (face) blass, bleich; (colour) hell

palm [pɑːm] n (of hand) Handfläche f; **~ (tree)** Palme f; **palmtop (computer)** n Palmtop(computer) m

pamper ['pæmpə°] vt
verhätscheln

pan [pæn] n (saucepan) Topf m;
(frying pan) Pfanne f; **pancake**
['pænkeɪk] n Pfannkuchen m;
Pancake Day n (Brit)
Fastnachtsdienstag m

pandemic [pæn'demɪk] n Pandemie f

panel ['pænl] n (of wood) Tafel f;
(in discussion) Diskussionsteilnehmer pl; (in jury) Jurymitglieder
pl

panic ['pænɪk] n Panik f ▷ vi in
Panik geraten; **panicky** ['pænɪkɪ]
adj panisch

pansy ['pænzɪ] n (flower)
Stiefmütterchen nt

panties ['pæntɪz] npl (Damen)slip m

pantomime ['pæntəmaɪm] n
(Brit) um die Weihnachtszeit
aufgeführte Märchenkomödie

pants [pænts] npl Unterhose f;
(esp US: trousers) Hose f

pantyhose ['pæntɪhəʊz] npl
(US) Strumpfhose f; **panty-liner** n
Slipeinlage f

paper ['peɪpə°] n Papier nt;
(newspaper) Zeitung f; (exam)
Klausur f; (for reading at conference)
Referat nt; ~s pl (identity papers)
Papiere pl; ~ **bag** Papiertüte f;
~ **cup** Pappbecher m ▷ vt (wall)
tapezieren; **paperback** n
Taschenbuch nt; **paper clip** n
Büroklammer f; **paper feed** n (of
printer) Papiereinzug m; **paper
round** n **to do a** ~ Zeitungen
austragen; **paperwork** n
Schreibarbeit f

parachute ['pærəʃuːt] n Fallschirm m ▷ vi abspringen

paracetamol [pærə'siːtəmɒl] n
(tablet) Paracetamoltablette
f

parade [pə'reɪd] n (procession)

Umzug m; (Mil) Parade f ▷ vi
vorbeimarschieren

paradise ['pærədaɪs] n Paradies
nt

paragliding ['pærəglaɪdɪŋ] n
Gleitschirmfliegen nt

paragraph ['pærəgrɑːf] n Absatz
m

parallel ['pærəlel] adj parallel
▷ n (Math, fig) Parallele f

paralyze ['pærəlaɪz] vt lähmen;
(fig) lahmlegen

paranoid ['pærənɔɪd] adj
paranoid

paraphrase ['pærəfreɪz] vt
umschreiben; (sth spoken) anders
ausdrücken

parasailing ['pærəseɪlɪŋ] n
Parasailing m

parasol ['pærəsɒl] n Sonnenschirm m

parcel ['pɑːsl] n Paket nt

pardon ['pɑːdn] n (Jur)
Begnadigung f; ~ **me/I beg your**
~ verzeih/verzeihen Sie bitte;
(objection) aber ich bitte dich/Sie; **I
beg your ~?/~ me?** wie bitte?

parent ['pɛərənt] n Elternteil m;
~**s** pl Eltern pl; ~**s-in-law** pl
Schwiegereltern pl; **parental**
[pə'rentl] adj elterlich, Eltern-

parish ['pærɪʃ] n Gemeinde f

park [pɑːk] n Park m ▷ vt, vi
parken; **parking** n Parken nt; "**no
~**" „Parken verboten"; **parking
brake** n (US) Handbremse f;
parking disc n Parkscheibe f;
parking fine n Geldbuße f für
falsches Parken; **parking lights**
npl (US) Standlicht nt; **parking lot**
n (US) Parkplatz m; **parking meter**
n Parkuhr f; **parking place**
n Parkplatz m; **parking space** n Parkplatz m;
parking ticket n Strafzettel m

parliament ['pɑːləmənt] n Parlament nt

parrot ['pærət] n Papagei m

parsley ['pɑːslɪ] n Petersilie f
parsnip ['pɑːsnɪp] n Pastinake f (längliches, weißes Wurzelgemüse)
part [pɑːt] n Teil m; (of machine) Teil nt; (Theat) Rolle f; (US: in hair) Scheitel m; **to take** ~ teilnehmen (in an +dat); **for the most** ~ zum größten Teil ▷ adj Teil- ▷ vt (separate) trennen; (hair) scheiteln ▷ vi (people) sich trennen
partial ['pɑːʃəl] adj (incomplete) teilweise, Teil-
participant [pɑːˈtɪsɪpənt] n Teilnehmer(in) m(f); **participate** [pɑːˈtɪsɪpeɪt] vi teilnehmen (in an +dat)
particular [pəˈtɪkjʊləʳ] adj (specific) bestimmt; (exact) genau; (fussy) eigen; (in ~) insbesondere ▷ n ~**s** pl (details) Einzelheiten pl; (about person) Personalien pl; **particularly** adv besonders
parting ['pɑːtɪŋ] n (farewell) Abschied m; (Brit: in hair) Scheitel m
partly ['pɑːtlɪ] adv teilweise
partner ['pɑːtnəʳ] n Partner(in) m(f); **partnership** n Partnerschaft f
partridge ['pɑːtrɪdʒ] n Rebhuhn nt
part-time ['pɑːtˈtaɪm] adj Teilzeit- ▷ adv: **to work** ~ Teilzeit arbeiten
party ['pɑːtɪ] n (celebration) Party f; (Pol, Jur) Partei f; (group) Gruppe f ▷ vi feiern
pass [pɑːs] vt (on foot) vorbeigehen an +dat; (in car etc) vorbeifahren an +dat; (time) verbringen; (exam) bestehen; (law) verabschieden; **to ~ sth to sb**, **to ~ sb sth** jdm etw reichen; **to ~ the ball to sb** jdm den Ball zuspielen ▷ vi (on foot) vorbeigehen; (in car etc) vorbeifahren; (years) vergehen; (in exam) bestehen ▷ n (document) Ausweis m; (Sport) Pass m; **pass**

away vi (die) verscheiden; **pass by** vi (on foot) vorbeigehen; (in car etc) vorbeifahren ▷ vt (on foot) vorbeigehen an +dat; (in car etc) vorbeifahren an +dat; **pass on** vt weitergeben (to an +akk); (disease) übertragen (to auf +akk); **pass out** vi (faint) ohnmächtig werden; **pass round** vt herumreichen
passage ['pæsɪdʒ] n (corridor) Gang m; (in book, music) Passage f; **passageway** n Durchgang m
passenger ['pæsɪndʒəʳ] n Passagier(in) m(f); (on bus) Fahrgast m; (on train) Reisende(r) mf; (in car) Mitfahrer(in) m(f)
passer-by ['pɑːsə'baɪ] (pl **passers-by**) n Passant(in) m(f)
passion ['pæʃən] n Leidenschaft f; **passionate** ['pæʃənɪt] adj leidenschaftlich; **passion fruit** n Passionsfrucht f
passive ['pæsɪv] adj passiv; ~ **smoking** Passivrauchen nt ▷ n: ~ **(voice)** (Ling) Passiv nt
passport ['pɑːspɔːt] n (Reise)pass m; **passport control** n Passkontrolle f
password ['pɑːswɜːd] n (Inform) Passwort nt
past [pɑːst] n Vergangenheit f ▷ adv (by) vorbei; **it's five** ~ es ist fünf nach ▷ adj (years) vergangen; (president etc) ehemalig; **in the** ~ **two months** in den letzten zwei Monaten ▷ prep (telling time) nach; **half** ~ **10** halb 11; **to go** ~ **sth** an etw dat vorbeigehen/-fahren
pasta ['pæstə] n Nudeln pl
paste [peɪst] vt (stick) kleben; (Inform) einfügen ▷ n (glue) Kleister m
pastime ['pɑːstaɪm] n Zeitvertreib m
pastry ['peɪstrɪ] n Teig m; (cake) Stückchen
pasty ['pæstɪ] n (Brit) Pastete f

patch [pætʃ] n (area) Fleck m; (for mending) Flicken ▸ vt flicken; **patchy** adj (uneven) ungleichmäßig

pâté ['pæteɪ] n Pastete f

paternal [pə'tɜːnl] adj väterlich; **~ grandmother** Großmutter f väterlicherseits; **paternity leave** [pə'tɜːnɪtɪliːv] n Elternzeit f (des Vaters)

path [pɑːθ] n (a. Inform) Pfad m; (a. fig) Weg m

pathetic [pə'θetɪk] adj (bad) kläglich, erbärmlich; **it's ~** es ist zum Heulen

patience ['peɪʃəns] n Geduld f; (Brit Cards) Patience f; **patient** adj geduldig ▸ n Patient(in) m(f)

patio ['pætɪəʊ] n Terrasse f

patriotic [pætrɪ'ɒtɪk] adj patriotisch

patrol car [pə'trəʊlkɑː°] n Streifenwagen m; **patrolman** (pl **-men**) n (US) Streifenpolizist m

patron ['peɪtrən] n (sponsor) Förderer m, Förderin f; (in shop) Kunde m, Kundin f

patronize ['pætrənaɪz] vt (treat condescendingly) von oben herab behandeln; **patronizing** adj (attitude) herablassend

pattern ['pætən] n Muster nt

pause [pɔːz] n Pause f ▸ vi (speaker) innehalten

pavement n (Brit) Bürgersteig m; (US) Pflaster nt

pay [peɪ] (**paid**, **paid**) vt bezahlen; **he paid (me) £20 for it** er hat (mir) 20 Pfund dafür gezahlt; **to ~ attention** Acht geben (to auf +akk); **to ~ sb a visit** jdn besuchen; **to ~** zahlen; (be profitable) sich bezahlt machen; **to ~ for sth** etw bezahlen ▸ n Bezahlung f, Lohn m; **pay back** vt (money) zurückzahlen; **pay in** vt (into account) einzahlen; **payable**

adj zahlbar; (due) fällig; **payday** n Zahltag m; **payee** [peɪ'iː] n Zahlungsempfänger(in) m(f); **payment** n Bezahlung f; (money) Zahlung f; **pay-per-view** adj Pay-per-View-; **pay phone** n Münzfernsprecher m; **pay TV** n Pay-TV nt

PC abbr = **personal computer** PC m; abbr = **politically correct** politisch korrekt

PDA abbr = **personal digital assistant** PDA m

PE abbr = **physical education** (school) Sport m

pea [piː] n Erbse f

peace [piːs] n Frieden m; **peaceful** adj friedlich

peach [piːtʃ] n Pfirsich m

peacock ['piːkɒk] n Pfau m

peak [piːk] n (of mountain) Gipfel m; (fig) Höhepunkt m; **peak period** n Stoßzeit f; (season) Hochsaison

peanut ['piːnʌt] n Erdnuss f; **peanut butter** n Erdnussbutter f

pear [peə°] n Birne f

pearl [pɜːl] n Perle f

pebble ['pebl] n Kiesel m

pecan [pɪ'kæn] n Pekannuss f

peck [pek] vt, vi picken; **peckish** adj (Brit fam) ein bisschen hungrig

peculiar [pɪ'kjuːlɪə°] adj (odd) seltsam; **~ to** charakteristisch für; **peculiarity** [pɪkjʊlɪ'ærɪtɪ] n (singular quality) Besonderheit f; (strangeness) Eigenartigkeit f

pedal ['pedl] n Pedal nt

pedestrian [pɪ'destrɪən] n Fußgänger(in) m(f); **pedestrian crossing** n Fußgängerüberweg m

pee [piː] vi (fam) pinkeln

peel [piːl] n Schale f ▸ vt schälen ▸ vi (paint etc) abblättern; (skin etc) sich schälen

peer [pɪə°] n Gleichaltrige(r) mf ▸ vi starren

peg [pɛg] n (for coat etc) Haken m; (for tent) Hering m; (clothes) ~ (Wäsche)klammer f

pelvis ['pɛlvɪs] n Becken nt

pen [pɛn] n (ball-point) Kuli m, Kugelschreiber; (fountain ~) Füller m

penalize ['piːnəlaɪz] vt (punish) bestrafen; **penalty** ['pɛnltɪ] n (punishment) Strafe f; (in football) Elfmeter m

pence [pɛns] pl of **penny**

pencil ['pɛnsl] n Bleistift m; **pencil sharpener** n (Bleistift)spitzer m

penetrate ['pɛnɪtreɪt] vt durchdringen; (enter into) eindringen in +akk

penfriend ['pɛnfrɛnd] n Brieffreund(in) m(f)

penguin ['pɛŋgwɪn] n Pinguin m

penicillin [pɛnɪ'sɪlɪn] n Penizillin nt

peninsula [pɪ'nɪnsjʊlə] n Halbinsel f

penis ['piːnɪs] n Penis m

penknife ['pɛnnaɪf] (pl **penknives**) n Taschenmesser nt

penny ['pɛnɪ] (pl **pence** o **pennies**) n (Brit) Penny m; (US) Centstück nt

pension ['pɛnʃən] n Rente f; (for civil servants, executives etc) Pension f; **pensioner** n Rentner(in) m(f); **pension plan**, **pension scheme** n Rentenversicherung f

penultimate [pɪ'nʌltɪmət] adj vorletzte(r, s)

people ['piːpl] npl (persons) Leute pl; (von Staat) Volk nt; (inhabitants) Bevölkerung f; **people carrier** n Minivan m

pepper ['pɛpə'] n Pfeffer m; (vegetable) Paprika m; **peppermint** n (sweet) Pfefferminz nt

per [pɜː'] prep pro; ~ **annum** pro Jahr; ~ **cent** Prozent nt

percentage [pə'sɛntɪdʒ] n Prozentsatz m

perceptible [pə'sɛptəbl] adj wahrnehmbar

percolator ['pɜːkəleɪtə'] n Kaffeemaschine f

percussion [pə'kʌʃən] n (Mus) Schlagzeug nt

perfect ['pɜːfɪkt] adj perfekt; (utter) völlig ▷ [pə'fɛkt] vt vervollkommnen; **perfectly** adv perfekt; (utterly) völlig

perform [pə'fɔːm] vt (task) ausführen; (play) aufführen; (Med: operation) durchführen ▷ vi (Theat) auftreten; **performance** n (show) Vorstellung f; (efficiency) Leistung f

perfume ['pɜːfjuːm] n Duft m; (substance) Parfüm nt

perhaps [pə'hæps] adv vielleicht

period ['pɪərɪəd] n (length of time) Zeit f; (in history) Zeitalter nt; (school) Stunde f; (Med) Periode f; (US: full stop) Punkt m; **for a ~ of three years** für einen Zeitraum von drei Jahren; **periodical** [pɪərɪ'ɒdɪkəl] n Zeitschrift f

peripheral [pə'rɪfərəl] n (Inform) Peripheriegerät nt

perjury ['pɜːdʒərɪ] n Meineid m

perm [pɜːm] n Dauerwelle f

permanent, **permanently** ['pɜːmənənt, -lɪ] adj, adv ständig

permission [pə'mɪʃən] n Erlaubnis f; **permit** ['pɜːmɪt] n Genehmigung f ▷ [pə'mɪt] vt erlauben, zulassen; **to ~ sb to do sth** jdm erlauben, etw zu tun

persecute ['pɜːsɪkjuːt] vt verfolgen

perseverance [pɜːsɪ'vɪərəns] n Ausdauer f

persist [pə'sɪst] vi (in belief etc) bleiben (in bei); (rain, smell) andauern; **persistent** adj beharrlich

person ['pɜːsn] n Mensch m; (in official context) Person f; **in ~** persönlich; **personal** adj persönlich; (private) privat; **personality** [pɜːsə'nælətɪ] n Persönlichkeit f; **personal organizer** n Organizer m; **personal stereo** (pl **-s**) n Walkman® m; **personnel** [pɜːsə'nel] n Personal nt

perspective [pə'spektɪv] n Perspektive f

persuade [pə'sweɪd] vt überreden; (convince) überzeugen; **persuasive** [pə'sweɪsɪv] adj überzeugend

perverse [pə'vɜːs] adj eigensinnig; abwegig; **pervert** ['pɜːvɜːt] n Perverse(r) mf ▷ [pə'vɜːt] vt (morally) verderben; **perverted** [pə'vɜːtɪd] adj pervers

pessimist ['pesɪmɪst] n Pessimist(in) m(f); **pessimistic** [pesɪ'mɪstɪk] adj pessimistisch

pest [pest] n (insect) Schädling m; (fig: person) Nervensäge f; (thing) Plage f; **pester** ['pestə°] vt plagen; **pesticide** ['pestɪsaɪd] n Schädlingsbekämpfungsmittel nt

pet [pet] n (animal) Haustier nt; (person) Liebling m

petal ['petl] n Blütenblatt nt

petition [pə'tɪʃən] n Petition f

petrol ['petrəl] n (Brit) Benzin nt; **petrol pump** n (at garage) Zapfsäule f; **petrol station** n Tankstelle f; **petrol tank** n Benzintank m

pharmacy ['fɑːməsɪ] n (shop) Apotheke f; (science) Pharmazie f

phase [feɪz] n Phase f

PhD abbr = **Doctor of Philosophy** Dr. phil; (dissertation) Doktorarbeit f; **to do one's ~** promovieren

pheasant ['feznt] n Fasan m

phenomenon [fɪ'nɒmɪnən] n (pl **phenomena**) n Phänomen nt

Philippines ['fɪlɪpiːnz] npl Philippinen pl

philosophical [fɪlə'sɒfɪkəl] adj philosophisch; (fig) gelassen; **philosophy** [fɪ'lɒsəfɪ] n Philosophie f

phone [fəʊn] n Telefon nt ▷ vt, vi anrufen; **phone book** n Telefonbuch nt; **phone bill** n Telefonrechnung f; **phone booth**, **phone box** (Brit) n Telefonzelle f; **phonecall** n Telefonanruf m; **phonecard** n Telefonkarte f; **phone-in** n Rundfunkprogramm, bei dem Hörer anrufen können; **phone number** n Telefonnummer f

photo ['fəʊtəʊ] (pl **-s**) n Foto nt; **photo booth** n Fotoautomat m; **photocopier** ['fəʊtəʊkɒpɪə°] n Kopiergerät nt; **photocopy** ['fəʊtəʊkɒpɪ] n Fotokopie f ▷ vt fotokopieren; **photograph** ['fəʊtəgrɑːf] n Fotografie f, Aufnahme f ▷ vt fotografieren; **photographer** [fə'tɒgrəfə°] n Fotograf(in) m(f); **photography** [fə'tɒgrəfɪ] n Fotografie f

phrase [freɪz] n (expression) Redewendung f, Ausdruck m; **phrase book** n Sprachführer m

physical ['fɪzɪkəl] adj (bodily) körperlich, physisch ▷ n ärztliche Untersuchung; **physically** adv (bodily) körperlich, physisch; **~ handicapped** körperbehindert

physics ['fɪzɪks] nsing Physik f

physiotherapy [fɪzɪə'θerəpɪ] n Physiotherapie f

physique [fɪ'ziːk] n Körperbau m

piano ['pjɑːnəʊ] (pl **-s**) n Klavier nt

pick [pɪk] vt (flowers, fruit) pflücken; (choose) auswählen; (team) aufstellen; **pick out** vt auswählen; **pick up** vt (lift up) aufheben; (collect) abholen; (learn) lernen

pickle ['pɪkl] n (food) (Mixed) Pickles pl ▷ vt einlegen

pickpocket ['pɪkpɒkɪt] n Taschendieb(in) m(f)

picnic ['pɪknɪk] n Picknick nt

picture ['pɪktʃə°] n Bild nt; **to go to the ~s** (Brit) ins Kino gehen ▷ vt (visualize) sich vorstellen; **picture book** n Bilderbuch nt; **picturesque** [pɪktʃə'resk] adj malerisch

pie [paɪ] n (meat) Pastete f; (fruit) Kuchen m

piece [pi:s] n Stück nt; (part) Teil nt; (in chess) Figur f; (in draughts) Stein m; **a ~ of cake** ein Stück Kuchen; **to fall to ~s** auseinanderfallen

pier [pɪə°] n Pier m

pierce [pɪəs] vt durchstechen, durchbohren; (cold, sound) durchdringen; **pierced** adj (part of body) gepierct; **piercing** adj durchdringend

pig [pɪg] n Schwein nt

pigeon ['pɪdʒən] n Taube f; **pigeonhole** n (compartment) Ablegefach nt

piggy ['pɪgɪ] adj (fam) verfressen; **pigheaded** ['pɪg'hedɪd] adj dickköpfig; **piglet** ['pɪglət] n Ferkel nt; **pigsty** ['pɪgstaɪ] n Schweinestall m; **pigtail** ['pɪgteɪl] n Zopf m

pile [paɪl] n (heap) Haufen m; (one on top of another) Stapel m; **pile up** vi (accumulate) sich anhäufen

piles [paɪlz] npl Hämorr(ho)iden pl

pile-up ['paɪlʌp] n (Auto) Massenkarambolage f

pilgrim ['pɪlgrɪm] n Pilger(in) m(f)

pill [pɪl] n Tablette f; **the ~** die (Antibaby)pille; **to be on the ~** die Pille nehmen

pillar ['pɪlə°] n Pfeiler m

pillow ['pɪləʊ] n (Kopf)kissen nt; **pillowcase** n (Kopf)kissenbezug m

pilot ['paɪlət] n (Aviat) Pilot(in) m(f)

pimple ['pɪmpl] n Pickel m

pin [pɪn] n (for fixing) Nadel f; (in sewing) Stecknadel f; (Tech) Stift m; **I've got ~s and needles in my leg** mein Bein ist mir eingeschlafen ▷ vt (fix with ~) heften (to an +akk)

PIN [pɪn] acr = **personal identification number** **~ (number)** PIN f, Geheimzahl f

pinch [pɪntʃ] n (of salt) Prise f ▷ vt zwicken; (fam: steal) klauen ▷ vi (shoe) drücken

pine [paɪn] n Kiefer f

pineapple ['paɪnæpl] n Ananas f

pink [pɪŋk] adj rosa

pinstripe(d) ['pɪnstraɪp(t)] adj Nadelstreifen-

pint [paɪnt] n Pint nt (Brit: 0,57 l, US: 0,473l); (Brit: glass of beer) Bier nt

pious ['paɪəs] adj fromm

pip [pɪp] n (of fruit) Kern m

pipe [paɪp] n (for smoking) Pfeife f; (for water, gas) Rohrleitung f

pirate ['paɪərɪt] n Pirat(in) m(f); **pirated copy** n Raubkopie f

Pisces ['paɪsi:z] nsing (Astr) Fische pl; **she's a ~** sie ist Fisch

piss [pɪs] vi (vulg) pissen ▷ n (vulg) Pisse f; **to take the ~ out of sb** jdn verarschen; **piss off** vi (vulg) sich verpissen; **~! I** verpiss dich!; **pissed** adj (Brit fam: drunk) sturzbesoffen; (US fam: annoyed) stocksauer

pistachio [pɪ'stɑ:ʃɪəʊ] (pl -s) n Pistazie f

piste [pi:st] n (Ski) Piste f

pistol ['pɪstl] n Pistole f

pit [pɪt] n (hole) Grube f; (coalmine) Zeche f; **the ~s** (motor racing) die Box, **to be the ~s** (fam) grottenschlecht sein

pitch [pɪtʃ] n (Sport) Spielfeld nt; (Mus: of instrument) Tonlage f; (of voice) Stimmlage f ▷ vt (tent)

aufschlagen; (throw) werfen;
pitch-black adj pechschwarz
pitcher ['pɪtʃə°] n (US: jug) Krug m
pitiful ['pɪtɪful] adj (contemptible)
jämmerlich
pitta bread ['pɪtə] n Pittabrot nt
pity ['pɪtɪ] n Mitleid nt; **what a
~** wie schade; **it's a ~** es ist schade
▷ vt Mitleid haben mit
pizza ['piːtsə] n Pizza f
place [pleɪs] n m (spot, in text)
Stelle f; (town etc) Ort; (house) Haus
nt; (position, seat, on course) Platz m;
~ of birth Geburtsort m; **at my
~** bei mir; **in third ~** auf dem dritten
Platz; **to three decimal ~s** bis auf
drei Stellen nach dem Komma; **out
of ~** nicht an der richtigen Stelle;
(fig: remark) unangebracht; **in ~ of**
anstelle von; **in the first ~** (firstly)
erstens; (immediately) gleich; (in any
case) überhaupt ▷ vt (put) stellen,
setzen; (lay flat) legen; (advertisement) setzen (in in +akk); (Comm:
order) aufgeben; **place mat** n Set nt
plague [pleɪg] n Pest f
plaice [pleɪs] n Scholle f
plain [pleɪn] adj (clear) klar,
deutlich; (simple) einfach; (not
beautiful) unattraktiv; (yoghurt)
Natur-; (Brit: chocolate)
(Zart)bitter- ▷ n Ebene f; **plainly**
adv (frankly) offen; (simply) einfach;
(obviously) eindeutig
plait [plæt] n Zopf m ▷ vt
flechten
plan [plæn] n Plan m; (for essay
etc) Konzept nt ▷ vt planen; **to
~ to do sth, to ~ on doing sth**
vorhaben, etw zu tun ▷ vi planen
plane [pleɪn] n (aircraft)
Flugzeug nt; (tool) Hobel m
planet ['plænɪt] n Planet m
plank [plæŋk] n Brett nt
plant [plɑːnt] n Pflanze f;
(equipment) Maschinen pl; (factory)
Werk nt ▷ vt (tree etc) pflanzen

plantation [plæn'teɪʃən] n Plan-
tage f
plaque [plæk] n Gedenktafel f;
(on teeth) Zahnbelag m
plaster ['plɑːstə°] n (Brit Med:
sticking ~) Pflaster nt; (on wall)
Verputz m; **to have one's arm in
~** den Arm in Gips haben
plastered ['plɑːstəd] adj (fam)
besoffen; **to get (absolutely)
~** sich besaufen
plastic ['plæstɪk] n Kunststoff m;
to pay with ~ mit Kreditkarte
bezahlen ▷ adj Plastik-; **plastic
bag** n Plastiktüte f; **plastic
surgery** n plastische Chirurgie f
plate [pleɪt] n (for food) Teller m;
(flat sheet) Platte f; (plaque) Schild
nt
platform ['plætfɔːm] n (Rail)
Bahnsteig m; (at meeting) Podium
nt
platinum ['plætɪnəm] n Platin nt
play [pleɪ] n Spiel nt; (Theat)
(Theater)stück nt ▷ vt spielen;
(another player or team) spielen
gegen; **to ~ the piano** Klavier
spielen; **to ~ a part in** (fig) eine
Rolle spielen bei ▷ vi spielen;
play at vt: **what are you ~ing at?**
was soll das?; **play back** vt
abspielen; **play down** vt
herunterspielen
playacting n Schauspielerei f;
playback n Wiedergabe f; **player**
n Spieler(in) m(f); **playful** adj
(person) verspielt; (remark)
scherzhaft; **playground** n
Spielplatz m; (in school) Schulhof m;
playgroup n Spielgruppe f;
playing card n Spielkarte f;
playing field n Sportplatz m;
playmate n Spielkamerad(in)
m(f); **playwright** n
Dramatiker(in) m(f)
plc abbr = **public limited company**
AG f

plea [pliː] n Bitte f (for um)

plead [pliːd] vi dringend bitten (with sb jdn); (Jur) **to ~ guilty** sich schuldig bekennen

pleasant, pleasantly ['pleznt, -lı] adj, adv angenehm

please [pliːz] adv bitte; **more tea? - yes, ~** noch Tee? - ja, bitte ▷ vt (be agreeable to) gefallen +dat; **~ yourself** wie du willst/Sie wollen; **pleased** adj zufrieden; (glad) erfreut; **~ to meet you** freut mich, angenehm; **pleasing** adj erfreulich; **pleasure** ['pleʒə*] n Vergnügen nt, Freude f, **it's a ~** gern geschehen

pledge [pledʒ] n (promise) Versprechen nt ▷ vt (promise) versprechen

plenty ['plentı] n; **~ of** eine Menge, viel(e); **to be ~** genug sein, reichen; **I've got ~** ich habe mehr als genug ▷ adv (US fam) ganz schön

pliable ['plaıəbl] adj biegsam

pliers ['plaıəz] npl (Kombi)zange f

plimsoll ['plımsəl] n (Brit) Turnschuh m

plonk [plɒŋk] n (Brit fam: wine) billiger Wein ▷ vt: **to ~ sth (down)** etw hinknallen

plot [plɒt] n (of story) Handlung f; (conspiracy) Komplott nt; (of land) Stück nt Land, Grundstück nt ▷ vi ein Komplott schmieden

plough, plow (US) [plaʊ] n Pflug m ▷ vt, vi (Agr) pflügen; **ploughman's lunch** n (Brit) in einer Kneipe serviertes Gericht aus Käse, Brot, Mixed Pickles etc

pluck [plʌk] vt (eyebrows, guitar) zupfen; (chicken) rupfen; **pluck up** vt: **to ~ (one's) courage** Mut aufbringen

plug [plʌg] n (for sink, bath) Stöpsel m; (Elec) Stecker m; (Auto)

(Zünd)kerze f; (fam: publicity) Schleichwerbung f ▷ vt (fam: advertise) Reklame machen für; **plug in** vt anschließen

plum [plʌm] n Pflaume f ▷ adj (fam: job etc) Super-

plumber ['plʌmə*] n Klempner(in) m(f); **plumbing** ['plʌmıŋ] n (fittings) Leitungen pl; (craft) Installieren nt

plump [plʌmp] adj rundlich

plunge [plʌndʒ] vt (knife) stoßen; (into water) tauchen ▷ vi stürzen; (into water) tauchen

plural ['plʊərəl] n Plural m

plus [plʌs] prep plus; (as well as) und ▷ adj Plus-; **20 ~** mehr als 20 ▷ n (fig) Plus nt

plywood ['plaıwʊd] n Sperrholz nt

pm abbr = **post meridiem**; **at 3 ~** um 3 Uhr nachmittags; **at 8 ~** um 8 Uhr abends

pneumonia [njuː'məʊnıə] n Lungenentzündung f

poached [pəʊtʃt] adj (egg) pochiert, verloren

PO Box abbr = **post office box** Postfach nt

pocket ['pɒkıt] n Tasche f ▷ vt (put in ~) einstecken; **pocketbook** n (US: wallet) Brieftasche f; **pocket calculator** n Taschenrechner m; **pocket money** n Taschengeld nt

poem ['pəʊəm] n Gedicht nt; **poet** ['pəʊıt] n Dichter(in) m(f); **poetic** [pəʊ'etık] adj poetisch; **poetry** ['pəʊıtrı] n (art) Dichtung f; (poems) Gedichte pl

point [pɔınt] n Punkt m; (spot) Stelle f; (sharp tip) Spitze f; (moment) Zeitpunkt m; (purpose) Zweck m; (idea) Argument nt; (decimal) Dezimalstelle f; **~s** pl (Rail) Weiche f; **~ of view** Standpunkt m; **three ~ two** drei Komma zwei; **at some ~** irgendwann (mal); **to get**

to the ~ zur Sache kommen;
there's no ~ es hat keinen Sinn; **I
was on the ~ of leaving** ich wollte
gerade gehen ▷ vt (gun etc)
richten (at auf +akk); **to ~ one's
finger at** mit dem Finger zeigen
auf +akk ▷ vi (with finger etc)
zeigen (at, to auf +akk); **point out**
vt (indicate) aufzeigen; (mention)
hinweisen auf +akk; **pointed** adj
spitz; (question) gezielt; **pointer** n
(on dial) Zeiger m; (tip) Hinweis m;
pointless adj sinnlos

poison ['pɔɪzn] n Gift nt ▷ vt
vergiften; **poisonous** adj giftig

poke [pəʊk] vt (with stick, finger)
stoßen, stupsen; (put) stecken

Poland ['pəʊlənd] n Polen nt

polar ['pəʊlə*] adj Polar-, polar;
~ bear Eisbär m

pole [pəʊl] n Stange f; (Geo, Elec)
Pol m

Pole [pəʊl] n Pole m, Polin f

pole vault n Stabhochsprung m

police [pə'liːs] n Polizei f; **police
car** n Polizeiwagen m; **policeman**
(pl **-men**) n Polizist m; **police
station** n (Polizei)wache f;
policewoman (pl **-women**) n
Polizistin f

policy ['pɒlɪsɪ] n (plan) Politik f;
(principle) Grundsatz m; (insurance
~) (Versicherungs)police f

polio ['pəʊlɪəʊ] n Kinderlähmung f

polish ['pɒlɪʃ] n (for furniture)
Politur f; (for floor) Wachs nt; (for
shoes) Creme f; (shine) Glanz m;
(fig) Schliff m ▷ vt polieren;
(shoes) putzen; (fig) den letzten
Schliff geben +dat

Polish ['pəʊlɪʃ] adj polnisch ▷ n
Polnisch nt

polite [pə'laɪt] adj höflich;
politeness n Höflichkeit f

political, politically [pə'lɪtɪkəl, -l]
adj, adv politisch; **~ly correct**
politisch korrekt; **politician**

[pɒlɪ'tɪʃən] n Politiker(in) m(f);
politics ['pɒlɪtɪks] nsing o pl
Politik f

poll [pəʊl] n (election) Wahl f;
(opinion) ~ Umfrage f

pollen ['pɒlən] n Pollen m,
Blütenstaub m; **pollen count** n
Pollenflug m

polling station ['pəʊlɪŋsteɪʃən]
n Wahllokal nt

pollute [pə'luːt] vt verschmutzen; **pollution** [pə'luːʃən] n
Verschmutzung f

pompous ['pɒmpəs] adj aufge-
blasen; (language) geschwollen

pond [pɒnd] n Teich m

pony ['pəʊnɪ] n Pony nt;
ponytail n Pferdeschwanz m

poodle ['puːdl] n Pudel m

pool [puːl] n (swimming ~)
Schwimmbad nt; (private)
Swimmingpool m; (of spilt liquid,
blood) Lache f; (game) Poolbillard
nt ▷ vt (money etc)
zusammenlegen

poor [pɔː*] adj arm; (not good)
schlecht ▷ npl: **the ~** die Armen
pl; **poorly** adv (badly) schlecht
▷ adj (Brit) krank

pop [pɒp] n (music) Pop m; (noise)
Knall m ▷ vt (put) stecken;
(balloon) platzen lassen ▷ vi
(balloon) platzen; (cork) knallen; **to
~ in** (person) vorbeischauen; **pop
concert** n Popkonzert nt;
popcorn n Popcorn nt

Pope [pəʊp] n Papst m

pop group ['pɒpgruːp] n
Popgruppe f; **pop music** n
Popmusik f

poppy ['pɒpɪ] n Mohn m

Popsicle® ['pɒpsɪkl] n (US) Eis
nt am Stiel

pop star ['pɒpstɑː*] n Popstar m

popular ['pɒpjʊlə*] adj (well-
-liked) beliebt (with bei);
(widespread) weit verbreitet

population [pɒpjʊˈleɪʃən] n
Bevölkerung f; (of town) Einwohner
pl

porcelain [ˈpɔːslɪn] n Porzellan
nt

porch [pɔːtʃ] n Vorbau m; (US:
verandah) Veranda f

porcupine [ˈpɔːkjʊpaɪn] n
Stachelschwein n

pork [pɔːk] n Schweinefleisch nt;
pork chop n Schweinekotelett;
pork pie n Schweinefleischpastete
f

porn [pɔːn] n Porno m;
pornographic [pɔːnəˈgræfɪk] adj
pornografisch; **pornography**
[pɔːˈnɒgrəfɪ] n Pornografie f

porridge [ˈpɒrɪdʒ] n Haferbrei m

port [pɔːt] n (harbour) Hafen m;
(town) Hafenstadt f; (Naut: left side)
Backbord nt; (wine) Portwein m;
(Inform) Anschluss m

portable [ˈpɔːtəbl] adj tragbar;
(radio) Koffer-

portal [ˈpɔːtl] n (Inform) Portal n

porter [ˈpɔːtə°] n Pförtner(in)
m(f); (for luggage) Gepäckträger m

porthole [ˈpɔːthəʊl] n Bullauge
nt

portion [ˈpɔːʃən] n Teil m; (of
food) Portion f

portrait [ˈpɔːtrɪt] n Porträt nt

portray [pɔːˈtreɪ] vt darstellen

Portugal [ˈpɔːtjʊgl] n Portugal
nt; **Portuguese** [pɔːtjʊˈgiːz] adj
portugiesisch ▷ n Portugiese m,
Portugiesin f; (language)
Portugiesisch nt

pose [pəʊz] n Haltung f ▷ vi
posieren ▷ vt (threat, problem)
darstellen

posh [pɒʃ] adj (fam) piekfein

position [pəˈzɪʃən] n Stellung f;
(place) Position f, Lage f; (job) Stelle
f; (opinion) Standpunkt m; **to be in
a ~ to do sth** in der Lage sein, etw
zu tun; **in third ~** auf dem dritten

Platz ▷ vt aufstellen; (Inform:
cursor) positionieren

positive [ˈpɒzɪtɪv] adj positiv;
(convinced) sicher

possess [pəˈzes] vt besitzen;
possession [pəˈzeʃən] n **~(s** pl)
Besitz m; **possessive** adj (person)
besitzergreifend

possibility [pɒsəˈbɪlɪtɪ] n
Möglichkeit f; **possible** [ˈpɒsəbl]
adj möglich; **if ~** wenn möglich; **as
big/soon as ~** so groß/bald wie
möglich; **possibly** adv (perhaps)
vielleicht; **I've done all I ~ can** ich
habe mein Möglichstes getan

post [pəʊst] n (mail) Post f; (pole)
Pfosten m; (job) Stelle f ▷ vt
(letters) aufgeben; **to keep sb ~ed**
jdn auf dem Laufenden halten;
postage [ˈpəʊstɪdʒ] n Porto nt;
~ and packing Porto und
Verpackung; **postal** adj Post-;
(Brit) **~ order** Postanweisung f;
postbox n Briefkasten m;
postcard n Postkarte f; **postcode**
n (Brit) Postleitzahl f

poster [ˈpəʊstə°] n Plakat nt,
Poster m

postgraduate [pəʊstˈgrædjʊɪt]
n jmd, der seine Studien nach dem
ersten akademischen Grad weiterführt

postman [ˈpəʊstmən] (pl **-men**)
n Briefträger m; **postmark** n
Poststempel m

postmortem [pəʊstˈmɔːtəm] n
Autopsie f

post office [ˈpəʊstɒfɪs] n Post® f

postpone [pəˈspəʊn] vt verschieben (till auf +akk)

posture [ˈpɒstʃə°] n Haltung f

pot [pɒt] n Topf m; (tea-, coffee ~)
Kanne f; (fam: marijuana) Pot nt
▷ vt (plant) eintopfen

potato [pəˈteɪtəʊ] (pl **-es**) n
Kartoffel f; **potato chips** (US) npl
Kartoffelchips pl; **potato peeler** n
Kartoffelschäler m

potent ['pəʊtənt] adj stark
potential [pəʊ'tenʃəl] adj
potenziell ▷ n Potenzial nt;
potentially adv potenziell
pothole ['pɒthəʊl] n Höhle f; (in
road) Schlagloch nt
potter about ['pɒtərəbaʊt] vi
herumhantieren
pottery ['pɒtərɪ] n (objects)
Töpferwaren pl
potty ['pɒtɪ] adj (Brit fam)
verrückt ▷ n Töpfchen nt
poultry ['pəʊltrɪ] n Geflügel
nt
pounce [paʊns] vi: **to ~ on** sich
stürzen auf +akk
pound [paʊnd] n (money) Pfund
nt; (weight) Pfund nt (0,454 kg); **a
~ of cherries** ein Pfund Kirschen;
ten-~ note Zehnpfundschein
m
pour [pɔː°] vt (liquid) gießen; (rice,
sugar etc) schütten; **to ~ sb sth**
(drink) jdm etw eingießen;
pouring adj (rain) strömend
poverty ['pɒvətɪ] n Armut f
powder ['paʊdə°] n Pulver nt;
(cosmetic) Puder m; **powdered
milk** n Milchpulver nt; **powder
room** n Damentoilette f
power ['paʊə°] n Macht f;
(ability) Fähigkeit f; (strength)
Stärke f; (Elec) Strom m; **to be in
~** an der Macht sein ▷ vt
betreiben, antreiben;
power-assisted steering n
Servolenkung f; **power cut** n
Stromausfall m; **powerful** adj
(politician etc) mächtig; (engine,
government) stark; (argument)
durchschlagend; **powerless** adj
machtlos; **power station** n
Kraftwerk nt
p&p abbr = **postage and packing**
PR abbr = **public relations** ▷ abbr =
proportional representation
practical, **practically** ['præktɪkəl,

-l] adj, adv praktisch; **practice**
['præktɪs] n (training) Übung f;
(custom) Gewohnheit f; (doctor's,
lawyer's) Praxis f; **in ~** (in reality) in
der Praxis; **out of ~** außer Übung;
to put sth into ~ etw in die Praxis
umsetzen ▷ vt, vi (US) see
practise, **practise** ['præktɪs] vt
(instrument, movement) üben;
(profession) ausüben ▷ vi üben;
(doctor, lawyer) praktizieren
Prague [prɑːɡ] n Prag nt
praise [preɪz] n Lob nt ▷ vt
loben
pram [præm] n (Brit)
Kinderwagen m
prawn [prɔːn] n Garnele f,
Krabbe f; **prawn crackers** npl
Krabbenchips pl
pray [preɪ] vi beten; **to ~ for sth**
(fig) stark auf etw akk hoffen;
prayer ['preə°] n Gebet nt
pre- [priː] pref vor-, prä-
preach [priːtʃ] vi predigen
prearrange [priːə'reɪndʒ] vt im
Voraus vereinbaren
precaution [prɪ'kɔːʃən] n Vor-
sichtsmaßnahme f
precede [prɪ'siːd] vt vorausgehen +dat; **preceding** adj
vorhergehend
precinct ['priːsɪŋkt] n (Brit:
pedestrian ~) Fußgängerzone f;
(Brit: shopping ~) Einkaufsviertel nt;
(US: district) Bezirk m
precious ['preʃəs] adj kostbar;
~ stone Edelstein m
précis ['preɪsiː] n Zusammenfassung f
precise, **precisely** [prɪ'saɪs, -lɪ]
adj, adv genau
precondition [priːkən'dɪʃən] n
Vorbedingung f
predecessor ['priːdɪsesə°] n
Vorgänger(in) m(f)
predicament [prɪ'dɪkəmənt] n
missliche Lage

predict [prɪ'dɪkt] vt voraussagen; **predictable** adj vorhersehbar; (person) berechenbar

predominant [prɪ'dɒmɪnənt] adj vorherrschend; **predominantly** adv überwiegend

preface ['prefɪs] n Vorwort nt

prefer [prɪ'fɜː°] vt vorziehen (to dat), lieber mögen (to als); **to ~ to do sth** etw lieber tun; **preferably** ['prefrəblɪ] adv vorzugsweise, am liebsten; **preference** ['prefərəns] n (liking) Vorliebe f; **preferential** [prefə'renʃəl] adj: **to get ~ treatment** bevorzugt behandelt werden

prefix ['priːfɪks] n (US Tel) Vorwahl f

pregnancy ['pregnənsɪ] n Schwangerschaft f; **pregnant** ['pregnənt] adj schwanger; **two months ~** im zweiten Monat schwanger

prejudice ['predʒʊdɪs] n Vorurteil nt; **prejudiced** adj (person) voreingenommen

preliminary [prɪ'lɪmɪnərɪ] adj (measures) vorbereitend; (results) vorläufig; (remarks) einleitend

premature ['premətʃʊə°] adj vorzeitig; (hasty) voreilig

premiere ['premɪeə°] n Premiere f

premises ['premɪsɪz] npl (offices) Räumlichkeiten pl; (of factory, school) Gelände nt

premium-rate [priːmiəmreɪt] adj (Tel) zum Höchsttarif

preoccupied [priː'ɒkjʊpaɪd] adj: **to be ~ with sth** mit etw sehr beschäftigt sein

prepaid [priː'peɪd] adj vorausbezahlt; (envelope) frankiert

preparation [prepə'reɪʃən] n Vorbereitung f; **prepare** [prɪ'peə°] vt vorbereiten (for auf +akk); (food)

zubereiten; **to be ~d to do sth** bereit sein, etw zu tun ⊳ vi sich vorbereiten (for auf +akk)

prerequisite [priː'rekwɪzɪt] n Voraussetzung f

prescribe [prɪ'skraɪb] vt vorschreiben; (Med) verschreiben; **prescription** [prɪ'skrɪpʃən] n Rezept nt

presence ['prezns] n Gegenwart f; **present** ['preznt] adj (in attendance) anwesend (at bei); (current) gegenwärtig; **~ tense** Gegenwart f, Präsens nt ⊳ n Gegenwart f; (gift) Geschenk nt; **at ~** zurzeit ⊳ ['preznt] vt (TV, Radio) präsentieren; (problem) darstellen; (report etc) vorlegen; **to ~ sb with sth** jdm etw überreichen; **present-day** adj heutig; **presently** adv bald; (at present) zurzeit

preservative [prɪ'zɜːvətɪv] n Konservierungsmittel nt; **preserve** [prɪ'zɜːv] vt erhalten; (food) einmachen, konservieren

president ['prezɪdənt] n Präsident(in) m(f); **presidential** [prezɪ'denʃəl] adj Präsidenten-; (election) Präsidentschafts-

press [pres] n (newspapers, machine) Presse f ⊳ vt (push) drücken; **to ~ a button** auf einen Knopf drücken ⊳ vi (push) drücken; **pressing** adj dringend; **press-stud** n Druckknopf m; **press-up** n (Brit) Liegestütz m; **pressure** ['preʃə°] n Druck m; **to be under ~** unter Druck stehen; **to put ~ on sb** jdn unter Druck setzen; **pressure cooker** n Schnellkochtopf m; **pressurize** ['preʃəraɪz] vt (person) unter Druck setzen

presumably [prɪ'zjuːməblɪ] adv vermutlich; **presume** [prɪ'zjuːm] vt, vi annehmen

presumptuous [prɪˈzʌmptʃʊəs] *adj* anmaßend

presuppose [priːsəˈpəʊz] *vt* voraussetzen

pretend [prɪˈtɛnd] *vt*: **to ~ that** so tun als ob; **to ~ to do sth** vorgeben, etw zu tun ▷ *vi*: **she's ~ing** sie tut nur so

pretentious [prɪˈtɛnʃəs] *adj* anmaßend; *(person)* wichtigtuerisch

pretty [ˈprɪtɪ] *adj* hübsch ▷ *adv* ziemlich

prevent [prɪˈvɛnt] *vt* verhindern; **to ~ sb from doing sth** jdn daran hindern, etw zu tun

preview [ˈpriːvjuː] *n* (Ciné) Voraufführung *f*; *(trailer)* Vorschau *f*

previous, **previously** [ˈpriːvɪəs, -lɪ] *adj, adv* früher

prey [preɪ] *n* Beute *f*

price [praɪs] *n* Preis *m* ▷ *vt*: **it's ~d at £10** es ist mit 10 Pfund ausgezeichnet; **priceless** *adj* unbezahlbar; **price list** *n* Preisliste *f*; **price tag** *n* Preisschild *nt*

prick [prɪk] *n* Stich *m*; *(vulg: penis)* Schwanz *m*; *(vulg: person)* Arsch *m* ▷ *vt* stechen in +*akk*; **to ~ one's finger** sich *dat* in den Finger stechen; **prickly** [ˈprɪklɪ] *adj* stachelig

pride [praɪd] *n* Stolz *m*; *(arrogance)* Hochmut *m* ▷ *vt*: **to ~ oneself on sth** auf etw *akk* stolz sein

priest [priːst] *n* Priester *m*

primarily [ˈpraɪmərɪlɪ] *adv* vorwiegend; **primary** [ˈpraɪmərɪ] *adj* Haupt-; **~ education** Grundschulausbildung *f*; **~ school** Grundschule *f*

prime [praɪm] *adj* Haupt-; *(excellent)* erstklassig ▷ *n*: **in one's ~** in den besten Jahren; **prime minister** *n* Premierminister(in) *m(f)*; **prime time** *n* (TV) Hauptsendezeit *f*

primitive [ˈprɪmɪtɪv] *adj* primitiv

primrose [ˈprɪmrəʊz] *n* Schlüsselblume *f*

prince [prɪns] *n* Prinz *m*; *(ruler)* Fürst *m*; **princess** [prɪnˈsɛs] *n* Prinzessin *f*; Fürstin *f*

principal [ˈprɪnsɪpəl] *adj* Haupt-, wichtigste(r, s) ▷ *n* (school) Rektor(in) *m(f)*

principle [ˈprɪnsəpl] *n* Prinzip *nt*; **in ~** im Prinzip; **on ~** aus Prinzip

print [prɪnt] *n* (picture) Druck *m*; (Foto) Abzug *m*; (made by feet, fingers) Abdruck *m*; **out of ~** vergriffen ▷ *vt* drucken; (photo) abziehen; (write in block letters) in Druckschrift schreiben; **print out** *vt* (Inform) ausdrucken; **printed matter** *n* Drucksache *f*; **printer** *n* Drucker *m*; **printout** *n* (Inform) Ausdruck *m*

prior [ˈpraɪə] *adj* früher; **a ~ engagement** eine vorher getroffene Verabredung; **~ to sth** vor etw *dat*; **~ to going abroad, she had ...** bevor sie ins Ausland ging, hatte sie ...

priority [praɪˈɒrɪtɪ] *n* (thing having precedence) Priorität *f*

prison [ˈprɪzn] *n* Gefängnis *nt*; **prisoner** *n* Gefangene(r) *mf*; **~ of war** Kriegsgefangene(r) *mf*

privacy [ˈprɪvəsɪ] *n* Privatleben *nt*; **private** [ˈpraɪvɪt] *adj* privat; *(confidential)* vertraulich ▷ *n* einfacher Soldat; **in ~** privat; **privately** *adv* privat; *(confidentially)* vertraulich; **privatize** [ˈpraɪvətaɪz] *vt* privatisieren

privilege [ˈprɪvɪlɪdʒ] *n* Privileg *nt*; **privileged** *adj* privilegiert

prize [praɪz] *n* Preis *m*; **prize money** *n* Preisgeld *nt*; **prizewinner** *n* Gewinner(in) *m(f)*; **prizewinning** *adj* preisgekrönt

pro [prəʊ] (pl **-s**) n (professional)
Profi m; **the ~s and cons** pl das Für
und Wider

pro- [prəʊ] pref pro-

probability [prɒbə'bɪlətɪ] n
Wahrscheinlichkeit f; **probable**,
probably ['prɒbəbl, -blɪ] adj, adv
wahrscheinlich

probation [prə'beɪʃən] n
Probezeit f; (Jur) Bewährung f

probe [prəʊb] n (investigation)
Untersuchung f ▷ vt untersuchen

problem ['prɒbləm] n Problem
nt; **no ~** kein Problem!

procedure [prə'siːdʒə°] n Verfahren nt

proceed [prə'siːd] vi (continue)
fortfahren; (set about sth) vorgehen
▷ vt: **to ~ to do sth** anfangen, etw
zu tun; **proceedings** npl (Jur)
Verfahren nt; **proceeds**
['prəʊsiːds] npl Erlös m

process ['prəʊses] n Prozess m,
Vorgang m; (method) Verfahren nt
▷ vt (application etc) bearbeiten;
(food, data) verarbeiten; (film)
entwickeln

procession [prə'seʃən] n Umzug m

processor ['prəʊsesə°] n (Inform)
Prozessor m; (Gastr)
Küchenmaschine f

produce [prə'djuːs] (Agr)
Produkte pl, Erzeugnisse pl
▷ [prə'djuːs] vt (manufacture)
herstellen, produzieren; (on farm)
erzeugen; (film, play, record)
produzieren; (cause) hervorrufen;
(evidence, results) liefern; **producer**
n (manufacturer) Hersteller(in)
m(f); (of film, play, record)
Produzent(in) m(f); **product**
['prɒdʌkt] n Produkt nt,
Erzeugnis nt; **production**
[prə'dʌkʃən] n Produktion f;
(Theat) Inszenierung f; **productive**
[prə'dʌktɪv] adj produktiv; (land)
ertragreich

prof [prɒf] n (fam) Prof m

profession [prə'feʃən] n Beruf
m; **professional** [prə'feʃənl] n
Profi m ▷ adj beruflich; (expert)
fachlich; (sportsman, actor etc)
Berufs-

professor [prə'fesə°] n Profes-
sor(in) m(f); (US: lecturer)
Dozent(in) m(f)

proficient [prə'fɪʃənt] adj
kompetent (in in +dat)

profile ['prəʊfaɪl] n Profil nt; **to
keep a low ~** sich rarmachen

profit ['prɒfɪt] n Gewinn m ▷ vi
profitieren (by, from von);
profitable adj rentabel

profound [prə'faʊnd] adj tief;
(idea, thinker) tiefgründig;
(knowledge) profund

program ['prəʊgræm] n (Inform)
Programm nt; (US) see **programme**
▷ vt (Inform) programmieren; (US)
see **programme**

programme ['prəʊgræm] n
Programm nt; (TV, Radio) Sendung f
▷ vt programmieren;
programmer n Program-
mierer(in) m(f); **programming**
(Inform) Programmieren nt;
~ language Programmiersprache f

progress ['prəʊgres] n Fortschritt m; **to make ~** Fortschritte
machen ▷ [prə'gres] vi (work,
illness etc) fortschreiten; (improve)
Fortschritte machen; **progressive**
[prə'gresɪv] adj (person, policy)
fortschrittlich; **progressively**
[prə'gresɪvlɪ] adv zunehmend

prohibit [prə'hɪbɪt] vt verbieten

project ['prɒdʒekt] n Projekt nt

projector [prə'dʒektə°] n Projektor m

prolong [prə'lɒŋ] vt verlängern

prom [prɒm] n (at seaside)
Promenade f; (Brit: concert) Konzert
nt (bei dem ein Großteil des Publikums
im Parkett Stehplätze hat); (US:

dance) Ball für die Schüler und
Studenten von Highschools oder
Colleges

prominent ['prɒmɪnənt] adj
(politician, actor etc) prominent;
(easily seen) auffallend

promiscuous [prə'mɪskjʊəs]
adj promisk

promise ['prɒmɪs] n Versprechen nt ▷ vt versprechen; **to
~ sb sth** jdm etw versprechen; **to
~ to do sth** versprechen, etw zu
tun ▷ vi versprechen; **promising**
adj vielversprechend

promote [prə'məʊt] vt (in rank)
befördern; (help on) fördern;
(Comm) werben für; **promotion**
[prə'məʊʃən] n (in rank)
Beförderung f; (Comm) Werbung f
(of für)

prompt [prɒmpt] adj prompt;
(punctual) pünktlich ▷ adv: **at two
o'clock ~** Punkt zwei Uhr ▷ vt
(Theat: actor) soufflieren +dat

prone [prəʊn] adj: **to be ~ to sth**
zu etw neigen

pronounce [prə'naʊns] vt
(word) aussprechen; **pronounced**
adj ausgeprägt; **pronunciation**
[prənʌnsɪ'eɪʃən] n Aussprache f

proof [pru:f] n Beweis m; (of
alcohol) Alkoholgehalt m

prop [prɒp] n Stütze f; (Theat)
Requisit nt ▷ vt: **to ~ sth
against sth** etw gegen etw
lehnen; **prop up** vt stützen; (fig)
unterstützen

proper ['prɒpə°] adj richtig;
(morally correct) anständig

property ['prɒpətɪ] n (possession)
Figentum nt; (house) Haus nt; (land)
Grundbesitz m; (characteristic)
Eigenschaft f

proportion [prə'pɔ:ʃən] n
Verhältnis nt; (share) Teil m; **~s** pl
(size) Proportionen pl; **in ~ to** im
Verhältnis zu; **proportional** adj

proportional; **~ representation**
Verhältniswahlrecht nt

proposal [prə'pəʊzl] n Vorschlag
m; **~ (of marriage)** (Heirats)antrag
m; **propose** [prə'pəʊz] vt
vorschlagen ▷ vi (offer marriage)
einen Heiratsantrag machen (to sb
jdm)

proprietor [prə'praɪətə°] n
Besitzer(in) m(f); (of pub, hotel)
Inhaber(in) m(f)

prose [prəʊz] n Prosa f

prosecute ['prɒsɪkju:t] vt verfolgen (for wegen)

prospect n ['prɒspekt] n Aussicht
f

prosperity [prɒ'sperɪtɪ] n
Wohlstand m; **prosperous** adj
wohlhabend; (business) gut
gehend

prostitute ['prɒstɪtju:t] n Prosti-
tuierte(r) mf

protect [prə'tekt] vt schützen
(from, against vor +dat, gegen);
protection [prə'tekʃən] n Schutz
m (from, against vor +dat, gegen);
protective adj beschützend;
(clothing etc) Schutz-

protein ['prəʊti:n] n Protein nt

protest n ['prəʊtest] n Protest m;
(demonstration)
Protestkundgebung f ▷ [prə'test]
vi protestieren (against gegen);
(demonstrate) demonstrieren

Protestant ['prɒtəstənt] adj
protestantisch ▷ n Protestant(in)
m(f)

proud **proudly** [praʊd, -lɪ] adj,
adv stolz (of auf +akk)

prove [pru:v] vt beweisen; (turn
out to be) sich erweisen als

proverb ['prɒvɜ:b] n Sprichwort
nt

provide [prə'vaɪd] vt zur
Verfügung stellen; (drinks, music
etc) sorgen für; (person) versorgen
(with mit); **provide for** vt (family

etc) sorgen für; **provided** *conj*: ~ **(that)** vorausgesetzt, dass; **provider** *n* (*Inform*) Provider *m*

provision [prə'vɪʒən] *n* (*condition*) Bestimmung *f*; **~s** *pl* (*food*) Proviant *m*

provisional, provisionally [prə'vɪʒənl, -l] *adj, adv* provisorisch

provoke [prə'vəʊk] *vt* provozieren; (*cause*) hervorrufen

proximity [prɒk'sɪmɪtɪ] *n* Nähe *f*

prudent ['pru:dənt] *adj* klug; (*person*) umsichtig

prudish ['pru:dɪʃ] *adj* prüde

prune [pru:n] *n* Backpflaume *f* ▷ *vt* (*tree etc*) zurechtstutzen

PS *abbr* = **postscript** PS *nt*

psalm [sɑ:m] *n* Psalm *m*

pseudo ['sju:dəʊ] *adj* pseudo-, Pseudo-; **pseudonym** ['sju:dənɪm] *n* Pseudonym *nt*

PST *abbr* = **Pacific Standard Time**

psychiatric [saɪkɪ'ætrɪk] *adj* psychiatrisch; (*illness*) psychisch; **psychiatrist** [saɪ'kaɪətrɪst] *n* Psychiater(in) *m(f)*; **psychiatry** [saɪ'kaɪətrɪ] *n* Psychiatrie *f*; **psychic** ['saɪkɪk] *adj* übersinnlich; **I'm not** ~ ich kann keine Gedanken lesen; **psychoanalysis** [saɪkəʊə'næləsɪs] *n* Psychoanalyse *f*; **psychoanalyst** [saɪkəʊ'ænəlɪst] *n* Psychoanalytiker(in) *m(f)*; **psychological** [saɪkə'lɒdʒɪkəl] *adj* psychologisch; **psychology** [saɪ'kɒlədʒɪ] *n* Psychologie *f*; **psychopath** ['saɪkəʊpæθ] *n* Psychopath(in) *m(f)*

pt *abbr* = **pint**

pto *abbr* = **please turn over** b.w.

pub [pʌb] *n* (*Brit*) Kneipe *f*

● **PUB**

● Ein **pub** ist ein Gasthaus mit
● einer Lizenz zum Ausschank von

● alkoholischen Getränken. Ein
● „Pub" besteht meist aus
● verschiedenen gemütlichen
● (**lounge, snug**) oder
● einfacheren (**public bar**)
● Räumen, in denen oft auch
● Spiele wie Darts, Domino und
● Poolbillard zur Verfügung
● stehen. In „Pubs" werden vor
● allem mittags auch Mahlzeiten
● angeboten (**pub lunch**). Die
● Sperrstunde wurde 2005
● aufgehoben. Dennoch sind
● „Pubs" oft nur von 11 bis 23 Uhr
● geöffnet. Nachmittags bleiben
● sie häufig geschlossen.

puberty ['pju:bətɪ] *n* Pubertät *f*

public ['pʌblɪk] *n*: **the (general)** ~ die (breite) Öffentlichkeit; **in** ~ in der Öffentlichkeit ▷ *adj* öffentlich; (*relating to the State*) Staats-; ~ **convenience** (*Brit*) öffentliche Toilette; ~ **holiday** gesetzlicher Feiertag; ~ **opinion** die öffentliche Meinung; ~ **relations** *pl* Öffentlichkeitsarbeit *f*, Public Relations *pl*; ~ **school** (*Brit*) Privatschule *f*; **publication** [pʌblɪ'keɪʃən] *n* Veröffentlichung *f*; **publicity** [pʌb'lɪsɪtɪ] *n* Publicity *f*; (*advertisements*) Werbung *f*; **publish** ['pʌblɪʃ] *vt* veröffentlichen; **publisher** *n* Verleger(in) *m(f)*; (*company*) Verlag *m*; **publishing** *n* Verlagswesen *nt*

pub lunch ['pʌb'lʌntʃ] *n* (*oft einfacheres*) Mittagessen in einer Kneipe

pudding ['pʊdɪŋ] *n* (*course*) Nachtisch *m*

puddle ['pʌdl] *n* Pfütze *f*

puff [pʌf] *vi* (*pant*) schnaufen

puffin ['pʌfɪn] *n* Papageientaucher *m*

puff paste (US), **puff pastry**
['pʌf'peɪstrɪ] n Blätterteig m

pull [pul] n Ziehen nt; **to give sth
a ~** an etw dat ziehen ▷ vt (cart,
tooth) ziehen; (rope, handle) ziehen
an +dat; (fam: date) abschleppen;
to ~ a muscle sich dat einen
Muskel zerren; **to ~ sb's leg** jdn
auf den Arm nehmen ▷ vi ziehen;
pull apart vt (separate)
auseinanderziehen; **pull down** vt
(blind) herunterziehen; (house)
abreißen; **pull in** vi hineinfahren;
(stop) anhalten; **pull off** vt (deal
etc) zuwege bringen; (clothes)
ausziehen; **pull out** vi (car from
lane) ausscheren; (train) abfahren;
(withdraw) aussteigen (of aus) ▷ vt
herausziehen; (tooth) ziehen;
(troops) abziehen; **pull round**, **pull
through** vi durchkommen; **pull
up** vt (raise) hochziehen; (chair)
heranziehen ▷ vi anhalten

pullover ['puləʊvə°] n Pullover m

pulp [pʌlp] n Brei m; (of fruit)
Fruchtfleisch nt

pulpit ['pulpɪt] n Kanzel f

pulse [pʌls] n Puls m

pump [pʌmp] n Pumpe f; (in
petrol station) Zapfsäule f; **pump up**
vt (tyre etc) aufpumpen

pumpkin ['pʌmpkɪn] n Kürbis m

pun [pʌn] n Wortspiel nt

punch [pʌntʃ] n (blow)
(Faust)schlag m; (tool) Locher m;
(hot drink) Punsch m; (cold drink)
Bowle f ▷ vt (strike) schlagen;
(ticket, paper) lochen

punctual, **punctually**
['pʌŋktjʊəl, -lɪ] adj, adv
pünktlich

punctuation [pʌŋktʊ'eɪʃən] n
Interpunktion f; **punctuation
mark** n Satzzeichen nt

puncture ['pʌŋktʃə°] n (flat tyre)
Reifenpanne f

punish ['pʌnɪʃ] vt bestrafen;
punishment n Strafe f; (action)
Bestrafung f

pupil ['pjuːpl] n (school)
Schüler(in) m(f)

puppet ['pʌpɪt] n Marionette f

puppy ['pʌpɪ] n junger Hund

purchase ['pɜːtʃɪs] n Kauf m ▷ vt
kaufen

pure [pjʊə°] adj rein; (clean)
sauber; (utter) pur; **purely**
['pjʊəlɪ] adv rein; **purify**
['pjʊərɪfaɪ] vt reinigen; **purity**
['pjʊərɪtɪ] n Reinheit f

purple ['pɜːpl] adj violett

purpose ['pɜːpəs] n Zweck m; (of
person) Absicht f; **on ~** absichtlich

purr [pɜː°] vi (cat) schnurren

purse [pɜːs] n Geldbeutel m; (US:
handbag) Handtasche f

pursue [pə'sjuː] vt (person, car)
verfolgen; (hobby, studies)
nachgehen +dat; **pursuit**
[pə'sjuːt] n (chase) Verfolgung f;
(occupation) Beschäftigung f;
(hobby) Hobby nt

pus [pʌs] n Eiter m

push [puʃ] n Stoß m ▷ vt (person)
stoßen; (car, chair etc) schieben;
(button) drücken; (drugs) dealen
▷ vi (in crowd) drängeln; **push in** vi
(in queue) sich vordrängeln; **push
off** vi (fam: leave) abhauen; **push
on** vi (with job) weitermachen;
push up vt (prices) hochtreiben;
pushchair n (Brit)
Sport(kinder)wagen m; **pusher** n
(of drugs) Dealer(in) m(f); **push-up**
n (US) Liegestütz m; **pushy** adj
(fam) aufdringlich, penetrant

put [put] (put, put) vt tun;
(upright) stellen; (flat) legen;
(express) ausdrücken; (write)
schreiben; **he ~ his hand in his
pocket** er steckte die Hand in die
Tasche; **he ~ his hand on her
shoulder** er legte ihr die Hand auf

die Schulter; **to ~ money into one's account** Geld auf sein Konto einzahlen; **put aside** vt (money) zurücklegen; **put away** vt (tidy away) wegräumen; **put back** vt zurücklegen; (clock) zurückstellen; **put down** vt (in writing) aufschreiben; (Brit: animal) einschläfern; (rebellion) niederschlagen; **to put the phone down** (den Hörer) auflegen; **to put one's name down for sth** sich für etw eintragen; **put forward** vt (idea) vorbringen; (name) vorschlagen; (clock) vorstellen; **put in** vt (install) einbauen; (submit) einreichen; **put off** vt (switch off) ausschalten; (postpone) verschieben; **to put sb off doing sth** jdn davon abbringen, etw zu tun; **put on** vt (switch on) anmachen; (clothes) anziehen; (hat, glasses) aufsetzen; (make-up, CD) auflegen; (play) aufführen; **to put the kettle on** Wasser aufsetzen; **to put weight on** zunehmen; **put out** vt (hand, foot) ausstrecken; (light, cigarette) ausmachen; **put up** vt (hand) hochheben; (picture) aufhängen; (tent) aufstellen; (building) errichten; (price) erhöhen; (person) unterbringen; **to ~ with** sich abfinden mit; **I won't ~ with it** das lasse ich mir nicht gefallen

putt [pʌt] vt, vi (Sport) putten
puzzle ['pʌzl] n Rätsel nt; (toy) Geduldsspiel nt; (jigsaw) ~ Puzzle nt ▷ vt vor ein Rätsel stellen; **it ~s me** es ist mir ein Rätsel; **puzzling** adj rätselhaft

pyjamas [pɪ'dʒɑːməz] npl Schlafanzug m
pylon ['paɪlən] n Mast m
pyramid ['pɪrəmɪd] n Pyramide f

quack [kwæk] vi quaken
quaint [kweɪnt] adj (idea, tradition) kurios; (picturesque) malerisch
qualification [kwɒlɪfɪ'keɪʃən] n (for job) Qualifikation f; (from school, university) Abschluss m; **qualified** ['kwɒlɪfaɪd] adj (for job) qualifiziert; **qualify** vt (limit) einschränken ▷ vi (finish training) seine Ausbildung abschließen; (contest etc) sich qualifizieren
quality ['kwɒlɪtɪ] n Qualität f; (characteristic) Eigenschaft f
quantity ['kwɒntɪtɪ] n Menge f, Quantität f
quarantine ['kwɒrəntiːn] n Quarantäne f
quarrel ['kwɒrəl] n Streit m ▷ vi sich streiten
quarter ['kwɔːtə] n Viertel nt;

(of year) Vierteljahr nt; (US: coin) Vierteldollar m; **a ~ of an hour** eine Viertelstunde; **~ to/past** (Brit) (o ~ **of/after** (US)) **three** Viertel vor/nach drei ▷ vt vierteln; **quarter final** n Viertelfinale nt; **quarters** npl (Mil) Quartier nt

quartet [kwɔːˈtet] n Quartett nt

quay [kiː] n Kai m

queasy [ˈkwiːzɪ] adj: **I feel ~** mir ist übel

queen [kwiːn] n Königin f; (in cards, chess) Dame f

queer [kwɪə°] adj (strange) seltsam, sonderbar; (esp: homosexual) schwul ▷ n (pej) Schwule(r) m

quench [kwentʃ] vt (thirst) löschen

query [ˈkwɪərɪ] n Frage f ▷ vt infrage stellen; (bill) reklamieren

question [ˈkwestʃən] n Frage f; **that's out of the ~** das kommt nicht infrage ▷ vt (interrogate) befragen; (suspect) verhören; (express doubt about) bezweifeln; **questionable** adj zweifelhaft; (improper) fragwürdig; **question mark** n Fragezeichen nt; **questionnaire** [kwestʃəˈnɛə°] n Fragebogen m

queue [kjuː] n (Brit) Schlange f; **to jump the ~** sich vordrängeln ▷ vi: **to ~ (up)** Schlange stehen

quibble [ˈkwɪbl] vi kleinlich sein; (argue) streiten

quiche [kiːʃ] n Quiche

quick [kwɪk] adj schnell; (short) kurz; **be ~** mach schnell!; **quickly** adv schnell

quid [kwɪd] (pl **quid**) n (Brit fam) Pfund nt; **20 ~** 20 Pfund

quiet [ˈkwaɪət] adj (not noisy) leise; (peaceful, calm) still, ruhig; **be ~** sei still!; **to keep ~ about sth** über etw akk nichts sagen ▷ n

Stille f, Ruhe f; **quiet down** (US), **quieten down** [ˈkwaɪətənˈdaʊn] vi sich beruhigen ▷ vt beruhigen; **quietly** adv leise; (calmly) ruhig

quilt [kwɪlt] n (Stepp)decke f

quit [kwɪt] (**quit** o **quitted, quit** o **quitted**) vt (leave) verlassen; (job) aufgeben; **to ~ doing sth** aufhören, etw zu tun ▷ vi aufhören; (resign) kündigen

quite [kwaɪt] adv (fairly) ziemlich; (completely) ganz, völlig; **I don't ~ understand** ich verstehe das nicht ganz; **a few** ziemlich viele; **~ so** richtig!

quits [kwɪts] adj: **to be ~ with sb** mit jdm quitt sein

quiver [ˈkwɪvə°] vi zittern

quiz [kwɪz] n (competition) Quiz nt

quota [ˈkwəʊtə] n Anteil m; (Comm, Pol) Quote f

quotation [kwəʊˈteɪʃən] n Zitat nt; (price) Kostenvoranschlag m; **quotation marks** npl Anführungszeichen pl; **quote** [kwəʊt] vt (text, author) zitieren; (price) nennen ▷ n Zitat nt; (price) Kostenvoranschlag m; **in ~s** in Anführungszeichen

r

rabbi ['ræbaɪ] n Rabbiner m

rabbit ['ræbɪt] n Kaninchen nt

rabies ['reɪbiːz] nsing Tollwut f

raccoon [rə'kuːn] n Waschbär m

race [reɪs] n (competition) Rennen nt; (people) Rasse f ▷ vt um die Wette laufen/fahren ▷ vi (rush) rennen; **racecourse** n Rennbahn f; **racehorse** n Rennpferd nt; **racetrack** n Rennbahn f

racial ['reɪʃəl] adj Rassen-; **~ discrimination** n Rassendiskriminierung f

racing ['reɪsɪŋ] n (horse) **~** Pferderennen nt; (motor) **~** Autorennen nt; **racing car** n Rennwagen m

racism ['reɪsɪzəm] n Rassismus m; **racist** n Rassist(in) m(f) ▷ adj rassistisch

rack [ræk] n Ständer m, Gestell nt ▷ vt: **to ~ one's brains** sich dat den Kopf zerbrechen

racket ['rækɪt] n (Sport) Schläger m; (noise) Krach m

radar ['reɪdɑː°] n Radar nt o m; **radar trap** n Radarfalle f

radiation [reɪdɪ'eɪʃən] n (radioactive) Strahlung f

radiator ['reɪdɪeɪtə°] n Heizkörper m; (Auto) Kühler m

radical ['rædɪkəl] adj radikal

radio ['reɪdɪəʊ] (pl -s) n Rundfunk m, Radio nt

radioactivity [reɪdɪəʊæk'tɪvɪtɪ] n Radioaktivität f

radio alarm ['reɪdɪəʊə'lɑːm] n Radiowecker m; **radio station** n Rundfunkstation f

radiotherapy [reɪdɪəʊ'θerəpɪ] n Strahlenbehandlung f

radish ['rædɪʃ] n Radieschen nt

radius ['reɪdɪəs] n Radius m; **within a five-mile ~** im Umkreis von fünf Meilen (of um)

raffle ['ræfl] n Tombola f; **raffle ticket** n Los nt

raft [rɑːft] n Floß nt

rag [ræg] n Lumpen m; (for cleaning) Lappen m

rage [reɪdʒ] n Wut f; **to be all the ~** der letzte Schrei sein ▷ vi toben; (disease) wüten

raid [reɪd] n Überfall m (on auf +akk); (by police) Razzia f (on gegen) ▷ vt (bank etc) überfallen; (by police) eine Razzia machen in +dat

rail [reɪl] n (on stairs, balcony etc) Geländer nt; (of ship) Reling f; (Rail) Schiene f; **railcard** n (Brit) = Bahncard® f Geländer nt; **~s** pl (fence) Zaun m; **railroad** n (US) Eisenbahn f; **railroad station** n (US) Bahnhof m; **railway** n (Brit) Eisenbahn f; **railway line** n Bahnlinie f; (track) Gleis m; **railway station** n Bahnhof m

rain [reɪn] n Regen m ▷ vi regnen; **it's ~ing** es regnet; **rainbow** n Regenbogen m;

raincoat n Regenmantel m;
rainfall n Niederschlag m;
rainforest n Regenwald m; **rainy**
adj regnerisch

raise [reɪz] n (US: of wages/salary)
Gehalts-/Lohnerhöhung f ▷ vt
(lift) hochheben; (increase)
erhöhen; (family) großziehen;
(livestock) züchten; (money)
aufbringen; (objection) erheben; **to
~ one's voice** laut werden

raisin ['reɪzən] n Rosine f

rally ['rælɪ] n (Pol) Kundgebung f;
(Aut) Rallye f; (Tennis) Ballwechsel
m

RAM [ræm] acr = **random access
memory** RAM m

ramble ['ræmbl] n Wanderung f
▷ vi (walk) wandern; (talk)
schwafeln

ramp [ræmp] n Rampe f

ran [ræn] pt of **run**

ranch [rɑːntʃ] n Ranch f

rancid ['rænsɪd] adj ranzig

random ['rændəm] adj
willkürlich ▷ n; **at ~** (choose)
willkürlich; (fire) ziellos

rang [ræŋ] pt of **ring**

range [reɪndʒ] n (selection)
Auswahl f (of an +dat); (Comm)
Sortiment n (of an +dat); (of
missile, telescope) Reichweite f; (of
mountains) Kette f; **in this price
~** in dieser Preisklasse ▷ vi; **to
~ from ... to ...** gehen von ... bis ...;
(temperature, sizes, prices) liegen
zwischen ... und ...

rank [ræŋk] n (Mil) Rang m; (social
position) Stand m ▷ vt einstufen

ransom ['rænsəm] n Lösegeld nt

rap [ræp] n (Mus) Rap m

rape [reɪp] n Vergewaltigung f
▷ vt vergewaltigen

rapid, rapidly ['ræpɪd, -lɪ] adj, adv
schnell

rapist n Vergewaltiger
m

rare [rɛə°] adj selten, rar;
(especially good) vortrefflich; (steak)
blutig; **rarely** adv selten; **rarity**
['rɛərɪtɪ] n Seltenheit f

rash [ræʃ] adj unbesonnen ▷ n
(Med) (Haut)ausschlag m

rasher ['ræʃə°] n: **~ (of bacon)**
(Speck)scheibe f

raspberry ['rɑːzbərɪ] n Himbeere f

rat [ræt] n Ratte f; (pej: person)
Schwein nt

rate [reɪt] n (proportion, frequency)
Rate f; (speed) Tempo nt; **~ (of
exchange)** (Wechsel)kurs m; **~ of
inflation** Inflationsrate f; **~ of
interest** Zinssatz m; **at any ~** auf
jeden Fall ▷ vt (evaluate)
einschätzen (as als)

rather ['rɑːðə°] adv (in preference)
lieber; (fairly) ziemlich; **I'd ~ stay
here** ich würde lieber hierbleiben;
I'd ~ not lieber nicht; **or ~** (more
accurately) vielmehr

ratio ['reɪʃɪəʊ] (pl -s) n Verhältnis
nt

rational ['ræʃənl] adj rational;
rationalize ['ræʃnəlaɪz] vt
rationalisieren

rattle ['rætl] n (toy) Rassel f ▷ vt
(keys, coins) klimpern mit; (person)
durcheinanderbringen ▷ vi (window) klappern; (bottles) klirren;
rattle off vt herunterrasseln;
rattlesnake n Klapperschlange
f

rave [reɪv] vi (talk wildly)
fantasieren; (rage) toben; (enthuse)
schwärmen (about von) ▷ n (Brit:
event) Raveparty f

raven ['reɪvn] n Rabe m

raving ['reɪvɪŋ] adv: **~ mad** total
verrückt

ravishing ['rævɪʃɪŋ] adj
hinreißend

raw [rɔː] adj (food) roh; (skin)
wund; (climate) rau

ray [reɪ] n (of light) Strahl m; **~ of
hope** Hoffnungsschimmer m

razor [ˈreɪzəʳ] n Rasierapparat
m; **razor blade** n Rasierklinge f

Rd n abbr = **road** Str.

re [riː] prep (Comm) betreffs +gen

RE abbr = **religious education**

reach [riːtʃ] n within/out of
(sb's) ~ in/außer (jds) Reichweite;
within easy ~ of the shops nicht
weit von den Geschäften ▷ vt
(arrive at, contact) erreichen; (come
down/up as far as) reichen bis zu;
(contact) **can you ~ it?** kommst
du/kommen Sie dran?; **reach for**
vt greifen nach; **reach out** vi die
Hand ausstrecken; **to ~ for** greifen
nach

react [riːˈækt] vi reagieren (to auf
+akk); **reaction** [riːˈækʃən] n
Reaktion f (to auf +akk); **reactor**
[riːˈæktəʳ] n Reaktor m

read [riːd] (read, read) vt lesen;
(meter) ablesen; **to ~ sth to sb** jdm
etw vorlesen ▷ vi lesen; **to ~ to sb**
jdm vorlesen; **it ~s well** es liest
sich gut; **it ~s as follows** es lautet
folgendermaßen; **read out** vt
vorlesen; **read through** vt
durchlesen; **read up on** vt
nachlesen über +akk; **readable** adj
(book) lesenswert; (handwriting)
lesbar; **reader** n Leser(in) m(f);
readership n Leserschaft f

readily [ˈrɛdɪlɪ] adv (willingly)
bereitwillig; **~ available** leicht
erhältlich

reading [ˈriːdɪŋ] n (action) Lesen
nt; (from meter) Zählerstand m;
reading glasses npl Lesebrille f;
reading lamp n Leselampe f;
reading list n Leseliste f; **reading
matter** n Lektüre f

readjust [riːəˈdʒʌst] vt (mechanism etc) neu einstellen ▷ vi sich
wieder anpassen (to an +akk)

ready [ˈrɛdɪ] adj fertig, bereit; **to**

be ~ to do sth (willing) bereit sein,
etw zu tun; **are you ~ to go?** bist
du so weit?; **to get sth ~** etw
fertig machen; **to get (oneself)**
~ sich fertig machen; **ready cash**
n Bargeld nt; **ready-made** adj
(product) Fertig-; (clothes)
Konfektions-; **~ meal**
Fertiggericht nt

real [rɪəl] adj wirklich; (actual)
eigentlich; (genuine) echt; (idiot etc)
richtig ▷ adv (fam, esp US) echt;
for ~ echt; **this time it's for**
~ diesmal ist es ernst; **get ~** sei
realistisch!; **real ale** n Ale nt; **real
estate** n Immobilien pl

realistic, realistically [rɪəˈlɪstɪk,
-əlɪ] adj, adv realistisch; **reality**
[riːˈælɪtɪ] n Wirklichkeit f; **in ~** in
Wirklichkeit; **reality TV** n
Reality-TV nt; **realization**
[rɪəlaɪˈzeɪʃən] n (awareness)
Erkenntnis f; **realize** [ˈrɪəlaɪz] vt
(understand) begreifen; (plan, idea)
realisieren; **I ~d (that)** ... mir
wurde klar, dass ...

really [ˈrɪəlɪ] adv wirklich

real time [rɪəlˈtaɪm] n (Inform)
in ~ in Echtzeit

realtor [ˈrɪəltəʳ] n (US)
Grundstücksmakler(in) m(f)

reappear [riːəˈpɪəʳ] vi wieder
erscheinen

rear [rɪəʳ] adj hintere(r, s),
Hinter- ▷ n (of building, vehicle)
hinterer Teil; **at the ~ of** hinter
+dat; (inside) hinten in +dat; **rear
light** n (Auto) Rücklicht nt

rearm [riːˈɑːm] vi wieder
aufrüsten

rearrange [riːəˈreɪndʒ] vt (furniture, system) umstellen; (meeting)
verlegen (for auf +akk)

rear-view mirror
[ˈrɪəvjuːˈmɪrəʳ] n Rückspiegel m;
rear window n (Auto)
Heckscheibe f

reason ['riːzn] n (cause) Grund m
(for für); (ability to think) Verstand
m; (common sense) Vernunft f; **for
some ~** aus irgendeinem Grund
▷ vi: **to ~ with sb** mit jdm
vernünftig reden; **reasonable** adj
(person, price) vernünftig; (offer)
akzeptabel; (chance) reell; (food,
weather) ganz gut; **reasonably** adv
vernünftig; (fairly) ziemlich

reassure [riːə'ʃuə*] vt beruhigen; **she ~d me that ...** sie
versicherte mir, dass ...

rebel ['rebl] n Rebell(in) m(f)
▷ [rɪ'bel] vi rebellieren; **rebellion**
[rɪ'beliən] n Aufstand m

reboot [riː'buːt] vt, vi (Inform)
rebooten

rebound [rɪ'baund] vi (ball etc)
zurückprallen

rebuild [riː'bɪld] irr vt wieder
aufbauen

recall [rɪ'kɔːl] vt (remember) sich
erinnern an +akk; (call back)
zurückrufen

recap ['riːkæp] vt, vi
rekapitulieren

receipt [rɪ'siːt] n (document)
Quittung f; (receiving) Empfang m;
~s pl (money) Einnahmen pl

receive [rɪ'siːv] vt (news etc)
erhalten, bekommen; (visitor)
empfangen; **receiver** n (Tel)
Hörer m; (Radio) Empfänger m

recent ['riːsnt] adj (event) vor
Kurzem stattgefunden; (photo)
neueste(r,s); (invention) neu; **in
~ years** in den letzten Jahren;
recently adv vor Kurzem; (in the
last few days or weeks) in letzter Zeit

reception [rɪ'sepʃən] n Empfang
m; **receptionist** n (in hotel)
Empfangschef m, Empfangsdame
f; (woman in firm) Empfangsdame f;
(Med) Sprechstundenhilfe f

recess [rɪ'ses] n (in wall) Nische
f; (US: in school) Pause f

recession [rɪ'seʃən] n Rezession
f

recharge [riː'tʃɑːdʒ] vt (battery)
aufladen; **rechargeable**
[riː'tʃɑːdʒəbl] adj wiederaufladbar

recipe ['resɪpɪ] n Rezept nt (for
für)

recipient [rɪ'sɪpɪənt] n
Empfänger(in) m(f)

reciprocal [rɪ'sɪprəkəl] adj
gegenseitig

recite [rɪ'saɪt] vt vortragen;
(details) aufzählen

reckless ['rekləs] adj leichtsinnig; (driving) gefährlich

reckon ['rekən] vt (calculate)
schätzen; (think) glauben ▷ vi: **to
~ with/on** rechnen mit

reclaim [rɪ'kleɪm] vt (baggage)
abholen; (expenses, tax)
zurückverlangen

recline [rɪ'klaɪn] vi (person) sich
zurücklehnen; **reclining seat** n
Liegesitz m

recognition [rekəg'nɪʃən] n
(acknowledgement) Anerkennung f;
in ~ of in Anerkennung +gen;
recognize ['rekəgnaɪz] vt
erkennen; (approve officially)
anerkennen

recommend [rekə'mend] vt
empfehlen; **recommendation**
[rekəmen'deɪʃən] n Empfehlung f

reconfirm [riːkən'fɜːm] vt (flight
etc) rückbestätigen

reconsider [riːkən'sɪdə*] vt noch
einmal überdenken ▷ vi es sich
dat noch einmal überlegen

reconstruct [riːkən'strʌkt] vt
wieder aufbauen; (crime)
rekonstruieren

record ['rekɔːd] n (Mus)
(Schall)platte f; (best performance)
Rekord m; **~s** pl (files) Akten pl; **to
keep a ~ of** Buch führen über +akk
▷ adj (time etc) Rekord- ▷ [rɪ'kɔːd]
vt (write down) aufzeichnen; (on

tape etc) aufnehmen; **~ed message**
Ansage *f*; **recorded delivery** *n*
(*Brit*) **by ~** per Einschreiben
recorder [rɪ'kɔ:də°] *n* (*Mus*)
Blockflöte *f*; (**cassette**)
~ (Kassetten)rekorder *m*;
recording [rɪ'kɔ:dɪŋ] *n* (*on tape
etc*) Aufnahme *f*; **record player**
['rekɔ:dpleɪə°] *n* Plattenspieler *m*
recover [rɪ'kʌvə°] *vt* (*money, item*)
zurückbekommen; (*appetite,
strength*) wiedergewinnen ▷ *vi*
sich erholen
recreation [rekrɪ'eɪʃən] *n*
Erholung *f*; **recreational** *adj*
Freizeit-; **~ vehicle** (*US*)
Wohnmobil *nt*
recruit [rɪ'kru:t] *n* (*Mil*)
Rekrut(in) *m(f)*; (*in firm,
organization*) neues Mitglied ▷ *vt*
(*Mil*) rekrutieren; (*members*)
anwerben; (*staff*) einstellen;
recruitment agency *n*
Personalagentur *f*
rectangle ['rektæŋgl] *n*
Rechteck *nt*; **rectangular**
[rek'tæŋgʊlə°] *adj* rechteckig
rectify ['rektɪfaɪ] *vt* berichtigen
recuperate [rɪ'ku:pəreɪt] *vi* sich
erholen
recyclable [ri:'saɪkləbl] *adj*
recycelbar, wiederverwertbar;
recycle [ri:'saɪkl] *vt* recyceln,
wiederverwerten; **~d paper**
Recyclingpapier *nt*; **recycling** *n*
Recycling *nt*, Wiederverwertung *f*
red [red] *adj* rot ▷ *n*: **in the ~** in
den roten Zahlen; **Red Cross** *n*
Rotes Kreuz; **red cabbage** *n*
Rotkohl *m*; **redcurrant** *n* (rote)
Johannisbeere
redeem [rɪ'di:m] *vt* (*Comm*)
einlösen
red-handed [red'hændɪd] *adj*:
to catch sb ~ jdn auf frischer Tat
ertappen; **redhead** *n*
Rothaarige(r) *mf*

redial [ri:'daɪəl] *vt, vi* nochmals
wählen
redirect [ri:daɪ'rekt] *vt* (*traffic*)
umleiten; (*forward*) nachsenden
red light [red'laɪt] *n* (*traffic
signal*) rotes Licht; **to go through
the ~** bei Rot über die Ampel
fahren; **red meat** *n*
Rind-, Lamm-, Rehfleisch
redo [ri:'du:] *irr vt* nochmals
machen
reduce [rɪ'dju:s] *vt* reduzieren
(*to* auf +*akk, by* um); **reduction**
[rɪ'dʌkʃən] *n* Reduzierung *f*; (*in
price*) Ermäßigung *f*
redundant [rɪ'dʌndənt] *adj*
überflüssig; **to be made ~**
entlassen werden
red wine [red'waɪn] *n* Rotwein
m
reef [ri:f] *n* Riff *nt*
reel [ri:l] *n* Spule *f*; (*on fishing rod*)
Rolle *f*; **reel off** *vt* herunterrasseln
ref [ref] *n* (*fam: referee*) Schiri *m*
refectory [rɪ'fektərɪ] *n* (*at
college*) Mensa *f*
refer [rɪ'fɜ:°] *vt*: **to ~ sb to sb/sth**
jdn an jdn/etw verweisen; **to
~ sth to sb** (*query, problem*) etw an
jdn weiterleiten ▷ *vi*: **to ~ to**
(*mention, allude to*) sich beziehen
auf +*akk*; (*book*) nachschlagen in
+*dat*
referee [refə'ri:] *n* Schiedsrich-
ter(in) *m(f)*; (*in boxing*) Ringrichter
m; (*Brit: for job*) Referenz *f*
reference ['refrəns] *n* (*allusion*)
Anspielung *f* (*to* auf +*akk*); (*for job*)
Referenz *f*; (*in book*) Verweis *m*;
~ (number) (*in document*)
Aktenzeichen *nt*; **with ~ to** mit
Bezug auf +*akk*; **reference book** *n*
Nachschlagewerk *nt*
referendum [refə'rendəm] *n* (*pl*
referenda) *n* Referendum *nt*
refill [ri:'fɪl] *vt* [ri:'fɪl] nachfüllen
▷ *n* (*for ballpoint pen*) Ersatzmine *f*

refine [rɪ'faɪn] vt (purify)
raffinieren; (improve) verfeinern;
refined adj (genteel) fein

reflect [rɪ'flekt] vt reflektieren;
(fig) widerspiegeln ▷ vi
nachdenken (on über +akk);
reflection [rɪ'flekʃən] n (image)
Spiegelbild nt; (thought)
Überlegung f; **on ~** nach reiflicher
Überlegung

reflex ['riːfleks] n Reflex m

reform [rɪ'fɔːm] n Reform f ▷ vt
reformieren; (person) bessern

refrain [rɪ'freɪn] vi: **to ~ from
doing sth** es unterlassen, etw zu
tun

refresh [rɪ'freʃ] vt erfrischen;
refresher course n
Auffrischungskurs m; **refreshing**
adj erfrischend; **refreshments** npl
Erfrischungen pl

refrigerator [rɪ'frɪdʒəreɪtə˚] n
Kühlschrank m

refuel [riː'fjʊəl] vt, vi auftanken

refugee [refjʊ'dʒiː] n Flüchtling
m

refund ['riːfʌnd] n (of money)
Rückerstattung f; **to get a ~ (on
sth)** sein Geld (für etw)
zurückbekommen ▷ [rɪ'fʌnd] vt
zurückerstatten

refusal [rɪ'fjuːzl] n (to do sth)
Weigerung f; **refuse** ['refjuːs] n
Müll m, Abfall m ▷ [rɪ'fjuːz] vt
ablehnen; **to ~ sb sth** jdm etw
verweigern; **to ~ to do sth** sich
weigern, etw zu tun ▷ vi sich
weigern

regain [rɪ'geɪn] vt wiedergewinnen, wiedererlangen; **to
~ consciousness** wieder zu
Bewusstsein kommen

regard [rɪ'gɑːd] vt (consider): **to ~
sb/sth as sth** jdn/etw als etw
betrachten; **as ~s** ... was ...
betrifft; **regarding** prep bezüglich
+gen; **regardless** adj: **~ of** ohne
Rücksicht auf +akk ▷ adv
trotzdem; **to carry on ~** einfach
weitermachen

regime [reɪ'ʒiːm] n (Pol) Regime
nt

region ['riːdʒən] n (of country)
Region f, Gebiet nt; **in the ~ of**
(about) ungefähr; **regional** adj
regional

register ['redʒɪstə˚] n Register
nt; (school) Namensliste f ▷ vt
(with an authority) registrieren
lassen; (birth, death, vehicle)
anmelden ▷ vi (at hotel, for course)
sich anmelden; (at university) sich
einschreiben; **registered** adj
eingetragen; (letter)
eingeschrieben; **by ~ post** per
Einschreiben; **registration**
[redʒɪ'streɪʃən] n (for course)
Anmeldung f; (at university)
Einschreibung f; (Auto: number)
(polizeiliches) Kennzeichen;
registration form n
Anmeldeformular nt; **registration
number** n (Auto) (polizeiliches)
Kennzeichen; **registry office**
['redʒɪstrɪfɪs] n Standesamt nt

regret [rɪ'gret] n Bedauern nt
▷ vt bedauern; **regrettable** adj
bedauerlich

regular ['regjʊlə˚] adj regelmäßig; (size) normal ▷ n (client)
Stammkunde m, Stammkundin f;
(in bar) Stammgast m; (petrol)
Normalbenzin nt; **regularly** adv
regelmäßig

regulate ['regjʊleɪt] vt
regulieren; (using rules) regeln;
regulation [regjʊ'leɪʃən] n (rule)
Vorschrift f

rehabilitation [riːəbɪlɪ'teɪʃən]
n Rehabilitation f

rehearsal [rɪ'hɜːsəl] n Probe f;
rehearse vt, vi proben

reign [reɪn] n Herrschaft f ▷ vi
herrschen (over über +akk)

reimburse [riːɪm'bɜːs] vt (person) entschädigen; (expenses)
zurückerstatten

reindeer ['reɪndɪə°] n Rentier nt

reinforce [riːɪn'fɔːs] vt
verstärken

reinstate [riːɪn'steɪt] vt
(employee) wieder einstellen;
(passage in text) wieder aufnehmen

reject ['riːdʒekt] n (Comm)
Ausschussartikel m ▷ [rɪ'dʒekt]
vt ablehnen; **rejection**
[rɪ'dʒekʃən] n Ablehnung f

relapse [rɪ'læps] n Rückfall m

relate [rɪ'leɪt] vt (story) erzählen;
(connect) in Verbindung bringen (to
mit) ▷ vi: **to ~ to** (refer) sich
beziehen auf +akk; **related** adj
verwandt (to mit); **relation**
[rɪ'leɪʃən] n (relative) Verwandte(r)
mf; (connection) Beziehung f; **~s** pl
(dealings) Beziehungen pl;
relationship n (connection)
Beziehung f; (between people)
Verhältnis nt

relative ['relətɪv] n Verwandte(r)
mf ▷ adj relativ; **relatively** adv
relativ, verhältnismäßig

relax [rɪ'læks] vi sich
entspannen; **~! reg** dich nicht auf!
▷ vt (grip, conditions) lockern;
relaxation [riːlæk'seɪʃən] n (rest)
Entspannung f; **relaxed** adj
entspannt; **relaxing** adj
entspannend

release [rɪ'liːs] n (from prison)
Entlassung f; **new/recent ~** (film,
CD) Neuerscheinung f ▷ vt
(animal, hostage) freilassen;
(prisoner) entlassen; (handbrake)
lösen; (news) veröffentlichen;
(film, CD) herausbringen

relent [rɪ'lent] vi nachgeben;

relentless, relentlessly adj, adv
(merciless) erbarmungslos;
(neverending) unaufhörlich

relevance ['reləvəns] n
Relevanz f (to für); **relevant** adj
relevant (to für)

reliable, reliably [rɪ'laɪəbl, -blɪ]
adj, adv zuverlässig; **reliant**
[rɪ'laɪənt] adj: **~ on** abhängig von

relic ['relɪk] n (from past) Relikt nt

relief [rɪ'liːf] n (from anxiety, pain)
Erleichterung f; (assistance) Hilfe f;
relieve [rɪ'liːv] vt (pain) lindern;
(boredom) überwinden; (take over
from) ablösen; **I'm ~d** ich bin
erleichtert

religion [rɪ'lɪdʒən] n Religion f;
religious [rɪ'lɪdʒəs] adj religiös

relish ['relɪʃ] n (for food) würzige
Soße f ▷ vt (enjoy) genießen; **I
don't ~ the thought of it** der
Gedanke behagt mir gar nicht

reluctant [rɪ'lʌktənt] adj
widerwillig; **to be ~ to do sth** etw
nur ungern tun; **reluctantly** adv
widerwillig

rely on [rɪ'laɪ ɒn] vt sich
verlassen auf +akk; (depend on)
abhängig sein von

remain [rɪ'meɪn] vi bleiben; (be
left over) übrig bleiben; **remainder**
n (a. Math) Rest m; **remaining** adj
übrig; **remains** npl Überreste pl

remark [rɪ'mɑːk] n Bemerkung f
▷ vt: **to ~ that** bemerken, dass
▷ vi: **to ~ on sth** über etw akk eine
Bemerkung machen; **remarkable,
remarkably** adj, adv
bemerkenswert

remarry [riː'mærɪ] vi wieder
heiraten

remedy ['remədɪ] n Mittel nt (for
gegen) ▷ vt abhelfen +dat

remember [rɪ'membə°] vt sich
erinnern an +akk; **to ~ to do sth**
daran denken, etw zu tun; **I
~ seeing her** ich erinnere mich

daran, sie gesehen zu haben; **I must ~ that** das muss ich mir merken ▷ *vi* sich erinnern

Remembrance Day [rɪˈmembrənsˈdeɪ] *n* (*Brit*) = Volkstrauertag *m*

● **REMEMBRANCE DAY**
●
● **Remembrance Sunday/Day** ist
● der britische Gedenktag für die
● Gefallenen der beiden
● Weltkriege und anderer Kriege.
● Er fällt auf einen Sonntag vor
● oder nach dem 11. November
● (am 11.11.1918 endete der Erste
● Weltkrieg) und wird mit einer
● Schweigeminute,
● Kranzniederlegungen an
● Kriegerdenkmälern und dem
● Tragen von Anstecknadeln in
● Form einer Mohnblume
● begangen.

remind [rɪˈmaɪnd] *vt*: **to ~ sb of/about sb/sth** jdn an jdn/etw erinnern; **to ~ sb to do sth** jdn daran erinnern, etw zu tun; **that ~s me** dabei fällt mir ein ...; **reminder** *n* (*to pay*) Mahnung *f*

reminisce [remɪˈnɪs] *vi* in Erinnerungen schwelgen (*about an +akk*); **reminiscent** [remɪˈnɪsənt] *adj*: **to be ~ of** erinnern an *+akk*

remittance *n* Überweisung *f* (*to an +akk*)

remnant [ˈremnənt] *n* Rest *m*

remote [rɪˈməʊt] *adj* (*place*) abgelegen; (*slight*) gering ▷ *n* (*TV*) Fernbedienung *f*; **remote control** *n* Fernsteuerung *f*; (*device*) Fernbedienung *f*

removal [rɪˈmuːvəl] *n* Entfernung *f*; (*Brit*: *move from house*) Umzug *m*; **removal firm** *n* (*Brit*) Spedition *f*; **remove** [rɪˈmuːv] *vt* entfernen; (*lid*) abnehmen;

(*clothes*) ausziehen; (*doubt, suspicion*) zerstreuen

rename [riːˈneɪm] *vt* umbenennen

renew [rɪˈnjuː] *vt* erneuern; (*licence, passport, library book*) verlängern lassen

renounce [rɪˈnaʊns] *vt* verzichten auf *+akk*; (*faith, opinion*) abschwören *+dat*

renovate [ˈrenəveɪt] *vt* renovieren

renowned [rɪˈnaʊnd] *adj* berühmt (*for für*)

rent [rent] *n* Miete *f*; **for ~** (*US*) zu vermieten ▷ *vt* (*as hirer, tenant*) mieten; (*as owner*) vermieten; **~ed car** Mietwagen *m*, **rent out** *vt* vermieten; **rental** *n* Miete *f*; (*for car, TV etc*) Leihgebühr *f* ▷ *adj* Miet-

reorganize [riːˈɔːgənaɪz] *vt* umorganisieren

rep [rep] *n* (*Comm*) Vertreter(in) *m(f)*

repair [rɪˈpeə°] *n* Reparatur *f* ▷ *vt* reparieren; (*damage*) wiedergutmachen; **repair kit** *n* Flickzeug *nt*

repay [riːˈpeɪ] *irr vt* (*money*) zurückzahlen; **to ~ sb for sth** (*fig*) sich bei jdm für etw revanchieren

repeat [rɪˈpiːt] *n* (*Radio, TV*) Wiederholung *f* ▷ *vt* wiederholen; **repetition** [repəˈtɪʃən] *n* Wiederholung *f*; **repetitive** [rɪˈpetɪtɪv] *adj* sich wiederholend

rephrase [riːˈfreɪz] *vt* anders formulieren

replace [rɪˈpleɪs] *vt* ersetzen (*with durch*); (*put back*) zurückstellen, zurücklegen; **replacement** *n* (*thing, person*) Ersatz *m*; (*temporarily in job*) Vertretung *f*; **replacement part** *n* Ersatzteil *nt*

replay [ˈriːpleɪ] *n*: (*action*)

~ Wiederholung f ▷ [ˌriːˈpleɪ] vt
(game) wiederholen

replica [ˈreplɪkə] n Kopie f

reply [rɪˈplaɪ] n Antwort f ▷ vi
antworten; **to ~ to sb/sth**
jdm/auf etw akk antworten ▷ vt:
to ~ that antworten, dass

report [rɪˈpɔːt] n Bericht m;
(school) Zeugnis nt ▷ vt (tell)
berichten; (give information against)
melden; (to police) anzeigen ▷ vi
(present oneself) sich melden; **to
~ sick** sich krankmelden; **report
card** n (US: school) Zeugnis nt;
reporter n Reporter(in) m(f)

represent [reprɪˈzent] vt darstellen; (speak for) vertreten;
representation [reprɪzenˈteɪʃən]
n (picture etc) Darstellung f;
representative [reprɪˈzentətɪv]
n Vertreter(in) m(f); (US Pol)
Abgeordnete(r) mf ▷ adj
repräsentativ (of für)

reprimand [ˈreprɪmɑːnd] n Tadel
m ▷ vt tadeln

reprint [ˈriːprɪnt] n Nachdruck m

reproduce [riːprəˈdjuːs] vt (copy)
reproduzieren ▷ vi (Bio) sich
fortpflanzen; **reproduction**
[riːprəˈdʌkʃən] n (copy)
Reproduktion f; (Bio)
Fortpflanzung f

reptile [ˈreptaɪl] n Reptil nt

republic [rɪˈpʌblɪk] n Republik f;
republican adj republikanisch
▷ n Republikaner(in) m(f)

repulsive [rɪˈpʌlsɪv] adj
abstoßend

reputable [ˈrepjʊtəbl] adj seriös

reputation [repjʊˈteɪʃən] n Ruf
m; **he has a ~ for being difficult**
er hat den Ruf, schwierig zu sein

request [rɪˈkwest] n Bitte f (for
um); **on ~** auf Wunsch ▷ vt bitten
um; **to ~ sb to do sth** jdn bitten,
etw zu tun

require [rɪˈkwaɪə] vt (need)

brauchen; (desire) verlangen; **what
qualifications are ~d?** welche
Qualifikationen sind
erforderlich?; **required** adj
erforderlich; **requirement** n
(condition) Anforderung f; (need)
Bedingung f

rerun [ˈriːrʌn] n Wiederholung f

rescue [ˈreskjuː] n Rettung f; **to
come to sb's ~** jdm zu Hilfe
kommen ▷ vt retten; **rescue
party** n Rettungsmannschaft f

research [rɪˈsɜːtʃ] n Forschung f
▷ vi forschen (into über +akk) ▷ vt
erforschen; **researcher** n
Forscher(in) m(f)

resemblance [rɪˈzembləns] n
Ähnlichkeit f (to mit); **resemble**
[rɪˈzembl] vt ähneln +dat

resent [rɪˈzent] vt übel nehmen

reservation [rezəˈveɪʃən] n
(booking) Reservierung f; (doubt)
Vorbehalt m; **I have a ~** (in hotel,
restaurant) ich habe reserviert;
reserve [rɪˈzɜːv] n (store) Vorrat m
(of an +dat); (manner)
Zurückhaltung f; (Sport)
Reservespieler(in) m(f); (game ~)
Naturschutzgebiet nt ▷ vt (book in
advance) reservieren; **reserved** adj
reserviert

reservoir [ˈrezəvwɑː°] n (for
water) Reservoir nt

reside [rɪˈzaɪd] vi wohnen;
residence [ˈrezɪdəns] n Wohnsitz m; (living) Aufenthalt m;
~ permit Aufenthaltsgenehmigung f; **~ hall** Studentenwohnheim nt; **resident**
[ˈrezɪdənt] n (in house)
Bewohner(in) m(f); (in town, area)
Einwohner(in) m(f)

resign [rɪˈzaɪn] vt (post)
zurücktreten von; (job) kündigen
▷ vi (from post) zurücktreten; (from
job) kündigen; **resignation**
[rezɪgˈneɪʃən] n (from post)

Rücktritt m; (from job) Kündigung f; **resigned** adj resigniert; **he is ~ to it** er hat sich damit abgefunden

resist [rɪ'zɪst] vt widerstehen +dat; **resistance** n Widerstand m (to gegen)

resit [riː'sɪt] (Brit) irr vt wiederholen ▷ ['riːsɪt] n Wiederholungsprüfung f

resolution [rezə'luːʃən] n (intention) Vorsatz m; (decision) Beschluss m

resolve [rɪ'zɒlv] vt (problem) lösen

resort [rɪ'zɔːt] n (holiday ~) Urlaubsort m; (health ~) Kurort m; **as a last ~** als letzter Ausweg ▷ vi: **to ~ to** greifen zu; (violence) anwenden

resources [rɪ'sɔːsɪz] npl (money) (Geld)mittel pl; (mineral ~) Bodenschätze pl

respect [rɪ'spekt] n Respekt m (for vor +dat); (consideration) Rücksicht f (for auf +akk); **with ~ to** in Bezug auf +akk; **in this ~** in dieser Hinsicht; **with all due ~** bei allem Respekt ▷ vt respektieren; **respectable** [rɪ'spektəbl] adj (person, family) angesehen; (district) anständig; (achievement, result) beachtlich; **respected** [rɪ'spektɪd] adj angesehen

respective [rɪ'spektɪv] adj jeweilig; **respectively** adv: **5 % and 10 %** = 5 % bzw. 10 %

respiratory [rɪ'spɪrətərɪ] adj: **~ problems** (o trouble) Atembeschwerden pl

respond [rɪ'spɒnd] vi antworten (to auf +akk); (react) reagieren (to auf +akk); (to treatment) ansprechen (to auf +akk); **response** [rɪ'spɒns] n Antwort f; (reaction) Reaktion f; **in ~ to** als Antwort auf +akk

responsibility [rɪspɒnsə'bɪlɪtɪ] n Verantwortung f; **that's her ~** dafür ist sie verantwortlich; **responsible** [rɪ'spɒnsəbl] adj verantwortlich (for für); (trustworthy) verantwortungsbewusst; (job) verantwortungsvoll

rest [rest] n (relaxation) Ruhe f; (break) Pause f; (remainder) Rest m; **to have** (o **take**) **a ~** sich ausruhen; (break) Pause machen; **the ~ of the wine/the people** der Rest des Weins/der Leute ▷ vi (relax) sich ausruhen; (lean) lehnen (on, against an +dat; gegen)

restaurant ['restərɒnt] n Restaurant nt; **restaurant car** n (Brit) Speisewagen m

restful ['restfʊl] adj (holiday etc) erholsam, ruhig; **restless** ['restləs] adj unruhig

restore [rɪ'stɔː] vt (painting, building) restaurieren; (order) wiederherstellen; (give back) zurückgeben

restrain [rɪ'streɪn] vt (person, feelings) zurückhalten; **to ~ oneself** sich beherrschen

restrict [rɪ'strɪkt] vt beschränken (to auf +akk); **restricted** adj beschränkt; **restriction** [rɪ'strɪkʃən] n Einschränkung f (on +gen)

rest room ['restruːm] n (US) Toilette f

result [rɪ'zʌlt] n (consequence) Folge f; Ergebnis nt; (consequence) Folge f; **as a ~ of** infolge +gen ▷ vi: **to ~ in** führen zu; **to ~ from** sich ergeben aus

resume [rɪ'zjuːm] vt (work, negotiations) wieder aufnehmen; (journey) fortsetzen

résumé ['rezjʊmeɪ] n Zusammenfassung f; (US: curriculum vitae) Lebenslauf m

resuscitate [rɪˈsʌsɪteɪt] vt
wiederbeleben

retail [ˈriːteɪl] adv im
Einzelhandel; **retailer** n
Einzelhändler(in) m(f)

retain [rɪˈteɪn] vt behalten; (heat)
halten

rethink [riːˈθɪŋk] irr vt noch
einmal überdenken

retire [rɪˈtaɪə*] vi (from work) in
den Ruhestand treten; (withdraw)
sich zurückziehen; **retired** adj
(person) pensioniert; **retirement** n
(time of life) Ruhestand m;
retirement age n Rentenalter nt

retrace [rɪˈtreɪs] vt
zurückverfolgen

retrain [riːˈtreɪn] vi sich
umschulen lassen

retreat [rɪˈtriːt] n (Mil) Rückzug
m (from aus); (refuge) Zufluchtsort
m ▷ vi (Mil) sich zurückziehen;
(step back) zurückweichen

retrieve [rɪˈtriːv] vt (recover)
wiederbekommen; (rescue) retten;
(data) abrufen

retrospect [ˈretrəʊspekt] n: in
~ rückblickend; **retrospective**
[retrəʊˈspektɪv] adj rückblickend;
(pay rise) rückwirkend

return [rɪˈtɜːn] n (going back)
Rückkehr f; (giving back)
Rückgabe f; (profit) Gewinn m;
(Brit: ~ ticket) Rückfahrkarte f;
(plane ticket) Rückflugticket nt;
(Tennis), Return m; **in ~** als
Gegenleistung (for für); **many
happy ~s (of the day)** herzlichen
Glückwunsch zum Geburtstag!
▷ vi (person) zurückkehren;
(doubts, symptoms) wieder
auftreten; **to ~ to school/work**
wieder in die Schule/die Arbeit
gehen ▷ vt (give back)
zurückgeben; **I -ed his call** ich
habe ihn zurückgerufen;
returnable adj (bottle) Pfand-;

return flight n (Brit) Rückflug m;
(both ways) Hin- und Rückflug m;
return key n (Inform)
Eingabetaste f; **return ticket** n
(Brit) Rückfahrkarte f; (for plane)
Rückflugticket nt

reunification [riːjuːnɪfɪˈkeɪʃən]
n Wiedervereinigung f

reunion [riːˈjuːnjən] n (party)
Treffen nt; **reunite** [riːjuːˈnaɪt] vt
wieder vereinigen

reusable [riːˈjuːzəbl] adj
wiederverwendbar

reveal [rɪˈviːl] vt (make known)
enthüllen; (secret) verraten; (show)
zeigen; **revealing** adj
aufschlussreich; (dress) freizügig

revenge [rɪˈvendʒ] n Rache f; (in
game) Revanche f; **to take ~ on sb
(for sth)** sich an jdm (für etw)
rächen

revenue [ˈrevənjuː] n Einnahmen pl

reverse [rɪˈvɜːs] n (back)
Rückseite f; (opposite) Gegenteil nt;
(Auto) ~ **(gear)** Rückwärtsgang m
▷ adj: **in ~ order** in umgekehrter
Reihenfolge ▷ vt (order)
umkehren; (decision) umstoßen;
(car) zurücksetzen; **to ~ the
charges** (Brit) ein R-Gespräch
führen ▷ vi (Auto)
rückwärtsfahren

review [rɪˈvjuː] n (of book, film
etc) Rezension f; Kritik f; **to be
under ~** überprüft werden ▷ vt
(book, film etc) rezensieren;
(re-examine) überprüfen

revise [rɪˈvaɪz] vt revidieren;
(text) überarbeiten; (Brit: in school)
wiederholen ▷ vi (Brit, in school)
(für eine Prüfung) lernen; **revision**
[rɪˈvɪʒən] n (of text)
Überarbeitung f; (Brit, in school)
Wiederholung f

revitalize [riːˈvaɪtəlaɪz] vt neu
beleben

revive [rɪ'vaɪv] vt (person) wiederbeleben; (tradition, interest) wieder aufleben lassen ▷ vi (regain consciousness) wieder zu sich kommen

revolt [rɪ'vəʊlt] n Aufstand m; **revolting** adj widerlich

revolution [revə'luːʃən] n (Pol, fig) Revolution f; (turn) Umdrehung f; **revolutionary** adj revolutionär ▷ n Revolutionär(in) m(f)

revolve [rɪ'vɒlv] vi sich drehen (around um); **revolver** n Revolver m; **revolving door** n Drehtür f

reward [rɪ'wɔːd] n Belohnung f ▷ vt belohnen; **rewarding** adj lohnend

rewind [riː'waɪnd] irr vt (tape) zurückspulen

rewrite [riː'raɪt] irr vt (write again; recast) umschreiben

rheumatism ['ruːmətɪzəm] n Rheuma nt

Rhine [raɪn] n Rhein m

rhinoceros [raɪ'nɒsərəs] n Nashorn nt

Rhodes [rəʊdz] n Rhodos nt

rhubarb ['ruːbɑːb] n Rhabarber m

rhyme [raɪm] n Reim m ▷ vi sich reimen (with auf +akk)

rhythm ['rɪðəm] n Rhythmus m

rib [rɪb] n Rippe f

ribbon ['rɪbən] n Band nt

rice [raɪs] n Reis m; **rice pudding** n Milchreis m

rich [rɪtʃ] adj reich; (food) schwer ▷ npl: **the ~** die Reichen pl

rickety ['rɪkɪtɪ] adj wackelig

rid [rɪd] (rid, rid) vt: **to get ~ of sb/sth** jdn/etw loswerden

ridden ['rɪdn] pp of **ride**

riddle ['rɪdl] n Rätsel nt

ride [raɪd] (rode, ridden) vt (horse) reiten; (bicycle) fahren ▷ vi

(on horse) reiten; (on bike) fahren ▷ n (in vehicle, on bike) Fahrt f; (on horse) (Aus)ritt m; **to go for a ~** (in car, on bike) spazieren fahren; (on horse) reiten gehen; **to take sb for a ~** (fam) jdn verarschen; **rider** n (on horse) Reiter(in) m(f); (on bike) Fahrer(in) m(f)

ridiculous [rɪ'dɪkjʊləs] adj lächerlich; **don't be ~** red keinen Unsinn!

riding ['raɪdɪŋ] n Reiten nt; **to go ~** reiten gehen ▷ adj Reit-

rifle ['raɪfl] n Gewehr nt

rig [rɪg] n: **oil ~** Bohrinsel f ▷ vt (election etc) manipulieren

right [raɪt] adj (correct, just) richtig; (opposite of left) rechte(r, s); (clothes, job etc) passend; **to be ~** (person) recht haben; (clock) richtig gehen; **that's ~** das stimmt! ▷ n Recht nt (to auf +akk); (side) rechte Seite; **the Right** (Pol) die Rechte; **to take a ~** (Auto) rechts abbiegen; **on the ~** rechts (of von) ▷ adv nach rechts; (on the ~) rechts (of von) ▷ adv (towards the ~) nach rechts; (directly) direkt; (exactly) genau; **to turn ~** (Auto) rechts abbiegen; **~ away** sofort; **~ now** im Moment; (immediately) sofort; **right angle** n rechter Winkel; **right-hand drive** n Rechtssteuerung f ▷ adj rechtsgesteuert; **right-handed** adj: **he is ~** er ist Rechtshänder; **right-hand side** n rechte Seite; **on the ~** auf der rechten Seite; **rightly** adv zu Recht; **right of way** n: **to have ~** (Auto) Vorfahrt haben; **right wing** n (Pol, Sport) rechter Flügel; **right-wing** adj Rechts-; **~ extremist** Rechtsradikale(r) mf

rigid ['rɪdʒɪd] adj (stiff) starr; (strict) streng

rigorous, rigorously [ˈrɪɡərəs, -lɪ] *adj, adv* streng

rim [rɪm] *n* (of cup etc) Rand *m*; (of wheel) Felge *f*

rind [raɪnd] *n* (of cheese) Rinde *f*; (of bacon) Schwarte *f*; (of fruit) Schale *f*

ring [rɪŋ] (**rang, rung**) *vt, vi* (bell) läuten; (Tel) anrufen ▷ *n* (on finger, in boxing) Ring *m*; (circle) Kreis *m*; (at circus) Manege *f*; **to give sb a ~** (Tel) jdn anrufen; **ring back** *vt, vi* zurückrufen; **ring up** *vt, vi* anrufen

ring binder *n* Ringbuch *nt*
ringleader *n* Anführer(in) *m(f)*
ring road *n* (Brit) Umgehungsstraße *f*
ringtone *n* Klingelton *m*
rink [rɪŋk] *n* (ice ~) Eisbahn *f*; (for roller-skating) Rollschuhbahn *f*

rinse [rɪns] *vt* spülen

riot [ˈraɪət] *n* Aufruhr *m*
to ~ sth open etw aufreißen ▷ *vi* reißen; **rip off** *vt* (fam: person) übers Ohr hauen; **rip up** *vt* zerreißen

ripe [raɪp] *adj* (fruit) reif; **ripen** *vi* reifen

rip-off [ˈrɪpɒf] *n*: **that's a ~** (fam: too expensive) das ist Wucher

rise [raɪz] (**rose, risen**) *vi* (from sitting, lying) aufstehen; (sun) aufgehen; (prices, temperature) steigen; (ground) ansteigen; (in revolt) sich erheben ▷ *n* (increase) Anstieg *m* (in +gen); (pay ~) Gehaltserhöhung *f*; (to power, fame) Aufstieg *m* (to zu); (slope) Steigung *f*; **risen** [ˈrɪzn] *pp of* **rise**

risk [rɪsk] *n* Risiko *nt* ▷ *vt* riskieren; **to ~ doing sth** es riskieren, etw zu tun; **risky** *adj* riskant

risotto [rɪˈzɒtəʊ] (*pl* **-s**) *n* Risotto *nt*

ritual [ˈrɪtjʊəl] *n* Ritual *nt* ▷ *adj* rituell

rival [ˈraɪvəl] *n* Rivale *m*, Rivalin *f* (for um); (Comm) Konkurrent(in) *m(f)*; **rivalry** *n* Rivalität *f*; (Comm, Sport) Konkurrenz *f*

river [ˈrɪvəʳ] *n* Fluss *m*; **the River Thames** (Brit), **the Thames River** (US) die Themse; **riverside** *n* Flussufer *nt* ▷ *adj* am Flussufer

road [rəʊd] *n* Straße *f*; (fig) Weg *m*; **on the ~** (travelling) unterwegs, mit dem Auto/Bus etc fahren; **roadblock** *n* Straßensperre *f*; **roadmap** *n* Straßenkarte *f*; **road rage** *n* aggressives Verhalten im Straßenverkehr; **roadside** *n*: **at** (*o* **by**) **the ~** am Straßenrand; **roadsign** *n* Verkehrsschild *nt*; **road tax** *n* Kraftfahrzeugsteuer *f*; **roadworks** *npl* Bauarbeiten *pl*; **roadworthy** *adj* fahrtüchtig

roar [rɔːʳ] *n* (of person, lion) Brüllen *nt*; (von Verkehr) Donnern *nt* ▷ *vi* (person, lion) brüllen (with *o* +dat)

roast [rəʊst] *n* Braten *m* ▷ *adj*: **~ beef** Rinderbraten *m*; **~ chicken** Brathähnchen *nt*; **~ pork** Schweinebraten *m*; **~ potatoes** *pl* im Backofen gebratene Kartoffeln ▷ *vt* (meat) braten

rob [rɒb] *vt* bestehlen; (bank, shop) ausrauben; **robber** *n* Räuber(in) *m(f)*; **robbery** *n* Raub *m*

robe [rəʊb] *n* (US: dressing gown) Morgenrock *m*; (of judge, priest etc) Robe *f*, Talar *m*

robin [ˈrɒbɪn] *n* Rotkehlchen *nt*

robot [ˈrəʊbɒt] *n* Roboter *m*

robust [rəʊˈbʌst] *adj* robust; (defence) stark

rock [rɒk] *n* (substance) Stein *m*; (boulder) Felsbrocken *m*; (Mus) Rock *m*; **stick of ~** (Brit) Zuckerstange *f*; **on the ~s** (drink)

mit Eis; *(marriage)* gescheitert
▷ vt, vi *(swing)* schaukeln; *(dance)*
rocken; **rock climbing** n Klettern
nt: **to go ~** klettern gehen
rocket ['rɒkɪt] n Rakete f; *(in
salad)* Rucola m
rocking chair ['rɒkɪŋtʃeə*] n
Schaukelstuhl m
rocky ['rɒkɪ] adj *(landscape)* felsig;
(path) steinig
rod [rɒd] n *(bar)* Stange f; *(fishing
)* Rute f
rode [rəʊd] pt of **ride**
rogue [rəʊg] n Schurke m,
Gauner m
role [rəʊl] n Rolle f; **role model** n
Vorbild nt
roll [rəʊl] n *(of film, paper etc)*
Rolle f; *(bread ~)* Brötchen nt ▷ vt
(move by ~ing) rollen; *(cigarette)*
drehen ▷ vi *(move by ~ing)* rollen;
(ship) schlingern; *(camera)* laufen;
roll out vt *(pastry)* ausrollen; **roll
over** vi *(person)* sich umdrehen;
roll up vi *(fam: arrive)* antanzen
▷ vt *(carpet)* aufrollen; **to roll
one's sleeves up** die Ärmel
hochkrempeln
roller n *(hair ~)* (Locken)wickler m;
Rollerblades® npl Inlineskates
pl; **rollerblading** n Inlineskaten
nt; **roller coaster** n Achterbahn f;
roller skates npl Rollschuhe pl;
roller-skating n Rollschuhlaufen
nt; **rolling pin** n Nudelholz nt;
roll-on *(deodorant)* n Deoroller
m

ROM [rɒm] acr = **read only
memory** ROM m
Roman ['rəʊmən] adj römisch
▷ n Römer(in) m(f); **Roman
Catholic** adj römisch-katholisch
▷ n Katholik(in) m(f)
romance [rəʊˈmæns] n Romantik f; *(love affair)* Romanze f
Romania [rəʊˈmeɪnɪə] n
Rumänien nt; **Romanian** adj

rumänisch ▷ n Rumäne m,
Rumänin f; *(language)* Rumänisch
nt
romantic [rəʊˈmæntɪk] adj
romantisch
roof [ruːf] n Dach nt: **roof rack** n
Dachgepäckträger m
rook [rʊk] n *(in chess)* Turm m
room [ruːm] n Zimmer nt, Raum
m; *(large, for gatherings etc)* Saal m;
(space) Platz m; *(fig)* Spielraum m;
to make ~ for Platz machen für;
roommate n Zimmergenosse m,
Zimmergenossin f;
Mitbewohner(in) m(f); **room
service** n Zimmerservice m;
roomy adj geräumig; *(garment)*
weit
root [ruːt] n Wurzel f; **root out** vt
(eradicate) ausrotten; **root
vegetable** n Wurzelgemüse nt
rope [rəʊp] n Seil nt; **to know
the ~s** *(fam)* sich auskennen
rose [rəʊz] pt of **rise** ▷ n Rose f
rosé ['rəʊzeɪ] n Rosé(wein) m
rot [rɒt] vi verfaulen
rota ['rəʊtə] n *(Brit)* Dienstplan m
rotate [rəʊˈteɪt] vt *(turn)* rotieren
lassen ▷ vi rotieren; **rotation**
[rəʊˈteɪʃən] n *(turning)* Rotation f;
in ~ abwechselnd
rotten ['rɒtn] adj *(decayed)* faul;
(mean) gemein; *(unpleasant)*
scheußlich; *(ill)* elend
rough [rʌf] adj *(not smooth)* rau;
(path) uneben; *(coarse, violent)*
grob; *(crossing)* stürmisch; *(without
comforts)* hart; *(unfinished,
makeshift)* grob; *(approximate)*
ungefähr; **~ draft** Rohentwurf m; **I
have a ~ idea** ich habe eine
ungefähre Vorstellung ▷ adv: **to
sleep ~** im Freien schlafen ▷ vt:
to ~ it primitiv leben ▷ n: **to
write sth in ~** etw ins Unreine
schreiben; **roughly** adv grob;
(approximately) ungefähr

round [raʊnd] adj rund ▷ adv: **all ~** (on all sides) rundherum; **the long way ~** der längere Weg; **I'll be ~ at 8** ich werde um acht Uhr da sein; **the other way ~** umgekehrt ▷ prep (surrounding) um (... herum); **~ (about)** (approximately) ungefähr; **~ the corner** um die Ecke; **to go ~ the world** um die Welt reisen; **she lives ~ here** sie wohnt hier in der Gegend ▷ n Runde f; (of bread, toast) Scheibe f; (of drinks) die Runde geht auf mich ▷ vt (corner) biegen um; **round off** vt abrunden; **round up** vt (number, price) aufrunden

roundabout n (Brit Auto) Kreisverkehr m; (Brit: merry-go-round) Karussell nt ▷ adj umständlich; **round-the-clock** adj rund um die Uhr; **round trip** n Rundreise f; **round-trip ticket** n (US) Rückfahrkarte f; (for plane) Rückflugticket nt

rouse [raʊz] vt (from sleep) wecken

route [ruːt] n Route f; (bus, plane etc service) Linie f; (fig) Weg m

routine [ruːˈtiːn] n Routine f ▷ adj Routine-

row¹ [rəʊ] n (line) Reihe f; **three times in a ~** dreimal hintereinander ▷ vt, vi (boat) rudern ▷ n (noise) Krach m; (dispute) Streit m

rowboat [ˈrəʊbəʊt] n (US) Ruderboot nt

row house [ˈrəʊhaʊs] n (US) Reihenhaus nt

rowing [ˈrəʊɪŋ] n Rudern nt; **rowing boat** n (Brit) Ruderboot nt; **rowing machine** n Rudergerät nt

royal [ˈrɔɪəl] adj königlich; **royalty** n (family) Mitglieder pl der königlichen Familie; **royalties** pl (from book, music) Tantiemen pl

RSPCA abbr = **Royal Society for the Prevention of Cruelty to Animals** britischer Tierschutzverein

RSPCC abbr = **Royal Society for the Prevention of Cruelty to Children** britischer Kinderschutzverein

RSVP abbr = **répondez s'il vous plaît** u. A. w. g.

rub [rʌb] vt reiben; **rub in** vt einmassieren; **rub out** vt (with eraser) ausradieren

rubber [ˈrʌbəə] n Gummi m; (Brit: eraser) Radiergummi m; (US fam: contraceptive) Gummi m; **rubber band** n Gummiband nt; **rubber stamp** n Stempel m

rubbish [ˈrʌbɪʃ] n Abfall m; (nonsense) Quatsch m; (poor-quality thing) Mist m; **don't talk ~** red keinen Unsinn!; **rubbish bin** n Mülleimer m; **rubbish dump** n Müllabladeplatz m

rubble [ˈrʌbl] n Schutt m

ruby [ˈruːbɪ] n (stone) Rubin m

rucksack [ˈrʌksæk] n Rucksack m

rude [ruːd] adj (impolite) unhöflich; (indecent) unanständig

rug [rʌg] n Teppich m; (next to bed) Bettvorleger m; (for knees) Wolldecke f

rugby [ˈrʌgbɪ] n Rugby nt

rugged [ˈrʌgɪd] adj (coastline) zerklüftet; (features) markant

ruin [ˈruːɪn] n Ruine f; (financial, social) Ruin m ▷ vt ruinieren

rule [ruːl] n Regel f; (governing) Herrschaft f; **as a ~** in der Regel ▷ vt, vi (govern) regieren; (decide) entscheiden; **ruler** n Lineal nt; (person) Herrscher(in) m(f)

rum [rʌm] n Rum m

rumble [ˈrʌmbl] vi (stomach) knurren; (train, truck) rumpeln

rummage [ˈrʌmɪdʒ] vi: **~ (around)** herumstöbern

rumor (US), **rumour** ['ruːmə] n
Gerücht nt

run [rʌn] (ran, run) vt (race,
distance) laufen; (machine, engine,
computer program, water) laufen
lassen; (manage) leiten, führen;
(car) unterhalten; **I ran her home**
ich habe sie nach Hause gefahren
▷ vi laufen; (move quickly) rennen;
(bus, train) fahren; (path etc)
verlaufen; (machine, engine,
computer program) laufen; (flow)
fließen; (colours, make-up)
verlaufen; **to ~ for President** für
die Präsidentschaft kandidieren;
to be ~ning low knapp werden;
my nose is ~ning mir läuft die
Nase; **it ~s in the family** es liegt in
der Familie ▷ n (on foot) Lauf m;
(in car) Spazierfahrt f; (series) Reihe
f; (sudden demand) Ansturm m (on
auf +akk); (in tights) Laufmasche f;
(in cricket, baseball) Lauf m; **to go
for a ~** laufen gehen; (in car) eine
Spazierfahrt machen; **in the long
~** auf die Dauer; **on the ~** auf der
Flucht (from vor +dat); **run about**
vi herumlaufen; **run away** vi
weglaufen; **run down** vt (with car)
umfahren; (criticize)
heruntermachen; **to be ~** (tired)
abgespannt sein; **run into** vt
(meet) zufällig treffen; (problem)
stoßen auf +akk; **run off** vi
weglaufen; **run out** vi (person)
hinausrennen; (liquid) auslaufen;
(lease, time) ablaufen; (money,
supplies) ausgehen; **he ran ~ of
money** ihm ging das Geld aus; **run
over** vt (with car) überfahren; **run
up** vt (debt, bill) machen

rung [rʌŋ] pp of **ring**

runner ['rʌnə'] n (athlete)
Läufer(in) m(f); **to do a ~** (fam)
wegrennen; **runner bean** n (Brit)
Stangenbohne f

running ['rʌnɪŋ] n (Sport) Laufen

nt; (management) Leitung f,
Führung f ▷ adj (water) fließend;
~ costs Betriebskosten pl; (for car)
Unterhaltskosten pl; **3 days ~** 3
Tage hintereinander

runny ['rʌnɪ] adj (food) flüssig;
(nose) laufend

runway ['rʌnweɪ] n Start- und
Landebahn f

rural ['rʊərəl] adj ländlich

rush [rʌʃ] n Eile f; (for tickets etc)
Ansturm m (for auf +akk); **to be in a
~** es eilig haben; **there's no ~** es
eilt nicht ▷ vt (do too quickly)
hastig machen; (meal) hastig
essen; **to ~ sb to hospital** jdn auf
dem schnellsten Weg ins
Krankenhaus bringen; **don't ~ me**
dräng mich nicht ▷ vi (hurry)
eilen; **don't ~** lass dir Zeit; **rush
hour** n Hauptverkehrszeit f

rusk [rʌsk] n Zwieback m

Russia ['rʌʃə] n Russland nt;
Russian adj russisch ▷ n Russe
m, Russin f; (language) Russisch nt

rust [rʌst] n Rost m ▷ vi rosten;
rustproof ['rʌstpruːf] adj rostfrei; **rusty** ['rʌstɪ] adj rostig

ruthless ['ruːθləs] adj rücksichtslos; (treatment, criticism)
schonungslos

rye [raɪ] n Roggen m; **rye bread**
n Roggenbrot nt

S

S abbr = **south** S

sabotage ['sæbətɑːʒ] vt sabotieren

sachet ['sæʃeɪ] n Päckchen nt

sack [sæk] n (bag) Sack m; **to get the ~** (fam) rausgeschmissen werden ▷ vt (fam) rausschmeißen

sacred ['seɪkrɪd] adj heilig

sacrifice ['sækrɪfaɪs] n Opfer nt ▷ vt opfern

sad [sæd] adj traurig

saddle ['sædl] n Sattel m

sadistic [sə'dɪstɪk] adj sadistisch

sadly ['sædlɪ] adv (unfortunately) leider

safari [sə'fɑːrɪ] n Safari

safe [seɪf] adj (free from danger) sicher; (out of danger) in Sicherheit; (careful) vorsichtig; **have a ~ journey** gute Fahrt! ▷ n Safe m; **safeguard** n Schutz m ▷ vt schützen (against vor +dat); **safely** adv sicher; (arrive) wohlbehalten; (drive) vorsichtig; **safety** n Sicherheit f; **safety belt** n Sicherheitsgurt m; **safety pin** n Sicherheitsnadel f

Sagittarius [sædʒɪ'tɛərɪəs] n (Astr) Schütze m

Sahara [sə'hɑːrə] n: **the ~ (Desert)** die (Wüste) Sahara

said [sed] pt, pp of **say**

sail [seɪl] n Segel nt; **to set ~** losfahren (for nach) ▷ vi (in yacht) segeln; (on ship) mit dem Schiff fahren; (ship) auslaufen (for nach) ▷ vt (yacht) segeln mit; (ship) steuern; **sailboat** n (US) Segelboot nt; **sailing** n: **to go ~** segeln gehen; **sailing boat** n (Brit) Segelboot nt; **sailor** n Seemann m; (in navy) Matrose m

saint [seɪnt] n Heilige(r) mf

sake [seɪk] n: **for the ~ of** um +gen ... willen; **for your ~** deinetwegen, dir zuliebe

salad ['sæləd] n Salat m; **salad cream** n (Brit) majonäseartige Salatsoße; **salad dressing** n Salatsoße f

salary ['sælərɪ] n Gehalt nt

sale [seɪl] n Verkauf m; (at reduced prices) Ausverkauf m; **the ~s** pl (in summer, winter) der Schlussverkauf; **for ~** zu verkaufen; **sales clerk** n (US) Verkäufer(in) m(f); **salesman** (pl **-men**) n Verkäufer m; (rep) Vertreter m; **sales rep** n Vertreter(in) m(f); **sales tax** n (US) Verkaufssteuer f; **saleswoman** (pl **-women**) n Verkäuferin f; (rep) Vertreterin f

salmon ['sæmən] n Lachs m

saloon [sə'luːn] n (ship's lounge) Salon m; (US: bar) Kneipe f

salt [sɔːlt] n Salz nt ▷ vt (flavour) salzen; (roads) mit Salz streuen; **salt cellar, salt shaker** (US) n Salzstreuer m; **salty** adj salzig

salvage ['sælvɪdʒ] vt bergen
(from aus); (fig) retten

same [seɪm] adj: the ~ (similar)
der/die/das gleiche, die gleichen
pl; (identical) der-/die-/dasselbe,
dieselben pl; **they live in the**
~ house sie wohnen im selben
Haus ▷ pron: **the ~** (similar)
der/die/das Gleiche, die Gleichen
pl; (identical) der-/die-/dasselbe,
dieselben pl, **all the ~** trotzdem;
the ~ to you gleichfalls; **it's all**
the ~ to me es ist mir egal ▷ adv:
the ~ gleich; **they look the ~** sie
sehen gleich aus

sample ['saːmpl] n Probe f; (of
fabric) Muster nt ▷ vt probieren

sanctions ['sæŋkʃənz] npl (Pol)
Sanktionen pl

sanctuary ['sæŋktjʊərɪ] n (refuge) Zuflucht f; (for animals)
Schutzgebiet n

sand [sænd] n Sand m

sandal ['sændl] n Sandale f

sandpaper n Sandpapier nt ▷ vt
schmirgeln

sandwich ['sænwɪdʒ] n Sandwich nt

sandy ['sændɪ] adj (full of sand)
sandig; **~ beach** Sandstrand m

sane [seɪn] adj geistig gesund,
normal; (sensible) vernünftig

sang [sæŋ] pt of **sing**

sanitary ['sænɪtərɪ] adj hygienisch; **sanitary napkin** (US),
sanitary towel n Damenbinde f

sank [sæŋk] pt of **sink**

Santa (Claus) ['sæntə('klɔːz)] n
der Weihnachtsmann

sarcastic [saːˈkæstɪk] adj
sarkastisch

sardine [saːˈdiːn] n Sardine f

Sardinia [saːˈdɪnɪə] n Sardinien
nt

sari [ˈsɑːrɪ] n Sari m (von indischen
Frauen getragenes Gewand)

sat [sæt] pt, pp of **sit**

Sat abbr = **Saturday** Sa.

satellite ['sætəlaɪt] n Satellit m;
satellite dish n
Satellitenschüssel f; **satellite TV** n
Satellitenfernsehen nt

satin ['sætɪn] n Satin m

satisfaction [sætɪsˈfækʃən] n
(contentment) Zufriedenheit f; **is**
that to your ~? bist du/sind Sie
damit zufrieden?; **satisfactory**
[sætɪsˈfæktərɪ] adj zufriedenstel-
lend; **satisfied** [ˈsætɪsfaɪd] adj
zufrieden (with mit); **satisfy**
['sætɪsfaɪ] vt zufriedenstellen;
(convince) überzeugen; (conditions)
erfüllen; (need, demand)
befriedigen; **satisfying** adj
befriedigend

Saturday ['sætədeɪ] n Samstag
m, Sonnabend m; see also **Tuesday**

sauce [sɔːs] n Soße f; **saucepan**
n Kochtopf m; **saucer** n
Untertasse f

saucy ['sɔːsɪ] adj frech

Saudi Arabia ['saʊdɪəˈreɪbɪə] n
Saudi-Arabien nt

sauna ['sɔːnə] n Sauna f

sausage ['sɒsɪdʒ] n Wurst f;
sausage roll n mit Wurst gefülltes
Blätterteigröllchen

save [seɪv] vt (rescue) retten (from
vor +dat); (money, time, electricity
etc) sparen; (strength) schonen;
(Inform) speichern; **to ~ sb's life**
jdm das Leben retten ▷ vi sparen
▷ n (in football) Parade f; **save up**
vi sparen (for auf +akk); **saving** n
(of money) Sparen nt; **~s** pl
Ersparnisse pl; **~s account**
Sparkonto nt

savory (US), **savoury** ['seɪvərɪ]
adj (not sweet) pikant

saw [sɔː] (**sawed, sawn**) vt, vi
sägen ▷ n (tool) Säge f ▷ pt of **see**;
sawdust n Sägemehl nt

saxophone ['sæksəfəʊn] n
Saxophon nt

say [seɪ] (**said, said**) vt sagen (to
sb jdm); (prayer) sprechen; **what
does the letter ~?** was steht im
Brief?; **the rules ~ that ...** in den
Regeln heißt es, dass ...; **he's said
to be rich** er soll reich sein ▷ n: **to
have a ~ in sth** bei etw ein
Mitspracherecht haben ▷ adv
zum Beispiel; **saying** n
Sprichwort nt

scab [skæb] n (on cut) Schorf m

scaffolding ['skæfəʊldɪŋ] n
(Bau)gerüst nt

scale [skeɪl] n (of map etc)
Maßstab m; (on thermometer etc)
Skala f; (of pay) Tarifsystem nt;
(Mus) Tonleiter f; (of fish, snake)
Schuppe f; **to ~** maßstabsgerecht;
on a large/small ~ in
großem/kleinem Umfang; **scales**
npl (for weighing) Waage f

scalp [skælp] n Kopfhaut f

scan [skæn] vt (examine) genau
prüfen; (read quickly) überfliegen;
(Inform) scannen ▷ n (Med)
Ultraschall m; **scan in** vt (Inform)
einscannen

scandal ['skændl] n Skandal m;
scandalous adj skandalös

Scandinavia [skændɪˈneɪvɪə] n
Skandinavien nt; **Scandinavian**
adj skandinavisch ▷ n Skandi-
navier(in) m(f)

scanner ['skænə°] n Scanner m

scapegoat ['skeɪpɡəʊt] n
Sündenbock m

scar [skɑː°] n Narbe f

scarce ['skeəs] adj selten; (in
short supply) knapp; **scarcely** adv
kaum

scare ['skeə°] n (general alarm)
Panik f ▷ vt erschrecken; **to be ~d**
Angst haben (of vor +dat)

scarf [skɑːf] n (pl **-scarves**) Schal
m; (on head) Kopftuch nt

scarlet ['skɑːlət] adj schar-
lachrot; **scarlet fever** n Scharlach
m

scary ['skeərɪ] adj (film, story)
gruselig

scatter ['skætə°] vt verstreuen;
(seed, gravel) streuen; (disperse)
auseinandertreiben

scene [siːn] n (location) Ort m;
(division of play) (Theat) Szene f;
(view) Anblick m; **to make a ~** eine
Szene machen; **scenery** ['siːnərɪ]
n (landscape) Landschaft f; (Theat)
Kulissen pl; **scenic** ['siːnɪk] adj
(landscape) malerisch; **~ route**
landschaftlich schöne Strecke

scent [sent] n (perfume) Parfüm
nt; (smell) Duft m

sceptical ['skeptɪkəl] adj (Brit)
skeptisch

schedule ['ʃedjuːl, 'skedʒʊəl] n
(plan) Programm nt; (of work)
Zeitplan m; (list) Liste f; (US: of
trains, buses, air traffic)
Fahr-, Flugplan m; **on
~** planmäßig; **to be behind ~ with
sth** mit etw in Verzug sein ▷ vt:
**the meeting is ~d for next
Monday** die Besprechung ist für
nächsten Montag angesetzt;
scheduled adj (departure, arrival)
planmäßig; **~ flight** Linienflug m

scheme [skiːm] n (plan) Plan m;
(project) Projekt nt; (dishonest)
Intrige f ▷ vi intrigieren

schizophrenic [skɪtsəˈfrenɪk]
adj schizophren

scholar ['skɒlə°] n Gelehrte(r)
mf; **scholarship** n (grant)
Stipendium nt

school [skuːl] n Schule f;
(university department) Fachbereich
m; (US: university) Universität f;
school bag n Schultasche f;
schoolbook n Schulbuch nt;
schoolboy n Schüler m; **school
bus** n Schulbus m; **schoolgirl** n

Schülerin f; **schoolteacher** n
Lehrer(in) m(f); **schoolwork** n
Schularbeiten pl

sciatica [saɪˈætɪkə] n Ischias m

science [ˈsaɪəns] n Wissenschaft
f; (natural ~) Naturwissenschaft f;
science fiction n Sciencefiction
f; **scientific** [saɪənˈtɪfɪk] adj
wissenschaftlich; **scientist**
[ˈsaɪəntɪst] n Wissenschaftler(in)
m(f); (in natural sciences)
Naturwissenschaftler(in) m(f)

scissors [ˈsɪzəz] npl Schere f

scone [skɒn] n kleines süßes
Teebrötchen mit oder ohne Rosinen,
das mit Butter oder Dickrahm und
Marmelade gegessen wird

scoop [sku:p] n (exclusive story)
Exklusivbericht m; **a ~ of
ice-cream** eine Kugel Eis ▷ vt: **to
~ (up)** schaufeln

scooter [ˈsku:tə⁎] n (Motor)-
roller m; (toy) (Tret)roller m

scope [skəʊp] n Umfang m;
(opportunity) Möglichkeit f

score [skɔ:⁎] n (Sport) Spielstand
m; (final result) Spielergebnis nt; (in
quiz etc) Punktestand m; (Mus)
Partitur f; **to keep (the)
~** mitzählen ▷ vt (goal) schießen;
(points) punkten ▷ vi (keep ~)
mitzählen; **scoreboard** n
Anzeigetafel f

scorn [skɔ:n] n Verachtung f;
scornful adj verächtlich

Scorpio [ˈskɔ:pɪəʊ] (pl **-s**) n (Astr)
Skorpion m

scorpion [ˈskɔ:pɪən] n Skorpion
m

Scot [skɒt] n Schotte m, Schottin
f; **Scotch** [skɒtʃ] n (whisky)
schottischer Whisky, Scotch m

Scotch tape® n (US) Tesafilm®
m

Scotland [ˈskɒtlənd] n Schottland nt; **Scotsman** (pl **-men**) n
Schotte m; **Scotswoman** (pl

-women) n Schottin f; **Scottish**
adj schottisch

scout [skaʊt] n (boy ~) Pfadfinder
m

scowl [skaʊl] vi finster blicken

scrambled eggs npl Rührei nt

scrap [skræp] n (bit) Stückchen
nt, Fetzen m; (metal) Schrott m ▷ vt
(car) verschrotten; (plan)
verwerfen; **scrapbook** n
Sammelalbum nt

scrape [skreɪp] n (scratch)
Kratzer m ▷ vt (car) schrammen;
(wall) streifen; **to ~ one's knee**
sich das Knie schürfen; **scrape
through** vi (exam) mit knapper
Not bestehen

scrap heap [ˈskræphi:p] n
Schrotthaufen m; **scrap metal** n
Schrott m; **scrap paper** n
Schmierpapier nt

scratch [skrætʃ] n (mark) Kratzer
m; **to start from ~** von vorne
anfangen ▷ vt kratzen; (car)
zerkratzen; **to ~ one's arm** sich
am Arm kratzen ▷ vi kratzen;
(~ oneself) sich kratzen

scream [skri:m] n Schrei m ▷ vi
schreien (with vor +dat); **to ~ at sb**
jdn anschreien

screen [skri:n] n (TV, Inform)
Bildschirm m; (Cine) Leinwand f
▷ vt (protect) abschirmen; (hide)
verdecken; (film) zeigen;
(applicants, luggage) überprüfen;
screenplay n Drehbuch nt;
screensaver n (Inform)
Bildschirmschoner m

screw [skru:] n Schraube f ▷ vt
(vulg: have sex with) ficken; **to ~ sth
to sth** etw an etw akk schrauben;
to ~ off/on (lid)
ab-/aufschrauben; **screw up** vt
(paper) zusammenknüllen; (make a
mess of) vermasseln; **screwdriver**
n Schraubenzieher m; **screw top**
n Schraubverschluss m

scribble ['skrɪbl] vt, vi kritzeln

script [skrɪpt] n (of play) Text m; (of film) Drehbuch nt; (style of writing) Schrift f

scroll down ['skrəʊl'daʊn] vi (Inform) runterscrollen; **scroll up** vi (Inform) raufscrollen; **scroll bar** n (Inform) Scrollbar f

scrub [skrʌb] vt schrubben; **scrubbing brush**, **scrub brush** (US) n Scheuerbürste f

scruffy ['skrʌfɪ] adj vergammelt

scrupulous, **scrupulously** ['skruːpjʊləs, -lɪ] adj, adv gewissenhaft; (painstaking) peinlich genau

scuba-diving ['skuːbədaɪvɪŋ] n Sporttauchen nt

sculptor ['skʌlptə°] n Bildhauer(in) m(f); **sculpture** ['skʌlptʃə°] n (Art) Bildhauerei f; (statue) Skulptur f

sea [siː] n Meer nt, See f; **seafood** n Meeresfrüchte pl; **sea front** n Strandpromenade f; **seagull** n Möwe f

seal [siːl] n (animal) Robbe f; (stamp, impression) Siegel nt; (Tech) Verschluss m; (ring etc) Dichtung f ▷ vt versiegeln; (envelope) zukleben

seam [siːm] n Naht f

search [sɜːtʃ] n Suche f (for nach); **to do a ~ for** (Inform) suchen nach; **in ~ of** auf der Suche nach ▷ vi suchen (for nach) ▷ vt durchsuchen; **search engine** n (Inform) Suchmaschine f

seashell ['siːʃel] n Muschel f; **seashore** n Strand m; **seasick** adj seekrank; **seaside** n: **at the ~** am Meer; **to go to the ~** ans Meer fahren; **seaside resort** n Seebad nt

season ['siːzn] n Jahreszeit f; (Comm) Saison f; **high/low**

~ Hoch-/Nebensaison f ▷ vt (flavour) würzen

seasoning n Gewürz nt

season ticket n (Rail) Zeitkarte f; (Theat) Abonnement nt; (Sport) Dauerkarte f

seat [siːt] n (place) Platz m; (chair) Sitz m; **take a ~** setzen Sie sich ▷ vt: **the hall ~s 300** der Saal hat 300 Sitzplätze; **please be ~ed** bitte setzen Sie sich; **to remain ~ed** sitzen bleiben; **seat belt** n Sicherheitsgurt m

sea view ['siːvjuː] n Seeblick m; **seaweed** n Seetang m

secluded [sɪ'kluːdɪd] adj abgelegen

second ['sekənd] adj zweite(r, s); **the ~ of June** der zweite Juni ▷ adv (in ~ position) an zweiter Stelle; (secondly) zweitens; **he came ~** er ist Zweiter geworden ▷ n (of time) Sekunde f; (moment) Augenblick m; **~ (gear)** der zweite Gang; (~ helping) zweite Portion; **just a ~** (einen) Augenblick!; **secondary** adj (less important) zweitrangig; **~ education** höhere Schulbildung f; **~ school** weiterführende Schule; **second-class** adj (ticket) zweiter Klasse; **~ stamp** Briefmarke für nicht bevorzugt beförderte Sendungen ▷ adv (travel) zweiter Klasse; **second-hand** adj, adv gebraucht; (information) aus zweiter Hand; **secondly** adv zweitens; **second-rate** adj (pej) zweitklassig

secret ['siːkrət] n Geheimnis nt ▷ adj geheim; (admirer) heimlich

secretary ['sekrətrɪ] n Sekretär(in) m(f); (minister) Minister(in) m(f); **Secretary of State** n (US) Außenminister(in) m(f); **secretary's office** n Sekretariat nt

secretive ['si:krətɪv] adj (person) geheimnistuerisch; **secretly** ['si:krətlɪ] adv heimlich
sect [sekt] n Sekte f
section ['sekʃən] n (part) Teil m; (of document) Abschnitt m; (department) Abteilung f
secure [sɪ'kjuə°] adj (safe) sicher (from vor +dat); (firmly fixed) fest ▷ vt (make firm) befestigen; (window, door) fest verschließen; **securely** adv fest; (safely) sicher; **security** [sɪ'kjuərɪtɪ] n Sicherheit f
sedative ['sedətɪv] n Beruhigungsmittel nt
seduce [sɪ'dju:s] vt verführen; **seductive** [sɪ'dʌktɪv] adj verführerisch; (offer) verlockend
see [si:] (saw, seen) vt (understand) verstehen; (check) nachsehen; (accompany) bringen; (visit) besuchen; (talk to) sprechen; **to ~ the doctor** zum Arzt gehen; **to ~ sb home** jdn nach Hause begleiten; **I saw him swimming** ich habe ihn schwimmen sehen; **~ you** tschüs!; **~ you on Friday** bis Freitag! ▷ vi sehen; (understand) verstehen; (you) ~ siehst du!; **we'll ~** mal sehen; **see about** vt (attend to) sich kümmern um; **see off** vt (say goodbye to) verabschieden; **see out** vt (show out) zur Tür bringen; **see through** vt **to see sth through** etw zu Ende bringen; **to ~ sb/sth** jdn/etw durchschauen; **see to** vt sich kümmern um; **~ it that ...** sieh zu, dass ...
seed [si:d] n (of plant) Samen m, (in fruit) Kern m; **seedless** adj kernlos
seedy ['si:dɪ] adj zwielichtig
seek [si:k] (sought, sought) vt suchen; (fame) streben nach; **to ~ sb's advice** jdn um Rat fragen

seem [si:m] vi scheinen; **he ~s (to be) honest** er scheint ehrlich zu sein; **it ~s to me that ...** es scheint mir, dass ...
seen [si:n] pp of **see**
seesaw ['si:sɔ:] n Wippe f
see-through adj durchsichtig
segment ['segmənt] n Teil m
seize [si:z] vt packen; (confiscate) beschlagnahmen; (opportunity, power) ergreifen
seldom ['seldəm] adv selten
select [sɪ'lekt] vt (exclusive) exklusiv ▷ vt auswählen; **selection** [sɪ'lekʃən] n Auswahl f (of an +dat); **selective** adj (choosy) wählerisch
self [self] (pl selves) n Selbst nt, Ich nt; **he's his old ~ again** er ist wieder ganz der Alte; **self-adhesive** adj selbstklebend; **self-assured** n selbstsicher; **self-catering** adj für Selbstversorger; **self-centred** adj egozentrisch; **self-confidence** n Selbstbewusstsein nt; **self-confident** adj selbstbewusst; **self-conscious** adj befangen, verklemmt; **self-contained** adj (flat) separat; **self-control** n Selbstbeherrschung f; **self-defence** n Selbstverteidigung f; **self-employed** adj selbstständig; **self-evident** adj offensichtlich
selfish, selfishly ['selfɪʃ, -lɪ] adj, adv egoistisch, selbstsüchtig; **selfless, selflessly** adj, adv selbstlos
self-pity [self'pɪtɪ] n Selbstmitleid nt; **self-portrait** n Selbstporträt nt; **self-respect** n Selbstachtung f; **self-service** n Selbstbedienung f ▷ adj Selbstbedienungs-
sell [sel] (sold, sold) vt verkaufen; **to ~ sb sth, to ~ sth to**

sb jdm etw verkaufen; **do you ~ postcards?** haben Sie Postkarten? ▷ vi (product) sich verkaufen; **sell out** vt: **to be sold ~** ausverkauft sein; **sell-by date** n Haltbarkeitsdatum nt

Sellotape® ['seləteɪp] n (Brit) Tesafilm® m

semester [sɪ'mestə°] n Semester nt

semi ['semɪ] n (Brit: house) Doppelhaushälfte f; **semicircle** n Halbkreis m; **semicolon** n Semikolon nt; **semidetached (house)** n (Brit) Doppelhaushälfte f; **semifinal** n Halbfinale nt

seminar ['semɪnɑː°] n Seminar nt

semiskimmed milk ['semɪskɪmd'mɪlk] n Halbfettmilch f

senate ['senət] n Senat m; **senator** n Senator(in) m(f)

send [send] (**sent, sent**) vt schicken; **to ~ sb sth, to ~ sth to sb** jdm etw schicken; **~ her my best wishes** grüße sie von mir; **send away** vt wegschicken ▷ vi: **to ~ for** anfordern; **send back** vt zurückschicken; **send for** vt (person) holen lassen; (by post) anfordern; **send off** vt (by post) abschicken; **send out** vt (invitations etc) verschicken ▷ vi: **to ~ for sth** etw holen lassen

sender ['sendə°] n Absender(in) m(f)

senior ['siːnɪə°] adj (older) älter; (high-ranking) höher; (pupils) älter; **he is ~ to me** er ist mir übergeordnet ▷ n: **he's eight years my ~** er ist acht Jahre älter als ich; **senior citizen** n Senior(in) m(f)

sensation [sen'seɪʃən] n Gefühl nt; (excitement, person, thing)

Sensation f; **sensational** adj sensationell

sense [sens] n (faculty, meaning) Sinn m; (feeling) Gefühl nt; (understanding) Verstand m; **~ of smell/taste** Geruchs-/ Geschmackssinn m; **to have a ~ of humour** Humor haben; **to make ~** (sentence etc) einen Sinn ergeben; (be sensible) Sinn machen; **in a ~** gewissermaßen ▷ vt spüren; **senseless** adj (stupid) sinnlos

sensible, sensibly ['sensəbl, -blɪ] adj, adv vernünftig

sensitive ['sensɪtɪv] adj empfindlich (to gegen); (easily hurt) sensibel; (subject) heikel

sensual ['sensjʊəl] adj sinnlich

sensuous ['sensjʊəs] adj sinnlich

sent [sent] pt, pp of **send**

sentence ['sentəns] n (Ling) Satz m; (Jur) Strafe f ▷ vt verurteilen (to zu)

sentiment ['sentɪmənt] n (sentimentality) Sentimentalität f; (opinion) Ansicht f; **sentimental** [sentɪ'mentl] adj sentimental

separate ['seprət] adj getrennt, separat; (individual) einzeln ▷ ['sepəreɪt] vt trennen (from von); **they are ~d** (couple) sie leben getrennt ▷ vi sich trennen; **separately** adv getrennt; (singly) einzeln

September [sep'tembə°] n September m; **in ~** im September; **on the 2nd of ~** am 2. September; **at the beginning/in the middle/at the end of ~** Anfang/Mitte/Ende September; **last/next ~** letzten/nächsten September

septic ['septɪk] adj vereitert

sequel ['siːkwəl] n (to film, book) Fortsetzung f (to von)

sequence ['si:kwəns] n (order)
Reihenfolge f

Serbia ['sɜ:bjə] n Serbien nt

sergeant ['sɑ:dʒənt] n Polizei-
meister(in) m(f); (Mil)
Feldwebel(in) m(f)

serial ['sɪərɪəl] n (TV) Serie f; (in
newspaper etc) Fortsetzungsroman
m ▷ adj (Inform) seriell; **~ number**
Seriennummer f

series ['sɪəri:z] nsing Reihe f; (TV,
Radio) Serie f

serious ['sɪərɪəs] adj ernst;
(injury, illness, mistake) schwer;
(discussion) ernsthaft; **are you ~?**
ist das dein Ernst?; **seriously** adv
ernsthaft; (hurt) schwer; **~? im**
Ernst?; **to take sb ~** jdn ernst
nehmen

sermon ['sɜ:mən] n (Rel) Predigt f

servant ['sɜ:vənt] n Diener(in)
m(f); **serve** [sɜ:v] vt (customer)
bedienen; (food) servieren; (one's
country etc) dienen +dat; (sentence)
verbüßen; **I'm being ~d** ich werde
schon bedient; **it ~s him right** es
geschieht ihm recht ▷ vi dienen
(as als), aufschlagen ▷ n
Aufschlag m

server n (Inform) Server m

service ['sɜ:vɪs] n (in shop, hotel)
Bedienung f; (activity, amenity)
Dienstleistung f; (set of dishes)
Service nt; (Auto) Inspektion f;
(Tech) Wartung f; (Rel)
Gottesdienst m, Aufschlag m;
train/bus ~ Zug-/Busverbindung
f; **"~ not included"** „Bedienung
nicht inbegriffen" ▷ vt (Auto, Tech)
warten; **service area** n (on
motorway) Raststätte f (mit
Tankstelle); **service charge** n
Bedienung f; **service provider** n
(Inform) Provider m; **service
station** n Tankstelle f

session ['seʃən] n (of court,
assembly) Sitzung f

set [set] (**set, set**) vt (place)
stellen; (lay flat) legen; (arrange)
anordnen; (table) decken; (trap,
record) aufstellen; (time, price)
festsetzen; (exam, alarm) stellen
(for auf +akk); **to ~ sb a task** jdm
eine Aufgabe stellen; **to ~ free**
freilassen; **to ~ a good example**
ein gutes Beispiel geben; **the
novel is ~ in London** der Roman
spielt in London ▷ vi (sun)
untergehen; (become hard) fest
werden; (bone)
zusammenwachsen ▷ n (collection
of things) Satz m; (of cutlery,
furniture) Garnitur f; (group of
people) Kreis m; (Radio, TV) Apparat
m, Satz m; (Theat) Bühnenbild nt;
(Cine) (Film)kulisse f ▷ adj (agreed,
prescribed) festgelegt; (ready)
bereit; **~ meal** Menü nt; **set aside**
vt (money) beiseitelegen; (time)
einplanen; **set off** vi aufbrechen
(for nach) ▷ vt (alarm) auslösen;
(enhance) hervorheben; **set out** vi
aufbrechen (for nach) ▷ vt (chairs,
chesspieces etc) aufstellen; (state)
darlegen; **to ~ to do sth** (intend)
beabsichtigen, etw zu tun; **set up**
vt (firm, organization) gründen;
(stall, tent, camera) aufbauen;
(meeting) vereinbaren ▷ vi: **to ~ up
as a doctor** sich als Arzt niederlassen

setback n Rückschlag m

settee [se'ti:] n Sofa nt, Couch f

setting ['setɪŋ] n (of novel, film)
Schauplatz m; (surroundings)
Umgebung f

settle ['setl] vt (bill, debt)
begleichen; (dispute) beilegen;
(question) klären; (stomach)
beruhigen ▷ vi: **to ~ (down)** (feel
at home) sich einleben; (calm down)
sich beruhigen; **settle in** vi (in
place) sich einleben; (in job) sich
eingewöhnen; **settle up** vi
(be)zahlen; **to ~ with sb** mit jdm

abrechnen; **settlement** n (of bill, debt) Begleichung f; (colony) Siedlung f; **to reach a ~** sich einigen

setup ['setʌp] n (organization) Organisation f; (situation) Situation f

seven ['sevn] num sieben ▷ n Sieben f; see also **eight; seventeen** ['sevn'tiːn] num siebzehn ▷ n Siebzehn f; see also **eight;**

seventeenth adj siebzehnte(r, s); see also **eighth; seventh** ['sevnθ] adj siebte(r, s) ▷ n (fraction) Siebtel nt; see also **eighth;**

seventieth ['sevntɪɪθ] adj siebzigste(r, s); see also **eight; seventy** ['sevntɪ] num siebzig; **~-one** einundsiebzig ▷ n Siebzig f; **to be in one's seventies** in den Siebzigern sein; see also **eight**

several ['sevrəl] adj, pron mehrere

severe [sɪ'vɪə°] adj (strict) streng; (serious) schwer; (pain) stark; (winter) hart; **severely** adv (harshly) hart; (seriously) schwer

sew [səʊ] (sewed, sewn) vt, vi nähen

sewage ['suːɪdʒ] n Abwasser nt; **sewer** ['svə°] n Abwasserkanal m

sewing ['səʊɪŋ] n Nähen nt; **sewing machine** n Nähmaschine f

sewn [səʊn] pp of **sew**

sex [seks] n Sex m; (gender) Geschlecht nt; **to have ~** Sex haben (with mit); **sexism** ['seksɪzəm] n Sexismus m; **sexist** ['seksɪst] adj sexistisch ▷ n Sexist(in) m(f); **sex life** n Sex(ual)leben nt

sexual ['seksjʊəl] adj sexuell; **~ discrimination/harassment** sexuelle Diskriminierung/ Belästigung; **~ intercourse** Geschlechtsverkehr m; **sexuality**

[seksju'ælɪtɪ] n Sexualität f; **sexually** adv sexuell

sexy ['seksɪ] adj sexy, geil

Seychelles ['seɪʃelz] npl Seychellen pl

shabby ['ʃæbɪ] adj schäbig

shack [ʃæk] n Hütte f

shade [ʃeɪd] n (shadow) Schatten m; (for lamp) (Lampen)schirm m; (colour) Farbton m; **~s** (US: sunglasses) Sonnenbrille f ▷ vt (from sun) abschirmen; (in drawing) schattieren

shadow ['ʃædəʊ] n Schatten m

shady ['ʃeɪdɪ] adj schattig; (fig) zwielichtig

shake [ʃeɪk] (shook, shaken) vt schütteln; (shock) erschüttern; **to ~ hands with sb** jdm die Hand geben; **to ~ one's head** den Kopf schütteln ▷ vi (tremble) zittern; (building, ground) schwanken; **shake off** vt abschütteln; **shaken** ['ʃeɪkn] pp of **shake; shaky** ['ʃeɪkɪ] adj (trembling) zittrig; (table, chair, position) wackelig; (weak) unsicher

shall [ʃæl] (should) vb aux werden; (in questions) sollen; **I ~ do my best** ich werde mein Bestes tun; **~ I come too?** soll ich mitkommen?; **where ~ we go?** wo gehen wir hin?

shallow ['ʃæləʊ] adj (a. fig) seicht; (person) oberflächlich

shame [ʃeɪm] n (feeling of ~) Scham f; (disgrace) Schande f; **what a ~!** wie schade!; **~ on you!** schäm dich/schämen Sie sich!; **it's a ~ that ...** schade, dass ...

shampoo [ʃæm'puː] n Shampoo nt; **to have a ~ and set** sich die Haare waschen und legen lassen ▷ vt (hair) waschen; (carpet) schamponieren

shandy ['ʃændɪ] n Radler m, Alsterwasser nt

shan't [ʃɑːnt] contr of **shall not**

shape [ʃeɪp] n Form f;
(unidentified figure) Gestalt f; **in
the ~ of** in Form +gen; **to be in
good ~** (healthwise) in guter
Verfassung sein; **to take ~** (plan,
idea) Gestalt annehmen ▷ vt (clay,
person) formen; **-shaped** [ʃeɪpt]
suf -förmig; **shapeless** adj
formlos

share [ʃeəˢ] n Anteil +dat (in, of an
m); (Fin) Aktie f ▷ vt, vi teilen;
shareholder n Aktionär(in) m(f)

shark [ʃɑːk] n (Zool) Haifisch m

sharp [ʃɑːp] adj scharf; (pin) spitz;
(person) scharfsinnig; (nose) heftig;
(increase, fall) abrupt; **C/F ~** (Mus)
Cis/Dis nt ▷ adv: **at 2 o'clock
~** Punkt 2 Uhr; **sharpen** vt (knife)
schärfen; (pencil) spitzen;
sharpener n (pencil ~) Spitzer m

shatter [ˈʃætəˢ] vt zerschmet-
tern; (fig) zerstören ▷ vi
zerspringen; **shattered** adj
(exhausted) kaputt

shave [ʃeɪv] (shaved, shaved or
shaven) vt rasieren ▷ vi sich
rasieren ▷ n Rasur f; **that was a
close ~** (fig) das war knapp; **shave
off** vt: **to shave one's beard off**
sich den Bart abrasieren; **shaven**
[ˈʃeɪvn] pp of **shave** ▷ adj (head)
kahl geschoren; **shaver** n (Elec)
Rasierapparat m; **shaving brush**
n Rasierpinsel m; **shaving foam** n
Rasierschaum m; **shaving tackle**
n Rasierzeug nt

shawl [ʃɔːl] n Tuch nt

she [ʃiː] pron sie

shed [ʃed] (shed, shed) n
Schuppen m ▷ vt (tears, blood)
vergießen; (hair, leaves) verlieren

she'd [ʃiːd] contr of **she had; she
would**

sheep [ʃiːp] (pl -) n Schaf nt;
sheepdog n Schäferhund m;
sheepskin n Schaffell nt

sheer [ʃɪəˢ] adj (madness) rein;

(steep) steil; **by ~ chance** rein
zufällig

sheet [ʃiːt] n (on bed) Betttuch nt;
(of paper) Blatt nt; (of metal) Platte f;
(of glass) Scheibe f; **a ~ of paper**
ein Blatt Papier

shelf [ʃelf] (pl shelves) n
Bücherbord nt, Regal nt; **shelves** pl
(item of furniture) Regal nt

she'll [ʃiːl] contr of **she will; she
shall**

shell [ʃel] n (of egg, nut) Schale f;
(sea~) Muschel f ▷ vt (peas, nuts)
schälen; **shellfish** n (as food)
Meeresfrüchte pl

shelter [ˈʃeltəˢ] n (protection)
Schutz m; (accommodation)
Unterkunft f; (bus ~)
Wartehäuschen nt ▷ vt schützen
(from vor +dat) ▷ vi sich
unterstellen; **sheltered** adj (spot)
geschützt; (life) behütet

shelve [ʃelv] vt (fig) aufschieben;
shelves pl of **shelf**

shepherd [ˈʃepəd] n Schäfer m;
shepherd's pie n
Hackfleischauflauf mit Decke aus
Kartoffelpüree

sherry [ˈʃerɪ] n Sherry m

she's [ʃiːz] contr of **she is; she has**

shield [ʃiːld] n Schild m; (fig)
Schutz m ▷ vt schützen (from vor
+dat)

shift [ʃɪft] n (change)
Veränderung f; (period at work,
workers) Schicht f; (on keyboard)
Umschalttaste f ▷ vt (furniture etc)
verrücken; (stain) entfernen; **to
~ gear(s)** (US Aut) schalten ▷ vi
(move) sich bewegen; (move up)
rutschen; **shift key** n
Umschalttaste f

shin [ʃɪn] n Schienbein nt

shine [ʃaɪn] (shone, shone) vi
(be shiny) glänzen; (sun) scheinen;
(lamp) leuchten ▷ vt (polish)
polieren ▷ n Glanz m

shingles ['ʃɪŋlz] nsing (Med) Gürtelrose f

shiny ['ʃaɪnɪ] adj glänzend

ship [ʃɪp] n Schiff nt ▷ vt (send) versenden; (by ship) verschiffen; **shipment** n (goods) Sendung f; (sent by ship) Ladung f; **shipwreck** n Schiffbruch m; **shipyard** n Werft f

shirt [ʃɜːt] n Hemd nt

shit [ʃɪt] n (vulg) Scheiße f; (person) Arschloch nt; ~! Scheiße!; **shitty** ['ʃɪtɪ] adj (fam) beschissen

shiver ['ʃɪvə⁰] vi zittern (with vor +dat)

shock [ʃɒk] n (mental, emotional) Schock m; **to be in ~** unter Schock stehen; **to get a ~** (Elec) einen Schlag bekommen ▷ vt schockieren; **shock absorber** n Stoßdämpfer m; **shocked** adj schockiert (by über +akk); **shocking** adj schockierend; (awful) furchtbar

shoe [ʃuː] n Schuh m; **shoehorn** n Schuhlöffel m; **shoelace** n Schnürsenkel m; **shoe polish** n Schuhcreme f

shone [ʃɒn] pt, pp of **shine**

shook [ʃʊk] pt of **shake**

shoot [ʃuːt] (**shot, shot**) vt (wound) anschießen; (kill) erschießen; (Cine) drehen; (fam: heroin) drücken ▷ vi (with gun, move quickly) schießen; **to ~ at sb** auf jdn schießen ▷ n (of plant) Trieb m; **shooting** n (exchange of gunfire) Schießerei f; (killing) Erschießung f

shop [ʃɒp] n Geschäft nt, Laden m ▷ vi einkaufen; **shop assistant** n Verkäufer(in) m(f); **shopkeeper** n Geschäftsinhaber(in) m(f); **shoplifting** n Ladendiebstahl m; **shopper** n Käufer(in) m(f); **shopping** n (activity) Einkaufen nt; (goods) Einkäufe pl; **to do the**

~ einkaufen; **to go** ~ einkaufen gehen; **shopping bag** n Einkaufstasche f; **shopping cart** n (US) Einkaufswagen m; **shopping center** (US), **shopping centre** n Einkaufszentrum nt; **shopping list** n Einkaufszettel m; **shopping trolley** n (Brit) Einkaufswagen m; **shop window** n Schaufenster nt

shore [ʃɔː°] n Ufer nt; **on ~** an Land

short [ʃɔːt] adj kurz; (person) klein; **to be ~ of money** knapp bei Kasse sein; **to be ~ of time** wenig Zeit haben; **~ of breath** kurzatmig; **to cut ~** (holiday) abbrechen; **we are two ~** wir haben zwei zu wenig; **it's ~ for ...** das ist die Kurzform von ... ▷ n (drink, Elec) Kurze(r) m; **shortage** n Knappheit f (of an +dat); **shortbread** n Buttergebäck nt; **short circuit** n Kurzschluss m; **shortcoming** n Unzulänglichkeit f; (of person) Fehler m; **shortcut** n (quicker route) Abkürzung f; (Inform) Shortcut m; **shorten** vt kürzen; (in time) verkürzen; **shorthand** n Stenografie f; **shortlist** n **to be on the ~** in der engeren Wahl sein; **short-lived** adj kurzlebig; **shortly** adv bald; **shorts** npl Shorts pl; **short-sighted** adj (a. fig) kurzsichtig; **short-sleeved** adj kurzärmelig; **short-stay car park** n Kurzzeitparkplatz m; **short story** n Kurzgeschichte f; **short-term** adj kurzfristig; **short wave** n Kurzwelle f

shot [ʃɒt] pt, pp of **shoot** ▷ n (from gun, in football) Schuss m; (Foto, Cine) Aufnahme f; (injection) Spritze f; (of alcohol) Schuss m

should [ʃʊd] vb aux: **I ~ go now** ich sollte jetzt gehen; **what ~ I do?** was soll ich tun?; **you ~n't have said that** das hättest

du/hätten Sie nicht sagen sollen;
that ~ be enough das müsste
reichen

shoulder ['ʃəʊldə°] n Schulter f

shouldn't ['ʃʊdnt] contr of
should not

should've ['ʃʊdəv] contr of
should have

shout [ʃaʊt] n Schrei m; (call) Ruf
m ▷ vt rufen; (order) brüllen ▷ vi
schreien; **to ~ at** anschreien; **to
~ for help** um Hilfe rufen

shove [ʃʌv] vt (person) schubsen;
(car, table etc) schieben ▷ vi (in
crowd) drängeln

shovel ['ʃʌvl] n Schaufel f ▷ vt
schaufeln

show [ʃəʊ] (showed, shown) vt
zeigen; **to ~ sb sth, to ~ sth to sb**
jdm etw zeigen; **to ~ sb in** jdn
hereinführen; **to ~ sb out** jdn zur
Tür bringen ▷ n (Cine, Theat)
Vorstellung f; (TV) Show f;
(exhibition) Ausstellung f; **show off**
vi (pej) angeben; **show round** vt
herumführen; **to show sb round
the house/the town** jdm das
Haus/die Stadt zeigen; **show up**
vi (arrive) auftauchen

shower ['ʃaʊə°] n Dusche f;
(rain) Schauer m; **to have** (o
take) a ~ duschen ▷ vi (wash)
duschen

showing ['ʃəʊɪŋ] n (Cine)
Vorstellung f

shown [ʃəʊn] pp of **show**

showroom ['ʃəʊruːm] n
Ausstellungsraum m

shrank [ʃræŋk] pt of **shrink**

shred [ʃred] n (of paper, fabric)
Fetzen m ▷ vt (in shredder) (im
Reißwolf) zerkleinern; **shredder** n
(for paper) Reißwolf m

shrimp [ʃrɪmp] n Garnele f

shrink [ʃrɪŋk] (shrank, shrunk)
vi schrumpfen; (clothes) eingehen

shrivel ['ʃrɪvl] vi: **to ~ (up)**

schrumpfen; (skin) runzlig werden;
(plant) welken

Shrove Tuesday ['ʃrəʊv'tjuːzdeɪ]
n Fastnachtsdienstag m

shrub [ʃrʌb] n Busch m, Strauch
m

shrug [ʃrʌg] vt, vi: **to ~ (one's
shoulders)** die Achseln zucken

shrunk [ʃrʌŋk] pp of **shrink**

shudder ['ʃʌdə°] vi schaudern;
(ground, building) beben

shuffle ['ʃʌfl] vt, vi mischen

shut [ʃʌt] (shut, shut) vt
zumachen, schließen; **~ your face!**
(fam) halt den Mund! ▷ vi
schließen ▷ adj geschlossen;
we're ~ wir haben geschlossen;
shut down vt schließen;
(computer) ausschalten ▷ vi
schließen; (computer) sich
ausschalten; **shut in** vt
einschließen; **shut out** vt (lock
out) aussperren; **to shut oneself
out** sich aussperren; **shut up** vt
(lock up) abschließen; (silence) zum
Schweigen bringen ▷ vi (keep
quiet) den Mund halten; **~I** halt den
Mund!; **shutter** n (on window)
(Fenster)laden m; **shutter release**
n Auslöser m; **shutter speed** n
Belichtungszeit f

shuttle bus ['ʃʌtlbʌs] n
Shuttlebus m

shuttlecock ['ʃʌtlkɒk] n
Federball m

shuttle service ['ʃʌtlsɜːvɪs] n
Pendelverkehr m

shy [ʃaɪ] adj schüchtern; (animal)
scheu

Siberia [saɪˈbɪərɪə] n Siberien nt

Sicily ['sɪsɪlɪ] n Sizilien nt

sick [sɪk] adj krank; (joke)
makaber; **to be ~** (Brit: vomit) sich
übergeben; **to be off ~** wegen
Krankheit fehlen; **I feel ~** mir ist
schlecht; **to be ~ of sb/sth**
jdn/etw satthaben; **it makes me**

~ (fig) es ekelt mich an; **sickbag** n
Spucktüte f; **sick leave** n: **to be
on ~** krankgeschrieben sein;
sickness n Krankheit f; (Brit:
nausea) Übelkeit f; **sickness
benefit** n (Brit) Krankengeld nt

side [saɪd] n Seite f; (of road) Rand
m; (of mountain) Hang m; (Sport)
Mannschaft f; **by my ~** neben mir;
~ by ~ nebeneinander ▷ adj (door,
entrance) Seiten-; **sideboard** n
Anrichte f; **sideburns** npl
Koteletten pl; **side dish** n Beilage
f; **side effect** n Nebenwirkung f;
sidelight n (Brit Auto) Parklicht
nt; **side order** n Beilage f; **side
road** n Nebenstraße f; **side street**
n Seitenstraße f; **sidewalk** n (US)
Bürgersteig m; **sideways** adv
seitwärts

sieve [sɪv] n Sieb nt

sift [sɪft] vt (flour etc) sieben

sigh [saɪ] vi seufzen

sight [saɪt] n (power of seeing)
Sehvermögen nt; (view, thing seen)
Anblick m; **~s** pl (of city etc)
Sehenswürdigkeiten pl; **to have
bad ~** schlecht sehen; **to lose ~ of**
aus den Augen verlieren; **out of
~** außer Sicht; **sightseeing** n: **to
go ~** Sehenswürdigkeiten
besichtigen; **~ tour** Rundfahrt f

sign [saɪn] n Zeichen nt; (notice,
road ~) Schild nt ▷ vt
unterschreiben ▷ vi unterschreiben; **to ~ for sth** den
Empfang einer Sache gen
bestätigen; **to ~ in/out** sich
ein-/austragen; **sign on** vi (Brit:
register as unemployed) sich
arbeitslos melden; **sign up** vi (for
course) sich einschreiben; (Mil) sich
verpflichten

signal ['sɪɡnl] n Signal nt ▷ vi
(car driver) blinken

signature ['sɪɡnətʃə°] n Unterschrift f

significant [sɪɡ'nɪfɪkənt] adj
(important) bedeutend, wichtig;
(meaning sth) bedeutsam;
significantly adv (considerably)
bedeutend

sign language ['saɪnlæɡwɪdʒ]
n Zeichensprache f; **signpost** n
Wegweiser m

silence ['saɪləns] n Stille f; (of
person) Schweigen nt; **~!** Ruhe! ▷ vt
zum Schweigen bringen; **silent**
adj still; (taciturn) schweigsam;
she remained ~ sie schwieg

silk [sɪlk] n Seide f ▷ adj Seiden-

silly ['sɪlɪ] adj dumm, albern;
don't do anything ~ mach keine
Dummheiten; **the ~ season** das
Sommerloch

silver ['sɪlvə°] n Silber nt; (coins)
Silbermünzen pl ▷ adj
Silber-, silbern; **silver-plated** adj
versilbert; **silver wedding** n
silberne Hochzeit

similar ['sɪmɪlə°] adj ähnlich (to
dat); **similarity** [sɪmɪ'lærɪtɪ] n
Ähnlichkeit f (to mit); **similarly**
adv (equally) ebenso

simple ['sɪmpl] adj einfach; (un-
sophisticated) schlicht; **simplify**
['sɪmplɪfaɪ] vt vereinfachen;
simply adv einfach; (merely) bloß;
(dress) schlicht

simulate ['sɪmjʊleɪt] vt
simulieren

simultaneous, simultaneously
[sɪmal'teɪnɪəs, -lɪ] adj, adv
gleichzeitig

sin [sɪn] n Sünde f ▷ vi sündigen

since [sɪns] adv seitdem; (in the
meantime) inzwischen ▷ prep seit
+dat; **ever ~ 1995** schon seit 1995
▷ conj (time) seit, seitdem;
(because) da, weil; **ever ~ I've
known her** seit ich sie kenne; **it's
ages ~ I've seen him** ich habe
ihn seit Langem nicht mehr
gesehen

sincere [sɪn'sɪə°] *adj* aufrichtig;
sincerely *adv* aufrichtig;
Yours ~ mit freundlichen
Grüßen

sing [sɪŋ] **(sang, sung)** *vt, vi*
singen

Singapore [sɪŋgə'pɔ:°] *n* Singapur *nt*

singer ['sɪŋə°] *n* Sänger(in) *m(f)*

single ['sɪŋgl] *adj* (one only)
einzig; (not double) einfach; (bed,
room) Einzel-; (unmarried) ledig;
(Brit: ticket) einfach ▷ *n* (Brit:
ticket) einfache Fahrkarte; (Mus)
Single *f*; **a ~ to London, please**
(Brit Rail) nach London
bitte; **single out** *vt* (choose)
auswählen; **single-handed**,
single-handedly *adv* im
Alleingang; **single parent** *n*
Alleinerziehende(r) *mf*; **single
supplement** *n* (for hotel room)
Einzelzimmerzuschlag *m*

singular ['sɪŋgjʊlə°] *n* Singular
m

sinister ['sɪnɪstə°] *adj*
unheimlich

sink [sɪŋk] **(sank, sunk)** *vt* (ship)
versenken ▷ *vi* sinken ▷ *n*
Spülbecken *nt*; (in bathroom)
Waschbecken *nt*

sip [sɪp] *vt* nippen an +dat

sir [sɜ:°] *n*: **yes, ~** ja(, mein Herr);
can I help you, ~? kann ich Ihnen
helfen?; **Sir James** (title) Sir James

sister ['sɪstə°] *n* Schwester *f*;
(Brit: nurse) Oberschwester *f*;
sister-in-law (pl **sisters-in-law**) *n*
Schwägerin *f*

sit [sɪt] **(sat, sat)** *vi* (be sitting)
sitzen; (~ down) sich setzen;
(committee, court) tagen ▷ *vt* (Brit:
exam) machen; **sit down** *vi* sich
hinsetzen; **sit up** *vi* (from lying
position) sich aufsetzen

sitcom ['sɪtkɒm] *n* Situ-
ationskomödie *f*

site [saɪt] *n* Platz *m*; (building ~)
Baustelle *f*; (web~) Site *f*

sitting ['sɪtɪŋ] *n* (meeting, for
portrait) Sitzung *f*; **sitting room** *n*
Wohnzimmer *nt*

situated ['sɪtjʊeɪtɪd] *adj*: **to be
~** liegen

situation [sɪtjʊ'eɪʃən] *n* (circum-
stances) Situation *f*, Lage *f*; (job)
Stelle *f*; **"~s vacant/wanted"** (Brit)
„Stellenangebote/Stellengesuche"

six [sɪks] *num* sechs ▷ *n* Sechs *f*;
see also **eight**; **sixpack** *n* (of beer
etc) Sechserpack *m*; **sixteen**
['sɪks'ti:n] *num* sechzehn ▷ *n*
Sechzehn *f*; see also **eight**;
sixteenth *adj* sechzehnte(r, s); see
also **eighth**; **sixth** [sɪksθ] *adj*
sechste(r, s); **~ form** (Brit) =
Oberstufe *f* ▷ *n* (fraction) Sechstel
nt; see also **eighth**; **sixtieth**
['sɪkstɪɪθ] *adj* sechzigste(r, s); see
also **eighth**; **sixty** ['sɪkstɪ] *num*
sechzig; **~-one** einundsechzig ▷ *n*
Sechzig *f*; **to be in one's sixties** in
den Sechzigern sein; see also **eight**

size [saɪz] *n* Größe *f*; **what ~ are
you?** welche Größe hast du/haben
Sie?; **a ~ too big** eine Nummer zu
groß

sizzle ['sɪzl] *vi* (Gastr) brutzeln

skate [skeɪt] *n* Schlittschuh *m*;
(roller~) Rollschuh *m* ▷ *vi*
Schlittschuh laufen; (roller~)
Rollschuh laufen; **skateboard** *n*
Skateboard *nt*; **skating** *n* Eislauf
m; (roller~) Rollschuhlauf *m*;
skating rink *n* Eisbahn *f*; (for
roller-skating) Rollschuhbahn *f*

skeleton ['skelɪtn] *n* (a. fig)
Skelett *nt*

skeptical *n* (US) see **sceptical**

sketch [sketʃ] *n* Skizze *f*; (Theat)
Sketch *m* ▷ *vt* skizzieren;
sketchbook *n* Skizzenbuch *nt*

ski [ski:] *n* Ski *m* ▷ *vi* Ski laufen;
ski boot *n* Skistiefel *m*

skid [skɪd] vi (Aut) schleudern

skier ['skiːə°] n Skiläufer(in) m(f); **skiing** n Skilaufen nt; **to go ~** Ski laufen gehen; **~ holiday** Skiurlaub m; **skiing instructor** n Skilehrer(in) m(f)

skilful, skilfully ['skɪlful, -fəlɪ] adj, adv geschickt

ski-lift ['skiːlɪft] n Skilift m

skill [skɪl] n Geschick nt; (acquired technique) Fertigkeit f; **skilled** adj geschickt (at, in in +dat); (worker) Fach-; (work) fachmännisch

skim [skɪm] vt: **to ~ (off)** (fat etc) abschöpfen; **to ~ (through)** (read) überfliegen; **skimmed milk** n Magermilch f

skin [skɪn] n Haut f; (fur) Fell nt; (peel) Schale f; **skin diving** n Sporttauchen nt; **skinny** adj dünn

skip [skɪp] vi hüpfen; (with rope) seilspringen ▷ vt (miss out) überspringen; (meal) ausfallen lassen; (school, lesson) schwänzen

ski pants ['skiːpænts] npl Skihose f; **ski pass** n Skipass m; **ski pole** n Skistock m; **ski resort** n Skiort m

skirt [skəːt] n Rock m

ski run ['skiːrʌn] n (Ski)abfahrt f; **ski stick** n Skistock m; **ski tow** n Schlepplift m

skittle ['skɪtl] n Kegel m; **~s** (game) Kegeln nt

skive [skaɪv] vi: **to ~ (off)** (Brit) (from school) schwänzen; (from work) blaumachen

skull [skʌl] n Schädel m

sky [skaɪ] n Himmel m; **skydiving** n Fallschirmspringen nt; **skylight** n Dachfenster nt; **skyscraper** n Wolkenkratzer m

slam [slæm] vt (door) zuschlagen; **slam on** vt: **to slam the brakes on** voll auf die Bremse treten

slander ['slɑːndə°] n Verleumdung f ▷ vt verleumden

slang [slæŋ] n Slang m

slap [slæp] n Klaps m; (across face) Ohrfeige f ▷ vt schlagen; **to ~ sb's face** jdn ohrfeigen

slash [slæʃ] n (punctuation mark) Schrägstrich m ▷ vt (face, tyre) aufschlitzen; (prices) stark herabsetzen

slate [sleɪt] n (rock) Schiefer m; (roof -) Schieferplatte f

slaughter ['slɔːtə°] vt (animals) schlachten; (people) abschlachten

Slav [slɑːv] adj slawisch ▷ n Slawe m, Slawin f

slave [sleɪv] n Sklave m, Sklavin f; **slave away** vi schuften; **slave-driver** n (fam) Sklaventreiber(in) m(f); **slavery** ['sleɪvərɪ] n Sklaverei f

sleaze [sliːz] n (corruption) Korruption f; **sleazy** adj (bar, district) zwielichtig

sledge [slɛdʒ] n Schlitten m

sleep [sliːp] (slept, slept) vi schlafen; **to ~ with sb** mit jdm schlafen ▷ n Schlaf m; **to put to ~** (animal) einschläfern; **sleep in** vi (lie in) ausschlafen; **sleeper** n (Rail: train) Schlafwagenzug m; (carriage) Schlafwagen m; **sleeping bag** n Schlafsack m; **sleeping car** n Schlafwagen m; **sleeping pill** n Schlaftablette f; **sleepless** adj schlaflos; **sleepy** adj schläfrig; (place) verschlafen

sleet [sliːt] n Schneeregen m

sleeve [sliːv] n Ärmel m; **sleeveless** adj ärmellos

sleigh [sleɪ] n (Pferde)schlitten m

slender ['slɛndə°] adj schlank; (fig) gering

slept [slɛpt] pt, pp of **sleep**

slice [slaɪs] n Scheibe f; (of cake, tart, pizza) Stück nt ▷ vt: **to ~ (up)** in Scheiben schneiden; **sliced bread** n geschnittenes Brot

slid [slɪd] pt, pp of **slide**

slide [slaɪd] (**slid, slid**) vt gleiten lassen; (push) schieben ▷ vi gleiten; (slip) rutschen ▷ n (Foto) Dia nt; (in playground) Rutschbahn f; (Brit: for hair) Spange f

slight [slaɪt] adj leicht; (problem, difference) klein; **not in the ~est** nicht im Geringsten; **slightly** adv etwas; (injured) leicht

slim [slɪm] adj (person) schlank; (book) dünn; (chance, hope) gering ▷ vi abnehmen

slime [slaɪm] n Schleim m, **slimy** adj schleimig

sling [slɪŋ] (**slung, slung**) vt werfen ▷ n (for arm) Schlinge f

slip [slɪp] n (mistake) Flüchtigkeitsfehler m; **~ of paper** Zettel m ▷ vt (put) stecken; **to ~ on/off** (garment) an-/ausziehen; **it ~ped my mind** ich habe es vergessen ▷ vi (lose balance) (aus)rutschen; **slip away** vi (leave) sich wegstehlen; **slipper** n Hausschuh m; **slippery** adj (path, road) glatt; (soap, fish) glitschig; **slip-road** n (Brit: onto motorway) Auffahrt f; (off motorway) Ausfahrt f

slit [slɪt] (**slit, slit**) vt aufschlitzen ▷ n Schlitz m

slope [sləʊp] n Neigung f; (side of hill) Hang m ▷ vi (be sloping) schräg sein; **sloping** adj (floor, roof) schräg

sloppy [ˈslɒpɪ] adj (careless) schlampig; (sentimental) rührselig

slot [slɒt] n (opening) Schlitz m; (Inform) Steckplatz m; **we have a ~ free at 2** (free time) um 2 ist noch ein Termin frei; **slot machine** n Automat m; (for gambling) Spielautomat m

Slovak [ˈsləʊvæk] adj slowakisch ▷ n (person) Slowake m, Slowakin f; (language) Slowakisch nt; **Slovakia** [sləʊˈvækɪə] n Slowakei f

Slovene [ˈsləʊviːn], **Slovenian** [sləʊˈviːnɪən] adj slowenisch ▷ n (person) Slowene m, Slowenin f; (language) Slowenisch nt; **Slovenia** [sləʊˈviːnɪə] n Slowenien nt

slow [sləʊ] adj langsam; (business) flau; **to be ~** (clock) nachgehen; (stupid) begriffsstutzig sein; **slow down** vi langsamer werden; (when driving/walking) langsamer fahren/gehen; **slowly** adv langsam; **slow motion** n: **in ~** in Zeitlupe

slug [slʌg] n (Zool) Nacktschnecke f

slum [slʌm] n Slum m

slump [slʌmp] n Rückgang m (in an ~ adj) ▷ vi (onto chair etc) sich fallen lassen; (prices) stürzen

slung [slʌŋ] pt, pp of **sling**

slur [slɜː] n (insult) Verleumdung f; **slurred** [slɜːd] adj undeutlich

slush [slʌʃ] n (snow) Schneematsch m; **slushy** adj matschig; (fig) schmalzig

slut [slʌt] n (pej) Schlampe f

smack [smæk] n Klaps m ▷ vt: **to ~ sb** jdm einen Klaps geben ▷ vi: **to ~ of** riechen nach

small [smɔːl] adj klein; **small ads** n (Brit) Kleinanzeigen pl; **small change** n Kleingeld nt; **small letters** npl: **in ~** in Kleinbuchstaben; **smallpox** n Pocken pl; **small print** n: **the ~ das** Kleingedruckte; **small-scale** adj (map) in kleinem Maßstab; **small talk** n Konversation f, Smalltalk m

smart [smɑːt] adj (elegant) schick; (clever) clever; **smartarse, smartass** (US) n (fam) Klugscheißer (in) m(f); **smart card** n Chipkarte f; **smartly** adv (dressed) schick

smash [smæʃ] n (car crash) Zusammenstoß m, Schmetterball

m ▷ vt (break) zerschlagen; (fig: record) brechen, deutlich übertreffen ▷ vi (break) zerbrechen; **to ~ into** (car) krachen gegen

smear [smɪə°] n (mark) Fleck m; (Med) Abstrich m; (fig) Verleumdung f ▷ vt (spread) schmieren; (make dirty) beschmieren; (fig) verleumden

smell [smɛl] (**smelt** o **smelled**, **smelt** o **smelled**) vt riechen ▷ vi riechen (of nach); (unpleasantly) stinken ▷ n Geruch m; (unpleasant) Gestank m; **smelly** adj übel riechend; **smelt** [smɛlt] pt, pp of **smell**

smile [smaɪl] n Lächeln nt ▷ vi lächeln; **to ~ at sb** jdn anlächeln

smock [smɒk] n Kittel m

smog [smɒg] n Smog m

smoke [sməʊk] n Rauch m ▷ vt rauchen; (food) räuchern ▷ vi rauchen; **smoke alarm** n Rauchmelder m; **smoked** adj (food) geräuchert; **smoke-free** adj (zone, building) rauchfrei; **smoker** n Raucher(in) m(f); **smoking** n Rauchen nt; **"no ~"** „Rauchen verboten"

smooth [smuːð] adj glatt; (flight, crossing) ruhig; (movement) geschmeidig; (without problems) reibungslos; (pej: person) aalglatt ▷ vt (hair, dress) glatt streichen; (surface) glätten; **to run ~** (engine) ruhig laufen

smudge [smʌdʒ] vt (writing, lipstick) verschmieren

smug [smʌg] adj selbstgefällig

smuggle ['smʌgl] vt schmuggeln; **to ~ in/out** herein-/herausschmuggeln

smutty ['smʌtɪ] adj (obscene) schmutzig

snack [snæk] n Imbiss m; **to have**

a **~** eine Kleinigkeit essen; **snack bar** n Imbissstube f

snail [sneɪl] n Schnecke f; **snail mail** n (fam) Schneckenpost f

snake [sneɪk] n Schlange f

snap [snæp] n (photo) Schnappschuss m ▷ adj (decision) spontan ▷ vt (break) zerbrechen; (rope) zerreißen ▷ vi (break) brechen; (rope) reißen; (bite) schnappen (at nach); **snap off** vt (break) abbrechen; **snap fastener** n (US) Druckknopf m; **snapshot** n Schnappschuss m

snatch [snætʃ] vt schnappen

sneak [sniːk] vi (move) schleichen; **sneakers** npl (US) Turnschuhe pl

sneeze [sniːz] vi niesen

sniff [snɪf] vi schniefen; (smell) schnüffeln (at an +dat) ▷ vt schnuppern an +dat; (glue) schnüffeln

snob [snɒb] n Snob m; **snobbish** adj versnobt

snog [snɒg] vi, vt knutschen

snooker ['snuːkə°] n Snooker nt

snoop [snuːp] vi: **to ~ (around)** (herum)schnüffeln

snooze [snuːz] n, vi: **to (have a) ~** ein Nickerchen machen

snore [snɔː°] vi schnarchen

snorkel ['snɔːkl] n Schnorchel m; **snorkelling** n Schnorcheln nt; **to go ~** schnorcheln gehen

snout [snaʊt] n Schnauze f

snow [snəʊ] n Schnee m ▷ vi schneien; **snowball** n Schneeball m; **snowboard** n Snowboard nt; **snowboarding** n Snowboarding nt; **snowdrift** n Schneewehe f; **snowdrop** n Schneeglöckchen nt; **snowflake** n Schneeflocke f; **snowman** (pl **-men**) n Schneemann m; **snowplough**,

snowplow (US) n Schneepflug m;
snowstorm n Schneesturm m;
snowy adj (region) schneereich;
(landscape) verschneit
snug [snʌg] adj (person, place)
gemütlich
snuggle up vi: to
~ to sb sich an jdn ankuscheln

⊙ KEYWORD

so [səʊ] adv 1 (thus) so; (likewise)
auch; **so saying he walked away**
indem er das sagte, ging er; **if so**
wenn ja; **I didn't do it — you did
so!** ich hab das nicht gemacht —
hast du wohll; **so do I, so am I** etc
ich auch; **so it is!** tatsächlich!; **I
hope/think so** hoffentlich/ich
glaube schon; **so far** bis jetzt
2 (in comparisons etc: to such a
degree) so; **so quickly/big (that)**
so schnell/groß, dass; **I'm so glad
to see you** ich freue mich so,
dich/Sie zu sehen
3 **so many** so viele; **so much work**
so viel Arbeit; **I love you so much**
ich liebe dich so sehr
4 (phrases) **10 or so** etwa 10; **so
long!** (inf) (goodbye) tschüss!
▷ conj 1 (expressing purpose) **so as to**
um ... zu; **so (that)** damit
2 (expressing result) also; **so I was
right after all** ich hatte also doch
recht; **so you see ...** wie du
siehst/Sie sehen ...

soak [səʊk] vt durchnässen;
(leave in liquid) einweichen; **I'm ~ed**
ich bin klatschnass; **soaking** adj:
~ **(wet)** klatschnass
soap [səʊp] n Seife f; **soap
(opera)** n Seifenoper f; **soap
powder** n Waschpulver nt
sob [sɒb] vi schluchzen
sober ['səʊbə°] adj nüchtern;
sober up vi nüchtern werden

so-called ['səʊ'kɔːld] adj
sogenannt
soccer ['sɒkə°] n Fußball m
sociable ['səʊʃəbl] adj gesellig
social ['səʊʃəl] adj sozial;
(sociable) gesellig; **socialist** adj
sozialistisch ▷ n Sozialist(in)
m(f); **socialize** vi unter die Leute
gehen; **social security** n (Brit)
Sozialhilfe f; (US)
Sozialversicherung f
society [sə'saɪətɪ] n Gesellschaft
f; (club) Verein m
sock [sɒk] n Socke f
socket ['sɒkɪt] n (Elec) Steckdose
f
soda ['səʊdə] n (water) Soda f;
(US: pop) Limo f; **soda water** n
Sodawasser nt
sofa ['səʊfə] n Sofa nt; **sofa bed**
n Schlafcouch f
soft [sɒft] adj weich; (quiet) leise;
(lighting) gedämpft; (kind)
gutmütig; (weak) nachgiebig;
~ **drink** alkoholfreies Getränk;
softly adv sanft; (quietly) leise;
software n (Inform) Software f
soil [sɔɪl] n Erde f; (ground) Boden
m
solar ['səʊlə°] adj Sonnen-, Solar-
solarium [sə'leəriəm] n
Solarium nt
sold [səʊld] pt, pp of **sell**
soldier ['səʊldʒə°] n Soldat(in)
m(f)
sole [səʊl] n Sohle f; (fish)
Seezunge f ▷ vt besohlen ▷ adj
einzig; (owner, responsibility)
alleinig; **solely** adv nur
solemn ['sɒləm] adj feierlich;
(person) ernst
solicitor [sə'lɪsɪtə°] n (Brit)
Rechtsanwalt m, Rechtsanwältin f
solid ['sɒlɪd] adj (hard) fest; (gold,
oak etc) massiv; (well built) solide;
(meal) kräftig; **three hours** ~ drei
volle Stunden

solitary ['sɒlɪtərɪ] *adj* einsam; (*single*) einzeln; **solitude** ['sɒlɪtjuːd] *n* Einsamkeit *f*

solo ['səʊləʊ] *n* (*Mus*) Solo *nt*

soluble ['sɒljʊbl] *adj* löslich; **solution** [sə'luːʃən] *n* Lösung *f* (*to +gen*); **solve** [sɒlv] *vt* lösen

somber (*US*), **sombre** ['sɒmbə°] *adj* düster

⬤ KEYWORD

some [sʌm] *adj* **1** (*a certain amount o number of*) einige; (*a few*) ein paar; (*with singular nouns*) etwas; **some tea/biscuits** etwas Tee/ein paar Kekse; **I've got some money, but not much** ich habe ein bisschen Geld, aber nicht viel
2 (*certain: in contrasts*) manche(r, s); **some people say that ...** manche Leute sagen, dass ...
3 (*unspecified*) irgendein(e); **some woman was asking for you** da hat eine Frau nach dir/Ihnen gefragt; **some day** eines Tages; **some day next week** irgendwann nächste Woche
▷ *pron* **1** (*a certain number*) einige; **have you got some?** hast du/haben Sie welche?
2 (*a certain amount*) etwas; **I've read some of the book** ich habe das Buch teilweise gelesen
▷ *adv*: **some 10 people** etwa 10 Leute

somebody *pron* jemand; **~ (or other)** irgendjemand; **~ else** jemand anders; **someday** *adv* irgendwann; **somehow** *adv* irgendwie; **someone** *pron see* **somebody**; **someplace** *adv* (*US*) *see* **somewhere**; **something** ['sʌmθɪŋ] *pron* etwas; **~ (or other)** irgendetwas; **~ else** etwas anderes; **~ nice** etwas Nettes;

would you like ~ to drink? möchtest du/möchten Sie etwas trinken? ▷ *adv*: **~ like 20** ungefähr 20; **sometime** *adv* irgendwann; **sometimes** *adv* manchmal; **somewhat** *adv* ein wenig; **somewhere** *adv* irgendwo; (*to a place*) irgendwohin; **~ else** irgendwo anders; (*to another place*) irgendwo anders hin

son [sʌn] *n* Sohn *m*

song [sɒŋ] *n* Lied *nt*; Song *m*

son-in-law ['sʌnɪnlɔː] (*pl* **sons-in-law**) *n* Schwiegersohn *m*

soon [suːn] *adv* bald; (*early*) früh; **too ~** zu früh; **as ~ as I ... should** ich ...; **as ~ as possible** so bald wie möglich; **sooner** *adv* (*time*) früher; (*for preference*) lieber

soot [sʊt] *n* Ruß *m*

soothe [suːð] *vt* beruhigen; (*pain*) lindern

sophisticated [sə'fɪstɪkeɪtɪd] *adj* (*person*) kultiviert; (*machine*) hoch entwickelt; (*plan*) ausgeklügelt

sophomore ['sɒfəmɔː°] *n* (*US*) College-Student(in) *m(f)* im zweiten Jahr

soppy ['sɒpɪ] *adj* (*fam*) rührselig

soprano [sə'prɑːnəʊ] *n* Sopran *m*

sore [sɔː°] *adj*: **to be ~** wehtun; **to have a ~ throat** Halsschmerzen haben ▷ *n* wunde Stelle

sorrow ['sɒrəʊ] *n* Kummer *m*

sorry ['sɒrɪ] *adj* (*sight, figure*) traurig; (**I'm**) **~** (*excusing*) Entschuldigung!; **I'm ~** (*regretful*) es tut mir leid; **~?** wie bitte?; **I feel ~ for him** er tut mir leid

sort [sɔːt] *n* Art *f*; **what ~ of film is it?** was für ein Film ist das?; **a ~ of** eine Art *+gen*; **all ~s of things** alles Mögliche; **~ of** (*fam*) irgendwie ▷ *vt* sortieren; **everything's ~ed** (*dealt with*) alles

ist geregelt; **sort out** vt (classify etc) sortieren; (problems) lösen

sought [sɔːt] pt, pp of **seek**

soul [səʊl] n Seele f; (music) Soul m

sound [saʊnd] adj (healthy) gesund; (safe) sicher; (sensible) vernünftig; (theory) stichhaltig; (thrashing) tüchtig ⊳ n (noise) Geräusch nt; (Mus) Klang m; (TV) Ton m ⊳ vt: **to ~ the alarm** Alarm schlagen; **to ~ one's horn** hupen ⊳ vi (seem) klingen (like wie); **soundcard** n (Inform) Soundkarte f; **sound effects** npl Klangeffekte pl; **soundproof** adj schalldicht; **soundtrack** n (of film) Filmmusik f, Soundtrack m

soup [suːp] n Suppe f

sour [ˈsaʊə°] adj sauer; (fig) mürrisch

source [sɔːs] n Quelle f; (fig) Ursprung m

sour cream [saʊəˈkriːm] n saure Sahne

south [saʊθ] n Süden m; **to the ~ of** südlich von ⊳ adv (go, face) nach Süden ⊳ adj Süd-; **South Africa** n Südafrika nt; **South African** adj südafrikanisch ⊳ n Südafrikaner(in) m(f); **South America** n Südamerika nt; **South American** adj südamerikanisch ⊳ n Südamerikaner(in) m(f); **southbound** adj (in) Richtung Süden; **southern** [ˈsʌðən] adj Süd-, südlich; **~ Europe** Südeuropa nt; **southwards** [ˈsaʊθwədz] adv nach Süden

souvenir [suːvəˈnɪə°] n Andenken nt (of an +akk)

sow [səʊ] (**sowed, sown** o **sowed**) vt (a. fig) säen; (field) besäen ⊳ [saʊ] n (pig) Sau f

soya bean [ˈsɔɪəbiːn] n Sojabohne f

soy sauce [ˈsɔɪsɔːs] n Sojasoße f

spa [spaː] n (place) Kurort m

space [speɪs] n (room) Platz m, Raum m; (outer ~) Weltraum m; (gap) Zwischenraum m; (for parking) Lücke f; **space bar** n Leertaste f; **spacecraft** (pl -) n Raumschiff nt; **space ship** n Raumschiff nt; **space shuttle** n Raumfähre f

spacing [ˈspeɪsɪŋ] n (in text) Zeilenabstand m; **double ~** zweizeiliger Abstand

spacious [ˈspeɪʃəs] adj geräumig

spade [speɪd] n Spaten m; **~s** Pik nt

spaghetti [spəˈɡetɪ] n/sing Spaghetti pl

Spain [speɪn] n Spanien nt

spam [spæm] n (Inform) Spam m

Spaniard [ˈspænɪəd] n Spanier(in) m(f); **Spanish** [ˈspænɪʃ] adj spanisch ⊳ n (language) Spanisch nt

spanner [ˈspænə°] n (Brit) Schraubenschlüssel m

spare [speə°] adj (as replacement) Ersatz-; **~ part** Ersatzteil m; **~ room** Gästezimmer nt; **~ time** Freizeit f; **~ tyre** Ersatzreifen m ⊳ n (~ part) Ersatzteil m ⊳ vt (lives, feelings) verschonen; **can you ~ (me) a moment?** hättest du/hätten Sie einen Moment Zeit?

spark [spaːk] n Funke m; **sparkle** [ˈspaːkl] vi funkeln; **sparkling wine** n Schaumwein m, Sekt m; **spark plug** [ˈspaːkplʌɡ] n Zündkerze f

sparrow [ˈspærəʊ] n Spatz m

sparse [spaːs] adj spärlich; **sparsely** adv: **~ populated** dünn besiedelt

spasm [ˈspæzəm] n Krampf m

spat [spæt] pt, pp of **spit**

speak [spiːk] (**spoke, spoken**) vt sprechen; **can you ~ French?** sprechen Sie Französisch?; **to**

~ one's mind seine Meinung sagen ▷ vi sprechen (to mit, zu); (make speech) reden; ~ing (Tel) am Apparat; **so to ~** sozusagen; **~ for yourself** das meinst auch nur dul; **speak up** vi (louder) lauter sprechen; **speaker** n Sprecher(in) m(f); (public ~) Redner(in) m(f); (loud~) Lautsprecher m, Box f

special ['speʃəl] adj besondere(r, s), speziell ▷ n (on menu) Tagesgericht nt; (TV, Radio) Sondersendung f; **special delivery** n Eilzustellung f; **special effects** npl Spezialeffekte pl; **specialist** n Spezialist(in) m(f); (Tech) Fachmann m, Fachfrau f; (Med) Facharzt m, Fachärztin f; **speciality** [speʃɪˈælɪtɪ] n Spezialität f; **specialize** vi sich spezialisieren (in auf +akk); **specially** adv besonders; (specifically) extra; **special offer** n Sonderangebot nt; **specialty** n (US) see **speciality**

species ['spiːʃiːz] nsing Art f

specific [spəˈsɪfɪk] adj spezifisch; (precise) genau; **specify** ['spesɪfaɪ] vt genau angeben

specimen ['spesɪmən] n (sample) Probe f; (example) Exemplar nt

specs [speks] npl (fam) Brille f

spectacle [ˈspektəkl] n Schauspiel nt

spectacles npl Brille f

spectacular [spekˈtækjʊləˈ] adj spektakulär

spectator [spekˈteɪtəˈ] n Zuschauer(in) m(f)

sped [sped] pt, pp of **speed**

speech [spiːtʃ] n (address) Rede f; (faculty) Sprache f; **to make a ~** eine Rede halten; **speechless** adj sprachlos (with vor +dat)

speed [spiːd] (**sped** ◊ **speeded**, **sped** ◊ **speeded**) vi rasen; (exceed

~ limit) zu schnell fahren ▷ n Geschwindigkeit f; (of film) Lichtempfindlichkeit f; **speed up** vt beschleunigen ▷ vi schneller werden/fahren; (drive faster) schneller fahren; **speedboat** n Rennboot nt; **speed bump** n Bodenschwelle f; **speed camera** n Blitzgerät nt; **speed limit** n Geschwindigkeitsbegrenzung f; **speedometer** [spɪˈdɒmɪtəˈ] n Tachometer m; **speed trap** n Radarfalle f; **speedy** adj schnell

spell [spel] (**spelt** ◊ **spelled**, **spelt** ◊ **spelled**) vt buchstabieren; **how do you ~ ...?** wie schreibt man ...? ▷ n (period) Weile f; (enchantment) Zauber m; **a cold/hot ~** (weather) ein Kälteeinbruch/eine Hitzewelle; **spellchecker** n (Inform) Rechtschreibprüfung f; **spelling** n Rechtschreibung f; (of a word) Schreibweise f; **~ mistake** Schreibfehler m

spelt [spelt] pt, pp of **spell**

spend [spend] (**spent, spent**) vt (money) ausgeben (on für); (time) verbringen; **spending money** n Taschengeld nt

spent [spent] pt, pp of **spend**

sperm [spɜːm] n Sperma nt

sphere [sfɪəˈ] n (globe) Kugel f; (fig) Sphäre f

spice [spaɪs] n Gewürz nt; (fig) Würze f ▷ vt würzen; **spicy** ['spaɪsɪ] adj würzig; (fig) pikant

spider [ˈspaɪdəˈ] n Spinne f

spike [spaɪk] n (on railing etc) Spitze f; (on shoe, tyre) Spike m

spill [spɪl] (**spilt** ◊ **spilled**, **spilt** ◊ **spilled**) vt verschütten

spin [spɪn] (**spun, spun**) vi (turn) sich drehen; (washing) schleudern; **my head is ~ning** mir dreht sich alles ▷ vt (turn) drehen; (coin) hochwerfen ▷ n (turn) Drehung f

spinach ['spɪnɪtʃ] n Spinat m

spin doctor n Spindoktor m
(Verantwortlicher für die
schönrednerische Öffentlichkeitsarbeit
besonders von Politikern)

spin-drier ['spɪndraɪə'] n
Wäscheschleuder f; **spin-dry** vt
schleudern

spine [spaɪn] n Rückgrat nt; (of
animal, plant) Stachel m; (of book)
Rücken m

spiral ['spaɪrəl] n Spirale f ▷ adj
spiralförmig; **spiral staircase** n
Wendeltreppe f

spire ['spaɪə'] n Turmspitze f

spirit ['spɪrɪt] n (essence, soul)
Geist m; (humour, mood) Stimmung
f; (courage) Mut m; (verve) Elan m;
~s pl (drinks) Spirituosen pl

spiritual ['spɪrɪtjʊəl] adj geistig;
(Rel) geistlich

spit [spɪt] (spat, spat) vi
spucken ▷ n (for roasting)
(Brat)spieß m; (saliva) Spucke f;
spit out vt ausspucken

spite [spaɪt] n Boshaftigkeit f; **in
~ of** trotz +gen; **spiteful** adj
boshaft

spitting image ['spɪtɪŋ'ɪmɪdʒ]
n: **he's the ~ of you** er ist
dir/Ihnen wie aus dem Gesicht
geschnitten

splash [splæʃ] vt (person, object)
bespritzen ▷ vi (liquid) spritzen;
(play in water) planschen

splendid ['splendɪd] adj herrlich

splinter ['splɪntə'] n Splitter
m

split [splɪt] (split, split) vt (stone,
wood) spalten; (share) teilen ▷ vi
(stone, wood) sich spalten; (seam)
platzen ▷ n (in stone, wood) Spalt
m; (in clothing) Riss m; (fig)
Spaltung f; **split up** vi (couple) sich
trennen ▷ vt (divide up) aufteilen;
split ends npl (Haar)spliss m;
splitting adj (headache) rasend

spoil [spɔɪl] (spoiled o spoilt,

spoiled o **spoilt**) vt verderben,
(child) verwöhnen ▷ vi (food)
verderben

spoilt [spɔɪlt] pt, pp of **spoil**

spoke [spəʊk] pt of **speak** ▷ n
Speiche f

spoken ['spəʊkən] pp of **speak**

spokesperson ['spəʊkspɜːsən]
(pl **-people**) n Sprecher(in) m(f)

sponge [spʌndʒ] n (for washing)
Schwamm m; **sponge bag** n
Kulturbeutel m; **sponge cake** n
Biskuitkuchen m

sponsor ['spɒnsə'] n (of event,
programme) Sponsor(in) m(f) ▷ vt
unterstützen; (event, programme)
sponsern

spontaneous, **spontaneously**
['spɒn'teɪnɪəs, -lɪ] adj, adv
spontan

spool [spuːl] n Spule f

spoon [spuːn] n Löffel m

sport [spɔːt] n Sport m; **sports
car** n Sportwagen m; **sports
centre** n Sportzentrum nt;
sports club n Sportverein m;
sportsman (pl **-men**) n Sportler
m; **sportswear** n Sportkleidung f;
sportswoman (pl **-women**) n
Sportlerin f; **sporty** adj sportlich

spot [spɒt] n (dot) Punkt m; (of
paint, blood etc) Fleck m; (place)
Stelle f; (pimple) Pickel m; **on the
~** vor Ort; (at once) auf der Stelle
▷ vt (notice) entdecken; (difference)
erkennen; **spotless** adj (clean)
blitzsauber; **spotlight** n (lamp)
Scheinwerfer m; **spotty** adj
(pimply) pickelig

spouse [spaʊs] n Gatte m,
Gattin f

spout [spaʊt] n Schnabel m

sprain [spreɪn] n Verstauchung
f ▷ vt: **to ~ one's ankle** sich den
Knöchel verstauchen

sprang [spræŋ] pt of **spring**

spray [spreɪ] n (liquid in can)

Spray nt o m; (~ (can)) Spraydose f
▷ vt (plant, insects) besprühen;
(car) spritzen

spread [spred] (**spread, spread**)
vt (open out) ausbreiten; (news,
disease) verbreiten; (butter, jam)
streichen; (bread, surface)
bestreichen ▷ vi (news, disease,
fire) sich verbreiten ▷ n (of disease,
religion etc) Verbreitung f; (for bread)
Aufstrich m; **spreadsheet** n
(Inform) Tabellenkalkulation f

spring [sprɪŋ] (**sprang, sprung**)
vi (leap) springen ▷ n (season)
Frühling m; (coil) Feder f; (water)
Quelle f; **springboard** n
Sprungbrett nt; **spring onion** n
(Brit) Frühlingszwiebel f; **spring
roll** n (Brit) Frühlingsrolle f;
springy adj (mattress) federnd

sprinkle ['sprɪŋkl] vt streuen;
(liquid) (be)träufeln; **to ~ sth with
sth** etw mit etw bestreuen; (with
liquid) etw mit etw besprengen;
sprinkler n (for lawn)
Rasensprenger m; (for fire)
Sprinkler m

sprint [sprɪnt] vi rennen; (Sport)
sprinten

sprout [spraʊt] n (of plant) Trieb
m; (from seed) Keim m; (**Brussels**)
~s pl Rosenkohl m ▷ vi sprießen

sprung [sprʌŋ] pp of **spring**

spun [spʌn] pt, pp of **spin**

spy [spaɪ] n Spion(in) m(f) ▷ vi
spionieren; **to ~ on sb** jdm
nachspionieren ▷ vt erspähen

squad [skwɒd] n (Sport) Kader m;
(police ~) Kommando nt

square [skweə°] n (shape)
Quadrat nt; (open space) Platz m;
(on chessboard etc) Feld nt ▷ adj (in
shape) quadratisch; **2 ~ metres** 2
Quadratmeter; **2 metres ~** 2 Meter
im Quadrat ▷ vt: **3 ~d** 3 hoch 2;
square root n Quadratwurzel f

squash [skwɒʃ] n (drink)

Fruchtsaftgetränk nt; (Sport)
Squash nt; (US: vegetable) Kürbis m
▷ vt zerquetschen

squat [skwɒt] vi (be crouching)
hocken; **to ~ (down)** sich
(hin)hocken

squeak [skwiːk] vi (door, shoes
etc) quietschen; (animal) quieken

squeal [skwiːl] vi (person)
kreischen (with vor +dat)

squeeze [skwiːz] vt drücken;
(orange) auspressen ▷ vi: **to ~ into
the car** sich in den Wagen
hineinzwängen; **squeeze up** vi
(on bench etc) zusammenrücken

squid [skwɪd] n Tintenfisch m

squint [skwɪnt] vi schielen; (in
bright light) blinzeln

squirrel ['skwɪrəl] n Eichhörnchen nt

squirt [skwɜːt] vt, vi (liquid)
spritzen

Sri Lanka [sriːˈlæŋkə] n Sri
Lanka nt

st abbr = **stone** Gewichtseinheit (6,35
kg)

St abbr = **saint** St.; abbr = **street** Str.

stab [stæb] vt (person) einstechen
auf +akk; (to death) erstechen;
stabbing adj (pain) stechend

stabilize ['steɪbəlaɪz] vt
stabilisieren ▷ vi sich
stabilisieren

stable ['steɪbl] n Stall m ▷ adj
stabil

stack [stæk] n (pile) Stapel m
▷ vt: **to ~ (up)** (auf)stapeln

stadium ['steɪdɪəm] n Stadion
nt

staff [stɑːf] n (personnel) Personal
nt, Lehrkräfte pl

stag [stæg] n Hirsch m

stag night n (Brit)
Junggesellenabschied m

stage [steɪdʒ] n (Theat) Bühne f;
(of project, life etc) Stadium nt; (of
journey) Etappe f; **at this ~** zu

diesem Zeitpunkt ▷ vt (Theat)
aufführen, inszenieren;
(demonstration) veranstalten

stagger ['stægə°] vi wanken ▷ vt
(amaze) verblüffen; **staggering**
adj (amazing) umwerfend; (amount,
price) schwindelerregend

stagnate [stæg'neɪt] vi (fig)
stagnieren

stain [steɪn] n Fleck m;
stained-glass window n
Buntglasfenster nt; **stainless steel**
n rostfreier Stahl; **stain remover**
n Fleck(en)entferner m

stair [steə°] n (Treppen)stufe f; **~s**
pl Treppe f; **staircase** n Treppe
f

stake [steɪk] n (post) Pfahl m; (in
betting) Einsatz m; (Fin) Anteil m (in
an +dat); **to be at ~** auf dem Spiel
stehen

stale [steɪl] adj (bread) alt; (beer)
schal

stalk [stɔːk] n Stiel m ▷ vt (wild
animal) sich anpirschen an +akk;
(person) nachstellen +dat

stall [stɔːl] n (in market)
(Verkaufs)stand m; (in stable) Box f;
~s pl (Theat) Parkett nt ▷ vt
(engine) abwürgen ▷ vi (driver) den
Motor abwürgen; (car) stehen
bleiben; (delay) Zeit schinden

stamina ['stæmɪnə] n Durch-
haltevermögen nt

stammer ['stæmə°] vi, vt
stottern

stamp [stæmp] n (postage ~)
Briefmarke f; (for document)
Stempel m ▷ vt (passport etc)
stempeln; (mail) frankieren;
stamped addressed envelope n
frankierter Rückumschlag

stand [stænd] (stood, stood) vi
stehen; (as candidate) kandidieren
▷ vt (place) stellen; (endure)
aushalten; **I can't ~ her** ich kann
sie nicht ausstehen ▷ n (stall)

Stand m; (seats in stadium) Tribüne
f; (for coats, bicycles) Ständer m; (for
small objects) Gestell nt; **stand
around** vi herumstehen; **stand
by** vi (be ready) sich bereithalten;
(be inactive) danebenstehen ▷ vt
(fig: person) halten zu; (decision,
promise) stehen zu; **stand for** vt
(represent) stehen für; (tolerate)
hinnehmen; **stand in for** vt
einspringen für; **stand out** vi (be
noticeable) auffallen; **stand up** vi
(get up) aufstehen ▷ vt (girlfriend,
boyfriend) versetzen; **stand up for**
vt sich einsetzen für; **stand up to**
vt: **to ~ sb** jdm die Stirn bieten

standard ['stændəd] n (norm)
Norm f; **~ of living**
Lebensstandard m ▷ adj
Standard-

standardize ['stændədaɪz] vt
vereinheitlichen

stand-by ['stændbaɪ] n (thing in
reserve) Reserve f; **on ~** in
Bereitschaft ▷ adj (flight, ticket)
Stand-by-; **standing order** n (at
bank) Dauerauftrag m; **standpoint**
['stændpɔɪnt] n Standpunkt m;
standstill ['stændstɪl] n Stillstand m; **to come to a ~** stehen
bleiben; (fig) zum Erliegen
kommen

stank [stæŋk] pt of stink

staple ['steɪpl] n (for paper)
Heftklammer f ▷ vt heften (to an
+akk); **stapler** n Hefter m

star [stɑː°] n Stern m; (person)
Star m ▷ vt: **the film ~s Hugh
Grant** der Film zeigt Hugh Grant
in der Hauptrolle ▷ vi die
Hauptrolle spielen

starch [stɑːtʃ] n Stärke f

stare [steə°] vi starren; **to ~ at**
anstarren

starfish ['stɑːfɪʃ] n Seestern m

star sign ['stɑːsaɪn] n
Sternzeichen nt

start [stɑːt] n (beginning) Anfang m, Beginn m; (Sport) Start m; (lead) Vorsprung m; **from the ~** von Anfang an ▷ vt anfangen; (car, engine) starten; (business, family) gründen; **to ~ to do sth, to ~ doing sth** anfangen, etw zu tun ▷ vi (begin) anfangen; (car) anspringen; (on journey) aufbrechen; (Sport) starten; (jump) zusammenfahren; **~ing from Monday** ab Montag; **start off** vt (discussion, process etc) anfangen, beginnen ▷ vi (begin) anfangen, beginnen; (on journey) aufbrechen; **start over** vi (US) wieder anfangen; **start up** vi (in business) anfangen ▷ vt (car, engine) starten; (business) gründen; **starter** n (Brit: first course) Vorspeise f; (Auto) Anlasser m; **starting point** n (a. fig) Ausgangspunkt m

startle ['stɑːtl] vt erschrecken; **startling** adj überraschend

starve [stɑːv] vi hungern; (to death) verhungern; **I'm starving** ich habe einen Riesenhunger

state [steɪt] n (condition) Zustand m; (Pol) Staat m; **the (United) States** die (Vereinigten) Staaten ▷ adj Staats-; (control, education) staatlich ▷ vt erklären; (facts, name etc) angeben; **stated** adj (fixed) festgesetzt

statement ['steɪtmənt] n (official declaration) Erklärung f; (to police) Aussage f; (from bank) Kontoauszug m

state-of-the-art [steɪtəvðiːˈɑːt] adj hochmodern, auf dem neuesten Stand der Technik

static ['stætɪk] adj (unchanging) konstant

station ['steɪʃən] n (for trains, buses) Bahnhof m; (underground ~) Station f; (police ~, fire ~) Wache f;

(TV, Radio) Sender m ▷ vt (Mil) stationieren

stationer's ['steɪʃənəz] n: **~ (shop)** Schreibwarengeschäft nt; **stationery** n Schreibwaren pl

station wagon ['steɪʃənwægən] n (US) Kombiwagen m

statistics [stəˈtɪstɪks] nsing (science) Statistik f; (figures) Statistiken pl

statue ['stætjuː] n Statue f

status ['steɪtəs] n Status m; (prestige) Ansehen nt; **status bar** n (Inform) Statuszeile f

stay [steɪ] n Aufenthalt m ▷ vi bleiben; (with friends, in hotel) wohnen (with bei); **to ~ the night** übernachten; **stay away** vi wegbleiben; **to ~ from sb** sich von jdm fernhalten; **stay behind** vi zurückbleiben; (at work) länger bleiben; **stay in** vi (at home) zu Hause bleiben; **stay out** vi (not come home) wegbleiben; **stay up** vi (at night) aufbleiben

steady ['stedɪ] adj (speed) gleichmäßig; (progress, increase) stetig; (job, income, girlfriend) fest; (worker) zuverlässig; (hand) ruhig; **they've been going ~ for two years** sie sind seit zwei Jahren fest zusammen ▷ vt (nerves) beruhigen; **to ~ oneself** Halt finden

steak [steɪk] n Steak nt; (of fish) Filet nt

steal [stiːl] (**stole, stolen**) vt stehlen; **to ~ sth from sb** jdm etw stehlen

steam [stiːm] n Dampf m ▷ vt (Gastr) dämpfen; **steam up** vi (window) beschlagen; **steamer** n (Gastr) Dampfkochtopf m; (ship) Dampfer m; **steam iron** n Dampfbügeleisen nt

steel [stiːl] n Stahl m ▷ adj Stahl-

steep [stiːp] adj steil

steeple ['stiːpl] n Kirchturm m

steer [stɪə°] vt, vi steuern; (car, bike etc) lenken; **steering** n (Auto) Lenkung f; **steering wheel** n Steuer nt, Lenkrad nt

stem [stem] n (of plant, glass) Stiel m

step [step] n Schritt m; (stair) Stufe f; (measure) Maßnahme f; **~ by ~** Schritt für Schritt ▷ vi treten; **~ this way, please** hier entlang bitte; **step down** vi (resign) zurücktreten

stepbrother n Stiefbruder m; **stepchild** (pl -children) n Stiefkind nt; **stepfather** n Stiefvater m

stepladder n Trittleiter f

stepmother n Stiefmutter f; **stepsister** n Stiefschwester f

stereo ['steriəʊ] (pl -s) n; **~ (system)** Stereoanlage f

sterile ['sterail] adj steril; **sterilize** ['sterilaiz] vt sterilisieren

sterling ['stɜːlɪŋ] n (Fin) das Pfund Sterling

stew [stjuː] n Eintopf m

steward ['stjuːəd] n (on plane, ship) Steward m; **stewardess** n Stewardess f

stick [stɪk] (stuck, stuck) vt (with glue etc) kleben; (pin etc) stecken; (fam: put) tun ▷ vi (get jammed) klemmen; (hold fast) haften ▷ n Stock m; (hockey ~) Schläger m; (of chalk) Stück nt; (of celery, rhubarb) Stange f; **stick out** vt: **to stick one's tongue out (at sb)** (jdm) die Zunge herausstrecken ▷ vi (protrude) vorstehen; (ears) abstehen; **stick to** vt (rules, plan etc) sich halten an +akk; **sticker** n Aufkleber m; **sticky** ['stɪkɪ] adj klebrig;

(weather) schwül; **~ label** Aufkleber m; **~ tape** Klebeband nt

stiff [stɪf] adj steif

stifle ['staifl] vt (yawn etc, opposition) unterdrücken; **stifling** adj drückend

still [stɪl] adj still; (drink) ohne Kohlensäure ▷ adv (yet, even now) (immer) noch; (all the same) immerhin; (sit, stand) still; **he ~ doesn't believe me** er glaubt mir immer noch nicht; **keep ~** halt still; **bigger/better ~** noch größer/besser

still life (pl still lives) n Stillleben nt

stimulate ['stɪmjʊleit] vt anregen; **stimulating** adj anregend

sting [stɪŋ] (stung, stung) vt (wound with ~) stechen ▷ vi (eyes, ointment etc) brennen ▷ n (insect wound) Stich m

stingy ['stɪndʒɪ] adj (fam) geizig

stink [stɪŋk] (stank, stunk) vi stinken (of nach) ▷ n Gestank m

stir [stɜː°] vt (mix) (um)rühren; **stir up** vt (mob) aufhetzen; (memories) wachrufen, **to ~ trouble** Unruhe stiften; **stir-fry** vt (unter Rühren) kurz anbraten

stitch [stɪtʃ] n (in sewing) Stich m; (in knitting) Masche f; **to have a ~ (pain)** Seitenstechen haben; **he had to have ~s** er musste genäht werden; **she had her ~s out** ihr wurden die Fäden gezogen; **to be in ~s** (fam) sich kaputtlachen ▷ vt nähen; **stitch up** vt (hole, wound) nähen

stock [stɒk] n (supply) Vorrat m; (of an +dat); (of shop) Bestand m; (for soup etc) Brühe f; **~s and shares** n Aktien und Wertpapiere pl; **to be in/out of ~** vorrätig/nicht vorrätig sein; **to**

take ~ Inventur machen; *(fig)* Bilanz ziehen ▷ vt *(keep in shop)* führen; **stock up** vi sich eindecken *(on, with* mit)

stockbroker n Börsenmakler(in) m(f)

stock cube n Brühwurfel m

stock exchange n Börse f

stocking ['stɒkɪŋ] n Strumpf m

stock market ['stɒkmɑːkɪt] n Börse f

stole [stəʊl] pt of **steal**; **stolen** ['stəʊlən] pp of **steal**

stomach ['stʌmək] n Magen m; *(belly)* Bauch m; **on an empty** ~ auf leeren Magen; **stomach-ache** n Magenschmerzen pl; **stomach upset** n Magenverstimmung f

stone [stəʊn] n Stein m; *(seed)* Kern m, Stein m; *(weight)* britische Gewichtseinheit (6,35 kg) ▷ adj Stein-, aus Stein; **stony** adj *(ground)* steinig

stood [stʊd] pt, pp of **stand**

stool [stuːl] n Hocker m

stop [stɒp] n Halt m; *(for bus, tram, train)* Haltestelle f; **to come to a** ~ anhalten ▷ vt *(vehicle, passer-by)* anhalten; *(put an end to)* ein Ende machen +dat; *(cease)* aufhören mit; *(prevent from happening)* verhindern; *(bleeding)* stillen; *(engine, machine)* abstellen; *(payments)* einstellen; *(cheque)* sperren; **to** ~ **doing sth** aufhören, etw zu tun; **to** ~ **sb (from) doing sth** jdn daran hindern, etw zu tun; ~ **it!** hör auf (damit)! ▷ vi *(vehicle)* anhalten; *(during journey)* Halt machen; *(pedestrian, clock, heart)* stehen bleiben; *(rain, noise)* aufhören; *(stay)* bleiben; **stop by** vi vorbeischauen; **stop over** vi *(overnight)* übernachten; **stop gap** n Provisorium nt, Zwischenlösung f; **stopover** n *(on journey)*

Zwischenstation f; **stopper** n Stöpsel m; **stop sign** n Stoppschild nt; **stopwatch** n Stoppuhr f

storage ['stɔːrɪdʒ] n Lagerung f; **store** [stɔː°] n *(supply)* Vorrat m *(of an +dat)*; *(place for storage)* Lager nt; *(large shop)* Kaufhaus nt; *(US: shop)* Geschäft nt ▷ vt lagern; *(Inform)* speichern; **storecard** n Kundenkreditkarte f; **storeroom** n Lagerraum m

storey ['stɔːrɪ] n *(Brit)* Stock m, Stockwerk nt

storm [stɔːm] n Sturm m; *(thunder~)* Gewitter nt ▷ vt, vi *(with movement)* stürmen; **stormy** adj stürmisch

story ['stɔːrɪ] n Geschichte f; *(plot)* Handlung f; *(US: of building)* Stock m, Stockwerk nt

stout [staʊt] adj *(fat)* korpulent

stove [stəʊv] n Herd m; *(for heating)* Ofen m

stow [stəʊ] vt verstauen; **stowaway** n blinder Passagier

straight [streɪt] adj *(not curved)* gerade; *(hair)* glatt; *(honest)* ehrlich *(with* zu); *(fam: heterosexual)* hetero ▷ adv *(directly)* direkt; *(immediately)* sofort; *(drink)* pur; *(think)* klar; ~ **ahead** geradeaus; **to go** ~ **on** geradeaus weitergehen/ weiterfahren; **straightaway** adv sofort; **straightforward** adj einfach; *(person)* aufrichtig, unkompliziert

strain [streɪn] n Belastung f ▷ vt *(eyes)* überanstrengen; *(rope, relationship)* belasten; *(vegetables)* abgießen; **to** ~ **a muscle** sich einen Muskel zerren; **strained** adj *(laugh, smile)* gezwungen; *(relations)* gespannt; ~ **muscle** Muskelzerrung f; **strainer** n Sieb nt

strand [strænd] n *(of wool)* Faden

m; (of hair) Strähne f ▷ vt: **to be (left) ~ed** (person) festsitzen

strange [streɪndʒ] adj seltsam; (unfamiliar) fremd; **strangely** adv seltsam; **~ enough** seltsamerweise; **stranger** n Fremde(r) mf; **I'm a ~ here** ich bin hier fremd

strangle ['stræŋgl] vt (kill) erdrosseln

strap [stræp] n Riemen m; (on dress etc) Träger m; (on watch) Band nt ▷ vt (fasten) festschnallen (to an +dat); **strapless** adj trägerlos

strategy ['strætɪdʒɪ] n Strategie f

straw [strɔː] n Stroh nt; (drinking ~) Strohhalm m

strawberry n Erdbeere f

stray [streɪ] n streunendes Tier ▷ adj (cat, dog) streunend ▷ vi streunen

streak ['striːk] n (of colour, dirt) Streifen m; (in hair) Strähne f; (in character) Zug m

stream [striːm] n (flow of liquid) Strom m; (brook) Bach m ▷ vi strömen; **streamer** n (of paper) Luftschlange f

street [striːt] n Straße f; **streetcar** n (US) Straßenbahn f; **street lamp, street light** n Straßenlaterne f; **street map** n Stadtplan m

strength [streŋθ] n Kraft f, Stärke f; **strengthen** vt verstärken; (fig) stärken

strenuous ['strenjʊəs] adj anstrengend

stress [stres] n Stress m; (on word) Betonung f; **to be under ~** im Stress sein ▷ vt betonen; (put under ~) stressen; **stressed** adj: **~ (out)** gestresst

stretch [stretʃ] n (of land) Stück nt; (of road) Strecke f ▷ vt (material, shoes) dehnen; (rope, canvas)

spannen; (person in job etc) fordern; **to ~ one's legs** (walk) sich die Beine vertreten ▷ vi (person) sich strecken; (area) sich erstrecken (to bis zu); **stretch out** vt: **to stretch one's hand/legs out** die Hand/die Beine ausstrecken, ausstrecken ▷ vi (reach) sich strecken; (lie down) sich ausstrecken; **stretcher** n Tragbahre f

strict, **strictly** [strɪkt, -lɪ] adj, adv (severe(ly)) streng; (exact(ly)) genau; **~ speaking** genauer gesagt

strike [straɪk] (**struck, struck**) vt (match) anzünden; (hit) schlagen; (find) finden; **it struck me as strange** es kam mir seltsam vor ▷ vi (stop work) streiken; (attack) zuschlagen; (clock) schlagen ▷ n (by workers) Streik m; **to be on ~** streiken; **strike up** vt (conversation) anfangen; (friendship) schließen; **striking** adj auffallend

string [strɪŋ] n (for tying) Schnur f; (Mus, Tennis) Saite f; **the ~s** pl (section of orchestra) die Streicher pl

strip [strɪp] n Streifen m; (Brit: of footballer etc) Trikot nt ▷ vi (undress) sich ausziehen, strippen

stripe [straɪp] n Streifen m; **striped** adj gestreift

stripper ['strɪpə] n Stripper(in) m(f); (paint) Farbentferner m

strip-search ['strɪpsɜːtʃ] n Leibesvisitation f (bei der man sich ausziehen muss)

striptease ['strɪptiːz] n Striptease m

stroke [strəʊk] n (Med, Tennis etc) Schlag m; (of pen, brush) Strich m ▷ vt streicheln

stroll [strəʊl] n Spaziergang m ▷ vi spazieren; **stroller** n (US: for baby) Buggy m

strong [strɒŋ] adj stark; (healthy)

robust; (wall, table) stabil; (shoes) fest; (influence, chance) groß; **strongly** adv stark; (believe) fest; (constructed) stabil

struck [strʌk] pt, pp of **strike**

structural, structurally ['strʌktʃərəl, -lɪ] adj strukturell; **structure** ['strʌktʃə°] n Struktur f; (building, bridge) Konstruktion f, Bau m

struggle ['strʌgl] n Kampf m (for um) ▷ vi (fight) kämpfen (for um); (do sth with difficulty) sich abmühen; **to ~ to do sth** sich abmühen, etw zu tun

stub [stʌb] n (of cigarette) Kippe f; (of ticket, cheque) Abschnitt m ▷ vt: **to ~ one's toe** sich dat den Zeh stoßen (on an +dat)

stubble ['stʌbl] n Stoppelbart m; (field) Stoppeln pl

stubborn ['stʌbən] adj (person) stur

stuck [stʌk] pt, pp of **stick** ▷ adj: **to be ~** (jammed) klemmen; (at a loss) nicht mehr weiterwissen; **to get ~** (car in snow etc) stecken bleiben

student ['stjuːdənt] n Student(in) m(f), Schüler(in) m(f)

studio ['stjuːdɪəʊ] (pl **-s**) n Studio nt

studious ['stjuːdɪəs] adj fleißig

study ['stʌdɪ] n (investigation) Untersuchung f; (room) Arbeitszimmer nt ▷ vt, vi studieren

stuff [stʌf] n Zeug nt, Sachen pl ▷ vt (push) stopfen; (Gastr) füllen; **to ~ oneself** (fam) sich vollstopfen; **stuffing** n (Gastr) Füllung f

stuffy ['stʌfɪ] adj (room) stickig; (person) spießig

stumble ['stʌmbl] vi stolpern; (when speaking) stocken

stun [stʌn] vt (shock) fassungslos

machen; **I was ~ned** ich war fassungslos (o völlig überrascht)

stung [stʌŋ] pt, pp of **sting**

stunk [stʌŋk] pp of **stink**

stunning ['stʌnɪŋ] adj (marvellous) fantastisch; (beautiful) atemberaubend; (very surprising, shocking) überwältigend; unfassbar

stunt [stʌnt] n (Cine) Stunt m

stupid ['stjuːpɪd] adj dumm; **stupidity** [stjuːˈpɪdɪtɪ] n Dummheit f

sturdy ['stɜːdɪ] adj robust; (building, car) stabil

stutter ['stʌtə°] vi, vt stottern

stye [staɪ] n (Med) Gerstenkorn nt

style [staɪl] n Stil m ▷ vt (hair) stylen; **styling mousse** n Schaumfestiger m; **stylish** ['staɪlɪʃ] adj elegant, schick

subconscious [sʌbˈkɒnʃəs] adj unterbewusst ▷ n: **the ~** das Unterbewusstsein

subdivide ['sʌbdɪvaɪd] vt unterteilen

subject ['sʌbdʒɪkt] n (topic) Thema nt; (in school) Fach nt; (citizen) Staatsangehörige(r) mf; (of kingdom) Untertan(in) m(f); (Ling) Subjekt nt; **to change the ~** das Thema wechseln ▷ adj [səbˈdʒekt] **to be ~ to** (dependent on) abhängen von; (under control of) unterworfen sein +dat

subjective [səbˈdʒektɪv] adj subjektiv

sublet [sʌbˈlet] irr vt untervermieten (to an +akk)

submarine [sʌbməˈriːn] n U-Boot nt

submerge [səbˈmɜːdʒ] vt (put in water) eintauchen ▷ vi tauchen

submit [səbˈmɪt] vt (application, claim) einreichen ▷ vi (surrender) sich ergeben

subordinate [səˈbɔːdɪnət] adj

untergeordnet (to +dat) ▷ n
Untergebene(r) mf

subscribe ['sʌb'skraɪb] vi: **to
~ to** (magazine etc) abonnieren;
subscription [səb'skrɪpʃən] n (to
magazine etc) Abonnement nt; (to
club etc) (Mitglieds)beitrag m

subsequent ['sʌbsɪkwənt] adj
nach(folgend); **subsequently** adv
später, anschließend

subside [səb'saɪd] vi (floods)
zurückgehen; (storm) sich legen;
(building) sich senken

substance ['sʌbstəns] n Substanz f

substantial [səb'stænʃəl] adj
beträchtlich; (improvement)
wesentlich; (meal) reichhaltig;
(furniture) solide

substitute ['sʌbstɪtjuːt] n Ersatz
m; (Sport) Ersatzspieler(in) m(f)
▷ vt: **to ~ A for B** B durch A
ersetzen

subtitle ['sʌbtaɪtl] n Untertitel
m

subtle ['sʌtl] adj (difference, taste)
fein; (plan) raffiniert

subtotal ['sʌbtəʊtl] n
Zwischensumme f

subtract [səb'trækt] vt abziehen
(from von)

suburb ['sʌbɜːb] n Vorort m; **in
the ~s** am Stadtrand; **suburban**
[sə'bɜːbən] adj vorstädtisch,
Vorstadt-

subway ['sʌbweɪ] n (Brit)
Unterführung f; (US Rail) U-Bahn f

succeed [sək'siːd] vi erfolgreich
sein; **he ~ed (in doing it)** es gelang
ihm(, es zu tun) ▷ vt nachfolgen
+dat; **succeeding** adj
nachfolgend; **success** [sək'ses] n
Erfolg m; **successful, successfully**
adj, adv erfolgreich

successive [sək'sesɪv] adj
aufeinanderfolgend; **successor** n
Nachfolger(in) m(f)

succulent ['sʌkjʊlənt] adj saftig

succumb [sə'kʌm] vi erliegen (to
+dat)

such [sʌtʃ] adj solche(r, s); **~ a
book** so ein Buch, ein solches
Buch; **it was ~ a success that ...**
es war solch ein Erfolg, dass ...;
~ as wie ▷ adv so; **~ a hot day** so
ein heißer Tag ▷ pron: **as ~** als
solche(r, s)

suck [sʌk] vt (toffee etc) lutschen;
(liquid) saugen; **it ~s** (fam) das ist
beschissen

Sudan [suː'dɑːn] n: **(the) ~** der
Sudan

sudden ['sʌdn] adj plötzlich; **all
of a ~** ganz plötzlich; **suddenly**
adv plötzlich

sue [suː] vt verklagen

suede [sweɪd] n Wildleder nt

suffer ['sʌfə°] vt erleiden ▷ vi
leiden; **to ~ from** (Med) leiden an
+dat

sufficient, sufficiently
[sə'fɪʃənt, -lɪ] adj, adv
ausreichend

suffocate ['sʌfəkeɪt] vt, vi
ersticken

sugar ['ʃʊgə°] n Zucker m ▷ vt
zuckern; **sugar bowl** n
Zuckerdose f; **sugary** adj (sweet)
süß

suggest [sə'dʒest] vt vorschlagen; (imply) andeuten; **I ~ saying
nothing** ich schlage vor, nichts zu
sagen; **suggestion** [sə'dʒestʃən]
n (proposal) Vorschlag m;
suggestive adj vielsagend;
(sexually) anzüglich

suicide ['suːɪsaɪd] n (act)
Selbstmord m; **suicide bomber** n
Selbstmordattentäter(in) m(f);
suicide bombing n
Selbstmordattentat nt

suit [suːt] n (man's clothes) Anzug
m; (lady's clothes) Kostüm nt; (Cards)
Farbe f ▷ vt (be convenient for)

passen +dat; (clothes, colour) stehen +dat; (climate, food) bekommen +dat; **suitable** adj geeignet (for für); **suitcase** n Koffer m

suite [swi:t] n (of rooms) Suite f; (sofa and chairs) Sitzgarnitur f

sulk [sʌlk] vi schmollen; **sulky** adj eingeschnappt

sultana [sʌl'tɑ:nə] n (raisin) Sultanine f

sum [sʌm] n Summe f; (money a.) Betrag m; (calculation) Rechenaufgabe f; **sum up** vt, vi (summarize) zusammenfassen

summarize ['sʌmaraiz] vt, vi zusammenfassen; **summary** n Zusammenfassung f

summer ['sʌmə°] n Sommer m; **summer camp** n (US) Ferienlager nt; **summer holidays** n Sommerferien pl; **summertime** n: **in (the)** ~ im Sommer

summit ['sʌmit] n (a. Pol) Gipfel m

summon ['sʌmən] vt (doctor, fire brigade etc) rufen; (to one's office) zitieren; **summon up** vt (courage, strength) zusammennehmen

summons ['sʌmənz] nsing (Jur) Vorladung f

sumptuous ['sʌmptjuəs] adj luxuriös; (meal) üppig

sun [sʌn] n Sonne f ▶ vt: **to ~ oneself** sich sonnen

Sun abbr = **Sunday** So.

sunbathe vi sich sonnen; **sunbathing** n Sonnenbaden nt; **sunbed** n Sonnenbank f; **sunblock** n Sunblocker m; **sunburn** n Sonnenbrand m; **sunburnt** adj: **to be/get** ~ einen Sonnenbrand haben/bekommen

sundae ['sʌndei] n Eisbecher m

Sunday ['sʌndi] n Sonntag m; see also **Tuesday**

sung [sʌŋ] pp of **sing**

sunglasses ['sʌnɡlɑ:siz] npl

Sonnenbrille f; **sunhat** n Sonnenhut m

sunk [sʌŋk] pp of **sink**

sunlamp ['sʌnlæmp] n Höhensonne f; **sunlight** n Sonnenlicht nt; **sunny** ['sʌni] adj sonnig; **sun protection factor** n Lichtschutzfaktor m; **sunrise** n Sonnenaufgang m; **sunroof** n (Auto) Schiebedach nt; **sunscreen** n Sonnenschutzmittel nt; **sunset** n Sonnenuntergang m; **sunshade** n Sonnenschirm m; **sunshine** n Sonnenschein m; **sunstroke** n (Sonnen)Stich m; **suntan** n (Sonnen)bräune f: **to get/have a** ~ braun werden/sein; ~ **lotion** (o **oil**) Sonnenöl nt

super ['su:pə°] adj (fam) toll

superb [su:'pə:b, -lι] adj, adv ausgezeichnet

superficial, superficially [su:pə'fiʃəl, -lι] adj, adv oberflächlich

superfluous [su'pə:fluəs] adj überflüssig

superglue ['su:pəglu:] n Sekundenkleber m

superior [su'piəriə°] adj (better) besser (to als); (higher in rank) höhergestellt (to als), höher ▶ n (in rank) Vorgesetzte(r) mf

supermarket ['su:pəmɑ:kit] n Supermarkt m

supersede [su:pə'si:d] vt ablösen

supersonic [su:pə'sɒnik] adj Überschall-

superstition [su:pə'stiʃən] n Aberglaube m; **superstitious** [su:pə'stiʃəs] adj abergläubisch

superstore ['su:pəstɔ:°] n Verbrauchermarkt m

supervise ['su:pəvaiz] vt beaufsichtigen; **supervisor** ['su:pəvaizə] n Aufsicht f; (at university) Doktorvater m

supper ['sʌpə*] n Abendessen nt; (late-night snack) Imbiss

supplement ['sʌplɪmənt] n (extra payment) Zuschlag m; (of newspaper) Beilage f ▷ vt ergänzen; **supplementary** [sʌplɪ'mentərɪ] adj zusätzlich

supplier [sə'plaɪə*] n Lieferant(in) m(f); **supply** [sə'plaɪ] vt (deliver) liefern; (drinks, music etc) sorgen für; **to ~ sb with sth** (provide) jdn mit etw versorgen ▷ n (stock) Vorrat m (of an +dat)

support [sə'pɔːt] n Unterstützung f; (Tech) Stütze f ▷ vt (hold up) tragen, stützen; (provide for) ernähren, unterhalten; (speak in favour of) unterstützen; **he ~s Manchester United** er ist Manchester-United-Fan

suppose [sə'pəʊz] vt (assume) annehmen; **I ~ so** ich denke schon; **I ~ not** wahrscheinlich nicht; **you're not ~d to smoke here** du darfst/Sie dürfen hier nicht rauchen; **supposedly** [sə'pəʊzɪdlɪ] adv angeblich; **supposing** conj angenommen

suppress [sə'pres] vt unterdrücken

surcharge ['sɜːtʃɑːdʒ] n Zuschlag m

sure [ʃʊə*] adj sicher; **I'm (not)** ~ ich bin mir (nicht) sicher; **make** ~ **you lock up** vergiss/vergessen Sie nicht abzuschließen ▷ adv: ~! klar!; ~ **enough** tatsächlich; **surely** adv: ~ **you don't mean it?** das ist nicht dein/Ihr Ernst, oder?

surf [sɜːf] n Brandung f ▷ vi (sport) surfen ▷ vt: **to ~ the net** im Internet surfen

surface ['sɜːfɪs] n Oberfläche f ▷ vi auftauchen; **surface mail** n: **by** ~ auf dem Land-/Seeweg

surfboard ['sɜːfbɔːd] n Surfbrett nt; **surfer** n Surfer(in) m(f);

surfing n Surfen nt; **to go** ~ surfen gehen

surgeon ['sɜːdʒən] n Chirurg(in) m(f); **surgery** ['sɜːdʒərɪ] n (operation) Operation f; (room) Praxis f, Sprechzimmer nt; (consulting time) Sprechstunde f; **to have** ~ operiert werden

surname ['sɜːneɪm] n Nachname m

surpass [sɜː'pɑːs] vt übertreffen

surplus ['sɜːpləs] n Überschuss m (of an +dat)

surprise [sə'praɪz] n Überraschung f ▷ vt überraschen; **surprising** adj überraschend, **surprisingly** adv überraschenderweise, erstaunlicherweise

surrender [sə'rendə*] vi sich ergeben (to +dat) ▷ vt (weapon, passport) abgeben

surround [sə'raʊnd] vt umgeben; (stand all round) umringen; **surrounding** adj (countryside) umliegend ▷ n ~s pl Umgebung f

survey ['sɜːveɪ] n (opinion poll) Umfrage f; (of literature etc) Überblick m (of über +akk); (of land) Vermessung f ▷ [sɜː'veɪ] vt (look out over) überblicken; (land) vermessen

survive [sə'vaɪv] vt, vi überleben

susceptible [sə'septəbl] adj empfänglich (to für); (Med) anfällig (to für)

sushi ['suːʃɪ] n Sushi nt

suspect ['sʌspekt] n Verdächtige(r) mf ▷ adj verdächtig ▷ [sə'spekt] vt verdächtigen (of +gen); (think likely) vermuten

suspend [sə'spend] vt (from work) suspendieren; (payment) vorübergehend einstellen; (player) sperren; (hang up) aufhängen; **suspender** n (Brit) Strumpfhalter

m; ~s *pl* (US: for trousers)
Hosenträger *pl*
suspense [sə'spens] *n* Spannung *f*
suspicious [sə'spɪʃəs] *adj*
misstrauisch *(of sb/sth)* jdm/etw
gegenüber); *(causing suspicion)*
verdächtig
swallow ['swɒləʊ] *n* (bird)
Schwalbe *f* ▷ *vt, vi* schlucken
swam [swæm] *pt of* swim
swamp [swɒmp] *n* Sumpf *m*
swan [swɒn] *n* Schwan *m*
swap [swɒp] *vt, vi* tauschen; to
~ sth for sth etw gegen etw
eintauschen
sway [sweɪ] *vi* schwanken
swear [sweə°] *(swore,*
sworn) *vi (promise)* schwören;
(curse) fluchen; to ~ at sb jdn
beschimpfen; **swear by** *vt (have*
faith in) schwören auf +kkk;
swearword *n* Fluch *m*
sweat [swet] *n* Schweiß *m* ▷ *vi*
schwitzen; **sweatband** *n*
Schweißband *nt;* **sweater** *n*
Pullover *m;* **sweatshirt** *n*
Sweatshirt *nt;* **sweaty** *adj*
verschwitzt
swede [swi:d] *n* Steckrübe *f*
Swede [swi:d] *n* Schwede *m,*
Schwedin *f;* **Sweden** *n* Schweden
nt; **Swedish** *adj* schwedisch ▷ *n*
(language) Schwedisch *nt*
sweep [swi:p] *(swept, swept)*
vt, vi (with brush) kehren, fegen;
sweep up *vt (dirt etc)*
zusammenkehren,
zusammenfegen
sweet [swi:t] *n* (Brit: candy)
Bonbon *nt;* (dessert) Nachtisch *m*
▷ *adj* süß; (kind) lieb;
sweet-and-sour *adj* süßsauer;
sweetcorn *n* Mais *m;* **sweeten** *vt*
(tea etc) süßen; **sweetener** *n*
(substance) Süßstoff *m;* **sweet**
potato *n* Süßkartoffel *f*

swell [swel] *(swelled, swollen o*
swelled) *vi:* to ~ (up)
(an)schwellen ▷ *adj* (US fam) toll;
swelling *n* (Med) Schwellung *f*
sweltering ['sweltərɪŋ] *adj* (heat)
drückend
swept [swept] *pt, pp of* sweep
swift, swiftly [swɪft] *adj, adv*
schnell
swig [swɪg] *n* (fam) Schluck *m*
swim [swɪm] *(swam, swum)* *vi*
schwimmen ▷ *n:* to go for a
~ schwimmen gehen; **swimmer** *n*
Schwimmer(in) *m(f);* **swimming** *n*
Schwimmen *nt;* to go
~ schwimmen gehen; **swimming**
cap *n* (Brit) Badekappe *f;*
swimming costume *n* (Brit)
Badeanzug *m;* **swimming pool** *n*
Schwimmbad *nt;* (private, in hotel)
Swimmingpool *m;* **swimming**
trunks *npl* (Brit) Badehose *f;*
swimsuit *n* Badeanzug *m*
swindle ['swɪndl] *vt* betrügen
(out of um)
swine [swaɪn] *n* (person)
Schwein *nt*
swing [swɪŋ] *(swung, swung)*
vt, vi (object) schwingen ▷ *n* (for
child) Schaukel *f*
swipe [swaɪp] *vt (credit card etc)*
durchziehen; *(fam: steal)* klauen;
swipe card *n* Magnetkarte *f*
Swiss [swɪs] *adj* schweizerisch
▷ *n* Schweizer(in) *m(f)*
switch [swɪtʃ] *n* (Elec) Schalter *m*
▷ *vi (change)* wechseln (to zu);
switch off *vt* abschalten,
ausschalten; **switch on** *vt*
anschalten, einschalten;
switchboard *n* (Tel) Vermittlung *f*
Switzerland ['swɪtsələnd] *n* die
Schweiz
swivel ['swɪvl] *vi* sich drehen
▷ *vt* drehen; **swivel chair** *n*
Drehstuhl *m*
swollen ['swəʊlən] *pp of* swell

▷ *adj* (*Med*) geschwollen; (*stomach*)
aufgebläht

swop [swɒp] *see* **swap**

sword [sɔːd] *n* Schwert *nt*

swore [swɔːʳ] *pt of* **swear**

sworn [swɔːn] *pp of* **swear**

swot [swɒt] *vi* (*Brit fam*) büffeln
(*for* für)

swum [swʌm] *pp of* **swim**

swung [swʌŋ] *pt, pp of* **swing**

syllable ['sɪləbl] *n* Silbe *f*

syllabus ['sɪləbəs] *n* Lehrplan *m*

symbol ['sɪmbəl] *n* Symbol *nt*;
symbolic [sɪm'bɒlɪk] *adj* sym-
bolisch; **symbolize** *vt*
symbolisieren

symmetrical [sɪ'metrɪkəl] *adj*
symmetrisch

sympathetic [sɪmpə'θetɪk] *adj*
mitfühlend; (*understanding*)
verständnisvoll; **sympathize**
['sɪmpəθaɪz] *vi* mitfühlen (*with sb*
mit jdm); **sympathy** ['sɪmpəθɪ]
n Mitleid *nt*; (*after death*) Beileid
nt; (*understanding*) Verständnis *nt*

symphony ['sɪmfənɪ] *n* Sinfonie
f

symptom ['sɪmptəm] *n* (*a. fig*)
Symptom *nt*

synagogue ['sɪnəgɒg] *n* Synagoge *f*

synonym ['sɪnənɪm] *n* Synonym
nt; **synonymous** [sɪ'nɒnɪməs]
adj synonym (*with* mit)

synthetic [sɪn'θetɪk] *adj*
(*material*) synthetisch

syphilis ['sɪfɪlɪs] *n* Syphilis *f*

Syria ['sɪrɪə] *n* Syrien *nt*

syringe [sɪ'rɪndʒ] *n* Spritze *f*

system ['sɪstəm] *n* System *nt*;
systematic [sɪstə'mætɪk] *adj*
systematisch; **system disk** *n*
(*Inform*) Systemdiskette *f*;
system(s) software *n* (*Inform*)
Systemsoftware *f*

tab [tæb] *n* (*for hanging up coat etc*)
Aufhänger *m*; (*Inform*) Tabulator *m*;
to pick up the ~ (*fam*) die
Rechnung übernehmen

table ['teɪbl] *n* Tisch *m*; (*list*)
Tabelle *f*; **~ of contents**
Inhaltsverzeichnis *nt*; **tablecloth**
n Tischdecke *f*; **tablelamp** *n*
Tischlampe *f*; **tablemat** *n* Set *nt*;
tablespoon *n* Servierlöffel *m*; (*in
recipes*) Esslöffel *m*

tablet ['tæblət] *n* (*Med*) Tablette *f*

table tennis ['teɪbltenɪs] *n*
Tischtennis *nt*; **table wine** *n*
Tafelwein *m*

tabloid ['tæblɔɪd] *n* Boulevard-
zeitung *f*

taboo [tə'buː] *n* Tabu *nt* ▷ *adj*
tabu

tacit, tacitly ['tæsɪt, -lɪ] *adj, adv*
stillschweigend

tack [tæk] *n* (*small nail*) Stift *m*;
(*US: thumb~*) Reißzwecke *f*

tackle ['tækl] n (Sport) Angriff m; (equipment) Ausrüstung f ▷ vt (deal with) in Angriff nehmen; (Sport) angreifen; (verbally) zur Rede stellen (about wegen)

tacky ['tækɪ] adj trashig, heruntergekommen

tact [tækt] n Takt m; **tactful**, **tactfully** adj, adv taktvoll; **tactic(s)** ['tæktɪk(s)] n(pl) Taktik f; **tactless**, **tactlessly** ['tæktləs, -lɪ] adj, adv taktlos

tag [tæg] n (label) Schild nt; (with maker's name) Etikett nt

Tahiti [tɑːˈhiːtɪ] n Tahiti nt

tail [teɪl] n Schwanz m; **heads or ~s?** Kopf oder Zahl?; **tailback** n (Brit) Rückstau m; **taillight** n (Auto) Rücklicht nt

tailor ['teɪlə*] n Schneider(in) m(f)

tailpipe ['teɪlpaɪp] n (US Auto) Auspuffrohr nt

tainted ['teɪntɪd] adj (US: food) verdorben

Taiwan [taɪˈwæn] n Taiwan nt

take [teɪk] (took, taken) vt nehmen; (~ along with one) mitnehmen; (~ to a place) bringen; (subtract) abziehen (from von); (capture: person) fassen; (gain, obtain) bekommen; (Fin, Comm) einnehmen; (train, taxi) nehmen, fahren mit; (trip, walk, holiday, exam, course, photo) machen; (bath) nehmen; (phone call) entgegennehmen; (decision, precautions) treffen; (risk) eingehen; (advice, job) annehmen; (consume) zu sich nehmen; (tablets) nehmen; (heat, pain) ertragen; (react to) aufnehmen; (have room for) Platz haben für; **I'll ~ it** (item in shop) ich nehme es; **how long does it ~?** wie lange dauert es?; **it ~s 4 hours** man braucht 4 Stunden; **do you ~ sugar?** nimmst

du/nehmen Sie Zucker?; **I ~ it that ...** ich nehme an, dass ...; **to ~ part in** teilnehmen an; **to ~ place** stattfinden; **take after** vt nachschlagen +dat; **take along** vt mitnehmen; **take apart** vt auseinandernehmen; **take away** vt (remove) wegnehmen (from sb jdm); (subtract) abziehen (from von); **take back** vt (return) zurückbringen; (retract) zurücknehmen; (remind) zurückversetzen (to in +akk); **take down** vt (picture, curtains) abnehmen; (write down) aufschreiben; **take in** vt (understand) begreifen; (give accommodation to) aufnehmen; (deceive) hereinlegen; (include) einschließen; (show, film etc) mitnehmen; **take off** vi (plane) starten ▷ vt (clothing) ausziehen; (hat, lid) abnehmen; (deduct) abziehen; (Brit: imitate) nachmachen; **to take a day off** sich einen Tag freinehmen; **take on** vt (undertake) übernehmen; (employ) einstellen; (Sport) antreten gegen; **take out** vt (wallet etc) herausnehmen; (person, dog) ausführen; (insurance) abschließen; (money from bank) abheben; (book from library) ausleihen; **take over** vt übernehmen ▷ vi: **he took over (from me)** er hat mich abgelöst; **take to** vt: **I've taken to her/it** ich mag sie/es; **to ~ doing sth** (begin) anfangen, etw zu tun; **take up** vt (carpet) hochnehmen; (space) einnehmen; (time) in Anspruch nehmen; (hobby) anfangen mit; (new job) antreten; (offer) annehmen

takeaway n (Brit: meal) Essen nt zum Mitnehmen

taken ['teɪkn] pp of **take** ▷ adj

(seat) besetzt; **to be ~ with** angetan sein von

takeoff ['teɪkɒf] n (Aviat) Start m; (imitation) Nachahmung f;

takeout (US) see **takeaway**

takeover n (Comm) Übernahme f

takings ['teɪkɪŋz] npl Einnahmen pl

tale [teɪl] n Geschichte f

talent ['tælənt] n Talent nt; **talented** adj begabt

talk [tɔːk] n (conversation) Gespräch nt; (rumour) Gerede nt; (to audience) Vortrag m ▷ vi sprechen, reden; (have conversation) sich unterhalten; **to ~ to** (o **with**) sb (about sth) mit jdm (über etw akk) sprechen; (nonsense) reden; (politics, business) reden über +akk; **to ~ sb into doing/out of doing sth** jdn überreden/jdm ausreden, etw zu tun; **talk over** vt besprechen

talkative adj gesprächig; **talk show** n Talkshow f

tall [tɔːl] adj groß, (building, tree) hoch; **he is 6ft ~** er ist 1,80m groß

tame [teɪm] adj (tame), (joke, story) fade ▷ vt (animal) zähmen

tampon ['tæmpɒn] n Tampon m

tan [tæn] n (on skin) (Sonnen)bräune f; **to get/have a ~** braun werden/sein ▷ vi braun werden

tangerine [tændʒəˈriːn] n Mandarine f

tango ['tæŋɡəʊ] n Tango m

tank [tæŋk] n Tank m; (for fish) Aquarium nt; (Mil) Panzer m

tanker ['tæŋkəʳ] n (ship) Tanker m; (vehicle) Tankwagen m

tanned [tænd] adj (by sun) braun

tantalizing ['tæntəlaɪzɪŋ] adj verlockend

Tanzania [tænzəˈnɪə] n Tansania nt

tap [tæp] n (for water) Hahn m ▷ vt (strike) klopfen; **to ~ sb on the shoulder** jdm auf die Schulter klopfen; **tap-dance** vi steppen

tape [teɪp] n (adhesive) Klebeband nt; (for tape recorder) Tonband nt; (cassette) Kassette f; (video) Video nt ▷ vt (record) aufnehmen; **tape up** vt (parcel) zukleben; **tape measure** n Maßband nt; **tape recorder** n Tonbandgerät nt

tapestry ['tæpɪstrɪ] n Wandteppich m

tap water ['tæpwɔːtəʳ] n Leitungswasser nt

target ['tɑːɡɪt] n Ziel nt; (board) Zielscheibe f; **target group** n Zielgruppe f

tariff ['tærɪf] n (price list) Preisliste f; (tax) Zoll m

tarmac ['tɑːmæk] n (Aviat) Rollfeld nt

tart [tɑːt] n (fruit ~) (Obst)kuchen m; (small) (Obst)törtchen nt; (fam, pej: prostitute) Nutte f; (fam: promiscuous person) Schlampe f

tartan ['tɑːtən] n (material) Schottenstoff m

tartar(e) sauce ['tɑːtəˈsɔːs] n Remouladensoße f

task [tɑːsk] n Aufgabe f; (duty) Pflicht f; **taskbar** n (Inform) Taskbar f

Tasmania [tæzˈmeɪnɪə] n Tasmanien nt

taste [teɪst] n Geschmack m; (sense of ~) Geschmackssinn m; (small quantity) Kostprobe f; **it has a strange ~** es schmeckt komisch ▷ vt schmecken; (try) probieren ▷ vi (food) schmecken (of nach); **to ~ good/strange** gut/komisch schmecken; **tasteful, tastefully** adj, adv geschmackvoll; **tasteless** adj, adv geschmacklos; **tasty** adj lecker

tattered ['tætəd] adj (clothes) zerlumpt; (fam: person) angespannt; **I'm absolutely ~** ich bin mit den Nerven am Ende

tattoo [tə'tu:] n (on skin) Tätowierung f

taught [tɔ:t] pt, pp of **teach**

Taurus ['tɔ:rəs] n (Astr) Stier m

tax [tæks] n Steuer f (on auf +akk) ▷ vt besteuern; **taxable** adj steuerpflichtig; **taxation** [tæk'seɪʃən] n Besteuerung f; **tax bracket** n Steuerklasse f; **tax disc** n (Brit Auto) Steuermarke f; **tax-free** adj steuerfrei

taxi ['tæksɪ] n Taxi nt ▷ vi (plane) rollen; **taxi driver** n Taxifahrer(in) m(f); **taxi rank** (Brit), **taxi stand** n Taxistand m

tax return ['tæksɪ'tɜ:n] n Steuererklärung f

tea [ti:] n Tee m; (afternoon ~) = Kaffee und Kuchen; (meal) frühes Abendessen; **teabag** n Teebeutel m; **tea break** n (Brit) Teepause f

teach [ti:tʃ] (**taught**, **taught**) vt (person, subject) unterrichten; **to ~ sb (how) to dance** jdm das Tanzen beibringen ▷ vi unterrichten; **teacher** n Lehrer(in) m(f); **teaching** n (activity) Unterrichten nt; (profession) Lehrberuf m

teacup ['ti:kʌp] n Teetasse f

team [ti:m] n (Sport) Mannschaft f, Team nt; **teamwork** n Teamarbeit f

teapot ['ti:pɒt] n Teekanne f

tear [tɪə*] n (in eye) Träne f

tear [tɛə*] (**tore**, **torn**) vt zerreißen; **to ~ a muscle** sich einen Muskel zerren ▷ vi (in material etc) Riss m (in); **tear down** vt (building) abreißen; **tear up** vt (paper) zerreißen

tearoom ['ti:rʊm] n Teestube f,

Café, in dem in erster Linie Tee serviert wird

tease [ti:z] vt (person) necken (about wegen)

tea set ['ti:set] n Teeservice nt; **teashop** n Teestube f; **teaspoon** n Teelöffel m; **tea towel** n Geschirrtuch nt

technical ['teknɪkəl] adj technisch; (knowledge, term, dictionary) Fach-; **technically** adv technisch; **technique** [tek'ni:k] n Technik f

techno ['teknəʊ] n Techno f

technological [teknə'lɒdʒɪkəl] adj technologisch; **technology** [tek'nɒlədʒɪ] n Technologie f, Technik f

tedious ['ti:dɪəs] adj langweilig

teen(age) ['ti:n(eɪdʒ)] adj (fashions etc) Teenager-; **teenager** n Teenager m; **teens** [ti:nz] npl: **in one's ~** im Teenageralter

teeth [ti:θ] pl of **tooth**

teetotal ['ti:'təʊtl] adj abstinent

telegraph pole ['telɪgra:fpəʊl] n (Brit) Telegrafenmast m

telephone ['telɪfəʊn] n Telefon nt ▷ vi telefonieren ▷ vt anrufen; **telephone banking** n Telefonbanking nt; **telephone book** n Telefonbuch nt; **telephone booth**, **telephone box** (Brit) n Telefonzelle f; **telephone call** n Telefonanruf m; **telephone directory** n Telefonbuch nt; **telephone number** n Telefonnummer f

telephoto lens ['telɪfəʊtəʊ'lenz] n Teleobjektiv nt

telescope ['telɪskəʊp] n Teleskop nt

televise ['telɪvaɪz] vt im Fernsehen übertragen; **television** ['telɪvɪʒən] n Fernsehen nt; **television programme** n Fernsehsendung f; **television (set)** n Fernseher m

teleworking ['teliwɜːkɪŋ] n
Telearbeit f

tell [tel] vt (told, told) (say,
inform) sagen (sb sth jdm etw);
(story) erzählen; (truth) sagen;
(difference) erkennen; (reveal secret)
verraten; **to ~ sb about sth** jdm
von etw erzählen; **to ~ sth from
sth** etw von etw unterscheiden
▷ vi (be sure) wissen; **tell apart** vt
unterscheiden; **tell off** vt
schimpfen

telling adj aufschlussreich

telly ['teli] n (Brit fam) Glotze f; **on
(the) ~** in der Glotze

temp [temp] n Aushilfskraft f
▷ vi als Aushilfskraft arbeiten

temper ['tempə*] n (anger) Wut f;
(mood) Laune f; **to lose one's ~** die
Beherrschung verlieren; **to have a
bad ~** jähzornig sein;
temperamental
[temprə'mentl] adj (moody)
launisch

temperature ['temprɪtʃə*] n
Temperatur f; (Med: high ~) Fieber
nt; **to have a ~** Fieber haben

temple ['templ] n Tempel m;
(Anat) Schläfe f

temporarily ['tempərərɪlɪ] adv
vorübergehend, **temporary**
['tempərərɪ] adj vorübergehend;
(road, building) provisorisch

tempt [tempt] vt in Versuchung
führen; **I'm ~ed to accept** ich bin
versucht anzunehmen;
temptation [temp'teɪʃən] n
Versuchung f; **tempting** adj
verlockend

ten [ten] num zehn ▷ n Zehn f;
see also **eight**

tenant ['tenənt] n Mieter(in)
m(f); (of land) Pächter(in) m(f)

tend [tend] vi: **to ~ to do sth**
(person) dazu neigen, etw zu tun;
to ~ towards neigen zu;
tendency ['tendənsɪ] n Tendenz

f; **to have a ~ to do sth** (person)
dazu neigen, etw zu tun

tender ['tendə*] adj (loving)
zärtlich, (sore) empfindlich; (meat)
zart

tendon ['tendən] n Sehne f

Tenerife [tenə'riːf] n Teneriffa f

tenner ['tenə*] n (Brit fam: note)
Zehnpfundschein m; (amount) zehn
Pfund

tennis ['tenɪs] n Tennis nt;
tennis ball n Tennisball m; **tennis
court** n Tennisplatz m; **tennis
racket** n Tennisschläger m

tenor ['tenə*] n Tenor m

tenpin bowling, **tenpins** (US)
['tenpɪn'bəʊlɪŋ, 'tenpɪnz] n
Bowling nt

tense [tens] adj angespannt;
(stretched tight) gespannt; **tension**
['tenʃən] n Spannung f; (strain)
Anspannung f

tent [tent] n Zelt nt

tenth [tenθ] adj zehnte(r, s) ▷ n
(fraction) Zehntel nt; see also **eighth**

tent peg ['tentpeg] n Hering m;
tent pole n Zeltstange f

term [tɜːm] n (in school, at
university) Trimester nt; (expression)
Ausdruck m; **~s** pl (conditions)
Bedingungen pl; **to be on good ~s
with sb** mit jdm gut auskommen;
to come to ~s with sth sich mit
etw abfinden; **in the long/short
~** langfristig/kurzfristig; **in ~s
of ...** was ... betrifft

terminal ['tɜːmɪnl] n (bus ~ etc)
Endstation f; (Aviat) Terminal m;
(Inform) Terminal m; (Elec) Pol m
▷ adj (Med) unheilbar; **terminally**
adv (ill) unheilbar

terminate ['tɜːmɪneɪt] vt (contract) lösen; (pregnancy) abbrechen
▷ vi (train, bus) enden

terminology [tɜːmɪ'nɒlədʒɪ] n
Terminologie f

terrace ['terəs] n (of houses)

Häuserreihe f; (in garden etc)
Terrasse f; **terraced** adj (garden)
terrassenförmig angelegt;
terraced house n (Brit)
Reihenhaus nt

terrible ['tɛrəbl] adj schrecklich

terrific [tə'rɪfɪk] adj (very good)
fantastisch

terrify ['tɛrɪfaɪ] vt erschrecken;
to be terrified schreckliche Angst
haben (of vor +dat)

territory ['tɛrɪtərɪ] n Gebiet nt

terror ['tɛrə°] n Schrecken m;
(Pol) Terror m; **terrorism** n
Terrorismus m; **terrorist** n
Terrorist(in) m(f)

test [tɛst] n Test m, Klassenarbeit
f; (driving ~) Prüfung f; **to put to
the ~** auf die Probe stellen ▷ vt
testen, prüfen; (patience, courage
etc) auf die Probe stellen

Testament ['tɛstəmənt] n: **the
Old/New ~** das Alte/Neue
Testament

test-drive ['tɛstdraɪv] vt Probe
fahren

testicle ['tɛstɪkl] n Hoden m

testify ['tɛstɪfaɪ] vi (Jur)
aussagen

test tube ['tɛsttjuːb] n
Reagenzglas nt

tetanus ['tɛtənəs] n Tetanus m

text [tɛkst] n Text m; (of
document) Wortlaut m; (sent by
mobile phone) SMS f ▷ vt (message)
simsen, SMSen; **to ~ sb** jdm
simsen, jdm eine SMS schicken;
I'll ~ it to you ich schicke es dir per
SMS

textbook n Lehrbuch nt

texting ['tɛkstɪŋ] n SMS-
Messaging nt; **text message** n
SMS f; **text messaging** n
SMS-Messaging nt

texture ['tɛkstʃə°] n
Beschaffenheit f

Thailand ['taɪlənd] n Thailand nt

Thames [tɛmz] n Themse f

than [ðæn] prep, conj als;
bigger/faster~ me
größer/schneller als ich; **I'd rather
walk ~ drive** ich gehe lieber zu
Fuß als mit dem Auto

thank [θæŋk] vt danken +dat;
~ you danke; **~ you very much**
vielen Dank; **thankful** adj
dankbar; **thankfully** adv (luckily)
zum Glück; **thankless** adj
undankbar; **thanks** npl Dank m;
~ dankel; **~ to dank +gen

● **THANKSGIVING DAY**
●
● **Thanksgiving (Day)** ist ein
● Feiertag in den USA, der auf den
● vierten Donnerstag im
● November fällt. Er soll daran
● erinnern, wie die Pilgerväter die
● gute Ernte im Jahre 1621
● feierten. In Kanada gibt es einen
● ähnlichen Erntedanktag (der
● aber nichts mit den Pilgervätern
● zu tun hat) am zweiten Montag
● im Oktober.

○ KEYWORD

that [ðæt, ðət] adj (demonstrative)
(pl those) der/die/das, jene(r, s);
that one das da
▷ pron 1 (demonstrative) (pl those)
das; **who's/what's that?** wer ist
da/was ist das?; **is that you?** bist
du/sind Sie das?; **that's what he
said** genau das hat er gesagt;
what happened after that? was
passierte danach?; **that is** das
heißt
2 (relative) (subj) der/die/das, die;
(direct obj) den/die/das, die;
(indirect obj) dem/der/dem, denen;
all (that) I have alles, was ich
habe
3 (relative) (of time); **the day (that)**

an dem Tag; als, **the winter (that) he came** in dem Winter, in dem er kam
▷ *conj* dass; **he thought that I was ill** er dachte, dass ich krank sei, er dachte, ich sei krank
▷ *adv* (*demonstrative*) so; **I can't work that much** ich kann nicht so viel arbeiten

that's [ðæts] *contr of* **that is; that has**

thaw [θɔː] *vi* tauen; (*frozen food*) auftauen ▷ *vt* auftauen lassen

KEYWORD

the [ðə, ðiː] *def art* 1 der/die/das; **to play the piano/violin** Klavier/Geige spielen; **I'm going to the butcher's/the cinema** ich gehe zum Fleischer/ins Kino; **Elizabeth the First** Elisabeth die Erste
2 (+*adj to form noun*) das, die; **the rich and the poor** die Reichen und die Armen
3 (*in comparisons*) **the more he works the more he earns** je mehr er arbeitet, desto mehr verdient er

theater (US), **theatre** ['θɪətə°] *n* Theater *nt*; (*for lectures etc*) Saal *m*

theft [θeft] *n* Diebstahl *m*

their [ðɛə°] *adj* ihr; (*unidentified person*) sein; **they cleaned ~ teeth** sie putzten sich die Zähne; **someone has left ~ umbrella here** jemand hat seinen Schirm hier vergessen; **theirs** *pron* ihre(r, s); (*unidentified person*) seine(r, s); **it's ~** es gehört ihnen; **a friend of ~** ein Freund von ihnen; **someone has left ~ here** jemand hat seins hier liegen lassen

them [ðem, ðəm] *pron* (*direct object*) sie; (*indirect object*) ihnen;

(*unidentified person*) ihn/ihm, sie/ihr; **do you know ~?** kennst du/kennen Sie sie?; **can you help ~?** kannst du/können Sie ihnen helfen?; **it's ~** sie sind's; **if anyone has a problem you should help ~** wenn jemand ein Problem hat, solltest du/sollten Sie ihm helfen

theme [θiːm] *n* Thema *nt*; (*Mus*) Motiv *nt*; **~ park** Themenpark *m*; **~ song** Titelmusik *f*

themselves [ðəm'selvz] *pron* sich; **they hurt ~** sie haben sich verletzt; **they ~ were not there** sie selbst waren nicht da; **they did it ~** sie haben es selbst gemacht; **they are not dangerous in ~** an sich sind sie nicht gefährlich; (**all**) **by ~** allein

then [ðen] *adv* (*at that time*) damals; (*next*) dann; (*therefore*) also; (*furthermore*) ferner; **from ~ on** von da an; **by ~** bis dahin
▷ *adj* damalig

theoretical, theoretically [θɪə'retɪkəl, -ɪ] *adj, adv* theoretisch

theory ['θɪərɪ] *n* Theorie *f*; **in ~** theoretisch

therapy ['θerəpɪ] *n* Therapie *f*

KEYWORD

there [ðɛə°] *adv* 1 **there is/there are** es o da ist/sind; (*there exists/exist also*) es gibt; **there are 3 of them** (*people, things*) es gibt 3 davon; **there has been an accident** da war ein Unfall
2 (*place*) da, dort; (*direction*) dahin, dorthin; **put it in/on there** leg es dahinein/dorthinauf
3 **there, there** (*esp to child*) na, na

thereabouts *adv* (*approximately*) so ungefähr; **therefore** *adv* daher, deshalb

thermometer [θəˈmɒmɪtəˀ] n
Thermometer m

Thermos® [ˈθɜːməs] n: **~ (flask)**
Thermosflasche® f

these [ðiːz] pron, adj diese; **I
don't like ~ apples** ich mag diese
Äpfel nicht; **~ are not my books**
das sind nicht meine Bücher

thesis [ˈθiːsɪs] (pl **theses**) n (for
PhD) Doktorarbeit f

they [ðeɪ] pron pl sie; (people in
general) man; (unidentified person)
er/sie; **~ are rich** sie sind reich;
~ say that ... man sagt, dass ...; **if
anyone looks at this, ~ will see
that ...** wenn sich jemand dies
ansieht, wird er erkennen, dass ...

they'd [ðeɪd] contr of **they had;
they would**

they'll [ðeɪl] contr of **they will;
they shall**

they've [ðeɪv] contr of **they have**

thick [θɪk] adj dick; (fog) dicht;
(liquid) dickflüssig; (fam: stupid)
dumm; **thicken** vi (fog) dichter
werden; (sauce) dick werden ▷ vt
(sauce) eindicken

thief [θiːf] (pl **thieves**) n
Dieb(in) m(f)

thigh [θaɪ] n Oberschenkel m

thimble [ˈθɪmbl] n Fingerhut m

thin [θɪn] adj dünn

thing [θɪŋ] n Ding nt; (affair)
Sache f; **my ~s** pl meine Sachen pl;
how are ~s? wie geht's?; **I can't
see a ~** ich kann nichts sehen; **he
knows a ~ or two about cars** er
kennt sich mit Autos aus

think [θɪŋk] (**thought, thought**)
vt, vi denken; (believe) meinen; **I
~ so** ich denke schon; **I don't ~ so**
ich glaube nicht; **think about** vt
denken an +akk; (reflect on)
nachdenken über +akk; (have
opinion of) halten von; **think of** vt
denken an +akk; (devise) sich
ausdenken; (have opinion of) halten

von; (remember) sich erinnern an
+akk; **think over** vt überdenken;
think up vt sich ausdenken

third [θɜːd] adj dritte(r, s); **the
Third World** die Dritte Welt ▷ n
(fraction) Drittel nt; **in ~ (gear)** im
dritten Gang; see also **eighth**;
thirdly adv drittens; **third-party
insurance** n Haftpflichtversicherung f

thirst [θɜːst] n Durst m (for nach);
thirsty adj: **to be ~** Durst haben

thirteen [ˈθɜːtiːn] num dreizehn
▷ n Dreizehn f; see also **eight**;
thirteenth adj dreizehnte(r, s);
see also **eighth**; **thirtieth** [ˈθɜːtiːθ]
adj dreißigste(r, s); see also **eighth**;
thirty [ˈθɜːtɪ] num dreißig;
~-one einunddreißig ▷ n Dreißig
f; **to be in one's thirties** in den
Dreißigern sein; see also **eight**

🔘 **KEYWORD**

this [ðɪs] adj (demonstrative) (pl
these) diese(r, s); **this evening**
heute Abend; **this one** diese(r, s)
(da)
▷ pron (demonstrative) (pl these)
dies, das; **who/what is this?**
wer/was ist das?; **this is where I
live** hier wohne ich; **this is what
he said** das hat er gesagt; **this is
Mr Brown** dies ist Mr Brown; (on
telephone) hier ist Mr Brown
▷ adv (demonstrative) **this
high/long** etc so groß/lang etc

thistle [ˈθɪsl] n Distel f

thong [θɒŋ] n String m

thorn [θɔːn] n Dorn m, Stachel m

thorough [ˈθʌrə] adj gründlich;
thoroughly adv gründlich; (agree
etc) völlig

those [ðəʊz] pron die da, jene;
~ who diejenigen, die ▷ adj die,
jene

though [ðəʊ] *conj* obwohl; **as ~ als ob ~ als ob; even ~ aber**

thought [θɔːt] *pt, pp of* **think** ▷ *n* Gedanke *m*; (*thinking*) Überlegung *f*; **thoughtful** *adj* (*kind*) rücksichtsvoll; (*attentive*) aufmerksam; (*in Gedanken versunken*) nachdenklich; **thoughtless** *adj* (*unkind*) rücksichtslos, gedankenlos

thousand ['θaʊzənd] *num* (**one**) **~, a ~** tausend; **five ~** fünftausend; **~s of** Tausende von

thrash [θræʃ] *vt* (*hit*) verprügeln; (*defeat*) vernichtend schlagen

thread [θred] *n* Faden *m* ▷ *vt* (*needle*) einfädeln; (*beads*) auffädeln

threat [θret] *n* Drohung *f*; (*danger*) Bedrohung *f* (to für); **threaten** *vt* bedrohen; **threatening** *adj* bedrohlich

three [θriː] *num* drei ▷ *n* Drei *f*; *see also* **eight**; **three-dimensional** *adj* dreidimensional; **three-piece suit** *n* Anzug *m* mit Weste; **three-quarters** *npl* drei Viertel *pl*

threshold ['θreʃhəʊld] *n* Schwelle *f*

threw [θruː] *pt of* **throw**

thrifty ['θrɪftɪ] *adj* sparsam

thrilled [θrɪld] *adj*: **to be ~ (with sth)** sich (über etw *akk*) riesig freuen; **thriller** *n* Thriller *m*; **thrilling** *adj* aufregend

thrive [θraɪv] *vi* gedeihen (on bei); (*fig, business*) florieren

throat [θrəʊt] *n* Hals *m*, Kehle *f*

throbbing ['θrɒbɪŋ] *adj* (pain, headache) pochend

thrombosis [θrɒm'bəʊsɪs] *n* Thrombose *f*; **deep vein ~** tiefe Venenthrombose *f*

throne [θrəʊn] *n* Thron *m*

through [θruː] *prep* durch; (*time*) während +*gen*; (*because of*) aus, durch; (*US: up to and including*) bis;

arranged ~ him durch ihn arrangiert ▷ *adv* durch; **to put sb ~** (*Tel*) jdn verbinden (to mit) ▷ *adj* (*ticket, train*) durchgehend; **~ flight** Direktflug *m*; **to be ~ with sb/sth** mit jdm/etw fertig sein; **throughout** [θruː'aʊt] *prep* (place) überall in +*dat*; (*time*) während +*gen*; **~ the night** die ganze Nacht hindurch ▷ *adv* überall; (*time*) die ganze Zeit

throw [θrəʊ] (**threw, thrown**) *vt* werfen; (*rider*) abwerfen; (*party*) geben; **to ~ sth to sb, to ~ sb sth** jdm etw zuwerfen; **I was ~ by his question** seine Frage hat mich aus dem Konzept gebracht ▷ *n* Wurf *m*; **throw away** *vt* wegwerfen; **throw in** *vt* (*include*) dazugeben; **throw out** *vt* (*unwanted object*) wegwerfen; (*person*) hinauswerfen (of aus); **throw up** *vt, vi* (*fam: vomit*) sich übergeben; **throw-in** *n* Einwurf *m*

thrown [θrəʊn] *pp of* **throw**

thru (*US*) *see* **through**

thrush [θrʌʃ] *n* Drossel *f*

thrust [θrʌst] (**thrust, thrust**) *vt, vi* (*push*) stoßen

thruway ['θruːweɪ] *n* (*US*) Schnellstraße *f*

thumb [θʌm] *n* Daumen *m* ▷ *vt*: **to ~ a lift** per Anhalter fahren; **thumbtack** *n* (*US*) Reißzwecke *f*

thunder ['θʌndə*] *n* Donner *m* ▷ *vi* donnern; **thunderstorm** *n* Gewitter *nt*

Thur(s) *abbr* = **Thursday** Do.

Thursday ['θɜːzdɪ] *n* Donnerstag *m*; *see also* **Tuesday**

thus [ðʌs] *adv* (*in this way*) so; (*therefore*) somit, also

thyme [taɪm] *n* Thymian *m*

Tibet [tɪ'bet] *n* Tibet *nt*

tick [tɪk] *n* (*Brit: mark*) Häkchen *nt* ▷ *vt* (*name*) abhaken; (*box, answer*) ankreuzen ▷ *vi* (*clock*) ticken

ticket ['tɪkɪt] n (for train, bus)
(Fahr)karte f; (for plane etc) Flugschein
m, Ticket nt; (for theatre, match,
museum etc) (Eintritts)karte f; (price
~) (Preis)schild nt; (raffle ~) Los nt;
(for car park) Parkschein m; (for
traffic offence) Strafzettel m; **ticket
collector**, **ticket inspector** (Brit)
n Fahrkartenkontrolleur(in) m(f);
ticket machine n (for public
transport) Fahrscheinautomat m;
(in car park) Parkscheinautomat m;
ticket office n (Rail)
Fahrkartenschalter m; (Theat)
Kasse f

tickle ['tɪkl] vt kitzeln; **ticklish**
['tɪklɪʃ] adj kitzlig

tide [taɪd] n Gezeiten pl; **the ~ is
in/out** es ist Flut/Ebbe

tidy ['taɪdɪ] adj ordentlich ▷ vt
aufräumen; **tidy up** vt, vi
aufräumen

tie [taɪ] n (neck~) Krawatte f;
(Sport) Unentschieden nt; (bond)
Bindung f ▷ vt (attach, do up)
binden (to an +akk); (~ together)
zusammenbinden; (knot) machen
▷ vi (Sport) unentschieden spielen;
tie down vt festbinden (to an
+dat); (fig) binden; **tie up** vt (dog)
anbinden; (parcel) verschnüren;
(shoelace) binden; (boat)
festmachen; **I'm tied up** (fig) ich
bin beschäftigt

tiger ['taɪɡə⁰] n Tiger m

tight [taɪt] adj (clothes) eng;
(knot) fest; (screw, lid) fest sitzend;
(control, security measures) streng;
(timewise) knapp; (schedule) eng
▷ adv (shut) fest; (pull) stramm;
hold ~ festhalten!; **sleep ~** schlaf
gut!; **tighten** vt (knot, rope, screw)
anziehen; (belt) enger machen;
(restrictions, control) verschärfen;
tights npl (Brit) Strumpfhose
f

tile [taɪl] n (on roof) Dachziegel m;

(on wall, floor) Fliese f; **tiled** adj
(roof) Ziegel-; (floor, wall) gefliest

till [tɪl] n Kasse f ▷ prep, conj see
until

tilt [tɪlt] vt kippen; (head) neigen
▷ vi sich neigen

time [taɪm] n Zeit f; (occasion)
Mal nt; (Mus) Takt m; **local
~** Ortszeit; **what ~ is it?**, **what's
the ~?** wie spät ist es?, wie viel Uhr
ist es?; **to take one's ~** (over sth)
sich (bei etw) Zeit lassen; **to have
a good ~** Spaß haben; **in two
weeks' ~** in zwei Wochen; **at ~s**
manchmal; **at the same
~** gleichzeitig; **all the ~** die ganze
Zeit; **by the ~ he ...** bis er ...; (in
past) als er ...; **for the ~ being**
vorläufig; **in ~** (not late)
rechtzeitig; **on ~** pünktlich; **the
first ~** das erste Mal; **this
~** diesmal; **five ~s** fünfmal; **five ~s
six** fünf mal sechs; **four ~s a year**
viermal im Jahr; **three at a ~** drei
auf einmal ▷ vt (with stopwatch)
stoppen; **you ~d that well** das
hast du/haben Sie gut getimt;
time difference n
Zeitunterschied m; **time limit** n
Frist f; **timer** n Timer m; (switch)
Schaltuhr f; **time-saving** adj
zeitsparend; **time switch** n
Schaltuhr f; **timetable** n (for
public transport) Fahrplan m;
(school) Stundenplan m; **time zone**
n Zeitzone f

timid ['tɪmɪd] adj ängstlich

timing ['taɪmɪŋ] n (coordination)
Timing nt, zeitliche Abstimmung

tin [tɪn] n (metal) Blech nt; (Brit:
can) Dose f; **tinfoil** n Alufolie f;
tinned [tɪnd] adj (Brit) aus der
Dose; **tin opener** n (Brit)
Dosenöffner m

tinsel ['tɪnsəl] n ~ Lametta nt

tint [tɪnt] n (Farb)ton m; (in hair)
Tönung f; **tinted** adj getönt

tiny ['taɪnɪ] adj winzig

tip [tɪp] n (money) Trinkgeld nt; (hint) Tipp m; (end) Spitze f; (of cigarette) Filter m; (Brit: rubbish ~) Müllkippe f ▷ vt (waiter) Trinkgeld geben +dat; **tip over** vt, vi (overturn) umkippen

tipsy ['tɪpsɪ] adj beschwipst

tiptoe ['tɪptəʊ] n: **on ~** auf Zehenspitzen

tire ['taɪə°] n (US) see **tyre** ▷ vt müde machen ▷ vi müde werden; **tired** adj müde; **to be ~ of sth/sb** jdn/etw satthaben; **to be ~ of doing sth** es satthaben, etw zu tun; **tireless, tirelessly** adv unermüdlich; **tiresome** adj lästig; **tiring** adj ermüdend

Tirol [tɪ'rəʊl] see **Tyrol**

tissue ['tɪʃuː] n (Anat) Gewebe nt; (paper handkerchief) Tempotaschentuch® nt, Papier(taschen)tuch nt; **tissue paper** n Seidenpapier nt

tit [tɪt] n (bird) Meise f; (fam: breast) Titte f

title ['taɪtl] n Titel m

titter ['tɪtə] vi kichern

KEYWORD

to [tuː, tə] prep 1 (direction) zu, nach; **I go to France/school** ich gehe nach Frankreich/zur Schule; **to the left** nach links
2 (as far as) bis
3 (with expressions of time) vor; **a quarter to 5** Viertel vor 5
4 (for, of) für; **secretary to the director** Sekretärin des Direktors
5 (expressing indirect object) **to give sth to sb** jdm etw geben; **to talk to sb** mit jdm sprechen; **I sold it to a friend** ich habe es einem Freund verkauft
6 (in relation to) zu; **30 miles to the gallon** 30 Meilen pro Gallone

7 (purpose, result) zu; **to my surprise** zu meiner Überraschung
▷ with vb 1 (infin) **to go/eat** gehen/essen; **to want to do sth** etw tun wollen; **to try/start to do sth** versuchen/anfangen, etw zu tun; **he has a lot to lose** er hat viel zu verlieren
2 (with vb omitted) **I don't want to** ich will (es) nicht
3 (purpose, result) **I did it to help you** ich tat es, um dir/Ihnen zu helfen
4 (after adj etc) ready to use gebrauchsfertig; **too old/young to ...** zu alt/jung, um ... zu ...
▷ adv: **push/pull the door to** die Tür zuschieben/zuziehen

toad [təʊd] n Kröte f; **toadstool** n Giftpilz m

toast [təʊst] n (bread, drink) Toast m; **a piece** (o **slice**) **of ~** eine Scheibe Toast; **to propose a ~ to sb** einen Toast auf jdn ausbringen ▷ vt (bread) toasten; (person) trinken auf +akk; **toaster** n Toaster m

tobacco [tə'bækəʊ] n (pl -es) n Tabak m; **tobacconist's** [tə'bækənɪsts] n: **~ (shop)** Tabakladen m

toboggan [tə'bɒgən] n Schlitten m

today [tə'deɪ] adv heute; **a week ~** heute in einer Woche; **~'s newspaper** die Zeitung von heute

toddler ['tɒdlə°] n Kleinkind nt

toe [təʊ] n Zehe f, Zeh m; **toenail** n Zehennagel m

toffee ['tɒfɪ] n (sweet) Karamellbonbon nt; **toffee apple** n kandierter Apfel; **toffee-nosed** adj hochnäsig

tofu ['təʊfuː] n Tofu m

together [tə'geðə°] adv

zusammen; **I tied them ~** ich habe sie zusammengebunden

toilet ['tɔɪlət] n Toilette f; **to go to the ~** auf die Toilette gehen; **toilet bag** n Kulturbeutel m; **toilet paper** n Toilettenpapier nt; **toiletries** ['tɔɪlətrɪz] npl Toilettenartikel pl; **toilet roll** n Rolle f Toilettenpapier

token ['təʊkən] n Marke f; (in casino) Spielmarke f; (voucher, gift ~) Gutschein m; (sign) Zeichen nt

Tokyo ['təʊkjəʊ] n Tokio nt

told [təʊld] pt, pp of **tell**

tolerant ['tɒlərənt] adj tolerant (of gegenüber); **tolerate** ['tɒləreɪt] vt tolerieren; (noise, pain, heat) ertragen

toll [təʊl] n (charge) Gebühr f; **the death ~** die Zahl der Toten; **toll-free** adj, adv (US Tel) gebührenfrei; **toll road** n gebührenpflichtige Straße

tomato [tə'mɑːtəʊ] (pl -es) n Tomate f; **tomato juice** n Tomatensaft m; **tomato ketchup** n Tomatenketchup m o nt; **tomato sauce** n Tomatensoße f; (Brit: ketchup) Tomatenketchup m o nt

tomb [tuːm] n Grabmal nt; **tombstone** n Grabstein m

tomorrow [tə'mɒrəʊ] adv morgen; **~ morning** morgen früh; **~ evening** morgen Abend; **the day after ~** übermorgen; **a week (from) ~/~ week** morgen in einer Woche

ton [tʌn] n (Brit) Tonne f (1016 kg); (US) Tonne f (907 kg); **~s of books** (fam) eine Menge Bücher

tone [təʊn] n Ton m; **tone down** vt mäßigen; **tone** ['təʊnə] n (for printer) Toner m; **toner cartridge** n Tonerpatrone f

tongs [tɒŋz] npl Zange f; (curling ~) Lockenstab m

tongue [tʌŋ] n Zunge f

tonic ['tɒnɪk] n (Med) Stärkungsmittel nt; **~ (water)** Tonic nt; **gin and ~** Gin m Tonic

tonight [tə'naɪt] adv heute Abend; (during night) heute Nacht

tonsils ['tɒnslz] n Mandeln pl; **tonsillitis** [tɒnsɪ'laɪtɪs] n Mandelentzündung f

too [tuː] adv zu; (also) auch; **~ fast** zu schnell; **~ much/many** zu viel/viele; **me ~** ich auch; **she liked it ~** ihr gefiel es auch

took [tʊk] pt of **take**

tool [tuːl] n Werkzeug nt; **toolbar** n (Inform) Symbolleiste f; **toolbox** n Werkzeugkasten m

tooth [tuːθ] (pl **teeth**) n Zahn m; **toothache** n Zahnschmerzen pl; **toothbrush** n Zahnbürste f; **toothpaste** n Zahnpasta f; **toothpick** n Zahnstocher m

top [tɒp] n (of tower, class, company etc) Spitze f; (of mountain) Gipfel m; (of tree) Krone f; (of street) oberes Ende; (of tube, pen) Kappe f; (of box) Deckel m; (of bikini) Oberteil nt; (sleeveless) Top nt; **at the ~ of the page** oben auf der Seite; **at the ~ of the league** an der Spitze der Liga; **on ~** oben; **on ~ of** auf +dat; (in addition to) zusätzlich zu; **in ~ (gear)** im höchsten Gang; **over the ~** übertrieben ▷ adj (floor, shelf) oberste(r, s); (price, note) höchste(r, s); (best) Spitzen-; (pupil, school) beste(r, s) ▷ vt (exceed) übersteigen; (be better than) übertreffen; (league) an erster Stelle liegen in +dat; **~ped with cream** mit Sahne obendrauf; **top up** vt auffüllen; **can I top you up?** darf ich dir nachschenken?

topic ['tɒpɪk] n Thema nt; **topical** adj aktuell

topless ['tɒpləs] *adj, adv* oben ohne

topping ['tɒpɪŋ] *n* (on top of pizza, ice-cream etc) Belag *m*, Garnierung *f*

top-secret ['tɒp'siːkrət] *adj* streng geheim

torch [tɔːtʃ] *n* (Brit) Taschenlampe *f*

tore [tɔː*] *pt of* tear

torment [tɔː'ment] *vt* quälen

torn [tɔːn] *pp of* tear

tornado [tɔː'neɪdəʊ] (*pl* **-es**) *n* Tornado *m*

torrential [tə'renʃəl] *adj* (rain) sintflutartig

tortoise ['tɔːtəs] *n* Schildkröte *f*

torture ['tɔːtʃə*] *n* Folter *f*; (fig) Qual *f* ▷ *vt* foltern

Tory ['tɔːrɪ] (Brit) *n* Tory *m*, Konservative(r) *mf* ▷ *adj* Tory-

toss [tɒs] *vt* (throw) werfen; (salad) anmachen; **to ~ a coin** eine Münze werfen ▷ *n*: **I don't give a ~** (fam) es ist mir scheißegal

total ['təʊtl] *n* (of figures, money) Gesamtsumme *f*; **a ~ of 30** insgesamt 30; **in ~** insgesamt ▷ *adj* total; (sum etc) Gesamt- ▷ *vt* (amount to) sich belaufen auf +akk; **totally** *adv* total

touch [tʌtʃ] *n* (act of ~ing) Berührung *f*; (sense of ~) Tastsinn *m*; (trace) Spur *f*; **to be/keep in ~ with sb** mit jdm in Verbindung stehen/bleiben; **to get in ~ with sb** sich mit jdm in Verbindung setzen; **to lose ~ with sb** den Kontakt zu jdm verlieren ▷ *vt* (feel) berühren; (emotionally) bewegen; **touch on** *vt* (topic) berühren; **touchdown** *n* (Aviat) Landung *f*; (Sport) Touchdown *m*; **touching** *adj* (moving) rührend; **touch screen** *n* Touchscreen *m*, Berührungsbildschirm *m*; **touchy** *adj* empfindlich, zickig

tough [tʌf] *adj* hart; (meat) zäh; (material) robust; (meat) zäh

tour ['tʊə*] *n* Tour *f* (of durch); (of town, building) Rundgang *m* (of durch); (of pop group etc) Tournee *f* ▷ *vt* eine Tour/einen Rundgang, eine Tournee machen durch ▷ *vi* (on holiday) umherreisen; **tour guide** *n* Reiseleiter(in) *m(f)*

tourism ['tʊərɪzəm] *n* Tourismus *m*, Fremdenverkehr *m*; **tourist** *n* Tourist(in) *m(f)*; **tourist class** *n* Touristenklasse *f*; **tourist guide** *n* (book) Reiseführer *m*; (person) Fremdenführer(in) *m(f)*; **tourist office** *n* Fremdenverkehrsamt *nt*

tournament ['tʊənəmənt] *n* Turnier *nt*

tour operator ['tʊərɒpəreɪtə*] *n* Reiseveranstalter *m*

tow [təʊ] *vt* abschleppen; (caravan, trailer) ziehen; **tow away** *vt* abschleppen

towards [tə'wɔːdz] *prep*: **~ me** mir entgegen, auf mich zu; **we walked ~ the station** wir gingen in Richtung Bahnhof; **my feelings ~ him** meine Gefühle ihm gegenüber; **she was kind ~ me** sie war nett zu mir

towel ['taʊəl] *n* Handtuch *nt*

tower ['taʊə*] *n* Turm *m*; **tower block** *n* (Brit) Hochhaus *nt*

town [taʊn] *n* Stadt *f*; **town center** (US), **town centre** *n* Stadtmitte *f*, Stadtzentrum *nt*; **town hall** *n* Rathaus *nt*

towrope ['təʊrəʊp] *n* Abschleppseil *nt*; **tow truck** *n* (US) Abschleppwagen *m*

toxic ['tɒksɪk] *adj* giftig, Gift-

toy [tɔɪ] *n* Spielzeug *nt*; **toy with** *vt* spielen mit; **toyshop** *n* Spielwarengeschäft *nt*

trace [treɪs] *n* Spur *f*; **without**

~ spurlos ▷ vt (find) ausfindig machen; **tracing paper** n Pauspapier nt

track [træk] n (mark) Spur f; (path) Weg m; (Rail) Gleis nt; (on CD, record) Stück nt; **to keep/lose ~ of sb/sth** jdn/etw im Auge behalten/aus den Augen verlieren; **track down** vt ausfindig machen; **trackball** n (Inform) Trackball m; **tracksuit** n Trainingsanzug m

tractor ['træktə°] n Traktor m

trade [treɪd] n (commerce) Handel m; (business) Geschäft nt; (skilled job) Handwerk nt ▷ vi handeln (in mit) ▷ vt (exchange) tauschen (for gegen); **trademark** n Warenzeichen nt; **tradesman** (pl **-men**) n (shopkeeper) Geschäftsmann m; (workman) Handwerker m; **trade(s) union** n (Brit) Gewerkschaft f

tradition [trə'dɪʃən] n Tradition f; **traditional, traditionally** adj, adv traditionell

traffic ['træfɪk] n Verkehr m; (pej: trading) Handel m (in mit); **traffic circle** n (US) Kreisverkehr m; **traffic island** n Verkehrsinsel f; **traffic jam** n Stau m; **traffic lights** npl Verkehrsampel f; **traffic warden** n (Brit) = Politesse f

tragedy ['trædʒədɪ] n Tragödie f; **tragic** ['trædʒɪk] adj tragisch

trail [treɪl] n Spur f; (path) Weg m ▷ vt (follow) verfolgen; (drag) schleppen; (drag behind) hinter sich herziehen; (Sport) zurückliegen hinter +dat ▷ vi (hang loosely) schleifen; (Sport) weit zurückliegen; **trailer** n Anhänger m; (US: caravan) Wohnwagen m; (Cine) Trailer m

train [treɪn] n (Rail) Zug m ▷ vt (teach) ausbilden; (Sport) trainieren

▷ vi (Sport) trainieren; **to ~ as** (o to be) **a teacher** eine Ausbildung als Lehrer machen; **trained** adj (person, voice) ausgebildet; **trainee** n Auszubildende(r) mf; (academic, practical) Praktikant(in) m(f); **traineeship** n Praktikum nt; **trainer** n (Sport) Trainer(in) m(f); **~s** (Brit: shoes) Turnschuhe pl; **training** n Ausbildung f; (Sport) Training nt; **train station** n Bahnhof m

tram ['træm] n (Brit) Straßenbahn f

tramp [træmp] n Landstreicher(in) m(f) ▷ vi trotten

tranquillizer ['træŋkwɪlaɪzə°] n Beruhigungsmittel nt

transaction n (piece of business) Geschäft nt

transatlantic ['trænzət'læntɪk] adj transatlantisch; **~ flight** Transatlantikflug m

transfer ['trænsfə°] n (of money) Überweisung f; (US: ticket) Umsteigekarte f ▷ [træns'fз:°] vt (money) überweisen (to sb an jdn); (patient) verlegen; (employee) versetzen; (Sport) transferieren ▷ vi (on journey) umsteigen; **transferable** [træns'fз:rəbl] adj übertragbar

transform [træns'fɔ:m] vt umwandeln; **transformation** [trænsfə'meɪʃən] n Umwandlung f

transfusion [træns'fju:ʒən] n Transfusion f

transistor [træn'zɪstə°] n Transistor m; **~ (radio)** Transistorradio nt

transition [træn'zɪʃən] n Übergang m (from ... to von ... zu)

transit lounge ['trænzɪtlaʊndʒ] n Transitraum m; **transit passenger** n Transitreisende(r) mf

translate [trænz'leɪt] vt, vi übersetzen; **translation** [trænz'leɪʃən] n Übersetzung f; **translator** [trænz'leɪtə°] n Übersetzer(in) m(f)

transmission [trænz'mɪʃən] n (Auto) Getriebe nt

transparent [træns'pærənt] adj durchsichtig; (fig) offenkundig

transplant [træns'plɑːnt] (Med) vt transplantieren ▷ n ['trænsplɑːnt] n (operation) Transplantation f

transport [ˈtrænspɔːt] n (of goods, people) Beförderung f; **public ~** öffentliche Verkehrsmittel pl ▷ [træns'pɔːt] vt befördern, transportieren; **transportation** [trænspɔː'teɪʃən] n see **transport**

trap [træp] n Falle f ▷ vt: **to be ~ped** (in snow, job etc) festsitzen

trash [træʃ] n (book, film etc) Schund m; (US: refuse) Abfall m; **trash can** n (US) Abfalleimer m; **trashy** adj niveaulos; (novel) Schund-

traumatic [trɔː'mætɪk] adj traumatisch

travel [ˈtrævl] n Reisen nt ▷ vi (journey) reisen ▷ vt (distance) zurücklegen; (country) bereisen; **travel agency, travel agent** n (company) Reisebüro nt; **traveller** (US) see **traveller**; **traveler's check** (US) see **traveller's cheque**; **travel insurance** n Reiseversicherung f; **traveller** n Reisende(r) mf; **traveller's cheque** n (Brit) Reisescheck m; **travelsick** n reisekrank

tray [treɪ] n Tablett nt; (for mail etc) Ablage f; (of printer, photocopier) Fach nt

tread [tred] n (on tyre) Profil nt, **tread on** [ued] (**trod, trodden**) vt treten auf +akk

treasure [ˈtreʒə°] n Schatz m ▷ vt schätzen

treat [triːt] n besondere Freude; **it's my ~** das geht auf meine Kosten ▷ vt behandeln, **to ~ sb (to sth)** jdn (zu etw) einladen; **to ~ oneself to sth** sich etw leisten; **treatment** [ˈtriːtmənt] n Behandlung f

treaty [ˈtriːtɪ] n Vertrag m

tree [triː] n Baum m

tremble [ˈtrembl] vi zittern

tremendous [trəˈmendəs] adj gewaltig; (fam: very good) toll

trench [trentʃ] n Graben m

trend [trend] n Tendenz f; (fashion) Mode f; **Trend** m, **trendy** adj trendig

trespass [ˈtrespəs] vi: **"no ~ing"** „Betreten verboten"

trial [ˈtraɪəl] n (Jur) Prozess m; (test) Versuch m; **by ~ and error** durch Ausprobieren; **trial period** n (for employee) Probezeit f

triangle [ˈtraɪæŋgl] n Dreieck nt; (Mus) Triangel m; **triangular** [traɪˈæŋgjʊlə°] adj dreieckig

tribe [traɪb] n Stamm m

trick [trɪk] n Trick m; (mischief) Streich m ▷ vt hereinlegen

tricky [ˈtrɪkɪ] adj (difficult) schwierig, heikel; (situation) verzwickt

trifle [ˈtraɪfl] n Kleinigkeit f; (Brit Gastr) Trifle nt (Nachspeise aus Biskuit, Wackelpudding, Obst, Vanillesoße und Sahne)

trigger [ˈtrɪgə°] n (of gun) Abzug m ▷ vt: **to ~ (off)** auslösen

trim [trɪm] vt (hair, beard) nachschneiden; (nails) schneiden; (hedge) stutzen ▷ n: **just a ~, please** nur etwas nachschneiden, bitte; **trimmings** npl (decorations) Verzierungen pl; (extras) Zubehör nt; (Gastr) Beilagen pl

trip [trɪp] n Reise f; (outing) Ausflug m ▷ vi stolpern (over über +akk)

triple ['trɪpl] adj dreifach ▷ adv:
~ **the price** dreimal so teuer ▷ vi
sich verdreifachen; **triplet**
['trɪplɪt] n Drilling m

tripod ['traɪpɒd] n (Foto) Stativ
nt

trite [traɪt] adj banal

triumph ['traɪʌmf] n Triumph m

trivial ['trɪvɪəl] adj trivial

trod [trɒd] pt of **tread**

trodden pp of **tread**

trolley ['trɒlɪ] n (Brit: in shop)
Einkaufswagen m; (for luggage)
Kofferkuli m; (serving ~) Teewagen
m

trombone [trɒm'bəʊn] n
Posaune f

troops [truːps] npl (Mil) Truppen
pl

trophy ['trəʊfɪ] n Trophäe f

tropical ['trɒpɪkl] adj tropisch

trouble ['trʌbl] n (problems)
Schwierigkeiten pl; (worry) Sorgen
pl; (effort) Mühe f; (unrest) Unruhen
pl; (Med) Beschwerden pl; **to be in
~ in** Schwierigkeiten sein; **to get
into ~** (with authority) Ärger
bekommen; **to make
~** Schwierigkeiten machen ▷ vt
(worry) beunruhigen; (disturb)
stören; **my back's troubling me**
mein Rücken macht mir zu
schaffen; **sorry to ~ you** ich muss
dich/Sie leider kurz stören;
troubled adj (worried)
beunruhigt; **trouble-free** adj
problemlos; **troublemaker** n
Unruhestifter(in) m(f);
troublesome adj lästig

trousers ['traʊzəz] npl Hose f;
trouser suit n (Brit) Hosenanzug
m

trout [traʊt] n Forelle f

truck [trʌk] n Lastwagen m; (Brit
Rail) Güterwagen m; **trucker** n
(US: driver) Lastwagenfahrer(in)
m(f)

true [truː] adj (factually correct)
wahr; (genuine) echt; **to come
~** wahr werden

truly ['truːlɪ] adv wirklich; **Yours
~** (in letter) mit freundlichen
Grüßen

trumpet ['trʌmpɪt] n Trompete

trunk [trʌŋk] n (of tree) Stamm
m; (Anat) Rumpf m; (of elephant)
Rüssel m; (piece of luggage)
Überseekoffer m; (US Auto)
Kofferraum m; **trunks** npl:
(**swimming**) ~ Badehose f

trust [trʌst] n (confidence)
Vertrauen nt (in sb) ~ vt vertrauen
+dat; **trusting** adj vertrauensvoll;
trustworthy adj
vertrauenswürdig

truth [truːθ] n Wahrheit f;
truthful adj ehrlich; (statement)
wahrheitsgemäß

try [traɪ] n Versuch m ▷ vt
(attempt) versuchen; (~ out)
ausprobieren; (sample) probieren;
(Jur: person) vor Gericht stellen;
(courage, patience) auf die Probe
stellen ▷ vi versuchen; (make
effort) sich bemühen; **~ and come**
versuch zu kommen; **try on** vt
(clothes) anprobieren; **try out** vt
ausprobieren

T-shirt ['tiːʃɜːt] n T-Shirt nt

tub [tʌb] n (for ice-cream,
margarine) Becher m

tube [tjuːb] n (pipe) Rohr nt; (of
rubber, plastic) Schlauch m; (for
toothpaste, glue etc) Tube f; **the
Tube** (in London) die U-Bahn

tube station ['tjuːbsteɪʃən] n
U-Bahn-Station f

tuck [tʌk] vt (put) stecken; **tuck
in** vt (shirt) in die Hose stecken;
(blanket) feststecken; (person)
zudecken ▷ vi (eat) zulangen

Tue(s) abbr = **Tuesday** Di.

Tuesday ['tjuːzdɪ] n Dienstag m;

on ~ (am) Dienstag; **on ~s dienstags:** **this/last/next ~** diesen/letzten/nächsten Dienstag; **(on) ~ morning/afternoon/evening** (am) Dienstagmorgen/-nachmittag/-abend; **every ~** jeden Dienstag; **a week on ~/~ week** Dienstag in einer Woche

tug [tʌg] vt ziehen; **she ~ged his sleeve** sie zog an seinem Ärmel ▷ vi ziehen *(at an +dat)*

tuition [tjuːˈɪʃən] n Unterricht m; *(US: fees)* Studiengebühren pl; **~ fees** pl Studiengebühren pl

tulip [ˈtjuːlɪp] n Tulpe f

tumble [ˈtʌmbl] vi *(person, prices)* fallen; **tumble dryer** n Wäschetrockner m; **tumbler** n *(glass)* (Becher)glas n

tummy [ˈtʌmɪ] n *(fam)* Bauch m; **tummyache** n *(fam)* Bauchweh nt

tumour (US), **tumour** [ˈtjuːmə*] n Tumor m

tuna [ˈtjuːnə] n Thunfisch m

tune [tjuːn] n Melodie f; **to be in/out of ~** *(instrument)* gestimmt/verstimmt sein; *(singer)* richtig/falsch singen ▷ vt *(instrument)* stimmen; *(radio)* einstellen *(to auf +akk)*; **tuner** n *(in stereo system)* Tuner m

Tunisia [tjuːˈnɪzɪə] n Tunesien nt

tunnel [ˈtʌnl] n Tunnel m; *(under road, railway)* Unterführung f

turban [ˈtɜːbən] n Turban m

turbulence [ˈtɜːbjʊləns] n *(Aviat)* Turbulenzen pl; **turbulent** adj stürmisch

Turk [tɜːk] n Türke m, Türkin f

turkey [ˈtɜːkɪ] n Truthahn m

Turkey [ˈtɜːkɪ] n die Türkei; **Turkish** adj türkisch ▷ n *(language)* Türkisch nt

turmoil [ˈtɜːmɔɪl] n Aufruhr m

turn [tɜːn] n *(rotation)* Drehung f; *(performance)* Nummer f; **to make a left ~** nach links abbiegen; **at the ~ of the century** um die Jahrhundertwende; **it's your ~** du bist/Sie sind dran; **in ~, by ~s** abwechselnd; **to take ~s** sich abwechseln ▷ vt *(wheel, key, screw)* drehen; *(to face other way)* umdrehen; *(corner)* biegen um; *(page)* umblättern; *(transform)* verwandeln *(into in +akk)* ▷ vi *(rotate)* sich drehen; *(to face other way)* sich umdrehen; *(change direction: driver, car)* abbiegen; *(become)* werden; *(weather)* umschlagen; **to ~ into sth** *(become)* sich in etw akk verwandeln; **to ~ cold/green** kalt/grün werden; **to ~ left/right** links/rechts abbiegen; **turn away** vt *(person)* abweisen; **turn back** vt *(person)* zurückweisen ▷ vi *(go back)* umkehren; **turn down** vt *(refuse)* ablehnen; *(radio, TV)* leiser stellen; *(heating)* kleiner stellen; **turn off** vi abbiegen ▷ vt *(switch off)* ausschalten; *(tap)* zudrehen; *(engine, electricity)* abstellen; **turn on** vt *(switch on)* einschalten; *(tap)* aufdrehen; *(engine, electricity)* anstellen; *(fam: person)* anmachen, antörnen; **turn out** vt *(light)* ausmachen; *(pockets)* leeren ▷ vi *(develop)* sich entwickeln; **as it turned out** wie sich herausstellte; **turn over** vt umdrehen; *(page)* umblättern ▷ vi *(car)* sich überschlagen; *(TV)* umschalten *(to auf +akk)*; **turn round** vt *(to face other way)* umdrehen ▷ vi *(person)* sich umdrehen; *(go back)* umkehren; **turn to** vt sich zuwenden *(to +dat)*; **turn up** vi *(person, lost object)* auftauchen ▷ vt *(radio, TV)* lauter stellen; *(heating)*

höher stellen; **turning** n (in road) Abzweigung f; **turning point** n Wendepunkt m

turnip ['tɜːnɪp] n Rübe f

turnover ['tɜːnəʊvə°] n (Fin) Umsatz m

turnpike ['tɜːnpaɪk] n (US) gebührenpflichtige Autobahn

turntable ['tɜːnteɪbl] n (on record player) Plattenteller m

turn-up ['tɜːnʌp] n (Brit: on trousers) Aufschlag m

turquoise ['tɜːkwɔɪz] adj türkis

turtle ['tɜːtl] n (Brit) Wasserschildkröte f; (US) Schildkröte f

tutor ['tjuːtə°] n (private) Privatlehrer(in) m(f); (Brit: at university) Tutor(in) m(f)

tux [tʌks], **tuxedo** [tʌk'siːdəʊ] (pl -s) n (US) Smoking m

TV ['tiː'viː] n Fernsehen nt; (~ set) Fernseher m; **to watch ~** fernsehen; **on ~** im Fernsehen ▷ adj Fernseh-; **~ programme** Fernsehsendung f

tweed [twiːd] n Tweed m

tweezers ['twiːzəz] npl Pinzette f

twelfth [twelfθ] adj zwölfte(r, s); see also **eighth**; **twelve** [twelv] num zwölf ▷ n Zwölf f; see also **eight**

twentieth ['twentɪɪθ] adj zwanzigste(r, s); see also **eighth**; **twenty** ['twentɪ] num zwanzig; **~-one** einundzwanzig ▷ n Zwanzig f; **to be in one's twenties** in den Zwanzigern sein; see also **eight**

twice [twaɪs] adv zweimal; **~ as much/many** doppelt so viel/viele

twig [twɪg] n Zweig m

twilight ['twaɪlaɪt] n (in evening) Dämmerung f

twin [twɪn] n Zwilling m ▷ adj (brother etc) Zwillings-; **~ beds** zwei

Einzelbetten ▷ vt: **York is ~ned with Münster** York ist eine Partnerstadt von Münster

twinge [twɪndʒ] n (pain) stechender Schmerz

twinkle ['twɪŋkl] vi funkeln

twin room ['twɪn'ruːm] n Zweibettzimmer nt; **twin town** n Partnerstadt f

twist [twɪst] vt (turn) drehen, winden; (distort) verdrehen; **I've ~ed my ankle** ich bin mit dem Fuß umgeknickt

two [tuː] num zwei; **to break sth in ~** etw in zwei Teile brechen ▷ n Zwei f; **the ~ of them** die beiden; see also **eight**; **two-dimensional** adj zweidimensional; (fig) oberflächlich; **two-faced** adj falsch, heuchlerisch; **two-piece** adj zweiteilig; **two-way** adj: **~ traffic** Gegenverkehr

type [taɪp] n (sort) Art f; (typeface) Schrift(art) f; **what ~ of car is it?** was für ein Auto ist das?; **he's not my ~** er ist nicht mein Typ; **typeface** n Schrift(art) f; **typewriter** n Schreibmaschine f

typhoid ['taɪfɔɪd] n Typhus m

typhoon [taɪ'fuːn] n Taifun m

typical ['tɪpɪkəl] adj typisch (of für)

typing error ['taɪpɪŋerə°] n Tippfehler m

tyre [taɪə°] n (Brit) Reifen m; **tyre pressure** n Reifendruck m

Tyrol [tɪ'rəʊl] n: **the ~** Tirol nt

u

UFO [ˈjuːfəʊ] *acr* = **unidentified flying object** Ufo *nt*

Uganda [juːˈgændə] *n* Uganda *nt*

ugly [ˈʌglɪ] *adj* hässlich

UHT *adj abbr* = **ultra-heat treated ~ milk** H-Milch *f*

UK *abbr* = **United Kingdom**

Ukraine [juːˈkreɪn] *n*: **the ~** die Ukraine

ulcer [ˈʌlsə°] *n* Geschwür *nt*

ulterior [ʌlˈtɪərɪə°] *adj*: **~ motive** Hintergedanke *m*

ultimate [ˈʌltɪmət] *adj* (*final*) letzte(r, s); (*authority*) höchste(r, s); **ultimately** *adv* letzten Endes; (*eventually*) schließlich; **ultimatum** [ʌltɪˈmeɪtəm] *n* Ultimatum *nt*

ultra- [ˈʌltrə] *pref* ultra-

ultrasound [ˈʌltrəsaʊnd] *n* (*Med*) Ultraschall *m*

umbrella [ʌmˈbrelə] *n* Schirm *m*

umpire [ˈʌmpaɪə°] *n* Schieds-richter(in) *m(f)*

umpteen [ˈʌmptiːn] *num* (*fam*) zig; **~ times** zigmal

un- [ʌn] *pref* un-

UN *nsing abbr* = **United Nations** VN, Vereinte Nationen *pl*

unable [ʌnˈeɪbl] *adj*: **to be ~ to do sth** etw nicht tun können

unacceptable [ʌnəˈkseptəbl] *adj* unannehmbar

unaccountably [ʌnəˈkaʊntəblɪ] *adv* unerklärlicherweise

unaccustomed [ʌnəˈkʌstəmd] *adj*: **to be ~ to sth** etw nicht gewohnt sein

unanimous, unanimously [juːˈnænɪməs, -lɪ] *adj, adv* einmütig

unattached [ʌnəˈtætʃt] *adj* (*without partner*) ungebunden

unattended [ʌnəˈtendɪd] *adj* (*luggage, car*) unbeaufsichtigt

unauthorized [ʌnˈɔːθəraɪzd] *adj* unbefugt

unavailable [ʌnəˈveɪləbl] *adj* nicht erhältlich; (*person*) nicht erreichbar

unavoidable [ʌnəˈvɔɪdəbl] *adj* unvermeidlich

unaware [ʌnəˈweə°] *adj*: **to be ~ of sth** sich einer Sache *dat* nicht bewusst sein; **I was ~ that ...** ich wusste nicht, dass ...

unbalanced [ʌnˈbælənst] *adj* unausgewogen; (*mentally*) gestört

unbearable [ʌnˈbeərəbl] *adj* unerträglich

unbeatable [ʌnˈbiːtəbl] *adj* unschlagbar

unbelievable [ʌnbɪˈliːvəbl] *adj* unglaublich

unblock [ʌnˈblɒk] *vt* (*pipe*) frei machen

unbutton [ʌnˈbʌtn] *vt* aufknöpfen

uncertain [ʌn'sɜːtən] *adj*
unsicher

uncle [ˈʌŋkl] *n* Onkel *m*

uncomfortable [ʌnˈkʌmfətəbl]
adj unbequem

unconditional [ʌnkənˈdɪʃənl]
adj bedingungslos

unconscious [ʌnˈkɒnʃəs] *adj*
(Med) bewusstlos; **to be ~ of sth**
sich einer Sache *dat* nicht bewusst
sein; **unconsciously** *adv*
unbewusst

uncork [ʌnˈkɔːk] *vt* entkorken

uncover [ʌnˈkʌvə°] *vt*
aufdecken

undecided [ʌndɪˈsaɪdɪd] *adj*
unschlüssig

undeniable [ʌndɪˈnaɪəbl] *adj*
unbestreitbar

under [ˈʌndə°] *prep* (beneath)
unter +*dat*; (with motion) unter
+*akk*; **children ~ eight** Kinder
unter acht; **~ an hour** weniger als
eine Stunde ▷ *adv* (beneath)
unten; (with motion) darunter;
children aged eight and ~ Kinder
bis zu acht Jahren; **under-age** *adj*
minderjährig

undercarriage [ˈʌndəkærɪdʒ] *n*
Fahrgestell *nt*

underdog [ˈʌndədɒg] *n* (outsider)
Außenseiter(in) *m(f)*

underdone [ʌndəˈdʌn] *adj*
(Gastr) nicht gar, durch;
(deliberately) nicht durchgebraten

underestimate [ʌndər-
ˈestɪmeɪt] *vt* unterschätzen

underexposed [ʌndərɪksˈpəʊzd]
adj (Foto) unterbelichtet

undergo [ʌndəˈgəʊ] *irr vt*
(experience) durchmachen;
(operation, test) sich unterziehen
+*dat*

undergraduate [ʌndəˈgrædjuət]
n Student(in) *m(f)*

underground [ˈʌndəgraʊnd] *adj*
unterirdisch ▷ *n* (Brit Rail) U-Bahn

f; **underground station** *n*
U-Bahn-Station *f*

underlie [ʌndəˈlaɪ] *irr vt*
zugrunde liegen +*dat*

underline [ʌndəˈlaɪn] *vt*
unterstreichen

underlying [ʌndəˈlaɪɪŋ] *adj*
zugrunde liegend

underneath [ʌndəˈniːθ] *prep*
unter; (with motion) unter +*akk*
▷ *adv* darunter

underpants [ˈʌndəpænts] *npl*
Unterhose *f*; **undershirt**
[ˈʌndəʃɜːt] *n* (US) Unterhemd *nt*;
undershorts [ˈʌndəʃɔːts] *npl* (US)
Unterhose *f*

understand [ʌndəˈstænd] *irr vt*,
vi verstehen; **I ~ that ...** (been told)
ich habe gehört, dass ...;
(sympathize) ich habe Verständnis
dafür, dass ...; **to make oneself
understood** sich verständlich
machen; **understandable** *adj*
verständlich; **understanding** *adj*
verständnisvoll

undertake [ʌndəˈteɪk] *irr vt*
(task) übernehmen; **to ~ to do sth**
sich verpflichten, etw zu tun;
undertaker *n* Leichenbestat-
ter(in) *m(f)*; **~'s (firm)**
Bestattungsinstitut *nt*

underwater [ʌndəˈwɔːtə°] *adv*
unter Wasser ▷ *adj* Unterwasser-

underwear [ˈʌndəweə°] *n*
Unterwäsche *f*

undesirable [ʌndɪˈzaɪərəbl] *adj*
unerwünscht

undo [ʌnˈduː] *irr vt* (unfasten)
aufmachen; (work)
zunichtemachen; (Inform)
rückgängig machen

undoubtedly [ʌnˈdaʊtɪdlɪ] *adv*
zweifellos

undress [ʌnˈdres] *vt* ausziehen;
to get ~ed sich ausziehen ▷ *vi*
sich ausziehen

undue [ʌnˈdjuː] *adj* übermäßig

unduly [ʌn'dju:lɪ] adv übermäßig

unearth [ʌn'ɜ:θ] vt (dig up) ausgraben; (find) aufstöbern

unease [ʌn'i:z] n Unbehagen nt; **uneasy** adj (person) unbehaglich; **I'm ~ about it** mir ist nicht wohl dabei

unemployed [ʌnɪm'plɔɪd] adj arbeitslos ▷ b npl: **the ~** die Arbeitslosen pl; **unemployment** [ʌnɪm'plɔɪmənt] n Arbeitslosigkeit f; **unemployment benefit** n Arbeitslosengeld nt

unequal [ʌn'i:kwəl] adj ungleich

uneven [ʌn'i:vən] adj (surface, road) uneben; (contest) ungleich

unexpected [ʌnɪk'spektɪd] adj unerwartet

unfair [ʌn'feə°] adj unfair

unfamiliar [ʌnfə'mɪljə°] adj: **to be ~ with sb/sth** jdn/etw nicht kennen

unfasten [ʌn'fɑ:sn] vt aufmachen

unfit [ʌn'fɪt] adj ungeeignet (for für); (in bad health) nicht fit

unforeseen [ʌnfɔ:'si:n] adj unvorhergesehen

unforgettable [ʌnfə'ɡetəbl] adj unvergesslich

unforgivable [ʌnfə'ɡɪvəbl] adj unverzeihlich

unfortunate [ʌn'fɔ:tʃnət] adj (unlucky) unglücklich; **it is ~ that ...** es ist bedauerlich, dass ...; **unfortunately** adv leider

unfounded [ʌn'faʊndɪd] adj unbegründet

unhappy [ʌn'hæpɪ] adj (sad) unglücklich, unzufrieden; **to be ~ with sth** mit etw unzufrieden sein

unhealthy [ʌn'helθɪ] adj ungesund

unheard-of [ʌn'hɜ:dɒv] adj

(unknown) gänzlich unbekannt; (outrageous) unerhört

unhelpful [ʌn'helpfʊl] adj nicht hilfreich

unhitch [ʌn'hɪtʃ] vt (caravan, trailer) abkoppeln

unhurt [ʌn'hɜ:t] adj unverletzt

uniform ['ju:nɪfɔ:m] n Uniform f ▷ adj einheitlich

unify ['ju:nɪfaɪ] vt vereinigen

unimportant [ʌnɪm'pɔ:tənt]- adj unwichtig

uninhabited [ʌnɪn'hæbɪtɪd] adj unbewohnt

uninstall [ʌnɪn'stɔ:l] vt (Inform) deinstallieren

unintentional [ʌnɪn'tenʃənl] adj unabsichtlich

union ['ju:njən] n (uniting) Vereinigung f; (alliance) Union f; **Union Jack** n Union Jack m (britische Nationalflagge)

unique [ju:'ni:k] adj einzigartig

unit ['ju:nɪt] n Einheit f; (of system, machine) Teil m; (in school) Lektion f

unite [ju:'naɪt] vt vereinigen; **the United Kingdom** das Vereinigte Königreich; **the United Nations** pl die Vereinten Nationen pl; **the United States (of America)** pl die Vereinigten Staaten (von Amerika) pl ▷ vi sich vereinigen

universe ['ju:nɪvɜ:s] n Universum m

university [ju:nɪ'vɜ:sɪtɪ] n Universität f

unkind [ʌn'kaɪnd] adj unfreundlich (to zu)

unknown [ʌn'nəʊn] adj unbekannt (to +dat)

unleaded [ʌn'ledɪd] adj bleifrei

unless [ən'les] conj es sei denn, wenn ... nicht; **don't do it ~ I tell you to** mach das nicht, es sei denn, ich sage es dir; **~ I'm**

mistaken ... wenn ich mich nicht irre ...

unlicensed [ʌnˈlaɪsənst] adj (to sell alcohol) ohne Lizenz

unlike [ʌnˈlaɪk] prep (in contrast to) im Gegensatz zu; **it's ~ her to be late** es sieht ihr gar nicht ähnlich, zu spät zu kommen; **unlikely** [ʌnˈlaɪklɪ] adj unwahrscheinlich

unload [ʌnˈləʊd] vt ausladen

unlock [ʌnˈlɒk] vt aufschließen

unlucky [ʌnˈlʌkɪ] adj unglücklich; **to be ~** Pech haben

unmistakable [ʌnmɪˈsteɪkəbl] adj unverkennbar

unnecessary [ʌnˈnesəsərɪ] adj unnötig

unobtainable [ʌnəbˈteɪnəbl] adj nicht erhältlich

unoccupied [ʌnˈɒkjʊpaɪd] adj (seat) frei; (building, room) leer stehend

unpack [ʌnˈpæk] vt, vi auspacken

unpleasant [ʌnˈpleznt] adj unangenehm

unplug [ʌnˈplʌg] vt: **to ~ sth** den Stecker von etw herausziehen

unprecedented [ʌnˈpresɪdəntɪd] adj beispiellos

unpredictable [ʌnprɪˈdɪktəbl] adj (person, weather) unberechenbar

unreasonable [ʌnˈriːznəbl] adj unvernünftig; (demand) übertrieben

unreliable [ʌnrɪˈlaɪəbl] adj unzuverlässig

unsafe [ʌnˈseɪf] adj nicht sicher; (dangerous) gefährlich

unscrew [ʌnˈskruː] vt abschrauben

unsightly [ʌnˈsaɪtlɪ] adj unansehnlich

unskilled [ʌnˈskɪld] adj (worker) ungelernt

unsuccessful [ʌnsəkˈsesfʊl] adj erfolglos

unsuitable [ʌnˈsuːtəbl] adj ungeeignet (for für)

until [ənˈtɪl] prep bis; **not ~** erst; **from Monday ~ Friday** von Montag bis Freitag; **he didn't come home ~ midnight** er kam erst um Mitternacht nach Hause; **~ then** bis dahin ▷ conj bis; **she won't come ~ you invite her** sie kommt erst, wenn du sie einlädst/wenn Sie sie einladen

unusual, unusually [ʌnˈjuːʒʊəl, -ɪ] adj, adv ungewöhnlich

unwanted [ʌnˈwɒntɪd] adj unerwünscht, ungewollt

unwell [ʌnˈwel] adj krank; **to feel ~** sich nicht wohlfühlen

unwilling [ʌnˈwɪlɪŋ] adj: **to be ~ to do sth** nicht bereit sein, etw zu tun

unwind [ʌnˈwaɪnd] irr vt abwickeln ▷ vi (relax) sich entspannen

unwrap [ʌnˈræp] vt auspacken

unzip [ʌnˈzɪp] vt den Reißverschluss aufmachen an +dat; (Inform) entzippen

O KEYWORD

up [ʌp] prep: **to be up sth** oben auf etw dat sein; **to go up sth** (auf) etw akk hinaufgehen; **go up that road** gehen Sie die Straße hinauf

▷ adv **1** (upwards, higher) oben; **put it up a bit higher** stell es etwas weiter nach oben; **up there** oben, dort oben; **up above** hoch oben

2 to be up (out of bed) auf sein; (prices, level) gestiegen sein; (building, tent) stehen

3 up to (as far as) bis; **up to now** bis jetzt

4 to be up to (depending on): **it's up to you** das hängt von dir ab; (equal to): **he's not up to it** (job, task etc) er ist dem nicht gewachsen; (inf: be doing) (showing disapproval, suspicion) **what is he up to?** was führt er im Schilde?; **it's not up to me to decide** die Entscheidung liegt nicht bei mir; **his work is not up to the required standard** seine Arbeit entspricht nicht dem geforderten Niveau
▷ n: **ups and downs** (in life, career) Höhen und Tiefen pl

upbringing ['ʌpbrɪŋɪŋ] n Erziehung f

update [ʌp'deɪt] n (list etc) Aktualisierung f; (software) Update nt ▷ vt (list etc, person) auf den neuesten Stand bringen, aktualisieren

upgrade [ʌp'greɪd] vt (computer) aufrüsten; **we were ~d** das Hotel hat uns ein besseres Zimmer gegeben

upheaval [ʌp'hiːvəl] n Aufruhr m; (Pol) Umbruch m

uphill [ʌp'hɪl] adv bergauf

upon [ə'pɒn] prep see **on**

upper ['ʌpə*] adj obere(r, s); (arm, deck) Ober-

upright ['ʌpraɪt] adj, adv aufrecht

uprising ['ʌpraɪzɪŋ] n Aufstand m

uproar ['ʌprɔː*] n Aufruhr m

upset [ʌp'set] irr vt (overturn) umkippen; (disturb) aufregen; (sadden) bestürzen; (offend) kränken; (plans) durcheinanderbringen ▷ adj (disturbed) aufgeregt; (sad) bestürzt; (offended) gekränkt; • **stomach** ['ʌpset] Magenverstimmung f

upside down [ʌpsaɪd'daʊn]

adv verkehrt herum; (fig) drunter und drüber; **to turn sth ~** (box etc) etw umdrehen/durchwühlen

upstairs [ʌp'steəz] adv oben; (go, take) nach oben

up-to-date ['ʌptə'deɪt] adj modern; (fashion, information) aktuell; **to keep sb ~** jdn auf dem Laufenden halten

upwards ['ʌpwədz] adv nach oben

urban ['ɜːbən] adj städtisch, Stadt-

urge [ɜːdʒ] n Drang m ▷ vt: **to ~ sb to do sth** jdn drängen, etw zu tun; **urgent, urgently** ['ɜːdʒənt, -lɪ] adj, adv dringend

urine ['jʊərɪn] n Urin m

us [ʌs] pron uns; **do they know ~?** kennen sie uns?; **can he help ~?** kann er uns helfen?; **it's ~** wir sind's; **both of ~** wir beide

US, USA nsing abbr = **United States (of America)** USA pl

use [juːs] n (using) Gebrauch m; (for specific purpose) Benutzung f; **to make ~ of** Gebrauch machen von; **in/out of ~** in/außer Gebrauch; **it's no ~** (doing that) es hat keinen Zweck(, das zu tun); **it's (of) no ~ to me** das kann ich nicht brauchen ▷ [juːz] vt benutzen, gebrauchen; (for specific purpose) verwenden; (method) anwenden; **use up** vt aufbrauchen

used [juːd] adj (secondhand) gebraucht ▷ vb aux: **to be ~d to sb/sth** jdn/etw gewöhnt sein, **to get ~d to sth** sich an jdn/etw gewöhnen; **she ~d to live here** sie hat früher mal hier gewohnt; **useful** adj nützlich; **useless** adj nutzlos; (unusable) unbrauchbar; (pointless) zwecklos; **user** ['juːzə*] n Benutzer(in) m(f);

user-friendly *adj* benutzerfreundlich

usual ['juːʒʊəl] *adj* üblich, gewöhnlich; **as ~** wie üblich; **usually** *adv* normalerweise

utensil [juːˈtensl] *n* Gerät *nt*

uterus ['juːtərəs] *n* Gebärmutter *f*

utilize ['juːtɪlaɪz] *vt* verwenden

utmost ['ʌtməʊst] *adj* äußerst; **to do one's ~** sein Möglichstes tun

utter ['ʌtə⁰] *adj* völlig ▷ *vt* von sich geben; **utterly** *adv* völlig

U-turn ['juːtɜːn] *n* (Auto) Wende *f*; **to do a ~** wenden; (*fig*) eine Kehrtwendung machen

vacancy ['veɪkənsɪ] *n* (*job*) offene Stelle; (*room*) freies Zimmer; **vacant** ['veɪkənt] *adj* (*room, toilet*) frei; (*post*) offen; (*building*) leer stehend; **vacate** [vəˈkeɪt] *vt* (*room, building*) räumen; (*seat*) frei machen

vacation [vəˈkeɪʃən] *n* (US) Ferien *pl*, Urlaub *m*; (*at university*) (Semester)ferien *pl*; **to go on ~** in Urlaub fahren; **~ course** Ferienkurs *m*

vaccinate ['væksɪneɪt] *vt* impfen; **vaccination** [væksɪˈneɪʃən] *n* Impfung *f*; **~ card** Impfpass *m*

vacuum ['vækjʊm] *n* Vakuum *nt* ▷ *vt, vi* (staub)saugen; **vacuum (cleaner)** *n* Staubsauger *m*

vagina [vəˈdʒaɪnə] *n* Scheide *f*

vague [veɪg] *adj* (*imprecise*) vage; (*resemblance*) entfernt; **vaguely** *adv* in etwa, irgendwie

vain [veɪn] *adj* (*attempt*)
vergeblich; (*conceited*) eitel; **in
~** vergeblich, umsonst; **vainly** *adv*
(*in vain*) vergeblich

valentine (card)
['væləntaɪn(kɑːd)] *n* Valentins-
karte *f*; **Valentine's Day** *n*
Valentinstag *m*

valid ['vælɪd] *adj* (*ticket, passport
etc*) gültig; (*argument*) stichhaltig;
(*claim*) berechtigt

valley ['vælɪ] *n* Tal *nt*

valuable ['væljuəbl] *adj* wertvoll;
(*time*) kostbar; **valuables** *npl*
Wertsachen *pl*

value ['væljuː] *n* Wert *m* ▷ *vt*
(*appreciate*) schätzen; **value added
tax** *n* Mehrwertsteuer *f*

valve [vælv] *n* Ventil *nt*

van [væn] *n* (*Auto*) Lieferwagen *m*

vanilla [və'nɪlə] *n* Vanille *f*

vanish ['vænɪʃ] *vi* verschwinden

vanity ['vænɪtɪ] *n* Eitelkeit *f*;
vanity case *n* Schminkkoffer *m*

vapor (*US*), **vapour** ['veɪpə*] *n*
(*mist*) Dunst *m*; (*steam*) Dampf
m

variable ['veərɪəbl] *adj* (*weather,
mood*) unbeständig; (*quality*)
unterschiedlich; (*speed, height*)
regulierbar; **varied** ['veərɪd] *adj*
(*interests, selection*) vielseitig;
(*career*) bewegt; (*work, diet*)
abwechslungsreich; **variety**
[və'raɪətɪ] *n* (*diversity*)
Abwechslung *f*; (*assortment*)
Vielfalt *f* (*of* an +*dat*); (*type*) Art *f*;
various ['veərɪəs] *adj*
verschieden

varnish ['vɑːnɪʃ] *n* Lack *m* ▷ *vt*
lackieren

vary ['veərɪ] *vt* (*alter*) verändern
▷ *vi* (*be different*) unterschiedlich
sein; (*fluctuate*) sich verändern;
(*prices*) schwanken

vase [vɑːz, ?? veɪz] (*US*) *n* Vase *f*

vast [vɑːst] *adj* riesig; (*area*) weit

VAT [væt] *abbr* = **value added tax**
Mehrwertsteuer *f*, MwSt.

Vatican ['vætɪkən] *n*: **the ~** der
Vatikan

VCR [viːsiːˈɑː°] *abbr* = **video
cassette recorder** Videorekorder
m

VD [viːˈdiː] *abbr* = **venereal
disease** Geschlechtskrankheit *f*

VDU [viːdiːˈjuː] *abbr* = **visual
display unit**

veal [viːl] *n* Kalbfleisch *nt*

vegan ['viːgən] *n* Veganer(in)
m(f)

vegetable ['vedʒtəbl] *n* Gemüse
nt

vegetarian [vedʒɪ'teərɪən] *n*
Vegetarier(in) *m(f)* ▷ *adj*
vegetarisch

veggie ['vedʒɪ] *n* (*fam*)
Vegetarier(in) *m(f)*; Gemüse *nt*
▷ *adj* vegetarisch; **veggieburger**
n Veggieburger *m*, Gemüseburger
m

vehicle ['viːɪkl] *n* Fahrzeug *nt*

veil [veɪl] *n* Schleier *m*

vein [veɪn] *n* Ader *f*

Velcro® ['velkrəʊ] *n* Klettband
nt

velvet ['velvɪt] *n* Samt *m*

vending machine
['vendɪŋməʃiːn] *n* Automat *m*

venetian blind [vɪˈniːʃən'blaɪnd]
n Jalousie *f*

Venezuela [vene'zweɪlə] *n*
Venezuela *n*

Venice ['venɪs] *n* Venedig *nt*

venison ['venɪsn] *n* Rehfleisch
nt

vent [vent] *n* Öffnung *f*

ventilate ['ventɪleɪt] *vt* lüften;
ventilation [ventɪ'leɪʃən] *n*
Belüftung *f*; **ventilator**
['ventɪleɪtə°] *n* (*in room*)
Ventilator *m*; **to be on a ~** (*Med*)
künstlich beatmet werden

venture ['ventʃə°] *n* (*project*)

Unternehmung f; (Comm)
Unternehmen nt ▷ vi (go) (sich)
wagen

venue ['venju:] n (for concert etc)
Veranstaltungsort m; (Sport)
Austragungsort m

verb [vɜ:b] n Verb nt; **verbal** adj
(agreement) mündlich; (skills)
sprachlich; **verbally** adv
mündlich

verdict ['vɜ:dɪkt] n Urteil nt

verge [vɜ:dʒ] n (of road)
(Straßen)rand m; **to be on the ~ of**
doing sth im Begriff sein, etw zu
tun ▷ vi: **to ~ on** grenzen an +akk

verification [verɪfɪˈkeɪʃən] n
(confirmation) Bestätigung f;
(check) Überprüfung f; **verify**
['verɪfaɪ] vt (confirm) bestätigen;
(check) überprüfen

vermin ['vɜ:mɪn] npl Schädlinge
pl; (insects) Ungeziefer nt

verruca [veˈruːkə] n Warze f

versatile ['vɜ:sətaɪl] adj
vielseitig

verse [vɜ:s] n (poetry) Poesie f;
(stanza) Strophe f

version ['vɜ:ʃən] n Version f

versus ['vɜ:səs] prep gegen

vertical ['vɜ:tɪkəl] adj senkrecht,
vertikal

very ['verɪ] adv sehr; **~ much** sehr
▷ adj: **the ~ book I need** genau
das Buch, das ich brauche; **at that**
~ moment gerade in dem
Augenblick; **at the ~ top** ganz
oben; **the ~ best** der/die/das
Allerbeste

vest [vest] n (Brit) Unterhemd nt;
(US: waistcoat) Weste f

vet [vet] n Tierarzt m, Tierärztin f

veto ['vi:təʊ] (pl -es) n Veto nt
▷ vt sein Veto einlegen gegen

VHF abbr = **very high frequency**
UKW

via ['vaɪə] prep über +akk

viable ['vaɪəbl] adj (plan)

realisierbar; (company) rentabel

vibrate [vaɪˈbreɪt] vi vibrieren;
vibration [vaɪˈbreɪʃən] n Vibration f

vicar ['vɪkə°] n Pfarrer(in) m(f)

vice [vaɪs] n (evil) Laster nt; (Tech)
Schraubstock m ▷ pref Vize-;
~chairman stellvertretender
Vorsitzender; **~president**
Vizepräsident(in) m(f)

vice versa ['vaɪsˈvɜ:sə] adv
umgekehrt

vicinity [vɪˈsɪnɪtɪ] n: **in the ~** in
der Nähe (of +gen)

vicious ['vɪʃəs] adj (violent)
brutal; (malicious) gemein; **vicious**
circle n Teufelskreis m

victim ['vɪktɪm] n Opfer nt

Victorian [vɪkˈtɔ:rɪən] adj
viktorianisch

victory ['vɪktərɪ] n Sieg m

video ['vɪdɪəʊ] (pl -s) adj Video-
▷ n Video nt; (recorder)
Videorekorder m ▷ vt (auf Video)
aufnehmen; **video camera** n
Videokamera f; **video cassette** n
Videokassette f; **video clip** n
Videoclip m; **video game** n
Videospiel nt; **video recorder** n
Videorekorder m; **video shop** n
Videothek f; **videotape** n
Videoband nt ▷ vt (auf Video)
aufnehmen

Vienna [vɪˈenə] n Wien nt

Vietnam [vjetˈnæm] n Vietnam
nt

view [vju:] n (sight) Blick m (of auf
+akk); (vista) Aussicht f; (opinion)
Ansicht f, Meinung f; **in ~ of**
angesichts +gen ▷ vt (situation,
event) betrachten; (house)
besichtigen; **viewer** n (for slides)
Diabetrachter m; (TV)
Zuschauer(in) m(f); **viewpoint** n
(fig) Standpunkt m

vigilant ['vɪdʒɪlənt] adj
wachsam

vile [vaɪl] adj abscheulich; (weather, food) scheußlich

village ['vɪlɪdʒ] n Dorf nt; **villager** n Dorfbewohner(in) m(f)

villain ['vɪlən] n Schurke m; (in film, story) Bösewicht m

vine [vaɪn] n (Wein)rebe f

vinegar ['vɪnɪgə°] n Essig m

vineyard ['vɪnjɑːd] n Weinberg m

vintage ['vɪntɪdʒ] n (of wine) Jahrgang m; **vintage wine** n edler Wein

vinyl ['vaɪnɪl] n Vinyl nt

viola [vɪ'əʊlə] n Bratsche f

violate ['vaɪəleɪt] vt (treaty) brechen; (rights, rule) verletzen

violence ['vaɪələns] n (brutality) Gewalt f; (of person) Gewalttätigkeit f; **violent** adj (brutal) brutal; (death) gewaltsam

violet ['vaɪələt] n Veilchen nt

violin [vaɪə'lɪn] n Geige f, Violine f

VIP abbr = **very important person** VIP mf

virgin ['vɜːdʒɪn] n Jungfrau f

Virgo ['vɜːgəʊ] n (Astr) Jungfrau f

virile ['vɪraɪl] adj (man) männlich

virtual ['vɜːtjʊəl] adj (Inform) virtuell; **virtually** adv praktisch; **virtual reality** n virtuelle Realität

virtue ['vɜːtjuː] n Tugend f; **by ~ of** aufgrund +gen; **virtuous** ['vɜːtjʊəs] adj tugendhaft

virus ['vaɪərəs] n (Med, Inform) Virus nt

visa ['viːzə] n Visum nt

visibility [vɪzɪ'bɪlɪtɪ] n (Meteo) Sichtweite f; **good/poor ~** gute/schlechte Sicht; **visible** ['vɪzəbl] adj sichtbar; (evident) sichtlich; **visibly** adv sichtlich

vision ['vɪʒən] n (power of sight) Sehvermögen nt; (foresight) Weitblick m; (dream, image) Vision f

visit ['vɪzɪt] n Besuch m; (stay) Aufenthalt m ▷ vt besuchen; **visiting hours** npl Besuchszeiten pl; **visitor** n Besucher(in) m(f); **~'s book** Gästebuch nt; **visitor centre** n Informationszentrum nt

visor ['vaɪzə°] n (on helmet) Visier nt; (Auto) Blende f

visual ['vɪzjʊəl] adj Seh-; (image, joke) visuell; **~ aid** n Anschauungsmaterial nt; **~ display unit** Monitor m; **visualize** vt sich vorstellen; **visually** adv visuell; **~ impaired** sehbehindert

vital ['vaɪtl] adj (essential) unerlässlich, wesentlich; (argument, moment) entscheidend; **vitality** [vaɪ'tælɪtɪ] n Vitalität f; **vitally** adv äußerst

vitamin ['vɪtəmɪn] n Vitamin nt

vivacious [vɪ'veɪʃəs] adj lebhaft

vivid ['vɪvɪd] adj (description) anschaulich; (memory) lebhaft; (colour) leuchtend

V-neck ['viːnek] n V-Ausschnitt m

vocabulary [vəʊ'kæbjʊlərɪ] n Wortschatz m, Vokabular nt

vocal ['vəʊkəl] adj (of the voice) Stimm-; (group) Gesangs-; (protest, person) lautstark

vocation [vəʊ'keɪʃən] n Berufung f; **vocational** adj Berufs-

vodka ['vɒdkə] n Wodka m

voice [vɔɪs] n Stimme f ▷ vt äußern; **voice mail** n Voicemail f

void [vɔɪd] n Leere f ▷ adj (Jur) ungültig; **~ of** (ganz) ohne

volcano [vɒl'keɪnəʊ] n (pl **~es**) n Vulkan m

volley ['vɒlɪ] n (Tennis) Volley m; **volleyball** n Volleyball m

volt [vəʊlt] n Volt nt; **voltage** n Spannung f

volume ['vɒljuːm] n (of sound) Lautstärke f; (space occupied by sth)

Volumen nt; (*size, amount*) Umfang m; (*book*) Band m; **volume control** n Lautstärkeregler m

voluntary, voluntarily ['vɒləntərɪ, -lɪ] adj, adv freiwillig; (*unpaid*) ehrenamtlich; **volunteer** [vɒlən'tɪə°] n Freiwillige(r) mf ▷ vi sich freiwillig melden ▷ vt: **to ~ to do sth** sich anbieten, etw zu tun

voluptuous [və'lʌptjʊəs] adj sinnlich

vomit ['vɒmɪt] vi sich übergeben

vote [vəʊt] n Stimme f; (*ballot*) Wahl f; (*result*) Abstimmungsergebnis nt; (*right to vote*) Wahlrecht nt ▷ vt (*elect*) wählen; **they ~d him chairman** sie wählten ihn zum Vorsitzenden ▷ vi wählen; **to ~ for/against sth** für/gegen etw stimmen; **voter** n Wähler(in) m(f)

voucher ['vaʊtʃə°] n Gutschein m

vow [vaʊ] n Gelöbnis nt ▷ vt: **to ~ to do sth** geloben, etw zu tun

vowel ['vaʊəl] n Vokal m

voyage ['vɔɪdʒ] n Reise f

vulgar ['vʌlgə°] adj vulgär, ordinär

vulnerable ['vʌlnərəbl] adj verwundbar; (*sensitive*) verletzlich

vulture ['vʌltʃə°] n Geier m

W

W abbr = **west** W

wade [weɪd] vi (*in water*) waten

wafer ['weɪfə°] n Waffel f; (*Rel*) Hostie f; **wafer-thin** adj hauchdünn

waffle ['wɒfl] n Waffel f; (*Brit fam: empty talk*) Geschwafel nt ▷ vi (*Brit fam*) schwafeln

wag [wæg] vt (*tail*) wedeln mit

wage [weɪdʒ] n Lohn m

waggon (*Brit*), **wagon** ['wægən] n (*horse-drawn*) Fuhrwerk nt; (*Brit Rail*) Waggon m; (*US Auto*) Wagen m

waist [weɪst] n Taille f; **waistcoat** n (*Brit*) Weste f; **waistline** n Taille f

wait [weɪt] n Wartezeit f ▷ vi warten (*for* auf +*akk*); **to ~ and see** abwarten; **~ a minute** Moment mal!; **wait up** vi aufbleiben

waiter n Kellner m; **~!** Herr Ober!

waiting n: **"no ~"** „Halteverbot";

waiting list n Warteliste f;
waiting room n (Med)
Wartezimmer nt; (Rail) Wartesaal
m
waitress n Kellnerin f
wake [weɪk] (**woke** o **waked**,
woken o **waked**) vt wecken ▷ vi
aufwachen; **wake up** vt
aufwecken ▷ vi aufwachen;
wake-up call n (Tel) Weckruf m
Wales ['weɪlz] n Wales nt
walk [wɔːk] n Spaziergang m;
(ramble) Wanderung f; (route) Weg
m; **to go for a ~** spazieren gehen;
it's only a five-minute ~ es sind
nur fünf Minuten zu Fuß ▷ vi
gehen; (stroll) spazieren gehen;
(ramble) wandern ▷ vt (dog)
ausführen; **walking** n: **to go
~ wandern; walking shoes** npl
Wanderschuhe pl; **walking stick** n
Spazierstock m
Walkman® [ˈwɔːkmən] n Walkman®
m
wall [wɔːl] n (inside) Wand f;
(outside) Mauer f
wallet ['wɒlɪt] n Brieftasche
f
wallpaper ['wɔːlpeɪpə'] n
Tapete f; (Inform)
Bildschirmhintergrund m ▷ vt
tapezieren
walnut ['wɔːlnʌt] n (nut)
Walnuss f
waltz [wɔːlts] n Walzer m
wander [ˈwɒndə'] vi (person)
herumwandern
want [wɒnt] n (lack) Mangel m
(of an +dat); (need) Bedürfnis n; **for
~ of** aus Mangel an +dat ▷ vt
(desire) wollen; (need) brauchen; **I
~ to stay here** ich will hier
bleiben; **he doesn't ~ to** er will
nicht
WAP phone ['wæpfəʊn] n
WAP-Handy nt
war [wɔː'] n Krieg m

ward [wɔːd] n (in hospital)
Station f; (child) Mündel nt
warden [ˈwɔːdən] n Aufseher(in)
m(f); (in youth hostel) Herbergsvater
m, Herbergsmutter f
wardrobe ['wɔːdrəʊb] n
Kleiderschrank m
warehouse ['wɛəhaʊs] n
Lagerhaus nt
warfare ['wɔːfɛə'] n Krieg m;
(techniques) Kriegsführung f
warm [wɔːm] adj warm;
(welcome) herzlich; **I'm ~** mir ist
warm ▷ vt wärmen; (food)
aufwärmen; **warm over** vt (US:
food) aufwärmen; **warm up** vt
(food) aufwärmen; (room)
erwärmen ▷ vi (food, room) warm
werden; (Sport) sich aufwärmen;
warmly adv warm; (welcome)
herzlich; **warmth** n Wärme f; (of
welcome) Herzlichkeit f
warn [wɔːn] vt warnen (of,
against vor +dat); **to ~ sb not to do
sth** jdn davor warnen, etw zu tun;
warning n Warnung f; **warning
light** n Warnlicht nt; **warning
triangle** n (Auto) Warndreieck nt
warranty ['wɒrəntɪ] n Garantie f
wart [wɔːt] n Warze f
wary ['wɛərɪ] adj vorsichtig;
(suspicious) misstrauisch
was [wɒz, wəz] pt of **be**
wash [wɒʃ] n: **to have a ~** sich
waschen; **it's in the ~** es ist in der
Wäsche ▷ vt waschen; (plates,
glasses etc) abwaschen; **to ~ one's
hands** sich dat die Hände
waschen; **to ~ the dishes** (das
Geschirr) abwaschen ▷ vi (clean
oneself) sich waschen; **wash off** vt
abwaschen; **wash up** vt (Brit:
wash dishes) abwaschen; (US: clean
oneself) sich waschen; **washable**
adj waschbar; **washbag** n (US)
Kulturbeutel m; **washbasin** n

Waschbecken nt; **washcloth** n (US) Waschlappen m; **washer** n (Tech) Dichtungsring m; (washing machine) Waschmaschine f; **washing** n (laundry) Wäsche f; **washing machine** n Waschmaschine f; **washing powder** n Waschpulver nt; **washing-up** n (Brit) Abwasch m; **to do the ~** abwaschen; **washing-up liquid** n (Brit) Spülmittel nt; **washroom** n (US) Toilette f

wasn't ['wɒznt] contr of **was not**
wasp [wɒsp] n Wespe f
waste [weɪst] n (materials) Abfall m; (wasting) Verschwendung f; **it's a ~ of time** das ist Zeitverschwendung ▷ adj (superfluous) überschüssig ▷ vt verschwenden (on an +akk); (opportunity) vertun; **waste bin** n Abfalleimer m; **wastepaper basket** n Papierkorb m
watch [wɒtʃ] n (timepiece) (Armband)uhr f ▷ vt (observe) beobachten; (guard) aufpassen auf +akk; (film, play, programme) sich dat ansehen; **to ~ TV** fernsehen ▷ vi zusehen; (guard) Wache halten; **to ~ for** sich nach jdm/etw Ausschau halten; **~ out** pass auf!; **watchdog** n Wachhund m; (fig) Aufsichtsbehörde f; **watchful** adj wachsam
water ['wɔːtə°] n Wasser nt ▷ vt (plant) gießen ▷ vi (eye) tränen; **my mouth is ~ing** mir läuft das Wasser im Mund zusammen; **water down** vt verdünnen; **watercolor** (US), **watercolour** n (painting) Aquarell nt; (paint) Wasserfarbe f; **watercress** n (Brunnen)kresse f; **waterfall** n Wasserfall m; **watering can** n Gießkanne f; **water level** n

Wasserstand m; **watermelon** n Wassermelone f; **waterproof** adj wasserdicht; **water-skiing** n Wasserskilaufen nt; **water sports** npl Wassersport m; **watertight** adj wasserdicht; **water wings** npl Schwimmflügel pl; **watery** adj wässerig

wave [weɪv] n Welle f ▷ vt (move to and fro) schwenken; (hand, flag) winken mit ▷ vi (person) winken; (flag) wehen; **wavelength** n Wellenlänge f; **to be on the same ~** (fig) die gleiche Wellenlänge haben; **wavy** ['weɪvɪ] adj wellig
wax [wæks] n Wachs nt; (in ear) Ohrenschmalz nt
way [weɪ] n Weg m; (direction) Richtung f; (manner) Art f; **can you tell me the ~ to ... ?** wie komme ich (am besten) zu ... ?; **we went the wrong ~** wir sind in die falsche Richtung gefahren/gegangen; **to lose one's ~** sich verirren; **to make ~ for** sb/sth jdm/etw Platz machen; **to get one's own ~** seinen Willen durchsetzen; **"give ~"** (Auto) „Vorfahrt achten"; **the other ~ round** andersherum; **one ~ or another** irgendwie; **in a ~** in gewisser Weise; **in the ~** im Weg; **by the ~** übrigens; **"~ in"** „Eingang"; **"~ out"** „Ausgang"; **no ~** (fam) kommt nicht infrage!
we [wiː] pron wir
weak [wiːk] adj schwach; **weaken** vt schwächen ▷ vi schwächer werden
wealth [welθ] n Reichtum m; **wealthy** adj reich
weapon ['wepən] n Waffe f
wear [weə°] (wore, worn) vt (have on) tragen; **what shall I ~?** was soll ich anziehen? ▷ vi (become worn) sich abnutzen ▷ n: **~ (and tear)** Abnutzung f; **wear**

off vi (diminish) nachlassen; **wear out** vt abnutzen; (person) erschöpfen ▷ vi sich abnutzen

weather ['weðə°] n Wetter nt; **I'm feeling under the ~** ich fühle mich nicht ganz wohl; **weather forecast** n Wettervorhersage f

weave [wi:v] (wove o weaved, woven o weaved) vt (cloth) weben; (basket etc) flechten

web [web] n (a. fig) Netz nt; **the Web** das Web, das Internet; **webcam** ['webkæm] n Webcam f; **web page** n Webseite f; **website** n Website f

we'd [wi:d] contr of **we had; we would**

Wed abbr = **Wednesday** Mi.

wedding ['wedɪŋ] n Hochzeit f; **wedding anniversary** n Hochzeitstag m; **wedding dress** n Hochzeitskleid nt; **wedding ring** n Ehering m

wedding shower n (US) Party für die zukünftige Braut

wedge [wedʒ] n (under door etc) Keil m; (of cheese etc) Stück nt, Ecke f

Wednesday ['wenzdeɪ] n Mittwoch m; see also **Tuesday**

wee [wi:] adj klein ▷ vi (fam) Pipi machen

weed [wi:d] n Unkraut nt ▷ vt jäten

week [wi:k] n Woche f; **twice a ~** zweimal in der Woche; **a ~ on Friday/Friday ~** Freitag in einer Woche; **a ~ last Friday** letzten Freitag vor einer Woche; **in two ~s' time, in two ~s** in zwei Wochen; **for ~s** wochenlang; **weekday** n Wochentag m; **weekend** n Wochenende nt; **weekend break** n Wochenendurlaub m; **weekly** adj,

adv wöchentlich; (magazine) Wochen-

weep [wi:p] (**wept, wept**) vi weinen

weigh [weɪ] vt, vi wiegen; **it ~s 20 kilos** es wiegt 20 Kilo; **weigh up** vt abwägen; (person) einschätzen; **weight** [weɪt] n Gewicht nt; **to lose/put on ~** abnehmen/zunehmen; **weightlifting** n Gewichtheben nt; **weight training** n Krafttraining nt; **weighty** adj (important) schwerwiegend

weird [wɪəd] adj seltsam; **weirdo** ['wɪədəʊ] n Spinner(in) m(f)

welcome ['welkəm] n Empfang m ▷ adj willkommen; (news) angenehm; **~ to London** willkommen in London! ▷ vt begrüßen; **welcoming** adj freundlich

welfare ['welfeə°] n Wohl nt; (US: social security) Sozialhilfe f; **welfare state** n Wohlfahrtsstaat m

well [wel] n Brunnen m ▷ adj (in good health) gesund; **are you ~?** geht es dir/Ihnen gut?; **to feel ~** sich wohlfühlen; **get ~ soon** gute Besserung! ▷ interj nun; **~, I don't know** nun, ich weiß nicht ▷ adv gut; **~ done** gut gemacht!; **it may ~ be** das kann wohl sein; **as ~** (in addition) auch; **~ over 60** weit über 60

we'll [wi:l] contr of **we will; we shall**

well-behaved [welbɪ'heɪvd] adj brav; **well-being** n Wohl nt; **well-built** adj (person) gut gebaut; **well done** adj (steak) durchgebraten; **well-earned** adj wohlverdient

wellingtons ['welɪŋtənz] npl Gummistiefel pl

well-known [wel'nəʊn] adj bekannt; **well-off** adj (wealthy)

wohlhabend; **well-paid** adj gut
bezahlt

Welsh [welʃ] adj walisisch ▷ n
(language) Walisisch nt; **the ~** pl die
Waliser pl; **Welshman** (pl **-men**) n
Waliser m; **Welshwoman** (pl
-women) n Waliserin f

went [went] pt of **go**

wept [wept] pt, pp of **weep**

were [wɜ:] pt of **be**

we're [wɪə] contr of **we are**

weren't [wɜ:nt] contr of **were not**

west [west] n Westen m; **the
West** (Pol) der Westen ▷ adv (go,
face) nach Westen ▷ adj West-;
westbound adj (in) Richtung
Westen; **western** adj
West-, westlich; **Western Europe**
Westeuropa nt ▷ n (Cine) Western
m; **West Germany** n: **(the
former) ~** (das ehemalige)
Westdeutschland,
Westdeutschland n; **westwards**
['westwədz] adv nach Westen

wet [wet] **(wet, wet)** vt: **to
~ oneself** in die Hose machen
▷ adj nass, feucht; **"~ paint"**
„frisch gestrichen"; **wet suit** n
Taucheranzug m

we've [wi:v] contr of **we have**

whale [weɪl] n Wal m

wharf [wɔ:f] (pl **-s** o **wharves**) n
Kai m

KEYWORD

what [wɒt] adj **1** (in questions)
welche(r, s) was für ein(e);
what size is it? welche Größe ist
das?
2 (in exclamations) was für ein(e);
what a mess! was für ein
Durcheinander!
▷ pron (interrogative/relative) was;
what are you doing? was machst
du/machen Sie gerade?; **what are
you talking about?** wovon redest

du/reden Sie?; **what's your
name?** wie heißt du/heißen Sie?;
what is it called? wie heißt das?;
what about ...? wie wär's mit ...?;
I saw what you did ich habe
gesehen, was du gemacht
hast/Sie gemacht haben
▷ excl (disbelieving) wie, was;
what, no coffee! wie, kein
Kaffee?; **I've crashed the car —
what!** ich hatte einen
Autounfall — was!

whatever pron: **I'll do ~ you
want** ich tue alles, was du
willst/Sie wollen; **~ he says** egal,
was er sagt

what's [wɒts] contr of **what is;
what has**

wheat [wi:t] n Weizen m

wheel [wi:l] n Rad nt; (steering
wheel) Lenkrad nt ▷ vt (bicycle,
trolley) schieben; **wheelbarrow** n
Schubkarren m; **wheelchair** n
Rollstuhl m; **wheel clamp** n
Parkkralle f

KEYWORD

when [wen] adv wann
▷ conj **1** (at, during, after the time
that) wenn; (in past) als; **she was
reading when I came in** sie las,
als ich hereinkam; **be careful
when you cross the road** sei
vorsichtig, wenn du über die
Straße gehst/seien Sie vorsichtig,
wenn Sie über die Straße gehen
2 (on, at which) als; **on the day
when I met him** an dem Tag, an
dem ich ihn traf
3 (whereas) wo ... doch

whenever adv (every time) immer
wenn; **come ~ you like** komm,
wann immer du willst/kommen
Sie, wann immer sie wollen

where [wɛəʳ] adv wo; ~ **are you going?** wohin gehst du/gehen Sie?; ~ **are you from?** woher kommst du/kommen Sie? ▷ conj wo; **that's ~ I used to live** da habe ich früher gewohnt; **whereabouts** [wɛərəˈbaʊts] adv wo ▷ n [ˈwɛərəbaʊts] Aufenthaltsort m; **whereas** [wɛərˈæz] conj während, wohingegen; **whereby** adv wodurch; **wherever** [wɛərˈɛvəʳ] conj wo immer; ~ **that may be** wo immer das sein mag; ~ **I go** überall, wohin ich gehe

whether [ˈwɛðəʳ] conj ob

⦿ KEYWORD

which [wɪtʃ] adj 1 (interrogative) (direct, indirect) welche(r, s); **which one?** welche? ▷ pron
~ **in which case** in diesem Fall; **by which time** zu dieser Zeit
▷ pron 1 (interrogative) welche(r, s); (of people also) wer
2 (relative) der/die/das; (referring to people) was; **the apple which you ate/which is on the table** der Apfel, den du gegessen hast/der auf dem Tisch liegt; **he said he saw her, which is true** er sagte, er habe sie gesehen, was auch stimmt

whichever adj, pron welche(r, s) auch immer

while [waɪl] n: **a** ~ eine Weile; **for a** ~ eine Zeit lang; **a short** ~ **ago** vor Kurzem ▷ conj während; (although) obwohl

whine [waɪn] vi (person) jammern

whip [wɪp] n Peitsche f ▷ vt (beat) peitschen; **~ped cream** Schlagsahne f

whirl [wɜːl] vt, vi herumwirbeln;

whirlpool n (in river, sea) Strudel m; (pool) Whirlpool m

whisk [wɪsk] n Schneebesen m ▷ vt (cream etc) schlagen

whisker [ˈwɪskəʳ] n (of animal) Schnurrhaar nt; **~s** pl (of man) Backenbart m

whisk(e)y [ˈwɪskɪ] n Whisky m

whisper [ˈwɪspəʳ] vi, vt flüstern; **to ~ sth to sb** jdm etw zuflüstern

whistle [ˈwɪsl] n Pfiff m; (instrument) Pfeife f ▷ vt, vi pfeifen

white [waɪt] n (of egg) Eiweiß nt; (of eye) Weiße nt ▷ adj weiß; (with fear) blass; (coffee) mit Milch/Sahne; **White House** n: **the** ~ das Weiße Haus; **white lie** n Notlüge f; **white meat** n helles Fleisch; **white sauce** n weiße Soße; **white water rafting** n Rafting nt; **white wine** n Weißwein m

Whitsun [ˈwɪtsn] n Pfingsten nt

⦿ KEYWORD

who [huː] pron 1 (interrogative) wer; (akk) wen; (dat) wem; **who is it?, who's there?** wer ist da? 2 (relative) der/die/das; **the woman/man who spoke to me** die Frau/der Mann, die/der mit mir sprach

whoever [huːˈɛvəʳ] pron wer auch immer; ~ **you choose** wen auch immer du wählst/Sie wählen

whole [həʊl] adj ganz ▷ n Ganze nt; **the ~ of my family** meine ganze Familie; **on the ~** im Großen und Ganzen; (*in) ~**foodfood** n (Brit) Vollwertkost f; **~ store** Bioladen m; **wholeheartedly** adv voll und ganz; **wholemeal** adj (Brit) Vollkorn-; **wholesale** adv (buy, sell) im Großhandel; **wholesome**

adj gesund; **whole wheat** adj
Vollkorn-; **wholly** ['həʊlɪ] adv
völlig

 KEYWORD

whom [hu:m] pron 1
(*interrogative*) (*akk*) wen; (*dat*) wem;
whom did you see? wen hast
du/haben Sie gesehen?; **to whom
did you give it?** wem hast
du/haben Sie es gegeben?
2 (*relative*) (*akk*) den/die/das; (*dat*)
dem/der/dem; **the man whom
I saw/to whom I spoke** der
Mann, den ich sah/mit dem ich
sprach

whooping cough ['hu:pɪŋkɒf]
n Keuchhusten m
whose [hu:z] adj (*in questions*)
wessen; (*in relative clauses*)
dessen/deren/dessen, deren pl;
~ bike is that? wessen Fahrrad ist
das? ▷ pron (*in questions*) wessen;
~ is this? wem gehört das?

 KEYWORD

why [waɪ] adv warum, weshalb
▷ conj warum, weshalb; **that's
not why I'm here** ich bin nicht
deswegen hier; **that's the reason
why** deshalb
▷ excl (*expressing surprise, shock*) na
so was; (*explaining*) also dann;
why, it's you! na so was, du
bist/Sie sind es!

wicked ['wɪkɪd] adj böse; (*fam:
great*) geil
wide [waɪd] adj breit; (*skirt,
trousers*) weit; (*selection*) groß
▷ adv weit; **wide-angle lens** n
Weitwinkelobjektiv nt;
wide-awake adj hellwach;
widely adv weit; **~ known**

allgemein bekannt; **widen** vt
verbreitern; (*fig*) erweitern;
wide-open adj weit offen;
widescreen TV n
Breitbildfernseher m; **widespread**
adj weit verbreitet

widow ['wɪdəʊ] n Witwe f;
widowed adj verwitwet;
widower n Witwer m
width [wɪdθ] n Breite f
wife [waɪf] (pl **wives**) n
(Ehe)frau f
wig [wɪg] n Perücke f
wiggle ['wɪgl] vt wackeln mit
wild [waɪld] adj (*violent*)
heftig; (*plan, idea*) verrückt ▷ n: **in
the ~** in freier Wildbahn; **wildlife**
n Tier- und Pflanzenwelt f; **wildly**
adv wild; (*exaggerated*) maßlos

 KEYWORD

will [wɪl] vb aux 1 (*forms future
tense*) werden; **I'll finish it
tomorrow** ich mache es morgen
zu Ende
2 (*in conjectures, predictions*) **he will**
o **he'll be there by now** er dürfte
jetzt da sein; **that will be the
postman** das wird der Postbote
sein
3 (*in commands, requests, offers*) **will
you be quiet!** sei/seien Sie
endlich still!; **will you help me?**
hilfst du/helfen Sie mir?; **will you
have a cup of tea?** trinkst
du/trinken Sie eine Tasse Tee?; **I
won't put up with it!** das lasse ich
mir nicht gefallen!
▷ vt wollen
▷ n Wille m; (*jur*) Testament
nt

willing adj bereitwillig; **to be ~ to
do sth** bereit sein, etw zu tun;
willingly adv gern(e)
willow ['wɪləʊ] n Weide f

willpower ['wɪlpauə°] n Willenskraft f

wimp [wɪmp] n Weichei nt

win [wɪn] (**won, won**) vt, vi gewinnen ▷ n Sieg m; **win over, win round** vt für sich gewinnen

wind [waɪnd] (**wound, wound**) vt (rope, bandage) wickeln; **wind down** vt (car window) herunterkurbeln; (clock) aufziehen; **wind up** vt (clock) aufziehen; (car window) hochkurbeln; (meeting, speech) abschließen; (person) aufziehen, ärgern

wind [wɪnd] n Wind m; (Med) Blähungen pl

wind instrument ['wɪndɪnstrəmənt] n Blasinstrument nt; **windmill** n Windmühle f

window ['wɪndəʊ] n Fenster nt; (counter) Schalter m; **~ of opportunity** Chance f, Gelegenheit f; **window box** n Blumenkasten m; **windowpane** n Fensterscheibe f; **window-shopping** n: **to go ~** einen Schaufensterbummel machen; **windowsill** n Fensterbrett nt

windpipe ['wɪndpaɪp] n Luftröhre f; **windscreen** n (Brit) Windschutzscheibe f; **windscreen wiper** n (Brit) Scheibenwischer m; **windshield** n (US) Windschutzscheibe f; **windshield wiper** n (US) Scheibenwischer m; **windsurfer** n Windsurfer(in) m(f); (board) Surfbrett nt; **windsurfing** n Windsurfen nt

windy ['wɪndɪ] adj windig

wine [waɪn] n Wein m; **wine bar** n Weinlokal nt; **wineglass** n Weinglas nt; **wine list** n Weinkarte f; **wine tasting** n (event) Weinprobe f

wing [wɪŋ] n Flügel m; (Brit Auto) Kotflügel m; **~s** pl (Theat) Kulissen pl

wink [wɪŋk] vi zwinkern; **to ~ at sb** jdm zuzwinkern

winner ['wɪnə°] n Gewinner(in) m(f); (Sport) Sieger(in) m(f); **winning** adj (team, horse etc) siegreich; **~ number** Gewinnzahl f ▷ n **~s** pl Gewinn m

winter ['wɪntə°] n Winter m; **winter sports** npl Wintersport m; **wint(e)ry** ['wɪntrɪ] adj winterlich

wipe [waɪp] vt abwischen; **to ~ one's nose** sich dat die Nase putzen; **to ~ one's feet** (on mat) sich dat die Schuhe abtreten; **wipe off** vt abwischen; **wipe out** vt (destroy) vernichten; (data, debt) löschen; (epidemic etc) ausrotten

wire [waɪə°] n Draht m; (Elec) Leitung f; (US: telegram) Telegramm nt ▷ vt (plug in) anschließen; (US Tel) telegrafieren (sb sth jdm jdm etw); **wireless** ['waɪələs] adj drahtlos

wisdom ['wɪzdəm] n Weisheit f; **wisdom tooth** n Weisheitszahn m

wise, wisely [waɪz, -lɪ] adj, adv weise

wish [wɪʃ] n Wunsch m (for nach); **with best ~es** (in letter) herzliche Grüße ▷ vt wünschen, wollen; **to ~ sb good luck/Merry Christmas** jdm viel Glück/frohe Weihnachten wünschen; **I ~ I'd never seen him** ich wünschte, ich hätte ihn nie gesehen

witch [wɪtʃ] n Hexe f

O KEYWORD

with [wɪð] prep **1** (accompanying, in the company of) mit; **we stayed with friends** wir übernachteten

bei Freunden; **I'll be with you in a minute** einen Augenblick, ich bin sofort da; **I'm not with you** (I don't understand) das verstehe ich nicht; **to be with it** (inf) (up-to-date) auf dem Laufenden sein; (alert) (voll) da sein if **2** (descriptive, indicating manner etc) mit; **the man with the grey hat** der Mann mit dem grauen Hut; **red with anger** rot vor Wut

withdraw [wɪð'drɔː] irr vt zurückziehen; (money) abheben; (comment) zurücknehmen ▷ vi sich zurückziehen

wither ['wɪðə°] vi (plant) verwelken

withhold [wɪð'həʊld] irr vt vorenthalten (from sb jdm)

within [wɪð'ɪn] prep innerhalb +gen; **~ walking distance** zu Fuß erreichbar

without [wɪð'aʊt] prep ohne; **~ asking** ohne zu fragen

withstand [wɪð'stænd] irr vt standhalten +dat

witness ['wɪtnəs] n Zeuge m, Zeugin f ▷ vt Zeuge sein; **witness box, witness stand** (US) n Zeugenstand m

witty ['wɪtɪ] adj geistreich

wives [waɪvz] pl of **wife**

WMD abbr = **weapon of mass destruction** Massenvernichtungswaffe

wobble ['wɒbl] vi wackeln; **wobbly** adj wackelig

wok [wɒk] n Wok m

woke [wəʊk] pt of **wake**

woken ['wəʊkn] pp of **wake**

wolf [wʊlf] (pl **wolves**) n Wolf m

woman ['wʊmən] (pl **women**) n Frau f

womb [wuːm] n Gebärmutter f

women ['wɪmɪn] pl of **woman**

won [wʌn] pt, pp of **win**

wonder ['wʌndə°] n (marvel) Wunder nt; (surprise) Staunen nt ▷ vt, vi (speculate) sich fragen; **I ~ what/if ...** ich frage mich, was/ob ...; **wonderful** adj, adv wunderbar

won't [wəʊnt] contr of **will not**

wood [wʊd] n Holz nt; **~s** Wald m; **wooden** adj Holz-; (fig) hölzern; **woodpecker** n Specht m; **woodwork** n (wooden parts) Holzteile pl; (in school) Werken nt

wool [wʊl] n Wolle f; **woollen, woollens** (US) adj Woll-

word [wɜːd] n Wort nt; (promise) Ehrenwort nt; **~s** pl (of song) Text m; **to have a ~ with sb** sprechen; **in other ~s** mit anderen Worten ▷ vt formulieren; **wording** n Wortlaut m, Formulierung f; **word processing** n Textverarbeitung f; **word processor** n (program) Textverarbeitungsprogramm nt

wore [wɔː°] pt of **wear**

work [wɜːk] n Arbeit f; (of art, literature) Werk nt; **~ of art** Kunstwerk nt; **he's at ~** er ist in/auf der Arbeit; **out of ~** arbeitslos ▷ vi arbeiten (at, on an +dat); (machine, plan) funktionieren; (medicine) wirken; (succeed) klappen ▷ vt (machine) bedienen; **work out** vi (plan) klappen; (sum) aufgehen; (person) trainieren ▷ vt (price, speed etc) ausrechnen; (plan) ausarbeiten; **work up vi: to get worked up** sich aufregen; **workaholic** [wɜːkə'hɒlɪk] n Arbeitstier nt; **worker** n Arbeiter(in) m(f); **working class** n Arbeiterklasse f; **workman** (pl **-men**) n Handwerker m; **workout** n (Sport) Fitnesstraining nt, Konditionstraining nt; **work permit** n Arbeitserlaubnis f;

workplace n Arbeitsplatz m; **workshop** n Werkstatt f; (meeting) Workshop m; **work station** n (Inform) Workstation f

world [wɜːld] n Welt f; **world championship** n Weltmeisterschaft f; **World War** n: ~ I/II, the First/Second ~ der Erste/Zweite Weltkrieg; **world-wide** adj, adv weltweit; **World Wide Web** n World Wide Web nt

worm [wɜːm] n Wurm m

worn [wɔːn] pp of **wear** ▷ adj (clothes) abgetragen; (tyre) abgefahren; **worn-out** adj abgenutzt; (person) erschöpft

worried [ˈwʌrɪd] adj besorgt; be ~ about sich dat Sorgen machen um; **worry** [ˈwʌrɪ] n Sorge f ▷ vt Sorgen machen +dat ▷ vi sich Sorgen machen (about um); **don't ~!** keine Sorge!; **worrying** adj beunruhigend

worse [wɜːs] adj comparative of **bad**: schlechter; (pain, mistake etc) schlimmer ▷ adv comparative of **badly**: schlechter; **worsen** vt verschlechtern ▷ vi sich verschlechtern

worship [ˈwɜːʃɪp] vt anbeten, anhimmeln

worst [wɜːst] adj superlative of **bad**: schlechteste(r, s); (pain, mistake etc) schlimmste(r, s) ▷ adv superlative of **badly**: am schlechtesten ▷ n: **the ~ is over** das Schlimmste ist vorbei; **at (the) ~** schlimmstenfalls

worth [wɜːθ] n Wert m; **£10 ~ of food** Essen für 10 Pfund ▷ adj: **it is ~ £50** es ist 50 Pfund wert; **~ seeing** sehenswert; **it's ~ it** (rewarding) es lohnt sich; **worthless** adj wertlos; **worthwhile** adj lohnend, lohnenswert; **worthy** [ˈwɜːðɪ]

adj (deserving respect) würdig; **to be ~ of sth** etw verdienen

KEYWORD

would [wʊd] vb aux **1** (conditional tense) **if you asked him he would do it** wenn du ihn fragtest/Sie ihn fragten, würde er es tun; **if you had asked him he would have done it** wenn du ihn gefragt hättest/Sie ihn gefragt hätten, hätte er es getan

2 (in offers, invitations, requests) **would you like a biscuit?** möchtest du/möchten Sie einen Keks?; **would you ask him to come in?** würdest du/würden Sie ihn bitte hereinbitten?

3 (in indirect speech) **I said I would do it** ich sagte, ich würde es tun

4 (emphatic) **it WOULD have to snow today!** es musste ja ausgerechnet heute schneien!

5 (insistence) **she wouldn't behave** sie wollte sich partout nicht anständig benehmen

6 (conjecture) **it would have been midnight** es mag ungefähr Mitternacht gewesen sein; **it would seem so** es sieht wohl so aus

7 (indicating habit) **he would go there on Mondays** er ging jeden Montag dorthin

wouldn't [ˈwʊdnt] contr of **would not**

would've [ˈwʊdəv] contr of **would have**

wound [wuːnd] n Wunde f ▷ vt verwunden; (fig) verletzen ▷ [waʊnd] pt, pp of **wind**

wove [wəʊv] pt of **weave**

woven [ˈwəʊvn] pp of **weave**

wrap [ræp] vt (parcel, present) einwickeln; **to ~ sth round sth**

etw um etw wickeln; **wrap up** vt
(parcel, present) einwickeln ▷ vi
(dress warmly) sich warm anziehen;
wrapper n (of sweet) Papier nt;
wrapping paper n Packpapier nt;
(giftwrap) Geschenkpapier nt
wreath [riːθ] n Kranz m
wreck [rek] n (ship, plane, car)
Wrack nt; **a nervous ~** ein
Nervenbündel m ▷ vt (car) zu
Schrott fahren; (fig) zerstören;
wreckage ['rekɪdʒ] n Trümmer pl
wrench [rentʃ] n (tool)
Schraubenschlüssel m
wrestling ['reslɪŋ] n Ringen nt
wring out ['rɪŋ'aʊt] (**wrung,
wrung**) vt auswringen
wrinkle ['rɪŋkl] n Falte f
wrist [rɪst] n Handgelenk nt;
wristwatch n Armbanduhr f
write [raɪt] (**wrote, written**) vt
schreiben; (cheque) ausstellen ▷ vi
schreiben; **to ~ to sb** jdm
schreiben; **write down** vt
aufschreiben; **write off** vt (debt,
person) abschreiben; (car) zu
Schrott fahren ▷ vi: **to ~ off for
sth** etw anfordern; **write out** vt
(name etc) ausschreiben; (cheque)
ausstellen; **write-protected** adj
(Inform) schreibgeschützt; **writer**
n Verfasser(in) m(f); (author)
Schriftsteller(in) m(f); **writing** n
Schrift f; (profession) Schreiben nt;
in ~ schriftlich; **writing paper** n
Schreibpapier nt
written ['rɪtən] pp of **write**
wrong [rɒŋ] adj (incorrect) falsch;
(morally) unrecht; **you're ~** du
hast/Sie haben unrecht; **what's
~ with your leg?** was ist mit
deinem/Ihrem Bein los?; **you've
got the ~ number** du bist/Sie sind
falsch verbunden; **I dialled the
~ number** ich habe mich
verwählt; **don't get me
~** versteh/verstehen Sie mich

nicht falsch; **to go ~** (plan)
schiefgehen; **wrongly** adv falsch;
(unjustly) zu Unrecht
wrote [rəʊt] pt of **write**
WWW abbr = World Wide Web
WWW

X y

xenophobia [zenəˈfəʊbɪə] *n* Ausländerfeindlichkeit *f*

XL *abbr* = **extra large** XL, übergroß

Xmas [ˈkrɪsməs] *n* Weihnachten *nt*

X-ray [ˈeksreɪ] *n* (*picture*) Röntgenaufnahme *f* ▷ *vt* röntgen

xylophone [ˈzaɪləfəʊn] *n* Xylo

yacht [jɒt] *n* Jacht *f*; **yachting** *n* Segeln *nt*; **to go ~** segeln gehen

yam [jæm] *n* (US) Süßkartoffel *f*

yard [jɑːd] *n* Hof *m*; (US: *garden*) Garten *m*; (*measure*) Yard *nt* (0,91 m)

yawn [jɔːn] *vi* gähnen

yd *abbr* = **yard(s)**

year [ˈjɪə°] *n* Jahr *nt*; **this/last/next ~** dieses/letztes/nächstes Jahr; **he is 28 ~s old** er ist 28 Jahre alt; **~s ago** vor Jahren; **a five-year-old** ein(e) Fünfjährige(r); **yearly** *adj, adv* jährlich

yearn [jɜːn] *vi* sich sehnen (*for* nach +dat); **to ~ to do sth** sich danach sehnen, etw zu tun

yeast [jiːst] *n* Hefe *f*

yell [jel] *vi, vt* schreien; **to ~ at sb** jdn anschreien

yellow [ˈjeləʊ] *adj* gelb; **~ card**

(Sport) gelbe Karte; **~ fever** Gelbfieber nt; **~ line** (Brit) = Halteverbot nt; **double ~ line** (Brit) = absolutes Halteverbot; **the Yellow Pages®** pl die Gelben Seiten pl

yes [jes] adv ja; (answering negative question) doch; **to say ~ to sth** ja zu etw sagen ▷ n Ja nt

yesterday ['jestədeɪ] adv gestern; **~ morning/evening** gestern Morgen/Abend; **the day before ~** vorgestern; **~'s newspaper** die Zeitung von gestern

yet [jet] adv (still) noch; (up to now) bis jetzt; (in a question: already) schon; **he hasn't arrived ~** er ist noch nicht gekommen; **have you finished ~?** bist du/sind Sie schon fertig?; **~ again** schon wieder; **as ~** bis jetzt ▷ conj doch

yield [jiːld] n Ertrag m ▷ vt (result, crop) hervorbringen; (profit, interest) bringen ▷ vi nachgeben (to +dat); (Mil) sich ergeben (to +dat); **"~"** (US Auto) „Vorfahrt beachten"

yoga ['jəʊɡə] n Yoga nt

yog(h)urt ['jɒɡət] n Jog(h)urt m

yolk [jəʊk] n Eigelb nt

Yorkshire pudding ['jɔːkʃə'pʊdɪŋ] n gebackener Eierteig, der meist zum Roastbeef gegessen wird

KEYWORD

you [juː] pron 1 (subj, in comparisons) (familiar form) (sg) du; (pl) ihr; (in letters) Du, Ihr; (polite form) Sie; **you Germans** ihr Deutschen; **she's younger than you** sie ist jünger als du/ihr/Sie
2 (direct object, after prep +akk) (familiar form) (sg) dich; (pl) euch; (in letters) Dich, Euch; (polite form)

Sie; **I know you** ich kenne dich/euch/Sie
3 (indirect object, after prep +dat) (familiar form) (sg) dir; (pl) euch; (in letters) Dir, Euch; (polite form) Ihnen; **I gave it to you** ich gab es dir/euch/Ihnen
4 (impers) (one) (subj) man; (direct object) einen; (indirect object) einem; **fresh air does you good** frische Luft tut (einem) gut

you'd [juːd] contr of **you had; you would; ~ better leave** du solltest/Sie sollten gehen

you'll [juːl] contr of **you will; you shall**

young [jʌŋ] adj jung ▷ n **the ~ pl** (~ people) die jungen Leute pl; (animals) die Jungen pl; **youngster** ['jʌŋstə'] n Jugendliche(r) mf

your ['jɔː'] adj sing dein; polite form Ihr; pl euer; polite form Ihr; **have you hurt ~ leg?** hast du dir/haben Sie sich das Bein verletzt?

you're ['jʊə'] contr of **you are**

yours ['jɔːz] pron sing deine(r, s); polite form Ihre(r, s); pl eure(r, s); polite form Ihre(r, s); **is this ~?** gehört das dir/Ihnen?; **a friend of ~** ein Freund von dir/Ihnen

yourself [jɔː'self] pron sing dich; polite form dir; **have you hurt ~?** hast du dich/haben Sie sich verletzt?; **did you do it ~?** hast du/haben Sie es selbst gemacht?; **(all) by ~** allein; **yourselves** pron pl euch; polite form Sie; **have you hurt ~?** habt ihr euch/haben Sie sich verletzt?; **did you do it ~?** habt ihr/haben Sie es selbst gemacht?; **(all) by ~** allein

youth [juːθ] n (period) Jugend f; (young man) junger Mann; (young people) Jugend f; **youth group** n

Jugendgruppe f; **youth hostel** *n*
Jugendherberge f
you've [juːv] *contr of* **you have**
yucky [ˈjʌkɪ] *adj (fam)* eklig
yummy [ˈjʌmɪ] *adj (fam)* lecker
yuppie, yuppy [ˈjʌpɪ] *n* Yuppie
m

zap [zæp] *vt (Inform)* löschen; *(in
computer game)* abknallen ▷ *vi (TV)*
zappen; **zapper** *n (TV)*
Fernbedienung f; **zapping** *n (TV)*
ständiges Umschalten, Zapping *nt*
zebra [ˈzebrə, ?? ˈziːbrə] *(US) n*
Zebra *nt*; **zebra crossing** *n (Brit)*
Zebrastreifen *m*
zero [zɪərəʊ] *n (pl -es) n* Null f; **10
degrees below** ~ 10 Grad unter
null
zest [zest] *n (enthusiasm)*
Begeisterung f
zigzag [ˈzɪɡzæɡ] *n* Zickzack *m*
▷ *vi (person, vehicle)* im Zickzack
gehen/fahren; *(path)* im Zickzack
verlaufen
zinc [zɪŋk] *n* Zink *nt*
zip [zɪp] *n (Brit)* Reißverschluss *m*
▷ *vt:* **to ~ (up)** den Reißverschluss
zumachen; *(Inform)* zippen; **zip
code** *n (US)* Postleitzahl f; **zip
disk®** *n (Inform)* ZIP-Diskette® f;

Zip drive® n (Inform)
ZIP-Laufwerk® nt; **Zip file®** n
(Inform) ZIP-Datei® f; **zipper** n
(US) Reißverschluss m

zit [zɪt] n (fam) Pickel m

zodiac ['zəʊdɪæk] n Tierkreis m;
  sign of the ~ Tierkreiszeichen
  nt

zone [zəʊn] n Zone f; (area)
  Gebiet nt; (in town) Bezirk m

zoo [zuː] n Zoo m

zoom [zuːm] vi (move fast)
  brausen, sausen ▷ n: **~ (lens)**
  Zoomobjektiv nt; **zoom in** vi
  (Foto) heranzoomen (on an +akk)

zucchini [zuːˈkiːnɪ] (pl **-(s)**) n
  (US) Zucchini f

Kleines Reise-ABC

Mini Phrasefinder

THEMEN | TOPICS

THEMEN | TOPICS

KENNENLERNEN | MEETING PEOPLE

Guten Tag!	Hello!
Guten Abend!	Good evening!
Gute Nacht!	Good night!
Auf Wiedersehen!	Goodbye!
Wie heißen Sie?	What's your name?
Mein Name ist ...	My name is ...
Das ist ...	This is ...
meine Frau.	*my wife.*
mein Mann.	*my husband.*
mein Partner/meine Partnerin.	*my partner.*
Wo kommen Sie her?	Where are you from?
Ich komme aus ...	I come from ...
Wie geht es Ihnen?	How are you?
Danke, gut.	Fine, thanks.
Und Ihnen?	And you?
Sprechen Sie Englisch?	Do you speak English?
Ich verstehe kein Deutsch.	I don't understand German.
Vielen Dank!	Thanks very much.

AUTO | CARS

Autovermietung — Car hire

Ich möchte ... mieten.	I want to hire ...
ein Auto	a car.
ein Moped	a moped.
ein Motorrad	a motorbike.
Ein Auto mit Automatikgetriebe, bitte.	An automatic, please.
Was kostet das für ...?	How much is it for ...?
einen Tag	one day
eine Woche	a week
Verlangen Sie eine Kilometergebühr?	Is there a kilometre charge?
Was ist alles im Preis inbegriffen?	What is included in the price?
Ich möchte einen Kindersitz für ein ... Jahre altes Kind.	I'd like a child seat for a ...-year-old child.
Bitte erklären Sie mir die Schalter.	Please show me the controls.
Was tue ich bei einem Unfall/einer Panne?	What do I do if I have an accident/if I break down?

Pannen — Breakdowns

Ich habe eine Panne.	My car has broken down.
Ich bin Mitglied in einem Automobilklub.	I'm a member of a rescue service.
Ich bin allein.	I'm on my own.
Ich habe Kinder dabei.	I have children in the car.
Bitte schleppen Sie mich zur nächsten Werkstatt.	Can you tow me to the next garage, please?
Wo ist die nächste Werkstatt?	Where is the next garage?
Der Auspuff	The exhaust
Das Getriebe	The gearbox
Die Windschutzscheibe	The windscreen
... ist kaputt.	... is broken.
Die Bremsen	The brakes

AUTO | CARS

Die Scheinwerfer	*The headlights*
Die Scheibenwischer	*The windscreen wipers*
... funktionieren nicht.	... are not working.
Die Batterie ist leer.	The battery is flat.
Der Motor springt nicht an.	The car won't start.
Der Motor wird zu heiß.	The engine is overheating.
Die Ölwarnlampe geht nicht aus.	The oil warning light won't go off.
Ich habe einen Platten.	I have a flat tyre.
Können Sie das reparieren?	Can you repair it?
Wann ist das Auto fertig?	When will the car be ready?

Parken | Parking

Kann ich hier parken?	Can I park here?
Brauche ich eine Parkscheibe?	Do I need a parking disc?
Muss ich einen Parkschein lösen?	Do I need to buy a (car-parking) ticket?
Wo ist der Parkscheinautomat?	Where is the ticket machine?
Der Parkscheinautomat funktioniert nicht.	The ticket machine isn't working.

Tankstelle | Petrol Station

Wo ist die nächste Tankstelle?	Where is the nearest petrol station?
Voll tanken bitte.	Fill it up, please.
Für 40 Euro ... bitte.	40 euros worth of ..., please.
Diesel	*diesel*
Normalbenzin	*(unleaded economy petrol)*
Super	*premium unleaded*
Säule Nummer ... bitte.	Pump number ... please.
Bitte überprüfen Sie ...	Please check ...
das Wasser.	*the water.*
den Reifendruck.	*the tyre pressure.*

AUTO | CARS

das Öl.	*the oil.*
Eine Marke für die Wasch-anlage bitte.	A token for the car wash, please.

Unfall | Accident

Bitte rufen Sie ...	Please call ...
die Polizei.	*the police.*
den Notarzt.	*the emergency doctor.*
Hier sind meine Ver-sicherungsangaben.	Here are my insurance details.
Bitte geben Sie mir Ihre Versicherungsangaben.	Give me your insurance details, please.
Würden Sie das bezeugen?	Can you be a witness for me?
Sie sind zu schnell gefahren.	You were driving too fast.
Sie haben die Vorfahrt nicht beachtet.	It wasn't your right of way.

Unterwegs mit dem Auto | Car Travel

Wie kommt man am besten nach/zu ...?	What's the best route to ...?
Wo kann ich die Maut bezahlen?	Where can I pay the toll?
Ich möchte einen Aufkleber für die Autobahngebühr/ eine Vignette ...	I'd like a motorway tax sticker ...
für eine Woche.	*for a week.*
für einen Monat.	*for a month.*
für ein Jahr.	*for a year.*
Haben Sie eine Straßenkarte von dieser Gegend?	Do you have a road map of this area?

BANK | CHANGING MONEY

Wo kann ich hier Geld wechseln?	Where can I change money?
Gibt es hier eine Bank/eine Wechselstube?	Is there a bank/bureau de change here?
Wann ist die Bank/Wechselstube geöffnet?	When is the bank/bureau de change open?
Ich möchte ... Euro/Franken in Pfund/Dollar umtauschen.	I'd like to change ... euros/francs into pounds/dollars.
Ich möchte diese Reiseschecks/Euroschecks einlösen.	I'd like to cash these traveller's cheques/eurocheques.
Wie hoch ist die Gebühr?	What's the commission?
Kann ich hier mit meiner Kreditkarte Bargeld bekommen?	Can I use my credit card to get cash?
Wo gibt es hier einen Geldautomaten?	Where is the nearest cash machine?
Der Geldautomat hat meine Karte geschluckt.	The cash machine swallowed my card.
Bitte geben Sie mir etwas Kleingeld.	Can you give me some change, please?

BEHINDERTE | DISABLED TRAVELLERS

Kann man ... auch im Rollstuhl besuchen?	Is it possible to visit ... with a wheelchair?
Wo ist der Eingang für Rollstuhlfahrer?	Where is the wheelchair-accessible entrance?
Ist Ihr Hotel rollstuhlgerecht?	Is your hotel accessible to wheelchairs?
Ich brauche ein Zimmer ...	I need a room ...
im Erdgeschoss.	*on the ground floor.*
für Rollstuhlfahrer.	*with wheelchair access.*
Haben Sie einen Aufzug für Rollstühle?	Do you have a lift for wheelchairs?
Haben Sie Rollstühle?	Do you have wheelchairs?
Wo ist die Behindertentoilette?	Where is the disabled toilet?
Kann ich als Rollstuhlfahrer in diesem Zug mitfahren?	Is the train wheelchair accessible?
Bitte helfen Sie mir beim Einsteigen/Aussteigen.	Can you help me get on/off, please?
Wo gibt es hier eine Werkstatt für Rollstühle?	Where is the nearest repair shop for wheelchairs?
Ein Reifen ist geplatzt.	A tyre has burst.
Die Batterie ist leer.	The battery has run down.
Die Räder blockieren.	The wheels lock.

BESICHTIGUNGEN | SIGHTSEEING

Wo ist die Touristeninformation?	Where is the tourist office?
Haben Sie Broschüren über ...?	Do you have any leaflets about ...?
Welche Sehenswürdigkeiten gibt es hier?	What sights can you visit here?
Gibt es eine Stadtrundfahrt/ einen Stadtrundgang auf Englisch?	Is there a guided tour in English?
Wann ist ... geöffnet?	When is ... open?
das Museum	*the museum*
die Kirche	*the church*
das Schloss	*the castle*
Was kostet der Eintritt?	How much does it cost to get in?
Gibt es eine Ermäßigung ...?	Are there any reductions ...?
für Studenten	*for students*
für Kinder	*for children*
für Rentner	*for pensioners*
für Arbeitslose	*for the unemployed*
Ich möchte einen Katalog.	I'd like a catalogue.
Kann ich hier fotografieren?	Can I take photos here?
Kann ich hier filmen?	Can I film here?

DIENSTREISE | BUSINESS TRAVEL

Ich möchte eine Besprechung mit ... ausmachen.	I'd like to arrange a meeting with ...
Ich habe einen Termin mit Herrn/Frau ...	I have an appointment with Mr/Ms ...
Hier ist meine Karte.	Here is my card.
Ich arbeite für ...	I work for ...
Wie komme ich ...?	How do I get to ...?
zu Ihrem Büro	*your office*
zum Büro von Herrn/Frau ...	*Mr/Ms ...'s office*
zur Kantine	*the canteen*
Ich brauche einen Dolmetscher.	I need an interpreter.
Bitte kopieren Sie das für mich.	Can you copy that for me, please?
Darf ich ... benutzen?	May I use ...?
Ihr Telefon	*your phone*
Ihren Computer	*your computer*
Ihren Schreibtisch	*your desk*

EINKAUFEN | SHOPPING

Ich suche ...	I'm looking for ...
Ich möchte ...	I'd like ...
Haben Sie ...?	Do you have ...?
Haben Sie das ...?	Do you have this ...?
in einer anderen Größe	*in another size*
in einer anderen Farbe	*in another colour*
mit einem anderen Muster	*in another design*
Ich trage Größe ...	I take size ...
Ich nehme das.	I'll take it.
Haben Sie noch etwas anderes?	Do you have anything else?
Das ist zu teuer.	That's too expensive.
Ich sehe mich nur um.	I'm just looking.
Nehmen Sie ...?	Do you take ...?
Kreditkarten	*credit cards*

Lebensmittel	Food shopping
Wo ist hier ...?	Where is the nearest ...?
ein Supermarkt	*supermarket*
eine Bäckerei	*baker's*
eine Metzgerei	*butcher's*
ein Obst- und Gemüseladen	*greengrocer's*
Wo ist der Markt?	Where is the market?
Wann ist Markt?	When is the market on?
ein Kilo ...	a kilo of ...
ein Pfund ...	a pound of ...
200 Gramm ...	200 grams of ...
... Scheiben ...	... slices ...
ein Liter ...	a litre of ...
eine Flasche ...	a bottle of ...
ein Päckchen ...	a packet of ...

ERKUNDIGUNGEN | ASKING THE WAY

Wo ist der/die/das nächste ...?	Where is the nearest ...?
Wie komme ich dahin?	How do I get there?
Wie komme ich zum/zur/ nach ...?	How do I get to ...?
Ist es weit?	Is it far?
Wie weit ist es?	How far is it?
Bin ich hier richtig zum/ zur/nach ...?	Is this the right way to ...?
Ich habe mich verlaufen/ verfahren.	I'm lost.
Können Sie mir das auf der Karte zeigen?	Can you show me on the map?
Welchen Hinweisschildern muss ich folgen?	Which signs should I follow?
Kehren Sie um.	You have to turn round.
Fahren Sie geradeaus.	Go straight on.
Biegen Sie nach links/rechts ab.	Turn left/right.
Nehmen Sie die zweite Straße links/rechts.	Take the second street on the left/right.

FOTO UND VIDEO | PHOTOS AND VIDEOS

Einen Farbfilm/Diafilm bitte.	A colour film/slide film, please.
Mit 24/36 Bildern.	With 24/36 exposures.
Batterien für diesen Apparat bitte.	Can I have batteries for this camera, please?
Der Apparat klemmt.	The camera is sticking.
Bitte nehmen Sie den Film heraus.	Take the film out, please.
Bitte entwickeln Sie diesen Film.	Can you develop this film, please?
Ich hätte die Bilder gern ...	I'd like the photos ...
matt.	*matt.*
Hochglanz.	*glossy.*
im Format 10 mal 15.	*10 by 15 centimetres.*
Die Dias ... bitte.	I'd like the slides ..., please.
mit Rahmung	*mounted*
ohne Rahmung	*developed only*
Bitte helfen Sie mir, den Umschlag auszufüllen.	Can you help me to fill out the envelope, please?
Wann sind die Fotos fertig?	When will the photos be ready?
Wie viel kosten die Bilder?	How much do the photos cost?
Darf man hier fotografieren?	Are you allowed to take photos here?
Könnten Sie bitte ein Foto von uns machen?	Could you take a photo of us, please?

GESUNDHEIT | HEALTH

Apotheke	Pharmacy
Wo gibt es hier eine Apotheke?	Where is the nearest pharmacy?
Welche Apotheke hat Bereitschaft?	Which pharmacy provides emergency service?
Ich möchte etwas gegen ...	I'd like something for ...
Durchfall.	*diarrhoea.*
Fieber.	*a temperature.*
Reisekrankheit.	*travel sickness.*
Kopfschmerzen.	*a headache.*
Erkältung.	*a cold.*
Ich möchte ...	I'd like ...
Pflaster.	*plasters.*
einen Verband.	*a bandage.*
ein Dreieckstuch.	*a triangular bandage.*
Ich vertrage kein ...	I can't take ...
Aspirin.	*aspirin.*
Penizillin.	*penicillin.*
Kann man das Kindern geben?	Is it safe to give children?
Wie soll ich das einnehmen?	How should I take it?

Beim Arzt	At the doctor
Ich brauche einen Arzt.	I need a doctor.
Wo ist die Notaufnahme?	Where is casualty?
Ich habe hier Schmerzen.	I have a pain here.
Mir ist ...	I feel ...
heiß.	*hot.*
kalt.	*cold.*
übel.	*sick.*
schwindlig.	*dizzy.*
Ich bin allergisch gegen ...	I'm allergic to ...
Ich bin ...	I am ...
schwanger.	*pregnant.*
Diabetiker.	*diabetic.*

GESUNDHEIT | HEALTH

HIV-positiv.	*HIV-positive.*
Ich nehme dieses Medikament.	I'm on this medication.
Meine Blutgruppe ist ...	My blood group is ...

Krankenhaus | At the hospital

Auf welcher Station liegt ...?	Which ward is ... in?
Wann ist die Besuchszeit?	When are visiting hours?
Ich möchte mit ... sprechen.	I'd like to speak to ...
einem Arzt	*a doctor*
einer Krankenschwester	*a nurse*
Ich möchte ein Telefon mieten.	I'd like to hire a phone.
Ich möchte Kopfhörer für das Fernsehen, bitte.	I'd like headphones for the TV, please.
Wann werde ich entlassen?	When will I be discharged?

Beim Zahnarzt | At the dentist

Ich brauche einen Zahnarzt.	I need a dentist.
Dieser Zahn tut weh.	This tooth hurts.
Mir ist eine Füllung herausgefallen.	One of my fillings has fallen out.
Ich habe einen Abszess.	I have an abscess.
Ich möchte eine/keine Spritze gegen die Schmerzen.	I want/don't want an injection for the pain.
Können Sie mein Gebiss reparieren?	Can you repair my dentures?
Ich brauche eine Quittung für die Versicherung.	I need a receipt for the insurance.

NOTFALLDIENSTE | EMERGENCY SERVICES

Hilfe!	Help!
Feuer!	Fire!
Bitte rufen Sie ...	Please call ...
den Notarzt.	the emergency doctor.
die Feuerwehr.	the fire brigade.
die Polizei.	the police.
Ich muss dringend telefonieren.	I need to make an urgent phone call.
Ich brauche einen Dolmetscher.	I need an interpreter.
Wo ist die Polizeiwache?	Where is the police station?
Wo ist das nächste Krankenhaus?	Where is the nearest hospital?
Ich möchte einen Diebstahl melden.	I want to report a theft.
... ist gestohlen worden.	... has been stolen.
Es ist ein Unfall passiert.	There's been an accident.
Es gibt ... Verletzte.	There are ... people injured.
Mein Standort ist ...	My location is ...
Ich bin ... worden.	I've been ...
beraubt	robbed
überfallen	attacked
vergewaltigt	raped
Ich möchte mit meiner Botschaft sprechen.	I'd like to phone my embassy.

PASS/ZOLL | PASSPORT/CUSTOMS

Hier ist ...	Here is ...
mein Pass.	*my passport.*
mein Personalausweis.	*my identity card.*
mein Führerschein.	*my driving licence.*
meine grüne Versicherungskarte.	*my green card.*
Hier sind meine Fahrzeug-papiere.	Here are my vehicle documents.
Die Kinder stehen in diesem Pass.	The children are on this passport.
Muss ich das verzollen?	Do I have to pay duty on this?
Das ist ...	This is ...
ein Geschenk.	*a present.*
ein Warenmuster.	*a sample.*
Das ist für meinen persönlichen Gebrauch.	This is for my own personal use.
Ich bin auf der Durchreise nach ...	I'm on my way to ...

FAHRRAD | CYCLING

Gibt es eine Fahrradkarte von dieser Gegend?	Is there a cycle map of this area?
Wo ist der Radwanderweg nach ...?	Where is the cycle path to ...?
Wie weit ist es noch bis ...?	How far is it now to ...?
Kann ich hier mein Fahrrad unterstellen?	Can I keep my bike here?
Bitte verschließen Sie mein Fahrrad an einem sicheren Ort.	Please lock my bike in a secure place.
Mein Fahrrad ist gestohlen worden.	My bike has been stolen.
Wo gibt es hier eine Fahrradwerkstatt?	Where is the nearest bike repair shop?
Der Rahmen ist verbogen.	The frame is twisted.
Die Bremse funktioniert nicht.	The brake isn't working.
Die Gangschaltung funktioniert nicht.	The gears aren't working.
Die Kette ist gerissen.	The chain is broken.
Ich habe einen Platten.	I've got a flat tyre.
Ich brauche Reifenflickzeug.	I need a puncture repair kit.

REISEN MIT KINDERN | TRAVELLING WITH CHILDREN

Können wir die Kinder mitbringen?	Is it ok to bring children here?
Ist der Eintritt auch Kindern gestattet?	Are children allowed in, too?
Gibt es eine Ermäßigung für Kinder?	Is there a reduction for children?
Haben Sie Kinderportionen?	Do you have children's portions?
Haben Sie ...?	Do you have ...?
einen Kinderstuhl	*a high chair*
ein Kinderbett	*a cot*
einen Kindersitz	*a child's seat*
einen Wickeltisch	*a baby's changing table*
Wo kann ich das Baby wickeln?	Where can I change the baby?
Wo kann ich das Baby stillen?	Where can I breast-feed the baby?
Können Sie das bitte aufwärmen?	Can you warm this up, please?
Was können Kinder hier unternehmen?	What is there for children to do?
Wo gibt es hier einen Spielplatz?	Where is the nearest playground?
Gibt es hier eine Kinderbetreuung?	Is there a childminding service?
Mein Sohn/meine Tochter ist krank.	My son/daughter is ill.

RESTAURANT | FOOD AND DRINK

Einen Tisch für ... Personen bitte.	A table for ... people, please.
Die Speisekarte bitte.	The menu, please.
Die Weinkarte bitte.	The wine list, please.
Was empfehlen Sie?	What do you recommend?
Haben Sie ...?	Do you have ...?
vegetarische Gerichte	*any vegetarian dishes*
Kinderportionen	*children's portions*
Enthält das ...?	Does that contain ...?
Erdnüsse	*peanuts*
Alkohol	*alcohol*
Bitte bringen Sie (noch) ...	Can you bring (more) ..., please?
Ich nehme ...	I'll have ...
Zahlen bitte.	The bill, please.
Bitte alles zusammen.	All together, please.
Getrennte Rechnungen bitte.	Separate bills, please.
Stimmt so.	Keep the change.
Das habe ich nicht bestellt.	I didn't order this.
Die Rechnung stimmt nicht.	The bill is wrong.
Das Essen ist kalt/versalzen.	The food is cold/too salty.

SPORT | SPORT

Ski	Skiing
Wo kann ich eine Skiausrüstung ausleihen?	Where can I hire skiing equipment?
Ich möchte ... ausleihen.	I'd like to hire ...
Abfahrtski	*downhill skis.*
Langlaufski	*cross-country skis.*
Skischuhe	*ski boots.*
Wo kann ich einen Skipass kaufen?	Where can I buy a ski pass?
Ich möchte einen Skipass ...	I'd like a ski pass ...
für einen Tag.	*for a day.*
für fünf Tage.	*for five days.*
für sieben Tage.	*for seven days.*
Wie viel kostet der Skipass?	How much is a ski pass?
Haben Sie eine Pistenkarte?	Do you have a map of the ski runs?
Wo sind die Abfahrten für Anfänger?	Where are the beginners' slopes?
Welchen Schwierigkeitsgrad hat diese Abfahrt?	How difficult is this slope?
Gibt es eine Skischule?	Is there a ski school?
Wie ist der Wetterbericht?	What's the weather forecast?
Wie ist der Schnee?	What's the snow like?
Besteht Lawinengefahr?	Is there a danger of avalanches?

Sport	Sport
Wo kann man hier ...?	Where can we ...?
Tennis/Golf spielen	*play tennis/golf*
schwimmen	*go swimming*
reiten	*go riding*
Wie viel kostet es pro Stunde?	How much is it per hour?
Wo kann ich einen Platz buchen?	Where can I book a court?

SPORT | SPORT

Wo kann ich Schläger ausleihen?	Where can I hire rackets?
Wo kann ich ein Ruderboot/ ein Tretboot mieten?	Where can I hire a rowing boat/ a pedal boat?
Braucht man einen Angelschein?	Do you need a fishing permit?
Ich möchte ... ansehen.	I'd like to see ...
ein Fußballspiel	*a football match.*
ein Pferderennen	*a horse race.*

AM STRAND | AT THE BEACH

Kann man hier/in diesem See baden?	Can you swim here/in this lake?
Wo gibt es hier einen ruhigen Strand?	Where is the nearest quiet beach?
Gibt es einen bewachten Strand?	Is there a beach with lifeguards?
Wie tief ist das Wasser?	How deep is the water?
Wie viel Grad hat das Wasser?	What is the water temperature?
Gibt es hier Strömungen?	Are there currents?
Gibt es hier einen Rettungsschwimmer?	Is there a lifeguard?
Wo kann man hier ...?	Where can you ...?
surfen	*go surfing*
Wasserski fahren	*go waterskiing*
tauchen	*go diving*
Gleitschirm fliegen	*go paragliding*
Ich möchte ... mieten.	I'd like to hire ...
einen Strandkorb	*a beach chair.*
einen Liegestuhl	*a deckchair.*
einen Sonnenschirm	*a sunshade.*
Ich möchte ... ausleihen.	I'd like to hire ...
ein Surfbrett	*a surfboard.*
einen Jetski	*a jet-ski.*
ein Ruderboot	*a rowing boat.*
ein Tretboot	*a pedal boat.*

TELEFON | TELEPHONE

Wo kann ich hier telefonieren?	Where can I make a phone call?
Wo ist das nächste Kartentelefon?	Where is the nearest card phone?
Wo ist der nächste Münzfernsprecher?	Where is the nearest coin box?
Ich möchte eine Telefonkarte für 10 Euro.	I'd like a ten euro phone card.
Ich möchte Münzen für das Telefon bitte.	I'd like some coins for the phone, please.
Ich möchte ein R-Gespräch anmelden.	I'd like to make a reverse charge call.
Hallo.	Hello.
Hier ist ...	This is ...
Wer spricht dort bitte?	Who's speaking, please?
Kann ich bitte mit Herrn/Frau ... sprechen?	Can I speak to Mr/Ms ..., please?
Apparat ... bitte.	Extension ..., please.
Ich rufe später wieder an.	I'll phone back later.
Wo kann ich mein Handy aufladen?	Where can I charge my mobile phone?
Ich brauche einen neuen Akku.	I need a new battery.
Hier ist kein Netz.	I can't get a network.
Die Verbindung ist sehr schlecht.	You're breaking up.

UNTERHALTUNG | ENTERTAINMENT

Was kann man hier unternehmen?	What is there to do here?
Haben Sie einen Veranstaltungskalender?	Do you have a list of events?
Wo kann man hier ...?	Where can we ...?
tanzen gehen	go dancing
Livemusik hören	hear live music
Wo gibt es hier ...?	Where is there ...?
eine nette Kneipe	a nice pub
eine gute Disko	a good disco
Was gibt es heute Abend ...?	What's on tonight ...?
im Kino	at the cinema
im Theater	at the theatre
in der Oper	at the opera
in der Konzerthalle	at the concert hall
Wo kann ich Karten für ... kaufen?	Where can I buy tickets for ...?
das Theater	the theatre
das Konzert	the concert
die Oper	the opera
das Ballett	the ballet
Was kostet der Eintritt?	How much is it to get in?
Ich möchte eine Karte/ ... Karten für ...	I'd like a ticket/... tickets for ...
Gibt es eine Ermäßigung für ...?	Are there any reductions for ...?
Kinder	children
Rentner	pensioners
Studenten	students
Arbeitslose	the unemployed

UNTERKUNFT | ACCOMMODATION

Camping	Camping
Gibt es hier einen Camping-platz?	Is there a campsite here?
Wir möchten einen Platz für ...	We'd like a site for ...
ein Zelt.	*a tent.*
ein Wohnmobil.	*a camper van.*
einen Wohnwagen.	*a caravan.*
Wir möchten eine Nacht/ ... Nächte bleiben.	We'd like to stay one night/ ... nights.
Was kostet die Nacht?	How much is it per night?
Wo sind ...?	Where are ...?
die Toiletten	*the toilets*
die Duschen	*the showers*
Wo ist ...?	Where is ...?
der Laden	*the shop*
die Verwaltung	*the site office*
Können wir über Nacht hier zelten?	Can we camp here overnight?

Ferienwohnung/-haus	Self-Catering
Wo bekommen wir den Schlüssel für die Wohnung/ das Haus?	Where do we get the key for the apartment/house?
Müssen wir Strom/Gas extra bezahlen?	Do we have to pay extra for electricity/gas?
Wie funktioniert ...?	How does ... work?
die Waschmaschine	*the washing machine*
der Herd	*the cooker*
die Heizung	*the heating*
An wen kann ich mich bei Problemen wenden?	Whom do I contact if there are any problems?
Wir brauchen ...	We need ...
einen zweiten Schlüssel.	*a second key.*
mehr Bettwäsche.	*more sheets.*

UNTERKUNFT | ACCOMMODATION

Das Gas ist alle.	The gas has run out.
Es gibt keinen Strom.	There is no electricity.
Wo geben wir die Schlüssel bei der Abreise ab?	Where do we hand in the keys when we're leaving?
Müssen wir die Wohnung/ das Haus vor der Abreise sauber machen?	Do we have to clean the apartment/the house before we leave?

Hotel	Hotel
Haben Sie ein ... für heute Nacht?	Do you have a ... for tonight?
Einzelzimmer	*single room*
Doppelzimmer	*double room*
mit Bad/Dusche	with bath/shower
Ich möchte eine Nacht/ ... Nächte bleiben.	I want to stay for one night/ ... nights.
Ich habe ein Zimmer auf den Namen ... reserviert.	I booked a room in the name of ...
Ich möchte ein anderes Zimmer.	I'd like another room.
Wann gibt es Frühstück?	What time is breakfast?
Wo gibt es Frühstück?	Where is breakfast served?
Können Sie mir das Frühstück aufs Zimmer bringen?	Can I have breakfast in my room?
Wo ist ...?	Where is ...?
das Restaurant	*the restaurant*
die Bar	*the bar*
der Fitnessraum	*the gym*
der Swimmingpool	*the swimming pool*
Bitte wecken Sie mich morgen früh um ...	I'd like an alarm call for tomorrow morning at ...
Den Schlüssel bitte.	The key, please.
Sind Nachrichten für mich da?	Are there any messages for me?

VERKEHRSMITTEL | TRANSPORT

Eisenbahn | Train

Eine einfache Fahrt nach ... bitte.	A single to ..., please.
Zweimal hin und zurück nach ... bitte.	Two returns to ..., please.
Gibt es eine Ermäßigung ...?	Is there a reduction ...?
für Studenten	*for students*
für Rentner	*for pensioners*
mit diesem Pass	*with this pass*
Eine Platzkarte für den Zug nach ... bitte.	I'd like to reserve a seat on the train to ..., please.
In Fahrtrichtung bitte.	Facing the front, please.
Ich möchte einen Liegewagenplatz/Schlafwagenplatz nach ... buchen.	I want to book a couchette/a berth to ...
Wann geht der nächste Zug nach ...?	When is the next train to ...?
Muss ich einen Zuschlag kaufen?	Is there a supplement to pay?
Muss ich umsteigen?	Do I need to change?
Wo muss ich umsteigen?	Where do I change?
Ist das der Zug nach ...?	Is this the train for ...?
Ich habe eine Platzkarte/ Reservierung.	I have a reservation.
Ist dieser Platz noch frei?	Is this seat free?
Wo ist der Speisewagen?	Where is the buffet car?
Wo ist Wagen Nummer ...?	Where is coach number ...?

Fähre | Ferry

Gibt es eine Fähre nach ...?	Is there a ferry to ...?
Wann geht die nächste Fähre nach ...?	When is the next ferry to ...?
Wann geht die erste/letzte Fähre nach ...?	When is the first/last ferry to ...?

VERKEHRSMITTEL | TRANSPORT

Was kostet ...?	How much is ...?
die einfache Fahrt	*a single*
die Hin- und Rückfahrt	*a return*
Was kostet es für ein Auto/ Wohnmobil mit ... Personen?	How much is it for a car/ camper with ... people?
Wo fährt das Schiff ab?	Where does the boat leave from?
Wie lange dauert die Überfahrt?	How long does the crossing take?
Wo ist ...?	Where is ...?
das Restaurant	*the restaurant*
der Dutyfreeshop	*the duty-free shop*
Wie komme ich zum Autodeck?	How do I get to the car deck?
Wo ist Kabine Nummer ...?	Where is cabin number ...?

Flugzeug	Plane
Wo ist ...?	Where is ...?
der Taxistand	*the taxi rank*
die Bushaltestelle	*the bus stop*
die Information	*the information office*
Mein Gepäck ist nicht angekommen.	My luggage hasn't arrived.
Wo ist der Check-in für den Flug nach ...?	Where do I check in for the flight to ...?
Von welchem Ausgang geht der Flug nach ...?	Which gate for the flight to ...?
Wann beginnt das Einsteigen?	When does boarding begin?
Fenster/Gang bitte.	Window/aisle, please.
Ich habe meine Einsteigekarte/meinen Flugschein verloren.	I've lost my boarding pass/ my ticket.
Ich möchte meinen Flug umbuchen/stornieren.	I'd like to change/cancel my flight.

VERKEHRSMITTEL | TRANSPORT

Öffentlicher Nahverkehr	Local public transport
Wie komme ich zum/zur/ nach ...?	How do I get to ...?
Welche Linie fährt zum/zur/ nach ...?	Which number goes to ...?
Wo ist die nächste ...?	Where is the nearest ...?
Bushaltestelle	*bus stop*
Straßenbahnhaltestelle	*tram stop*
U-Bahn-Station	*underground station*
Wo ist der Busbahnhof?	Where is the bus station?
Gibt es eine Ermäßigung ...?	Is there a reduction ...?
für Studenten	*for students*
für Rentner	*for pensioners*
mit diesem Ausweis	*with this card*
Gibt es Mehrfahrtenkarten/ Tageskarten?	Do you have multi-journey tickets/day tickets?
Haben Sie eine Karte mit dem Streckennetz?	Do you have a map of the rail network?
Was ist die nächste Halte- stelle?	What is the next stop?

Taxi	Taxi
Wo bekomme ich hier ein Taxi?	Where can I get a taxi?
Bitte rufen Sie mir ein Taxi.	Call me a taxi, please.
Bitte bestellen Sie mir ein Taxi für ... Uhr.	Please order me a taxi for ... o'clock.
Zum Flughafen/Bahnhof bitte.	To the airport/station, please.
Ich habe es sehr eilig.	I'm in a hurry.
Was kostet die Fahrt?	How much is it?
Ich brauche eine Quittung.	I need a receipt.
Stimmt so.	Keep the change.
Bitte halten Sie hier.	Stop here, please.

BESCHWERDEN | COMPLAINTS

Ich möchte mich beschweren.	I'd like to make a complaint.
Bei wem kann ich mich beschweren?	To whom can I complain?
Ich möchte mit dem Geschäftsführer sprechen.	I'd like to speak to the manager, please.
... funktioniert nicht.	... doesn't work.
Das Licht	*The light*
Die Heizung	*The heating*
Die Toilette	*The toilet*
Das Zimmer ist ...	The room is ...
schmutzig.	*dirty.*
zu klein.	*too small.*
zu kalt.	*too cold.*
Bitte machen Sie das Zimmer sauber.	Can you clean the room, please?
Bitte stellen Sie den Fernseher/das Radio leiser.	Can you turn down the TV/the radio, please?
Das Essen ist ...	The food is ...
kalt.	*cold.*
versalzen.	*too salty.*
Das habe ich nicht bestellt.	This isn't what I ordered.
Wir warten schon sehr lange.	We've been waiting for a very long time.
Die Rechnung stimmt nicht.	The bill is not correct.
Ich möchte mein Geld zurück.	I want my money back.
Ich möchte das umtauschen.	I'd like to exchange this.
Ich bin damit nicht zufrieden.	I'm not satisfied with this.